Corporate Restructuring
Volume I

The International Library of Critical Writings in Financial Economics

Series Editor: Richard Roll
Allstate Professor of Economics
The Anderson School at UCLA, USA

This major series presents by field outstanding selections of the most important articles across the entire spectrum of financial economics – one of the fastest growing areas in business schools and economics departments. Each collection has been prepared by a leading specialist who has written an authoritative introduction to the literature. A full list of published and future titles in this series is printed at the end of this volume.

Wherever possible, the articles in these volumes have been reproduced as originally published using facsimile reproduction, inclusive of footnotes and pagination to facilitate ease of reference.

For a list of all Edward Elgar published titles visit our site on the World Wide Web at www.e-elgar.com

Corporate Restructuring
Volume I

Edited by

John J. McConnell

Emanuel T. Weiler Distinguished Professor (Finance)
Purdue University, USA

and

David J. Denis

Burton D. Morgan Chair of Private Enterprise and Professor of Finance
Purdue University, USA

THE INTERNATIONAL LIBRARY OF CRITICAL WRITINGS IN FINANCIAL ECONOMICS

An Elgar Reference Collection
Cheltenham, UK • Northampton, MA, USA

Published by
Edward Elgar Publishing Limited
Glensanda House
Montpellier Parade
Cheltenham
Glos GL50 1UA
UK

Edward Elgar Publishing, Inc.
136 West Street
Suite 202
Northampton
Massachusetts 01060
USA

A catalogue record for this book is available from the British Library.

ISBN 1 84376 727 9 (2 volume set)

Printed and bound in Great Britain by MPG Books Ltd, Bodmin, Cornwall.

Contents

Acknowledgements

The editors and publishers wish to thank the authors and the following publishers who have kindly given permission for the use of copyright material.

American Economic Association for articles: Michael C. Jensen (1986), 'Agency Costs of Free Cash Flow, Corporate Finance, and Takeovers', *American Economic Review, Papers and Proceedings*, **76** (2), May, 323–9; Gregg A. Jarrell, James A. Brickley and Jeffry M. Netter (1988), 'The Market for Corporate Control: The Empirical Evidence Since 1980', *Journal of Economic Perspectives*, **2** (1), Winter, 49–68; E. Han Kim and Vijay Singal (1993), 'Mergers and Market Power: Evidence from the Airline Industry', *American Economic Review*, **83** (3), June, 549–69.

Blackwell Publishing Ltd for articles: John J. McConnell and Timothy J. Nantell (1985), 'Corporate Combinations and Common Stock Returns: The Case of Joint Ventures', *Journal of Finance*, **XL** (2), June, 519–36; Randall Morck, Andrei Shleifer and Robert W. Vishny (1990), 'Do Managerial Objectives Drive Bad Acquisitions?', *Journal of Finance*, **XLV** (1), March, 31–48; Tim Opler and Sheridan Titman (1993), 'The Determinants of Leveraged Buyout Activity: Free Cash Flow vs. Financial Distress Costs', *Journal of Finance*, **XLVIII** (5), December, 1985–99; Philip G. Berger and Eli Ofek (1996), 'Bustup Takeovers of Value-Destroying Diversified Firms', *Journal of Finance*, **LI** (4), September, 1175–200.

Elsevier for articles: Michael Bradley, Anand Desai and E. Han Kim (1988), 'Synergistic Gains from Corporate Acquisitions and Their Division Between the Stockholders of Target and Acquiring Firms', *Journal of Financial Economics*, **21** (1), May, 3–40; Steven Kaplan (1989), 'The Effects of Management Buyouts on Operating Performance and Value', *Journal of Financial Economics*, **24** (2), October, 217–54; Paul M. Healy, Krishna G. Palepu and Richard S. Ruback (1992), 'Does Corporate Performance Improve After Mergers?', *Journal of Financial Economics*, **31** (2), April, 135–75; Kathryn L. Dewenter (1995), 'Does the Market React Differently to Domestic and Foreign Takeover Announcements? Evidence from the U.S. Chemical and Retail Industries', *Journal of Financial Economics*, **37** (3), March, 421–41; Julian Franks and Colin Mayer (1996), 'Hostile Takeovers and the Correction of Managerial Failure', *Journal of Financial Economics*, **40** (1), January, 163–81; Susan Chaplinsky, Greg Niehaus and Linda Van de Gucht (1998), 'Employee Buyouts: Causes, Structure, and Consequences', *Journal of Financial Economics*, **48**, 283–332; P. Raghavendra Rau and Theo Vermaelen (1998), 'Glamour, Value and the Post-acquisition Performance of Acquiring Firms', *Journal of Financial Economics*, **49**, 223–53; Myron B. Slovin and Marie E. Sushka (1998), 'The Economics of Parent-subsidiary Mergers: An Empirical Analysis', *Journal of Financial Economics*, **49**, 255–79; Andrei Shleifer and Robert W. Vishny (2003), 'Stock Market Driven Acquisitions', *Journal of Financial Economics*, **70**, 295–311; Gregor Andrade and Erik Stafford (2004), 'Investigating the Economic Role of Mergers', *Journal of Corporate Finance*, **10**, 1–36.

Journal of Financial and Quantitative Analysis for article: John D. Leeth and J. Rody Borg (2000), 'The Impact of Takeovers on Shareholder Wealth during the 1920s Merger Wave', *Journal of Financial and Quantitative Analysis*, **35** (2), June, 217–38.

Journal of Law and Economics, University of Chicago for article: Harry DeAngelo, Linda DeAngelo and Edward M. Rice (1984), 'Going Private: Minority Freezeouts and Stockholder Wealth', *Journal of Law and Economics*, **27** (2), October, 367–401.

RAND for article: John G. Matsusaka (1993), 'Takeover Motives During the Conglomerate Merger Wave', *RAND Journal of Economics*, **24** (3), Autumn, 357–79.

University of Chicago Press for articles: Henry G. Manne (1965), 'Mergers and the Market for Corporate Control', *Journal of Political Economy*, **73**, 110–20; Richard Roll (1986), 'The Hubris Hypothesis of Corporate Takeovers', *Journal of Business*, **59** (2, Part 1), April, 197–216.

John Wiley and Sons Ltd for article: Diane Kowalski Denis (1994), 'Evidence on the Effects of Hostile and Friendly Tender Offers on Employment', *Managerial and Decision Economics*, **15** (4), July/August, 341–57.

Every effort has been made to trace all the copyright holders but if any have been inadvertently overlooked the publishers will be pleased to make the necessary arrangement at the first opportunity.

In addition the publishers wish to thank the Library of Indiana University at Bloomington, USA for their assistance in obtaining these articles.

We dedicate this book with love to our families: Karen, Matt, and Josh, and Diane, Matt, and Ellen

Foreword

Richard Roll

Corporate restructurings are sudden macroscopic changes in corporate form. The classic restructuring is a merger involving two (or sometimes more) formerly independent firms who henceforth operate under a single management team. Other types of restructuring include buyouts, major alterations in assets, defensive and distressed-induced changes in the corporate charter or the corporation's ownership structure.

Scholars have long puzzled about these significant corporate events. Why do they occur? What are the motives of managers and shareholders? How do they affect market value? McConnell and Denis have collected papers from peer-reviewed scholarly journals, almost all published during last two decades, which offer answers to these questions. They divide this literature into two major parts: Volume I covers mergers, tender offers, joint ventures and buyouts. Volume II focuses on events that involve only a single corporation; defensive, internal asset, and distressed restructurings.

In Part I of Volume I, McConnell and Denis have collected papers about mergers and tender offers. These are further subdivided into papers about the motives for corporate combinations, the sources of gains and losses, and two papers on joint ventures. Even the motives are controversial.

Some scholars see corporate combinations as manifestations of the market for corporate control. Of course, stockholders of a single corporation could, in principle, rise up and replace management. This sometimes happens after a proxy contest. But mergers and corporate takeovers appear to be a more effective control mechanism in that they occur more frequently. Others have suggested that takeovers are motivated by managers who are reluctant to pay excess cash out to shareholders, or managers who are infected with overconfidence in their ability to value potential takeover targets, or simply by managers who realize that their own shares are over-inflated by an irrational stock market.

Empirical studies of the value creation or destruction around takeover events have not settled the controversies about motives. McConnell and Denis summarize these findings as follows:

> The bottom line appears to be that regardless of time period, shareholders of target firms benefit from takeovers, while shareholders of acquirers earn returns that are close to zero.

This raises an obvious question about motivation since acquiring firm management, not target firm management, initiates the undertaking. Since acquisitions gain little or nothing for their shareholders, why bother? Possible explanations are (1) takeovers are colossal blunders or (2) managers gain personally even though shareholders do not and shareholders are unable or unwilling to prevent managers from engaging in such activities, perhaps because it does not cost them all that much.

Joint ventures, unlike takeovers, do not result in the elimination of a management team. They are consequently more likely to result from purely synergistic motives. Empirical papers about joint ventures seem to support this idea in that these agreements generally create value. Buyout transactions also have more transparent motives, at least in some cases. For example, buyouts by employee groups can result in better labor relations for both managers and stockholders/employees. Leveraged buyouts and other management buyouts are likely to reduce agency costs.

Part I of Volume II is divided into two sections; Defensive Restructurings and Internal Asset Restructurings.

Defensive restructurings, such as 'anti-takeover' corporate charter amendments, are obviously intended to make it more costly for a potential acquirer to seize control. Is this bad or good for shareholders? The empirical evidence is mixed. Although the probability of a takeover bid might be reduced to some extent, the takeover premium might very well be increased. According to some studies, there is a negative market reaction to the adoption of an anti-takeover device. But other studies have found countervailing evidence.

Internal asset restructurings usually involve 'divesting divisional units in some way.' Generally, the empirical evidence indicates that the market reacts favorably to such events, sometimes by an impressive amount. For example, voluntary corporate liquidations, which eliminate the company entirely, result in announcement period returns averaging 20 per cent. There are many interesting details in these papers about the impact of partial divestitures of assets, equity carveouts, and corporate refocusing on narrower lines of business.

Part II of Volume II is devoted to restructurings prompted by corporate distress. These include comparisons between firms under bankruptcy (Chapter 11) and non-distressed firms. In addition, firms suffering major declines in operating profit are sometimes obliged to sell off assets; the experiences of such firms differ by country. There are some curiosities too, such as the empirical finding that aircraft are sold cheaper by airlines in distress; one might have thought that used aircraft in the same condition would have a market value independent of the seller.

Overall, these two volumes portray a rich scholarly literature about corporate events, a literature that is by no means complete. The articles collected here are probably the most important and enduring among those published since the early 1980s. As such, they are essential reading for future students, scholars, and practitioners in this fascinating and complex field.

Introduction

John J. McConnell and David J. Denis

In this two-book series, we provide a collection of scholarly studies on the topic of corporate restructuring. The papers that we have chosen trace the development of scholarly research on restructuring topics from the earliest seminal contributions through the most recent 'state-of-the-art' contributions. As such, we hope that a reader of these two books will come away with a thorough understanding of the development of critical thinking on corporate restructuring.

The collection comprises research in four general topic areas: corporate combinations, corporate buyouts, asset restructurings, and distressed restructurings. The selected articles highlight the motives for restructuring transactions as well as the wealth consequences of such transactions. The studies are primarily empirical in nature, and study restructuring phenomena in different periods of time and in a variety of market settings.

In this introduction, we provide a brief overview of the selected studies. Our goal in doing so is not to provide readers with a substitute for reading the articles themselves. Rather, we hope to simply introduce readers to the topics that are covered in the series and to provide some sense of how the various articles fit together.

Part I of the first book contains 19 studies that analyze various types of corporate combinations. Section A consists of seven articles that study the motives for mergers and tender offers, Section B consists of ten articles that study the sources of gains and losses in mergers and tender offers, and Section C consists of two articles that study alternative types of corporate combinations.

The articles in Section A put forth a variety of possible motives for mergers and tender offers. Manne (Volume I, Chapter 1) argues that control of a corporation is a valuable asset and that the market for this control provides shareholders with power and protection from inefficient management teams. If a company is poorly managed, its stock price declines, thereby creating a capital gain opportunity for another, more efficient management team. Manne suggests that a great many mergers are the result of the successful workings of this market for corporate control.

While Manne's arguments specifically target managerial inefficiency as the source of economic gains in mergers, Bradley, Desai, and Kim (Volume I, Chapter 2) argue more generally that the combination of two firms can create synergistic gains. These gains might come from more efficient management, but also might arise from economies of scale, improved production techniques, combination of complementary resources, redeployment of certain assets to more profitable uses, exploitation of market power, or any of a number of other value-creating corporate synergies. Consistent with the synergy view of takeovers, Bradley, Desai, and Kim report evidence that successful tender offers produce, on average, a 7.4 per cent increase in the combined wealth of the stockholders of target and acquiring firms.

The papers by Jensen (Volume I, Chapter 3) and Roll (Volume I, Chapter 4) argue that many corporate combinations represent mistakes rather than value-creating transactions. Such mistakes, therefore, represent transfers of wealth from the shareholders of the acquiring firm to those of the target firm. According to Jensen, managers are reluctant to pay out free cash flow – cash flow in excess of that required to fund all positive net present value opportunities – to the company's shareholders because doing so reduces the resources under managerial control. Consequently, managers of firms with large free cash flows and unused borrowing capacity are more likely to undertake value-destroying mergers. Roll (Volume I, Chapter 4) argues that observed takeovers can be the result of managerial hubris. That is, observed takeovers are those in which the bidding company managers overestimate synergistic gains from the corporate combination.

The above articles all assume that financial markets are rational. An alternative approach proposed by Shleifer and Vishny (Volume I, Chapter 5) is that mergers are due to stock market misvaluations of the merging firms. Under their model, managers understand stock market inefficiencies and take advantage of them by undertaking stock-financed mergers when the market overestimates the synergies from the corporate combination.

Finally, the last two articles in Section A empirically explore two other wealth-transfer motives for mergers and tender offers. Kim and Singal (Volume I, Chapter 6) explore the possibility that mergers increase market power and, therefore, lead to wealth transfers from consumers to shareholders. Using a sample of airline mergers between 1985 and 1988, a period characterized by relaxed antitrust policy, Kim and Singal find evidence that airline mergers led to higher airfares. Denis (Volume I, Chapter 7) examines whether successful tender offers result in wealth transfers from employees of the target and acquiring firms. She finds no significant decreases in the combined number of employees of the target and acquiring firm. However, she does report significant reductions in employment for a subset of 'hostile' transactions.

Section B of Part I contains a number of studies that document the wealth effects of takeovers and provide evidence on several potential sources of gains and losses in these transactions. The first three papers in this section document shareholder wealth effects from takeovers during three different merger waves: the 1920s, the 1960s, and the 1980s. Leeth and Borg (Volume I, Chapter 8) study takeovers in the 1920s, a period characterized by few legal constraints on takeovers. They report that during the month of takeover announcement, target shareholders earn abnormal returns of 15.57 per cent, while acquiring shareholders earn abnormal returns of 2.43 per cent. Matsusaka (Volume I, Chapter 9) studies the 1960s, a period characterized by a large number of conglomerate mergers. He reports that shareholders of acquiring firms earned positive abnormal returns of 1.2 per cent in conglomerate mergers and 0.4 per cent in related mergers. Jarrell, Brickley, and Netter (Volume I, Chapter 10) survey the empirical evidence on stockholder wealth effects of takeovers in the 1980s, a period of rapid deregulation, weaker antitrust enforcement, and financing innovations such as junk bonds. They report that shareholders of target firms in the 1980s earned large, positive abnormal returns while shareholders of acquiring firms earned abnormal returns that were statistically insignificant. The bottom line appears to be that, regardless of time period, shareholders of target companies benefit from takeovers, while shareholders of acquirers earn returns that are close to zero.

Jarrell, Brickley, and Netter (Volume I, Chapter 10) also offer insights into the sources of shareholder gains from takeovers. In particular, they summarize the findings of several studies that explore the possibility that shareholder gains are offset by economic losses to other parties including the government through tax reductions. The evidence is consistent with taxes playing a role in explaining merger and acquisition activity. However, there is little evidence that shareholder gains come from economic losses to bondholders or to labor.

Andrade and Stafford (Volume I, Chapter 11) and Healy, Palepu, and Ruback (Volume I, Chapter 12) provide further evidence on the economic role of mergers. Andrade and Stafford (Volume I, Chapter 11) show that mergers are often a response to industry shocks. During expansionary periods, mergers are a means by which companies can expand their capital base. During periods of contraction, mergers help facilitate industry consolidation. The Healy, Palepu, and Ruback (Volume I, Chapter 12) evidence implies that the asset reallocations effected by mergers appear to be efficient. Specifically, merged firms exhibit significant improvements in operating cash flows in the five years following the merger.

Most of the evidence on shareholder wealth effects of takeovers comes from short-run event studies of abnormal returns conducted on samples of US companies. The study by Rau and Vermaelen (Volume I, Chapter 13) extends this evidence by considering longer-run post-acquisition stock returns, while Dewenter (Volume I, Chapter 14) considers whether target shareholder wealth gains differ between domestic and foreign acquisitions. Defining long-run abnormal returns as three-year post-merger stock returns adjusted for size and book-to-market effects, Rau and Vermaelen report that, on average, acquirers in mergers earn significantly negative abnormal returns while acquirers in tender offers earn significantly positive abnormal returns. Because the negative abnormal returns following mergers are driven by the poor performance of low book-to-market firms, Rau and Vermaelen argue that both the market and acquiring firm managers overextrapolate the acquirer's past performance when assessing the desirability of a merger. Dewenter (Volume I, Chapter 14) finds no difference between the shareholder wealth gains of foreign and domestic takeovers. This finding contrasts with that of many prior studies which appear to indicate that foreign acquirers pay higher premia than do domestic acquirers. Unlike prior studies, however, Dewenter's analysis compares takeover premia within an industry. Her findings imply that the prior evidence of higher premia for foreign acquisitions is due to studies having aggregated transactions across multiple industries.

The final three papers in Section B investigate whether shareholder gains and losses in acquisitions are connected in some way to poor managerial performance. Morck, Shleifer, and Vishny (Volume I, Chapter 15) consider whether bad acquisitions – i.e. those that reduce the wealth of acquiring firm shareholders – are a result of managers pursuing their own objectives. They hypothesize that acquisitions might benefit managers by contributing to the long-term growth of the firm, by allowing the manager to diversify the risk of his or her human capital, or by improving his or her job security. If an acquisition offers these private benefits to managers, they may pursue an acquisition even if it reduces shareholder wealth. Consistent with this view, Morck et al. report that acquiring firm returns are lower when acquisitions represent unrelated diversification, when the target is a higher growth firm, and when the prior industry-adjusted performance of the acquiring firm is poor. They conclude that 'bad' acquisitions are driven by managerial objectives.

By contrast, Franks and Mayer (Volume I, Chapter 16) and Berger and Ofek (Volume I, Chapter 17) explore whether takeovers are a byproduct of prior managerial failure and report conflicting findings. Using a sample of hostile takeovers in the UK, Franks and Mayer (Volume I, Chapter 16) report strong evidence of post-takeover board turnover and asset restructuring. However, because they find little evidence of poor pre-bid performance for targets of hostile acquisitions, Franks and Mayer conclude that the market for corporate control does not serve a disciplinary role for poorly performing companies. Berger and Ofek (Volume I, Chapter 17), however, ascribe an important role to takeovers in disciplining managers. They examine a sample of diversified firms and report that the likelihood of the firm being taken over is directly related to a measure of the 'diversification discount,' i.e. the value loss attributed to the firm's diversification strategy. Moreover, those firms with a higher pre-takeover diversification discount are more likely to be broken up following the takeover. From these findings, Berger and Ofek conclude that 'bustup' takeovers are motivated by a desire to recapture value that was previously destroyed by combining business units whose values are greater as stand-alone entities.

While Sections A and B focus on mergers and tender offers, Section C of Part I contains two articles that study alternative types of corporate combinations. McConnell and Nantell (Volume I, Chapter 18) study a sample of joint ventures. Because joint ventures are corporate combinations that join together the management of two or more companies, they represent a useful laboratory for isolating the role of synergy, as opposed to management displacement, in generating stockholder gains from corporate combinations. McConnell and Nantell report that like mergers, joint ventures increase the combined wealth of the participating firm's shareholders. Moreover, the stockholder gains in joint ventures are similar in magnitude to those earned by shareholders of merging companies. McConnell and Nantell interpret their findings as supporting the 'synergy' hypothesis of gains from corporate combinations. Slovin and Sushka (Volume I, Chapter 19) study a sample of parent-subsidiary mergers. These transactions differ from other corporate combinations because of an absence of voluntary arms-length bargaining between the buyer and seller. Because the parent company has control, it initiates the merger and sets the terms. Despite this potential for parent self-dealing, Slovin and Sushka report that minority and parent shareholder returns in these mergers do not differ from those observed in third-party buyouts of parent-controlled subsidiaries. Slovin and Sushka also report a substantial amount of post-merger restructuring in the subsidiaries. These findings are consistent with the view that parent-subsidiary buyouts facilitate the reallocation of subsidiary assets to higher-valued uses.

The articles in Part II of the book examine buyout transactions. These transactions differ from those in Part I in that there is no corporate combination. Rather, the target company's shares are 'bought out' by either the existing management team (sometimes in combination with a third-party investor) or a group of the company's employees. Because there is no combination of the company's assets with those of another company, there can be no synergies. Thus, one question surrounding these transactions is whether they create any value at all. Moreover, because in management buyouts, managers are themselves the purchaser of the shares, there is the potential for managers to structure the buyout in a manner that transfers wealth from the public stockholder to themselves.

The articles by DeAngelo, DeAngelo and Rice (Volume I, Chapter 20) and Kaplan (Volume I, Chapter 21) address these issues in the context of management buyouts. DeAngelo, DeAngelo and Rice report evidence of 30.4 per cent abnormal returns in the two months surrounding management buyout proposals. Their findings indicate that management buyout proposals generate substantial shareholder gains for public stockholders. Kaplan (Volume I, Chapter 21) complements this evidence by reporting substantial operating improvements over the three years following management buyouts. Kaplan notes that these operating improvements could come from a reduction in agency costs following the buyout, from wealth transfers from employees, or from managers initiating buyouts when they possess inside information about future profitability. After conducting further tests, Kaplan concludes that the operating improvements are best explained by the reduced agency cost hypothesis.

During the 1980s a large number of buyout transactions were financed almost exclusively with debt. Although these 'leveraged buyouts' might create value by reducing agency costs of free cash flow, they might also destroy wealth in periods of economic distress. Opler and Titman (Volume I, Chapter 22) examine these issues by studying the characteristics of firms that undertake leveraged buyouts (LBOs). They show that firms undertaking leveraged buyouts tend to have high cash flow and relatively poor growth opportunities (as measured by Tobin's q). These findings are consistent with a free cash flow motivation for LBOs. However, Opler and Titman also find that LBO firms tend to have relatively low research and development expenditures and are less likely to operate in machinery and equipment industries. These findings imply that firms with high potential financial distress costs are deterred from LBO activity.

While most studies of buyouts focus on management-led transactions, a number of US companies have undergone private transactions in which a group of the company's employees purchase a substantial portion of the company's equity. Chaplinsky, Niehaus and Van de Gucht (Volume I, Chapter 23) empirically examine the factors that motivate employee participation by comparing employee buyouts to management ones. Their analysis is consistent with three broad motivations for employee participation in buyouts. First, employee participation can facilitate optimal labor contracts by altering employee incentives and control rights over firm-specific human capital. Second, employee participation can facilitate the financing of the buyout by providing a tax-advantaged source of funds or by reducing cash commitments of employee compensation costs. Third, employee participation can be used by incumbent managers to maintain or enhance their control.

The second book contains two parts. Part I includes 13 studies that analyze various types of asset restructurings. Section A of Part I comprises three articles that study defensive maneuvers by firms that are or may become the targets of takeover attempts by outside parties, while Section B consists of ten articles that examine internal asset restructurings that firms undertake in apparent attempts to improve operating performance.

The defensive maneuvers considered by the articles in Section A include such tactics as divesting valuable assets, acquiring redundant assets, repurchasing shares, or instituting various types of 'anti-takeover' charter amendments. Dann and DeAngelo (Volume II, Chapter 1) analyze four types of restructurings that managers attempt when confronted with an unwelcome takeover offer. These include acquisitions of unrelated companies, divestitures of valuable assets (sometimes termed the 'crown jewels'), share repurchases and share offerings. Among other findings, they report that there is an average decrease in share value of 2 per cent to 3 per cent when such restructurings plans are announced, the median asset restructuring constitutes 23 per cent of the target firm's equity value, 20 per cent to 30 per cent of targets of hostile takeovers undertake such restructurings, and hostile bidders rarely prevail in the face of this type of resistance. Denis and Denis (Volume II, Chapter 2) study leveraged recapitalizations, a specific form of financial restructuring that dramatically increases leverage and concentrates ownership in the hands of managers. The authors report that corporate performance improves and investment expenditures are reduced following a leveraged recapitalization and that share prices increase. Moreover, the gains in share value are positively correlated with the reduction in investment outlays. Although such tactics may reduce the likelihood of a takeover, shareholders gain from the restructuring.

Field and Karpoff (Volume II, Chapter 3) study takeover defenses in firms that undertake initial public offerings (IPOs). They discover that even at the IPO stage, 53 per cent of firms employ some form of takeover defense, including such devices as classified boards of directors, supermajority voting provisions, fair price charter provisions, and 'poison pills.' Such mechanisms are more likely to be employed when management compensation is higher and when management owns a smaller fraction of outstanding shares. They also report that such firms are less likely to be acquired and, when they are, the premium received is about the same as for firms with no defenses in place. They conclude that managers shift the cost of takeover defenses to outside shareholders.

The internal asset restructurings considered in Section B encompass various ways in which corporations streamline their business operations, usually by divesting divisional units. The forms of divestiture include asset sell-offs (i.e., the sale of a division or operating unit to another company), spinoffs (i.e., the establishment of a business unit as a freestanding company with the distribution of shares in the subsidiary to parent company shareholders), and equity carve-outs (i.e., the establishment of a business unit as a freestanding company with the sale of shares to the public).

Allen, Lummer, McConnell and Reed (Volume II, Chapter 4) study a sample of spinoffs that originated as aquisitions at an earlier date. They report that at the time of the acquisition announcement the stock price reaction is negative and statistically significant. By contrast, the stock price reaction to the announcement of the spinoff is positive and significant. Moreover, the spinoff announcement return is negatively correlated with the acquisition announcement period returns. Allen, Lummer, McConnell and Reed interpret this evidence as consistent with the conjecture that the positive returns at the announcement of the spinoff represent, in part, the re-creation of value destroyed at the time of the earlier acquisition. Comment and Jarrell (Volume II, Chapter 5) find that companies that shed assets to become more focused (i.e., reduce their level of diversification) have higher long-term stock returns. Thus, the virtue of some asset divestitures appears to be aimed at creating shareholder value by focusing the firm on a narrower mission. Berger and Ofek (Volume II, Chapter 6) study diversified firms that underwent major refocusing programs during the 1980s and early 1990s. They discover that 22 per cent of the refocusing programs were preceded by a major control event including management turnover, outside shareholder pressure, or financial distress. The refocusing programs typically involved major asset divestitures and were accompanied by significant increases in share price. Further, the share price increases were highest when the divestitures reduced corporate diversification. The conclusion is that focused firms are more valuable than similar diversified firms.

Contingent on the decision to make an asset sale, Schlingemann, Stulz and Walkling (Volume II, Chapter 7) find that the liquidity of the asset market plays a key role in determining which division is divested. The more liquid the market for a category of assets, the more likely that is the division that will be sold. Segments unrelated to the company's core business, poorly performing segments, and smaller segments are also more likely to be divested. Daley, Mehrota and Sivakumar (Volume II, Chapter 8) report that spinoffs of subsidiaries unrelated to the parent company's core business are associated with greater value creation at the announcement date of the spinoff than are spinoffs of related subsidiaries. They find that the operating performance of the parent improves after the spinoff, but that of the subsidiary is unchanged. Gertner, Powers and Scharfstein (Volume II, Chapter 9) examine changes in investment allocations in divisions that are spun off and report that investment in the division is more sensitive to investment opportunities (as measured by industry q) following the spinoff. Vijh

(Volume II, Chapter 10) studies equity carve-outs. He determines that like spinoffs and sell-offs, announcement period stock returns are higher when the carved-out subsidiary is in a different industry segment than the parent, and that the motive most frequently cited for the carve-out is the lack of fit with the parent company.

Erwin and McConnell (Volume II, Chapter 11) study piecemeal voluntary corporate liquidations in which an entire company is split up and ceases to operate. Usually such liquidations involve the piecemeal sale of the company's assets to several different companies. They report that shareholders of the split-up company earn announcement period returns of roughly 20 per cent and that voluntary liquidations are more likely when the stock is closely held by the founding family.

Mulherin and Boone (Volume II, Chapter 12) and Maksimovic and Phillips (Volume II, Chapter 13) share the commonality that each article looks at both acquisitions and divestitures. Mulherin and Boone study these activities over the 1990s and report that both acquisitions and divestitures were associated with significant increases in shareholder value. They also report significant industry clustering in both types of activities. Maksimovic and Phillips examine plant level, as opposed to full firm, acquisitions and sales. They conclude that this market is highly active, involving about 7 per cent of assets in any given year, and that both types of plant-level transfers lead to efficiencies in asset utilization.

Part IV includes seven articles that examine various aspects of liability and asset restructurings by firms in the throes of financial distress. Gilson, John and Lang (Volume II, Chapter 14) compare distressed firms that restructure their debt in bankruptcy with those that restructure outside of Chapter 11 of the US Bankruptcy Code. Firms that restructure privately are likely to have fewer tangible assets and more bank debt that those that enter Chapter 11. Further, shareholders appear to fare better when firms restructure out of court.

Kang and Shivdasani (Volume II, Chapter 15) and Denis and Kruse (Volume II, Chapter 16) study the types of asset restructurings that occur following major declines in operating performance. The first paper considers firms in Japan, while the second considers firms in the US. Both find that declines in performance are followed by major asset sales and reductions in workforce. However, these restructurings are less dramatic in Japan than in the US. A further difference between the two countries is that firms in the US are more likely to be confronted with a challenge to managerial control than their Japanese counterparts.

Using plant level data, Maksimovic and Phillips (Volume II, Chapter 17) study the divestment and investment decisions of firms that file for bankruptcy under Chapter 11 of the US Bankruptcy Code. They find that industry-wide conditions are a more important factor in determining the asset reallocation decisions of bankrupt firms than Chapter 11 status. They conclude that Chapter 11 neither facilitates nor hinders asset reallocation, which implies that bankruptcy *per se* does not increase the cost of financial distress. Thorburn (Volume II, Chapter 18) studies the unique bankruptcy procedure in Sweden in which the assets of bankrupt firms are quickly auctioned off. She finds that such a procedure has lower costs and fewer deviations from the rules of absolute priority than US bankruptcy proceedings. Pulvino (Volume II, Chapter 19) analyzes secondary market prices of aircraft. He documents that aircraft sold by airlines in financial distress sell for lower prices than otherwise similar aircraft sold by healthy airlines. He concludes that distressed asset sales represent a real cost of financial distress. Eberhart, Altman and Aggarwal (Volume II, Chapter 20) analyze stock returns of firms that emerge from Chapter 11. They report that these stocks outperform various risk-adjusted benchmarks over the first year following emergence indicating that firms that reorganize in bankruptcy tend to perform better than investors had expected.

As we noted at the outset, this introduction is intended only as an overview of the topics that are covered in this two-book series. We hope that it has given the reader a general idea of how the chosen articles fit together and that it motivates the reader to pursue a more careful reading of these excellent papers.

Part I
Corporate Combinations

A
Mergers and Tender Offers: Motives

[1]

MERGERS AND THE MARKET FOR CORPORATE CONTROL[1]

HENRY G. MANNE
George Washington University Law School

IN RECENT years many of the traditional economic justifications of our antitrust laws have been seriously questioned. A new sophistication has developed, and economic activities frequently held illegal by the courts are now thought by many to be consistent with our antitrust goals. The rules against tie-ins, vertical mergers, predatory competition, among others, have to a greater or lesser degree had their theoretical foundations considerably weakened. Recently even cartels, the most venerable victim of American antitrust laws, have found their near champion.[2]

One practice, however, remains generally condemned in both the economic literature and the most recent Supreme Court rulings. Mergers among competitors would seem to have no important saving grace. The position has gained considerable legal currency that any merger between competing firms is at least suspect and perhaps per se illegal. The latter result seems especially likely when one of the combining firms already occupies a substantial position in the relevant market. Antitrust problems in the merger field seem more and more to be confined to discussions of relevant product and geographic markets and perhaps to the issue of quantitative substantiality.[3]

Presumably there is still a so-called failing-company defense to an illegal merger charge. The announced justification for this doctrine was that, if indeed the merged company was failing, then it was not actually a competitor in the industry.[4] But there are strong suggestions that even that defense may be unavailable when a large corporation is making the acquisition, or when there is any chance of absorption by a non-competing firm, or when the acquired company has not "failed" enough.[5]

[1] Helpful criticisms and suggestions on this article by Professors Armen A. Alchian, Joseph Aschheim, Donald Dewey, and Joseph P. McKenna are gratefully acknowledged.

A companion article to this one by the same author, entitled "Some Theoretical Aspects of Share Voting," appears in *Columbia Law Review*, LXIV (1964), 1427–45. That article analyzes the strategies available to shareholders when different techniques for taking over control of a corporation are used.

[2] Donald Dewey, "The Economic Theory of Anti-Trust: Science or Religion?" *Virginia Law Review*, L (1964), 413–34. This article also contains references to the other iconoclastic literature (pp. 426–27).

[3] Among the recent articles and cases bearing out this conclusion are the following: Donald Dewey, *op. cit.*; Richard E. Day, "Conglomerate Mergers and the 'Curse of Bigness,'" *North Carolina Law Review*, XLII (1964), 511–66; James A. Rahl, "Current Anti-Trust Developments in the Merger Field," *Anti-Trust Bulletin*, VIII (1963), 493–515; United States v. El Paso Natural Gas Company, 376 U.S. 651 (1964); and United States v. First National Bank and Trust Company of Lexington, 376 U.S. 665 (1964).

[4] International Shoe Company v. Federal Trade Commission, 280 U.S. 291, 294 (1929); but see Derek C. Bok, "Section 7 of the Clayton Act and the Merging of Law and Economics," *Harvard Law Review*, LXXIV (1960), 226–355, esp. p. 340, where concern for the interests in the failing company is argued to be the most likely reason for the doctrine.

[5] Derek C. Bok, *op. cit.*, pp. 339–47; and see cases cited in anonymous comment, "An Updating of the 'Failing Company' Doctrine in the Amended Section 7 Setting," *Michigan Law Review*, LXI (1963), 566–83.

There is also a "solely for investment" defense to Clayton Act charges. This appears as an explicit proviso in the third paragraph of Section 7, 15 U.S.C.A. sec. 18 (1962). But the famous du Pont–

There is general agreement among economists that the courts' approach to horizontal mergers is correct.[6] Professor Donald Dewey, who appears slightly regretful about the severe treatment of mergers by our courts and administrative agencies, concedes that no important economies can be attained through a merger which cannot be gained either by internal growth or, at worst, by a cartel, if that were legal. But Dewey is certainly not as severe in his personal indictment of horizontal mergers as most other economists. He has argued that most mergers "have virtually nothing to do with either the creation of market power or the realization of scale economies. They are merely a civilized alternative to bankruptcy or the voluntary liquidation that transfers assets from falling to rising firms."[7]

Consistent with his alternative-to-bankruptcy explanation of mergers, Dewey points out that, "[i]f the capital market were perfect and a merger conferred no monopoly power, a rising firm would be indifferent between the two forms of expansion."[8] Thus a rapidly expanding industry with a relatively short life cycle of its firms would be characterized by substantial external growth of successful firms. Mergers then would "most commonly indicate not the decline of competition but its undoubted vigor."[9]

Dewey's argument is, however, only a partial redemption of mergers, since a great many have occurred in industries in which the life cycle of firms is not as short as in the southern textile industry, which he mentions as his example. Further, Dewey's defense of mergers seems to be limited to those cases in which bankruptcy or liquidation is imminent. But, if a merger can be justified at this stage of the firm's life, presumably it is also desirable before bankruptcy becomes imminent in order to avoid that eventuality. If, as Dewey suggests, mergers actually are superior to bankruptcy as a method of "shifting assets from fall-

G. M. case, United States v. E. I. Du Pont de Nemours and Company, 353 U.S. 586 (1957), seems to have very substantially weakened the force of this proviso. Also see Swift and Co. v. F.T.C., 8 Fed. 2d 595, 599, reversed on other grounds, 272 U.S. 554 (1925), where it is stated: "It would be difficult to conceive of any case where one corporation purchased all the stock of its competitor solely for investment. Such a case would be a rare one."

There was once thought to be an illegal purpose requirement for convictions under the Sherman Act. See Eugene V. Rostow, "Monopoly under the Sherman Act: Power or Purpose?" *Illinois Law Review*, XLIII (1949), 745–92. But recent Supreme Court decisions in the merger field have left little vitality to that notion. Cf. United States v. First National Bank and Trust Company of Lexington, 376 U.S 665, 669 (1964).

[6] See George J. Stigler, "Mergers and Preventive Anti-Trust Policy," *Pennsylvania Law Review*, CIV (1955), 176–84 (Stigler too recognizes the possibility that some mergers may increase competition, but he finds it "most uncommon" [p. 181]); M. A. Adelman, "The Anti-Merger Act, 1950–60," *American Economic Review*, LI (May, 1961), 236–54 ("The horizontal elements of mergers . . . have been treated severely and—if maintaining competition is the object—rationally" [p. 238]).

[7] "Mergers and Cartels: Some Reservations about Policy," *Market Economic Review*, LI (May, 1961), 257. Dewey analyzed four relatively unimportant cases of scale economies that can be realized only through a consolidation, but he concluded, in substantial agreement with Stigler and Adelman, "that the present experiment discouraging growth by mergers should be continued" with a ban in any industry not generally considered a good example of workable competition (p. 261).

Jesse W. Markham has remarked that some mergers are the "means by which some entrepreneurs make their exit from the industry, selling their undepreciated assets to other entrepreneurs. . . . Since 1930 most mergers appear to have been of the ordinary business variety in that they had neither monopoly nor promotional gains as their objective" ("Survey of the Evidence and Findings on Mergers," in *Business Concentration and Price Policy* [New York: National Bureau of Economic Research, 1955], p. 181). He concluded that "while some mergers impair a competitive enterprise system, others may be an integral part of it" (p. 182).

[8] "Mergers and Cartels . . . ," *op. cit.*, p. 257.

[9] *Ibid.*

ing to rising firms," and if mergers were completely legal, we should anticipate relatively few actual bankruptcy proceedings in any industry which was not itself contracting. The function so wastefully performed by bankruptcies and liquidations would be economically performed by mergers at a much earlier stage of the firm's life.

THE CORPORATE-CONTROL MARKET

The conventional approach to a merger problem takes corporations merely as decision-making units or firms within the classical market framework. This approach dictates a ban on many horizontal mergers almost by definition. The basic proposition advanced in this paper is that the control of corporations may constitute a valuable asset; that this asset exists independent of any interest in either economies of scale or monopoly profits; that an active market for corporate control exists; and that a great many mergers are probably the result of the successful workings of this special market.

Basically this paper will constitute an introduction to a study of the market for corporation control. The emphasis will be placed on the antitrust implications of this market, but the analysis to follow has important implications for a variety of economic questions. Perhaps the most important implications are those for the alleged separation of ownership and control in large corporations. So long as we are unable to discern any control relationship between small shareholders and corporate management, the thrust of Berle and Means's famous phrase remains strong. But, as will be explained below, the market for corporate control gives to these shareholders both power and protection commensurate with their interest in corporate affairs.

A fundamental premise underlying the market for corporate control is the existence of a high positive correlation between corporate managerial efficiency and the market price of shares of that company.[10] As an existing company is poorly managed—in the sense of not making as great a return for the shareholders as could be accomplished under other feasible managements—the market price of the shares declines relative to the shares of other companies in the same industry or relative to the market as a whole. This phenomenon has a dual importance for the market for corporate control.

In the first place, a lower share price facilitates any effort to take over high-paying managerial positions. The com-

[10] The claim of a positive correlation between managerial efficiency and the market price of shares would seem at first blush to raise an empirical question. In fact, however, the concept of corporate managerial efficiency, with its overtones of an entrepreneurial function, is one for which there are no objective standards. But there are compelling reasons, apart from empirical data, for believing that this correlation exists. Insiders those who have the most reliable information about corporate affairs, are strongly motived financially to perform a kind of arbitrage function for their company's stock. That is, given their sense of what constitutes efficient management, they will cause share prices to rise or decline in accordance with that standard.

The contention is often made that stock-market prices are not accurate gauges, since far more trades take place without reliable information than with it. But there is reason to believe that intelligence rather than ignorance ultimately determines the course of individual share prices. Stock-market decisions tend to be of the one-out-of-two-alternatives variety, such as buy or not buy, hold or sell, or put or call. To the extent that decisions on these questions are made by shareholders or potential shareholders operating without reliable information, over a period of time the decisions will tend to be randomly distributed and the effect will therefore be neutral. Decisions made by those with a higher degrees of certainty will to that extent not meet a canceling effect since they will not be made on a random basis. Over some period of time it would seem that the average market price of a company's shares must be the "correct" one.

pensation from these positions may take the usual forms of salary, bonuses, pensions, expense accounts, and stock options. Perhaps more important, it may take the form of information useful in trading in the company's shares; or, if that is illegal, information may be exchanged and the trading done in other companies' shares. But it is extremely doubtful that the full compensation recoverable by executives for managing their corporations explains more than a small fraction of outsider[11] attempts to take over control. Take-overs of corporations are too expensive generally to make the "purchase" of management compensation an attractive proposition.[12]

It is far more likely that a second kind of reward provides the primary motivation for most take-over attempts. The market price of shares does more than measure the price at which the normal compensation of executives can be "sold" to new individuals. Share price, or that part reflecting managerial efficiency, also measures the potential capital gain inherent in the corporate stock. The lower the stock price, relative to what it could be with more efficient management, the more attractive the take-over becomes to those who believe that they can manage the company more efficiently. And the potential return from the successful take-over and revitalization of a poorly run company can be enormous.[13]

Additional leverage in this operation can be obtained by borrowing the funds with which the shares are purchased, although American commercial banks are generally forbidden to lend money for this purpose. A comparable advantage can be had from using other shares rather than cash as the exchange medium. Given the fact of special tax treatment for capital gains, we can see how this mechanism for taking over control of badly run corporations is one of the most important "get-rich-quick" opportunities in our economy today.

But the greatest benefits of the take-over scheme probably inure to those least conscious of it. Apart from the stock market, we have no objective standard of managerial efficiency. Courts, as indicated by the so-called business-judgment rule, are loath to second-guess business decisions or remove directors from office. Only the take-over scheme provides some assurance of competitive efficiency among corporate managers and thereby affords strong protection to the interests of vast numbers of small, non-controlling shareholders. Compared to this mechanism, the efforts of the SEC and the courts to protect shareholders through the development of a fiduciary duty concept and the shareholder's derivative suit seem small indeed. It is true that sales by dissatisfied shareholders are necessary to trigger the mechanism and that these shareholders may suffer considerable losses. On the other hand, even greater capital losses are prevented by the existence of a competitive market for corporate control.[14]

11 "Outsider" here refers to anyone not presently controlling the affairs of the corporation, even though it may include one or more individuals on the corporation's board of directors.

12 To the extent that executive compensation increases with higher share prices, the take-over is most attractive at the time when it is also most expensive. Indeed, the danger of a take-over may account for managers' voluntarily decreasing their compensation when the company's share price is down.

13 The clearest modern illustration is probably furnished by Louis Wolfson's successful venture into Montgomery Ward. For details of this and other large stock price gains associated with corporation "raids" see David Karr, *Fight for Control* (New York: Ballantine Books, 1956).

14 Unfortunately the suppression of this market would be the consequence of proposals made by sev-

There are several mechanisms for taking over the control of corporations. The three basic techniques are the proxy fight, direct purchase of shares, and the merger. The costs, practical difficulties, and legal consequences of these approaches vary widely. The selection of one or another or some combination of these techniques frequently represents a difficult strategy decision. An attempt will be made in this paper to analyze some of the considerations involved in a selection of one device over another.

PROXY FIGHTS

The most dramatic and publicized of the take-over devices is the proxy fight; it is also the most expensive, the most uncertain, and the least used of the various techniques. Indeed it is somewhat difficult to describe the necessary conditions under which a proxy fight rather than some other take-over form will be indicated. At first blush, the proxy fight appears to be inexpensive since one does not have to own a large number of shares (or for that matter any shares) in order to wage a fight. But this fact is most relevant when the take-over is for the purpose of gaining the incumbents' compensation. If the outsider wants capital gains, he will be interested in owning more, not fewer, shares. This suggests that proxy fights will be relatively more often used when the issue is not one of management policies but of distribution of insiders' compensation.[15]

Even as a device for settling internal power struggles, actual proxy fights constitute only a small percentage of threatened fights.[16] The parties will generally prefer to negotiate a settlement in accordance with their respective strengths than incur the costs of soliciting proxies. The more reliable the information about relative strengths available, the more will settlement be likely to occur. This suggests that proxy fights will be relatively more common when there is widespread distribution of the company's shares than when there are relatively large holdings.

In a number of cases the outsider would probably like to own more shares and take over control without waging or threatening a proxy fight. But if he is unable to accumulate sufficient capital to purchase control directly, he may settle for half a loaf. In effect he indicates his willingness to share the capital-gain potential with all other shareholders in exchange for enough of their votes to put him into control.

When a proxy fight is announced, the shares tend to rise in price, reflecting a rise in both the market value of the vote and the discounted value of potential gain in the underlying share interest if

---

eral writers in the field. For a review and a criticism of this literature see Henry G. Manne, "The 'Higher Criticism' of the Modern Corporation," *Columbia Law Review*, LXII (1962), 399–432. For another defense of this market see Harry G. Johnson, *The Canadian Quandary* (Toronto: McGraw-Hill Book Co., 1963), pp. xvii–xviii.

[15] The courts draw a similar distinction for purposes of determining when contestants in a proxy fight may recover their expenses from the corporate treasury. Generally they may recover if the contest is found to be one of policy rather than a "purely personal power contest" (Rosenfeld v. Fairchild Engine & Airplane Corp., 309 N.Y. 168, 129 N.E. 2d 291 [1955]). It does not seem to be too difficult, however, to establish the existence of a "policy" controversy to the court's satisfaction.

[16] In the SEC's fiscal year 1962 seventeen companies were involved in proxy contests, while a total of 253 persons, both management and non-management, filed statements as participants. The respective figures for 1961 were thirty-two proxy contests and 463 participant filings. Many non-management filings are multiple; that is, several people are involved in the same fight. But no breakdown beyond the total number of participants is available. Therefore, it is impossible to prove the point made in the text from published data. See *27th and 28th Annual Reports* (Washington: Securities and Exchange Commission, 1961 and 1962).

the outsider wins.[17] Other outsiders will find it in their interest to retain their shares or purchase shares, to vote for the outsider seeking control, and to share in the capital appreciation. It may be cheaper to elicit the support of these voters through expenditures on persuasion than through outright purchase of the shares. But to the outsider seeking control, every voter represents another person with whom he must share the potential gain resulting from his more efficient management. These voters are analogous to, or substitutes for, the capital or credit with which the outsider would otherwise purchase control directly.

Proxy-fight expenses have always included direct expenses of mailings, advertising, telephone calls, and visits to large shareholders. But since the Securities Exchange Act of 1934, the cost of waging a proxy fight has probably increased substantially. Prior to the act, the proxy system operated largely through broker intermediaries acting as full agents for the beneficial owners of the shares. To the brokers was delegated not merely the ministerial job of voting but the more important responsibility of deciding how to vote. That practice has been largely replaced because of the SEC philosophy that the proxy system should duplicate actual meetings of shareholders as closely as possible. Thus, today, "giving a proxy" is really tantamount to voting. And, since the shareholder himself is voting, it is also felt that he should be fully and truthfully informed about all aspects of the corporation's affairs. This has tremendously increased the cost of soliciting proxies. But while the incumbents finance the bulk of their proxy solicitation expenses from corporate funds, the outsider will have this advantage only if he wins.[18]

DIRECT PURCHASE OF SHARES

The second mechanism for taking over control of a corporation is the direct purchase of the requisite number of shares of the corporations. There are several techniques that may be used in the direct

[17] See Henry G. Manne, *op. cit.*, pp. 410–13. It is possible, of course, for the vote price to be rising while the market value of the underlying investment interest is declining, though this would seem to be uncommon.

[18] The SEC rules on proxy solicitations have aided the insiders in unexpected and curious ways. Outsiders in a proxy fight are not privy to the particulars of corporate information as are the insiders, so they must frequently "guess" why the company is not doing as well as it should. These "guesses" will take the form of broad accusations and innuendoes directed at the incumbents. Outsiders would like the opportunity to include in their proxy solicitation such general statements as "the incumbents are wasting corporate assets"; "the incumbents are paying themselves fraudulently high salaries"; or "the officers of the company have been negligent in failing to acquire new opportunities for the corporation." The SEC generally refuses to allow such statements to be mailed to shareholders unless the insurgents can prove the truthfulness of the allegations. Frequently there is no way the insurgents can find that proof, short of discovery proceedings in a suit, though they might in all good faith suspect the facts alleged. Therefore, the practice has developed of filing shareholder derivative suits when a proxy fight is decided upon. Then the solicitation materials may legally say, "A shareholder's derivative suit is presently pending in the Federal District Court for the Southern District of New York charging the officers and directors with waste of corporate assets"; or "a suit to force the officers to pay back part of their salaries has been filed by a shareholder in Delaware"; etc.

Not only has the Securities Exchange Act increased the cost of waging a proxy fight because of the additional materials that must be cleared through the SEC, but it has also increased uncertainty because of the panoply of SEC regulations. For instance, the Chicago and North Western Railroad's successful fight against the Union Pacific's first bid for control of the Rock Island Railroad was recently voided on the grounds, among others, that unsolicited advice by a broker to his customer advising acceptance of the C. & N.W.'s offer constituted an illegal solicitation of proxies (Union Pacific Railroad Company v. Chicago and North Western Railway Company, 226 F. Supp. 400 [N.D., Ill., 1964]).

purchase of shares. The most obvious is outright purchase on the open market of the requisite percentage of shares.[19] The outsider might also try to buy the shares from large individual owners, thus preserving secrecy and allowing negotiation on price. Finally, he may make a bid for tenders, that is, a request that shareholders make an offer to sell their shares to him at a certain price, usually above the market. This last form of direct purchase is most apposite when the shares are widely held and there is a chance of a fast increase in market price if the news spreads that there is a heavy buyer in the market for the company's shares. A tender bid is usually stated to be effective only if a minimum percentage of shares is offered at the announced price. Also, the bid will ordinarily be for less than 100 per cent of the shares in order to avoid the problem of many individual shareholders trying to be the sole hold-out. In practice, private negotiation for large blocks of shares may be combined with either open-market purchases or a tender bid.

There are few serious legal problems with any of the direct purchase techniques. In fact, about the only one which has arisen with any regularity in recent years results from Professor Adolf A. Berle's contention that control is a corporate asset.[20] The implication of this notion is that any premium received by an individual for a sale of control belongs in equity to all of the shareholders. As a general proposition, the courts have refused to follow this thesis; and there are numerous judicial statements to the effect that one may claim a premium for control.[21]

A number of legal writers, following Berle, continue to press for a rule of equality in share purchase price when an outsider buys control in a corporation.[22] The economic results of such a rule could be most unfortunate. Many holders of

[19] This percentage may range from less than 51 per cent if the purchaser is only interested in establishing a foundation for a proxy fight; to 51 per cent when only simple control is desired; to 66⅔ or 75 per cent, when state law requires that percentage for approval of a merger or reorganization; to 80 per cent, the figure required for consolidation of income statements under the Internal Revenue Code as well as for tax-free reorganizations; to 90 per cent, the figure required for simplified mergers of subsidiaries into parent companies in Delaware (95 per cent in New York); or 100 per cent if no minority interests are wanted.

[20] Adolf A. Berle and Gardiner C. Means, *The Modern Corporation and Private Property* (New York: Macmillan Co., 1933), p. 244; Adolf A. Berle, "'Control' in Corporate Law," *Columbia Law Review*, LVIII (1958), 1212–25, esp. 1221.

[21] The difficult cases have been those in which control carried with it peculiar advantages not normally assumed to be part of the standard compensation of corporate managers. The problem is illustrated by the now classic case of Perlman v. Feldmann, 219 F. 2d 172 (2d Cir., 1955), in which only a controlling block of shares was purchased, but at a price reflecting the value of the right to allocate the company's steel production to the purchaser at a time when quasi-official price controls existed. The court found the control seller liable to the other shareholders for a part of the premium received over the normal market price of the shares. The most convincing factor, not emphasized by the court, was that the company had probably been receiving a full free-market price for its steel, with the difference over the controlled price taken in the form of interest-free loans and guaranteed future orders. Indications were that the new controllers would sell to themselves at the "quasi-legal" price and discontinue these other valuable practices. Thus the premium paid for the control block of shares was given partly in exchange for a right more appropriately thought of as belonging equally to each share than to the control group. That is, if a "gray-market" profit was to be made, it should go to all the shareholders. The court was explicit, however, that the seller could retain that part of the premium received for control not covering the power to allocate steel.

[22] Richard W. Jennings, "Trading in Corporate Control," *California Law Review*, XLIV (1956), 1–39; and Noyes Leech, "Transactions in Corporate Control," *University of Pennsylvania Law Review*, CIV (1956), 725–839. For a sharply opposing viewpoint see Wilbur G. Katz, "The Sale of Corporate Control," *Chicago Bar Record*, XXXVIII (1957), 376–80; also Alfred Hill, "The Sale of Controlling Shares," *Harvard Law Review*, LXX (1957), 986–1039.

control blocks of shares would refuse to sell at a share price which did not pay them a premium at least sufficient to compensate them for the loss of net values presently being received from their position in the corporation. If all non-controlling shareholders must accordingly be paid a premium over the market price of their shares, then in a substantial number of cases the purchaser will not conclude the bargain. This further suggests that, if control is securely held in one block, the "market price" of traded shares is the price for an underlying share interest without an aliquot portion of control. That is, if one person owns 51 per cent of the shares of a company, nothing will be paid for the vote attached to the other shares,[23] no matter how actively the shares may be traded on the market. The less securely control is held in one block, the more likely are non-controlling shareholders to participate in the "premium," and the less will an outsider be willing to pay one shareholder for control. Both proxy fights and competitive tender bids are more likely to occur under these conditions, since each of them gives shareholders the power to sell their votes at a premium.

MERGERS

The third major mechanism for taking over control of the corporation is the merger. Here, by definition, the acquiring concern will be a corporation and not an individual, and the medium of exchange used to buy control will typically be shares of the acquiring company rather than cash. Another major difference between the merger and other take-over forms is that, almost without exception, a merger requires the explicit approval of those already in control of the corporation.[24] And most statutes require more than a simple majority vote by shareholders to effectuate a merger. If the merger occurs after an acquisition of shares in a tender bid, then the tender bid and not the merger is the actual mechanism for changing control.

The requirement of management's approval for a merger generates some peculiar results. Generally speaking, managers' incentives and interests coincide with those of their shareholders in every particular except one: they have no incentive, as managers, to buy management services for the company at the lowest possible price.[25] Even if the market for corporate control is working perfectly, so long as the cost to the corporation of the incumbent managers' inefficiency is below the cost to an outsider of taking over control, the insiders will remain secure in the positions with protected high salaries.[26]

In the case of tender bids, as we have seen, a premium for control may be paid; and in the proxy fight situation, in one

[23] This holds true only to the extent that 51 per cent is the relevant majority. If a higher percentage is necessary for some purpose, minority votes will have some value so long as the requisite percentage is not already controlled.

[24] There is a slight possibility that outsiders might be able to force a merger vote by shareholders under the Securities Exchange Act's "Stockholder's Proposal" Rule, although the SEC seems to take the position that such a proposal may only be advisory, not mandatory, on the board, if passed. See Louis Loss, *Securities Regulation* (Boston: Little, Brown & Co., 1961), p. 908.

[25] To the extent that the same individuals are also shareholders, their motivation will reflect a conflict. If their ownership interest is great enough, they may sacrifice the emoluments of management in order to improve their position as shareholders. The decision will simply reflect the greater of the two conflicting interests.

[26] This may furnish some proof for the notion that executive compensation is a function of size. If the cost of taking over control is a function of the number of shareholders, as it certainly is in the case of proxy fights, it is likely that managers may be able to claim larger compensation to the extent of the higher cost to outsiders of buying control.

sense at least, the premium is paid in the form of expenditures necessary to persuade shareholders to vote a certain way. But the merger has considerable cost advantages over the other two forms of take-over, not the least being the ability to use shares rather than cash as the purchasing medium.

The shareholders should ordinarily be willing to accept any offer of a tax-free exchange of new marketable shares worth more than their old shares. But the managers are in a position to claim almost the full market value of control, since they have it in their power to block the merger by voting against it.[27] When we find incumbents recommending a control change, it is generally safe to assume that some side payment is occurring.

Side payments are often not simple transactions at law because of the rule that directors and officers may not sell their positions shorn of the share interest necessary to insure a transfer of control.[28] The most obvious kind of side payment to managers is a position within the new structure either paying a salary or making them privy to valuable market information.[29] This arrangement, easily established with mergers, can look like normal business expediency, since the argument can always be made that the old management provides continuity and a link with the past experience of the corporation.

There is still another very important reason why mergers may be more desirable than proxy fights or take-over bids as a way of operating in the corporate-control market. This is a market in which reliable information about valuable opportunities will be extremely difficult to discover. For reasons already mentioned, the corporate insiders will generally have no incentive to advertise this kind of information. Blatant cases will, of course, be evident from casual observation of industrial affairs and the stock market.[30]

The great problem in the corporate-control market is finding reliable information about new opportunities. There have generally been a few individual operators in this market, and perhaps they have found the more obvious cases of bad management. But to guarantee effective competitition in the market for corporate control, it seems clear that corporations must be allowed to function therein. Managers of a competing firm, unlike free-wheeling individual participants in the market for corporate control, almost automatically know a great deal of the kind of information crucial to a take-over decision. Careful analysis of cost conditions in their own firm and the market price of shares of other corporations in the same industry will provide information that can be relied upon with some degree of confidence.

Since, in a world of uncertainty, profitable transactions will be entered into

[27] The greater the shareholdings of mangement, the more likely they are to approve a merger offer with little or no side payment.

[28] Essex Universal Corp. v. Yates 305 F.2d (2d Cir., 1962).

[29] See, e.g., Smith v. The Good Music Station, 129 A.2d 242 (Del. Ch. 1957), and Borak v. J. I. Case Co., 317 Fed. 2d 838, at 844 (7th Cir., 1963), aff'd 377 U.S. 426 (1964). There are no reported cases of differential numbers of shares being offered controlling and non-controlling shareholders in a merger. Such an arrangement may be illegal under state statutes, and it is not likely to receive the high-majority-share vote required for most mergers.

[30] The most obvious example is that of a corporation whose total assets in liquidation would be worth more than the aggregate market value of all of its shares. This situation can continue to exist only because no individual shareholder believes there is any way of claiming the premium, since the managers will take no step toward liquidation and there is no indication that the corporation will not continue to be badly run. Perhaps the classic case of this sort was the take-over by Louis Wolfson of the Capital Transit Corporation. For this and other examples see Karr, *op. cit.*, p. 150.

more often by those whose information is relatively more reliable,[31] it should not surprise us that mergers within the same industry have been a principal form of changing corporate control. Reliable information is often available to suppliers and customers as well. Thus many vertical mergers may be of the control take-over variety rather than of the "foreclosure of competitors" or scale-economies type. Undoubtedly many more mergers, both horizontal and vertical, would have occurred but for our antitrust laws. The managers of corporations have considerable incentive to exploit such opportunities for their corporation, just as they are motivated to find any good new investment opportunity. And there are both legal and practical barriers to the individuals' utilizing such opportunities for themselves.

CONCLUSIONS

Mergers seem in many instances to be the most efficient of the three devices for corporate take-overs. Consequently, they are of considerable importance for the protection of individual non-controlling shareholders and are desirable from a general welfare-economics point of view. Certainly they are more desirable than the increased number of bankruptcies that would undoubtedly ensue if this avenue of taking over control were totally closed.

This is not to suggest that the antitrust norm of competition in the product market need be entirely sacrificed to the norm of competition in the market for corporate control. Rather it points up some of the serious problems with current antitrust doctrine. The market for corporate control implies a number of important advantages which must be compared to those existing in present antitrust enforcement. Among the advantages of the former, as we have seen, are a lessening of wasteful bankruptcy proceedings, more efficient management of corporations, the protection afforded non-controlling corporate investors, increased mobility of capital, and generally a more efficient allocation of resources.

The greatest difficulty in assessing the proper role for the market for corporate control comes in the area of horizontal mergers, where, as previously indicated, this market may operate most effectively.[32] It may be that, so long as entry into an industry is kept open, there is no reason at all for rules against mergers, at least short of a monopolization charge under Section 2 of the Sherman Act. It is extremely unlikely, however, that Congress or the courts would ever adopt such a rule.

Far more likely is an *ad hoc* recognition of the importance of the market for corporate control in individual cases.[33] Courts or agencies might begin to look at such factors as the average life cycle of firms in the industry, the amount of total new investment in the industry, the condition of the acquired firms in terms of both financial and managerial strength, the number of bankruptcies in the industry, and the amount of proxy-fight and tender-bid activity. These fac-

[31] Cf. H. B. Malmgren, "Information, Expectations, and the Theory of the Firm," *Quarterly Journal of Economics*, LXXIX (1961), 399–421; and George J. Stigler, "The Economics of Information," *Journal of Political Economy*, LXIX (1961), 213–25.

[32] The case for a free market in corporate control as between supplier and customer firms seems quite strong, since the arguments in favor of present anti-merger policy are perhaps weakest there. See Robert Bork, "Vertical Integration and the Sherman Act: The Legal History of an Economic Misconception," *University of Chicago Law Review*, XXII (1954), 157–201.

[33] This might be done either through the resurrection of the "business-purpose" doctrine or, in Clayton Act cases, by beefing up the "solely-for-investment" proviso. See n. 5 above.

tors would then have to be weighed on the scales with the more traditional approach in terms of number of firms in the industry, concentration ratios, size of the acquiring firm, and its acquisitions history. But no longer does the tendency to hold most mergers illegal per se seem justified.

One real problem will be in devising statistical methods for distinguishing mergers motivated by a quest for monopoly profit from those merely trying to establish more efficient management in poorly run companies. But if the theoretical aspects of these transactions are well enough understood, this should not be insuperable. There may be different effects on the prices of shares depending on the motive behind the merger. In the normal merger for acquisition of control, something will be paid by the acquiring company for the control opportunity. Since this factor does not figure largely in the market price of even badly run companies until the possibility of a takeover is known, the exchange ratio in the merger will appear to be too favorable to the acquired company, judged by the relative premerger announcement prices. The price of the shares of the acquiring company in such a merger should then tend to decrease and those of the acquired company to increase upon the announcement of the merger. If, on the other hand, the merger is motivated by a quest for market power, or by economies of scale available to both corporations, then the price of stock of each company should increase on the announcement of the merger terms. The first of these two results conforms to what seems most frequently to occur when mergers are announced, though no data are presently available on this subject.[34] The study of the economics of the market for corporate control is still in its infancy.

[34] A study of the effect of mergers on stock prices has been completed by the staff of the Subcommittee on Anti-Trust and Monopoly of the Senate Judiciary Committee. That study was unavailable at the time of writing this article.

Another possible approach to proof in this area is to determine if actual changes in the management personnel ultimately follow the merger. In mergers for market power, there is little reason to believe that this will occur very quickly; whereas, if the position is in the nature of a side payment, as it would be if the merger was motivated more by the control potential, we might anticipate somewhat earlier efforts to "ease out" the old managers of the acquired company.

[2]

Journal of Financial Economics 21 (1988) 3–40. North-Holland

SYNERGISTIC GAINS FROM CORPORATE ACQUISITIONS AND THEIR DIVISION BETWEEN THE STOCKHOLDERS OF TARGET AND ACQUIRING FIRMS*

Michael BRADLEY

University of Michigan, Ann Arbor, MI 48109, USA

Anand DESAI

University of Florida, Gainesville, FL 32611, USA

E. Han KIM

University of Michigan, Ann Arbor, MI 48109, USA

Received August 1984, final version received December 1987

This paper documents that a successful tender offer increases the combined value of the target and acquiring firms by an average of 7.4%. We also provide a theoretical analysis of the process of competition for control of the target and empirical evidence that competition among bidding firms increases the returns to targets and decreases the returns to acquirers, that the supply of target shares is positively sloped, and that changes in the legal/institutional environment of tender offers have had no impact on the total (percentage) synergistic gains created but have significantly affected their division between the stockholders of the target and acquiring firms.

1. Introduction

There is empirical evidence that corporate acquisitions effected through tender offers are wealth-increasing transactions for the stockholders of both the target and acquiring firms [Dodd and Ruback (1977) and Bradley (1980)]. Moreover, Bradley, Desai, and Kim (1983) show that these gains are not due to the market's reassessment of previously undervalued securities. They docu-

*This paper is a substantially revised version of earlier drafts entitled 'Specialized Resources and Competition in the Market for Corporate Control' (September 1982) and 'Determinants of the Wealth Effects of Corporate Acquisitions via Tender Offers: Theory and Evidence' (September 1983). We have received valuable comments and criticism from participants of finance workshops at Buffalo, Berkeley–Stanford, Concordia, Indiana, Michigan, Minnesota, Northwestern, NYU, Ohio State, Purdue, Rutgers, SMU, Toronto, UCLA, USC, VPI, Washington University, Wharton, and Wisconsin/Madison. In addition we would like to thank Cliff Ball, Robert Comment, Gregg Jarrell, Stanley Kon, Richard Leftwich (a referee of earlier drafts), John McConnell, Philip Perry, Myron Scholes, an anonymous referee of the most recent draft and, especially, Michael Jensen (the editor) for their helpful comments. This research was supported by Michigan Business School Summer Research Grants.

0304-405X/88/$3.50

ment that the positive revaluation of the target's shares is permanent only if the offer is successful, i.e., only if the resources of the two firms are combined. This evidence is consistent with the synergy theory of tender offers, which posits that the acquisition of control over the target enables the acquirer to redeploy the combined assets of the two firms toward higher-valued uses.

None of the above studies, however, documents the magnitude of the synergistic gains that result from successful acquisitions achieved through tender offers. Indeed, whether or not such acquisitions result in synergistic gains is still a contentious issue in the literature. For example, Roll (1986) has proposed the 'Hubris Hypothesis', which posits that the gains to target shareholders represent wealth transfers from acquiring firms' shareholders and not necessarily synergistic gains. To test this hypothesis, it is necessary to measure synergistic gains using matched pairs of target and acquiring firms. None of the earlier studies impose this requirement on their samples.

In this paper, we estimate the magnitude of the synergistic gains, using the revaluation of the combined wealth of target-firm and acquiring-firm shareholders as a basis. We also examine the factors that determine the division of these gains between the stockholders of the two firms and document how the division and the total gains created have changed with the changing environment of the tender offer process.

This paper is organized as follows. In section 2 we estimate the synergistic gains created by successful tender offers. In section 3 we analyze how these gains are divided between the stockholders of the target and acquiring firms. Section 3 also summarizes our analysis of competition among bidding firms, which is presented more fully in the appendix. We present our empirical results on competition and the division of gains in section 4. A summary and concluding remarks are presented in section 5.

2. Synergistic gains

2.1. Definition of synergy

We assume that a tender offer is an attempt by the bidding firm to exploit a profit opportunity created by a change in economic conditions. This change may be the result of an exogenous change in supply and/or demand, technological innovations, or purposeful investments by the bidding firm. The value created by the combination may result from more efficient management, economies of scale, improved production techniques, the combination of complementary resources, the redeployment of assets to more profitable uses, the exploitation of market power, or any number of value-creating mechanisms that fall under the general rubric of corporate synergy. We define the total synergistic gain from a successful tender offer as the sum of the change in the wealth of the stockholders of the target and acquiring firms:

$$\Delta \Pi = \Delta W_{\mathrm{T}} + \Delta W_{\mathrm{A}}, \tag{1}$$

where

$\Delta\Pi$ = total synergistic gain,
ΔW_T = change in target-firm shareholders' wealth, and
ΔW_A = change in acquiring-firm stockholders' wealth.

This definition assumes that corporate acquisitions effected through interfirm tender offers have no effect on the wealth of the senior claimants (e.g., bondholders and other creditors) of the firms involved. Kim and McConnell (1977) and Asquith and Kim (1982) provide evidence that is consistent with this assumption for a sample of firms involved in corporate mergers.

2.2. Sample description

Our study is based on a sample of successful tender offer contests occurring over the period 1963–1984. We identify the beginning of a tender offer contest with the announcement of a bid for a given target. If there is only one bid, the contest ends when the offer is executed. The average duration between the announcement and the execution of a tender offer is three to four weeks. If additional bids are made by the same or another firm while the initial bid is outstanding, our definition of the contest is extended through the execution of the last bid made. The duration of a contest is also extended if a subsequent bid is made within 14 trading days of the expiration of a previous bid.

The primary data base consists of 921 interfirm tender offers, reflecting contests for 721 target firms between October 1958 and December 1984.[1] From this data base we select our sample according to the following criteria: (1) The winning bidder in each contest purchased at least some of the outstanding target shares, (2) the acquisition took place after 1963, and (3) the shares of *both* the target and acquiring firms were traded on the New York Stock Exchange (NYSE) or the American Stock Exchange (AMEX) at the time of the acquisition. The first criterion is imposed because our definition of synergistic gains applies only to successful tender offers.[2] The last two criteria enable us to use the CRSP (Center for Research in Security Prices) daily stock return data to calculate the total synergistic gain from an acquisition.

These selection criteria reduce our initial sample of 721 tender offer contests to 236. Summary statistics for the percentage of target shares held, sought, and

[1]Tender offers through 1977 were identified with the help of the data bases compiled by Bradley (1980) and Dodd and Ruback (1977). Relevant information for all offers was collected and/or verified with citations in the *Wall Street Journal* (index and newspaper).

[2]Rather than imposing some arbitrary cut-off point for the definition of a successful tender offer, we include in our sample all offers in which the bidding firm bought any number of target shares. The smallest percentage of shares purchased is 2.0. Although this may appear small, one should recognize that the control of a corporation lies along a continuum from none for those who own no shares to complete for those who own 100% of the firm's voting shares. From this perspective, the acquisition of even 2.0% may significantly alter the power of voting coalitions and affect the operations of the firm.

Table 1

Descriptive statistics of the percentage of target shares held, sought, and purchased by the acquiring firms in 236 successful tender offer contests effected over the period 1963–1984.[a]

	Percent of target shares[b]		
	Held	Sought	Purchased
Mean	9.8	66.2	60.4
Standard deviation	18.2	32.2	30.2
Median	0	67.2	62.8
Minimum	0	5.4	2.0
Maximum	78.0	100.0	100.0

[a]We define a successful tender offer as one in which the bidding firm buys some (however few) of the target shares pursuant to the terms of the bid.
[b]The denominator of all these percentages is the total number of shares outstanding.

purchased in the 236 successful tender offers are reported in table 1. Of the 236 acquiring firms, 155 held no target shares prior to the offer. The 236 acquiring firms sought, on average, 66.2% of the target shares. The mean as well as the median fraction of target shares ultimately purchased in our total sample is in excess of 50%. Thus the 'typical' acquiring firm in our sample held no target shares prior to the offer but held a majority of the outstanding target shares upon successful execution of the offer.

2.3. *Methodology*

Our estimates of the gains created by tender offers are based on market model prediction errors. Under the assumption of multivariate normality, the abnormal return (prediction error) to firm i on day t can be written as

$$AR_{it} = R_{it} - \hat{\alpha}_i - \hat{\beta}_i R_{mt}, \tag{2}$$

where

AR_{it} = abnormal return to firm i on day t,
R_{it} = realized return to firm i on day t,
$\hat{\alpha}_i, \hat{\beta}_i$ = market model parameter estimates, and
R_{mt} = return to the equally-weighted CRSP market portfolio on day t.

The market model parameter estimates for each target firm are obtained using a maximum of 240 trading days of daily returns data beginning 300 days before the announcement of the first tender offer bid in the contest. Estimates for the acquiring firms are obtained using 240 trading days of returns data beginning 300 days before the first bid made for the target by this firm.[3]

For each of the 472 firms in our sample, we cumulate the daily abnormal return over a contest-specific interval to obtain the cumulative abnormal return (*CAR*). The *CAR* is computed from five trading days before the announcement of the first bid through five days after the announcement of the ultimately successful bid. We begin to cumulate the *CAR* five days before the announcement of the initial bid in order to capture any anticipatory price behavior (leakage of information) that may occur before the actual public announcement.

Ideally, we would like to extend our *CAR* window until the day just before the offer is executed. Reliable execution dates are not available, however, for most of the offers in our sample. The postannouncement interval of five trading days is consistent with the requirement in the 1968 Williams Amendment that tendered shares can be withdrawn within seven calendar days (five trading days). The seven-calendar-day withdrawal period was extended to 15 business days in 1970, and starting in 1978 the regulation required that all tender offers remain open for 20 business days.

We do not extend the *CAR* window through the execution of the offer because this would cause a downward bias in the measured returns to target shareholders. This downward bias stems from the necessary condition for a successful tender offer that the offer price, P_{T}, be greater than the expected postexecution price of the remaining target shares, P_{E}. (See the appendix.) The premium $(P_{\mathrm{T}} - P_{\mathrm{E}})$ can be likened to a dividend paid to tendering

[3]In a recent paper Loderer and Mauer (1986) argue that the market model parameter estimates for acquiring firms will be biased if the estimation period is confined to the period just before the acquisition. Specifically, they argue that the estimate of the constant α will be biased upward because many acquiring firms initiate acquisition programs – indeed, investment programs in general – following a period of earnings growth. This overstimate of α for acquiring firms will result in a negative bias in the market model residuals (prediction errors) after the acquisition. Clearly, whether using preoffer data biases the estimate of the constant is an empirical issue.

To examine this issue, we estimated the market model parameters for the acquiring firms twice: first, using preoffer data as described above, and second, using 240 days beginning 20 days following the execution of the offer. The mean of the preoffer α's is -0.01% ($\sigma = 0.13\%$) and the mean of the postoffer α's is -0.02% ($\sigma = 0.13\%$). Although the mean of the preoffer α's is larger (a less negative number) than the mean of the postoffer α's, neither estimate is significantly different from zero or significantly different from the other. Moreover, if the preoffer α's are systematically greater than the postoffer α's, a linear regression of preoffer α's on the postoffer α's should yield either a slope coefficient greater than one and/or a positive constant. Contrary to this prediction, a simple linear regression yields the following results:

$$\text{Pre}\,\alpha_i = \underset{(t=-1.4)}{-0.00012} + \underset{(t=1.9)}{0.126}\,\text{Post}\,\alpha_i, \qquad R^2 = 0.015.$$

With these results and because our typical estimation period for cumulative abnormal returns is only 11 days, we feel that our results will not be significantly biased by using the preoffer α's. We should note that the Loderer and Mauer analysis is based on monthly data whereas ours is based on daily data. Perhaps the misestimation of the α of acquiring firms is important (significant) only when monthly data are used.

stockholders. As such, the target shares will trade 'cum-dividend' after the announcement until just before the execution and 'ex-dividend' after the execution. The 'cum-dividend' return is the relevant measure of the gain to target stockholders.

Ending the *CAR* window before the execution of the offer subjects our estimates to two potential biases. On the one hand, there is still a positive probability of failure after the end of the *CAR* window, and hence, our estimate of returns might be downward biased. On the other hand, to the extent that the market assigns a positive probability that the outstanding offer will be topped by a higher-valued bid, the measure will be an overestimate. We feel that the choice of five trading days after the announcement of the ultimately successful offer as the end of the window represents a reasonable tradeoff between these possible sources of bias.[4]

[4] We recognize that our *CAR* statistic is but one measure of the increase in the wealth of target stockholders. An alternative measure has been proposed by Jensen (1985) and Comment and Jarrell (1987). These authors employ what has become known as the blended premium (*BP*), which is defined as

$$BP = [(F)(P_T - P_0) + (1 - F)(P_E - P_0)]/P_0,$$

where F is the fraction of target shares purchased at P_T and P_0 is the pre-offer market price of the target shares.

As mentioned above, the necessary data for some of the variables in this equation are not available. However, for the 52 tender offers in our sample that were effected over the period 1981–1984, we were able to obtain all the necessary data from Robert Comment and Gregg Jarrell. For each of the offers in this subsample, we calculate a blended premium, using the closing price six days prior to the public announcement of the offer as a measure of P_0.

The mean *BP* for these 52 firms is 43.03%. In comparison, our *CAR* measure for this portfolio of firms is 35.34% (see table 2). A simple linear regression of *CAR* on *BP* yields the following results:

Model:	$CAR = \gamma_0$	$+ \gamma_1 (BP)$
Coefficient:	0.018	0.779
Standard error:	0.019	0.037
R^2 and F-statistic:	0.902	442.3

Although the estimate of the constant (γ_0) in this regression is insignificantly different from zero, the estimate of the slope coefficient (γ_1) is significantly less than 1.0. Thus, both the regression results and the difference in means indicate that our *CAR* measure is systematically less than *BP* by roughly 7.7%.

There are a number of reasons why we would expect *CAR* to be systematically less than *BP*. As discussed above, there still may be a positive probability that the outstanding offer will be unsuccessful even five days after the announcement of the ultimately successful offer, which is the end of our *CAR* window. If this were the reason for the discrepancy, however, we would expect to see the *CAR* to single-bidder targets rise after our cutoff date. No such increase is observed (see table 3 and fig. 2). Moreover, there are at least two computational reasons why *CAR* is systematically less than *BP*, and these explanations can easily account for the 7.7% difference.

First, *CAR* is, by design, net of market movements. The average duration of the offers in this sample is 22 trading days or one trading month. The average monthly return to the CRSP equally-weighted market portfolio between 1981 and 1984 is roughly 1.7%. Since the average Beta of the firms in this sample is 0.996, 1.7% of the 7.7% difference between *BP* and *CAR* can be attributed to general market movements.

A second reason for the disparity between *CAR* and *BP* is that the former is a sum of (abnormal) returns whereas the latter is essentially a continuously compounded return. Given that

Our *CAR* algorithm generates an 11-day window for all but 15 tender offers in which there is only one bidder. For tender offer contests in which there is more than one bidder, the window for targets varies, with a mean of 43 trading days and a standard deviation of 52 trading days.

Using these variable-window *CAR*s, we estimate the dollar gain to the target and acquiring firms in each tender offer contest i as

$$\Delta\hat{W}_{\mathrm{T}i} = W_{\mathrm{T}i} \cdot CART_i, \qquad \Delta\hat{W}_{\mathrm{A}i} = W_{\mathrm{A}i} \cdot CARA_i, \tag{3}$$

where

$W_{\mathrm{T}i}$ = market value of the target equity as of the end of six trading days prior to the first announcement for the target, minus the value of the target shares held by the acquirer,

$CART_i$ = cumulative abnormal return to the target firm from five trading days before the announcement of the first bid through five trading days after the announcement of the ultimately successful bid,

$W_{\mathrm{A}i}$ = market value of the acquiring firm as of the end of six days prior to the first announcement made by the acquiring firm,

$CARA_i$ = cumulative abnormal return to the acquiring firm from five trading days before the announcement of the first offer made by this firm through five trading days after the announcement of the ultimately successful bid.

Conceptually, an empirical measure of the total percentage synergistic gains created by the ith tender offer would be a weighted average of *CART* and *CARA*. Since *CART* and *CARA* are based on different event windows, however, they are not directly comparable. Moreover, we have no information on the statistical properties of such a weighted average.

To circumvent these statistical problems, our estimate of the total percentage synergistic gains is based on the *CAR* to a value-weighted *portfolio* of the ith target and the ith acquiring firm, where the weights used are $W_{\mathrm{T}i}$ and $W_{\mathrm{A}i}$ as defined above. Market model parameter estimates for each of the 236 value-weighted portfolios are obtained using 240 trading days of portfolio returns beginning 300 days before the first tender offer bid in the contest. The

---

the returns to the targets are predominantly positive over the tender offer period, it follows that the sum of the daily (abnormal) returns will be strictly less than a continuously compounded return. For example, the sum of 2% per day for 22 days is 44%, whereas the continuously compounded return of 2% for 22 days is 55%.

In sum, our *CAR* measure is less than the *BP* measure used by Jensen and by Comment and Jarrell. However, it is not at all clear which is superior. One obvious advantage of the *CAR* statistic is that it has known statistical properties and therefore can be used in hypothesis testing.

combined percentage synergistic gain created by a successful tender offer, $CARC_i$, is measured by cumulating the abnormal returns to this portfolio from five trading days before the announcement of the first bid through five days after the announcement of the ultimately successful bid. Using this percentage measure, we estimate the total dollar synergistic gain, $\Delta\hat{\Pi}_i$, as

$$\Delta\hat{\Pi}_i = \Pi_i \cdot CARC_i, \tag{4}$$

where

$$\Pi_i = W_{\mathrm{T}i} + W_{\mathrm{A}i}.$$

2.4. Estimate of synergistic gains

Table 2 reports our measures of the synergistic gains created by tender offers, as well as the changes in the wealth of the stockholders of the target and acquiring firms. The data in the last column of the top panel of table 2 (labeled *Combined*) show that the combined value of the target and acquiring firms increased, on average, by 7.43%, with 75% of the combined revaluations being positive. Our estimate of this percentage synergistic gain is statistically greater than zero ($z = 19.95$).[5]

The mean total dollar gain created by the acquisitions in our sample is $117 million (expressed in December 1984 dollars). Since the distribution of our

[5]This z-statistic is computed following Patell's (1976) eq. (11). Specifically, we compute the standardized abnormal return to the ith portfolio on day t, SAR_{it}, defined as

$$SAR_{it} = AR_{it} \Bigg/ \left[\sigma_i \left(1 + \frac{1}{T_i} + \frac{(R_{mt} - \bar{R}_m)^2}{\sum_{\tau}^{T_i} (R_{m\tau} - \bar{R}_m)^2} \right)^{1/2} \right],$$

where

σ_i = standard deviation of the residuals in the market model estimation period,
T_i = number of days in the estimation period, and
$\bar{R}_m$ = mean return to the market portfolio over the estimation period.

The SAR_{it} is then used to obtain the standardized CAR_i over K_i event days:

$$SCAR_i = \left[\sum_{t=1}^{K_i} SAR_{it} \right] \Bigg/ \sqrt{K_i}\,.$$

Finally, the z-statistic for the portfolio of N_p firms in the sample is computed as

$$z = \sum_{i=1}^{N_p} SCAR_i \Bigg/ \left[\sum_{i=1}^{N_p} ((T_i - 2)/(T_i - 4)) \right]^{1/2}$$

Table 2

Mean percentage and dollar synergistic gains to 236 successful tender offer contests effected between 1963 and 1984 for combined, target, and acquiring firms. All dollar figures are stated in millions of 1984 dollars.[a]

	Subperiod			Total
	7/63–6/68	7/68–12/80	1/81–12/84	7/63–12/84
No. of contests	51	133	52	236
Combined				
% $CARC$	7.78[b]	7.08[b]	8.00[b]	7.43[b]
$\$\Delta\hat{\Pi}$	91.08	87.45	218.51	117.11
% Positive	78	74	73	75
Targets				
% $CART$	18.92[b]	35.29[b]	35.34[b]	31.77[b]
$\$\Delta\hat{W}_T$	70.71	71.59	233.53	107.08
% Positive	94	98	90	95
Acquirers				
% $CARA$	4.09[b]	1.30	−2.93[b]	0.97[b]
$\$\Delta\hat{W}_A$	24.96	31.80	−27.28	17.30
% Positive	59	48	35	47

[a] $\Delta\hat{W}_T = W_T * CART$; $\Delta\hat{W}_A = W_A * CARA$; and $\Delta\hat{\Pi} = (W_T + W_A) * CARC$; where W_T = preoffer market value of target equity, excluding shares held by the acquirer; W_A = preoffer market value of equity of acquiring firm; $CART$ = cumulative abnormal return from five days before the first offer to five days after the last offer made for this target; $CARA$ = cumulative abnormal return from five days before the first offer to five days after the last offer made by this bidding firm; $CARC$ = cumulative abnormal return to the value-weighted portfolio of the target and the acquiring firm, measured over the same interval as $CART$.

[b] Significantly different from zero at the 0.01 level.

dollar measure $\Delta\hat{\Pi}$ is extremely leptokurtic and skewed to the right (the skewness and kurtosis coefficients are 6.70 and 62.38, respectively), we conduct the nonparametric Wilcoxon Signed Rank test to test if the median $\Delta\hat{\Pi}$ of \$26.9 million for the total sample is statistically greater than zero. This test yields a z-statistic of 9.30, which is significant at the 1% level.

Table 2 also reports data for three subperiods: 1963–1968, 1968–1980, and 1981–1984. Although this division is somewhat arbitrary, there have been some dramatic changes in the tender offer process during the 22-year period under study, and these three subperiods correspond roughly to the three distinct regimes that have existed in the legal and institutional environment of tender offers since 1963.

The first period (1963–1968) is important because before 1968, cash tender offers were free of government regulation. They were considered private transactions between the acquiring firm and the stockholders of the target firm. In July 1968 Congress passed the Williams Amendment, which brought the tender offer within the purview of the Securities and Exchange Commission (SEC). In the same year, Virginia enacted the first state antitakeover statute; by 1978, 36 states had enacted their own takeover regulations. By isolating the offers that occurred in the unregulated period, we can examine the effects of government regulation on the magnitude and division of the synergistic gains from tender offers.

The last period (1981–1984) is distinguished by three factors that have drastically changed the environment in which tender offers take place. First is the avowed laissez-faire attitude of the Reagan Administration toward corporate takeovers in general.[6] Second is the development of sophisticated tactics to repel takeovers (poison pills, targeted share repurchases, lock-up provisions, and supermajority and fair-price amendments). The third factor is the advent of investment banking firms that specialize in raising funds to finance corporate takeovers. We are interested in how these recent developments in the market for corporate control have affected the gains created by tender offers.

The data in the top panel of table 2 indicate that the percentage synergistic gains created by tender offers have remained remarkably constant, between 7% and 8%, over the three subperiods. The dollar gains, however, have increased dramatically from the first two subperiods to the third; expressed in December 1984 dollars, the average synergistic gain has grown from $91 million and $87 million in the first two subperiods to $219 million in the 1981–1984 subperiod.

This increase in the dollar synergistic gains, but not in the percentage synergistic gains, is due to the increase in the size of target firms. The mean preoffer market value of targets increased from $379 million in the first period to $550 million in the last period, while the average size of acquiring firms actually dropped from $1,624 million to $1,477 million.

The increase in the size of the target firms in the third period may be due to the laissez-faire attitude of the Reagan Administration and innovative financing methods of investment banking firms. Also, the popularity of two-tier offers has reduced the cash outlays required of bidding firms.[7] These developments in the takeover arena have made it easier for bidding firms to seek control of larger targets.

In the next section we identify the factors that determine how the synergy gains created by tender offers are divided between the stockholders of the target and acquiring firms. The data presented in the last two panels of table 2 allow us to draw some preliminary conclusions on this issue.

[6]See the Economic Report of the President, 1985, especially ch. 6.

[7]In the typical two-tier offer, the bidding firm makes a cash offer for a fraction of the target shares (usually 51% or more) and agrees to purchase the remainder if the offer is successful. Often, the remaining shares are purchased by an exchange of securities. Thus, the cash outlay for the shares purchased through a fractional tender offer is less than the outlay necessary for an any-or-all cash offer.

The overwhelming conclusion is that target stockholders capture the majority of the gains from tender offers. Ninety-five percent of the targets in the total sample experienced a positive abnormal return. The average abnormal return is 32% and the ratio of the mean dollar gain to targets to the mean dollar total gain ($\Delta\hat{W}_T/\Delta\hat{\Pi}$) is 91%. In contrast, the average abnormal return to acquiring firms is 0.97%, only 47% of the observations are positive, and the ratio of the mean dollar gain to the mean total gain ($\Delta\hat{W}_A/\Delta\hat{\Pi}$) is 15%. Whether measured as rates of return or dollar gains, the lion's share of the gains from tender offers is captured by target shareholders.

The data in table 2 also indicate that the returns to acquiring firms have decreased over time, whereas the returns to targets have increased. The mean abnormal return to acquiring firms is 4.09% ($z = 5.88$) in the first period and -2.93% ($z = -2.79$) in the last. In contrast, the mean abnormal return to targets has increased from 18.92% ($z = 26.2$) to 35.34% ($z = 26.2$).

In sum, the data in table 2 compel the following conclusions:

(1) Successful tender offers generate significant synergistic gains and lead to a more efficient allocation of corporate resources.[8]

(2) The stockholders of both target and acquiring firms realize significant positive abnormal returns. However, most of the gains are captured by the stockholders of target firms.

(3) Both the rate of return and dollar gains to target stockholders have increased over time, whereas the returns to the stockholders of acquiring firms have decreased. In fact, in the most recent subperiod, acquiring firms actually suffered a significant abnormal loss.

3. A model of the division of the gains from interfirm tender offers

In the previous section we documented that corporate acquisitions made through tender offers generate significantly positive synergistic gains. In this section we attempt to identify the factors that determine the division of the synergistic gains between the stockholders of the target and acquiring firms. We begin by reviewing the important legal and institutional aspects of this capital market transaction. We then summarize and extend our analysis of the tender offer process, which is presented in the appendix. This summary and extension provide a framework within which we develop implications regarding the division of the gains from tender offers.

[8] We recognize that, theoretically, the gains from tender offers may stem from the creation of market power and not necessarily from increased allocative efficiency. However, the work of Eckbo (1983, 1985) and Stillman (1983) indicates that corporate acquisitions have no measurable effect on the degree of market power in the economy.

3.1. Regulation of tender offers

As discussed earlier, interfirm cash tender offers were not regulated by federal securities law until July 1968 when Congress passed the Williams Amendment and brought cash tender offers within the purview of the SEC.[9] Provisions of the Williams Amendment require bidding firms to provide detailed information about how the tender offer will be financed and what changes in the operations of the target will be made if the offer is successful. The regulations also specify a minimum number of days that a tender offer must remain open and a minimum number of days before the target shares can be purchased. Target stockholders who have tendered their shares to one bidding firm are allowed to withdraw their shares if a higher-valued offer is made by another firm before the required number of days for the initial offer has elapsed. Furthermore, if an outstanding offer is revised upward, then all target stockholders, even those who tendered their shares at the previous terms, must receive the higher price.

The 'disclosure and delay' requirements of federal regulations make the tender offer process similar to an open auction for the target shares. The regulations force bidding firms to reveal information about the target company and delay the offer long enough so that other potential bidding firms can discover this information. Moreover, the delay and withdrawal provisions of the regulations allow target stockholders to take advantage of competing offers similar to that which occurs in open auction markets. The delay requirements permit further production of information that may generate higher-valued bids, and the withdrawal privilege allows target stockholders to recontract and tender their shares to the firm that makes the highest-valued offer.[10]

3.2. Assumptions

To be consistent with the institutional setting of the tender offer process, we assume that competition for the target shares is effected through a tatônnement process. We also assume that there are no transactions costs in bidding, that target shareholders are wealth maximizers, and that managers of bidding firms seek to maximize their shareholders' wealth.

From the evidence presented in section 2, we view a tender offer as an attempt by the bidding firm to gain control of the target resources and to

[9] Stock tender offers (exchange offers) are regulated under the original Securities and Exchange Act of 1933 because the transaction typically involves the issuance of new stock.

[10] Fifty-one (22%) of the offers in our sample were effected prior to the passage of the Williams Amendment and were thus free of its constraints. However, voluntary practices and/or the rules of the NYSE or AMEX during the 1960s produced offers not unlike those in the post-Williams era. Thus, in most of the pre-Williams offers in our sample the bidding firm was identified, target stockholders were given at least one week to tender their shares, and oversubscribed offers were effected on a pro-rata basis.

allocate the combined resources of the two firms to higher-valued uses. We assume that to generate synergistic gains the bidding firm must secure control, which requires acquisition of at least N_C of the N_0 target shares outstanding.[11] We do not analyze the determinants of N_C. Rather, we assume that N_C is target-specific. We can, however, speculate on several factors that would affect its magnitude. The most obvious include the number of target shares outstanding, the concentration of these shares among the target stockholders, the predisposition of the target stockholders toward the takeover, and provisions in the firm's charter about the number of shares (votes) required to make fundamental changes in the firm's operations.

3.3. The tender offer process

In the appendix we present an analysis of the tender offer process within the context of the above assumptions and institutional and legal setting. We demonstrate that competition among rival management teams, including the managers of the target firm, ensures that the total value of the successful offer must be greater than or equal to the next-highest-valued allocation of the target resources.[12] Thus, given competition by target managers, the minimum value of the offer is bounded by the total preoffer market value of the target shares.

Our analysis implies a certain structure for the bidding process. In the appendix we show that a successful tender offer must be front-end loaded, i.e.,

$$P_T > P_E, \tag{5}$$

where

P_T = front-end price, and

P_E = back-end price.[13]

We also show that the winning bid in a tender offer contest will be the bid that maximizes the difference between P_T and P_E. By this criterion, bidding

[11] It cannot be the case that the bidding firm can simply 'package' its value-creating ideas and sell them to the target firm. If this were possible, the bidding firm would never bother with the costly process of acquiring the target shares through a public tender offer. The control assumption is consistent with the finding of Bradley, Desai, and Kim (1983) that the permanent positive revaluation of target shares requires a successful acquisition of the target shares by the bidding firm.

[12] In this respect our notion of competition in the market for corporate control parallels that of Ruback (1983).

[13] If the bidding firm makes a partial offer without specifying the back-end price, we define P_E as the market's expectation of the postacquisition price of the target shares not purchased.

firms have an incentive to minimize P_E, regardless of their valuation of the target firm. In the appendix, we argue that the minimum P_E will be determined by statutes and legal standards. Thus, rival bidders will compete for control of the target by setting the back-end price to the minimum 'allowable' level and bidding for a controlling interest with their front-end price.

There is empirical evidence to support this view of the bidding process. As predicted by our analysis, the vast majority of successful tender offers are front-end loaded. Of the 52 tender offer contests for which we have estimates of P_T and P_E (see footnote 4), 32 satisfy the condition $P_T > P_E$. In 19 cases the two prices are (nominally) equivalent. Only in two instances is $P_T < P_E$; in one case the back-end price is \$.25 higher and in the other it is \$1.00 more. Note that the estimate of P_E is the (ex-post) market price of unpurchased target shares two days after the execution of the front-end offer. Thus, nominally equivalent front- and back-end prices do not vitiate our prediction that successful tender offers must be front-end loaded. The time value of money between the execution of the front and back ends makes the present value of P_E less than P_T. Moreover, general market movements between these two dates could account for the two aberrant cases where our measure of P_E is greater than P_T.[14]

Also, there is evidence that of the three parameters of a tender offer, rival bidding firms typically compete with each other on the front-end price, P_T, rather than on the back-end price, P_E, or the fraction of target shares sought, F. In our sample of 236 tender offer contests, we can identify a total of 408 bids: 236 initial bids and 172 revised bids. Of these 172 revised bids, 127 (74%) involved an increase only in P_T. Four bids involved an increase in the fraction of shares sought, F, alone and 28 bids involved an increase in both P_T and F. In the remaining 13 bids, the changes in P_T and F were in the opposite directions.

Our analysis of the tender offer process in the appendix is based on two unrealistic assumptions: (1) there are no tax consequences from tendering and (2) target stockholders have homogeneous beliefs about the outcome of the offer and about the postexecution market price of the target shares not purchased. These assumptions imply that all target stockholders have the same reservation price and hence the supply of target shares is perfectly elastic.

[14] In section 4.1 we provide further evidence that successful tender offers are front-end loaded. Data reported in that section show that the *CAR* to the targets of single-bidder tender offers begins to decline 18 days after the announcement of the ultimately successful bid. This period roughly coincides with the average duration of the tender offers in our sample. We interpret this price decline as the ex-dividend effect discussed above. The ex-dividend effect will result in a price decline of the target shares on the execution date only if $P_T > P_E$. Bradley (1980) and Comment and Jarrell (1987) also provide evidence that the average front-end price in successful tender offers is significantly greater than the average back-end price.

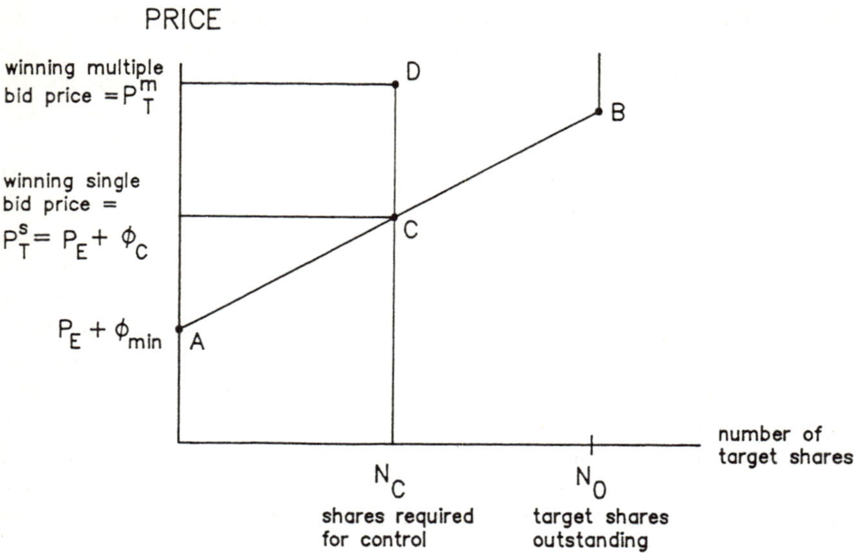

Fig. 1. The postannouncement supply of target shares with heterogeneous capital-gains tax positions and/or expectations about future takeover bids.
P_E = back-end price of the outstanding offer, ϕ_i = premium demanded by the owner of the ith share, P_T^s = winning price in a single-bidder acquisition = the minimum price to elicit N_C shares, P_T^m = winning price in a multiple-bidder acquisition, ABC = postannouncement supply of target shares.

Relaxing these two assumptions requires us to modify inequality (5) as follows: The owner of the ith target share will not tender unless

$$P_T > P_E + \phi_i, \tag{6}$$

where ϕ_i is the premium demanded by the owner of the ith share above P_E. The premium ϕ_i varies across target shareholders and represents differences in capital-gains tax positions and in expectations regarding the possibility of future acquisition activity. When tendering shares results in a realization of taxable gains, the shareholder loses an option to defer the capital-gains tax to a future date [Rosenfeld (1982)]. With heterogeneous capital-gains tax positions among target shareholders, the option will have a different value for different shareholders; hence, the premium ϕ_i will vary across target shareholders.

Another component of ϕ_i stems from differing expectations about the outcome of an outstanding offer and the probability of receiving future takeover bids. For example, all market participants may not agree that the outstanding offer represents the highest-valued bid that will be made. Some target stockholders may believe there is a positive probability that a higher-valued bidder might materialize after they tender their shares and the outstanding offer is executed.[15] From this perspective, ϕ_i may be thought of as the premium individual i must be paid to give up the (expected) benefit from a subsequent, higher-valued takeover bid.

Given the vector ϕ_i, the supply of target shares will be upward sloping as represented by the line ACB in fig. 1. We also assume that all bidders know the minimum price required to elicit N_C shares but do not know each other's maximum offer price. The minimum price required to elicit N_C target shares is denoted in fig. 1 by $P_E + \phi_C$, where ϕ_C is the premium demanded by the owner of the N_Cth share. This reservation price of the marginal tendering shareholder determines the minimum synergistic gain (MSG) that a bidding firm must be able to generate to win control of the target firm and still make a profit.

When only one firm can create synergistic gains in excess of MSG, that firm will bid $P_T^s = P_E + \phi_C$ and win control of the target. (See point C in fig. 1.) If at least one more firm can generate synergistic gains in excess of MSG, an auction will ensue. As discussed above, rival bidding firms will compete by raising P_T. Thus, competition among bidding firms will move the target stockholders vertically off their supply curve (e.g., to point D in fig. 1) and, as a consequence, the offer will be oversubscribed.[16]

Because the successful offer price in a multiple-bidder contest, P_T^m, will be greater than the offer price in a successful single-bidder offer, i.e., $P_T^m > P_T^s$ (compare points D and C in fig. 1), the dollar gains to target stockholders will be greater in multiple-bidder contests than in single-bidder contests. Specifically, the dollar gains can be written as

$$\Delta W_T = (P_T - P_0)(N_C) + (P_E - P_0)(N_0 - N_C), \tag{7}$$

where P_0 is the preoffer market price of target shares. The first term on the right side of eq. (7), $(P_T - P_0)(N_C)$, represents the premium paid to target stockholders for the shares purchased on the front end. The second term, $(P_E - P_0)(N_0 - N_C)$, represents the premium paid for the remaining shares on the back end. Because $P_T^m > P_T^s$ and by the assumption that the other terms in eq. (7) are independent of the occurrence of a multiple-bidder contest, ΔW_T will be greater in a multiple-bidder contest than in a single-bidder offer.

[15]Of course if a higher-valued bid materializes before the offer is executed, provisions in the Williams Amendment allow target stockholders to withdraw their shares from the lower bidder and tender them to the higher bidder.

[16]Consistent with this implication, the frequency of oversubscribed offers is greater in our multiple-bidder sample (90%) than in our single-bidder sample (67%).

This prediction in dollar terms will hold also in percentage terms if we make certain independence assumptions about the occurrence of a multiple-bidder contest and the preoffer values of the target and bidding firms. Specifically, assuming that the occurrence of a multiple-bidder contest is independent of the preoffer value of the target, W_T, it follows that the rate of return to target stockholders will be greater in multiple-bidder contests than in single-bidder contests. Moreover, assuming that $\Delta\Pi$, the total synergistic gains created by the combination, and W_A, the preoffer value of the acquiring firm, are independent of the occurrence of a multiple-bidder contest, it follows that the rate of return to acquirers will be greater in single-bidder contests than in multiple-bidder contests.

An alternative hypothesis is that multiple-bidder contests arise when the initial bid is 'too low' and that there is no difference between the premiums ultimately paid for targets in single- and multiple-bidder contests. According to this scenario, the gains to the targets of multiple-bidder contests would start out low on the announcement of the initial bid and rise to the level of the gains in single-bidder offers. The eventual gains to both targets and acquirers would be unaffected by the number of bidding firms.

Finally, an upward sloping supply of target shares implies a positive relation between the return to target stockholders and the fraction of shares purchased. Consider once again fig. 1. By our analysis, successful single-bidder acquisitions will take place along the (positively sloped) line ACB and the successful price in multiple-bidder acquisitions will always lie above this supply curve. Thus, the gain (return) to target stockholders will be positively related to the number (fraction) of target shares purchased.

4. Empirical evidence on the determinants of the division of the gains from tender offers

We begin our empirical analysis by examining the time series of cumulative abnormal returns (*CAR*s) to the portfolios of 236 targets and 236 acquiring firms, classified by the observed level of competition among bidding firms. Although the time-series analysis provides insights into the intertemporal behavior of the returns from tender offers, it is unidimensional and hence does not allow us to examine the simultaneous effects of the factors identified by our analysis. Furthermore, when the first bid for the target shares is announced, the eventual outcome of the bid is uncertain. This uncertainty is resolved over time when either new information about the acquisition is revealed to the market or when competing, higher-valued bids for the target are announced. The period over which this uncertainty is resolved varies across the sample, and the *CAR*s to the portfolios cannot account for these differences. Thus, we also conduct cross-sectional analyses using the variable window return measures defined in section 2.

4.1. Time-series analysis

The time series of *CAR*s are computed for three portfolios of the target firms: 163 targets of single-bidder tender offers, 73 targets of multiple-bidder tender offer contests, and the total sample of 236 targets. Similarly, three *CAR* series are computed for the corresponding portfolios of the acquiring firms.

To be classified as a multiple-bidder contest, a tender offer contest must involve an identifiable second bidder – i.e., the firm's name is mentioned in the press and it must be actively seeking target shares by engaging in at least one of the following activities: (1) making a formal tender offer or a merger proposal, (2) negotiating a merger possibility with the target management, or (3) announcing its plans to make a bid. The activities of competing bidding firms were obtained from citations in the *Wall Street Journal*.[17]

For each portfolio p consisting of N_t firms on day t, the abnormal return for day t is defined as

$$AR_{pt} = (1/N_t) \sum_{i=1}^{N_t} AR_{it}. \tag{8}$$

The K-day *CAR* for each portfolio is defined as

$$CAR_{pK} = \sum_{t=-\tau}^{K-\tau-1} AR_{pt}, \tag{9}$$

where τ is the number of days before the relevant event day. To test the significance of this K-day cumulative abnormal return to the portfolio, we compute a standardized portfolio cumulative abnormal return, $SCAR_{pK}$, in a manner analogous to the $SCAR_i$ computation described in footnote 5. This $SCAR_{pK}$ has a t-distribution with 238 degrees of freedom.

The *CAR* series for the three portfolios of the target firms in our sample are presented in table 3 and plotted in fig. 2. The *CAR* series are cumulated from event day -20 through event day $+80$, where event day 0 is the day on which

[17] Classifying a tender offer as a single- or multiple-bidder contest based on the number of identifiable bidding firms becomes ambiguous when an initial bidding firm revises its bid and there is no identifiable competing bidder. On the one hand, the revision may have been triggered by the realization (on the part of the bidding firm) that the initial offer was too low to induce the target shareholders to tender their shares. On the other hand, it may have been a response to a competing offer by another firm or the anticipation thereof that we were unable to identify. Since it is impossible to distinguish between these two cases, the empirical tests were run twice. One set of results is based on a multiple/single-*bidder* classification (the number of firms bidding for the target); a second set of results is based on a multiple/single-*bid* classification scheme (the number of bids made for the target). Since the results are qualitatively indistinguishable, we report results based only on the multiple/single-*bidder* classification.

Table 3

Percentage abnormal returns (AR) and cumulative abnormal returns (CAR) to the portfolio of target firms involved in 236 tender offer contests, 163 single-bidder contests and 73 multiple-bidder contests between 1963 and 1984.

	Single-bidder subsample				Multiple-bidder subsample				Total sample			
Event day	NT[a]	NP[b]	AR	CAR	NT	NP	AR	CAR	NT	NP	AR	CAR
−20	163	72	−0.13	−0.13	71	33	0.11	0.11	234	105	−0.05	−0.05
⋮												
−15	163	87	0.19	0.38	71	30	−0.27	1.46	234	117	0.05	0.70
⋮												
−10	162	78	0.28	1.26	73	39	1.60	4.04	235	117	0.69	2.12
⋮												
−5	162	85	0.21	3.01	73	44	0.60	6.12	235	129	0.33	3.97
−4	160	83	1.09	4.10	73	40	0.92	7.04	233	123	1.03	5.01
−3	162	94	0.98	5.08	73	38	1.09	8.13	235	132	1.01	6.02
−2	159	103	1.57	6.64	73	44	1.46	9.59	232	147	1.53	7.56
−1	147	101	2.63	9.27	72	52	2.27	11.86	219	153	2.51	10.07
0	163	139	14.67	23.95	73	66	14.12	25.98	236	205	14.50	24.57
1	135	95	4.71	28.66	56	41	4.42	30.40	191	136	4.63	29.19
2	156	78	0.79	29.44	61	29	0.81	31.21	217	107	0.79	29.99
3	159	72	0.69	30.14	66	29	0.96	32.17	225	101	0.77	30.76
4	159	80	0.13	30.27	71	41	1.79	33.96	230	121	0.65	31.41
5	160	76	0.05	30.33	70	34	0.88	34.85	230	110	0.31	31.71
⋮												
10	162	79	−0.28	30.46	70	32	−0.07	37.82	232	111	−0.22	32.72
⋮												
15	160	76	−0.12	30.40	68	37	0.53	40.94	228	113	0.07	33.63
⋮												
20	152	71	−0.43	29.17	70	35	0.09	41.70	222	106	−0.27	33.02
⋮												
30	130	59	−0.24	27.84	69	33	−0.18	44.92	199	92	−0.22	33.19
⋮												
40	117	45	−0.25	26.65	63	30	0.09	46.12	180	75	−0.13	32.85
⋮												
50	108	50	0.25	25.80	59	27	−0.13	45.47	167	77	0.12	32.06
⋮												
60	97	41	−0.06	26.04	53	33	0.17	44.70	150	74	0.02	31.95
⋮												
70	89	41	−0.06	26.14	43	19	0.01	44.26	132	60	−0.04	31.87
⋮												
80	84	42	−0.35	24.65	41	24	0.46	45.50	125	66	−0.08	31.28

[a] NT = total number of firms.
[b] NP = number of firms with positive abnormal returns.

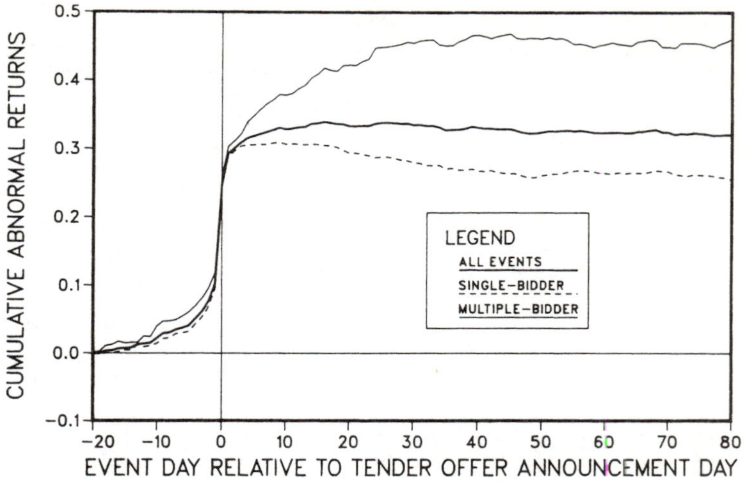

Fig. 2. Cumulative abnormal returns to the portfolio of target firms involved in 236 contests, 163 single-bidder contests and 73 multiple-bidder contests, 1963–1984. Event day relative to tender offer announcement day.

the announcement of the first offer for the target appeared in the *Wall Street Journal*.

The *CAR* for the portfolio of all 236 target firms from event day −5 through event day +5 is 28.07% with a *t*-statistic of 51.24, showing once again that an acquisition by tender offer is a wealth-increasing event for the stockholders of the target firm.

The *AR* and the *CAR* of the single-bidder subsample on day 0 (14.67% and 23.95%) are approximately equal to those of the multiple-bidder subsample (14.12% and 25.98%). Thus when a target receives an initial offer, the average value of this offer does not depend on whether it will be followed by other bids. Only when competing bids are actually announced do additional returns accrue to the targets of multiple-bidder contests. The additional returns are reflected in the gradual rise of the *CAR* series for the multiple-bidder sample. The difference in the *CAR* between the multiple-bidder and single-bidder subsamples reaches about 20% by day +40.[18] Clearly, target shareholders earn greater returns from multiple-bidder contests than from single-bidder offers.

These findings are not consistent with the alternative hypothesis that multiple-bidder contests arise because the initial bid was too low. Rather, they

[18]Some of this difference can be attributed to the postexecution drop in the price of the remaining target shares. Of the 163 single-bidder offers, 119 (or 73%) were executed within 40 trading days of the initial announcement. By contrast, only 32 of the 73 multiple-bidder offers (44%) were executed during this 40-day period. Since the time-series analysis cannot account for the differences in the duration of the tender offers in the sample, formal tests for the effect of competition on the returns to targets and acquirers must await the cross-sectional tests in the next section.

Table 4

Percentage abnormal returns (*AR*) and cumulative abnormal returns (*CAR*) to the portfolio of acquiring firms involved in 236 tender offer contests, 163 single-bidder contests and 73 multiple-bidder contests between 1963 and 1984.

	Single-bidder subsample				Multiple-bidder subsample				Total sample			
Event day	*NT*[a]	*NP*[b]	*AR*	*CAR*	*NT*	*NP*	*AR*	*CAR*	*NT*	*NP*	*AR*	*CAR*
−20	163	84	0.12	0.12	73	33	−0.07	−0.07	236	117	0.06	0.06
−15	163	74	−0.17	0.20	73	30	−0.22	−0.66	236	104	−0.19	−0.06
−10	163	85	0.25	0.66	73	36	0.14	−0.05	236	121	0.22	0.44
−5	163	79	0.12	1.05	73	32	−0.30	0.23	236	111	−0.01	0.80
−4	163	73	0.04	1.09	73	39	0.14	0.37	236	112	0.07	0.87
−3	163	92	0.50	1.59	73	38	0.34	0.71	236	130	0.45	1.32
−2	163	84	0.50	2.09	72	29	0.23	0.95	235	113	0.42	1.74
−1	163	86	0.19	2.29	72	28	−0.39	0.56	235	114	0.02	1.76
0	163	80	0.62	2.91	73	30	−0.65	−0.09	236	110	0.23	1.99
1	162	76	−0.16	2.75	71	34	−0.41	−0.51	233	110	−0.24	1.75
2	163	79	0.16	2.91	73	34	−0.33	−0.83	236	113	0.01	1.76
3	163	73	−0.24	2.67	73	35	−0.12	−0.96	236	108	−0.20	1.55
4	163	73	0.17	2.84	72	39	0.05	−0.91	235	112	0.13	1.69
5	163	66	−0.35	2.50	73	36	0.49	−0.43	236	102	−0.09	1.60
10	163	93	0.02	2.71	73	38	0.20	−1.13	236	131	0.08	1.53
15	163	77	0.31	3.33	73	33	0.15	−1.04	236	110	0.26	1.98
20	163	83	0.37	3.69	73	33	0.04	−0.17	236	116	0.27	2.51
30	163	72	−0.03	3.29	73	32	−0.35	0.56	236	104	−0.13	2.46
40	163	80	0.12	2.97	73	30	−0.21	0.64	236	110	0.02	2.26
50	163	77	−0.01	2.70	73	34	−0.08	0.42	236	111	−0.03	2.00
60	163	81	−0.08	2.73	73	37	−0.20	0.61	236	118	−0.12	2.09
70	163	80	−0.08	2.22	73	37	−0.11	−0.55	236	117	−0.09	1.37
80	163	73	−0.04	2.02	73	36	0.16	0.70	236	109	0.02	1.62

[a] *NT* = total number of firms.
[b] *NP* = number of firms with positive abnormal returns.

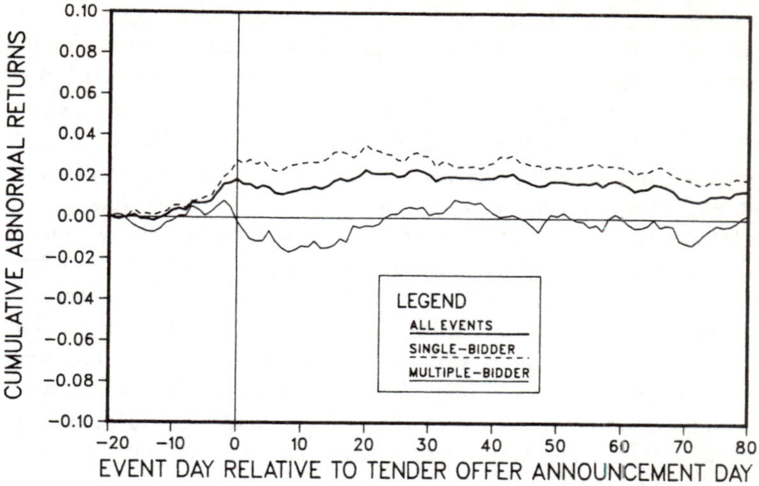

Fig. 3. Cumulative abnormal returns to the portfolios of acquiring firms involved in 236 contests, 163 single-bidder contests and 73 multiple-bidder contests, 1963–1984. Event day relative to tender offer announcement day.

suggest that the premiums paid to the target shareholders in multiple-bidder contests are, as implied by our model, above the supply curve of target shares.

The *CAR* series for the three portfolios of acquiring firms are presented in table 4 and plotted in fig. 3. Event day 0 is the day of the announcement of the first offer made by the acquiring firm. The *CAR* to the portfolio of all 236 acquiring firms from event day −5 through +5 is 0.79% with a t-statistic of 1.69. This is not significantly different from zero at the 5% level. However, the *CAR* from day −5 through day +20 is 1.70% ($t = 2.36$), which is significant at the 5% level. Thus, unlike for target firms, there is mixed evidence concerning the returns to acquiring firms.

Classifying the portfolios of acquiring firms by the level of competition reveals that the *CAR* from day −5 through day +20 to the single-bidder portfolio is 2.8% ($t = 2.94$), whereas the return to the multiple-bidder portfolio is −0.70% ($t = -0.56$) over the same period. Thus, significant positive returns accrue to the stockholders of acquiring firms in single-bidder tender offers but not in multiple-bidder contests.

To examine the behavior of the *CAR*s to the multiple-bidder portfolio more closely, we divide the sample into two groups: first-bidder, ultimately successful acquirers, and those acquirers who entered the contest after some other firm initiated the bidding process. Of the 73 acquirers in the multiple-bidder portfolio, 24 are first-bidder acquirers, and 49 are late-bidder acquirers. The *CAR* from day −5 to day +1 for the portfolio of first-bidder acquirers is

2.0%, whereas the *CAR* for the portfolio of late-bidder acquirers is −2.5% over the same interval. Apparently, the market's reaction to the first bid of first-bidder acquirers in multiple-bidder contests is similar to its reaction to bids made in single-bidder tender offers. Thus the negative *CAR* from day −5 to day +1 to the portfolio of acquirers in multiple-bidder contests is due primarily to the negative returns to late-bidder acquirers, more commonly known as white knights. In other words, our data indicate that the average white knight pays 'too much' for the target it acquires.

In sum, our time-series analysis indicates that the net effect of multiple-bidder contests is to increase the returns to target firms and decrease the returns to acquiring firms. The market's average reaction to the bid that initiates a tender offer contest does not depend on whether the bid eventually leads to a multiple-bidder contest. This is true for both target and bidding firms. Only when competing bids are actually made do we observe greater returns to target shareholders and a dissipation of the initial gains to the stockholders of bidding firms.

4.2. *Cross-sectional analysis*

In this section we use variable-window *CAR*s to examine the cross-sectional differences in the returns to the stockholders of target and acquiring firms. Specifically, we examine the effects of (1) changes in the tender offer environment, (2) competition, and (3) the fraction of target shares purchased on the rates of return to these stockholders. We also examine the effects of the above variables on the total value-weighted percentage synergistic gains.

Our cross-sectional regression model is given by eq. (10) and the variables are defined in table 5,

$$CAR = \gamma_0 + \gamma_1 T_1 + \gamma_2 T_2 + \gamma_3 M + \gamma_4 F. \tag{10}$$

The dummy variables T_1 and T_2 indicate the time period (environment) in which the tender offer is made. T_1 equals one if the offer is made between July 1, 1968 and December 1980, and zero otherwise. It is included to account for the effect of the passage of the Williams Amendment. T_2 equals one if the offer is made after December 1980, and zero otherwise. It is included to account for the changes in the acquisitions arena that have occurred in the 1980s.

The dummy variable M, which equals one if the offer is made in a multiple-bidder contest and zero otherwise, reflects the level of competition. We restrict our analysis of competition to a simple single/multiple-bidder classification instead of the number of bidders, because our multiple-bidder sample consists of 65 contests with two bidding firms and only 8 with more

Table 5

Weighted least-squares estimates of the effects of time-period, multiple-bidder contests, and fraction of shares purchased on the abnormal returns to the stockholders of the targets ($CART$), acquirers ($CARA$), and combined ($CARC$) involved in 236 successful tender offers between 1963 and 1984 (t-statistics in parentheses).[a]

Model: $CAR = \gamma_0 + \gamma_1 T_1 + \gamma_2 T_2 + \gamma_3 M + \gamma_4 F.$

Dependent Variable	$\hat{\gamma}_0$	$\hat{\gamma}_1$	$\hat{\gamma}_2$	$\hat{\gamma}_3$	$\hat{\gamma}_4$	F-statistic
$CART$	0.098	0.080	0.053	0.130	0.167	14.84[b]
	(3.89)	(3.22)	(1.40)	(4.23)	(4.26)	
$CARA$	0.035	−0.025	−0.055	−0.017	0.005	4.20[c]
	(2.65)	(−2.07)	(−3.43)	(−1.32)	(0.27)	
$CARC$	0.069	(−0.012)	−0.018	0.024	0.006	0.66[d]
	(4.60)	(−0.87)	(−0.91)	(1.35)	(0.28)	

[a]$CART$ = cumulative abnormal return to the target shares from five trading days before the announcement of the first bid through five trading days after the announcement of the ultimately successful bid; $CARA$ = cumulative abnormal return to the acquiring firm from five trading days before the announcement of the first offer made by this firm through five trading days after the announcement of the ultimately successful bid; $CARC$ = cumulative abnormal return to the value-weighted portfolio of the target and the acquiring firms from five trading days before the announcement of the first offer made for the target through five days after the announcement of the ultimately successful bid; T_1 = dummy variable that equals one if the offer is made between July 1, 1968 and December 1980, and zero otherwise; T_2 = dummy variable that equals one if the offer is made after December 1980, and zero otherwise; M = dummy variable that equals one if the offer is made in a multiple-bidder contest, and zero otherwise; F = fraction of target shares purchased in the offer by the successful bidder.

[b]Significant at the 0.01 level.

[c]Significant at the 0.05 level.

[d]Insignificantly different from zero.

than two bidding firms. Our analysis in section 3 indicates that the estimate of γ_3 will be positive for targets and negative for acquirers.

The final independent variable included in our regression model is F, the fraction of target shares purchased by the successful bidding firm. A positively sloping supply of target shares implies that the return to target stockholders will be positively related to F.[19]

Finally, to account for the possibility of heteroskedasticity in the data, all observations are divided by the standard error of the K_i-day CAR. This is equivalent to using weighted least squares to estimate the regression parameters, where the standard error of the firm's CAR is the relevant weight. This

[19]We perform all our cross-sectional tests using two definitions of F. In the first, the denominator is simply the total number of shares outstanding; in the second, we adjust the denominator by subtracting the number of shares held by the acquirer (prior to the offer) from the total number of shares outstanding. The results are virtually identical using these alternative measures. In the text we only report results based on the first definition.

standard error is computed as the square root of the sum of the variances of the prediction errors over the K_i days.[20]

4.2.1. Returns to target stockholders

The results of our regression analysis for the sample of target firms are reported in the first row of table 5. The estimates of γ_0 and γ_1 are both statistically greater than zero. These statistics imply that the average abnormal return to target stockholders is significantly positive ($\hat{\gamma}_0 = 9.8\%$, $t = 3.89$) and even more so after the passage of the Williams Amendment ($\hat{\gamma}_1 = 8.0\%$, $t = 3.22$).[21] The point estimate of γ_2 is also positive ($\hat{\gamma}_2 = 5.3\%$, $t = 1.40$) but is not significantly different from zero.[22]

The estimated coefficient of the single/multiple-bidder dummy variable is significantly greater than zero ($\hat{\gamma}_3 = 13.0\%$, $t = 4.23$). Consistent with the earlier results, the marginal impact of a multiple-bidder contest is to increase the return to the target stockholders.

The estimated coefficient on the fraction of target shares purchased, F, is significantly positive ($\hat{\gamma}_4 = 16.7\%$, $t = 4.26$). This is consistent with a positively sloping supply of target shares.

4.2.2. Returns to the stockholders of acquiring firms

The second row of table 5 reports the results of our cross-sectional regression analysis for acquiring firms.[23] The estimate of the constant is significantly

[20]Specifically, the standard error of CAR is given by $(\sum_t^{K_i} \sigma_i^2 C_{it})^{1/2}$, where $C_{it} = (1 + 1/T + ((R_{mt} - \bar{R}_m)^2 / \sum_\tau^T (R_{m\tau} - \bar{R}_m)^2))$, σ_i is the standard deviation of the residuals from the estimation period of T days, and $\bar{R}_m$ is the mean return on the market over the estimation period.

[21]This result is consistent with the findings of Jarrell and Bradley (1980). They find that the passage of the Williams Amendment is associated with an increase in the returns to targets and a decrease in the returns to acquirers.

[22]The lack of statistical significance of the estimate of γ_2 may be due to the positive relation between the second time-period dummy variable, T_2, and the multiple/single-bidder dummy variable, M. The simple correlation between these two independent variables is 0.18 ($P = 0.007$). Multicollinearity between two independent variables biases the t-statistics of the estimated coefficients toward zero.

[23]Earlier studies suggest that the average rate of return to *all* acquiring firms may not be an appropriate measure of the gains from tender offers because of the disparity between the values of the target and acquiring firms. The acquisition of a very small firm by a very large firm may have an imperceptible effect on the return to the acquiring firm regardless of the profitability of the acquisition. Consistent with this observation, Asquith, Bruner, and Mullins (1983) show that the measured returns to acquiring firms are positively related to a dummy variable that indicates whether the target is at least 10% of the value of the acquiring firm. Jarrell (1983) generalizes this finding and shows that the return to acquiring firms is a continuous positive function of the relative value of the target. Kim and McConnell (1977) and Asquith and Kim (1982) limit their analysis to acquisitions involving targets that are at least 10% of the value of their respective acquiring firms. Thus, the regressions for acquiring firms were run on two data sets: the entire 236-observation sample and a subsample in which the targets are at least 10% of the value of their acquirers. (There are 171 tender offer events in which the relative size of the target is 10% or more.) Because none of our empirical results are materially different for the reduced sample, we report only results for the total sample.

positive ($\hat{\gamma}_0 = 3.5\%$, $t = 2.65$) which indicates that the average return to acquiring firms in single-bidder tender offers effected before passage of the Williams Amendment was significantly positive. The estimates of γ_1 and γ_2 are both significantly negative ($\hat{\gamma}_1 = -2.5\%$, $t = -2.07$ and $\hat{\gamma}_2 = -5.5\%$, $t = -3.43$, respectively). Thus, bidding firms earn significantly lower returns in the post-Williams Amendment era. Moreover, the estimate of γ_2 is less than the estimate of γ_1, which is consistent with our earlier results in table 2 that the returns to acquiring firms have decreased over time and that in the most recent subperiod acquiring firms actually suffered a significant loss.

The point estimate of the coefficient on the single/multiple-bidder dummy variable ($\gamma_3 = -1.7\%$, $t = -1.32$) shows that the marginal impact of multiple-bidder contests is to reduce the returns to acquiring firms, but this estimate is not significantly different from zero.[24] Note that higher returns to targets from multiple-bidder contests do not translate into corresponding lower returns to acquiring firms unless the total synergistic gains are the same in multiple-bidder and single-bidder contests. We return to this issue in the next subsection.

Finally, we note without much elaboration that the return to acquiring firms is unrelated to F, the fraction of shares purchased; the estimate of γ_4 has a t-statistic of 0.27. By our analysis this relation (estimate) should be negative: all else constant, the greater F, the greater the returns to targets and the smaller the returns to acquirers. However, this implication is based on the assumption that the total synergy created and the preoffer values of the target and acquiring firms are all independent of F. Violation of any of these independence assumptions would negate the prediction of a negative relation between F and $CARA$. No attempt was made to pursue this issue further.

To provide a more intuitive presentation of the separate effects of regulation and competition on the returns to acquiring firms, we report the $CARA$ by time period and our multiple/single-bidder classification in table 6. The data show that acquiring firms gained most (4.62%, $z = 5.99$) in single-bidder contests effected during the unregulated period of 1963–1968; they lost the most (−5.10%, $z = -2.87$) in multiple-bidder contests effected in the most recent period (1981–1984).

Perhaps the most notable of the data reported in table 6 is that the 52 acquiring firms in the most recent period (1981–1984) realized a significant abnormal loss of −2.93% ($z = -2.79$). This period is associated with an increase in the extent and degree of Congressional regulations, the tolerance of Reagan Administration towards large-scale mergers, the advent of investment banking firms that specialize in raising funds to finance takeover battles, and the development of sophisticated defensive tactics. We believe that all of these

[24] Once again we note that the multicollinearity between T_2 and M biases the t-statistics of the estimated coefficients of each toward zero. See footnote 22.

Table 6

Percent mean abnormal return to acquirers involved in 236 successful tender offers between 1963 and 1984, by time period and multiple/single-bidder classification (z-statistics in parentheses).

	Subperiod			Total
	7/63–6/68	7/68–12/80	1/81–12/84	7/63–12/84
Single bidder	4.62[a] (5.99) $N = 42$	1.74[b] (2.04) $N = 93$	−1.08 (−1.14) $N = 28$	2.00[a] (4.11) $N = 163$
Multiple bidder	1.62 (1.05) $N = 9$	0.27 (0.22) $N = 40$	−5.10[a] (−2.87) $N = 24$	−1.33 (−1.44) $N = 73$
Total	4.09[a] (5.88) $N = 51$	1.30 (1.58) $N = 133$	−2.93[a] (−2.79) $N = 52$	0.97[a] (2.61) $N = 236$

[a]Significant at the 0.01 level.
[b]Significant at the 0.01 level.

factors have contributed to an increase in competition among bidding firms. Consistent with this conjecture, the data in the table indicate an increasing trend in the relative frequency of multiple-bidder contests over time; 18%, 30%, and 46%, in subperiods 1963–1968, 1968–1980, and 1981–1984, respectively. Obviously, an increase in competition among bidders does not explain negative returns to acquirers. However, if every successful bidder is pushed to its maximum valuation of the target, there is a greater probability that overvaluations will occur and the acquirer's shareholders will suffer a capital loss. This adverse effect was most severe during the period 1981–1984, when the shareholders on average lost 5.10% ($z = -2.87$) as a result of successful acquisitions in multiple-bidder contests.

In light of these results, we note our earlier finding [Bradley, Desai, and Kim (1983)] that the *un*successful bidders in multiple-bidder contests during the period 1963–1980 on average lost 8% of their preoffer value. In contrast, the data in table 6 show that the average gain to the successful bidders in multiple-bidder contests during the same period (1963–1980) is not significantly different from zero. Thus, it appears that once a firm finds itself in a bidding war, it is better to win than lose, even though in winning, the firm's stockholders may suffer a capital loss.

On the basis of our time-series analysis in section 4.1, we conjectured that the low returns to acquiring firms in multiple-bidder contests are driven by the negative returns to so-called white knights. The results of our cross-sectional analysis reinforce this conclusion. As reported in table 6, the mean *CARA* of the 73 successful bidders in our multiple-bidder sample is −1.33% ($z = -1.44$). The mean *CARA* to the 24 first-bidder acquirers is 0.81% ($z = 0.41$), whereas the mean *CARA* for the 49 late-bidder acquirers (white knights) is −2.38%

($z = -2.05$). Clearly, the evidence is consistent with our contention that white knights, on average, pay 'too much' for the targets they acquire.

4.2.3. Total percentage synergistic gains

The results of our cross-sectional regression analysis for the relative synergistic gains (*CARC*) are presented in the third row of table 5. The data show that only the estimate of γ_0 is significantly different from zero. The estimate of the constant indicates that the average unregulated, single-bidder tender offer results in an increase in the combined values of the two firms.

The estimate of the coefficient on the multiple/single-bidder dummy variable is positive but the t-statistic is only 1.35. We interpret this as weak evidence that competition among bidding firms generates additional information that leads to a higher-valued allocation of the combined resources of the two firms.[25] Alternatively, it may be that the potential for large synergistic gains attracts multiple bidders. At any rate, the positive relation between our measure of synergistic gains and our multiple/single-bidder dummy variable partially explains the lack of a significant negative relation between the returns to acquiring firms and the multiple/single-bidder dummy variable.

Finally, neither of the estimated coefficients on the time dummy variables is significantly different from zero. This suggests that the effects of increased regulation, developments in the investment banking industry, and the use of defensive tactics have been a zero sum game. That is, the increased gains to the stockholders of target firms have come at the expense of the gains to the stockholders of acquired firms.

5. Summary and conclusions

This paper provides a theoretical and empirical analysis of interfirm tender offers. We analyze the mechanics of the tender offer process and demonstrate how this capital market transaction allocates corporate resources to their highest-valued use. Our empirical analysis documents the synergistic gains created by tender offers and how these gains are divided between the stockholders of the target and acquiring firms.

Our analysis of the tender offer process, which is presented in the appendix, demonstrates that a successful tender offer must be front-end loaded. More importantly, we show that two-tier, front-end loaded tender offers are not coercive and do not impede the (optimal) allocation of the target resources. Indeed, we argue that all successful offers, even partial and any and all offers,

[25] The positive correlation between the time-period dummy variables (T_1 and T_2) and the multiple/single-bidder dummy variable (M) biases the t-statistics of the estimated coefficients toward zero.

are front-end loaded. We also argue that although there are three parameters of any tender offer, rival bidding firms compete on the front-end offer price rather than the back-end price or the fraction of shares sought. The data are consistent with both conjectures.

On the basis of this characterization of the tender offer process, we show that the bidding firm that can effect the highest-valued reallocation of the target resources can always fashion the highest-valued (winning) bid. We also show that target managers are always able to structure an intrafirm tender offer that can defeat a value-decreasing interfirm tender offer. Thus, the management team that can effect the highest-valued allocation of the target resources will acquire (maintain) control of the target.

Our empirical investigation is based on an exhaustive sample of successful tender offers effected between 1963 and 1984 in which both the target and acquiring firms were listed on either the NYSE or AMEX at the time of the acquisition. The average synergistic gain created by the 236 offers in our sample is $117 million (in December 1984 dollars), representing a 7.4% increase in the combined wealth of the stockholders of the target and acquiring firms. This finding is consistent with the synergy hypothesis advanced by Bradley, Desai, and Kim (1983) and inconsistent with Roll's (1986) 'Hubris Hypothesis'.

We find that target stockholders have captured the lion's share of the gains from tender offers, and their share of the gains has increased significantly since the passage of the Williams Amendment in 1968. Acquiring firms, on the other hand, realized a significant positive gain only during the unregulated period 1963–1968 and, in fact, suffered a significant loss during the most recent subperiod, 1981–1984. We also find that the total percentage synergistic gains from tender offers have remained remarkably constant over time. Thus, government regulations and other changes that have occurred in the tender offer environment have been a zero sum game: the increase in the gains to the target stockholders has come at the expense of the stockholders of acquiring firms.

Our empirical analysis confirms our contention that competition among bidding firms increases the returns to targets and decreases the returns to acquirers. However, competition is not a zero sum game: total synergistic gains are larger in multiple-bidder acquisitions. Thus, the targets of multiple-bidder contests realize greater gains not only at the expense of the shareholders of acquiring firms but also from the greater synergistic gains that accompany these transactions.

We find that competition among bidding firms reduces the average gain to acquirers to a level that is not significantly different from zero. This adverse effect of competition is most severe for late-bidder acquirers, more commonly known as white knights. On average, the white knights in our sample pay 'too much' for the targets they acquire.

Our data also show that the return to target firms is positively related to the fraction of target shares purchased. This is consistent with our contention that tax considerations and/or heterogeneous expectations among target shareholders generate a positively sloped supply of target shares.

In sum, our theoretical analysis implies that interfirm tender offers are efficient mechanisms to channel corporate resources to higher-valued uses. Our empirical results are consistent with this implication. We therefore see no justification for the continuing efforts by those in Washington to 'reform' the tender offer process.[26] Rather, we believe that public policy should be directed toward facilitating this capital market transaction.

Appendix: An analysis of the tender offer process[27]

The objective of this appendix is to demonstrate analytically the contentions made in section 3.3. To this end, we develop a stylized model of the tender offer process that is consistent with existing legal and institutional constraints.[28] We analyze the mechanics of the tender offer process and demonstrate how market forces arise to solve various problems posed by this capital market transaction. Specifically, we show (1) how bidding firms use front-end loaded offers to solve the free-rider problem and (2) how the potential for competing bids by target managers solves the prisoner's dilemma and ensures that successful tender offers will be value-increasing transactions for target stockholders. More important, we demonstrate how market forces ensure that the management team that can effect the highest-valued allocation of the target resources will acquire (maintain) control of the target. Although some of these issues have been discussed elsewhere in the literature, we do provide some new insights into the mechanics of the tender offer and the process of competition in the market for corporate control.

A.1. Tender offers and the free-rider problem

A.1.1. The problem

The free-rider problem associated with tender offers has been analyzed by several authors.[29] The issue can be illustrated by means of a simple numerical example. Consider an all-equity target firm with ten shares outstanding, each selling at \$40: a \$400 firm. Assume that if a potential acquiring firm were to

[26] Lehn and Jones (1987) document that over the past three years, at least 74 bills have been introduced by more than 100 senators or congressmen to further regulate corporate takeovers.

[27] This appendix is a revised version of a model developed in Bradley and Kim (1984). In revising this portion of the paper, we have benefited greatly from helpful discussions with Elazar Berkovitch.

[28] For alternative modeling of tender offers, see Berkovitch and Khanna (1986), Fishman (1986), Khanna (1986), and Shleifer and Vishny (1986).

[29] See Bradley (1980) and Grossman and Hart (1980).

secure control of the target, it could reallocate the firm's resources in such a way that the market value of the target firm's assets would increase to \$600. Thus the acquisition would generate a \$200 synergistic gain.

Assume that in an attempt to exploit the available synergies, a potential acquirer makes the following offer. It will purchase five of the outstanding target shares (a controlling interest) at \$50 per share (a 25% premium). If the offer is successful, the market price per share will rise to \$60 (= \$600/10). If fewer than five shares are tendered, the offer will be withdrawn and the target's share price will fall back to the preoffer level of \$40 per share.[30]

If we assume that the target stockholders behave as atomistic wealth maximizers, their optimal response to this offer is clear. They will hold on to their shares because the payoff will be greater if they wait until others tender their shares and the value of the target is increased by the takeover. As a consequence, no one will tender, even though by tendering they would all realize a substantial capital gain. This result is nothing more than a manifestation of the free-rider problem. The inability of target stockholders to write and enforce a contract that all will tender leads each separately not to tender. Each hopes that the others will tender so that the value of the target will be increased by the takeover, but none will tender for \$50 if the postexecution market value of the target shares is (expected to be) \$60. Those who do not tender will hope to free ride on those who do, but because all target stockholders will feel this way, no shares will be tendered.

A.1.2. The solution

The obvious solution to the free-rider problem is for the bidding firm to make a two-tier bid and front-end load the offer. Specifically, the bidding firm must set P_T, the offer price, greater than P_E, the (expected) postoffer price. In our example, the bidding firm could offer to buy five shares at \$60 and stipulate that if five shares (a controlling block) were obtained, it would effect a takeout merger and redeem the remaining five shares for \$50 a piece.

The dominating response for any target stockholder to this revised bid is to tender. By assumption, if the offer is unsuccessful, each stockholder's wealth will remain at its preoffer level. If the offer is successful and a target stockholder does not tender, however, he will forego the takeover premium, $P_T - P_E$. Since all target stockholders will evaluate the offer in the same manner, all will tender and the offer will be successful.

The implication of the foregoing analysis is clear. A necessary condition for a successful tender offer is that it be front-end loaded, i.e., $P_T > P_E$. By front-end loading the offer, the bidding firm provides an incentive for target stockholders to tender and thus solves the free-rider problem.

[30] Bradley, Desai, and Kim (1983) document that the market price of the shares of a target of an unsuccessful tender offer falls back to the pretender offer level if the target is not taken over within the next five years.

A.2. The prisoner's dilemma and corporate raiders

A.2.1. The problem

Critics of the tender offer process often claim that front-end loaded offers are coercive in that target stockholders have no real choice but to tender under such terms. Further, critics argue that the coercive nature of front-end loaded, two-tier offers allows so-called corporate raiders to acquire the assets of a target for something less than their preoffer market value. To illustrate this point, we return to the numerical example in which the hypothetical target has 10 shares outstanding, each worth \$40. Assume that a potential corporate raider makes the following two-tier bid. The raider will pay \$50 per share (a 25% premium) for five target shares. Having obtained control of the target, it will then redeem the remaining target shares for \$20 per share. If fewer than five shares are tendered, the offer will be withdrawn. In terms of our earlier notation, $P_T = \$50$ and $P_E = \$20$.

The 'corporate-raiding' aspect of the above offer lies in the fact that the bidding firm is attempting to buy a \$400 firm for \$350: \$250 on the front end and \$100 on the back end. Table 7 illustrates the payoff matrix faced by a target stockholder with two shares. The two possible responses are to hold or to tender. Without any loss in generality, we consider three possible aggregate market responses: fewer than five shares are tendered, in which case the offer will be withdrawn and the price of the target shares will fall to their preoffer level; exactly five shares are tendered and all are accepted by the bidding firm; and all outstanding shares are tendered and, following federal regulations, five shares are accepted on a pro-rata basis. The entries in table 7 reflect the changes from preoffer wealth of \$80.

Reading the entries across the first row of table 7, if the stockholder does not tender and the offer is unsuccessful, his wealth will be unaffected. If the offer is successful, however, he will lose \$40. Each of his two shares will be redeemed in the back end of the offer for \$20.

If the stockholder tenders and the offer is unsuccessful, his wealth will be unaffected. If exactly five shares are tendered, the stockholder will receive \$100: \$50 for each share tendered. This will increase his wealth by \$20. If all outstanding shares are tendered, the offer will be executed on a pro rata basis and the stockholder will receive \$50 for one share (the front end) and \$20 for the other (the back end). Thus, he will receive \$70 for his two-share portfolio for a net loss of \$10.

The entries in table 7 indicate that the dominant strategy is to tender: if the offer is successful, the shareholder's wealth will be greater; and if the offer is unsuccessful, his wealth will be no different. Thus, each target stockholder acting in his self-interest will tender all of his shares. As a result, the offer will be successful and the acquiring firm will have obtained a \$400 firm for \$350.

Table 7

Wealth changes for a target stockholder (owning two shares) contingent on aggregate stockholder response and his individual response. Rows indicate stockholder response; columns indicate aggregate stockholder response; and cells indicate change in wealth. *Assumptions*: Target is an all-equity firm with ten shares outstanding and stockholder owns two shares with a preoffer value of \$40 each. Tender offer is for 50% of the target shares; offer (front-end) price is \$50; (implicit) back-end price is \$20; pro-rata execution.

Individual shareholder response	Aggregate shareholder response: Unsuccessful offer	Successful offer	
	Fewer than five shares tendered	Five shares tendered	All other shares tendered
Hold	0	\$ − 40	\$ − 40
Tender	0	\$ + 20	\$ − 10

The preceding numerical example is general in its application. As long as $P_T > P_E$, target stockholders will find it in their interest to tender. Note that this tendering decision is independent of P_0, the preoffer market price of the target shares. Once a firm receives a takeover bid the behavior of the target stockholders is determined by the relation between P_T and P_E and is independent of P_0.

The potential for a corporate raider to acquire the target assets at less than their market value stems from the inability of the target stockholders to act collectively. The presumption is that it is prohibitively costly for the target stockholders to write and enforce a contract that guarantees that no one will tender and attempt to realize the 25% front-end premium.

A.2.2. Institutional / legal solutions to the Prisoner's Dilemma

Clearly, if target stockholders could act collectively or if arbitrageurs could secure a controlling block of the firm's shares, front-end loaded offers would pose no problem (dilemma). Under these circumstances, the target stockholders or market arbitrageurs would collectively analyze the entire value of each bid according to the equation

$$V = [F \times P_T] + [(1 - F) \times P_E],$$

where F is the fraction of target shares purchased on the front end. That is, they would evaluate each bid in terms of the fraction of shares purchased at the offer price and the fraction purchased (redeemed) at the back-end price. They would then tender collectively to the bidder who offered the highest-valued total bid. Thus, collective action on the part of target stockholders or arbitrageurs could solve the prisoner's dilemma.

Another solution to the prisoner's dilemma stems from the legal/institutional constraints imposed on bidding firms in setting the back-end or takeout price, P_E. Note that corporate 'raiding' requires bidding firms to be able to set P_E below the preoffer price, P_0. The latitude afforded bidding firms in setting the back-end price (P_E) is governed by state statutes and charter provisions. Many states have fair-price *statutes* dictating that the back-end price cannot be lower than the front-end price. Fair-price *charter amendments* impose the same constraints on bidders.[31] Finally, target stockholders can seek an appraisal remedy from the courts if the back-end price is less than 'fair'. The appraisal remedy exists to prevent the exploitation of a minority by a majority of a firm's stockholders. For example, suppose that a bidding firm secures a majority of the firm's shares in the front end of a two-step tender offer. Appraisal statutes exist to insure that the majority will not 'cash out' the minority at an 'unfair' price. In sum, these legal and institutional arrangements impose a limit on the minimum P_E that the bidder can set, and thereby limit the extent to which corporate raiders can ply their trade.

A.2.3. A market solution to the prisoner's dilemma

Even when target stockholders cannot act collectively or they are not 'protected' by legal/institutional sanctions, there will be a market solution to

[31] The constraints imposed by fair-price statutes and fair-price amendments do not vitiate our necessary condition for a successful tender offer that P_T be greater than P_E. Even when these legal and institutional constraints require the back-end price to be nominally equal to the front-end price, there are economic forces at work that make even these offers front-end loaded.

To begin with, fair-price provisions are relevant only in two-step takeovers. Thus, one way to negate their effects is for bidding firms to buy a controlling interest in the target at the stated offer price and never buy the remaining target shares. In other words, the bidding firm could secure a controlling interest in the target and run it as a subsidiary. As long as the bidding firm does not buy the remaining shares in a two-step takeover, fair-price provisions cannot guarantee that the back-end market price will be as great as the front-end offer price.

A second reason why fair-price provisions do not affect our necessary condition for a successful offer is the time value of money. If there is a significant delay between the first and the second steps of a two-step takeover, the value of the front end will be greater than the (present) value of the back end even if the dollar amounts of the two are the same.

Finally, transactions costs may make the front-end price more valuable than the back-end price even when the two are nominally the same. Typically, target stockholders who tender to the front end of a two-step offer do not pay brokerage fees. However, if a significant number of shares are purchased in the front end and, as a result, the major exchanges delist the firm's stock, target stockholders will have to incur transactions costs to have their shares redeemed at the back-end price.

In sum, although fair-price provisions constrain the degree to which bidding firms can effect a front-end loaded acquisition, these constraints do not negate our necessary condition for a successful offer. For many of these same reasons, even any-and-all offers, in which the bidding firm is willing to buy all target shares at a given price, are, for all intents and purposes, front-end loaded offers. For a further analysis of the constraints imposed on bidding firms in setting the back-end or takeout price, see Bradley and Rosenzweig (1986 a, b).

the prisoner's dilemma. Recall that in section A.2.1, the bid of the 'raider' was \$50 each for five shares on the front end and \$20 each for the remaining five shares on the back end; and that in the absence of an alternative bid, target stockholders were induced to tender their shares to this bidder.

Consider now a share repurchase (an intrafirm tender offer) with the following terms. The target managers will pay \$60 each for all shares tendered up to five shares. If more than five shares are tendered, they will effect the offer on a pro-rata basis, and hence, the *implicit* back-end price of this offer is \$20. The question now becomes; how will target stockholders respond to these two competing bids?

We employ the logic of game theory to deduce the 'optimal' response by target stockholders. Assume first that target stockholders believe that the 'raider' will be successful; i.e., the 'raider' will be successful in attracting at least five of the ten target shares. (Note that in our example we assume that the 'raider' will be able to secure control of the target with five shares. To be technically correct we should be talking about securing 51% of the outstanding target shares.) With these beliefs, target stockholders will also believe that the target management will purchase every share tendered at \$60. Consequently, they will not tender to the raider; instead, they will tender to the target management. Clearly, this does not constitute a Nash equilibrium.

Assume now that target stockholders believe that the target managers will be successful in their share repurchase program. Under this set of beliefs, target stockholders will tender to the target managers and the repurchase program will in fact succeed. This is a Nash equilibrium – the beliefs of target stockholders are fulfilled.

Table 8 illustrates the response/outcome payoff matrix facing our two-share target stockholder in the wake of the bid by the 'raider' and the intrafirm tender offer. The entries in the table illustrate that tendering to the share repurchase is the dominant strategy. The obvious outcome of this game is that all target stockholders will tender their shares to the repurchase program and, as indicated in the table, aggregate stockholder wealth will be unchanged.

The importance of the preceding numeric example lies in its generality. Target managers are always able to structure an intrafirm tender offer that dominates the bid of a corporate raider who attempts to acquire the target at below its preoffer market value. The potential for such a dominating intrafirm tender offer solves the prisoner's dilemma.[32] As a result, value-decreasing bids will never be successful and therefore probably are never made.

[32]Another defensive mechanism available to target management is to liquidate the firm and pay out the proceeds as a liquidating dividend. Thus, the firm's liquidation value represents the ultimate lower bound for the value of a successful raiding bid. Kim and Schatzberg (1987) examine a sample of firms that voluntarily liquidated and document that the shareholder wealth increased by an average of 34 percent.

Table 8

Wealth changes for a target stockholder (owning two shares) contingent on aggregate stockholder response and his individual response. Rows indicate stockholder response; columns indicate aggregate shareholder response; and cells indicate change in wealth. *Assumptions*: Target is an all-equity firm with ten shares outstanding and stockholder owns two shares with a preoffer value of $40 each. One tender offer outstanding: bidder offers to buy 50% of the target shares for $50 on the front end and $20 on the back end; a repurchase program outstanding: offer to repurchase up to 50% of the target shares for $60 (on the front end) with an implicit back-end price of $20; pro-rata execution.

	Aggregate market response				
	Repurchase successful		Bidder successful		
Individual shareholder response	50% tendered	All other shares tendered	50% tendered	All other shares tendered	Neither offer successful
Hold	$ − 40	$ − 40	$ − 40	$ − 40	0
Tender to bidder	− 40	− 40	+ 20	− 10	0
Tender repurchase	+ 40	0	+ 40	+ 40	0

A.3. Tender offers with synergistic gains

The analysis presented in the preceding section implies that only value-increasing tender offers will be made. In this section we argue that if there is more than one firm that can effect a value-increasing allocation of the target resources, the firm that can effect the highest synergistic gain will win control of the target. To see this, consider two firms that are able to effect synergistic gains by combining with the target. Assume that bidder 1 can increase the value of the target to $500 and bidder 2 can increase its value to $600. As we will see, both firms will attempt to set as high a front-end price as possible and will try to minimize its back-end price. As discussed earlier, the minimum P_E that a bidding firm can set is determined by legal and institutional factors. Thus we assume that the minimum P_E is specific to the target – as opposed to the bidding firm. For expositional convenience, we assume that the minimum P_E that either bidder can set is the preoffer value of the target firm, which is $40 in our example. With a $40 back-end price, bidder 1 can offer $60 on the front end (for five shares) and bidder 2 can offer $80. The question now becomes: if both bidding firms make their respective maximum offers, how would target stockholders respond?

It is clear that there is no dominant strategy for target stockholders to pursue. There is no unique Nash equilibrium. If target stockholders believe that bidder 1 will win, the optimal strategy is to tender to bidder 1. However, if they believe bidder 2 will win, they will tender to bidder 2. In short, with front-end loaded tender offers it is always better to have tendered to the winning bidder. Thus, each target stockholder will tender to the bidding firm that he believes will win.

Given the above assumptions, bidder 2 (the one that can effect the highest-valued synergy) can make the following revised bid. It can make a firm commitment to purchase up to five (51%) of the target shares for $1 more than bidder 1's offer price ($61), regardless of the number of shares tendered to bidder 1. We now examine the possible equilibria of this revised game.

Assume that target stockholders believe that bidder 2 will win the contest. With this set of beliefs, target stockholders will tender to bidder 2 and bidder 2 will in fact win. This is a Nash equilibrium.

Now assume that target stockholders believe that bidder 1 will win the contest (secure 51% of the target shares). Under these circumstances target stockholders would eschew bidder 1's offer and tender to bidder 2's firm commitment to buy up to 51% of the shares at $61 per share. Since, by assumption, target stockholders believe that bidder 1 will receive at least 51%, they will also believe that bidder 2 will purchase every share tendered for $61 each. Thus, when target stockholders believe that bidder 1 will win, they will tender to bidder 2 instead. Consequently, this is not a Nash equilibrium. Thus, by the above analysis, the only set of beliefs that are consistent with the outcome of the 'game' is that bidder 2, the higher-valued bidder with the firm commitment offer, will win the tender offer contest.

Note that bidder 1 (the lower-valued bidder) will never make an offer with a front-end price greater than $60 a share, nor will it make an unconditional (firm-commitment) offer at $60 a share. Given a minimum back-end price of $40, the acquisition of five shares at greater than $60 a share will result in a value-decreasing transaction for its shareholders. (Recall that bidder 1 can effect only $100 in total synergistic gains.) Moreover, it will never offer a firm commitment at $60 a share, because bidder 1 knows that every share it purchases at $60 will be worth only $40 when bidder 2 inevitably gains control of the target.

The analysis of this appendix generates several important implications. First, in tender offer contests, the successful bidder will be the one that can effect the highest synergistic gains. Second, the total value of the winning offer must be at least equal to the next-highest-valued allocation of the target resources, which is bounded from below by the preoffer market value of the target shares. Thus, successful tender offers will be value-increasing transactions for the stockholders of target firms and will result in the optimal allocation of the target resources.

References

Asquith, P., R. Bruner, and D. Mullins, 1983, The gains to bidding firms from merger, Journal of Financial Economics 11, 121–140.

Asquith, P. and E.H. Kim, 1982, The impact of merger bids on the participating firms' security holders, Journal of Finance 37, 1209–1228.

Berkovitch, E. and N. Khanna, 1986, A theory of acquisition markets: Mergers versus tender offers: Golden parachutes and greenmail, Working paper (University of Michigan, Ann Arbor, MI).

Bradley, M., 1980, Interfirm tender offers and the market for corporate control, Journal of Business 53, 345–376.

Bradley, M. and E.H. Kim, 1984, The advent and mechanics of the tender offer: An analysis of ownership structure and prisoner's dilemma, Proceedings of Seminar on the Analysis of Security Prices 29, 277–302.

Bradley, M. and M. Rosenzweig, 1986a, Defensive stock repurchases, Harvard Law Review 99, 1378–1430.

Bradley, M. and M. Rosenzweig, 1986b, Defensive stock repurchases and the appraisal remedy, Yale Law Journal 96, 322–338.

Bradley, M., A. Desai, and E.H. Kim, 1983, The rationale behind interfirm tender offers: Information or synergy?, Journal of Financial Economics 11, 183–206.

Comment, R. and G. Jarrell, 1987, Two-tier and negotiated tender offers: The imprisonment of the free-riding shareholder, Journal of Financial Economics 19, 283–310.

Dodd, P. and R. Ruback, 1977, Tender offers and stockholder returns, Journal of Financial Economics 5, 351–373.

Eckbo, B.E., 1983, Horizontal mergers, collusion, and stockholder wealth, Journal of Financial Economics 11, 241–274.

Eckbo, B.E., 1985, Mergers and the market concentration doctrine: Evidence from the capital market, Journal of Business 58, 325–349.

Economic report of the President, Feb. 1985.

Fishman, M., 1986, A theory of preemptive takeover bidding, Working paper (Northwestern University, Evanston, IL).

Grossman, S. and O. Hart, 1980, Takeover bids, the free rider problem, and the theory of the corporation, Bell Journal of Economics 11, 42–64.

Jarrell, G., 1983, Do acquirers benefit from corporate acquisitions?, Working paper (University of Chicago, Chicago, IL).

Jarrell, G. and M. Bradley, 1980, The economic effects of federal and state regulations of cash tender offers, Journal of Law and Economics 23, 371–407.

Jensen, M.C., 1985, When Unocal won over Mesa, shareholders and society lost, The Financier 9, 30–52.

Khanna, N., 1986, Optimal bidding for tender offers, Working paper (University of Michigan, Ann Arbor, MI).

Kim, E.H. and J. McConnell, 1977, Corporate merger and the 'co-insurance' of corporate debt, Journal of Finance 32, 349–365.

Kim, E.H. and J. Schatzberg, 1987, Voluntary corporate liquidations, Journal of Financial Economics 19, 311–328.

Lehn, K. and J.W. Jones, 1987, The legislative politics of hostile corporate takeovers, Paper presented at the conference on political economy and business (Washington University, St. Louis, MO).

Loderer, C.F. and D.C. Mauer, 1986, Acquiring firms in corporate mergers: The postmerger performance, Working paper (Purdue University, W. Lafayette, IN).

Patell, J.M., 1976, Corporate forecasts of earnings per share and stock price behavior: Empirical tests, Journal of Accounting Research 14, 246–276.

Roll, R., 1986, The Hubris hypothesis of corporate takeovers, Journal of Business 59, 197–216.

Rosenfeld, A., 1982, Repurchase offers, information adjusted premiums and shareholder response, MERC monograph series MP-8201 (University of Rochester, Rochester, NY).

Ruback, R., 1983, Assessing competition in the market for corporate control, Journal of Financial Economics 11, 141–153.

Shleifer, A. and R.W. Vishny, 1986, Large shareholders and corporate control, Journal of Political Economy 94, 461–488.

Stillman, R., 1983, Examining antitrust policy towards horizontal mergers, Journal of Financial Economics 11, 225–240.

[3]

Agency Costs of Free Cash Flow, Corporate Finance, and Takeovers

By MICHAEL C. JENSEN*

Corporate managers are the agents of shareholders, a relationship fraught with conflicting interests. Agency theory, the analysis of such conflicts, is now a major part of the economics literature. The payout of cash to shareholders creates major conflicts that have received little attention.[1] Payouts to shareholders reduce the resources under managers' control, thereby reducing managers' power, and making it more likely they will incur the monitoring of the capital markets which occurs when the firm must obtain new capital (see M. Rozeff, 1982; F. H. Easterbrook, 1984). Financing projects internally avoids this monitoring and the possibility the funds will be unavailable or available only at high explicit prices.

Managers have incentives to cause their firms to grow beyond the optimal size. Growth increases managers' power by increasing the resources under their control. It is also associated with increases in managers' compensation, because changes in compensation are positively related to the growth in sales (see Kevin Murphy, 1985). The tendency of firms to reward middle managers through promotion rather than year-to-year bonuses also creates a strong organizational bias toward growth to supply the new positions that such promotion-based reward systems require (see George Baker, 1986).

Competition in the product and factor markets tends to drive prices towards minimum average cost in an activity. Managers must therefore motivate their organizations to increase efficiency to enhance the probability of survival. However, product and factor market disciplinary forces are often weaker in new activities and activities that involve substantial economic rents or quasi rents.[2] In these cases, monitoring by the firm's internal control system and the market for corporate control are more important. Activities generating substantial economic rents or quasi rents are the types of activities that generate substantial amounts of free cash flow.

Free cash flow is cash flow in excess of that required to fund all projects that have positive net present values when discounted at the relevant cost of capital. Conflicts of interest between shareholders and managers over payout policies are especially severe when the organization generates substantial free cash flow. The problem is how to motivate managers to disgorge the cash rather than investing it at below the cost of capital or wasting it on organization inefficiencies.

The theory developed here explains 1) the benefits of debt in reducing agency costs of free cash flows, 2) how debt can substitute

*LaClare Professor of Finance and Business Administration and Director of the Managerial Economics Research Center, University of Rochester Graduate School of Management, Rochester, NY 14627, and Professor of Business Administration, Harvard Business School. This research is supported by the Division of Research, Harvard Business School, and the Managerial Economics Research Center, University of Rochester. I have benefited from discussions with George Baker, Gordon Donaldson, Allen Jacobs, Jay Light, Clifford Smith, Wolf Weinhold, and especially Armen Alchian and Richard Ruback.

[1] Gordon Donaldson (1984) in his study of 12 large *Fortune* 500 firms concludes that managers of these firms were not driven by maximization of the value of the firm, but rather by the maximization of "corporate wealth," defined as "*the aggregate purchasing power available to management for strategic purposes during any given planning period*" (p. 3). "In practical terms it is cash, credit, and other corporate purchasing power by which management commands goods and services" (p. 22).

[2] Rents are returns in excess of the opportunity cost of the resources to the activity. Quasi rents are returns in excess of the short-run opportunity cost of the resources to the activity.

for dividends, 3) why "diversification" programs are more likely to generate losses than takeovers or expansion in the same line of business or liquidation-motivated takeovers, 4) why the factors generating takeover activity in such diverse activities as broadcasting and tobacco are similar to those in oil, and 5) why bidders and some targets tend to perform abnormally well prior to takeover.

I. The Role of Debt in Motivating Organizational Efficiency

The agency costs of debt have been widely discussed, but the benefits of debt in motivating managers and their organizations to be efficient have been ignored. I call these effects the "control hypothesis" for debt creation.

Managers with substantial free cash flow can increase dividends or repurchase stock and thereby pay out current cash that would otherwise be invested in low-return projects or wasted. This leaves managers with control over the use of future free cash flows, but they can promise to pay out future cash flows by announcing a "permanent" increase in the dividend. Such promises are weak because dividends can be reduced in the future. The fact that capital markets punish dividend cuts with large stock price reductions is consistent with the agency costs of free cash flow.

Debt creation, without retention of the proceeds of the issue, enables managers to effectively bond their promise to pay out future cash flows. Thus, debt can be an effective substitute for dividends, something not generally recognized in the corporate finance literature. By issuing debt in exchange for stock, managers are bonding their promise to pay out future cash flows in a way that cannot be accomplished by simple dividend increases. In doing so, they give shareholder recipients of the debt the right to take the firm into bankruptcy court if they do not maintain their promise to make the interest and principle payments. Thus debt reduces the agency costs of free cash flow by reducing the cash flow available for spending at the discretion of managers. These control effects of debt are a potential determinant of capital structure.

Issuing large amounts of debt to buy back stock also sets up the required organizational incentives to motivate managers and to help them overcome normal organizational resistance to retrenchment which the payout of free cash flow often requires. The threat caused by failure to make debt service payments serves as an effective motivating force to make such organizations more efficient. Stock repurchase for debt or cash also has tax advantages. (Interest payments are tax deductible to the corporation, and that part of the repurchase proceeds equal to the seller's tax basis in the stock is not taxed at all.)

Increased leverage also has costs. As leverage increases, the usual agency costs of debt rise, including bankruptcy costs. The optimal debt-equity ratio is the point at which firm value is maximized, the point where the marginal costs of debt just offset the marginal benefits.

The control hypothesis does not imply that debt issues will always have positive control effects. For example, these effects will not be as important for rapidly growing organizations with large and highly profitable investment projects but no free cash flow. Such organizations will have to go regularly to the financial markets to obtain capital. At these times the markets have an opportunity to evaluate the company, its management, and its proposed projects. Investment bankers and analysts play an important role in this monitoring, and the market's assessment is made evident by the price investors pay for the financial claims.

The control function of debt is more important in organizations that generate large cash flows but have low growth prospects, and even more important in organizations that must shrink. In these organizations the pressures to waste cash flows by investing them in uneconomic projects is most serious.

II. Evidence from Financial Restructuring

The free cash flow theory of capital structure helps explain previously puzzling results on the effects of financial restructuring. My paper with Clifford Smith (1985, Table 2) and Smith (1986, Tables 1 and 3) summarize more than a dozen studies of stock price changes at announcements of transactions which change capital structure. Most leverage-increasing transactions, including stock repurchases and exchange of debt or preferred for common, debt for preferred, and income bonds for preferred, result in significantly positive increases in common stock prices. The 2-day gains range from 21.9 percent (debt for common) to 2.2 percent (debt or income bonds for preferred). Most leverage-reducing transactions, including the sale of common, and exchange of common for debt or preferred, or preferred for debt, and the call of convertible bonds or convertible preferred forcing conversion into common, result in significant decreases in stock prices. The 2-day losses range from −9.9 percent (common for debt) to −.4 percent (for call of convertible preferred forcing conversion to common). Consistent with this, free cash flow theory predicts that, except for firms with profitable unfunded investment projects, prices will rise with unexpected increases in payouts to shareholders (or promises to do so), and prices will fall with reductions in payments or new requests for funds (or reductions in promises to make future payments).

The exceptions to the simple leverage change rule are targeted repurchases and the sale of debt (of all kinds) and preferred stock. These are associated with abnormal price declines (some of which are insignificant). The targeted repurchase price decline seems to be due to the reduced probability of takeover. The price decline on the sale of debt and preferred stock is consistent with the free cash flow theory because these sales bring new cash under the control of managers. Moreover, the magnitudes of the value changes are positively related to the change in the tightness of the commitment bonding the payment of future cash flows, for example, the effects of debt for preferred exchanges are smaller than the effects of debt for common exchanges. Tax effects can explain some of these results, but not all, for example, the price increases on exchange of preferred for common, which has no tax effects.

III. Evidence from Leveraged Buyout and Going Private Transactions

Many of the benefits in going private and leveraged buyout (*LBO*) transactions seem to be due to the control function of debt. These transactions are creating a new organizational form that competes successfully with the open corporate form because of advantages in controlling the agency costs of free cash flow. In 1984, going private transactions totaled $10.8 billion and represented 27 percent of all public acquisitions (by number, see W. T. Grimm, 1985, Figs. 36 and 37). The evidence indicates premiums paid average over 50 percent.[3]

Desirable leveraged buyout candidates are frequently firms or divisions of larger firms that have stable business histories and substantial free cash flow (i.e., low growth prospects and high potential for generating cash flows)—situations where agency costs of free cash flow are likely to be high. The *LBO* transactions are frequently financed with high debt; 10 to 1 ratios of debt to equity are not uncommon. Moreover, the use of strip financing and the allocation of equity in the deals reveal a sensitivity to incentives, conflicts of interest, and bankruptcy costs.

Strip financing, the practice in which risky nonequity securities are held in approximately equal proportions, limits the conflict of interest among such securities' holders and therefore limits bankruptcy costs. A somewhat oversimplified example illustrates the point. Consider two firms identical in every respect except financing. Firm *A* is entirely financed with equity, and firm *B* is highly leveraged with senior subordinated debt, convertible debt and preferred as well

[3]See H. DeAngelo et al. (1984), and L. Lowenstein (1985). Lowenstein also mentions incentive effects of debt, but argues tax effects play a major role in explaining the value increase.

as equity. Suppose firm *B* securities are sold only in strips, that is, a buyer purchasing *X* percent of any security must purchase *X* percent of all securities, and the securities are "stapled" together so they cannot be separated later. Security holders of both firms have identical unlevered claims on the cash flow distribution, but organizationally the two firms are very different. If firm *B* managers withhold dividends to invest in value-reducing projects or if they are incompetent, strip holders have recourse to remedial powers not available to the equity holders of firm *A*. Each firm *B* security specifies the rights its holder has in the event of default on its dividend or coupon payment, for example, the right to take the firm into bankruptcy or to have board representation. As each security above the equity goes into default, the strip holder receives new rights to intercede in the organization. As a result, it is easier and quicker to replace managers in firm *B*.

Moreover, because every security holder in the highly levered firm *B* has the same claim on the firm, there are no conflicts among senior and junior claimants over reorganization of the claims in the event of default; to the strip holder it is a matter of moving funds from one pocket to another. Thus firm *B* need never go into bankruptcy, the reorganization can be accomplished voluntarily, quickly, and with less expense and disruption than through bankruptcy proceedings.

Strictly proportional holdings of all securities is not desirable, for example, because of IRS restrictions that deny tax deductibility of debt interest in such situations and limits on bank holdings of equity. However, riskless senior debt needn't be in the strip, and it is advantageous to have top-level managers and venture capitalists who promote the transactions hold a larger share of the equity. Securities commonly subject to strip practices are often called "mezzanine" financing and include securities with priority superior to common stock yet subordinate to senior debt.

Top-level managers frequently receive 15–20 percent of the equity. Venture capitalists and the funds they represent retain the major share of the equity. They control the board of directors and monitor managers. Managers and venture capitalists have a strong interest in making the venture successful because their equity interests are subordinate to other claims. Success requires (among other things) implementation of changes to avoid investment in low return projects to generate the cash for debt service and to increase the value of equity. Less than a handful of these ventures have ended in bankruptcy, although more have gone through private reorganizations. A thorough test of this organizational form requires the passage of time and another recession.

IV. Evidence from the Oil Industry

Radical changes in the energy market since 1973 simultaneously generated large increases in free cash flow in the petroleum industry and required a major shrinking of the industry. In this environment the agency costs of free cash flow were large, and the takeover market has played a critical role in reducing them. From 1973 to the late 1970's, crude oil prices increased tenfold. They were initially accompanied by increases in expected future oil prices and an expansion of the industry. As consumption of oil fell, expectations of future increases in oil prices fell. Real interest rates and exploration and development costs also increased. As a result the optimal level of refining and distribution capacity and crude reserves fell in the late 1970's and early 1980's, leaving the industry with excess capacity. At the same time profits were high. This occurred because the average productivity of resources in the industry increased while the marginal productivity decreased. Thus, contrary to popular beliefs, the industry had to shrink. In particular, crude oil reserves (the industry's major asset) were too high, and cutbacks in exploration and development (*E&D*) expenditures were required (see my 1986 paper).

Price increases generated large cash flows in the industry. For example, 1984 cash flows of the ten largest oil companies were \$48.5 billion, 28 percent of the total cash flows of the top 200 firms in Dun's *Business Month* survey. Consistent with the agency costs of free cash flow, management did not pay out the excess resources to shareholders. Instead, the industry continued to spend heavily on *E&D* activity even though average returns were below the cost of capital.

Oil industry managers also launched diversification programs to invest funds outside the industry. The programs involved purchases of companies in retailing (Marcor by Mobil), manufacturing (Reliance Electric by Exxon), office equipment (Vydec by Exxon), and mining (Kennecott by Sohio, Anaconda Minerals by Arco, Cyprus Mines by Amoco). These acquisitions turned out to be among the least successful of the last decade, partly because of bad luck (for example, the collapse of the minerals industry) and partly because of a lack of managerial expertise outside the oil industry. Although acquiring firm shareholders lost on these acquisitions, the purchases generated social benefits to the extent they diverted cash to shareholders (albeit to target shareholders) that otherwise would have been wasted on unprofitable real investment projects.

Two studies indicate that oil industry exploration and development expenditures have been too high since the late 1970's. John McConnell and Chris Muscarella (1986) find that announcements of increases in *E&D* expenditures by oil companies in the period 1975–81 were associated with systematic *decreases* in the announcing firm's stock price, and vice versa. These results are striking in comparison with their evidence that the opposite market reaction occurs to changes in investment expenditures by industrial firms, and similar SEC evidence on increases in *R&D* expenditures. (See Office of the Chief Economist, SEC, 1985.) B. Picchi's study of returns on *E&D* expenditures for 30 large oil firms indicates on average the industry did not earn "...even a 10% return on its pretax outlays" (1985, p. 5) in the period 1982–84. Estimates of the average ratio of the present value of future net cash flows of discoveries, extensions, and enhanced recovery to *E&D* expenditures for the industry ranged from less than 60 to 90 cents on every dollar invested in these activities.

V. Takeovers in the Oil Industry

Retrenchment requires cancellation or delay of many ongoing and planned projects. This threatens the careers of the people involved, and the resulting resistance means such changes frequently do not get made in the absence of a crisis. Takeover attempts can generate crises that bring about action where none would otherwise occur.

Partly as a result of Mesa Petroleum's efforts to extend the use of royalty trusts which reduce taxes and pass cash flows directly through to shareholders, firms in the oil industry were led to merge, and in the merging process they incurred large increases in debt, paid out large amounts of capital to shareholders, reduced excess expenditures on *E&D* and reduced excess capacity in refining and distribution. The result has been large gains in efficiency and in value. Total gains to shareholders in the Gulf/Chevron, Getty/Texaco, and Dupont/Conoco mergers, for example, were over $17 billion. More is possible. Allen Jacobs (1986) estimates total potential gains of about $200 billion from eliminating inefficiencies in 98 firms with significant oil reserves as of December 1984.

Actual takeover is not necessary to induce the required retrenchment and return of resources to shareholders. The restructuring of Phillips and Unocal (brought about by threat of takeover) and the voluntary Arco restructuring resulted in stockholder gains ranging from 20 to 35 percent of market value (totaling $6.6 billion). The restructuring involved repurchase of from 25 to 53 percent of equity (for over $4 billion in each case), substantially increased cash dividends, sales of assets, and major cutbacks in capital spending (including *E&D* expenditures). Diamond-Shamrock's reorganization is further support for the theory because its market value *fell* 2 percent on the announcement day. Its restructuring involved, among other things, *reducing* cash dividends by 43 percent, repurchasing 6 percent of its shares for $200 million, selling 12 percent of a newly created master limited partnership to the public, and *increasing* expenditures on oil and gas exploration by $100 million/year.

VI. Free Cash Flow Theory of Takeovers

Free cash flow is only one of approximately a dozen theories to explain takeovers, all of which I believe are of some relevance (see my 1986 paper). Here I sketch out some empirical predictions of the free cash flow theory, and what I believe are the facts that lend it credence.

The positive market response to debt creation in oil industry takeovers (as well as elsewhere, see Robert Bruner, 1985) is consistent with the notion that additional debt increases efficiency by forcing organizations with large cash flows but few high-return investment projects to disgorge cash to investors. The debt helps prevent such firms from wasting resources on low-return projects.

Free cash flow theory predicts which mergers and takeovers are more likely to destroy, rather than to create, value; it shows how takeovers are both evidence of the conflicts of interest between shareholders and managers, and a solution to the problem. Acquisitions are one way managers spend cash instead of paying it out to shareholders. Therefore, the theory implies managers of firms with unused borrowing power and large free cash flows are more likely to undertake low-benefit or even value-destroying mergers. Diversification programs generally fit this category, and the theory predicts they will generate lower total gains. The major benefit of such transactions may be that they involve less waste of resources than if the funds had been internally invested in unprofitable projects. Acquisitions not made with stock involve payout of resources to (target) shareholders and this can create net benefits even if the merger generates operating inefficiencies. Such low-return mergers are more likely in industries with large cash flows whose economics dictate that exit occur. In declining industries, mergers within the industry will create value, and mergers outside the industry are more likely to be low- or even negative-return projects. Oil fits this description and so does tobacco. Tobacco firms face declining demand due to changing smoking habits but generate large free cash flow and have been involved in major acquisitions recently. Forest products is another industry with excess capacity. Food industry mergers also appear to reflect the expenditure of free cash flow. The industry apparently generates large cash flows with few growth opportunities. It is therefore a good candidate for leveraged buyouts and these are now occurring. The $6.3 billion Beatrice *LBO* is the largest ever. The broadcasting industry generates rents in the form of large cash flows on its licenses and also fits the theory. Regulation limits the supply of licenses and the number owned by a single entity. Thus, profitable internal investments are limited and the industry's free cash flow has been spent on organizational inefficiencies and diversification programs—making these firms takeover targets. CBS's debt for stock restructuring fits the theory.

The theory predicts value increasing takeovers occur in response to breakdowns of internal control processes in firms with substantial free cash flow and organizational policies (including diversification programs) that are wasting resources. It predicts hostile takeovers, large increases in leverage, dismantlement of empires with few economies of scale or scope to give them economic purpose (for example, conglomerates), and much controversy as current managers object to loss of their jobs or the changes in organizational policies forced on them by threat of takeover.

The debt created in a hostile takeover (or takeover defense) of a firm suffering severe agency costs of free cash flow is often not permanent. In these situations, levering the firm so highly that it cannot continue to exist in its old form generates benefits. It creates the crisis to motivate cuts in expansion programs and the sale of those divisions which are more valuable outside the firm. The proceeds are used to reduce debt to a more normal or permanent level. This process results in a complete rethinking of the organization's strategy and its structure. When successful a much leaner and competitive organization results.

Consistent with the data, free cash flow theory predicts that many acquirers will tend to have exceptionally good performance prior to acquisition. (Again, the oil industry fits well.) That exceptional performance generates the free cash flow for the acquisition. Targets will be of two kinds: firms with poor management that have done poorly prior to the merger, and firms that have done exceptionally well and have large free cash flow which they refuse to pay out to shareholders. Both kinds of targets seem to exist, but more careful analysis is desirable (see D. Mueller, 1980).

The theory predicts that takeovers financed with cash and debt will generate larger benefits than those accomplished through exchange of stock. Stock acquisitions tend to be different from debt or cash acquisitions and more likely to be associated with growth opportunities and a shortage of free cash flow; but that is a topic for future consideration.

The agency cost of free cash flow is consistent with a wide range of data for which there has been no consistent explanation. I have found no data which is inconsistent with the theory, but it is rich in predictions which are yet to be tested.

REFERENCES

Baker, George, "Compensation and Hierarchies," Harvard Business School, January 1986.

Bruner, Robert F., "The Use of Excess Cash and Debt Capacity as a Motive for Merger," Colgate Darden Graduate School of Business, December 1985.

DeAngelo, H., DeAngelo, L. and Rice, E., "Going Private: Minority Freezeouts and Stockholder Wealth," *Journal of Law and Economics*, October 1984, *27*, 367–401.

Donaldson, Gordon, *Managing Corporate Wealth*, New York: Praeger, 1984.

Easterbrook, F. H., "Two Agency-Cost Explanations of Dividends," *American Economic Review*, September 1984, *74*, 650–59.

Grimm, W. T., *Mergerstat Review*, 1985.

Jacobs, E. Allen, "The Agency Cost of Corporate Control," MIT, February 6, 1986.

Jensen, Michael C., "The Takeover Controversy: Analysis and Evidence," Managerial Economics Research Center, Working Paper No. 86-01, University of Rochester, March 1986.

______, "When Unocal Won Over Pickens, Shareholders and Society Lost," *Financier*, November 1985, *9*, 50–52.

______ **and Smith, C. W., Jr.,** "Stockholder, Manager and Creditor Interests: Applications of Agency Theory," in E. Altman and M. Subrahmanyam, eds., *Recent Advances in Corporate Finance*, Homewood: Richard Irwin, 1985, 93–131.

Lowenstein, L., "Management Buyouts," *Columbia Law Review*, May 1985, *85*, 730–84.

McConnell, John J. and Muscarella, Chris J., "Corporate Capital Expenditure Decisions and the Market Value of the Firm," *Journal of Financial Economics*, forthcoming 1986.

Mueller, D., *The Determinants and Effects of Mergers*, Cambridge: Oelgeschlager, 1980.

Murphy, Kevin J., "Corporate Performance and Managerial Remuneration: An Empirical Analysis," *Journal of Accounting and Economics*, April 1985, *7*, 11–42.

Picchi, B., "Structure of the U.S. Oil Industry: Past and Future," Salomon Brothers, July 1985.

Rozeff, M., "Growth, Beta and Agency Costs as Determinants of Dividend Payout Ratios," *Journal of Financial Research*, Fall 1982, *5*, 249–59.

Smith, Clifford W., "Investment Banking and the Capital Acquisition Process," *Journal of Financial Economics*, Nos. 1–2, *15*, forthcoming, 1986.

***Dun's Business Month*,** "Cash Flow: The Top 200," July 1985, 44–50.

Office of the Chief Economist, SEC, "Institutional Ownership, Tender Offers, and Long-Term Investments," April 1985.

[4]

Richard Roll
University of California, Los Angeles

The Hubris Hypothesis of Corporate Takeovers*

The hubris hypothesis is advanced as an explanation of corporate takeovers. Hubris on the part of individual decision makers in bidding firms can explain why bids are made even when a valuation above the current market price represents a positive valuation error. Bidding firms infected by hubris simply pay too much for their targets. The empirical evidence in mergers and tender offers is reconsidered in the hubris context. It is argued that the evidence supports the hubris hypothesis as much as it supports other explanations such as taxes, synergy, and inefficient target management.

> Finally, knowledge of the source of takeover gains still eludes us. [Jensen and Ruback 1983, p. 47]

I. Introduction

Despite many excellent research papers, we still do not fully understand the motives behind mergers and tender offers or whether they bring an increase in aggregate market value. In their comprehensive review article (from which the above quote is taken), Jensen and Ruback (1983) summarize the empirical work presented in over 40

* The earlier drafts of this paper elicited many comments. It is a pleasure to acknowledge the benefits derived from the generosity of so many colleagues. They corrected several conceptual and substantive errors in the previous draft, directed my attention to other results, and suggested other interpretations of the empirical phenomena. In general, they provided me with an invaluable tutorial on the subject of corporate takeovers. The present draft undoubtedly still contains errors and omissions, but this is due mainly to my inability to distill and convey the collective knowledge of the profession. Among those who helped were C. R. Alexander, Peter Bernstein, Thomas Copeland, Harry DeAngelo, Eugene Fama, Karen Farkas, Michael Firth, Mark Grinblatt, Gregg Jarrell, Bruce Lehmann, Paul Malatesta, Ronald Masulis, David Mayers, John McConnell, Merton Miller, Stephen Ross, Richard Ruback, Sheridan Titman, and, especially, Michael Jensen, Katherine Schipper, Walter A. Smith, Jr., and J. Fred Weston. I also benefited from the comments of the finance workshop participants at the University of Chicago, the University of Michigan, and Dartmouth College, and of the referees.

(*Journal of Business*, 1986, vol. 59, no. 2, pt. 1)

0021-9398/86/5902-0001$01.50

papers. There are many important details in these papers, but Jensen and Ruback interpret them to show overall "that corporate takeovers generate positive gains, that target firm shareholders benefit, and that bidding firm shareholders do not lose" (p. 47).

My purpose here is to suggest a different and less conclusive interpretation of the empirical results. This interpretation may not turn out to be valid, but I hope to show that it has enough plausibility to be at least considered in further investigations. It will be argued here that takeover gains may have been overestimated if they exist at all. If there really are no aggregate gains associated with takeovers, or if they are small, it is not hard to understand why their sources are "elusive."

The mechanism by which takeover attempts are initiated and consummated suggests that at least part of the large price increases observed in target firm shares might represent a simple transfer from the bidding firm, that is, that the observed takeover premium (tender offer or merger price less preannouncement market price of the target firm) overstates the increase in economic value of the corporate combination. To see why this could be the case, let us follow the steps undertaken in a takeover.

> First, the bidding firm identifies a potential target firm.
>
> Second, a "valuation" of the equity of the target is undertaken. In some cases this may include nonpublic information. The valuation definitely would include, of course, any estimated economies due to synergy and any assessments of weak management et cetera that might have caused a discount in the target's current market price.
>
> Third, the "value" is compared to the current market price. If value is below price, the bid is abandoned. If value exceeds price, a bid is made and becomes part of the public record. The bid would not generally be the previously determined "value" since it should include provision for rival bids, for future bargaining with the target, and for valuation errors inter alia.

The key element in this series of events is the valuation of an asset (the stock) that already has an observable market price. The preexistence of an active market in the identical item being valued distinguishes takeover attempts from other types of bids, such as for oil-drilling rights and paintings. These other assets trade infrequently and no two of them are identical. This means that the seller must make his own independent valuation. There is a symmetry between the bidder and the seller in the necessity for valuation.

In takeover attempts, the target firm shareholder may still conduct a valuation, but it has a lower bound, the current market price. The bidder knows for certain that the shareholder will not sell below that; thus when the valuation turns out to be below the market price, no offer is made.

Consider what might happen if there are no potential synergies or other sources of takeover gains but when, nevertheless, some bidding firms believe that such gains exist. The valuation itself can then be considered a random variable whose mean is the target firm's current market price. When the random variable exceeds its mean, an offer is made; otherwise there is no offer. Offers are observed only when the valuation is too high; outcomes in the left tail of the distribution of valuations are never observed. The takeover premium in such a case is simply a random error, a mistake made by the bidding firm. Most important, the observed error is always in the same direction. Corresponding errors in the opposite direction are made in the valuation process, but they do not enter our empirical samples because they are not made public.

If there were no value at all in takeovers, why would firms make bids in the first place? They should realize that any bid above the market price represents an error. This latter logic is alluring because market prices do seem to reflect rational behavior. But we must keep in mind that prices are averages. There is no evidence to indicate that every individual behaves as if he were the rational economic human being whose behavior seems revealed by the behavior or market prices. We may argue that markets behave as if they were populated by rational beings. But a market actually populated by rational beings is observationally equivalent to a market characterized by grossly irrational individual behavior that cancels out in the aggregate, leaving the trace of the only systematic behavioral component, the small thread of rationality that all individuals have in common. Indeed, one possible definition of irrational or aberrant behavior is independence across individuals (and thus disappearance from view under aggregation).

Psychologists are constantly bombarding economists with empirical evidence that individuals do not always make rational decisions under uncertainty. For example, see Oskamp (1965), Tversky and Kahneman (1981), and Kahneman, Slovic, and Tversky (1982). Among psychologists, economists have a reputation for arrogance mainly because this evidence is ignored; but psychologists seem not to appreciate that economists disregard the evidence on individual decision making because it usually has little predictive content for market behavior. Corporate takeovers are, I believe, one area of research in which this usually valid reaction of economists should be abandoned; takeovers reflect individual decisions.

There is little reason to expect that a particular individual bidder will refrain from bidding because he has learned from his own past errors. Although some firms engage in many acquisitions, the average individual bidder/manager has the opportunity to make only a few takeover offers during his career. He may convince himself that the valuation is right and that the market does not reflect the full economic value of the combined firm. For this reason, the hypothesis being offered in this paper to explain the takeover phenomenon can be termed the "hubris hypothesis." If there actually are no aggregate gains in takeover, the phenomenon depends on the overbearing presumption of bidders that their valuations are correct.

Even if gains do exist for some corporate combinations, at least part of the average observed takeover premium could still be caused by valuation error and hubris. The left tail of the distribution of valuations is truncated by the current market price. To the extent that there are errors in valuation, fewer negative errors will be observed other than positive errors. When gains exist, a smaller fraction of the distribution will be truncated than when there are no gains at all. Nonetheless, truncation will occur in every situation in which the gain is small enough to allow the distribution of valuations to have positive probability below the market price.

Rational bidders will realize that valuations are subject to error and that negative errors are truncated in repeated bids. They will take this into account when making a bid. Takeover attempts are thus analogous to the auctions discussed in bidding theory wherein the competing bidders make public offers. In the takeover situation, the initial bidder is the market, and the initial public offer is the current price. The second bidder is the acquiring firm who, conscious of the "winner's curse," biases his bid downward from his estimate of value. In fact, he frequently abandons the auction altogether, allowing the first bidder to win.

In a standard auction, we would observe all cases, including those in which the initial bid was victorious. Theory predicts that the winning bid is an accurate assessment of value. In takeovers, however, if the initial bid (by the market) wins the auction, we throw away the observation. If all bidders accounted properly for the "winner's curse," there would be no particular bias associated with discarding bids won by the market; but if bidders are infected by hubris, the standard bidding theory conclusion would not be valid. Empirical evidence from repeated sealed bid auctions (Capen, Clapp, and Campbell 1971; and Dougherty and Lohrenz 1976), indicates that bidders do not fully incorporate the winner's curse. Unless there is something curative about the public nature of corporate takeover auctions, we should at least consider the possibility that the same phenomenon exists in them.

The hubris hypothesis is consistent with strong-form market efficiency. Financial markets are assumed to be efficient in that asset prices reflect all information about individual firms. Product and labor markets are assumed efficient in the sense that (*a*) no industrial reorganization can bring gains in an aggregate output at the same cost or reductions in aggregate costs with the same output and (*b*) management talent is employed in its best alternative use.

Most other explanations of the takeover phenomenon rely on strong-form market inefficiency of at least a temporary duration. Either financial markets are ignorant of relevant information possessed by bidding firms, or product markets are inefficiently organized so that potential synergies, monopolies, or tax savings are being ineffectively exploited (at least temporarily), or labor markets are inefficient because gains could be obtained by replacement of inferior managers. Although perfect strong-form efficiency is unlikely, the concept should serve as a frictionless ideal, the benchmark of comparison by which other degrees of efficiency are measured. This is, I claim, the proper role for the hubris hypothesis of takeovers; it is the null against which other hypotheses of corporate takeovers should be compared.

Section II presents the principal empirical predictions of the hubris hypothesis and discusses supportive and disconfirming empirical results. Section III concludes the paper by summarizing the results and by discussing various objections to the hypothesis.

II. Evidence for and against the Hubris Hypothesis

If there are absolutely no gains available to corporate takeovers, the hubris hypothesis implies that the average increase in the target firm's market value should then be more than offset by the average decrease in the value of the bidding firm. Takeover expenses would constitute the aggregate net loss. The market price of a target firm should increase when a previously unanticipated bid is announced, and it should decline to the original level or below if the first bid is unsuccessful and if no further bids are received.

Implications for the market price reaction of a bidding firm are somewhat less clear. If we could be sure that (*a*) the bid was unanticipated and (*b*) the bid conveys no information about the bidder other than that it is seeking a combination with a particular target, then the hubris hypothesis would predict the following market price movements in bidding firms:

1. a price decline on announcement of a bid;
2. a price increase on abandoning a bid or on losing a bid; and
3. a price decline on actually winning a bid.

It has been pointed out by several authors, most forcefully by Schipper and Thompson (1983), that condition *a* above is by no means assured in all cases. Bids are not always surprises. As Jensen and Ruback (1983, pp. 18–20) observe, this alone complicates the measurement of bidder firm returns.

The possibility that a bid conveys information about the bidding firm's own operations, that is, violation of condition *b*, is an equally serious problem (cf. Jensen and Ruback 1983, p. 19 and n. 14). For example, the market might well interpret a bid as signaling that the bidding firm's immediate past or expected future cash flows are higher than previously estimated, that this has actually prompted the bid, and that, although the takeover itself has a negative value, the combination of takeover and new information is on balance positive.

Similarly, abandoning a previous bid could convey negative information about the bidding firm's ability to pay for the proposed acquisition, perhaps because of negative events in its own operations. Losing a bid to rivals could signal limited resources. These problems of contaminating information make it difficult to interpret bidding firm price movements and to interpret the combined price movements of bidder and target.

A. *The Evidence about Target Firms*

Let us first examine, therefore, the more straightforward implications of the hubris hypothesis for target firms. Bradley, Desai, and Kim (1983*b*) present results for target firms in tender offers that are consistent with the implications. Target firms display increases in value on the announcement of a tender offer, and they fall back to about the original level if no combination occurs then or later.

A similar pattern is observed in Asquith's (1983) sample of target firms in unsuccessful mergers. These firms were targets in one or more merger bids that were later abandoned and for whom no additional merger bids occurred during the year after the last original bid was withdrawn. The original merger bid announcement was accompanied by a 7.0% average increase in target firm value that appears to be almost entirely reversed within 60 days (fig. 1, p. 62). By the date when the last bid is abandoned, the target's price decline amounts to 8.1% (table 9, p. 81), slightly more than offsetting the original increase.

The result may be partially compromised by the following problem. The "outcome date" of an unsuccessful bid is the withdrawal date of the final offer following which no additional bid is received for 1 year. Thus as of the outcome date the market could not have known for certain that other bids would not arrive. However, if the market had known that no other bids would arrive, the price decline would likely have been ever larger, so perhaps this partial use of hindsight was not material. In summary, target firm share behavior, as presented in Bradley et al. (1983*b*) for tender offers and in Asquith (1983) for mergers, is consistent with the hubris hypothesis.

B. *The Evidence about Total Gains*

The central prediction of the hubris hypothesis is that the total combined takeover gain to target and bidding firm shareholders is nonpositive. None of the evidence using returns can unambiguously test this prediction for the simple reason that average returns of individual firms do not measure average dollar gains, especially in the typical takeover situation in which the bidding firm is much larger (cf. Jensen and Ruback 1983, p. 22). In some cases, the observed price increase in the target would correspond to such a trivial loss to the bidder that the loss is bound to be hidden in the bid/ask spread and in the noise of daily return volatility.

In an attempt to circumvent the problem that returns cannot measure takeover gains when bidder and target have different sizes, Asquith, Bruner, and Mullins (1983) take the unique approach of regressing the bidder announcement period return on the relative size of target to bidder. They reason that, if acquisitions benefit bidder firms, large acquisitions should show up as having larger return effects on bidder firm returns. They do find this positive relation for bidding firms. The same relation is not significant for target firms, although, as usual, target firms have much larger average returns. The positive relation for bidding firms is consistent with more than one explanation. It is consistent with the bidding firm losing on average, but losing less the larger the target. Perhaps a more accurate valuation is conducted when the stakes are large and this results in a smaller percentage loss to the bidder. Perhaps large targets are less closely held so that the takeover premium can be smaller relative to the preoffer price and still convince shareholders to deliver their shares. Perhaps bidders for larger targets have fewer rivals and can thus get away with a bidder-perceived "bargain."

The absence of any relation for target firms is puzzling under every hypothesis unless the entire gain accrues to the target firm shareholders (and Asquith et al. [1983] interpret their results to indicate that takeover gains are shared). If synergy is the source of gains, for example, target shareholder's returns would increase with the relative size of its bidder-partner.

Several studies have attempted to measure aggregate dollar gains directly. Halpern (1973) finds average market adjusted gains of \$27.35 million in a sample of mergers between New York Stock Exchange–listed firms (p. 569); the gain was calculated over a period 7 months prior to the first public announcement of the merger through the merger consummation month. The standard error of this average gain, assuming cross-sectional independence, was \$19.7 ($\$173.2/\sqrt{77}$ [see table 3, p. 569]). In 53 cases out of 77, there was a dollar gain.

Bradley, Desai, and Kim (1982) present dollar returns for a sample of 162 successful tender offers from 20 days before the announcement until 5 days after completion. The average combined dollar increase in value of bidder plus target was \$17 million, but this was not statistically significant. The \$17 million gain was divided between a \$34 million average gain by targets and a \$17 million average loss to bidders. The authors note that the equally weighted average rate of return to bidders is positive, though the dollar change is a loss; they argue that this can be explained by skewness in the distribution of dollar changes.

In a revision of their 1982 paper, Bradley, Desai, and Kim (1983*a*) present slightly different results. The sample is expanded from 162 and 183 tender offer events, although the underlying data base appears to be the same (698 tender offers from October 1958 to December 1980). The only stated difference in the selection of samples is that the earlier paper excludes offers that are not "control oriented" (cf. Bradley et al. 1982, p. 13; and Bradley et al. 1983*a*, pp. 35–36). This sample change resulted in an average gain to targets of $28.1 million and to bidders to +$5.8 million (table 9). The authors say, however, that "the distributional properties of our dollar gain measures preclude any meaningful inferences about their significance" (p. 58).

Malatesta (1983) examines the combined change in target and bidder firms before, during, and after a merger. Jensen and Ruback summarize Malatesta's results as follows: "Malatesta examines a matched sample of targets and their bidders in 30 successful mergers and finds a significant average increase of $32.4 million ($t$ = 2.07) in their combined equity value in the month before and the month of outcome announcement. . . . This evidence indicates that changes in corporate control increase the combined market value" (1983, p. 22).

Malatesta (1983) himself does not reach so definite a conclusion. In fact, his overall interpretation of the evidence is that "the immediate impact of merger per se is positive and highly significant for acquired firms but *larger in absolute value and negative* for acquiring firms" (p. 155; emphasis added). Jensen and Ruback were referring to smaller samples of matching pairs. Even for this sample, Malatesta says, the results "provide *weak* evidence that successful resolution of these mergers had a positive impact on combined shareholder wealth" (p. 170; emphasis added). In 2 months culminating in board approval of the merger, the combined gain was positive, but "over the entire interval −60 to 0 [months], the cumulative dollar return is a trivial 0.29 million dollars" (p. 171). Of course, this could be due to selection bias; bidding or acquired firms or both may tend to be involved in mergers after a period of poor performance. According to Asquith's (1983) results, however, this is true only for targets. The opposite is true for bidders; they tend to display superior performance prior to the merger bid announcement. During the culminating merger months, the acquiring firms' gains in Malatesta's sample were not statistically significant (although the acquired firms' were).

Malatesta's month zero is when the board announced merger approval, not when the merger proposal first reached the public. Even if the merger per se has no aggregate value, the price reaction on approval could be positive because it signals that court battles, further bids to overcome rivals, and other costly events associated with hostile mergers will not take place in this case, although their possibility was signaled originally by the merger proposal. Malatesta does not present evidence about the dollar reactions of the combined firm on the first announcement of the merger proposal.

Firth (1980) presents the results of a study of takeovers in the United Kingdom. In his sample, target firms gain, and bidding firms lose, both statistically significantly. The average total change in market value of the two firms in a successful combination, from a month prior to the takeover bid through the month of acceptance of the offer, is £−36.6 million. No t-statistic is given for this number, but we can obtain a rough measure of significance by using the fact that 224 of 434 cases displayed aggregate losses. If these cases were independent, the t-statistic that the true proportion of losing takeovers is greater than 50% is about .67.

The relative division of losses was examined by Firth (1980) in an ingenious calculation that strongly suggests the presence of bidding errors. The premium paid to the target firm (in £) as a fraction of the size of the bidding firm was cross-sectionally related to the percentage loss in the bidding firm's shares around the takeover period. The regression coefficient was −.89 (t = −5.94). Firth concludes (p. 254), "This supports the view that the stock market expects zero benefits from a takeover, that the gains to the acquired firm represent an 'overpayment' and that the acquiring company's shareholders suffer corresponding losses."

Using dollar-based matched pairs of firms, Varaiya (1985) finds that the aggregate abnormal dollar gain of targets is $189.4 million while the average abnormal dollar loss of bidders is $128.7 million for 121 days around the takeover announcement. The aggregate gain of $60.7 ($189.4 − 128.7) is not statistically significant, on the basis of a parametric test, though a nonparametric test does indicate significance. Varaiya also reports a cross-sectional regression that indicates that, the larger the target's dollar gain, the larger the bidder's dollar loss. The regression coefficient was −.81 (t = −2.81).

To summarize, the evidence about total gains in takeovers must be judged inconclusive. Results based on returns are unreliable. Malatesta's dollar-based results show a small aggregate gain in the months just around merger approval in a small matched sample and an aggregate loss in a larger unmatched sample. The interpretation of Malatesta's results is rendered difficult by the possibility of losses or gains in prior months, after announcement of a merger possibility but before final approval is a certainty. Dollar-based results presented by Bradley et al. (1982, 1983*a*) show a small and insignificant aggregate gain. Firth's (1980) British results show an insignificant aggregate loss. Both Firth (1980) and Varaiya (1985) present persuasive evidence for the existence of overbidding. But, on balance, the existence of either gains or losses to the combined firms involved in corporate combinations remains in doubt.

This mixed and insignificant evidence is made even less conclusive (if that is possible) by potential measurement biases. There is a potential upward bias in the measured price reaction of bidding firms (and thus of the aggregate) caused by contaminating information. There is a potential downward bias due to prior anticipation of the takeover event, as explained by Schipper and Thompson (1983), and another potential downward bias in some studies due to an improper computation of abnormal returns (Chung and Weston 1985). These biases will be discussed in detail next, in connection with the empirical findings for bidding firms.

C. Evidence about Bidding Firms: The Announcement Effect

The hubris hypothesis predicts a decrease in the value of the bidding firm. As pointed out previously, this decrease may not be completely reflected in a market price decline because of contaminating information in a bid, because the bid has been (partly) anticipated, or simply because the economic loss is too small to be reliably reflected in prices.

The data contain several interesting patterns. Asquith (1983) finds that bidding firm shares show "no consistent pattern" around the announcement date, but, "in summary, bidding firms appear to have small but insignificant positive excess returns at the press day" (p. 66). Some of Asquith's other results are understandable under the hubris hypothesis. Before the first merger bid, for instance, firms who become successful bidders have much larger price increases than firms whose bids are unsuccessful. One would expect a higher level of hubris and thus more aggressive pursuit of a target in firms that had experienced recent good times.

Asquith's results are in conflict with those of Dodd (1980), who finds statistically significant negative returns at the bid announcement. Jensen and Ruback (1983) noted the difference in results, and they asked Dodd to check his data and computer program, which they report (Jensen and Ruback 1983, p. 17, n. 12) he did without finding an error.[1]

Negative bidder returns were also found by Eger (1983) in her study of pure exchange (noncash) mergers. Bidding firm stock prices de-

1. Recently, Chung and Weston (1985) suggested that part of the difference in results could be explained by an improper calculation of "abnormal" returns around the merger announcement. Chung and Weston point out that the premerger period generally displays statistically significant positive returns for bidding firms. If data from this period are used to estimate abnormal returns at merger announcement, the measured announcement effect will be biased downward. The reported diffrence between, say, Dodd (1980) and Asquith (1983) would be reduced by a recalculation by Dodd excluding the preannouncement period. However, it probably would not be entirely eliminated; the bias appears to be only a small fraction of Dodd's observed announcement effect.

clined, on average by about 4%, from 5 days prior to merger bid announcement to 10 days afterward (Eger 1983, table 4, p. 563). The decline was statistically significant. Eger suggests that the difference between her results and Asquith's (1983) might be attributable to a difference between mergers involving cash and pure stock exchange mergers; and she notes that tender offers, which often involve cash, seem to display more positive bidder stock price reactions (see below).

In his study of United Kingdom takeovers, Firth (1980) reports statistically significant negative bidding firm returns in the month of the takeover announcement. Eighty percent of the bidders had negative abnormal returns during that month, and the *t*-statistic for the average return was about −5.0 (cf. Firth 1980, table 5, p. 248).

Varaiya (1985) also finds statistically significant negative returns for bidding firms on the announcement day. He reports also that the bidder's loss is significantly larger when there are rival bidders.

A recent paper by Ruback and Mikkelson (1984) documents announcement effects of corporate purchases of another corporation's shares according to the stated purpose of the acquisition (filed on form 13-D with the Securities and Exchange Commission). The 2-day announcement effect for acquiring firms was positive and statistically significant for the 370 firms whose stated purpose was not a takeover. In contrast, for 134 acquiring firms indicating an intention to effect a takeover, the announcement effect was negative and significant (table 4, p. 17).

Studies of individual cases have been mixed. For example, Ruback (1982) argues that DuPont's large stock price decline in announcing a bid to take over Conoco could be an indication that managers (of DuPont) "had an objective function different from that of shareholder wealth maximization" (p. 24). However, he rejects this explanation because of "the magnitude of Conoco's revaluation and the lack of evidence that DuPont's management benefitted from the acquisition" (p. 24). He also rejects every other explanation except inside information possessed by DuPont and not yet appreciated by the market; but even this hypothesis "cannot be confirmed since the nature of the information is unknown" (p. 25).

One interesting aspect of the DuPont/Conoco case is that DuPont's decline was more than offset by Conoco's gain; that is, the total gain was positive (although the bidding firm lost). This suggests that nonhubris factors were indeed present, bringing a total gain to the corporate combination, but that overbidding was present too, resulting in a loss to DuPont shareholders.

The other case study by Ruback (1983) finds only a small negative effect for Occidental Petroleum in its bid for Cities Service. Cities Service's stock price increased by a relatively small amount for a target firm, and the total effect was positive. Apparently, there was little significant hubris evidenced by Occidental (who offered only a small premium). An interesting sidelight was the performance of Gulf Oil, a rival bidder who withdrew. It suffered a loss far in excess of Cities Service's gain.

Schipper and Thompson (1983) find a positive price reaction around the announcement that a firm is embarking on a program of conglomerate acquisitions. Also they observe negative price reactions of such firms to antimerger regulatory events. The two findings are interpreted as at least consistent with the proposition that acquisitions are positive net present value projects for the bidding firm. However, the authors emphasize the tentative nature of their conclusion (pp. 109–11). For example, they note that the announcement of an acquisition program is sometimes accompanied by "announcements of related policy decisions, such as de-emphasis of old lines of business, changes in management, changes in capital structure or specific merger proposals" (p. 89). Even without such explicit contaminating information, announcement of the program could be interpreted as good news about the future profitability of the bidder's current assets rather than about the prospect of an undisclosed future target firm to be obtained at a bargain price.

The possibility of contaminating information is a central problem in interpreting the price movement of a bidding firm on the announcement date of an intended acquisition. Bidders are activists in the takeover situation, and their announcements may convey as much information about their own prospects as about the takeover. To mention one example of the measurement problem, mergers are usually leverage-increasing events. It is well documented from studies of other leverage-increasing events, such as exchange offers (Masulis 1980) and share repurchases (Vermaelen 1981), that positive price movements are to be expected. Thus to measure properly that part of the gain of a bidding firm in a merger that is attributable to the merger per se and not to an increase in leverage, we ought to deduct the price increase that would have been obtained by the same firm through independently increasing its leverage by the same amount.[2]

The measurement problem induced by the disparate sizes of target and bidder is the subject of a paper by Jarrell (1983). Jarrell argues that, when a bidder is several times larger than a target, a gain to the bidder equal in size to the gain observed in the target can be hidden in the noise of the bidder's return variability; that is, the t-statistic for the bidder's effect is likely to be much smaller than for the target's effect. Jarrell suggests solving this problem by adjusting the bidder's t-statistic upward by a factor proportional to the relative sizes of bidder and target. When he makes the adjustment in his sample, bidding firms

2. I am grateful to Sheridan Titman for pointing out this possibility.

display significantly positive price movements from 30 days prior to 10 days after the takeover announcement. The mean abnormal return prior to adjustment is 2.3%; after adjustment it is 9.2%. Similarly, the combined bidder and target returns become more statistically significant.

The problem with the Jarrell adjustment is that it can be applied to any sample in order to render a sample mean of either sign statistically significant. For example, if Firth (1980) had adjusted his bidding firm returns downward according to the relative sizes of bidder and target, he could have concluded that British takeovers had significant aggregate negative effects on shareholders. This does not imply that Jarrell's conclusions are incorrect, but we are certainly entitled to remain skeptical. Several studies have reported positive bidder gains, and several others have reported losses. Applying the Jarrell technique indiscriminately to all of them could make the gains or losses more "significant," but this would simply create more confusion since the now "significant" results would disagree across studies.

D. Evidence about Bidding Firms: Resolution of Doubtful Success

There is some evidence available to help isolate the reevaluation of a bidding firm's own assets induced by the bid but not caused by the proposed corporate combination itself. Asquith's (1983) sample of bidding firms in mergers is separated into successful and unsuccessful bidders, and both samples are examined prior to bid announcement, between announcement and merger outcome, and after outcome. For the successful group, merger outcome is the actual date when the target firm is delisted; this is presumably the effective date of the merger. At the original bid announcement, the market cannot know for sure whether such firms actually will consummate the merger, that is, be in the "successful" group. There is only a probability of success. Between the bid announcement and the final outcome this probability goes to 1.0 for firms in the successful group. Thus if the combination itself has value for the bidder, these bidding firms should increase in value over this interim period. They do not. On average, successful bidding firms decline in value by .5% over the interim period (see Asquith 1983, fig. 4, p. 71; table 9, p. 81). The decrease in value is small and statistically insignificant, but the result has economic significance because the opposite sign must be observed if the corporate combination per se has value. If the combination has substantial value, one might have expected to observe a statistically significant upward price movement between bid announcement and outcome, provided, of course, that the upward revision in probability of success is large enough to show up.

Firms in Asquith's successful bidder group have very large prebid returns; abnormal returns average 14.3% over a 460-day period ending

20 days before the bid announcement. They have small positive returns (.2%) on the announcement date. The entire sequence of returns for successful bidding firms is consistent with the hubris hypothesis. In the prebid period, excellent performance endows management with both hubris and cash. A target is selected. The bid itself signals a small upward revision in the market's estimate of the bidding firm's current assets that is not completely offset by the prospect of paying too much for the target. Then there is a small downward revision in bidder firm value as it becomes more probable and then certain that the target will be acquired (at too high a price).

Eckbo (1983) reports a small and insignificant decline during the 3 days subsequent to the initial merger bid. But Eckbo's "successful" bidder is defined as one who is unchallenged on antitrust grounds; this may be a less relevant representation of actual success for our purposes here.

Eger (1983, p. 563) finds significant negative bidder firm returns averaging −3.1% in the 20 days after the original announcement of a merger that is ultimately successful. Most of this decline occurs in the first 10 days after the merger announcement. The bonds of these firms also decline slightly in price over the same period. This is consistent with a price decline in the total value of the bidding firm as it becomes more certain that the merger will succeed.

The most significant price decline between merger proposal and outcome is reported by Dodd (1980). Successful bidding firms decline in value by 7.22% from 10 days before the bid is announced until 10 days after the merger outcome, where outcome is defined as target stockholder approval of merger bid. The price decline is statistically significant. In the 20 days prior to the outcome date, successful bidder firms in Dodd's sample fall in price by about 2% (p. 124).

Evidence from papers using monthly data is more difficult to interpret, but the patterns do seem consistent with a negative price movement between merger announcement and successful outcome. For example, Langetieg's (1978, p. 377) bidding firms show a significant price decline continuing in the combined firm after the merger outcome. Similarly, Chung and Weston (1982, p. 334) report price declines between merger announcement month and merger completion in pure conglomerate mergers. However, the decline is not statistically significant.

Similar evidence is given in Malatesta (1983, table 4, p. 172). Acquiring firms in this sample have significant negative price performance in the period after the first announcement of a merger proposal. Since the data are monthly, the merger outcome date could be included somewhere in the sample period. This means that part of the puzzling post-outcome negative performance detected by Langetieg (1978) and Asquith (1983) might be included in Malatesta's table 4 results. In tables 5 and 6 Malatesta presents performance results for acquiring firms after the "first announcement of board/management approval of the merger" (p. 170). The returns are strongly negative in this period. This might not be such a puzzle if "board/management approval" still leaves open the possibility of withdrawal, for then the absolute certainty of merger (and the concomitant price drop expected under the hubris hypothesis) would occur sometime after this particular event date.

In summary, during the interim period between initial bid and successful outcome, the average price movement of successful merger bids is small, so it is not possible to draw strong implications. However, the pattern is generally consistent with the hubris hypothesis, which predicts the observed loss in value of bidding firm's shares. The loss is statistically insignificant in Asquith's sample but is significant in the samples of Dodd (1980) and Eger (1983) and in the monthly data samples of Langetieg (1978) and Malatesta (1983).

Evidence about the interim period from tender offer studies is mixed. One study seems to be clearly inconsistent with hubris alone; Bradley's (1980) sample of 88 successful bidding firms shows a price rise after the announcement data and before the execution date. The number is not given, but the plot of the mean abnormal price index (p. 366) indicates that the gain is approximately 2%–3%.

The interim price movement of the successful acquiring firm is reported by Ruback and Mikkelson (1984) as −1.07% with a t-statistic of −2.34 (table 6). Their sample is not dichotomized by merger versus tender offers, however, and it probably contains some of both types of takeovers.

The results given by Kummer and Hoffmeister (1978) for a 17-firm matched sample of tender offers are more difficult to interpret because the data are monthly and, apparently because of the small size of the cross-sectional sample, the time series of prices relative to the event data appears to be more variable. Abnormal returns are positive and largest in the announcement month but are also positive in months +1 and +2. If the tender offer is revolved sometime during these 2 months, the results are basically the same as Bradley's (1980). Months +3 to +12 witness a decline of about 4%. If the success of the tender offer is not known until sometime during this period, an interpretation could be made similar to the one discussed above concerning Asquith's and Dodd's samples of successful merger bids.

An identical set of nonconclusive inferences can be drawn from the monthly data of Dodd and Ruback (1977). There appears to be a positive price movement by successful bidders just after the announcement month followed by a price decline later. The decline over the 12 months after a bid amounts to −1.32%, but it is not statistically significant.

Bradley's daily results probably represent the best available evidence against the hubris hypothesis. The detected movement is small, but, unlike the case of merger's, the bidding firm's price does increase on average in Bradley's sample. This is consistent with the proposition that tender offers increase aggregate value and that some of the increase accrues to tender offer bidders. Whether the evidence is sufficiently compelling, particularly when balanced against evidence of an opposite character, is up to further investigation to decide definitely.

One other piece of evidence from the interim period between announcement and outcome is worthy of comtemplation. This is the price behavior of the first bidder's stock on the announcement of a rival bid. In their study of unsuccessful tender offers, Bradley et al. (1983*b*) report a significant price drop in the first bidder's stock. In contrast, Ruback and Mikkelson (1984) report a significant price increase (table 5); however, the latter sample consists not only of ultimately unsuccessful bidders in tender offers but of all corporate investors in other stock (including many who are not contemplating a takeover).

A price drop in the first takeover bidder's stock on the announcement of a rival bid is explainable by hubris. The rival bid may set off a bidding war that the market expects to result in a large loss for the winner. It would be extremely informative to observe the price reaction of the first bidder when it becomes evident that the rival bidder has won.

Finally, it should be noted that the price change after the resolution of a successful bid (either merger or tender offer) is almost uniformly negative (cf. Jensen and Ruback 1983, table 4, p. 21) and is relatively large in magnitude. This is a result that casts doubt on all estimates of bidding firm returns because it suggests the presence of substantial measurement problems.

III. Summary and Discussion

The purpose of this paper is to bring attention to a possible explanation of the takeover phenomenon of mergers and tender offers. This explanation, the hubris hypothesis, is very simple: decision makers in acquiring firms pay too much for their targets on average in the samples we observe. The samples, however, are not random. Potential bids are abandoned whenever the acquiring firm's valuation of the target turns up with a figure below the current market price. Bids are rendered when the valuation exceeds the price. If there really are no gains in takeovers, hubris is necessary to explain why managers do not abandon these bids also since reflection would suggest that such bids are likely to represent positive errors in valuation.

The hubris hypothesis can serve as the null hypothesis of corporate takeovers because it asserts that all markets are strong-form efficient.

Financial markets are aware of all information. Product markets are efficiently organized. Labor markets are characterized by managers being employed in their best operational positions.

Hubris predicts that, around a takeover, (*a*) the combined value of the target and bidder firms should fall slightly, (*b*) the value of the bidding firm should decrease, and (*c*) the value of the target should increase. The available empirical results indicate that the measured combined value has increased in some studies and decreased in others. It has been statistically significant in none. Measured changes in the prices of bidding firms have been mixed in sign across studies and mostly of a very small order of magnitude. Several studies have reported them to be significantly negative, and other studies have reported the opposite. Target firm prices consistently display large increases, but only if the initial bid or a later bid is successful. There is no permanent increase in value for target firms that do not eventually enter a corporate combination.

The interpretation of bidding firm returns is complicated by several potential measurement problems. The bid can convey contaminating information, that is, information about the bidder rather than about the takeover itself. The bid can be partially anticipated and thus result in an announcement effect smaller in absolute value than the true economic effect. Since bidders are usually much larger than targets, the effect of the bid can be buried in the noise of the bidder's return volatility. There is weak evidence from the interim period between the announcement of a merger and the merger outcome that the merger itself results in a loss to the bidding firm's shareholders; but the interim period in tender offers shows some results that favor the opposite view. Both findings have minimal statistical reliability.

The final impression one is obliged to draw from the currently available results is that they provide no really convincing evidence against even the extreme (hubris) hypothesis that all markets are operating perfectly efficiently and that individual bidders occasionally make mistakes. Bidders may indicate by their actions a belief in the existence of takeover gains, but systematic studies have provided little to show that such beliefs are well founded.

Finally, I should mention several issues that have arisen as objections by others to the hubris idea. First, the hubris hypothesis might seem to imply that managers act consciously against shareholder interests. Several recent papers that have examined nontakeover corporate control devices have concluded that the evidence is consistent with conscious management actions against the best interests of shareholders.[3] But the hubris hypothesis does not rely on this result. It is

3. See Bradley and Wakeman (1983), Dann and DeAngelo (1983), and DeAngelo and Rice (1983). Linn and McConnell (1983) disagree with the last paper. The possibility that managers do not act in the interest of stockholders has frequently been associated with the takeover phenomenon. For example, in a recent review, Lev (1983, p. 15) concludes

sufficient that managers act, de facto, against shareholder interests by issuing bids founded on mistaken estimates of target firm value. Management intentions may be fully consistent with honorable stewardship of corporate assets, but actions need not always turn out to be right.

Second, it might seem that the hubris hypothesis implies systematic biases in market prices. One correspondent argued that stock prices would be systematically too high for reasons similar to those advanced in E. M. Miller's (1977) paper. This implication is not correct, however, for the simple reason that firms can be either targets or bidders. If bidders offer too much, their stock price will fall ex post while their target's price will rise. On average over all stocks, this cancels. Unless one can predict which firms will be targets and which will be bidders, there is no bias in any individual firm, and there is certainly no bias on average over all firms.

Third, an argument can be advanced that the hubris hypothesis implies an inefficiency in the market for corporate control. If all takeovers were prompted by hubris, shareholders could stop the practice by forbidding managers ever to make any bid. Since such prohibitions are not observed, hubris alone cannot explain the takeover phenomenon.

The validity of this argument depends on the size of deadweight takeover costs. If such costs are relatively small, stockholders would be indifferent to hubris-inspired bids because target firm shareholders would gain what bidding firm shareholders lose. A well-diversified shareholder would receive the aggregate gain, which is close to zero.

Fourth, and finally, a frequent objection is that hubris itself is based on a market inefficiency defined in a particular way; in the words of one writer, "It seems to me that your hypothesis does not rest on strong form efficiency, because it presumes that one set of market bidders is systematically irrational" (private correspondence). This argument contends that a market is inefficient if some market participants make systematic mistakes. Perhaps one of the long-term benefits of studying takeovers is to clarify the notion of market efficiency. Does efficiency mean that every individual behaves like the rational, maximizing ideal? Or does it mean instead that market interactions generate prices and allocations indistinguishable from those that would have been generated by rational individuals?

References

Asquith, P. 1983. Merger bids, uncertainty, and stockholder returns. *Journal of Financial Economics* 11 (April): 51–83.

by saying, I think we are justified in doubting . . . the argument that mergers are done to maximize stockholder wealth." Foster (1983) seems to share this view or at least the view that bidders make big mistakes. Larcker (1983) presents interesting results that managers in large takeovers are more likely to have short-term, accounting-based compensation contracts. He finds that, the more accounting-based the compensation, the more negative is the market price reaction to a bid. Larcker also suggests that managers who own less stock in their own company are more likely to make bids.

Asquith, P.; Bruner, R. F.; and Mullins, D. W., Jr. 1983. The gains to bidding firms from merger. *Journal of Financial Economics* 11 (April): 121–39.

Bradley, M. 1980. Interfirm tender offers and the market for corporate control. *Journal of Business* 53 (October): 345–76.

Bradley, M.; Desai, A.; and Kim, E. H. 1982. Specialized resources and competition in the market for corporate control. Typescript. Ann Arbor: University of Michigan, Graduate School of Business.

Bradley, M.; Desai, A.; and Kim, E. H. 1983*a*. Determinants of the wealth effects of corporate acquisition via tender offers: Theory and evidence. Typescript. Ann Arbor: University of Michigan, Graduate School of Business.

Bradley, M.; Desai, A.; and Kim, E. H. 1983*b*. The rationale behind interfirm tenders offers: Information or synergy? *Journal of Financial Economics* 11 (April): 183–206.

Bradley, M., and Wakeman, L. Mac. 1983. The wealth effects of targeted share repurchases. *Journal of Financial Economics* 11 (April): 301–28.

Capan, E. C.; Clapp, R. V.; and Campbell, W. M. 1971. Competitive bidding in high risk situations. *Journal of Petroleum Technology* (June), pp. 641–53.

Chung, K. S., and Weston, J. F. 1982. Diversification and mergers in a strategic long-range planning framework. In M. Keenan and L. I. White (eds.), *Mergers and Acquisitions*. Lexington, Mass.: D. C. Heath.

Chung, K. S., and Weston, J. F. 1985. Model-created bias in residual analysis of mergers. Working paper. Los Angeles: University of California, Los Angeles, Graduate School of Management.

Dann, L. Y., and DeAngelo, H. 1983. Standstill agreements, privately negotiated stock repurchases, and the market for corporate control. *Journal of Financial Economics* 11 (April): 275–300.

DeAngelo, H., and Rice, E. M. 1983. Antitakeover charter amendments and stockholder wealth. *Journal of Financial Economics* 11 (April): 329–60.

Dodd, P. 1980. Merger proposals, managerial discretion and stockholder wealth. *Journal of Financial Economics* 8 (June): 105–38.

Dodd, P., and Ruback, R. 1977. Tender offers and stockholder returns: An empirical analysis. *Journal of Financial Economics* 5 (December): 351–74.

Dougherty, F. L., and Lohrenz, J. 1976. Statistical analysis of bids for Federal offshore leases. *Journal of Petroleum Technology* (November), pp. 1377–90.

Eckbo, B. E. 1983. Horizontal mergers, collusion and stockholder wealth. *Journal of Financial Economics* 11 (April): 241–73.

Eger, C. E. 1983. An empirical test of the redistribution effect in pure exchange mergers. *Journal of Financial and Quantitative Analysis* 18 (December): 547–72.

Firth, M. 1980. Takeovers, shareholder returns and the theory of the firm. *Quarterly Journal of Economics* (March): 235–60.

Foster, G. 1983. Comments on M & A analysis and the role of investment bankers. *Midland Corporate Finance Journal* 1 (Winter): 36–38.

Halpern, P. J. 1973. Empirical estimates of the amount and distribution of gains to companies in mergers. *Journal of Business* 46 (October): 554–75.

Jarrell, G. A. 1983. Do acquirers benefit from corporate acquisition? Typescript. Chicago: University of Chicago, Center for the Study of the Economy and the State.

Jensen, M. C., and Ruback, R. S. 1983. The market for corporate control. *Journal of Financial Economics* 11 (April): 5–50.

Kahneman, D.; Slovic, P.; and Tversky, A. 1982. *Judgment under Uncertainty: Heuristics and Biases*. New York: Cambridge University Press.

Kummer, D. R., and Hoffmeister, J. R. 1978. Valuation consequences of cash tender offers. *Journal of Finance* 33 (May): 505–16.

Langetieg, T. C. 1978. An application of a three-factor performance index to measure stockholder gains from merger. *Journal of Financial Economics* 6 (December): 365–83.

Larcker, D. 1983. Managerial incentives in mergers and their effect on shareholder wealth. *Midland Corporate Finance Journal* 1 (Winter): 29–35.

Lev, B. 1983. Observations on the merger phenomenon and review of the evidence. *Midland Corporate Finance Journal* 1 (Winter): 6–16.

Linn, S. C., and McConnell, J. J. 1983. An empirical investigation of the impact of "antitakeover" amendments on common stock prices. *Journal of Financial Economics* 11 (April): 361–99.

Malatesta, P. H. 1983. The wealth effect of merger activity and the objective functions of merging firms. *Journal of Financial Economics* 11 (April): 155–81.
Masulis, R. W. 1980. The effects of capital structure change on security prices: A study of exchange offers. *Journal of Financial Economics* 8 (June): 139–77.
Miller, E. M. 1977. Risk, uncertainty and the divergence of opinion. *Journal of Finance* 32 (September): 1151–68.
Oskamp, S. 1965. Overconfidence in case study judgments. *Journal of Consulting Psychology* 29 (June): 261–65.
Ruback, R. S. 1982. The Conoco takeover and stockholder returns. *Sloan Management Review* 14 (Winter): 13–33.
Ruback, R. S. 1983. The Cities Service takeover: A case study. *Journal of Finance* 38 (May): 319–30.
Ruback, R. S., and Mikkelson, W. H. 1984. Corporate investments in common stock. Working paper. Cambridge: Massachusetts Institute of Technology, Sloan School of Business.
Schipper, K., and Thompson, R. 1983. Evidence on the capitalized value of merger activity for acquiring firms. *Journal of Financial Economics* 11 (April): 85–119.
Tversky, A., and Kahneman, D. 1981. The framing of decisions and the psychology of choice. *Science* 211 (January 30): 453–58. Reprinted in Peter Diamond and Michael Rothschild. 1978. *Uncertainty in Economics*. New York: Academic Press.
Varaiya, N. 1985. A test of Roll's Hubris Hypothesis of corporate takeovers. Working paper. Dallas, Tex.: Southern Methodist University, School of Business.
Vermaelen, T. 1981. Common stock repurchase and marketing signalling: An empirical study. *Journal of Financial Economics* 9 (June): 139–84.

Available online at www.sciencedirect.com
SCIENCE @ DIRECT•

ELSEVIER

Journal of Financial Economics 70 (2003) 295–311

JOURNAL OF Financial ECONOMICS

www.elsevier.com/locate/econbase

Stock market driven acquisitions ☆

Andrei Shleifer[a,*], Robert W. Vishny[b]

[a] *Department of Economics, Harvard University, Littauer Center, Cambridge, MA 02138, USA*
[b] *University of Chicago, Graduate School of Business, 1101 East 58th Street, Chicago, IL 60637, USA*

Received 24 June 2002; accepted 1 December 2002

Abstract

We present a model of mergers and acquisitions based on stock market misvaluations of the combining firms. The key ingredients of the model are the relative valuations of the merging firms and the market's perception of the synergies from the combination. The model explains who acquires whom, the choice of the medium of payment, the valuation consequences of mergers, and merger waves. The model is consistent with available empirical findings about characteristics and returns of merging firms, and yields new predictions as well.

JEL classification: G34

Keywords: Takeover; Synergy; Merger

1. Introduction

In the late 1990s, the U.S. and world economies experienced a large wave of mergers and acquisitions. Most of these deals were for stock, and the acquirers were typically in the same industry as the targets (Andrade et al., 2001). This wave of acquisitions was very different from the "hostile" takeover wave of the 1980s, when many acquirers were financiers, and the medium of payment was often cash rather

☆We are grateful to Malcolm Baker, Amar Bhide, Gene D'Avolio, John Friedman, Robin Greenwood, Michael Jensen, Steven Kaplan, Rafael La Porta, Mark Mitchell, Raghu Rajan, Antoinette Schoar, Jeremy Stein, René Stulz, Luigi Zingales, students in Stein's Economics 2725, two anonymous referees, and especially Jeffrey Wurgler for helpful comments, and to the National Science Foundation for financial support of this research.

*Corresponding author. Tel.: +1-617-495-5046; fax: +1-617-496-1708.
E-mail address: ashleifer@harvard.edu (A. Shleifer).

0304-405X/$ - see front matter
doi:10.1016/S0304-405X(03)00211-3

than stock. These acquisitions also differed from the "conglomerate" wave in the 1960s, when mergers typically involved firms from different industries. At the same time, the waves of the 1960s and 1990s were similar in that the medium of payment was generally stock and both occurred during periods of very high stock market valuations. In the 1980s, in contrast, the valuations were lower.

Neoclassical theory sees mergers as an efficiency-improving response to various industry shocks, such as antitrust policy or deregulation (Mitchell and Mulherin, 1996; Jovanovic and Rousseau, 2002). In the conglomerate mergers of the 1960s, well-managed bidders built up diversified groups by adding capital and know-how to the targets (Gort, 1962; Rumelt, 1974; Meeks, 1977; Steiner, 1975). In the bust-up takeovers of the 1980s, raiders financed by bank debt and junk bonds acquired and split up the very same conglomerates assembled in the 1960s, because the conglomerate organization was no longer efficient (Jensen, 1986; Blair, 1993; Bhagat et al., 1990). The wave of related acquisitions in the 1990s, which still does not have a name, was part consolidation of major industries, and part response to deregulation (Holmstrom and Kaplan, 2001; Andrade et al., 2001).

The neoclassical theory of mergers has considerable explanatory power, but it is incomplete. Because it focuses on industry-specific shocks, it does not explain aggregate merger waves unless, of course, several industries experience shocks at the same time. The neoclassical theory also does not explain whether cash or stock is used to pay target shareholders, even though there are distinct patterns in the data on means of payment in mergers. On the central prediction of the neoclassical theory that mergers increase profitability, the evidence is inconclusive. Ravenscraft and Scherer (1987), focusing on the period of conglomerate mergers, fail to find evidence of improvements in profitability, whereas Healy et al. (1992), focusing on the period of hostile takeovers, do find such evidence.

Last but not least, the neoclassical theory is difficult to reconcile with some stock market evidence. Loughran and Vijh (1997) find that the market does not react correctly to the news of a merger, with acquirers making cash tender offers earning positive long-run abnormal returns, and those making stock acquisitions earning negative long-run abnormal returns. Rau and Vermaelen (1998) show that this pattern of returns remains even after the correction for size and book-to-market ratio recommended by Fama and French (1993). Mitchell and Stafford (2000) and Andrade et al. (2001), however, challenge this evidence on the grounds that merger observations are not statistically independent, and present long-run bidder returns that are lower in absolute value and statistically insignificant.

We propose a theory of acquisitions related to the neoclassical theory, but also able to accommodate the additional evidence. In this theory, transactions are driven by stock market valuations of the merging firms. The fundamental assumption of the model is that financial markets are inefficient, so some firms are valued incorrectly. In contrast, managers are completely rational, understand stock market inefficiencies, and take advantage of them, in part through merger decisions. Mergers in this model are a form of arbitrage by rational managers operating in inefficient markets. This theory is in a way the opposite of Roll's (1986) hubris hypothesis of corporate takeovers, in which financial markets are rational, but corporate managers are not. In our theory, managers rationally respond to less-than-rational markets.[1]

Our theory helps explain who acquires whom, the choice of the medium of payment, the valuation consequences of mergers, and merger waves. We show that the key ingredients of the answers are the relative valuations of the combining firms and the synergies that the market perceives in the merger. Our simple model is consistent with the available evidence, and yields several new predictions, including the following: (1) acquisitions are disproportionately for stock when aggregate or industry valuations are high, and for cash when they are low; (2) the volume of stock acquisition increases with the dispersion of valuations among firms; (3) targets in cash acquisitions earn low prior returns, whereas bidders in stock acquisitions earn high prior returns; (4) bidders in stock acquisitions exhibit signs of overvaluation, such as earnings manipulation and insider selling; (5) long-run returns to bidders are likely to be negative in stock acquisitions, and positive in cash acquisitions; (6) despite negative long-run returns, acquisitions for stock serve the interest of long-term shareholders of the bidder; (7) acquiring a firm in another industry may yield higher long-run returns than a related acquisition; (8) management resistance to some cash tender offers is in the interest of shareholders; (9) managers of targets in stock acquisitions are likely to have relatively short horizons or, alternatively, get paid for agreeing to the deal. Some of these predictions, such as the second and third, also follow from the neoclassical theory; others are more distinctive.

In Sections 2, 3, and 4, we present a simple model. Section 5 discusses the evidence. Section 6 concludes.

2. A simple model of acquisitions

We consider two firms, 0 and 1, with capital stocks K and K_1, and stock market valuations per unit of capital of Q and Q_1. We assume that Q and Q_1 are not efficient valuations of these firms, but rather reflect investor sentiment about them. We do not model the sources of market inefficiency explicitly, relying on a growing theoretical and empirical literature describing the circumstances under which security prices deviate from fundamental values (Shleifer, 2000). Without loss of generality, we assume that $Q_1 > Q$.

The investor sentiment affecting valuations can but need not be idiosyncratic: it may reflect over- or undervaluations of entire industries, sectors, or groups of firms with similar characteristics. For example, all diversified firms (conglomerates) can be

[1] The idea that stock market valuations shape merger activity dates back at least to Nelson's (1959) study of merger waves in the U.S.: "It appears that merger expansion was not only a phenomenon of prosperity, but that it was also closely related to the state of the capital market. Two reference cycle expansions, unaccompanied by a strong upswing in stock prices, were marked by the absence of a merger revival." Our theory is part of the growing body of research on behavioral corporate finance, including Stein (1988, 1989, 1996), Morck et al. (1990a), Shleifer and Vishny (1990), Baker and Wurgler (2000, 2002, 2003), Baker et al. (2003), Jenter (2002), and Polk and Sapienza (2002), which sees corporate financial policies as a response to market misvaluations.

in or out of favor, as can all technology stocks, all basic industry stocks, or all European stocks.

If the two firms merge, the short-run valuation of the combined equity per unit of capital is denoted by S, so the market value of the two firms together is $V=S(K+K_1)$. We call S the "perceived synergy" of the merger. In effect, S is the story that the market consensus holds about the benefits of the merger. It could be a story about industrial diversification, or consolidation, or European integration. For example, S could be high when the market favors diversification and the two firms come from different industries. Alternatively, S could be high when a well-performing firm (high Q_1) merges with a poorly performing firm (low Q). Lang et al. (1989) find that short-run announcement returns are consistent with the latter scenario. In our model, S is just the lubricant that greases the wheels of the M&A process—it might be invented by investment bankers or academics and have little to do with the reality of what drives actual acquisitions.

The case $S=Q$ corresponds to the market valuing the combination at the same value per unit of capital as the less valuable firm, and $S=Q_1$ to the market valuing the combination as the more valuable firm. It is possible that $S>Q_1$, in which case the combination of the two firms is perceived by the "euphoric" market to be more valuable (again, per unit of capital) than even the more valuable firm is on its own. It is also possible that $S<Q$, although we are unlikely to see mergers in this case (since, as we show below, both short- and long-run bidder returns are negative). We think that typically $Q<S<Q_1$. Under these assumptions, the total short-run gains from two firms merging are given by $S(K+K_1)-KQ-K_1Q_1$. We call the synergy level S^* at which $S^*(K+K_1)-KQ-K_1Q_1=0$ the no-synergy point. For $S>S^*$, there is a positive perceived synergy and the combined short-run return is positive.

We make the extreme assumption that, in the long run, all assets are worth q per unit of capital (q is best thought of as the cost of capital). In the long run, then, firm 0 is worth qK as a stand-alone entity, firm 1 is worth qK_1, and the combination, if it materializes, is worth $q(K+K_1)$. This assumption implies that there are no long-run gains from a merger (regardless of whether cash or stock is used): no synergies in combining the two firms, and no managerial improvements.

This specification allows for the maximum contrast between ours and the neoclassical theory of mergers (Mitchell and Mulherin, 1996). This is not to suggest that, empirically, mergers are always pure financial plays that create no long-run value. The wave of hostile takeovers in the 1980s has almost surely created efficiency gains (Jensen, 1986). In contrast, the wave of acquisitions in the 1990s might have destroyed value (Fuller and Jensen, 2002). In general, there is a great deal of doubt, especially outside the period of hostile takeovers, that mergers increase profitability (Meeks, 1977; Ravenscraft and Scherer, 1987; but see Healy et al., 1992, for the period 1979–1984). We make the stark simplifying assumption that mergers have no long-run real consequences to see how far it takes us.

Whereas we assume that the stock market is inefficient, managers are perfectly rational and informed. They know precisely with respect to both their own firms and the prospective merger partners how the short-run valuation deviates from efficiency, what the perception of synergies is, and what the long-run valuation will be. They then maximize their personal wealth given their horizons and their knowledge of market inefficiencies.

3. The arithmetics of returns

We consider first the more valuable firm 1 acquiring the less valuable firm 0, and examine the consequences of this acquisition for both long- and short-term shareholders of the target and the acquirer, depending on whether the means of payment is cash or stock. Rather than adopt a specific model of takeover bids, such as Grossman and Hart (1980), we assume that the acquirer pays a price P per unit of capital of the target. We interpret P as the relative bargaining strength of the lower-valuation firm. Thus if $P=Q$, there is no takeover premium. If $P=S$, the price reflects the merged short-run valuation of the combined entity. We assume that P in many instances is lower than S because there are many potential targets around and, moreover, acquirers can compensate target managers personally for agreeing to merge at $P<S$.

We make the simplifying assumption that, aside from having a theory of perceived synergy, the market draws no inferences from the announcement of an acquisition. The announcement does not cause prices to converge to long-term values, or to move in that direction. Put differently, neither the merger itself, nor the choice of cash versus stock, conveys any information about management's valuation of assets in place (Myers and Majluf, 1984) or the severity of any agency problems (Morck et al., 1990b). Market beliefs are specified completely by Q, Q_1, and S, and traders stick to these beliefs in the short run.

Except for simplicity, we do not need to assume no learning by the market. All that is necessary is that learning be incomplete, and the adjustment to rational valuations from the announcement of a merger or a security issue be partial. The conclusion that, in equilibrium, the market puts some weight on the beliefs of rational investors and some on investor sentiment is standard in models of inefficient markets (e.g., DeLong et al., 1990). As long as investor sentiment influences prices, the results we obtain survive.

Consider first short-run gains to acquisitions (in terms of dollar amounts rather than percentages). In the short run, since there is no information entering the market other than the news of the merger, observed returns are due entirely to this news. Moreover, since the market draws the same inferences from acquisitions for cash and for stock, it is obvious that the bidder, the target, and the total short-run changes in value are invariant to whether the means of payment is cash or stock. We trivially establish the following proposition.

Proposition 1. *The immediate effect of the acquisition on the combined market value is*

$$S(K+K_1)-K_1Q_1-KQ; \tag{1}$$

the immediate effect on the short-run target value is

$$(P-Q)K; \tag{2}$$

and the immediate effect on the short-run bidder value is

$$(S - P)K + (S - Q_1)K_1. \tag{3}$$

In the short run, the combined entity benefits from the perception that the combination of the two firms is synergistic, in that some of the value of the more valuable one spills over on the less valuable one. Eq. (2) shows that P governs how much of that gain in the short run accrues to the target firm. When $P = Q$, target shareholders do not gain; when $P = S$, they gain proportionately to their capital. Finally, Eq. (3) shows that, in the short run, bidding shareholders gain insofar as they pay $P < S$ for the target and thus collect some of the gains from its higher valuation, but lose insofar as the valuation of their own capital is diluted from Q_1 to S.

This analysis suggests that at least some takeover activity is driven purely by short-run stock market perceptions. When $S > Q_1$, there is a money machine available to the bidding firm, which can buy assets and get its own capital revalued upwards. Presumably, such opportunities are limited. Even if the market is not euphoric, but believes in positive synergies ($S > S^*$) from a merger, both the target and the acquirer could gain in the short run.

The results for the long-run valuation consequences of mergers are more interesting. Here we treat acquisitions for cash and stock separately. The results for cash are summarized in the following proposition.

Proposition 2. *The long-run effect of a cash acquisition on the combined value of the two firms is zero, the effect on the value of the target is* $K(P - q)$, *and the effect on the value of the acquirer is* $K(q - P)$.

By construction, there are no long-term profitability gains from making acquisitions. What the target gains, the bidder loses. The only long-run reason for making acquisitions for cash is the undervaluation of the target. It is still likely that, if the bidder is overvalued, its preferred medium of payment for an undervalued target is stock. This choice, as we show below, depends on P relative to S. In this model, the target's undervaluation is a necessary, but not a sufficient, condition for cash deals.

Proposition 2 raises two related questions. Why does not a cash acquirer simply buy a diversified portfolio of undervalued firms? First, the acquirer may know a lot about a particular target, and would have more confidence about its undervaluation than that of a portfolio. Second, the realization of gains from undervaluation might require taking actions, such as a bust-up and a sale of divisions, for which gaining control is necessary. A related question is why the acquirer's manager does not simply get into the business of buying undervalued assets, and give up the business of managing the firm. The answer is that we actually saw in the 1980s so-called raiders, who specialized in acquiring and busting up undervalued firms. But one can also imagine the benefits of conducting such business through a company with a balance sheet, perhaps to make it easier to raise cash for acquisitions.

In our model, managers of takeover targets benefit their long-term shareholders by resisting tender offers at a premium if $Q < P < q$. The interest of long-term shareholders is not just an excuse for resistance, as it has been portrayed in agency models. Shareholders actually benefit from resistance in the long run as share prices return to fundamentals, even though prices decline in the short run when offers are turned down.

In the case of acquisitions for stock, the share x of the combined firm's equity that the target shareholders end up owning after the exchange of shares is given by

$$x = PK/[S(K + K_1)]. \tag{4}$$

In the long run, this share is worth $xq(K+K_1)=q(P/S)K$. We can establish the following proposition.

Proposition 3. *The net long-run gain to the shareholders of the target firm from being acquired for stock is* $q(P/S)K - qK = qK(P/S - 1)$, *and that to the bidding shareholders is the opposite, i.e.,* $qK(1 - P/S)$.

In the long run, bidding shareholders gain if and only if $P<S$, i.e., shares are exchanged on terms better (from bidder viewpoint) than the market's short-run assessment of synergy. Bidders can only benefit if they increase their shareholders' claim on physical capital, which happens when $P<S$. Since all capital is worth the same in the long run, they end up better off. When the price is below the blended short-run valuation of the two companies, bidding shareholders redistribute wealth away from the target shareholders to themselves.

In this model, there is an important difference between the effect of an acquisition on the long-run value and the observed long-run returns. The acquirer's long-run returns without making an acquisition would have been $K_1(q - Q_1)$, which is negative when the firm is initially overpriced. The acquirer's long run *incremental* return from making the acquisition is given by $qK(1 - P/S)$, which is positive when $P<S$. The total observed return may still be negative, especially if initial overvaluation is significant, but this does not mean that the acquisition does not serve the interest of the bidding shareholders. Indeed, when $P<S$, bidding shareholders gain in the long run even when the observed stock returns are negative: returns are just not as negative as they would have been without the acquisition.

This distinction between long-run gains from a stock merger and observed long-run returns raises a number of interesting possibilities. To begin, it may be in the long-term, but not the short-term, interest of shareholders of firm 1 to acquire firm 0. When $P<S$ but $(S - P)K + (S - Q_1)K_1 <0$, the shares of firm 1 drop on the announcement of the deal, but the acquisition still benefits its long-run shareholders because in the long run the shares would have fallen even more. Indeed, both short- and long-run observed returns in this range may be negative, but the acquisition still serves the interest of the long-term shareholders of the acquirer. Using overvalued shares as a means of payment enhances the claim on capital of the bidding shareholders, and thereby cushions the collapse of the shares in the long run.

4. Discussion

Why would a firm make an acquisition for stock, rather than just issue equity and invest in either cash or its own business? To address this question, we need to consider the long-run payoffs to the three alternative strategies. For all three strategies, we make the same simplifying assumption that the market learns nothing from the firm's issuance decision, contrary to Myers and Majluf (1984). We also assume that investors know exactly how the issuer will use the funds raised in an equity issuance; the management cannot trick investors by changing the way it uses funds.

Conceptually, acquisitions for stock and greenfield investment financed by equity issues are identical. Compare the acquisition of K units of capital at a price P per unit with an investment of K units of capital acquired at a price R per unit. Suppose that both are equity financed, and that the former results in a valuation of the combined firm of S per unit of capital, while the latter results in the post-issuance valuation of T per unit of capital. We have shown before that the acquisition serves the interest of acquirer shareholders as long as $P < S$. Likewise, the share issuance financed investment serves the interest of long-term shareholders as long as $R < T$. It is trivial to show that acquisition is more likely to be preferred to investment the lower is P relative to R, and the higher is S relative to T.

When is this likely to occur? Generally speaking, new capital probably costs less than whole firms ($R < P$), unless there are significant bottlenecks in the capital goods industry that make is cheaper to buy old capital than to install new capital. It is more likely, however, that $S > T$. This would happen, for example, if a high-valuation firm has enough capacity to meet the market demand for its existing product, so market participants believe that it can only grow by extending its product line. In this case, the valuation of new investment is low, but a perceived synergy from an acquisition is higher. The bottom line is that investing is not necessarily better than making acquisitions, and in equilibrium we expect to see some of each. How far additional investment or acquisitions will go depends, of course, on how fast S and T fall relative to the costs with each additional transaction.

An extreme version of investing in capital that is cheaper than acquisitions in an overvalued market is issuing equity to hold cash. Assume again that the acquisition has synergy S, and takes place at price P, and compare this to raising PK by issuing equity and holding PK in cash. In this case, the condition that the acquisition is preferred by long-term shareholders is

$$\frac{S(K + K_1) - PK}{S(K + K_1)}[q(K + K_1)] > \frac{Q_1 K_1}{PK + Q_1 K_1}[PK + qK_1]. \qquad (5)$$

In this case, it is still possible that an acquisition is better as long as S is high enough. One special case is that of a large share issuance for holding cash or making an acquisition, so we can take the limit as K_1/K approaches zero. In this case, an acquisition is preferred as long as $S > P$, i.e., the perceived synergy is greater than the price paid for the target. This condition makes intuitive sense: since the perceived synergy applies to the valuation of the whole company, as long as it is higher than the price paid for the acquisition, the transfer of capital in the long run to the old shareholders is high enough to outweigh the benefits of a fair-priced investment in cash. The point here, as before, is that, with high enough perceived synergies, making acquisitions might be the best strategy for the shareholders of the bidding firm.

Issuing shares and investing in cash can also have an adverse signaling effect that leads to a reduction in Q_1. This signaling effect is distinct from Myers and Majluf (1984) in that the signal comes from the investment policy rather than from capital structure. The advantage of making acquisitions, aside from the positive perceived synergies, is that they contribute to the growth in earnings of the firm, and thereby help justify the high valuations. As the policies of Cisco and other technology firms illustrate, acquisitions become part of a growth strategy justifying high market multiples in a way that cash accumulation cannot. For this reason as well, it might be better to use overvalued equity to buy other overvalued firms than to invest in cash.

A second important question is why would the target agree to a stock merger? In this model, combined long-run benefits of an acquisition are always zero, so what the bidder gains the target loses. If the bidder acts in the interest of its long-term shareholders by making the acquisition, the target must be hurting *its* long-term shareholders by consenting to it. Put differently, who would agree to be a target?

We can think of two related answers. The first concerns the difference in the horizons of the various managers (see Stein, 1988,1989; Shleifer and Vishny, 1990). If $Q<P<S$, then target shareholders gain in the short-run but lose in the long run. Bidder shareholders, in contrast, might lose in the short-run, but gain in the long run. Target shareholders receive a premium, and as long as they sell the shares they obtain in the exchange, they are better off. The acquirer shareholders (or their management), who for whatever reason keep their shares, benefit in the long run if $P<S$. The losers are those holding onto shares in an overvalued market.

Under this view, we expect target firms to be those whose managers want to "sell out," for reasons of retirement or ownership of illiquid stock options. In contrast, we expect bidding firms to be controlled by shareholders who cannot as easily get out: irreplaceable executives with large equity stakes or managers who are young or locked in. The examples of family firms selling out to conglomerates in the 1960s and of entrepreneurial firms selling out to Cisco and Intel in the 1990s fit nicely with this view.

A second reason for target management's consent is that the acquirer pays them for it. This can be done through the acceleration in the exercise of stock options (which could be very valuable if the target is overvalued), severance pay, or even by keeping the managers of the target in top positions (as was done, for example, in the AOL acquisition of Time Warner). Both the target and the acquirer managers benefit: the former by cashing out or keeping a good job, the latter by increasing the long-run value of their equity. When target managers sell out, both they and the bidder managers in effect get rid of overvalued equity: one through a personal sale, the other through issuance. The absence of such gains from trade (at the expense of the new bidder shareholders) is precisely why we see more hostility in cash tender offers than in stock mergers. Consistent with this analysis, Hartzell et al. (2003) present compelling evidence that managers of target firms obtain significant wealth increases in acquisitions, and that those receiving extraordinary personal treatment agree to lower acquisition premia.

This analysis gives us a map of when we are likely to see acquisitions, and what kind. To begin, we expect targets of cash acquisitions to be undervalued firms, and moreover, we predict that such acquisitions are more likely to be hostile than those for stock. We are likely to see acquisitions for stock under a combination of three circumstances. First, market valuations must be high, and there must be a supply of highly overvalued firms (bidders) as well as of relatively less overvalued ones (targets). This condition is more likely to obtain when the dispersion of valuations in the market is also high. Second, the market should perceive a synergy, which makes the mergers relatively more attractive in the short-run, and enables the acquirers to pay a premium yet still enhance their long-run claim on capital. Third, either target managers have short-horizons, or alternatively they are paid off to consent to a merger.

Finally, we return to the possibility of firm 0, the less valuable one, acquiring firm 1. If we denote the price that firm 0 pays for firm 1 by P, we must have $P \geqslant Q_1$ for firm 1 to agree to a takeover. Since any bidder only benefits in the long run from an acquisition for cash if $P < q$, we could see such acquisitions when $Q < Q_1 < P < q$, i.e., in a highly undervalued market. This is possible, and indeed we saw some such deals in the 1980s. However, such deals are likely to be limited because extreme undervaluation is probably temporary and, moreover, such low-valuation bidders might be unable to raise capital to finance acquisitions. The lower-valuation bidder benefits from an acquisition for stock if $P < S$, which means $S > P > Q_1 > Q$. Such acquisitions require fantastic perceived synergies, which seem unlikely to materialize very often, especially when the lower-valuation firm rather than the high-flying firm assumes control.

5. Implications

In this section, we discuss the empirical implications of the analysis. We divide the discussion into three parts. First, we examine the theory in light of the available empirical evidence on short- and long-run stock returns. Second, we look at the relationship between the aggregate merger activity and the stock market by considering the three U.S. merger waves in the last 40 years. Third, we review some of the untested implications of the model.

5.1. Implications for the cross-section of returns

Recent evidence on long- and short-term stock returns around acquisition announcements is carefully summarized by Agrawal and Jaffe (2000) and Andrade et al. (2001) and we rely on their summaries of the evidence rather than on individual studies. Andrade et al. show that in a sample of 3,688 mergers between 1973 and 1998, target firms gain 23.8% in the window beginning 20 days before the acquisition announcement and ending on the close. Acquirer firms lose 3.8% over the same interval, and the combined value change is a statistically insignificant 1.9%. If we translate the returns in the propositions into percentage returns rather than dollar amounts, our model can easily mimic this pattern of returns. In fact, the simple case of equal-sized firms with $S=P=1.25$, $Q=1$, and $Q_1=1.3$ generates a 25% gain for the target firm, a 5% loss for the acquirer, and a 2.5% loss in the combined value.

The evidence on long-run returns is more interesting. Our model suggests that the more highly valued acquirer would only make a cash bid if the target is undervalued even at the bid price, i.e., $P<q$. This is most likely to happen with seriously undervalued targets, which must have experienced low returns prior to being acquired. The evidence on this is limited, although Schwert (2000) documents lower valuations of targets of hostile takeovers than of average targets, whereas Andrade et al. (2001) show that in 66% of mergers between 1973 and 1998, the acquirer's Q exceeded the target's Q. More importantly, our model predicts that long-run bidder returns from cash acquisitions should be positive. Loughran and Vijh (1997) find that, after a size and book-to-market adjustment, tender offers result in positive abnormal bidder returns of 43% in the five years following the merger. Rau and Vermaelen (1998) use a larger sample of 316 tender offers between 1980 and 1991, and find that acquirers experience long-run excess returns of 8.5% in the three years following the merger. This evidence is supportive of our model.

The crucial case is of course acquisitions for stock. The model suggests that such acquisitions are made by overvalued acquirers of relatively less overvalued targets. Moreover, in the model, such acquisitions are likely to result in negative long-run returns, but—as long as $P<S$—not as negative as would have obtained without the acquisition. This prediction is consistent with Rau and Vermaelen (1998), who find that acquirers in mergers earn a statistically significant negative 4% return relative to a size and book-to-market benchmark in the three years after the merger.[2] Agrawal and Jaffe (2000) list earlier papers corroborating this finding. Rau and Vermaelen also show that value bidders outperform glamour bidders in the three years after the completion of the merger, and that glamour bidders pay more frequently with stock than do value bidders. Both of these findings are consistent with our view that acquisitions completed with stock arise from the overvaluation of the bidder relative to the target. Acquisitions for stock by the glamour bidders indeed appear to be a defensive strategy we model.

Interestingly, the key studies of long-run bidder returns, such as Loughran and Vijh (1997), Rau and Vermaelen (1998), and Agrawal and Jaffe (2000), treat the two predictors of negative long-run bidder returns—higher bidder valuation (measured in various ways) and the use of stock as a means of payment—as evidence for two different hypotheses, which they call the method of payment hypothesis and the performance extrapolation hypothesis.

In our model, these results are part of the same story. The performance extrapolation hypothesis states that the market wrongly extrapolates the past

[2] Strictly speaking, this statement is only true when bidders in stock acquisitions are overvalued even relative to their book-to-market benchmark, which is plausible. As noted in the introduction, there is also a statistical controversy over this evidence (Mitchell and Stafford, 2000).

performance of the bidder in determining the combined value of the two firms. This corresponds to positive synergy in our model. According to the means of payment hypothesis, if managers are better informed about the firm's prospects than the market, they acquire with stock when stock is overpriced, and use cash otherwise. In our model, both the decision to acquire and the means of payment derive from market timing. Stock acquisitions are used specifically by overvalued bidders who expect to see negative long-run returns on their shares, but are attempting to make these returns less negative.

In these acquisitions for stock, a high level of perceived synergy can be essential because the condition for both short- and long-run attractiveness for the bidder is $P<S$. Even if such synergies do not exist, there is a strong incentive to "invent" them.

5.2. *Merger waves*

In his original study, Nelson (1959) pointed out that mergers are highly concentrated in time, that they cluster during periods of high stock market valuations, and that the means of payment is generally stock. Andrade et al. (2001) confirm this picture but also show that the preponderance of stock acquisitions is greater in high-valuation markets, consistent with our model. Thus acquisitions where *any* stock was used as payment represent 45.6% of total in the 1980s, versus 70.9% in the 1990s. The share of acquisitions that were *all* for stock rose from 32.9% in the 1980s to 57.8% in the 1990s. Verter (2002) presents systematic evidence of higher levels of merger activity in higher-valuation markets. He also finds, consistent with the model, that (1) this correlation is driven by acquisitions for stock, (2) a high incidence of acquisitions for stock predicts low subsequent market returns, suggesting overvaluation, and (3) high levels of merger activity are associated with a higher dispersion in valuations.

We can use the model to say a bit more about the American M&A experience of the last 40 years. In our framework, the conglomerate merger wave of the 1960s is the case of prototypical acquisitions by the more overvalued firms of the less overvalued ones for stock. A commonly given reason why these acquisitions took the form of diversification is that the antitrust policy restricted related acquisitions (e.g., Shleifer and Vishny, 1991). Our model suggests a different reason. For long-term shareholders of high-valuation bidders, it might have been advantageous to issue new stock to diversify and to build conglomerates so as to raise their claim to long-term capital. Such acquisitions might have been more attractive than those in the same industry because within-industry target valuations were too high to justify acquisitions, even when perceived synergies were higher than those for diversification. All that was required was a good story, S, for the benefits of diversification.

Conveniently, such a story was invented: the efficiency gains from conglomeration through better management. Thanks to this story, positive short-run returns accrued to both the acquirers and the targets (Matsusaka, 1990). Moreover, even though conglomerates have not increased profits (Ravenscraft and Scherer, 1987), and the long-run stock market returns to the acquirers have been negative (Agrawal and Jaffe 2000), such acquisitions were still preferable to doing nothing. In our model, negative bidder returns are not evidence of a failure to serve shareholder interests—conglomerate values would have fallen even more without them

The acquisition of smaller family firms by conglomerates such as ITT, and the vertical integration of franchisee-owned restaurants by McDonald's, illustrate this logic. In our model, because the targets were so much smaller than the acquirers, we can think of conglomeration as diversification with $S = Q_1$. Indeed, discussions of the 1960s acquisitions often argue that the purpose of these combinations was to transfer the high multiple of the acquirer to the earnings of the target. From this angle, the focus on efficiency aspects of conglomerates in most discussions of the 1960s is just window dressing; the fundamental economics have to do with buying hard capital using overvalued shares. A final point has to do with horizons. The targets in conglomerate mergers were often family-run firms, whose owners wished to sell out and retire. This is exactly what the model predicts: a merger requires a coincidence of short-term objectives of the target managers with longer-run objectives of the bidders.

In the 1980s, following a decade of miserable stock market performance, the market saw a wave of bust-up takeovers. As our model predicts, these were likely to target undervalued firms, and to take place for cash rather than stock. Moreover, the incidence of hostility was higher in the 1980s than in any other major merger wave—as the model predicts for takeovers of low-valuation firms for cash. The common finding that the bust-up value of the acquired firms was higher than the acquisition price is broadly consistent with our view that market undervaluation of targets was central to the 1980s takeovers (Kaplan, 1989; Bhagat et al., 1990). Also consistent with the model, the 1980s acquisitions were not followed by negative long-run acquirer returns, unlike the acquisitions from the earlier period.

Some other aspects of the 1980s takeover wave also fit the model. The model implies that, for these acquisitions to earn good short-run returns for acquiring shareholders, a story of perceived synergy, or of benefits to the valuation of combined firms, is needed. It is possible that the free cash flow theory of Jensen (1986), with its emphasis on the elimination of agency problems through takeovers, provided the necessary story for that period. Our model also provides an alternative interpretation of why the takeover wave of the 1980s petered out toward the end of that decade. The traditional explanation is that corporate, state, and federal antitakeover policies, as well as legal action against Drexel and other financiers of hostile deals, raised the costs of takeover bids to acquirers to the point that the activity was no longer profitable. In our model, in contrast, the more important culprit is the rising stock market prices, which eliminated undervaluation—the fundamental reason for the takeover wave of the 1980s. Like the conglomerate merger wave of the 1960s, the 1980s wave fits nicely into our framework.

The rising stock market valuations of the 1990s, particularly the second half, stimulated another massive takeover wave. The acquisitions were generally for stock, and the acquirers were often more highly valued firms than the targets, even when both belonged to the same industry. The story of perceived synergies changed to a combination of technological synergies, industry consolidation, and European integration, although in some instances the spin did not rescue the short-run acquirer returns.

A classic merger of this period is the acquisition of Time Warner by America Online for stock (although in this instance, S was not as high as AOL management hoped: the company lost a third of its market value in the few months following the announcement).[3] From our perspective, the central feature of this acquisition is not technological synergies, but rather the attempt by the management of overvalued AOL to buy the hard assets of Time Warner to avoid even worse returns in the long run. In this acquisition, as in other deals involving high-technology acquirers with overvalued stock prices, long-run acquirer returns appear to be poor. However, according to our model, these returns are not as negative as they would have been had the acquisitions not taken place. When future writers condemn the merger spree of the late 1990s as manifesting misguided policies on the part of the acquirers, they should focus on the alternative of not making these acquisitions. Indeed, the fact that many of the high-tech acquirers during this period were entrepreneurial firms, with managers owning substantial equity stakes, is prima facie evidence that the motive for these acquisitions was not agency, but overvaluation.

5.3. Untested predictions

Before concluding this section, we reiterate three very distinctive predictions of the model that have not yet been tested directly, but which are testable.

First, the model predicts that targets in cash acquisitions are undervalued in absolute terms (i.e., relative to fundamentals), but targets in stock acquisitions are undervalued *relative* to the bidders. A corollary of this prediction is that the pace of stock mergers should be higher in industries and markets with a large dispersion of valuations.

Second, bidders in stock acquisitions should exhibit signs of overvaluation relative to fundamentals. Recent research proposes several measures of overvaluation, including abnormally high insider sales, earnings manipulation through accruals, and negative post-formation returns (Jenter, 2002; Polk and Sapienza, 2002; Baker et al., 2003). Erickson and Wang (1999) actually find that, between 1985 and 1990, acquiring firms in stock deals managed earnings prior to merger agreement so as to raise their stock prices. It remains to be tested more systematically whether acquirers in stock deals exhibit signs of overvaluation.

Third, the model makes a prediction that bidders in stock acquisitions either have relatively longer horizons than those of the targets, or alternatively pay off target managers to agree to the stock merger. Since horizons of corporate managers can be measured using data on age or stock options, and data on the personal deals that target managers get are also available (Hartzell et al., 2003), this prediction is testable.

[3] This material was originally written in 2000, before the AOL Time Warner merger publicly became recognized as a disaster for the shareholders of Time Warner who kept the AOL stock.

6. Conclusion

This paper has presented a model of stock-market-driven acquisitions. It falls into the rapidly growing field of behavioral corporate finance, which sees corporate policies such as debt and equity issuance, share repurchases, dividends, and investment as a response to market mispricing. A good deal of empirical evidence appears to be consistent with this view.

Our model takes mispricing as given. But it also points to a powerful incentive for firms to get their equity overvalued, so that they can make acquisitions with stock. In a more general framework, firms with overvalued equity might be able to make acquisitions, survive, and grow, while firms with undervalued, or relatively less overvalued, equity become takeover targets themselves.[4] The benefit of having a high valuation for making acquisitions also points to an incentive to raise a firm's stock price even through earnings manipulation, a phenomenon whose prevalence is becoming increasingly apparent (D'Avolio et al., 2001).

This model is not intended to deny a role for real rather than just valuation factors, noted in recent surveys by Holmstrom and Kaplan (2001) and Andrade et al. (2001). Still, the model helps interpret a good deal of evidence, and yields new predictions. As such, it may add to the set of frameworks that financial economists use to examine mergers and acquisitions.

References

Agrawal, A., Jaffe, J., 2000. The post-merger performance puzzle. In: Cooper, C., Gregory, A., (Eds.), Advances in Mergers and Acquisitions, Vol. 1. Elsevier, Amsterdam, pp. 7–41.

Andrade, G., Mitchell, M., Stafford, E., 2001. New evidence and perspectives on mergers? Journal of Economic Perspectives 15, 103–120.

Andrews, E., 2002. Becoming less German. New York Times, Section C, p. 1, May 21.

Baker, M., Wurgler, J., 2000. The equity share in new issues and aggregate stock returns. Journal of Finance 55, 2219–2258.

Baker, M., Wurgler, J., 2002. Market timing and capital structure. Journal of Finance 57, 1–32.

Baker, M., Wurgler, J., 2003. A catering theory of dividends. Journal of Finance, forthcoming.

Baker, M., Stein, J., Wurgler, J., 2003. When does the market matter? Stock prices and the investment of equity-dependent firms. Quarterly Journal of Economics 118, 969–1005.

Bhagat, S., Shleifer, A., Vishny, R., 1990. Hostile takeovers in the 1980s: the return to corporate specialization. Brookings Papers on Economic Activity: Microeconomics 0, 1–72.

Blair, M., 1993. The deal decade: what takeovers and leveraged buyouts mean for Corporate governance. Brookings Institution, Washington.

D'Avolio, G., Gildor, E., Shleifer, A., 2001. Technology, information production, and market efficiency. In: Federal Reserve Bank of Kansas City, Economic Policy and the Information Economy.

DeLong, B., Shleifer, A., Summers, L., Waldmann, R., 1990. Noise trader risk in financial markets. Journal of Political Economy 98, 703–738.

[4] A recent article in the New York Times notes, in line with this reasoning, that Deutsche Bank might not survive as an independent entity because its valuation is much lower than that of its competitors, and that it is making efforts to raise its valuation both to survive and to make acquisitions for stock (Andrews, 2002).

Erickson, M., Wang, S., 1999. Earnings management by acquiring firms in stock for stock acquisitions. Journal of Accounting and Economics 27, 149–176.

Fama, E., French, K., 1993. Common risk factors in the returns on stock and bonds. Journal of Financial Economics 33, 3–56.

Fuller, J., Jensen, M., 2002. Just say no to Wall Street. Journal of Applied Corporate Finance 14, 41–46.

Gort, M., 1962. Diversification and Integration in American Industry. Princeton University Press, Princeton, NJ.

Grossman, S., Hart, O., 1980. Takeover bids, the free rider problem, and the theory of the corporation. Bell Journal of Economics 11, 42–64.

Hartzell, J., Ofek, E., Yermack, D., 2003. What's in it for me? CEOs whose firms are acquired. Review of Financial Studies, forthcoming.

Healy, P., Palepu, K., Ruback, R., 1992. Does corporate performance improve after mergers? Journal of Financial Economics 31, 135–176.

Holmstrom, B., Kaplan, S., 2001. Corporate governance and merger activity in the U.S.: making sense of the 80's and the 90's. Journal of Economic Perspectives 15, 121–144.

Jensen, M., 1986. Agency cost of free cash flow, corporate finance and takeovers. American Economic Review Papers and Proceedings 76, 323–329.

Jenter, D., 2002. Market timing and managerial portfolio decisions. Unpublished working paper, Harvard University.

Jovanovic, B., Rousseau, P., 2002. The q-theory of mergers. American Economic Review Papers and Proceedings 92, 198–204.

Kaplan, S., 1989. The effects of management buyouts on operating performance and value. Journal of Financial Economics 24, 217–254.

Lang, L., Stulz, R., Walkling, R., 1989. Managerial performance, Tobin's q, and the gains from successful tender offers. Journal of Financial Economics 24, 137–154.

Loughran, T., Vijh, A., 1997. Do long-term shareholders benefit from corporate acquisitions? Journal of Finance 52, 1765–1790.

Matsusaka, J., 1990. Takeover motives during the conglomerate merger wave. Unpublished working paper, University of Chicago.

Meeks, G., 1977. Disappointing Marriage: a Study of the Gains of the Merger. University of Cambridge Occasional Paper 51, Cambridge University Press, Cambridge.

Mitchell, M., Mulherin, H., 1996. The impact of industry shocks on takeover and restructuring activity. Journal of Financial Economics 41, 193–230.

Mitchell, M., Stafford, E., 2000. Managerial decisions and long term stock price performance. Journal of Business 73, 287–329.

Morck, R., Shleifer, A., Vishny, R., 1990a. The stock market and investment: is the market a sideshow? Brookings Papers on Economic Activity 2, 157–215.

Morck, R., Shleifer, A., Vishny, R., 1990b. Do managerial objectives drive bad acquisitions? Journal of Finance 45, 31–48.

Myers, S., Majluf, N., 1984. Corporate financing and investment decisions when firms have information that investors do not have. Journal of Financial Economics 13, 187–221.

Nelson, R., 1959. Merger Movements in the American Industry. NBER, New York.

Polk, C., Sapienza, P., 2002. The real effects of investor sentiment. Unpublished working paper, Kellogg Graduate School of Business.

Rau, R., Vermaelen, T., 1998. Glamour, value, and the post-acquisition performance of acquiring firms. Journal of Financial Economics 49, 223–254.

Ravenscraft, D., Scherer, F., 1987. Mergers, Selloffs, and Economic Efficiency. Brookings Institution, Washington.

Roll, R., 1986. The hubris hypothesis of corporate takeovers. Journal of Business 59, 197–216.

Rumelt, R., 1974. Strategy, Structure, and Economic Performance. Harvard Business School Press, Boston.

Schwert, W., 2000. Hostility in takeovers: in the eye of the beholder? Journal of Finance 55, 2599–2640.

Shleifer, A., 2000. Inefficient Markets: An Introduction to Behavioral Finance. Oxford University Press, Oxford, UK.

Shleifer, A., Vishny, R., 1990. Equilibrium short horizons of investors and firms. American Economic Review Papers and Proceedings 80, 148–153.

Shleifer, A., Vishny, R., 1991. Takeovers in the '60s and '80s: evidence and implications. Strategic Management Journal 12, 51–59.

Stein, J., 1988. Takeover threats and managerial myopia. Journal of Political Economy 96, 61–80.

Stein, J., 1989. Efficient capital markets, inefficient firms: a model of myopic corporate behavior. Quarterly Journal of Economics 104, 655–669.

Stein, J., 1996. Rational capital budgeting in an irrational world. Journal of Business 69, 429–455.

Steiner, P., 1975. Mergers: Motives, Effects, Policies. University of Michigan Press, Ann Arbor.

Verter, G., 2002. Timing merger waves. Harvard University Mimeo.

[6]

Mergers and Market Power: Evidence from the Airline Industry

By E. HAN KIM AND VIJAY SINGAL*

This paper examines price changes associated with airline mergers during 1985–1988, a period of natural experimentation in which mergers were not contested by the government. The results show that prices increased on routes served by the merging firms relative to a control group of routes unaffected by the merger. Mergers may lead to more efficient operations, but on the whole, the impact of efficiency gains on airfares is more than offset by exercise of increased market power. (*JEL* L13, G34, L93)

It is well documented that corporate acquisitions via mergers and tender offers are wealth-increasing events for shareholders. The existing evidence shows that shareholders of acquired firms almost always gain, while the shareholders of acquiring firms do not lose.[1] When the wealth effects of acquired and acquiring firms are combined, evidence shows that the combined firm value in successful tender offers increases significantly, by 7–8 percent (Michael Bradley et al., 1988).

This increase in the stock-market value of the merging firms may represent either value creation or wealth transfers from other stakeholders of the firm. Value creation may arise from economies of scale or scope, increases in managerial efficiency, improvements in production techniques, or other synergistic gains. Wealth transfers from other stakeholders may include losses suffered by bondholders due to an increase in the default risk of outstanding debt, loss of jobs by employees or a reduction in wages, reduction in prices paid to suppliers, decreases in government tax revenue, or higher prices paid by consumers due to the exercise of increased market power.

The existence of these potential wealth transfers remains a contentious issue.[2] One

*Kim: Fred M. Taylor Professor of Business Administration, School of Business Administration, University of Michigan, Ann Arbor, MI 48109-1234; Singal: Assistant Professor of Finance, R. B. Pamplin College of Business, Virginia Polytechnic Institute and State University, Blacksburg, VA 24061-0221. This paper has benefited from helpful comments and suggestions from workshop participants at the University of Chicago, the University of Colorado at Denver, Concordia University, the University of Dayton, London Business School, Michigan State University, the University of Rochester, the University of Toronto, the U.S. Department of Justice, and Virginia Polytechnic Institute and State University and from Jim Bodurtha, Michael Bradley, Jim Brickley, Bob Comment, Dan Ebels, David Graham, Gloria Hurdle, Richard Johnson, Alfred Kahn, Gautam Kaul, Arun Kumar, Patrick Murphy on behalf of the U.S. Department of Transportation, Dan O'Brien, Sam Peltzman, John Scott, Roger Sherman, An Jen Tai, two anonymous referees, and especially Ted Snyder. We also thank Severin Borenstein for generously providing data which were used for a pilot study in earlier stages of this project and for facilitating our understanding of the data base. The usual disclaimer applies.

[1]The shareholders of acquired firms in mergers and successful tender offers gain, on average, 20 percent and 32 percent, respectively. For the acquiring-firm shareholders, the gains are either small or not significantly different from zero. For a summary of empirical evidence see Michael C. Jensen and Richard S. Ruback (1983), Clifford W. Smith (1986) and Gregg A. Jarrell et al. (1988).

[2]On the issue of wealth transfers from bondholders, see Kim and John J. McConnell (1977), Paul Asquith and Kim (1982), Debra K. Dennis and John J. McConnell (1986), Kenneth Lehn and Annette B. Poulsen (1988), and Asquith and Thierry A. Wizman (1990). For the impact of mergers on employees, see Charles Brown and James L. Medoff (1987), Andrei Shleifer and Lawrence H. Summers (1988), Sanjai Bhagat et al. (1990), and Diane K. Denis (1990). Finally, on the issue of government tax revenue, see Alan J. Auerbach and David Reishus (1988) and Lehn and Poulsen (1988).

school of thought rejects the notion of wealth transfers from other stakeholders and attributes stockholder gains primarily to value creation. For example, Jensen (1988, p. 23) argues that "Takeovers do not waste credit or resources.... [The] value gains represent gains to economic efficiency, not redistribution between various parties.... Takeover gains do not come from creation of monopoly power." This rejection of monopoly power is based on previous studies that examine the impact of mergers on stock prices (B. Espen Eckbo, 1983, 1985; Robert Stillman, 1983; Eckbo and Peggy Wier, 1985).

The purpose of this study is to reexamine the question of whether mergers increase market power and lead to wealth transfers from consumers.[3] We provide a more direct test by using product price data instead of stock price data; specifically, we investigate the extent to which airline mergers have affected airfares. We recognize that any changes in the product prices of merging firms reflect the joint effect of increased efficiency, which may decrease airfares, and the exercise of increased market power, which may increase airfares. The direction of price changes will indicate which of these two effects dominates. Severin Borenstein (1990) has studied the effect on airfares of two airline mergers: the TWA-Ozark and Northwest-Republic mergers. He finds a significant increase in relative airfares on routes affected by the Northwest-Republic merger, but no evidence of fare increases associated with the TWA-Ozark merger.

Our study examines all airline mergers during 1985–1988 and all routes affected by those mergers for which data are available. We study not only fare changes, but also the relation between fare changes and changes in the degree of concentration, as well as the pricing behavior of rival firms operating in the same markets. We stratify the sample according to the financial health of the acquired firm and construct observation periods and subsamples of routes for which we expect different levels of efficiency gains. The results provide insights into how market power and efficiency gains interact in mergers and have important public policy implications.

In brief, we find that airline mergers during the 1985–1988 sample period led to higher fares, creating wealth transfers from consumers. Over the period from merger talks through merger completion, the merging firms increased airfares by an average of 9.44 percent relative to other routes unaffected by the merger. Rival firms responded by raising their prices by an average of 12.17 percent. The price effects of efficiency gains and market power vary across routes. For example, on routes where the merging firms used the same airport as a hub prior to the merger, the effect of efficiency gains is at least as pronounced as the effect of market power. For the total sample, however, efficiency gains are dominated by the exercise of increased market power. We conclude that, at least for airline mergers, wealth gains to the stockholders of merging firms do not arise through value creation alone, and relaxation of antitrust policy may result in nontrivial wealth transfers from consumers.

This paper is organized as follows. Section I reviews studies based on stock-market data and explains why we chose airline mergers to evaluate the role of market power. Section II describes the data and methodology. Section III develops the hypotheses, reports the relative price changes, and examines how the fare changes are related to changes in concentration. Section IV contains the summary and concluding remarks.

I. Background

A. *Previous Research Based on Stock Price Data*

Eckbo (1983, 1985), Stillman (1983), and Eckbo and Wier (1985) test for market power by examining the stock price reactions of rival firms in challenged mergers.

[3]In this paper, the term "mergers" is used synonymously with "successful tender offers."

They recognize that exercise of market power benefits rival firms, whereas efficiency gains have an adverse impact on the rival firms by placing them at a competitive disadvantage in the product market. These authors find that the announcement of mergers increases the market price of rival firms' shares. However, they characterize this increase in stock prices as an information effect; namely, rival firms are now more likely to be takeover targets. Since the announcement of an antitrust challenge reduces the probability of mergers, they reason that if mergers increase market power, an antitrust challenge should have a negative impact on the stock prices of rival firms. The authors find no statistically significant decreases in the stock prices of rival firms and reject the market-power hypothesis.

These studies are subject to several criticisms. First, the tests are weak. Even at the time of merger announcement, when the impact on rival firms should be most pronounced, the abnormal returns to rival firms are small relative to those of the merging firms. For instance, Eckbo (1983) finds that the average abnormal returns to target, bidding, and rival firms at the time of merger announcement are 18.58 percent, 2.68 percent, and 0.91 percent, respectively.[4] Thus, the negative impact that an antitrust challenge can have on rival firms' stock prices is likely to be very small. In addition, the period from the merger announcement to the antitrust challenge, during which the forthcoming antitrust challenge can be anticipated and discounted in stock prices is, on average, ten months.[5] This is too long to allow for a meaningful inference regarding the impact of an antitrust challenge on rival firms' stock prices.

Second, an antitrust challenge, by reducing the probability that the proposed merger will be successful, reduces both the positive effect of market power and the negative effect of efficiency gains. Since we can only observe the net effect through stock prices, the evidence of insignificant stock price reaction can be interpreted as either the absence of *both* market power and efficiency effects or their offsetting presence.[6]

Third, stock-market data aggregate a firm's performance in all of its markets. If a merger affects market power in a small fraction of the markets served by the rival (merging) firms, its influence on the rival (merging) firms' overall profits may be too small to generate a significant impact on the stock prices.

In short, the tests based on stock-market prices are at best indirect and probably weak.[7] A more direct test of market power requires an examination of product price changes. However, such a test will require controlling for a multitude of factors affecting product prices, such as changes in raw-material costs, labor costs, market demand, and general economic conditions. There is also the problem of scarcity of reliable product price and cost data.

B. *The Airline Industry*

The airline industry provides a unique opportunity to test for market power using product prices. In the airline industry, each route can be considered a separate market. The routes not affected by mergers can serve as a control group to capture industry-wide factors such as changes in fuel costs, labor costs, and seasonal variations in demand, as well as economy-wide factors that influence airfares. Thus, airfare changes on routes affected by a merger, computed relative to the control group, can be attributed to the

[4]These gains are measured from ten days before to five days after the announcement.

[5]The time period between announcement of a merger and filing of complaint varies from a few days to more than four years.

[6]R. Preston McAfee and Michael A. Williams (1988) examine the merger of Xidex Corporation with Kalvar Corporation, a challenged merger known to be *ex post* anticompetitive. Using the same methodology as Eckbo and Stillman, they demonstrate that the methodology leads to the conclusion that the merger was *not* anticompetitive. See also David M. Barton and Roger Sherman (1984).

[7]See Michael A. Salinger and Laurence Schumann (1988) and Bhagat et al. (1990) for further criticism of using stock-market data for testing market power.

merger. There are, on average, 196 unaffected routes for each route affected by a merger. Furthermore, there are hundreds of routes affected by each merger. Thus, each merger generates a large number of observations, each of which can be compared with its control group.

The airline industry offers several other attractive features. First, the Airline Deregulation Act of 1978 led to many new carriers entering on profitable routes, followed by price-cutting and reduced operating margins, with losing carriers filing for bankruptcy and consolidating through mergers. The restructuring process during the 1980's gave rise to many mergers. Second, the Department of Transportation has compiled a comprehensive data base on airfares by carriers and routes, which makes this empirical study feasible. Third, there are no easy substitutes for airline travel. Road and rail travel are potential substitutes, but mainly for short-distance nonbusiness travel.

Moreover, during 1985–1988, the airline industry was governed by the Department of Transportation,[8] and the DOT did not deny any of the mergers proposed for approval.[9] This environment provides a controlled experiment for the question: what would happen if the antitrust policy toward mergers were relaxed?

II. Data and Methodology

Our sample of routes is obtained from 14 airline mergers that were initiated during the period 1985–1988.[10] Although 27 airline mergers were identified during the sample period,[11] 13 have been dropped from the study because of inadequate data.[12] Table 1 lists the names of the acquired and acquir-

[8]The airline industry was governed by the Civil Aeronautics Board from 1938 to 1984. Under the Airline Deregulation Act of 1978, the industry was deregulated in stages. Effective January 1, 1982, all controls on entry and exit were removed, while airfares were deregulated from January 1, 1983. On January 1, 1985, the governance of the airline industry was transferred from the Civil Aeronautics Board to the Department of Transportation, which had the authority over proposed airline mergers until 1988.

[9]We cannot find any mergers that were disapproved by the Department of Transportation during 1985–1988. In addition, Paul S. Dempsey (1990 p. 13) states: "the DOT approved *every* airline merger submitted to it...." Similarly, Steven Berry (1989 p. 176) states: "After that decision [Northwest-Republic approval], many mergers were proposed and approved quickly before the DOT's power in the area ran out at the end of 1988." Finally, Alfred E. Kahn, former chairman of Civil Aeronautics Board and the architect of airline deregulation, was quoted in *Fortune* (1986 p. 64) as saying, "DOT never met an airline merger it didn't like."

[10]We choose the sample period of 1985–1988 for two reasons. First, as noted above, no proposed mergers were denied during this period, reflecting the relaxation of antitrust policy. Second, out of the 41 airline mergers that could be identified following the 1978 Airline Deregulation Act until 1988, 27 occurred during 1985–1988.

[11]Airline mergers were identified from several sources including (i) *Wall Street Journal Index* (*General News*), (ii) *Mergers and Acquisitions Journal*, (iii) Compustat Research file, (iv) CRSP (Center for Research in Security Prices) stock files, and (v) trade journals such as *Air Transport World* and *Aviation Week and Space Technology*. The *Wall Street Journal Index* was searched to find relevant information concerning these mergers, such as announcement dates, merger completion dates, government approvals, and financial status of merging firms. These reports were supplemented with the information contained in company annual reports, *Predicasts F&S Index*, *The New York Times Index*, *Antitrust and Trade Regulation Reporter*, and *Aviation Week and Space Technology*. When in doubt, we searched the text service of Dow Jones Retrieval Service.

[12]The mergers in which either the acquirer or acquired has the following characteristics are excluded from the sample:

(i) Airlines providing charter services only. Two mergers involving Key Airlines are dropped.
(ii) Airlines that are so small in size that no data on airfares are available for the quarter prior to their merger. Three mergers involving Colgan, Business Express, and Chapparal are excluded.
(iii) Airlines with extensive code-sharing arrangements. Some smaller airlines use the codes of a larger airline, making the two airlines indistinguishable in the data base. For example, "AA", the code for American Airlines was used by Command Air, which makes it impossible to determine whether the carrier was American Airlines or Command Air. There are eight airlines with extensive code-sharing arrangements: Command Air, Simmons, Wings West, Ransome, Britt Air, Rocky Airways, Provincetown–Boston Airlines, and Mississippi Valley Airlines.

ing firms, the number of passengers carried by each, the relevant announcement dates of merger bids, and the merger completion dates. The sample of 14 mergers generates 21,351 affected routes, which provide the basis for construction of our sample.

A. *Product Market Data, Sample Routes, and Control Groups*

Raw product market data are obtained from the Department of Transportation's Ticket Dollar Value Origin and Destination data bank, where they are reported on a quarterly basis.[13] From this data base we obtain domestic economy-class airfares and numbers of passengers by routes and carriers, which allow us to compute other relevant information, such as route distance, market shares of different airlines, concentration, and fare per mile. We exclude all foreign-travel tickets, first-class tickets, and any tickets that involve more than one connecting point on any directional trip.[14] We also exclude tickets for which the fare cannot be directly attributed to a route and airline.[15]

These data are used for construction of the sample. To be included in the sample, a route has to be served by at least one of the merging airlines with at least 1,200 passengers per year.[16] These criteria reduce the number of sample routes to 11,629.[17]

We define rival firms as those airlines that serve the 11,629 sample routes. When more than one rival firm operates on a route, we compute the average fare of rival firms (weighted by passenger-miles) and treat it as a single observation. Using the same criteria applied to the merging-firm

[13]The raw data base is very large with 1–2 million records per quarter. Although there are edited versions of the data base, we process it ourselves to construct a data base best suited to our requirements. The raw data base contains all of the data as reported by participating air carriers. The carriers are required to report every tenth ticket (i.e., 10 percent of all tickets issued by them). Each record identifies the point of origin, the airline carrier code(s), intermediate airports, the point of destination, the dollar fare, the number of passengers, the distance(s), and the fare class(es).

When airlines fly under different carrier codes but are controlled by the same parent, we change the carrier codes to reflect the control status of the carriers. The same changes are made when the acquired firm's carrier code continues to be used after the merger.

In addition, tickets with abnormally high fares are excluded to eliminate tickets with data-entry errors. The Department of Transportation calculates a "Standard Industry Fare Level" (SIFL), which is designed to check the reasonableness of airfares. During 1980–1989, the maximum SIFL for a 250-mile trip was 29 cents per mile. Allowing for a wide margin of error, we eliminate tickets when the fare is equal to or in excess of $3.00 per mile. This same upper limit is used by DOT to identify suspect fares. We also delete frequent-flyer tickets (with indicated price of zero) because frequent-flyer awards may have been earned on different routes during different quarters. In addition, if the fare per mile on any sample route is less (greater) than or equal to one-tenth (ten times) the fare per mile in its control group, then those routes are removed from further analysis.

[14]Thus, we include only direct flights and flights that involve a single change of plane. We do not distinguish between direct flights and single-connection flights. These flights could represent different markets, as a connecting flight requires the passenger to wait for a connection. We do not believe that ignoring the value of a passenger's waiting time would significantly bias our results, because our analysis is based on a comparison between sample routes and the control groups. There is no reason to believe that ignoring the value of passengers' time imparts a greater bias for sample routes than for the control groups.

[15]Specifically, we exclude (i) tickets with missing carrier codes, (ii) tickets that involve more than one carrier, (iii) tickets for which travel is neither one-way nor round-trip, and (iv) round-trip tickets with different intermediate stops on outward and return journeys.

[16]Note that 1,200 passengers per year is equivalent to 300 passengers per quarter. Since the data base contains only 10 percent of the population, 300 passengers will provide 30 observations, which we feel is the minimum required to draw reasonable statistical inferences about the population. Gloria J. Hurdle et al. (1989) and Borenstein (1990) use 1,000 passengers and 3,650 passengers, respectively, as their screens.

[17]These sample routes include cases in which more than one merger took place in the same quarter. This will overstate the impact of mergers on airfares if we examine only the unconditional fare changes. However, our formal test is conducted on the relation between fare changes and concentration changes. Because the concentration changes also reflect the impact of multiple mergers, the regression results will not overstate the significance of the relation between the two variables.

TABLE 1—THE SAMPLE OF AIRLINE MERGERS

Acquired firm-acquirer	Passengers (thousands) Acquired firm	Passengers (thousands) Acquirer	Dates: First bid for acquired firm	Dates: First bid by acquirer	Dates: Final bid	Dates: Completion
Muse Air-Southwest	1,980	10,698	85/03/11	85/03/11	85/03/11	85/06/25
Empire-Piedmont	1,084	14,274	85/09/26	85/10/03	85/10/03	86/02/01
Frontier-People	7,068	9,100	85/09/20	85/10/09	85/10/09	85/11/22
Republic-Northwest	17,465	14,539	86/01/24	86/01/24	86/01/24	86/08/12
Eastern-Texas	41,662	19,640	86/02/24	86/02/24	86/02/24	86/11/25
Ozark-TWA	5,541	20,876	86/02/28	86/02/28	86/02/28	86/09/12
People-Texas	11,907	19,640	86/07/03	86/07/03	86/09/16	86/12/30
Jet America-Alaska	774	3,132	86/08/07	86/08/07	86/09/08	86/09/30
Western-Delta	9,062	39,804	86/09/10	86/09/10	86/09/10	86/12/17
Air Cal-American	4,451	41,165	86/11/18	86/11/18	86/11/18	87/04/30
Horizon-Alaska Air	942	3,132	86/11/20	86/11/20	86/11/20	86/12/29
Pacific SW-US Air	9,049	19,278	86/12/09	86/12/09	86/12/09	87/05/29
Piedmont-US Air	22,800	21,725	87/01/28	87/02/18	87/03/06	87/11/05
Florida Ex-Braniff	1,415	2,557	87/10/23	87/10/23	87/12/15	88/06/15[a]

Notes: The numbers of passengers given are for the year prior to the merger. Dates are shown as year/month/date. Completion date refers to the date when the acquirer obtained control.

[a]This date may not be exact.

routes, we obtain 8,109 routes for the rival firms.[18]

For each route in the sample, we construct a control group. The control group consists of all routes on which neither of the merging firms operated during the period of analysis and on which the distance falls within 7.5 percent of that of the sample route (i.e., 92.5–107.5 percent of the sample route distance).[19] The average number of routes in the control group is 196.6 for merging-firm routes and 199.1 for rival-firm routes. The fare for the control group is the mean of the fares on the individual routes weighted by passenger-miles.

B. *Relative Fare Changes*

To identify price changes that can be attributed to mergers, we compare the fare change of a sample route with the average fare change in its control group. Industry-wide changes like fluctuations in fuel prices, changes in labor cost, and seasonal or cyclical variations in demand are likely to have an equivalent effect on routes of a similar distance.[20] We isolate the effect of the merger by comparing routes where a merger has taken place with routes where the merger has not taken place. Specifically, relative fare changes are computed as

$$(1)\quad \text{Lfarchg} = \log\left(\frac{\text{Fare}_e^s}{\text{Fare}_b^s}\right) - \log\left(\frac{\text{Fare}_e^c}{\text{Fare}_b^c}\right)$$

where the subscripts on Fare denote the ending (e) and beginning (b) of a period, while the superscripts denote the sample (s) and the control (c) routes. The expressions on the right-hand side of the equation are the continuously compounded rates of

[18]The only difference in selection criteria is that the requirement of 1,200 passengers per year is imposed on the sum of the passengers carried by the rival firms on each route.

[19]To the extent that there may be other mergers affecting the routes in the control group, the distinction between the control group and the sample routes will be diminished. This will weaken the power of the test and biases against finding a significant difference in airfares between the sample and the control routes.

[20]Local economic conditions may affect some routes differently. We hope the large number of observations in our sample averages out the noise.

change in fares for the sample route and for the control group. Thus Lfarchg represents the difference in the percentage change in fares between the sample and the control routes.

III. Hypotheses and Empirical Results

In this section, we develop hypotheses concerning the effect of mergers on the product prices of merging and rival firms and their relation to changes in concentration. We then present empirical results using the data and methodology described above.

A. *Hypotheses*

If a merger generates efficiency gains, it will reduce the marginal cost of the merged firm. In the absence of a change in market power, the decrease in marginal cost will lead to a lower price. If, on the other hand, there are no efficiency gains and the primary effect is the exercise of greater market power, the merger will lead to a higher product price. If both effects are present, then the direction of change in observed prices will indicate which of the two effects dominates. An increase in price implies that the market-power effect dominates efficiency gains; a decrease in price implies the dominance of efficiency gains. Thus, we first examine *whether or not mergers lead to an increase in airfares of merging firms relative to the control group*.

We expect that the greater the increase in market concentration resulting from a merger, the greater is the potential for the exercise of market power, and the greater is the increase in airfares. Notice, however, that the increase in concentration measures the extent to which a market is previously served jointly by the merging firms (i.e., the degree of overlap). By serving the same proportion of a market with one firm instead of two, it is possible to achieve efficiency gains through economies of scale. Since efficiency gains should lead to a price decrease, we would expect to see a negative correlation between price changes and changes in concentration, if the effect of efficiency gains dominates the market-power effect. On the other hand, if the market-power effect dominates the efficiency effect, the correlation should be positive. Thus, our primary test investigates *the correlation between price changes of merging firms and changes in concentration*.

A price change by the merging (or merged) firms may affect other firms serving the same market. If the merging (or merged) firms increase their price and the rival firms cooperate, we will observe an increase in the prices of rival firms. If the efficiency gain dominates and the merged firm decreases its price, rival firms are likely to reduce their prices to maintain their market share. Thus, a price increase by rival firms is consistent with market power dominating efficiency gains, while a price decrease implies that efficiency gains dominate market power. Likewise, the correlation between the price changes of rival firms and concentration changes will be positive if market power is the primary effect and negative if efficiency gains dominate market power.

To separate the effect of efficiency gains from the market-power effect, we consider two subperiods: the announcement period and the completion period. The announcement period is the quarter in which the potential or actual bid by the successful bidder could be identified in the press; the completion period is the quarter in which the successful bidder acquires control of the target. The "full period" extends from the announcement quarter to the merger-completion quarter. For each period, we compute relative fare changes from the quarter preceding the period to the quarter following the period.

The potential sources of efficiency gains include economies of scale or scope, improved production techniques, the combination of complementary resources, the redeployment of assets to more profitable uses, and more efficient management. Such synergies cannot be realized until the firms actually merge.[21] Since the marginal cost

[21] Michael Bradley et al. (1983) present evidence that the synergistic gains are not realized unless targets are successfully acquired by the bidder.

will not decrease until these synergies are realized, we expect the impact of efficiency gains to prevail only during the completion period.[22]

In contrast, exercise of market power does not have to wait until merger completion. Getting the two management teams together to discuss merger possibilities provides a relatively safe and convenient forum to arrive at mutually beneficial pricing strategies. Even without an explicit price-fixing agreement, the mere anticipation of a merger would make the participating firms more cooperative.[23] Further exercise of market power may take place during the completion period, if the exercise of market power during the announcement period is tempered by the uncertainty regarding the eventual outcome of merger discussions. In sum, we hypothesize that *fare changes during the announcement period are primarily due to the market-power effect, whereas the fare changes during the completion period reflect the joint, and offsetting, effects of market power and efficiency gains*.

To buttress the results from the subperiod analysis, we also examine subsamples that are constructed according to the potential sources of efficiency gains and market power. The hypotheses concerning the subsample analysis will be described later in the results section.

B. *Mergers Involving Financially Distressed Firms*

Some of the acquired firms in our sample were in financial distress prior to the merger. Since these firms may have pricing strategies different from firms not in financial distress, we choose to treat them separately. For firms in financial distress, for example, the need to raise cash for current operations may dominate the long-term benefits from cooperating with other airlines.[24] In addition, the possibility of suspension of service or the perception that airlines in financial distress provide poor service may make travelers reluctant to choose those airlines. One way to attract these customers is to discount airfares. We expect such pricing behavior to prevail until a failing firm is taken over by a more solvent firm.

We classify a firm as financially distressed if reports in the financial press indicate serious financial problems (such as denial of additional credit, debt postponement, and asset sales) or if *Moody's Transportation Manual* contains remarks by external auditors implying financial difficulty of the firm. In our sample, there are five such firms: Frontier Airlines, People Express, Eastern Airlines, Jet America, and Muse Air. Mergers involving these firms are defined as "failing-firm mergers"; mergers not involving these firms are defined as "normal firm mergers."

C. *Relative Fare Changes*

Table 2 reports the average beginning and ending relative fares and the mean value of Lfarchg for announcement, completion, and full periods.[25] The relative fare is de-

[22] Further efficiency gains may materialize even after the completion period. Obviously, these additional efficiency gains can be accounted for by increasing the length of the completion period. A longer sample period, however, will increase the noise in the data. We believe that the choice of one quarter after merger completion represents a reasonable trade-off.

[23] The same argument does not apply for efficiency gains. If the merging firms reduce prices in anticipation of efficiency gains, but without actually realizing the gains, they may end up losing money, because realization of efficiency gains is contingent upon the merger being successful. In contrast, collusion in anticipation of a merger is beneficial to both airlines, irrespective of whether the merger is ultimately successful or not.

[24] A management team, in order to avoid immediate bankruptcy or liquidation, may pursue a policy of revenue maximization rather than profit maximization. The revenue maximum occurs where demand is unit-elastic, which is a profit maximum only if marginal cost is zero. If marginal cost is greater than zero, the profit maximum will occur at a higher price, where demand is elastic. Thus, the price for revenue maximization is always less than or equal to the price for profit maximization.

[25] The full period is divided into announcement and completion periods only for those mergers where there is a gap of at least one quarter between the announcement and completion periods. For example, the Western-Delta merger was announced and completed in the third and fourth quarters of 1986, respectively. Since it is not possible to separate the effect of announcement from the effect of completion, such merg-

fined as the ratio of the fare on the sample route to the fare in the control group. To account for the possibility that high-density routes are estimated with greater precision, we also report (in parentheses) means weighted by the total number of passengers for each route. The overall conclusions that emerge from Table 2 are that airline mergers increase fares by about 10 percent,[26] mergers involving financially troubled firms result in distinctly different pricing behavior from mergers involving normal firms, and the rival firms closely mimic the merging firms.

The results are generally insensitive to whether or not the means are weighted by the number of passengers. The only exception is that the weighted-average relative fares are consistently lower than the unweighted averages, indicating that the relative fares are generally lower in high-density routes.

Whichever averages we use in the comparison, Table 2 shows that, at the beginning of the full period, routes in failing-firm mergers have considerably lower relative fares than routes in normal-firm mergers: the unweighted-mean relative fares are 0.76 and 1.03, respectively. This means that financially distressed airlines were initially setting prices well below the industry average (the industry average is equal to 1). Table 2 also shows a similar pricing difference among the rivals.

During the announcement period, both merging and rival firms in failing-firm mergers cut their prices by an average of 19 percent, further increasing the gap between their prices and the industry average. In contrast, merging and rival firms in normal-firm mergers increase their fares by 11 percent and 13 percent. This price increase suggests that discussions culminating in a possible merger between normal firms are conducive to cooperative pricing behavior. For the failing firm, however, the need to discount fares to attract reluctant customers or to raise cash for survival appears to outweigh the motive to collude.

During the completion period, both the merging and rival firms *decrease* their relative fares, by 9 percent and 5 percent, in normal-firm mergers. This price decline suggests that efficiency gains dominate any additional market power that may arise due to resolution of uncertainty. In contrast, the merging and rival firms in failing-firm mergers increase their fares, by 40 percent and 45 percent. These large price increases suggest that, having merged with presumably a more solvent acquirer, the failing firm no longer has the incentive to undercut prices. Furthermore, the exit of the failing firm enables greater collusion among the remaining airlines. The dual effect of these considerations appears overwhelmingly to dominate any efficiency gains that may arise in these mergers.

In sum, agreements to merge that are not motivated by financial distress are conducive to exercise of market power. These mergers result in large increases in relative airfares during the announcement period; but upon merger completion, efficiency gains offset much, but not all, of the impact of market power.[27] In contrast, the financially distressed firms continue to cut prices during the announcement period. It is only when the merger is successfully completed that they stop undercutting and dramatically increase fares to bring them closer to the industry level. These different pricing strategies are closely matched by rival firms operating on the same routes.

ers are included only in the full period. Thus, the full period has all 14 mergers, while the announcement and completion periods consist of only seven mergers.

[26]The relative fare changes are measured by Lfarchg. The skewness and kurtosis coefficients of Lfarchg are 0.85 and 3.32, which do not indicate serious departures from normality. Nevertheless, we test for the significance of Lfarchg using the sign test. The results for Table 2 are the same, except for two cells: Lfarchg values for "all mergers" during the completion period become significantly negative.

[27]Borenstein (1990) also reports that a substantial portion of the price increases in the Northwest-Republic merger took place before merger completion.

TABLE 2—CHANGES IN RELATIVE FARES OF MERGING AND RIVAL FIRMS

	Merging firms			Rival firms		
Variable	All mergers	Mergers between normal firms	Mergers with a failing firm	All mergers	Mergers between normal firms	Mergers with a failing firm
Full period:						
Sample size	11,629	8,511	3,118	8,109	5,578	2,531
Relative fares, beginning	0.9602** (0.8238**)	1.0325** (0.8982**)	0.7626** (0.6883**)	0.9140** (0.8645**)	0.9745** (0.9218**)	0.7807** (0.7588**)
Relative fares, ending	1.0159** (0.8850**)	1.0529** (0.9309**)	0.9148** (0.8015**)	0.9831** (0.9287**)	1.0085 (0.9472**)	0.9272** (0.8944**)
Relative fare changes: Lfarchg (percentage)	9.44** (9.75**)	3.25** (3.76**)	26.35** (20.66**)	12.17** (11.20**)	5.94** (4.42**)	25.90** (23.71**)
Announcement Period:						
Sample size	7,214	5,832	1,382	4,891	3,730	1,161
Relative fares, beginning	0.9792** (0.8575**)	0.9855** (0.8636**)	0.9530** (0.8376**)	0.9444** (0.8945**)	0.9499** (0.9093**)	0.9268** (0.8487**)
Relative fares, ending	1.0270** (0.8947**)	1.0754** (0.9440**)	0.8228** (0.7337**)	0.9807** (0.9208**)	1.0345** (0.9634**)	0.8079** (0.7882**)
Relative fare, changes: Lfarchg (percentage)	5.54** (3.81**)	11.32** (10.38**)	−18.85** (−17.66**)	5.06** (3.77**)	12.64** (9.73**)	−19.28** (−14.80**)
Completion Period:						
Sample size	7,557	6,140	1,417	5,304	4.105	1,199
Relative fares, beginning	0.9874** (0.8657**)	1.048** (0.9273**)	0.7247** (0.6528**)	0.9496** (0.8938**)	1.0201** (0.9507**)	0.7081** (0.7046**)
Relative fares, ending	0.9640** (0.8683**)	0.9652** (0.8724**)	0.9590** (0.8541**)	0.9764** (0.9296**)	0.9776** (0.9286**)	0.9725** (0.9332**)
Relative fare changes: Lfarchg (percentage)	0.21 (3.31**)	−9.00** (−6.82**)	40.11** (38.36**)	6.10** (7.13**)	−5.36** (−3.72**)	45.34** (43.24**)

Notes: Relative fare is the ratio of the fare on the sample route to the weighted average fare in the control group. The relative fares are measured at the start and end of each observation period. Lfarchg is the mean of the differences between the sample and control routes in the natural logs of the ratio of fares at the end to the beginning of each period. All numbers not in parentheses represent unweighted means of the variable. All numbers in parentheses are means weighted by the number of passengers on each route. For relative fares, statistical significance is tested using the t statistic with reference to a mean of 1.00, and for Lfarchg the significance is with reference to a mean of zero.

**Statistically significant at the 1-percent level (two-tailed test).

D. *Relation Between Fares and Concentration*

The relative fare changes examined in the preceding section suggest that airline mergers have an important impact on pricing behavior. In this section, we provide estimates of the relation between these price changes and changes in concentration.

Specification.—We measure level of concentration by the Herfindahl-Hirschman index (HHI).[28] Janusz A. Ordover et al. (1982) demonstrate that changes in the HHI can be useful indicators of the effect of mergers

[28]The Herfindahl-Hirschman index is calculated for each route as the sum of squares of the market shares of all airlines operating on the route.

when such changes are evaluated in light of other evidence—in this case, the other evidence being the relative fare changes. Like the relative fare change, the change in the concentration (Lhhichg) is measured relative to the control group. The Lhhichg is calculated using equation (1), with HHI instead of fares. For the complete sample of routes served by the merging firms, the mean Lhhichg for the full period is 5.62 percent if unweighted, and it is 10.16 percent if weighted by the total number of passengers. For the rival firms, the means are 6.50 percent and 10.15 percent.

We examine the relation between the fare changes and the changes in concentration by regressing Lfarchg on the following independent variables: (i) Lhhichg, a relative percentage change in HHI from the beginning to the end of a sample period, (ii) Fail, a dummy variable for mergers involving financially distressed firms, (iii) Normal, a dummy variable for mergers involving normal firms, and (iv) Ldist, the natural log of distance.

We use interaction terms between the Fail dummy and Lhhichg and between the Normal dummy and Lhhichg. This allows for different relations between changes in concentration and fare changes for failing-firm mergers and normal-firm mergers. Ldist is included in the regression to measure the effect of distance on fare changes. Since the substitution effect between air travel and rail or road travel would be greater for shorter distances, we use the natural log of distance.[29]

The regression relations are estimated using ordinary least squares under the following two specifications:

$$(2)\quad \text{Lfarchg}_i = \alpha + \beta_1 \text{Normal}_i \times \text{Lhhichg}_i + \beta_2 \text{Fail}_i \times \text{Lhhichg}_i + \beta_3 \text{Ldist}_i + \varepsilon_i$$

$$(3)\quad \text{Lfarchg}_i = \alpha + \beta_1 \text{Normal}_i \times \text{Lhhichg}_i + \beta_2 \text{Fail}_i \times \text{Lhhichg}_i + \varepsilon_i$$

Regression Results, Total Sample.—The regression results for the full, announcement, and completion periods for merging and rival firms are reported in Table 3.[30] All standard errors are adjusted for heteroscedasticity using Halbert White's (1980) correction. For the full period, the results portray a significant positive relation between fare changes and changes in concentration. This is true for rival firms as well as for merging firms in both failing- and normal-firm mergers. On the whole, the market-power effects dominate whatever efficiency gains are achieved in these mergers.

In addition, the regression coefficient on Ldist is significantly positive for both merging and rival firms for all periods. Road and rail travel become less of a substitute for air travel as distance increases; consequently, firms have greater latitude for the exercise of market power on longer routes. The positive coefficient on the distance variable indicates that airlines exploit more market power on routes for which there are fewer substitutes; namely, longer-distance routes.

During the announcement period, the regression coefficients on Lhhichg are significantly positive for normal-firm mergers and insignificant for failing-firm mergers. Apparently, firms in normal-firm mergers start to take full advantage of increased market power during the announcement period. Firms in failing-firm mergers, on the other hand, show no such inclination. These firms show a large and significantly positive regression coefficient on Lhhichg only during the completion period. This suggests that the failing firms are restrained from exercising market power until merger completion,

[29] Hurdle et al. (1989) also use log of the distance to measure a nonlinear relation between airfare and distance.

[30] The regression relations reported in Table 3 are based on ordinary least squares (OLS). Regressions are also estimated using weighted least squares, where the weight is equal to the number of passengers on each route. This is done to account for the possibility that variables are measured with greater precision for high-density routes. These regressions have a slightly higher explanatory power, but the results are generally consistent with the OLS results. For the sake of simplicity, we report only the OLS results.

TABLE 3—ORDINARY LEAST SQUARES REGRESSIONS FOR THE TOTAL SAMPLE

Models:

(2) $\text{Lfarchg}_i = \alpha + \beta_1 \text{Normal}_i \times \text{Lhhichg}_i + \beta_2 \text{Faii}_i \times \text{Lhhichg}_i + \beta_3 \text{Ldist}_i + \varepsilon_i$

(3) $\text{Lfarchg}_i = \alpha + \beta_1 \text{Normal}_i \times \text{Lhhichg}_i + \beta_2 \text{Fail}_i \times \text{Lhhichg}_i + \varepsilon_i$

Period and model	Regression coefficient (*t* statistic)					
	Constant	Normal× Lhhichg	Fail× Lhhichg	Ldist	R^2_{adj}	Sample size
A. *Merging Firms:*						
Full period						
Model (2)	−0.6864 (−23.22)	0.0942 (7.14)	0.2331 (6.99)	0.1154 (25.00)	0.051	11,629
Model (3)	0.0855 (21.78)	0.1072 (8.09)	0.2438 (7.10)	—	0.013	11,629
Announcement period						
Model (2)	−0.2409 (−8.03)	0.2178 (10.44)	0.0094 (0.19)	0.0437 (9.28)	0.030	7,214
Model (3)	0.0511 (12.86)	0.2364 (11.16)	0.0220 (0.45)	—	0.022	7,214
Completion period						
Model (2)	−0.3173 (−10.75)	−0.0118 (−1.08)	0.4233 (7.06)	0.0465 (10.06)	0.035	7,557
Model (3)	−0.0046 (−1.10)	−0.0179 (−1.69)	0.4233 (6.92)	—	0.026	7,557
B. *Rival Firms:*						
Full period						
Model (2)	−0.7311 (−18.56)	0.1203 (6.47)	0.2253 (6.89)	0.1233 (20.64)	0.052	8,109
Model (3)	0.1098 (22.85)	0.1455 (7.76)	0.2333 (6.92)	—	0.016	8,109
Announcement period						
Model (2)	−0.3523 (−8.49)	0.3293 (12.05)	0.0210 (0.38)	0.0571 (9.14)	0.052	4,891
Model (3)	0.0378 (7.10)	0.3509 (12.65)	0.0409 (0.76)	—	0.042	4,891
Completion period						
Model (2)	−0.2132 (−5.32)	−0.0193 (−1.19)	0.3967 (6.31)	0.0387 (6.41)	0.028	5,304
Model (3)	0.0528 (9.85)	−0.0214 (−1.36)	0.3928 (6.18)	—	0.024	5,304

Notes: Lfarchg(Lhhichg) is the difference in the logs of the ratio of fares (concentrations) at the end to the beginning of each period between the sample and control routes. Ldist is the natural log of the route distance. The Fail (Normal) dummy is 1 (0) for failing-firm mergers and 0 (1) otherwise.

and they start to catch up aggressively with the industry level once the merger is completed.[31]

The results for the normal-firm mergers during the completion period are mixed; although the regression coefficient on Lhhichg turns negative, the significance level is low. We suspect that there are systematic differences across routes which are masked by the regression on the total sample. For this reason, we conduct a subsample analysis in the next subsection.

Finally, the regression coefficients for rival firms are almost indistinguishable from those of merging firms for all periods and under both regression specifications. Apparently, the joint effect of market power and efficiency gains due to mergers has similar pricing implications for both merging and rival firms. The parallel movement in prices and correlations leads us to suspect that some kind of tacit cooperation exists among airlines in setting prices.

E. *Subsample Analysis*

To further separate market-power effects from efficiency effects, we divide the sample into four subsamples according to the potential sources of operating synergies and market power. If the merging firms have a common hub at the same airport prior to the merger, then all routes to or from the hub are called "Hub" routes. If a route is served by both firms prior to the merger, then that route is called an "Overlapping" route. Given these distinctions, we divide our sample of routes into four subsamples: subsample Hub/Overlap consists of overlapping routes with a common hub; subsample Hub Only consists of a common hub with no overlapping routes; subsample Overlap Only contains overlapping routes with no common hub; and subsample Neither consists of routes which are neither overlapping nor have a common hub.

Subsample Hub/Overlap represents the set of routes with the maximum potential for operating efficiency, because the merged firm can better realize both "in the air" and "on-the-ground" synergies.[32] These are also the routes from which the merging firms can derive the maximum increase in market power, because they have the greatest degree of joint operation on these routes. Routes in subsample Hub Only can realize on-the-ground synergies, and the merged firm may also be able to exercise some additional market power because it is now in a better position to control the choices available to the traveler from the hub airport. Routes in subsample Overlap Only can realize in-the-air synergies and also have the potential for exercising additional market power by virtue of having reduced the num-

[31] For the announcement period, it is not clear which Lhhichg is the most appropriate measure to use. The first and most obvious one is the actual change in relative concentration during the announcement period, which is the one used for Tables 3 and 4. This measure, however, ignores the possibility of anticipatory pricing behavior. For instance, airlines may set prices based on the expected changes in market structure. Thus, an alternative approach is to assume that airlines have perfect foresight and use the Lhhichg of the full period. Yet another approach is to use a simulated Lhhichg assuming that the merger will occur with certainty, after which all services on overlapping routes will be consolidated with no other changes taking place in market structure. Such a simulation approach does not consider the rivals' reactions, nor does it account for the effect of the change in the relative power of merging airlines due to common hubs or multimarket contact (see footnote 35). Thus, we use the actual (rather than simulated) changes in concentration.

When the regressions are rerun using the full period's Lhhichg for the announcement period, (i.e., the perfect-foresight approach), the results for normal-firm mergers are qualitatively the same for both merging and rival firms. For failing-firm mergers, however, the coefficient on Fail × Lhhichg becomes significantly negative. This may be interpreted as evidence that the failing firms cut prices more, the greater the ultimate change in concentration. A possible explanation is that the causality is in the reverse; namely, when failing firms cut prices more they capture greater market shares, and when they are ultimately acquired, the change in concentration is greater. Since we are interested in the effect of concentration changes on airfares, we rely on the results using contemporaneous changes in concentration.

[32] "In the air" synergies may arise from use of fewer aircraft and a better load factor. "On the ground" synergies may arise from better use of gates/slots and ground crews.

ber of competitors by one. Routes in subsample Neither have no potential for direct operating synergies or for any increase in direct market power.[33]

We assume that company-wide, nonoperating synergies have no differential effect on fares between routes and that no cross-subsidization of operating synergies takes place across markets. Thus, we hypothesize that the airfare changes on routes in subsample Hub/Overlap will be most affected by efficiency gains and market power, and airfares in subsample Neither will be the least affected.

Table 4 reports the mean relative fare changes, the mean relative concentration changes, and the ordinary-least-squares results using the regression specification in equation (2) for each of the four subsamples.[34] As would be expected, the changes in concentration are larger for overlapping routes than for nonoverlapping routes,[35] and also larger during the completion period than during the announcement period.

The results reveal important differences for normal-firm mergers in pricing behavior across subsamples. During the announcement period, both the relative fare changes and the regression coefficients on Normal × Lhhichg are significantly positive for all subsamples except for the subsample Hub Only: for this subsample, neither the fare change nor the coefficient is significantly different from zero. Evidently, firms exercise greater market power during merger discussion on most routes, except on routes where they only share a common hub.

For the completion period, normal-firm mergers exhibit significantly negative regression coefficients for all subsamples that have either common hubs or overlapping routes; in contrast, the same coefficient for subsample Neither is significantly positive. This is consistent with our hypothesis that mergers generate direct operating synergies on routes with common hubs or overlapping routes. Clearly, these efficiency gains dominate any residual market power obtained during this period. For subsample Neither, such efficiency gains are neither expected nor observed.

The results for the two subperiods are aggregated in the full period.[36] For the three subsamples with common-hub routes or overlapping routes, the price effect during the completion period appears to offset (and sometimes dominate) the effect during the announcement period; namely, the efficiency gains seem to play at least as important a role as market power. For the subsample Neither, on the other hand, the exercise of increased market power during the completion period reinforces the price effect during the announcement period. Indeed, these results reveal that the positive relation between fare changes and concentration changes for normal-firm mergers reported in Table 3 is driven by subsample Neither, which represents 76 percent of the sample. Apparently, it is only when there are no obvious sources of direct operating synergies, as is the case for subsample Neither, that increased market power leads to

[33]Subsample Neither may result in an increase in market power indirectly through multimarket contact. We will discuss this issue later.

[34]We run both ordinary least squares and weighted least squares for each of the two regression models, (2) and (3). All of the four regression results are qualitatively similar. Hence we report only the ordinary-least-squares results for regression model (2), because the variable Ldist does not facilitate distinction between the market-power and efficiency effects. The coefficient of Ldist is positive and significant at the 1-percent level in nine out of 12 ordinary-least-squares regressions, insignificantly different from zero for one, and significantly negative for two at the 1-percent level.

[35]The HHI's in the two subsamples with no overlapping routes may still change because the relative power of merging firms can increase due to common hubs or multimarket contact. Common hubs and multimarket contact can increase control/availability of routes for travelers and can increase control over rival firms through the threat of retaliation. Such increases in power may lead to an increase in market share. Also, because we measure the concentration changes relative to the control group, the relative concentration ratios can change if there is a change in the concentration for the control group.

[36]Notice that the full period contains a larger set of routes than the announcement and completion periods, as mentioned in footnote 25. For this reason, the results in the announcement period and the completion period may not add up exactly to those in the full period.

TABLE 4—ORDINARY-LEAST-SQUARES REGRESSIONS FOR SUBSAMPLES
$\text{Lfarchg}_i = \alpha + \beta_1 \text{Normal}_i \times \text{Lhhichg}_i + \beta_2 \text{Fail}_i \times \text{Lhhichg}_i + \varepsilon_i$

	Mean Lfarchg, percentage [sample size]		Mean Lhhichg, percentage [sample size]		Regression coefficient (t statistic)			
Period and subsample	Merger between normal firms	Merger with a failing firm	Merger between normal firms	Merger with a failing firm	Constant	Normal× Lhhichg	Fail× Lhhichg	R^2_{adj}
A. *Merging Firms:*								
Full period								
Hub/Overlap	−0.33	48.91**	36.35**	20.13**	0.3174	−0.4891	0.0920	0.101
	[193]	[180]	[193]	[180]	(9.00)	(−6.69)	(1.00)	
Hub Only	−11.01**	40.23**	1.89	5.81**	0.1604	−0.0461	0.0837	−0.002
	[291]	[331]	[291]	[331]	(6.99)	(−0.45)	(0.72)	
Overlap Only	3.92**	40.12**	22.49**	19.92**	0.1535	−0.1370	0.3512	0.044
	[1,205]	[566]	[1,205]	[566]	(11.89)	(−4.56)	(5.28)	
Neither	3.84**	18.28**	0.84**	4.02**	0.0690	0.1945	0.1548	0.016
	[6,822]	[2,041]	[6,822]	[2,041]	(16.59)	(12.12)	(3.38)	
Announcement period								
Hub/Overlap	7.18**	−13.63**	2.74[a]	−0.69	−0.0110	0.5359	−0.0329	0.080
	[186]	[101]	[186]	[101]	(0.61)	(4.16)	(−0.31)	
Hub Only	1.15	−14.96**	−1.67	−2.30	−0.0435	0.0258	0.0507	−0.004
	[278]	[147]	[278]	[147]	(−2.81)	(0.21)	(0.52)	
Overlap Only	12.09**	−21.88**	3.00**	5.30**	0.0430	0.1780	−0.0716	0.009
	[1,106]	[311]	[1,106]	[311]	(4.40)	(3.48)	(−0.70)	
Neither	11.96**	−19.03**	2.24**	−0.47	0.0649	0.2468	0.0622	0.027
	[4,262]	[823]	[4,262]	[823]	(13.92)	(10.37)	(0.87)	
Completion period								
Hub/Overlap	−5.69**	56.52**	31.45**	17.04**	0.2395	−0.4590	0.3689	0.139
	[190]	[110]	[190]	[110]	(6.17)	(−6.09)	(2.42)	
Hub Only	−10.23**	34.92**	3.68*	2.74	0.0549	−0.1550	−0.1276	0.004
	[283]	[144]	[283]	[144]	(2.71)	(−2.24)	(−0.64)	
Overlap Only	−7.47**	55.71**	18.30**	15.88**	0.0846	−0.2052	0.5213	0.071
	[1,143]	[357]	[1,143]	[357]	(6.06)	(−7.95)	(4.53)	
Neither	−9.45**	31.88**	−1.41**	6.13**	−0.0346	0.0374	0.3330	0.015
	[4,524]	[806]	[4,524]	[806]	(−7.94)	(2.45)	(3.96)	
B. *Rival Firms:*								
Full period								
Hub/Overlap	4.29	44.10**	33.06**	18.65**	0.2837	−0.3316	0.2499	0.062
	[135]	[160]	[135]	[160]	(7.77)	(−3.59)	(2.38)	
Hub Only	−6.17[a]	44.33**	5.20*	6.36**	0.2469	−0.0009	0.1570	0.001
	[157]	[260]	[157]	[260]	(9.15)	(−0.01)	(1.36)	
Overlap Only	2.49*	37.36**	14.74**	18.12**	0.1533	−0.0613	0.2299	0.014
	[790]	[528]	[790]	[528]	(10.42)	(−1.43)	(3.36)	
Neither	7.02**	17.21**	2.97**	5.20**	0.0897	0.2118	0.1742	0.020
	[4,496]	[1,583]	[4,496]	[1,583]	(17.50)	(9.55)	(4.05)	
Announcement period								
Hub/Overlap	11.48**	−21.79**	4.54*	−0.86	−0.0445	0.8197	0.1394	0.135
	[134]	[95]	[134]	[95]	(−1.79)	(5.31)	(0.92)	

TABLE 4—*Continued.*

Period and subsample	Mean Lfarchg, percentage [sample size]		Mean Lhhichg, percentage [sample size]		Regression coefficient (*t* statistic)			
	Merger between normal firms	Merger with a failing firm	Merger between normal firms	Merger with a failing firm	Constant	Normal × Lhhichg	Fail × Lhhichg	R^2_{adj}
Hub Only	−0.97	−17.47**	−0.02	−1.70	−0.0831	0.4019	0.2415	0.043
	[150]	[126]	[150]	[126]	(−4.10)	(2.63)	(2.76)	
Overlap Only	12.65**	−23.29**	5.79**	5.29**	0.0049	0.3828	−0.0737	0.033
	[699]	[297]	[699]	[297]	(0.39)	(5.64)	(−0.68)	
Neither	13.44**	−17.41**	4.78**	0.10	0.0637	0.3155	0.0414	0.040
	[2,747]	[643]	[2,747]	[643]	(10.19)	(10.16)	(0.53)	
Completion period								
Hub/Overlap	−6.25**	62.37**	28.27**	17.03**	0.3091	−0.6046	0.3483	0.155
	[131]	[103]	[131]	[103]	(6.72)	(−5.86)	(2.22)	
Hub Only	−6.11**	43.97**	6.39**	3.32	0.1522	−0.1151	−0.0698	−0.004
	[169]	[120]	[169]	[120]	(5.42)	(−1.47)	(−0.32)	
Overlap Only	−6.07**	56.99**	8.23**	14.83**	0.1320	−0.1394	0.4415	0.035
	[705]	[343]	[705]	[343]	(7.85)	(−3.53)	(3.69)	
Neither	−5.12**	36.51**	−1.18**	6.70**	0.0160	0.0176	0.3143	0.015
	[3,100]	[633]	[3,100]	[633]	(3.07)	(0.31)	(3.63)	

Notes: Lfarchg (Lhhichg) is the difference between the sample and control routes in the logs of the ratio of fares (concentrations) at the end to the beginning of each period. The mean Lfarchg and Lhhichg reported are the unweighted means. The Fail (Normal) dummy is 1 (0) for failing mergers and 0 (1) otherwise. Sample sizes are given in brackets below the mean Lfarchg and mean Lhhichg; *t* statistics are given in parentheses under the coefficients.

[a]Statistically significant at the 10-percent level.

*Statistically significant at the 5-percent level.

**Statistically significant at the 1-percent level.

higher prices. We explain how market power can increase in mergers with no overlapping routes or common hubs within the context of multimarket contact in the next section.

For the failing-firm mergers, the change in concentration has no significant impact for any of the subsamples during the announcement period, although the decreases in relative fares are large and significant for all subsamples. Apparently, the failing firms are more interested in cutting prices than in exercising market power until the merger is consummated. During the completion period, the concentration coefficient becomes significantly positive in three out of four subsamples. Thus, even in mergers involving failing airlines, the market power seems to play an important role once the financially troubled firm is successfully merged with a presumably more solvent acquirer.[37]

Finally, the results for rival firms reported in panel B of Tables 3 and 4 are generally consistent with those for merging firms. This again confirms our claim that the joint effect of market power and efficiency gains

[37]The only exception to the above generalization is again the subsample Hub Only; its concentration coefficient is not significantly different from zero during the completion period. Like normal-firm mergers during the announcement period, subsample Hub Only does not show evidence of increased market power when all other subsamples do. Thus, when routes affected by a merger have only common hubs, the market-power effect does not dominate efficiency gains. This is true regardless of the financial situation of the acquired firm.

has similar pricing implications for both merging and rival firms.

F. *Multimarket Contact*

In the preceding subsection we documented that airfares increase with increases in concentration for subsample Neither, which consists of nonoverlapping routes with no common hubs. This is surprising because, unless the merging firms serve the same route or have indirect control of a route through a common hub, a merger should leave the level of competition and prices in that market unaffected.

A possible explanation for this apparent puzzle can be found in the literature on multimarket contact.[38] Alfred E. Kahn (1950) and Corwin D. Edwards (1955) advance the notion that when firms face each other in a web of markets, they compete less vigorously by allowing each other more or less exclusive spheres of influence. More recently, John T. Scott (1982) suggests that multimarket contact can increase the recognition of mutual dependence and make oligopolistic consensus more likely, and B. Douglas Bernheim and Michael D. Whinston (1990) show that increased multimarket contact relaxes the incentive constraints that limit the extent of collusion, increasing the probability of tacit collusion under most circumstances.[39] The influence of multimarket contact on pricing behavior can also be applied to airline mergers. When airlines face each other in several markets they may compete less vigorously due to the fear of retaliation. Acquisition of a competitor has the effect of extending and creating alliances on routes where either of the merging firms was operating previously. Thus, multimarket contact will increase market power even on routes where the merging firms do not have direct contact.

To illustrate, consider three separate routes, AB, CD, and EF, and three airlines X, Y, and Z. Assume that X and Y operate on route AB with 80 percent and 20 percent shares, respectively. They also operate on CD with 20 percent and 80 percent shares, respectively. On route EF, airlines Y and Z operate with 20 percent and 80 percent shares, respectively. First consider routes AB and CD. Assume that Y, which has a small presence in AB, can increase its market share by reducing the fare. However, X may retaliate, not by reducing fares in AB, but by reducing fares on CD, where Y is dominant. The threat of such retaliation may prevent X and Y from competing vigorously on routes AB and CD; but there is nothing to restrain Y from cutting fares on route EF, because there is no retaliatory threat from Z. Therefore the fares on route EF will be more competitive than the fares on routes AB and CD. However, a merger between X and Z will put X in a position to retaliate if Y reduces fares on EF. This may restrain the competitive intentions of Y and raise the price on route EF even though X and Z have no direct contact on route EF.

The case of Northwest and Midway is illustrative. In 1989, Midway Airlines cut its prices in Milwaukee, an important market for Northwest. Northwest retaliated, not by matching fare cuts in Milwaukee, but by slashing fares at Midway's Chicago hub, where the fare cuts would hurt Midway the

[38]There are other possible explanations. First, creation of a larger firm due to a merger may result in a frequent-flyer program that is greater than the sum of frequent-flyer tickets issued by the two premerger firms. Because we exclude frequent flyers from our analysis, the fare changes could be overstated. However, frequent-flyer tickets constitute only about 1 percent of the tickets written in our data base.

A second and more plausible explanation is that, even for routes in subsample Neither, a merger can reduce the number of airlines with gates on either side of the route, if the merging airlines operate from the same airport. To the extent that airlines with gates on either side of the route pose a greater threat of new entry than others, a merger reduces the threat of potential competition due to new entry. This explanation is not mutually exclusive with multimarket contact.

[39]Scott (1982) uses data for manufacturing firms and John E. Martinez (1990) uses data for banking firms to show that the firms which have grown interdependent in several markets compete less vigorously. Scott (1989, 1991) also provides evidence of how multimarket contact reduces rivalry among firms through *conglomerate* mergers.

most. The retaliation prompted Midway to end its Milwaukee fare cut earlier than planned. Passengers sued Northwest for denying them lower fares. Northwest settled the suit in 1991 without admitting wrongdoing.[40] In addition to this anecdotal evidence, William N. Evans and Ioannis N. Kessides (1991) show that fares in airline markets are positively correlated with the level of multimarket contact.

G. *Other Considerations*

Although we attribute documented price increases to a greater exercise of market power, at least two competing explanations exist. One explanation is that an excess supply of air transportation service existed prior to (or during) the sample period, and mergers provided a means by which the industry could restore a competitive price equilibrium by reducing the supply. However, there is no evidence of a reduction in supply for the industry as a whole over the sample period. According to *Aerospace Facts and Figures 1989/1990*, the available seat-miles (number of seats in a plane multiplied by the distance traveled) for all certificated carriers show a steady increase from 1984 through 1988.[41] There was also a steady increase in demand over the same years.[42] A study by the U.S. Department of Transportation (1990), which is based on the same data base as ours, reports an increase in daily revenue passenger-miles from 183 million for the year ending December 1984 to 243 million for the year ending September 1988. If the mergers during the sample period were merely correcting an oversupply, we should not have observed such an increase in both the supply of and demand for air transportation.

The other possible explanation is that the price increases may reflect an improvement in quality. Although quality is difficult to measure, the quantifiable measures of quality include number of customer complaints, frequency of direct flights,[43] and time required to fly from origin to destination. As noted earlier, out of the 41 mergers that could be identified following the 1978 Airline Deregulation Act until 1988, nearly two-thirds took place during 1985–1988. Moreover, most of the major airlines were involved in a merger during this period.[44] Thus, if mergers result in quality improvements, we should detect a quality enhancement as measured in these dimensions during our sample period. On the contrary, the number of complaints filed with the governing agency increased almost threefold, from 1.49 per 100,000 passengers in 1984 to 4.43 per 100,000 passengers in 1988.[45]

Furthermore, mergers do not appear to have helped passengers in flying directly to their destinations. The study by the U.S. Department of Transportation (1990) shows a small decline in the number of direct markets (routes served by airlines without a change of plane), from 5,412 in July 1984 to 5,314 in July 1988. Also, in 1984, 71.5 percent of the passengers flew on direct flights, whereas by September 1988 this proportion had declined to 65.6 percent. In terms of revenue passenger-miles, the figures are 60.7 percent and 54.1 percent.

[40] For more details, see the *Wall Street Journal* (17 May 1991). In addition, according to the *Wall Street Journal* (9 October 1990, p. B1), an internal pricing policy memo of Northwest states, "Attempts to use price to improve market share will be countered immediately and rendered ineffective."

[41] The available seat-miles were 516 billion in 1984, 548 billion in 1985, 607 billion in 1986, 649 billion in 1987, and 677 billion in 1988.

[42] The number of revenue passenger-miles (number of passengers multiplied by the number of miles traveled) were 305 billion in 1984, 337 billion in 1985, 366 billion in 1986, 405 billion in 1987, and 423 billion in 1988. Comparison of these revenue passenger-miles with available seat-miles, reported in footnote 41, indicates that capacity utilization improved from 59.1 percent in 1984 to 62.5 percent in 1988.

[43] Direct flights refer to flights which do not involve a change of plane. They include both nonstop and stopping flights. The data base does not distinguish between the two types of direct flights.

[44] The only notable exceptions are Pan Am and United Airlines.

[45] The data are compiled based on statistics reported in *Air Transport World*. The consumer complaints peaked to 8.59 per 100,000 passengers in 1987 when the Airline Passenger Protection Bill was passed by the Congress.

Finally, on the time required to fly from origin to destination, Stephen A. Morrison and Clifford Winston (1986) report that the average time for air travel on similar routes increased by 5.4 percent from 1977 to 1983, which they attribute to the "hub-and-spoke" operations and the concomitant increase in airport congestion.[46] Mergers may lead to larger hub-and-spoke operations at the common hubs of the merging airlines (see Jan K. Brueckner et al., 1990). Thus, in terms of the three quantifiable measures of quality, there is no evidence of quality improvement in the service provided by airlines during the sample period.

IV. Summary and Conclusions

Our examination of price changes associated with airline mergers reveals evidence of the exercise of increased market power. In general, routes affected by mergers show significant increases in airfares relative to the control group. These price increases are positively correlated with changes in concentration and do not appear to be the result of an improvement in quality or of an industry-wide contraction of air services to rectify a supply–demand imbalance. The fare changes are also positively related to the distance of routes, suggesting that airlines exploit greater market power on longer routes for which substitution by other modes of transport is less likely.

We observe distinctly different pricing effects between mergers that involve financially distressed firms and those that do not. When mergers involve only "normal" firms, most of the effect of increased market power takes place during merger discussion. Efficiency gains start to kick in after merger completion, mainly for routes with potential sources of direct operating synergies, such as routes on which the merging firms have common hubs or provide overlapping service. For these routes, efficiency gains offset much of the impact of increased market power.

For routes on which the merging firms have neither common hubs nor overlapping service, we observe no such offsetting effect of efficiency gains. We only observe a persistent exercise of market power throughout merger discussion and merger completion. While the absence of efficiency gains is expected, the presence of market power is surprising. One might expect that, unless the merging firms serve the same route or have indirect control of a route through a common hub, a merger should leave the level of competition and prices in that market unaffected. We explain this apparent puzzle in the context of multimarket contact. Airlines face each other in several markets and hence may compete less vigorously in one market due to the fear of retaliation in another. Acquisition of a competitor, even when it has no direct contact with the acquirer, has the effect of strengthening existing alliances or creating new ones on routes where the merging firms are operating.

For mergers in which the acquired firm was in financial distress, we observe airfares well below the industry level prior to merger discussions, with further reductions throughout merger talks until merger completion. Upon merger completion, the merged firm raises fares drastically, though the increased fares still remain below the industry level. This pricing pattern is closely matched by the rival firms. Presumably, the exit of a noncooperative firm enables greater collusion among the remaining airlines.

The parallel pricing behavior between merging and rival firms is evident for all mergers for all periods under all regression specifications. Apparently, the joint effect of market power and efficiency gains due to mergers has similar pricing implications for both merging and rival firms. The parallel movement in prices raises the possibility that tacit cooperation exists among airlines in setting prices.

Finally, the results of this study have important policy implications. They show that relaxation of the antitrust policy for airline mergers during the sample period did per-

[46]A hub-and-spoke operation is a system in which flights from numerous points (spokes) arrive at and then depart from a common point (hub) to their ultimate destinations. In this manner, feed traffic from spoke points is collected at hubs and then consolidated. The earlier system was a linear system in which a carrier provides crisscrossing flights between cities serviced by it.

mit greater exercise of market power. On the whole, market power dominated efficiency gains, making the consumer worse off. In addition, the results demonstrate that the market power derived from multimarket contact deserves attention from the regulators. While market power derived from an increase in concentration is moderated by efficiency gains, the exercise of market power due to multimarket contact has no redeeming features.

REFERENCES

Asquith, Paul and Kim, E. Han, "The Impact of Mergers Bids on the Participating Firms' Security Holders," *Journal of Finance*, December 1982, *37*, 1209–28.

______ **and Wizman, Thierry A.,** "Event Risk, Covenants, and Bondholder Returns in Leveraged Buyouts," *Journal of Financial Economics*, September 1990, *27*, 195–213.

Auerbach, Alan J. and Reishus, David, "Taxes and the Merger Decision," in John C. Coffee, Louis Lowenstein, and Susan Rose-Ackerman, eds., *Knights, Raiders and Targets: The Impact of the Hostile Takeover*, New York: Oxford University Press, 1988, pp. 300–13.

Barton, David M. and Sherman, Roger, "The Price and Profit Effects of Horizontal Merger: A Case Study," *Journal of Industrial Economics*, December 1984, *33*, 165–77.

Bernheim, B. Douglas and Whinston, Michael D., "Multimarket Contact and Collusive Behavior," *Rand Journal of Economics*, Spring 1990, *21*, 1–26.

Berry, Steven, "Entry into Deregulated Airline Markets," in Leonard Weiss, ed., *Concentration and Price*, Cambridge, MA: MIT Press, 1989, pp. 167–78.

Bhagat, Sanjai, Shleifer, Andrei and Vishny, Robert W., "Hostile Takeovers in the 1980s: The Return to Corporate Specialization," *Brookings Papers on Economic Activity: Microeconomics*, Special Issue, 1990, 1–72.

Borenstein, Severin, "Airline Mergers, Airport Dominance, and Market Power," *American Economic Review*, May 1990 (*Papers and Proceedings*), *80*, 400–4.

Bradley, Michael, Desai, Anand and Kim, E. Han, "The Rationale Behind Interfirm Tender Offers: Information or Synergy?" *Journal of Financial Economics*, April 1983, *11*, 183–206.

______, ______ **and** ______, "Synergistic Gains from Corporate Acquisitions and their Division between Stockholders of Target and Acquiring Firms," *Journal of Financial Economics*, May 1988, *21*, 3–40.

Brown, Charles and Medoff, James L., "The Impact of Firm Acquisitions on Labor," National Bureau of Economic Research (Cambridge, MA) Working Paper No. 2273, 1987.

Brueckner, Jan K., Dyer, Nichola J. and Spiller, Pablo T., "Fare Determination in Airline Hub-and-Spoke Networks," working paper, University of Illinois, 1990.

Dempsey, Paul S., *Flying Blind: The Failure of Airline Deregulation*, Washington, DC: Economic Policy Institute, 1990.

Denis, Diane K., "Evidence on the Effects of Hostile and Friendly Tender Offers on Employment," Ph.D. dissertation, University of Michigan, 1990.

Dennis, Debra K. and McConnell, John J., "Corporate Mergers and Security Returns," *Journal of Financial Economics*, June 1986, *16*, 143–87.

Eckbo, B. Espen, "Horizontal Mergers, Collusion and Stockholder Wealth," *Journal of Financial Economics*, April 1983, *11*, 241–73.

______, "Mergers and the Market Concentration Doctrine: Evidence from the Capital Market," *Journal of Business*, July 1985, *58*, 325–49.

______ **and Wier, Peggy,** "Antimerger Policy under the Hart-Scott-Rodino Act: A Reexamination of the Market Power Hypothesis," *Journal of Law and Economics*, April 1985, *28*, 119–49.

Edwards, Corwin D., "Conglomerate Bigness as a Source of Power," in *Business Concentration and Price Policy*, National Bureau of Economic Research Report, Princeton, NJ: Princeton University Press, 1955, pp. 331–52.

Evans, William N. and Kessides, Ioannis N., "Living by the 'Golden Rule': Multimarket Contact in the U.S. Airline Industry," working paper, University of Maryland, 1991.

Hurdle, Gloria J., Johnson, Richard L., Joskow, Andrew S., Werden, Gregory J. and Williams, Michael A., "Concentration, Potential Entry, and Performance in the Airline Industry," *Journal of Industrial Economics*, December 1989, *38*, 119–39.

Jarrell, Gregg A., Brickley, James A. and Netter, Jeffry M., "The Market for Corporate Control: The Empirical Evidence Since 1980," *Journal of Economic Perspectives*, Winter 1988, *2*, 49–68.

Jensen, Michael C., "Takeovers: Their Causes and Consequences," *Journal of Economic Perspectives*, Winter 1988, *2*, 21–48.

Jensen, Michael C. and Ruback, Richard S., "The Market for Corporate Control: The Scientific Evidence," *Journal of Financial Economics*, 1983, *11*, 5–50.

Kahn, Alfred E., "The Chemicals Industry," in Walter Adams, ed., *The Structure of American Industry: Some Case Studies*, New York: Macmillan, 1950, pp. 197–230.

Kim, E. Han and McConnell, John J., "Corporate Mergers and the Co-insurance of Corporate Debt," *Journal of Finance*, May 1977, *32*, 349–65.

Lehn, Kenneth and Poulsen, Annette B., "Leveraged Buyouts: Wealth Created or Wealth Redistributed?" in Murray L. Weidenbaum and Kenneth W. Chilton, eds., *Public Policy Toward Corporate Takeovers*, New Brunswick, NJ: Transaction Publishers, 1988, pp. 46–62.

Martinez, John E., "The Linked Oligopoly Concept: Recent Evidence from Banking," *Journal of Economic Issues*, June 1990, *24*, 589–95.

McAfee, R. Preston and Williams, Michael A., "Can Event Studies Detect Anticompetitive Mergers?" *Economics Letters*, 1988, *28* (2), 199–203.

Morrison, Stephen A. and Winston, Clifford, *The Economic Effects of Airline Deregulation*, Washington, DC: Brookings Institution, 1986.

Ordover, Janusz A., Sykes, Alan O. and Willig, Robert D., "Herfindahl Concentration, Rivalry and Mergers," *Harvard Law Review*, June 1982, *95*, 1857–74.

Salinger, Michael A. and Schumann, Laurence, "Horizontal Mergers and the Market Value of Rivals: The 'In Play' Effect," working paper, Columbia University, 1988.

Scott, John T., "Multimarket Contact and Economic Performance," *Review of Economics and Statistics*, August 1982, *64*, 368–75.

______, "Purposive Diversification as a Motive for Merger," *International Journal of Industrial Organization*, March 1989, *7*, 35–47.

______, "Multimarket Contact among Diversified Oligopolists," *International Journal of Industrial Organization*, June 1991, *9*, 225–38.

Shleifer, Andrei and Summers, Lawrence H., "Breach of Trust in Hostile Takeovers," in Alan J. Auerbach, ed., *Papers in Corporate Takeovers: Causes and Consequences*, Chicago: University of Chicago Press, 1988, pp. 33–56.

Smith, Clifford W., Jr., "Investment Banking and the Capital Acquisition Process," *Journal of Financial Economics*, January/February 1986, *15*, 3–29.

Stillman, Robert, "Examining Antitrust Policy Towards Horizontal Mergers," *Journal of Financial Economics*, April 1983, *11*, 225–40.

White, Halbert, "A Heteroskedasticity-Consistent Covariance Matrix Estimator and a Direct Test for Heteroskedasticity," *Econometrica*, May 1980, *48*, 817–38.

***Fortune*,** "Yes, Antitrust Can Still Say No" [by Craig C. Carter], 1 September 1986, *114* (5), 63–64.

U.S. Department of Transportation, *Report of Secretary's Task Force on Competition in the U.S. Domestic Airline Industry*, Washington, DC: U.S. Department of Transportation, February 1990.

MANAGERIAL AND DECISION ECONOMICS, VOL. 15, 341–357 (1994)

Evidence on the Effects of Hostile and Friendly Tender Offers on Employment

Diane Kowalski Denis

Virginia Polytechnic Institute and State University, Blacksburg, VA, USA

This paper provides evidence on the effects of successful tender offers on the number of target and acquiring firm employees. No significant change in combined employment is observed, on average, over the three-year period following offer completion. However, hostile tender offers completed between 1980 and 1984 are followed by an average 17.2% decline in employment. Net divestitures of operations over the period are responsible for some of the observed employment decrease; however, an estimated −12.2% change remains, on average, after adjusting for divestiture activity. Information contained in firm annual reports and in the Wall Street Journal indicates that the tender offers in the sample are often followed by considerable restructuring activity with respect to both target and acquiring firm operations. The findings suggest that acquiring firm managements may acquire new operations when the need to restructure their existing operations frees up resources, e.g. cash and/or managerial time and talent. The evidence also suggests that the corporate control market must be viewed as an integral part of the process by which US firms restructure to meet changing circumstances.

INTRODUCTION

There is considerable evidence that successful tender offers result in significant gains to the shareholders of target firms and to the shareholders of target and acquiring firms combined.[1] Yet tender offers and other transactions in the corporate control market have been drastically curtailed in the past several years. A number of factors have potentially contributed to the dearth of corporate control activity: the economic recession, the demise of Drexel, Burnham, Lambert and the junk bond market, and a significant reduction in net lending to the corporate sector by commercial banks.[2]

Jensen (1991) also emphasizes the role of intense political pressures in curbing the corporate control market. In his words, 'The current controversy pitting Main Street against Wall Street has been wrought to a pitch that recalls the intensity of the 1930s'. Concern about the fates of employees, communities and other potential 'victims' of control changes are emotional issues that have received a great deal of media attention. Romano (1992) notes that in the most recent wave of state anti-takeover legislation, over half of the states adopted statutes that permit boards of directors to consider the interests of nonshareholder groups in deciding how to react to a bid for control of their firm.

The overall economic consequences of corporate control transactions are indeed influenced by the fates of all affected parties. The current lull in corporate control activity provides an opportunity to step back and consider these consequences carefully. Future policies governing the control market should be based on scientific evidence about what happens as a result of control market transactions and why it happens.

In this study we address one aspect of the controversy: the effect of tender offers on target and acquiring firm employees. We document changes in employment following 117 tender offers completed between 1975 and 1984. In addition, we extensively examine the post-tender offer actions that accompany these changes, both to increase our understanding of the context in which the observed employment changes occur and to document more generally the circumstances surrounding the tender offers in the sample.

CCC 0143–6570/94/040341–17

Several recent studies examine the employment effects of changes in the ownership of firms or parts of firms. They document no significant change in employment levels following mergers (Brown and Medoff, 1987) and management buy-outs (Kaplan, 1989; Smith, 1990); reductions in white-collar employment following changes in the ownership of individual plants (Lichtenberg and Siegel, 1990); and reductions in target firm employment following hostile tender offers (Bhide, 1989; Bhagat *et al.*, 1989).

We examine hostile and friendly tender offers in which both the acquiring firm and the target firm are publicly traded corporations. This excludes the majority of the highly leveraged 'raider' transactions that have dominated the corporate control market in more recent years. The subsample of tender offers by public corporations is interesting for at least two reasons. First, it is possible that these transactions differ systematically in motivation and/or in employment effects because they involve the combination of two separate operating entities. Second, the recent weakening of the junk bond market has led some to predict that 'strategic' tender offers, those made by corporations, will again dominate.[3]

Extensive analysis of the post-tender offer actions of the 117 combined target and acquiring firms reveals that, on average, hostile and friendly transactions in the 1975–79 subperiod and friendly transactions in the 1980–84 subperiod are not followed by significant changes in employment. Hostile tender offers completed between 1980 and 1984 are followed by an average 17.2% decrease in combined employment through the end of the first full year following completion of the tender offers.

Divestitures of target and acquiring firm operations can account for some of the employment reductions; however, they cannot fully explain the observed decreases in employment. We also find no evidence that employment decreases reflect more general trends in the firms or in their industries.

The observed employment decreases are accompanied by considerable restructuring of the operations of both target and acquiring firms. Staff reductions and plant closings are common; their incidence is greater for acquiring firm operations than for target firm operations. The fact that acquirers are more likely to close their own plants is consistent with Blackwell *et al.* (1990), who find that firms tend to close plants due to declining profitability and not because they have become targets of a takeover. The extent of restructuring of acquiring firms' operations casts doubt on the hypothesis that the primary motivation for the tender offers in the sample is the expropriation of the targets' resources (including employees). Rather, the tender offers appear to be just one part of a broader restructuring program undertaken by the acquiring firm.

MEASURING THE CHANGE IN EMPLOYMENT

The Sample

The sample represents all tender offers completed between 1975 and 1984 that are contained in the Managerial Economics Research Center (MERC) tender offer database and meet the following criteria:

- The tender offer was successful[4], defined here to mean that some number of shares of the target firm were acquired by the bidder[5];
- The numbers of target and acquiring firm employees are listed on Compustat.[6]

These requirements yield 119 tender offers. We cannot verify one of these in the *Wall Street Journal Index*; another acquiring firm made a change in consolidation principles in the offer completion year such that its pre- and post-tender offer employment figures are not comparable. The final sample consists of 117 tender offers.

The sample firms represent 21 different broad industry categories.[7] The most highly represented of these is the machinery manufacturing industry; 17 target and 18 acquiring firms fall into this category. Sixteen target firms and 14 acquiring firms are in the retail industry. There are 22 firms each in the electronics and natural resources industries. Food products, chemical products, metals, transportation equipment and non-financial services are also well represented; there are 10 or more sample firms in each of these industries. Finally, there are 12 industries in which there are less than 10 firms each.

We classify each transaction in the sample as

either hostile or friendly. Recent evidence suggests that there are differences in the characteristics of targets of hostile and friendly control changes. Morck *et al.* (1988) interpret these differences as evidence that target management/board response to a tender offer is related to the motivation for the offer. If this is true and if employment changes are related to tender offer motivations, then there will be a relationship between employment effects and target management response.

We define an offer as hostile if the *Wall Street Journal Index* provides any evidence that the target board and/or management made any public statement of opposition to any offer made during the time period examined. Sixty-two of the 117 offers in the sample are hostile and 55 are friendly.

Table 1 presents descriptive characteristics of the target and acquiring firms and of the tender offers. Acquiring firms are considerably larger than target firms, on average. Targets of hostile offers are significantly larger than friendly targets, in terms of both market value of equity and number of employees. Hostile and friendly contests do not differ significantly in any of the other characteristics.

Labor Changes Following Successful Tender Offers

We measure the change in number employed by comparing the total number of target and acquirer employees at the end of the year prior to bid completion (year −1) to the combined number of employees at the ends of each of the three full years following tender offer completion (years 1, 2, and 3).[8] Table 2 presents mean and median percentage changes in number of employees.[9] The

Table 1. Mean and Median Target and Acquiring Firm Size and Bid Characteristics[a]

	Hostile		Friendly	
	Mean	Median	Mean	Median
Market value of target firm equity ($000)	$424,088[d]	$91,892[c]	$138,738[d]	$45,071[c]
Market value of acquiring firm equity ($000)	$1,137,678	$306,510	$1,279,802	$375,616
Number of employees in target firm	10,151	5,024[c]	6,473	2,200[c]
Number of employees in acquiring firm	36,845	20,348	42,129	13,648
Target firm capital per employee ($000)	$102.71	$21.16	$51.84	$16.84
Acquiring firm capital per employee ($000)	$67.70	$24.44	$102.48	$18.10
% Target common sought	76.16	92.40	77.92	95.70
% Target common purchased via the tender offer	67.50	72.60	74.21	87.50
% Target common held by acquirer prior to bid	7.24	0.00	7.22	0.00

[a] Market values of target and acquiring firms are collected from the Standard and Poor's *Security Owners' Stock Guide* as of the month-end that is at least two and not more than three months prior to the bid announcement. Target and acquiring firm number of employees are taken from Compustat. Capital is measured as Compustat gross property, plant, and equipment. Employee numbers and capital are as of the year-end prior to bid completion, with the exception of 18 target firm numbers. In these 18 cases target firm information was provided only through the end of the year two years prior to completion; the last numbers given were used. The percentages of target common stock that the acquirer sought, purchased and held prior to the bid are taken from the MERC database.

[b–d] Significance of difference between hostile and friendly subsamples' means or medians at the 0.01, 0.05, and 0.10 levels, respectively.

Table 2. Mean and Median Percentage Changes in combined Number of Target and Acquiring Firm Employees from the End of Year −1 until the Ends of Years 1, 2, and 3 where Year 0 is the Year the Offer is Completed (*P*-values in parentheses)

	Total sample		Hostile		Friendly	
From the end of	Mean	Median	Mean	Median	Mean	Median
Panel A: Percentage changes in number of employees						
Year −1 to year 1	−1.84	0.31	−6.55[b]	−7.40[b]	3.54[b]	4.15[b]
	(0.4452)	(0.4446)	(0.0542)	(0.0281)	(0.2954)	(0.1089)
	[*n* = 105]		[*n* = 56]		[*n* = 49]	
Year −1 to year 2	−0.24	−1.15	−6.54[b]	−6.30[b]	7.20[b]	4.20[b]
	(0.9399)	(0.7141)	(0.1364)	(0.0770)	(0.1306)	(0.1603)
	[*n* = 96]		[*n* = 52]		[*n* = 44]	
Year −1 to year 3	0.91	−5.82	−6.19[c]	−10.19[b]	9.43[c]	7.32[b]
	(0.8247)	(0.5858)	(0.2847)	(0.0349)	(0.0992)	(0.1608)
	[*n* = 88]		[*n* = 48]		[*n* = 40]	
Panel B: Percentage changes following tender offers completed between 1975 and 1979						
Year −1 to year 1	4.97	5.93	6.67	5.78	3.67	6.38
	(0.0886)	(0.0247)	(0.1735)	(0.2497)	(0.3112)	(0.0466)
	[*n* = 58]		[*n* = 25]		[*n* = 33]	
Year −1 to year 2	8.94	9.76	8.56	6.17	9.26	10.63
	(0.0319)	(0.0201)	(0.1921)	(0.1764)	(0.0930)	(0.0572)
	[*n* = 51]		[*n* = 23]		[*n* = 28]	
Year −1 to year 3	13.11	9.32	8.87	4.45	16.54	15.33
	(0.0342)	(0.0618)	(0.3941)	(0.6502)	(0.0305)	(0.0409)
	[*n* = 47]		[*n* = 21]		[*n* = 26]	
Panel C: Percentage changes following tender offers completed between 1980 and 1984						
Year −1 to year 1	−10.24	−8.32	−17.21[b]	−13.65[a]	3.26[b]	−0.63[a]
	(0.0084)	(0.0001)	(0.0001)	(0.0001)	(0.6624)	(0.8603)
	[*n* = 47]		[*n* = 31]		[*n* = 16]	
Year −1 to year 2	−10.66	−14.20	−18.52[b]	−17.03[b]	3.59[b]	−5.77[b]
	(0.0293)	(0.0042)	(0.0008)	(0.0005)	(0.6964)	(0.8603)
	[*n* = 45]		[*n* = 29]		[*n* = 16]	
Year −1 to year 3	−13.08	−18.88	−17.90	−19.82	−3.79	−5.43
	(0.0069)	(0.0041)	(0.0035)	(0.0020)	(0.6339)	(0.7148)
	[*n* = 41]		[*n* = 27]		[*n* = 14]	

[a–c]Significance of difference between hostile and friendly subsamples' means or medians at the 0.01, 0.05, and 0.10 levels, respectively.

change as of the end of year 1 is negative and insignificant for the overall sample; the changes through the ends of years 2 and 3 are positive and insignificant. On average, the number of employees does not change following a takeover.

The overall changes in employment mask differences between hostile and friendly acquisitions. Following hostile acquisitions, total employees are reduced an average of 6.6% by the end of year 1. Cumulative changes through the ends of year 2 and 3 are −6.5% and −6.2%, respectively, indicating that combined employment increases slightly during years 2 and 3. The −6.6% change through year 1 represents the loss of a mean (median) of 3,893 (1, 288) jobs following successful hostile control contests.

Friendly acquisitions are followed by steady increases in employment in the combined target and acquiring firms. However, only the mean 9.4% increase through the end of the year 3 is significant at conventional levels. The mean and median number of employees added through the end of the first full year following completion of friendly combinations are 352 and 356, respectively. The differences between mean and median employment changes for the hostile and friendly subsamples are all statistically significant at at least the 10% level. Sixty-two per cent of hostile transactions are followed by employment decreases through the end of year 1, while 32.0% of firms involved in friendly transactions experience reductions in employment. Approximately 40% of hostile changes are followed by large changes in employment (increases or decreases > 20%); the comparable figure for the friendly group is 20.0%. These findings suggest that there are systematic differences in post-acquisition actions taken following hostile and friendly tender offers.

Previous studies of corporate control transactions (Bradley *et al.*, Morck *et al.*, 1990) have suggested that there may be systematic differences in these transactions in the 1980s. They cite a more relaxed antitrust policy in the 1980s, more sophisticated financing technology and disillusionment with the diversification-motivated takeovers of the 1970s as potential reasons for such differences. Panels B and C of Table 2 present percentage employment changes separately for tender offers completed during the 1975–79 and the 1980–84 periods.

The employment decreases observed following hostile tender offers are driven by those transactions completed during the 1980s. Employment changes following hostile tender offers in the 1970s are essentially the same as those following friendly transactions in both periods: generally positive, though not significantly different from zero. Hostile tender offers completed from 1980 to 1984, however, are followed by significant decreases in employment: a mean (median) change of −17.2% (−13.7%) through the end of year 1. These results suggest that some combination of relaxed antitrust policy, more sophisticated financing technology and/or the trend away from diversification led to important differences in the nature of hostile tender offers between the late 1970s and the early 1980s.

Tender Offers by Multiple Bidders

The acquiring firms in the sample are those firms that ultimately acquire the sample target firms. In 41 of the 117 transactions examined there were two or more bidders for the target firm. The incidence of multiple bidders is much greater in the hostile subsample: 34 of 62 hostile transactions involve multiple bidders, as compared to seven of 55 friendly transactions.

Bradley *et al.* (1988) present evidence that returns to acquirers are lower in multiple bidder contests; these returns are significantly negative in their 1981–4 sample period. They suggest that competition increases the likelihood that an acquirer will be driven to pay 'too much' for a target firm. If this leads to more drastic post-tender offer restructuring then decreases in employment will be more likely following multiple bidder contests. It is possible, therefore, that the differences in employment changes between the hostile and friendly subsamples actually stem from differences in multiple and single bidder contests. However, we find that there is not a statistically significant correlation between the percentage change in employment and the presence of more than one bidder.

Bradley *et al.* find that the negative returns to acquirers in multiple bid contests are driven by negative returns to those acquirers that act as white knights. It may be that target firm managements seek to protect the wealth of employees and agree to be acquired only by a firm that will do so. If this is the case then, *ceteris paribus*, employees will fare better following the white knights tender offers that target management negotiates.

We further split the hostile subsample into tender offers in which the target firm initially objected to the bid of the sample acquiring firm and those in which the sample acquiring firm acted as a white knight and acquired the target firm with management's blessing. Sample tender offers are considered white knight transactions if:

- There was a previous bid by an alternative bidder to which target management voiced opposition;
- There was never any public objection by target management to a bid by the sample acquiring firm; and
- There is evidence that the target and acquiring firm boards met prior to announcement of *the acquirer's tender offer for the target.*

Panel A of Table 3 presents percentage employment changes by subperiod for white knight and non-white knight transactions. It is interesting that the incidence of white knight transactions is much higher in the later time period; 24% of the acquirers in the 1975–9 hostile subsample are white knights, while 64.5% of the acquirers in the 1980–84 hostile transactions acted as white knights.

The panel A results indicate that employees fare better following acquisitions by white knights, at least in terms of maintaining their positions with the sample firms. Differences in raw mean and median employment changes for the two groups are significant. The average transaction in which a white knight does not acquire the target firm is followed by a 26.9% drop in employment, while white knight transactions in this period are followed by an average 11.9% drop. Thus, one possible explanation for white knights' negative returns is that they take fewer potentially value-increasing restructuring actions following combination of the firms than do hostile acquirers.

Horizontal versus Unrelated Tender Offers

If an employment decrease following the combination of two firms stems from the elimination of duplicate positions, then, *ceteris paribus*, combinations of firms in the same industry (horizontal combinations) should be followed by greater employment decreases, on average, than combinations of unrelated firms.

We establish the existence of overlap in the target and acquiring firms' businesses by examining entries for the two firms in the *Standard and Poor's Register of Corporations* in the year prior to the takeover. The *Register* lists all 4-digit SIC

Table 3. Mean and Median Percentage Changes in Combined Number of Target and Acquiring Firm Employees from the End of Year −1 until the End of Year 1 for Horizontal versus Unrelated Transactions and for White Knight versus Non-White Knight Transactions (*P*-values in parentheses)

	White knight		Non-white knight	
	Mean	Median	Mean	Median
Panel A: White knight transactions versus non-white knight transactions[a]				
1975–9	13.81	12.68	4.42	0.90
	(0.0141)	(0.0313)	(0.4785)	(0.7680)
	[n = 6]		[n = 19]	
1980–84	−11.87[c]	−10.13[d]	−26.92[c]	−30.26[d]
	(0.0143)	(0.0073)	(0.0009)	(0.0010)
	[n = 20]		[n = 11]	

	Horizontal transactions		Unrelated transactions	
	Mean	Median	Mean	Median
Panel B: Horizontal versus unrelated transactions				
1975–9	−1.76	0.36	8.24	8.84
	(0.6809)	(0.9843)	(0.0301)	(0.0110)
	[n = 19]		[n = 39]	
1980–4	−12.57	−5.25	−8.36	−11.22
	(0.0328)	(0.0558)	(0.1153)	(0.0005)
	[n = 21]		[n = 26]	

[a] Only the hostile transactions are classified as to whether or not they are white knight transactions.

[b–d] Significance of difference between horizontal and unrelated transactions or between white knight and non-white knight transactions means or medians at the 0.01, 0.05, and 0.10 levels, respectively.

codes relevant to a particular firm. We define the target and acquirer's businesses as overlapping if there is any 4-digit SIC code that is common to the two firms.

Panel B of Table 3 presents both raw and adjusted employment changes for horizontal and unrelated transactions by subperiod. The results indicate that economies of scale with respect to employment are not an important factor in explaining employment changes. The mean changes in employment following horizontal combinations are less than those following unrelated combinations but the differences are not statistically significant. Median employment changes in the 1975–9 period are lower following horizontal tender offers, as predicted by scale economies; the difference is significant at the 10% level. However, greater employment loss is observed following unrelated combinations in 1980–84, contrary to prediction.[10]

A CLOSER LOOK AT THE OBSERVED CHANGES IN EMPLOYMENT

The previous section established that hostile tender offers completed between 1980 and 1984 are followed by significant decreases in the number of people employed by the firms involved. In this section we examine the economic climate and the actions of the acquiring firms following the sample acquisitions to shed some light on how and why the sample employment changes are accomplished.

Divestitures and Other Acquisitions

The employment changes documented in the previous section represent the net change in the number of people employed by the target and acquiring firms. This is not an accurate measure of the jobs that are actually lost or created. If the combined firm sells operations to new owners who maintain some employees in their original positions then these results overstate the number of jobs lost. Similarly, if an increase in measured employment stems from further acquisitions then observed employment changes will overstate the number of jobs gained as a result of the sample acquisition.

Our information about divestitures and other acquisitions comes from two sources:[11] the narrative sections of the year 0 and year 1 annual reports of the acquiring firms[12] and the year 0 and year 1 *Wall Street Journal* articles concerning both the target and acquiring firms. Narrative sections of the firms' annual reports typically include management's letter to the shareholders, management's summary of operations, notes to the financial statements, and various sections describing the firm and its business activities.

The combined target/acquirer firms in the sample are involved in numerous divestitures and other acquisitions following the sample tender offers. Other acquisitions range as high as 40% of the combined firm, while the maximum relative divestiture observed in the sample is 82% of the combined firm. On the other hand, 32 of 105 combinations are not followed by any acquisitions and 36 are not followed by any divestitures.

Firms that undertake hostile tender offers appear to be generally more inclined to acquire and divest operations. The average hostile combination is followed by over three divestitures and almost three other acquisitions, while friendly combinations are followed by approximately one divestiture and two other acquisitions, on average.

Table 4 presents mean and median percentage divestitures and other acquisitions undertaken by the sample firms in years 0 and 1. We calculate these percentages as the ratio of the prices the units are sold/bought for to the combined year −1 value[13] of the target and acquiring firms for the 301 transactions for which we are able to identify a price. We use the ratio of the year −1 sales revenue of the units being acquired/divested to the combined year −1 sales revenue of the target and acquiring firms for another 38 transactions. There are 85 acquisitions and 100 divestitures for which we are unable to identify either price or sales revenue. The majority of these 185 are disclosed only in annual reports and referred to as small. The remainder are reported in the *Wall Street Journal* but no terms are disclosed.

The Table 4 results suggest that the observed employment changes documented in Table 2 may be at least partially explained by changes in asset ownership. The average increases in employment observed following the 1970s transactions are accompanied by average net acquisitions of assets. The observed increase in employment following friendly 1980s transactions is accompanied by an average net divestiture of assets. None of these changes differs significantly from zero. Hostile 1980s transactions are followed by a 5.1% net divestiture, on average, significantly different from zero at the 0.05 level.

These results suggest that the employment changes in the previous section should be adjusted for jobs that were transferred to and from the sample firms via changes in their asset structure. Unfortunately, the actual numbers employed by acquired and divested units are available for less than 10% of the transactions. We estimate these employment figures by assuming that relative employment is constant across the units of a firm. This is admittedly a strong assumption and the results must be interpreted with caution. If the firms in the sample are inclined to divest their more (less) labor-intensive operations and/or acquire operations which are less (more) labor-intensive than average then the estimated net transfer of jobs out of the sample firms will be biased downward (upward).[14]

We estimate the number of employees associated with the acquired/divested units as follows:

(1) The actual number of employees involved is known for 29 of 270 acquisitions and 21 of 254 divestitures.
(2) For 152 of 270 acquisitions and 119 of 254 divestitures we calculate the ratio of the purchase/sales price of the unit to the value[15] of the appropriate firm (target or acquirer) and multiply it by the total number employed by the target or acquiring firm.
(3) We estimate employment in nine of 270

Table 4. Mean and Median Percentage Divestitures and Other Acquisitions Made by Target/acquiring Firm Pairs During Years 0 and 1[a] (*P*-values in parentheses)

Transaction Type	Total sample Mean	Total sample Median	Hostile Mean	Hostile Median	Friendly Mean	Friendly Median
Panel A: Percentage divestitures and other acquisitions following 1975–9 tender offers						
	[$n = 56$]		[$n = 23$]		[$n = 33$]	
Divestitures	1.91	0.00	2.75	0.00[d]	1.32	0.00[d]
	(0.0080)	(0.0001)	(0.0089)	(0.0020)	(0.1817)	(0.0078)
Other acquisitions	7.51	2.28	11.57[c]	3.37[d]	4.68[c]	1.55
	(0.0001)	(0.0001)	(0.0006)	(0.0001)	(0.0005)	(0.0001)
Net	5.60	1.38	8.82	0.78	3.36	1.43
	(0.0015)	(0.0006)	(0.0128)	(0.0663)	(0.0508)	(0.0028)
Panel B: Percentage divestitures and other acquisitions following 1980–84 tender offers						
	[$n = 47$]		[$n = 31$]		[$n = 16$]	
Divestitures	9.79	2.52	9.13	3.44	11.05	2.14
	(0.0002)	(0.0001)	(0.0005)	(0.0001)	(0.0665)	[illegible]
Other acquisitions	4.35	0.63	4.03	1.39	4.97	0.31
	(0.0001)	(0.0001)	(0.0010)	(0.0001)	(0.0263)	(0.0039)
Net	−5.44	−0.94	−5.10	−2.52	−6.08	0.00
	(0.0303)	(0.0229)	(0.0373)	(0.0139)	(0.2992)	(0.5693)

[a]The percentage for a given target/acquirer pair is calculated using either: (1) (divestiture or acquisition price)/(target + acquirer year −1 value) for transactions for which the price is available; or (2) (year −1 sales revenue of divested or acquired unit)/target + acquirer year −1 sales revenue) for transactions for which price is not available but sales revenue of the affected unit is known. There were 301 transactions for which relative values was used and 38 transactions for which relative sales revenue was used. Neither price nor sales revenue was known for 185 transactions.

[b-d]Significance of difference between hostile and friendly transactions' means or medians at the 0.01, 0.05, and 0.10 levels, respectively.

acquired units and 25 of 254 divested units using the ratio of the sales revenue of the affected unit to total firm sales revenue.

(4) Finally, we exclude 80 acquisitions and 89 divestitures from the adjustment because no information is available.[16]

We then use these estimates of the number employed by acquired and divested units to calculate a net adjustment to the employment change following each tender offer. Net divestitures result in an addition to the change in number employed because these jobs were transferred rather than lost. The reverse is true for net acquisitions.[17]

Table 5 presents both the raw year −1 to year 1 percentage employment changes from Table 2 and the adjusted percentage changes calculated here. Changes in asset ownership appear to account for only some of the observed employment change. The magnitude of the adjusted employment change is less than that of the raw employment change for all but the friendly 1980–84 tender offers. Average adjusted employment change following the 1980s hostile tender offers, for example, is −12.2%, as compared to a −17.2% unadjusted change.

Thus, even after adjusting for asset restructurings in the post-combination firm, hostile tender offers in the 1980s appear to be followed by a loss of jobs, on average. This impression is strengthened by the fact that the mean (median) employment change among the six firms in this subsample that were not followed by any acquisitions or divestitures is −16.2% (−8.1%). Five of the six experienced employment decreases.

Divestitures of Target Firm Operations

One criticism often leveled against hostile takeovers is that they serve as occasion for the acquiring firm to 'bust up' the operations of the

Table 5. Raw and Adjusted Mean and Median Percentage Changes in Combined Number of Target and Acquiring Firm Employees from the End of Year −1 until the End of Year 1 (*P*-values in parentheses)

	Raw change		Adjusted change	
	Mean	Median	Mean	Median
Panel A: Percentage changes in number of employees following 1975–9 transactions				
Total sample	4.97	5.93	1.17	3.35
[$n = 58$]	(0.0886)	(0.0247)	(0.6144)	(0.2946)
Hostile subsample	6.67	5.78	1.77	3.78
[$n = 25$]	(0.1735)	(0.2497)	(0.6094)	(0.5735)
Friendly subsample	3.67	6.38	0.71	2.59
[$n = 33$]	(0.3112)	(0.0466)	(0.8232)	(0.3561)
Panel B: Percentage changes in number of employees following 1980–84 transactions				
Total sample	−10.24	−8.32	−4.73	−6.48
[$n = 47$]	(0.0084)	(0.0001)	(0.2445)	(0.0022)
Hostile subsample	−17.21	−13.65	−12.23	−9.56
[$n = 31$]	(0.0001)	(0.0001)	(0.0002)	(0.0001)
Friendly subsample	3.26	−0.63	9.80	−0.87
[$n = 16$]	(0.6624)	(0.8603)	(0.3242)	(1.0000)

[a] Raw percentages are based on the changes in Compustat employment numbers over this period. Adjusted changes begin with the Compustat employment change and exclude estimated decreases/increases in employment that are associated with divestitures/other acquisitions of operations during years 0 and 1.

target firm. Target firm management may resist such takeovers to protect the interests of other firm stakeholders, such as employees. Abstracting from the issue of whether or not such actions are efficient, this study provides an opportunity to assess the extent to which target firms are dismantled following tender offers.

We examined *Moody's Manuals'* business descriptions of the target and acquiring firms prior to their combinations to identify whether post-acquisition divestitures involve operations that were part of the target or the acquirer prior to the combination. We can reliably identify operations as belonging to one firm or the other for 190 of 254 divestiture transactions. The price of the unit sold is available for 103 of these and sales revenues are available for a further 23 divested units. There are 64 transactions for which neither price nor revenue can be found.

Table 6 reveals that target firm operations are often shed following hostile takeovers. Acquirers sell an average of 8.1% of the target firm following 1970s hostile takeovers and 9.4% following 1980s hostile takeovers.[18] On the other hand, 23 of the 55 hostile transactions are not followed by divestitures of any target firm operations. Friendly combinations are followed by the divestiture of 2.6% of the target firm, on average, in the 1975–9 period and 0.9% in the 1980–84 period. Thirty-six of the 49 friendly tender offers are not followed by any divestitures of target firm operations.[19]

Acquiring firms also undertake significant di-

Table 6. Mean[a] Percentage Divestitures of Target and Acquiring Firm Operations During Years 0 and 1[b] (*P*-values in parentheses)

	Hostile Mean % divested	Friendly Mean % divested
	[n = 24]	[n = 34]
Panel A: Percentage divestitures of operations following 1975–9 acquisitions		
Divestitures of target operations	8.08 (0.1466)	2.59 (0.0606)
Divestitures of acquirer operations	1.82 (0.0540)	0.53 (0.3165)
P-value for difference between target and acquirer means	(0.2620)	(0.1589)
Panel B: Percentage divestitures of operations following 1980–84 acquisitions		
	[n = 31]	[n = 16]
Divestitures of target operations	9.36[c] (0.0005)	0.92[c] (0.2089)
Divestitures of acquirer operations	8.12 (0.0086)	12.96 (0.0754)
P-value for difference between target and acquirer means	(0.7427)	(0.0975)

[a]All medians for the 1975–1984 period are equal to zero.

[b]The percentage for a given target or acquirer is calculated as the sum of (1) (divestiture price)/(target or acquirer year −1 value) for transactions for which the price is available; and (2) (year −1 sales revenue of divested unit)/target or acquirer year −1 sales revenue) for transactions for which price is not available but sales revenue of the affected unit is known. There were 254 total divestiture transactions; information necessary to identify the transaction as involving either target or acquiring firm operations was available for 190 of these. Relative values were used to measure 103 of these transactions and relative sales revenues were used for 23 transactions. Neither price nor sales revenue was known for 64 transactions.

[c-e]Significance of difference between hostile and friendly transactions' means at the 0.01, 0.05, and 0.10 levels, respectively.

vestitures of their own operations following tender offers completed in the 1980s. The average 1980s hostile transaction is followed by the sale of 8.1% of the pre-tender offer acquiring firm. Friendly tender offers during this period are followed by the sale of an average 13.0% of the pre-tender offer acquiring firm.

These results suggest that the 1980–84 acquisitions of the target firms in the sample are often one facet of larger restructuring programs undertaken by the acquiring firms and cast doubt on the conjecture that the purpose of hostile tender offers is to bust up the target firm.[20]

Other Influences on Employment

If employment changes following the sample tender offers are similar to pre-tender offer changes in the separate firms then it is more difficult to attribute the observed changes to the tender offer. Table 7 presents mean and median percentage changes in the number employed by the target and acquiring firms between the ends of years −3 and −1. These results suggest that the employment changes observed in the sample firms over the year −1 to 1 period are not simply continuations of established trends. For example, the 1980s hostile transactions in the sample are followed by average declines in employment. The Table 7 results indicate that the average hostile target and acquirer experienced a positive, though insignificant, employment change between the ends of years −3 and −1.

If observed employment changes are precipitated by more general economic conditions then employment changes in the sample firms should not differ significantly from concurrent employment changes in similar firms that have not been involved in control contests. Table 8 presents means and medians of the median percentage changes in the number of individuals employed by the firms in the target and acquiring firms' 4-digit SIC code industries.[21] The results indicate that the average firm in the target or acquiring firm industry does not experience significant declines in employment, on average, at any point over the 4-year period from the end of year −3 to the end of year 1. The industry changes for the 1980–84 hostile subsample are insignificantly positive, suggesting that the employment change observed in the sample firms cannot be attributed to factors that affect other similar firms.[22]

Table 7. Mean and Median Percentage Changes in the Number of People Employed by the Target and Acquiring Firms from the End of Year −3 to the End of Year −1 (*P*-values in parentheses)

	Total sample		Hostile		Friendly	
	Mean	Median	Mean	Median	Mean	Median
Panel A: Percentage changes in employment prior to 1975–9 transactions						
Target firm	2.07	10.04	4.80	3.16	17.89	11.68
	(0.0099)	(0.0029)	(0.4896)	(0.3572)	(0.0050)	(0.0024)
	[n = 54]		[n = 24]		[n = 30]	
Acquiring firm	5.43	3.61	3.42	5.04	7.00	2.34
	(0.0336)	(0.0186)	(0.3618)	(0.2266)	(0.0485)	(0.0270)
	[n = 57]		[n = 25]		[n = 32]	
Panel B: Percentage changes in employment prior to 1980–84 transactions						
Target firm	5.95	2.37	3.07	0.62	11.52	10.99
	(0.2310)	(0.2818)	(0.5266)	(0.7161)	(0.3174)	(0.3303)
	[n = 47]		[n = 31]		[n = 16]	
Acquiring firm	6.27	0.00	10.75	0.36	−2.41	−5.26
	(0.1923)	(0.7593)	(0.1134)	(0.4194)	(0.6455)	(0.5995)
	[n = 47]		[n = 31]		[n = 16]	

a–c Significance of difference between hostile and friendly subsamples' means or medians at the 0.01, 0.05, and 0.10 levels, respectively.

Thus, the employment changes that occur following the sample tender offers cannot be explained by more general employment trends. This suggests that the observed employment changes are related to the tender offers themselves and to the general restructuring programs undertaken by the individual acquiring firms in the sample.

Other Post-acquisition Restructuring Activity

Table 9 summarizes the incidence of various categories of actions that potentially influence changes in employment. They include: expanding existing operations, closing existing operations, reducing or relocating staff, consolidating operations, and undertaking various productive efficiency measures. We separate the sample transactions into two groups: those with positive adjusted percentage changes in employment between the ends of years −1 and 1 and those with negative changes. This information comes from the year 0 and year 1 annual reports of the sample firms and from *Wall Street Journal* articles pertaining to the target and acquiring firms.

Most of the information regarding the inci-

Table 8. Means and Medians of the Median Percentage Changes in the Number of People Employed by Firms in the Target and Acquiring Firms' 4-digit SIC Code Industries from the Ends of Years −3 to −1 and Years −1 to 1 (*P*-values in parentheses)

	Total sample		Hostile		Friendly	
	Mean	Median	Mean	Median	Mean	Median
Panel A: Percentage changes in industry employment for the transactions completed 1975						
Year −3 to year −1						
Target firm industry	8.27 (0.0001)	8.02 (0.0001)	9.08 (0.0020)	8.90 (0.0020)	7.65 (0.0013)	6.75 (0.0004)
	[n = 58]		[n = 25]		[n = 33]	
Acquiring firm industry	5.35 (0.0001)	5.00 (0.0001)	4.43 (0.0139)	3.97 (0.0106)	6.08 (0.0002)	6.21 (0.0001)
	[n = 57]		[n = 25]		[n = 32]	
Year −1 to year 1						
Target firm industry	12.00 (0.0001)	8.56 (0.0001)	9.33 (0.0016)	8.78 (0.0016)	14.02 (0.0001)	8.33 (0.0001)
	[n = 58]		[n = 25]		[n = 33]	
Acquiring firm industry	9.39 (0.0001)	8.02 (0.0001)	8.68 (0.0002)	6.62 (0.0001)	9.94 (0.0001)	8.70 (0.0001)
	[n = 57]		[n = 25]		[n = 32]	
Panel B: Percentage changes in industry employment for the transactions completed 1980–84						
Year −3 to year −1						
Target firm industry	2.34 (0.1763)	2.97 (0.0522)	3.53 (0.0775)	2.97 (0.0569)	0.04 (0.9908)	1.71 (0.5416)
	[n = 47]		[n = 31]		[n = 16]	
Acquiring firm industry	1.41 (0.2660)	0.00 (0.4790)	1.53 (0.3919)	−0.27 (0.6880)	1.16 (0.4244)	0.76 (0.3662)
	[n = 47]		[n = 31]		[n = 16]	
Year −1 to year 1						
Target firm industry	0.58 (0.7880)	0.48 (0.8513)	−2.75[b] (0.2982)	−1.40[b] (0.2079)	7.04[b] (0.0576)	7.77[b] (0.0577)
	[n = 47]		[n = 31]		[n = 16]	
Acquiring firm industry	3.33 (0.1111)	0.48 (0.2710)	0.97 (0.7115)	−2.15[b] (0.7865)	7.91 (0.0223)	5.30[b] (0.0246)
	[n = 47]		[n = 31]		[n = 16]	

[a–c]Significance of difference between hostile and friendly subsamples' means or medians at the 0.01, 0.05, and 0.10 levels, respectively.

Table 9. Incidence of Sample Firms Taking Various Actions During Years 0 and 1 that are Potentially Employment-influencing

	Number (fraction) of firms					
	Employment decrease group [n = 57]			Employment increase group [n = 48]		
Action taken	Total[b]	Target	Acquirer	Total[b]	Target	Acquirer
Expanded existing operations	38 (0.67)	25 (0.44)	17 (0.30)	38 (0.79)	21 (0.44)	18 (0.38)
Closed operations	28 (0.49)	9 (0.16)	16 (0.28)	18 (0.38)	7 (0.15)	13 (0.27)
Reduced staff	27 (0.47)	8 (0.14)	18 (0.32)	13 (0.27)	6 (0.13)	4 (0.08)
Relocated staff	13 (0.23)	5 (0.09)	7 (0.12)	9 (0.19)	6 (0.13)	2 (0.04)
Consolidated operations	27 (0.47)	8 (0.14)	14 (0.25)	13 (0.27)	7 (0.15)	7 (0.15)
Productive efficiency measures[c]	48 (0.84)	18 (0.32)	23 (0.40)	25 (0.52)	12 (0.25)	13 (0.27)

[a] Firms are grouped according to whether the percentage change in employment from year −1 to year 1 after adjusting for divestitures and other acquisitions is negative or positive. Information is taken from the firm annual reports and the *Wall Street Journal*.

[b] Information about actions taken is not always specific enough to determine whether target and/or acquiring firms' operations were affected. This is true for 21 of the firms that expanded operations, eight that closed operations, 10 that reduced staff, three that relocated staff, 13 that consolidated operations, and 30 that took productive efficiency measures.

[c] Productive efficiency measures are considered to have been taken if any reference is made to cost reductions, productivity increases, streamlining, and/or automation.

dence of the actions we consider here is specific enough to determine whether the actions taken affect operations that were originally part of the target firm, the acquiring firm, or both. Table 9 presents the number of tender offers in each group that are followed by each specified action.

The table indicates that relatively more of the employment increase firms expand existing operations than do firms in the employment decrease group. It is surprising, however, that the difference is as small as it is. Sixty-seven per cent of the employment decrease firms expand operations, as compared to 79% of the employment increase firms. Target firm operations are more likely to have been expanded than are acquiring firm operations in both groups. Exploiting target firm growth opportunities appears to be one motivation for a number of the tender offers in the sample. Some portion of target firm operations is expanded following over 40% of the sample offers.

Firms in the employment decrease group are more likely to close operations than are those in the employment increase group, 49% versus 38%, respectively. Acquiring firm operations are nearly twice as likely to be closed as are target firm operations.

The staff-reduction category includes reductions via layoffs, early retirements, and/or attrition. The majority of staff reductions reported are carried out via employee layoffs. Six firms specifically indicate that there was elimination of duplicate employees following the combination of the target and acquiring firms, consistent with some employment-related economies of scale.

Staff reductions occur more frequently in the employment decrease group (47%) than in the employment increase group (27%). They are more likely to affect acquiring firm employees than target firm employees in the employment decrease group. The reverse is true in the employment increase group, although the difference is smaller in this group.

The final two categories are consolidation of operations and productive efficiency measures. The latter include programs to cut costs, increase operating efficiency, modernize/automate, or streamline. In the short term, these groups of actions are more likely to result in decreases in the number of employees.

Table 9 indicates that firms in the employment decrease group are more likely to have made specific announcements of programs to consolidate and/or increase efficiency. Such actions are more likely to affect acquiring firm operations than target firm operations.

Overall, the results indicate that structural changes are common following successful tender offers.[23] These changes involve both target and acquiring firm operations; target firm operations are more likely to have been expanded and acquiring firm operations are more likely to have been contracted. There is little support for the notion that tender offers provide occasion to raid the target firm operations. Rather, the acquisition of the target firm appears to often be one facet of a larger restructuring program undertaken by the acquiring firm.

CONCLUSION

The evidence presented here suggests that acquisitions by public corporations are often facets of broader restructuring programs by the acquiring firms. This is especially true of hostile acquisitions made between 1980 and 1984. Successful hostile tender offers during this period are followed by average 17.2% reductions in combined employment through the end of the first full year following offer completion. Hostile 1975–9 tender offers and friendly tender offers in both periods are followed by insignificant average increases in employment.

The observed employment changes are not simply the result of jobs being transferred to and from the combined firms via other acquisitions and divestitures; neither can the employment changes observed be attributed either to prior employment trends in the target and acquiring firms or to concurrent trends in their industries.

We find evidence of significant restructuring activity following the tender offers in the sample: divestiture and acquisition of operations, expansion or closing of existing operations, and reductions in staff, primarily via layoffs. Hostile combinations are followed by greater restructuring than friendly combinations.

The results do not indicate that restructuring activity and the resulting employment changes following control changes are driven solely by the acquisitions of the target firms. Rather, in the 1980–84 subperiod in which large employment changes are observed these restructuring activities are as likely to involve operations which belonged to the acquiring firm prior to the tender offer as to the target firm. The evidence in this study cannot address the question of the net effects of such restructuring on the economy. It does suggest, however, that policy makers and others should not view the corporate control market in isolation but consider it as an integral part of the process of adapting US business to changing circumstances.

The evidence presented here suggests that managerial motivations of firms making acquisitions remain an interesting area for future research. In particular, the fact that acquiring firms in the 1980–84 subperiod are, on average, selling a significant portion of their own operations raises the possibility that some acquisitions are made when it is expected that corporate resources will become available. Such a motivation may or may not be in shareholders' interest. The expected reduction in an acquiring firm's current level of operations may free up valuable managerial time and talent to be applied to newly acquired operations. Alternatively, management may primarily be concerned with avoiding the resultant reduction in the scope of assets under its control. The latter motivation seems less likely; a management team that is primarily concerned with the level of assets under its control would not be expected to divest significant amounts of assets.

Acknowledgements

This paper is adapted from the author's dissertation at the University of Michigan. She would like to thank her committee members: Charles Brown, Harry DeAngelo, E. Han Kim, and Scott Masten, and especially her chairman, Michael Bradley. She would also like to thank Susan Chaplinsky, Dave Denis, Tom George, Rob Hansen, Dana Johnson, Wayne Marr, Greg Niehaus, Nejat Seyhun, Dilip Shome, and workshop participants at the University of Michigan, the University of Houston, Virginia Tech, the University of Iowa, and the Securities and Exchange Commission. The author is grateful to Keith Ingels for very competent research assistance. Any remaining errors are her own responsibility.

NOTES

1. See, for example, Dodd and Ruback (1977), Kummer and Hoffmeister (1978), Bradley (1980) and Bradley *et al.* (1983, 1988).
2. Putnam (1991) reports that net new lending to the nonfinancial corporate sector by commercial banks fell from $33 billion in 1989 to $2 billion in 1990.
3. For example, the *Wall Street Journal* quotes a leveraged buyout analyst as saying: 'The day of the great acquisition motivated by financial considerations is over. It will be replaced by strategic acquisitions.' 'In other words,' as the *Wall Street Journal* article added, 'corporations will replace 'LBO types' as

buyers.' ('Heard on the street: stock prices might trip over a pile of junk', *Wall Street Journal*, 15 September 1989, p. C1.)

4. We focus on successful tender offers in this study. Employment changes following unsuccessful tender offers are potentially of interest as well. For example, they may provide evidence on the extent to which an unsuccessful tender offer provides target management with a 'kick-in-the-pants'; i.e. does a failed attempt to take over a firm spur that firm to make any of the changes that the acquiring firm would have made?
5. There are only five sample transactions in which the acquirer does not acquire a new majority of the target firm between the ends of years −1 and 1. One acquirer increases its ownership of the target firm from 22% to 29.5% via the tender offer. One acquirer returned the target shares it had purchased to the target firm in exchange for the target's major division, and three acquiring firms owned a majority of their respective target firms prior to the end of year −1. The employment change results after excluding these transactions from the sample do not differ qualitatively from those presented in Table 2.
6. We require target firm employee numbers for at least one of the two year-ends just prior to the completion year. Acquiring firm information is required for the year-end prior to the completion year.
7. We define industry categories using the firm's primary two-digit SIC codes. Where consecutive two-digit industry groups represent different facets of business within the same general industry, I group these together as a broad industry group.
8. This study focuses only on changes in the number of people employed, as conventional data sources do not allow systematic detection of compensation changes in the sample firms. Rosett (1990) uses data from union contracts to estimate the influences of takeovers on the real wage growth of union employees, assuming no change in employment level. He finds decreases in real wage growth following friendly takeovers and increased growth following hostile takeovers. He concludes that decreases in compensation of union employees can explain, at best, a small portion of takeover premiums.
9. The number of target/acquirer pairs for which employee changes are calculated decreases each year. The original 117 pairs becomes 115 because two acquirers had two sample acquisitions each in one year. These transactions were consolidated to one for each acquirer. Information on 11 pairs is lost when the acquiring firm acquires another firm and the latter acquisition is included in the sample; 12 acquirers are themselves acquired or taken private within the three years following; two acquirers have employee numbers missing at some point during the period; one target firm is taken over by an alternative acquirer; and one target firm's results are not included with the acquirer's results and are not separately available.
10. The panel A tests were also performed separately for the hostile and friendly subsamples. The conclusions drawn from the separate results do not differ significantly from those drawn above; therefore they are not presented here. The difference in employment changes following horizontal versus unrelated transactions is more pronounced in the friendly subsample but that difference still does not differ significantly from zero.
11. The Table 2 results indicate that most of the employment changes observed occur by the end of the first full year following tender offer completion. Consequently, the analyses presented in this section and in all subsequent sections focus on the employment change between the ends of years −1 and 1.
12. In the small number of cases in which the target and acquiring firms' results are not consolidated, annual reports of both firms were read.
13. Firm value is the end of year market value of equity plus the book value of long-term debt and preferred stock, all taken from Compustat.
14. Year −1 to year 1 percentage changes in the sample firms' capital to labor ratios reveal that the dollar value of capital per employee increases significantly for all subsamples, where capital is defined as Compustat gross property, plant, and equipment. The increase is greatest in the hostile 1980–84 subsample, where the ratio increases by over 30%, on average. These results are difficult to interpret as they could result from either the divestiture of more labor-intensive operations or reductions in the labor force of the remaining operations. Also, it is not clear whether gross property, plant, and equipment is an effective proxy for the replacement value of the firms' capital assets.
15. The value of the firm is estimated as the market value of its equity plus the book value of its long-term debt and preferred stock, all taken from Compustat. If the acquisition/divestiture occurred during year 0 then year-end −1 value and employment are used. If it occurred during year 1 then the figures as of the end of year 0 are used.
16. The transactions for which the number of employees and either the value or the sales revenue of the affected unit are known provide an opportunity to test the estimation procedure. There are 37 such transactions, nine divestitures and 28 acquisitions. Regression of the actual number of employees on the number predicted using the estimation procedure produces the following equation (t-statistics in parentheses):

$$ACTUAL = -20.47 + 0.53\ PREDICTED \quad R^2 = 0.83$$
$$(-0.03)\ (11.71)$$

17. In using this methodology we are implicitly assuming that all employees of acquired or divested firms and units retain their jobs under new ownership. In fact, Lichtenberg and Siegel (1989) find

that when an average individual operation of a firm changes owners, the number of administrative employees typically falls by 16% and the number of production employees falls by 3%. In addition, employees who do remain employed may or may not retain comparable positions following the change.

18. Bhagat *et al.* (1989) find that an average 29.6% of the target firm is divested in years 0, 1, and 2. They indicate that divestitures are most prevalent following the LBO and 'raider' transactions in their sample. The sample studied here includes only offers made by publicly traded firms.
19. Information about a further nine of the hostile combinations and three of the friendly combinations indicates that target firm operations had been divested but did not provide the details necessary to include them in the calculations.
20. Gulf and Western's 1984 acquisition of Prentice Hall provides a good illustration of the acquisition and divestiture results presented here. Gulf and Western, a highly diversified concern, announced its intention to focus on three areas, including publishing. As a part of this strategy the firm acquired Prentice Hall, a publishing concern. Employment in the combined firm fell 63.1% between the end of year −1 and the end of year 1. Over that time period Gulf and Western sold $1.5 billion of operations, $1.4 billion of which were its own operations prior to acquiring Prentice Hall. Gulf and Western also made other acquisitions totaling $338 million, primarily small publishing firms.
21. A potential problem with an industry comparison is that the extent to which SIC codes are indicative of economic markets is controversial. (See, for example, Clarke, 1989.) Target and acquiring firm employment change over the years −3 to −1 were compared with median employment change in the appropriate 4-digit SIC code industry over the same period. The results, which are not presented here, indicate that, on average, the sample firms' −3 to −1 employment changes do not differ significantly from average industry employment changes.
22. Industry firms' employment changes are not adjusted for acquisitions or divestitures. Median percentage changes in number employed are useful because they will not be driven by outlier firms that engaged in significant restructuring activity.
23. One caveat regarding the results presented in Table 9 concerns the potential underreporting of the activities of the firm. Although considerable detail about firm actions appears to be provided, there remains the possibility that important actions are undertaken and are not mentioned in the annual report or in the *Wall Street Journal*.

REFERENCES

S. Bhagat., A. Shleifer and R. W. Vishny (1989). The aftermath of hostile takeovers. Brookings Institution Paper.

A. Bhide (1989). The causes and consequences of hostile takeovers. *Journal of Applied Corporate Finance*, **2**, 36–59.

D. W. Blackwell, M. W. Marr and M. F. Spivey (1990). Plant-closing decisions and the market value of the firm. *Journal of Financial Economics*, **26**, 277–88.

M. Bradley (1980). Interfirm tender offers and the market for corporate control. *Journal of Business*, **53**, 345–76.

M. Bradley, A. Desai and E. H. Kim (1983). The rationale behind interfirm tender offers: information or synergy? *Journal of Financial Economics*, **11**, 183–206.

M. Bradley, A. Desai and E. H. Kim (1988). Synergistic gains from corporate acquisitions and their division between the stockholders of target and acquiring firms. *Journal of Financial Economics*, **21**, 3–40.

C. Brown and J. L. Medoff (1987). The impact of firm acquisitions on labor. In *Corporate Takeovers: Causes and Consequences* (edited by A. J. Auerbach), University of Chicago Press.

R. N. Clarke (1989) SICs as delineators of economic markets. *Journal of Business*, **62**, 17–31.

L. Y. Dann and H. DeAngelo (1988). Corporate financial policy and corporate control: a study of defensive adjustments in asset and ownership structure. *Journal of Financial Economics*, **20**, 87–128

P. Dodd and R. Ruback (1977). Tender offers and stockholder returns: an empirical analysis. *Journal of Financial Economics*, **5**, 351–74.

C. G. Holderness and D. P. Sheehan (1985). Raiders or saviors? The evidence on six controversial investors. *Journal of Financial Economics*, **14**, 555–80.

M. Jensen (1984). Takeovers: folklore and science. *Harvard Business Review*, **62** (1984).

M. C. Jensen (1986). Agency costs of free cash flow, corporate finance, and takeovers. *American Economic Review*, **76**, 323–9.

M. C. Jensen (1987). The takeover controversy: analysis and evidence. In, eds. *Takeovers and Contests for Corporate Control* (edited by J. Coffee, L. Lowenstein and S. Rose-Ackerman), Oxford: Oxford University Press.

M. C. Jensen (1991). Corporate control and the politics of finance. *Journal of Applied Corporate Finance*, **4**, 13–33.

M. C. Jensen and W. H. Meckling (1976). Theory of the firm: managerial behavior, agency costs, and ownership structure. *Journal of Financial Economics*, **3**, 305–60.

M. C. Jensen and R. S. Ruback (1983). The market for corporate control: the scientific evidence. *Journal of Financial Economics*, **11**, 5–50.

S. Kaplan (1989). The effects oi management buyouts on operating performance and value. *Journal of Financial Economics*, **24**, 217–54.

D. Kummer and R. Hoffmeister (1978). Valuation consequences of cash tender offers. *Journal of Finance*, **33**, 505–16.

F. R. Lichtenberg and D. Siegel (1989). The effect of control changes on the productivity of US manufacturing plants. *Journal of Applied Corporate Finance*, **2**, 60–67.

F. R. Lichtenberg and D. Siegel (1990). The effect of

takeovers on the employment and wages of central-office and other personnel. First Boston Working Paper Series.

M. L. Mitchell and K. Lehn (1990). Do bad bidders become good targets?. *Journal of Political Economy* **98**, 372–398.

R. Morck, A. Shleifer, and R. Vishny (1988). Characteristics of hostile and friendly takeover targets. In, *Corporate Takeovers: Causes and Consequences* (edited by A. J. Auerbach), University of Chicago Press.

R. Morck, A. Shleifer and R. Vishny (1989). Alternative mechanisms for corporate control. *American Economic Review*, **79**, 842–52.

R. Morck, A. Shleifer and R. Vishny (1989). Do managerial objectives drive bad acquisitions? *Journal of Finance*, **45**, 31–48.

B. H. Putnam (1991). Regulation and capital market efficiency: some evidence from the US credit crunch of 1990. *Journal of Applied Corporate Finance*, **4**, 92–5.

R. Romano (1992). Rethinking takeover regulation *Journal of Applied Corporate Finance*, **5**, 47–57.

J. G. Rosett (1990). Do union wealth concessions explain takeover premiums? The evidence on contract wages. *Journal of Financial Economics*, **27**, 263–82.

A. Shleifer and L. H. Summers (1988). Breach of trust in hostile takeover. In *Corporate Takeovers: Causes and Consequences* (edited by A. J. Auerbach), University of Chicago Press.

A. Shleifer and R. W. Vishny (1988). Value maximization and the acquisition process. *Journal of Economic Perspectives*, **2**, 7–20.

A. Shleifer and R. W. Vishny (1989). Management entrenchment: the case of manager-specific investments. *Journal of Financial Economics*, **25**, 123–39.

A. Smith (1990). Corporate ownership structure and performance: the case of management buyouts. *Journal of Financial Economics*, **27**, 143–64.

R. S. Walkling and M. S. Long (1984). Agency theory, managerial welfare, and takeover bid resistance. *Rand Journal of Economics*, **15**, 54–68.

B
Mergers and Tender Offers: Sources of Gains and Losses

[8]

JOURNAL OF FINANCIAL AND QUANTITATIVE ANALYSIS VOL. 35, NO. 2, JUNE 2000

The Impact of Takeovers on Shareholder Wealth during the 1920s Merger Wave

John D. Leeth and J. Rody Borg*

Abstract

We examine the impact of merger announcements on portfolios of acquiring firm and target firm common stock from 1919 to 1930. Despite vast changes in the economic and regulatory environment, overall acquisition profitability has remained remarkably constant over the last 70 to 80 years. Target firm shareholders in the 1920s clearly gained from takeovers, averaging abnormal returns in excess of 15%, while acquiring firm shareholders essentially broke even. Synergistic or monopolistic gains from consolidation were minimal. Unlike the more recent experience, target firm and acquiring firm abnormal returns were largely unaffected by the mode of acquisition, the means of financing, or the degree of industrial relatedness.

I. Introduction

The economic and regulatory environment surrounding takeovers in the 1920s varied greatly from the current environment. No legislation meant to protect stockholders from stock manipulators, raiders, and unscrupulous managers existed. Antitrust laws had been written but Justice Department enforcement was lax. The Securities and Exchange Commission (SEC) had not been created. And, until passage of the Celler-Kefauver Act in 1950, the Federal Trade Commission had little power to regulate mergers. Financial markets and the market for corporate control were at early stages of development.

Studies of contemporary takeovers generally find large target firm returns, small acquiring firm returns, and positive, but small total gains (Roll (1986)). Many also uncover significant differences in returns depending on the mode of acquisition, the means of financing, and the degree of industrial relatedness (Franks, Harris, and Mayer (1988), Jensen and Ruback (1983), Matsusaka (1993)). In this paper, we examine the shareholder wealth effects of takeovers from 1919 to 1930, the period roughly encompassing the second great merger wave in U.S. history, to

*Bentley College, Department of Economics, 175 Forest Street, Waltham, MA 02452, and Jacksonville University, Davis College of Business, 2800 University Boulevard North, Jacksonville, FL 32211, respectively. We thank Patrick Byrne, Jay Fletcher, Ronald Fontaine, Breton Hanley, and Tara Nussman for help in collecting the financial data, and Ralph Nelson for permitting us to use his and Carl Eis's worksheets on merger activity from 1919 to 1930. We also thank T. Randolph Beard, Steve Grubaugh, David Gulley, Jonathan Karpoff (the editor), Lori Leeth, John Matsusaka (the referee), Dennis Mueller, Rexford Santerre, and Scott Sumner for their helpful comments.

determine if the pattern of returns observed on contemporary acquisitions also existed more than 70 years ago when financial markets and the market for corporate control were considerably less regulated and advanced than today.

Our results show that shareholder gains in the 1920s match closely the gains observed on more recent takeovers. Target firm shareholders experienced large increases in wealth, acquiring firm shareholders broke even, and combined gains were small. The average publicly traded target firm in the 1920s recorded a cumulative abnormal return of 15.57% and a market value gain of $30.12 million (1998 dollars) from one month before announcement to completion. In contrast, the typical publicly traded acquiring firm substantially outperformed the market years before a takeover, but earned less than a 3% cumulative abnormal return and posted no significant increase in market value from one month before announcement to completion and then lost value the following year. We find no evidence of synergistic or monopolistic gains from takeovers in the 1920s or evidence that mode of acquisition or means of payment affected target firm or acquiring firm gains. Our results do show target firm returns on diversifying acquisitions exceeding those from related acquisitions, but with only four diversifying target firm events in our sample any population inference is questionable.

From the 1960s to the 1980s, target firm returns rose and acquiring firm returns fell. Jarrell and Poulsen (1989) contend that this secular trend in takeover gains reflects the increased competition in the market for corporate control caused by changes in the regulatory environment and innovations in financial markets and takeover defenses. Foremost among the regulatory changes was passage of the Williams Act in 1968, which brought cash tender offers under the control of the SEC. By imposing delays and forcing disclosure of private information, the Williams Act fostered multiple bidder contests and preemptive bidding, slanting gains in the 1980s away from bidders and toward targets (Jarrell, Brickley, and Netter (1988)).

By detailing how securities could be issued and financial information released, the Securities Act of 1933 and the Securities and Exchange Act of 1934 also may have served to transfer wealth away from bidders and toward targets. Alternatively, the expanding regulation of securities issues may have simply raised acquisition costs and truncated the distribution of takeover gains. As explained by Jensen and Ruback (1983), higher costs eliminate low valued acquisitions and thereby raise the average measured gain. Our results provide no evidence that the institutional changes from the 1920s to the 1960s served to either transfer wealth from bidders to targets or truncate the distribution of takeover gains. Target firm, acquiring firm, and combined gains in the 1920s are well in line with similar gains in the 1960s. Instead, our results conform more closely with a view discussed by Malatesta and Thompson (1993), which holds that acquiring firms have various means of taking over other companies, all of roughly equivalent costs, and financial regulations simply alter the acquisition form and not the total gain or its division between merging parties.

II. Data

A. Target Firm and Acquiring Firm Samples

Previous financial research on historical takeovers has ignored target firms entirely and relied on samples of acquiring firms conditioned on the absence of previous merger activity (Borg, Borg, and Leeth (1989) and Leeth and Borg (1994)). In this paper, we examine both sides of the takeover market and investigate a comprehensive sample of acquiring firms. By including targets in our analysis, we are able to provide information on an important segment of the market for corporate control and develop estimates of total or synergistic gains. Additionally, by including all acquisitions regardless of previous merger activity, we are able to generate shareholder wealth estimates comparable to the vast majority of financial studies that also examine unrestricted samples of acquisitions. Equally important, the expansion of the acquiring firm sample allows us to examine the variability of gains across acquisition forms. Because relatively few takeovers in the 1920s were achieved through tender offers, financed with cash, or took place between firms producing unrelated products, it is impossible to determine the impact of acquisition form without a sufficiently large sample.

Table 1 presents summary information on the financial characteristics of the target and acquiring firm samples we examine. Most of the target and acquiring firm events are between firms producing related products. Tender offers are relatively rare and stock is the primary means of payment. Not surprisingly, the average and median pre-acquisition market values of acquiring firms exceed those for targets by considerable margins.

The sample of 466 acquisitions represents 37.5% of all acquisitions completed from 1919 to 1930 and accounts for the disappearance of 755 firms, 39.4% of all firm disappearances. Of the 188 firms, the average firm completed 2.53 acquisitions—one company made 24 separate acquisitions, and 96 companies made only a single acquisition.

The target firm sample tracks 72 companies or 3.8% of all firm disappearances through merger from 1919 to 1930. As should be expected with any financial study, the availability of stock price data gears our investigation toward relatively large firms. The average target firm in our sample has a book value of assets of $365.3 million (1998 dollars), 5.6 times greater than the $64.7 million average for the population (Eis (1977)). The exclusion of small targets is not unique to the 1920s. As Ravenscraft and Scherer (1987) document, even in the 1960s and 1970s relatively few targets were sufficiently large to have publicly available stock price data.

B. Sample Selection

Carl Eis's worksheets represent the starting point of our research. In background work for his 1977 study on merger movements in American industry, Eis compiled a thorough reporting of mergers in manufacturing and mining from 1919 to 1930. From his list of completed acquisitions and multiple firm consolidations, we limit our investigation to acquisitions. Current theoretical and empirical evidence suggests large differences in motives between acquiring and acquired com-

TABLE 1

Sample Characteristics

	Target Firm Sample ($n = 72$)		Acquiring Firm Sample ($n = 466$)	
Variable	Mean [Median]	Standard Deviation	Mean [Median]	Standard Deviation
Dummy = 1 if related acquisition	0.944	0.231	0.895	0.307
Dummy = 1 if diversifying acquisition	0.056	0.231	0.060	0.238
Dummy = 1 if industrial relatedness unknown	0	0	0.045	0.208
Dummy = 1 if target was acquired through a tender offer	0.181	0.387	0.060	0.238
Dummy = 1 if target shareholders offered cash	0.097	0.298	0.088	0.284
Dummy = 1 if target shareholders offered stock	0.611	0.491	0.335	0.472
Dummy = 1 if target shareholders offered notes, bonds, or preferred stock	0.014	0.118	0.034	0.182
Dummy = 1 if target shareholders offered a combination of cash, stock, notes, bonds, and preferred stock	0.167	0.375	0.146	0.353
Dummy = 1 if financial offer undisclosed	0.083	0.278	0.397	0.490
Pre-acquisition market value (millions of 1998 dollars)	$273.057 [135.208]	$356.699	$1,489.445 [427.178]	$3,529.691

We categorize an acquisition as related if the target and acquiring firm shared at least one two-digit SIC code and diversifying if they did not. SIC codes are determined using Eis's worksheets and company descriptions in *Moody's* and the financial press. In some instances, SIC codes cannot be assigned. We determine whether the takeover was achieved through a tender offer or some other means (such as a merger, an acquisition of assets, or a stock purchase from a majority stockholder) based on descriptions in the financial press. We also rely on the financial press to determine the financial consideration offered target firm shareholders. We calculate pre-acquisition market values using the number of outstanding shares and share price as of six months before the first press report of an impending acquisition. The absence of information on the number of outstanding shares prevents determining the market value of one target firm. We rely on *Moody's* for the number of outstanding shares and the *Commercial and Financial Chronicle: Bank and Quotation Section* for the end-of-month stock price. Dollar values are adjusted for inflation to 1998 using the Consumer Price Index.

panies making the categorization of firms extremely important. Because multiple firm consolidations preclude this determination, we exclude them from the analysis. Unlike the situation during the turn of the century merger wave, the simultaneous consolidation of multiple firms was relatively rare after 1916 (Scherer (1980)). Acquisitions accounted for roughly 65% of the total number and 70% of the value of assets of firms disappearing through merger from 1919 to 1930 (Eis (1977)).

Many companies in the 1920s announced the simultaneous takeover of several firms. In the most extreme case, on July 13, 1929, Borden announced the purchase of 25 companies. To ensure a few firms' returns do not overwhelm the results, we treat the announcement of multiple acquisitions by one firm in a single month as a single event. Using this convention, 1,242 acquisition events were completed from 1919 to 1930 resulting in the disappearance of 1,916 firms.

From the two populations of acquiring and target firms, we exclude from further analysis any firm with insufficient financial data to calculate monthly holding period returns on common stock for at least two years before the first press report of a possible acquisition and any takeover lacking a clear announcement date. The absence of published stock prices eliminates 705 acquiring firm and 1,830 target firm events, while other stock price problems eliminate 14 acquiring firm and 10 target firm events. The inability to discover announcement dates reduces the acquiring firm sample by 53 and the target firm sample by one. We also ignore four acquiring firm and three target firm events because only a partial sell-off of assets occurred or because target firm assets were sold in bankruptcy.

C. Financial Data

We measure stock prices using the mean of the end-of-month bid and ask prices reported in the *Commercial and Financial Chronicle: Bank and Quotation Section.*[1] By relying on the *Commercial and Financial Chronicle,* instead of the Center for Research in Securities Prices (CRSP) tapes, we are able to examine acquisitions completed before 1926 and include firms with stock traded on the New York Curb Market and on the major regional exchanges. To reduce measurement problems, we exclude any company with four or more consecutive months of missing bid and ask prices in the two-year period before merger completion or with fewer than half the months with both prices reported.

Moody's and the *Commercial and Financial Chronicle* provide dividend information for each firm in the sample. We add cash dividends to the end-of-month stock price to determine monthly holding period returns based on the holding-of-record date reported in the weekly dividend column of the *Commercial and Financial Chronicle.* We also adjust stock returns for the issuance of stock rights, stock splits, and stock dividends. For those companies with stock rights listed in the *Capital Changes Reporter* or *Moody's*, we add the market value of the right to the end-of-month stock price to determine the total holding period return. For stock dividends and stock splits, we adjust the end-of-month share price to reflect the increased number of shares held.[2]

[1] In those months where one price is missing, we calculate the missing value by grossing up the bid price or deflating the asking price using the average percentage bid/ask spread computed for the firm. In those months where both prices are missing, we determine stock value by allocating to each month the average monthly capital gain earned over the period of unreported prices. The sole exception is for missing bid and ask prices caused by the closing of the stock market at the outbreak of World War I. Because all stock prices are missing from August 1914 to November 1914, we make no attempt to calculate monthly holding period returns during the period. Instead, the series of monthly returns ends July 1914 and resumes January 1915.

[2] In several instances during World War I, companies paid dividends in the form of Liberty and Victory bonds. We treat these as cash dividends equal to the market value reported in the financial press. Two firms also distributed stock in subsidiary companies; and Reynolds Tobacco issued script in lieu of cash dividends. In each case, we treat the market value of the assets as a cash dividend. We use book values if market values are unreported. If the market value of a right is unreported, we set the value equal to the market price per share minus the exercise price multiplied by the number of shares the right permits the stockholder to purchase. We assume rights where the exercise price is above the market price to be worthless. It should be noted that by imposing an immediate exercise value on the rights, our procedure understates their true worth.

D. Industrial Relatedness, Mode of Acquisition, and Means of Payment

Following on the work of Matsusaka (1993) and Hubbard and Palia (1999), we define an acquisition as "related" if the target and acquiring firm produced products within the same two-digit SIC code and "diversifying" if they did not. Eis's worksheets provide the primary source of SIC information for most firms. In situations where Eis fails to assign an SIC code, we rely on company descriptions in *Moody's* or the financial press to assign SIC codes. For most firms, Eis lists only a single two-, three-, or four-digit SIC code to indicate the company's primary business. In all cases where an acquisition is diversifying based on information from Eis, we determine the full array of target and acquiring firm products by reviewing company descriptions in *Moody's* and the financial press. If the review indicates that the firms produced any product within the same two-digit SIC code, then we reclassify the acquisition as related. The absence of product line information from any source prevents us from classifying 21 acquiring firm events as either related or diversifying.

We determine mode of acquisition and means of payment using reports in the financial press. To be classified as a tender offer, the acquiring firm must have made a general proposal to target firm shareholders to purchase their shares for cash or exchange them for securities in another firm. We do not consider stock purchases on the open market or from majority shareholders or proposals to acquire minority stock interests after control had been obtained to be tender offers.

III. Empirical Method

We use standard event study methods to calculate abnormal returns. Specifically, following the normal convention we define abnormal return for stock i in month t as

$$\text{AR}_{it} = R_{it} - E(R_{it}), \quad (1)$$

where R_{it} is the stock's realized return for month t and $E(R_{it})$ is its expected return in the absence of a merger.

We measure abnormal returns relative to two dates: i) the month the acquisition is first announced to the general public (AD), and ii) the month the acquisition is formally completed (CD). Negative time values represent the number of months before the event, while positive values represent the number of months after the event.

We determine announcement dates using the *Commercial and Financial Chronicle* and the *New York Times*, the only periodicals with indexes covering the period from 1919 to 1930. To parallel studies of more contemporary acquisitions, we use the month of the first confirmed report that either negotiations were under way or a formal plan of consolidation had been adopted as the announcement date. The empirical results do not change if the date of the first publication of any merger information is used as the announcement date.

For the completion date, we use the latter of the two votes by acquiring firm or target firm shareholders approving the consolidation if the takeover were handled as a formal merger. In cases where the financial press fails to note shareholder approval, we treat the first report that a company had been acquired or a merger had been completed as the completion date. For the tender offers in our sample, we use the last date target firm shareholders could deposit their shares to receive the acquiring firm offer of cash, stock, and/or bonds. In some cases, the financial press reports acquisitions that had been formally completed many months previously. Lacking a good announcement date, we exclude them from the analysis.

We calculate expected returns using two methods. In the first, the simple market adjustment, we ignore the variation in financial risk among companies and set each stock's expected return equal to the realized return on a market index of common stocks ($E(R_{it}) = R_{mt}$). In the second, the market model procedure, we regress each stock's monthly holding period return against the market's return over the 54-month period beginning five years before the merger announcement. We then use the estimated parameters from the regression and the market's realized return to forecast the firm's monthly expected return ($E(R_{it}) = \widehat{\alpha}_i + \widehat{\beta}_i R_{mt}$).

As recommended by Schwert (1990), we measure market returns before 1926 using a modified Dow Jones index of common stock. Specifically, we determine pre-1926 market returns by combining the capital gains calculated using a weighted average of the Dow Jones Transportation and Industrial portfolios with the dividend yield of the Cowles All-Stock Index (Cowles and Associates (1939)). After 1926, we measure market returns using the CRSP value-weighted portfolio of New York Stock Exchange (NYSE) stocks.

To eliminate problems caused by the number of companies varying over time, we determine portfolio performance by computing a company-specific abnormal return (CAR_i), and then averaging across companies. More formally, we calculate the average cumulative abnormal return from $t = J$ to $t = K$ as

$$\text{ACAR} = \frac{1}{N}\sum_{i=1}^{N}\text{CAR}_i = \frac{1}{N}\sum_{i=1}^{N}\sum_{t=J}^{K}\text{AR}_{it}, \tag{2}$$

where N represents the number of firms in the merger portfolio during the period. We estimate dollar merger gains by multiplying each firm's cumulative abnormal return from $t = J$ to $t = K$ by its market value at the end of the previous month, $t = J - 1$.[3]

[3] We test the statistical significance of abnormal returns by averaging abnormal returns across all stocks in each month and calculating the standard deviation of the monthly averages, σ, from 60 to six months before merger announcement, a time period likely unaffected by merger news. For individual monthly returns, we divide the monthly average abnormal return by σ. The ratio follows a Student t-distribution with $N - 1$ degrees of freedom, N representing the number of firms in the portfolio, assuming monthly abnormal returns are normal, independent, and identically distributed across time. For cumulative returns, we divide the average cumulative monthly abnormal return by $\sigma\sqrt{M}$, where M equals the cross company average number of months in the period. The ratio is approximately normally distributed assuming a zero mean average cumulative abnormal return and statistical independence of monthly average abnormal returns (Franks and Harris (1989)). We determine the statistical significance of average dollar wealth gains using a cross-sectional t-statistic and median cumulative abnormal returns and dollar wealth gains using a signs test.

IV. Results

A. Target Firms

Figure 1 graphs target firm average cumulative monthly market-adjusted abnormal returns from 60 months before announcement to completion. The figure shows cumulative returns remaining relatively flat for the first three and a half years, falling for six months, leveling off for about a year, and then rising dramatically starting a few months before announcement and continuing through completion.

FIGURE 1

Target Firm Average Cumulative Monthly Market-Adjusted Abnormal Common Stock Returns from Takeover, 1919 to 1930

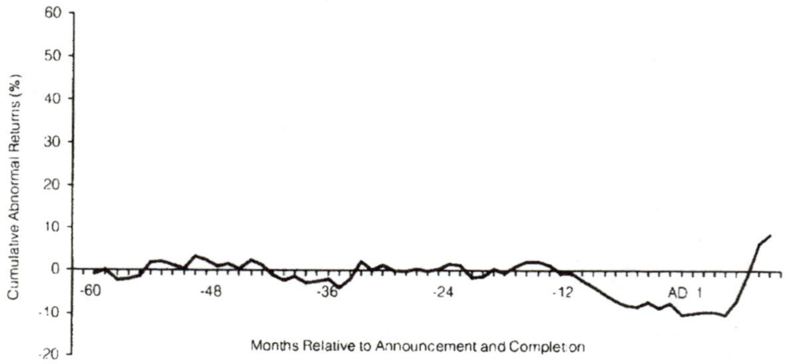

Negative time values represent the number of months before the first press report of an impending takeover (AD) and positive values represent the number of months after completion. Market-adjusted returns are the stock's returns minus the market's returns ($AR_{it} = R_{it} - R_{mt}$).

Table 2 quantifies the gains shown in Figure 1. The first grouping of columns in Panel A report measures of market-adjusted abnormal returns for target firms over various subintervals beginning five years before announcement and continuing through completion. The same columns in Panel B report wealth gains from AD −1 to CD and from AD −5 to CD measured in 1998 dollars. Because of the similarity between market-adjusted and market model abnormal returns, the table displays only the results using the simpler of the two estimating procedures.

Panel A of Table 2 shows target firms averaged only slightly lower returns than stocks in general over the entire pre-merger period from AD −60 to AD −6. They broke even relative to the market the next three months, but then began posting strong positive gains two months before merger announcement. Target firms averaged significant market-adjusted abnormal returns of 2.89% in AD −2, 6.53% in AD −1, and 6.74% in the announcement month. Although insignificant, the average target gained another 3.25% in the interim period from AD +1 to CD.

TABLE 2

Acquisition Gains from 1919 to 1930 on Target Firm and Acquiring Firm Common Stock

Panel A. Monthly Abnormal Returns

	Target Firms (sample size = 72)				Acquiring Firms (sample size = 466)							
	Market-Adjusted ($AR_{it} = R_{it} - R_{mt}$)				Market-Adjusted ($AR_{it} = R_{it} - R_{mt}$)				Market Model ($AR_{it} = R_{it} - \alpha_i - \beta_i R_{mt}$)			
Event Month	Mean	Test Statistic	Median	% Positive	Mean	Test Statistic	Median	% Positive	Mean	Test Statistic	Median	% Positive
AD −60 to AD −6	−9.81%	−0.96	−5.38%	48.6%	41.74%***	10.60	34.24%***	72.3%				
AD −5	0.32	0.21	−0.54	43.1	0.43	0.79	−0.39	47.0	−0.48%	−0.85	−1.28%***	41.2%
AD −4	0.06	0.04	−0.99	41.7	0.33	0.61	−0.40*	45.7	−0.49	−0.88	−1.36***	42.1
AD −3	−0.44	−0.30	−1.97*	38.9	1.28**	2.34	0.21	51.3	0.37	0.65	−1.14**	44.0
AD −2	2.89*	1.96	0.07	51.4	1.67***	3.05	0.07	50.4	0.65	1.16	−0.70***	43.8
AD −1	6.53***	4.43	4.23*	61.1	1.85***	3.39	0.26	51.5	0.94*	1.66	−0.71*	45.9
AD	6.74***	4.58	1.64*	61.1	1.27**	2.33	−0.01	49.8	0.17	0.30	−1.14**	44.4
AD +1 to CD	3.25	1.36	−0.88	49.0	−3.00**	−2.18	−2.58***	33.0	−4.11***	−3.07	−3.35***	29.4
AD −1 to CD	15.57***	5.91	10.30***	76.4	2.43***	2.86	0.48	52.8	0.14	0.16	−1.62	46.1
AD −5 to CD	18.40***	4.64	10.70***	70.8	6.14***	4.44	4.35***	58.8	0.19	0.13	−2.03*	45.9
CD +1 to CD +12					−5.28***	−2.79	−1.39	47.0	−17.88***	−9.18	−12.10***	33.0
CD +1 to CD +36					1.10	0.34	4.72	52.4	−34.89***	10.37	−30.80***	35.0

(continued on next page)

TABLE 2 (continued)

Acquisition Gains from 1919 to 1930 on Target Firm and Acquiring Firm Common Stock

Panel B. Wealth Changes (millions of 1998 dollars)

	Target Firms (sample size = 71)				Acquiring Firms (sample size = 466)							
	Market-Adjusted ($AR_{it} = R_{it} - R_{mt}$)				Market-Adjusted ($AR_{it} = R_{it} - R_{mt}$)				Market Model ($AR_{it} = R_{it} - \alpha_i - \beta_i R_{mt}$)			
Event Month	Mean	Test Statistic	Median	% Positive	Mean	Test Statistic	Median	% Positive	Mean	Test Statistic	Median	% Positive
AD −1 to CD	$30.12**	2.55	$9.95***	76.1%	$4.67	0.24	$1.79	52.8%	−$42.52	−1.60	−$3.28	46.1%
AD −5 to CD	43.25***	3.42	7.45***	71.8	20.54	0.50	8.67***	58.8	−104.91	−1.64	−2.35*	45.9

Event months are measured relative to the date of the first formal announcement of an impending acquisition in the financial press (AD) and the date the acquiring firm controlled target firm assets (CD). Wealth changes are calculated as the product of each firm's market value immediately before the event window and its excess return over the event window. The absence of information on the number of outstanding shares prevents determining the market value of one target firm. Test statistics for monthly abnormal returns follow a Student t-distribution with $N - 1$ degrees of freedom, N representing the number of firms in the portfolio. For cumulative abnormal returns, the test statistic is approximately normally distributed. We calculate the Z-statistics for the period from AD +1 to CD using the standard deviation of the time-series abnormal return performance of the 51 target firms and 109 acquiring firms where the announcement and completion month differed. We use a cross-sectional t-statistic to determine the significance of average wealth changes and a signs test to determine the significance of median values.

*, **, *** Represent statistical significance at the 10, 5, and 1% levels, respectively.

Table 2 evaluates merger gains over two extended event windows, from AD −1 to CD and from AD −5 to CD. The shorter window starts one month before announcement because merger information published near the beginning of the month in the *Commercial and Financial Chronicle*, a weekly publication, may have already been known to the market before the end of the previous month. The longer window starts five months before announcement to capture possible pre-announcement leakage of information.

Over the two merger event windows, target firms strongly outperformed other stocks averaging significant cumulative market-adjusted abnormal returns of 15.57% from AD −1 to CD and 18.40% from AD −5 to CD. More than 70% of target firms rose in value and the median firm recorded a market-adjusted abnormal return exceeding 10% in both event windows. Dollar wealth gains paint a consistent picture of target firm success. Panel B of Table 2 shows a takeover in the 1920s raised the average market value of target firm stock from between $30.12 million and $43.25 million and the median market value from between $7.45 million and $9.95 million.

The size and the timing of target firm gains in Table 2 duplicate returns observed from more contemporary acquisitions. While it is tempting to credit the gains of more than 9% in the two months before announcement to the absence of insider trading prohibitions in the 1920s, studies of more contemporary takeovers also discover similar stock price run-ups (Magenheim and Muller (1988) and Schwert (1996)). They also find the average target firm shareholder earning about a 20% abnormal return from a merger, about a 20% abnormal return from a tender offer in the 1960s, and over a 30% abnormal return from a tender offer in the 1970s and 1980s (Bradley, Desai, and Kim (1988), Jensen and Ruback (1983), and Jarrell, Brickley, and Netter (1988)).

B. Acquiring Firms

Figure 2 graphs acquiring firm average cumulative market-adjusted abnormal returns from 60 months before announcement to 36 months after completion. The figure shows cumulative abnormal returns rising steadily from AD −60 to the announcement month, falling from the announcement month to one year after completion, leveling off for about 12 months, and then rising during the final 12 months.

The last two groupings of columns in Panel A of Table 2 report measures of market-adjusted and market model abnormal returns over various time intervals beginning five years before announcement and continuing through completion. The same columns in Panel B present wealth gains over the two merger event windows measured in 1998 dollars.

Corresponding to the strong upward movement of cumulative returns in Figure 2, Panel A of Table 2 shows acquiring firms substantially outperforming the market in the pre-merger period with the average and median firm earning significant abnormal returns exceeding 34% from AD −60 to AD −6. Studies of contemporary mergers also find acquiring firms earning positive abnormal returns years before a takeover attempt (Asquith (1983), Magenheim and Muller (1988),

FIGURE 2

Acquiring Firm Average Cumulative Monthly Market-Adjusted Abnormal Common Stock Returns from Takeover, 1919 to 1930

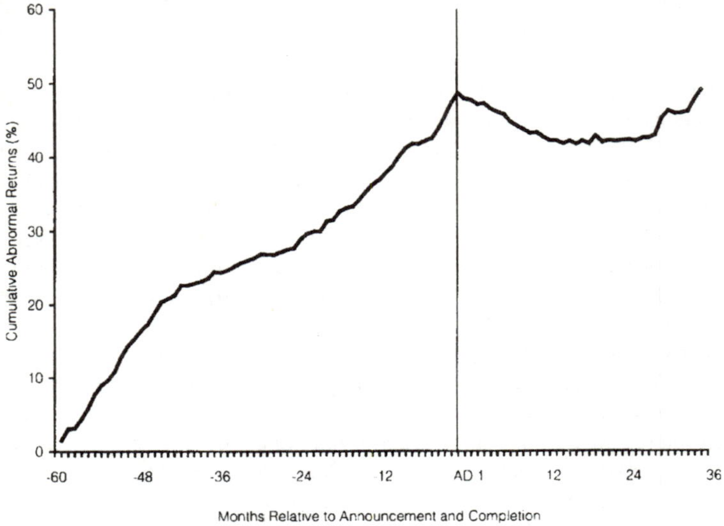

Negative time values represent the number of months before the first press report of an impending takeover (AD) and positive values represent the number of months after completion. Market-adjusted returns are the stock's returns minus the market's returns ($AR_{it} = R_{it} - R_{mt}$).

and Malatesta (1983)). Franks and Harris (1989) argue companies time mergers coincide with historically high profits. The unexpected increase in profits both causes investors to bid up the price of the stock creating the abnormal returns during the pre-merger period and provides the funds necessary for the company to take over other firms. Mergers do not cause the gains; instead, the gains reflect events permitting companies to make acquisitions.

As Panel A, Table 2 shows, the two methods of controlling for expected returns produce quite sizable differences in estimated merger gains. Market-adjusted abnormal returns indicate shareholders in the 1920s anticipated synergistic and/or monopolistic gains from the typical acquisition. The average acquiring firm significantly outperformed the market by over 1% every month from AD -3 to AD. Although acquiring firms lost value from AD +1 to CD, the losses were insufficient to outweigh earlier gains. Acquiring firms recorded significant average cumulative market-adjusted abnormal returns of 2.43% from AD -1 to CD and 6.14% from AD -5 to CD. The median acquiring firm also gained, but the gain is significant only in the longer event window.

Based on market model abnormal returns, investors in the 1920s viewed acquisitions as zero net present value projects. The average acquiring firm earned insignificantly positive market model abnormal returns starting three months before and continuing through announcement but then lost a significant 4.11% from AD +1 to CD. Over the two merger event windows, the average acquiring firm earned small but insignificant market model gains. The median acquiring firm fell in value in both periods, but the loss is significant only in the longer window.

The tremendous stock price run up from AD −60 to AD −6, the period used to estimate the market model, makes evaluating acquiring firm merger success problematic. Gains during the estimation period pull α coefficients upward and calculated market model abnormal returns downward. In particular, the average acquiring firm in our sample has an estimated α of 0.92 and β of 0.95. These parameters imply that market model returns will fall short of market-adjusted returns by almost 1% per month. By way of comparison, the target firm portfolio earned essentially normal returns from AD −60 to AD −6 and the average estimated α and β coefficients for the 72 firms are 0.12 and 0.87, respectively. Only small differences exist between target firm market-adjusted and market model abnormal returns.

Panel B of Table 2 shows the two methods used to control for expected returns also produce quite sizable differences in estimated acquiring firm wealth gains. Over the two event windows, the simple market adjustment procedure indicates the average market value of acquiring firm stock rose from between \$4.67 million and \$20.54 million and the median market value rose from between \$1.79 million and \$8.67 million. In contrast, the market model procedure implies the average market value of acquiring firm stock fell from between \$42.52 million and \$104.91 million and the median market value fell from between \$2.35 million and \$3.28 million.[4] Further confounding interpretation, all of the estimates are insignificant except for the two median values calculated from AD −5 to CD and they provide conflicting evidence on whether the typical takeover raised or lowered shareholder wealth.

At best, the results in Table 2 show the typical takeover in the 1920s created only a relatively small gain for acquiring firm shareholders. Most studies of contemporary acquisitions likewise find only modest returns (Jensen and Ruback (1983), Franks and Harris (1989), Magenheim and Mueller (1988), Roll (1986)). A few indicate that the rewards to acquiring firm shareholders have fallen since the 1960s (Jarrell, Brickley, and Netter (1988), Jarrell and Poulsen (1989), Loderer and Martin (1990)). The results in Table 2 provide no evidence the decline originated 40 years earlier. The largest estimates for the 1920s are in line with the 2% to 5% average abnormal return earned in the 1960s, while the smallest estimates are similar to the zero gains in the 1980s.

The post-completion returns reported in Table 2 also duplicate more modern results. Many studies observe acquiring firms losing value after completion (Agrawal, Jaffe, and Mandelker (1992) and Franks, Harris, and Titman (1991)). Panel A shows the average acquiring firm in the 1920s recorded a 5.28% loss relative to stocks in general and a 17.88% loss relative to market model projections

[4]By weighting larger firms more greatly than smaller firms, wealth gains serve to magnify the impact of exaggerated α coefficients. Companies with substantial stock price growth from AD −60 to AD −6 have both large calculated α coefficients and large market values. As one indication of how sensitive the results are to possible misestimation, the average dollar wealth loss from AD −5 to CD drops more than 80% from \$104.91 million to \$18.59 million ($t = -0.45$) by simply setting $\alpha = 0$ for the top 10% of firms by pre-merger market value.

the year after completion.[5] Over the entire three post-completion years, the pattern of gains and losses varies by type of return. The average acquiring firm from CD +1 to CD +36 earned an insignificant market-adjusted gain of 1.10%, but a highly significant market model loss of 34.89%.

The post-merger results should be interpreted with caution. Research by Barber and Lyon (1997) and Kothari and Warner (1997) shows long horizon tests for abnormal return performance to be misspecified, resulting in substantially more frequent findings of abnormal return performance than justified. Their work indicates the reported test statistics in Table 2 seriously overstate the true statistical significance of post-merger returns.

C. Matched Sample of Target and Acquiring Firms

Table 3 examines a matched sample of target and acquiring firms to determine total synergistic or monopolistic gains in the 1920s. Following along the lines of Bradley, Desai, and Kim (1988), we create a single return series for each of the 53 mergers for which share price information exists on both sides of the market by weighting each firm's returns by its market value six months before merger announcement. Essentially, the technique merges the two companies in a stock portfolio, thereby creating a financial baseline to evaluate the gains from consolidation. We then multiply cumulative abnormal return estimates generated using the single return series by the pre-event market value of target and acquiring firm stock to estimate combined gains.

Table 3 provides limited evidence mergers between publicly traded firms from 1919 to 1930 created net shareholder wealth. All four estimates of average combined gains are insignificantly positive. Median combined gains are either positive or negative depending on the estimating technique used, but none are significant. From the point estimates, the average merger increased the combined market value of target and acquiring firms measured in 1998 dollars from between $18.13 million and $122.95 million while the median merger increased the combined market value from between −$12.09 million and $20.15 million. Similar work examining more recent matched samples of target and acquiring firms also finds only modest gains from consolidation (Berkovitch and Narayanan (1993), Bradley, Desai, and Kim (1988), Malatesta (1983), and Varaiya (1986)).

The individual target and acquiring firm results shown in Table 3 mirror closely the estimates presented earlier. A takeover increased the market value of the average target firm in the matched sample from between $28.81 million and $49.40 million but had no significant impact on the market value of the average acquiring firm.

D. Industrial Relatedness, Mode of Acquisition, and Means of Payment

Table 4 examines the impact of industrial relatedness, mode of acquisition, and means of payment on target and acquiring firm shareholder gains. Panel A

[5]Acquisitions may systematically change β coefficients creating a possible ex-post bias if researchers use pre-merger βs to estimate post-merger expected returns. When we use the final two years of data to estimate the market model for each company, average market model cumulative abnormal returns rise the year after completion to −7.84% but remain statistically significant, $z = -3.97$.

TABLE 3

Wealth Changes on a Matched Sample of 53 Acquiring and Target Firms Completing Acquisitions from 1919 to 1930 (millions of 1998 dollars)

	Target Firms				Acquiring Firms				Combined			
Event Time	Mean	Test Statistic	Median	% Positive	Mean	Test Statistic	Median	% Positive	Mean	Test Statistic	Median	% Positive
Panel A. Market-Adjusted ($AR_{it} = R_{it} - R_{mt}$)												
AD −1 to CD	$33.19**	2.18	$10.59***	75.5%	$56.63	0.97	−$6.80	41.5%	$86.84	1.40	$13.21	56.6%
AD −5 to CD	49.40***	3.14	9.24***	69.8	73.53	1.01	−11.00	47.2	122.95	1.66	20.15	52.8
Panel B. Market Model ($AR_{it} = R_{it} - \alpha_i - \beta_i R_{mt}$)												
AD −1 to CD	$28.81*	1.91	$7.49***	69.8%	$15.38	0.22	−$17.58*	35.8%	$40.08	0.55	−$12.09	41.5%
AD −5 to CD	37.67**	2.47	8.03**	66.0	−21.59	−0.22	−10.64	39.6	18.13	0.19	−6.08	49.1

Event months are measured relative to the date of the first formal announcement of an impending acquisition in the financial press (AD) and the date the acquiring firm controlled target firm assets (CD). Wealth changes are calculated as the product of each firm's market value immediately before the event window and its excess return over the event window. Returns for the combined sample are generated using a market value-weighted average return of target and acquiring firm shares. Market value weights are determined using the number of outstanding shares and share price at the end of AD −6. We use a cross-sectional t-statistic to determine the significance of average wealth changes and a signs test to determine the significance of median values.

*, **, *** Represent statistical significance at the 10, 5, and 1% levels, respectively.

estimates market model abnormal returns and wealth gains from AD −1 to CD for six portfolios of target and acquiring firm stock and then calculates t-statistics for equality of means between adjacent portfolios. Although the method used to benchmark expected returns alters acquiring firm abnormal return and wealth gain estimates considerably, the table presents only the results using the market model procedure. Calculated differences between portfolios are unaffected by the estimating technique employed.

Panel A of Table 4 shows target firm shareholders in the 1920s averaged 60.85% higher abnormal returns from diversifying acquisitions than from related acquisitions. With only four diversifying acquisitions, one may question whether the observed difference in sample means accurately reflects the true difference in population means. The inclusion of a single outlier in a small sample can dramat-

TABLE 4

The Impact of Industrial Relatedness, Mode of Acquisition, and Means of Payment on Acquiring Firm and Target Firm Gains from 1919 to 1930

Panel A. Portfolio effects using market model gains measured from one month before takeover to the month of completion (AD −1, CD). The numbers in each cell represent the mean, (z-statistic), [median, % positive], and sample size. Wealth gains are measured in millions of 1998 dollars.

	Target Firms		Acquiring Firms	
	Abnormal Returns	Wealth Gains	Abnormal Returns	Wealth Gains
Related Acquisition	12.87%*** (4.74) [10.05%***, 72.1%] n = 68	$25.22** (2.07) [$6.10***, 71.6%] n = 67	0.61% (0.66) [−1.17%, 47.0%] n = 417	−$50.53* (−1.78) [−$2.06, 47.0%] n = 417
Diversifying Acquisition	73.72%*** (7.83) [79.71%, 100%] n = 4	$55.14*** (2.58) [$43.96, 100%] n = 4	−2.30% (−1.08) [−6.20%, 35.7%] n = 28	$32.67 (0.26) [−$30.85, 35.7%] n = 28
t-statistic for Equality of Means	−4.42***	−0.59	1.23	−0.66
Tender Offer	7.31% (1.39) [8.07%, 69.2%] n = 13	$5.82 (0.24) [$30.39, 69.2%] n = 13	−3.62% (−1.13) [−1.63%, 46.4%] n = 28	−$150.27 (−1.48) [−$10.16, 46.4%] n = 28
Non-Tender Offer	18.22%*** (6.47) [11.45%***, 74.6%] n = 59	$31.63** (2.42) [$5.61***, 74.1%] n = 58	0.38% (0.45) [−1.62%, 46.1%] n = 438	−$35.63 (−1.30) [−$3.26, 46.1%] n = 438
t-statistic for Equality of Means	−1.19	−0.86	−1.13	−1.09
Cash Offer	25.27%*** (2.77) [16.69%, 57.1%] n = 7	$1.25 (0.15) [$0.58, 57.1%] n = 7	2.47% (0.86) [0.94%, 56.1%] n = 41	−$40.97 (−0.90) [$1.53, 56.1%] n = 41
Stock Offer	12.61%*** (4.37) [9.00%***, 70.5%] n = 44	$12.15 (1.35) [$7.51***, 70.5%] n = 44	−1.12% (−0.94) [−3.52%***, 38.5%] n = 156	−$121.96* (−1.90) [−$11.11***, 38.5%] n = 156
t-statistic for Equality of Means	1.00	−0.47	1.27	1.03

(continued on next page)

TABLE 4 (continued)

The Impact of Industrial Relatedness, Mode of Acquisition, and Means of Payment on Acquiring Firm and Target Firm Gains from 1919 to 1930

Panel B. Regression estimates using market model gains measured from one month before takeover to the month of completion (AD −1, CD). The numbers in each cell represent the estimated parameter value and (*t*-statistic). Wealth gains are measured in millions of 1998 dollars.

	Target Firms (sample size = 72)		Acquiring Firms (sample size = 466)	
Variable	Abnormal Returns	Wealth Gains	Abnormal Returns	Wealth Gains
Intercept	73.297*** (3.60)	18.253 (0.59)	−2.765 (−0.79)	−30.710 (−0.23)
Dummy = 1 if related acquisition	−58.461*** (−2.98)	−19.164 (−0.56)	3.409 (1.49)	−64.755 (−0.52)
Dummy = 1 if industrial relatedness unknown			−2.226 (−0.42)	10.423 (0.07)
Dummy = 1 if tender offer	−5.960 (−0.77)	−26.033 (−1.02)	−5.268 (−1.53)	−91.105 (−0.88)
Dummy = 1 if target shareholders offered stock	−3.390 (−0.39)	18.698** (2.03)	−3.077 (−1.1[illegible])	−65.449 (−0.90)
Dummy = 1 if target shareholders offered notes, bonds, or preferred stock	8.176 (1.19)	3.214 (0.58)	1.186 (0.26)	45.253 (0.72)
Dummy = 1 if target shareholders offered a combination of cash, stock, notes, bonds, and preferred stock	8.469 (0.97)	110.142** (2.00)	−2.098 (−0.64)	43.940 (0.48)
Dummy = 1 if financial offer undisclosed	−2.783 (−0.22)	17.797 (0.94)	−0.666 (−0.24)	74.365 (1.30)
Dummy = 1 if acquirer firm size/target firm size > 0.096			4.058** (1.98)	73.274 (1.29)
Dummy = 1 if first acquisition within three years			0.835 (0.60)	20.906 (0.54)
R^2	0.248	0.152	0.033	0.016

We categorize an acquisition as related if the target and acquiring firm shared at least one two-digit SIC code and diversifying if they did not. SIC codes are determined using Eis's worksheets and company descriptions in *Moody's* and the financial press. In some instances, SIC codes cannot be assigned. We determine whether the takeover was achieved through a tender offer or some other means based on descriptions in the financial press. We also rely on the financial press to determine the financial consideration offered target firm shareholders. We measure the relative size of the target firm to the acquiring firm using the book value of total assets the year before the acquisition, if available, or the book value of outstanding capital, if not. In situations where *Moody's* fails to report any accounting information on the target, we use the purchase price of the target as reported in Eis's worksheets or the financial press relative to the market value of acquiring firm equity at the end of AD −6. In many cases, the total absence of information on the target or the acquirer prevents calculating any measure of relative size. Wealth changes are calculated as the product of each firm's market value two months before announcement and its excess return from AD −1 to CD. The absence of information on the number of outstanding shares prevents determining the market value of one target firm. Market values are adjusted for inflation to 1998 using the Consumer Price Index. We determine *t*-statistics for differences in means using a pooled sample standard deviation for cell sizes under 28 and a non-pooled sample standard deviation for cell sizes over 28. We calculate regression *t*-statistics using heteroskedasticity-consistent standard errors (see White (1980)).

*, **, *** Represent statistical significance at the 10, 5, and 1% levels, respectively.

ically skew the results, indicating a significant difference when none really exists. In the case at hand, only three target firms earned market-adjusted abnormal returns of more than 100% and two of the three were diversifying acquisitions.

The wealth gain estimates also call into question the superior profitability of diversifying acquisitions. The average diversifying acquisition created a greater dollar gain than the average related acquisition but the difference is insignificant. The two diversifying target firm outliers had fairly small market values, which diminished their importance in the dollar value estimates.

None of the other target firm portfolio differences in Table 4 are significant. Based on point estimates, target firm shareholders in the 1920s averaged lower abnormal returns and lower dollar gains from tender offers than non-tender offers and higher average abnormal returns but lower dollar gains from cash offers than stock offers. The results for the 1920s are in marked contrast to the more recent experience where gains from tender offers have generally exceeded those from other types of takeovers and where cash offers have usually produced larger returns than stock offers (Franks, Harris, and Mayer (1988), Huang and Walkling (1987), Jensen and Ruback (1983)).

Table 4 provides no evidence that industrial relatedness, mode of acquisition, or means of payment affected acquiring firm gains in the 1920s. None of the six differences in means pass traditional thresholds of significance. The table shows acquiring firm shareholders averaging higher abnormal returns but lower dollar gains from related acquisitions than diversifying acquisitions, lower abnormal returns and dollar gains from tender offers than non-tender offers, and higher abnormal returns and dollar gains from cash offers than stock offers. Other studies generally find acquiring firm shareholders earning smaller gains from tender offers than non-tender offers and larger gains from cash offers than stock offers (Franks and Harris (1989), Franks, Harris, and Mayer (1988)). The impact of industrial relatedness has varied over time with acquiring firm shareholders on average gaining from diversifying acquisitions in the early 1970s, breaking even in the late 1970s, and losing in the 1980s (Matsusaka (1993)).

Panel B of Table 4 presents regression estimates of the impact of industrial relatedness, mode of acquisition, and means of payment on target and acquiring firm shareholder gains. For both groups of firms, we include a series of dummy variables for industrial relatedness, type of offer, and means of payment. For the acquiring firm sample, we also include two other control variables. The first is a dummy variable that equals one for acquisitions where the ratio of target firm size to acquiring firm size exceeds 0.096 and zero otherwise; 0.096 is the median for all acquisitions with non-missing values.[6] Takeovers of small targets should produce minimal gains. The second variable attempts to control for partial anticipation by measuring takeover frequency. The more mergers a company makes, the more likely investors are to anticipate additional acquisitions; hence, abnormal returns should be the greatest on first acquisitions, which were likely surprises, rather than on other acquisitions, which may have been anticipated (Asquith, Bruner, and Mullins (1983)). We measure takeover frequency using

[6]We determine relative size using the book value of total assets reported in *Moody's* the year before the acquisition, if available, or the book value of outstanding capital, if not. If *Moody's* fails to report any accounting information on the target, then we use the purchase price of the target as reported in Eis's worksheets or the financial press relative to the market value of acquiring firm equity six months before takeover announcement. For 31.3% of the sample, the total absence of information prevents us from calculating any measure of relative size.

a dummy variable that equals one if the takeover was the first within the previous three years for the acquiring firm and zero otherwise.

The results presented in Panel B of Table 4 correspond closely to the portfolio effects presented in Panel A. Target firm shareholders averaged a significant 58.5% lower market model abnormal return from AD −1 to CD on related acquisitions than on diversifying acquisitions, all else equal. Once again, the small number of diversifying acquisitions in the 1920s and the absence of any significant dollar value impact make this result questionable. Target firm shareholders also earned insignificantly lower abnormal returns and wealth gains on tender offers than non-tender offers and they earned insignificantly lower abnormal returns, but significantly higher dollar gains from stock offers than cash offers, after controlling for other factors. Offers of a combination of cash, stock, notes, bonds, and/or preferred stock created both higher abnormal returns and higher dollar gains for target firm shareholders than did straight cash offers, but only the dollar gains are significant. The differing abnormal return and dollar gain impacts for stock and combination financing suggest that acquiring firms in the 1920s used cash to purchase smaller targets and stock or a combination of stock and other assets to purchase larger targets.[7]

Except for relative size, none of the acquiring firm coefficients in Panel B are significant. The pattern of returns and dollar gains by industrial relatedness, mode of acquisition, and means of payment match exactly the portfolio effects discussed previously. All else equal, acquiring firm shareholders earned insignificantly higher returns but smaller dollar gains on related acquisitions than diversifying acquisitions, lower returns and smaller dollar gains on tender offers than non-tender offers, and lower returns and smaller dollar gains on stock offers than cash offers. First takeovers created insignificantly larger gains than subsequent acquisitions and takeovers of large targets created significantly higher abnormal returns but insignificantly higher dollar gains than takeovers of small targets.[8]

The regression estimates in Table 4 are robust across many empirical specifications. Measuring takeover gains using a simple market adjustment or differentiating between related and diversifying acquisitions at the three-digit SIC code level alters the results only slightly. Target firm abnormal returns are consistently lower on related acquisitions than diversifying acquisitions regardless of how returns are calculated or relatedness measured. Still, it should be noted that even at the three-digit SIC code level, only seven target firm events are unrelated. Tender offers produce marginally lower market model abnormal returns than non-tender offers, all else equal, using the more narrow definition of industrial relatedness. For acquiring firms, all of the variables measuring industrial relatedness, mode

[7]The average market value of targets acquired with cash in our sample is $169.5 million (1998 dollars), while the averages of targets acquired with stock or a combination of cash, stock, notes, bonds, and preferred stock are $283.6 million and $443.3 million, respectively.

[8]The coefficient on relative size suggests that investors in the 1920s may have viewed acquisitions as positive net present value projects but that the inclusion of a large number of small acquisitions in the overall portfolio masks this assessment. Nevertheless, even for acquisitions with a relative size measure exceeding 0.096 the average takeover produced minimal shareholder gains, cumulative market model abnormal returns of 2.42% ($z = 2.03$) from AD −1 to CD. By way of comparison, the average market model abnormal return for the remaining 306 acquiring firms is −1.05% ($z = -1.02$), creating a difference in means of 3.47% ($t = 1.99$).

of acquisition, and means of payment remain insignificant using either market-adjusted gains or measuring relatedness at the three-digit level. Excluding small acquisitions, those unlikely to have created substantial shareholder gains, also produces only minimal changes in the acquiring firm results. When we limit the sample to events where the ratio of target firm to acquiring firm assets is 5% or larger, all but two of the independent variables are insignificant. In the restricted sample, acquiring firm dollar wealth gains are smaller on stock offers than cash offers and market model abnormal returns are larger on related than diversifying acquisitions at the two-digit level. The significance of industrial relatedness disappears using either market-adjusted abnormal returns or a three-digit SIC code measure of relatedness.[9]

V. Conclusions

Compared to today, takeovers in the 1920s faced few legal constraints. The Securities and Exchange Commission did not exist, antitrust enforcement was minimal, and state blue-sky laws were largely ineffective. Financial information was sketchy. Only 44% of the 545 leading industrial corporations in the U.S. reported gross income in 1929 and, even for these companies, the wide variation in their treatment of balance sheet and income statement items made it difficult for investors to compare data across firms. A Twentieth Century Fund study concludes that the financial disclosure in prospectuses for new securities issues ranged from adequate to overblown to "material omissions and outright misstatements" (as quoted in Du Boff and Herman (1989), p. 116). The market for corporate control was at an early stage of development. Sophisticated antitakeover defenses did not exist, but then hostile tender offers were unknown.

Our research examines the shareholder wealth effects of takeovers during the 1920s merger wave to determine if the pattern of returns typically observed on contemporary acquisitions prevailed when financial markets were less regulated and the market for corporate control less evolved. Overall, the gains in the 1920s look surprisingly familiar. Target firm shareholders clearly gained, acquiring firm shareholders did not lose, and combined gains were modest. From one month before announcement to completion, the average target firm recorded a cumulative abnormal return of 15.57% and a market value gain of $30.12 million. Over the same period, the average acquiring firm posted a market-adjusted abnormal return of 2.43%, a market model abnormal return of nearly zero, and no significant change in market value. The combined market value gains of target and acquiring firms were insignificant across all estimating techniques and event windows. Similar to the more recent experience, the typical acquiring firm in the 1920s substantially outperformed the market years before a takeover, but then lost value after merger completion.

Studies of more contemporary takeovers generally find target firm shareholders earning significantly larger returns and acquiring firm shareholders earning significantly smaller returns on tender offers than non-tender offers and both groups of shareholders earning significantly larger returns on cash offers than

[9]The results of the sensitivity analysis can be obtained by e-mailing Jleeth@Bentley.edu.

stock offers. In contrast, we discover no significant differences in either target firm or acquiring firm abnormal returns in the 1920s by type of acquisition or means of payment. We also fail to uncover any significant difference in acquiring firm gains by the degree of industrial relatedness between the acquiring and target firms. Although our results do show substantially larger target firm gains on diversifying acquisitions than related acquisitions, the limited sample size makes any population inference questionable.

The introduction of more stringent financial market regulation may alter the form of acquisition but leave the decision to acquire, the total gain created, and the division of the gains unchanged if companies have a multitude of ways to take over other firms, all of roughly equivalent costs. The closeness of target firm, acquiring firm, and combined gains in the 1920s to gains in the 1960s suggests that acquiring firms adjusted to regulations detailing how securities could be issued and financial information released by substituting one form of takeover for another form. The results are inconsistent with early financial regulations either causing a transfer of takeover profits from acquiring firms to target firms or increasing acquisition costs and truncating the distribution of takeover gains.

References

Agrawal, A.; J. F. Jaffe; and G. N. Mandelker. "The Post-Merger Performance of Acquiring Firms: A Re-Examination of an Anomaly." *Journal of Finance,* 47 (1992), 1605–1621.

Asquith, P. "Merger Bids, Uncertainty, and Stockholder Returns." *Journal of Financial Economics,* 11 (1983), 51–83.

Asquith, P.; R. F. Bruner; and D. W. Mullins, Jr. "The Gains to Bidding Firms from Merger." *Journal of Financial Economics,* 11 (1983), 121–139.

Barber, B. M., and J. D. Lyon. "Detecting Long-Run Abnormal Stock Returns: The Empirical Power and Specification of Test Statistics." *Journal of Financial Economics,* 43 (1997), 341–372.

Berkovitch, E., and M. P. Narayanan. "Motives for Takeovers: An Empirical Investigation." *Journal of Financial and Quantitative Analysis,* 28 (1993), 347–362.

Borg, J. R.; M. O. Borg; and J. D. Leeth. "The Success of Mergers in the 1920s: A Stock Market Appraisal of the Second Merger Wave." *International Journal of Industrial Organization,* 7 (1989), 117–131.

Bradley, M.; A. Desai; and E. H. Kim. "Synergistic Gains from Corporate Acquisitions and Their Division between the Stockholders of Target and Acquiring Firms." *Journal of Financial Economics,* 21 (1988), 3–40.

Cowles, A., 3rd, and Associates. *Common Stock Indexes: 1871–1939.* Bloomington, IN: Principia Press, Inc. (1939).

Du Boff, R. B., and E. S. Herman. "The Promotional-Financial Dynamic of Merger Movements: A Historical Perspective." *Journal of Economic Issues,* 23 (1989), 107–133.

Eis, C. *The 1919–1930 Merger Movement in American Industry.* New York, NY: Arno Press (1977).

Franks, J. R., and R. S. Harris. "Shareholder Wealth Effects of Corporate Takeovers: The U.K. Experience 1955–1985." *Journal of Financial Economics,* 23 (1989), 225–249.

Franks, J. R.; R. S. Harris; and C. Mayer. "Means of Payment in Takeovers: Results for the United Kingdom and the United States." In *Corporate Takeovers: Causes and Consequences,* A. Auerbach, ed. Chicago, IL: Univ. of Chicago Press (1988).

Franks, J.; R. Harris; and S. Titman. "The Postmerger Share-Price Performance of Acquiring Firms." *Journal of Financial Economics,* 29 (1991), 81–96.

Huang, Y., and R. A. Walkling. "Target Abnormal Returns Associated with Acquisition Announcements: Payment, Acquisition Form, and Managerial Resistance." *Journal of Financial Economics,* 19 (1987), 329–349.

Hubbard, R. G., and D. Palia. "A Re-Examination of the Conglomerate Merger Wave in the 1960s: An Internal Capital Markets View." *Journal of Finance,* 54 (1999), 1131–1152.

Jarrell, G. A.; J. A. Brickley; and J. M. Netter. "The Market for Corporate Control: The Empirical Evidence since 1980." *Journal of Economic Perspectives,* 2 (1988), 49–68.

Jarrell, G. A., and A. B. Poulsen. "The Returns to Acquiring Firms in Tender Offers: Evidence from Three Decades." *Financial Management,* 18 (1989), 12–19.

Jensen, M. C., and R. S. Ruback. "The Market for Corporate Control: The Scientific Evidence." *Journal of Financial Economics,* 11 (1983), 5–50.

Kothari, S. P., and J. B. Warner. "Measuring Long-Horizon Security Price Performance." *Journal of Financial Economics,* 43 (1997), 301–339.

Leeth, J. D., and J. R. Borg. "The Impact of Mergers on Acquiring Firm Shareholder Wealth: The 1905–1930 Experience." *Empirica,* 21 (1994), 221–244.

Loderer, C., and K. Martin. "Corporate Acquisitions by Listed Firms: The Experience of a Comprehensive Sample." *Financial Management,* 19 (1990), 17–33.

Magenheim, E. B., and D. C. Mueller. "Are Acquiring-Firm Shareholders Better Off after an Acquisition?" In *Knights, Raiders, and Targets: The Impact of the Hostile Takeover,* J. C. Coffee, Jr., L. Lowenstein, and S. Rose-Ackerman, eds. New York, NY: Oxford Univ. Press (1988).

Malatesta, P. H. "The Wealth Effect of Merger Activity and the Objective Functions of Merging Firms." *Journal of Financial Economics,* 11 (1983), 155–181.

Malatesta, P. H., and R. Thompson. "Government Regulation and Structural Change in the Corporate Acquisitions Market: The Impact of the Williams Act." *Journal of Financial and Quantitative Analysis,* 28 (1993), 363–379.

Matsusaka, J. G. "Takeover Motives during the Conglomerate Merger Wave." *Rand Journal of Economics,* 24 (1993), 357-379.

Ravenscraft, D. J., and F. M. Scherer. *Mergers, Sell-offs, and Economic Efficiency.* Washington, DC: Brookings Institution (1987).

Roll, R. "The Hubris Hypothesis of Corporate Takeovers." *Journal of Business,* 59 (1986), 197–216.

Scherer, F. M. *Industrial Market Structure and Economic Performance,* 2nd ed. Chicago, IL: Rand McNally College Publishing Co. (1980).

Schwert, G. W. "Indexes of U.S. Stock Prices from 1802 to 1987." *Journal of Business,* 63 (1990), 399–426.

_______________. "Markup Pricing in Mergers and Acquisitions." *Journal of Financial Economics,* 41 (1996), 153–192.

Varaiya, N. P. "An Empirical Investigation of the Bidding Firms' Gains from Corporate Takeovers." *Research in Finance,* 6 (1986), 149–178.

White, H. "A Heteroskedasticity-Consistent Covariance Matrix Estimator and a Direct Test for Heteroskedasticity." *Econometrica,* 48 (1980), 817–838.

[9]

RAND Journal of Economics
Vol. 24, No. 3, Autumn 1993

Takeover motives during the conglomerate merger wave

John G. Matsusaka*

This article examines the stock market response to acquisition announcements during and immediately after the conglomerate merger wave of the late 1960s. The main finding is that acquirer shareholders benefited from diversification acquisitions, which implies that diversification was not driven by managerial objectives. It is also shown that the market responded positively to bidders who retained the management of target companies and negatively to bidders who replaced target management. This is consistent with the hypothesis that the market favored acquisitions intended to exploit managerial synergies. It suggests that the market disliked takeovers that were motivated to discipline target management. Evidence on buyer and target price-earnings ratios is presented that is inconsistent with the conjecture that conglomerates were able to mislead investors by earnings-per-share manipulation.

1. Introduction

■ One of the major business developments of the last half century has been the diversification of American firms. The process reached its zenith during the merger wave of the late 1960s and was carried to its logical extreme by the conglomerate firms that rose to prominence at that time. Recent research has suggested that the postwar movement toward increased diversification has ended and a return to specialization has begun (Comment and Jarrell, 1991; Liebeskind, Opler, and Hatfield, 1992). The 1980s saw a wave of consolidating mergers aimed at undoing the conglomeration of the previous two decades (Shleifer and Vishny, 1990). It was not uncommon in the 1980s for the assets of a diversified target company to be sold off to management or firms in related industries (Bhagat, Shleifer, and Vishny, 1990) or for a firm to divest unrelated businesses (Kaplan and Weisbach, 1992).

Understanding what drove managers to diversify during the conglomerate merger wave is important in evaluating the 1980s merger wave. If diversification was motivated by managers' desires to found corporate empires or entrench themselves, then deconglomeration was a good thing, reversing the value-reducing actions of previous managers. On the other

* University of Southern California.

I received helpful suggestions from Gary Becker, Thomas Gilligan, Barbara McCutcheon, Vikram Nanda, James Poterba, Jaffer Qamar, Andrei Shleifer, Lester Telser, Robert Vishny, and an anonymous referee, and I learned much from the comments of workshop participants at Harvard Business School, MIT, Northwestern University, Stanford University, University of Chicago, University of Southern California, and University of Washington. F. M. Scherer kindly provided his merger sample. I am grateful to the Bradley Foundation (through a grant to the Center for the Study of the Economy and the State at the University of Chicago) and the University of Chicago for financial support.

hand, if conglomeration was pursued to maximize shareholder wealth, then deconglomeration is more difficult to explain and evaluate.

There are theoretical reasons to suspect that managers may have pursued a diversification strategy even when it hurt shareholders. They may have entered new lines of business to protect their organization-specific human capital (Amihud and Lev, 1981) or entrench themselves (Shleifer and Vishny, 1989). Alternatively, they may have been pursuing size as an end and because of strict antitrust opposition to horizontal and vertical mergers had to expand by buying into unrelated industries (Baumol, 1967; Mueller, 1969; Ravenscraft and Scherer, 1987).

Perhaps the most direct way to evaluate whether a manager was diversifying for his own benefit or in the interest of shareholders is to examine the effect of diversification on the value of his firm's equity. The premise of this article is that if the value of a firm declined upon announcement of an acquisition, then its management was not acting to maximize shareholder wealth. The article's most striking finding is that during the conglomerate merger wave, bidder shareholders earned significantly positive announcement-period returns from diversifying acquisitions and negative returns from related acquisitions. This evidence is inconsistent with the hypothesis that managers diversified to achieve personal objectives. Together with the findings of Morck, Shleifer, and Vishny (1990), it documents a dramatic reversal in investor sentiment toward diversification—positive in the 1960s, neutral in the 1970s, and negative in the 1980s.

If managers were diversifying to maximize shareholder value, where did they (and the market) think the increased value was going to come from? The men who founded the conglomerates were sometimes considered the vanguard of a new generation of managers. It was thought that these "supermanagers" were experts in general concepts of management and their skills could be applied to any business—detailed knowledge of a firm's particular products and industry was not essential.

One possible explanation for conglomeration, then, is basically a reworking of the familiar managerial-discipline theory: firms were taken over to discipline or replace their bad managers. A second explanation is the flip side of managerial discipline, call it the "managerial synergy" theory: bidder management wanted to work with target management, not replace it. According to this explanation, acquirer management believed it had valuable managerial expertise that would be complementary to the skills of target management. For example, the buyer would provide expertise at raising capital, and the target would provide product development and manufacturing talents.[1]

Takeovers in which the target's management was replaced are consistent with a managerial-discipline motive—one way to discipline managers is to fire them. Takeovers in which the target's management was retained are consistent with a managerial-synergy motive—target management is the key asset in a managerial-synergy acquisition. A second, perhaps surprising, finding is that the market reacted positively to bidders who retained target management and negatively to bidders who removed target management. This evidence suggests that the market subscribed to the managerial-synergy theory. In addition, it suggests that buyers who replaced target management were believed to have overpaid or overestimated their own abilities.

The premerger profitability of the target firm potentially can shed some light on the takeover motive. Managerial-discipline targets were likely to have had low profits—why discipline a good firm?—while managerial-synergy targets were likely to have had high

[1] The idea that conglomerates exploited capital market inefficiencies has received considerable attention, with mixed results (McCutcheon, 1991). The idea of general managerial synergies, however, has enjoyed more popularity in the business press than in the economic press, for example, Berg (1969), Sobel (1984), and Holland (1989). Matsusaka (1991) is an attempt to formalize the managerial synergy theory.

profits—talented managers are better able to exploit complementarities. However, the evidence indicates that the market did not attach a premium to bidders depending on the profitability of their targets.

In addition to determining why the market liked certain acquisitions, it is instructive to investigate why the market disliked others. In particular, why did some firms make acquisitions that reduced shareholder value? A third finding of the article is that governance structure matters: the market reaction to a takeover announcement was negatively related to the ratio of insiders to outsiders on the bidder's board of directors. This is consistent with the hypothesis that insider-dominated firms had been captured by managers, freeing them to pursue non-value-creating objectives. The market's reaction to acquisitions by family-run firms is also considered.

A different explanation for conglomeration is that buyers were driven by earnings-per-share (EPS) manipulation. This explanation plays off the observation that conglomerates tended to have a high price-earnings ratio (P/E). It is an algebraic fact that when one firm acquires another with a lower P/E, its EPS rises—called "bootstrapping." If the market sets the price of a stock at a constant multiple of EPS, then a firm can increase its stock price by buying firms with lower P/Es than its own. According to this explanation of conglomeration, bidder management was playing a bootstrapping game by buying firms with low P/Es; diversification was largely coincidental.

There are logical objections to this explanation—in particular, it assumes that investors could be manipulated with accounting numbers. A simple way to evaluate this explanation is to observe the returns to bidders who appeared to be playing the bootstrapping game. If it worked, bidders should have earned positive returns when they bought firms with lower P/Es than their own. Another finding of the article is that there is no evidence that bidders profited from EPS manipulation. Although not statistically significant, high-P/E buyers of low-P/E firms earned negative returns, while other buyers earned positive returns.

The remainder of this article takes an in-depth look at these and other issues pertaining to takeover motives during the conglomerate merger wave. The next section discusses construction of the dataset and defines the variables. Section 3 reports the returns to diversifying and related acquisitions, and investigates the source of the diversification premium. Section 4 evaluates the returns to EPS manipulation. Section 5 presents evidence on the returns to managerial-discipline and managerial-synergy takeovers. Section 6 summarizes and offers some conclusions.

2. Data and variables

■ Construction of the dataset began with a list of mergers from the sample of 1968, 1971, and 1974 manufacturing sector acquisitions used to study premerger target profitability by Ravenscraft and Scherer (1987, 1989). Ravenscraft and Scherer identified their sample of takeovers from New York Stock Exchange listing statements. Corporations wishing to list securities on the stock exchange in relation to a merger are required to submit a recent balance sheet and income statement for the target. An advantage of this data source, as opposed to the Federal Trade Commission's large-merger series and Center for Research in Security Prices (CRSP) delistings, is that it allows an inside look at privately owned targets (most of the sample). By construction, all observations are in part equity-financed. This may be relevant to the extent that all-cash transactions have different motivations than security transactions (Carleton et al., 1983). An additional 212 mergers were identified from the listing statements, which increased the basic list to 855 observations, 71.2% from 1968, 13.7% from 1971, and 15.1% from 1974.[2]

[2] Ravenscraft and Scherer collected observations in these three years to look for systematic variations in merger behavior in different periods. The 1974 observations occur after the conglomerate merger wave, so I considered

Once the basic set of mergers was identified, detailed information about each takeover was hand-collected from a variety of sources. The *Wall Street Journal Index* and various unindexed issues of the *Wall Street Journal* were searched for articles discussing the sample mergers. Announcement articles were found for 429 of them, and the date of the article was linked to the appropriate observation. The dataset was then carefully cleaned; each observation was examined for its quality, and 131 were dropped for one of the following reasons: the same acquisition appeared twice in the dataset; subsidiaries of the target that had been entered as separate observations in the Ravenscraft and Scherer sample were consolidated with the parent; the target was a majority-owned subsidiary of the buyer; the *Wall Street Journal* story was not the first public announcement of the merger; other news more important than the merger concerning the acquirer was reported in the announcement article;[3] the acquirer announced another acquisition in the preceding or following week; or there was not enough CRSP information on the acquirer to compute bidder returns (for example, Zurn Industries was not listed when it made its first acquisition announcements). One observation was dropped because the target was not in manufacturing. Finally, acquisitions where the book value of the target's assets was less than $5 million (68.3% of the targets) were dropped.[4] Inclusion of very small acquisitions only adds noise to the estimates. The Appendix lists the sources of the data and indicates how many observations were deleted for each reason. It also discusses some minor changes and corrections to the Ravenscraft and Scherer sample.

□ **Measuring the return to the bidder's shareholders.** There are several ways to measure the announcement-period return to the acquiring firm's shareholders. The measure that seems to be most appropriate for the following tests is the "dollar return," the cumulated residual rates of return from a market model weighted by the value of the firm (Malatesta, 1983). If r_t is the abnormal rate of return on the firm's common stock on day t and V_t is the firm's value at the start of day t, then the dollar return over a T-day event window is defined to be $\sum_{t=1}^{T} r_t V_t$. Price changes were calculated from five days before the announcement to five days after.[5] Market-model coefficients were estimated in the usual way over a 240-day interval beginning 300 days before the event using an equally weighted market portfolio with dividends (Bradley, Desai, and Kim, 1988). Dollar returns were then normalized to 1968 dollars using the consumer price index. The mean announcement-period return for the sample using this measure was −$0.517 million, insignificantly different from zero (t = 0.179). Thus, the sample conforms to other event studies that find zero abnormal returns to bidders on average.

A more common way to measure the stockholder return is as a percentage return on the acquirer's equity; the change in the bidder's price is divided by its preannouncement

excluding them from the estimates. In the end I retained them for the following reasons: (1) their inclusion or exclusion has substantive effects only on the standard errors, not the signs or magnitudes, of the estimates; (2) although the overall number of mergers peaked in 1968–1969, the percentage of conglomerate mergers remained high into the mid-1970s; (3) Ravenscraft and Scherer do not find systematic differences between mergers in the three periods; (4) in the final event study sample, 1974 provides only 15% of the observations.

[3] To be specific, I consulted the earliest mention of each merger in the *Wall Street Journal*. If the story mentioned the acquisition *after* mentioning something else about the buyer—for example, resignation of its CEO or introduction of a new product—the observation was dropped. If the acquisition led the story, the observation was retained.

[4] I also tried cutoff points based on the ratio of the target's assets to the value of the buyer's equity, with essentially the same results.

[5] The results did not differ in substance when a [−4, +4] event window was used, but the standard errors were much larger with a [−1, +1] window.

price, usually approximated as $\sum_{t=1}^{T} r_t$. This is sometimes called the cumulative abnormal residual, here simply the "percentage return." An undesirable feature of this measure is that if a large and a small corporation acquire identical firms and each experiences a $1 million increase in value, the percentage return to the small corporation exceeds the percentage return to the large corporation, implying the small company made a better acquisition. In addition, the percentage return reflects the payoff to investment strategies that are not, in general, feasible to the firm's shareholders as a group (Malatesta, 1983).

Morck, Shleifer, and Vishny (1990) use a third measure: the change in the value of the bidder is divided by the purchase price, in effect treating each acquisition as an investment equal to the purchase price and computing the return on the project. According to this "investment" measure, the two acquisitions above are equally good. However, suppose a firm makes two acquisitions, one that costs $10 million and results in a $1 million value increase and another that costs $100 million and increases value by $5 million. The investment measure rates the takeovers at 10% and 5%, respectively, but the latter adds more value and is a better acquisition for the stockholders. Because the change in the buyer's value impounds the purchase price, it seems redundant to rescale by the purchase price. The dollar measure does not have this problem; according to it, a takeover that increases shareholder wealth by $\$X$ is equally good for all sizes of buyer and seller. However, it tends to weight large acquisitions heavily.

There is some disagreement about which of these measures is appropriate. Accordingly, although I concentrate on the dollar return throughout the article, I also report estimates using the percentage return and the investment return for the main results. All three measures generally tell the same story.

□ **Relatedness of the buyer and target.** To determine which acquisitions were diversifying moves and which were not, the industries of each buyer and target were identified. Industry classifications were drawn from product-line descriptions in the listing statements and from *Poor's* (later *Standard and Poor's*) *Register of Corporations, Directors, and Executives* for 1968 and 1974 and Dun and Bradstreet's *Million Dollar Directory* for 1971 and 1974. I have four-digit SIC codes for about 85 percent of the targets and the primary two-digit industry for all of them. Many of the corporations operated multiple divisions that *Poor's* and the *Million Dollar Directory* reported separately. Entire product lines were not attributed to the parent in such cases. Subsidiaries were found either with the 1974 *Directory of Corporate Affiliations* or by searching the original volumes.

For most of this article, a takeover is defined to be a "diversification acquisition" if the buyer and the target did not have a two-digit SIC code in common. An acquisition is defined to be "related," then, if the buyer and target shared a two-digit SIC code.

Morck, Shleifer, and Vishny (1990) call a merger related if the buyer and target shared a four-digit SIC among their top three activities. This article's relatedness measure differs from their measure by examining whether the buyer and target were related in *any* activity and by measuring relatedness at the two-digit level. A large diversified corporation like Textron may have done only a small fraction of its business in a given industry, say, zippers. As a result, zippers would not have appeared as one of its top three SICs. If it acquired another zipper maker it should be considered a related acquisition, but this would be classified as unrelated by the Morck, Shleifer, and Vishny measure. This problem is especially acute in my sample because the average target was fairly small (the median target in the final sample had assets worth $20 million).

Second, goods defined at the four-digit level are fairly specific. For example, SICs 3721, 3722, 3723, and 3729 are Aircraft, Aircraft engines and engine parts, Aircraft propellers and propeller parts, and Aircraft parts and auxiliary equipment not elsewhere classified, respectively. It is probably not overstating things to view mergers of firms in these four-digit industries as related. The main advantage of measuring relatedness broadly, as this article does, is that we can be reasonably confident that "unrelated" mergers are in fact unrelated.

If anything, the requirement that firms have a two-digit industry in common is probably too restrictive. For example, SIC 3537 is Industrial trucks, tractors, trailers, and stackers, while SIC 3713 and 3715 are Truck and bus bodies and Truck trailers, respectively. Both relatedness measures would classify mergers of 3537 and 3715 as unrelated. Similarly, it is not hard to imagine production complementarities between Guided missiles and space vehicles (SIC 1925) and Aircraft (SIC 3721), but they are unrelated even with the two-digit definition.

Information was also collected on vertical relationships. First, the flow of goods in the economy in 1972 was identified with the Census Bureau's input-output matrices of the United States. These tables report what fraction of each industry's input was purchased from each industry and what fraction of output was sold to each industry. Industries were classified at roughly the three-digit level (the classification system featured 52 manufacturing industries). Following other researchers, I classified two industries as vertically related if they either bought 5% of their input or sold 5% of their output to each other.[6] This roughly parallels the recent comprehensive study by McGuckin, Nguyen, and Andrews (1992), with the difference that they looked at the input-requirements side but not at the output-sales side.

A merger was classified as vertically related if the buyer and target operated in any SIC industries that were vertically related as defined above. If the only vertical relation was between a manufacturing SIC and a wholesale trade or retail trade SIC, it was not coded as vertically related. The wholesale and retail trade industries are classified so broadly that almost every manufacturing firm would have been classified as vertically related to any wholesale or retail firm.

□ **Retention of the target's management after the merger.** For each acquisition I attempted to ascertain the fate of the target's top managers after the merger. Top management is said to have been "retained" if either (i) the *Wall Street Journal* reported an announcement that the company would continue to be operated under the same management, (ii) the buyer's listing statement indicated the target's management would be retained, or (iii) at least one of the top three executives of the target firm in the year of the merger was still managing the firm three years later or was associated with the acquirer (as either a vice president or director), according to *Poor's* or the *Million Dollar Directory.* According to this definition, 61.8% of the managers in the sample were retained. For a subset of the sample I compared the cases where the buyer announced that the target's management would be retained with *Poor's* and the *Million Dollar Directory* to see if the announcements were credible; I failed to find any discrepancies.

When the *Wall Street Journal* announced that the managers were to be replaced or the same two corporate registers revealed that the managers were different three years later, the management is listed as "replaced." Only 3.5% of the acquisitions fell in this category. This number is drastically lower than the 37.5% reported by Comment (1985) and the 60.9% reported by Martin and McConnell (1991).

One reason for the difference is that both Comment and Martin and McConnell look at turnover of individuals, while this article tries to focus on teams. Martin and McConnell show that many mergers occur when the target's CEO is near retirement. I use the retention variable to capture the buyer's confidence in the target's top management team—not natural

[6] Specifically, the "5% of input" was taken from the commodity-by-industry direct requirements table (Table 3), and the "5% of output" was taken from the use table (Table 1) in Ritz (1979). SIC codes for 1968 were converted to 1972 according to the 1972 *Standard Industrial Classification Manual.*

attrition or departures due to merger-related job redundancies—so as long as any of the top three officers continued to run the company, the management is said to have been retained. This seems to be appropriate for studying the managerial-discipline and managerial-synergy theories.

The fate of management could not be determined for 34.7% of the sample. The main reason was that the target was so small relative to the buyer that its management could not be determined after the merger.

□ **Profitability of the target before the merger.** The target's premerger performance is proxied by its operating profit. Specifically, the target's net operating revenue before interest and federal income taxes, drawn from its income statement, is divided by the book value of its assets, drawn from its balance sheet, as reported in the listing statements:

OPERATING PROFIT

= (NET OPERATING REVENUE)/(BOOK VALUE OF ASSETS).

Target operating profit ranged from a low of −2.87% to a high of 54.7%, with a mean of 17.2%.

It is useful to adjust for the profitability of the target's industry. The "excess" operating profit is calculated by subtracting the average operating profit earned by all firms in the target's primary two-digit industry in the appropriate quarter from the target's operating profit:

EXCESS OPERATING PROFIT

= (OPERATING PROFIT) − (INDUSTRY OPERATING PROFIT).

For example, a firm that had a 12% profit rate in an industry with an average profit rate of 10% had a 2% excess operating profit. Because this measure nets out industry-specific influences, it proxies for the quality of the underlying management and assets and is well-suited for examining the managerial-discipline and managerial-synergy theories. If the market liked discipline it should have reacted positively to acquisitions of firms performing below their industry average. The industry averages were computed from two-digit information in the *Quarterly Financial Report*. The excess operating profit ranged from a low of −14.8% to a high of 44.9%, with a mean of 5.4%.

□ **Price/earnings multiples.** EPS values were collected from *Moody's Industrial Manual* for the years 1967 through 1974 and Compustat for both bidders and publicly traded targets. The analysis below uses primary (undiluted) EPS where earnings are measured after taxes but before extraordinary items and, for comparison, primary EPS after extraordinary items and diluted EPS before extraordinary items. The numbers are EPS before the merger, usually taken from the previous year's income statement. Unfortunately, reported EPS sometimes used year-end shares outstanding and sometimes used average shares.

Prices were drawn from CRSP when possible. Because most of the targets ceased to be traded in 1968, CRSP information on many of them is incomplete; in these cases I use the stock's high price from the previous year as reported in *Moody's*. Care was taken to adjust reported EPS for stock splits that occurred between filing of the income statement and the merger announcement.

□ **Inside directors and family-run firms.** Two variables are considered to control for the effect of corporate governance. One variable is equal to the number of inside directors on the board divided by the number of outside directors, following Baysinger and Butler (1985). The mean insider/outsider ratio was .87 and ranged from a low of .09 to a high of 13. The second variable, which tries to capture Chandler's (1980) idea of family-run firms, is a dummy variable set equal to one if one of the top three executives had the same last name as the company, if the top executive founded the company, or if more than two people with the same name were top executives and directors. According to this definition, 26.6% of acquisitions were made by family-run firms. The information on executives and board members was taken from *Poor's* and the *Million Dollar Directory.* Board members who were listed with a title were defined to be inside directors (this usually included the chairman of the board), while untitled directors were defined to be outside directors.

3. Bidder returns to diversification

■ **Diversification and managerial objectives.** Diversification was the salient fact of the conglomerate merger wave. A primary objective of this article is to document the market's response to determine whether managers diversified to maximize value or to achieve personal goals. If diversifying acquisitions resulted in negative announcement-period returns to acquirers, it can be concluded that diversification was driven by managerial objectives.

Table 1 presents the central evidence on this question. Each column reports the results of a regression of bidder returns on two dummy variables, one for diversification acquisitions and the other for related acquisitions. Of the 199 sample acquisitions, 67 were diversification acquisitions and 132 were related acquisitions. Diversification here implies that the buyer and the target did not have a two-digit SIC code in common. The coefficient estimates represent the mean returns to the given type of takeover. All regressions here and below are corrected for heteroskedasticity using White standard errors.

Column (1) presents a regression using the dollar-return measure, which, as is argued in the previous section, is the best way to measure the consequences to bidder shareholders. The main finding is that the return to a diversification acquisition was significantly positive. When bidders made a diversification acquisition, on average their shareholders enjoyed an $11.0 million value increase in value after correcting for market movements. This rejects the hypothesis that diversification hurt shareholders and is thus inconsistent with the idea that diversification was driven by managerial objectives.

In contrast, bidders who made related acquisitions cost their shareholders $6.4 million on average, statistically significant at the 10% level. If anything, it appears that managerial objectives were driving horizontal expansion during the conglomerate merger wave. The hypothesis that the market's reaction to diversification and related acquisitions was the same can be rejected at better than the 1% level, suggesting that there was a market "premium" to diversification.

TABLE 1 Mean Bidder Returns to Diversification and Related Acquisitions

Type of Acquisition	(1)	(2)	(3)	(4)
Diversification	11.036**	1.233**	61.86	12.95
	(4.960)	(.673)	(39.41)	(12.79)
Related	−6.380***	.354	−34.09***	−36.72
	(3.422)	(.662)	(20.57)	(28.58)
p-value for the hypothesis that coefficients are equal	.004	.351	.031	.113
Observations	199	199	199	71

Note: Each column in this table reports coefficient estimates from a regression of bidder returns on two dummy variables, one for diversification and one for related acquisitions. A merger is coded "diversification" if the buyer and target did not have a two-digit SIC code in common, otherwise it is coded "related." The regressions are corrected for heteroskedasticity using White standard errors. The dependent variables are the dollar return (1), percentage return (2), dollar return divided by the book value of target assets (3), and dollar return divided by target stock value (4).

** Significant at the 5% level.

*** Significant at the 10% level.

To check the robustness of the dollar-return measure, column (2) reports estimates for the same regression using the percentage-return measure. Under this measure, bidder stock prices increased 1.2% over the announcement period after adjusting for market movements when they made diversification acquisitions. This value is significant at the 5% level. Thus, the hypothesis that bidder shareholders suffered from diversification can be rejected with the percentage-return measure as well. The return to a related acquisition under this measure was positive and cannot be statistically distinguished from zero.

Column (3) reports regression estimates using a return measure similar to Morck, Shleifer, and Vishny's (1990) investment return—the dollar return divided by the book value of the target's assets. The big limitation of this measure is that the book value of target assets is only tenuously related to the purchase price. The effect of this should be to introduce additional noise, making the estimates less precise. Indeed, although the bidder return to diversification is still estimated to have been positive with this measure, the standard error is too large for the estimate to achieve statistical significance. Even so, the return to a diversification acquisition was larger than the return to a related acquisition at the 5% level.

Column (4) reports estimates for the regression using a measure virtually identical to Morck, Shleifer, and Vishny's investment return—the dollar return divided by the market value of the target's stock five days after the announcement. Because most of the targets were not publicly traded, the denominator of this return measure can be computed for only 71 observations. Nevertheless, the general pattern is the same: bidders earned positive returns when they diversified and negative returns when they bought in their own industry. The coefficients are not too far from being statistically different ($p = .113$).

A consistent return pattern is visible no matter how returns are measured: the market liked diversification. Bidders who made diversification acquisitions helped their shareholders, and the market attached a premium to diversification acquisitions. There is no evidence for the theory that diversification was driven by managerial objectives and pursued at shareholder expense.[7]

Some theoretical work suggests that there may be opportunities for value creation in vertical mergers that are not present in other mergers. It is natural to ask if the observed positive reaction to diversification mergers is driven by vertical diversification. Table 2 gives evidence on this question. In this table and all subsequent tables, bidder returns are measured with the dollar measure.

As in Table 1, the regression column reports coefficient estimates of bidder dollar returns on dummy variables. Separate dummies are included for diversification acquisitions, where the buyer and target operated in vertically related industries, and "pure" diversification, where there was no apparent vertical or horizontal link between the buyer and seller. In addition, the related acquisitions are broken down into those where the buyer and target had a three-digit SIC code in common[8] and those where they had only a two-digit SIC code in common. Presumably, the former were more closely related than the latter. The last three columns of the table report the chi-squared statistic for tests of equality between the coefficients. For example, the chi-squared statistic for the hypothesis that the return to pure diversification and vertical diversification was the same is .073, which is not statistically significant.

---

[7] Elgers and Clark (1980) find that returns to conglomerate acquirers exceeded returns to nonconglomerate acquirers in the 1957–1975 period, the most analogous evidence. They do not distinguish between related and unrelated acquisitions, and half of their sample lies outside the conglomerate merger wave. In addition, they consider only acquisitions where the buyer made no other takeovers in the previous and subsequent two years, in effect deleting all the conglomerating acquisitions. Related estimates have been made in the strategy literature, for example, Seth (1990).

[8] More precisely, the 52 approximately three-digit industries from the input-output tables are used rather than true three-digit industries.

TABLE 2 Mean Bidder Returns to Subdivided Diversification and Related Acquisitions

Type of Acquisition	Regression	Diversification, Vertical	Related, 2-digit	Related, 3-digit
Diversification, pure	9.774	.073	4.952**	4.152**
(N = 36)	(6.118)			
Diversification, vertical	12.502	—	4.958**	3.839***
(N = 31)	(8.019)			
Related, 2-digit	−13.409	—	—	.869
(N = 24)	(8.433)			
Related, 3-digit	−4.819	—	—	—
(N = 108)	(3.722)			

Note: The Regression column reports coefficient estimates from a regression of bidder dollar returns on four dummy variables, one each for pure diversification, vertical diversification, related (2-digit), and related (3-digit). A merger is coded pure diversification if the buyer and target did not have a two-digit SIC code in common and were not vertically related, vertical diversification if they did not have a two-digit SIC code in common but had SIC codes in vertically related industries, related (2-digit) if they had a two-digit SIC code but not a three-digit SIC code in common, and related (3-digit) if they had a three-digit SIC code in common. N is the number of mergers of a given type. The regression is corrected for heteroskedasticity using White standard errors. The regression has 199 observations. The table also reports the chi-squared values for tests of equality between coefficients.

** Significant at the 5% level.

*** Significant at the 10% level.

The estimates indicate that the market's enthusiasm for diversification extended to both vertical and pure diversification—as long as the bidder was entering a new industry, the market reacted favorably. The return to both types of diversification acquisition was positive, and the coefficients are not statistically different from each other. Both types of diversification acquisition earned bidder shareholders significantly greater returns than both types of related acquisition. In short, the positive return to diversification was not driven by vertical relations. It can also be seen that both of the related-acquisition coefficients are negative, and they cannot be statistically distinguished from each other. Neither the diversification nor the related subdivisions add much information.

Morck, Shleifer, and Vishny report that bidder returns to diversification acquisitions were significantly negative in 1980–1987 and not different from zero in 1975–1979. Their evidence supports the idea that deconglomeration was beneficial to shareholders. Table 3 pieces together a long view of the returns to diversification from their estimates and the estimates above. For each of the three time periods it is reported whether returns were statistically positive, negative, or not different from zero for related and unrelated acquisitions. The table documents what appears to be a dramatic reversal in the market's reaction to diversification over the last two decades. In the late 1960s and early 1970s the market looked favorably on diversification. By the late 1970s it was indifferent. In the 1980s it reacted negatively to unrelated acquisitions. I offer this as a puzzle awaiting resolution, and make some speculative comments regarding it in the conclusion.

□ **The diversification premium.** The preceding section establishes that the market reacted favorably to diversification acquisitions. This section investigates whether the market liked diversification per se, or if the buyers who made these acquisitions were just doing something better. For example, did diversifying buyers choose better-run targets?

One way to address this question is to determine if the firms that made diversifying acquisitions and their targets were different from the firms that made related acquisitions and their targets. Table 4 presents statistical summaries of diversification and related mergers. The mean value of variables characterizing the acquirer and the target are calculated for the sample of diversification mergers and the sample of related mergers, and the t-value is given for the test that the means are the same.

TABLE 3 Summary of Bidder Returns to Diversification over Time

Period	Diversification Return	Related Return	Significant Difference?	Source
1968–1974 ($N = 199$)	*POSITIVE*	*ZERO*	Yes	This article
1975–1979 ($N = 154$)	*ZERO*	*ZERO*	No	MSV
1980–1987 ($N = 172$)	*NEGATIVE*	*ZERO*	Yes	MSV

Note: This table reports the returns to acquirers when they bought related and unrelated firms using the results in Morck, Shleifer, and Vishny (1990) (MSV) and this article. "*POSITIVE*" indicates the average return was positive and statistically different from zero at the 5% level; "*NEGATIVE*" indicates it was negative and statistically different from zero; "*ZERO*" indicates it was not statistically different from zero. The sample sizes are indicated beneath the years.

Consider first the characteristics of targets. Both diversifying and horizontal buyers preferred to buy profitable firms. The average operating profit for targets of both types of acquisition was 17%, more than 5% in excess of the target's industry average. The popularity of high-profit targets argues against the importance of a managerial-discipline motive for both types of acquisition and in favor of a managerial-synergy motive. Managerial-discipline takeovers should have been directed at low-profit firms, which were to be cleaned up and restored to profitability. Managerial-synergy takeovers should have been directed at high-profit firms because synergy-motivated managers were looking for good partners (Matsusaka, 1993).

A second variable linked to the managerial-discipline and managerial-synergy theories is whether or not the target's management was retained. The quality of management is a crucial consideration in a merger motivated by managerial synergies. Under the synergy hypothesis, top management, as a valuable resource, was retained after a merger. The discipline hypothesis predicts that target managers were replaced.

TABLE 4 Mean Characteristics of Diversification and Related Acquisitions

Variable	Diversification	Related	t-value
Target operating profit	17.007	17.312	.228
	(1.001)	(.891)	
Target excess operating profit	5.726	5.257	.347
	(1.017)	(.891)	
Dummy = 1 if the target's management was retained after the merger	.872	.988	2.299**
	(.049)	(.012)	
Insiders/outsiders on bidder's board	.807	.882	.524
	(.096)	(.106)	
Dummy = 1 if bidder was family-run	.299	.250	.724
	(.056)	(.038)	

Note: This table reports the mean value of each variable for diversification and related acquisitions. In parentheses below each mean is the standard error of the estimate. The rightmost column gives the t-value for the test of equality between the means. There are 67 diversification observations and 132 related observations for all variables except managerial retention, for which there are 47 diversification observations and 83 related observations. A merger is coded "diversification" if the buyer and seller did not have a two-digit SIC code in common.

** Significant at the 5% level.

Table 4 reveals that firms which bought in their own industry were more likely to retain target management, a difference significant at the 5% level. This suggests that managerial discipline may have been more important in diversification acquisitions, although it should be noted that removal of target management was rare in either case; 87.2% of target management teams in diversification takeovers and 98.8% in related takeovers were retained. Again, managerial discipline does not appear to have been an important factor in most of these takeovers.

Turning to bidder characteristics, it can be seen that related buyers tended to have higher insider/outsider ratios and were less likely to be family-run. However, neither of these differences is significant. As far as this set of variables goes, acquisitions by diversifiers were basically the same as horizontal acquisitions, except when it came to the fate of target management.

It is not possible to test directly whether the positive return to diversification is a response to diversification per se or whether diversification was a proxy for some other variable. But Table 5 addresses the related issue of the diversification premium, that is, the premium bidders enjoyed from diversification compared to related acquisitions. The table presents a series of regressions where the dependent variable is the bidder dollar return. A dummy variable equal to one for diversifying acquisitions is included as an explanatory variable, and a series of other explanatory variables is then introduced. If the diversification premium vanishes when a control variable is included, it can be concluded that the diversification premium is actually a proxy for the control variable.

Both the managerial-discipline and managerial-synergy theories offer an explanation for the diversification premium and guide the choice of controls. The first variable examined is the target's premerger profitability. Column (1) presents a regression including the diversification dummy, a constant, and the target's operating profit. Column (2) is the same except that the target's excess operating profit is used to measure profitability. In both

TABLE 5 **Regressions of Bidder Returns on Diversification, Target Characteristics, and Buyer Characteristics**

Variable	(1)	(2)	(3)	(4)	(5)	(6)
Constant	−8.771	−7.207***	−23.750*	−1.259	−18.508***	−20.189**
	(7.004)	(3.974)	(8.813)	(3.538)	(11.047)	(9.344)
Dummy = 1 if	17.459*	17.343*	13.734***	11.103***	13.502***	13.483***
diversification	(6.040)	(5.984)	(7.032)	(6.710)	(7.053)	(7.039)
Target operating profit	.138	—	—	—	−.143	—
	(.314)				(.341)	
Target excess operating profit	—	.157	—	—	—	−.078
		(.293)				(.325)
Dummy = 1 if the target's	—	—	22.765*	—	23.831*	23.383*
management was retained			(8.387)		(8.801)	(8.897)
Insiders/outsiders on bidder's	—	—	—	—	−5.138*	−5.146*
board					(2.010)	(1.969)
Dummy = 1 if the bidder	—	—	—	—	3.980	4.205
was family-run					(5.529)	(5.629)
R^2	.042	.042	.043	.023	.077	.076
Observations	199	199	130	130	130	130

Note: Each column of the table reports coefficient estimates of a regression where bidder dollar returns are the dependent variable. Standard errors are in parentheses beneath each estimate. Regressions are corrected for heteroskedasticity using White standard errors. A merger is coded "diversification" if the buyer and seller did not have a two-digit SIC code in common.

* Significant at the 1% level.

** Significant at the 5% level.

*** Significant at the 10% level.

regressions the diversification premium remains and is significant at the 1% level. Target profitability does not appear to affect the bidder's return. The R^2's are low in these and the following regressions, in part because most of the explanatory variables are dummies while the dependent variable is continuous.

The second variable examined is managerial retention. Column (3) presents a regression that includes a dummy variable equal to one if the target's management was retained after the merger and zero if the management was removed. Because the fate of the target's management could not be determined in 69 cases, the number of observations falls to 130.

In contrast to target profitability, the managerial-retention variable is a highly significant predictor of bidder announcement-period returns. The coefficient estimate indicates that shareholder value rose $22.8 million more for bidders who retained target management compared to bidders who removed target management. Evidently the market preferred that target managers continue to run their companies.

When the managerial-retention variable is included, the diversification premium falls to $13.7 million but remains significantly greater than zero. There is still a diversification effect after controlling for the fate of the target's management. A natural question is whether the premium is lower in regression (3) because of the inclusion of the managerial-retention variable or because of the 69 deleted observations.

Column (4) reports a regression designed to answer this question. The regression is run on the same 130 observations used in column (3), but the managerial-retention variable is excluded. A statistically significant diversification premium can be observed, but it is smaller than in regressions (1) and (2). This implies that the smaller premium in regression (3) is a consequence of the managerial-retention sample, not the managerial-retention variable. If anything, it appears that the diversification premium is larger after controlling for the fate of management.

Columns (5) and (6) present regressions that include both target profitability and managerial retention. Column (5) uses target operating profit and column (6) uses excess operating profit. In addition, the two governance controls are included. These controls are not linked to theories of diversification but to theories of acquisition in general, and they are not expected to remove the diversification effect.[9]

It can be seen that a positive and significant diversification premium remains even after the controls are included. The additional controls also have no effect on the managerial-retention variable. The market's preference for retention of target management remains large and statistically significant. Another interesting finding is that the market assessed a penalty to bidders whose boards were dominated by inside directors. This is consistent with the idea that insider-dominated boards represent entrenched managers who are able to pursue acquisitions for reasons other than maximization of shareholder value.

To summarize, this section investigates whether there was a premium to diversification per se, or if diversifying bidders were simply doing something else the market liked. I examine a set of variables describing the target and the buyer that, while not exhaustive, is closely linked to factors that theory suggests might be driving bidder returns. I show that diversification and related mergers were similar, and that a diversification premium remains even after controlling for these variables. Thus, until additional variables are explored it can be tentatively concluded that the market was favorably disposed to diversification per se.

□ **Which diversification acquisitions did the market like best?** The regressions in Table 5 suggest that the market subscribed to a managerial-synergy theory and rejected a managerial-

[9] The regressions were also estimated with controls for whether the acquisition was hostile or made by a white knight, and for choice of accounting technique (pooling versus purchase). Neither variable had a significant effect, so for ease of exposition they are not included in the final regressions.

discipline theory. However, the regressions lump together diversification and related acquisitions. Perhaps the market used different criteria to evaluate the two types of takeovers.

Table 6 presents a set of regressions addressed to the question "What kind of diversification acquisition did the market like best?" Columns (1)–(4) present the usual regressions for the subsample of diversification acquisitions. Columns (1) and (2) include target profitability and the governance variables. The managerial-retention variable is added to the regressions in columns (3) and (4), which are reported separately because of the smaller managerial-retention sample size.

The only variable that has a statistically significant effect on the return to diversification acquisitions is managerial retention. As in the full regressions, retention of target management is associated with an announcement-period premium to bidder shareholders in excess of $20 million. This is strong evidence that the market evaluated diversification through the lens of a managerial-synergy theory, not a managerial-discipline theory. The market's reaction to a diversification announcement was not significantly related to the insider/outsider ratio or the presence of family influences. It cannot be determined whether the effect is absent for diversification or the sample size is too small to detect it. Schipper and Thompson (1983) have given evidence that the market reacted to announcements of acquisition *programs;* if the diversifiers were the firms that announced acquisition programs, then we might expect to see bidder-specific factors taken into account when the program was announced, so that the response to actual acquisitions depended only on target-specific factors.

Columns (5) and (6) are the analogs to columns (1) and (2) for related acquisitions. It is not possible to run these regressions including the managerial-retention variable because there is only one case of a related acquisition where target management was removed. This attenuates but does not completely negate what can be learned about how the market evaluated related acquisitions.

Columns (5) and (6) contain an interesting finding. As opposed to diversification acquisitions, the bidder return to a horizontal acquisition was heavily influenced by the

TABLE 6 Explaining Bidder Returns to Diversification and Related Acquisitions

	Diversification				Related	
Variable	(1)	(2)	(3)	(4)	(5)	(6)
Constant	1.534	11.596***	−26.248	−12.513	−4.839	−5.482
	(11.605)	(6.398)	(17.570)	(9.425)	(7.983)	(4.758)
Target operating profit	.788	—	1.122	—	−.014	—
	(.642)		(.891)		(.344)	
Target excess operating profit	—	.583	—	.629	—	.098
		(.578)		(.851)		(.331)
Dummy = 1 if the target's management was retained	—	—	21.505**	23.891**	—	—
			(9.747)	(9.924)		
Insiders/outsiders on bidder's board	−5.646	−5.313	.020	.199	−5.511*	−5.613*
	(5.321)	(5.519)	(8.092)	(8.378)	(1.753)	(1.687)
Dummy = 1 if the bidder was family-run	2.193	1.299	−9.991	−10.068	14.247**	14.143*
	(11.264)	(11.535)	(10.826)	(11.357)	(6.306)	(6.296)
R^2	.029	.018	.102	.069	.042	.042
Observations	67	67	47	47	132	132

Note: Each column of the table reports coefficient estimates of a regression where bidder dollar returns are the dependent variable. Standard errors are in parentheses beneath each estimate. Regressions are corrected for heteroskedasticity using White standard errors. A merger is coded "diversification" if the buyer and seller did not have a two-digit SIC code in common.

* Significant at the 1% level.

** Significant at the 5% level.

*** Significant at the 10% level.

bidder's governance. On average, insider-dominated firms imposed $5.5-million costs on their shareholders when they announced acquisitions. The market responded positively to family-run firms, resulting in $14-million value increases from their acquisitions. A possible reason the market liked horizontal acquisitions by family-run firms is that a large fraction of the equity of these firms remained in the hands of top management or relatives of top management, reducing agency problems. While intriguing, without data on actual equity holdings this is speculation.

Bearing in mind the data contraints, Table 6 suggests that the market's reaction to an acquisition announcement during the conglomerate merger wave can be summarized in the following way. First, diversification acquisitions were evaluated on the basis of how they were operationalized—if management was retained, consistent with a managerial-synergy motive, the market reaction was positive. Second, related acquisitions were evaluated on the basis of the buyer—insider-dominated buyers were disliked and family-run firms were favored.

4. EPS manipulation

■ The basic idea behind EPS manipulation can be seen with an example. Suppose firm A has $1 million in earnings, 1 million shares outstanding, and a price of $20. Its EPS is $1.00. Firm B has $1 million in earnings, 1 million shares outstanding, and a price of $10. Firm A has a P/E of 20 and firm B has a P/E of 10. Firm A plays the game by buying firm B. Firm A exchanges one of its shares for two of firm B's, increasing its outstanding shares to 1.5 million. However, its total earnings rise to $2 million, for a new EPS of $1.33. If investors watch EPS, so the argument goes, they observe a 33% increase and bid up the price of firm A. Lynch (1971) provides an extensive discussion of this idea and useful background information. He cites the CEOs of "Automatic" Sprinkler, Whittaker, City Investing, and TRW as saying they would never make acquisitions that diluted EPS. In effect, they claimed never to buy firms with higher P/Es than their own.

Table 7 reports the mean P/E ratios for the 111 observations where target price data was available (with two exceptions, the rest of the targets were privately owned). The table reports mean bidder P/E ratios, mean target P/E ratios, and the fraction of acquisitions where the bidder's P/E exceeded the target's P/E.

The numbers are reported with three different measures of EPS. Measure (a) is earnings per common share before extraordinary items, measure (b) is earnings per common share after extraordinary items, and measure (c) is earnings before extraordinary items assuming full conversion of common stock equivalent securities (fully diluted EPS). The price of the buyer is the market price five days before the acquisition announcement. The target's price is the market price five days after the announcement; this is the relevant price for computing the purchase P/E. When I could not find the target's price on this day (usually because it traded over the counter), I used instead its high price for the previous year. Comparing the previous year's high price with the five-day-later market price for the subsample where both are available indicates this is not a bad approximation. At any rate, the results do not change if the previous year's low or average price is used instead.

The first thing to note is that diversification buyers were more willing to dilute EPS than horizontal buyers. Bidder P/E ratios exceeded target P/E ratios in roughly 50% of the diversification acquisitions and over 70% of the related acquisitions. This difference is statistically significant.

The reason for this pattern was that targets of related takeovers had significantly lower P/E ratios (the mean was roughly 15) than targets of diversification takeovers (the mean was roughly 21). Bidder P/E ratios averaged about 20 for both related and diversification acquisitions. This is not the pattern that would be predicted by the EPS-bootstrapping explanation for conglomeration. Taking related acquisitions as the normal case, the boot-

TABLE 7 Mean P/E Ratios for Diversification and Related Acquisitions

Variable	Diversification	Related	*t*-value
Dummy = 1 if bidder P/E > target P/E (a)	.528 (.084)	.720 (.052)	1.937***
Dummy = 1 if bidder P/E > target P/E (b)	.556 (.084)	.733 (.051)	1.805***
Dummy = 1 if bidder P/E > buyer P/E (c)	.472 (.084)	.773 (.049)	3.091*
Bidder P/E (a)	19.654 (1.464)	21.957 (1.907)	.958
Bidder P/E (b)	20.660 (1.631)	22.697 (1.900)	.813
Bidder P/E (c)	19.354 (1.479)	20.748 (1.216)	.728
Target P/E (a)	21.000 (2.201)	15.447 (.881)	2.342**
Target P/E (b)	21.000 (2.201)	15.541 (.886)	2.301**
Target P/E (c)	20.959 (2.190)	15.045 (.852)	2.517*

Note: This table reports the mean value of each variable for diversification and related acquisitions. In parentheses below each mean is the standard error of the estimate. EPS are calculated as follows: (a) primary earnings before extraordinary items, (b) diluted earnings before extraordinary items, and (c) primary earnings after extraordinary items. The rightmost column gives the *t*-value for the test of equality between the means. There are 36 diversification observations and 75 related observations. A merger is coded "diversification" if the buyer and seller did not have a two-digit SIC code in common.

* Significant at the 1% level.

** Significant at the 5% level.

*** Significant at the 10% level.

strapping explanation predicts that firms that bought outside their industries had higher P/E ratios than firms that bought within their own industries, and were less likely to buy firms with high P/E ratios.

But ultimately the proof is in the pudding: Did bidders who played the bootstrapping game increase the price of their stock? Table 8 reports a set of regressions to answer this. Columns (1)–(3) report regressions of bidder dollar returns on two dummy variables. One dummy is for acquisitions where the bidder's P/E exceeded the target's P/E—the candidate bootstrappers—and the other is for acquisitions that diluted bidder EPS. According to the

TABLE 8 Bidder Returns Regressed on Relative P/E Dummies

Variable	(1)	(2)	(3)	Diversification (4)	Related (5)
Dummy = 1 if bidder P/E was greater than target P/E	−3.549 (4.656)	−3.595 (4.533)	−3.493 (4.583)	5.611 (4.476)	−6.773 (6.033)
Dummy = 1 if bidder P/E was less than or equal to target P/E	4.125 (6.027)	4.647 (6.345)	4.434 (6.194)	11.389 (11.884)	−1.756 (4.764)
p-value for the hypothesis that coefficients are equal	.314	.291	.304	.649	.514
Observations	111	111	111	36	75

Note: Each column of the table reports coefficient estimates of a regression of bidder dollar returns on two dummy variables, one if the bidder's P/E was greater than the target's P/E, and the other if it was less than or equal to the target's P/E. Standard errors are in parentheses beneath each estimate. Regressions are corrected for heteroskedasticity using White standard errors.

bootstrapping theory, the candidate bootstrappers should have experienced positive returns while the diluters experienced negative returns. Column (1) measures EPS as primary earnings before extraordinary items, column (2) uses primary earnings after extraordinary items, and column (3) uses diluted earnings before extraordinary items (as in Table 7).

There is no evidence in support of the bootstrapping explanation. In all three regressions, candidate bootstrappers earned negative returns while diluters earned positive returns, contrary to predictions. Bidders who bought firms with lower P/E ratios than their own lost about \$3.5 million on average. Bidders who bought firms with higher P/E ratios than their own gained over \$4.1 million on average. None of the coefficients is significantly different from zero, nor can they be distinguished from each other. Because the results are nowhere significant it is not possible to reject the bootstrapping hypothesis in a statistical sense, but it appears to have no explanatory power.

It is possible that EPS manipulation might have some explanatory power for diversification acquisitions that cannot be detected in the full sample (or there may be an effect only for the related acquisitions). Columns (4) and (5) investigate this possibility by running the regressions separately for the diversification and related samples. In these regressions EPS is primary earnings before extraordinary items. In both cases the mean returns are inconsistent with the hypothesis that EPS bootstrapping increased bidder value. Indeed, it is still the case that acquisitions which diluted EPS were more beneficial to bidder shareholders than acquisitions which inflated EPS, although again the coefficients are not statistically different at conventional levels of significance.

5. Managerial discipline and managerial synergy

■ The regressions in the preceding sections suggest that the market did not reward bidders who made acquisitions in order to discipline target management. This is a surprising finding, to some extent, in light of the academic literature's emphasis on discipline as a value-creating takeover motive.

In this section I address the managerial-discipline theory more directly by focusing on takeovers of publicly traded firms. It is not always appreciated that the managerial-discipline theory would seem to apply only to acquisitions of publicly traded firms. The heart of the managerial-discipline theory is the idea that shareholders may fail to discipline managers because of free-riding problems (the basic idea goes back to Berle and Means (1968)). In a firm with many shareholders and diffuse ownership, the argument goes, each individual captures only a fraction of the benefit to disciplining managers and so is willing to pay only a fraction of the monitoring and enforcing cost. In such a situation it may pay for an outside investor to buy a majority of the firm's stock and effect a change in management. The conditions that lead to a breakdown in shareholder monitoring in public companies are not present in private companies, which tend to have concentrated ownership and a small number of shareholders. If there are managerial-discipline effects, then, they will be observed only in the subsample of publicly traded targets.

Following this logic, this section looks for systematic differences between acquisitions of public and private targets that might support the managerial-discipline theory. Targets are defined to be public if they were traded on the NYSE, AMEX, a regional exchange, or over the counter. The primary source was *Moody's Industrial Manual.* Additional public firms were identified from the *Wall Street Journal* and the listing statements. A decision was made to classify targets that were divisions or subsidiaries of another company as private. They were similar to private firms in two respects: first, they were not subject to a hostile takeover, and second, they had few (usually only one) shareholders.

Table 9 presents mean target and buyer characteristics for takeovers of public and private firms. The t-value is reported for the test of equality between means. The managerial-discipline theory predicts that public targets had low profits and their managers were unlikely

TABLE 9 **Mean Characteristics of Public and Private Acquisitions**

Variable	Public Target	Private Target	t-value
Target operating profit	16.578	18.037	1.043
	(.843)	(1.117)	
Target excess operating profit	4.668	6.396	1.226
	(.828)	(1.140)	
Dummy = 1 if the target's management was retained	.943	.953	.244
	(.025)	(.032)	
Insiders/outsiders on bidder's board	.911	.785	.872
	(.123)	(.077)	
Dummy = 1 if bidder was family-run	.212	.337	1.944***
	(.039)	(.051)	
Dummy = 1 if diversification	.319	.360	.601
	(.044)	(.052)	
Mean bidder dollar return in millions	−.549	−.475	.013
	(3.689)	(4.615)	

Note: This table reports the mean value of each variable for diversification and related acquisitions. In parentheses below each mean is the standard error of the estimate. The rightmost column gives the t-value for the test of equality between the means. There are 113 public-target observations and 86 private-target observations for all variables except managerial retention, for which there are 87 public-target observations and 43 private-target observations. A merger is coded "diversification" if the buyer and seller did not have a two-digit SIC code in common.

*** Significant at the 10% level.

to be retained, at least compared to private targets. The mean operating profit, excess operating profit, and rate of managerial retention all conform to this pattern, but none of the public-private means are significantly different from each other. Moreover, even within the class of public targets, buyers tended to purchase highly profitable firms (the mean excess operating profit was 4.7%) and rarely removed target management (only 5.7% were removed).

The firms that bought public targets had higher insider/outsider ratios on average, and fewer of them were family-run. The family-run difference is significant at the 10% level, but the insider/outsider difference is not significant at conventional levels. The table also shows that private targets were more often involved in diversification acquisitions than public targets were, but again the difference is not significant. Finally, the mean announcement-period returns to acquisitions of both target types were not significantly different from zero or each other. The impression left by Table 9 is more one of similarity between public and private takeovers than difference.

Table 10 reports a set of regressions in which, as above, the dependent variable is the bidder dollar return. The regressions in columns (1)–(3) are run on only the public-target subsample, which should provide a more congenial environment for detection of managerial-discipline effects. A diversification dummy is included in all regressions as a control because the preceding sections show that it is an important independent factor contributing to the bidder return. Only the excess-operating-profit measure of target profitability is included—both measures lead to the same conclusions.

The regression reported in column (1) includes excess operating profits and the controls. Discipline targets should have had low profits, so if the market liked discipline-motivated buyers there should be a negative coefficient on this variable. The estimated coefficient is negative, but it is quantitatively trivial and statistically insignificant.

The regression reported in column (2) adds managerial retention to the list of explanatory variables. This is done in a separate regression because of the reduction in sample size when managerial retention is included. If the market liked managerial discipline, then the coefficient on managerial retention should be negative. To the contrary, the managerial-retention coefficient is large and significantly greater than zero at the 5% level. The market

TABLE 10 **Bidder Returns from Acquisitions of Publicly Traded Targets**

Variable	(1)	(2)	(3)	(4)
Constant	.166	−20.345***	−20.711***	−20.647**
	(5.903)	(11.581)	(11.279)	(9.439)
Target excess operating profit	−.079	−.230	—	—
	(.376)	(.370)		
Dummy = 1 if the target's management was retained	—	25.284**	—	—
		(11.476)		
Dummy = 1 if target's management was retained and excess profit was greater than zero	—	—	22.914**	22.009*
			(11.047)	(9.097)
Dummy = 1 if target's management was retained and excess profit was less than zero	—	—	28.572**	26.100**
			(14.330)	(11.011)
Dummy = 1 if diversification	12.007	11.500	11.766	13.939***
	(7.551)	(8.547)	(8.491)	(7.134)
Insider/outsiders on bidder's board	−6.152*	−6.633*	−6.592*	−5.023*
	(1.155)	(1.314)	(1.255)	(2.039)
Dummy = 1 if the bidder was family-run	6.747	11.562	11.152	4.314
	(6.910)	(7.441)	(7.723)	(5.704)
R^2	.066	.108	.110	.078
Observations	113	87	87	130

Note: Each column of the table reports coefficient estimates of a regression where bidder dollar returns are the dependent variable. Standard errors are in parentheses beneath each estimate. Regressions are corrected for heteroskedasticity using White standard errors. Columns (1)–(3) include only acquisitions of public targets while column (4) includes acquisitions of public and private targets. A merger is coded "diversification" if the buyer and seller did not have a two-digit SIC code in common.

* Significant at the 1% level.

** Significant at the 5% level.

*** Significant at the 10% level.

clearly preferred that target management be retained, even for public targets. This finding leaves little to commend the managerial-discipline theory. Rather, it adds to the support for the managerial-synergy theory. The coefficient on excess operating profit remains insignificant.

There is one more possibility to consider. Mergers where the target firm was underperforming its industry, that is, where its excess profit was less than zero and where the target's managers were subsequently removed, were the most likely to be intended to discipline bad managers. If the market subscribed to the discipline theory, such takeovers should have earned acquirer shareholders positive announcement-period returns. Suppose the market liked managerial discipline when the target was doing poorly and liked managerial synergy when the target was doing well. If true, then the regressions in columns (1) and (2), which treat all managerial retention the same, would not be able to detect a managerial-discipline effect.

Column (3) reports a regression that allows for this possibility. In the regression, two managerial-retention dummies are included, one for targets whose excess operating profit was positive and one for targets whose excess operating profits were negative. This comes close to providing an ideal environment for observation of a positive market response to managerial discipline. If the market liked bidders who replaced managers of poorly performing firms, then the coefficient on managerial retention for low-profit firms should be negative. As can be seen, even this attempt to isolate a managerial-discipline effect meets with failure. The coefficient of interest is positive and significant at the 5% level. The message is clearly that the market liked retention of target management regardless of whether the target was profitable or losing money. The conclusion that the market rewarded managerial retention and punished managerial removal appears to be fairly robust. The last column

(4) reports the same regression for the full (public and private) sample. The results are unchanged.

These estimates argue against the managerial-discipline theory and in favor of the synergy theory. They show that the market disliked buyers who removed target management. Whether this pattern holds for other time periods remains to be seen. Lang, Stulz, and Walkling (1989) report positive event-window returns for bidders who acquired a target with a low Tobin's Q, which they argue is a proxy for management quality, and they take this as evidence for the managerial-discipline hypothesis. The results from Table 10 lead to a different conclusion and suggest that a low Q may not mean that management was bad.

The magnitudes of the managerial-retention coefficients indicate that bidders who replaced target management tended to reduce their shareholders' value. Why would they do this? One explanation is that they were pursuing managerial objectives, perhaps empire building. A second possibility is that they overpaid, or almost equivalently, that they overestimated their own ability to make improvements in the target, at least in the eyes of the market. This is consistent with the hubris hypothesis proposed by Roll (1986). It may be that the negative returns to related mergers on the whole are attributable to hubris rather than empire building.

6. Conclusion

■ The rise and (possible) decline of corporate diversification is one of the major business developments of the last 50 years. Even so, our understanding of the motives and consequences of diversification is very incomplete. This article makes three contributions to the study of diversification: it directly tests and refutes one popular explanation for the conglomerate merger wave, it provides some indirect evidence on three other explanations, and it presents an empirical puzzle concerning the market's changing sentiments over time.

The main finding is that buyers earned significantly positive announcement-period returns during the conglomerate merger wave when they made diversifying acquisitions. The hypothesis that conglomerates were driven by empire building or some other managerial objective can be rejected because such explanations imply value decreases to unrelated acquisitions. The simple view that the 1980s "bust-ups" were a corrective to past managerial excesses is untenable.

It appears the market expected diversification to increase value. A natural question is, "What did the market think would be the source of the value increase?" The evidence suggests the market was following a managerial-synergy theory and not a managerial-discipline theory: buyers who retained target management earned the highest returns.

Another explanation of the conglomerate merger wave is that mergers were driven by an accounting gimmick rather than anticipated efficiencies. According to this explanation, investors watched EPS; when they saw EPS go up they bid up the price of the stock. Conglomerates, according to this argument, tended to buy companies with lower P/E ratios than their own in order to increase their EPS and boost their stock prices. I find no evidence that firms which inflated EPS in this way earned positive returns.

The empirical puzzle is the time pattern of investor sentiment regarding diversification (Table 3). In conjunction with the estimates of Morck, Shleifer, and Vishny (1990), it can be seen that buyers who diversified earned significantly positive returns in 1968–1974, approximately zero returns in 1975–1979, and significantly negative returns in 1980–1987. There is a dramatic reversal in market sentiment over the last 20 years. This is an interesting empirical finding that begs explanation. By way of concluding, I sketch out three possible explanations that would seem to be worth pursuing.

First, it may be that something in the world changed between the 1960s and the 1980s. Some have pointed to antitrust regimes—there was tight enforcement in the 1960s and lax enforcement in the 1980s under the Reagan administration. According to this explanation, diversification was always a second-best choice, but in the constrained world of the 1960s it was the best available option (Shleifer and Vishny, 1991). Another suggested change is financial innovation. One theory of conglomerates is that they served to internalize certain capital market transactions. If capital markets are now much improved, then the need for businesses to internalize them may be gone (Comment and Jarrell, 1991). Still others have pointed to "globalization" as a factor, although the links between this and the return to unrelated acquisitions have yet to be clearly spelled out.

A second explanation for the change in market sentiment has to do with first-mover advantages and learning. It may be that the early conglomerators earned significantly positive returns simply because they were first; they may have captured some rents to organizational innovation that were subsequently driven to zero. Perhaps the men who built the first conglomerates had a special talent for diversification, which the market rewarded, but they were followed by a second wave of imitators who saw the big gains but did not really understand the mechanics of the form.

A third and final explanation is that the market simply made a mistake about diversification. This need not imply irrationality or less-than-efficient use of information. (Indeed, there is some evidence the market is right about mergers on average: see Healy, Palepu, and Ruback (1992) and Ravenscraft and Pascoe (1988).) In the 1960s, the conglomerate was considered a radical innovation in corporate organization. We expect that investors made rational forecasts based on their information, but because there was no historical precedent, their information was very limited and their estimates correspondingly noisy. In support of this, compare the generally favorable attitude of the business press[10] and the conventional wisdom in many of the top business schools in the late 1960s with the current opinion of both that diversification is bad—that businesses should "stick to their knitting."

Once we entertain the possibility that the market's enthusiasm for an innovation may bear little relation to the innovation's eventual success, we are forced to entertain a discouraging hypothesis about today's situation. It may be that the market's enthusiasm for a return to specialization in the 1980s was excessive as well. The positive returns from dismantling the companies of the 1960s may just reflect the latest fad.

Appendix

■ **Construction of the dataset.** This table lists the number of observations by source and gives the number of observations that were deleted for various reasons.

Observations used in Ravenscraft and Scherer (1987, 1989)	634
Collected but not used by Ravenscraft and Scherer	9
Added by the author from NYSE listings	212
Basic dataset	855
No announcement in the *Wall Street Journal*	−426
Duplicate, consolidated with parent, or target not in manufacturing	−16
Target was a subsidiary of the buyer	−11
Wall Street Journal story was not the first announcement	−58
Other important announcement during event window	−34
Not enough CRSP information	−12
Target assets were less than $5 million	−99
Final dataset	199

[10] For example: "Like the men who run them and staff them, the newer-type corporation is cocky. At first, timidly, it was called 'diversification.' Later on, somewhat scornfully, it was called 'conglomerization.' It now appears that the cross-industry corporation is in some ways the most efficient sort" (from a September 15, 1967, *Forbes* story entitled "The Changing Nature of the Corporation"). Or the *Wall Street Journal*'s citation of a comment by an investment research service that the quintessential conglomerate Gulf & Western was "the prototype of what the American corporation of the future is all about" (from a front-page story entitled "The Conglomerates: Antitrusters, Investors Eye Combines Warily, But Firms Still Grow," July 25, 1968).

Changes in the Ravenscraft and Scherer sample.

1. Industry average operating profit was recomputed for the Food and Kindred Products industry for the three quarters 72:IV–73:II to account for data revisions.
2. Target industries were reclassified to conform to *Poor's Register* or the *Million Dollar Directory* for 50 observations.
3. Data-entry errors were corrected for three observations.
4. When computing target excess operating profit, Ravenscraft and Scherer consolidated the Furniture and Fixtures, Lumber and Wood Products, and Miscellaneous Manufacturing and Ordnance Industries. For 1968 and 1971 I computed Miscellaneous Manufacturing and Ordnance separately from the other two industries. The *Quarterly Financial Report* does not report the industries separately in 1974.
5. The Amphenol–Bunker Ramo merger was recoded so that Bunker Ramo was the (white knight) acquirer and Amphenol the target.

References

AMIHUD, Y. AND LEV, B. "Risk Reduction as a Managerial Motive for Conglomerate Mergers." *Bell Journal of Economics*, Vol. 12 (1981), pp. 605–617.

BAUMOL, W.J. *Business Behavior, Value and Growth* (revised). New York: Harcourt, Brace & World, 1967.

BAYSINGER, B.D. AND BUTLER, H.N. "Corporate Governance and the Board of Directors: Performance Effects of Changes in Board Composition." *Journal of Law, Economics, and Organization*, Vol. 1 (1985), pp. 101–124.

BERG, N.A. "What's Different About Conglomerate Management?" *Harvard Business Review*, Vol. 47 (1969), pp. 112–120.

BERLE, A.A. AND MEANS, G.C. *The Modern Corporation and Private Property*. New York: Harcourt, Brace, & World, 1968.

BHAGAT, S., SHLEIFER, A., AND VISHNY, R.W. "Hostile Takeovers in the 1980s: The Return to Corporate Specialization." *Brookings Papers on Economic Activity: Microeconomics*, Special Issue (1990), pp. 1–72.

BRADLEY, M., DESAI, A., AND KIM, E.H. "Synergistic Gains from Corporate Acquisitions and Their Division between the Stockholders of Target and Acquiring Firms." *Journal of Financial Economics*, Vol. 21 (1988), pp. 3–40.

CARLETON, W.T., GUILKEY, D.K., HARRIS, R.F., AND STEWART, J.F. "An Empirical Analysis of the Role of the Medium of Exchange in Mergers." *Journal of Finance*, Vol. 38 (1983), pp. 813–826.

CHANDLER, A.D., JR. "The United States: Seedbed of Managerial Capitalism." In A.D. Chandler, Jr. and H. Daems, eds., *Managerial Hierarchies: Comparative Perspectives on the Rise of Modern Industrial Enterprise*. Cambridge, Mass.: Harvard University Press, 1980.

COMMENT, R. "The Effects of Firm-Specific Human Capital on Management Equity Investment and Turnover." Ph.D. dissertation, University of Michigan, 1985.

——— AND JARRELL, G.A. "Corporate Focus and Stock Returns." University of Rochester, May 1991.

ELGERS, P.T. AND CLARK, J.J. "Merger Types and Shareholder Returns: Additional Evidence." *Financial Management*, Vol. 9 (1980), pp. 66–72.

HEALY, P.M., PALEPU, K.G., AND RUBACK, R.S. "Does Corporate Performance Improve after Mergers?" *Journal of Financial Economics*, Vol. 31 (1992), pp. 133–175.

HOLLAND, M. *When the Machine Stopped*. Boston: Harvard Business School Press, 1989.

KAPLAN, S.N. AND WEISBACH, M.S. "The Success of Acquisitions: Evidence from Divestitures." *Journal of Finance*, Vol. 47 (1992), pp. 107–138.

LANG, L.H.P., STULZ, R., AND WALKLING, R.A. "Managerial Performance, Tobin's *Q*, and the Gains from Successful Tender Offers." *Journal of Financial Economics*, Vol. 24 (1989), pp. 137–154.

LIEBESKIND, J., OPLER, T.C., AND HATFIELD, D.E. "Corporate Restructuring and the Consolidation of U.S. Industry." University of Southern California, Southern Methodist University, UCLA, April 1992.

LYNCH, H.H. *Financial Performance of Conglomerates*. Division of Research, Harvard Business School, 1971.

MALATESTA, P.H. "The Wealth Effect of Merger Activity and the Objective Functions of Merging Firms." *Journal of Financial Economics*, Vol. 11 (1983), pp. 155–181.

MARTIN, K.J. AND MCCONNELL, J.J. "Corporate Performance, Corporate Takeovers, and Management Turnover." *Journal of Finance*, Vol. 46 (1991), pp. 671–687.

MATSUSAKA, J.G. "Headhunts, Mergers and Acquisitions: The Implications of Synergy." University of Southern California, 1991.

———. "Target Profits and Managerial Discipline during the Conglomerate Merger Wave." *Journal of Industrial Economics*, Vol. 41 (1993), pp. 179–189.

MCCUTCHEON, B.J. "What Caused Conglomerate Formation? An Examination of Managerial Behavior and Internal Capital Markets in the 1960s Conglomerates." Ph.D. dissertation, The University of Chicago, June 1991.

MCGUCKIN, R.H., NGUYEN, S.V., AND ANDREWS, S.H. "The Relationships among Acquiring and Acquired Firms' Product Lines." *Journal of Law and Economics*, Vol. 34 (1992), pp. 477–502.

MORCK, R., SHLEIFER, A., AND VISHNY, R.W. "Do Managerial Objectives Drive Bad Acquisitions?" *Journal of Finance*, Vol. 45 (1990), pp. 31–48.

MUELLER, D.C. "A Theory of Conglomerate Mergers." *Quarterly Journal of Economics,* Vol. 83 (1969), pp. 643–659.

RAVENSCRAFT, D.J. AND PASCOE, G.A., JR. "Can the Stock Market Predict Merger Success?" Federal Trade Commission, July 1988.

——— AND SCHERER, F.M. *Mergers, Sell-offs, and Economic Efficiency.* Washington, D.C.: The Brookings Institution, 1987.

——— AND ———. "The Profitability of Mergers." *International Journal of Industrial Organization,* Vol. 7 (1989), pp. 101–116.

RITZ, P.M. "The Input-Output Structure of the U.S. Economy, 1972." *Survey of Current Business,* Vol. 59 (1979), pp. 34–72.

ROLL, R. "The Hubris Hypothesis of Corporate Takeovers." *Journal of Business,* Vol. 59 (1986), pp. 197–216.

SCHIPPER, K. AND THOMPSON, R. "Evidence on the Capitalized Value of Merger Activity for Acquiring Firms." *Journal of Financial Economics,* Vol. 11 (1983), pp. 85–119.

SETH, A. "Value Creation in Acquisitions: A Reexamination of Performance Issues." *Strategic Management Journal,* Vol. 11 (1990), pp. 99–115.

SHLEIFER, A. AND VISHNY, R.W. "Management Entrenchment: The Case of Manager-Specific Investments." *Journal of Financial Economics,* Vol. 25 (1989), pp. 123–139.

——— AND ———. "The Takeover Wave of the 1980s." *Science,* Vol. 249 (1990), pp. 745–749.

——— AND ———. "Takeovers in the '60s and the '80s: Evidence and Implications." *Strategic Management Journal,* Vol. 12 (1991), pp. 51–59.

SOBEL, R. *The Rise and Fall of the Conglomerate Kings.* New York: Stein and Day, 1984.

[10]

Journal of Economic Perspectives—Volume 2, Number 1—Winter 1988—Pages 49–68

The Market for Corporate Control: The Empirical Evidence Since 1980

Gregg A. Jarrell, James A. Brickley, and Jeffry M. Netter

Corporate takeovers have been very big business in the 1980s. The Office of the Chief Economist (OCE) of the Securities and Exchange Commission estimates that shareholders of target firms in successful tender offers from 1981 through 1986 received payments in excess of $54 billion over the value of their holdings before the tender offers. Almost $38 billion of the total was received after 1984. If we include the increased wealth of target firm shareholders resulting from leveraged buyouts, mergers, and corporate restructurings (prompted in large part by the threat of takeovers) these numbers are even larger. W. T. Grimm & Co. collects similar data for a larger sample of change-of-control transactions, including mergers and leveraged buyouts. They estimate that from 1981 to 1986 the total dollar value of the premiums over the pre-announcement price paid for securities involved in change-of-control transactions was $118.4 billion.[1] Corporate restructurings have created even more

[1]These estimates understate the total premiums (dollar value of the percentage increase in the target's stock price caused by the takeover) paid in change-of-control transactions. OCE's sample is limited to the first successful tender offer for a firm. Thus, if an "auction" for the firm develops, resulting in an even higher offer price, they do not capture that additional premium. In addition, no account is made for tender offers that do not ultimately succeed. Shareholders may sell their shares in the market at the premium induced by the offer before it is known that the offer fails. The W. T. Grimm data also understates the total profits earned by stockholders because they calculate the premium based on the market price only five days before the initial public announcement and do not capture the premium attributable to increases in share prices that occur more than five days in advance of a public announcement.

■ *Gregg A. Jarrell is Senior Vice-President, Alcar Group Inc., Skokie, Illinois; James A. Brickley is Associate Professor, William E. Simon Graduate School of Business Administration, University of Rochester, Rochester, New York; Jeffry M. Netter is Senior Financial Economist, Office of the Chief Economist, United States Securities and Exchange Commission, Washington, DC.*

wealth. For example, Jensen (1986) estimated that the restructurings of Phillips, Unocal and Arco created total gains to shareholders of $6.6 billion by reducing investment in negative net present value projects.

There are numerous factors behind the high level of takeover activity in the 1980s. For example, antitrust regulators have come to understand that in the increasingly competitive international marketplace U.S. interests are well-served by domestic mergers that could be objectionable in a more closed economy. Today's antitrust regulators almost never object to vertical combinations, and even horizontal mergers between industry leaders—completely taboo before the 1980s—are often allowed today.

Deregulation also has induced merger and acquisition activity by calling forth new skills and strategies, and new management teams to implement them. Many of the mergers, takeovers, and restructurings over the last ten years have occurred in industries that recently were deregulated such as airlines and transportation, financial services, broadcasting, and oil and gas. For example, transportation and broadcasting together accounted for 20 percent of all mergers and acquisition activity from 1981 and 1984 while oil and gas accounted for another 26.3 percent (Jensen, 1986).

Other factors motivating the high level of takeover and restructuring activity in the 1980s include innovations in takeover financing, less potent state antitakeover regulations, the retreat by the Federal courts and regulatory agencies from protecting besieged target firms, and learning about the possible returns to this type of activity. These factors are critical to understanding why firms that were considered "untouchable" not long ago have been the targets of hostile takeovers with increasing frequency. This growing list includes USX, CBS, Phillips, and TWA, to name just a few.

The Council of Economic Advisors (CEA) in the 1985 *Economic Report of the President* provides data on the extent of the takeover activity in the 1980s and the importance of large transactions in explaining this activity. The CEA states that the increase in merger and acquisition activity in the 1980s is due to a large increase in the size of the largest transactions. Their evidence indicates that in the period 1981 to 1984 the average annual reported real value of mergers and acquisitions was 48 percent greater than in any four year period from the late 1960s to the early 1970s. In addition, of the 100 largest acquisition transactions recorded through 1983, 65 occurred after 1982 and only 11 took place prior to 1979.

Returns to Bidders and Targets

Critics of takeovers question whether tender offers, mergers, and leveraged buyouts produce net gains to society. Critics argue any gains to a given party are simply redistributions resulting from losses to someone else (or more colorfully put, a pirating of assets by modern financial buccaneers). Also critics contend that battles for corporate control divert energy from more productive endeavors.[2] In this section, we find that such criticisms are ill founded, and thus conclude that battles for corporate control serve a beneficial function for the economy.

The market for corporate control is the market for the right to control the management of corporate resources. In a takeover, an outside party seeks to obtain control of a firm. There are several types of takeovers, including mergers, hostile and friendly tender offers, and proxy contests. In a merger the bidder negotiates an agreement with target management on the terms of the offer for the target and then submits the proposed agreement to a vote of the shareholders. In a tender offer, a bidder makes an offer directly to shareholders to buy some or all of the stock of the target firm. A "friendly" tender offer refers to offers that are supported by target management. The most controversial type of takeovers are "hostile" tender offers, which are tender offers that are opposed by target managements. In a proxy contest, a dissident group attempts through a vote of shareholders to obtain control of the board of directors. Finally, leveraged buyouts are buyouts of shareholder's equity, heavily financed with debt by a group that frequently includes incumbent management.

Many of the studies reviewed in this paper are event studies that measure the effects of certain unanticipated events (such as a takeover or other control contest) on stock prices, after correcting for overall market influence on security returns. Any finding of abnormal returns, therefore, shows how the stock market views the impact of the event on the firm's common stockholders. (See Brown and Warner, 1985, for a more thorough review of event study methods.)

Returns to Shareholders of Target Companies

Shareholders of target companies clearly benefit from takeovers. Jarrell and Poulsen (1987a) estimate the premiums paid in 663 successful tender offers from 1962 to December 1985. They find that premiums averaged 19 percent in the 1960s, 35 percent in the 1970s, and from 1980 to 1985 the average premium was 30 percent. These figures are consistent with the 13 studies of pre-1980 data contained in Jensen and Ruback (1983) which agree that targets of successful tender offers and mergers before 1980 earned positive returns ranging from 16 percent to 30 percent for tender offers.[3]

Similar results are contained in studies of leveraged buyouts and going private transactions. Lehn and Poulsen (1987) find premiums of 21 percent to shareholders in

[2]Many critics of acquisition activity (such as the Business Roundtable) are primarily concerned with alleged abuses arising from hostile takeovers. The other types of acquisition activity are approved by target firms' management who allegedly are the individuals most concerned with the welfare of the target firm and its shareholders.

[3]Jensen and Ruback (1983) review 13 studies published between 1977 and 1983—six on mergers and seven on tender offers. Their survey provides a concise summary of the pre-1980 data. But because of the lengthy review process for academic journals, the most up-to-date sample used in these studies ends in 1981, and most do not go beyond the late 1970s. This paper can be considered an update of Jensen and Ruback with a focus on recent empirical studies that cover takeovers made in the 1980s.

93 leveraged buyouts taking place from 1980 to 1984. DeAngelo, DeAngelo and Rice (1984) find an average 27 percent gain for leveraged buyouts between 1973 and 1980.

OCE (1985a) measures premiums paid by comparing the price per share offered by the bidder to the trading price of the stock one month before the offer, not adjusting for changes in the market index (also see Comment and Jarrell, forthcoming). Using a comprehensive sample of 225 successful tender offers from 1981 through 1984, including over-the-counter targets, OCE finds the average premium to shareholders to be 53.2 percent. OCE has updated these figures for 1985 and 1986 and finds a decrease over the last two years. OCE finds that the average premium is 37 percent in 1985 and 33.6 percent in 1986.[4]

While the evidence reported thus far indicates substantial gains to target shareholders, it probably understates the total gains to these shareholders. In many cases events occur before a formal takeover offer, so studies that concentrate on the stock price reactions to formal offers will understate the total gains to shareholders.

Several recent empirical studies examine the stock market reaction to events that often precede formal steps in the battle for corporate control. Mikkelson and Ruback (1985a) provide information on the stock price reaction to Schedule 13D filings. Schedule 13D must be filed with the SEC by all purchasers of 5 percent of a corporation's common stock, requiring disclosure of, among other things, the investor's identity and intent. Mikkelson and Ruback find significant price reactions around the initial announcement of the filing, and that the returns depend on the intent stated in the 13D. The highest returns, an increase of 7.74 percent, occurred when the filer in the statement of intent indicated some possibility of a control change. However, the abnormal returns were only 3.24 percent if the investor reported the purchase was for investment purposes. Holderness and Sheehan (1985) find a differential stock market effect to 13D filings depending on the identity of the filer. They show the filings of six "corporate raiders" increased target share prices by a significantly greater amount than a sample of other filers (5.9 percent to 3.4 percent).

More direct evidence that significant stock price increases occur prior to formal announcements of corporate events is contained in OCE (1987c) which finds a significant increase in the stock price of target firms in 172 successful tender offers in the period before any announcement of the offer. OCE finds a run-up in stock prices of 38.8 percent of the total control premium by the close of day *before* the offer announcement. The announcement date is, in the parlance of Wall Street, the date the target firm was put "in play" and represents some event having significant implications for corporate control. For example, the in-play date in some cases is the formal offer but in other cases is the eventual bidder's filing of a Schedule 13D with corporate control implications for the target.

[4] The OCE (1985a) study also explicitly tests and rejects the popular theory that two-tier tender offers disadvantage target shareholders. Some observers argue that two-tier offers—in which the bidder first makes an offer for control of the firm and then makes a "clean-up" offer for remaining shares at a lower price—coerces shareholders to tender to avoid the clean-up price. OCE finds that two-tier offers have overall premiums that are nearly identical to the average for any-or-all offers and that there is no evidence that two-tier offers "stampede" shareholders into unwise trading decisions.

Table 1

Cumulative excess returns to successful bidders for tender offers during 1960 to 1985, by decade

Trading-day Interval	Cumulative excess returns in percent			
	All	*1960s*	*1970s*	*1980s*
− 10 to + 5	1.14	4.40	1.22	− 1.10
(*t*-stat.)	(2.49)	(4.02)	(2.12)	(− 1.54)
− 10 to + 20	2.04	4.95	2.21	− 0.04
(*t*-stat.)	(3.31)	(3.52)	(2.87)	(− 0.04)
Number of observations	405	106	140	159

Source: Jarrell and Poulsen (1987a)

While some commentators argue that price run-up before the formal announcements of tender offers indicates the presence of illegal insider trading, OCE's evidence demonstrates that the legal market for information can explain much of the run-up. OCE shows that a significant portion of the run-up can be explained by three readily identifiable influences on pre-bid trading: media speculation, the bidder's foothold acquisition in the target, and whether the bid is friendly or hostile. Systematic relations between these factors and run-up in target share prices indicate that there is an active market for information about impending takeover bids and a large portion of the run-up can be explained by factors other than illegal insider trading. OCE's results on pre-bid market activity are supported by Comment (1986).

Returns to Shareholders of Acquiring Companies

The 1980s evidence on bidders comes from Jarrell and Poulsen (1987a), with data on 663 successful tender offers covering 1962 to 1985. Table 1 summarizes the excess returns to 440 NYSE and AMEX bidders. For the entire sample period bidders on average realized small, but statistically significant, gains of about 1 to 2 percent in the immediate period around the public announcement. Most interesting is the apparent secular decline in the gains to successful bidders in tender offers. Consistent with the previous studies reviewed by Jensen and Ruback (1983), Table 1 shows positive excess returns of five percent during the 1960s, and a lower, but still significantly significant, positive average of 2.2 percent over the 1970s. However, the 159 cases from the 1980s show statistically insignificant losses to bidders.

How the Distribution of Takeover Gains Is Determined

Companies that are targets of takeovers receive the bulk of the value created by corporate combinations and these gains are not offset by losses to acquirers. As one might predict, an important factor in determining how these takeover gains are split seems to be how many bidders are trying to acquire the target company. In fact, the secular decline in the stock returns to bidders probably reflects the increased competition among bidders and the rise of auction-style contests during the 1980s.[5]

Conditions which foster an increase in multiple bidding tend to increase target premiums and reduce bidder returns. For example, Jarrell and Bradley (1980) demonstrate that Federal (Williams Act) and state regulations of tender offers have this effect because they impose disclosure and delay rules that foster multiple-bidder, auction contests and preemptive bidding.[6] In addition to greater regulation, other factors contributing to this increased competition include court rulings protecting defensive tactics, the inventions of several defenses against takeovers, and the increase in sophisticated takeover advisers to implement them.

Interesting support for this theory in the banking industry is provided by James and Wier (1987). Federal and state banking regulations effectively limit the number of eligible acquisition partners, thus affecting the number of potential substitutes for bidders or targets in particular transactions. For 39 proposed banking acquisitions, James and Wier measure a positive relation between the bidder's share of the takeover gains and the number of alternative targets, and a negative relation between the bidder's share and the number of alternative bidders.[7]

The Source of Takeover Gains

Shareholders of target companies definitely gain from mergers and tender offers. But much uneasiness has been expressed at who might be paying for those gains. In their summary several years ago, Jensen and Ruback (1983, p. 47) were forced to conclude that "knowledge of the sources of takeover gains still eludes us."[8] The studies they reviewed did not allow them to judge the many redistributive theories, which suggest that shareholder gains are offset by economic losses to others. Since then, many popular "redistributive theories" have been examined. The evidence has led many financial economists like Jensen (1986, p. 6) to attribute takeovers, leveraged buyouts, and restructurings to "productive entrepreneurial activity that improves the control and management of assets and helps move assets to more productive uses." We now turn to a review of the most important of these redistributive theories.

[5]Bradley, Desai, and Kim (1984) show that targets gain more in multiple bidder than single bidder contests.
[6]The Williams Act contains the Federal regulations of tender offers and was enacted in July 1968. Its main components are disclosure requirements, a regulated minimum offer period, and antifraud provisions that give target management standing to sue for injunctive relief.
[7]Other evidence supporting this point includes a recent paper by Guerin-Calvert, McGuckin, and Warren-Boulton (1986) that reexamines the effects of state and Federal regulations of tender offers. They also find the regulations increase the incidence of multiple-bidder auction takeovers among all control contests. Also consistent with this result is the evidence on the French experience presented by Eckbo and Langohr (1986). They show that the imposition of disclosure-only (not delay) rules governing tender offers in France significantly shifted the gains in French takeovers from acquirers to targets.
[8]Jensen and Ruback review the empirical work testing the market power theory of takeovers by Eckbo (1983) and Stillman (1983). This theory is that increased monopoly power in product markets explains takeover gains. Jensen and Ruback conclude the evidence rejects this theory as the source of gains from takeovers. Recent papers by Eckbo and Wier (1985) and by Eckbo (1985) provide empirical support for the conclusion that except in isolated cases, increased market power cannot explain the gains from takeovers.

Short-Term Myopia and Inefficient Takeovers. This theory is based on an allegation that market participants, and particularly institutional investors, are concerned almost exclusively with short-term earnings performance and tend to undervalue corporations engaged in long-term activity. From this viewpoint, any corporation planning for long-term development will become undervalued by the market as its resource commitments to the long-term depress its short-term earnings, and thus will become a prime takeover candidate.

Critics of this theory point out that it is blatantly inconsistent with an efficient capital market. Indeed, if the market systematically undervalues long-run planning and investment, it implies harmful economic consequences that go far beyond the costs of inefficient takeovers. Fortunately, no empirical evidence has been found to support this theory. In fact, a study of 324 high research and development firms and of all 177 takeover targets during 1981–84 by the SEC's Office of the Chief Economist (OCE, 1985b) shows evidence that (1) increased institutional stock holdings are not associated with increased takeovers of firms; (2) increased institutional holdings are not associated with decreases in research and development; (3) firms with high research and development expenditures are not more vulnerable to takeovers; and (4) stock prices respond positively to announcements of increases in research and development expenditures.

Further evidence opposing the myopia theory is provided by Hall (1987) in an NBER study and by McConnell and Muscarella (1985). Hall studies data on acquisition activity among manufacturing firms from 1977 to 1986. She presents evidence that much acquisition activity has been directed towards firms and industries which are less intensive in R&D activity. She also finds that firms involved in mergers show little difference in their pre- and postmerger R&D performance compared with industry peers. McConnell and Muscarella, in a study of 658 capital expenditure announcements, show that stock prices respond positively to announcements of increased capital expenditures, on average, except for exploration and development announcements in the oil industry.

Undervalued Target Theory. Recalcitrant target management and other opponents of takeovers often contend that because targets are "undervalued" by the market, a savvy bidder can offer substantial premiums for target firms while still paying far below the intrinsic value of the corporation. By this theory, it becomes the duty of target managements to defend vigorously against even high premium offers since remaining independent, it is argued, can offer shareholders greater rewards over the long term than are offered by opportunistic bidders seeking short-term gains.

However, the evidence shows the promised long-term gains from remaining independent do not usually materialize. When a target defeats a hostile bid, its post-defeat value reverts to approximately the (market adjusted) level obtaining before the instigation of the hostile bid (Bradley, Desai and Kim, 1983; Easterbrook and Jarrell 1984; Jarrell 1985; Ruback, 1986). Bhagat, Brickley and Lowenstein (1987) used option pricing theory to show that the announcement period returns around cash tender offers are too large to be explained by revaluations due to information about undervaluation.

This evidence indicates that the market does not, on average, learn much of anything that is new or different about target firms' intrinsic values through the tender offer process, despite the tremendous attention lavished on targets, and the huge amounts of information traded among market participants during takeover contests. If undervaluation had indeed been present, then the deluge of new information on the intrinsic value of targets should have caused fundamental price corrections even in the event of takeover defeats. But in the overwhelming majority of cases studied, prices dropped rather than increased for target firms that fought off takeovers.

Do Tax Effects Motivate Mergers and Takeovers? Tax motives have long been suspected as an important cause of merger and acquisition activity. Indeed, the Tax Reform Act of 1986 contains several provisions aimed at reducing the tax benefits available through mergers.[9] Most recent studies, however, assign tax benefits a minor role in explaining merger and takeover activity. Auerbach and Reishus (1987a) study 318 mergers and acquisitions during 1968–83 to estimate the tax benefits available in these transactions from increased use of tax losses and credits. They found that these tax benefits in general were not a significant factor in the majority of large acquisitions. In a fair number of transactions, however (potentially 20 percent of the mergers), tax factors did appear to be significant enough to affect the decision to merge.[10] Lehn and Poulsen (1987) find, in their study of leveraged buyouts from 1980–84, that the premiums paid are directly related to potential tax benefits associated with these transactions, suggesting that in part these leveraged buyouts are motivated by tax considerations.

In summary, acquiring firms' tax losses and credits, and the option to step-up the basis of targets' assets without paying corporate level capital gains, are two tax benefits that appear to have had some impact on merger activity. However, the evidence suggests that much of the takeover activity in the last twenty years was not tax motivated.

Do Bondholders Lose From Takeovers? Some critics of takeovers suggest that the premiums paid by bidders are not a result of any wealth enhancing changes, but instead represent a redistribution from the holders of the target's bonds and preferred equity. For example, the bonds of an acquiring firm can drop in value if the acquiring firm pays cash for a riskier target firm. Given that the combined value of the two firms remains unchanged, the decline in the bond value will be captured as a gain by

[9] A review of the effects on the takeover market of the change of the 1986 Tax Reform Act is contained in Steindel (1986). The 1986 Tax Reform Act repeals the General Utilities doctrine, which states that corporations liquidating their businesses are not subject to capital gains tax on the value of their assets. A firm using General Utilities in a liquidation (the purchaser of at least 80 percent of the stock of a corporation may treat the transaction for tax purposes as a liquidation) avoids the tax liability that comes with appreciated assets. Steindel argues that the repeal of the General Utilities doctrine combined with the changes in corporate tax rates reduces the attractiveness of many mergers and acquisitions. Other tax changes with effects on takeover activity include the increase in the personal capital gains tax and new rules on the transfer of net operating loss carryforwards.

[10] However, Auerbach and Reishus (1987b) compare actual mergers over 1968–1983 with a control group of nonmerging firms and conclude that the potential increase in interest deductions and unused tax losses and tax credits of the acquired firms have not driven acquisitions.

some other class of security holder (such as common stockholders).[11] However, the empirical evidence does not support this argument.

Denis and McConnell (1986) examine the returns on various classes of the securities of a sample of 132 mergers in the period 1962 to 1980. Denis and McConnell's results are consistent with earlier studies in that they find gains to mergers and no losses to bondholders. Their results indicate that on average holders of common stock, convertible and nonconvertible preferred stock, and convertible bonds in the acquired firm gain from a merger. Those who hold nonconvertible bonds in the acquired firm and convertible bonds, nonconvertible bonds, and nonconvertible preferred stock in the acquiring firm neither gain nor lose in a merger. Denis and McConnell also find some evidence that the acquiring firms' common shareholders do not lose and may gain from mergers, especially in the days immediately following the announcement. Lehn and Poulsen's (1987) study of 108 leveraged buyouts from 1980 to 1984 finds no support for the redistribution theory. They find no evidence that the shareholder value created by the leveraged buyouts comes at the expense of preferred shareholders or bondholders. In sum, the evidence provides no support for the hypothesis that the supposed gains from acquisitions are actually transfers from the holders of senior securities to the holders of common stock.

Do Labor's Losses Finance Takeovers? Recent takeovers in the airline industry have involved conflict between acquiring-firm management and the (usually) unionized labor of the target firm. These conflicts have contributed to the popular generalization that shareholder premiums from takeovers come largely at the expense of labor. Shleifer and Summers (1987) articulate this view more rigorously focusing on implicit long-term contracts between labor and incumbent (target) management. They argue raiders can sometimes exploit these contracts by buying a controlling share of the equity and financing the premium by using pressure tactics to force significant wage concessions. In theory, this activity can be socially inefficient by ruining the market for these implicit long-run labor contracts and forcing labor and management to use less efficient contracting devices.

This redistributive theory from labor to shareholders has not been tested widely, but a recent NBER study by Brown and Medoff (1987) presents statistical evidence based on Michigan's employment and wages that fails to support it. Although this close look at Michigan is not necessarily indicative of the U.S. experience (for example, it contains few large mergers or hostile tender offers), the results are that wages and employment rise on average for firms that are involved in acquisitions.

Summary of Source of Gains

The various redistribution theories of takeover gains have been the subject of considerable empirical work since the Jensen and Ruback (1983) review. Most convincing is the empirical rejection of the undervaluation theory: target firms cannot be depicted generally as being "undervalued" by the stock market. Also soundly

[11] The senior security holders of the target firm can also lose depending on the takeover's effect on the riskiness of their claims.

rejected by the data is the short-term myopia theory. The evidence gives tax-benefits theories at least a minor role in explaining merger and tender offer activity. Finally, evidence is inconsistent with the theories that the stock-price gains to shareholders come from bondholders and labor.

Although some individuals (incumbent management, for example) obviously lose in at least some takeovers, the literature, while not conclusive, offers little or no support for the notion that the redistribution theories explain a major portion of the apparent gains from takeovers. It has been impossible so far to find systematic losses which could offset the enormous gains to target and bidding firm shareholders from mergers, tender offers, and other corporate-control activities. We therefore conclude that evidence is consistent with the notion that these corporate transactions reflect economically beneficial reshufflings of productive assets.

The Effects of Defending Against Hostile Takeovers

Defensive strategies against hostile takeovers have always been controversial since they pose a conflict of interest for target management. After all, takeovers can impose significant welfare losses on managers, who may be displaced and lose their organization-specific human capital. These conflicts may tempt some managers to erect barriers to hostile takeovers, thus insulating themselves from the discipline of the outside market for control at the expense of their shareholders and the efficiency of the economy.

However, providing target management with the power to defend against hostile takeover bids might also help target shareholders during a control contest. Target management can in certain cases defeat bids that are "inadequate." Although this rationale is popular, the evidence discussed earlier shows that in very few cases do these alleged long-term gains of independence actually materialize. The other benefit of resistance comes when resistance by target management helps promote a takeover auction. Litigation and other blocking actions can provide the necessary time for the management of the target firm to "shop" the target and generate competing bids. This auction rationale for resistance is harder to reject statistically. Evidence on occasional shareholder losses after the defeat of a takeover attempt does not in itself disprove the auction theory. This negotiating leverage can be expected to fail in some cases, with the sole bidder becoming discouraged and withdrawing. It is a gamble. The hypothesis is rejected only if the harmful outcome of defeating all bids is sufficiently frequent and costly to offset the benefits of inducing higher takeover prices. One must also consider the social cost of tender offers that never occur because of the presence of defensive devices. Unfortunately, this deterrence effect is very difficult to measure and we present no direct evidence of the extent of these costs.

Evidence on the effects of defensive measures by target management is obtained mainly from two approaches, the event-type study and the outcomes-type study. The event-type study recognizes that an efficient market must judge this cost-benefit tradeoff when it adjusts the market value of a firm in response to the adoption of a charter amendment or some other kind of resistance. Alternatively, the outcomes-type study examines the actual outcomes of control contests over a significant time horizon among firms using a common kind of resistance—say all firms adopting poison pills. That is, an event study measures the stock price reaction to the introduction of defensive devices while outcomes studies follow the use of defensive devices in control contests to determine their effects on the outcomes of the contests.

Many defensive measures must be approved by a vote of the shareholders. Hence, voting has the potential to block management-sponsored proposals that harm shareholders, depending on the costs and benefits to individual shareholders from collecting relevant information and voting. In general, a shareholder with a small amount of shares will not invest heavily in the voting process since a small number of shares will not generally affect the outcome regardless of how they are voted. However, if individual voting and information costs are near zero even the shareholder with few shares can be expected to vote against management on value-decreasing proposals. Alternatively, large outside block holders (like institutional investors) internalize more of the benefits from participation in the voting process and can be expected to take an active interest in voting on antitakeover proposals even when the information gathering and voting costs are positive. Since voting rights can block harmful measures, we distinguish between two broad categories of defensive measures, those receiving approval by voting shareholders and those adopted unilaterally by management.

Defensive Measures Approved by Shareholders

Antitakeover amendments generally operate by imposing new conditions that must be satisfied before changing managerial control of the corporation. They are almost always proposed by management and they usually require majority voting approval by shareholders. Proposed antitakeover amendments are very rarely rejected by voting shareholders; Brickley, Lease, and Smith (forthcoming) find for a sample of 288 management-sponsored antitakeover proposals in 1984 that about 96 percent passed.

Supermajority Amendments. Most state corporation laws set the minimum approval required for mergers and other important control transactions at either one-half or two-thirds of the voting shares. Supermajority amendments require the approval by holders of at least two-thirds and sometimes as much as nine-tenths of the voting power of the outstanding common stock. These provisions can apply either to mergers and other business combinations or to changing the firm's board of directors or to both. Pure supermajority provisions are very rare today, having been replaced by similar provisions that are triggered at the discretion of the board of directors. This allows the board to waive the supermajority provisions allowing friendly mergers to proceed unimpeded.

Five years ago, Jensen and Ruback (1983) found mixed evidence on the effect of supermajority amendments passed before 1980. However, a more recent study by Jarrell and Poulsen (1987b), derived from OCE (1985c), covers 104 supermajority amendments passed since 1980 and reports significant negative stock-price effects of over 3 percent around the introduction of the proposals. They also show that firms passing supermajority amendments have relatively low institutional stockholdings (averaging 19 percent) and high insider holdings (averaging 18 percent), which they interpret as helping to explain how these amendments received voting approval despite their harmful wealth effect. That is, firms proposing these amendments have fewer blockholders with incentives to invest in the voting process. Jarrell and Poulsen further conjecture that the increased shareholder resistance to harmful supermajority amendments helps explain their declining popularity in contrast to the success of the fair price amendment which appear less likely to harm shareholders (as discussed below).

Fair Price Amendments. The fair price amendment is a supermajority provision that applies only to nonuniform, two-tier takeover bids that are opposed by the target's board of directors. Uniform offers that are considered "fair" circumvent the supermajority requirement, even if target management opposes them. Fairness of the offer is determined in several ways. The most common fair price is defined as the highest price paid by the bidder for any of the shares it has acquired in the target firm during a specified period of time. Jarrell and Poulsen (1987b) report that 487 firms adopted fair price charter provisions between 1979 and May 1985, with over 90 percent of these coming in the very recent period of 1983 to May 1985.

The stock price effects reflect the low deterrence value of the fair price amendment. Jarrell and Poulsen (1987b) report an average loss of 0.73 percent around the introduction of these amendments, which is not statistically significant. They also show that firms adopting fair price amendments have roughly normal levels of insider holdings (12 percent) and of institutional holdings (30 percent). They interpret this evidence as supporting the view that shareholder voting retards adoption of harmful amendments, especially when insider holdings are low and institutional holdings are high. Further support for this view is provided by Brickley, Lease, and Smith (forthcoming) who document that "no" votes on antitakeover amendments (especially ones that harm shareholders) increase with institutional and other outside blockholdings, while "no" votes decrease with increases in managerial holdings.

Dual-Class Recapitalizations. These plans restructure the equity of a firm into two classes with different voting rights. Although several methods are used, the common goal is to provide management or family owners with voting power disproportionately greater than provided by their equity holdings under a "one share-one vote" rule.[12]

Evidence before and after 1980 has confirmed that the market generally values shares with voting power more than those without. Lease, McConnell, and Mikkelson (1983) examine 30 firms having dual-class common stock and show that voting stock on average trades at a significant premium, ranging from one to seven percent. A recent paper by OCE (1987a) examines the monthly stock prices of 26 OTC and

[12]For over 60 years, the New York Stock Exchange did not allow any member firm to have a dual-class capitalization structure, but it has recently proposed a liberalization to allow dual-class listings in response to competitive pressures from Amex and OTC markets. Amex currently allows dual-class listings with some restrictions, and the OTC market has no restrictions beyond usual state-law requirements.

AMEX firms having dual-class common and shows an average discount of four to five percent for low-vote common, though the discount is reduced when the low-vote stock has rights to preferential dividends.

Of course, the fact that the market values voting power does not demonstrate that dual-class recapitalizations reduce the overall price of stock. DeAngelo and DeAngelo (1985) examine in detail 45 firms that had dual-voting common stock as of 1980. They find that, after restructuring, management and family insiders control a median of 57 percent of the votes and 24 percent of the common stock cash flows. This confirms that dual-class structures often confer substantial voting powers on incumbent management. However, DeAngelo and DeAngelo also suggest that the shareholders of the firms in this sample found it beneficial to contract with incumbent management to limit the competition for management of their firms. They argue that shareholders rationally accept a reduced potential for hostile takeovers in return for other benefits, such as greater incentives for incumbents to make specific long-term investments in human capital.

Two recent studies have addressed the empirical question of whether dual-voting structures are beneficial, as DeAngelo and DeAngelo suggest, or harmful to outside shareholders. Partch (1987) examines the stock-price reaction around the announcement of the proposed dual-class recapitalizations for 44 firms. She reports nonnegative share-price effects. However, for more recent recapitalizations, Jarrell and Poulsen (forthcoming, extending OCE 1987a, 1987d) find negative effects at the announcement of dual-class recapitalizations. For a sample of 89 firms delisting from 1976 through 1987, they report an average abnormal stock price effect of −.93 percent.

If dual-class recapitalization proposals are viewed primarily as takeover defenses, their announcement should cause negative stock price reactions, similar to those observed at the announcement of supermajority amendments. However, firms announcing dual-class recapitalizations have some unusual characteristics. Jarrell and Poulsen (forthcoming) find that the average net-of-market return to their 94 dual-class firms over the year preceding the recapitalization is over 37 percent. Jarrell and Poulsen and Partch both find that insider holdings average 44 percent before the recapitalization, and that recapitalization significantly increases insider voting control. These two characteristics suggest that the typical dual-class firm is already controlled by insiders and the recapitalization provides a means to raise needed capital for positive net present value projects without the dilution of control.

Changes in the State of Incorporation. Changing the state of incorporation can affect the contractual arrangements between management and shareholders. For example, some states such as Ohio, Indiana, and New York have elements in their corporate codes that make takeovers more difficult than in other states. Dodd and Leftwich (1980) find that firms change their state of incorporation after a period of superior performance and that the change itself is associated with small positive excess returns. More recently, Romano (1985) finds a statistically significant price increase around the reincorporation announcement in a sample of firms that reincorporate for various reasons. However, in the subsample of 43 firms who reincorporated as an antitakeover device she found a small statistically insignificant price increase at the announcement of a reincorporation. The evidence is not conclusive but it does indicate that reincorporating in a new state does not on average harm shareholders.

Reduction in Cumulative Voting Rights. Cumulative voting makes it possible for a group of minority shareholders to elect directors even if the majority of shareholders oppose their election. Dissidents in hostile takeovers and proxy contests will often attempt to elect some board members through the use of cumulative voting. Bhagat and Brickley (1984) examine the stock price reaction to 84 management sponsored charter amendments that either eliminate or reduce the effect of cumulative voting. Since these amendments decrease the power of dissident shareholders to elect directors, they increase management's ability to resist a tender offer. Bhagat and Brickley find statistically significant negative abnormal returns of about one percent at the introduction of these charter amendments.

Defensive Measures That Do Not Require Shareholder Approval

Four general kinds of defensive measures do not require voting approval by shareholders: general litigation, greenmail, poison pills, and the use of state antitakeover laws. With the exception of general litigation, these defensive actions are associated on average with negative stock-price reactions indicating that in most cases they are economically harmful to stockholders of companies whose management enacted them.

Litigation by Target Management. As described earlier, litigation can be expected to hurt shareholders of some target companies by eliminating takeovers and to help shareholders of other companies by giving their management time and weapons to cut a better deal. Jarrell (1985) examines 89 cases involving litigation against a hostile suitor based on charges of securities fraud, antitrust violations, and violations of state or Federal tender offer regulations. His results show that litigation usually delays the control contest significantly and that litigating targets are frequently the beneficiaries of auctions. The 59 auction-style takeovers produced an additional 17 percent excess return to shareholders over the original bid, while the 21 targets that remained independent lost nearly all of the original average premium of 30 percent. Overall, Jarrell concludes that this evidence cannot reject the theory that on average target litigation is consistent with shareholder wealth maximization.[13]

However, harm can result from certain types of defensive litigation. Netter (1987) finds that litigation based in part on a claim alleging the filing of a false Schedule 13D Item 4 can be detrimental to target shareholders. In an exhaustive sample of all cases where target management filed a suit alleging (among other things) that a bidder filed a false 13D Item 4, he finds that target shareholders are better off if their management loses the case than if they win. If the target firm wins the case its share price declines by a significant amount (an abnormal return of negative 3.37 percent in the two-day window around the decision) while if the bidder wins, the stock price of the target firm increases by a significant amount (positive 3.15 percent abnormal return in the two-day window.

[13] Jarrell also notes that while defensive litigation redistributes premiums it also, by reducing incentives to engage in takeovers and through the cost of the litigation itself, can reduce social welfare.

Targeted Block Stock Repurchases (Greenmail). Greenmail occurs when target management ends a hostile takeover threat by repurchasing at a premium the hostile suitor's block of target stock. This controversial practice has been challenged in federal courts, in congressional testimony, and in SEC hearings, and it has brought negative publicity both to payers and to receivers of greenmail. In reviewing earlier studies, Jensen and Ruback (1983) conclude that greenmail repurchases are associated with significantly negative abnormal stock returns for the shareholders of the repurchasing firms (probably because they eliminate potential takeover bids) and significantly positive abnormal stock returns for shareholders of the selling firms. These negative effects of greenmail repurchases contrast sharply with the normally positive stock-price effects associated with nontargeted offers to repurchase a company's own stock.

Since then, three new empirical studies have contributed to a more complex and less conclusive discussion of greenmail transactions. These studies indicate that it is not necessarily in the interests of shareholders to ban greenmail payments. Such a ban has the potential to discourage outside investment in the potential target's stock by investors anticipating greenmail payments and hence reduces the incentives of outsiders to monitor managers.

Mikkelson and Ruback (1985a) examine 39 cases of greenmail (based on 13Ds filed during 1978–80). They find a significant stock-price loss of 2.3 percent upon the announcement of the repurchases. However, they also report an average gain of 1.7 percent over the entire period including the original stock purchase by the hostile suitors. Holderness and Sheehan's (1985) outcome-type study includes 12 cases of greenmail, and they report a pattern of returns consistent with the evidence of Mikkelson and Ruback. Although the greenmail transaction itself harms target shareholders, the net returns to stockholders resulting from the initial purchase and related events is positive. A more comprehensive sample of targeted block stock repurchases is covered by OCE (1984). This study includes 89 cases of large repurchases (blocks greater than 3 percent of the outstanding common stock) from 1979 to 1983. The initial announcement of investor interest induces a positive return averaging 9.7 percent, while the greenmail transaction is associated with a stock price loss of 5.2 percent.

Poison Pills. Since its introduction in late 1982, the "poison pill" has become the most popular and controversial device used to defend against hostile takeover attempts. Poison pill describes a family of shareholder rights agreements that, when triggered by an event such as a tender offer for control or the accumulation of a specified percentage of target shares by an acquirer, provide target shareholders with rights to purchase additional shares or to sell shares to the target at very attractive prices. These rights, when triggered, impose significant economic penalties on a hostile acquirer.

Poison pills are considered very effective deterrents against hostile takeover attempts because of two striking features. First, pills can be cheaply and quickly altered by target management if a hostile acquirer has not pulled the trigger. This feature pressures potential acquirers to negotiate directly with the target's board. Second, if not redeemed, the pill makes hostile acquisitions exorbitantly expensive in most cases. As an obstacle to hostile takeover attempts, the poison pill is unmatched except by dual-voting recapitalizations or direct majority share ownership by incumbent management. The concern over poison pills was heightened by the Delaware Supreme Court's 1985 ruling in *Moran v. Household International*[14] that poison pills do not require majority voting approval by shareholders.

The most comprehensive study of poison pills is Ryngaert (forthcoming), which is an outgrowth of OCE (1986). The Ryngaert study features an exhaustive collection of 380 poison pills adopted from 1982 to December 25, 1986. Over 80 percent of these were adopted after the *Household* decision. Ryngaert divides his sample into discriminatory pills (the most restrictive) and flip-over pills (the least restrictive). He also accounts for whether firms are subject to takeover speculation and whether confounding events occur close to the announcement of the pill that contaminate the data. The stock-price effect over the 283 cases with no confounding events is a statistically significant −.34 percent. Focusing on 57 cases subject to takeover speculation, the average loss is 1.51 percent, also statistically significant. These results are supported by the findings of Malatesta and Walkling (forthcoming).

Discriminatory pills have more harmful effects on shareholder wealth than do flip-over pills. Also, the discriminatory pills that threaten the hostile suitor with severe dilution have become increasingly popular. Ryngaert reports that pill-adopting managements own a surprisingly low average of around 3.0 percent of their firms' outstanding stock. This fact, together with high institutional holdings, suggest that many of these firms would have difficulty obtaining shareholder voting approval if it were required.

Ryngaert also examines the stock-price effects of important court decisions emanating from legal battles involving pill defenses during 1983–86. He shows that 15 of 18 pro-target, pro-poison pill decisions have negative effects on the target's stock price, and 6 of 11 pro-acquirer decisions have positive effects on the target stock price. This evidence is inconsistent with the theory that pill defenses improve shareholder wealth by strengthening management's bargaining position in control contests.

Although these losses are not large in percentage terms, these empirical tests suggest that poison pills are harmful to target shareholders.

State Antitakeover Amendments. In addition to the Williams Act at the Federal level, tender offers are regulated by many states. So-called first-generation state antitakeover regulations are antitakeover laws that were passed by the states before the 1982 Supreme Court decision in *Edgar v. Mite*.[15] The Jarrell and Bradley (1980) study of state and Federal regulation of tender offers finds that first generation state regulations significantly increase the premiums paid in tender offers. Smiley (1981) illustrates the deterrent effects of these early state takeover regulations.

However, first generation antitakeover laws were generally extinguished in *Edgar v. Mite* when the Supreme Court ruled the Illinois antitakeover law unconstitutional. Justice White's opinion held the Illinois takeover statute was preempted by the Williams Act and constituted an undue and direct burden on interstate commerce. As

[14] *Moran v. Household International*, 490 A.2d 1059 (1985).
[15] *Edgar v. Mite*, 457 U.S. 624, 102 S. Ct. 2629 (1982).

a result over 20 states passed second generation antitakeover laws to attempt to pass constitutional muster under the Supreme Court's reasoning. While some of them have also been ruled unconstitutional, the Supreme Court in 1987 (*CTS v. Dynamics Corp. of America*) ruled the Indiana antitakeover law constitutional.[16] This decision already is leading states to pass third generation antitakeover laws that would be constitutional under the CTS reasoning.

Two recent studies, Ryngaert and Netter (1987, based on OCE, 1987c) and Schumann (1987) provide more direct evidence on the wealth effects of state antitakeover regulations. Ryngaert and Netter examine the stock price effects of the passage of the Ohio antitakeover law on shareholders of firms chartered in Ohio. This act was passed during (and apparently motivated by) Sir James Goldsmith's attempted hostile takeover of Goodyear. They find that the passage of the law was accompanied by a significant stock-price loss of up to 3.24 percent to the shareholders of firms incorporated in Ohio with less than 30 percent inside ownership. This evidence on the impact of state takeover laws is supported by Schumann (1987) who finds a decline of approximately one percent to shareholders of New York firms on the announcement and passage of a New York antitakeover law. While these laws potentially could be beneficial to the individual states (if jobs are kept in the state by preventing takeovers), shareholders are harmed by state antitakeover regulations.

Summing Up Defensive Tactics

Four years ago Jensen and Ruback (1983) reviewed empirical studies of antitakeover charter amendments, shark repellents, changes of incorporation, and greenmail. They conclude (p. 47): "It is difficult to find managerial actions related to corporate control that harm stockholders; the exception are those actions that eliminate an actual or potential bidder, for example, through the use of targeted large block repurchases or standstill agreements."

Since their review, the defensive arsenal available to target management has been strengthened. These defensive tactics have been developed through a fascinating process of sequential innovations, as specific defenses arise to counter improved bidder finances and other tactics. In 1983, the now common fair-price amendment was a novel idea and the poison pill was not yet invented. Financial economists in academia and government have kept close pace with these developments, providing timely analyses of new charter amendments, poison pill defenses, greenmail transactions, and so on. While Jensen and Ruback were correct in predicting this area would be a "growth industry," we cannot reiterate their then-accurate conclusion that harmful defensive tactics are rare.

Conclusion

In the 1980s, the market for corporate control has been increasingly active, and the quantity of output of academic researchers studying corporate control questions

[16] *CTS v. Dynamics Corp. of America*, 107 S. Ct. 1637 (1987).

has mirrored the market activity. This review has confirmed the basic conclusions of Jensen and Ruback's (1983) review article and has shed light on some questions Jensen and Ruback were forced to leave unanswered. Financial researchers continue to find larger premiums being paid to target shareholders for later tender offers than for earlier tender offers. Acquirers, however, receive at best modest increases in their stock price, and the winners of bidding contests suffer stock-price declines as often as they do gains. This pro-target division of takeover gains appears to be partially a result of improved defensive tactics that can effectively delay execution of the bid and allow the target to receive improved bids from others or fashion a defensive restructuring and stock buyback. The evidence further suggests that the premiums in takeovers represent real wealth gains and are not simply wealth redistributions.

Prominent in the 1980s are new studies of defensive measures, such as antitakeover charter amendments, targeted block stock repurchases (greenmail), dual-voting recapitalizations, state antitakeover laws, and poison pills. The general finding, although it is far from conclusive, is that defensive measures that require shareholder voting approval are less likely to be harmful to shareholder wealth than are defensive measures not subject to shareholder approval. Fair-price charter amendments and dual-class recapitalizations that require shareholder approval are not shown to be harmful to stock value, while poison pills and greenmail-type repurchases that do not need shareholder approval appear on average to reduce shareholder value. However, some proposals that require a favorable vote from shareholders to implement (e.g., supermajority provisions and the elimination of cumulative voting) on average appear to reduce shareholder wealth. These findings raise serious questions about whether the business judgment rule is operating too broadly as a shield for defensive actions by target managements.

■ *We are especially grateful to Joseph Stiglitz, Timothy Taylor, and Annette Poulsen for their many helpful comments and suggestions. The Securities and Exchange Commission as a matter of policy disclaims responsibility for any private publication or statement by any of its employees. The views expressed here are those of the authors and do not necessarily reflect the views of the Commission or the authors' colleagues on the Staff of the Commission.*

References

Auerbach, Alan J. and David Reishus, "Taxes and the Merger Decision." In Coffee, J. and Louis Lowenstein, eds., *Takeovers and Contests for Corporate Control*, Oxford: Oxford University Press, 1987a.

Auerbach, Alan J. and David Reishus, "The Effects of Taxation on the Merger Decision," NBER Working Paper, 1987b.

Bhagat, Sanjai, and James Brickley, "The Value of Minority Shareholder Voting Rights," *Journal of Law and Economics*, 1984, *27*, 339–365.

Bhagat, Sanjai, James Brickley, and Uri Lowenstein, "The Pricing Effects of Inter-Firm Cash Tender Offers, *Journal of Finance*, 1987, *42*, 965–986.

Bradley, Michael, Amand Desai, and E. Han Kim, "Determinants of the Wealth Effects of Corporate Acquisitions," working paper, The University of Michigan, 1984.

Bradley, Michael, Amand Desai, and E. Han Kim, "The Rationale Behind Interfirm Tender Offers: Information or Synergy?" *Journal of Financial Economics*, 1983, *11*, 183–206.

Brickley, James, Ronald Lease, and Clifford Smith, "Ownership Structure and the Voting on Antitakeover Amendments," *Journal of Financial Economics*, forthcoming.

Brown, Charles and James L. Medoff, "The Impact of Firm Acquisitions on Labor," NBER Working paper, 1987.

Brown, Stephen J. and Jerold B. Warner, "Using Daily Stock Returns: The Case of Event Studies," *Journal of Financial Economics*, 1985, *14*, 3–31.

Comment, Robert, "Price and Volume Before Tender Offers: Market Anticipation Activity or Inside Trading, working paper New York University, 1986.

Comment, Robert and Gregg A. Jarrell, "Two-Tier Tender Offers: The Imprisonment of the Free Riding Shareholder," *Journal of Financial Economics*, forthcoming.

Council of Economic Advisors, "The Market for Corporate Control," *Economic Report of the President*, 1985, 187–216.

DeAngelo, Harry, and Linda DeAngelo, "Managerial Ownership of Voting Rights: A Study of Public Corporations With Dual Classes of Common Stock," *Journal of Financial Economics*, 1985, *14*, 33–69.

DeAngelo, Harry, Linda DeAngelo, and Edward M. Rice, "Going Private: Minority Freezeouts and Stockholder Wealth," *Journal of Law and Economics*, 1984, *27*, 367–402.

Denis, Debra K., and John J. McConnell, "Corporate Mergers and Security Returns," *Journal of Financial Economics*, 1986, *16*, 143–187.

Dodd, Peter, and Richard Leftwich, "The Market for Corporate Charters: 'Unhealthy Competition' Versus Federal Regulation," *Journal of Business*, 1980, *53*, 259–283.

Easterbrook, Frank H., and Gregg A. Jarrell, "Do Targets Gain From Defeating Tender Offers?" *New York University Law Review*, 1984, *59*, 277–299.

Eckbo, B. Espen, "Merger and the Market Concentration Doctrine: Evidence from the Capital Market," *Journal of Business*, 1985, *58*, 325–349.

Eckbo, B. Espen, and Herwig Langohr, "The Effect of Disclosure Regulations and the Medium of Exchange on Takeover Bids," Working paper, 1986.

Guerin-Calvert, Margaret, Robert H. McGuckin, and Frederick R. Warren-Boulton, "State and Federal Regulation in the Market for Corporate Control," U.S. Department of Justice, Economic Analysis Group Discussion Paper 86-4, 1986.

Hall, Bronwyn H., "The Effect of Takeover Activity on Corporate Research and Development," working paper, NBER, 1987.

Holderness, Clifford G. and Dennis P. Sheehan, "Raiders or Saviors? The Evidence on Six Controversial Investors," *Journal of Financial Economics*, 1985, *14*, 555–579.

James, Christopher M., and Peggy Weir, "Determinants of the Division of Gains in Corporate Acquisitions: Evidence from the Banking Industry, working paper, University of Oregon, 1987.

Jarrell, Gregg A., "The Wealth Effects of Litigation by Targets: Do Interests Diverge in a Merge?" *Journal of Law and Economics*, 1985, *28*, 151–177.

Jarrell, Gregg A., and Michael Bradley, "The Economic Effects of Federal and State Regulations of Cash Tender Offers," *Journal of Law and Economics*, 1980, *23*, 371–407.

Jarrell, Gregg A., and Annette B. Poulsen, "Bidder Returns," working paper, 1987a.

Jarrell, Gregg A., and Annette B. Poulsen, "The Effects of Recapitalization with Dual Classes of Common Stock on the Wealth of Shareholders," *Journal of Financial Economics*, forthcoming.

Jarrell, Gregg A., and Annette B. Poulsen, "Shark Repellents and Stock Prices: The Effects of Antitakeover Amendments Since 1980," *Journal of Financial Economics*, 1987b, *19*, 127–168.

Jensen, Michael C., "The Takeover Controversy: Analysis and Evidence," *Midland Corporate Finance Journal*, 1986, 6–32.

Jensen, Michael C., and Richard S. Ruback, "The Market for Corporate Control: The Scientific Evidence," *Journal of Financial Economics*, 1983, *11*, 5–50.

Lease, Ronald C., John J. McConnell, and Wayne H. Mikkelson, "The Market Value of Control in Publicly Traded Corporations," *Journal of Financial Economics*, 1983, *11*, 439–472.

Lehn, Kenneth, and Annette B. Poulsen, "Sources of Value in Leveraged Buyouts." In *Public Policy Towards Corporate Takeovers*. New Brunswick, NJ: Transaction Publishers, 1987.

Malatesta, Paul H., and Ralph A. Walkling, "Poison Pill Securities: Stockholder Wealth, Profitability, and Ownership Structure," *Journal of Financial Economics*, forthcoming.

McConnell, John J. and Chris J. Muscarella, "Capital Expenditure Decisions and Market Value of the Firm," *Journal of Financial Economics*, 1985, *14*, 399–422.

Mikkelson, Wayne H. and Richard S. Ruback, "An Empirical Analysis of the Interfirm Equity Investment Process," *Journal of Financial Economics*, 1985, *14*, 523–553.

Netter, Jeffry M. "Shareholder Wealth Effects of Litigation Based on Allegedly False Schedule 13D Item 4 Disclosure," working paper, 1987.

Office of the Chief Economist, Securities and Exchange Commission, "The Economics of Any-or-All, Partial, and Two-Tier Tender Offers," 1985a.

Office of the Chief Economist, Securities and Exchange Commission, "Update—The Effects of Dual-Class Recapitalizations on Shareholder Wealth: Including Evidence from 1986 and 1987," 1987d.

Office of the Chief Economist, Securities and Exchange Commission, "The Effects of Poison Pills on the Wealth of Target Shareholders," 1986.

Office of the Chief Economist, Securities and Exchange Commission, "The Impact of Targetted Share Repurchases (Greenmail) on Stock Prices," 1984.

Office of the Chief Economist, Securities and Exchange Commission, "Institutional Ownership, Tender Offers and Long Term Investment," 1985b.

Office of the Chief Economist, Securities and Exchange Commission, "Shareholder Wealth Effects of Ohio Legislation Affecting Takeovers," 1987b.

Office of the Chief Economist, Securities and Exchange Commission, "Shark Repellents and Stock Prices: The Effects of Antitakeover Amendments Since 1980," 1985c.

Office of the Chief Economist, Securities and Exchange Commission, "Stock Trading Before the Announcement of Tender Offers: Insider Trading or Market Anticipation?" 1987c.

Office of the Chief Economist, Securities and Exchange Commission, "The Effects of Dual-Class Recapitalizations on the Wealth Of Shareholders," 1987a.

Partch, Megan. "The Creation of A Class of Limited Voting Common Stock and Shareholders" Wealth," *Journal of Financial Economics*, 1987, *18*, 313–339.

Romano, Roberta, "Law as a Product: Some Pieces of the Incorporation Puzzle," *Journal of Law Economics and Organization*, 1985, *1*, 225–267.

Ruback, Richard S., "An Overview of Takeover Defenses," working paper #1836-86, Massachusetts Institute of Technology, 1986.

Ryngaert, Michael, "The Effect of Poison Pill Securities on Shareholder Wealth," *Journal of Financial Economics*, forthcoming.

Ryngaert, Michael, and Nettter Jeffry, "Shareholder Wealth Effects of the Ohio Antitakeover Law," working paper, 1987.

Schumann, Laurence, "State Regulation of Takeovers and Shareholder Wealth: The Effects of New York's 1985 Takeover Statutes," Bureau of Economics Staff Report to the Federal Trade Commission, March 1987.

Shleifer, Andrei and Lawrence Summers, "Hostile Takeovers as Breaches of Trust," working paper, NBER, 1987.

Smiley, Robert, "The Effect of State Securities Statutes on Tender Offer Activity," *Economic Inquiry*, 1981, *19*, 426–435.

Steindel, Charles, "Tax Reform and the Merger and Acquisition Market: The Repeal of General Utilities," *Federal Reserve Bulletin of New York*, Autumn 1986, 31–35.

[11]

ELSEVIER

Journal of Corporate Finance 10 (2004) 1–36

Journal of CORPORATE FINANCE

www.elsevier.com/locate/econbase

Investigating the economic role of mergers

Gregor Andrade *, Erik Stafford

Harvard Business School, Soldiers Field, Boston, MA 02163, USA

Received 31 May 2000; accepted 17 May 2002

Abstract

We investigate the economic role of mergers by performing a comparative study of mergers and internal corporate investment at the industry and firm levels. We find strong evidence that merger activity clusters through time by industry, whereas internal investment does not. Mergers play both an "expansionary" and "contractionary" role in industry restructuring. During the 1970s and 1980s, excess capacity drove industry consolidation through mergers, while peak capacity utilization triggered industry expansion through non-merger investments. In the 1990s, this phenomenon is reversed, as industries with strong growth prospects, high profitability, and near capacity experience the most intense merger activity.

JEL classification: G34
Keywords: Mergers; Acquisitions; Restructuring; Corporate governance

1. Introduction

This paper investigates the economic role of corporate mergers and acquisitions by studying both the firm and industry level forces that motivate them. We classify these forces broadly as either "expansionary," in which case mergers are similar in spirit to internal investment, adding to the capital stock of a firm or industry; or "contractionary," whereby mergers facilitate consolidation and reduction of the asset base.

From the point of view of the acquiring company, the first-order effect of mergers is a net addition to the firm's stock of assets. This has two implications. Firstly, a significant portion of merger activity should be explained by factors that motivate firms to expand and

* Corresponding author.
E-mail addresses: gandrade@hbs.edu (G. Andrade), estafford@hbs.edu (E. Stafford).

0929-1199/$ - see front matter © 2002 Elsevier Science B.V. All rights reserved.
doi:10.1016/S0929-1199(02)00023-8

grow. Secondly, mergers and internal investment should be related, since they are similar ways of adding to a firm's asset base and productive capacity. Therefore, the choice between investing internally and acquiring another firm boils down to considering the relative net benefits of the alternatives.

Industry-wide forces can also precipitate mergers, for example, a reaction to a change in the industry structure, in response to some fundamental shock. This somewhat intuitive view has gained prominence in recent years. Jensen (1993) proposes that most merger activity since the mid-1970s has been caused by technological and supply shocks, which resulted in excess productive capacity in many industries. He argues that mergers are the principal way of removing this excess capacity, as faulty internal governance mechanisms prevent firms from "shrinking" themselves. Mitchell and Mulherin (1996) document that a substantial portion of takeover activity in the 1980s could be explained by industries reacting to major shocks, such as deregulation, increased foreign competition, financial innovations, and oil price shocks. In addition, Morck et al. (1988) suggest that hostile takeovers are "responses to adverse industry-wide shocks."

When mergers are due to industry-wide causes, their association with expansion becomes less clear-cut. In particular, at the industry level, the immediate effect of own-industry mergers is the reallocation of existing assets. Clearly, this reallocation can occur in the context of an industry-wide expansion, as firms may attempt to increase their size and scale in order to afford large capital investments.[1] However, it is also clear that to the extent that mergers within an industry allow firms to remove duplicate functions and rationalize operations, they often result in an overall decrease in the industry's asset base. These are two fundamentally different types of merger activity, and the tension between their effects on industry-level productive capacity, growth in one case and neutral or reduction in the other, suggests that merger activity can be decomposed into two fundamental roles: "expansion" and "contraction."

While the notion that mergers play different economic roles has been previously cited, and to some extent intuitively held by many merger researchers, there is scant empirical work linking these disparate roles. This paper is aimed at filling this gap. We examine the determinants of mergers and internal corporate investment, within a framework that allows us to test for the incidence of different types of mergers, expansionary or contractionary, over time and across industries. Also, by performing the analysis both at the industry- and firm-level, we can empirically verify our premise that merger activity is related to both firm-specific and industry-wide causes.

Given our previous definitions, we test for the expansionary role of mergers at the firm and industry-level by determining the extent to which mergers and internal investment both respond to the same external incentives to add assets. In particular, this story predicts that both merger and non-merger investment should be increasing in estimates of growth opportunities, such as Tobin's q. We also expect that the incentives to expand are stronger in times when existing capacity is near exhaustion, and thus both merger and non-merger investment should be positively related to capacity utilization. In contrast, the contractio-

[1] This explanation is often cited as the main reason behind the media and telecommunications mergers of the 1990s.

nary role implies that merger activity should be negatively related to capacity utilization, particularly at the industry level.

Regression analysis on the industry-level determinants of merger and non-merger investment finds that industry capacity utilization has significant and opposite effects on merger and non-merger investment. Excess capacity drives industry consolidation through mergers, while peak capacity utilization induces industry expansion through non-merger investments.[2] Further analysis reveals that the negative relationship between mergers and capacity utilization is restricted to the 1970s and 1980s, while in the 1990s, the relation is positive and significant, indicating that the role of mergers in facilitating expansion and contraction changes over time. The evidence suggests that in the mid-1970s and 1980s, as the economy adjusted to a variety of shocks to capacity and competition (see Mitchell and Mulherin, 1996), industries restructured and consolidated via mergers. However, during the 1990s, merger activity appears more related to industry expansion, as industries near capacity, with high q, and increased profitability are more likely to experience intense merger activity. In addition, we find a strong positive relation between industry shocks and own-industry mergers in the 1990s. This is consistent with recent findings by Mulherin and Boone (2000) and Andrade et al. (2001) who each find significantly higher merger activity in recently deregulated industries in the 1990s.

We also perform clustering tests, which indicate significant time series clustering of mergers by industry of the acquirer. In particular, industry rankings of merger activity are essentially independent through time, while similar rankings for non-merger forms of investment show strong persistence from one 5-year sub-period to the next. Also, on average, half of an industry's mergers occur within a span of 5 years during our sample period from 1970 to 1994. This evidence is suggestive of mergers resulting from industry shocks, unlike non-merger investments. These results on acquirer industry clustering are similar to those found for target firms by Mitchell and Mulherin (1996), and for both mergers and divestitures in the 1990s by Mulherin and Boone (2000). In a separate test, we find that in four out of five sub-periods, industry rankings of merger and non-merger investment are independent of each other, indicating a lack of either complementarity or substitutability between merger and other types of investment.

At the firm level, we find further evidence of an important expansionary component to mergers. In particular, we find that firms classified as "high q" are significantly more likely to undertake both mergers and non-merger investment projects than "low q" firms, as would be predicted by the q-theory of investment. Moreover, we find a strong positive relation between sales growth and both mergers and non-merger investment. Therefore, both merger and non-merger investments seem to respond similarly to firm-level incentives to grow.

The sample used in our study is described in the next section. Section 3 characterizes industry level merger and non-merger investment activity. Section 4 reports firm-level analysis. The final section summarizes our results and concludes.

[2] The positive relation between internal investment and industry capacity utilization is also reported in Kovenock and Phillips (1997).

2. Data sources and sample description

One of the main difficulties in performing industry-level empirical work is deciding on relevant industry classifications and allocating firms to them. Both CRSP and Compustat report SIC codes for most firms they cover, but these data are fraught with errors. In fact, recent studies (see for example, Kahle and Walkling, 1996, Guenther and Rosman, 1994 and the CRSP documentation manuals) indicate that more than one-third of firms on both databases do not match at the two-digit level of SIC code, which for many industries is already an excessive level of aggregation.[3] In addition, since Compustat only reports current SIC codes, while CRSP reports historical classifications, matching worsens as one goes further back in time.[4]

The data set we use for this paper is based on the universe of firms and industries covered by Value Line from 1970 to 1994. This provides a ready-made, widely accepted industry classification scheme, allowing us to sidestep the problems with SIC codes mentioned above. For each year during the sample period, we compile a list of all firms and their industry assignments from the fourth quarter edition of Value Line (see Appendix A for details on this procedure).

We exclude all firms classified under: (1) foreign industries (e.g., "Japanese Diversified," or "Canadian Energy"), (2) ADR's, (3) REIT's, and (4) investment funds and/or companies. We also eliminate 6 firms that were not in Compustat, as well as 67 firms that were classified as "Unassigned" or "Recent Additions" in some years but were not subsequently assigned to an industry. There are also 30 firms that, for at least 1 year, Value Line placed in two different industries, which we randomly assign to one of them. The resulting sample contains 2969 firms, representing 37,147 firm-years.

Merger data consist of a subset of the CRSP Merger Database including all mergers between CRSP-listed firms over the 1970–1994 period. The database includes transaction announcement and completion dates obtained from the Wall Street Journal Index for most mergers, where completion is defined as the earliest date in which control (+50% interest) is achieved. For 196 deals where a completion date is not available, it is estimated as 4 months following the announcement, which corresponds to the median time period elapsed between announcement and completion for the mergers that report both dates. We assign each merger a value based on the total market value of the target at completion, defined as the sum of total book debt and preferred stock [Compustat items 9, 34 and 56], market equity capitalization [from CRSP], less excess cash, estimated as total cash in the balance sheet [Compustat item 1] in excess of 5.5% of sales,[5] with all balance sheet items as of pre-completion fiscal year-end (see Appendix C for a listing of Compustat data items

[3] For example, SIC code 2800 includes firms which produce chemicals, drugs, and toiletries and cosmetics, all of which we classify separately.

[4] However, this should not lead one to conclude that since CRSP reports historical SIC codes, that it must be the preferred classification source, because as Kahle and Walkling (1996) show, Compustat classifies current firms more accurately. In fact, CRSP SIC code allocations have so many mistakes that they effectively offset any advantage from having historical numbers.

[5] 5.5% corresponds to the median ratio of cash to sales for all firms on Compustat from 1970 to 1994.

used in this paper). Targets in the financial sector are valued only at market equity. In addition, for 612 target firms not available in Compustat, we hand-collect capitalization figures from the annual Moody's Industrial, OTC, Transportation and Utilities manuals. As a result, only 66 mergers are not assigned a value, and are therefore excluded from the analysis. Our method for assigning deal values allows us to maximize use of the sample by not requiring the parties involved to disclose the price of the transaction. On the other hand, it assumes that the acquirer obtains 100% of the target at the completion date. While that may be true for most mergers in the sample, there are some for which the completion date merely represents acquisition of control, which was later followed by a "clean-up merger" at a different price. In addition, we exclude leveraged buyouts and other going-private deals, which were very common in the 1980s. This is because our analysis focuses on acquirers that can and do engage in both mergers and non-merger investment, rather than firms whose sole purpose is to perform takeovers.[6]

Finally, we search through the merger data set for deals where the acquirer belonged to our industry sample at the time of the merger completion and the deal was completed after 1969. This procedure yields 1711 mergers, of which 1682 have estimated values that are allocated to the respective acquirer in the fiscal year of completion. Table A2 in Appendix B shows how the mergers are distributed by industry and year. In addition, for each of these mergers, we attempt to allocate the target firm to an industry at the time of the initial merger announcement, by searching in Value Line, or by matching combinations of CRSP, Compustat and Dun and Bradstreet Million Dollar Directory SIC codes (see Appendix B for details on the target industry assignment procedure). For the subset of target firms assigned to an industry, we classify the merger as diversifying or own-industry by comparing acquirer and target industry classifications at announcement. Diversifying mergers are defined as deals where the industry of the acquirer and the target differ, while the opposite is true for own-industry merger. In total, 1536 targets are successfully assigned to an industry, resulting in 656 diversifying and 880 own-industry mergers.

3. Mergers and non-merger investment at the industry level

The goal of this section is to gain insights into the industry-level forces behind merger and non-merger investment. Specifically, we test (1) the degree to which mergers and non-merger investment are related to shocks to industry structure, (2) whether mergers tend to occur in times of industry-wide excess capacity, and (3) whether mergers tend to occur in times of strong industry growth prospects.

Most industry-level empirical analysis we perform is based on industry-wide measures of annual merger and investment "intensities," which we define as the total value of merger and investment activity in the industry, scaled by the total book assets of all firms in the industry at year-end. This method is useful in two respects: (1) the intensities can be compared across time, industries, and types of merger and non-merger investment, since

[6] Excluding LBO's and other going-private deals makes our merger series different at the aggregate level from the ones used by other authors, who include all takeovers of domestic targets.

they are fairly insensitive to changes and/or differences in industry composition,[7] and (2) at the firm level, investment is aimed at replacing depreciated assets and/or adding new assets, therefore, it is natural to scale investment by some measure of the capital stock in place.[8] We estimate annual industry-level intensities for six types of expenditures: (1) Merger, (2) Diversifying Merger, (3) Own-Industry Merger, (4) CAPX, (5) R&D, and (6) Non-Merger Investment (defined as the sum of CAPX, R&D and advertising expenses). For merger-related intensities (1, 2 and 3 above), the denominator in the intensity measure includes all firms reporting non-missing book assets, whereas for non-merger investment intensities (4, 5 and 6), we also require firms to report non-missing CAPX to ensure that the same firms are included in the numerator and denominator. When calculating the non-merger investment intensities, R&D and advertising are set to zero whenever missing.

Table 1 reports summary statistics on the total level of investment by our sample firms between 1970 and 1994. This total includes both merger and non-merger investment, as defined above.[9] The table also displays the percentage of total investment made up of merger activity. Note that the relative importance of merger activity changes over time. This is seen more clearly in Fig. 1, which plots the average ratio of merger to total investment expenditures for our sample firms on an annual basis.[10] Firm-level expenditures on mergers relative to internal investment increased dramatically in the late 1980s, not surprising considering the period corresponds to a well-known economy-wide merger wave. However, it is interesting that even during the recession that followed in the early 1990s, merger activity remained at a significantly higher level than in the 1970s. Perhaps this represents a shift in the overall propensity of firms to acquire others, which would also be consistent with the subsequent explosion in merger activity of the late 1990s, the largest merger wave ever (see Andrade et al., 2001).

3.1. Historical patterns in industry merger and non-merger investment

Mitchell and Mulherin (1996) document significant clustering of target firms by industry during the 1980s.[11] In this sub-section, we test for such industry clustering in both merger

[7] Furthermore, these intensities are later used as dependent variables in panel regressions, in which case the scaling provides a rough but somewhat effective means of controlling for heteroscedasticity.

[8] See Kaplan and Zingales (1997) and Mitchell and Mulherin (1996) for recent examples of empirical studies where proxies for firm value scale investment and merger expenditures.

[9] Aggregate investment peaks in the early 1980's but that is due mainly to changes in the composition of Value Line over the sample period. In particular, starting in the early 1980's, the banking and brokerage industries have constituted a larger portion of the sample relative to early periods (see Table A1 in Appendix A). As these industries perform little non-merger investment (especially CAPX and R&D), they reduce the overall level of investment in the total sample.

[10] Both Table 1 and Fig. 1 understate total merger activity, given the way we identify merger in this study. In particular, we only look at merger between Value Line acquirers and CRSP-listed targets. We ignore foreign acquirers and targets, acquisitions of plants and divisions, as well as LBO's and other going-private transactions.

[11] There is also evidence of clustering in earlier periods. Nelson (1959) identifies pronounced differences in takeover rates across industries over time, using data for the first half of the century. Gort (1969) confirms those results with data on takeovers in the 1950s, and suggests they are caused by "economic disturbances" due to rapid changes in technology and/or stock prices.

Table 1
Summary statistics on real investment expenditures by sample firms, and comparison of industry-level investment intensity rankings across 5-year sub-periods from 1970 to 1994

Summary Statistics:

	1970–1974	1975–1979	1980–1984	1985–1989	1990–1994
Real total investment (merger and non-merger) in billions of 1994 dollars	\$1377	\$1954	\$2340	\$2291	\$2168
Merger as of total investment (%)	3.8%	4.9%	9.4%	12.5%	7.9%

Sub-period correlations

	Spearman's rank correlation coefficient			
	1970–1974 vs. 1975–1979	1975–1979 vs. 1980–1984	1980–1984 vs. 1985–1989	1985–1989 vs. 1990–1994
Merger	0.376 (0.006)	0.331 (0.015)	0.114 (0.403)	0.175 (0.198)
CAPX	0.830 (0.000)	0.860 (0.000)	0.659 (0.000)	0.729 (0.000)
R&D	0.970 (0.000)	0.969 (0.000)	0.949 (0.000)	0.931 (0.000)
Non-merger investment	0.883 (0.000)	0.912 (0.000)	0.853 (0.000)	0.855 (0.000)

Total investment expenditures include both merger and non-merger investment, and are reported in constant 1994 dollars. Comparisons between pairs of consecutive sub-periods are based on Spearman's rank correlation coefficient. Industry rankings are based on investment intensities that are calculated for each industry as the average over the sub-period of the annual ratio of total investment of each type by firms in the industry to the total book assets of the industry at year-end. Industry merger values are the total value of all transactions in the CRSP Merger Database involving acquirers in the industry. Capital expenditures (CAPX), research and development (R&D) and advertising include all sample firms with Compustat data. Non-merger investment is the sum of CAPX, R&D, and advertising. CAPX rankings exclude financial sector firms. R&D rankings include only industries related to manufacturing and mining. *P*-values are in parentheses.

and non-merger investment activity. In contrast to those authors, we look at the industry of the acquirer, not the target. A finding that mergers cluster by industry over time would support the claim that, to some extent, merger activity is a result of industry shocks.

We divide the sample period (1970–1994) into five equal sub-periods, and calculate industry-level sub-period intensities for all six of the investment measures defined above,

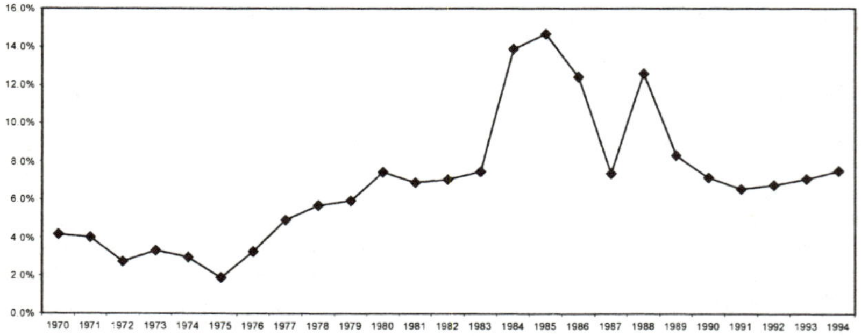

Fig. 1. Merger activity as the percentage of total firm-level investment (average across all firms).

by averaging the annual intensities within each sub-period.[12] Then, each of the industry-level investment intensity series is ranked within each sub-period, and we compare the rankings over time and across forms of investment.[13] Therefore, we are testing whether the relative ranking across industries, for each form of investment, is persistent over time.

For each of merger, CAPX, R&D and non-merger investment, we analyze the stability of rankings over time. We perform a Spearman's rank correlation test for each pair of consecutive sub-periods (see Gibbons, 1985 for details). Since the null hypothesis is that the rankings are independent each period, rejection indicates a strong level of stability in the rankings. Table 1 reports our results.

The first thing to note is the striking contrast between the stability of merger and non-merger rankings across sub-periods. While industry merger rankings, particularly in the 1980s, exhibit little correlation from one sub-period to the next, the rankings for CAPX, R&D and total non-merger investment intensity are nearly constant.[14] This is evident not only from the puny *p*-values, but the magnitude of the test statistics themselves, which can be loosely interpreted as correlation coefficients. The industry-rank correlations average 0.25 across sub-periods for mergers and 0.88 for non-merger investment. Additionally, the average industry has approximately 50% of its mergers occur within a 5-year sub-period over the 25-year sample period (see Table A2 in Appendix B). These results suggest strong time series clustering of industry merger activity, while rejecting the notion of clustering for non-merger investment. The result that non-merger investment does not cluster by industry is important, as it strengthens the restructuring interpretation of the evidence on mergers. In some sense, if both merger and non-merger investment clustered, we would be hard-pressed to argue that mergers play a distinct restructuring role, one that cannot be fulfilled by other forms of investment.[15]

Given the markedly different historical patterns in merger and non-merger investment, it is interesting to check whether at each point in time there is any relation, positive or negative, between the two. In particular, we want to know whether there is any evidence of complementarity or substitutability between internal and external investment, or its components. Towards that goal, within each sub-period, we compare the rankings between the following sets of investment intensity pairs: (1) merger and non-merger investment, (2) diversifying merger and non-merger investment, (3) own-industry merger and non-merger

---

[12] We also estimate business cycle-based sub-periods, using NBER's classification of expansions and contractions. This resulted in five cycles during our sample period: 1970–1974, 1975–1979, 1980–1982, 1983–1990, and 1991–1994 (this last period is not a complete cycle, since it has been a period of expansion only). Changing the sub-period definition did not impact the results, and the inferences remained unaltered, therefore, only the equal sub-periods are reported.

[13] For CAPX and R&D rankings, we exclude certain industries because: (1) Compustat does not report CAPX or R&D expense for them, or (2) by the very nature of their business, these firms do not perform R&D investment. As a result, CAPX rankings exclude firms in the financial sector, while the R&D rankings include only manufacturing and mining firms.

[14] If depreciation rates differ greatly across industries but are fairly constant through time, it can be argued that the stability in CAPX and non-merger investment intensity rankings is partly due to industries replacing depreciated assets.

[15] A separate impliction of the results on industry clustering is that merger event studies are poorly specified statistically. The assumption of independence across events is certainly violated, and is likely even more severe a problem for long-term performance studies (see Mitchell and stafford, 2000).

investment, and (4) diversifying merger and own-industry merger. The statistical procedure used is again the Spearman's rank correlation test. Note that under the null hypothesis, the rankings within each sub-period are independent—a rejection indicates some complementarity or substitutability between investment forms, depending on the sign.

Table 2 contains our results for these tests. In general, the merger and non-merger investment intensities are independent within sub-periods. Therefore, there is no persistent evidence that firms merge conditionally on high levels of internal investment in the industry, during our sample period. There is some indication that merger and non-merger investment in the late 1980s are complements, apparently driven by diversifying mergers. In other words, the industries that experienced high levels of merger activity in the late 1980s were also industries that were expanding via internal investment. Note that in addition, we find virtually no relation between own-industry and diversifying mergers, suggesting that it is important to analyze these separately.

In short, during the 1970–1994 sample period, merger intensities differed significantly through time by industry, and showed little relation to non-merger investment within any given sub-period. The picture that emerges is one where industry non-merger investment is fairly stable through time, while there are periods of intense merger activity at the industry level, perhaps in response to changing industry conditions that bring about broad restructuring.

3.2. Panel regressions: the determinants of industry merger and non-merger investment

In this section, we search for more specific evidence on the expansionary and contractionary motives for mergers by examining the relation between annual industry-level merger and non-merger investment activity, industry capacity utilization, shocks, and proxies for growth opportunities. The regression framework allows us to control for other

Table 2

Comparison within sub-periods of industry-level investment intensity rankings across investment types. Sub-periods are 5-year intervals from 1970 to 1994

Investment comparison	1970–1974	1975–1979	1980–1984	1985–1989	1990–1994
Merger vs. non-merger investment	0.009 (0.950)	− 0.021 (0.875)	0.210 (0.123)	0.308 (0.024)	0.057 (0.677)
Diversifying merger vs. non-merger investment	− 0.069 (0.614)	− 0.265 (0.051)	0.032 (0.813)	0.287 (0.035)	− 0.031 (0.822)
Own-industry merger vs. non-merger investment	− 0.008 (0.954)	0.107 (0.432)	0.073 (0.593)	0.108 (0.429)	0.064 (0.639)
Diversifying merger vs. own-industry merger	0.259 (0.057)	0.005 (0.972)	− 0.039 (0.777)	− 0.112 (0.409)	− 0.184 (0.177)

Comparisons are based on Spearman's rank correlation coefficients. Industry rankings are based on investment intensities that are calculated for each industry as the average over the sub-period of the annual ratio of total investment of each type by firms in the industry to the total book assets of the industry at year-end. Industry merger values are the total value of all transactions in the CRSP Merger Database involving acquirers in the industry. Capital expenditures (CAPX), research and development (R&D) and advertising include all sample firms with Compustat data. Non-merger investment is the sum of CAPX, R&D, and advertising. CAPX rankings exclude financial sector firms. R&D rankings include only industries related to manufacturing, mining and utilities. *P*-values are in parentheses.

determinants of merger and non-merger investment, such as business conditions and industry structure characteristics. The dependent variables in our panel regressions are "merger," "own-industry merger," and "non-merger investment" intensities. For the merger-based dependent variable, we have the problem that in many industry-years there are no mergers, as can be seen in Table A2 (Appendix B). Therefore, the intensity measure is censored at zero, which makes ordinary least squares (OLS) estimates inconsistent. We account for this by fitting Tobit specifications, which are designed to explicitly correct for this type of censoring.[16] For the non-merger-based dependent variables, censoring is not a problem, and simple OLS regressions are estimated. To allow comparable inferences from both Tobit and OLS specifications, only raw Tobit coefficients are reported, i.e., not conditioned on the dependent variable being strictly positive (for a discussion on this point, see Greene, 1993).

From Compustat, we create the following set of annual industry-level explanatory variables, which are all constructed as ratios of sums over firms in the industry at year-end:[17]

Variable	Definition	Requirements for inclusion of firm
Tobin's q (q)[18]	[book assets + market equity− book equity]/book assets	market equity, book equity>0 book assets>0
Cash flow (CF)	EBITDA/sales	sales>0
Sales growth (SALESGRO)	[sales(t)/cpi(t)]/[sales($t-2$)/ cpi($t-2$)] − 1	sales(t and $t-2$)>0, presence in industry at time t
Shock	abs[sales growth (t) − mean(sales growth in all t)]	same as sales growth
Industry concentration (INDCONC)[19]	sum[(sales/ total industry sales)^2]	sales>0[20]

Note that the above definition of 2-year sales growth is somewhat biased, since it only includes firms that are present at time t. Therefore, it underestimates industry growth if there has been entry, and industry decline if there has been exit. The same goes for the "shock" variable, which is based on the sales growth calculation.

[16] See Greene (1993) and Maddala (1983) for detailed discussions on Tobit estimation techniques, the form of the likelihood function, and the asymptotic variance matrix.

[17] Summing over all numerator and denominator firms before creating the ratio makes these independent variables "value-weighted" measures.

[18] This definition of q is flawed in many respects: (1) it assumes replacement value of assets and market value of liabilities is well proxied by book value, (2) it assumes average and marginal q are the same, (3) it ignores tax effects. Still, it is easy to calculate and it's minimal data requirements allow for maximal coverage on Compustat, which likely explains why it is commonly found in the macro and finance literatures (see Blanchard et al., 1994 and Kaplan and Zingales, 1997 for recent examples).

[19] We use the natural logarithm of INDCONC in all of our regressions. The industry concentration measure that we use is also known as the Hirshman–Herfindahl Index.

[20] For years, where less then two-thirds of the firms in the industry reported positive sales, we estimated the INDCONC using one of the following procedures: (1) if 1970 or 1994 is missing, we regress the valid INDCONC's on a time trend and predict the missing values for those 2 years, otherwise (2) we linearly interpolate using INDCONC's available on dates surrounding the missing year.

From CITIBASE, we obtain industry capacity utilization rates (CAPUTIL). Only figures for manufacturing, mining and utilities are available, therefore service and financial industries are assigned "missing" codes for this variable. Also, since the capacity utilization ratios are reported on the basis of two-digit SIC codes for the most part, wherever our industries are more finely classified than the figures on CITIBASE, we assign the same capacity utilization figure for all the industries covered by the classification (e.g., both the electrical equipment and electronics industries are given the CITIBASE "Electrical Equipment" capacity utilization rate).

All regression specifications exclude three financial sector industries[21] because: (a) Compustat does not report CAPX for these firms, making non-merger investment invalid, and (b) differences in accounting and the nature of the businesses themselves make it difficult to define variables comparable to cash flow, capacity, etc. In addition, the explanatory variables are always as of the beginning of the period, i.e., lagged by 1 year. This is done to accommodate the fact that variables such as q are forward-looking, so their effect must precede the investment, as well as the more practical point that depending on how investment is financed or a merger accounted for, accounting-based variables such as profitability and sales growth may be affected by the merger or investment itself, generating a spurious correlation. Finally, all regression specifications include both year and industry dummy variables.

Our choice of independent variables is motivated by the need to control for other factors which theory suggests should influence investment activity. On the other hand, since some of these theories, such as q-theory, are meant to describe firm-level investment, arguably they are better suited to the firm-level analysis of Section 4. Still, to the extent that growth prospects are correlated across firms in an industry, we might expect to see some industry-wide effects, and therefore the variables are included in the industry-level specifications. For example, assuming q-theory is well specified at the industry level, all forms of investment should be positively related to q. This is captured in our "base" specification, where q is measured as a continuous variable. However, another interpretation of the theory suggests that firms with good growth opportunities should be investing, while firms with poor growth opportunities should not. It is not clear what can be said about the relation between investment and q, conditional on having good or bad growth prospects. Therefore, we present specifications that also include the "high q" and "low q" dummy variables, which are meant to identify the industries with good and poor growth opportunities. Each year, we sort the industries on the basis of q, classifying the bottom third as "low q" and the top third as "high q," and then assigning them to dummy variables of the same name. In addition, this classification scheme helps get around some of the empirical problems with measures of q. Since our estimates of q likely have measurement error, we are more comfortable making inferences based on the broader classifications. This will be particularly important for the firm level analysis in Section 4, where measurement errors are more severe.

We also include a measure of industry profitability and cash flow (CF), which not only captures some measure of industry business conditions, but also helps pick up elements of growth prospects and "real q" that our noisy estimate of q might fail to measure.

---

[21] They are: (1) Bank and Thrift, (2) Brokerage, Leasing and Financial Services, and (3) Insurance.

Table 3

(a) Ordinary least squares panel regressions of annual non-merger investment intensities on industry-level variables

	Levels			Industry-adjusted		
Low q		− 13.28	− 9.08		− 17.07	− 16.27
		(− 5.71)***	(− 3.44)***		(− 5.92)***	(− 4.97)***
High q		6.26	9.54		8.74	22.87
		(2.62)***	(3.05)***		(2.62)***	(5.52)***
q	11.54	7.59	− 0.19	38.06	26.60	21.76
	(5.84)***	(3.61)***	(− 0.08)	(17.31)***	(9.29)***	(6.90)***
Cash flow	151.55	130.21	− 2.40	65.70	73.67	93.04
	(5.59)***	(4.83)***	(− 0.06)	(3.47)***	(3.95)***	(3.59)***
Sales growth	26.40	19.98	27.04	26.66	15.56	− 0.07
	(4.88)***	(3.68)***	(3.26)***	(3.53)***	(2.05)**	(− 0.01)
Industry shock	− 4.57	− 1.25	− 4.77			
	(− 0.57)	(− 0.16)	(− 0.45)			
Industry	2.89	4.45	2.80	13.82	13.58	20.51
concentration	(1.01)	(1.57)	(0.63)	(8.18)***	(8.17)***	(10.82)***
Capacity			0.78			0.40
utilization			(4.62)***			(1.86)*
R^2	0.76	0.77	0.83	0.34	0.37	0.54
N	1297	1297	699	1297	1297	699

(b) TOBIT panel regressions of annual merger intensities on industry-level variables

	Levels			Industry-adjusted		
Low q		− 0.06	1.55		− 2.65	− 3.14
		(− 0.02)	(0.34)		(− 0.82)	(− 0.89)
High q		6.37	2.16		4.50	5.44
		(1.50)	(0.41)		(1.21)	(1.24)
q	0.33	− 1.64	0.75	4.16	0.64	3.93
	(0.09)	(− 0.43)	(0.19)	(1.67)*	(0.19)	(1.16)
Cash flow	55.95	46.96	30.15	52.72	53.94	28.18
	(1.14)	(0.95)	(0.46)	(2.57)**	(2.62)***	(1.04)
Sales growth	16.68	14.73	40.90	15.66	12.39	33.48
	(1.63)	(1.42)	(2.83)***	(1.83)*	(1.41)	(2.61)***
Industry shock	25.11	25.99	29.27			
	(1.69)*	(1.75)*	(1.59)			
Industry	− 25.92	− 25.91	− 21.62	− 7.38	− 7.59	− 5.22
concentration	(− 4.87)***	(− 4.85)***	(− 2.66)***	(− 3.97)***	(− 4.07)***	(− 2.48)**
Capacity			− 0.47			− 0.39
utilization			(− 1.60)			(− 1.62)
Log-likelihood	828.31	829.44	554.42	753.24	754.59	535.55
N	1298	1298	700	1298	1298	700

continued over

Table 3 (*continued*)

(c) TOBIT panel regressions of annual own-industry merger intensities on industry-level variables

	Levels			Industry-adjusted		
Low q		0.07	− 1.57		− 1.25	− 6.07
		(0.02)	(− 0.34)		(− 0.40)	(− 1.67) *
High q		2.11	5.11		− 1.83	3.65
		(0.50)	(0.93)		(− 0.50)	(0.83)
q	1.11	0.51	0.26	3.57	4.04	0.58
	(0.33)	(0.14)	(0.07)	(1.49)	(1.29)	(0.17)
Cash Flow	28.59	25.97	45.09	56.47	57.27	67.20
	(0.59)	(0.54)	(0.68)	(2.79)* * *	(2.82)* * *	(2.37) * *
Sales Growth	15.54	14.92	41.65	− 1.24	− 1.04	36.68
	(1.56)	(1.46)	(2.83)* * *	(− 0.15)	(− 0.12)	(2.84)* * *
Industry Shock	26.67	26.79	17.53			
	(1.84) *	(1.84) *	(0.95)			
Industry	− 13.31	− 13.43	− 5.25	− 3.38	− 3.31	0.51
Concentration	(− 2.52) * *	(− 2.52) * *	(− 0.63)	(− 1.88) *	(− 1.83) *	(0.24)
Capacity			− 0.55			− 0.65
Utilization			(− 1.96) * *			(− 2.65)* * *
Log-Likelihood	560.04	560.16	392.82	466.67	466.84	373.80
N	1298	1298	700	1298	1298	700

Statistical significance at the 1%, 5%, and 10% levels are denoted by ***, **, and *, respectively.

Panel refers to 55 industries and 25 years covering 1970–1994. Annual (type) merger/investment intensities are calculated for each industry as the ratio of total value of (type) acquisitions/investments over the year by firms in the industry to the total book value of assets in the industry at year-end. Mergers are determined to be diversifying if the target and acquirer are in different industries at the time of announcement, or own-industry if both parties are in the same industry. Industry capital expenditures (CAPX), research and development (R&D), and advertising are based on sample firms with Compustat data. Non-merger investment is the sum of CAPX, R&D, and advertising. q is estimated as the ratio of the industry's total market value of assets (book value of assets + market value of common equity − book value of common equity) to its total book value of assets. Low (high) q is a dummy variable equal to one if the industry's q is below the 33rd (above the 67th) percentile of all industry q's during the year. Cash flow (CF) is calculated as the sum across firms in the industry of EBITDA divided by the sum across firms in the industry of sales. High CF is a dummy variable equal to one if the industry's CF is above the 67th percentile of all industry CFs during the year. Sales growth is the 2-year growth rate in industry sales, based on the firms assigned to the industry in year t. Industry shock is calculated as the absolute value of the deviation of industry sales growth from the mean sales growth for the industry over the sample period. The industry market concentration index is the natural logarithm of the sum of squared market shares (based on sales) calculated each year for each industry. Capacity utilization is the percentage of total industry capacity utilized (available for manufacturing, mining, and utilities). All specifications include year and industry dummies, although not reported. Industry-adjusted independent variables are net of the industry's own time series mean. N refers to the number of observations. t-statistics are in parentheses. All coefficients are multiplied by 1000.

Industrial organization theory suggests that the level of merger activity is affected by changing industry characteristics and/or conditions. Therefore, to control for differences in industry structure, we include the natural logarithm of the market concentration index (INDCONC).

We attempt to capture "shocks" to the industry by including lagged sales growth and the absolute deviation of sales growth from its long-term mean (our shock variable). This is arguably a very weak proxy, since it primarily captures shocks to demand, and fails to identify technological shocks that primarily affect costs of production, as well as any forward-looking industry changes, such as anticipated deregulation.

All of the regressions are estimated with independent variables measured both in levels and as deviations from their industry's time series mean. The level regressions are meant to capture the marginal effect of the industry-level variables on merger/investment intensity across all industries and time, while the industry-adjusted variables are designed to capture the marginal effect of the independent variables during periods when they are unusually high or low relative to the historical average for that industry.

Table 3 displays our results for both the entire panel of 55 industries, and the restricted panel of industries for which CAPUTIL data is available. The regression results are largely consistent with there being an important industry-restructuring component to merger activity. We find opposite signs on the capacity utilization coefficient for merger and non-merger investment. Consistent with the claim by Jensen (1993) that recent mergers have been largely motivated by the need to eliminate excess capacity, we find a significantly negative relation between own-industry merger and utilization rates. We also find some evidence that mergers are related to industry shocks. Mitchell and Mulherin (1996) show that industry shocks motivate industry restructuring and account for a significant portion of takeover activity from the target's perspective. Based on that evidence, we expect a positive relation between shocks and own-industry mergers, as industries undergoing restructuring consolidate, and indeed, find the effect of SHOCK to be restricted to own-industry mergers.

The positive and significant coefficient on q, which is predicted by q-theory, only appears in the specifications involving non-merger forms of investment. All of the coefficients on q, as well as the high and low q dummy variables, are significant and of the predicted sign for the non-merger investment specifications, both in levels and industry-adjusted. Together with the positive relation between non-merger investment and capacity utilization, this evidence suggests that there is a strong industry-wide component to firm-level growth prospects. We find no relation between merger intensity and q, although it is not clear that q-theory predicts such a relation for the industry in the first place.

We also find a strong positive relationship between merger and non-merger investment and both cash flow, as proxied by EBITDA/sales, and sales growth. This result is broadly consistent with the previous evidence on the link between cash flow and investment at the firm level (for a recent discussion see Kaplan and Zingales, 1997). It should be noted that EBITDA/sales and sales growth might proxy for components of "real q" which our measure for q does not capture. Alternatively, a positive relation between investment and cash flow is consistent with some degree of capital market imperfection, which forces industries to rely primarily on internally generated funds in order to invest.

The opposite signs of the coefficient on INDCONC for merger and non-merger investment intensity in the industry-adjusted specifications suggest an interesting interpretation. When industries are particularly concentrated, relative to their historical average, expansion is likely to occur via internal investment. On the other hand, the negative coefficient on INDCONC in the merger regressions suggests that high levels of industry concentration deter firms from pursuing acquisitions, perhaps due to antitrust regulations or even just a lack of targets. However, we caution that this latter result might also be due to problems with the coverage of our merger sample. We implicitly assume that all zero

Table 4
Panel regressions of annual industry investment intensities on industry-level variables split by decade—independent variables in LEVELS

	Non-merger investment			Mergers			Own-industry mergers		
	1970–1979	1980–1989	1990–1994	1970–1979	1980–1989	1990–1994	1970–1979	1980–1989	1990–1994
Low *q*	−0.73	−9.42	5.40	−0.23	14.02	−1.36	−0.17	2.63	−70.16
	(−0.17)	(−1.98)**	(1.27)	(−0.03)	(1.45)	(−0.11)	(−0.02)	(0.30)	(−2.45)**
High *q*	9.54	0.59	−0.03	−0.15	−5.94	12.82	2.30	3.17	115.58
	(1.76)*	(0.12)	(−0.01)	(−0.02)	(−0.58)	(1.00)	(0.25)	(0.36)	(2.42)**
q	1.18	34.26	35.49	7.53	50.99	−40.06	4.28	19.61	−307.81
	(0.42)	(3.23)***	(5.81)***	(1.71)*	(2.38)**	(−1.78)*	(0.94)	(1.04)	(−2.73)***
CF	72.98	−11.79	38.15	125.91	−2.62	335.14	76.85	77.84	2498.30
	(0.99)	(−0.20)	(0.50)	(1.08)	(−0.02)	(1.33)	(0.62)	(0.67)	(2.50)**
SALESGRO	−10.79	10.50	29.23	19.25	45.28	34.13	17.15	27.34	11.99
	(−0.82)	(0.87)	(1.71)*	(0.89)	(1.81)*	(0.66)	(0.74)	(1.24)	(0.14)
SHOCK	12.20	−8.87	21.20	34.58	40.80	7.27	51.61	−20.79	681.25
	(0.70)	(−0.56)	(1.04)	(1.20)	(1.21)	(0.12)	(1.66)*	(−0.68)	(2.39)**
INDCONC	−5.51	−1.98	12.84	10.46	−11.67	−41.55	14.48	12.04	−93.56
	(−0.36)	(−0.22)	(1.18)	(0.44)	(−0.61)	(−1.16)	(0.56)	(0.72)	(−1.48)
CAPUTIL	0.71	0.57	0.99	−0.83	−0.38	2.05	−0.79	−0.55	9.61
	(2.88)***	(2.15)**	(3.06)***	(−2.04)**	(−0.68)	(1.84)*	(−1.83)*	(−1.10)	(2.34)**
N	279	280	140	280	280	140	280	280	140

Statistical significance at the 1%, 5%, and 10% levels are denoted by ***, **, and *, respectively.

Panel refers to 55 industries and 25 years covering 1970–1994. Annual (type) merger/investment intensities are calculated for each industry as the ratio of total value of (type) acquisitions/investments over the year by firms in the industry to the total book value of assets in the industry at year-end. Mergers are determined to be diversifying if the target and acquirer are in different industries at the time of announcement, or own-industry if both parties are in the same industry. Industry capital expenditures (CAPX), research and development (R&D) and advertising are based on sample firms with Compustat data. Non-merger investment is the sum of CAPX, R&D, and advertising. *q* is estimated as the ratio of the industry's total market value of assets (book value of assets + market value of common equity − book value of common equity) to its total book value of assets. Low (high) *q* is a dummy variable equal to one if the industry's *q* is below the 33rd (above the 67th) percentile of all industry *q*'s during the year. Cash flow (CF) is calculated as the sum across firms in the industry of EBITDA divided by the sum across firms in the industry of sales. High CF is a dummy variable equal to one if the industry's CF is above the 67th percentile of all industry CFs during the year. Sales growth (SALESGRO) is the 2-year growth rate in industry sales, based on the firms assigned to the industry in year *t*. SHOCK is calculated as the absolute value of the deviation of industry sales growth from the mean sales growth for the industry over the sample period. The industry market concentration index (INDCONC) is the natural logarithm of the sum of squared market shares (based on sales) calculated each year for each industry. Capacity utilization (CAPUTIL) is the percentage of total industry capacity utilized (available for manufacturing, mining, and utilities). All specifications include year and industry dummies, although not reported. *N* refers to the number of observations. Specifications involving non-merger investment intensities are estimated using OLS, while merger-related specifications employ TOBIT. *t*-statistics are in parentheses. All coefficients are multiplied by 1000.

merger intensities represent no mergers in the industry over the year. Failure to identify mergers increases the probability of small industries (in terms of number of firms) reporting zero transactions in a given year. Since INDCONC is roughly inversely related to the number of firms, the negative relation between merger intensity and INDCONC might be spurious. Still, we do not believe that the significance of INDCONC is completely driven by measurement errors, as our merger sample is quite comprehensive.

The overall results suggest that mergers, particularly own-industry mergers, appear to play a key role in affecting major industry change. Own-industry mergers seem to follow industry shocks, and occur in times of excess capacity, consistent with the hypothesized contractionary motive for mergers. On the other hand, periods of peak utilization and good growth prospects require capacity expansion via increased internal investment. However, one must be careful not to generalize the results to all own-industry mergers through time. Jensen (1993) for example, explicitly notes that the industry restructuring role should refer primarily to mergers from the mid-1970s through the late 1980s, as this is the time "when excess capacity began to proliferate in the worldwide economy." Morck et al. (1988) suggest that a key determinant of merger, takeover and LBO activity in the 1980s is the need to restructure industries that have experienced adverse economic shocks. We allow for the possibility that the contractionary role of mergers is period-specific, by splitting the panel regressions by decade. Table 4 reports the results for these decade-by-decade specifications. For most variables, results are qualitatively consistent over the 1970s, 1980s, and 1990s. While statistical significance might be concentrated in just one decade, the signs tend to be preserved throughout. One major exception is industry capacity utilization. In particular, in specifications involving either mergers or own-industry mergers, the sign on CAPUTIL is negative (and sometimes statistically significant) during the 1970s and 1980s, while positive (and sometimes significant) in the 1990s. Note also the strongly positive sign on the high q dummy and CF for own-industry mergers during the 1990s. These results are consistent with Jensen (1993) and Morck et al. (1988), and suggest that the restructuring role for mergers is important during the 1970s and 1980s, as industries react to excess capacity by merging. However, during the 1990s merger activity appears more related to industry expansion, as industries with high q, increased profitability and near capacity, are more likely to experience increased merger activity.

4. Mergers and non-merger investment at the firm level

At the firm level, the net effect of a merger or an internal investment is largely the same, namely an increase in the firm's asset base and/or productive capacity. Therefore, we hypothesize that from the point of view of the investor–acquirer, both merger and non-merger investment will respond similarly to external incentives to invest. This section documents this expansionary motive for mergers, by examining the determinants of both corporate merger and non-merger investment. Moreover, we gain insights into the previously identified contractionary motive for mergers by analyzing the pre-merger characteristics of the acquirer and target companies, with the overall goal of better understanding who the buyers and sellers are.

4.1. Defining investment events

The decision to merge is inherently a "lumpy" one—mergers are discrete events, and as such cannot be modeled by a continuous variable. Therefore, to better capture the merger versus non-merger investment decisions of firms, we need to "discretize" the latter. For this purpose, we define a set of individual investment "events," which we calculate as "abnormal" firm-level changes in non-merger investment expenditures (relative to some trend). The rationale is that these large 1-year changes in investment are more likely to be the result of discrete choices by the firms, making them more comparable to mergers.

For each firm in the sample with at least 2 years of valid data on Compustat, we calculate a series of annual non-merger investment intensities, defined (as in Section 3) as the ratio of the sum of CAPX, R&D and advertising expense to the year-end total book assets of the firm. Firm-years with missing CAPX or book assets are excluded. We define annual "abnormal" investment as a deviation from the firm's average non-merger investment, that is, for firm j in year t:

$$\begin{aligned}&(\text{abnormal non} - \text{merger investment})_{jt}\\&\quad = (\text{non} - \text{merger intensity})_{jt} - \text{mean}(\text{non} - \text{merger intensity})_j\end{aligned}$$

Next, we combine all abnormal non-merger investment figures across firms and years into one panel, and rank them. The upper-tail of this distribution, more than one standard deviation above the mean, is defined as the set of non-merger events, which we will compare to mergers.[22] Note that this definition of events only includes large positive changes in non-merger investment, so that they represent net additions to assets. A total of 3876 events are classified by this procedure.

In an attempt to remain consistent with the above definition of investment events, we also exclude all mergers where the target value was less than 1% of the total value of the acquirer at the end of the pre-completion year. Again, the idea is to focus on a set of events which likely result from important individual decisions by firms, rather than normal day-to-day operations. This trimming results in 1090 merger events, with 645 classified as own-industry and 363 as diversifying.[23]

4.2. Logit analysis on the determinants of merger and non-merger events

The main econometric tool used in this section is the logit regression, which is designed specifically to analyze the determinants of discrete dependent variables, as is the case with our events. We create four panels of dependent variables, each of which consists of a set of dummy variables for different types of events. They are:

1. NON_MERGER = 1 for non-merger event, 0 otherwise
2. DIV_MERGER = 1 for diversifying merger event, 0 otherwise

[22] A plot of the ranked abnormal non-merger investment panel revealed the following properties of the distribution: (1) centered around zero, (2) near-perfect symmetry, (3) slightly "fatter" tails than a normal of similar mean and variance.

[23] The actual numbers of merger-related events used in the estimation are slightly smaller because some of the firms had missing values for the explanatory variables.

Table 5

(a) Panel regressions of annual individual firm non-merger investment events on firm-level independent variables from 1970 to 1994

	Levels (LOGIT)			Fama–MacBeth Levels (OLS)			Industry-adjusted (LOGIT)			Fama–MacBeth industry-adjusted (OLS)		
	1	2	3	1	2	3	1	2	3	1	2	3
Low q		− 160.7	− 115.2		− 9.5	− 6.0		− 187.2	− 148.6		− 9.4	− 5.9
		(0.00)***	(0.00)***		(− 2.04)**	(− 1.12)		(0.00)***	(0.00)***		(− 2.01)**	(− 1.06)
High q		59.5	62.5		18.3	18.4		115.0	117.7		19.9	20.0
		(0.00)***	(0.00)***		(2.79)***	(2.81)***		(0.00)***	(0.00)***		(2.92)***	(2.93)***
AGENCY			− 33.9			− 18.0			− 29.5			− 20.1
			(0.00)***			(− 2.42)**			(0.00)***			(− 2.40)**
q	230.0	51.7	46.9	15.5	3.3	3.1	17.5	− 6.8	− 6.9	15.7	2.4	2.2
	(0.00)***	(0.32)	(0.37)	(2.88)***	(0.53)	(0.50)	(0.00)***	(0.16)	(0.15)	(2.84)***	(0.35)	(0.32)
CF	494.3	433.4	462.6	316.6	301.8	312.0	13.3	10.6	11.4	316.4	300.7	311.2
	(0.00)***	(0.00)***	(0.00)***	(7.96)***	(7.43)***	(7.44)***	(0.00)***	(0.00)***	(0.00)***	(6.87)***	(6.47)***	(6.45)***
BOOKLEV	− 13.8	− 9.1	− 8.0	2.1	2.3	2.3	− 7.1	− 4.7	− 4.1	2.0	2.1	2.2
	(0.47)	(0.63)	(0.67)	(0.80)	(0.84)	(0.87)	(0.13)	(0.31)	(0.36)	(0.75)	(0.78)	(0.80)
SALESGRO	54.6	48.8	49.0	35.6	30.9	31.1	15.8	13.2	13.4	30.0	24.8	25.2
	(0.00)***	(0.00)***	(0.00)***	(2.68)***	(2.39)**	(2.39)**	(0.00)***	(0.00)***	(0.00)***	(2.21)**	(1.93)*	(1.96)**
SALESGRO^2	− 3.0	14.1	14.2	44.5	42.8	43.0	17.5	15.0	15.1	45.6	43.7	44.0
	16.0	(0.00)***	(0.00)***	(5.25)***	(5.28)***	(5.28)***	(0.00)***	(0.00)***	(0.00)***	(5.32)***	(5.33)***	(5.33)***
	(0.00)***											
CAPUTIL	21.7	18.8	18.9	23.3	22.0	21.9	15.0	11.5	11.7	22.9	21.5	21.3
	(0.00)***	(0.00)***	(0.00)***	(5.31)***	(4.98)***	(4.95)***	(0.00)***	(0.00)***	(0.00)***	(5.34)***	(5.05)***	(5.01)***
Number observed	28,592	28,592	28,592				28,580	28,580	28,580			
Number of events	2810	2810	2810				2805	2805	2805			

continued over

(b) Panel regressions of annual individual firm own-industry merger events on firm-level independent variables from 1970 to 1994

	Levels (LOGIT)			Fama–MacBeth levels (OLS)			Industry-adjusted (LOGIT)			Fama–MacBeth industry-adjusted (OLS)		
	1	2	3	1	2	3	1	2	3	1	2	3
Low q		− 22.1	− 58.8		− 2.7	− 4.8		− 28.4	− 66.7		− 3.6	− 5.5
		(0.57)	(0.16)		(− 1.53)	(−2.74)***		(0.47)	(0.11)		(− 1.90)*	(−2.99)***
High q		28.6	29.6		1.7	1.8		49.6	51.1		2.1	2.1
		(0.46)	(0.45)		(0.61)	(0.64)		(0.19)	(0.18)		(0.79)	(0.82)
AGENCY			39.5			11.1			41.5			10.1
			(0.01)***			(3.05)***			(0.01)***			(2.61)***
q	90.0	19.9	34.7	− 0.2	− 1.1	− 1.0	9.0	− 1.1	− 0.1	0.4	− 1.0	− 0.9
	(0.41)	(0.88)	(0.79)	(− 0.09)	(− 0.49)	(− 0.43)	(0.36)	(0.93)	(0.99)	(0.26)	(− 0.54)	(− 0.48)
CF	− 74.8	− 92.8	− 151.9	− 16.6	− 18.6	− 25.2	− 3.0	− 3.9	− 6.0	− 18.6	− 21.2	− 27.7
	(0.41)	(0.32)	(0.12)	(− 1.21)	(− 1.35)	(− 1.76) *	(0.34)	(0.23)	(0.08)*	(− 1.37)	(− 1.57)	(− 1.95) *
BOOKLEV	− 37.0	− 34.8	− 38.5	0.2	0.3	0.2	− 5.5	− 4.6	− 5.8	− 0.3	− 0.2	− 0.3
	(0.41)	(0.43)	(0.38)	(0.19)	(0.30)	(0.25)	(0.60)	(0.65)	(0.58)	(− 0.40)	(− 0.33)	(− 0.37)
SALESGRO	49.3	48.3	48.0	13.6	13.1	12.3	18.3	17.8	17.6	14.5	13.5	12.8
	(0.00)***	(0.00)***	(0.00)***	(2.53)**	(2.38)**	(2.24)**	(0.00)***	(0.00)***	(0.00)***	(2.74)***	(2.48)***	(2.35)**
SALESGRO^2	− 4.9	− 4.8	− 4.8	− 3.7	− 3.5	− 3.1	5.7	5.6	5.5	− 3.6	− 3.1	− 2.7
	(0.35)	(0.36)	(0.36)	(− 1.03)	(− 0.92)	(− 0.82)	(0.01)***	(0.01)***	(0.01)***	(− 0.97)	(− 0.79)	(− 0.71)
STOCKRET	3.5	3.2	3.1	3.9	3.3	3.1	1.8	1.2	1.1	3.4	2.7	2.5
	(0.34)	(0.40)	(0.41)	(1.06)	(0.91)	(0.84)	(0.67)	(0.78)	(0.80)	(0.97)	(0.76)	(0.70)
CAPUTIL	− 19.3	− 20.0	− 20.0	− 5.5	− 5.9	− 5.9	− 18.4	− 19.4	− 19.3	− 6.1	− 6.5	− 6.4
	(0.01)***	(0.00)***	(0.00)***	(−2.76)***	(−2.91)***	(−2.88)***	(0.00)***	(0.00)***	(0.00)***	(−3.19)***	(−3.41)***	(−3.40)***
Number observed	28,512	28,512	28,512				28,501	28,501	28,501			
Number of events	594	594	594				592	592	592			

(continued on next page)

Table 5 (*continued*)

(c) Panel regressions of annual individual firm diversifying merger events on firm-level independent variables from 1970 to 1994

	Levels (LOGIT)			Fama–MacBeth levels (OLS)			Industry-adjusted (LOGIT)			Fama–MacBeth industry-adjusted (OLS)		
	1	2	3	1	2	3	1	2	3	1	2	3
Low *q*		− 118.0	− 114.9		− 3.8	− 3.6		− 127.1	− 127.0		− 3.8	− 3.8
		(0.03)**	(0.05)**		(−2.68)***	(− 2.23)**		(0.02)**	(0.03)**		(−2.67)***	(− 2.29)**
High *q*		33.6	33.7		0.9	0.8		47.0	47.0		1.7	1.6
		(0.50)	(0.50)		(0.37)	(0.33)		(0.33)	(0.33)		(0.73)	(0.69)
AGENCY			− 3.1			− 1.6			− 0.1			− 0.5
			(0.89)			(− 0.55)			(1.00)			(− 0.16)
q	1.7	− 144.0	− 144.8	1.4	− 0.9	− 1.0	1.0	− 13.5	− 13.5	1.4	− 1.3	− 1.3
	(0.99)	(0.39)	(0.38)	(0.91)	(− 0.58)	(− 0.60)	(0.93)	(0.35)	(0.35)	(0.83)	(− 0.80)	(− 0.82)
CF	126.5	79.9	83.1	− 2.9	− 6.5	− 4.9	3.1	1.3	1.3	− 1.8	− 5.8	− 5.1
	(0.26)	(0.49)	(0.48)	(− 0.33)	(− 0.70)	(− 0.52)	(0.43)	(0.75)	(0.75)	(− 0.19)	(− 0.60)	(− 0.50)
BOOKLEV	− 153.4	− 146.0	− 146.1	− 0.7	− 0.8	− 0.8	− 29.9	− 27.7	− 27.7	− 0.6	− 0.6	− 0.6
	(0.04)***	(0.05)**	(0.05)**	(− 1.07)	(− 1.14)	(− 1.18)	(0.07)*	(0.09)*	(0.09)*	(− 0.75)	(− 0.77)	(− 0.82)
SALESGRO	55.8	52.9	52.9	11.9	11.2	11.2	24.5	23.5	23.5	12.3	11.4	11.4
	(0.00)***	(0.01)***	(0.01)***	(3.62)***	(3.52)***	(3.51)***	(0.00)***	(0.00)***	(0.00)***	(3.48)***	(3.29)***	(3.27)***
SALESGRO^2	3.2	3.4	3.4	− 4.5	− 3.9	− 3.9	− 2.8	− 3.1	− 3.1	− 4.6	− 4.0	− 3.9
	(0.30)	(0.27)	(0.27)	(− 2.31)**	(− 2.08)**	(− 2.03)**	(0.54)	(0.51)	(0.51)	(− 2.09)**	(− 1.81)*	(− 1.76)*
STOCKRET	10.0	8.9	8.9	7.1	6.5	6.5	11.5	10.1	10.1	7.4	6.7	6.7
	(0.03)**	(0.05)**	(0.05)**	(3.33)***	(3.23)***	(3.23)***	(0.02)**	(0.05)**	(0.05)**	3.66)***	(3.51)***	(3.52)***
CAPUTIL	− 4.4	− 6.2	− 6.2	− 2.6	− 3.0	− 3.0	− 4.4	− 6.4	− 6.4	− 2.1	− 2.5	− 2.5
	(0.59)	(0.46)	(0.46)	(− 1.69)*	(− 1.89)*	(− 1.90)*	(0.56)	(0.41)	(0.41)	(− 1.29)	(− 1.51)	(− 1.52)
Number observed	28,512	28,512	28,512				28,501	28,501	28,501			
Number of events	333	333	333				332	332	332			

(d) Panel regressions of annual individual firm merger events on firm-level independent variables from 1970 to 1994

	Levels (LOGIT)			Fama–MacBeth levels (OLS)			Industry-adjusted (LOGIT)			Fama–MacBeth industry-adjusted (OLS)		
	1	2	3	1	2	3	1	2	3	1	2	3
Low q		− 63.2	− 81.7		− 8.3	− 9.7		− 69.6	− 90.1		− 8.9	− 10.5
		(0.04)**	(0.01)***		(−3.26)***	(−3.47)***		(0.02)**	(0.01)***		(−3.48)***	(−3.58)***
High q		23.2	23.2		0.9	0.8		36.5	36.7		1.8	1.8
		(0.44)	(0.44)		(0.27)	(0.25)		(0.21)	(0.21)		(0.65)	(0.64)
AGENCY			20.2			7.5			22.4			7.7
			(0.11)			(1.53)			(0.07)*			(1.51)
q	44.8	− 49.4	− 42.9	0.6	− 2.3	− 2.2	5.9	− 4.7	− 4.2	1.7	− 2.0	− 1.9
	(0.58)	(0.62)	(0.67)	(0.23)	(− 0.73)	(− 0.70)	(0.43)	(0.60)	(0.63)	(0.60)	(− 0.66)	(− 0.65)
CF	− 30.6	− 60.6	− 87.2	− 26.4	− 33.0	− 36.8	− 1.5	− 2.7	− 3.7	− 27.4	− 34.7	− 39.3
	(0.66)	(0.40)	(0.24)	(− 1.44)	(− 1.83)*	(− 2.07)**	(0.53)	(0.27)	(0.14)	(− 1.43)	(− 1.86)*	(− 2.09)**
BOOKLEV	− 72.1	− 69.6	− 70.5	− 0.8	− 0.8	− 0.9	− 12.4	− 11.6	− 12.0	− 1.3	− 1.4	− 1.4
	(0.05)**	(0.05)**	(0.05)**	(− 0.67)	(− 0.67)	(− 0.72)	(0.14)	(0.16)	(0.15)	(− 1.18)	(− 1.21)	(− 1.29)
SALESGRO	56.4	54.6	54.5	27.3	26.0	25.4	22.5	21.8	21.8	29.5	27.6	27.1
	(0.00)***	(0.00)***	(0.00)***	(3.65)***	(3.43)***	(3.35)***	(0.00)***	(0.00)***	(0.00)***	(4.08)***	(3.77)***	(3.69)***
$SALESGRO^2$	− 0.6	− 0.5	− 0.5	− 7.4	− 6.8	− 6.4	3.2	3.1	3.1	− 7.9	− 6.9	− 6.5
	(0.81)	(0.85)	(0.85)	(− 1.58)	(− 1.41)	(− 1.33)	(0.07)*	(0.08)*	(0.09)*	(− 1.66)	(− 1.43)	(− 1.35)
STOCKRET	6.2	5.5	5.5	11.6	10.3	10.2	6.4	5.5	5.5	11.2	9.7	9.6
	(0.03)**	(0.05)**	(0.05)**	(2.47)**	(2.25)**	(2.21)**	(0.04)**	(0.08)*	(0.09)*	(2.60)***	(2.28)**	(2.24)**
CAPUTIL	− 15.6	− 16.9	− 16.9	− 9.5	− 10.3	− 10.3	− 14.3	− 15.7	− 15.8	− 9.6	− 10.4	− 10.4
	(0.00)***	(0.00)***	(0.00)***	(−2.94)***	(−3.18)***	(−3.19)***	(0.00)***	(0.00)***	(0.00)***	(−2.87)***	(−3.13)***	(−3.16)***
Number observed	28,592	28,592	28,592				28,580	28,580	28,580			
Number of events	995	995	995				991	991	991			

3. OWNIND_MERGER = 1 for own-industry merger event, 0 otherwise
4. MERGER = 1 for merger event, 0 otherwise

We refrain from defining all the independent variables, due to their similarity to the definitions used in Section 3 at the industry level. The key differences are: (1) all variables are now estimated at the firm level; (2) we no longer include INDCONC and SHOCK, the latter because it requires a long time series of sales growth to be estimated, something most individual firms do not have; (3) we include a measure of the excess returns earned by the firm's stock during the year (STOCKRET); and (4) since we do not have firm-level capacity utilization rates, we replace them with a sales to total book assets ratio, under the assumption that variations in this measure over time should be correlated with the "intensity" of asset use. Brealey and Myers (1996) state that "a high ratio (of sales to total assets) could indicate that the firm is working close to capacity." We adjust the sales to assets ratio for each firm-year by subtracting the median sales to assets ratio across all years of the industry, which is meant to adjust for differences in accounting and/or steady-state capacity utilization rates across industries.

Capital structure can also play a role in influencing investment activity. In particular, higher leverage can lead to under-investment (Myers, 1977) or reduce over-investment in firms with excess free cash flow (Jensen, 1986). In addition, both the agency costs of free cash flow and the financial constraints literature have found that measures of leverage appear significantly in investment regressions. Therefore, our specifications include

Note to Table 5:
Base specifications are estimated via LOGIT (we report adjusted coefficients—"slopes"—evaluated at the average value of the independent variables). Fama–MacBeth specifications are estimated via ordinary least squares, and involve estimating annual cross-sectional regressions, resulting in a time series for each coefficient, from which the mean is reported. Each independent variable is trimmed 1% (0.5% from each tail). Dependent variables are dummy variables set to 1 if the firm participated in the event during the year, and 0 otherwise. A firm is determined to have participated in a non-merger investment event if the firm's abnormal non-merger investment intensity is more than 1 standard deviation above the sample mean abnormal non-merger intensity across all firms and all years. Firm abnormal non-merger investment intensity is the deviation in non-merger investment intensity from its mean estimated over all years available for the firm. Non-merger investment intensity is estimated for each firm-year as the ratio of the sum of CAPX, R&D and advertising expense to total book assets. Mergers are classified as diversifying if the target and acquirer are in different industries at the time of announcement, and own-industry if both parties are in the same industry. Industry-adjusted independent variables for each firm-year are calculated as deviations from the industry median for that year. q is estimated as the ratio of the firm's total market value of assets (book value of assets + market value of common equity – book value of common equity) to its total book value of assets. Low (high) q is a dummy variable equal to one if the firm's q is below the 33rd (above the 67th) percentile of all firm q's during the year. Cash flow (CF) is calculated as EBITDA divided by sales. High CF is a dummy variable equal to one if the firm's CF is above the 67th percentile of all firm CFs during the year. AGENCY is the product of Low q and High CF. Book leverage (BOOKLEV) is calculated as the ratio of the firm's debt (long-term debt + short-term debt + preferred stock) to the firm's book value of common equity. Sales growth (SALESGRO) is the 2-year growth rate. Stock return (STOCKRET) is the net-of-market annual return for the firm's common stock. Capacity utilization (CAPUTIL) is proxied by the deviation of the firm's ratio of sales to book assets from the industry median over the entire period. All specifications include industry dummies and LOGIT specifications also include year dummies. P-values referring to unadjusted coefficients are reported in parentheses for the LOGIT specifications. t-statistics are reported in parentheses for the Fama–MacBeth specifications, based on the standard error of the time series mean of each coefficient. All coefficients are multiplied by 1000.

measures of firm-level financial leverage (BOOKLEV), estimated as the ratio of book debt plus preferred stock to book equity.

In order to reduce measurement error in the independent variables due to potential mistakes in the data reported by Compustat, we trim 1% off the tails (0.5% each) of all explanatory variables separately, which results in a small loss of firm-years with investment events (approximately 200), but a significant improvement in the maximized likelihood values for the fitted models. Finally, as is the case in Section 3, all regression specifications: (a) exclude three financial sector industries, (b) include dummy variables for year and industry (except Fama–MacBeth specifications), and (c) contain beginning-of-period values for the independent variables.

Table 5 displays the results for this section. It is divided into four panels (a through d), one for each of the dependent variables defined above. Explanatory variables can be expressed both in "levels" and in "industry-adjusted" form, where the latter are calculated as deviations from the firm's industry median for the same year, and the table displays results for both types. For all logit specifications, we report adjusted coefficients that are designed to measure the marginal impact of each explanatory variable[24] (see Greene, 1993, Chapter 21). One of the problems with large panel data sets is that often the standard errors are poorly estimated, and usual inference techniques are not valid, because the estimated covariance matrix fails to account for cross-correlations between dependent variables and/or residuals across time. In order to partially account for this, and therefore test the robustness of our logit p-values to these estimation problems, we re-estimate each specification using the procedure pioneered by Fama and MacBeth (see Fama, 1976). Our Fama–MacBeth procedure involves estimating annual cross-sectional OLS regressions, which results in a time series of coefficient estimates for each independent variable. The mean and standard error of this time series of estimates of each coefficient, allows us to construct a t-statistic for that coefficient, and test whether it significantly differs from zero. These results are displayed in Table 5 under the headings "Fama–MacBeth Levels" and "Fama–MacBeth Industry-Adjusted."

In order to make statements about firms' decisions based on the estimated coefficients of our regressions, we implicitly assume that in every firm-year, firms could have undertaken any form of investment. Therefore, a value of zero for the event dummy variable actually represents a decision not to invest. This assumption could be false if either: (a) there are missing mergers in our sample, or (b) firms were prevented from engaging in certain types of investment, for whatever reason. In an attempt to test the robustness of our results, we re-estimate some of the MERGER and NON-MERGER logit specifications, restricting the sample to firms that at some point engaged in each. The results are mostly unchanged, so we do not report these restricted sample estimates.

As in Section 3, for each dependent variable, the first model we run (which is labeled "1" in Table 5) includes q as a continuous variable, and corresponds to the traditional interpretation of q-theory as predicting that investment should increase with q. However, as we noted before, our reading of the theory suggests that the decision to invest based on

[24] In constructing the adjusted logit coefficients—"slopes"—we evaluate all the independent variables at their sample averages This procedure is meant to improve comparability between the logit estimates and their Fama–MacBeth counterparts, although the relationship is not perfect due to the existence of dozens of dummy variables in our various specifications.

Table 6

Panel regressions of annual individual firm investment events on firm-level variables split by decade

	Event = Merger			Event = Diversifying merger			Event = Own-industry merger			Event = Non-merger investment		
	1970–1979	1980–1989	1990–1994	1970–1979	1980–1989	1990–1994	1970–1979	1980–1989	1990–1994	1970–1979	1980–1989	1990–1994
Low q	− 60.1	− 56.5	− 508.5	− 24.7	− 62.9	− 682.1	− 25.7	− 79.7	− 459.6	− 27.9	− 117.7	− 23.1
	(0.23)	(0.24)	(0.00)***	(0.81)	(0.43)	(0.00)***	(0.67)	(0.21)	(0.02)**	(0.02)**	(0.00)***	(0.72)
High q	32.0	47.9	− 127.3	173.8	5.3	− 215.0	− 4.4	81.0	31.9	18.7	91.8	− 19.9
	(0.49)	(0.29)	(0.18)	(0.04)**	(0.94)	(0.14)	(0.94)	(0.19)	(0.81)	(0.05)**	(0.00)***	(0.72)
AGENCY	8.3	14.0	75.9	− 41.3	− 3.2	124.3	23.4	36.2	61.8	28.7	− 7.7	− 45.8
	(0.50)	(0.55)	(0.13)	(0.21)	(0.94)	(0.08)*	(0.08)*	(0.22)	(0.44)	(0.43)	(0.31)	(0.19)
q	201.1	− 519.1	18.2	329.5	− 574.2	74.4	188.8	− 597.8	− 10.7	− 0.3	80.9	162.6
	(0.11)	(0.01)***	(0.96)	(0.12)	(0.05)**	(0.88)	(0.22)	(0.04)**	(0.98)	(0.94)	(0.31)	(0.23)
CF	− 77.9	94.8	− 427.7	− 99.7	323.8	− 313.8	− 42.9	− 34.5	− 437.8	1893.3	289.4	711.1
	(0.56)	(0.36)	(0.03)**	(0.70)	(0.04)**	(0.27)	(0.79)	(0.81)	(0.12)	(0.00)***	(0.00)***	(0.00)***
BOOKLEV	− 18.3	− 148.5	34.5	− 4.1	− 242.9	− 172.6	− 29.9	− 126.6	149.5	2.7	− 70.6	− 114.7
	(0.74)	(0.01)***	(0.68)	(0.97)	(0.02)**	(0.40)	(0.67)	(0.10)	(0.13)	(0.01)***	(0.02)**	(0.05)**
SALESGRO	27.8	57.0	71.4	13.9	67.6	51.7	13.6	54.5	68.1	47.5	55.1	− 43.9
	(0.29)	(0.00)***	(0.00)***	(0.81)	(0.00)***	(0.12)	(0.67)	(0.12)	(0.01)***	(0.00)***	(0.00)***	(0.05)**
SALESGRO^2	− 1.6	− 0.4	2.9	− 36.9	4.6	7.2	0.0	− 9256.7	− 60.8	0.0	− 1.7	− 2.9
	(0.71)	(0.91)	(0.70)	(0.95)	(0.22)	(0.36)	(1.00)	(0.91)	(0.95)	(0.33)	(0.42)	(0.58)
STOCKRET	4.9	8.1	2.1	17.0	7.1	7.8	2.8	7.7	− 6.1	58.5	17.2	11.4
	(0.40)	(0.06)*	(0.51)	(0.10)	(0.31)	(0.07)*	(0.70)	(0.17)	(0.25)	(0.00)***	(0.00)***	(0.02)**
CAPUTIL	− 10.8	− 28.7	14.0	− 20.2	0.3	9.9	− 4.8	− 45.5	12.2	28.4	21.6	42.7
	(0.33)	(0.01)***	(0.04)**	(0.29)	(0.98)	(0.37)	(0.73)	(0.00)***	(0.18)	(0.00)***	(0.00)***	(0.00)***
Number observed	10,994	12,003	5595	10,965	11,961	5586	10,965	11,961	5586	10,994	12,003	5595
Number of events	413	476	106	114	170	49	275	271	48	1111	1366	333

q is really a discrete one, i.e., if q exceeds a certain threshold, investment should be undertaken, otherwise not. Empirically, this can be accomplished by classifying firms based on whether q exceeds that threshold or not. Another problem with the continuous measure of q is that there is likely to be a significant measurement error in our estimate of q, so we feel more confident grouping companies into broad categories, rather than relying on the estimates directly. As a result, each year we sort all firms by q and classify them as "high q" or "low q," depending on whether they fall in the top third or bottom third of the distribution. Based on this classification, we create dummy variables which are included in models "2" and "3."

Finally, we define an "AGENCY" dummy variable, which corresponds to those firms which, in a given year, belong to both "low q" and "high CF" (the latter corresponds to firms in the top third of the annual cross-section of firm cash-flow margins). By including this variable, we can test the prediction of the agency costs of free cash flow theory that firms with poor growth or investment prospects, but available cash flow, will over-invest. This test should be especially powerful in the models that include our "low q" dummy in addition to AGENCY, since here we are isolating the marginal effect of higher cash flow on the investment patterns of companies with no growth opportunities. The agency cost of free cash flow theory implies a significantly positive sign on AGENCY in these regressions.

The first striking results to emerge from Table 5 are the consistently positive signs on "high q" and negative signs on "low q," across all forms of investment, merger and non-merger. While the significance level varies across specifications, with "high q" appearing as significant in the non-merger investment regressions, and "low q" in the various

Note to Table 6:

Base specifications are estimated via LOGIT (we report adjusted coefficients—"slopes"—evaluated at the average value of the independent variables). Each independent variable is trimmed 1% (0.5% from each tail) to remove the effect of outliers. Dependent variables are dummy variables set to 1 if the firm participated in the event during the year, and 0 otherwise. A firm is determined to have participated in a non-merger investment event if the firm's abnormal non-merger investment intensity is more than 1 standard deviation above the sample mean abnormal non-merger intensity across all firms and all years. Firm abnormal non-merger investment intensity is the deviation in non-merger investment intensity from its mean estimated over all years available for the firm. Non-merger investment intensity is estimated for each firm-year as the ratio of the sum of CAPX, R&D and advertising expense to total book assets. Merger events are transactions in the CRSP Merger Database involving acquirers in the sample, and where the estimated target value exceeded 1% of the total market value of the acquirer at the end of the pre-completion fiscal year. Mergers are classified as diversifying if the target and acquirer are in different industries at the time of announcement, and own-industry if both parties are in the same industry. q is estimated as the ratio of the firm's total market value of assets (book value of assets + market value of common equity – book value of common equity) to its total book value of assets. Low (high) q is a dummy variable equal to one if the firm's q is below the 33rd (above the 67th) percentile of all firm's q during the year. Cash flow (CF) is calculated as EBITDA divided by sales. High CF is a dummy variable equal to one if the firm's CF is above the 67th percentile of all firm CFs during the year. AGENCY is the product of low q and high CF. Book leverage (BOOKLEV) is calculated as the ratio of the firm's debt (long-term debt + short-term debt + preferred stock) to the firm's book value of common equity. Sales growth (SALESGRO) is the 2-year growth rate. Stock return (STOCKRET) is the net-of-market annual return for the firm's common stock. Capacity utilization (CAPUTIL) is proxied by the deviation of the firm's ratio of sales to book assets from the industry median over the entire period. All specifications include industry and year dummy variables. P-values referring to unadjusted coefficients are reported in parentheses for the LOGIT specifications. All coefficients are multiplied by 1000.

merger-related specifications,[25] we consider the results to be supportive of the hypothesis that mergers have an important expansionary role.

The results on AGENCY are more inconsistent across investment types. For both diversifying mergers and non-merger investment, the coefficient estimates on AGENCY are negative, although only significant in the latter case. As stated above, this appears to be inconsistent with the basic predictions of the agency costs of free cash flow theory. In the case of diversifying mergers, the negative coefficient on "low *q*" and the weakly negative sign on AGENCY should serve to mitigate the concerns that these transactions are the result of rampant agency problems within the acquirers. Previous empirical evidence (e.g., Morck et al., 1990) has indicated that most diversifying mergers are value decreasing, a claim which cannot be addressed in our paper, as we focus on the decision to invest, rather than how much to spend. However, even if acquirers overpay and/or destroy value when diversifying, our evidence suggests that this is not necessarily related to a deliberate desire to overbuild and invest in negative NPV projects, simply due to an overabundance of available cash flow. In fact, the strongly positive coefficient estimates on SALESGRO and STOCKRET for these diversifying acquisitions are more consistent with managerial optimism rather than malice (see Heaton, 1999).

For own-industry mergers, the AGENCY dummy is significantly positive across all specifications. In conjunction with the results discussed above, we could interpret this as implying that own-industry mergers are the only type of major corporate investment activities motivated by costly agency problems within the firm. This might be evidence of a desire to increase market power, or self-serving behavior by managers, who wish to become dominant players in an industry, irrespective of the cost. However, an alternative interpretation of the results is suggested by the view, already expressed, that many of these own-industry mergers are precipitated by the need for industry contraction. In this case, in declining industries (low *q*) requiring consolidation, it is not surprising that the relatively cash-flow-rich companies (high CF) are the acquirers. For example, if Jensen's (1993) view is correct, then excess capacity generated by productivity shocks could induce both low values of *q* (since capital needs to exit, not enter these industries) and higher expenditures on own-industry acquisitions. We cannot distinguish between these two interpretations, i.e., agency costs of free cash flow or industry restructuring, although we do find evidence (see Section 4.3) that in own-industry mergers, acquirers tend to be more profitable and have higher *q* than target companies.

The significant and opposite signs on CAPUTIL are consistent with our evidence in Section 3.2 that own-industry mergers are often a tool for restructuring, where industries with excess capacity undergo consolidation via mergers. The picture that emerges is that

[25] The "high *q*" and "low *q*" dummy variables measure marginal effects of *q* relative to the middle third of the distribution. As we already pointed out, *q*-theory predicts that firms with *q* above a certain threshold should be investing, but due to the measurement error in our proxy, we cannot say where this "cut-off" value lies within our estimated values. For example, if the threshold is relatively low, then we would expect that all the "high *q*" and most "middle third" companies should be investing heavily. In that case, only the coefficient on "low *q*" would be significant (and negative), while the estimate on "high *q*" would be statistically insignificant, since there would be no marginal impact in going from the "middle third" to "high *q*". The opposite would be the case if the threshold is relatively high. Therefore, we consider that if either "low *q*" is significantly negative or "high *q*" is significantly positive, that is consistent with *q*-theory.

own-industry mergers often arise from the need to restructure the industry, perhaps in reaction to some shock. On the other hand, firms that initiate significant internal expansions can be characterized as having had strong operating performance and healthy growth prospects as evidenced by the positive relation between non-merger investment events and sales growth, profitability, and excess returns.

Jensen (1993) suggests that this excess capacity motivation for mergers was predominantly a mid-1970s and 1980s phenomenon. As in Section 3, we explicitly allow for this possibility by splitting the sample by decade, and re-running the logit regressions for each sub-period separately. The results, reported in Table 6, bear out Jensen's prediction, that is, the negative relationship between capacity utilization and either merger or own-industry merger, is restricted to the 1970s and 1980s, while the relationship is positive (and sometimes significant) in the 1990s. This evidence, combined with that of Section 3, strengthens our view that mergers can play two different roles for acquirers, contraction or expansion, and that while the former was more important through the late 1980s, as economic conditions forced a massive reallocation of assets among companies, the latter role seems to better describe merger activity in the 1990s.

Finally, we emphasize the remarkable consistency in the results discussed above across estimation methods. Whether one focuses on "Levels" or "Industry-Adjusted" specifications, the direction and significance of the coefficients is stable, and the same occurs with the "Fama–MacBeth" regressions, which occasionally lead to higher significance levels than the panel logits themselves. This stability and consistency gives us confidence that the effects we uncover are real, irrespective of whether the reader agrees with the interpretations we ascribe to them.

4.3. Acquirer and target characteristics

In this section, we analyze the relative characteristics of acquirer and target companies in different types of mergers. For all mergers used in the regressions of Section 4.2, we compile data on a variety of financial variables for both the acquirer and the target companies, as of the last fiscal year before deal closing. These variables are then differenced for each transaction (acquirer minus target), with the median values of these differences reported in Table 7, together with *p*-values for the test that these median differences are equal to zero.[26] The table contains three panels, for mergers, own-industry mergers and diversifying mergers, respectively. Each panel reports statistics on differences in characteristics both in absolute levels and industry-adjusted, where we subtract the industry median characteristic from the firm's.

Evidence on diversifying mergers is somewhat tricky to interpret. On one hand, acquirers have higher cash flows, consistent with diversifying acquisitions being related to agency problems in firms with excess cash. On the other hand, these acquirers also have higher leverage, which goes against the agency story. In addition, these results do not survive in the industry-adjusted analysis.

[26] The results are qualitatively similar for means of differences (rather than medians), although statistical significance is sometimes less, due to outliers in the observations, which is why we prefer the non-parametric Wilcoxon signed rank test for medians reported in Table 7.

Table 7
Differences in acquirer and target pre-merger characteristics

	Median acquirer characteristics	Panel 1		Panel 2		Panel 3	
		All mergers		Own-industry mergers		Diversifying mergers	
		Levels	Industry-adjusted	Levels	Industry-adjusted	Levels	Industry-adjusted
q	1.142	0.021	0.053	0.097	0.097	− 0.023	0.020
		(0.40)	(0.03)	(0.00)	(0.00)	(0.05)	(0.78)
CF	0.133	0.013	0.008	0.015	0.015	0.011	0.004
		(0.00)	(0.00)	(0.00)	(0.00)	(0.00)	(0.10)
BOOKLEV	0.606	0.034	− 0.010	− 0.057	− 0.057	0.075	0.042
		(0.09)	(0.60)	(0.01)	(0.01)	(0.00)	(0.19)
MKTLEV	0.434	0.010	− 0.022	− 0.060	− 0.060	0.046	0.019
		(0.89)	(0.04)	(0.00)	(0.00)	(0.07)	(0.86)
SALESGRO	0.116	− 0.003	0.021	0.010	0.010	− 0.010	0.025
		(0.64)	(0.07)	(0.47)	(0.47)	(0.90)	(0.08)
STOCKRET	0.022	0.053	0.132	0.184	0.184	− 0.061	0.051
		(0.21)	(0.02)	(0.00)	(0.00)	(0.26)	(0.83)
CAPUTIL	0.005	− 0.067	− 0.064	− 0.025	− 0.025	− 0.090	− 0.084
		(0.00)	(0.00)	(0.06)	(0.06)	(0.00)	(0.00)

Medians of differences between acquirer and target characteristics in the last fiscal year before transaction closing. Merger events are transactions in the CRSP Merger Database where the estimated target value exceeded 1% of the total market value of the acquirer at the end of the pre-completion fiscal year. Mergers are classified as diversifying if the target and acquirer are in different industries at the time of announcement, and own-industry if both parties are in the same industry. Industry-adjusted independent variables for each firm-year are calculated as deviations from the industry median for that year. *q* is estimated as the ratio of the firm's total market value of assets (book value of assets + market value of common equity − book value of common equity) to its total book value of assets. Cash flow (CF) is calculated as EBITDA divided by sales. Book leverage (BOOKLEV) is calculated as the ratio of the firm's debt (long-term debt + short-term debt + preferred stock) to the firm's book value of common equity. Market leverage (MKTLEV) is similar to BOOKLEV, but the denominator is the firm's market value of common equity. Sales growth (SALESGRO) is the 2-year growth rate. Stock return (STOCKRET) is the net-of-market annual return for the firm's common stock. Capacity utilization (CAPUTIL) is proxied by the deviation of the firm's ratio of sales to book assets from the industry median over the entire period. *P*-values for the Wilcoxon signed rank test for each coefficient are reported in parentheses.

The most interesting results pertain to own-industry mergers, as they tie in directly to the industry contraction role discussed above. Table 7 reports that for the sub-sample of own-industry deals, acquirers have significantly higher *q*, cash flows, and lagged stock returns, as well as lower leverage and capacity utilization, than their target companies. That is, within a given industry, the acquirers are firms that are better performers, at least in relative terms, and also have the ability to carry out the acquisition, in the sense of more debt capacity, and the operational slack to absorb their targets, consistent with the findings in Maksimovic and Phillips (2001). These mergers are also more likely to generate value, given the results of Lang et al. (1989) that mergers between high *q* and acquirers and low *q* targets result in the most overall gains. Overall, our findings suggest that industry restructuring results in a transfer of assets to the relatively effective users, and that the contractionary role of mergers leads to a more efficient allocation of resources and capacity within industries and the economy.

5. Conclusion

There is a growing empirical literature documenting that mergers are efficient means for assets to be reallocated within the economy. Large sample evidence on combined acquirer and target stock returns, as well as post-merger operating performance,[27] suggests that mergers on average increase value, and lead to improved profitability in subsequent years. Song and Walkling (2000) report that stock prices in a given industry tend to appreciate upon an announcement of a takeover, presumably in expectation of other mergers to come, and consistent with mergers being a tool for industries to generate synergies by consolidating and restructuring. In a recent paper, Maksimovic and Phillips (2001) show that mergers and acquisitions on average result in productivity gains for the assets acquired, and that the buyers tend to be relatively more productive firms. Our results add to the literature on the efficiency of merger activity, by suggesting a mechanism by which mergers help firms and industries grow and restructure, particularly in response to shocks.

Overall, our analysis indicates that mergers play a dual economic role. On one hand, mergers, like internal investments, are a means for companies to increase their capital base, in response to good growth prospects. Both merger and non-merger investment are positively related to the firm's Tobin's q and sales growth. On the other hand, mergers appear to facilitate industry contraction. The clustering of mergers by industry suggests that mergers are often a response to industry shocks. Our finding that own-industry mergers are negatively related to capacity utilization during the 1970s and 1980s, is consistent with the view that mergers are an effective means for industries with excess capacity to rationalize and induce exit. In addition, we find that within these contracting industries, acquirers tend to be the firms with better performance, perhaps even better management, and lower leverage and capacity utilization, suggesting that this industry rationalization and asset reallocation results in improved efficiency.

Acknowledgements

This paper was previously titled: "Investigating the Characteristics and Determinants of Mergers and Other Forms of Investment." We thank several anonymous referees, seminar participants at Wharton, Duke, Stanford, NYU and MIT, as well as Judy Chevalier, Doug Diamond, Eugene Fama, J.B. Heaton, Laurie Hodrick, Anil Kashyap, Owen Lamont, Raghuram Rajan, Robert Vishny, Tuomo Vuolteenaho, and Luigi Zingales for helpful comments and discussion, and Fai Tong Chung for assisting with data collection. We are particularly indebted to Steve Kaplan and Mark Mitchell for their support and valuable insights.

[27] See Healy et al. (1992) on operating performance, as well as Jarrell et al. (1988) and Andrade et al. (2001) for a review of the literature on announcement returns and long-term profitability.

Table A1
Value Line sample by year and industry classification. Includes all firms on Value Line from 1970 to 1994 which had data on COMPUSTAT and were not classified as: (1) foreign industries, (2) ADR's, (3) REIT's, (4) investment companies or funds, (5) "Unassigned." Industries are based on actual industry classifications from Value Line, with some modifications to adjust for changes in Value Line coverage, such as additions, deletions and mergers of industries and reclassifications of subsets of industries in different years (see Appendix A for details)

Industry Number	Industry Name	1970	1971	1972	1973	1974	1975	1976	1977	1978	1979	1980	1981	1982	1983	1984	1985	1986	1987	1988	1989	1990	1991	1992	1993	1994
1	Advertising, Publishing and Newspaper	24	27	27	31	32	36	36	38	39	38	38	40	40	41	39	40	40	38	34	34	35	37	37	36	36
2	Aerospace and Defense	21	22	21	20	20	24	24	27	26	26	30	31	30	32	33	33	33	30	31	31	32	29	32	35	34
3	Air Transport	16	16	15	15	15	17	17	17	19	23	23	25	24	25	24	24	20	19	17	14	14	11	11	11	11
4	Apparel and Shoe	35	40	38	39	38	38	39	40	38	36	34	37	39	38	35	34	30	30	26	29	25	25	24	22	23
5	Auto and Truck	5	5	6	6	6	5	5	6	6	6	6	6	7	6	6	9	8	7	6	5	4	4	4	4	4
6	Auto Parts	29	32	32	33	31	31	31	30	26	25	25	25	24	24	23	21	23	22	23	21	19	19	18	18	19
7	Bank and Thrift	46	48	48	60	63	64	65	70	71	71	71	74	73	70	67	78	86	82	81	84	90	89	85	82	80
8	Beverage	21	21	22	24	23	24	24	23	22	22	23	19	16	14	13	11	10	9	9	10	9	10	10	11	13
9	Broadcasting and Cable TV	7	6	6	6	5	8	8	8	8	7	7	11	15	16	15	16	14	12	12	11	10	10	10	10	10
10	Brokerage, Leasing and Financial Services	15	27	28	25	25	24	22	23	22	20	18	17	16	27	26	27	28	32	37	35	34	36	40	42	41
11	Building Materials, Cement, Furniture and Homebuilding	53	61	62	70	64	67	74	74	72	73	68	66	68	66	65	68	70	76	68	64	59	59	57	57	54
12	Chemical	43	44	45	45	46	47	52	52	48	49	49	53	52	54	55	52	53	53	56	58	65	64	62	62	63
13	Coal and Alternate Energy	8	7	7	6	6	9	9	11	11	10	12	12	11	11	10	10	9	11	9	7	8	7	7	5	4
14	Computer	8	18	18	19	19	19	23	25	25	27	30	34	40	50	52	50	57	59	61	54	55	58	62	66	72
15	Diversified	27	39	37	39	38	36	37	34	35	35	39	43	44	42	44	45	44	53	56	51	52	52	51	49	49
16	Drug	20	20	20	21	23	21	21	22	20	20	19	20	20	21	21	20	23	24	24	21	19	19	22	27	27
17	Drugstore	5	12	12	14	14	16	17	15	15	15	14	10	10	12	10	8	8	7	7	9	9	9	9	9	10
18	Electrical Equipment and Home Appliance	41	45	44	45	46	49	49	48	49	46	46	45	43	43	43	41	34	32	30	27	25	25	25	25	24
19	Electronics and Semiconductor	30	31	30	29	28	32	34	32	34	39	45	46	51	46	47	51	52	49	53	55	54	54	52	54	52
20	Food Processing	54	56	57	56	57	62	66	67	64	61	60	59	57	55	53	50	48	46	45	45	46	45	44	44	41
21	Food Wholesalers and Grocery Stores	20	25	26	27	27	25	25	24	23	25	25	29	32	34	30	29	29	28	30	25	30	30	28	28	29
22	Hotel and Gaming	7	8	8	12	12	14	13	14	15	14	12	12	12	13	14	14	13	14	15	15	15	15	15	16	15
23	Household Products	7	9	8	8	8	8	10	12	11	10	10	10	10	9	11	11	12	11	10	10	10	11	11	12	12

24	Industrial Services (Including Environmental)	5	10	10	17	16	19	18	18	16	18	19	19	22	20	20	23	24	23	29	35	38	41	42	41	38
25	Insurance	20	25	26	33	33	41	42	45	47	47	46	47	43	41	41	42	41	43	46	49	49	48	49	49	50
26	Machine Tool	15	15	15	17	17	18	17	17	16	16	15	15	14	14	14	13	11	15	11	11	9	8	9	7	7
27	Machinery	67	67	64	70	70	74	73	72	71	70	69	67	69	64	60	60	53	46	45	46	47	45	46	45	47
28	Manufactured Housing and Recreational Vehicles	8	7	8	9	9	8	10	11	11	11	11	11	9	9	9	8	10	8	9	8	7	7	7	8	8
29	Maritime	7	7	8	9	8	7	9	8	8	7	8	7	8	8	12	12	8	6	6	6	5	5	5	5	5
30	Medical Services	0	0	0	3	3	4	5	3	4	9	9	8	10	10	9	11	10	10	12	9	10	11	12	15	14
31	Medical Supplies	11	14	13	14	12	12	15	18	18	21	26	25	23	25	24	23	27	32	33	36	39	45	43	42	42
32	Metal Fabricating	20	20	20	21	21	21	18	19	19	19	20	20	18	18	18	20	18	19	16	16	14	14	14	14	13
33	Metals and Mining	43	43	43	45	44	44	43	40	36	34	36	33	33	33	32	31	31	28	28	28	28	30	29	28	27
34	Natural Gas	43	48	48	46	44	47	48	50	51	50	54	50	53	52	53	54	50	50	49	48	47	48	47	47	47
35	Office Equip. and Supplies	12	12	12	14	15	17	17	16	18	15	15	15	15	15	14	15	17	19	20	21	21	21	21	21	22
36	Oilfield Services and Equipment	10	12	13	15	14	19	19	19	23	29	27	32	34	33	34	32	26	21	19	20	19	17	18	18	17
37	Packaging and Container	19	21	21	26	26	26	27	27	23	22	22	23	25	24	19	19	17	17	16	18	17	17	17	13	13
38	Paper and Forest Products	18	19	19	20	19	22	25	26	26	27	28	27	25	25	28	29	25	28	30	30	29	29	29	29	30
39	Petroleum	41	46	43	46	49	54	58	64	62	63	64	63	61	54	47	45	45	45	46	42	42	44	42	42	42
40	Precision Instrument	23	27	28	28	28	31	31	32	36	35	22	23	27	26	26	24	26	26	25	25	24	23	22	22	20
41	Railroad	19	18	17	16	16	16	17	17	17	17	14	14	13	13	11	10	10	11	11	11	10	10	10	9	12
42	Real Estate	5	8	8	14	14	13	12	13	13	11	12	12	10	9	12	15	14	14	11	10	8	6	5	0	0
43	Recreation	15	17	19	22	21	24	22	21	21	22	20	18	20	18	18	19	21	22	22	21	19	19	20	20	19
44	Restaurant	3	4	4	4	4	13	19	19	19	17	16	16	15	16	16	16	21	20	21	18	17	17	17	19	19
45	Retail (Special Lines)	8	11	12	13	13	16	16	17	16	17	18	15	18	20	23	26	32	36	43	49	54	53	54	53	52
46	Retail Store	33	38	37	40	39	41	38	38	36	42	42	38	33	32	35	36	32	31	29	26	25	24	24	27	27
47	Steel	31	30	29	28	27	31	32	31	31	30	31	31	29	29	26	25	24	20	20	24	26	26	24	22	25
48	Telecommunications	11	12	12	12	12	13	13	14	14	14	16	18	20	22	30	32	34	36	34	35	36	33	33	33	35
49	Textile	19	19	20	22	22	21	21	18	19	20	19	17	14	15	12	9	8	9	11	10	9	9	9	9	11
50	Tire and Rubber	10	10	10	11	11	12	12	12	12	12	12	12	13	13	11	11	11	8	4	4	4	4	4	4	5
51	Tobacco	11	11	10	10	10	9	9	9	9	9	8	8	7	7	7	8	8	8	9	8	8	9	9	9	9
52	Toiletries and Cosmetics	14	12	12	11	11	12	13	14	15	15	15	15	16	16	15	14	11	12	11	10	9	9	10	10	9
53	Toys	6	8	8	8	8	7	7	8	10	11	10	10	6	6	5	6	6	5	6	7	7	6	7	6	4
54	Trucking and Transportation Leasing	16	18	17	20	20	21	21	23	23	18	21	17	13	12	11	12	14	17	12	12	12	12	12	11	12
55	Utilities	91	94	94	95	95	97	96	98	98	97	96	97	97	96	95	97	97	97	101	102	103	101	101	101	100
	Total	1196	1322	1317	1409	1397	1486	1524	1549	1537	1543	1545	1547	1547	1544	1523	1539	1526	1526	1525	1510	1511	1509	1507	1504	1504

Table A2

Mergers by acquirers in Value Line during the 1970 – 1994 period. Includes all deals where target was in CRSP and a transaction value could be estimated. Mergers are assigned to the industry of the acquirer in the year of completion. This sample is a subset of the CRSP Merger Database, including all mergers between CRSP-listed firms in the 1958 – 1994 period. Industries are based on actual industry classifications from Value Line, with some modifications to adjust for changes in Value Line coverage and classification, such as additions, deletions and mergers of industries, as well as reclassifications of subsets of industries in different years (see Appendix A for details)

Industry Number	Industry Name	1970	1971	1972	1973	1974	1975	1976	1977	1978	1979	1980	1981	1982	1983	1984	1985	1986	1987	1988	1989	1990	1991	1992	1993	1994	Total
1	Advertising, Publishing and Newspaper	0	1	0	2	1	0	0	3	4	7	1	1	0	0	3	1	1	3	2	0	2	0	1	1	0	34
2	Aerospace and Defense	0	1	0	0	1	0	2	3	3	2	5	0	0	2	3	3	4	2	0	2	1	1	0	0	0	35
3	Air Transport	1	1	0	1	0	0	0	0	0	2	2	0	1	0	0	3	6	5	4	0	0	0	0	0	0	26
4	Apparel and Shoe	0	1	1	1	1	2	1	0	1	3	1	1	0	0	3	0	1	1	0	0	0	0	0	1	1	20
5	Auto and Truck	0	0	0	0	0	1	0	0	0	0	0	1	0	0	1	2	0	4	2	1	1	0	0	0	0	13
6	Auto Parts	2	0	1	0	2	2	2	0	5	3	3	2	3	0	0	1	2	1	0	1	0	0	0	1	0	31
7	Bank and Thrift	2	0	0	3	3	2	1	0	1	0	1	1	12	9	8	8	24	18	14	12	13	10	23	31	21	217
8	Beverage	2	0	2	3	1	0	1	4	3	1	0	1	3	2	0	1	1	0	2	0	0	1	0	0	0	28
9	Broadcasting and Cable TV	0	0	0	0	1	1	0	1	2	1	0	0	3	1	0	0	2	0	2	1	0	0	1	0	2	18
10	Brokerage, Leasing and Financial Services	0	0	1	1	1	1	1	2	2	3	4	1	1	0	0	1	3	1	5	2	3	1	2	0	0	36
11	Building Materials, Cement, Furniture and Homebuilding	1	1	0	0	0	1	0	3	5	4	4	4	1	2	3	3	2	3	3	0	0	0	1	0	0	41
12	Chemical	3	2	1	2	3	1	1	4	5	3	4	8	3	7	1	6	2	4	3	3	1	0	0	1	0	68
13	Coal and Alternate Energy	0	0	0	0	3	0	0	0	2	1	0	1	0	0	0	0	0	1	2	0	0	0	0	0	0	10
14	Computer	0	0	0	0	0	1	2	2	3	1	3	2	2	0	3	1	1	4	4	3	1	4	2	5	0	44
15	Diversified	3	5	3	4	5	6	8	11	8	4	3	3	2	4	5	12	10	3	6	2	3	1	2	0	0	113
16	Drug	3	1	0	0	0	0	2	2	3	3	3	2	1	2	0	0	3	3	1	2	0	0	0	3	0	34
17	Drugstore	0	0	1	0	1	0	1	1	0	0	1	0	0	0	0	0	0	0	1	0	0	0	0	0	0	6
18	Electrical Equipment and Home Appliance	3	1	1	1	1	5	3	2	4	5	5	3	1	2	0	3	2	3	4	6	2	0	0	2	0	59
19	Electronics and Semiconductor	0	1	0	1	0	1	2	1	3	0	3	0	4	0	2	0	0	3	0	2	0	0	0	0	1	24
20	Food Processing	0	2	0	5	5	3	2	5	14	4	4	4	3	1	3	4	2	2	0	5	2	1	0	1	0	72
21	Food Wholesalers and Grocery Stores	0	0	0	0	1	0	1	0	0	2	1	0	1	2	2	2	2	0	2	0	0	0	1	0	0	17
22	Hotel and Gaming	0	0	0	0	0	0	0	0	0	0	1	0	2	0	0	1	2	0	0	1	0	1	0	0	0	8
23	Household Products	0	1	1	2	0	0	1	1	0	1	0	0	0	1	0	1	1	2	0	0	3	0	2	1	0	18
24	Industrial Services (Including Environmental)	0	0	0	0	0	0	0	0	1	0	0	0	1	0	0	0	0	3	2	1	3	2	1	1	0	15

25	Insurance	1	0	0	2	0	2	5	1	2	9	8	5	10	1	2	2	2	4	2	2	3	1	3	0	1	68
26	Machine Tool	0	0	0	0	0	0	0	1	1	1	0	0	1	1	0	0	0	0	0	0	0	0	1	0	0	6
27	Machinery	0	2	1	1	2	2	5	4	9	10	4	4	2	1	2	2	3	4	0	1	1	0	0	0	0	60
28	Manufactured Housing and Recreational Vehicles	0	0	0	0	0	0	0	0	0	0	0	1	0	0	0	0	0	0	0	0	0	0	0	0	0	1
29	Maritime	0	0	0	0	0	0	0	0	0	1	0	0	0	0	0	1	0	0	0	0	0	0	0	0	0	2
30	Medical Services	0	0	0	0	0	0	0	0	2	1	0	1	2	2	1	3	3	0	0	0	0	0	0	2	1	18
31	Medical Supplies	0	0	0	2	1	0	0	2	1	2	0	3	3	2	1	3	0	2	1	2	3	0	1	3	0	32
32	Metal Fabricating	0	0	0	0	0	0	2	1	2	1	0	1	0	0	2	0	0	1	0	2	0	0	0	0	0	12
33	Metals and Mining	1	2	1	2	1	0	0	2	1	0	1	1	0	0	4	2	0	3	0	0	0	2	1	1	0	25
34	Natural Gas	1	3	1	1	0	0	1	5	5	0	1	2	0	2	4	7	4	2	4	1	1	0	0	0	0	45
35	Office Equip. and Supplies	0	0	0	0	0	0	1	0	0	2	0	0	0	1	1	0	0	0	1	0	0	2	0	0	0	8
36	Oilfield Services and Equipment	0	0	1	0	0	1	0	0	0	2	2	1	2	0	2	0	0	0	1	0	0	0	0	0	1	13
37	Packaging and Container	1	0	1	0	0	0	1	3	3	3	3	0	3	3	2	1	1	0	0	0	0	0	1	3	0	29
38	Paper and Forest Products	0	0	0	0	1	2	1	3	1	2	2	1	1	1	2	0	3	3	0	0	1	1	0	0	0	25
39	Petroleum	0	1	1	0	2	3	1	6	3	6	4	7	4	1	3	0	4	0	3	0	0	2	1	1	0	53
40	Precision Instrument	0	0	0	1	0	1	4	1	0	2	2	3	0	0	0	2	1	1	1	0	1	1	1	1	0	23
41	Railroad	2	1	1	2	1	0	0	1	4	3	1	0	1	3	0	2	2	0	2	0	0	0	0	1	0	27
42	Real Estate	0	0	1	0	0	0	0	0	0	1	0	0	0	0	0	0	0	0	1	0	0	0	0	0	0	3
43	Recreation	1	0	0	1	2	1	0	5	2	2	0	1	0	0	0	1	0	0	1	0	0	0	2	0	0	19
44	Restaurant	0	0	0	0	0	0	0	0	0	0	0	0	0	0	0	1	0	0	1	1	0	0	0	0	0	3
45	Retail (Special Lines)	0	1	0	1	0	0	0	0	1	0	1	1	1	0	1	3	0	0	0	2	2	3	0	0	0	17
46	Retail Store	2	0	2	3	0	0	1	3	5	2	3	5	2	0	2	5	3	2	1	2	0	1	1	0	1	46
47	Steel	1	0	0	0	0	0	1	0	0	1	3	0	2	0	1	1	0	0	0	1	0	0	0	0	1	12
48	Telecommunications	0	0	0	1	0	1	0	0	0	5	3	1	4	3	1	2	3	2	4	4	7	6	2	3	2	54
49	Textile	0	0	0	1	0	0	0	1	0	0	0	0	0	0	0	2	1	0	1	0	0	0	0	2	0	8
50	Tire and Rubber	1	0	1	0	0	0	0	2	2	0	1	0	0	0	0	0	2	0	0	0	0	0	0	0	0	9
51	Tobacco	2	0	0	0	0	1	1	1	1	3	0	0	1	1	1	2	0	1	2	0	0	0	0	0	0	17
52	Toiletries and Cosmetics	0	0	0	1	0	1	1	0	1	1	2	0	1	0	1	1	1	1	0	0	0	0	0	0	0	12
53	Toys	0	0	0	0	0	0	0	0	0	1	0	0	0	0	1	0	0	1	0	2	1	1	1	2	0	10
54	Trucking and Transportation Leasing	2	0	0	0	0	0	1	0	2	0	1	0	0	0	0	1	1	0	1	1	0	0	0	1	0	11
55	Utilities	0	0	0	1	1	0	0	0	1	0	1	0	2	1	0	2	3	1	2	2	2	1	3	2	2	27
	Total	35	28	23	46	41	42	57	87	118	111	92	73	86	58	71	99	108	94	88	67	57	43	54	70	34	

Appendix A. Procedure for Creating Industries

Value Line industry classifications have not remained static since 1970, with industries dividing or merging over time. In order to create a single set of industries that could be followed continuously from 1970 to 1994, we generate a subset of 55 industry classifications, to which firms in Value Line are allocated.

We include each firm in our sample up to 3 years before its addition, in which case, the firm is included in the industry where it first appears, and up to 3 years after its exclusion, with the firm remaining in the last industry to which it belonged. This procedure mitigates some of the problems caused by increases in overall Value Line coverage in the early 1970s, which can be seen in the first few columns of Table A1.

For most cases, the following guidelines are followed in transforming Value Line industries into "our" industries:

• Most industries which exist in the same form throughout the entire 1970–1994 period, i.e., no other industries are merged into them or split off from them, are kept intact.

• Industries which differ merely by geographic classifications (e.g., "Utilities (East)" and "Utilities (West)"), or where the product lines seem particularly similar (e.g., "Auto Parts (OEM)" and "Auto Parts (Replacement)"), are merged.

• Some industries that are separate as of 1994, but are merged in earlier periods, and where re-classification is straightforward (e.g., "Computers" and "Office Equipment"), are split up in the early periods. Companies which existed both pre- and post-split are assigned to their post-split industry, while for companies that only exist pre-split, a description of the firm's product line from Value Line is used for classification.

• There are some subsets of firms that Value Line includes in different industries at various points in time (e.g., "Forest Products" firms are first included in "Building" and later become part of the "Paper and Forest Products" industry). In these cases, we transfer firms from their early period classifications to their later ones (e.g., all "Forest Products" firm are classified with "Paper Products" firms for the entire sample period). This also requires reading descriptions of firms which only exist in the early years, and deciding where to allocate them.

• In total, 60 firms are allocated manually after reading their descriptions on Value Line.

Appendix B. Procedure for assigning industries to merger targets

In an attempt to assign an industry to all the targets in mergers where the acquirer belonged to the sample, a total of 1711 transactions, we follow these steps in order:

(1) Check if the target is in Value Line, and assign it's corresponding industry. This results in 572 classifications.

(2) Create a conversion table of SIC codes to our industry classifications. This is based on our reading the descriptions of all four-digit SIC codes from the Standard Industrial Classification Manual (1987). For most cases, the appropriate industry assignment is obvious, but in case of doubt, we classify the four-digit code as "missing."

(3) Using the conversion table, assign industries to the remaining targets on the basis of both their CRSP and Compustat SIC codes. If the industries match, assign the target to it, which results in 456 additional classifications

(4) Hand-collect primary SIC codes for remaining unclassified targets from Dun and Bradstreet's Million Dollar Directory. Using the conversion table, assign industries to the targets found in the Directory. This results in 537 additional classifications.

Appendix C. Compustat data items

The following Compustat data items were used to construct the industry-level and firm-level variables in Sections 3 and 4:

Variable name	Compustat data item number
Advertising	45
CAPX	128
R&D	46
Cash	1
Sales	12
Total assets	6
Book equity	60
Market equity	199 × 25
EBITDA	13
Debt in current liabilities	34
Long-term debt	9
Preferred stock—redemption value	56

References

Andrade, G., Mitchell, M., Stafford, E., 2001. New evidence and perspectives on mergers. Journal of Economic Perspectives 15, 103–120.

Blanchard, O., Lopez-de-Silanes, F., Shleifer, A., 1994. What do firms do with cash windfalls? Journal of Financial Economics 36, 337–360.

Brealey, R., Myers, S., 1996. Principles of Corporate Finance, 5th edn. McGraw-Hill, New York, NY.

Fama, E., 1976. Foundations of Finance. Basic, New York.

Gibbons, J., 1985. Nonparametric Statistical Inference, 2nd edn. Marcel Dekker, New York, NY.

Gort, M., 1969. An economic disturbance theory of mergers. Quarterly Journal of Economics 83, 624–642.

Greene, W., 1993. Econometric Analysis, 2nd edn. Macmillan, New York, NY.

Guenther, D., Rosman, A., 1994. Differences between Compustat and CRSP SIC codes and related effects on research. Journal of Accounting and Economics 18, 115–128.

Healy, P., Palepu, K., Ruback, R., 1992. Does corporate performance improve after mergers? Journal of Financial Economics 31, 135–175.

Heaton, J.B., 1999. Managerial optimism and corporate finance. University of Chicago Working Paper.

Jarrell, G., Brickley, J., Netter, J., 1988. The market for corporate control: the empirical evidence since 1980. Journal of Economic Perspectives 2, 49–68.

Jensen, M., 1986. Agency costs of free cash flow, corporate finance and takeovers. American Economic Review 76, 323–329.

Jensen, M., 1993. The modern industrial revolution, exit, and control systems. Journal of Finance 48, 831–880.

Kahle, K., Walkling, R., 1996. The impact of industry classifications on financial research. Journal of Financial and Quantitative Analysis 31, 309–335.

Kaplan, S., Zingales, L., 1997. Do financing constraints explain why investment is correlated with cash flow? Quarterly Journal of Economics 112, 169–215.

Kovenock, D., Phillips, G., 1997. Capital structure and product market behavior: an examination of plant exit and investment decisions. Review of Financial Studies 10, 767–803.

Lang, L., Stulz, R., Walkling, R., 1989. Managerial performance, Tobin's q, and the gains from successful tender offers. Journal of Financial Economics 24, 137–154.

Maddala, G., 1983. Limited Dependent and Qualitative Variables in Econometrics. Cambridge Univ. Press, New York, NY.

Maksimovic, V., Phillips, G., 2001. The market for corporate assets: who engages in mergers and asset sales and are there efficiency gains? Journal of Finance 56, 2019–2065.

Mitchell, M., Mulherin, J., 1996. The impact of industry shocks on takeover and restructuring activity. Journal of Financial Economics 41, 193–229.

Mitchell, M., Stafford, E., 2000. Managerial decisions and long-term stock price performance. Journal of Business 73, 287–329.

Morck, R., Shleifer, A., Vishny, R., 1988. Characteristics of targets of hostile and friendly takeovers. In: Auerbach, A.J. (Ed.), Corporate Takeovers: Causes and Consequences. University of Chicago Press/NBER, Chicago, IL.

Morck, R., Shleifer, A., Vishny, R., 1990. Do managerial objectives drive bad acquisitions? Journal of Finance 45, 31–48.

Mulherin, J., Boone, A., 2000. Comparing acquisitions and divestitures. Journal of Corporate Finance 6, 117–139.

Myers, S., 1977. Determinants of corporate borrowing. Journal of Financial Economics 5, 147–175.

Nelson, R., 1959. Merger Movements in American Industry, 1895–1956. Princeton Univ. Press/NBER, Princeton, NJ.

Song, M., Walkling, R., 2000. Abnormal returns to rivals of acquisition targets: a test of the "acquisition probability hypothesis". Journal of Financial Economics 55, 143–172.

[12]

Journal of Financial Economics 31 (1992) 135–175. North-Holland

Does corporate performance improve after mergers?*

Paul M. Healy
Massachusetts Institute of Technology, Cambridge, MA 02139, USA

Krishna G. Palepu and Richard S. Ruback
Harvard Business School, Cambridge, MA 02163, USA

Received April 1990, final version received January 1992

We examine post-acquisition performance for the 50 largest U.S. mergers between 1979 and mid-1984. Merged firms show significant improvements in asset productivity relative to their industries, leading to higher operating cash flow returns. This performance improvement is particularly strong for firms with highly overlapping businesses. Mergers do not lead to cuts in long-term capital and R&D investments. There is a strong positive relation between postmerger increases in operating cash flows and abnormal stock returns at merger announcements, indicating that expectations of economic improvements underlie the equity revaluations of the merging firms.

1. Introduction

This study examines the postmerger cash flow performance of acquiring and target firms, and explores the sources of merger-induced changes in cash flow performance. Our research is motivated by the inability of stock price

*We acknowledge the helpful comments of the referee, Michael Jensen (the editor), Robin Cooper, George Foster, Robert Kaplan, Richard Leftwich, Mark Wolfson, Karen Wruck, and seminar participants at Baruch College, Carnegie Mellon University, Columbia University, Dartmouth College, Duke University, the Federal Reserve Bank (Washington, DC), Harvard University, the London School of Economics, the University of Michigan, Massachusetts Institute of Technology, New York University, Northwestern University, the University of Minnesota, the University of Rochester, Stanford University, the University of Southern California, the University of Alberta, and the U.S. Department of Justice. We are thankful to Chris Fox and Ken Hao, who provided research assistance, and the International Financial Services Center at MIT and the Division of Research at the Harvard Business School for financial support.

performance studies to determine whether takeovers create real economic gains and to identify the sources of such gains.

There is near-unanimous agreement that target stockholders benefit from mergers, as evidenced by the premium they receive for selling their shares. The stock price studies of takeovers also indicate that bidders generally breakeven, and that the combined equity value of the bidding and target firms increases as a result of takeovers. These increases in equity values are typically attributed to some unmeasured source of real economic gains, such as synergy. But researchers have had little success in relating the equity value gains to improvements in subsequent corporate performance.[1] Therefore, the equity value gains could also be due to capital market inefficiencies, arising simply from the creation of an overvalued security.

To determine whether the equity value increases in takeovers are from real economic gains or capital market inefficiencies, stock price studies have analyzed unsuccessful takeovers.[2] But these studies, too, are unable to distinguish between the real economic gains and the market inefficiency explanations. That the stock prices of unsuccessful merger targets return to their preoffer level is consistent with the loss of an anticipated premium – whatever its source. From the stock price perspective, the anticipation of real economic gains is observationally equivalent to market mispricing. It is therefore difficult to conceive of a pure stock price study that could resolve the ambiguity in the interpretation of the evidence.

Stock price studies are also unable to provide evidence on the sources of any merger-related gains. Yet differences of opinion about the source of the gains in takeovers underlie much of the public policy debate on their desirability. Gains from mergers could arise from a variety of sources, such as operating synergies, tax savings, transfers from employees or other stakeholders, or increased monopoly rents. Equity gains from only some of these sources are unequivocally beneficial at the social level.

Our approach is to use postmerger accounting data to test directly for changes in operating performance that result from mergers.[3] Our tests use accounting data collected from company annual reports, merger prospectuses, proxy statements, and analysts' reports for 50 large mergers between U.S. public industrial firms completed between 1979 and mid-1984. We recognize that accounting data are imperfect measures of economic perfor-

[1]See Caves (1989) for a review of the studies that examine the *ex post* performance of merged firms.

[2]Dodd (1980), Asquith (1983), Dodd and Ruback (1977), Bradley, Desai, and Kim (1983), and Ruback (1988).

[3]Three recent studies have examined earnings performance following management buyouts of corporations [Bull (1988), Kaplan (1990), and Smith (1990)]. Our paper focuses on acquisitions of one public company by another in either a merger or a tender offer, rather than on management buyouts.

mance and that they can be affected by managerial decisions. As we explain in section 2, we use cash flow measures of economic performance to mitigate the impact of the financing of the acquisition and the method of accounting for the transaction. We also recognize that our cash flow variables measure period-by-period performance, which is affected by firm-specific and industry factors. We therefore use industry performance as a benchmark to evaluate postmerger performance.

Results reported in section 3 show that the merged firms have increases in postmerger operating cash flow returns in comparison with their industries. These increases arise from postmerger improvements in asset productivity. We find no evidence that the improvement in postmerger cash flows is achieved at the expense of the merged firms' long-term viability, since the sample firms maintain their capital expenditure and R&D rates in relation to their industries. Our results differ from the findings reported by Ravenscraft and Scherer (1987) and Herman and Lowenstein (1988), who examine earnings performance after takeovers and conclude that merged firms have no operating improvements.

In section 4 we examine the relation between our cash flow measures of postmerger performance and stock market measures used in earlier studies. Postmerger improvements in operating cash flow returns explain a significant portion of the increase in equity values of the merging firms at the announcement of the merger. This suggests that the stock price reaction to mergers is driven by anticipated economic gains after the merger.

Section 5 discusses the implications of our primary findings and explores some popular hypotheses on factors that influence postmerger performance. There is little evidence that transaction characteristics such as the method of financing, whether the merger is hostile or friendly, or the size of the target firm explain cross-sectional variation in postmerger performance. We find some support, however, for the view that mergers between firms in overlapping businesses lead to better performance than other mergers.

2. Experimental design

2.1. Sample

The analysis in this study is based on the largest 50 acquisitions during the period January 1979 to June 1984. We limit the number of acquisitions studied to make the hand data collection tasks manageable. The largest acquisitions have several important advantages over a similarly sized random sample. First, although the sample consists of a small fraction of the total acquisitions in the sample period, the total dollar value of the 50 firms selected accounts for a significant portion of the dollar value of domestic merger activity.[4] Second, if there are economic gains from a takeover, they are most likely to be detected when the target firm is large. Third, it is less likely that the acquirers in the sample undertake equally large acquisitions before or after the events we study, reducing the probability of confounding events. Finally, public concern about the consequences of takeovers is typically triggered by the largest transactions, making them interesting in their own right.

The sample period is selected to focus on recent mergers and also to have sufficient postmerger performance data.[5] To select the acquisition sample, we identify the 382 merger-related delistings on the Center for Research in Security Prices (*CRSP*) database in the sample period. The names of the acquirers are identified from the *Wall Street Journal Index*. The sample comprises acquisitions involving the 50 largest targets that satisfy the following two criteria: the acquirer is a U.S. company listed on the New York Stock Exchange (NYSE) or the American Stock Exchange (Amex), and the target and acquirer are not financial or regulated companies. Target-firm size is computed from *Compustat* as the market value of common stock plus the book values of net debt and preferred stock at the beginning of the year before the acquisition. Acquisitions are deleted from the sample if the acquirers are non-U.S. or private companies, since post-acquisition financial information is not available for these mergers. Regulated (railroads and utilities) and financial firms are deleted because they are subject to special accounting and regulatory requirements, making them difficult to compare with other firms.

A summary of the sample is provided in the appendix. The information provided includes target and acquiring firms' names, a description of their businesses and industries from *Value Line* reports, target equity value before the merger, the target's assets as a percentage of the acquirer's assets, and the merger completion date. The sample targets and acquirers represent a wide cross-section of *Value Line* industries. The target firms belong to 27 industries; the acquiring firms come from 33 industries.

The transactions are approximately evenly distributed over the sample years: eight acquisitions in the sample were completed in 1979, seven in 1980, twelve in 1981, eleven in 1983, and two in 1984. Since we focus on mergers completed in only a few years, however, the sample firms' postmerger performance is likely to be influenced by economywide changes. Our tests, therefore, control for these factors by comparing sample firms' performance with their corresponding industries'.

[4]The aggregate market value of equity of the 50 target firms in our sample one year before the acquisition is $43 billion.

[5]The sample period ends in June 1984 to ensure that when the study was initiated, at least five years of postmerger data were available on *Compustat* for the sample firms. *Compustat* files end in June each year.

The sample acquisitions are significant economic events for purchasing firms. On average, target firms are 42% of the assets of acquirers, where assets are measured by the book value of net debt (long-term debt, plus short-term debt, less cash and marketable securities) plus the market value of equity one year prior to the merger.

2.2. Performance measurement

We use pretax operating cash flow returns on assets to measure improvements in operating performance. Conceptually, we focus on cash flows because they represent the actual economic benefits generated by the assets. Since the level of economic benefits is affected by the assets employed, we scale the cash flows by the assets employed to form a return measure that can be compared across time and across firms. We measure assets employed using market values, which represent the opportunity cost of the assets. In our opinion, market-based measures of asset values dominate accounting and other historical estimates in this context because they simplify intertemporal and cross-sectional comparisons. Our market-based measure has a potential limitation, however, because unexpected cash flow realizations can change expectations about future cash flows, and hence market values. The sensitivity tests in section 3.2 show no evidence of such a feedback effect for our sample of mergers.

We define operating cash flows as sales, minus cost of goods sold and selling and administrative expenses, plus depreciation and goodwill expenses. This measure is deflated by the market value of assets (market value of equity plus book value of net debt) to provide a return metric that is comparable across firms. Unlike accounting return on book assets, our return measure excludes the effect of depreciation, goodwill, interest expense and income, and taxes. It is therefore unaffected by the method of accounting for the merger (purchase or pooling accounting) and the method of financing (cash, debt, or equity). As discussed below, these factors make it difficult to compare traditional accounting returns of the merged firm over time and cross-sectionally.

2.2.1. Effects of purchase and pooling accounting

In our sample, 38 mergers (76%) use the purchase method and the remaining 12 use the pooling of interests method. The purchase method restates the assets and liabilities of target firms at their current market values. No such revaluation is permitted under the pooling method. Further, under the purchase method the acquirer records any difference between the acquisition price and the market value of identifiable assets and liabilities of the target company as goodwill, and amortizes it. No goodwill is recorded under the pooling-of-interests method. Finally, for the first year of the merger, the purchase method consolidates results of the target with those of the acquirer from the date the merger took place; the pooling method consolidates results for the two firms from the beginning of the year regardless of when the merger took place.

The same transaction typically results in lower postmerger earnings under purchase accounting than under pooling. The purchase method increases depreciation, cost of goods sold, and goodwill expenses after the takeover. Also, in the year of the merger, earnings are usually lower under purchase accounting because the target's and acquirer's earnings are consolidated for a shorter period than under pooling. The lower earnings reported under the purchase method are due to differences in the method of accounting for the merger and not to differences in economic performance. Further, postmerger book assets under the purchase method will be larger than those under pooling because of the asset write-up under the purchase method. It is therefore misleading to compare post- and premerger accounting rates of return for firms that use purchase accounting to infer whether there are economic gains from mergers.

Our operating cash flow performance measure – unlike earnings-based performance measures – is unaffected by depreciation and goodwill. It is comparable cross-sectionally and on a time-series basis when firms use different methods of accounting for the merger. We exclude the first year of the merger in our analysis because of the differences between the purchase and pooling methods in timing the consolidation of the target with the acquirer. Excluding the first year also mitigates the effect of inventory write-ups under the purchase method, since this inventory is usually included in cost of sales in the merger year.[6] Because the asset base in our return metric is the market value of assets, rather than book value, it is also unaffected by the accounting method used to record the merger.

2.2.2. Effects of method of financing mergers

The method used to finance the sample transactions varies considerably. Thirty percent of the sample mergers are stock transactions, 26% are financed by cash, and the remaining 14% are financed by combinations of cash, stock, and other securities. It is important to control for these financing differences in measuring postmerger performance. If an acquisition is financed by debt or cash, its post-acquisition profits will be lower than if the

[6]Firms using the LIFO inventory valuation method expense the written-up inventory as inventory layers are depleted, making it difficult to determine when to adjust earnings for the effect of the write-up. We therefore do not make any adjustments for these firms. This lack of adjustment will not lead to a serious downward bias in our earnings measure, however, since LIFO inventory liquidations are relatively infrequent.

same transaction is financed by stock, because income is computed after deducting interest expenses (the cost of debt), but before allowing for any cost of equity. Since the differences in earnings reflect the financing choice and not differences in economic performance, it is misleading to compare reported accounting earnings, which are computed after interest income and expense, for firms that use different methods of merger financing. We use operating cash flows before interest expense and income from short-term investments deflated by the market value of assets (net of short-term investments) to measure performance. This cash flow return is unaffected by the choice of financing.

2.3. *Performance benchmark*

We aggregate performance data of the target and bidding firms before the merger to obtain the pro forma premerger performance of the combined firms. Comparing the postmerger performance with this premerger benchmark provides a measure of the change in performance. But some of the difference between premerger and postmerger performance could be also due to economywide and industry factors, or to a continuation of firm-specific performance before the merger. Hence, we use abnormal industry-adjusted performance of the target and bidding firms as our primary benchmark to evaluate postmerger performance.

Abnormal industry-adjusted performance is measured as the intercept of a cross-sectional regression of postmerger industry-adjusted cash flow returns on the corresponding premerger returns. For each year and firm, industry-adjusted performance measures are calculated by subtracting the industry median from the sample firm value. The data for sample firms are excluded when calculating the industry median. *Value Line* industry definitions immediately before the merger are used for the target and acquirer in both the premerger and the postmerger analysis. Industry data are collected from *Compustat Industrial and Research* files.

2.4. *Comparison with prior research*

Earlier studies of postmerger performance have a number of methodological problems, making their findings difficult to interpret. Ravenscraft and Scherer (1987) examine the performance in 1974 to 1977 for firms acquired between 1950 and 1977. Since the postmerger years examined are not aligned with the merger, it is hard to know what to make of the performance comparisons.

Ravenscraft and Scherer focus exclusively on acquired firms' lines of business. It is not obvious why gains from mergers would be reflected only in the acquired segments; synergies are just as likely to improve the performance of the other lines of business of the acquiring firms. The authors also use FTC line-of-business data, which have several potential problems. Definitions of business segments may change systematically after mergers if acquirers restructure their operations. Results of tests using segment data reported to the FTC are also likely to be difficult to interpret, since reporting firms have incentives to use accounting discretion to mask superior performance, thereby reducing the likelihood of antitrust suits by the FTC [see Watts and Zimmerman (1986)].

Herman and Lowenstein (1988) examine postmerger performance using a sample of hostile acquisitions between 1975 and 1983. Complete postmerger data are unavailable for transactions after 1979, however, which limits the analysis to a small number of postmerger years for many sample firms. Further, the return on equity measure, which is used to judge postmerger performance, does not control for differences in pooling and purchase accounting, methods of merger financing, or the effect of common industry shocks. These limitations make it difficult to interpret the study's findings.

3. Cash flow return performance

3.1. Operating cash flow returns

As described in section 2, we aggregate pretax operating cash flows for the target and acquiring firms to determine pro forma cash flows for the combined firms in each of the five years before the merger (years -5 to -1). Postmerger operating cash flows are the actual values reported by the merged firm in years 1 to 5. We deflate the operating cash flows by the market value of assets. Operating cash flow returns are the ratio of operating cash flows during a given year to the market value of assets at the beginning of that year. The market value of assets is recomputed at the beginning of each year to control for changes in the size of the firm over time. For premerger years the market value of assets is the sum of the values for the target and acquiring firms. The market value of assets of the combined firm is used in the postmerger years.

We exclude the change in equity values of the target and acquiring firms at the merger announcement from the asset base in the postmerger years. For the target the change in equity value is measured from five days before the first offer is announced (not necessarily by the ultimate acquirer) to the date the target is delisted from trading on public exchanges. For the acquirer the change in equity value is measured from five days before its first offer is announced to the date the target is delisted from trading on public exchanges. In an efficient stock market these revaluations represent the capitalized value of any expected postmerger performance improvements. If merger announcement equity revaluations are included in the asset base, measured cash flow returns will not show any abnormal increase, even though the merger results in an increase in operating cash flows.

For example, consider an acquiring firm (company A) and a target (company T) with annual operating cash flows of $20 and $10 forever. Both firms have the same cost of capital (10%), implying that their market values are $200 and $100. Therefore, a portfolio comprising of A and T has a market value of $300 and cash flows of $30, producing an annual return of 10%. Suppose that when A acquires T combined cash flows increase to $35 per year. An efficient market capitalizes this $5 improvement at $50. If postmerger cash flow returns are computed as the ratio of postmerger cash flows ($35) and postmerger assets including the premium ($350), measured performance will be identical to the premerger operating return for the portfolio of A and T (10%). There is no improvement in the measured cash flow return even though cash flows per year have increased by $5. Our measure of performance is computed as the ratio of postmerger cash flows ($35) and postmerger assets excluding the asset revaluation ($350 – $50). This return measure (11.7%) correctly reflects the improvement in operating performance after the merger.

We also adjust the merging firms' performance for the impact of contemporaneous unrelated events by measuring industry cash flow returns during the same ten-year period. We use *Value Line* industry definitions, and exclude the target and acquiring firms' returns from the industry computations. Before the merger, industry values for the sample firms are constructed by weighting median performance measures for the target and acquiring firms' industries by the relative asset sizes of the two firms at the beginning of each year. In all of the postmerger years target and acquirer industry cash flow returns are weighted by the relative asset sizes of the two firms one year before the merger.

We focus our analysis on years −5 to −1 and 1 to 5. Year 0, the year of the merger, is excluded from the analysis for two reasons. First, many of the acquiring firms use the purchase accounting method, implying that in the year of the merger the two firms are consolidated for financial reporting purposes only from the date of the merger. Results for this year are therefore not comparable across firms or for industry comparisons. Second, year 0 figures are affected by one-time merger costs incurred during that year, making it difficult to compare them with results for other years.

3.1.1. Changes in cash flows and assets

Table 1 reports the changes in cash flows and assets in years 1 to 5 relative to the year before the merger. The merged firms have a median increase in cash flows of 14% in year 1, 17% in year 2, 16% in years 3 and 4, and 9% in year 5. This cash flow growth does not indicate that the merged firms

Table 1

Postmerger firm and industry growth in operating cash flows and market value of assets for 50 combined target and acquirer firms in mergers completed in the period 1979 to mid-1984.[a]

Growth period in relation to merger	Firm cash flow growth rate	Firm asset growth rate	Industry cash flow growth rate	Industry asset growth rate
Year −1 to 1	14%	15%	10%	20%
Year −1 to 2	17	20	11	33
Year −1 to 3	16	28	14	40
Year −1 to 4	16	23	22	43
Year −1 to 5	9	18	24	56

[a]Operating cash flows are sales less cost of goods sold, less selling and administrative expenses, plus depreciation. The market value of assets, measured at the beginning of the year, is the market value of equity plus the book values of preferred stock and net debt. Year −1 cash flow and asset values for the combined firm are weighted averages of target and acquirer values, with the weights being the relative asset values of the two firms. Postmerger values use data for the merged firms. Industry-adjusted cash flow and asset growth rates are computed for each firm and year as the difference between the sample-firm growth rate in that year and growth rates for aggregated cash flows and assets of other firms in the same industry (as defined by *Value Line* in year −1). Target and acquirer industry growth rates are weighted by the relative asset values of the acquirer and target firms in year −1.

[b]Significantly different from zero at the 1% level, using a two-tailed test.

[c]Significantly different from zero at the 5% level, using a two-tailed test.

performed better in the postmerger period, however, because assets also increased during this period. Asset values increase by 15% in year 1, 20% in year 2, 28% in year 3, 23% in year 4, and 18% in year 5. Also, the sample firms' industries experience growth in cash flows and assets in the postmerger period. The cash flow return measures we use to gauge performance adjust for changes in the size of the sample firms and their corresponding industries that are evident in table 1.

3.1.2. Raw cash flow returns

Panel A of table 2 reports median pretax unadjusted operating cash flow returns for the merged firms (column 2) in years −5 to −1 and 1 to 5. The median pretax operating returns range from 24.5% to 26.8% in the five years before the merger, with a median annual value of 25.3%.[7] After the merger, the median pretax operating returns are lower, ranging from 18.4% to 22.9% with a median annual value of 20.5% for the whole period. As indicated in table 1, this decline arises because cash flows grow more slowly than assets in

[7]To calculate the sample median pretax operating cash flow return for years −5 to −1, we first compute the median return in these years for each sample firm. The reported sample median is the median of these values. Sample median returns in the postmerger period are calculated the same way.

the postmerger period. These changes cannot be attributed to the merger, however, if there is a contemporaneous downward trend in industry cash flow returns. Industry-adjusted returns, which are differences between values for the merged firms and their weighted-average industry median estimates, correct for this problem.

3.1.3. Industry-adjusted cash flow returns

Columns 3 and 4 in panel A, table 2 show median industry-adjusted cash flow returns and the percentage of sample firms with positive industry-adjusted returns. Merged firms have higher operating cash flow returns on assets than their industries' in the postmerger period. Median industry-adjusted operating returns for the merged firms are 3.0% in year 1, 5.3% in year 2, 3.2% in year 3, and 3.0% in year 4, all significantly different from zero.[8] Year 5 also shows better performance than the industry, but is not statistically significant. The percentage of positive industry-adjusted returns is 67% in year 1, 79% in year 2, 70% in year 3, and 68% in year 4, all well above the value expected by chance alone (50%). Overall, the annual median return for the sample firms in the five postmerger years is 2.8%, about 16% larger than their industries' returns.[9]

The benchmark for the significant postmerger industry-adjusted returns depends on the relation between industry-adjusted returns before and after the merger. If there is no relation between pre- and postmerger industry-adjusted returns, the appropriate benchmark for the postmerger industry-adjusted returns is zero. Alternatively, the appropriate benchmark is the premerger industry-adjusted return if firms that perform above or below their industries before the merger are likely to realize the same performance after the merger.

For our sample, there is no evidence of superior industry-adjusted pretax operating cash flow returns in the premerger period. Median returns are not significantly different from zero in four of the five years. The percentage of positive industry-adjusted returns is not significantly different from the value expected by chance in four of the five years before the merger. The overall median annual return in the premerger period is only 0.3%, which is statistically insignificant. This suggests that, on average, the postmerger performance is not due to a continuation of superior premerger industry performance. In the next section we use a cross-sectional regression approach to compare performance before and after the merger.

[8]Throughout the paper we use a two-tailed test and a 10% or lower cutoff significance level. This is equivalent to a 5% cutoff one-tailed test for the many cases where the hypotheses examined are directional.

[9]We calculate the percentage increase relative to the industry as 2.8/(20.5 – 2.8).

Table 2

Median operating cash flow return on actual market value of assets for 50 combined target and acquirer firms in years surrounding mergers completed in the period 1979 to mid-1984.[a]

Panel A: Pre- and postmerger operating cash flow returns

Year relative to merger	Firm median	Industry-adjusted Median	Industry-adjusted % positive	Number of observations
−5	24.5%	0.4%	50%	48
−4	26.2	0.1	51	49
−3	26.8	2.1[d]	63[c]	49
−2	26.4	0.0	49	49
−1	25.4	1.2	54	46
Median annual performance for years −5 to −1	25.3%	0.3%	52%	50
1	21.5%	3.0%[b]	67%[c]	48
2	22.9	5.3[b]	79[b]	47
3	20.6	3.2[c]	70[b]	46
4	18.4	3.0[d]	68[b]	44
5	18.5	2.5	60	40
Median annual performance for years 1 to 5	20.5%	2.8%[b]	73%[b]	48

Panel B: Abnormal industry-adjusted postmerger operating cash flow returns (t-values in parentheses)

$$IACR_{post,i} = \underset{(2.4)^c}{2.8\%} + \underset{(2.3)^c}{0.37}\ IACR_{pre,i}, \quad R^2 = 0.10, \quad F\text{-statistic} = 5.3^c \quad N = 47$$

[a]Operating cash flow return on assets is sales less cost of goods sold, less selling and administrative expenses, plus depreciation, divided by the market value of assets at the beginning of the year. Change in equity values of the target and acquiring firms at the merger announcement are excluded from the market values of assets in the postmerger years. Industry-adjusted cash flow returns are computed for each firm and year as the difference between the sample firm value in that year and median values for other firms in the same industry (as defined by *Value Line* in year −1). Premerger returns for the combined firm are weighted averages of target and acquirer returns, with the weights being the relative asset values of the two firms. Postmerger returns use data for the merged firms. Premerger industry returns are weighted averages of target and acquirer industry median returns, with the weights being the relative asset values of the acquirer and target firms each year. In the postmerger period the weights used to compute industry returns are the relative asset values of the acquirer and target firms in year −1. $IACR_{post,i}$ and $IACR_{pre,i}$ are the median annual industry-adjusted operating cash flow returns in the post- and premerger periods for firm i.

[b]Significantly different from zero at the 1% level, using a two-tailed test.

[c]Significantly different from zero at the 5% level, using a two-tailed test.

[d]Significantly different from zero at the 10% level, using a two-tailed test.

3.1.4. Abnormal industry-adjusted cash flows returns

Our measure of abnormal industry-adjusted returns extends the industry-adjusted return measure to incorporate the relation between pre- and post-merger industry-adjusted returns. Abnormal industry-adjusted cash flow returns are estimated using the following cross-sectional regression:

$$IACR_{post,i} = \alpha + \beta\, IACR_{pre,i} + \varepsilon_i, \tag{1}$$

where $IACR_{post,i}$ is the median annual industry-adjusted cash flow return for company i from the postmerger years and $IACR_{pre,i}$ is the premerger median for the same company. Our measure of the abnormal industry-adjusted return is the intercept α from (1). The slope coefficient β captures any correlation in cash flow returns between the pre- and postmerger years so that $\beta\ IACR_{pre,i}$ measures the effect of the premerger performance on postmerger returns. The intercept α is therefore independent of premerger returns.

As shown in panel B of table 2, for our sample, the estimate of β is 0.37, indicating that industry-adjusted cash flow returns tend to persist over time. The estimate of α shows that there is a 2.8% per-year increase in postmerger cash flow returns after premerger performance is controlled for. This evidence indicates that there is a significant improvement in the merged firms' cash flow returns in the post-merger period.[10]

3.2. Sensitivity analysis

3.2.1. Use of Value Line industry definitions

The industry-adjusted results are strikingly different from the operating cash flow returns before industry adjustment. The industry-adjusted results show a significant *increase* in postmerger performance and the unadjusted returns show a *decrease*. We think that industry-adjusted returns are a more reliable measure of performance, since they control for industry events unrelated to the merger. But, they are also sensitive to the definitions of industries used in the analysis. To test whether the industry-adjusted results are sensitive to the particular industry definitions employed by *Value Line*, we use a market performance benchmark. We estimate the market index each year as the median operating cash flow return for all firms on the *Compustat Industrial and Research* tapes. Median market-adjusted cash flow returns for the sample firms are 1.3% (statistically insignificant) in the

[10] These results remain unchanged when we reestimate the model excluding outlier observations identified using Belsley, Kuh, and Welsch (1980) influence diagnostics. We also conduct specification tests for regression equation (1) to assess whether the residuals are homoskedastic [see White (1980)] and normally distributed. We cannot reject the hypotheses that the residuals are homoskedastic and normally distributed at the 5% level.

premerger period and 4.3% (statistically significant) in the postmerger years, confirming improvements in industry-adjusted performance. A reestimation of (1) using market-adjusted cash flow returns indicates that, on average, returns increase by 5.4% per year in the postmerger period after premerger performance is controlled for.

3.2.2. Change in market value of assets

Our measure of industry-adjusted returns can increase in the postmerger period if investors lower their assessment of merged firms' prospects in relation to their industries. Since we use the market value of equity in our computation of asset values, a postmerger decline in equity value will reduce our measure of asset values. If cash flows are held constant, such a decline in asset values would lead to an increase in cash flow returns, making the postmerger improvements documented in the previous section spurious. To examine this possibility, we compute the difference between annual stock returns for the sample firms and their industries in years surrounding the merger.

Summary statistics on equity returns in years surrounding the merger are reported in table 3. We compute both raw equity returns and industry-adjusted returns for years -5 to -1 and 1 to 5 using *Compustat* data. These same data are used to estimate the market value of assets to compute cash flow returns. Because daily data are not available on *Compustat*, we use *CRSP* returns to compute raw and industry-adjusted equity returns for three subperiods in year 0: the premerger period, the period from the merger announcement to completion, and the postmerger period.

Consistent with the evidence reported in the literature, the median returns in the preannouncement and announcement periods in year 0 are -3.0% and 7.7%, which are statistically significant. There is no evidence that the market value of equity for the sample firms declines in comparison with their industries in the postmerger period. Median industry-adjusted returns are insignificant in the postmerger period in years 0 to 4, and are significantly positive in year 5. Mean industry-adjusted returns, which are not reported here, are comparable to the sample medians. Therefore, the postmerger cash flow return improvements do not appear to be driven by a postmerger decline in equity value, which is used in the denominator of our return measure.

3.2.3. Use of market value of assets to compute returns

We also evaluate the sensitivity of the results to the use of the market value of equity in computing asset values by replicating the cash flow returns using an alternative asset measure. Market equity values incorporate investor's revaluations of firms' growth opportunities, as well as existing assets. We construct an alternative measure of equity values that excludes the effect of revisions in growth opportunities after the merger announcement.

Table 3

Median industry-adjusted and raw stock returns for combined target and acquirer companies in the five years before the merger, and for the merged firm for five years after the merger, for mergers completed in the period 1979 to mid-1984.[a]

Year relative to merger		Industry-adjusted returns	Raw returns	Number of observations
−5		2.8%	17.9%	48
−4		5.3[c]	22.6	49
−3		0.9	19.2	49
−2		−0.1	10.9	49
−1		−2.6	10.9	45
	Premerger	−3.0[c]	4.9	42
Year 0	Merger	7.7[b]	12.0	50
	Postmerger	−3.8	4.7	46
1		0.1	10.0	48
2		0.8	18.5	48
3		0.8	10.0	46
4		−2.5	9.8	41
5		7.1[c]	14.4	40

[a]Returns in years −5 to −1 and 1 to 5 are taken from *Compustat*, consistent with the equity values reported in table 1. Returns in year 0 are from *CRSP*. For target firms, the merger announcement period is the date from the first announcement of a takeover offer for the target to the date a merger is completed. For acquirers, the merger announcement period is the date from the first announcement of a takeover offer by the acquirer to the date a merger is completed. Premerger returns for the combined firm are weighted averages of target and acquirer values, with the weights being the relative equity values of the two firms. Postmerger performance measures use data for the merged firms. Industry-adjusted returns are computed for each firm and year as the difference between the sample-firm value in that year and median values for other firms in the same industry (as defined by *Value Line* in year −1). Premerger industry returns are weighted averages of target and acquirer industry median returns, with the weights being the relative equity values of the acquirer and target firms each year. In the postmerger period the weights used to compute industry returns are the relative equity values of the acquirer and target firms in year −1.

[b]Significantly different from zero at the 1% level, using a two-tailed test.

[c]Significantly different from zero at the 10% level, using a two-tailed test.

To compute the value of equity for the combined firm at the beginning of year 1, we start with the total market equity value for the target and acquirer at the beginning of year −1. We then add year −1 and year 0 values of the merged firm's after tax cash from operations (net of interest expense, nonoperating income, and cash taxes) and cash from new share issues, and subtract cash dividends to common and preferred stockholders and cash used to acquire treasury stock.[11] In each of years 2 through 5, we repeat this procedure using the estimated equity at the beginning of the prior year, and

[11]For firms that use purchase accounting, new debt or equity issued at the merger includes the merger premium for the target, whereas for firms that use the pooling method it does not. To make the measure comparable across firms, we deduct the target premium for the purchase accounting firms in computing the quasi-market values of equity.

adding changes in equity cash flows for the merged firm during the prior year. The resulting quasi-market equity measure captures changes in equity available for reinvestment, but does not reflect revaluations of growth opportunities after the merger announcement.

To provide a benchmark for evaluating the postmerger returns, we also compute comparable equity values at the beginning of years −5 to −1. For year −1 we use the actual market value of assets at the beginning of the year. To compute the pro forma equity value for the combined firm at the beginning of year −2, we start with the total market value of equity for the target and acquirer at the beginning of year −1. We then subtract year −2 values of the target's and acquirer's after-tax cash from operations (net of interest expense, nonoperating income, and cash taxes) and cash from new share issues, and add cash dividends to common and preferred stockholders and cash used to acquire treasury stock. This procedure is repeated for years −3 to −5.

We estimate the quasi-market value of assets in each of the years −5 to +5 as the sum of the quasi-market value of equity estimated as above and the book value of net debt. We then compute the ratio of operating cash flow to the estimated quasi-market value of assets in each year to provide an alternative return measure.

The main advantage of the cash flow return on the quasi-market value of assets is that it excludes postmerger equity market revaluations from the asset base. The measure preserves some important features of the original measure: it is unaffected by the method of merger financing or asset write-ups, and reflects funds invested in the firm in each year. But, it is not without limitations. The measure does not take into account reductions in asset values from economic depreciation. This can lead to a significant overstatement of asset values in the postmerger period, leading in turn to an understatement of measured postmerger performance. Also, for firms that use purchase accounting, cash from operations for the target in year 0 is reflected in the acquirers' records only from the date the merger is consummated. This leads to a small understatement of the postmerger asset values. Both these limitations are avoided by the market value of assets used in our original cash flow return measure.

Cash flow returns computed using the alternative measure of asset values are reported in table 4. The results are generally consistent with the findings reported in table 2. The merged firms continue to show higher cash flow returns on assets than their industries in the postmerger period. Median industry-adjusted pretax operating returns for the merged firms are 2.8% in year 1, 2.6% in year 2, and 2.1% in year 3, all significantly different from zero. The percentage of industry-adjusted returns that are positive is 67% in year 1, 62% in year 2, and 65% in year 3, all above the value expected by chance alone (50%). Overall, the annual median pretax return in the five postmerger years is 3.2%.

Table 4

Median operating cash flow return on quasi-market value of assets for 50 combined target and acquirer firms in years surrounding mergers completed in the period 1979 to mid-1984.[a]

Panel A: Pre- and postmerger operating cash flow returns

Year relative to merger	Firm median	Industry-adjusted Median	Industry-adjusted % positive	Number of observations
−5	31.7%	−2.5%	47%	43
−4	31.1	0.3	51	45
−3	32.5	2.7	59	46
−2	26.8	2.0	54	46
−1	25.4	1.2	54	46
Median annual performance for years −5 to −1	31.3%	2.1%	56%	49
1	23.9%	3.8%[b]	67%[c]	48
2	20.3	3.0[c]	62[c]	47
3	18.7	2.1[d]	65[c]	46
4	15.6	0.8	56	43
5	18.2	0.5	53	39
Median annual performance for years 1 to 5	17.9%	3.2%[c]	66%[c]	48

Panel B: Abnormal industry-adjusted postmerger operating cash flow returns (t-values in parentheses)

$$IACR_{post,i} = \underset{(2.0)^c}{2.7\%} + \underset{(1.5)}{0.18}\, IACR_{pre,i}, \quad R^2 = 0.05, \quad F\text{-statistic} = 2.3, \quad N = 46$$

[a]Pretax operating cash flow return on assets is sales less cost of goods sold, less selling and administrative expenses, plus depreciation, divided by quasi-market value of assets at the beginning of the year. The computation of quasi-market value of assets begins with market values in year −1 and adjusts for changes in capital available for reinvestment in other years. Premerger returns for the combined firm are weighted averages of target and acquirer values, with the weights being the relative asset values of the two firms. Postmerger returns are for the merged firm. Industry-adjusted cash flow returns are computed for each firm and year as the difference between the sample-firm value in that year and median values for other firms in the same industry (as defined by *Value Line* in year −1). Premerger industry returns are weighted averages of target and acquirer industry median returns, with the weights being the relative asset values of the acquirer and target firms each year. In the postmerger period the weights used to compute industry returns are the relative asset values of the acquirer and target firms in year −1. $IACR_{post,i}$ and $IACR_{pre,i}$ are the median annual industry-adjusted pretax operating cash flow returns in the post- and premerger periods for firm i.

[b]Significantly different from zero at the 1% level, using a two-tailed test.

[c]Significantly different from zero at the 5% level, using a two-tailed test.

[d]Significantly different from zero at the 10% level, using a two-tailed test.

In contrast to the postmerger performance, there is no strong evidence of superior industry-adjusted pretax operating cash flow returns in the premerger period. Median returns are not significantly different from zero in each of the five years. Also, the percentage of positive industry-adjusted returns is not significantly different from the value expected by chance in any of the five years before the merger. The overall median annual industry-adjusted return in the premerger period is 2.1%, which is statistically insignificant.

To examine whether there are abnormal postmerger industry-adjusted cash flow returns, we again estimate (1) using return on assets based on quasi-market equity values. The slope coefficient, which captures any persistence of performance between the pre- and postmerger years, is 0.18 and insignificant. The intercept, which captures postmerger performance controlling for premerger returns, is 2.7% and is statistically reliable. These results remain unchanged when we reestimate the model excluding outliers identified using Belsley, Kuh, and Welsch (1980) influence diagnostics.[12]

In summary, the evidence presented in this section indicates that the postmerger performance improvements are not driven by the use of market equity values in computing assets.

3.3. *Components of industry-adjusted cash flow returns*

The improvements in cash flow returns in the postmerger period can arise from a variety of sources. These include improvements in operating margins, greater asset productivity, or lower labor costs. Alternatively, they may be achieved by focusing on short-term performance improvements at the expense of the long-term viability of the firm. In this section we provide evidence on which of these sources contribute to the sample firms' postmerger cash flow return increases. The specific variables analyzed are italicized in the text and defined in table 5. The results are reported in table 6.

3.3.1. *Operating performance changes*

The operating cash flow return on assets can be decomposed into *cash flow margin on sales* and *asset turnover*. Cash flow margin on sales measures the pretax operating cash flows generated per sales dollar. Asset turnover measures the sales dollars generated from each dollar of investment in assets. The variables are defined so that their product equals the operating cash flow return on assets.

[12] We again conduct specification tests for (1) to assess whether the residuals are homoskedastic [see White (1980)] and normally distributed. We cannot reject the hypotheses that the residuals are homoskedastic and normally distributed at the 5% level.

Table 5

Definitions of variables used to analyze actual performance of 50 targets and 50 acquirers in years surrounding mergers.

Variable	Definition
	(A) *Operating characteristics*
Cash flow margin on sales	Earnings before depreciation, interest, and taxes as a percentage of sales
Asset turnover	Sales divided by market value of assets at the beginning of the year (the market value of common equity plus the book values of debt and preferred stock)
Employee growth rate	Change in number of employees as a percentage of number of employees in the previous year
Pension expense/employee	Pension expense per employee
	(B) *Investment characteristics*
Capital expenditure rate	Capital expenditures as a percentage of the market value of assets at the beginning of the year
Asset sale rate – Cash value	Cash receipts from asset sales as a percentage of the market value of assets at the beginning of the year
Asset sale rate – Book value	Book value of asset sales as a percentage of the market value of assets at the beginning of the year
R&D rate	Research and development expenditures as a percentage of the market value of assets at the beginning of the year

The results in table 6 suggest that the increase in industry-adjusted operating returns is attributable to an increase in asset turnover, rather than an increase in operating margins. In years −5 to −1 the merged firms have industry-adjusted median asset turnover of −0.2, implying that they generated 20 cents *less* in sales than their competitors for each dollar of assets. In years 1 to 5 they close this gap as they achieve asset turnovers comparable to their industries'. The intercept in the cross-sectional regression of postmerger industry-adjusted asset turnover on premerger turnover is 0.2 and is statistically significant. The evidence thus indicates that there is a significant improvement in sample firms' asset turnover in the postmerger period.

The merged firms also have higher pretax operating margins on sales than their industries in the postmerger years. But these cannot be attributed to the merger itself, because they are also higher in the premerger period. Before the merger, the higher operating margins are primarily due to higher industry-adjusted margins for acquirers. Targets do not show higher operating

Table 6

Firm and industry-adjusted operating performance and investment policy measures for 50 combined target and acquirer firms in years surrounding mergers completed in the period 1979 to mid-1984.[a]

Variable	Firm medians		Industry-adjusted medians		Abnormal industry-adjusted postmerger performance[b]	Number of observations
	Premerger	Postmerger	Premerger	Postmerger		
Operating characteristics						
Cash flow margin on sales	14.3%	13.3%	1.4%[c]	1.1%[d]	0.2%	46
Asset turnover	1.9x	1.9x	−0.2x	0.0x	0.2x[e]	48
Employee growth rate	3.0%	−3.0%	0.4%	−2.5%[d]	−2.3%[d]	44
Pension expense per employee	$796.3	$840.7	$101.1[c]	−$60.4	−$119.5	40
Investment characteristics						
Capital expenditure rate	14.4%	10.6%	1.0%	−0.1%	0.5%	47
Asset sale rate – Cash value	0.6	0.6	0.0	0.1	0.3	45
Asset sale rate – Book value	0.9	1.3	0.1[d]	0.6[c]	0.9[d]	42
R&D rate	2.0	2.1	0.1	0.0	0.1	33

[a]Operating performance and investment policy measures are defined in table 5. Industry-adjusted values of these variables are computed for each firm and year as the difference between the firm value in that year and the median value for other firms in the same industry (as defined by *Value Line* in year −1). Before the merger, performance measures for the merged firm are weighted averages of target and acquirer values, with the weights being the relative sizes of the two firms. Performance measures for the merged firm's industry in the premerger period are weighted averages of target industry and acquirer industry medians, with the weights being the relative sizes of the two test firms. Medians in the premerger (postmerger) period are the median values of the variables in years −5 to −1 (1 to 5).

[b]Postmerger industry-adjusted performance measures controlling for premerger performance are the estimated intercepts from regressing postmerger industry-adjusted performance on premerger values.

[c]Significantly different from zero at the 1% level, using a two-tailed test.

[d]Significantly different from zero at the 5% level, using a two-tailed test.

[e]Significantly different from zero at the 10% level, using a two-tailed test.

margins than their industries in these years. When we control for premerger operating margins, there is no evidence of a significant change in margins after the merger. Rather, merged firms seem to use their assets more productively.

Mergers also give the acquirer an opportunity to renegotiate explicit and implicit labor contracts to lower labor costs and achieve a more efficient mix of capital and labor [see Shleifer and Summers (1988)]. Because we are unable to obtain sufficient data on wages directly, we examine *employee growth rates* and *pension expense per employee* to analyze changes in labor costs in years surrounding the mergers.

The median number of employees declines in each of the postmerger years. Overall, the industry-adjusted employee growth rate is negative after we control for the growth rate in the premerger period. There is also evidence of a decline in pension expense per employee after the merger. Before the merger the sample firms have a significantly higher pension expense per employee than their industries. After the merger the pension expense of the merged firms is reduced to the industry level. There are two ways to view these findings. One interpretation is that mergers are followed by improvements in operating efficiency achieved through reduced labor costs. Alternatively, mergers lead to a wealth redistribution between employees and stockholders through renegotiations of explicit and implicit employment contracts. Whatever the explanation, the labor cost reductions in the postmerger period do not appear to be large, since they do not lead to significant changes in postmerger operating margins.[13]

3.3.2. *Investment policy changes*

Since our analysis is limited to five years after the merger, we cannot provide direct evidence on cash flows beyond this period. To assess whether the merged firms focus on short-term performance improvements at the expense of long-term investments, we examine their *capital outlays* and *research and development* (R&D) expense. These expenditure patterns are reported in table 6. The median capital expenditures as a percentage of assets is 14.4% in the premerger period and 10.6% in the postmerger years. The median R&D expense is 2% of assets in years -5 to -1 and 2.1% in years 1 to 5. The capital expenditures and R&D of the sample firms are not significantly different from those of their industry counterparts in either the pre- or the postmerger period.

[13]Pontiff, Shleifer, and Weisbach (1990) report that 11% of takeovers involve pension fund reversions, accounting for 10–13% of takeover premiums in these transactions. Thus for their sample as a whole pension fund reversions account for an average 1–2% of the takeover premium. Similarly, Rosett (1990) reports that labor union wealth changes in the six years following takeovers account for 1–2% of the premiums. Our conclusions are consistent with the results of both these studies.

Asset sales also reflect changes in merged firms' investment policies. It is possible that postmerger improvements in asset turnover arise from the sale of assets with low turnover. We therefore examine cash proceeds from asset sales and their book values in the pre- and postmerger years. Statistics on asset sales as a percentage of the market value of assets are reported in table 6. The median cash proceeds from asset sales for the merged firms is 0.6% of assets in both the pre- and postmerger periods, not significantly different from their industry level in either period. The book values of asset disposals before and after the merger are 0.9% and 1.3% of assets. Both of these rates are significantly higher than the rates for their industry counterparts. Further, controlling for the level of premerger book values of asset sales, there is an increase in asset sales in the postmerger period.

There are two potential explanations for the increase in book value of asset sales, but not in cash proceeds from disposals. First, the merged firms sell poorly performing assets after the merger. This could in part explain the improved asset productivity and the decline in employee growth rates.[14] Second, the assets sold are written up at the merger to a value higher than their true market value. Managers have considerable discretion in allocating merger premiums to assets and goodwill, and have incentives to write up assets as high as possible to increase depreciation tax shields. If these assets are subsequently sold, cash proceeds from the sale are likely to be below the written-up book values. Whatever the explanation, the effect of asset sales on postmerger performance is unlikely to be significant, because disposals in all years are very small in relation to capital expenditures or the market value of total assets. This is confirmed by the insignificant correlation between asset sales and postmerger cash flow return improvements.[15]

In summary, we find that improvements in cash flow operating returns in the five years following mergers arise from increased asset productivity. There is no evidence of decreased capital expenditures or R&D following mergers, indicating that the cash flow improvements do not come from policies that impede the long-term viability of the merged firms.

4. Relation between cash flow and stock price performance

Our postmerger data on cash flow performance are consistent with the hypothesis that the stock market revaluation of merging firms at merger announcements reflects expected future improvements in operations. A more powerful test of this hypothesis is to correlate the merger-related stock

[14]Kaplan and Weisbach (1992) find that acquirers of firms in unrelated businesses are more likely to later divest their targets than acquirers of related businesses. They find no evidence, however, that divested businesses are systematically poor performers.

[15]We reestimate (1) after including asset sales in the pre- and postmerger periods. The coefficients on both these variables are insignificant, and the intercept remains positive and significant.

Table 7

Unexpected equity and asset returns at merger announcements for target, acquirer, and combined firms, and tests of the relation between unexpected asset returns and ex post cash flow returns for 50 target and acquiring firms merging in the period 1979 to mid-1984.[a]

Panel A: Distribution of unexpected equity returns at merger announcement

	Target	Acquirer	Combined
Mean	45.6%[b]	−2.2%	9.1%[b]
First quartile	21.2%	−16.6%	−2.9%
Median	41.8%[b]	−3.6%	6.6%[b]
Third quartile	64.1%	3.4%	16.7%

Panel B: Distribution of unexpected asset returns at merger announcement

	Target	Acquirer	Combined
Mean	40.6%[b]	0.6%	8.8%[b]
First quartile	19.0%	−9.3%	−2.3%
Median	32.5%[b]	−2.2%	5.2%[b]
Third quartile	55.0%	6.1%	15.1%

Panel C: Relation between median postmerger industry-adjusted cash flow returns and unexpected asset returns at merger announcement (t-values in parentheses)

$$IACR_{post,i} = \underset{(1.6)}{1.9\%} + \underset{(1.7)^{c}}{0.26}\, IACR_{pre,i} + \underset{(3.4)^{b}}{0.24}\,(\Delta V/V^{i})$$

$R^2 = 0.30$, F-statistic $= 8.5$,[b] $N = 42$

[a]Unexpected merger announcement equity returns are the sum of market-adjusted changes in equity values for the target and acquirer firms in the merger announcement period as a percentage of the sum of the premerger equity values for the two firms. Unexpected merger announcement asset returns ($\Delta V/V$) are unlevered market-adjusted equity returns. $IACR_{post}$ and $IACR_{pre}$ are median industry-adjusted cash flow returns for each firm in the five years after and the five years before the merger.

[b]Significantly different from zero at the 1% level, using a two-tailed test.

[c]Significantly different from zero at the 10% level, using a two-tailed test.

market performance and the postmerger cash flow performance. If the stock market capitalizes expected improvements, there should be a significant positive correlation between the stock market revaluation of merging firms and the actual postmerger cash flow improvements.

4.1. Stock returns at merger announcements

Market-adjusted stock returns for the target and acquirer at the announcement of the merger are reported in panel A of table 7.[16] Returns for the target are measured from five days before the first offer is announced (not

[16]Risk-adjusted returns, computed using premerger market model estimates, are similar to the market-adjusted returns reported in the paper.

necessarily by the ultimate acquirer) to the date the target is delisted from trading on public exchanges. Returns for the acquirer are measured from five days before its first offer is announced to the date the target is delisted from trading on public exchanges. Much as earlier studies have found, target shareholders earn large positive returns from mergers (mean 45.6% and median 41.8%), and acquiring stockholders earn insignificant returns.

We also compute the aggregate market-adjusted return for the two firms in the merger announcement period. This return is the weighted average of the market-adjusted returns for the target and acquirer, where the weights are the relative market values of equity of the two firms before the merger announcement period. The mean aggregate return, reported in panel A of table 7, is 9.1%, and the median is 6.6%. Both these values are significantly different from zero. These findings are consistent with those of Bradley, Desai, and Kim (1988).

4.2. Asset returns at merger announcements

Our tests examine whether the change in equity values at merger announcements can be explained by cash flow return improvements in the postmerger period. In section 3 we measured postmerger performance using cash flow return on *assets*, whereas the merger announcement returns computed above are returns on *equity*. Therefore, before we correlate merger announcement returns and postmerger cash flow improvements, we compute *asset* returns at merger announcements from equity returns to ensure that the *anticipated* gains from mergers and the measured gains are comparable.

Asset returns at the merger announcement $\Delta V/V$ are weighted averages of returns to equity $\Delta E/E$ and debt $\Delta D/D$:

$$\frac{\Delta V}{V} = \frac{\Delta E}{E}\frac{E}{V} + \frac{\Delta D}{D}\frac{D}{V}. \qquad (2)$$

Assuming that the value of debt does not change at takeover announcements, asset returns equal the equity announcement returns multiplied by the equity-to-assets ratio E/V.[17] We use leverage at the beginning of the year of the takeover announcement to compute the equity-to-assets ratio. We use the book value of debt and the market value of equity to measure leverage.

Summary statistics on the estimated asset returns at the announcement of the merger for the target firms, acquiring firms, and combined firms are reported in panel B of table 7. The mean and median asset returns for the

[17]A number of studies, including Asquith and Kim (1982), report evidence consistent with this assumption.

targets are 40.6% and 32.5% and for the combined firms 8.8% and 5.2%. The asset returns for the bidding firm are insignificant.

4.3. Relation between announcement returns and postmerger cash flow improvements

The hypothesis that merger-induced abnormal returns reflect the capitalized value of future cash flow improvements implies:

$$\Delta V = \frac{\Delta CF}{\Theta}, \tag{3}$$

where ΔV is the change in the market value of assets at the merger announcement, $1/\Theta$ is the present value operator, and ΔCF is the vector of cash flow improvements. Transposing (3) and dividing both sides by V, to express both sides as returns:

$$\frac{\Delta CF}{V} = \Theta \frac{\Delta V}{V}. \tag{4}$$

We measure $\Delta CF/V$ as abnormal industry-adjusted cash flow returns [(1) in section 3]:

$$\frac{\Delta CF}{V} = \alpha = IACR_{post,i} - \beta\, IACR_{pre,i} - \varepsilon_i, \tag{5}$$

where $IACR_{post,i}$ and $IACR_{pre,i}$ are the median annual industry-adjusted operating cash flow returns in the post- and premerger periods for firm i. We measure asset returns, $\Delta V/V$, as unlevered market-adjusted stock returns for the combined target and acquirer firms at the merger announcement, discussed in section 4.2. Substituting these two measures for variables in (4) and rearranging yields:

$$IACR_{post,i} = \beta\, IACR_{pre,i} + \Theta \frac{\Delta V}{V^i} + \varepsilon_i. \tag{6}$$

Eq. (6) forms the basis for our tests of the relationship between ex post cash flow improvements and the *anticipated* gains represented by merger announcement returns. Since $\Delta V/V$ is the *capitalized* value of future cash flow return improvements and $IACR_{post}$ is the pretax cash flow return improvement *per year*, the coefficient Θ in (6) equals the pretax capitalization rate. For example, if the cash flow return improvements are permanent and the pretax capitalization rate is 20%, the coefficient Θ would be 0.20.

Although (6) does not have a constant, we estimate a regression equation with an intercept and test whether it is zero.

The regression results are shown in panel C of table 7. The estimated model has an R^2 of 30%. The estimated slope coefficient on asset returns at the merger announcement is 0.24 and is statistically reliable, implying that if cash flow return improvements are permanent, the pretax discount rate for the sample firms is 24%. This estimated discount rate is economically plausible, although it exceeds the pretax cost of capital for our sample firms assuming a 10% pretax risk-free rate and an 8% risk premium. Consistent with findings reported earlier, the estimated coefficient on premerger performance is positive and statistically significant. Finally, as predicted by (6), the intercept is insignificant.[18]

As an alternative specification, we estimate a regression equation with merger announcement returns, $\Delta V/V$, as the dependent variable and abnormal industry-adjusted cash flow returns from (1), $\Delta CF/V$, as the independent variable. The estimated coefficient for the abnormal industry-adjusted cash flow returns is 1.01 and is statistically significant with a t-statistic of 3.2. The implied capitalization rate from this specification is 100%. Since this specification, as well as the specification in (6), suffers from potential errors-in-variables problems, the actual rate at which the market capitalizes postmerger cash flow improvements is likely to be between 24% and 100%.

There are two interpretations of the statistically and economically significant relation between our measure of postmerger performance improvements and the market's revaluation of the merged firms' equity at the merger announcement. First, if equity markets are efficient, the findings indicate that our estimates of postmerger performance are reasonable. Alternatively, the findings can be viewed as evidence that the stock price gains at the merger announcement are related to expectations of subsequent cash flow improvements.

5. Discussion

Our finding that there are postmerger cash flow increases advances the debate on mergers from *whether* there are cash flow changes after these transactions to *why* these cash flow improvements occur. The improvements in sample firms' cash flow returns are primarily a result of increased asset

[18]Specification tests are conducted for (6) to assess whether the residuals are homoskedastic [see White (1980)] and normally distributed. We cannot reject the hypotheses that the residuals are homoskedastic and normally distributed at the 5% level. We also reestimated the regression excluding observations more than two standard deviations from the mean for each variable. The results are very similar to those reported. Finally, we estimate Spearman rank correlation coefficients between the median annual postmerger industry-adjusted cash flow return and unexpected asset returns at the merger announcement. The correlation is 0.41 and is significant at the 1% level.

productivity. The reported postmerger gains cannot be attributed to tax benefits, since the cash flow returns are pretax. Although there is some evidence that gains come at the expense of labor, reduced labor costs do not significantly increase sample firms' cash flows. Finally, there is no decrease in capital outlays and R&D expenditures after the merger, indicating that merged firms do not reduce their long-term investments.

Our findings raise two interesting questions. First, are the increases in cash flow returns and asset productivity caused by the merger, or would they have occurred without it? Mergers can lead to increased asset productivity if suboptimal policies pursued by the target or the acquirer before the merger are eliminated, or if they provide new opportunities to use existing resources of the merging firms. In contrast, if mergers arise from undervaluation of the target firms by the stock market, cash flow returns will improve whether or not there is a merger. Managers who anticipate the cash flow improvements will pay a premium to acquire the targets.

Our findings also raise another question: what economic factors explain the cross-sectional variation in postmerger cash flow changes? Although cash flow performance improves on average, a quarter of the sample firms have negative postmerger cash flow changes. These firms may have performed poorly because of bad luck. Alternatively, systematic business and managerial reasons may have led to these outcomes.

These questions, which have important managerial and public policy implications, can be answered only through development of structural models of how mergers improve cash flows. We do not attempt to undertake such an ambitious exercise in this paper, but, we do provide some preliminary evidence and suggest directions for future research.

5.1. Business overlap of merging firms and postmerger performance

One popular hypothesis on how mergers improve cash flows is that they provide opportunities for economies of scale and scope, synergy, or product market power. This implies that mergers by firms that have overlapping businesses will show greater cash flow improvements than mergers between firms with no overlap. We examine this proposition by classifying our sample mergers as those with high, medium, and low business overlap between the target and acquiring firms. This classification is made by reading the line of business discussion in the merging firms' annual reports, merger prospectuses, *Value Line* reports, and *Moody's Industrial Manuals*.

The following cases illustrate our classifications. The combination of Best Products and Modern Merchandising, both of which are catalog showroom retailers, is classified as a high overlap transaction. The merger between Holiday Inns and Harrahs is treated as a transaction with medium overlap because Holiday Inns operates a hotel chain and Harrahs operates casinos and associated hotels. Exxon Corp's acquisition of Reliance Electric is an unrelated transaction: Exxon is an oil company and Reliance Electric is a producer of industrial equipment. Classification of the degree of business overlap of each of the sample transactions is reported in the appendix, where we describe our sample mergers in detail.

To evaluate whether postmerger performance improvements differ by the degree of business overlap, we estimate the following regression:

$$IACR_{post,i} = \alpha + \beta\ IACR_{pre,i} + \theta\ MEDIUM_i + \psi\ HIGH_i + \varepsilon_i, \qquad (7)$$

where $IACR_{post,i}$ and $IACR_{pre,i}$ are the median annual industry-adjusted cash flow returns in the post- and premerger periods for firm i, *HIGH* is a dummy variable that is one if the target and acquirers are in highly overlapping businesses and zero otherwise, and *MEDIUM* is a dummy variable that is one if there is a medium overlap between the target and acquiring firms' businesses and zero otherwise. The intercept coefficient (α) represents the postmerger abnormal cash flow returns for firms in nonoverlapping businesses, whereas the coefficients θ and ψ show the differential postmerger returns of firms in medium and high overlapping businesses. As in (1), the variable $IACR_{pre}$ is included in the model to control for premerger performance.

The results are reported in panel A of table 8. The estimated coefficient on $IACR_{pre}$ is positive and significant, similar to that reported in earlier regressions. The estimated intercept and coefficients on *MEDIUM* and *HIGH* are not significant, indicating that the degree of business overlap has no impact on postmerger performance improvements. These results, however, are sensitive to two extreme observations identified using Belsley, Kuh, and Welsh (1980) outlier diagnostics. We reestimate the model excluding these observations and report the results in panel B of table 8. The intercept and the coefficient of *MEDIUM* remain insignificant, indicating that there is no performance improvement associated with mergers between firms with little or medium business overlap. Transactions with a high business overlap, however, have 5.1% improvements in postmerger performance. Mergers with a high business overlap, therefore, show significant postmerger improvement, whereas other types of mergers do not.

The two outliers in the above analysis are the LTV–Republic Steel merger and Penn Central's acquisition of G.K. Technologies. LTV and Republic Steel have highly overlapping businesses, yet the combination performed very poorly. In contrast, there is little overlap between the businesses of Penn Central and G.K. Technologies, yet the merger was followed by excellent performance. These two observations are obviously exceptions to the conclusion above, indicating that the relation between the merging firms' businesses is not the sole determinant of postmerger performance.

Table 8

Comparison of postmerger performance for mergers between firms whose industries have high, medium, and low overlap for 50 target and acquiring firms merging in the period 1979 to mid-1984.[a]

Panel A: Full sample
(t-values in parentheses)

$$IACFR_{post,i} = \underset{(0.9)}{0.018} + \underset{(0.2)}{0.005}\, MEDIUM_i + \underset{(1.3)}{0.033}\, HIGH_i + \underset{(2.2)^c}{0.35}\, IACR_{pre,i}$$

$R^2 = 0.13$, F-statistic $= 2.2,^d$ $N = 47$

Panel B: Sample excluding outliers[b]
(t-values in parentheses)

$$IACFR_{post,i} = \underset{(0.3)}{0.006} + \underset{(0.6)}{0.016}\, MEDIUM_i + \underset{(1.8)^d}{0.051}\, HIGH_i + \underset{(2.1)^c}{0.33}\, IACR_{pre,i}$$

$R^2 = 0.17$ F-statistic $= 2.9^c$ $N = 45$

[a] $IACR_{post}$ and $IACR_{pre}$ are median industry-adjusted cash flow returns for each firm in the five years after and the five years before the merger. *MEDIUM* and *HIGH* are dummy variables that take the value one if the merger is between two firms whose product markets have medium and high overlap.

[b] This sample excludes two observations identified as influential outliers using Belsey, Kuh, and Welsch (1980) diagnostics. These transactions are the LTV–Republic Steel and the Penn Central–GK Technologies mergers.

[c] Significantly different from zero at the 5% level, using a two-tailed test.

[d] Significantly different from zero at the 10% level, using a two-tailed test.

5.2. *Transaction characteristics of merging firms and postmerger performance*

Transaction characteristics, such as the form of financing, whether the transaction is hostile or friendly, and the size of the target firm, are frequently cited as important to the ultimate success of mergers. We use postmerger cash flow returns for different types of transactions to examine each of the hypotheses associated with these characteristics. We estimate a cross-sectional regression similar to (7) with dummy variables representing the form of financing and find no significant postmerger performance differences between transactions financed with equity, cash, or a mixture of securities. We also do not find any relation between the merger-related abnormal stock returns for the combined firm and the form of financing.[19]

A similar approach is used to test whether postmerger performance differs for hostile and friendly transactions. Using the information from *Wall Street Journal* articles that discuss the initial offer, we classify transactions as hostile, friendly, white knight, and indeterminate. We do not find any

[19] Previous studies examine the relation between stock returns and the form of financing for acquiring and target firms separately. See Huang and Walkling (1987) and Asquith, Bruner, and Mullins (1990).

evidence of postmerger cash flow performance or merger-related abnormal stock return differences among any of these transaction types.

Finally, we examine whether size of the acquisition influences postmerger performance. Two variables are used in this analysis: the log of target assets and the ratio of target assets to acquirer's assets, both one year prior to the acquisition. Neither variable explains cross-sectional variation in postmerger performance.

In summary, while there is some evidence that the degree of business overlap between merging firms influences postmerger performance, there is little evidence that transaction characteristics have a significant impact.[20] We view our analysis on the determinants of postmerger performance as preliminary, however, since our study is designed to examine whether performance improves after a merger.

Given the complexity and heterogeneity of reasons for mergers, we believe that large-sample studies will provide limited new insights into factors that influence the outcomes of mergers. A promising approach is to examine a smaller number of mergers in greater detail. These clinical studies can provide valuable evidence on the mechanisms through which mergers increase cash flows, and are likely to be fruitful avenues for future research.[21]

6. Summary

This paper examines the post-acquisition operating performance of merged firms using a sample of the 50 largest mergers between U.S. public industrial firms completed in the period 1979 to mid-1984. We develop a methodology to deal with a number of measurement issues that arise in studying the consequences of takeovers. Further, we integrate accounting and stock return data in a consistent fashion to permit richer tests of corporate control theories. This general approach has been adopted by several recent studies to examine mergers and acquisitions – Tehranian and Cornett (1991) and Linder and Crane (1991) analyze performance in bank mergers, and Jarrell (1991) investigates postmerger performance using analysts' forecasts of sales margins.

Our findings indicate that merged firms have significant improvements in operating cash flow returns after the merger, resulting from increases in asset productivity relative to their industries. These improvements are particularly strong for transactions involving firms in overlapping businesses. Postmerger cash flow improvements do not come at the expense of long-term perfor-

[20]The findings on the relation between transaction characteristics and postmerger performance are not sensitive to outliers.

[21]Recent examples of clinical studies on corporate control issues include Baker and Wruck (1989), Kaplan (1989), and Donaldson (1990).

mance, since sample firms maintain their capital expenditure and R&D rates relative to their industries after the merger. Finally, there is a strong positive relation between postmerger increases in operating cash flows and abnormal stock returns at merger announcements, indicating that expectations of economic improvements explain a significant portion of the equity revaluations of the merging firms.

Appendix

Acquiring / target firms and their industries

This appendix provides a detailed description of the sample used in the analysis. The business descriptions and industry classifications of acquirer and target firms are based on *Value Line* reports before the merger. The relation between the firms is a subjective classification by the authors of the degree of overlap between the target's and acquirer's businesses. Relative size of the target is the ratio of the target's assets to acquirer's assets one year before the merger. Assets are measured as the market value of common equity plus the book values of preferred stock and net debt. Acquisition date is the date the merger was completed and the target was delisted from the public exchange. Target equity values are the market value of common equity one year before the merger. Acquirer stock return is the market-adjusted stock return from five days before the acquirer's offer announcement to the merger completion. Target stock return is the market-adjusted stock return from five days before the first offer announcement (not necessarily by the ultimate acquirer) to the merger completion.

1. American Medical International / Lifemark (Acquirer / Target)

American Medical owns and operates proprietary hospitals and other health-care businesses (94% of revenue in 1982) and offers medical–technical support. Lifemark owns and manages general hospitals (90% of 1982 revenues) and provides cardiopulmonary, physical therapy, pharmacy, and clinical laboratory services.

Acquirer industry:	Medical services	Target industry:	Medical services
Acquisition date:	Jan. 20 1984	Relation between firms:	High overlap
Target equity value:	$808.0 million	Relative size of target:	34%
Acquirer stock return:	−16.0%	Target stock return:	55.1%

2. Anheuser-Busch Companies / Campbell Taggart Inc.

Anheuser-Busch is the world's largest brewer of beer. Campbell Taggart's business is baking and distributing bread, rolls, crackers, cake and other sweet products, and food products.

Acquirer industry:	Brewing	Target industry:	Food processing
Acquisition date:	Nov. 2 1982	Relation between firms:	Low overlap
Target equity value:	$536.3 million	Relative size of target:	15.8%
Acquirer stock return:	−3.0%	Target stock return:	−4.8%

3. Associated Dry Goods / Caldor Inc.
Associated Dry Goods operates general department stores in 25 states. Caldor operates 65 promotional discount department stores in five states.

Acquirer industry:	Retail stores	Target industry:	Retail stores
Acquisition date:	May 27 1981	Relation between firms:	High overlap
Target equity value:	$309.5 million	Relative size of target:	47.5%
Acquirer stock return:	9.3%	Target stock return:	36.7%

4. Avon Products Inc./Mallinckrodt
Avon is the world's largest manufacturer of cosmetics and toiletries, and also sells costume jewelry and ceramics. Mallinckrodt develops and manufactures fine chemicals, drugs and other health care products, and chemicals for the food, cosmetics, laboratory, petrochemical, and printing industries.

Acquirer industry:	Toiletries/cosmetics	Target industry:	Speciality chemical
Acquisition date:	March 8 1982	Relation between firms:	Low overlap
Target equity value:	$574.6 million	Relative size of target:	31.2%
Acquirer stock return:	−5.9%	Target stock return:	18.3%

5. Best Products / Modern Merchandising Inc.
Best Products and Modern Merchandising sell general merchandise through catalog showrooms.

Acquirer industry:	Retail–special lines	Target industry:	Retail–special lines
Acquisition date:	Sept. 15 1982	Relation between firms:	High overlap
Target equity value:	$114.3 million	Relative size of target:	55.6%
Acquirer stock return:	−16.7%	Target stock return:	15.7%

6. Brown-Forman Distillers / Lenox Inc.
Brown-Forman manufactures a wide variety of alcoholic beverages. Lenox produces home furnishings (including china and crystal) and personal-use products (including jewelry and luggage).

Acquirer industry:	Distilling and tobacco	Target industry:	Household products
Acquisition date:	July 21 1983	Relation between firms:	Low overlap
Target equity value:	$407.0 million	Relative size of target:	19.1%
Acquirer stock return:	−7.7%	Target stock return:	55.7%

7. Burroughs Corp./Memorex Corp.
Burroughs is a major participant in the data processing and business computer equipment industry. Memorex develops, manufactures, markets, and services a wide range of computer peripheral equipment systems, and products employed in the recording, retrieval, communication, and storage of information.

Acquirer industry:	Computer/data processing products	Target industry:	Computer/data processing products
Acquisition date:	Dec. 3 1981	Relation between firms:	High overlap
Target equity value:	$98.8 million	Relative size of target:	10.4%
Acquirer stock return:	−2.7%	Target stock return:	52.9%

8. Coca Cola Co./Columbia Pictures Industries Inc.
Coca Cola is the largest manufacturer and distributor of soft drink concentrates and syrups in the world. The company also manufactures citrus, coffee, tea, wine, and plastic products. Columbia Pictures produces and distributes theatrical motion pictures, television series and features, amusement games, and commercials.

Acquirer industry:	Soft drinks	Target industry:	Recreation
Acquisition date:	June 21 1982	Relation between firms:	Low overlap
Target equity value:	$704.3 million	Relative size of target:	11.4%
Acquirer stock return:	2.2%	Target stock return:	78.2%

9. Con Agra Inc./Peavey Co.
Con Agra is a diversified food processor engaged in agriculture (agricultural chemicals, formula feed, and fertilizers), grain (flour, by-products, and grain and feed merchandising), and food

(frozen foods, broiler chicken, eggs, seafood, and pet products) industries. Peavey is also a diversified food processor and retailer engaged in grain merchandising, food processing (flour, bakery mixes, and jams), and the operation of specialty retail stores.

Acquirer industry:	Food processing	Target industry:	Food processing
Acquisition date:	July 20 1982	Relation between firms:	High overlap
Target equity value:	$186.5 million	Relative size of target:	71.9%
Acquirer stock return:	2.7%	Target stock return:	58.1%

10. Cooper Industries / Gardner-Denver
Cooper is a diversified, international corporation that produces consumer and industrial tools, aircraft services, mining and construction, and energy services. Gardner-Denver makes portable and stationary air compressors, drilling equipment for above- and underground, and air-operated tools. Drilling equipment for mining, petroleum, and construction industries makes up 67% of sales.

Acquirer industry:	Machinery	Target industry:	Construction and mining machinery
Acquisition date:	April 30 1979	Relation between firms:	Medium overlap
Target equity value:	$605.5 million	Relative size of target:	66.7%
Acquirer stock return:	−5.2%	Target stock return:	49.7%

11. Dart Industries / Kraft Inc.
Dart is a diversified company that manufactures and markets consumer products (including Tupperware containers, Duracell batteries, and West Bend appliances), chemicals, plastics, and packaging products. Kraft manufactures food products and markets them to retail, industrial, and food service customers.

Acquirer industry:	Household products	Target industry:	Food processing
Acquisition date:	Sept. 25 1980	Relation between firms:	Low overlap
Target equity value:	$1,099.4 million	Relative size of target:	78.7%
Acquirer stock return:	−17.0%	Target stock return:	−6.6%

12. Diamond Shamrock / Natomas Co.
Diamond Shamrock is a domestic integrated oil and gas company with interests in coal and chemicals. Natomas is principally engaged in petroleum exploration and production. Its operations also include ocean shipping, coal, real estate, and geothermal energy.

Acquirer industry:	Integr. petroleum	Target industry:	Integr. petroleum
Acquisition date:	Aug. 31 1983	Relation between firms:	High overlap
Target equity value:	$1,610.0 million	Relative size of target:	86.2%
Acquirer stock return:	−1.6%	Target stock return:	66.7%

13. E. I. Du Pont de Nemours / Conoco Inc.
Du Pont manufactures diversified lines of chemicals, plastics, specialty products, and fibers. Conoco is engaged in the exploration, production, and transportation of crude oil, coal, and natural gas; petroleum refining; and the production, processing, and transportation of chemicals.

Acquirer industry:	Basic chemicals	Target industry:	Integr. petroleum
Acquisition date:	Sept. 30 1981	Relation between firms:	Low overlap
Target equity value:	$5,524.9 million	Relative size of target:	82.7%
Acquirer stock return:	−16.5%	Target stock return:	33.1%

14. Eaton Corp./ Cutler-Hammer Inc.
Eaton is engaged in areas of transportation, materials handling, industrial automation, security, construction, agriculture, and consumer durables. Cutler-Hammer designs and manufactures electronic and electrical components and systems for industrial, aerospace, air traffic control, semiconductor, housing, and consumer markets.

Acquirer industry:	Replacement auto parts	Target industry:	Electrical equipment
Acquisition date:	Jan. 2 1979	Relation between firms:	Low overlap
Target equity value:	$382.7 million	Relative size of target:	19.7%
Acquirer stock return:	−8.4%	Target stock return:	60.7%

15. Exxon Corp./Reliance Electric Co.
Exxon is engaged in the exploration, production, and transportation of crude oil and natural gas, and in the production and transportation of petroleum and chemicals. Reliance develops, manufactures, and services a broad line of industrial equipment, including electric motors and drives, mechanical power transmission components, industrial and retail scales and weighting systems, and telecommunications equipment.

Acquirer industry:	Integr. petroleum	Target industry:	Electrical equipment
Acquisition date:	Dec. 27 1979	Relation between firms:	Low overlap
Target equity value:	$1,133.2 million	Relative size of target:	2.5%
Acquirer stock return:	1.2%	Target stock return:	97.9%

16. Fairchild Industries / VSI Corp.
Fairchild produces military aircraft and parts, commercial aircraft and parts, spacecraft and parts, and domestic communications systems. VSI is a diversified manufacturer of a wide range of precision metal products, including fastening systems for aircraft and missiles, steel mold bases for the plastics industry, door knobs, stainless steel cabinets, and building hardware.

Acquirer industry:	Diversified aerospace	Target industry:	Machinery
Acquisition date:	Nov. 7 1980	Relation between firms:	Medium overlap
Target equity value:	$279.1 million	Relative size of target:	87.3%
Acquirer stock return:	19.1%	Target stock return:	71.2%

17. Fluor Corp./ St. Joe Minerals Corp.
Fluor designs, engineers, procures, and constructs complex manufacturing plants, processing plants, and related facilities for energy, natural resources, and industrial clients. St. Joe is a diversified producer of natural resources (principally lead, gold, zinc, silver, coal, oil and gas, and iron ore).

Acquirer industry:	Building	Target industry:	Lead, zinc & minor metals
Acquisition date:	Aug. 3 1981	Relation between firms:	Low overlap
Target equity value:	$2,011.7 million	Relative size of target:	86.0%
Acquirer stock return:	−19.3%	Target stock return:	60.9%

18. Fort Howard Paper Co./Maryland Cup Corp.
Fort Howard manufactures a broad line of disposable sanitary paper products, principally table napkins, paper towels, toilet tissue, industrial and automotive wipes, and boxed facial tissues. Maryland Cup manufactures a variety of single-use paper and plastic products for food and beverage service, including plates, cups, bowls, cutlery, drinking straws, and toothpicks. Maryland Cup markets its products to major fast-food chains, restaurants, vending operators, soft drink bottlers, contract feeders, and dairy and other food packagers.

Acquirer industry:	Paper and forest products	Target industry:	Packaging and container
Acquisition date:	Aug. 31 1983	Relation between firms:	Medium overlap
Target equity value:	$554.8 million	Relative size of target:	25.9%
Acquirer stock return:	−9.5%	Target stock return:	30.4%

19. Freeport Minerals Co./McMoran Oil & Gas Co.
Freeport Minerals is a diversified company engaged in exploration and development of natural resources, including agricultural minerals, uranium, oxide and kaolin, and oil and gas. (Oil and gas account for 3% of Freeport's sales.) McMoran is engaged in the acquisition, exploration, and development of oil and gas properties, and the production and sale of oil and natural gas.

Acquirer industry:	Metals and mining	Target industry:	Oil and gas
Acquisition date:	April 7 1981	Relation between firms:	Medium overlap
Target equity value:	$455.1 million	Relative size of target:	22.5%
Acquirer stock return:	14.7%	Target stock return:	27.4%

20. Gannett Co. Inc./Combined Communications Corp.
Gannett and its subsidiaries publish daily newspapers. Combined Communications Corporation is engaged in outdoor advertising (45% of revenues), television and radio broadcasting (30% of revenues), and newspaper publishing (25% of revenues).

Acquirer industry:	Newspaper	Target industry:	Broadcasting
Acquisition date:	June 7 1979	Relation between firms:	Medium overlap
Target equity value:	$309.6 million	Relative size of target:	30.8%
Acquirer stock return:	−1.4%	Target stock return:	−5.0%

21. General Foods Corp./Oscar Mayer & Co. Inc.
General Foods is a leading processor of packaged grocery products. Oscar Mayer operates in the meat packing and processing industry.

Acquirer industry:	Food processing	Target industry:	Food processing
Acquisition date:	May 5 1981	Relation between firms:	High overlap
Target equity value:	$460.8 million	Relative size of target:	16.7%
Acquirer stock return:	5.6%	Target stock return:	66.2%

22. Genstar Ltd./Flintkote Co.
Genstar manufactures building materials and cement (31% of revenues), and is engaged in housing and land development (36% of sales), construction (10% of sales), marine transportation, financial services, and venture capital investment. Flintkote is engaged in mining, and manufactures various building and construction materials, including gypsum wallboard, floor tile, sand and gravel products, concrete, cement, and various lime products.

Acquirer industry:	Building	Target industry:	Building
Acquisition date:	Jan. 3 1980	Relation between firms:	High overlap
Target equity value:	$400.1 million	Relative size of target:	38.7%
Acquirer stock return:	−23.8%	Target stock return:	47.6%

23. Gulf & Western Industries/Simmons Co.
Gulf & Western is a conglomerate with interests in the manufacture of automotive and air-conditioning components, paper products, leisure, financial services, automotive replacement parts, consumer products, sugar growing and processing, citrus farming, natural resources, and apparel. Simmons produces furnishings for home, commercial, and institutional customers.

Acquirer industry:	Conglomerate	Target industry:	Building
Acquisition date:	Jan. 5 1979	Relation between firms:	Low overlap
Target equity value:	$134.3 million	Relative size of target:	9.0%
Acquirer stock return:	−2.5%	Target stock return:	38.6%

24. Harris Corp./Lanier Business Products Inc.
Harris designs and produces voice and video communication, and information processing systems, equipment, and components. Lanier develops, manufactures, and services a broad line of dictating equipment, several models of video-display text-editing typewriters, and small-business computers.

Acquirer industry:	Electronics	Target industry:	Office equipment
Acquisition date:	Oct. 28 1983	Relation between firms:	Medium overlap
Target equity value:	$275.3 million	Relative size of target:	22.5%
Acquirer stock return:	0.4%	Target stock return:	30.4%

25. Holiday Inns Inc./Harrahs
Holiday Inns owns and operates hotels throughout the world. Harrahs operates two luxury casinos.

Acquirer industry:	Travel services	Target industry:	Recreation
Acquisition date:	Feb. 28 1980	Relation between firms:	Medium overlap
Target equity value:	$315.1 million	Relative size of target:	25.6%
Acquirer stock return:	−14.3%	Target stock return:	67.8%

26. Internorth Inc./Belco Petroleum Corp.
Internorth owns and operates natural gas businesses; produces, transports, and markets liquid fuels and petrochemicals; and is involved in the exploration and production of oil and gas. Belco

is engaged in the exploration and production of crude oil and natural gas and in the production of coal.

Acquirer industry:	Natural gas	Target industry:	Integr. petroleum
Acquisition date:	July 29 1983	Relation between firms:	High overlap
Target equity value:	$803.2 million	Relative size of target:	30.0%
Acquirer stock return:	50.4%	Target stock return:	17.1%

27. Kroger Inc./Dillon Companies Inc.
Kroger operates the country's second largest supermarket chain, manufactures and processes food for sale by these supermarkets, and operates one of the country's largest drugstore chains. Dillon distributes retail food through supermarkets and convenience stores.

Acquirer industry:	Grocery store	Target industry:	Grocery store
Acquisition date:	Jan. 25 1983	Relation between firms:	High overlap
Target equity value:	$593.9 million	Relative size of target:	42.6%
Acquirer stock return:	−17.3%	Target stock return:	21.4%

28. Litton Industries / Itek Corp.
Litton industries is a conglomerate. Its businesses include production of office equipment, material handling equipment, machine tools, microwave cookers, medical equipment, and oil drilling equipment. Litton is also engaged in geophysical exploration, ship building, and production of advanced electronics products for defense, industrial automation, and geophysical markets. Itek develops and manufactures a variety of aerial reconnaissance and surveillance products based on optical and electronic technologies.

Acquirer industry:	Conglomerate	Target industry:	Precision instruments
Acquisition date:	Feb. 15 1983	Relation between firms:	Medium overlap
Target equity value:	$196.2 million	Relative size of target:	14.0%
Acquirer stock return:	8.5%	Target stock return:	40.9%

29. LTV Group / Republic Steel
LTV is the nation's third largest steel producer. In addition, the company manufactures oil field equipment and commercial aerospace and defense products. Republic Steel is the nation's seventh largest steel producer. Republic Steel also produces coal that is used in its steel operations.

Acquirer industry:	Integrated steel	Target industry:	Integrated steel
Acquisition date:	June 29 1984	Relation between firms:	High overlap
Target equity value:	$408.7 million	Relative size of target:	58.4%
Acquirer stock return:	−23.5%	Target stock return:	−3.9%

30. Mapco Inc./Earth Resources Company
Mapco is a diversified energy company principally engaged in the exploration and production of coal, oil, natural gas, and natural gas liquids; pipeline transportation of natural gas liquids and anhydrous ammonia; and marketing of natural gas liquids, refined petroleum products, domestic and foreign crude oil, and liquid fertilizers. Earth Resources is a diversified energy and resources development company engaged primarily in refining, transporting, and marketing petroleum products.

Acquirer industry:	Coal/uranium/ geothermal	Target industry:	Integr. petroleum
Acquisition date:	Feb. 9 1981	Relation between firms:	Medium overlap
Target equity value:	$369.7 million	Relative size of target:	24.6%
Acquirer stock return:	−4.1%	Target stock return:	35.3%

31. McGraw-Edison Co./Studebaker Worthington Inc.
McGraw-Edison manufactures and distributes electrical appliances, tools, and other products for the consumer market; power-system and related equipment for electrical utilities and industry; and a wide range of services and equipment for industrial and commercial uses. Studebaker

Worthington has diversified business operations that deal with the manufacture of process equipment and industrial products.

Acquirer industry:	Home appliance	Target industry:	Diversified manufg.
Acquisition date:	Oct. 23 1979	Relation between firms:	Medium overlap
Target equity value:	$712.9 million	Relative size of target:	82.4%
Acquirer stock return:	2.9%	Target stock return:	92.1%

32. Motorola Inc./Four-Phase Systems Inc.

Motorola produces data communication equipment and systems, semiconductors, and other high-technology electronic equipment. Four-Phase produces clustered video display computer systems for distributed data processing applications.

Acquirer industry:	Electronics	Target industry:	Computer/data processing
Acquisition date:	March 2 1982	Relation between firms:	Medium overlap
Target equity value:	$234.7 million	Relative size of target:	6.8%
Acquirer stock return:	−6.2%	Target stock return:	42.7%

33. Morton-Norwich Products/Thiokol Corporation

Morton-Norwich produces ethical and proprietary drugs, salt for domestic and industrial uses, household cleaning and laundry products, and specialty chemicals. Thiokol manufactures specialty chemical products (44% of revenues), and propulsion and ordnance products and services for the government.

Acquirer industry:	Proprietary drug	Target industry:	Aerospace/diversified
Acquisition date:	Sept. 24 1982	Relation between firms:	Low overlap
Target equity value:	$564.4 million	Relative size of target:	69.3%
Acquirer stock return:	1.3%	Target stock return:	33.5%

34. Occidental Petroleum/Cities Service Company

Occidental produces and markets crude oil and coal, and manufactures industrial chemicals and plastics, metal finishes, agricultural chemicals, and fertilizers. Oil and gas business accounts for 70% of the company's sales. Cities Service is an integrated oil company.

Acquirer industry:	Integr. petroleum	Target industry:	Integr. petroleum
Acquisition date:	Dec. 2 1982	Relation between firms:	High overlap
Target equity value:	3,792.5 million	Relative size of target:	130.1%
Acquirer stock return:	−24.3%	Target stock return:	12.9%

35. Pan Am Corp./National Airlines Inc.

Pan Am is primarily an international commercial air carrier providing services to 73 cities in 43 foreign countries. National Airlines is a domestic air carrier with routes extending from its hub in Miami to New York, San Francisco, and Los Angeles. Although the company also has transatlantic service to London, Paris, Frankfurt, and Amsterdam, 96% of its revenues are derived from domestic routes.

Acquirer industry:	Air transportation	Target industry:	Air transportation
Acquisition date:	Jan. 7 1980	Relation between firms:	Medium overlap
Target equity value:	$426.0 million	Relative size of target:	29.8%
Acquirer stock return:	−27.8%	Target stock return:	158.4%

36. Penn Central Corp./GK Technologies Inc.

Penn Central is a diversified company whose primary businesses include oil refining, the transportation and marketing of refined petroleum products and crude, real estate development, operation of amusement parks, and production of offshore drilling rigs. GK Technologies produces wire and cable, primarily for the telecommunications industry, and electronic components, and provides engineering services for weapons systems and environmental products.

Acquirer industry:	Conglomerate	Target industry:	Electronics
Acquisition date:	May 14 1981	Relation between firms:	Low overlap
Target equity value:	$636.5 million	Relative size of target:	27.5%
Acquirer stock return:	96.3%	Target stock return:	73.7%

37. Phillips Petroleum / General American Oil of Texas

Phillips Petroleum is a fully integrated oil company engaged in petroleum exploration, production, and refining. General American is primarily engaged in oil and gas production and exploration.

Acquirer industry:	Integr. petroleum	Target industry:	Petroleum production
Acquisition date:	March 8 1983	Relation between firms:	High overlap
Target equity value:	$572.0 million	Relative size of target:	14.0%
Acquirer stock return:	−8.1%	Target stock return:	20.1%

38. Raytheon Corp./ Beech Aircraft Corp.

Raytheon develops and manufactures electronic systems for government and commercial use. Raytheon also supplies energy services, manufactures major home appliances, designs and manufactures heavy construction equipment, and publishes textbooks. Beech Aircraft designs, manufactures, and sells airplanes for the general aviation market. Beech is also a substantial aerospace contractor producing a variety of military aircraft, missile targets, and cryogenics systems for aerospace vehicles.

Acquirer industry:	Electrical equipment	Target industry:	Aerospace/ diversified
Acquisition date:	Feb. 8 1980	Relation between firms:	Medium overlap
Target equity value:	$740.7 million	Relative size of target:	42.1%
Acquirer stock return:	22.5%	Target stock return:	110.4%

39. Revlon Inc./ Technicon Corp.

Revlon is in the beauty products (65% of revenues) and health products and service business (35% of revenues). Technicon designs and produces automated testing systems for blood and other biological fluids, chemical reagents and consumables, industrial analytical instruments, and medical information systems.

Acquirer industry:	Toiletries/cosmetics	Target industry:	Health care/ hospital supplies
Acquisition date:	May 2 1980	Relation between firms:	Medium overlap
Target equity value:	$392.7 million	Relative size of target:	19.8%
Acquirer stock return:	−10.2%	Target stock return:	34.9%

40. R.J. Reynolds Corp./ Del Monte Corp.

R.J. Reynold's lines of business are the domestic and international manufacture and sale of tobacco products (64% of revenues), transportation (14% of revenues), energy (15% of revenues), food and beverage products (5% of revenues), and aluminum products and packaging (2% of revenues). Del Monte's principal business is in food products (primarily processed foods and fresh fruit) and related services (including transportation and institutional services).

Acquirer industry:	Tobacco	Target industry:	Food processing
Acquisition date:	Feb. 2 1979	Relation between firms:	Low overlap
Target equity value:	$583.0 million	Relative size of target:	13.5%
Acquirer stock return:	4.2%	Target stock return:	63.3%

41. Signal Companies / Wheelabrator Frye Inc.

Signal is a diversified, technology-based company that manufactures aerospace equipment, professional audio-video systems, and heavy trucks. Wheelabrator Frye's products and services include environmental, energy, and engineered products and services, and chemical and specialty products.

Acquirer industry:	Auto and trucks	Target industry:	Machinery
Acquisition date:	Feb. 1 1983	Relation between firms:	Low overlap
Target equity value:	$904.7 million	Relative size of target:	36.3%
Acquirer stock return:	8.5%	Target stock return:	15.6%

42. SmithKline Corp./ Beckman Instruments Inc.

SmithKline researches, develops, manufactures, and markets ethical drugs, proprietary medicines, animal health products, ethical and proprietary eye care products, and ultrasonic and electronic instruments. Beckman is an international manufacturer of laboratory analytical instruments and related chemical products that are used widely in medicine and science and in a broad range of industrial applications.

Acquirer industry:	Ethical drugs	Target industry:	Precision instruments
Acquisition date:	March 4 1982	Relation between firms:	Medium overlap
Target equity value:	$1,000.8 million	Relative size of target:	15.5%
Acquirer stock return:	3.1%	Target stock return:	85.4%

43. Sohio / Kennecott Corp.

Sohio is an integrated petroleum company engaged in all phases of the petroleum business. Kennecott produces copper, gold, silver, molybdenum, and lead; manufactures industrial abrasive and resistant materials; manufactures and markets industrial engineered systems; and owns two-thirds of a Canadian producer of titanium dioxide slag, high-purity iron, and iron powders.

Acquirer industry:	Integr. petroleum	Target industry:	General metals and mining
Acquisition date:	June 3 1981	Relation between firms:	Low overlap
Target equity value:	$1,760.4 million	Relative size of target:	11.6%
Acquirer stock return:	−21.4%	Target stock return:	140.3%

44. Standard Brands / Nabisco Inc.

Standard Brands is a manufacturer, processor, and distributor of food and related products. Nabisco is a manufacturer and marketer of food products (specializing in cookies and crackers, which account for 60% of total sales), toiletries, pharmaceuticals, and household accessories.

Acquirer industry:	Food processing	Target industry:	Food processing
Acquisition date:	July 2 1981	Relation between firms:	High overlap
Target equity value:	$929.0 million	Relative size of target:	81.4%
Acquirer stock return:	1.0%	Target stock return:	−5.7%

45. Tenneco / Houston Oil & Minerals Corp.

Tenneco is a diversified company. Its major businesses include natural gas, petrochemicals, construction and farm equipment, automotive components, shipbuilding, chemicals, packaging, agriculture and land management, and life insurance. The recent business emphasis of Houston Oil & Minerals has been on exploration for oil and natural gas on undeveloped properties, and the development of production upon discovery. In 1980, the breakdown of revenues was oil 21%, gas 61%, and pipeline and other 21%.

Acquirer industry:	Natural gas	Target industry:	Petroleum producing industry
Acquisition date:	April 23 1981	Relation between firms:	Medium overlap
Target equity value:	$1,447.0 million	Relative size of target:	13.9%
Acquirer stock return:	−21.4%	Target stock return:	−3.4%

46. Tosco Corp./AZL Resources Inc.

Tosco owns and operates petroleum refineries and related wholesale distribution facilities. Prior to the merger AZL had been in the process of changing its focus from agricultural-based businesses to oil and gas exploration and production.

Acquirer industry:	Integr. petroleum	Target industry:	Agricultural products
Acquisition date:	Dec. 31 1982	Relation between firms:	Low overlap
Target equity value:	$77.9 million	Relative size of target:	42.8%
Acquirer stock return:	−29.0%	Target stock return:	30.8%

47. U.S. Steel / Marathon Oil Co.

U.S. Steel's principal businesses include steel, chemicals, resource development, fabricating and engineering, and transportation. Marathon is an integrated petroleum company engaged in the production, refining, and transportation of crude oil, natural gas, and petroleum products.

Acquirer industry:	Integr. steel	Target industry:	Integr. petroleum
Acquisition date:	March 11 1982	Relation between firms:	Low overlap
Target equity value:	$4,438.3 million	Relative size of target:	145.0%
Acquirer stock return:	21.4%	Target stock return:	29.0%

48. United Technologies / Carrier Corp.
United Technologies designs and produces high-technology power systems, flight systems, and industrial products and services. Carrier's principal business is the manufacture and sale of air conditioning equipment.

Acquirer industry:	Aerospace/ diversified	Target industry:	Building
Acquisition date:	July 6 1979	Relation between firms:	Low overlap
Target equity value:	$757.1 million	Relative size of target:	42.8%
Acquirer stock return:	−21.3%	Target stock return:	44.7%

49. Westinghouse Electric / Teleprompter Corp.
Westinghouse Electric is a diversified corporation primarily engaged in the manufacture and sale of electrical equipment. Westinghouse's wholly owned subsidiary WBC operates six TV stations, 12 radio stations, and cable television systems. Teleprompter is the nation's largest cable television company and owns MUZAC, the leading supplier of music to offices and other commercial establishments.

Acquirer industry:	Electrical equipment	Target industry:	Broadcasting
Acquisition date:	Aug. 18 1981	Relation between firms:	Medium overlap
Target equity value:	$642.7 million	Relative size of target:	41.8%
Acquirer stock return:	4.8%	Target stock return:	44.5%

50. Williams Companies / Northwest Energy Company
Williams is primarily engaged in the chemical fertilizer (49% of revenues), natural gas (27% of sales), and metals (24% of sales) businesses. Northwest is primarily engaged in interstate natural gas transmission, oil and gas exploration, and the marketing of natural gas liquids.

Acquirer industry:	Chemical/ diversified	Target industry:	Natural gas
Acquisition date:	Nov. 30, 1983	Relation between firms:	Medium overlap
Target equity value:	$721.2 million	Relative size of target:	61.1%
Acquirer stock return:	−5.6%	Target stock return:	42.6%

References

Asquith, Paul, 1983, Merger bids, uncertainty, and stockholder returns, Journal of Financial Economics 11, 51–84.

Asquith, Paul and E. Han Kim, 1982, The impact of merger bids on participating firms' security holders, Journal of Finance 37, 1209–1228.

Asquith, Paul, Robert Bruner, and David Mullins, 1988, Merger returns and the form of financing, Working paper (MIT Sloan School, Cambridge, MA).

Baker, George and Karen Wruck, Organizational changes and value creation in leveraged buyouts: The case of The O.M. Scott & Sons Company, Journal of Financial Economics 25, 163–190.

Belsley, David, Edwin Kuh, and Roy Welsch, 1980, Regression diagnostics (Wiley, New York, NY).

Bradley, Michael, Anand Desai, and E. Han Kim, 1983, The rationale behind interfirm tender offers: Information or synergy?, Journal of Financial Economics 11, 183–206.

Bradley, Michael, Anand Desai, and E. Han Kim, 1988, Synergistic gains from corporate acquisitions and their division between the stockholders of target and acquiring firms, Journal of Financial Economics 21, 3–40.

Bull, Ivan, 1988, Management performance and leveraged buyouts: An empirical analysis, Unpublished paper (University of Illinois at Urbana-Champaign, IL).

Caves, Richard, 1989, Takeovers and economic efficiency: Foresight vs. hindsight, International Journal of Industrial Organization 7, 151–174.

Dodd, Peter, 1980, Merger proposals, management discretion and stockholder wealth, Journal of Financial Economics 8, 105–138.

Dodd, Peter and Richard Ruback, 1977, Tender offers and stockholder returns: An empirical analysis, Journal of Financial Economics 5, 351–374.
Donaldson, Gordon, Voluntary restructuring: The case of General Mills, Journal of Financial Economics 27, 117–142.
Herman, Edwin and Louis Lowenstein, 1988, The efficiency effects of hostile takeovers, in: John Coffee Jr., Louis Lowenstein, and Susan Rose-Ackerman, eds., Knights, raiders and targets: The impact of the hostile takeover (Oxford University Press, New York, NY).
Huang, Yen-Shong and Ralph Walkling, 1987, Target abnormal returns associated with acquisition announcements: Payment, acquisition form, and managerial resistance, Journal of Financial Economics 19, 329–349.
Jarrell, Sherry, 1991, Do takeovers generate value? Evidence on the capital market's ability to assess takeovers, Working paper (Southern Methodist University, Dallas, TX).
Kaplan, Steven, 1989a, The effects of management buyouts on operating performance and value, Journal of Financial Economics 24, 581–618.
Kaplan, Steven, 1989b, Campeau's acquisition of Federated: Value destroyed or value added?, Journal of Financial Economics 25, 191–212.
Kaplan, Steven and Michael Weisbach, 1992, Acquisitions and diversification: What is divested and how much does the market anticipate?, Journal of Finance, forthcoming.
Linder, Jane and Dwight Crane, 1991, Bank mergers: Integration and profitability, Working paper (Harvard Business School, Boston, MA).
Pontiff, Jeffrey, Andre Shleifer, and Michael Weisbach, 1990, Reversion of excess pension assets after takeovers, Rand Journal of Economics 21, 600–613.
Ravenscraft, David and Frederick M. Scherer, 1987, Mergers, selloffs, and economic efficiency (Brookings Institution, Washington, DC).
Rosett, Joshua, 1990, Do union wealth concessions explain takeover premiums? The evidence of contract wages, Journal of Financial Economics 27, 263–282.
Ruback, Richard, 1988, Do target shareholders lose in unsuccessful control contests?, in: Corporate takeovers: Causes and consequences (National Bureau of Economic Research, Cambridge, MA).
Shleifer, Andre and Larry Summers, 1988, Breach of trust in hostile takeovers, in: A. Auerbach, ed., Corporate takeovers: Causes and consequences (University of Chicago Press, Chicago, IL).
Smith, Abbie, 1990, Corporate ownership structure and performance: The case of management buyouts, Journal of Financial Economics 27, 143–164.
Tehranian, Hassan and Marcia Cornett, 1991, An investigation of the change in corporate performance associated with bank acquisitions, Journal of Financial Economics, forthcoming.
Watts, Ross and Jerold Zimmerman, Positive accounting theory (Prentice-Hall, Englewood Cliffs, NJ).
White, Halbert, 1980, A heteroskedasticity-consistent covariance covariance matrix estimator and a direct test for heteroskedasticity, Econometrica 48, 817–838.

[13]

ELSEVIER

Journal of Financial Economics 49 (1998) 223–253

JOURNAL OF Financial ECONOMICS

Glamour, value and the post-acquisition performance of acquiring firms[1]

P. Raghavendra Rau[a,*], Theo Vermaelen[b,c]

[a] *Krannert Graduate School of Management, Purdue University, West Lafayette, IN 47907, USA*

[b] *INSEAD, Fontainebleau Cedex, France*

[c] *Maastricht University, Maastricht, The Netherlands*

Received 26 September 1996; received in revised form 11 November 1997

Abstract

This paper uses a methodology robust to recent criticisms of standard long-horizon event study tests to show that bidders in mergers underperform while bidders in tender offers overperform in the three years after the acquisition. However, the long-term underperformance of acquiring firms in mergers is predominantly caused by the poor post-acquisition performance of low book-to-market "glamour" firms. We interpret this finding as evidence that both the market and the management overextrapolate the bidder's past performance (as reflected in the bidder's book-to-market ratio) when they assess the desirability of an acquisition. © 1998 Elsevier Science S.A. All rights reserved.

JEL classification: G14; G34

Keywords: Mergers; Post-acquisition performance; Long-horizon event studies; Bootstrapping

* Corresponding author. Tel.: 765/494-4488; fax: 765/494-9658; E-mail: rau@mgmt.purdue.edu.

[1] We would like to thank Eugene Fama for providing us with monthly factor returns. We would also like to thank Brad Barber, Chun Chang, Dave Denis, Eugene Fama, Kenneth French (the referee), Paolo Fulghieri, Gabriel Hawawini, Pierre Hillion, Ravi Jagannathan, Dave Ikenberry, Murgie Krishnan, Tim Loughran, Arijit Mukherji, Kevin Murphy, Abraham Ravid, Bill Schwert (the editor), Kiran Verma, and seminar participants at the 1996 Western Finance Association meetings, the 1996 European Finance Association meetings, the 1996 Financial Management Association meetings, the 1996 European Financial Management Association meetings, the 1996 French Finance Association meetings, Erasmus University, ESSEC, London Business School, Maastricht University, the University of Minnesota at Minneapolis Saint-Paul, University of North Carolina at Chapel Hill, Oxford University, Purdue University, Rice University, and Yale University for comments on previous drafts of this paper.

PII S0304-405X(98)00023-3

1. Introduction

Mergers and acquisitions have been extensively researched in finance. However, a number of issues still remain controversial, in particular the long-run price behavior of bidders in mergers and tender offers. We investigate two basic issues in this paper: bidders' underperformance (if any) in the long run after the acquisition and the determinants of this underperformance. These issues are important because the conclusion that mergers and acquisitions increase the combined wealth of bidder and target shareholders is based on the results of numerous short-term event studies that find returns to bidders to be small or at least insignificantly different from zero in the short run.

In their classic survey of the empirical research in this area, Jensen and Ruback (1983) summarize the results of six studies that examine the returns to bidders in the year following the takeover. The evidence shows that after tender offers, bidders earn statistically insignificant positive abnormal returns, while after mergers, bidding firms systematically underperform. However, this evidence on long-term post-merger bidder performance is controversial, with different researchers finding contrasting results. Bradley and Jarrell (1988), Langetieg (1978), and Franks, Harris and Titman (1991), for example, do not find significant underperformance in the two to three years after the acquisition. Others, such as Asquith (1983) and Agrawal et al. (1992), conclude that these firms do experience significantly negative abnormal returns in the first few years after the merger. Loderer and Martin (1992) find some evidence of negative returns in the first three years following the acquisition, but none after the fourth year. Also, they find that the negative abnormal performance progressively diminishes through the 1960s and the 1970s and disappears in the 1980s.

In contrast to event studies over short horizons, long-term event studies are sensitive to the model used for computing normal returns, which may partially explain the conflicting conclusions of past research. The most recent papers, Agrawal et al. (1992) and Loderer and Martin (1992), both adjust for firm size and beta risk. However, Fama and French (1992) have recently shown that beta does not capture much of the cross-sectional variation in average stock returns. Firm size and book-to-market equity combine to explain a much larger proportion of the variation in average stock returns. Consequently, Fama and French (1993) criticize the Agrawal, Jaffe, and Mandelker results for ignoring the book-to-market effect. They conjecture (pp. 54–55) that acquiring firms might tend to be large, successful firms with low book-to-market ratios. Hence, they argue that a methodology controlling for the below-average returns of low book-to-market firms would reveal no persistent negative abnormal returns.

Moreover, some studies (Kothari and Warner, 1997; Barber and Lyon, 1997) have recently questioned the validity of standard parametric tests in testing the statistical significance of long-horizon abnormal returns. Barber and Lyon, for example, document that long-horizon *t*-statistics are negatively biased, in many cases detecting significant abnormal performance when none is present.

The first contribution of this paper is to examine the issue of long-horizon bidder performance in mergers and acquisitions after explicitly adjusting for both firm size and book-to-market effects, as suggested by Fama and French (1993). We also test the statistical significance of these results using bootstrapping (see Ikenberry et al., 1995), a methodology that is robust to the problems that plague standard long-horizon tests of statistical significance. As Kothari and Warner (1997) point out, the bootstrap procedure represents a state-of-the-art procedure for recognizing and attempting to adjust for systematic biases in assessing statistical significance. Barber et al. (1998) prove that the bootstrap method not only yields well-specified test statistics but is also more powerful than the control firm method, a method that has also been used to detect abnormal performance in some recent long-horizon event studies.

We examine a sample of 3169 mergers and 348 tender offers with acquirors listed on both the Center for Research in Security Prices (CRSP) NYSE/AMEX/Nasdaq tapes and COMPUSTAT, and bids announced between January 1980 and December 1991. We find that bidding firms do *not* overwhelmingly tend to be successful firms with low book-to-market ratios. The distribution of bidding firms across the spectrum of book-to-market ratios of firms listed on CRSP is relatively uniform.

Adjusting for both firm size and book-to-market ratio, we find that, on average, acquirors in mergers underperform equally weighted control portfolios with similar sizes and book-to-market ratios by a statistically significant 4% over a period of three years after the merger completion date. On the other hand, acquirors in tender offers earn a statistically significant positive abnormal return of 9%, on average. Hence, in contrast to Fama and French's (1993) conjecture, the negative abnormal returns to bidding firms in mergers are not simply a result of not adjusting for book-to-market ratios.

To explain the cross-sectional variation in long-run bidder returns, we examine three hypotheses: the performance extrapolation hypothesis, the means of payment hypothesis, and the earnings per share (EPS) myopia hypothesis.

According to the performance extrapolation hypothesis, the market overextrapolates the past performance of the bidder when it assesses the value of an acquisition. At the same time, managers and other decision makers (such as large shareholders and the board of directors) who have to approve an acquisition, indirectly receive feedback on the quality of the bidder's management from the market. Specifically, we argue that in companies with low book-to-market ratios ('glamour' firms), managers are more likely to overestimate their own abilities to manage an acquisition, i.e., they will be infected by hubris (Roll, 1986). Indeed, glamour firms are firms with high past stock returns and high past growth in cash flow and earnings (see Lakonishok et al., 1994), which should presumably strengthen the management's belief in its own actions. Moreover, other stakeholders in these firms, such as the board of directors and large shareholders, are more likely to give the management the benefit of the doubt and approve its acquisition plans. On the other hand, in companies whose management has a poor track record, such as companies with high book-to-market ratios ('value' stocks), managers, directors, and large shareholders will be more prudent before approving a major transaction that may well determine the survival of the company. Because these acquisitions are not motivated by hubris, they should create shareholder value rather than destroy it.

The performance extrapolation hypothesis also assumes that the market only gradually reassesses the quality of the bidder as the results of the acquisition become clear. Hence, while in the short run, i.e., around the announcement of the acquisition, glamour bidders will experience higher abnormal returns than value bidders, in the long run this performance will reverse. Consistent with this extrapolation story, Lang et al. (1989) and Servaes (1991) report that short-term announcement returns are significantly negatively correlated with Tobin's Q (which is negatively correlated with the book-to-market ratio). Hayward and Hambrick (1995) also report that managerial behavior in acquisitions is influenced by past success, a crucial assumption in the performance extrapolation hypothesis. In a survey of 106 publicly traded American companies involved in large acquisitions in 1989 and 1992, they find that acquisition premiums are positively correlated to measures of recent organizational performance, CEO pay relative to the other executives in the firm, and recent media praise for the CEO. Moreover, the size of acquisition premiums is inversely related to shareholder losses following an acquisition.

If managers are better informed about the long-term prospects of their firm than is the market, they will tend to pay for their acquisitions with shares when they believe that their stock is overvalued and use cash otherwise. Hence, the means of payment hypothesis predicts that, on average, long-run abnormal returns to bidders will be negative in share-financed acquisitions and positive in cash-financed acquisitions. Note that such a timing strategy will only work if the market (and especially the target shareholders) underestimates the extent of over- or undervaluation of the bidder. This hypothesis also requires that the short-term negative announcement returns to bidders in all-stock mergers and positive announcement returns to bidders in all-cash mergers reported by Travlos (1987) do not fully reflect the extent of bidder mispricing. Loughran and Vijh (1997) find that acquirors paying for acquisitions by issuing shares earn significantly negative abnormal returns while cash acquirors earn significantly positive abnormal returns in the five years following the acquisition, which is consistent with the means of payment hypothesis.

Finally, the EPS myopia hypothesis predicts that mergers with a positive impact on EPS will *ceteris paribus*, perform the worst. Suppose both the market and the bidding firm's management are fixated on EPS. Merging with a company with a lower price–earnings ratio than the buyer's and paying for the acquisition with shares may inflate the buyer's EPS. Managers find it easier to justify an acquisition if it is accompanied by an EPS increase rather than a decrease. In fact, there is a widespread belief that companies should not acquire others with higher price–earnings ratios than their own (Brealey and Myers, 1996 pp. 921–923). Consequently, managers might be willing to pay higher prices (and possibly overpay) for target firms if the acquisition results in an increase in earnings per share. Alternatively, the market might overvalue acquiring firms when the acquisition results in an increase in EPS. In an analysis of AT&T's acquisition of NCR in 1991, Lys and Vincent (1995) report that AT&T was willing to pay as much as $500 million extra to satisfy pooling accounting, although the only effect of the accounting change was to boost EPS by around 17% without any cash flow implications. In an investigation of conglomerate and predatory acquisitions in the 1960s, Barber et al. (1995) find some evidence that friendly acquisitions in particular were concentrated along targets with low *P*/*E*s and high return on equity, which is consistent with the EPS myopia hypothesis.

These three hypotheses can be easily characterized in a simple manner. The means of payment hypothesis says that the bidder is mispriced before the merger, but the management is aware of the mispricing. Both the performance extrapolation hypothesis and the EPS myopia hypothesis say that the bidder is mispriced immediately after the acquisition announcement but the management is not aware of the mispricing. The EPS myopia hypothesis assumes that the mispricing occurs because the market is preoccupied with earnings per share, while the performance extrapolation hypothesis assumes that all parties involved (the market and the corporate decision makers) are too focused on past performance.

After testing the various hypotheses, we conclude that the performance extrapolation hypothesis is more consistent with the data than the other two hypotheses. Specifically, we find that value bidders far outperform glamour bidders in the three years after the completion of a merger or tender offer. After adjusting for size and book-to-market ratio, we find that value acquirors earn statistically significant positive abnormal returns of 8% in mergers and 16% in tender offers, while glamour acquirors earn statistically significant negative abnormal returns of − 17% in mergers and insignificant abnormal returns of 4% in tender offers. The finding that value bidders outperform glamour bidders is remarkably robust. Our conclusions are unchanged when we exclude small acquisitions, Nasdaq bidders, or periods when events are clustered.

We hasten to add that, although the performance extrapolation hypothesis is the most consistent with the data, many of the results are also consistent with the means of payment hypothesis. In particular, post-acquisition returns in mergers are negative while in tender offers they are positive. This is predicted by the means of payment hypothesis because in mergers, bidders tend to pay with shares, while in tender offers, they pay with cash. Moreover, at least in the merger sample, glamour bidders pay more frequently with stock than value bidders.

The remainder of the paper is organized as follows. In Section 2, we describe the data and our methodology. Section 3 reports the long-run performance of acquiring firms in mergers and tender offers and explores how the different hypotheses can explain the results. Section 4 concludes.

2. Data and methodology

2.1. The data

We examine the long-term underperformance (over the three years following the date of completion of the merger) of bidding firms in mergers and tender offers, with bids announced and completed between January 1980 and December 1991. Our sample is drawn from the Securities Data Corporation (SDC) on-line Mergers and Corporate Transactions database, using the following criteria:

- the transaction is classified either as a merger or an acquisition of majority interest (for mergers) or as a tender offer,
- the transaction is listed as completed, and
- the announcement date and effective date of the merger lie between January 1, 1980 and December 31, 1991, respectively.

Our full sample is composed of 3169 mergers and 348 tender offers. We classify cases as tender offers when the bidder first launches a tender offer to acquire control and this is followed by a merger agreement whereby the acquiring company agrees to purchase the remaining shares not tendered under the offer. (Reclassifying these situations as mergers does not significantly change the analysis.) We require acquirors to be on both CRSP's monthly NYSE/AMEX/Nasdaq tapes and COMPUSTAT. Targets in the full sample may be publicly or privately owned, but sometimes we consider only acquisitions in which the target is publicly traded. This requirement reduces the sample to 709 mergers and 278 tender offers. Almost all of the acquirors in tender offers trade on the NYSE, and over 35% of the acquirors in mergers trade on Nasdaq.

Table 1 shows the distribution of sizes and book-to-market ratios of the acquiring firms, relative to the universe of firms listed on the NYSE and AMEX covered by both CRSP and COMPUSTAT, with size and book-to-market deciles computed every month. Panel A ranks the acquiring firms into size deciles, with size deciles measured on the basis of market equity value relative to the universe of all NYSE, AMEX, and Nasdaq stocks covered by both CRSP and COMPUSTAT. Our sample of acquiring firms tilts towards large

Table 1
Descriptive statistics for mergers and tender offers announced and completed between January 1980 and December 1991

Panel A reports the distribution of size decile rankings of acquirors in mergers and tender offers for U.S. targets by acquirors listed on NYSE/AMEX and Nasdaq, covered by both COMPUSTAT and CRSP, listed on the SDC Mergers and Corporate Transactions on-line database, and announced and completed between January 1980 and December 1991. Each type of acquisition is listed for two sets of targets: all targets, irrespective of their public or private status, and only public targets, listed on CRSP as well as COMPUSTAT. Size deciles are computed every month for all firms in the universe of NYSE /AMEX and Nasdaq stocks. Decile 1 is the smallest. Panel B reports the distribution of book-to-market decile rankings, where book-to-market deciles are similarly computed every month for all firms in the universe of NYSE/AMEX and Nasdaq stocks.

Panel A: Size deciles of acquiror at the time of announcement of merger or tender offer

Size decile	Mergers[a]		Tender offers[a]	
	All targets	Only public targets	All targets	Only public targets
1–2	126 (4.2%)	24 (3.6%)	8 (2.5%)	7 (2.7%)
3–4	282 (9.4%)	52 (7.7%)	10 (3.1%)	6 (2.3%)
5–6	516 (17.2%)	84 (12.4%)	30 (9.3%)	22 (8.5%)
7–8	815 (27.2%)	156 (23.1%)	99 (30.6%)	74 (28.5%)
9–10	1258 (42.0%)	359 (53.2%)	177 (54.6%)	151 (58.1%)
Total	2997	675	324	260
Average[b] (Median)	\$986 (\$214)	\$1755 (\$380)	\$2161 (\$402)	\$2335 (\$583)

Panel B: Book-to-market deciles of acquiror at the time of announcement of merger or tender offer

Book-to-market decile	Mergers[c]		Tender offers[c]	
	All targets	Only public targets	All targets	Only public targets
1–2	557 (19.7%)	117 (18.2%)	27 (8.5%)	22 (8.6%)
3–4	741 (26.2%)	163 (25.3%)	72 (22.8%)	60 (23.5%)
5–6	685 (24.3%)	167 (26.0%)	94 (29.7%)	65 (25.5%)
7–8	518 (18.3%)	131 (20.4%)	79 (25.0%)	68 (26.7%)
9–10	322 (11.4%)	65 (10.1%)	44 (13.9%)	40 (15.7%)
Total	2823	643	316	255
Average (Median)	1.788 (0.576)	1.187 (0.582)	5.218 (0.675)	6.279 (0.670)

[a] Using the Wilcoxon rank-sum test, the null hypothesis that bidder sizes are distributed among the deciles in the same proportions for the unrestricted and the restricted samples can be rejected at the 1% level for mergers. Bidding firms for all targets, whether public or private, are smaller on average than those bidding for public targets only. For tender offers, we cannot reject the null even at the 10% level.
[b] In millions of dollars.
[c] Using the Wilcoxon rank-sum test, the null hypothesis that bidder book-to-market ratios are distributed among the deciles in the same proportions for the unrestricted and the restricted samples cannot be rejected at any reasonable level of significance for either mergers or tender offers.

acquirors – over 40% of the acquirors are in the largest two deciles. Bidders in mergers involving only public targets (our restricted sample) tend to be much larger than those involving both private and public targets (the unrestricted sample). On the other hand, for tender offers, there are no significant differences in the distribution of sizes across the two samples. Panel B ranks the acquiring firms on the basis of their book-to-market ratios, with the book-to-market quintiles similarly calculated relative to the universe of all NYSE, AMEX, and Nasdaq stocks covered by both CRSP and COMPUSTAT. There is no major bias in our sample towards low book-to-market acquirors; book-to-market ratios are relatively evenly distributed across deciles, though there is a relative paucity of bidding firms in the two highest deciles (with the highest book-to-market ratios). It is also interesting to note that in tender offers, there is less of a tendency for bidders to be glamour firms than in mergers.

We also measure the sizes of public targets relative to acquiror firms four weeks before the announcement date. Our targets are reasonably significant targets for the acquirors, with a median size ratio of 10% for mergers (383 firms) and 17% for tender offers (200 firms).

2.2. Methodology

To measure abnormal performance, we use the common technique of computing cumulative abnormal returns relative to a size- and book-to-market-based benchmark. (Using a size-based benchmark does not significantly alter the results.) To calculate abnormal returns based on size and book-to-market, we use the sequential sort procedure employed by Ikenberry et al. (1995), Barber and Lyon (1997), Barber et al. (1998), and Kothari and Warner (1997) among others. Specifically, we form ten size deciles at the end of every month on the basis of the market capitalization of NYSE and AMEX firms listed on both CRSP and COMPUSTAT. Then we rank each firm on the NYSE and AMEX listed on both CRSP and COMPUSTAT into one of ten portfolios formed on the basis of these breakpoints. This decile breakpoint formation and ranking procedure is repeated every month between January 1980 and December 1994. These deciles are further sorted into quintiles using book-to-market ratios. Portfolio returns are then formed every month by averaging the monthly returns for these 50 portfolios. These returns are then used as benchmarks to calculate abnormal performance. Abnormal returns are calculated for each firm relative to its size and book-to-market benchmark (as the difference between its monthly return and that of its control portfolio) every month for 36 months after the merger completion date. CARs are calculated by averaging across all acquiror firms every month and then summing these averages over time.

To estimate significance levels for the monthly CARs, we use the bootstrapping approach as applied by Ikenberry, Lakonishok, and Vermaelen. For each merger or tender offer in our sample, we randomly select, with replacement, a firm listed on NYSE or AMEX that has the same size and book-to-market ranking at that point in time. This matching firm is treated as though it had completed an acquisition at that point in time. We carry out this process for each firm in our acquiror sample, ending up with a pseudo-portfolio consisting of a randomly drawn firm matched in size, book-to-market, and time for each firm in our acquiror sample. We repeat this process till we have 1000 pseudo-portfolios and thus 1000 abnormal return observations. This gives us an empirical distribution for the abnormal returns drawn under the null model specific to our hypothesis. The significance levels we report represent the probability that a randomly drawn portfolio from our empirical distribution will have an abnormal return greater than our sample. For comparison purposes, we also report t-statistics using the crude dependence adjustment method as described by Brown and Warner (1980) and a 24-month holdout period (months -12 to -24 relative to the merger or tender offer completion date).

As has been noted in other studies (for example, Ikenberry, Lakonishok, and Vermaelen), the bootstrapping approach also avoids the problems associated with standard t-tests over long horizons, such as assumptions of normality, stationarity, and time independence of observations. If these problems exist in long-horizon returns, they are also present in our pseudo-portfolios and are thus controlled for in our tests.

There are, however, some important methodological issues connected with the monthly rebalancing procedure we use in our bootstrapping methodology, which have not been noted previously. Other studies use either an annual rebalancing method, whereby the size deciles and the book-to-market quintiles are formed once a year with monthly returns calculated for these portfolios for the following 12 months (see, for example, Ikenberry, Lakonishok, and Vermaelen), no rebalancing (see, for example, Mitchell and Stafford, 1997), or a control firm approach, whereby a matching firm is chosen on the basis of size and book-to-market characteristics and held for the period over which abnormal returns are calculated (see, for example, Loughran and Vijh, 1997). Monthly rebalancing avoids some problems associated with these alternative methods.

First, the book-to-market and size characteristics for our sample firms change over the year, as glamour firms perform poorly compared to value firms in the long term following the classification. Fig. 1 depicts the evolution of glamour and value status for acquirors in mergers and tender offers. It shows the average book-to-market decile ranking for the firms in our glamour and value merger and tender offer samples, relative to the universe of NYSE/AMEX and Nasdaq firms. Over the three years after acquisition completion, the average book-to-market decile ranking for glamour acquirors in mergers sharply increases from 2.37 to 4.57, while in tender offers, the ranking increases from 3.27 to 4.41. Hence, two years after the merger announcement, glamour bidders have lost most of their glamour status. In our 50 size and book-to-market portfolios, only 19% of the sample firms in our merger sample are classified in the same portfolio

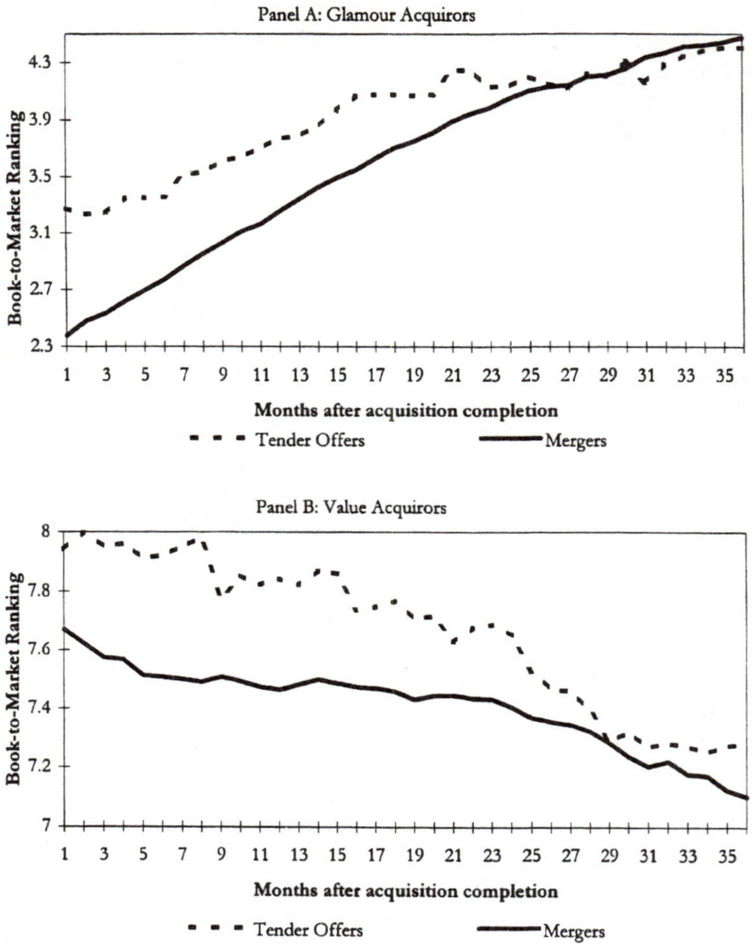

Fig. 1. Evolution of glamour and value status for acquirors in mergers and tender offers. This graph shows the average book-to-market decile rankings for glamour and value acquirors in mergers and tender offers, respectively. Acquirors are ranked into deciles relative to the universe of NYSE, AMEX, and Nasdaq firms every month for 36 months after the acquisition completion.

three years after the acquisition completion. Similarly, Mitchell and Stafford, in their analysis of the long-run abnormal performance of a sample of acquirors listed on the CRSP EVENTS database, report that most firms in their sample change portfolio assignments following the event. In particular, they report that only 25% of their sample firms remain in their original size and book-to-market portfolio three years after the event. Using either annual rebalancing, no rebalancing, or the control firm approach does not adequately control for the changing risk characteristics of our sample firms over time.

Second, in order to test the performance extrapolation hypothesis, we rank the firms in the acquiring firm sample into separate subsamples based on their book-to-market ratios at the time of announcement of the acquisition in some of our later analyses. As Barber et al. (1998) note, the bootstrap approach could yield biased measures of mean abnormal returns and test statistics when the sample firms are drawn from the subsamples consisting of the firms with the highest or the lowest book-to-market ratios. This is because sample firms with low book-to-market ratios will tend to cluster around the lower end of their size and book-to-market reference partition. The bootstrap approach assumes that all firms constituting a particular reference partition have the same expected return. On average, therefore, if there is a large difference between the returns of the firms with the largest and the smallest book-to-market ratio within each of the reference partitions, the pseudo-portfolios created for firms with low book-to-market ratios will tend to have higher returns than the sample firms, which leads to a negative bias in the abnormal returns and in the t-statistics. Similarly, firms with high book-to-market ratios will exhibit a positive bias in their abnormal returns and the *t*-statistics.

To estimate the possible magnitude of this bias, we further sort each of our 50 reference partitions on the basis of book-to-market ratio and measure the difference between the average return to the top half of the partition and the second half. This procedure is equivalent to creating a reference partition twice as fine as before. We find that over the entire 1980–1994 period, this difference is 0.64% per month on average for all reference partitions, ranging from a low of − 1.18% per month to a high of 1.1% per month. This could potentially lead to a bias in the returns of as much as ± 12% per year with annual rebalancing. Our monthly rebalancing method mitigates the extent of this bias. As can be seen from Fig. 1, both glamour and value firms experience changes in their original size and book-to-market characteristics after the completion of the acquisition. Hence, with monthly rebalancing, they will no longer cluster around the extreme ends of the reference partition.

Our methodology is nevertheless susceptible to some biases. First, the CARs we calculate over the three-year horizon after the acquisition completion are subject to the measurement, new listing, and skewness biases described by Barber and Lyon (1997). Using monthly rebalancing instead of annual rebalancing or the control firm approach exacerbates the total bias in long-horizon CARs, most notably by accentuating the new listing and rebalancing biases.

In addition, it creates yet another bias, which we refer to as the *momentum bias*.[2] Monthly rebalancing implies that the firms in the universe are reclassified

[2] Thanks are due to Dave Ikenberry for helpful discussions on this point.

into the glamour and value benchmarks every month. However, as Chan et al. (1996) note, the returns of glamour 'winner'and value 'loser' stocks exhibit positive and negative drifts, respectively, up to six months after their classification into winner and loser portfolios. Hence, firms that are classified as glamour firms in any month continue to be winner firms the following month, while firms classified as value firms continue to be loser firms. Consequently, CARs calculated with respect to the glamour benchmarks tend to be negatively biased while CARs calculated with respect to the value benchmarks are positively biased. Our empirical distribution therefore has a negative mean when we examine glamour firms, while the mean is positive when we examine value firms. Similarly, Ikenberry et al. (1995) find that the mean return for the bootstrap distribution for their glamour repurchasers sample is −4.31% (see Kothari and Warner, 1997, fn. 4). The bias decreases if we decrease the frequency with which we rebalance.

These three biases make it difficult to judge the economic significance of our long-horizon CARs. We therefore report in our tables a bias-adjusted CAR (BCAR) obtained in each case by subtracting the mean CAR for the empirical distribution from the CAR value for the sample. The BCAR value gives us a better idea of the economic significance of our results. Note however that the *p*-values computed through bootstrapping and the statistical significance of the results are unaffected by these biases.

Second, as noted by Kothari and Warner, another potential bias can occur if the universe of firms from which the pseudo-portfolios are formed does not have the same survival characteristics as the sample firms. A disproportionate number of IPOs, which perform poorly in the long run, are listed on Nasdaq. Consequently, including Nasdaq firms in the universe from which the pseudo-portfolios are drawn biases our empirical distribution of abnormal returns negatively. Loughran (1993) reports that small NYSE securities earn average annual returns that are 6% higher than those earned by similarly sized Nasdaq firms and concludes that this return differential is largely due to the preponderance of IPOs listing on Nasdaq. To alleviate this possible bias, we draw our pseudo-firms only from the universe of NYSE/AMEX stocks. An alternate approach might be to include, in addition to the NYSE/AMEX stocks, only Nasdaq stocks that had been in existence for at least three years at the time of inclusion in the pseudo-universe. However, this procedure would add tremendously to the computational requirements of the bootstrapping program. To check if our methodology is robust to excluding Nasdaq firms, we repeat the analysis excluding all Nasdaq acquirors from our sample. This does not affect our results (see Section 3.2.2).

The fact that long-horizon returns are sensitive to the methodology employed may explain the difference between our results and the conclusions drawn by Mitchell and Stafford (1997). They compute three-year buy-and-hold abnormal returns relative to a benchmark portfolio adjusted for size and book-to-market ratio (without rebalancing), include Nasdaq firms in their pseudo-universe, and do not distinguish between mergers and tender offers. Consequently, it is not surprising that they find different results from the ones reported in this paper.

3. The long-term performance of acquiring firms

3.1. Do bidders underperform?

Table 2 reports the long-term underperformance for both mergers and tender offers taken as a whole, for size- and book-to-market-adjusted returns. Unless specified otherwise, all the abnormal returns we report throughout the paper are computed over a period of three years after the completion of the acquisition

Table 2
Long-term performance for acquirors in mergers and tender offers announced and completed between January 1980 and December 1991

This table reports cumulative abnormal returns (in percent) for acquirors in mergers and tender offers. Results are reported for two sets of targets: all targets, irrespective of their public or private status, and only public targets, listed on CRSP as well as COMPUSTAT. Abnormal returns are computed with reference to a size- and book-to-market-based benchmark portfolio, consisting of stocks listed on the NYSE and AMEX exchanges (formed using size deciles computed every month for all firms in the universe of NYSE and AMEX stocks and then subdividing these size deciles into five quintiles based on book-to-market ratios). The abnormal returns are then adjusted for the bias in the empirical distribution by subtracting the mean of the empirical distribution in each case from the abnormal return for the sample. The first number in parentheses is the significance level, i.e., the probability that a random portfolio from the empirical distribution computed through bootstrapping will have an abnormal return greater than the sample abnormal return. The second number is the standard t-statistic, computed using the crude dependence adjustment method using a 24-month holdout period, i.e., $-12 \ldots -36$ months. With 23 degrees of freedom, the absolute value of the 5% confidence level for the t-test is 2.07 and the 1% level is 2.81.

Bias-adjusted CARs for acquiring firms in mergers and tender offers (in %)

Period	Mergers		Tender offers	
	Only public targets ($N = 643$)	All mergers ($N = 2823$)	Only public targets ($N = 255$)	All tender offers ($N = 316$)
1–12	−1.39 (0.84, −2.94)	−1.76 (1.00, −6.39)	3.78 (0.02, 1.17)	3.95 (0.01, 1.34)
13–24	−2.80 (0.98, −3.58)	−2.72 (1.00, −7.09)	2.26 (0.10, 0.78)	1.90 (0.14, 0.59)
25–36	1.61 (0.09, −0.61)	−0.44 (0.25, −2.76)	2.53 (0.10, 0.67)	3.00 (0.04, 1.07)
1–36	−2.58 (0.90, −4.12)	−4.04 (1.00, −9.39)	8.56 (0.00, 1.51)	8.85 (0.00, 1.73)

and are bias-adjusted by subtracting the mean of the empirical distribution from the CAR for the sample. Acquiring firms underperform an equally weighted control portfolio with a similar size and book-to-market ratio by a statistically significant 4.04% and outperform the control portfolio in tender offers, earning a statistically significant positive bias-adjusted abnormal return of 8.85% over a period of three years after the completion of the acquisition. It is interesting to note that these bias-adjusted CAR values are broadly consistent with the abnormal returns reported by Mitchell and Stafford, who find that acquiring firms in mergers and tender offers underperform their benchmarks by a statistically significant 4% in the three years following the acquisition.

In addition, the magnitude of our *unadjusted* CARs, − 15.23% and 4.94% for acquiring firms in mergers and tender offers, respectively, is broadly consistent with Agrawal et al. (1992), who find that acquiring firms in mergers earn a statistically significant negative cumulative average abnormal return of − 13.85% in the 36 months following merger completion. They also report that abnormal returns for tender offers are small and insignificantly different from zero.

However, the statistical significance of our results is different from those reported by other studies, which do not use bootstrapping. The standard *t*-statistics appear to be negatively biased. Calculating these statistics using the crude dependence approach leads us to the same conclusions as those obtained by Agrawal, Jaffe, and Mandelker. Bootstrapping, however, reveals that bidders in tender offers earn highly significant positive abnormal returns, outperforming *all* 1000 pseudo-portfolios in our unrestricted sample and 997 portfolios in the public targets sample. Similarly, bidders in mergers underperform *all* 1,000 pseudo-portfolios in the unrestricted sample. The reason standard *t*-statistics are biased can be seen when examining the mean of the empirical distribution. The distribution is not centered at zero: the average firm in the pseudo-universe of firms that did not make acquisitions earned negative abnormal returns of − 11.2% in mergers and − 3.92% in tender offers.

3.2. Test of the performance extrapolation hypothesis

We sort all acquirors in our sample into equal subsamples of 'glamour', 'neutral', and 'value' firms by sorting on book-to-market ratio measured in the month of the acquisition announcement. Book value is taken from COMPUSTAT (annual data item number 60) for the previous fiscal year while market value is taken from CRSP and computed as the number of shares outstanding times the price at the end of the announcement month. If firms do not have a book-to-market value reported at the time of acquisition, to minimize the loss of data, we use the last six months before the announcement and take the last available value as the book-to-market ratio for the firm.

Table 3 reports some descriptive statistics for glamour, neutral, and value bidders. It follows a pattern similar to Table 1, showing the distribution of sizes

Table 3
Descriptive statistics for glamour, neutral, and value acquirors in mergers and tender offers for acquisitions announced and completed between January 1980 and December 1991

Panel A reports the distribution of size decile rankings of acquirors in mergers and tender offers for U.S. firms. Acquirors are classified as glamour, neutral, and value based on their book-to-market ratio at the announcement date. Acquirors are NYSE/AMEX and Nasdaq firms, covered by both COMPUSTAT and CRSP, listed on the SDC Mergers and Corporate Transactions on-line database, and announced and completed between January 1980 and December 1991. Each type of acquisition is listed for all targets irrespective of their public or private status. Size deciles are computed every month for all firms in the universe of NYSE/AMEX and Nasdaq stocks. Decile 1 is the smallest. Panel B reports the distribution of book-to-market decile rankings, where book-to-market deciles are similarly computed every month for all firms in the universe of NYSE/AMEX and Nasdaq stocks. Panel C reports the sizes of publicly listed targets relative to glamour, neutral, and value acquirors four weeks before the announcement date of the merger or tender offer.

Panel A: Size deciles of glamour, neutral, and value acquirors at the time of announcement of merger or tender offer

Size Decile	All mergers[a]			All tender offers[a]		
	Glamour	Neutral	Value	Glamour	Neutral	Value
1–2	38	15	58	2	0	5
3–4	100	56	87	3	1	6
5–6	149	145	154	12	7	9
7–8	251	240	279	27	33	35
9–10	394	503	353	61	46	49
Total	932	959	931	105	107	104
Average[b]	$11901	$1129	$788	$3544	$1700	$1396
(Median)	($234)	($339)	($172)	($751)	($719)	($233)

Panel B: Book to market deciles of glamour, neutral, and value acquirors at the time of announcement of merger or tender offer

B/M Decile	All mergers			All tender offers		
	Glamour	Neutral	Value	Glamour	Neutral	Value
1–2	549	8	0	27	0	0
3–4	381	357	3	66	6	0
5–6	2	533	150	17	67	15
7–8	0	62	456	0	34	45
9–10	0	0	322	0	0	44
Total	932	960	931	105	107	104
Average	0.222	0.574	4.607[c]	0.302	0.662	14.870[c]
(Median)	(0.247)	(0.576)	(1.066)	(0.349)	(0.677)	(1.118)

continued over

Table 3. Continued.

Panel C: Sizes of publicly listed targets relative to glamour, neutral, and value acquirors four weeks before the announcement date of the merger or tender offer

	Public target mergers[d]			Public target tender offers[d]		
	Glamour ($N = 80$)	Neutral ($N = 130$)	Value ($N = 110$)	Glamour ($N = 68$)	Neutral ($N = 66$)	Value ($N = 64$)
Average	0.25	0.19	1.22	0.29	0.41	5.40
Maximum	5.50	1.20	89.27	2.11	3.24	105.30
Minimum	0.00	0.00	0.00	0.00	0.00	0.01
Median	0.08	0.09	0.11	0.10	0.15	0.30

[a] Using the Wilcoxon rank-sum test, the null hypothesis that bidder sizes are distributed among the deciles in the same proportions for the three types of acquirors can be rejected at the 1% level for both mergers and tender offers. Glamour acquirors are larger on average than neutral or value acquirors.

[b] In millions of dollars.

[c] The book-to-market ratios of the value firms are marked by several extreme outliers, which affect the average.

[d] Using the median score test, the null hypothesis that the three types of acquirors have the same median ratio of relative size of target to bidder cannot be rejected at the 5% level for tender offers and at any reasonable level of significance for mergers.

and book-to-market ratios of the acquiring firms relative to the universe of firms listed on the NYSE, AMEX, and Nasdaq covered by both CRSP and COMPUSTAT. As in Table 1, Panel A ranks the firms into size deciles, with size deciles again measured on the basis of market equity value relative to the universe of all NYSE/AMEX and Nasdaq stocks covered by both CRSP and COMPUSTAT. We see that glamour acquirors are, on average, much larger than value acquirors. Panel B ranks the firms on the basis of their book-to-market ratios, with the book-to-market quintiles calculated as before, relative to the universe of all NYSE/AMEX and Nasdaq stocks covered by both CRSP and COMPUSTAT. As can be seen, by construction, glamour acquirors have book-to-market ratios much lower than value acquirors and also tend to rank in the lowest deciles of book-to-market ratio in comparison to the universe of NYSE/AMEX and Nasdaq stocks.

Panel C reports statistics on the target-acquiror size ratio. The median target-acquiror size ratio is between 8% and 11% for the three types of acquirors in mergers and varies between 10% and 30% for tender offers. We cannot reject the hypothesis that the median target-acquiror size ratio is constant across the three types of acquirors. The pattern for the exchange listings of the acquirors is broadly the same as before, with most of the acquirors listed on the NYSE.

3.2.1. *Results for the total sample*

Consistent with the performance extrapolation hypothesis, the three types of bidders exhibit a striking pattern in their long-term performance after the acquisition. Table 4, Panel A, shows that glamour bidders in mergers significantly underperform other glamour firms in the 36 months following the acquisition, earning negative bias-adjusted abnormal returns of − 17% on average in our unrestricted sample. Glamour bidders in tender offers earn statistically insignificant bias-adjusted abnormal returns of 4% in the three years after the acquisition. Panel C shows that value acquirors, on the other hand, outperform other firms with similar sizes and book-to-market ratios, earning statistically significant positive bias-adjusted abnormal returns of 15.5% for tender offers and 7.64% for mergers. The relation between book-to-market ratio and subsequent performance is relatively smooth, with neutral acquirors performing neither as badly as glamour acquirors nor as well as value acquirors.

The negative bias in the standard t-statistics is again visible in this table. The negative abnormal performance found using standard t-statistics is not always confirmed by the bootstrapping methodology, unless the value for the t-statistic is strongly negative. Similarly, when we find statistically significant positive abnormal returns for tender offers using bootstrapping, we do not find statistical significance using the traditional methodology.

We also calculate abnormal returns based on the Fama and French (1993) three-factor model. The results of these three-factor regressions carried out on the full sample are broadly similar. The alphas show the same pattern as our results using the BCAR approach. Value stocks, for example, have an alpha of 0.11% per month while glamour stocks, have an alpha of − 0.27% per month. None of the alphas is statistically significant at the 5% level, though the alpha for glamour firms is significant at the 10% level. However, the Fama–French three-factor approach requires some unreasonable assumptions, most notably that the regression estimates are constant over the estimation period. It also assumes that the firm's size, book-to-market, and market characteristics are stable over time, a rather implausible assumption, especially if bidders experience significant abnormal returns subsequent to an acquisition (see Fig. 1). In addition, Barber and Lyon (1997) find that the model yields negatively biased estimates at a 12-month horizon and positively biased estimates at a 36-month horizon.

3.2.2. *Robustness check*

The pattern observed in our results is remarkably robust. We check the performance of glamour, neutral, and value acquirors for a subsample of the public targets sample in which the size of the target is greater than 20% of the size of the acquiror. This gives us a sample size of 171 mergers and 111 tender

Table 4
Long-term performance for acquirors in mergers and tender offers, classifying acquirors as glamour, neutral, or value firms

Panel A reports abnormal returns (in percent) for glamour acquirors in mergers and tender offers, while Panel B reports the same statistics for neutral acquirors and Panel C for value acquirors. Acquirors are classified as value, neutral, or glamour on the basis of their book-to-market ratios at the time of announcement. Results are reported for two sets of targets: all targets, irrespective of their public or private status, and only public targets, listed on CRSP as well as COMPUSTAT. Abnormal returns are computed with reference to a size- and book-to-market-based benchmark portfolio. The abnormal returns are then adjusted for the bias in the empirical distribution by subtracting the mean of the empirical distribution in each case from the abnormal return for the sample. The first number in parentheses is the significance level, i.e., the probability that a random portfolio from the empirical distribution computed through bootstrapping will have an abnormal return greater than the sample abnormal return. The second number is the standard t-statistic, computed using the crude dependence adjustment method, using a 24-month holdout period, i.e., $-12 \ldots -36$ months. With 23 degrees of freedom, the absolute value of the 5% confidence level for the t-test is 2.07 and the 1% level is 2.81.

Panel A: Bias-adjusted CARs for glamour acquiring firms in mergers and tender offers (in %)

Period	Mergers		Tender offers	
	Only public targets ($N = 213$)	All mergers ($N = 932$)	Only public targets ($N = 85$)	All tender offers ($N = 105$)
1–12	− 5.55 (0.98, − 3.98)	− 6.25 (1.00, − 9.35)	3.06 (0.15, − 2.32)	2.12 (0.23, − 3.12)
13–24	− 5.37 (0.98, − 3.75)	− 7.97 (1.00, − 9.66)	3.25 (0.15, − 1.99)	2.67 (0.16, − 2.55)
25–36	0.10 (0.47, − 2.00)	− 3.03 (0.99, − 6.03)	− 1.38 (0.67, − 3.07)	− 0.53 (0.58, − 3.29)
1–36	− 10.82 (1.00, − 5.63)	− 17.26 (1.00, − 14.45)	4.92 (0.18, − 4.26)	4.25 (0.18, − 5.17)

Panel B: Bias-adjusted CARs for neutral acquiring firms in mergers and tender offers (in %)

Period	Mergers		Tender offers	
	Only public targets ($N = 218$)	All mergers ($N = 960$)	Only public targets ($N = 86$)	All tender offers ($N = 107$)
1–12	− 5.59 (1.00, − 4.16)	− 1.37 (0.92, − 6.28)	5.23 (0.02, 0.84)	4.14 (0.05, 0.73)
13–24	− 1.19 (0.72, − 2.05)	− 1.70 (0.97, − 5.90)	0.38 (0.45, − 0.11)	− 1.10 (0.70, − 0.67)
25–36	− 0.34 (0.55, − 1.39)	− 1.23 (0.91, − 4.79)	2.64 (0.15, 0.85)	1.76 (0.23, 0.39)
1–36	− 7.12 (0.99, − 4.39)	− 4.29 (1.00, − 9.80)	8.24 (0.03, 0.70)	4.79 (0.10, 0.26)

Table 4. Continued.

Panel C: Bias-adjusted CARs for value acquiring firms in mergers and tender offers (in %)

Period	Mergers		Tender offers	
	Only public targets ($N = 212$)	All mergers ($N = 931$)	Only public targets ($N = 84$)	All tender offers ($N = 104$)
1–12	5.58 (0.00, 4.70)	1.83 (0.04, 8.52)	2.54 (0.26, 3.38)	4.93 (0.04, 4.21)
13–24	– 1.06 (0.68, 1.74)	0.88 (0.20, 6.69)	2.22 (0.27, 3.02)	3.48 (0.12, 3.72)
25–36	5.36 (0.01, 4.18)	4.93 (0.00, 9.45)	5.07 (0.08, 3.35)	7.13 (0.01, 4.16)
1–36	9.87 (0.00, 6.13)	7.64 (0.00, 14.23)	9.81 (0.05, 5.63)	15.53 (0.00, 6.98)

The absolute value of the t-statistic to test the null hypothesis that there is no difference between size and book-to-market adjusted abnormal returns for glamour mergers vs. value mergers is 17.92 (p-value: 0.0001). For glamour tender offers vs value tender offers, the absolute value of the t-statistic is 7.06 (p-value: 0.0001).

offers. We obtain broadly similar results in this sample, with glamour acquirors earning a statistically significant negative bias-adjusted abnormal return of – 22.8% in mergers and a statistically significant positive return of 17.24% in tender offers. Value acquirors earn a statistically significant positive bias-adjusted abnormal return of 14.45% in mergers and 23.25% in tender offers.

Similarly, as noted earlier, we also exclude Nasdaq acquirors from our analysis to see if our results are robust to our methodology of excluding Nasdaq stocks from our pseudo-universe while bootstrapping. This does not change our results significantly. Glamour acquirors earn a statistically significant negative bias-adjusted abnormal return of – 6.47% in mergers and an insignificant – 1.92% in tender offers. Value acquirors earn a statistically significant positive bias-adjusted abnormal return of 6.1% in mergers and 8.8% in tender offers.

Lastly, over 50% of the mergers in our sample were announced between 1982–85, while over 50% of our tender offers were announced between 1986–89. Brav (1996) shows that the nonparametric bootstrap method, which ignores residual covariation in the returns, can lead to biased inferences in periods when there is a significant clustering of the events. We therefore repeat the analysis excluding the two merger wave and tender offer wave periods. Again, we obtain broadly the same results, with glamour acquirors earning a statistically significant negative bias-adjusted abnormal return of – 20.2% in mergers and an insignificant 9.87% in tender offers, while value acquirors earn a statistically significant positive bias-adjusted abnormal return of 4.88% in mergers and 18.51% in tender offers.

3.3. The means of payment vs. the performance extrapolation hypothesis

In order to test whether the findings in Table 4 can be explained by the means of payment used by the bidding firms, we investigate the methods of payment used by bidders in the tender offers and mergers in our sample. For each firm in our sample, we check if the total value of the transaction as reported by SDC is equal to the value paid through common shares or through cash. If so, we classify the merger as 100% stock- or 100% cash-financed respectively. Otherwise, the ratio of the amount of common financing to the total value of the deal is used to judge the degree of stock financing of the merger or tender offer. Because we are interested in investigating whether glamour bidders exploit their overvaluation by paying with (overvalued) shares, we treat other methods of compensation, such as the value paid through preferred shares or through some form of debt securities, as equivalent to cash. For simplicity, we refer to all these mergers as cash-financed. Table 5 summarizes the results of the nonparametric tests we use in testing our various hypotheses.

As can be seen, we can reject the initial hypothesis that mergers and tender offers are financed in the same way, even at the 1% level. Consistent with other results in the literature (see, for example, Travlos, 1987; Agrawal et al., 1992 pp. 1611–1612), we find that mergers are much more likely than tender offers to be paid for by shares – the average merger in our sample is over 50% paid for by shares, while only 7% of the value of the average tender offer is payment in stock.

3.3.1. Glamour, value, and the means of payment

We cannot reject the hypothesis that tender offers are identical in their payment method across glamour, value, and neutral acquirors, even at the 10% level. All three types of acquirors in tender offers use insignificantly different and small proportions of stock financing in their acquisitions. In mergers, on the other hand, glamour acquirors use stock to a significantly greater degree than value acquirors, with 54% stock financing for glamour acquirors on average as opposed to only 38% for value acquirors. This is also consistent with Martin (1996), who finds that mergers and tender offers paid for in stock tend to have much higher market-to-book ratios than cash-financed acquisitions.

To some extent, the combined results of Tables 2, 4 and 5 are consistent with the predictions of the means of payment hypothesis. First, bidders in mergers typically pay with shares, while in tender offers they pay with cash. Hence, as predicted by the means of payment hypothesis, the post-acquisition return is significantly negative in the merger sample, but significantly positive in the tender offer sample (Table 2). Second, glamour bidders in mergers pay more frequently with stock than do value bidders, which explains why glamour

Table 5
Nonparametric tests for differences in payment mechanisms across mergers and tender offers

This table reports Wilcoxon two-sample rank-sum z-scores (or the Kruskal-Wallis H-test χ^2 approximation for more than two samples) for comparing methods of financing of different combinations of merger and tender offers. The method of financing is computed using the value paid through common shares, VCOM, and the value of the transaction, VAL, reported in the SDC database. Acquirors are classified as value or glamour on the basis of their book-to-market ratios at the time of announcement.

Samples/analyzed	Mean proportion financed through stock (%)	Z (p-value)	χ^2 (p-value)
1. All tender offers ($N = 247$)	7.5	− 12.92	166.93
All mergers ($N = 971$)	50.7	(0.00)	(0.00)
2. *Public targets sample*:			
Glamour mergers ($N = 145$)	62.1		16
Neutral mergers ($N = 151$)	56.8		(0.00)
Value mergers ($N = 103$)	38.9		
3. *Public targets sample*:			
Glamour tenders ($N = 79$)	8.3		3.07
Neutral tenders ($N = 78$)	8.9		(0.22)
Value tenders ($N = 61$)	3.8		
4. *All targets sample*:			
Glamour mergers ($N = 336$)	54.5	− 4.08	16.64
Value mergers ($N = 212$)	37.6	(0.00)	(0.00)
5. *All targets sample*:			
Glamour tenders ($N = 92$)	11.0	− 1.60	2.56
Value tenders ($N = 59$)	3.9	(0.11)	(0.11)

bidders significantly underperform value bidders (Table 4, Panel A). However, the significant difference between value bidders and glamour bidders in tender offers cannot be explained by the means of payment hypothesis: although both bidder types typically pay with cash, glamour bidders perform significantly worse than value bidders (compare Panels A and C of Table 4).

To test further the relation between the method of payment and performance, we classify all firms in the unrestricted targets subsample into three groups on the basis of whether they were 100% stock-financed, 100% cash-financed, or financed using a mixture of stock and cash. For mergers, this gives us 409 cash-financed mergers, 332 stock-financed mergers, and 970 mixtures. For tender offers, the numbers are 217, 7, and 247, respectively. Owing to the lack of data on stock-financed tender offers, we do not analyze this subsample. We then classify the firms in each sample into glamour or value stocks based on their book-to-market ratio at the time of announcement.

Table 6 shows size and book-to-market adjusted BCARs for stock- and cash-financed mergers and cash-financed tender offers. The results for mixtures

Table 6
Long-term performance for acquirors in stock- or cash-financed mergers and tender offers, classifying acquirors as glamour or value firms

Panel A reports abnormal returns (in percent) for glamour and value acquirors in mergers which are 100% stock-financed, while Panel B reports the same statistics for tender offers and mergers which are 100% cash-financed. The method of financing is computed using the VCOM and VAL variables in the SDC database. Acquirors are classified as value or glamour on the basis of their book-to-market ratios at the time of announcement. Targets are all targets, whether public or private. Abnormal returns are computed with reference to a size- and book-to-market-based benchmark portfolio. The abnormal returns are then adjusted for the bias in the empirical distribution by subtracting the mean of the empirical distribution in each case from the abnormal return for the sample. The first number in parentheses is the significance level, i.e., the probability that a random portfolio from the empirical distribution computed through bootstrapping will have an abnormal return greater than the sample abnormal return. The second number is the standard t-statistic, computed using the crude dependence adjustment method, using a 24-month holdout period, i.e., − 12 ... − 36 months. With 23 degrees of freedom, the absolute value of the 5% confidence level for the t-test is 2.07 and the 1% level is 2.81.

Panel A: Bias-adjusted CARs for acquiring firms in 100% *stock-financed Mergers** (*in* %)

Period	Mergers	
	Glamour acquirors (N = 150)	Value acquirors (N = 150)
1–12	− 7.03 (0.99, − 4.53)	− 4.80 (0.98, − 1.30)
13–24	− 1.49 (0.68, − 3.30)	1.25 (0.32, 0.96)
25–36	5.49 (0.03, − 0.93)	2.19 (0.17, 1.19)
1–36	− 3.05 (0.73, − 5.06)	− 1.37 (0.63, 0.49)

Panel B: Bias-adjusted CARs for acquiring firms in 100% *cash-financed merger and tender offers* (*in* %)

Period	Mergers[a]		Tender offers[a]	
	Glamour (N = 187)	Value (N = 187)	Glamour (N = 100)	Value (N = 100)
1–12	− 1.25 (0.69, − 4.00)	3.97 (0.05, 2.63)	4.95 (0.03, − 1.21)	3.95 (0.10, 3.84)
13–24	− 9.45 (1.00, − 6.38)	0.61 (0.39, 1.50)	4.89 (0.04, − 0.86)	2.57 (0.20, 3.41)
25–36	− 0.81 (0.61, − 2.87)	7.12 (0.00, 3.37)	− 1.34 (0.68, − 2.42)	5.94 (0.04, 3.88)
1–36	− 11.51 (0.99, − 7.65)	11.69 (0.00, 4.33)	8.49 (0.04, − 2.59)	12.43 (0.01, 6.43)

*100% stock-financed tender offers are not analyzed as there were only seven such offers in the sample. The absolute value of the t-statistic to test the null hypothesis that there is no difference between size- and book-to-market-adjusted abnormal returns for glamour mergers vs. value mergers is 3.46 (p-value: 0.001).

[a]The absolute value of the t-statistic to test the null hypothesis that there is no difference between size and book-to-market adjusted abnormal returns for glamour mergers vs. value mergers is 8.27 (p-value: 0.0001). For glamour tender offers vs value tender offers, the absolute value of the t-statistic is 5.08 (p-value: 0.0001).

are similar and are not reported. As can be seen, glamour firms perform worse than value firms in every case, regardless of the payment method. In stock-financed mergers, value acquirors earn a statistically insignificant three-year positive abnormal return, while glamour acquirors earn a statistically insignificant three-year negative abnormal return. In the first 12 months after the merger completion, however, both value and glamour bidders earn statistically significant negative abnormal returns and the return to glamour acquirors (− 7%) is worse than the return to value acquirors (− 4.8%). In addition, we can reject the hypothesis that the three-year abnormal returns earned by value acquirors are identical to those earned by glamour acquirors. In cash-financed acquisitions, value acquirors far outperform glamour acquirors in both mergers and tender offers. Specifically, in cash-financed mergers, value acquirors earn significant positive three-year abnormal returns of 11.7%, in contrast to a significant negative three-year abnormal return of − 11.51% for glamour acquirors. We conclude that, while all results presented so far are consistent with the performance extrapolation hypothesis, many results are inconsistent with the hypothesis that the post-acquisition returns of bidders are simply driven by the method of payment.

We also investigate why the long-term abnormal returns for bidders in tender offers are higher than the returns to bidders in mergers by dividing a sample of 100% cash-financed mergers and tender offers into glamour, neutral, and value bidders depending on whether the book-to-market ratios of the bidders at the time of announcement was less than 0.47, between 0.47 and 0.73, and higher than 0.73, respectively (the cutoff points divide the sample roughly at the 33rd and the 67th percentile, respectively). Interestingly, even after controlling for both method of payment and the book-to-market ratio of the bidder, bidders in tender offers continue to perform better than bidders in mergers, with glamour bidders earning statistically significant negative bias-adjusted abnormal returns of − 9.9% in mergers and significant bias-adjusted positive abnormal returns of 10.9% in tender offers over the three years after the acquisition completion. Neutral bidders earn statistically insignificant three-year bias-adjusted abnormal returns of − 5.6% in mergers but strongly significant positive three-year bias-adjusted abnormal returns of 11.3% in tender offers. Value bidders in both mergers and tender offers earn significant positive three-year bias-adjusted abnormal returns of 15.5% and 9.6%, respectively. Why this difference in performance remains is a puzzle, which the data do not allow us to investigate in this paper. For example, as opposed to mergers, tender offers tend to be more hostile transactions. Perhaps this leads to more fundamental change in the target and consequently results in greater value creation after the acquisition.

3.3.2. Determinants of takeover premiums: glamour status or means of payment

According to the performance extrapolation hypothesis, glamour firms should pay higher takeover premiums than value firms. Indeed, managers of glamour firms will tend to overestimate their ability to create synergies in the target and should therefore be willing to pay more than managers of value firms. This should be particularly relevant in tender offers because there is typically more competition for the target. The means of payment hypothesis would predict that acquirors will pay higher premiums in acquisitions paid with shares than in acquisitions paid with cash. Indeed, if the bidder believes its shares are overvalued, it can afford to pay a higher 'apparent' premium in a stock-financed transaction, as the 'real' premium is much smaller. Moreover, if target shareholders are concerned about the bidders' opportunistic behavior, they may require a higher premium if the bidder chooses to pay with shares.

We therefore investigate the acquisition premiums paid by bidders in the tender offers and mergers in our sample. We measure the acquisition premium as the difference between the highest price paid per share in the transaction and the target share price four weeks before the announcement of the acquisition, as a percentage of the target share price four weeks before the announcement date. Table 7 consolidates the results of our tests of these hypotheses.

As can be seen from Table 7, there is no evidence in mergers as a whole that acquisition premiums differ across types of acquiror. In tender offers, however, we can reject at the 3% level the hypothesis that tender offers pay similar acquisition premiums. In tender offers, glamour bidders pay premiums of 66% on average, while value bidders pay premiums of only 47%. Tender offers tend to be cash-financed while mergers tend to be more stock-financed. To distinguish between our two main hypotheses, we divide our sample as before into 100% cash-financed and 100% stock-financed acquisitions. While glamour and value bidders in cash-financed mergers tend to pay similar acquisition premiums of around 52% for their targets, glamour bidders in stock-financed mergers tend to pay far higher acquisition premiums than value bidders, paying 58% as opposed to 37%. Our results for cash-financed tender offers remain similar.

The results for tender offers are consistent with the performance extrapolation hypothesis. Glamour firms pay significantly higher takeover premiums than value firms. However, the results for mergers are not consistent with this hypothesis: on average, the takeover premium is independent of the book-to-market ratio of the bidder. Only in 100% stock-financed acquisitions do glamour firms pay larger takeover premiums than value firms. Note, however, that the results are generally not consistent with the means of payment hypothesis: on average, bidders do not pay higher takeover premiums in stock-financed acquisitions than in acquisitions financed with cash.

3.4. Are glamour bidders myopic about EPS?

With their tendency towards high P/E ratios and stock financing of acquisitions, (the Pearson correlation coefficient between market-to-book ratio

Table 7
Nonparametric tests for differences in acquisition premiums across mergers and tender offers

This table reports Wilcoxon two-sample rank-sum z-scores (or the Kruskal-Wallis H-test χ^2 approximation for more than two samples) for comparing acquisition premiums for different combinations of merger and tender offers. Acquisition premiums are defined as the difference between the highest price paid per share and the target share price four weeks before the announcement date as a percentage of the target share price four weeks before the announcement date, measured by the PREM4WK variable in the SDC database. Acquirors are classified as value, neutral, or glamour on the basis of their book-to-market ratios at the time of announcement.

Samples analyzed	Mean (Median) acquisition premium (%)	Z (p-value)	χ^2 (p-value)
1. *Public targets sample*:			
Glamour mergers (N = 127)	52.36 (41.8)		0.122
Neutral mergers (N = 124)	51.74 (40.8)		(0.94)
Value mergers (N = 103)	51.69 (42.9)		
2. *Public targets sample*:			
Glamour tenders (N = 68)	66.29 (60.9)		6.90
Neutral tenders (N = 63)	53.70 (49.5)		(0.03)
Value tenders (N = 60)	47.16 (43.9)		
3. *Acquirors in 100% cash-financed mergers*:			
Glamour mergers (N = 47)	51.58 (39.5)	0.67	0.46
Value mergers (N = 38)	51.54 (42.0)	(0.50)	(0.50)
4. *Acquirors in 100% stock-financed mergers*:			
Glamour mergers (N = 50)	57.99 (53.2)	2.73	7.49
Value mergers (N = 51)	37.35 (28.8)	(0.01)	(0.01)
5. *Acquirors in 100% cash-financed tender offers*:			
Glamour tender offers (N = 76)	62.64 (60.75)	− 1.88	3.56
Value tender offers (N = 66)	49.63 (46.35)	(0.05)	(0.05)

and P/E ratio is 0.61 for tender offers and 0.47 for mergers), glamour acquirors seem most likely to exhibit an EPS fixation. A firm with a high P/E buying a company with a lower P/E ratio and financing the acquisition through shares may inflate its EPS. This will be easier for the firm's managers to justify and can cause them to overpay for an acquisition.

To test if this EPS myopia is also a determinant of glamour bidder underperformance, we use a subsample of our public targets sample with the criterion that the target is 100% owned by the bidder after the completion of the merger. This leaves us with 613 mergers. Results for tender offers are similar and are not reported. We then measure the impact on acquiror EPS for each transaction. To do this, we adopt a procedure similar to the procedure outlined by Lys and Vincent (1995).

Under generally accepted accounting principles (GAAP), acquirors can record business combinations in one of two ways: pooling of interests or purchase. The two methods differ in their treatment of intangible assets. The pooling method simply uses the book value of net assets of the target as the basis for the target. Under the purchase method, the difference between the market value paid for the target and the book value of net assets of the target is recorded as goodwill and has to be amortized over the life of the acquired assets. SEC permission to use the pooling of interests method rather than the purchase method depends on the structure of the transaction and the history of the two companies.

The *non-merger EPS* of the acquiror is defined as the EPS if the acquiror had not carried out the merger. It is computed as the net income in the year before the merger completion year divided by the last available value for number of shares outstanding for the acquiror between the announcement date and six months before the merger completion date. The reason for this definition is that if the bidder used its common shares as (part) payment for the acquisition, we rarely have data on exactly when and how many of these shares were first issued for the transaction, especially if the acquiror makes another acquisition in the same period.

If the pooling method is used in the merger, then the *merger EPS* is defined as the sum of the acquiror net income and the target net income in the last 12 months before the acquisition divided by the last available figure for the number of shares outstanding for the acquiror up to one month after the merger completion date. If the pooling method is not used, we subtract from the sum of the acquiror and target net incomes (above) the difference between the value of the transaction and the book value of net assets amortized over a period of ten years and then divide the result by the number of shares of the acquiror outstanding one month after the merger completion. This assumes that the entire difference between the transaction value and the book value of net assets is purchased goodwill. Inasmuch as we ignore the tax effects on depreciation of the target's assets, we underestimate the resulting change in EPS. If part of the transaction is financed either by borrowing or through an issue of debt securities, we assume that the entire non-common-stock portion of the payment is financed with debt at an interest rate of 8% and the tax rate is the tax actually paid by the company in the previous year. If the tax rate figure is missing, the federal statutory tax rate of 34% is assumed.

The growth in EPS (calculated as the difference between the merger EPS after the above adjustments and the non-merger EPS, normalized by the absolute value of the non-merger EPS) is taken as the *EPS impact* of the acquiror.

A high-EPS-impact merger would therefore be a merger with a large growth in the EPS of the acquiror as a result of the merger.[3]

Rejecting companies for lack of availability of data on the value of the transaction, the value paid for through shares, and the book value of net assets leads to a sample of 333 mergers. We divide these into low-, medium-, and high-EPS-impact categories, ranking on the EPS impact for the acquiror as computed above. Table 8 reports our results for our normal CAR analysis. As can be seen, the results do not support the EPS myopia hypothesis. All three types of companies earn statistically insignificant abnormal returns. Results for tender offers (not reported) are similar.

To check whether the high-EPS-impact mergers are in fact composed largely of high *P/E* companies buying companies with lower *P/E*s, an indicator that the high-EPS-impact mergers are perhaps partially motivated by EPS fixation, we examine the *P/E*s of the acquiring and acquired companies directly. These are reported in the footnotes to Table 8. In the range of the worst-performing companies, 19% of the bidders had, in fact, a *P/E* higher than the target while 22% of the bidders had a *P/E* smaller than the target *P/E*. For the best-performing companies, 30% of the companies had a *P/E* higher than the target *P/E*, while 22% of the companies had a lower *P/E* than that of their target. We also carry out a sign test on the differences between acquiror *P/E* and target *P/E* (reported in the footnotes). However, we are unable to reject the null hypothesis that acquiror *P/E* is on average no different from target *P/E*, for any of the merger types. Hence, our results do not support the EPS myopia hypothesis.

4. Conclusions

Using a methodology robust to the criticisms of the standard long-horizon event study methodology, we find that acquirors in mergers underperform in the three years after the acquisition while acquirors in tender offers earn a small but

---

[3] To illustrate these calculations, consider the takeover of Monolithic Memories Inc by Advanced Micro Devices Inc. announced on April 30, 1987 and completed on August 13, 1987. The value of the transaction was $441 million, entirely paid for through common shares and with the assumption of the options and warrants of the target by the acquiror. The net assets of the target were $236.8 million and the net income (latest 12 months) for Advanced Micro Devices and Monolithic Memories were − $95.87 and $12.7 million, respectively. Advanced Micro Devices had 57.159 million shares outstanding six months before the merger completion date and 77.300 million shares outstanding one month after the completion date. The non-merger EPS of Barnett is therefore − 1.677. Since this was not classified as a pooling-of-assets transaction, the difference between the value of the target and its net assets ($204.2) was amortized over ten years, which implies that the merger EPS is S1.34. Therefore, the EPS grew by 20.1% as a result of the merger and this is taken as the merger impact.

Table 8
Long-term performance for acquirors in mergers, classifying acquirors on the basis of the impact on their EPS due to the acquisition

This table reports abnormal returns (in percent) for acquirors in mergers that have the smallest growth in merger EPS as opposed to the EPS had the merger not taken place, mergers with intermediate EPS impact, and mergers with the highest growth in merger EPS as compared to the non-merger EPS. Targets are listed on CRSP as well as COMPUSTAT. Abnormal returns are computed with reference to a size- and book-to-market-based benchmark portfolio, and adjusted for the bias in the empirical distribution by subtracting the mean of the empirical distribution in each case from the abnormal return for the sample. The number in parentheses reports the significance level, i.e., the probability that a random portfolio from the empirical distribution computed through bootstrapping will have an abnormal return greater than the sample abnormal return. To facilitate the analysis, we assume that the acquisition takes place on December 31 of the year preceding the actual completion date of the merger (because after the merger only consolidated financial statements are issued and it is impossible to construct separate financials for each company in the year); if the pooling method is not used, we assume that the excess of the value paid for the transaction (VAL) over the net assets of the target (NETASS) is amortized over ten years; if debt securities or borrowings are used to finance the acquisition, we assume that the non-common stock portion of the compensation (VAL-VCOM) is financed through debt at an interest rate of 8%. We use the tax rate actually paid by the company for the previous year if available; otherwise, the federal statutory tax rate of 34% is used. Footnotes to the table give details on the P/E ratios of the bidder and target and the results of a sign test under the null hypothesis that there is no difference in the two. The significance level in the test reports the probability of a greater absolute value for the sign statistic under the null hypothesis of no difference.

Bias-adjusted CARs for acquiring firms in mergers (in %)

Period	Low EPS impact ($N = 110$)[a]	Medium EPS impact ($N = 114$)[b]	High EPS impact ($N = 109$)[c]
1–12	– 2.97 (0.78)	– 2.22 (0.81)	0.19 (0.44)
12–24	– 4.92 (0.92)	0.31 (0.45)	0.15 (0.46)
24–36	2.02 (0.25)	– 1.67 (0.25)	1.15 (0.34)
1–36	– 5.88 (0.85)	– 0.24 (0.53)	1.50 (0.35)

[a] Sample size: 110 firms, of which 21(19%) had an acquiror P/E greater than the target's P/E four weeks before the date of announcement and 24 (22%) had an acquiror P/E less than the target's P/E four weeks before the date of announcement. For 65 firms there is no information on one or both of the acquiror or target P/Es four weeks before the announcement date. Sign Test: M(Sign): – 1.5 Significance level: 75%

[b] Sample size: 114 firms, of which 30 (26%) had an acquiror P/E greater than the target's P/E four weeks before the date of announcement and 27 (24%) had an acquiror P/E less than the target's P/E four weeks before the date of announcement. For 57 firms there is no information on one or both of the acquiror or target P/Es four weeks before the announcement date. Sign Test: M(Sign): 0.5 Significance level: 100%

[c] Sample size: 109 firms, of which 33 (30%) had an acquiror P/E greater than the target's P/E four weeks before the date of announcement and 24 (22%) had an acquiror P/E less than the target's P/E four weeks before the date of announcement. For 52 firms there is no information on one or both of the acquiror or target P/Es four weeks before the announcement date. Sign Test: M(Sign): 5.5 Significance level: 17%.

statistically significant positive abnormal return. However, the long-term underperformance of acquiring firms in mergers is not uniform across firms. It is predominantly caused by the poor post-acquisition performance of low book-to-market 'glamour' acquirors, who perform much worse than other glamour stocks and earn significant negative bias-adjusted abnormal returns of − 17% in mergers. This conclusion is independent of the method of payment. Specifically, in contrast to value bidders, glamour bidders in both 100% cash-financed and 100% equity-financed mergers significantly underperform after the merger. The fact that glamour bidders in tender offers perform significantly worse than value bidders suggests that companies with low book-to-market ratios tend to make relatively poor acquisition decisions, in general. Our results are also very robust. They hold up when we exclude smaller acquisitions, Nasdaq bidders, or periods when events are clustered.

We argue that these findings are consistent with the hypothesis that the market overextrapolates the past performance of the bidder management when it assesses the benefits of an acquisition decision. As a result, the market, as well as the management, the board of directors and large shareholders overestimate the ability of the glamour bidder to manage other companies. At the same time, the market tends to be too pessimistic about the managerial capacities of bidders with poor past performance (value firms). Unlike in glamour firms, bidder managers are not affected by hubris and are likely to face tougher scrutiny from directors and large shareholders before they are allowed to engage in an acquisition. This performance extrapolation hypothesis is also consistent with the fact that in the short run, stock prices of glamour bidders increase much more than stock prices of value bidders around the announcement of the acquisition (Lang et al., 1989; Servaes, 1991). It is also consistent with the results of Hayward and Hambrick (1995), who report that takeover premiums are positively correlated with proxies for past managerial performance such as recent organizational success and media praise for the CEO. In some ways, the market fails to understand that past managerial performance is not necessarily a good indicator of future performance, at least in the case of acquisitions.

Although, glamour bidders in mergers exhibit a much stronger tendency than value bidders to finance their acquisitions by issuing shares, one cannot explain the results of this paper by the hypothesis that glamour firms 'time' their acquisitions by paying with overvalued shares. The means of payment hypothesis cannot explain (1) why, both in mergers and tender offers, glamour acquirors perform worse than value acquirors, even when they pay for their acquisitions with cash, (2) why, in tender offers and in 100% equity-financed mergers, glamour bidders tend to pay higher takeover premiums than value bidders, and (3) why, in general, bid premiums are uncorrelated with the method of financing. Moreover, because post-acquisition returns are uncorrelated with the short-term impact on earnings per share, one cannot simply explain the results by earnings per share myopia. So we conclude that, although the three hypotheses are not mutually exclusive, the performance extrapolation hypothesis is more consistent with the data than either of the others.

The paper also adds to a growing body of evidence that short-term measurements of abnormal performance do not capture the full effects of the market reaction to an event, a common assumption in many event studies. Examples of such delayed reactions occur with share repurchases, IPOs, SEOs, proxy contests, etc. Ritter (1991) for example, finds poor long-term stock performance following initial public offerings. Loughran and Ritter (1997) and Spiess and Affleck-Graves (1995) find similar underperformance for seasoned equity offerings. Dharan and Ikenberry (1995) find that firms switching stock exchanges subsequently underperform. Ikenberry et al. (1995) find that value stocks announcing open market share repurchases outperform other value stocks in the four years following the announcement. Concerns about the appropriateness of short-term measurements of abnormal performance are justified. Hence, future research must explain why market participants systematically tend to react sluggishly to corporate financial and strategic decisions. This paper also offers some evidence that standard long-horizon *t*-statistics are biased, detecting abnormal performance when none is present and failing to detect abnormal performance when it is present. Such tests should be used with caution.

References

Agrawal, A., Jaffe, J.F., Mandelker, G.N., 1992. The post-merger performance of acquiring firms: a re-examination of an anomaly. Journal of Finance 47, 1605–1621.

Asquith, P., 1983. Merger bids, uncertainty and stockholder returns. Journal of Financial Economics 11, 51–83.

Barber, B.M., Lyon, J.D., 1997. Detecting long-run abnormal stock returns: the empirical power and specification of test statistics. Journal of Financial Economics 43, 341–372.

Barber, B.M., Lyon, J.D., Tsai, C.-L., 1998. Improved methods for tests of long-run abnormal stock returns. Journal of Finance, forthcoming.

Barber, B.M., Palmer, D.A., Wallace, J., 1995. Determinants of conglomerate and predatory acquisitions: evidence from the 1960's. Journal of Corporate Finance 1, 283–318.

Bradley, M., Jarrell, G., 1988. Comment. In: Coffee, J., Lowenstein, L., Rose-Ackerman, S. (Eds.), Knights, Raiders and Targets. Oxford University Press, Oxford, UK, pp. 252–259.

Brav, A., 1996. Inference in long-horizon event studies: a parametric bootstrap approach with application to initial public offerings. Unpublished working paper, University of Chicago, Chicago, IL.

Brealey, R.A., Myers, S.C., 1996. Principles of Corporate Finance. McGraw-Hill, New York.

Brown, S.J., Warner, J.B., 1980. Measuring security price performance. Journal of Financial Economics 8, 205–258.

Chan, L.K.C., Jegadeesh, N., Lakonishok, J., 1996. Momentum strategies. Journal of Finance 51, 1681–1714.

Dharan, B.G., Ikenberry, D., 1995. The long run negative drift of post-listing stock returns. Journal of Finance 50, 1547–1574.

Fama, E.F., French, K.R., 1992. The cross-section of expected stock returns. Journal of Finance 47, 427–465.

Fama, E.F., French, K.R., 1993. Common risk factors in the returns on stocks and bonds. Journal of Financial Economics 33, 3–56.
Franks, J., Harris, R., Titman, S., 1991. The postmerger share-price performance of acquiring firms. Journal of Financial Economics 29, 81–96.
Hayward, M.L.A., Hambrick, D.C., 1995. Explaining premiums paid for large acquisitions: evidence of CEO hubris. Unpublished working paper, Columbia University, New York, NY.
Ikenberry, D., Lakonishok, J., Vermaelen, T., 1995. Market underreaction to open market share repurchases. Journal of Financial Economics 39, 181–208.
Jensen, M.C., Ruback, R.S., 1983. The market for corporate control: the scientific evidence. Journal of Financial Economics 11, 5–50.
Kothari, S.P., Warner, J.B., 1997. Measuring long-horizon security price performance. Journal of Financial Economics 43, 301–339.
Lakonishok, J., Shleifer, A., Vishny, R.W., 1994. Contrarian investment, extrapolation, and risk. Journal of Finance 49, 1541–1578.
Lang, L., Stulz, R., Walkling, R., 1989. Managerial performance, Tobin's Q and the gains from successful tender offers. Journal of Financial Economics 24, 137–154.
Langetieg, T.C., 1978. An application of a three-factor performance index to measure stockholder gains from merger. Journal of Financial Economics 6, 365–383.
Loderer, C., Martin, K., 1992. Postacquisition performance of acquiring firms. Financial Management 19, 69–79.
Loughran, T., 1993. NYSE vs NASDAQ returns: market microstructure or the poor performance of initial public offerings? Journal of Financial Economics 33, 241–260.
Loughran, T., Ritter, J.R., 1997. The operating performance of firms conducting seasoned equity offerings. Journal of Finance 52, 1823–1850.
Loughran, T., Vijh, A.M., 1997. Do long-term shareholders benefit from corporate acquisitions? Journal of Finance 52, 1765–1790.
Lys, T., Vincent, L., 1995. An analysis of value destruction in AT&T's acquisition of NCR. Journal of Financial Economics 39, 353–378.
Martin, K.J., 1996. The method of payment in corporate acquisitions, investment opportunities, and management ownership. Journal of Finance 51, 1227–1246.
Mitchell, M.L., Stafford, E., 1997. Managerial decisions and long-term stock performance. Unpublished working paper CRSP WP 453, University of Chicago, Chicago, IL.
Ritter, J.R., 1991. The long-run performance of initial public offerings. Journal of Finance 46, 3–27.
Roll, R., 1986. The hubris hypothesis of corporate takeovers. Journal of Business 59, 197–216.
Servaes, H., 1991. Tobin's Q and the gains from takeovers. Journal of Finance 46, 409–419.
Spiess, D.K., Affleck-Graves, J., 1995. Underperformance in long-run stock returns following seasoned equity offerings. Journal of Financial Economics 38, 243–268.
Travlos, N.G., 1987. Corporate takeover bids, methods of payment and bidding firms' stock returns. Journal of Finance 42, 943–963.

[14]

ELSEVIER Journal of Financial Economics 37 (1995) 421–441

JOURNAL OF Financial ECONOMICS

Does the market react differently to domestic and foreign takeover announcements? Evidence from the U.S. chemical and retail industries

Kathryn L. Dewenter

University of Washington, Seattle, WA 98195, USA

(Received August 1993; final version received May 1994)

Abstract

This paper examines shareholder wealth gains from domestic and foreign takeover announcements in the U.S. chemical and retail industries. Contrary to results in several recent papers, these data indicate there is no significant difference in within industry mean takeover premia levels. There is evidence, though, that the sensitivity of takeover premia levels to standard transaction characteristics does differ across buyers: Foreign investors do pay more than domestic investors in hostile transactions, but pay less when there are rival bidders. The results indicate the market's reaction to buyer nationality is closely tied to the transaction's characteristics.

Key words: Takeover premia; Foreign acquisitions
JEL classification: G34

1. Motivation

Recently, several empirical papers have compared target shareholder wealth gains in domestic and foreign takeovers. See Kang (1993), Swenson (1993), Harris and Ravenscraft (1991), Cebenoyan, Papaioannou, and Travlos (1992), Marr, Mohta, and Spivey (1991). The results of these papers provide insight into both the domestic takeover literature and the foreign direct investment (FDI)

This paper is based on the third chapter of my dissertation. I appreciate helpful comments from John Huizinga (my chairman), Wayne Ferson, Steve Kaplan, seminar participants at University of Chicago and University of Washington, Mark Wolfson and Carl Kester (the referees), and Michael Jensen (the editor).

0304-405X/95/$09.50
SSDI 0304405X9400795 3

literature. For example, Cebenoyan et al. (1992) show that target shareholder wealth gains are higher in the industries with the highest levels of FDI, consistent with domestic evidence on rival bidders (see Bradley, Desai, and Kim, 1988). Harris and Ravenscraft (1991) and Swenson (1993) show that takeover premia levels in foreign acquisitions are sensitive to the exchange rate, consistent with imperfect capital markets explanations of FDI (see Froot and Stein, 1991).

All of these papers employ a similar approach. They compare abnormal returns to shareholders of takeover targets in a cross-sectional regression, controlling for factors from both the domestic and FDI literature that may affect returns. All of these studies find that the mean takeover premia paid by foreign investors are significantly higher than those paid by domestic investors. Evidence to explain only part of the difference has been found in exchange rates (Harris and Ravenscraft, 1991; Swenson, 1993), the intensity or level of foreign investment (Cebenoyan et al., 1992), bidder and transaction characteristics (Kang, 1993), and target relatedness (Marr et al., 1991).

This paper has the same goal, to examine shareholder wealth gains in domestic and foreign takeovers. I use a different approach, however, that provides different results. Rather than base the analysis on a sample of takeovers from all industries, I compare shareholder wealth gains within an industry. Rather than focus on mean takeover premia conditional on several explanatory variables, I focus on the explanatory variables themselves, testing whether or not the sensitivity of takeover premia to those variables differs between domestic and foreign buyers. For example, I look to see if the presence of rival bidders affects takeover premia in the same manner for both domestic and foreign buyers.

Studies that use target takeover premia to compare the marginal value added of different bidder groups assume that the fixed window measure of abnormal returns to target shareholders reflects the same information for each of the bidder groups. More specifically, they assume that the ex ante probability of acquisition as of the window's opening day, the impact of the acquisition announcement on the probability of deal completion, and the distribution of marginal value added between the bidder and target do not systematically differ across the groups of interest. If all of these assumptions hold, then the observed differences in target abnormal returns should reflect different adjustments to the distribution of expected gains. I do not address these assumptions in this paper. Instead, my focus is on the empirical issue of whether or not target shareholder wealth gains differ across buyer groups. This paper provides evidence on the robustness of prior test results, not on the validity of their premise that target shareholder wealth gains is an appropriate measure of marginal value added.

The paper's major finding is that within the two industries studied here there is no evidence that foreign mean takeover premia are higher than domestic mean takeover premia. This result contradicts the findings of all five papers cited above. The primary explanation for the different result is in the aggregation process. The other papers aggregate transactions across multiple industries. If takeover premia levels vary by industry, and if the domestic and foreign transaction samples are not evenly distributed across industries, aggregation might indicate higher average premia for one set of buyers. The tests in this paper show that within industry mean takeover premia levels, unconditional or conditional on standard transaction characteristics such as hostile and rival bidders, are insignificantly different.

The second finding is that the sensitivity of takeover premia levels to standard transaction characteristics does differ across buyers: Foreign investors do pay more than domestic investors in hostile transactions, but pay less when there are rival bidders. No prior paper has simultaneously tested for differences across all of these variables. These results indicate that the market's reaction to buyer nationality is closely tied to the transaction characteristics.

The final set of results concerns explanatory variables often mentioned in the FDI literature. I confirm results in Kang (1993) and Harris and Ravenscraft (1991) that the two U.S. tax changes in the 1980s provide no explanatory power for the difference in domestic and foreign takeover premia levels. Unlike results in other papers (see Kang, 1993; Harris and Ravenscraft, 1992; Swenson, 1993) these takeover premia show no significant exchange rate elasticity.

The paper proceeds as follows. Section 2 explains the approach used in these tests. Section 3 describes the sample set and provides summary statistics. The test results are covered in Section 4. Section 5 reviews what we have learned from these tests and discusses some possible next steps.

2. Literature review and empirical approach

If the goal is to gain insight into the domestic takeover and/or FDI literature through a comparison of domestic and foreign takeover premia, then the ideal model specification would be

$$Takeover\ premia = \sum_{\substack{i=buyer\\country}} \sum_{\substack{j=target\\industry}} \beta_{ij} + \sum_{\substack{i=buyer\\country}} \sum_{\substack{j=target\\industry}} \sum_{\substack{z=expl.var.\\index}} \alpha_{ijz} x_z \,. \quad (1)$$

This specifications allows both the intercept (β's) and slope (α's) coefficients to vary by buyer country and target industry.

The FDI literature provides several possible reasons why the attractiveness of U.S. targets may vary by investor country. Hymer (1960) argues that foreign investors are at a cost disadvantage relative to domestic investors. Two key components of this disadvantage, cultural differences and geographic distance, vary by country. This suggests investors from countries such as Canada and the U.K. may face lower cost barriers than investors from Japan or Spain. Aliber (1970, 1983) looks at 'separable currency areas' and argues that investors from strong currency areas enjoy a distinct funding or financial advantage. Neither of these theories explicitly links their arguments to target takeover premia.

Both the domestic and FDI literature indicate the level of shareholder wealth gains could vary across industries. For example, industries undergoing rapid change, with high acquisition activity, might have higher levels of gains due to higher numbers of potential bidders. See James and Weir (1987) for evidence from the banking industry. Jensen's (1986) free cash flow model suggests that free cash flow opportunities may vary by industry. He points to oil, forest, food, and pharmaceutical companies as likely candidates for excess cash flow. The FDI literature (Hymer, 1960; Dunning, 1988) argues that a firm's ability to compete profitably in a foreign country depends on its market power, which varies systematically across industries. This view is supported by noting that foreign investment flows are concentrated in industries with relatively high levels of R&D and advertising, two proxies for market power. It seems reasonable to assume that the opportunities and threats that drive acquisition activity are not uniformly distributed across industries.

In addition, the sensitivity of shareholder wealth gains to certain factors may vary across industries. Cushman (1985) argues that the effect of exchange rate changes on foreign investors depends on the configuration of their costs and revenues.[1] Revenga (1992) shows that the terms of trade impact of the dollar's movements in the 1980s varied considerably across industries. The impact of tax changes should also differ across industries. Swenson (1989) shows that, over the 1979–87 period, average taxes paid by industry varied from 5.8% in banking to 38.2% in food and allied products. (The standard deviation of taxes paid also varies widely across industries.) Looking within an industry controls for the differential inter-industry impact of these and other factors.

Numerous explanatory variables could be used in this 'ideal' specification. Jensen and Ruback's (1983) and Jarrell, Brickley, and Netter's (1988) reviews of the domestic literature on the market for corporate control indicate that the most consistently powerful explanatory variables are method of payment, level of competition, and hostile or delaying actions by management. Other variables that might affect the level of takeover premia, discussed in these two summary papers, are federal and state regulations that affect the bidding environment, taxes, certain defensive strategies, such as super majority amendments and poison pills, and block shareholdings by institutions or insiders.

The FDI literature suggests finance variables such as the exchange rate (Froot and Stein, 1991) and taxes (Scholes and Wolfson, 1990) might help explain takeover premia levels. It also indicates industrial organization variables such as buyer and target R&D and advertising may provide some explanatory power (Hymer, 1960; Swenson, 1993).

[1]Cushman also discusses the role of exchange rate expectations.

While the above specification may be ideal, it is clearly not practical. There are only approximately 600 foreign acquisitions over the 1975–89 period for which takeover premia data are available. As a result, I must do a constrained estimation. I select the model constraints based on two criteria: First, I focus on those variables and relationships that the theory or empirical evidence suggests will have the greatest impact on takeover premia. Second, I only include variables that are available for all transactions. As a first step, these tests are constructed to identify the basic differences in how the market reacts to domestic versus foreign takeover announcements.

To begin, I distinguish only between domestic versus foreign transactions. There are not enough observations within industries to break out more than one or two foreign countries. Also, as noted above, most FDI theories that focus on country differences do not have a direct link to takeover premia. In the one case where there is a direct link (taxes), I do separate foreign countries into different tax policy groups for the tests. (Preliminary tests on these data indicate that takeover premia levels may vary by country, but the pattern varies across industries. For example, the British appear to pay the highest average takeover premia for chemical targets, while the Canadians pay the highest for retail targets. This suggests that country differences do not confer systematic benefits or disadvantages to their investors.)

I look at results for two industries: chemical and retail. These two industries comprise a significant portion of overall (16%) and foreign (17%) acquisition activity.[2] Chemical and retail targets are also more easily identified than those in, for example, machinery or business services. Chemical and retail also provide an opportunity to compare results for a manufacturing and a service industry. To the extent that these two industries represent unique configurations of characteristics and trends, the results cannot be generalized. I will return to this issue in the conclusion.

The explanatory variables are restricted to the transaction characteristics: hostile, equity, and rival bidders. Hostile is a binary variable equal to one in transactions where management or shareholders take any steps to delay or stop the takeover. Huang and Walkling (1987) show that resisted offers are associated with insignificantly higher returns than unresisted offers. Jarrell (1985) shows that target litigation against hostile suitors results in additional excess returns to shareholders in successful auction-style takeovers. Equity is a binary variable equal to one in transactions where the buyer's equity is used for all or part of the purchase. Huang and Walkling (1987) show that abnormal returns are significantly higher for cash offers than for stock offers. Rival bidders is a binary variable equal to one in transactions where one or more rival bidders

[2]The source for overall merger activity is the W.T. Grimm Mergerstat Review, 1981–89; for foreign activity is my data set on foreign acquisitions in the U.S., over 1978–89.

are explicitly mentioned in the press. Bradley, Desai, and Kim (1988) show that competition among bidding firms increases returns to targets.

One variable from the domestic takeover literature that I do not control for is tender offers. Huang and Walkling (1987) and Franks, Harris, and Mayer (1988) show that once the method of payment and degree of resistance are controlled for, the distinction between tender offers and mergers is uninformative.[3]

Other domestic literature variables not controlled for are target equity owned by management or other block shareholders, the form of management compensation, or defense mechanisms such as poison pills. These data are not readily available, and I have no evidence they vary systematically across domestic and foreign targets.

I also include the two explanatory variables that have received the most attention in recent FDI literature: exchange rates and taxes. Froot and Stein (1991) build an imperfect capital markets model that indicates that lower (real) values of the dollar should raise the level of foreign acquisition bids. A lower value of the dollar increases the U.S. dollar value of a foreign investor's assets or wealth. Credit-constrained foreign investors can use this higher wealth to raise their (constrained) acquisition bids closer to the U.S. target's expected net present value.

Scholes and Wolfson (1990) argue that due to the asymmetric effect of implicit and explicit taxes on domestic versus foreign investors, the 1981 and 1986 tax reforms should have altered the relative attractiveness of U.S. investments to these two groups. They note the 1981 Economic Recovery Tax Act (ERTA) encouraged domestic mergers through such measures as accelerated depreciation schedules and investment tax credits. The Tax Reform Act (TRA) of 1986 discouraged domestic mergers through less generous depreciation schedules, elimination of investment tax credits, and higher corporate and personal capital gains tax. According to their argument, the relative position of foreign investors was harmed by ERTA in 1981 and helped by the 1986 TRA. They note that (p. S156) 'fewer assets will bear *implicit* taxes under the 1986 act. Since more taxes will be explicit, the before-tax rates of return on U.S. investment should increase. Given the increase in explicit taxes, this does not make investment to U.S. investors more attractive, but it does make investment to high-tax non-U.S. investors more attractive. For a highly taxed foreign investor, most explicit taxes paid in the United States will be fully refunded upon repatriation of U.S. earnings (through foreign tax credit mechanisms), whereas implicit taxes are

[3]With these data, tender offers have no explanatory power for the level of domestic or foreign target takeover premia in the chemical industry. In the retail industry, domestic target takeover premia levels are positively related to the existence of a tender offer, while takeover premia for foreign targets exhibit no significant links to tender offers. The explanatory power of other variables is not significantly affected when tender offers are controlled for in either industry.

often only tax deductible but not creditable against taxes paid in the home country.'

The primary omission from the FDI literature is buyer and target characteristics. My preliminary research here has shown that while the distribution of these variables (e.g., target market share and R&D levels) does vary across the domestic and foreign transactions, the variables have no significant explanatory power for differences between domestic and foreign takeover premia. These findings are consistent with results in Harris and Ravenscraft (1991), who look at target industry R&D and selling expenses, and Swenson (1993), who looks at (target/industry) intangibles. Neither of these papers can show that the sensitivity of takeover premia to these variables differs between domestic and foreign buyers.

One factor that is often suggested as a potential cause of differences in domestic and foreign takeover premia levels is national differences in goodwill policies. Preliminary work with these data suggests that the pattern of takeover premia across countries does *not* conform to the differences in goodwill policies. The data do not show that investors from countries with immediate write-off or tax deductibility of goodwill expenses systematically pay higher takeover premia than investors from countries which require amortization of goodwill against reported earnings, or where investors are not allowed to deduct goodwill expenses for tax purposes.

As a result of the above constraints, I estimate Eq. (1) by breaking out domestic and foreign [for buyer countries (i)] and chemical and retail [for target industries (j)]. The explanatory variables (x_z) are hostile, equity, rival bidder, FX, and tax regimes.

3. Data sources and summary statistics

The source for the domestic acquisitions of U.S. targets is Mergers & Acquisitions Journal of Corporate Venture magazine acquisition rosters, M&A. The sources for foreign acquisitions of U.S. targets are the M&A rosters, the W.T. Grimm Mergerstat Review, Commerce Department FDI in the U.S. Transactions Lists, and Japan's Expanding U.S. Manufacturing Presence (1988) from the Japan Economic Institute. These additional sources for foreign transactions are used because the M&A rosters, particularly in the early years, do not capture all foreign transactions (see Dewenter, 1991). Approximately 19% of the foreign transactions (12% of the value) are from the non-M&A sources.

These transaction sources provide the target and buyer names, locations, major product lines, and transaction details such as value and ownership interest acquired. Announcement dates are found in the Wall Street Journal Index or, if no reference is given there, in F&S Predicasts.

From these sources, all transactions that fit the following criteria are included in the tests:

- Transaction is announced and completed within 1978–89.
- Target produces chemicals (SIC code 2800–2899) or has retail operations (SIC code 5000–5999).
- Buyer acquires at least 20% equity interest; transaction value, when announced, is at least $1 million.
- Target is listed on NYSE, AMEX, or NASDAQ over a sufficient period to calculate abnormal returns (see below).

The above sources and restrictions yield a total of 116 chemical (81 domestic and 35 foreign) and 268 retail (213 domestic and 55 foreign) acquisitions. One chemical transaction was deleted because an unfavorable government ruling on one of its major products was announced the same week as the takeover announcement. An additional screen, three years of target data on Compustat, was also employed to allow tests of the impact of target characteristics, such as R&D levels, on takeover premia. None of these tests is included in this paper.

Table 1 has a breakdown of these chemical and retail acquisitions over time. Both industries experienced increases in activity in the mid 1980s. This parallels overall merger and acquisition activity in the U.S.

Table 1
Distribution of U.S. acquisition targets over 1978–89, separated by domestic and foreign acquirers

The sample includes acquisitions of chemical (SIC code 2800–2899) and retail (SIC code 5000–5999) targets for which CRSP cumulative abnormal return data are available. Transactions are sorted by announcement date.

	Chemical targets		Retail targets	
Year	Domestic acquirer	Foreign acquirer	Domestic acquirer	Foreign acquirer
1978	13	1	15	4
1979	10	2	22	5
1980	6	1	14	5
1981	6	4	17	7
1982	6	5	21	5
1983	4	0	10	0
1984	4	2	17	7
1985	10	5	22	5
1986	4	4	19	7
1987	3	2	25	1
1988	7	2	18	8
1989	8	7	13	1
Total transactions	81	35	213	55

I use cumulative abnormal returns (CAR) to measure takeover premia:

$$R_{it} = \alpha_i + \beta_i R_{mt} + \varepsilon_{it}$$

$$= \text{daily stock return for company } i,$$

$$\mathrm{E}(R_{it}) = \hat{\alpha}_i + \hat{\beta}_i R_{mt}$$

$$= \text{expected daily stock return for company } i,$$

$$AR_{it} = R_{it} - \mathrm{E}(R_{it}) = R_{it} - \hat{\alpha}_i - \hat{\beta}_i R_{mt}$$

$$= \text{daily abnormal, or excess return for company } i,$$

$$(t = 0) = \text{takeover announcement date}\,,$$

and

$$CAR_i = \sum_{t=-20}^{+10} AR_{it} = \sum_{t=-20}^{+10} R_{it} - \hat{\alpha}_i - \hat{\beta}_i R_{mt}\,. \tag{2}$$

This measure uses the standard market model to compute abnormal returns over a window around the announcement date. Expected returns are based on stock performance over a 250-day window prior to takeover announcement. Tests were conducted with both a 'large' 31-day (− 20, 10) and 'small' 5-day (− 3, 1) fixed window. Only the large window results are reported, with any significant differences noted. Throughout the paper, I use the terms 'cumulative abnormal returns', 'takeover premia', and 'shareholder wealth gain' interchangeably.

Brown and Warner (1980, 1985) show that variations of this measure have minimal impact on event study findings of this type. In addition to the two fixed-window takeover premia measures above, I have conducted the tests in this paper with two other measures: variable window and share price paid. The variable window measure cumulates abnormal returns from 20 days prior to announcement date up to the deal closing or effective date. The share price paid measure equals [(actual share price paid *minus* listed share price) *divided by* listed share price *minus* expected returns]. This measure is only available for about 2/3 of the transactions. Test results using these two alternative measures are consistent with those reported in the tests that follow. None of the measures reject equality of domestic and foreign takeover premia levels.

The top half of Table 2 shows how the three transaction variables are distributed across domestic and foreign transactions. Significantly more domestic acquirers use equity: 28.4% of domestic chemical acquirers compared to 5.7% of the foreign chemical acquirers; and 20.2% of the domestic retail acquirers compared to 1.8% of the foreign acquirers. There is no significant difference in the incidence of hostile and rival bidders across domestic and foreign acquisitions.

Table 2
Transaction characteristics and cumulative abnormal returns (*CAR*)

Sample includes acquisitions of U.S. chemical (SIC code 2800–2899) and retail (SIC code 5000–5999) targets over 1978–89. The mean (μ) and standard deviation of the mean (std. dev.) values for each variable are provided for domestic and foreign acquirers. The test statistic for the difference in means ($\mu_D - \mu_F$) is from a two-tailed t-test assuming unequal variances. ***denotes significance at the 1% level.

	Chemical targets			Retail targets		
	Domestic acquirers $N = 81$	Foreign acquirers $N = 35$	$(\mu_D - \mu_F)$ t-stat.	Domestic acquirers $N = 213$	Foreign acquirers $N = 55$	$(\mu_D - \mu_F)$ t-stat.
Transaction characteristics						
Hostile[a]						
μ	0.074	0.057	0.017	0.080	0.109	– 0.029
(std. dev.)	(0.029)	(0.040)	0.347	(0.019)	(0.042)	0.630
Equity[b]						
μ	0.284	0.057	0.227	0.202	0.018	0.184
(std. dev.)	(0.050)	(0.040)	3.547***	(0.028)	(0.018)	5.576***
Rival bidder[c]						
μ	0.185	0.086	0.099	0.099	0.109	– 0.010
(std. dev.)	(0.043)	(0.048)	1.547	(0.020)	(0.042)	0.213
CAR[d]						
μ	0.235	0.213	0.022	0.206	0.222	– 0.016
(std. dev.)	(0.031)	(0.046)	0.458	(0.019)	(0.038)	0.381

[a]*Hostile* is a binary variable set equal to one for transactions where management or shareholders take any action to delay or stop the bid.

[b]*Equity* is a binary variable set equal to one for transactions where the acquirer uses its equity for all or part of the purchase price.

[c]*Rival bidder* is a binary variable set equal to one for transactions where another bidder is explicitly mentioned in the press.

[d]*CAR* is the cumulative abnormal return, from standard market model calculations, of the target's stock price over a (– 20, 10) window around the initial transaction announcement date.

4. Test results

4.1. Unconditional mean takeover premia

A comparison of unconditional mean takeover premia levels indicates that for these two industries, shareholder wealth gains are not statistically higher when the buyer is foreign.[4] The bottom row of Table 2 shows that the difference in

[4]The distributions of cumulative abnormal returns (*CAR*s) are slightly skewed to the right, means greater than medians, with no great outliers. In both industries, the median *CAR* for domestic acquirers is slightly larger than the median *CAR* for foreign acquirers.

mean takeover premia levels ($\mu_D - \mu_F$) is less than one standard error and never significant. These results differ from prior papers that find a significant difference in domestic versus foreign takeover premia levels for transactions aggregated across industries. The estimated difference in unconditional mean takeover premia levels is 0.134 in Harris and Ravenscraft's (1991) paper, which measures *CAR* over a (– 20, 4) window for 1,114 domestic and 159 foreign acquisitions, and 0.108 in Swenson's (1993) paper, which measures *CAR* over a (– 20, 10) window for 477 domestic and 226 foreign acquisitions.[5]

One possible explanation for the different findings is aggregation bias. If takeover premia vary by industry and if the industry mix of domestic and foreign acquisition targets differs, then aggregation of transactions across multiple industries may yield the false conclusion that one group pays higher average premia. For this argument to be true, foreign acquisitions must be concentrated in relatively high takeover premia industries. This could happen if the presence of foreign bidders raises the level of competition in a given industry, resulting in higher wealth gains to all targets in that industry. Cebenoyan, Papaioannou, and Travlos (1992) document a significant positive link between the relative dollar volume of foreign acquisitions in a particular industry and the target shareholder wealth gains in that industry.

Another possible source of aggregation bias is the time series distribution of acquisitions. Table 1 shows that the distribution of domestic and foreign acquisitions across time differs in both industries. Forty-one percent of the domestic chemical acquisitions, compared to 23% of the foreign chemical acquisitions, were announced in the three years that had the highest average (across all buyers) cumulative abnormal returns (1978, 1979, 1985). The respective shares in the retail industry are 24% of the domestic and 25% of the foreign acquisitions in the high *CAR* years (1978, 1979, 1980). Inclusion of year dummy variables in the regression analysis that follows, however, does not materially affect any of the results. Moreover, both Swenson (1993) and Harris and Ravenscraft (1991) include year dummies in their tests that find significantly higher wealth gains in foreign acquisitions. Therefore, it seems that industry (rather than time) aggregation bias is the more likely explanation for the different takeover premia levels found in prior tests.

Systematic evidence on different takeover premia levels across industries is difficult to find. The means in these two industries appear indistinguishable. Mergerstat Review provides an industry breakdown of mean takeover premia paid for all acquisitions of U.S. targets. Their measure is a percent premia paid over the target's market price five business days prior to the initial announcement, unadjusted for expected returns. They do not provide standard errors or

[5]Harris and Ravenscraft (1991) report unconditional mean *CAR* in domestic acquisitions of 0.263, while Swenson (1993) reports 0.301.

test for significant differences across industries. Nevertheless, their numbers do provide strong evidence of different takeover premia levels across industries. For example, in 1989, takeover premia across 50 industries ranged between a high of 1.833 in broadcasting to a low of 0.082 in mining and minerals. The average was 0.410. Six industries had means above 0.600, while seven had means below 0.200. In 1985, the range was a high of 0.834 (broadcasting), a mean of 0.317, and a low of 0.099 (furniture). Five industries had means above 0.600, six industries had means below 0.200.

Harris and Ravenscraft (1991) do not provide an industry breakdown of their sample. They do show, however, that their takeover premia levels appear to vary by industry. They include industry dummies, without distinguishing domestic versus foreign buyers, in one takeover premia regression. An *F*-statistic for these industry identifiers is significant at the 1% level. They find that even when the industry identifiers are included, a foreign dummy is positive and significant, indicating higher foreign takeover premia.

Swenson (1993) provides an industry breakdown of her sample. It indicates that the distribution of domestic and foreign transactions across industries is not the same. For example, 0.59 of the foreign transactions are in four industries: machinery (except electric), chemicals, food, and instruments. These same four industries represent only 0.41 of the domestic sample. She also provides mean takeover premia levels across industries, without testing for significant differences. The foreign means range from 1.077 in apparel to 0.007 in leather. The domestic means range from 0.528 in stone, clay, and glass to 0.246 in primary metals. Swenson has confirmed that, while the aggregated sample results reported in her paper indicate takeover premia are significantly higher for foreign buyers, separate tests conducted later on intraindustry subsamples show no significant difference between domestic and foreign takeover premia levels.

Based on the test results in this paper, I cannot conclude that foreign acquirers systematically pay more than domestic acquirers for U.S. targets.

4.2. Transaction variables

Table 3 provides the results of weighted least squares (WLS) regressions of the cumulative abnormal return measure (*CAR*) against the transaction characteristics. To control for heteroskedasticity, weights equal the standard deviation of the market model residuals. Initially, I focus on the results in columns 1 and 2, where I separate the chemical and retail transactions to allow for a different structure in the error terms. Different foreign slope terms are included for each variable. *P*-values are reported in parentheses.

All *Constant* coefficient estimates are significantly different from zero at the 1% level. The coefficient estimates on the binary identifiers for foreign investors (*Foreign*) are never significantly different from zero. Again, I cannot show that

Table 3
Weighted least squares (WLS) regression analysis of U.S. target cumulative abnormal returns (*CAR*) on explanatory variables

The dependent variable, *CAR*, is from standard market model calculations for a fixed (– 20, 10) window around the initial transaction announcement date. To control for heteroskedasticity, weights equal the standard deviation of market model residuals. *P*-values are in parentheses. The sample in column 1 includes domestic and foreign acquisitions of U.S. chemical (SIC code 2800–2899) targets over 1978–89. The sample in column 2 includes domestic and foreign acquisitions of U.S. retail (SIC code 5000–5999) targets over 1978–89. The sample in column 3 includes foreign acquisitions of all U.S. targets over 1975–89.

Variables	Targets: Acquirers: Dates:	Chemical industry Domestic & foreign 1978–89	Retail industry Domestic & foreign 1978–89	All industry Foreign 1975–89
Constant		0.233 (0.000)	0.209 (0.000)	—
Foreign[a]		– 0.009 (0.876)	– 0.026 (0.543)	0.217 (0.000)
Hostile[b]		– 0.015 (0.882)	– 0.002 (0.981)	—
*Foreign * Hostile*		0.429 (0.035)	0.294 (0.016)	0.106 (0.015)
Equity[c]		0.072 (0.288)	0.020 (0.659)	—
*Foreign * Equity*		– 0.234 (0.194)	0.081 (0.809)	– 0.132 (0.070)
Rival bidder[d]		0.066 (0.400)	0.138 (0.031)	—
*Foreign * Rival bidder*		– 0.316 (0.093)	– 0.232 (0.075)	0.059 (0.140)
N		116	268	601
Adj. R^2		0.122	0.081	0.050
Wald test: All *Foreign ** coefficients = 0		2.346 (0.077)	2.488 (0.061)	—

[a]*Foreign* is a binary variable set equal to one for transactions with a buyer headquartered outside the U.S.

[b]*Hostile* is a binary variable set equal to one for transactions where management or shareholders take any action to delay or stop the bid.

[c]*Equity* is a binary variable set equal to one for transactions where the acquirer uses its equity for all or part of the purchase price.

[d]*Rival bidder* is a binary variable set equal to one for transactions where another bidder is explicitly mentioned in the press.

the mean takeover premia paid by foreign investors exceeds the domestic mean premia.

In contrast, in his sample of Japanese targets, which includes mergers and tender offers, partial acquisitions (< 50%), and acquisitions of units, Kang (1993) finds that Japanese bidders pay significantly higher returns than domestic bidders for U.S. targets in majority interest acquisitions only. The data in this paper's tests do not include acquisitions of units or ownership interests of < 20%. If the intercept coefficients in Table 3, columns 1 and 2, are split to differentiate acquisitions where the buyer takes full ownership (100%) versus less than full ownership (between 20% and 100%), the chemical transactions still show no significant difference between domestic and foreign takeover premia levels for either transaction type. The retail transactions, though, indicate takeover premia paid by foreign investors are significantly higher than those paid by domestic investors when full ownership (100%) is acquired, and significantly less when less than 100% of the target's equity is acquired. However, this distinction only holds for the large (– 20, 10) window *CAR* measure.

Neither of the *Hostile* coefficient estimates is significantly different from zero. [If the small (– 3, 1) window *CAR* measure is used, the retail *Hostile* coefficient estimate is positive and significant at the 10% level. It indicates maneuvering by management or shareholders to delay or block the bid raises the conditional mean takeover premia from 0.312 to 0.394, all else constant.] When the buyer is foreign, delaying tactics by management or shareholders appear to have a much larger effect. Both *Foreign*Hostile* coefficient estimates are significantly different from zero at the 5% level. The size of these coefficients is quite large, exceeding the intercepts in both regressions. Hostile maneuvering by target management or shareholders appears to be extracting larger incremental returns from foreign investors than from domestic investors.

Neither of the *Equity* coefficients is significantly different from zero. [If the small (– 3, 1) window *CAR* measure is used, the chemical *Equity* coefficient estimate is 0.098 (0.087).] The chemical *Foreign*Equity* coefficient estimate is negative, with a *p*-value of (0.194). The sign of this coefficient is consistent with results in Huang and Walkling (1987), which indicate the transactions with equity usually lower target shareholder returns. The retail coefficient estimate is positive, but not significant. (There is only one foreign retail transaction with equity, so this coefficient equals the regression residual.) The chemical results provide weak evidence that the use of equity by foreign investors may depress returns to target shareholders more than the use of equity by domestic investors.

The two *Rival bidder* coefficient estimates are positive; the retail estimate is significant at the 5% level. Cumulative abnormal returns for retail targets are higher when there are rival bidders. This is consistent with domestic studies (see Bradley, Desai, and Kim, 1988). Both *Foreign*Rival bidder* coefficients are negative, and significant at the 10% level. [When the small (– 3, 1) window *CAR* measure is used, both *Foreign*Rival bidder* coefficient estimates are negative with p-values between 0.2 and 0.3.] When the ultimate buyer is foreign, the presence of rival bidders appears to depress target shareholder returns.[6] This is one of the most puzzling results in the paper. Why would the presence of rival bidders boost target returns when the buyer is domestic, but depress them when the buyer is foreign? One possible explanation, that foreign investors with low bids *attract* competitive bidders, is not consistent with these transactions. There is no distinct timing pattern here. The foreign investors with rival bidders are not always the first, or the last, bidder to enter the contest. (This sample only includes bidders that win.)

Another possible explanation concerns the likelihood of deal completion. Suppose the probability of successfully closing an acquisition is lower for foreign than for domestic investors. The number of government reviews the transactions must go through supports this assumption. Twenty percent of the foreign chemical transactions had to be reviewed by a government entity, compared to 4% of the domestic chemical transactions. (The comparable retail numbers are 5.5% foreign and 5.4% domestic.) A lower probability of successful deal completion would lower the expected net present value of the takeover. This uncertainty would rise with rival bidders or equity, as discussed in Huang and Walkling (1987). Alternatively, suppose foreign investors incur higher costs to become informed about U.S. targets. The entrance, or presence, of a (lower-cost) U.S. bidder may significantly reduce the probability that the high-cost foreign bidder will win a bidding contest. This finding deserves further study.

The bottom row of Table 3 reports the result of a Wald test of whether all three (*Foreign∗*) slope coefficients equal zero. The F-statistic rejects the null in both regressions at the 10% level. These regressions indicate the market is reacting differently to domestic and foreign investors.

One possible concern with these results is the small number of foreign transactions with the characteristics of interest. The number of foreign acquisitions of chemical targets with these characteristics is two hostile, two equity, and three rival bidders. For retail targets, the numbers are six hostile, one equity, and six rival bidders. Despite the small number of observations, these results appear to be robust. First, the results are consistent across takeover premia measures and across industries, except for the retail equity estimate. If the chemical and retail transactions are combined and Table 3 regressions re-estimated, the foreign identifiers are positive for hostile (significant at the 10% level), and negative for equity (not significant) and rival bidders (significant at the 5% level).

Second, none of the transactions with these characteristics represent the maximum or minimum takeover premia paid. The results are not driven by outliers.

---

[6] When Swenson (1993) breaks out the domestic versus foreign impact from rival bidders, she finds positive, yet insignificant coefficient estimates on the *Foreign∗Rival bidder* variables.

Third, WLS regressions of the takeover premia paid by foreign investors across all industries yield similar coefficient estimates. Column 3 in Table 3 provides the results of regressions of takeover premia paid by foreign investors across all industries over 1975–89. These transactions were collected in the same manner, and with the same criteria, as the chemical and retail transactions used in this paper. The sample in column 3 includes all foreign acquisitions over 1975–89 for which takeover premia are available. In other words, the foreign chemical and retail acquisitions in columns 1 and 2 are a subset of those in column 3.

The coefficient estimates in column 3 indicate target takeover premia paid by foreign investors across all industries are positively related to hostile maneuvering by management and negatively related to equity. The positive 0.059 *Foreign∗Rival bidder* coefficient estimate in the (– 20, 10) window regression is still consistent with foreigners paying less than domestic investors in multiple-bidder contests. In Bradley, Desai, and Kim's (1988) sample of 125 takeovers over 1963–84, the cumulative abnormal returns for a (– 20, 10) window are 0.3046 for single-bidder targets and 0.3782 for multiple-bidder targets. Within a WLS regression, using a (– 5, 5) window takeover premia as the dependent variable, their estimated coefficient on a binary identifier for multiple bidders is 0.130. Harris and Ravenscraft's (1991) coefficient estimate for the multiple-bidder identifier ranges between 0.1019 and 0.1129. [This is for a (– 20, 4) window, without breaking out domestic and foreign transactions.] If the regression in column 3 is run with the small (– 3, 1) window *CAR*, the rival bidder coefficient estimate equals – 0.055 (0.082). Column 3 confirms that the coefficient estimates in columns 1 and 2 are consistent with the experience across all foreign acquisitions.

4.3. Variables from the FDI literature

Several recent papers have suggested that exchange rates and taxes may affect the level of takeover premia. Scholes and Wolfson (1990) argue that foreign investors should have been hurt by the 1981 ERTA and helped by the 1986 TRA. Froot and Stein (1991) build an imperfect capital markets model that indicates a depreciated dollar might raise the level of foreign acquisition bids. They use an auction model to study the impact of exchange rates on credit-constrained foreign investors.

Table 4 reports the results from WLS regressions of the takeover premia against the transaction characteristics and the levels of the real exchange rate index. To test the Scholes and Wolfson (1990) tax story, the foreign binary identifier is split into four dummy variables. First, I break out the worldwide tax regime (*WWTax*) investors from the other foreign investors. Worldwide tax regime countries tax repatriated earnings with a credit for foreign taxes paid. The U.K. and Japan are worldwide tax regime countries with higher statutory

Table 4
Weighted least squares (WLS) regression analysis of U.S. target cumulative abnormal returns (*CAR*)

The sample includes acquisitions of chemical (SIC code 2800–2899) and retail (SIC code 5000–5999) targets of domestic and foreign acquirers over 1978–89. The dependent variable, *CAR*, is from standard market model calculations for a fixed (– 20, 10) window around the initial transaction announcement date. To control for heteroskedasticity, weights equal the standard deviation of market model residuals. *P*-values are in parentheses.

Variables	Chemical targets	Retail targets
Constant	0.449	0.317
	(0.016)	(0.016)
WWTax: 1978/80[a]	—	0.298
		(0.282)
WWTax: 1981/86	0.084	0.184
	(0.866)	(0.568)
WWTax: 1987/89	– 0.022	0.146
	(0.956)	(0.627)
Other foreign[b]	– 0.222	0.153
	(0.583)	(0.600)
Hostile[c]	– 0.017	– 0.004
	(0.866)	(0.952)
*Foreign * Hostile*	0.239	0.253
	(0.274)	(0.043)
Equity[d]	0.048	0.015
	(0.481)	(0.743)
*Foreign * Equity*	– 0.230	0.171
	(0.212)	(0.615)
Rival bidder[e]	0.075	0.131
	(0.329)	(0.041)
*Foreign * Rival bidder*	– 0.311	– 0.192
	(0.112)	(0.147)
FX[f]	– 0.003	– 0.001
	(0.228)	(0.402)
*Foreign * FX*	0.002	– 0.002
	(0.738)	(0.484)
N	116	268
Adj. R^2	0.165	0.081

[a]*WWTax*:1978/80, *WWTax*:1981/86, and *WWTax*:1987/89 are binary variables set equal to one for U.K. and Japanese buyers (the two countries with worldwide tax systems) for transactions completed in 1978–80, 1981–86, and 1987–89, respectively.

[b]*Other foreign* is a binary variable set equal to one for transactions with foreign buyers other than U.K. or Japanese.

[c]*Hostile* is a binary variable set equal to one for transactions where management or shareholders take any action to delay or stop the bid.

[d]*Equity* is a binary variable set equal to one for transactions where the acquirer uses its equity for all or part of the purchase price.

[e]*Rival bidder* is a binary variable set equal to one for transactions where another bidder is explicitly mentioned in the press.

[f]*FX* equals the real, trade weighted index of the U.S. dollar exchange rate. It is matched to each transaction according to deal announcement date.

corporate tax rates than the U.S. (except for the U.K. from 1984–88). Foreign buyers from 'territorial' tax countries (e.g., Netherlands and France) or from countries with applicable tax treaties with the U.S. (e.g., Canada and Germany) are not subject to home taxes on repatriated earnings. Therefore, these investors should be on an equal footing with domestic investors vis-a-vis taxes. Second, I split the *WWTax* transactions into three periods, corresponding to 1978–80, the ERTA (1981–86), and the TRA (1987–89). (Note: Some of the TRA's changes were retroactive to January 1, 1986. If these tests are adjusted to include 1986 in the post-TRA period, however, the results do not change. All foreign binary variables are still insignificantly different than zero.) Transactions are classified according to deal completion, not deal announcement, dates. If the takeover premia paid by investors from worldwide tax countries are lower in 1981–86 and higher post-1986 than takeover premia paid by the domestic and other foreign investors, then the results are consistent with the Scholes and Wolfson tax story. The *FX* variable equals the level of the real, trade-weighted U.S. dollar exchange rate. A rise indicates a dollar appreciation. The Froot and Stein (1991) model predicts no link between the exchange rate and domestic takeover premia levels, and higher values of the dollar associated with lower foreign takeover premia levels.

The *Constant* coefficient estimates in Table 4 are larger, with lower significant levels than those in Table 3. None of the foreign binary identifiers is significantly different from zero. (Note: There are no *WWTax*:1978/80 transactions in chemicals.) None of the *WWTax*:1981/86 coefficient estimates are negative, as predicted in the Scholes and Wolfson (1990) model. The retail *WWTax*:1987/89 coefficient estimate is positive, as predicted, but has a *p*-value of 0.627. These results are consistent with those in Harris and Ravenscraft (1991) and Kang (1993), who also find no support for the Scholes and Wolfson tax story.

The transaction variable estimates are consistent with those in Table 3, yet with lower significance levels. They again indicate that hostile maneuvering may boost shareholder wealth gains with foreign investors more than with domestic investors, and that the presence of rival bidders is more often associated with lower returns when the buyer is foreign than when it is domestic.

These two samples provide no evidence of a significant link between the level of U.S. target takeover premia and the level of the real exchange rate; however, this finding may be due to the relatively small sample size. In a separate paper (Dewenter, 1993), using transactions across all U.S. targets (sample size is 601 targets of foreign acquirers), I estimate a significant exchange rate elasticity of between -0.69 and -1.38, compared to these estimates in Table 4 of -0.35 for chemical and -1.02 for retail.[7]

[7] The average value of *FX* over this period is 75.5. The average foreign *CAR* are 0.213 in chemical and 0.222 in retail. The coefficient estimates in column one indicate a 10% change in *FX* yields a change in the chemical *CAR* of $[(0.10*75.5)*(-0.003+0.002)/0.213] = -0.035$. The coefficient

The new finding in Table 4 is that takeover premia paid by domestic acquirers may be just as, or more, sensitive to exchange rates as foreign takeover premia. This implies that the exchange rate impact may have more to do with general factors (cost and revenue exposure, market growth prospects) than with market imperfections or asymmetries that only affect cross-border investors.

Marr et al. (1991) do not test for exchange rate effects. Harris and Ravenscraft (1991), Kang (1993), and Cebenoyan et al. (1992) test for exchange rate effects in the foreign acquisitions only. Swenson (1993) tests for an exchange rate effect on domestic investors by separating the domestic intercept term into strong and weak dollar periods. She finds no significant differences across the periods. Swenson tests for an exchange rate effect on foreign buyers by separating the foreign binary identifier into strong and weak (and appreciating/depreciating) periods. She finds that wealth gains of foreign target shareholders are larger in weak dollar years. When I redo the regressions in Table 3, splitting the foreign binary identifier into three periods corresponding to the mixed (1978–1980), strong (1981–1985), and weak (1986–1989) dollar, none of the foreign identifier coefficient estimates are significantly different from zero at the 5% level.

5. Conclusion

This paper employs a different approach to examine whether or not the market's reaction to takeover announcements differs with buyer nationality. I have compared takeover premia within industries and have shifted the focus of analysis to the sensitivity of takeover premia to various explanatory variables.

Contrary to results in prior papers, these data indicate no significant difference in the mean level of target shareholder wealth gains in domestic versus foreign acquisitions. The lack of any significant exchange rate sensitivity in these abnormal returns also contradicts prior results. A new finding in this paper is that the sensitivity of takeover premia to standard transaction characteristics does appear to vary with buyer nationality. Foreign investors do appear to pay more in hostile transactions, and less with rival bidders and (perhaps) equity. Finally, the results confirm prior work that shows the U.S. tax regime changes in the 1980s provide no explanatory power for the difference between domestic and foreign takeover premia levels.

---

estimates in column two indicate a 10% change in FX yields a change in the retail CAR of $[(0.10*75.5)*(-0.001-0.002)/0.222] = -0.102$. Note, if the chemical and retail transactions are combined into one regression with the same coefficients as in Table 4, plus four FX coefficients (*Domestic∗Chemical∗FX*, *Foreign∗Chemical∗FX*, *Domestic∗Retail∗FX*, *Foreign∗Retail∗FX*), I cannot show a significant difference in exchange rate sensitivity across industries, for either the domestic or foreign buyers.

While the chemical and retail industries do comprise a significant portion (16%) of overall acquisition activity in the U.S., the first and most obvious extension for this research is to incorporate other industries. Adding industries will confirm the robustness of these results and provide more evidence on the strength and possible interindustry differences in the exchange rate effect.

The other obvious next step is to expand the number of explanatory variables. From the domestic takeover literature, block shareholdings or defense mechanisms could be explored. The most interesting result here might be to find that there is a significant difference in the incidence of these characteristics between domestic and foreign targets. From the FDI literature, consideration of buyer and target characteristics, such as buyer R&D levels, product relatedness, and target market share, might help illuminate the motives for cross-border acquisitions.

References

Aliber, R.Z., 1970, A theory of foreign direct investment, in: C.P. Kindleberger, ed., The international corporation (MIT Press, Cambridge, MA).

Aliber, R.Z., 1983, Money, multinationals, and sovereigns, in: ed. C.P. Kindleberger and D.B. Audretsch, eds., The multinational corporation in the 1980s (MIT Press, Cambridge, MA).

Bradley, M., A. Desai, and E.H. Kim, 1988, Synergistic gains from corporate acquisitions and their division between the stockholders of target and acquiring firms, Journal of Financial Economics 21, 3–40.

Brown, S.J. and J.B. Warner, 1980, Measuring security price performance, Journal of Financial Economics 8, 205–258.

Brown, S.J. and J.B. Warner, 1985, Using daily stock returns: The case of event studies, Journal of Financial Economics 14, 3–31.

Cebenoyan, A.S., G.J. Papaioannou, and N.G. Travlos, 1992, Foreign takeover activity in the U.S. and wealth effects on target firm shareholders, Financial Management, Autumn, 58–68.

Cushman, D.O., 1985, Real exchange rate risk, expectations, and the level of direct investment, Review of Economics and Statistics 67, 297–308.

Dewenter, K.L., 1991, A review of sources of foreign direct investment data, Mimeo.

Dewenter, K.L., 1993, Do exchange rate changes drive foreign direct investment?, Mimeo.

Dunning, J.H., 1988, The eclectic paradigm of international production: A restatement and some possible extensions, Journal of International Business Studies, 1– 31.

Franks, J.R., R.S. Harris, and C. Mayer, 1988, Means of payment in takeovers: Results for the United Kingdom and the United States, in: A.J. Auerbach, ed., Corporate takeovers: Causes and consequences (University of Chicago Press, Chicago, IL) 221–264.

Froot, K.A. and J.C. Stein, 1991, Exchange rates and foreign direct investment: An imperfect capital markets approach, Quarterly Journal of Economics, 1191–1217.

Harris, R.S. and D. Ravenscraft, 1991, The role of acquisitions in foreign direct investment: Evidence from the US stock market, Journal of Finance XLVI, 825–844.

Huang, Y.S. and R.A. Walkling, 1987, Target abnormal returns associated with acquisitions announcements: Payment, acquisitions form, and managerial resistance, Journal of Financial Economics 19, 329–350.

Hymer, S.H., 1960, The international operations of national firms: A study of direct foreign investment, Ph.D. dissertation (Massachusetts Institute of Technology, Cambridge, MA).

James, C.M. and P. Weir, 1987, Returns to acquirers and competition in the acquisition market: The case of banking, Journal of Political Economy 95, 355–370.

Jarrell, G.A., 1985, The wealth effects of litigation by targets: Do interests diverge in a merge?, Journal of Law and Economics 28, 151–177.

Jarrell, G.A., J.A. Brickley, and J.M. Netter, 1988, The market for corporate control: The empirical evidence since 1980, Journal of Economic Perspectives 2, 49–68.

Jensen, M.C., 1986, The takeover controversy: Analysis and evidence, Midland Corporate Finance Journal, Summer, 6–32.

Jensen, M.C. and R.S. Ruback, 1983, The market for corporate control: The scientific evidence, Journal of Financial Economics 11, 5–50.

Kang, J.K., 1993, The international market for corporate control: Mergers and acquisitions of U.S. firms by Japanese firms, Journal of Financial Economics 34, 345–372.

Marr, M.W., S. Mohta, and M.F. Spivey, 1991, Foreign takeovers in the US: An analysis of the pre-takeover, takeover, and post-takeover stages, Mimeo.

Revenga, A.L., 1992, Exporting jobs? The impact of import competition on employment and wages in US manufacturing, Quarterly Journal of Economics CVII, 255–284.

Scholes, M.S. and M.A. Wolfson, 1990, The effects of changes in tax laws on corporate reorganization activity, Journal of Business 63, S141–S164.

Swenson, D., 1989, The impact of US tax reforms on foreign investment in the US, Mimeo.

Swenson, D., 1993, Foreign mergers and acquisitions in the United States, in: K.A. Froot, ed., Foreign direct investment (University of Chicago Press, Chicago, IL) 255–286.

Data sources

Foreign Direct Investment in the United States, Transactions Lists, 1974–1988 (International Trade Administration, U.S. Department of Commerce, Washington, DC).

Japan's Expanding US Manufacturing Presence, 1988 Update, 1989 (Japan Economic Institute of America, Washington, DC).

Mergers & Acquisitions, The Journal of Corporate Venture, 1975–1990 (MLR Publishing Co., PA).

Mergerstat Review, W.T. Grimm & Co., Pub: 1981–1987, Merrill Lynch Business Brokerage & Valuation, Pub: 1988–1989 (IL).

Moody's International Manual, 1981–1989 (Moody's Investor Service, The Dun & Bradstreet Corp., NY).

Morgan Stanley Capital International Perspectives Data Base, 1990 (Morgan Stanley, NY).

Predicasts F&S Index, 1975–1990 (Predicasts, OH).

Wall Street Journal Index, 1975–1990 (Dow Jones & Co., NY).

[15]

THE JOURNAL OF FINANCE • VOL. XLV, NO. 1 • MARCH 1990

Do Managerial Objectives Drive Bad Acquisitions?

RANDALL MORCK, ANDREI SHLEIFER, and ROBERT W. VISHNY*

ABSTRACT

In a sample of 326 US acquisitions between 1975 and 1987, three types of acquisitions have systematically lower and predominantly negative announcement period returns to bidding firms. The returns to bidding shareholders are lower when their firm diversifies, when it buys a rapidly growing target, and when its managers performed poorly before the acquisition. These results suggest that managerial objectives may drive acquisitions that reduce bidding firms' values.

THERE IS NOW CONSIDERABLE evidence that making acquisitions is a mixed blessing for shareholders of acquiring companies. Average returns to bidding shareholders from making acquisitions are at best slightly positive, and significantly negative in some studies (Bradley, Desai and Kim 1988, Roll 1986). Some have suggested that negative bidder returns are purely a consequence of stock financing of acquisitions that leads to a release of adverse information about acquiring firms (Asquith, Bruner, and Mullins 1987). In this case, negative bidder returns are not evidence of a bad investment. An alternative interpretation of poor bidder performance is that bidding firms overpay for the targets they acquire. In this paper, we present evidence that some types of bidders *systematically* overpay.

There are at least two reasons why bidding firms' managers might overpay in acquisitions, thereby truly reducing the wealth of their shareholders as opposed to just revealing bad news about their firm. According to Roll (1986), managers of bidding firms are infected by hubris, and so overpay for targets because they overestimate their own ability to run them. Another view of overpayment is that managers of bidding firms pursue personal objectives other than maximization of shareholder value. To the extent that acquisitions serve these objectives, managers of bidding firms are willing to pay more for targets than they are worth to bidding firms' shareholders.

Our view is that when a firm makes an acquisition or any other investment, its manager considers both his personal benefits from the investment and the consequences for the market value of the firm. Some investments are particularly attractive from the former perspective: they contribute to long term growth of the firm, enable the manager to diversify the risk on his human capital, or

* University of Alberta, University of Chicago, and University of Chicago, respectively. We are indebted for comments to Steve Kaplan, Wayne Marr, Wayne Mikkelson, Sam Peltzman, Rene Stulz and an anonymous referee and for financial support to the Russell Sage Foundation, the Center for the Study of the Economy and the State, the National Center for Management Research and Development, the William S. Fishman and the Dimensional Fund Advisers Faculty Research Funds at the Graduate School of Business, University of Chicago.

improve his job security (Shleifer and Vishny, 1990). When an investment provides a manager with particularly large personal benefits, he is willing to sacrifice the market value of the firm to pursue that investment. Other things equal, the net present value of an acquisition with high private benefits should be lower than that of an acquisition with no such benefits. Put differently, managers will overpay for targets with high private benefits.

If shareholders could perfectly monitor and control the investment decisions of managers, acquisitions that reduce shareholder wealth because they deliver managerial benefits would not be allowed (or would be allowed on a small scale only when they are an efficient form of compensation (Shleifer and Vishny, 1988)). However, managers of large public corporations are typically subject to only loose scrutiny. Boards of directors give managers considerable leeway in choosing investment projects, and do not use negative stock market reactions to investment or acquisition announcements as the definitive indicator of long-run value consequences. There is some ex post settling up in that firms pursuing value-decreasing acquisitions are taken over with a higher frequency themselves (Mitchell and Lehn, 1990), but these takeovers are too expensive and infrequently used to provide the necessary deterrence. Management ownership of shares may be the most effective deterrent to investments that dissipate market value,[1] but in most large corporations top managers own only a small stake. In sum, while it is incorrect to say that managers make investment decisions without regard for market value consequences, it is also incorrect to say that existing monitoring and control devices keep managers from pursuing personal non-value-maximizing objectives. We therefore expect some observed investments to reflect pursuit of these objectives. Our methodology is designed to uncover the hypothesized negative relation between the managerial benefits of an acquisition and its consequences for the market value of the acquiring firm.

Specifically, we try to find out which acquisitions are bad investments for bidding shareholders and determine whether those acquisitions appear to provide private benefits to bidding managers. We focus on two aspects of acquisition strategies that can be readily understood in terms of managerial objectives: buying growth and diversification. We also look at the relationship between bidders' past performance and their returns from acquisitions. This relationship sheds light on the bidding managers' motives for acquiring. Before presenting the evidence, we briefly summarize the literature on managerial objectives to justify looking at relatedness, target growth and past performance of the bidder to uncover managerial objectives in making acquisitions.

Relatedness

Several models predict that managers would pursue unrelated diversification even when it hurts shareholders. First, if managers themselves are not properly diversified, they would diversify the holdings of the firm to reduce the risk to their human capital even when diversification offers few if any benefits to shareholders (Amihud and Lev 1981). Second, to assure the survival and conti-

[1] Lewellyn, Loderer and Rosenfeld (1985) find that returns to acquiring firms are positively correlated with the equity stake of the acquirer's top management.

nuity of the firm even when shareholder wealth maximization dictates shrinkage or liquidation, managers would try to enter new lines of business (Donaldson and Lorsch, 1983). Third, when poor performance of the firm threatens a manager's job, he has an incentive to enter new businesses at which he might be better (Shleifer and Vishny, 1990). In all these cases, managers might be willing to overpay for targets outside the bidding firm's industry, reducing the wealth of their shareholders.

Buying Growth

Many authors argue that managers want their firms to grow even at a cost to market value. Baumol (1959) simply assumes that growth of sales is part of the manager's utility function. Donaldson (1984) suggests that growth of the firm creates attractive promotion opportunities for its junior managers, enabling the firm to attract young managers concerned with upward mobility. By buying a growing firm, a mature firm ensures that its younger managers do not have to compete for only a few top positions. Growth of this sort can be value maximizing if it serves to attract and retain required managerial talent. It can also be wasteful if managers overpay for growing targets just to promote their proteges. Finally, pursuit of growth can be part of a strategy of ensuring long run survival of the corporation as an independent entity (Donaldson and Lorsch 1983), a goal likely to be more important to managers than to shareholders.

On these views, managers maximize growth, and not just pure size, to create attractive opportunities for the insiders and to assure the survival of the firm. Managers spend corporate resources to buy rapidly growing firms, even if such investments have a negative present value.

Past Performance of Acquirer Management

Bad managers might make bad acquisitions simply because they are bad managers. Alternatively, bad managers have more incentive to acquire to assure the survival of the firm or to find new businesses they might be good at. The prediction is that acquisitions by bad managers are particularly disastrous. In contrast, a plausible version of Roll's hubris hypothesis predicts that the worst acquisitions are made by well performing firms, since their managers are most likely to be infected by hubris.

The evidence presented below evaluates the importance of diversification, buying growth, and past bidder performance for bidder returns in acquisitions. We also evaluate and control for alternative explanations of negative bidder returns. In particular, we control for the form of payment in the acquisition since the announcement of stock financing may release information, as well as be correlated with our variables. In addition, we test a particular version of Roll's hubris hypothesis, according to which managers of bidding firms are infected by hubris and so overpay for targets because they overestimate their own ability at running them. A plausible version of this hypothesis predicts that the worst acquisitions are made by well-performing firms, since their managers are the most likely ones to be infected by hubris. Our prediction is the opposite.

Our evidence suggests that bad acquisitions are driven by managerial objectives;

they are not just cases of information release via stock financing or of hubris of successful managers. We find that unrelated diversification and buying growth reduce the returns to making an acquisition. We also find that bad managers are also bad acquirers, consistent with the notion that poor performance drives managers to try something new. Finally, we find that the market penalizes unrelated diversification much more heavily in the 1980's than in the 1970's, coincident with the rise of hostile bust-up takeovers.

These results fit well with some recent findings of others. Lang, Stulz and Walkling (1989) find that having a low Tobin's Q, which might stand for poor quality of the bidding firm's management, reduces the bidder's return in a takeover. They also find that a low Tobin's Q of the target, which is likely to be correlated with low sales growth, is associated with a higher bidder return. The latter finding is also obtained by Servaes (1988). Lewellen, Loderer and Rosenfeld (1985) and You, Caves, Henry and Smith (1986) show that low management ownership in the bidding firm is associated with lower returns from making acquisitions. This result suggests that managers who have little incentive to maximize market value make bad acquisitions. Mitchell and Lehn (1990) find that firms making acquisitions that reduce their market value are subsequently more likely to be acquired than firms not making bad acquisitions. Although neither these papers nor our own work identify managerial objectives precisely, the importance of these objectives in determining acquisition choices seems well supported.

Section I of the paper describes the data we use in the analysis. Sections II and III present our empirical results. Section IV concludes.

I. The Sample and Construction of Variables

The Sample

Our data set is obtained by combining Bronwyn Hall's (1988) sample of mergers based on deletions of firms from Compustat with Jarrell and Poulsen's (1988) sample of acquisitions. We only consider acquisitions in which the bidder has actually obtained control. Table I presents the details of sample construction. The main reasons we lose observations include unavailability of stock price data on CRSP, absence of data in COMPUSTAT needed to construct our bidder performance variables, and missing data in the *Dun and Bradstreet Million Dollar Directory* (MDD) on the lines of business in which each firm operates. We use these lines of business to construct our diversification measures. We also omit 63 observations because the equity value of the target is less than 5% of the equity value of the bidder. These observations would only add noise to the results. Finally, we omit one outlier firm whose market value dropped more than 150% of the price it paid for the acquisition. Table I shows that our full sample consists of 326 acquisitions.

Return Variable

The traditional measure of the bidder's payoff from making an acquisition is the percentage change in the bidder's equity value at or around the time the

Table I

Construction of the 1975–1987 Sample of Acquisitions

Panel A: Construction of the Basic Full Sample

Bronwyn Hall Sample	
1095	Partial list of firms that disappeared from Compustat
−322	Name changes/bankruptcies/LBOs/foreign bidder/reorganizations/consolidations/disappearance before 1975
−296	Bidder or target not in CRSP, or bidder not in Compustat
−2	No *Wall Street Journal* event date
−79	No listing of bidder or target in Million Dollar Directory
396	Usable mergers from Bronwyn Hall's sample
Jarrell-Poulsen Sample	
657	Bids
−584	Toeholds but not takeovers/bidder or target not in CRSP/bidder not in Compustat/disappearance before 1975 or duplicate entry with Bronwyn Hall sample
−17	No listing of bidder or target in Million Dollar Directory
56	
+396	From Bronwyn Hall sample
452	Total from Bronwyn Hall and Jarrell-Poulsen samples
−44	Bidder or target data missing from CRSP on the event date
−18	Date of first bid is 1974, even though firm disappeared from Compustat in 1975 or later
−63	Target < 5% of the equity value of the bidder
−1	Outlier: bidder price declined over 150% of the purchase price of the target around announcement
326	Basic full sample

Panel B: Construction of More Restricted Sample for Empirical Work

1. Quality of Bidder Management Measured by Relative Income Growth	
326	Basic full sample
−26	Bidder income missing in 1 of the 2 years needed to construct bidder income growth variable
−1	Outlier: 250% income growth due to end of lawsuit writeoffs
299	Sample for income growth means in Table II
−33	Target sales missing in 1 of the 2 years needed to construct target sales growth
266	Sample for relative income growth regressions
2. Quality of Bidder Management Measured by Relative Equity Return	
326	Basic full sample
−37	Bidder returns missing in more than 33 of 36 months needed to construct bidder equity return
289	Sample for relative equity return means in Table II
−35	Target sales missing in 1 of the 2 years needed to construct target sales growth
254	Sample for relative equity return regressions.
3. Target Sales Growth Analysis	
326	Basic full sample
−39	Target sales missing in 1 of the 2 years needed to construct target sales growth
287	Sample for target sales means in Table II

acquisition is announced. This measure is somewhat unsatisfactory because it makes equally good acquisitions differentially good to firms of different sizes. When a firm with an equity value of $1000 buys another firm for $200 and as a result loses $50 in equity value, its return is −5%. But when a firm with an equity value of $500 makes the very same acquisition for $200 and loses $50 in equity value, its return is −10%. In this calculation, the same bad investment is evaluated differently depending on the initial equity value of the bidding firm. A good return measure should make the quality of the investment independent of the equity value or other characteristics of the bidding firm.

A measure not suffering from this problem is the ratio of the change in the market value of the bidder to the acquisition price of the target. This variable is equal to the ratio of the acquisition's net present value to its price. This measure is obviously −25% in both cases mentioned above. Using the price paid for the target as the normalizing factor seems more natural than using the initial market value of the bidder.

We use the date on which the acquirer's first bid is announced in the *Wall Street Journal* as our event date. We then compute the change in the bidder's equity value from two trading days before to one trading day after the event date.[2] We get a proxy for the acquisition price by looking at the equity value of the target on the first trading day following the last bid mentioned in the *Wall Street Journal.* Our return variable is then the ratio of the change in the bidder equity value to the acquisition price.[3]

While we prefer this approach to the traditional approach of just looking at the percentage change in the bidder's share price upon announcement of the acquisition as a means of evaluating the acquisition decision, the traditional approach is not completely without merit. In particular, it may be that acquiring managers are primarily concerned with the impact of an acquisition on their share price and not so much with the market's view of the wisdom of the acquisition itself. In that case, when a large corporation grossly overpays for a small target, the traditional measure's treatment of this action is not that worrisome for management may not be far off base. Accordingly, we have done our analysis using the traditional return measure for the bidder as well as the measure discussed above. The results for the two measures are quite similar. Results for the traditional measure are available from the authors upon request.[4]

Another measure of the value consequences of the acquisition would be the

[2] We have repeated the analysis using various event windows other than −2 to +1 and have found similar results. In particular, we have looked at (−1,+1), (−2,+2), (−3,+3) and (−4,+4).

[3] The target's value after the bid is announced is only a proxy for the acquisition price since that value may reflect only probabilistic success of the bid as well as the possibility of future higher bids. In addition, not all bids are for 100% of the target's stock (although experience suggests that second tier "cleanup offers" at prices in the range of the initial bid are the rule rather than the exception). Deflating by the target's post-bid value is just intended to give a better normalization factor by which to gauge the change in the bidder's market value.

[4] In the regressions using the traditional measure of the bidder's stock return as the dependent variable, a variable corresponding to the ratio of the market values of the target and the bidder prior to any bidding for the target is also included as a regressor. This relative size variable enters positively in the regression using the traditional bidder return measure and is statistically significant. On the other hand, this variable neither enters significantly nor changes the results for any of the other variables using our bidder return measure.

sum of the market value changes of the target and the bidder surrounding the takeover contest. A decline in the combined value of the two firms as the market learns about the acquisition would be evidence of diseconomies or a bad expected match between the target and the bidding management team, as when a conglomerate becomes so diversified that top management's expertise gets spread too thinly. This is not the focus of our study. Even when the combined value of the two firms rises because of the existence of a synergy, we are still interested in the regularity with which the bidder's value actually declines and in relating those declines to the managerial benefits flowing to bidding management. Hence, when we talk about overpayment we are referring to the negative reaction of the bidder's share price only. It is interesting, however, that our estimate of the change in combined value for the target and bidder is negative in roughly 25% of the cases.[5] This suggests that many of these acquisitions are not only ill-advised from the standpoint of bidding shareholders but also that there may be negative synergies associated with these combinations.

Relatedness Measures

One of the main issues addressed in this paper is the relative attractiveness of related and unrelated acquisitions. We construct two measures of relatedness. The first measures whether the target has any lines of business in common with the bidder. For each target and bidder in the sample, we use the *Dun and Bradstreet Million Dollar Directory* (MDD) to obtain the 4-digit SIC codes of the three main lines of business (by sales) that the firm operates in.[6] If the firm operates in fewer than three 4-digit industries, we use all its industries. All the data are for the year prior to the acquisition. If the bidder and the target have a 4-digit industry in common among the top three they operate in, we call the acquisition related. Otherwise we call the acquisition unrelated. This procedure leaves us reasonably confident that a related acquisition really falls in the firm's field of expertise.[7]

The second measure of relatedness is the correlation coefficient of monthly stock returns between the target and the bidder over the three years prior to the acquisition. The data are taken from both the NYSE/AMEX and the OTC files of CRSP. Although this variable is highly correlated with the previous measure, it is perhaps better for asking whether managers make acquisitions to diversify either their personal risk or the firm's risk.

Target Growth Measure

To evaluate the value consequences of buying growing firms, we must measure the growth rate of the target. We use the total growth rate of sales between 5

[5] Our estimate of the sum of the two value changes is obtained as follows. The change in target value is calculated as the difference between its market value two days before any bid for the target and one day after the successful bidder's first bid. The successful bidder's market value change is the same as the numerator of our bidder return measure. It is the change from 2 days before that bidder's first bid to 1 day after that bid. These two market value changes are then added to get the net value consequences of the acquisition.

[6] SIC code 6711, used for holding companies, is not treated as a separate line of business.

[7] We have also conducted the analysis using 2-digit SIC codes to measure relatedness. Not surprisingly, the difference between related and unrelated acquisitions is much smaller in this case.

years before the acquisition and the year before, defined as log(S(t-1)) − log(S(t-6)), where t is the year of the acquisition, and S(x) is constant dollar sales in year x from COMPUSTAT using the CPI as the deflator.

Measures of Past Performance of the Bidder

We use two measures of the past performance of the bidding firm: one based on stock returns (including dividends) and one based on growth of income. We use the firm's performance relative to its industry because the industry component of performance is presumably not under the management's control. Use of industry-adjusted performance to measure the quality of management is supported by the finding that firms underperforming their industries have more internally-precipitated management turnover (Morck, Shleifer and Vishny 1989).

Our measure of the bidding firm's industry-adjusted stock return is the difference between the cum dividend stock return of the bidder (from CRSP) and that of its "industry" over the three-year period ending in December of the year before the acquisition. To define the average stock return of the bidder's industry, we use the top three 4-digit SIC codes that the bidder operates in, discussed above. For each code, we take up to 10 other firms operating in the same 4-digit SIC code, making sure that for each of these firms this SIC code is one of its two most important in terms of sales. We take 10 firms in alphabetical order from the list of firms operating in each 4-digit SIC code that the MDD provides. When there are fewer than 10 firms, we take all the ones the MDD offers. When a firm does not have return data going four years back, we take a substitute that does. Using this procedure, we can construct an equally weighted average stock return for each 4-digit industry in which each bidder operates. Last, we take the simple arithmetic average of the industry stock returns for the top three 4-digit industries that each bidder operates in to arrive at the equity return of the bidder's "industry."

A similar procedure gives us 3-year bidder income growth relative to industry. Three-year income growth is defined as $\log(I(t-1)) - \log(I(t-4))$, where t is the year of the acquisition and I is defined as the sum of net income, interest and deferred taxes taken from COMPUSTAT.[8]

Other Variables Used in the Analysis

We use three other variables in the analysis. First, we use a dummy variable equal to 1 when multiple bidders are involved in the contest, since it has been documented that bidders do worse when they are involved in an open contest for

[8] An alternative earnings based measure of past performance is the level of earnings (normalized by value of assets) relative to industry rather than recent growth in earnings relative to industry. We tried this measure at the suggestion of the referee, with mixed results. We think there are two reasons for this. First, the level of earnings relative to asset value is a noisier measure of how the current management team is doing than is the recent change in earnings. This is true because the level of earnings is probably more a result of decisions made by previous managements than are recent changes in earnings and also because extra noise is introduced by the need to normalize by some measure of assets-in place. Second, the level of earnings may proxy for the amount of free cash flow available to management. According to Jensen's free cash flow theory, all other things equal, one would expect more negative returns on the investments of firms in which management had access to more free cash flow.

the target (Bradley, Desai and Kim 1988). Second, we examine whether the returns to bidders in related and unrelated acquisitions have changed in the 1980s. At least two changes have occurred under the Reagan administration. First, the antitrust policy has become laxer, presumably raising the returns to related diversification by allowing some extremely profitable matches to occur. Second, investors have apparently become disillusioned with unrelated diversification, which has led to the advent of hostile bustup takeovers. Finally, we include a dummy variable for whether the bidder's offer included any stock. In light of Asquith, Bruner and Mullins (1987) we want to be sure that the acquisition announcement effects that we observe are not explained by information conveyed through the choice of whether or not to issue stock to finance an acquisition. Table II contains summary statistics for all of the variables that we use in our analysis.

II. Preliminary Evidence

In this section, we present some simple statistics on bidder returns in acquisitions. In the next section, we present the regressions.

Recall that we define the bidder return as the ratio of the 3-day change in the bidding firm's equity value around the announcement date to the price of the target's equity. The mean value of bidder return in the 326 acquisitions is −.70%, with a standard error of 1.22%; and 41.4% of the returns are positive. Hereafter we use the notation −.70% (1.22, .414 > 0). Although we define the bidder return variable differently from previous studies, the common finding that the average bidder return is not significantly different from zero obtains in our data set as well. The question is: which properties of the match make this return (more) negative? The three properties we look at are the growth rate of the target, the past performance of the bidding firm, and relatedness of the acquisition. Table III presents mean bidder returns for various categories of firms, as well as t-tests of the difference in means across categories and chi-squared tests of the difference in percent positive.

As a preliminary look at the effects of the growth rate of target's sales, we divide the sample into faster than the median and slower than the median growing targets. For fast growing targets, the mean bidder return is −2.43% (2.35, .389 > 0). For slow growing targets, the mean bidder return in 2.15% (1.91, .448 > 0). Buying a fast growing company is unattractive relative to buying a slow growing one. However, neither mean is significantly different from 0, and their difference, equal to 4.58%, is not quite significant at conventional levels (t = 1.51). The more precise regression tests of the effect on the bidder's return from buying growth do reject the null hypothesis of no effect (see Section III).

Recall that we measure the quality of bidding firm's management in two distinct ways: 3-year income growth relative to industry and 3-year cum dividend equity returns relative to industry. For both income and equity value, we split the sample into firms that do better than their industry and firms that do worse than their industry. Bidders with fast relative income growth earn an average return of 3.02% (2.24, .473 > 0). Bidders with slow relative income growth earn an average return of −5.02% (1.80, .338 > 0). According to this measure, bad

Table II

Summary Statistics for the Variables Used in the Analysis

Sample of 326 acquisitions between 1975 and 1987. The variables are defined in the text.

	Median	Mean	Standard Deviation	Minimum	Maximum	Sample Size
Bidder's Return on Acquisition of Target	−.0156	−.0070	.252	−.866	1.22	326
Dummy = 1 if Acquisition Is at Least Partly Equity-Financed	0	.485	.501	0	1	326
5-Year Target Real Sales Growth	.143	.179	.482	−1.37	2.74	287
Bidder 3-Year Income Growth Relative to Industry	.0608	.0969	.627	−2.78	3.00	299
Bidder 3-Year (cum dividend) Stock Return Relative to Industry	.0522	.165	1.35	−4.80	7.81	289
Dummy = 1 if Deal Is in 1980–1987	1	.528	.500	0	1	326
Dummy = 1 if Bidder and Target Share a 4-Digit SIC Industry	0	.279	.449	0	1	326
Correlation Coefficient of Bidder and Target Stock Returns over 3 Years Prior to Takeover	.365	.343	.206	−.706	.878	326
Dummy = 1 if Deal Is in 1980–1987 *and* Bidder/Target Share 4-Digit SIC Industry	0	.175	.380	0	1	326
Dummy = 1 if Deal Is in 1980–1987 Times Correlation Coefficient of Target and Bidder Returns	0	.164	.211	−.184	.878	326
Dummy = 1 if there Are Multiple Bidders	0	.239	.427	0	1	326

Table III

A Comparison of Mean Bidder Return on Acquisition by Characteristics of the Match

Characteristics of the match covered include target sales growth prior to the acquisition, bidder's income growth prior to the acquisition, bidder's stock return prior to the acquisition, measures of relatedness of the target and the bidder, and the time period during which the acquisition occurred. Sample of 326 acquisitions between 1975 and 1987.

	5-Year Target Sales Growth			3-Year Bidder Income Growth			3-Year Bidder Stock Return		
	Faster Than Sample Median	Slower Than Sample Median	Tests of Difference in Means & in % > 0	Faster Than Industry Average	Slower Than Industry Average	Tests of Difference in Means & in % > 0	Higher Than Industry Average	Lower Than Industry Average	Tests of Difference in Means & in % > 0
Mean Bidder Return	−2.43	2.15	$t = 1.51$	3.02	−5.02	$t = 2.67$	2.12	−2.12	$t = 1.39$
(Standard Error)	(2.35)	(1.91)	$(p = .132)$	(2.24)	(1.80)	$(p = .0078)$	(2.25)	(2.02)	$(p = .167)$
Number of Observations	144	143	$\chi^2 = 1.01$	169	130	$\chi^2 = 5.47$	153	136	$\chi^2 = .20$
Percent Positive	38.9	44.8	$(p = .314)$	47.3	33.8	$(p = .0194)$	43.8	41.2	$(p = .654)$
	Bidder and Target Share 4-Digit SIC Industry			3-Year Bidder and Target Correlation of Stock Returns			Year of the Acquisition		
	Yes	No	Tests of Difference in Means & in % > 0	Below Sample Median	Above Sample Median	Tests of Difference in Means & in % > 0	1975–1979	1980–1987	Tests of Difference in Means & in % > 0
Mean Bidder Return	2.38	−1.89	$t = 1.37$	.983	−2.37	$t = 1.20$	.517	−1.78	$t = .821$
(Standard Error)	(2.41)	(1.70)	$(p = .171)$	(2.21)	(1.70)	$(p = .230)$	(1.86)	(2.06)	$(p = .412)$
Number of Observations	91	235	$\chi^2 = .69$	163	163	$\chi^2 = .62$	154	172	$\chi^2 = 3.42$
Percent Positive	45.1	40.0	$(p = .406)$	43.6	39.3	$(p = .431)$	46.8	36.6	$(p = .064)$

managers earn significantly negative returns from making acquisitions. Moreover, they earn significantly less than do good managers. The return difference of 8.04% has a t-statistic of 2.67.

A similar result obtains using the bidder's past equity returns relative to industry, except now we cannot as reliably conclude that firms underperforming their industries lose from making acquisitions. The difference between returns to good and bad managers from making an acquisition, at 4.24%, is different from 0 with a p-value of .167.

Our first measure of relatedness is defined above through commonality of 4-digit SIC industries that the target and the bidder operate in. The evidence in Table III shows that the average bidder return in a related acquisition is 2.38% (2.41, .451 > 0), and in an unrelated acquisition it is −1.89% (1.70, .400 > 0). Although the two mean returns are of opposite signs and differ by 4.2%, they are not statistically significantly different from 0 or from each other. A similar picture emerges when we measure relatedness by correlation of bidder and target returns. The average bidder return in the subsample with above median correlation of bidder/target stock returns is .938% (2.21, .436 > 0) and that in the subsample with below median correlation is −2.37% (1.70, .393 > 0). The two mean returns are not significantly different from 0 or from each other.

The results become sharper when we distinguish between the 1970s and the 1980s, as is done in Table IV. Table IV shows that the difference between returns to related and unrelated acquisitions is both statistically and substantively more pronounced in the 1980s than in the 1970s. In Panel A of Table IV we call an acquisition related if the target and the bidder operate in the same 4-digit SIC industry. The panel shows that the returns to both related and unrelated acquisitions have changed from the 1970s to the 1980s. The mean return to related acquisitions has risen (insignificantly) by 1.3% in the 1980s, while the mean return to unrelated acquisitions has declined (also insignificantly) by 4.3%. Note that the sharp decrease over time in the fraction of returns that are positive in unrelated acquisitions is statistically significant. This evidence indicates that unrelated diversification became unattractive in the 1980s.

We can also see this point by comparing related to unrelated acquisitions in the two subperiods separately. Mean returns in related vs unrelated acquisitions are not statistically or substantively different in the 1970s, but are different in the 1980s. In the 1980s, the difference in mean returns in related and unrelated acquisitions is 6.97%, with a t-statistic of 1.60 (p = .11). During this period, in 45.6% of related acquisitions bidder returns are positive, but in only 32.2% of unrelated acquisitions are bidder returns positive (p = .09). Not surprisingly, the rise in the relative attractiveness of related acquisitions has led to an increase in the fraction of acquisitions that are related, from 22% in the 1970s to 33% in the 1980s.

These results are qualitatively confirmed using correlation of stock returns as a measure of relatedness, although the evidence is much weaker. One reason the results are weaker is that we split the sample at the median, and call acquisitions with above median stock return correlation related, even though according to our previous measure of relatedness over two thirds of the acquisitions are unrelated. The finding that the consequences of diversification are different in the two

Table IV

A Comparison of Mean Bidder Returns in Related and Unrelated Acousitions in the 1970s and 1980s

Each panel consists of 3 main rows corresponding to related acquisitions, unrelated acquisitions, and tests of equality of bidder returns between these two types of acquisitions. Within each row, there is a column of four numbers. They correspond to the mean bidder return on acquisition for that cell, the standard error of that mean return, the number of observations in the cell, and the percentage of observations in that cell for which the bidder's return on acquisition is positive (as in Table III). Sample of 326 acquisitions between 1975 and 1987.

Panel A: Diversification Measured Using 4-Digit SIC Industries in Which Bidder and Target Operate

	1975–1979	1980–1987	Tests of Equality of Means & of % > 0 in Two Periods
Bidder and Target Share a 4-Digit SIC Industry	1.54	2.88	$t = .268$
	(3.82)	(3.12)	($p = .7897$)
	34	57	$\chi^2 = .02$
	44.1	45.6	($p = .8896$)
Bidder and Target Do Not Share a 4-Digit SIC Industry	.227	−4.09	$t = 1.27$
	(2.13)	(2.65)	($p = .2037$)
	120	115	$\chi^2 = 5.69$
	47.5	32.2	($p = .0171$)
Tests of Equality of Means & of % > 0 between Related and Unrelated	$t = .293$	$t = 1.60$	
	($p = .770$)	($p = .112$)	
	$\chi^2 = .12$	$\chi^2 = 2.94$	
	($p = .728$)	($p = .0865$)	

Panel B: Diversification Measured Using Correlation Coefficient of Bidder and Target Monthly Stock Returns over 3 Years Prior to the Year of the Bid

	1975–1979	1980–1987	Tests of Equality of Means & of % > 0 in Two Periods
Correlation of Bidder and Target Stock Returns above Sample Median	.770	1.27	$t = .111$
	(2.62)	(3.83)	($p = .9120$)
	93	70	$\chi^2 = .63$
	46.2	40.0	($p = .4270$)
Correlation of Bidder and Target Stock Returns below Sample Median	.132	−3.87	$t = 1.14$
	(2.47)	(2.28)	($p = .2558$)
	61	102	$\chi^2 = 2.78$
	47.5	34.3	($p = .0955$)
Tests of Equality of Means & of % > 0 between Related and Unrelated	$t = .168$	$t = 1.23$	
	($p = .8672$)	($p = .2220$)	
	$\chi^2 = .03$	$\chi^2 = .58$	
	($p = .8739$)	($p = .4474$)	

periods guides our regression analysis, in that we distinguish between the 1970s and the 1980s in measuring the effect of diversification on returns to the bidding firms.

III. Regressions

Table V presents the regressions of bidder returns (change in value of bidder divided by target value) on the characteristics of the match. The left panel of Table V uses 3-year income growth relative to industry as a measure of the quality of bidder management, and the right panel uses 3-year stock returns relative to industry. The three regressions on each side use commonality of 4-digit industries between the bidder and the target, correlation coefficient of bidder and target returns, and both of them at the same time as measures of relatedness. In all regressions, we use both a time dummy for the 1980s and an

Table V

Regressions of Bidder's Return on Acquisition on Characteristics of the Match

These regressions for our 1975–1987 sample of acquisitions estimate the effect of target sales growth, bidder's prior performance, and relatedness of the bidder and target on the acquisition return to the bidder. The regression allows for the 1970s and 1980s to have a separate intercept and separate relatedness effects. The use of equity as a method of payment and the presence of competing bidders are also included as control variables. Numbers in brackets are standard errors. White (1980) adjustments are used in regressions where a χ^2 test indicates significant heteroskedasticity.

	Quality of Bidder Management Measured by 3-Year Income Growth Relative to Industry			Quality of Bidder Management Measured by 3-Year Equity Return Relative to Industry		
Variable Name	I	II	III	I	II	III
Intercept	.0769[b]	.0871[c]	.0878[c]	.0871[b]	.0887[c]	.0928[c]
	(.0340)	(.0456)	(.0451)	(.0352)	(.0487)	(.0478)
Dummy = 1 if Acquisition Is at Least Partly Equity-Financed	−.0340	−.0424	−.0376	−.0314	−.0407	−.0354
	(.0336)	(.0324)	(.0326)	(.0345)	(.0338)	(.0336)
5-Year Target Sales Growth	−.101[a]	−.0947[b]	−.102[a]	−.0953[a]	−.0900[b]	−.0996[b]
	(.0348)	(.0392)	(.0394)	(.0345)	(.0396)	(.0399)
Quality of Bidder Management	.0519[b]	.0530[b]	.0511[b]	.0230[c]	.0268[c]	.0231
	(.0257)	(.0233)	(.0220)	(.0128)	(.0164)	(.0153)
Dummy = 1 if Deal Is in 1980–87	−.0813[b]	−.126[b]	−.143[b]	−.0762[c]	−.104[c]	−.127[b]
	(.0376)	(.0548)	(.0562)	(.0392)	(.0601)	(.0624)
Dummy = 1 if Bidder and Target Share a 4-Digit SIC Industry	−.0163		−.0145	−.0254		−.0248
	(.0531)		(.0470)	(.0544)		(.0484)
Dummy = 1 if Deal Is in 1980–87 *and* Target and Bidder Share a 4-Digit SIC Industry	.127[c]		.113	.122[c]		.115[c]
	(.0737)		(.0731)	(.0743)		(.0696)
Correlation Coefficient of Bidder and Target Monthly Stock Returns over 3 Years Prior to Takeover		−.0278	−.0196		−.0140	−.0047
		(.0930)	(.100)		(.103)	(.107)
Dummy = 1 if Deal Is in 1980–87 Times Correlation Coefficient of Bidder and Target Stock Returns		.250[b]	.203		.190	.157
		(.126)	(.132)		(.130)	(.135)
Dummy = 1 if there Are Multiple Bidders	−.0988[b]	−.0970[a]	−.104[a]	−.0918[b]	−.0850[a]	−.0944[a]
	(.0389)	(.0259)	(.0265)	(.0395)	(.0264)	(.0267)
Number of Observations	266	266	266	254	254	254
R^2	.09	.08	.10	.08	.07	.08

[a] Significant at 1%.
[b] Significant at 5%.
[c] Significant at 10%.

interaction of that dummy with the relatedness measure to allow for different returns to diversification in the 1970s and the 1980s.

In all regressions, the coefficient on the dummy equal to 1 when there are multiple bidders is highly significant and is equal to about −0.1. This means that entry by additional bidders reduces the winning bidder's market value by 10 cents on each dollar paid for the target. The second control variable, the dummy equal to 1 if the acquisition is at least partly equity financed, is not statistically significant in any of the regressions.

Depending on the specification, estimated bidder return falls between 9.0% and 10.2% as the target's change in log sales over the five years prior to the year of the acquisition goes from 0 to 1. In all specifications, this estimate of the cost of buying growth is highly statistically significant. To interpret the magnitude of this effect better, note that the value of 0 for the 5-year change in log sales represents 35th percentile sales growth performance, while the value of 1 represents 95th percentile performance. In our data, buying rapidly growing firms is extremely costly to the bidders.

Whether we measure past performance of the bidder by income growth relative to industry or by stock returns relative to industry, its effect is significant. When the industry-adjusted 3-year change in the log of bidder income goes from 0 to 1, the average return from making an acquisition rises by somewhere between 5.1% and 5.3% depending on the specification. An industry-adjusted change in the log of income of 0 represents median relative income growth, while a value of 1 represents growth at the 95th percentile.

Similarly, when the industry adjusted 3-year bidder's stock return goes from 0 to 100%, the average return from making an acquisition rises by somewhere between 2.3% and 2.7%, depending on the specification. An industry-adjusted 3-year stock return of 0 is about median, and a return of 100% is at about the 85th percentile.

As do the findings of Lang, Stulz and Walkling (1989), these results show that firms with better managers are also better acquirers. These results are inconsistent with a particular version of Roll's hubris hypothesis, in which managers of better performing firms are more arrogant and therefore overestimate the target's value under their control by more.

Comparing the effect of diversification on bidding firm's returns in the 1970s and the 1980s requires looking at three variables: the measure of relatedness, the time period dummy, and the interaction of the two. We do not discuss the regressions with both measures of relatedness included at the same time, since the strong correlation between the two measures makes the results insignificant and difficult to interpret. We also focus, for concreteness, on the left panel, where past bidder performance is measured by 3-year relative income growth. The results for the right panel are very similar. Note finally that the correlation coefficient of stock returns can be interpreted similarly to the shared 4-digit SIC codes dummy. We can think of unrelated acquisitions as those for which the value of the correlation of stock returns is 0, and of related acquisitions as those for which this correlation is 1.

When the relatedness measure, the time period dummy, and the interaction are all equal to 0, we are in the benchmark case of unrelated acquisitions in the

1970s. The coefficient on the 1980s dummy therefore captures the difference in returns on *unrelated* acquisitions between the 1980s and the 1970s. In regression I, the return on unrelated acquisitions was 8.1% lower in the 1980s than in the 1970s (t = 2.16). In regression II, the return from aquiring a target whose stock returns are uncorrelated with the bidder's was 12.6% lower in the 1980s than in the 1970s (t = 2.30). Using the zero correlation of stock returns to define unrelatedness yields bigger magnitudes simply because this is a more extreme form of unrelatedness than non-sharing of a 4-digit SIC industry. The results confirm our earlier finding that returns to unrelated acquisitions have declined substantially in the 1980s.

To see what happened to returns in *related acquisitions* between the 1970s and the 1980s, we add the coefficient on the relatedness measure to the coefficient on the interaction between the relatedness measure and the 1980s dummy. In regression I, the return on related acquisitions is 12.7% − 8.1% = 4.6% higher in the 1980s than in the 1970s (t = .78). In regression II, the return from acquiring a firm with a perfectly correlated stock return is 25.0% − 12.6% = 12.4% higher in the 1980s than in the 1970s (t = 1.34). In contrast to the statistically significant decline in returns to *unrelated* acquisitions over this period, the returns to *related* acquisitions have risen, but not significantly. The apparent overall decline of returns to acquisitions from the 1970s to the 1980s documented in Table III is completely a consequence of the large decline in returns to unrelated diversification.

The coefficient on the interaction of the 1980s dummy and the relatedness measure describes the change from the 1970s to the 1980s of the returns difference in related and unrelated acquisitions. In regression I, the return from doing a related as opposed to an unrelated deal has gone up by 12.7% from the 1970s to the 1980s (t = 1.72, p-value = .085). In regression II, the return from buying a target whose stock returns are perfectly correlated with the bidder's rather than a target with uncorrelated stock returns has gone up by 25.0% (t = 1.98, p-value = .048) from the 1970s to the 1980s. In the 1980s, the penalty for diversification relative to making a related acquisition has gone way up.

Similar results obtain when we use industry-adjusted stock returns to measure past performance of the bidding firm. In the 1980s, returns to related acquisitions have gone (insignificantly) up, returns to diversification have gone (significantly) down, and the cost of diversifying relative to buying related has risen significantly. The overall verdict on diversification is clear: it is a bad idea in the 1980s.

The results in Table V support the proposition that managerial objectives drive acquisitions. For example, they show that buying growth is a bad idea from the point of view of bidding firm's shareholders. Of course, growth is one of the much discussed managerial objectives, pursued either for its own sake or for the sake of assuring the survival of the bidding firm and the continuity of its top management.

The results in Table V also suggest that unrelated diversification is a bad idea from the point of view of the bidding firm's shareholders in the 1980s. Like pursuit of growth, diversification can be understood as serving the objectives of managers.

Perhaps surprisingly, we do not find that diversification reduces bidding firms' shareholder wealth in the 1970s. We take this to mean one of two things. First, there might have been some efficiency reasons for diversification in the earlier period, such as imperfect capital markets, foreclosure of related acquisitions due to antitrust policy, or the attractiveness of conglomerate control. Second, the market might have favored diversification during this period given the information it had, even though ex post diversification proved unattractive and by the 1980s the market caught on.

Finally, the results in Table V demonstrate that firms with bad managers (identified by poor firm performance relative to its industry) do much worse in making acquisitions than firms with good managers. The negative return to acquisitions by poorly performing acquirers is evidence that bad acquisitions are a manifestation of agency problems in the firm.

IV. Implications

Although this paper has focused on managerial objectives in making mostly friendly acquisitions, the results may also shed light on the source of gains in hostile bust-up takeovers, leveraged buyouts, and defensive recapitalizations involving large scale divestitures. Our finding that in the 1980s the stock market punishes unrelated diversification is consistent with the view that the source of bust-up gains in the 1980s is the reversal of the unrelated diversification of the 1960s and the 1970s. Hostile bust-up takeovers simply undo past conglomeration.

At the same time, our finding that managerial objectives drive bad acquisitions suggests a different interpretation of the gains from bustup takeovers. Raiders in these deals facilitate the sale of each piece of the target to the highest bidder. Part of the gain from this activity is doubtless the improvement in the operations of particular divisions under a more talented or a better motivated management team. But part of the gain from bustups may come from the willingness of other non-value-maximizing managers to buy the pieces of the target for their own empires. By allowing each buyer to overpay only for the piece of the target he really wants, the raider can collect more than any single bidder would pay for the whole target. This suggests that takeover premia may overestimate the efficiency gains from hostile bustup takeovers.

REFERENCES

Amihud, Yakov and Baruch Lev, 1981, Risk reduction as a managerial motive for conglomerate mergers, *Bell Journal of Economics* 12, 605–617.

Asquith, Paul R., R. F. Bruner, and David W. Mullins, Jr., 1987, Merger returns and the form of financing, Working paper, Harvard Business School.

Baumol, William J., 1959, *Business Behavior, Value and Growth* (Macmillan, New York).

Bradley, Michael, A. Desai, and E. Han Kim, 1988, Synergistic gains from corporate acquisitions and their division between the stockholders of target and acquiring firms, *Journal of Financial Economics* 21, 3–40.

Donaldson, Gordon, 1984, *Managing Corporate Wealth* (Praeger, New York).

——— and Jay Lorsch, 1983, *Decision Making at the Top* (Basic Books, New York).

Dun and Bradstreet, 1974–1987, *Million Dollar Directory* (Dun and Bradstreet, New York).

Hall, Bronwyn H., 1988, The effect of takeover activity on corporate research and development, in

Alan J. Auerbach, ed.: *Corporate Takeovers: Causes and Consequences* (University of Chicago Press, Chicago, IL).

Jarrell, Gregg and Anette Poulsen, 1988. The returns to acquiring firms: Evidence from three decades, Working paper, University of Rochester.

Jensen, Michael C., 1986, Agency cost of free cash flow, corporate finance, and takeovers, *American Economic Review* 76, 323–329.

Lang, Larry, René M. Stulz, and Ralph A. Walkling, 1989, Tobin's q and the gains from successful tender offers, *Journal of Financial Economics* 24, 137–154.

Lewellen, Wilbur, Claudio Loderer, and Ahron Rosenfeld, 1985, Merger decisions and executive stock ownership in acquiring firms, *Journal of Accounting and Economics* 7, 209–231.

Mitchell, Mark L. and Kenneth Lehn, 1990, Do bad bidders become good targets?, *Journal of Political Economy*, Forthcoming.

Morck, Randall, Andrei Shleifer, and Robert W. Vishny, 1989, Alternative mechanisms for corporate control, *American Economic Review* 79, 842–852.

Roll, Richard, 1986, The hubris hypothesis of corporate takeovers, *Journal of Business* 59, 197–216.

Servaes, Henri, 1988, Tobin's Q, agency costs and corporate control, Working paper, University of Chicago.

Shleifer, Andrei and Robert W. Vishny, 1988, Value maximization and the acquisition process, *Journal of Economic Perspectives* 2, 7–20.

——— and Robert W. Vishny, 1990, Managerial entrenchment: The case of manager-specific investments, *Journal of Financial Economics,* Forthcoming.

You, Victor L., Richard E. Caves, James S. Henry, and Michael M. Smith, 1986, Mergers and bidders' wealth: Managerial and strategic factors, in L. G. Thomas, ed.: *The Economics of Strategic Planning* (Lexington Books, Boston, MA).

[16]

ELSEVIER Journal of Financial Economics 40 (1996) 163–181

JOURNAL OF Financial ECONOMICS

Hostile takeovers and the correction of managerial failure

Julian Franks*,[a], Colin Mayer[b]

[a]London Business School, Regent's Park, London NW1 4SA, United Kingdom
[b]School of Management Studies, University of Oxford, Oxford OX2 6HE, United Kingdom

(Received March 1992; final version received April 1995)

Abstract

This paper examines the disciplining function of hostile takeovers in the U.K. in 1985 and 1986. We report evidence of high board turnover and significant levels of post-takeover restructuring. Large gains are anticipated in hostile bids as reflected in high bid premiums. However, there is little evidence of poor performance prior to bids, suggesting that the high board turnover does not derive from past managerial failure. Hostile takeovers do not therefore perform a disciplining function. Instead, rejection of bids appears to derive from opposition to post-takeover redeployment of assets and renegotiation over the terms of bids.

Key words: Hostile takeovers; Executive dismissals
JEL classification: G34

*Corresponding author.

This paper is part of an ESRC funded project, number W102251003, on 'Capital Markets, Corporate Governance, and the Market for Corporate Control'. We are grateful to Nick Carrick, Luis Correia da Silva, and Marc Goergen for valuable research assistance. We wish to thank John Chown for financial assistance on this project and for helpful discussions.

The paper has been presented at the 1993 Annual Meeting of the American Finance Association in Anaheim, at the Annual Meeting of the French Finance Association in Paris, at the Annual Meeting of the European Finance Association in Athens, at a conference on European Restructuring at INSEAD and at seminars in Essex, Keele, Oxford, Paris, and Warwick. We are particularly grateful to discussants Patrick Bolton, Stuart Gilson, Kristian Rydqvist, and Paul Seabright for valuable suggestions. We are also grateful for comments from Swami Bhaskaran, Michael Brennen, Michel Habib, David Hirshleifer, Ernst Maug, Narayan Naik, Kjell Nyborg, and Walter Torous. We also wish to thank Richard Ruback (the editor) and John Pound (the referee) for many helpful comments in the revision of the manuscript.

SSDI 0304405X9500840 B

1. Introduction

Hostile takeovers are controversial. To some, takeovers are an important method of correcting managerial failure. Rappaport (1990), for example, believes that the recent wave of takeover activity 'has changed the attitudes and practices of U.S. managers'. He argues (p. 100) that 'it represents the most effective check on management autonomy ever devised. And it is breathing new life into the public corporation'. Grossman and Hart (1980, p. 329) associate this discipline with hostile takeovers: '... since the threat of raids encourages good management and raids only occur in events where the company is worth more to the raider than it is currently worth, there is no reason on efficiency grounds for society to restrict raids'.

To others, takeovers are a poor form of corporate governance. Peter Drucker has declared that 'there can be absolutely no doubt that hostile takeovers are exceedingly bad for the economy.' Herzel and Shepro (1990, p. 3) believe that they are 'a tremendously expensive and imprecise solution.' Shleifer and Summers (1988, p. 37) take a wider social perspective and 'see hostile takeovers as destructions of valuable corporate cultures . . . which have extremely serious allocative consequences'.

This paper addresses the disciplining function of takeovers, specifically examining whether hostile takeovers are associated with the dismissal of the management and prior poor performance. Evidence on poor performance of target firms comes from pre-bid measures of financial performance as well as bid premiums and post-takeover restructurings. We find clear evidence of high board turnover and significant levels of restructuring in hostile takeovers. Large gains are anticipated, as reflected in high bid premiums paid to target shareholders. However, using a number of different benchmarks, we find little evidence that hostile takeovers are motivated by poor performance prior to bids. We therefore reject the view that hostile takeovers perform a disciplinary role. Instead, we argue that opposition to bids by incumbent management reflects disagreement over the price the bidder is willing to pay and its intentions to restructure the company.

Section 2 describes the sample and the methodology. Section 3 reports results on hostile takeovers and managerial control changes. Section 4 provides evidence on the bidding process in hostile bids. Section 5 concludes the paper.

2. Data, hypotheses, and methodology

The U.K. and U.S., unlike many other countries, have active markets for corporate control. In 1985 and 1986 there were 80 hostile bids in the U.K. Jensen (1988) reports that there were 40 hostile tender offers in the U.S. in 1986. In contrast, Germany has had just three cases of hostile acquisitions of nonfinancial corporations in the whole of the post-Second World War period. The absence of a market for corporate control in most of continental Europe is attributable to the structure of capital markets, with small numbers of quoted companies and ownership of quoted companies concentrated in the hands of a small number of investors (see Franks and Mayer, 1994).

The U.K. is thus one of the few countries other than the U.S. whose market for corporate control can be studied. In fact, the U.K. has certain advantages over the U.S. in that there are fewer antitakeover provisions enshrined in either corporate charters or state legislation. For example, the Takeover Code in the U.K. explicitly prevents the application of poison pills once a takeover bid has been launched.

This paper examines hostile takeovers in the U.K. in 1985 and 1986. A hostile takeover is defined as one in which the first offer is opposed by the incumbent management. A bid is successful if the bidder acquires the target on the basis of its first or a revised offer. A bid is unsuccessful if the target firm remains independent or is subsequently acquired by another bidder in a later bid battle. There were a total of 325 bids for listed companies, including unsuccessful bids. Of the 80 hostile bids, 35 were successful, 23 remained independent (to July 1990), and 22 were subsequently acquired. In five cases there were multiple bids involving more than one bidder. If two companies bid for one target and the target management rejected one bid but accepted the other, then the former bid was classified as 'rejected' and the latter as 'accepted'. This occurred only once in our sample. The level of hostile takeover activity is similar to prior years: according to the annual report of the U.K. Takeover Panel, 23% of bids for publicly listed targets in 1969–1971 were classified as hostile. The level of hostile takeover activity is also not dissimilar to that recorded in the U.S. by Bhagat, Shleifer, and Vishny (1990), who find 63 successful hostile takeover bids and 22 unsuccessful contests during the three years 1984–1986.[1]

The sample data is drawn from AMDATA, a database of takeover bids, buyouts, and divestments. The sample includes all 35 successful hostile takeovers, all 23 unsuccessful hostile takeovers, a set of 35 randomly selected accepted bids from AMDATA, and a group of nonmerging firms over the performance period 1980 to 1986. The nonmerging sample was matched by industry (London Stock Exchange Industry Classification) and size (equity market capitalization in 1990) with the targets of hostile bids (and of uncontested bids) using the London Share Price Data Base (LSPD).

The unsuccessful hostile takeovers, the randomly selected accepted bids, and the nonmerging firms provide benchmarks of comparative performance for the

[1]Their sample includes hostile takeovers for targets with a value greater than $50 million. The definition of hostility is similar to that in this paper, where the target management initially expressed opposition to the bid.

sample of successful hostile takeovers. We compare the performance of firms involved in successful hostile bids with the performance of firms involved in other takeovers (accepted bids). We also compare targets of hostile takeovers and nonmerging firms to see how firms that become hostile takeover targets perform relative to other firms of similar size in the same industry. Finally, we compare successful hostile takeovers and failed hostile takeovers. Failed takeovers provide evidence of target management's response to the threat of a hostile bid and can be compared with the bidder's response in a successful takeover.

2.1. Board turnover and post-takeover restructuring

If hostile takeovers perform a disciplinary role, we should see a high level of managerial turnover followed by large-scale restructuring. These actions are necessary but not sufficient conditions for takeovers to be disciplinary because they could reflect disagreement over a strategic redeployment of assets. To evaluate management turnover, we collect data on all members of the board of directors of the target firm, including the name of the director, the date of resignation or retirement, and the eventual position of the director in the merged company.

Our information comes from company accounts of the target and bidder firms and from company announcements issued by the Stock Exchange. The number of target company board members promoted to the acquiring company's board comes from accounts of the target company and the acquiring firm. Telephone interviews with company representatives corroborated and supplemented the data. The directors' histories were followed for two years after the takeover.

We use two measures of post-takeover restructuring. The first measure is significant sales of assets during the two years after takeover. Asset sales for successful hostile and friendly bids are classified as significant if more than 10% of the total fixed assets of the merged firm are sold in the corresponding year. Data on asset sales are based on annual accounts and telephone interviews with company secretaries to the board of directors or equivalent persons.

Post-bid studies of successful takeovers suffer from the difficulty of separately identifying asset sales in the target firms from those of the bidder, since the financial accounts are reported on a consolidated basis. In contrast, the post-bid asset sales of targets of unsuccessful bids are readily observable. Consequently, we also analyze the asset sales of targets of unsuccessful bids over a period of five years around the bid.

2.2. Anticipated bid benefits and prebid performance measures

If hostile bids serve a disciplinary function there must also be evidence of anticipated gains associated with the restructurings and poor performance prior to the takeover. Anticipated merger benefits are measured using bid premiums based on abnormal share price returns in the month of the first bid. If bids are revised, we examine the month of the first bid to the month of the last bid.

We use four measures of pre-bid financial performance. The first is share price returns over five years prior to the month of the announcement of the initial bid. The bid announcement date is from Financial Times Mergers & Acquisitions (FTM&A). If bids are revised, the date of the first bid is obtained from FTM&A, London Stock Exchange Microfiches, and Textline. Textline provides extracts from newspapers such as the *Financial Times*. Returns are based upon share price and dividend data collected from LSPD and Datastream. Abnormal returns are calculated using a market model ($\alpha = 0$, $\beta = 1$). The second measure of financial performance is based on changes in dividends per share and dividend omissions in each of the two years prior to the financial year in which the takeover occurred. The third measure of pre-bid financial performance is the cash flow rate of return on assets employed in 1980 and in the last accounting year before the bid, calculated from the cash flow gross of interest and depreciation divided by the sum of the market value of equity and the book value of debt. The last measure is based on Tobin's Q ratio, the ratio of the market value to replacement cost of a firm's assets. The ratio is calculated for 1980 (or the first year of the listing) and the last accounting year before the bid. The market value of equity and book value of debt proxy for the numerator. The replacement cost of each company's assets was taken from its annual accounts. Until 1985, companies in the U.K. were required to report the current cost of their assets. Current cost is the replacement cost based on an up-to-date cost of the assets, after providing for depreciation to reflect the age and usage of the assets. Replacement costs are based on an index of prices of new assets.

3. Test results

Sections 3.1 and 3.2 examine the extent to which hostile takeovers give rise to management board turnover and post-takeover restructuring. Sections 3.3 and 3.4 evaluate the extent to which hostility and managerial control changes are associated with higher bid premiums and poor pre-bid performance.

3.1. Board turnover

Table 1 reports that 50% of the directors resign after accepted bids, compared with 90% after successful hostile bids. If outside directors are excluded, the difference barely changes. According to panel 2, the differences in proportions between successful hostile and accepted bids are significant at the 1% level for both total and inside board resignations.

Table 1
Proportion of directors who resigned in the targets of accepted and successful and unsuccessful hostile bids (size of sample, *n*, in parentheses)

Panel 1. Resignations

	Accepted	Successful hostile	Unsuccessful hostile
All directors	50% (34)	90% (31)	39% (23)
Inside directors	50% (26)	88% (26)	36% (22)

Panel 2: t-statistic: difference in proportions

	All directors	Inside directors
Successful hostile vs. accepted	3.52[a]	3.00[a]
Unsuccessful hostile vs. successful hostile	– 4.01[a]	– 3.76[a]

Source: Annual reports, Stock Exchange microfiches. Part of the source data for 1986 is contained in appendices A and B of Franks and Mayer (1990). It includes resignations in the two years subsequent to takeover.

[a]Significant at the 1% level.

The levels of inside director resignations in both successful and unsuccessful hostile bids are higher than in nonmerging firms. For example, in a sample of ten nonmerging firms drawn from the lowest decile of share price performance in 1985, only 19% of the board resigned during the year of bad performance and the subsequent year, compared with 90% in successful hostile bids and 39% in unsuccessful bids. Clearly, hostile takeovers are associated with a high level of board turnover. These results are consistent with Klein and Rosenfeld (1988) who find that firms successfully defending themselves through greenmail experience above-average management turnover. The high turnover of the executive members of the boards in unsuccessful hostile bids is also consistent with Hirshleifer and Thakor's (1994) prediction that hostile bids reveal information about the quality of management to the monitors of the firm.

3.2. Post-takeover asset sales

Hostile takeovers are also associated with restructurings. Based on accounts of merged companies and telephone interviews, asset sales exceed 10% of the value of total fixed assets of the merged firms in 53% of successful hostile bids. In contrast, only 26% of accepted bids had significant asset sales, a difference that is statistically significant at greater than the 5% level. The high level of asset disposals is consistent with the results of Dann and DeAngelo (1988, p. 88), who

Table 2
Asset disposals for a five-year period around the bid for unsuccessful bids occurring in 1985 and 1986 (size of sample, t-statistic, and proportion > 10% in parentheses)

	$B-1$[a]	B	$B+1$	$B+2$	$B+3$	*Average*[b]
Asset disposals as a % of tangible fixed assets	8.5% (32, – 1.0,0)	9.2% (24, – 0.4,25)	13.3% (19,1.0,42)	17.2% (17,1.6,53)	19.4% (15,2.2,60)	11.0% (33,0.7,42)

Source: Annual reports. t-statistic indicates whether the figure is different from 10%.

[a]B is the year of the bid.

[b]Firms for which data do not exist for some of the five years have been included for the calculation of the average.

find that 'the median restructuring involves assets constituting 23% of the target's pre-offer equity value'. It is also consistent with Bhide (1989) who finds more evidence of sales of assets arising from past acquisitions of targets in hostile than in friendly bids.

Table 2 provides a detailed examination of the proportion of asset disposals for unsuccessful hostile bids. The table suggests that prior to the bid and in the year of the bid, annual sales of assets total 8–9% of total fixed assets. Post-bid asset sales are larger, with the proportion increasing from 13% in the year after the acquisition to 19% three years after takeover. In the third year after the acquisition, asset sales are significantly greater than 10% (at the 5% significance level), with 60% of companies having sold more than 10% of their assets. This finding is consistent with the observation of Dann and DeAngelo (1988, p. 88) that 'hostile bids rarely prevail in cases in which the planned restructurings were implemented by target managers'.

3.3. *Anticipated benefits and bid premiums*

It might be expected that the higher levels of restructurings in hostile takeovers would create greater shareholder value than in other takeovers. Furthermore, if takeovers are disciplinary, then takeovers which give rise to managerial control changes should have higher bid premiums than those which do not. Table 3 finds that anticipated benefits are higher in successful hostile bids than in other bids: bid premiums average 30% in the month of a bid compared with only 18% for accepted bids. [By way of comparison, Franks and Harris (1989) report premiums of 42% for hostile bids and 28% for uncontested and unrevised bids in the U.S.] The difference of 12 percentage points is statistically significant at the 5% level. When bid premiums are computed for a period which includes any bid revisions, the difference is 15 percentage points and is significant at the 1% level. There is therefore some support for the proposition that bid

Table 3
Bid premiums for three samples: targets of accepted bids, successful hostile bids, and unsuccessful hostile bids (sample size, t-statistic, and proportion positive in parentheses)

Panel 1. Bid premiums

	Accepted	Successful hostile	Unsuccessful hostile
Bid month	18.44%	29.76%	21.50%
	(34, 6.09, 88)	(32, 8.30, 100)	(43, 6.27, 87)
Initial bid to final bid month	18.44%	33.88%	22.40%
	(34, 6.09, 88)	(33, 7.39. 97)	(46, 5.98, 89)

Panel 2: t-statistic: difference in bid premiums

	Bid month	Initial bid to final bid month
Successful hostile vs. accepted	2.29[a]	2.80[b]
Unsuccessful hostile vs. successful hostile	– 1.41	– 1.94[c]

Source: LSPD. Bid premiums in panel 1 are calculated using a market model with parameter values of $\beta = 1$ and $\alpha = 0$.

[a]Significant at the 5% level.
[b]Significant at the 1% level.
[c]Significant at the 10% level.

premiums are higher in hostile bids. Bradley, Desai, and Kim (1988) suggest that competition in the bidding market may produce benefits to the target shareholders at the expense of the shareholders of the bidder.

Unsuccessful hostile bids have bid premiums that are considerably lower than those in successful hostile bids. In fact, they are much closer to the bid premiums in accepted bids, suggesting that the market is anticipating some restructuring after unsuccessful bids but not at as high a level as in successful hostile bids.

We also examine whether the high level of board turnover in hostile bids (reported earlier) is associated with high bid premiums. We define a change in managerial control as occuring when either the chief executive or the chairman of the target firm resigns *or* when there are no promotions from the target to the main board of the acquiring firm. This happens in 88% of successful hostile bids and 60% of accepted bids. The difference is statistically significant at the 2% level. We also repeat the analysis using an alternative definition: a control change occurs when either the chief executive or the chairman resigns *and* there are no promotions to the main board of the acquiring firm. According to this definition, there are control changes in 24% of accepted bids and 66% of successful hostile bids. Since the subsequent results are similar we report the evidence from the first test only.

Bid premiums for targets with control changes are almost identical to those without control changes: 25.23% versus 25.25%. This result is similar to Martin and McConnell (1991) who report abnormal returns of 31.33% for the sample in which there is turnover of the top manager and 33.77% when there is no change; they find that the difference is not statistically significant. Thus, while hostile takeovers give rise to higher bid premiums, the higher premiums are not attributable to the high level of managerial control changes. This evidence is not consistent with a disciplinary role for hostile takeovers. Section 4 provides an alternative explanation for the high bid premiums in hostile takeovers based on bargaining over the terms of the offer.

3.4. Pre-bid performance

Finally, if hostile bids are disciplinary, we would expect high board turnover to be associated with poor performance of the target prior to the bid. We use four measures of performance: share prices, dividend changes, cash flow rates of return, and Tobin's Q.

3.4.1. Pre-bid share price performance

The first panel of Table 4 reports abnormal share price performance for successful hostile bids, unsuccessful hostile bids, and accepted bids, as well as for two samples of nonmerging firms paired by industry and size with the samples of accepted bids and successful hostile bids. Abnormal returns are shown for five years, two years, and one year prior to the date when the market first began to anticipate the bid which is assumed to be three months prior to the announcement date as reported by the London Stock Exchange. Results are reported on an equally weighted basis. The t-statistics in the second panel test the hypothesis that the average abnormal returns in the two relevant samples are equal. The t-statistics are calculated as $t = (M_1 - M_2)/SD$, where M stands for the cell mean $SD = \sqrt{(S_1^2/N_1 + S_2^2/N_2)}$, with N the number of observations averaged in a cell mean and S the cross-sectional deviation about the cell mean.

A comparison of accepted bids with successful hostile bids in panel 1 suggests that the pre-bid performance of targets of successful hostile bids is worse than that of accepted bids: in each of the periods described as one and two years prior to the bid, the difference is around 14 percentage points. Although economically meaningful, panel 2 records that this difference is not significant at the 5% level. The difference in returns is reduced to less than 5 percentage points when abnormal returns are estimated over the five years prior to the bid.

When matching the accepted and hostile bids with nonmerging firms of equivalent size and industry, nonmerging firms record almost identical performance to successful hostile bids over the five years prior to a bid and somewhat

Table 4
Abnormal share price returns for the period up to five years before the bid for various samples of merging and nonmerging firms (size of sample, *t*-statistic, and proportion positive in parentheses)

Panel 1. Abnormal returns

	Accepted bids	Matched nonmerging sample[a]	Successful hostile bids	Matched nonmerging sample[a]	Unsuccessful hostile bids
Average over 5 years[b]	4.53% (28, 0.99, 64)	0.83%[b] (19, 0.23, 53)	− 0.14% (32, − 0.04, 50)	0.14% (26, 0.03, 38)	2.71% (34, 0.72, 50)
2 years prior	7.75% (32, 1.10, 53)	− 7.84% (18, − 0.67, 50)	− 6.09% (34, − 0.84, 38)	2.26% (25, − 0.84, 38)	5.07% (44, 0.78, 41)
1 year prior	7.77% (35, 1.11, 51)	1.99% (19, 0.22, 58)	− 7.68% (34, − 1.17, 41)	7.90% (26, 1.14, 54)	− 2.84% (44, − 0.57, 48)

Panel 2. t-statistic: difference in abnormal returns

	Average over 5 years	2 years prior	1 year prior
Successful hostile less accepted	− 0.79	− 1.37	− 1.61
Accepted less nonmerging	0.46	1.14	0.51
Successful hostile less nonmerging	− 0.05	− 0.83	− 1.63
Successful hostile less unsuccessful hostile	− 0.53	1.15	0.60

Source: LSPD and own calculations. Abnormal returns in panel 1 are calculated using a market model with parameter values of $\alpha = 0$ and $\beta = 1$.

[a]Based upon the same industry using the Stock Exchange Industrial Classification and the company with the closest market equity capitalisation.

[b]Some companies had incomplete data for the five years because they were not listed at the beginning of the period.

[c]One company has been excluded because it was an outlier showing an abnormal return of 161% over five years.

worse (but not statistically significantly so) performance than accepted bids. Abnormal returns are higher for unsuccessful bids than for successful bids, although the difference over five years is small and none of the differences are statistically significant. An analysis of medians discloses similar differences between accepted and successful hostile bids on an equally weighted basis two years prior to a bid and a smaller difference one year before a bid. Using the Wilcoxon test, the differences in medians are significant at the 13% level two years before a bid and at the 14% level one year before a bid.

3.4.2. Dividend changes

The second measure of financial performance reports firms' dividend decisions in each of the two years prior to a bid using four classifications: omission, increase, decrease, or no change. Poor performance should be associated with reductions and omissions in dividends. Panel 1 of Table 5 shows that in the two years prior to a bid a majority of companies in all three samples of bids (successful hostile, unsuccessful hostile, and accepted bids) increased their dividends; very few reduced them. The dividend was omitted entirely in only six cases. A similar pattern emerges in the second panel for dividends declared over the one prior to a bid. The dividend behavior of targets of unsuccessful hostile bids is very similar to targets of successful bids.

Differences in dividend policy may reflect changes in payout policy rather than differences in underlying performance. However, the payout ratios of the three samples calculated for the six-year period 1980–85 (or 1981–86 for 1986 bids) are similar: 38.3% for accepted bids, 40.4% for successful hostile bids, and 43.3% for unsuccessful hostile bids. The differences in the payout ratios between the three samples are not statistically significant and the *t*-statistics are all less than one. The results suggest that there is little difference in performance between the samples.

Table 5
Proportion of companies omitting or changing dividends in accepted and hostile bids (size of sample, *n*, in parentheses)

Panel 1. 2 years prior

	Accepted	Successful hostile	Unsuccessful hostile
Omitted	5.6% (3)	5.9% (2)	2.8% (1)
Decrease	14.3% (5)	2.9% (1)	5.7% (2)
No change	22.9% (8)	14.7% (5)	17.1% (6)
Increase	51.4% (18)	73.5% (25)	71.4% (25)
N/A	2.9% (1)	2.9% (1)	2.8% (1)

Panel 2. 1 year prior

	Accepted	Successful hostile	Unsuccessful hostile
Omitted	2.9% (1)	5.9% (2)	2.9% (1)
Decrease	8.6% (3)	5.9% (2)	5.7% (2)
No change	11.4% (4)	11.8% (4)	11.4% (4)
Increase	77.1% (27)	76.5% (26)	74.3% (26)
N/A	0.0% (0)	0.0% (0)	5.7% (2)

Source: Annual reports.

This result stands in marked contrast to the dividend behavior of a sample of 80 firms in the lowest quintile of shareprice performance reported by LSPD in 1985. The sample had an average abnormal return of − 63%. Dividends were omitted or reduced in 41% of cases compared with 12% for successful hostile bids. In the remaining cases, dividends were held constant (29%) or increased (30%) For 80 firms with zero abnormal returns, dividends were omitted and reduced in 9% of cases and increased in 77% of the cases. These results are remarkably similar to the dividend performance of the sample of hostile takeover targets reported in Table 5. This evidence suggests that when there is poor performance as measured by share prices, dividends are more likely to be omitted or reduced. The results strongly suggest that the sample of targets of hostile bids with its very low level of dividend reductions or omissions is not representative of firms with poor share price performance.

3.4.3. Pre-bid cash flow rates of return

Table 6 reports cash flow rates of return on capital for 1980 and 1985/86. Rates of return for targets for successful hostile bids (17.82%) are similar to those of accepted bids (20.25%) as well as to their matched sample of nonmerging companies (17.15%). None of the differences is statistically significant. Rates of return for targets for successful hostile bids are not statistically different from those of unsuccessful bids.

3.4.4. Tobin's Q

The failure to uncover differences in pre-bid rates of return between targets of hostile bids and other firms may be due to the stock market capitalizing poor performance at the start of the period. If this is the case, then there will be differences in the Tobin's Q ratios, the ratio of market to replacement cost valuations of firms. Table 7 shows that the Q ratios of targets of successful and unsuccessful hostile bids in 1980 are similar to those of accepted bids. Thus the difference in abnormal returns between hostile and accepted bids revealed in Table 4 is not a consequence of differences in initial market values. However, the nonmerging sample has a significantly higher Tobin's Q than the successful hostile bids. There is, therefore, some evidence that poor performance is being capitalized in the targets of hostile bids when the comparison is made with firms in the same industry.

For 1985 and 1986 the Tobin's Q ratios of targets of hostile bids are lower than those of accepted bids in the year of the merger (1.04 versus 1.35); the t-statistic for the difference is − 2.95. In addition, the Q ratio of successful hostile bids is lower than that for the targets of unsuccessful hostile bids (1.04 versus 1.22, t-statistic = − 2.2). Thus, the performance of targets of hostile takeover bids is significantly worse than that for the other two samples. However, the average Q ratios of the targets of accepted and hostile bids are both

Table 6
Cash flow to asset ratios in 1980 and 1985/1986 for various samples of merging and nonmerging firms (size of sample, *t*-statistic, and proportion positive in parentheses)

Panel 1. Cash flow/(market value of equity + book value of debt)

	Accepted bids	Matched nonmerging sample[a]	Successful hostile bids	Matched nonmerging sample[a]	Unsuccessful hostile bids
1980	28.20%	21.74%	22.28%	18.24%	24.49%[b]
	(23, 6.04, 96)	(18, 8.81, 100)	(27, 6.69, 100)	(23, 6.42, 100)	(26, 8.66, 100)
1985, 1986	20.25%	21.61%	17.82%	17.15%	17.50%
	(30, 5.73, 97)	(18, 5.27, 94)	(29, 8.72, 100)	(24, 10.3, 100)	(30, 13.67, 100)

Panel 2. t-statistic: difference in cash flow ratio of two samples

	1980	1985, 1986
Sccessful hostile less accepted	−1.03	−0.60
Accepted less nonmerging	1.28	−0.25
Successful hostile less nonmerging	0.92	0.25
Successful hostile less unsuccessful hostile	−0.51	0.13

Source: Datastream, LSPD, own calculations.

Definitions: Cash flow = Profit after tax + Depreciation + Interest payments, Book value of debt = ST loans + LT loans − Cash balances + Deferred tax.

[a]Based upon the same industry, using the Stock Exchange Industrial Classification and the company with the closest market equity capitalization.

[b]One company has been excluded from the sample because it showed a cash flow ratio of 306.64%.

greater than one, providing evidence of poor relative, rather than poor absolute, performance.

3.5. *Summary of findings*

To summarize, three different measures indicate that the pre-bid financial performance of targets of hostile bids is not easily distinguished from that of targets of accepted bids. The performance of targets of hostile bids is not inferior to that of a nonmerging sample of firms matched on the basis of size and industry; the only exception is for *Q* ratios. This evidence is consistent with Martin and McConnell (1991) who find no difference in pre-bid performance of targets of accepted and rejected bids.

These findings raise the question of whether poor pre-bid performance is more closely associated with managerial control changes than with the hostility of bids. We examine this proposition by repeating the above pre-performance

Table 7
Tobin's Q for 1980 (or first year of listing) and 1985/1986 (or last year of listing/annual report) for various samples of merging and nonmerging firms (size of sample, t-statistic, and proportion with Tobin's $Q > 1$ in parentheses)

Panel 1. Tobin's Q

	Accepted bids	Matched nonmerging sample[a]	Successful hostile bids	Matched nonmerging sample[a]	Unsuccessful hostile bids
1980	0.72%	0.92%	0.82%	1.12%	0.80
	(23, – 3.8, 26)	(17, – 1.0, 47)	(27, – 2.7, 19)	(24, 1.0, 38)	(24, – 3.1, 25)
1985, 1986	1.35	1.25	1.04	1.11	1.22
	(29, 3.7, 76)	(18, 2.1, 73)	(29, 1.0, 55)	(25, 2.0, 60)	(27, 3.0, 74)

Panel 2. t-statistic: difference in Tobin's Q of two samples

	1980	1985, 1986
Successful hostile less accepted	0.92	– 2.95[c]
Accepted less nonmerging	– 1.73[b]	0.67
Successful hostile less nonmerging	– 2.12[d]	– 1.06
Successful hostile less unsuccessful hostile	– 0.21	– 2.20[d]

Source: Datastream, LSPD, own calculations. t-statistic indicates whether Tobin's Q is different from one.

Definition: Tobin's Q = (Market value of equity + Book value of debt)/Replacement cost of assets.

[a]Based upon the same industry using the Stock Exchange Industrial Classification and the company with the closest market equity capitalization.
[b]Significant at the 10% level.
[c]Significant at the 1% level.
[d]Significant at the 5% level.

tests on the sample of all takeovers partitioned by control changes. A very similar picture to that described for the hostile and accepted partition emerges. (Tables relating to this section are available from the authors on request.)

Over five and two years prior to the bid, takeovers with control changes display superior abnormal share price performance to those without control changes, the opposite of the result predicted by evidence of managerial failure. Only in the year prior to the bid is there worse performance although the difference is not statistically significant. [Kini, Kracaw, and Mian (1993) record an inverse relation between performance and CEO turnover for insider-dominated boards and no relation for outsider-dominated boards.] The proportion of firms cutting or omitting dividends is very small in relation to the proportion raising dividends for both samples. There is slightly more evidence that firms omit dividends prior to control change bids but no evidence that they cut them. Cash flow rates of return are lower in the control change sample both five years before the bid and in the year of the bid. However, the differences are not statistically significant. Finally, five years prior to the bid the Tobin's Q ratio of control change targets is slightly higher (0.79) than that of noncontrol change targets (0.70), although in the year of the bid it is lower (1.17 versus 1.32); the differences are not statistically significant. In both cases, the Q ratios are greater than one and therefore suggest profitable investment opportunities rather than poor performance.

In summary, there is little evidence that takeovers with control changes are the result of poor past performance. Several studies examine the relation between board turnover and performance. Weisbach (1988) finds a strong association between prior performance and the probability of director resignations for companies with outsider-dominated boards. Warner, Watts, and Wruck (1988) only find an inverse relation between the probability of a management change and a firm's share price performance when the latter is extremely good or bad. Gilson (1989) finds a significantly higher level of executive turnover in financially distressed than nondistressed firms.

Whereas the last two studies find a relation between very poorly performing companies and high board turnover, we show that the targets of hostile takeovers are performing neither poorly nor worse than the targets of accepted bids. However, Martin and McConnell's (1991) finding of worse pre-bid performance in takeovers where there are high executive changes stands in contrast to our results for the U.K.

4. Revised bids

The previous section reports a high level of board turnover in hostile takeovers, associated with high levels of sales of assets and high bid premiums. However, there is no evidence of high bid premiums when takeovers are partitioned on the basis of control changes. In addition, neither hostile takeovers nor control changes are associated with poor pre-bid performance. The evidence therefore strongly suggests that hostile takeovers are not associated with a disciplinary role in this sample of U.K. takeovers.

The evidence of a high level of post-takeover restructuring in conjunction with high board turnover is more consistent with board dismissal being a result of disagreement with the bidder over the future restructuring of the company. Another explanation, consistent with the high bid premiums in hostile bids, is that rejection of bids is part of the process of negotiating the terms of bids. To evaluate this possibility, we collected data on bid revisions for our sample of successful and unsuccessful bids. In Table 8, we show that hostile bids were

Table 8
Number of bids subject to revision partitioned by hostility of bid

	Revised	Unrevised
Accepted	0	35
Successful hostile: finally accepted	13[b]	0
Successful hostile: contested to the end	12[c]	10
Unsuccessful hostile bids[a]	15[d]	20

Source: Financial Times Mergers & Acquisitions, Extel and Textline.

[a]Some data on revisions of unsuccessful bids missing.

[b]Average length of the window: approximately 45 days.

[c]Average length of the window: approximately 75 days. In three cases, the length was greater than 100 days. One of them was referred to the Monopolies and Mergers Commission, another was referred to the Takeover Panel because of alleged irregularities with the offer, and the other was subject to multiple bidders.

[d]Average length of the window: approximately 78 days. In two of them the length was greater than 100 days. One of them was referred to the Monopolies and Mergers Commission and the other was subject to multiple bidders.

revised in 25 out of the 35 successful hostile bids. When the hostile bidder did not revise the terms after rejection by the target, there was a high rate of bid failure (20 out of 30 cases).

If rejection of bids were a matter of negotiation over price, we would expect to observe bids being rejected, revised, and then accepted (if the bid succeeded); alternatively, the bid would fail because other bidders would emerge in the same or in a subsequent bid. The 13 successful hostile bids that were finally accepted (and therefore recommended) by target management can be interpreted in this way. However, we also observe 12 successful hostile bids being rejected to the end, even after the bids were revised. For this sample, rejection may reflect the breakdown of the bargaining process or outright hostility towards the particular bidder. The latter is consistent with a disciplinary role for takeovers or disagreement over the redeployment of assets after the takeovers.

A further test of the disciplining function involves examining whether a sample of hostile bids that were ultimately rejected had worse performance than a sample of revised bids that were ultimately accepted. Table 9 reports three measures of performance: Tobin's Q, abnormal share price returns, and cash flow rates of return. If initial rejection but ultimate acceptance of bids has to do with bargaining over price, then we would predict (i) higher Q ratios for bids that are ultimately accepted (S.2 in table 9), (ii) larger abnormal returns, and (iii) higher cash flow rates of return.

Table 9

Tobin's Q, abnormal returns, and cash flow rates of return for (i) revised successful hostile bids which are ultimately rejected by the incumbent management (S.1), and (ii) revised successful hostile bids which are ultimately accepted by the incumbent management (S.2) (size of sample, t-statistic, and proportion with Tobin's $Q > 1$ or abnormal returns and cash flow rates of return > 0 in parentheses)

Panel 1. Tobin's Q, abnormal returns, and cash flow rates of return

	Tobin's Q		Abnormal returns			Cash flow rates of return	
	1980	1985/86	− 5 years	− 2 years	− 1 year	1980	1985/86
S.1: Ultimately rejected bids	0.73% (10, − 3.1, 10)	1.02% (11, 0.2, 45)	0.50% (12, − 0.28, 47)	− 5.31% (12, − 0.58, 46)	0.85% (12, 0.09, 31)	18.72% (10, 7.07, 100)	21.60% (11, 4.79, 100)
S.2: Ultimately accepted bids	0.87% (10, − 1.0, 30)	1.08% (11, 1.2, 64)	− 4.20% (13, − 1.40, 47)	− 3.00% (13, − 0.28, 47)	− 8.33% (13, − 0.87, 40)	27.12% (10, 3.06, 100)	13.92% (11, 7.82, 100)

Panel 2. t-statistic

	Tobin's Q		Abnormal returns			Cash flow rates of return	
	1980	1985/86	− 5 years	− 2 years	− 1 year	1980	1985/86
S.1 less S.2	− 0.87	− 0.64	0.98	− 0.14	0.69	− 0.91	1.59

Source: Datastream, LSPD, own calculations. Abnormal returns are based on a market model with parameter values $\alpha = 0$ and $\beta = 1$.

Definitions: Tobin's Q = (Market value of equity + Book value of debt)/Replacement cost of assets, Cash flow = Profit after tax + Depreciation + Interest payments, Book value of debt = ST loans + LT loans − Cash balances + Deferred tax, Cash flow rates of return = Cash flow/(Market value of equity + Book value of debt).

The sample sizes are small, between 10 and 15 for each partition of hostile bids. Table 9 reports that the pattern of results is not consistent for any of the three measures, except that the Q ratios for contested bids that are ultimately accepted are greater (0.87) than for the sample of bids that are ultimately rejected (0.73) in 1980. In 1985/86, the Q ratios are almost identical. Abnormal returns are smaller for ultimately accepted bids over five years, though the difference in averages is not statistically significant. Cash flow rates of return are higher in ultimately accepted than in rejected bids in 1980 but lower in 1985/86.

In sum, there is no evidence of poor pre-bid performance in ultimately rejected bids. Continuing opposition to the bid appears to reflect a breakdown over negotiations or disagreement over the redeployment of assets after the takeover. The fact that post-takeover restructuring is significantly higher in hostile than accepted takeovers points to the latter as being an important consideration.

5. Conclusion

This paper examines whether hostile takeovers act as a discipline on management. Evidence comes from the performance of targets of hostile takeovers before, during, and after acquisition. We report that hostile takeovers are associated with high levels of boardroom changes, higher in hostile than accepted bids and higher in targets of successful than unsuccessful hostile bids. There are also larger asset disposals and bid premiums in hostile takeovers. However, targets of hostile takeovers do not perform worse prior to bids than either targets of other acquisitions or nonmerging firms. By only one measure (Tobin's Q) is there any evidence of statistically significant worse performance of targets of hostile bids. There is no evidence of either high bid premiums or poor pre-bid performance when takeovers involve managerial control changes. The market for corporate control does not therefore function as a disciplinary device for poorly performing companies.

Rejection of bids is more consistent with opposition to the anticipated redeployment of assets by the bidder and negotiation over the terms of bids. We find that there is a high level of bid revisions and large bid premiums in hostile takeovers but no evidence of poor performance where negotiations over the terms of the bid break down. Thus, our results provide a picture of a market for corporate control in the U.K. that is more consistent with dissatisfaction over the bid terms and the redeployment of assets after the takeover than with a disciplinary role.

References

Bhagat, Sanjay, Andrei Shleifer, and Robert W. Vishny, 1990, Hostile takeovers in the 80s: The return to corporate specialization, Brookings Papers on Economic Activity, 1–72.

Bhide, Amar, 1989, The causes and consequences of hostile takeovers, Journal of Applied Corporate Finance 2, 36–59.

Bradley, Michael, Anand Desai, and E. Han Kim, 1988, Synergistic gains from corporate acquisitions and their division between the stockholders of target and acquiring firms, Journal of Financial Economics 21, 183–206.

Dann, Larry and Harry DeAngelo, 1988, Corporate financial policy and corporate control: A study of defensive adjustments in asset and ownership structure, Journal of Financial Economics 20, 87–127.

Franks, Julian R. and Robert Harris, 1989, Shareholder wealth effects of corporate takeovers: The UK experience 1955–1985, Journal of Financial Economics 23, 225–249.

Franks, Julian R. and Colin P. Mayer, 1990, Capital markets and corporate control: A study of France, Germany and the UK, Economic Policy 10, 191–230.

Franks, Julian R. and Colin P. Mayer, 1994, Ownership and control in Germany, Working paper (London Business School, London).

Gilson, Stuart C., 1989, Management turnover and financial distress, Journal of Financial Economics 25, 241–267.

Grossman, Sanford J. and Oliver D. Hart, 1980, Takeover bids, the free rider problem, and the theory of the corporation, Bell Journal of Economics 11, 42–64.

Herzel, Leo and Richard W. Shepro, 1990, Bidders and targets: Mergers and acquisitions in the U.S. (Blackwell, Oxford).

Hirshleifer, David and Anjan Thakor, 1994, Managerial performance, boards of directors and takeover bidding, Journal of Corporate Finance 1, 63–90.

Jensen, Michael, 1988, Takeovers: Their causes and consequences, Journal of Economic Perspectives 2, 21–48.

Klein, April and James Rosenfeld, 1988, Targeted share repurchases and top management changes, Journal of Financial Economics 20, 493–506.

Kini, Omesh, William Kracaw, and Shehzad Mian, 1993, Corporate takeovers, firm performance, and board composition, Working paper (Pennsylvania State University, University Park, PA).

Martin, Kenneth J. and John J. McConnell, 1991, Corporate performance, corporate takeovers and management turnover, Journal of Finance 46, 671–687.

Rappaport, Alfred, 1990, The staying power of the public corporation, Harvard Business Review 1, 96–104.

Shleifer, Andrei and Larry H. Summers, 1988, Breach of trust in hostile takeovers, in: A.J. Auerbach, ed., Corporate takeovers: Causes and consequences (National Bureau of Economic Research, Chicago, IL).

Warner, Jerold B., Ross L. Watts, and Karen H. Wruck, 1988, Stock prices and top management changes, Journal of Financial Economics 20, 461–492.

Weisbach, Michael S., 1988, Outside directors and CEO turnover, Journal of Financial Economics 20, 431–460.

[17]

THE JOURNAL OF FINANCE • VOL. LI, NO. 4 • SEPTEMBER 1996

Bustup Takeovers of Value-Destroying Diversified Firms

PHILIP G. BERGER and ELI OFEK*

ABSTRACT

We examine whether the value loss from diversification affects takeover and breakup probabilities. We estimate diversification's value effect by imputing stand-alone values for individual business segments and find that firms with greater value losses are more likely to be taken over. Moreover, those acquired firms whose losses are greatest are most likely to be bought by LBO associations, which frequently break up their targets. For a subsample of large diversified targets: (1) higher value losses increase the extent of post-takeover bustup; and (2) post-takeover bustup generally results in divested divisions being operated as part of a focused, stand-alone firm.

BERGER AND OFEK (1995) CONFIRM recent evidence by Lang and Stulz (1994) of a value loss from diversification in the 1980s, which Servaes (1996) finds also occurred in the 1960s, and, to a lesser extent, in the 1970s. Berger and Ofek use segment-level data to estimate the magnitude of the loss and find that, during 1986–1991, the average diversified firm destroyed about 15 percent of the value its lines of business would have had if operated as stand-alone businesses. The evidence that diversification represents a suboptimal managerial strategy suggests that internal control systems do not prevent managers from destroying significant amounts of value. The value destruction does, however, generate large profit opportunities for outsiders. The natural question that arises is whether these profit opportunities result in takeovers disciplining the management of firms with large and persistent value losses from diversification.

The U.S. market for corporate control reached its zenith during the last half of the 1980s. The many takeovers and leveraged buyouts (LBOs) during this period transferred control over corporate resources which, in many cases, had been under the control of diversified corporations. Marris (1963) and Manne (1965) argue that the difference between actual and potential stock prices in firms operated suboptimally creates incentives for outsiders to acquire these firms and improve operations. Jensen (1986) extends this reasoning to value-

* Berger is from The Wharton School, University of Pennsylvania. Ofek is from Stern School of Business, New York University. We appreciate capable research assistance from Franco Wong and helpful comments from Andrew Alford, Brad Barber, Robert Comment, Bob Holthausen, Edi Hotchkiss, Henri Servaes, and participants at the NBER's Conference on Corporate Finance, the Western Finance Association meetings, the American Finance Association meetings, and workshops at New York University and the University of Pennsylvania. We are especially grateful for the many constructive comments of the anonymous referee. Berger acknowledges the financial support of Coopers & Lybrand.

destroying diversification by contending that many takeovers are designed to undo previous unprofitable acquisitions by target firms. Given the persistence of the value losses documented by Berger and Ofek (1995) and Lang and Stulz (1994) for diversified companies, the takeover and LBO wave of the 1980s may partially represent an attempt to break up diversified firms that destroy value.

Breakups of target assets occur regularly following mergers or acquisitions. Bhagat, Shleifer, and Vishny (1990) find that sell-offs occur frequently following 62 large hostile takeovers undertaken between 1984 and 1986. Kaplan and Weisbach (1992) examine divestitures of target company assets following large acquisitions and find that almost 44 percent of the target companies are later divested. Moreover, they find that acquirers of firms in unrelated businesses are more likely to later divest their targets than acquirers of related businesses. They also document that the most frequently announced reason for the divestitures is to refocus the acquiring company. Mitchell and Lehn (1990) show that firms that subsequently become takeover targets are more likely to have made bad acquisitions (i.e., ones that significantly reduce their equity value). In addition, they find that the worst acquisitions made by targets are those that are later divested either in bustup takeovers or restructuring programs to thwart takeover.[1]

Berger and Ofek (1995) find that overinvestment in, and excessive subsidization of, poorly performing segments contributes to the value loss from diversification. Such managerial decisions are reversible, and selling off the divisions of a diversified firm to buyers who will operate them as stand-alone, focused businesses, may facilitate the necessary changes in management structure. For example, managers can more easily be given high equity ownership in a broken-off piece of a conglomerate than in the conglomerate itself, and board members can monitor a focused business more closely. Recent evidence shows that increasing focus is value-enhancing. John and Ofek (1995) provide evidence that increase in focus is a major factor in explaining seller gains from asset sales, and Comment and Jarrell (1995) find a positive relation between abnormal stock returns and increases in focus as measured by either the number of segments reported by management or by accounting-based Herfindahl indices.

Potential acquirers have an incentive to take over and break up the most value-reducing diversified targets, because empirical evidence indicates that bidders do better when they target poorly managed targets. Lang, Stulz, and Walking (1989) and Servaes (1991) find that bidders earn higher returns when their targets have lower Tobin's q ratios. Interpreting q as a measure of managerial performance, these results are consistent with bidders earning greater profits when their targets' managers have destroyed more value.

[1] Contrasting evidence is provided by Healy, Palepu, and Ruback (1992), who find a modest increase in book value of asset sales, but not in cash proceeds from disposals, from the *combined* target and acquirer firms in years following the 50 largest mergers completed during 1979 to mid-1984. Healy, Palepu, and Ruback also find that asset sales by the *combined* target and acquirer in the years before and after the merger are a small portion of the market value of total assets.

Consistent with the greater profit potential of more poorly managed targets, prior research shows that firms with lower q ratios have greater takeover probabilities (Hasbrouck (1985), Morck, Shleifer, and Vishny (1988), and Barber, Palmer, and Wallace (1995)).

The value loss from diversification, the use of break-ups after takeover, the ability to create value by increasing focus, bidders' ability to earn higher returns by targeting poorly managed firms, and poorly managed firms' higher probability of being taken over are all established in the extant literature. Our contribution is to investigate how these strands of evidence may be linked in the context of takeovers and breakups of diversified firms.

To test the relation between value destruction and takeover probability, we follow Berger and Ofek (1995) in comparing the sum of the imputed stand-alone values of the segments of diversified companies to the actual values of those companies. The resulting construct, which we measure in 1984 and 1987, is designed to capture the value loss from diversification. We then identify all takeovers of these diversified companies in the four-year period following each base year and relate the magnitude of the value loss to the likelihood of takeover. We find that, after controlling for other determinants of takeover, greater value losses are associated with higher takeover probabilities.

As a check on whether the value losses we measure are actually associated with firms' diversification strategies, we also impute values for stand-alone firms and calculate differences between actual and imputed values for these firms in 1984 and 1987. We then identify all takeovers of these stand-alone firms during the four-year periods following the measurement of value loss. We use both binomial and multinomial logistic regressions to compare value destruction's effect on takeover probability between diversified and stand-alone firms. The binomial logit results show that variation in value loss affects takeover likelihood somewhat more for multi-segment than one-segment firms, although the difference is not significant at conventional levels. These results show that diversified firms' takeover probabilities are at least as sensitive as those of single-line firms to variation in value loss, but they do not provide any information about the effect on takeover likelihood of the much greater average level of value loss for diversified companies. The multinomial logits do so, and their results show that the effect of value destruction on the probability of being a takeover target is significantly greater when comparing diversified targets to all nontargets than it is when comparing stand-alone targets to all nontargets. Overall, because value loss and diversification are correlated, it is impossible to completely disentangle the extent to which general value loss versus value loss associated with diversification policy affects the takeover likelihood of diversified companies. The binomial logits cannot reject the hypothesis that general value loss alone affects takeover likelihood, but they do not take account of the correlation between value loss and diversification. The results from the multinomial logits are consistent with *value destruction associated with diversification policy* affecting takeover likelihood, but these results may overcorrect for the correlation between value loss and diversification by comparing each type of target firm (diversified and stand-alone) against all nontarget firms.

We use both indirect and direct evidence to investigate further whether the opportunity to reverse value destruction through bustup underlies the relation we document between value destruction and subsequent takeover. First, for the diversified firms that are subsequently taken over, we compare those acquired by LBO associations to the rest. Jensen (1989) argues that the organizational changes associated with LBOs makes them particularly likely to take value-increasing actions, such as breaking apart lines of business that are more valuable when separated. Moreover, LBOs often need to sell off acquired assets to pay down acquisition debt. We find that, among subsequently acquired diversified firms, greater value losses enhance the likelihood that the acquirer is an LBO, consistent with LBO associations being more likely than other bidders to break-up the target.

Second, we examine in detail the subsample of targets which had values exceeding $250 million before being taken over. For this subsample of large targets, we examine whether the value loss from diversification is related to the extent of post-takeover bustup. Defining bustup dichotomously, based on the number of target divisions sold following takeover, we find that 50 percent of the large diversified targets are broken up, and that the mean value effect of diversification is −21 percent to −37 percent for these firms. In contrast, those firms not broken up after takeover have a significantly smaller mean valuation effect from diversification of −5 percent. Measuring the extent of bustup continuously, as the proportion of target value subsequently divested, we find that the value effect of diversification is significantly negatively related to the extent of bustup.

Finally, for the subsample of large targets, we examine the buyers of divisions divested from diversified targets after takeovers. We classify LBOs and single-line firms in a business related to that of the divested division as likely to operate the acquired division as a focused business, and find that 75 percent of the identifiable buyers are either LBOs or focused, related firms. Overall, our results are consistent with the market for corporate control targeting and breaking-up combinations of business lines which have greater value when each line is operated on a stand-alone basis.

Section I presents sample selection details, describes the sample, and explains our empirical approach. Section II tests the relation between value destruction from diversification and the probabilities of subsequent takeover and break-up. Section III examines who the buyers are in post-takeover breakups, and Section IV concludes. The Appendix provides additional details on our empirical approach and variable construction.

I. Sample Selection and Estimation of Segment Values

A. Sample Selection and Description

FASB No. 14 and Securities and Exchange Commission (SEC) Regulation S-K require firms to report segment information for fiscal years ending after

December 15, 1977. Firms must report audited footnote information for segments whose sales, assets, or profits exceed 10 percent of consolidated totals. The COMPUSTAT Industry Segment (CIS) database (active and research files) reports segment information for all COMPUSTAT firms other than utility subsidiaries.

For our main sample (diversified firms), we obtain data for all firms on the CIS database during either 1984 or 1987 that have at least two segments, total sales of at least $20 million, and no segments in the financial services industry (Standard Industrial Classification (SIC) codes between 6000 and 6999). We require firms to have sales of at least $20 million to avoid distorted valuation multiples for firms with sales or assets near zero. Firms with financial services segments are removed from consideration because applying the valuation methods we use is problematic for such firms. To be included in the final sample, diversified corporations must have available data on the CIS, Compustat, and Center for Research in Security Prices (CRSP) data files. Additionally, total capital (measured as market value of common equity plus book value of debt) for the firm must be available. Unlike assets, sales are usually completely allocated among the reported segments of a diversified firm; therefore, we require that the sum of segment sales must be within 1 percent of total sales for the firm. Panel A of Table I shows that these procedures result in a total sample of 1,513 multi-segment firms, with 1,192 observations in 1984 and 1,085 observations in 1987.

We also use a secondary sample of single-segment companies, which are selected using the same selection criteria described above for the multi-segment firms (except for the requirement of multiple segments). The stand-alone sample we obtain, but do not describe in Table I, contains 1,558 firms, with 1,038 observations in 1984 and 798 observations in 1987.[2]

We determine which sample firms had takeovers that were announced in the four fiscal years following the base year, and identify which takeovers are by LBO groups. We document which sample firms have CRSP delisting dates prior to December 31, 1993, the last date with available information on CRSP at the time we conducted our tests. For all such firms, we investigate whether the reason for delisting was a takeover, and what the announcement date of the takeover was, by examining the *W.T. Grimm Mergerstat Review* and the Investment Dealer's Digest U.S. M&A (IDDMA) file of the Lexis/Nexis database. LBO acquirers are separately identified by both sources. As Table I shows, these procedures identify a total of 334 takeovers of diversified firms, of which 47 are LBOs. The four-year period following 1984 contains 251 announcements of successful takeovers (28 LBOs), whereas the period following 1987 has 127 (25).

[2] The sample selection criteria result in twice as many observations for both 1984 and 1987, of which we eliminate half to reduce the data collection needed to identify firms subsequently taken over. The eliminations are achieved by sorting the sample by SIC code, then eliminating every second firm. The remaining single-segment firms thus have industry representation proportional to the full sample of single-line companies.

Table I

Takeover and LBO Frequencies for the Sample of Diversified Firms

The sample of diversified firms includes 2,277 observations for 1,513 firms from the Compustat Industry Segment (CIS) database for fiscal years 1984 and 1987 that have at least two segments, total sales of at least $20 million, and no segments in the financial services industry (Standard Industrial Classification (SIC) codes 6000–6999). All sample firms have available data on the CIS, COMPUSTAT, and Center for Research in Security Prices (CRSP) data files, and have the sum of segment sales within 1 percent of total sales for the firm. Panel A displays the frequencies with which sample observations were subsequently taken over during the following four fiscal years by any acquirer, and by an LBO acquirer, for the total sample and for the 1984 and 1987 subsamples. Panel B displays the frequencies with which sample observations were taken over by any acquirer, and by an LBO acquirer, during each year 1985–1991, and in total.

Panel A: Sample Takeover/LBO Frequencies for the Total Sample and the 1984 and 1987 Base Years

	Total	1984	1987
Number of firms	1513	1192	1085
Takeovers	334	251	127
Takeover Frequency	22%	21%	12%
LBOs	47	28	25
LBO Frequency	3%	2%	2%

Panel B: Takeovers and LBOs by Year of Announcement

Fiscal Year Announced	Takeovers	LBOs
1985	61	5
1986	63	6
1987	62	9
1988	80	15
1989	44	11
1990	17	1
1991	7	0
Total	334	47

Panel A of Table I shows that takeover frequency is high among our sample of multi-segment firms, especially during 1985–1988. Twenty-one percent of the diversified firms from 1984 are taken over in the following four year period, whereas, for the 1987 sample, the frequency is 12 percent. For single-line firms, the corresponding rates are 13 percent in 1984 and 19 percent in 1987 (not reported in a table). Panel B shows the distribution of takeovers and LBOs during the 1985–1991 period. The 80 takeovers and 15 LBOs in 1988 make it the most active year for acquisitions of the firms in our sample. Takeover frequency begins to decline sharply after 1989, with just 17 takeovers of sample firms in 1990 and seven in 1991. Acquisitions by LBOs decrease even more rapidly than other takeovers after the demise of Drexel Burnham Lambert, with just one of the 24 takeovers in 1990–1991 performed by an LBO.

B. Estimating Segment Values Using Multipliers

To measure diversification's value effect, we follow the procedures described in Berger and Ofek (1995). We measure the percentage difference between a firm's total value and the sum of imputed values for its segments as stand-alone entities (see the Appendix for additional details not described below). We calculate the imputed value of each segment by multiplying the median ratio, for single-segment firms in the same industry, of total capital to one of two accounting items (assets or sales) by the segment's level of the accounting item. The industry median ratios are based on the narrowest SIC grouping that includes at least five single-line businesses with at least $20 million of sales and sufficient data for computing the ratios.

The sum of the imputed values of a company's segments estimates the value of the firm if all of its segments are operated as stand-alone businesses. The natural log of the ratio of a firm's actual value to its imputed value is our measure of excess value, or the gain or loss in value from diversification. Negative excess value indicates that diversification reduces the value of segments below that of their stand-alone counterparts.

C. Tying the Value Loss to Takeover Probability

We examine the association between the value loss from diversification in two base years, 1984 and 1987, and the likelihood of subsequent takeover in the following four-year periods. A four-year period is a relatively short one in which to follow takeover activity. As discussed below, we identify takeovers over a relatively short period in order to ensure that variation in base year value losses reflects variation in value losses throughout the potential takeover period.

We examine the validity of our assumption that diversified firms with greater value losses in a base year continue to have greater value losses from diversification during the following four years. We calculate autocorrelation coefficients for lags of one to five years for excess value measures based on multiples of assets, sales, and earnings before interest and taxes (EBIT). The autocorrelation results (which are not presented in a table) show that the excess value measures using both the asset and sales multipliers are highly correlated over time. The average correlation between a firm's value losses in adjacent years is 0.80 for both multipliers. The autocorrelation decreases with the time lag, yet even for observations four years apart, it averages 0.46 to 0.48. The stability over time of the excess value measure obtained with the EBIT multiplier is, however, much smaller. We therefore use only the asset and sales multipliers in our tests.[3]

[3] We also examine whether, for diversified firms subsequently taken over, the value loss varies systematically with the time between the base year and the date of takeover. We group the targets into those acquired one, two, three, and four years after the base year. We find no systematic relation between the amount of excess value in the base year and the time lag until takeover. For example, the mean excess value using the asset (sales) multiplier ranges from −17 percent (−22

The autocorrelation results, combined with the sample frequencies in Panel A of Table I, illustrate a research design trade-off between measuring excess value near the time of takeover versus a possible lack of independence from measuring values for the same firm at different times. The autocorrelations show that the longer the time lag between measuring excess value and the date of takeover, the less the association between the value loss at the time of takeover and the value loss in the base year. Panel A of Table I shows that using two base years results in many firms entering the sample in both years. The sample contains 1,513 firms, but 2,277 observations (the sum of the observations in the 1984 and 1987 subsamples). To address the independence concern that arises from some firms entering the sample twice, we report results separately for each base year, and we report the sensitivity of the inferences from the combined-years sample to a conservative standard error adjustment.

II. Value Loss from Diversification and Subsequent Takeover

A. *Total Value Destruction and Subsequent Takeovers*

To investigate whether the market for corporate control acts to undo the persistent value losses from diversification, we see whether diversified firms in which more value is being destroyed are more likely to be taken over. Table II shows that value destruction is greater among diversified firms subsequently taken over than it is among firms that do not experience a control change. Using the asset (sales) multiplier, the mean value loss among firms subsequently taken over is 22.2 percent (31.8 percent), which is 5 percent (10.6 percent) more than the loss among other diversified firms. The differences in mean value destruction between targets and nontargets are significant at better than the 0.05 level. These results are consistent with acquirers targeting those multi-segment firms whose diversification policies result in greater value losses. The difference in value destruction between targets and nontargets is negative in both 1984 and 1987, consistent with acquirers targeting value destroying firms in both the 1985–1988 and the 1988–1991 periods. The inferences remain similar when the median value destruction of targets and nontargets is compared. For the full sample, future targets destroy 2.6 percent more value based on the asset multiplier and 9.3 percent more (significant at the 0.01 level) using the sales multiplier. The only case in which targets do not have greater median value destruction is for the 1987 sample using the asset multiplier.

The preceding univariate tests do not control for factors, other than excess value, that may affect takeover likelihood. We therefore perform multivariate logit regressions in which a takeover indicator is the dependent variable, and the nontakeover group includes both stand-alone and diversified firms. The independent variables are previously identified explanators of takeover prob-

percent) to −29 percent (−40 percent), with the greatest value loss for targets acquired two years after the base year and the smallest value loss for targets acquired three years after the base year.

Table II

Comparison of Value Destruction Between Diversified Firms That Do and Do Not Become Takeover Targets

The table presents mean and median excess value measures for the sample of 2,277 observations of diversified firms from fiscal years 1984 and 1987. Sample observations are grouped into those that were taken over during the subsequent four fiscal years and those that were not taken over during that period. The asset multiplier measure of excess value is the natural logarithm of actual value/imputed value where: actual value is total book value of debt plus market value of equity, and imputed value is the sum of imputed values of the firm's segments. Each segment's imputed value is the segment's assets multiplied by its industry median capital-to-assets ratio. The sales multiplier measure of excess value is the natural logarithm of actual value/imputed value with each segment's imputed value equal to the segment's sales multiplied by its industry median capital-to-sales ratio.

	Means			Medians		
Sample	No takeover	Takeover	Difference	No takeover	Takeover	Difference
Excess value, asset multiplier						
Full sample	−0.172	−0.222	−0.050[b]	−0.204	−0.230	−0.026
1984 sample	−0.189	−0.220	−0.031	−0.199	−0.243	−0.044[c]
1987 sample	−0.155	−0.224	−0.069[c]	−0.214	−0.180	0.034
Excess value, sales multiplier						
Full sample	−0.213	−0.318	−0.106[a]	−0.230	−0.323	−0.093[a]
1984 sample	−0.245	−0.318	−0.073[c]	−0.277	−0.338	−0.061[c]
1987 sample	−0.182	−0.316	−0.134[a]	−0.179	−0.266	−0.087

[a,b,c] denotes that the mean (median) difference is significantly different from zero at the 0.01, 0.05, and 0.10 two-tailed probability level, respectively.

ability taken from Palepu (1986), two interactive variables set equal to excess value if the observation is for a multi-segment firm in the first case, and for a stand-alone firm in the second case, and the number of segments reported by management. The interactive variables separate the effects on takeover likelihood of variation in excess value for the diversified versus single-line companies, whereas the number of segments variable controls for any additional effect of the extent of diversification on takeover probability. All independent variables are measured in the base year (1984 or 1987) for the observation.

We modify those Palepu (1986) variables, which use the book value of equity, by either replacing it with the book value of total assets or by placing it in the numerator (rather than the denominator) of ratios. We make these modifications in order to avoid negative figures in the denominators of ratios and in quantities where we use log transformations. Palepu's original measures are noted in parentheses when they differ from ours. Return on assets (return on equity) is the ratio of earnings before interest, taxes, and depreciation to total assets. Size is the log of total assets (net book value of assets). Liquidity is the ratio of net liquid assets to total assets. The net liquid assets are defined as the cash plus the marketable securities less the current liabilities. Book-to-market (market-to-book) ratio is book equity over market value of common equity. Growth is the annual rate of change in sales. Leverage is the ratio of debt to assets (long-term debt to equity). Palepu finds that growth, leverage, and size are significantly negatively related to acquisition likelihood.

Table III presents estimations of the takeover likelihood models. We use the takeover likelihood estimations to evaluate the economic importance of the explanatory variables. The magnitudes of the coefficients from a discrete choice model are, however, difficult to interpret because the marginal effects of each variable on the choice probability depend on all of the data in a nonlinear manner. To aid in interpretation, we present "standardized elasticities" for each variable in Tables III–V. The standardized elasticities are calculated by first determining the probability of takeover at an evaluation point on the cumulative logistic distribution. We use the point that results when all of the explanatory variables have their median values.[4] The elasticity for a given variable is then the amount by which the probability of takeover increases above this evaluation point when the variable's median is replaced with either its 25th or 75th percentile (whichever leads to a probability increase).

Table III shows that excess value has a strong negative relation with takeover probability for the multi-segment firms, indicating that firms destroying more value with their diversification strategy are more likely to be taken over.[5] For the overall, the 1984, and the 1987 samples, the estimate on excess value from diversified firms is always negative for both the asset and sales multiplier measures. The multi-segment firm value loss coefficient estimates are significant at the 0.01 level for the full sample, and at better than the 0.10 level for the 1984 and 1987 samples. The relation between excess value and takeover probability is somewhat weaker for the single-line firms. The estimates on excess value are always smaller for stand-alone companies than for diversified firms, and the estimates for the one-segment sample are significant at better than the 0.10 level in only two of the six regressions. A chi-squared test for the equality of the estimates on the two interactive variables shows, however, that they are not significantly different at better than the 0.10 level in any of the six regressions. The evidence thus indicates that variation in excess value has an equal (or, perhaps, marginally greater) effect on takeover likelihood for diversified versus single-line firms.

Note that significance levels for the full sample in Table III may be overstated because observations for the same firm are sometimes included for both 1984 and 1987. Therefore, we compute conservatively adjusted standard errors for all full sample binomial logits reported in the paper. The adjusted standard errors result from reestimation in which a weighted residual sum of squares is minimized, with the observations of firms that enter the sample twice, assigned half the weight of other observations. For the Table III full sample, the

[4] Note that the nonlinearity of the logit model could make inferences sensitive to the evaluation point chosen.

[5] Note that all of the reported inferences are insensitive to excluding related diversified firms from the sample, where related diversified firms are those in which all segments report the same main two-digit SIC code. All reported inferences are also unchanged when firms that are diversified in the base year, but not at the time of takeover, are excluded.

Table III

Logit Regressions Relating Takeover Likelihood to Excess Value and Other Firm Characteristics

The sample includes 2,277 observations of diversified firms from fiscal years 1984 and 1987, and 1,836 observations of firms reporting one segment in these years. The top number for each variable is the parameter estimate, the middle number is the elasticity, and two-tailed p-values are in parentheses. All independent variables are measured in the observation's base year (1984 or 1987). Variable definitions are as follows. The asset and sales multiplier measures of excess value are as defined in Table II. Return on assets is the ratio of net income before extraordinary items and discontinued operations to total assets. Size is the log of total assets. Liquidity is the ratio of net liquid assets to total assets. Book/market ratio is book value of equity over market value of common equity. Number of segments is the number of segments listed by the firm on the COMPUSTAT Industry Segment database. Sales growth is the annual rate of change in sales. Leverage is the ratio of debt to assets. The elasticities for the explanatory variables are defined as the percentage increase in the probability of takeover above the evaluation point (see definition below) when the variable's median is replaced with either its 25th or 75th percentile (whichever leads to a probability increase). The probability of takeover at the evaluation point is defined as the probability of takeover at the point on the cumulative logistic distribution that results when all of the explanatory variables have their median values.

Sample	All	All	1984	1984	1987	1987
Observations = 0, no takeover	2673	2966	1221	1357	1452	1609
Observations = 1, takeover	554	618	323	370	231	248
Probability of takeover at evaluation point	18.580	18.045	22.309	22.577	14.792	13.498
Intercept	−1.369[a]	−1.497[a]	−1.067[a]	−1.203[a]	−1.676[a]	−1.791[a]
	(0.000)	(0.000)	(0.000)	(0.000)	(0.000)	(0.000)
Excess value, asset multiplier for multisegment firms	−0.566[a]		−0.428[c]		−0.742[b]	
	2.076		1.874		2.086	
	(0.004)		(0.090)		(0.021)	
Excess value, asset multiplier for single-segment firms	−0.363[b]		−0.133		−0.618[b]	
	1.470		0.566		2.239	
	(0.031)		(0.554)		(0.018)	
Excess value, sales multiplier for multisegment firms		−0.384[a]		−0.396[a]		−0.386[c]
		2.140		2.468		1.800
		(0.002)		(0.010)		(0.055)
Excess value, sales multiplier for single-segment firms		−0.182		−0.221		−0.198
		1.093		1.548		0.943
		(0.151)		(0.210)		(0.279)
Return on assets	1.274[b]	1.012[b]	1.012	0.803	1.383[c]	0.940
	0.660	0.737	0.703	0.677	0.528	0.547
	(0.017)	(0.042)	(0.156)	(0.228)	(0.099)	(0.220)
Size	−0.112[a]	−0.088[a]	−0.096[b]	−0.076[c]	−0.103[b]	−0.068
	2.046	1.559	2.010	1.594	1.558	0.941
	(0.001)	(0.004)	(0.029)	(0.064)	(0.034)	(0.138)
Liquidity	0.261	0.267	0.576[c]	0.611[c]	−0.009	0.015
	0.399	0.399	0.986	1.056	0.013	0.018
	(0.277)	(0.256)	(0.093)	(0.063)	(0.980)	(0.966)
Book/market ratio	−0.058	0.062	−0.111	−0.018	−0.025	0.118
	0.246	0.338	0.571	0.093	0.089	0.473
	(0.529)	(0.419)	(0.379)	(0.865)	(0.858)	(0.305)
Number of segments	0.039	0.015	0.062	0.041	−0.076	−0.121[c]
	0.597	0.223	1.093	0.725	0.984	1.476
	(0.341)	(0.693)	(0.230)	(0.395)	(0.288)	(0.075)
Sales growth	−0.275[b]	−0.244[b]	−0.492[b]	−0.352[b]	−0.092	−0.145
	0.377	0.327	0.734	0.528	0.116	0.170
	(0.027)	(0.040)	(0.014)	(0.050)	(0.560)	(0.374)
Leverage	0.709[a]	0.673[a]	0.736[b]	0.770[b]	0.935[a]	0.865[b]
	1.464	1.358	1.721	1.817	1.632	1.396
	(0.005)	(0.005)	(0.041)	(0.027)	(0.010)	(0.013)

[a,b,c] denotes that the coefficient estimate is significantly different from zero at the 0.01, 0.05, and 0.10 two-tailed probability level, respectively.

multi-segment company value loss coefficient estimates are significant at the 0.05 level using the conservatively adjusted standard errors.

The effect of value destruction on takeover likelihood appears to be important economically as well as statistically. For the full sample, changing the diversified firm asset (sales) multiplier measure of excess value from its median to its 25th percentile increases the acquisition probability by 2.1 percent (2.1 percent) from its evaluation point of 18.6 percent (18 percent). Consistent with Palepu (1986), the only control variables significant at the 0.10 level in more than half of the regressions are size, growth, and leverage. Leverage's positive effect is, however, opposite in direction to that found by Palepu for the 1971–1979 period. Palepu did not hypothesize a directional relation between leverage and takeover probability, but subsequent theoretical papers by Stulz (1988) and Israel (1991) predict that leverage is negatively related to takeover probability. Our findings do not provide empirical support for this prediction during the 1985–1991 period, although, as Harris and Raviv (1991, p. 325) caution, these and related theoretical papers "should be viewed as theories of short-term changes in capital structure taken in response to imminent takeover threats . . . ." The size and leverage control variables appear to have economically important effects on takeover probability. For the asset (sales) multiplier estimation using the full sample, the elasticities of takeover likelihood with respect to size and leverage are 2 percent (1.6 percent), and 1.5 percent (1.4 percent).

The binomial logits show that variation in value destruction is always significantly related to takeover likelihood within multi-segment businesses, but has at most a marginally greater effect on takeover probability within the diversified sample than it does in the single-line sample. It is important, however, to incorporate the fact that the average level of value destruction is much larger in diversified firms than in stand-alone companies (Berger and Ofek (1995)). Allowing for the greater value destruction of diversified firms requires separately comparing multi-segment targets to all nontargets and single-line targets to all nontargets. We therefore use multinomial logits to incorporate the large average difference in value destruction into the assessment of the effect of value destruction on the takeover probability of diversified versus stand-alone firms.

Table IV presents the results. Observations are assigned a value of zero if the firm is not taken over, and one (two) if the firm is one-segment (multi-segment) and is taken over. The nontakeover group again includes both stand-alone and diversified firms. Two columns of results are reported for each estimation. The first column (stand-alone targets) provides information on the impact of the independent variables on the likelihood of takeover for single-segment firms relative to the non-takeover group, whereas the second column (multi-segment targets) reports the independent variables' effect on takeover likelihood for multi-segment firms relative to the nontakeover group. Panel A presents results using the asset multiplier measure of excess value, whereas Panel B reports results using the sales multiplier measure.

Table IV

Multinomial Logit Regressions Relating Takeover Likelihood to Excess Value and Other Firm Characteristics

The sample includes 2,277 observations of diversified firms from fiscal years 1984 and 1987, and 1,836 observations of firms reporting one segment in these years. The top number for each variable is the parameter estimate, the middle number is the elasticity, and two-tailed p-values are in parentheses. All independent variables are measured in the observation's base year (1984 or 1987). Variable definitions are as follows. The asset and sales multiplier measures of excess value are as defined in Table II. Return on assets is the ratio of net income before extraordinary items and discontinued operations to total assets. Size is the log of total assets. Liquidity is the ratio of net liquid assets to total assets. Book/market ratio is book value of equity over market value of common equity. Sales growth is the annual rate of change in sales. Leverage is the ratio of debt to assets. The elasticities for the explanatory variables are defined as the percentage increase in the probability of takeover above the evaluation point (see definition below) when the variable's median is replaced with either its 25th or 75th percentile (whichever leads to a probability increase). The probability of takeover at the evaluation point is defined as the probability of takeover at the point on the cumulative logistic distribution which results when all of the explanatory variables have their median values. The line labeled *Significance of multiplier diff.* provides the two-tailed probability level that the coefficient estimate on the excess value variable for single-segment firms is significantly different from the estimate for multi-segment firms.

Panel A: Multinomial Logit Estimation of Takeover Probability, with Asset Multiplier

Sample	All		1984		1987	
	Single seg	Multiseg	Single seg	Multiseg	Single seg	Multiseg
Observations = 0, no takeover	2673		1221		1452	
Observations = 1 or 2, takeover	271	283	136	187	135	96
Probability of takeover at evaluation point	10.215	10.377	11.557	14.195	9.032	6.779
Intercept	−0.881[a]	−3.224[a]	−0.587	−2.575[a]	−1.197[a]	−4.174[a]
	(0.002)	(0.000)	(0.155)	(0.000)	(0.003)	(0.000)
Excess value, asset multiplier	−0.170	−0.816[a]	0.031	−0.554[b]	−0.388	−1.162[a]
	0.413	1.904	0.095	1.812	0.902	1.725
	(0.373)	(0.000)	(0.905)	(0.021)	(0.171)	(0.001)
Return on assets	0.492	2.738[a]	0.977	1.240	0.036	4.625[a]
	0.250	1.167	0.598	0.682	0.016	1.446
	(0.435)	(0.001)	(0.292)	(0.201)	(0.968)	(0.003)
Size	−0.306[a]	0.060[c]	−0.340[a]	0.085[c]	−0.274[a]	0.044
	2.804	0.847	3.440	1.579	2.234	0.436
	(0.000)	(0.096)	(0.000)	(0.069)	(0.000)	(0.471)
Liquidity	0.691[b]	−0.259	1.149[b]	0.033	0.368	−0.540
	0.785	0.221	1.462	0.034	0.363	0.326
	(0.025)	(0.432)	(0.014)	(0.939)	(0.389)	(0.347)
Book/market ratio	−0.159	0.066	−0.208	0.008	−0.118	0.112
	0.427	0.215	0.603	0.034	0.278	0.238
	(0.241)	(0.562)	(0.289)	(0.957)	(0.527)	(0.542)
Sales growth	−0.059	−0.712[a]	−0.312	−0.743[b]	0.106	−0.687[c]
	0.057	0.576	0.328	0.747	0.170	0.396
	(0.673)	(0.002)	(0.194)	(0.017)	(0.532)	(0.059)
Leverage	0.864[a]	0.616[c]	1.106[b]	0.471	0.852[c]	1.139[b]
	1.236	0.704	1.631	0.736	1.148	0.831
	(0.008)	(0.074)	(0.023)	(0.312)	(0.062)	(0.031)
Significance of multiplier diff.	(0.013)		(0.080)		(0.074)	

Table IV (*continued*)

Panel B: Multinomial Logit Estimation of Takeover Probability, with Sales Multiplier

Sample	All		1984		1987	
	Single seg	Multiseg	Single seg	Multiseg	Single seg	Multiseg
Observations = 0, no takeover	2996		1357		1609	
Observations = 1 or 2, takeover	266	352	133	237	133	115
Probability of takeover at evaluation point	9.124	11.148	10.340	15.720	8.107	6.861
Intercept	−1.045[a]	−3.004[a]	−0.689[c]	−2.426[a]	−1.421[a]	−3.782[a]
	(0.000)	(0.000)	(0.095)	(0.000)	(0.000)	(0.000)
Excess value, sales multiplier	0.084	−0.607[a]	0.091	−0.599[a]	0.059	−0.629[a]
	0.247	2.360	0.043	2.924	0.153	1.688
	(0.526)	(0.000)	(0.622)	(0.000)	(0.755)	(0.003)
Return on assets	0.714	1.498[b]	1.035	0.593	0.417	2.102[c]
	0.330	0.665	0.576	0.351	0.170	0.633
	(0.262)	(0.033)	(0.259)	(0.489)	(0.649)	(0.088)
Size	−0.332[a]	0.071[b]	−0.368[a]	0.080[c]	−0.295[a]	0.079
	2.786	1.073	3.423	1.609	2.202	0.810
	(0.000)	(0.031)	(0.000)	(0.057)	(0.000)	(0.155)
Liquidity	0.378	0.216	0.765[c]	0.557	0.069	0.002
	0.382	0.186	0.869	0.628	0.061	0.001
	(0.230)	(0.494)	(0.099)	(0.182)	(0.880)	(0.997)
Book/market ratio	−0.006	0.136	−0.129	0.058	0.098	0.165
	0.014	0.477	0.337	0.273	0.254	0.357
	(0.959)	(0.151)	(0.460)	(0.636)	(0.526)	(0.284)
Sales growth	−0.014	−0.648[a]	−0.251	−0.487[c]	0.141	−0.991[a]
	0.012	0.557	0.239	0.528	0.206	0.585
	(0.920)	(0.002)	(0.284)	(0.056)	(0.397)	(0.009)
Leverage	0.756[b]	0.665[b]	0.964[c]	0.669	0.722	1.047[b]
	0.972	0.810	1.282	1.146	0.875	0.769
	(0.022)	(0.035)	(0.053)	(0.124)	(0.120)	(0.028)
Significance of multiplier diff.	(0.000)		(0.002)		(0.012)	

[a,b,c] denotes that the coefficient estimate is significantly different from zero at the 0.01, 0.05, and 0.10 two-tailed probability level, respectively.

In both panels, the excess value measures have significantly more impact on takeover likelihood for diversified than for stand-alone firms. Because all six sets of results in Table IV are similar, we focus on those for the full sample using the asset multiplier measure of excess value. These results, presented in the first two columns of Panel A, show that the coefficient estimate of −0.816 on excess value for the multi-segment targets is significant at the 0.01 level, whereas the corresponding estimate of −0.170 for the stand-alone targets does not differ significantly from zero. Thus, value loss significantly affects the probability that an observation is a diversified target rather than a (diversified or stand-alone) nontarget, but does not significantly affect the probability that an observation is a stand-alone target rather than a nontarget. Moreover, a chi-squared test for the equality of the coefficient estimates on the excess value variable between the multi-segment targets and the stand-alone targets, reported in the bottom row of Table IV, is significant at the 0.05 level. This result shows that the effect of value loss on the probability of being a target firm is significantly greater when comparing diversified targets to all nontargets than it is when comparing stand-alone targets to all nontargets. This result indicates that it is not merely value loss per se that increases takeover likelihood among the sample of diversified firms, but rather value loss *associated with the diversification discount*.

The other five estimations reported in Table IV provide results very similar to those for the full sample using the asset multiplier. Excess value is always the economically most important variable for the multi-segment targets, and it is never so for the stand-alone targets. The coefficient estimates on the control variables generally have the same sign for both the stand-alone targets and the multi-segment targets. One exception is the size variable, which is always signed negatively for the former group and positively for the latter. The positive sign for the multi-segment targets reflects the inclusion of the naturally smaller stand-alone firms in the nontakeover group.

The combined results from Tables III and IV provide support for both value destruction in general, and *value loss associated with diversification policy* affecting takeover probabilities for diversified firms. Because value loss and diversification policy are correlated, it is impossible to completely disentangle the extent to which general versus diversification-specific value destruction is affecting takeover likelihood. The Table III results cannot reject the hypothesis that general value loss alone affects the probability of takeover, but these tests make no attempt to address the correlation between the level of value loss and whether the firm is diversified. The Table IV results strongly support diversification-specific value loss affecting takeover likelihood, but these tests may over-adjust for the correlation between value destruction and diversification by comparing each type of target (diversified and stand-alone) to all nontargets.

We corroborate the evidence from the multinomial logits by examining whether diversification increases the probability of takeover, after controlling for other determinants. Diversification is measured by an indicator variable set to one if the firm has multiple segments, and to zero otherwise. The control variables are the same ones used in Tables III and IV. We perform estimations for the full, 1984, and 1987 samples. Consistent with the hypothesis that diversification provides acquirers with more opportunity to profit from value creation, the diversification indicator is significantly positively (0.05 level) related to takeover likelihood for the full and the 1984 samples (results not reported in a table). Our evidence extends univariate results presented by Comment and Jarrell (1995). They find that, among firms with a market capitalization above $500 million, the annual takeover rate among multi-segment firms is 2.6 percent, versus only 1.7 percent for their single-line counterparts.

B. LBOs Versus Other Acquirers of Diversified Targets

Although the results in Tables III and IV show that acquirers tend to target diversified firms in which more value can be added through breakup, we do not know whether acquirers actually breakup, or otherwise enhance the value of, their targets. Therefore, we turn to an examination of the LBO acquirers, which have been argued to be particularly likely to undertake value-enhancing actions. For example, Jensen (1989) argues that the management, compensation, and financial structures of LBO associations lead to efficiency gains and high-return asset sales. He views high leverage as an important LBO advantage, in part because the need to service debt increases the incentive to produce cash by selling assets. Empirical evidence provides support for the preceding arguments. Kaplan (1989) documents the high frequency with which LBOs break-up targets. He notes that 16 of 42 sample LBOs make divestitures (or acquisitions) of at least 10 percent of the buyout capital within one year of the LBO.[6] Bhagat, Shleifer, and Vishny (1990) provide evidence that divestitures are more common following LBO acquisitions than non-LBO takeovers. They find that the median portion of the acquisition price realized through selloffs is 40.7 percent following the seven LBO buyouts in their sample versus 12.3 percent for the 55 non-LBO acquisitions.

Table V presents, for the diversified firms subsequently taken over, estimations of the likelihood their takeover was by an LBO group. The only control reported is growth, which is the only control variable consistently significant in the Table V regressions. The Table V estimations are similar across both excess value measures, with the signs of the excess value coefficient estimates negative in all six estimations, and significant at the 0.01 (0.10) level using the asset (sales) multiplier for the full and the 1987 samples. Significance levels for the full sample continue to exceed the 0.01 (0.10) level when we use the conservatively adjusted standard errors. Finally, when (unreported) regressions using the same variables as those in Table V are performed on the sample of one-segment firms subsequently taken over, the estimates on the excess value variables are not consistent in sign and are never significant at the 0.10 level.

The elasticities also suggest that value destruction has an economically significant effect on the conditional probability that, given takeover, the acquirer is an LBO. For the full sample of takeovers, decreasing the asset (sales) multiplier measure of excess value from its median to its 25th percentile increases takeover probability by 3.9 percent (3 percent) from its evaluation point of 10.1 percent (12.1 percent). Comparing the 1984 and 1987 samples, it is apparent that the economic impact of value destruction on the likelihood the acquirer is an LBO is greater in the later period. The 8.1 percent elasticity on the asset multiplier measure in 1987 is particularly striking. The smaller elasticities for the 1984 sample, and their lack of significance (at the 0.10 level), are consistent with three possible explanations. First, there is less likelihood that the value losses of 1987 firms change drastically prior to the

[6] Jensen (1993) contends that LBOs are more likely than other acquirers to take other value-increasing actions in addition to break-ups. For example, he notes that LBO associations are characterized by limited partnership agreements that prohibit headquarters from cross-subsidizing one division with cash from another.

Table V

Logit Regressions Relating the Likelihood of LBO Versus Non-LBO Takeover to Excess Value and Sales Growth

The sample includes all observations with two or more segments on the COMPUSTAT Industry Segment database in 1984 or 1987 that were taken over during the four fiscal years following the observation year. The top number for each variable is the parameter estimate, the middle number is the elasticity, and two-tailed p-values are in parentheses. All independent variables are measured in the observation's base year (1984 or 1987). Variable definitions are as follows. The asset and sales multiplier measures of excess value are as defined in Table II. Sales growth is the annual rate of change in sales. The elasticities for the explanatory variables are defined as the percentage increase in the probability of takeover above the evaluation point (see definition below) when the variable's median is replaced with either its 25th or 75th percentile (whichever leads to a probability increase). The probability of takeover at the evaluation point is defined as the probability of takeover at the point on the cumulative logistic distribution which results when all of the explanatory variables have their median values.

Dependent variable LBO logit Sample	All	All	1984	1984	1987	1987
Observations = 0, no LBO	249	309	170	211	79	98
Observations = 1, LBO	39	49	18	27	21	22
Probability of takeover at evaluation point	10.068	12.079	7.077	9.847	14.607	16.014
Intercept	−2.819[a]	−2.323[a]	−3.103[a]	−2.525[a]	−2.483[a]	−2.050[a]
	(0.000)	(0.000)	(0.000)	(0.000)	(0.000)	(0.000)
Excess value, asset multiplier	−1.496[a]		−1.068		−2.237[a]	
	3.862		2.171		8.109	
	(0.005)		(0.129)		(0.007)	
Excess value, sales multiplier		−0.567[c]		−0.426		−0.840[c]
		2.989		1.705		6.592
		(0.060)		(0.276)		(0.086)
Sales growth	2.816[a]	1.507[a]	2.772[a]	1.520[b]	2.896[b]	1.684[c]
	2.353	1.410	1.734	1.221	3.281	1.983
	(0.000)	(0.004)	(0.010)	(0.010)	(0.010)	(0.088)

[a,b,c] denotes that the coefficient estimate is significantly different from zero at the 0.01, 0.05, and 0.10 two-tailed probability level, respectively.

LBO date than is true for 1984 companies. Table I shows that all but one of the LBOs of 1987 firms occurs within two years of the measurement of value loss, whereas most of the LBOs of 1984 firms do not occur within two years. Second, the elasticities in 1987 must be about twice as high as those in 1984 in order to provide an equal proportional increase in takeover probability. This is so because the probability of takeover at the evaluation point is about twice as high in 1987 as in 1984, but this explanation can only partially explain the fact that the elasticities are roughly four times as large in 1987. A final possibility is that LBOs became more likely to make break-up acquisitions, rather than strategic ones, in the late 1980s. This possibility is intriguing, since Kaplan and Stein (1993) show that the ratio of buyout price to target fundamentals (as measured by cash flow) rose significantly in the late 1980s. They comment that such a pattern is consistent with an "overheating phenomenon" in the buyout market. Our evidence suggests that some of the apparent overpayment in later LBOs could reflect an increased emphasis on taking extreme value-destroying firms private.

III. Value Loss from Diversification and Subsequent Breakup

A. Value Destruction and Post-Takeover Breakup

The preceding analysis suggests that takeovers of diversified firms often lead to breakups. To provide evidence on this issue, and to examine the difference between targets that are broken up and those that are not, we document the post-takeover sales of target assets following large acquisitions. We define large acquisitions as those in which the target's pre-takeover total capital exceeded $250 million. We also require the targets to have complete information available for calculating both excess value measures.

We obtain information on post-takeover divestitures from the IDDMA file and the PR Newswire M&A file of the Lexis/Nexis database. We gather information on the number of target divisions divested in the acquisition year plus the two following years and, when available, the value of the consideration received for the divested divisions. Post-takeover information is typically disseminated for the merged firm, making attribution of sold-off divisions to the target difficult. We label a post-takeover selloff as a breakup of the target's divisions only when the division sold is described as having been a part of the target. This conservatism, and the tendency for reporting on selloffs to be incomplete, mean that the selloffs we document are likely to underestimate the amount of post-takeover divestiture activity.

Panel A of Table VI provides comparisons of the value destruction in targets subsequently broken up and those not broken up. Some of the 1988 targets enter both the 1984 and 1987 base year samples, and therefore have two value destruction measures. We eliminate these cases of double-counting by deleting the 1987 measure of target excess value when the takeover announcement occurs during the first three months of 1988 and the 1984 measure of target excess value otherwise.[7]

We define a bustup as occurring when the number of divested divisions is either: 1) at least three, or 2) at least one less than the number of segments reported by the target on the CIS database in the base year. The Panel A results show a striking difference in the value loss between targets that are broken up and those that are not. Measuring excess value with the asset multiplier, the mean value loss of 20.8 percent for the 50 targets subsequently broken up exceeds the value loss for the 50 targets not broken up by 16.2

[7] Table VII shows that target stock prices three months prior to the takeover announcement are much smaller than the final purchase price. This evidence is consistent with excess value measures for a given year not being distorted by a following year takeover as long as the takeover occurs at least three months into the following year.

Table VI

The Relation Between Excess Value and Post-Takeover Bust-Up

The sample consists of 100 large, diversified firms that were taken over. Panel A groups the sample into targets that were busted-up after takeover and those that were not. In this panel, we define a bustup as occurring when the number of divested divisions is either: 1) at least three, or 2) at least one less than the number of segments reported by the target on the COMPUSTAT Industry Segment database in the base year. Panel B uses a continuous measure of the extent of post-takeover breakup: the proportion of the target's acquisition value that was subsequently divested. The asset and sales multiplier measures of excess value are as defined in Table II. The divestitures with value/total variable in Panel B is a control for the proportion of the firm's divestitures for which values are reported. If the firm has no divestitures (i.e., the denominator is zero), the ratio is set equal to one.

Panel A: Value Loss for Firms Later Busted-up Versus Those Not Busted-up

	Means			Medians		
Excess Value	No Bustup	Bustup	Difference	No Bustup	Bustup	Difference
Asset multiplier	−0.046	−0.208	−0.162[b]	−0.059	−0.226	−0.167[b]
Sales multiplier	−0.045	−0.367	−0.322[a]	0.043	−0.367	−0.410[a]
Number of segments	3.5	3.5	0.0	3.0	3.0	0.0
Observations	50	50		50	50	

Panel B: Regressions of the Proportion of Target's Value Subsequently Divested on the Excess Value Measures

Dependent Variable	Minimum Value Divested/Acquisition Price	
Observations	100	100
Adj R^2	0.080	0.073
Intercept	0.055	0.055
	(0.860)	(0.849)
Excess value, asset multiplier	−0.192[b]	
	(0.031)	
Excess value, sales multiplier		−0.127[b]
		(0.048)
Divestitures with value/total	0.218[b]	0.216[b]
	(0.011)	(0.012)

[a,b] denotes, in Panel A, that the mean (median) difference is significantly different from zero at the 0.01 and 0.05 two-tailed probability level, respectively. In Panel B, denotes that the coefficient estimate is significantly different from zero at the 0.01, and 0.05 two-tailed probability level, respectively.

percent. With the sales multiplier, the broken up targets have a mean value loss of 36.7 percent, and the remaining targets have a mean value loss of 4.5 percent. These results are consistent with breakup takeovers targeting value-destroying firms and strategic takeovers targeting relatively better-performing diversified companies.

Absent measurement error, a more powerful test of the relation of value loss to post-takeover divestitures is achieved by using a continuous measure of the value of such divestitures. In Panel B of Table VI, we construct such a measure by summing, for each target, all available selling prices of the divested divisions, then dividing this total by the purchase price the bidder paid for the target. The resulting ratio measures the proportion of the target's value for which information on values divested by the bidder is available. Unfortunately, of the 234 target divisions we know were divested by bidders in the two years following the acquisitions, just 124 have information about the value of the divisions sold. There is thus considerable measurement error in using the ratio we construct to proxy for the proportion of target value subsequently divested.

We regress the ratio of minimum value divested to acquisition price on excess value and a control for the proportion of the firm's divestitures for which values are reported.[8] We find that, using both measures of excess value, a greater portion of the acquisition price is divested when the target is destroying more value. The coefficient estimates on the excess value measures are significant at better than the 0.05 level in both regressions. Even with the large amount of noise in our proxy, we still find that firms destroying more value have a greater portion of their assets divested after takeovers.

Table VII provides details on the sample of 100 large acquisitions used in the Table VI tests. The second and third columns provide the takeover announcement date (i.e., the date of the first bid by the bidder who gained control of the target) and the purchase price of the target's equity. The information in these columns demonstrates that the sample of large acquisitions has some differences from the remainder of our sample. For example, eight of the 100 takeovers are announced in 1990, and three in 1991. Thus, 11 percent of the large acquisitions occur in these two years, versus 7.2 percent for the full sample.

The premiums paid by the acquirers, defined as the final equity purchase price divided by the target's market value of equity three months before the takeover announcement, range from −1.4 percent for Ausimont N.V. to 379.5 percent for GCA Corp., with an average of 58.8 percent. These premia are slightly larger than those previously documented for takeovers during the 1980s (see Jensen (1991)). The number of target divisions divested by the acquirer by the end of the second year after acquisition ranges from zero to 15, with an average of 2.3. Twenty-six of the 50 acquisitions we classify as non-bustups have no divested divisions, whereas the remaining 24 have one or two divisions divested. In those cases where one or more divested divisions had a disclosed selling price, the value of divested assets as a portion of the target's purchase price ranged from 0.6 percent for Contel to 155.2 percent for Stauffer Chemical, with an average of 42.5 percent. These figures are similar to those reported by Bhagat, Shleifer, and Vishny (1990), who report a range of 0.4 percent to 131.8 percent, with an average of 43.7 percent. Their measurement differs slightly from ours, in that they include the value of acquired debt in

[8] If the firm has no divestitures (i.e., the denominator of the control variable is zero), the ratio is set equal to one. If we instead set the ratio to zero for these cases, the significance of the coefficient estimate on the control variable is increased, but our inferences on the excess value variables remain unchanged.

Table VII

Summary of 100 Takeovers of Large, Diversified Firms

The sample consists of 100 large, diversified firms that were taken over. The information referred to by each column heading is as follows. Target refers to the name of the firm taken over. Announced refers to the announcement day of the first bid by the bidder who gained control over the target. Purchase price is the final price per share offered by the bidder multiplied by the number of shares outstanding. Premium is the excess of the final purchase price over the stock price three months before the announcement. Divest refers to the number of divisions divested from the target in the year of the acquisition and the following two years. Min val divested is the total value divested for divisions whose sale price is reported, divided by the purchase price of the target. Selloffs w/ value reports the number of divisions divested with available selling prices. Segn refers to the number of segments reported by the firm in the year its excess value is measured.

Target	Announced	Purchase Price	Premium	Divest	Min Val Divested	Selloffs w/ Value	Segn
A G S COMPUTERS INC	880613	407	82.35%	2	23.6%	1	2
A M F INC	850426	631	48.8%	9	82.4%	5	7
ADOBE OIL & GAS CORP	850214	284	7.58%	2	23.6%	2	3
AMERICAN BROADCASTING COS	850319	3517	91.7%	0	0.0%	0	4
AMFAC INC	880127	834	81.5%	7	67.3%	7	7
AMSTED INDUSTRIES INC	851104	512	3.33%	5	0.0%	0	4
ANCHOR HOCKING CORP	861106	337	1.19%	1	0.0%	0	3
ASAMERA INC	880226	375	63.23%	2	10.1%	1	3
ASSOCIATED DRY GOODS CORP	860623	1908	45.4%	4	34.6%	2	2
AUSIMONT N V	880928	640	−1.4%	3	27.2%	1	2
BECOR WESTERN INC	870217	280	34.65%	1	43.2%	1	3
BIG THREE INDS INC	860813	1093	13.2%	1	0.0%	0	3
BLAIR JOHN & CO	860601	251	47.62%	4	143.7%	3	5
C N W CORP	890606	814	28.2%	0	0.0%	0	3
C P NATIONAL CORP	880725	315	60.19%	1	27.0%	1	5
CAMPBELL RED LAKE MINES LT	870606	NA	NA	0	0.0%	0	2
CATALYST ENERGY DEV CORP	880726	189	23.3%	1	0.0%	0	3
CENTRAL SOYA INC	850314	342	45.86%	4	31.6%	3	3
CESSNA AIRCRAFT CO	850916	592	31.9%	0	0.0%	0	2
CHESEBROUGH PONDS INC	861201	2478	63.8%	9	88.1%	4	9
CHICAGO PACIFIC CORP	881025	562	27.3%	1	37.9%	1	2
CHIEFTAIN DEVELOPMENT LTD	880608	230	43.12%	0	0.0%	0	3
COLEMAN INC	890320	521	80.49%	4	15.0%	2	2
COLLINS & AIKMAN CORP	861110	1155	42.76%	1	0.0%	0	3
CONTEL CORP	900712	6191	58.3%	5	0.6%	1	3
COX COMMUNICATION INC	850409	2116	37.3%	2	7.3%	2	4
DAY INTERNATIONAL	870707	359	64.81%	1	10.3%	1	4
DENNISON MANUFACTURING CO	900525	497	43.8%	2	0.0%	0	4
DIVERSIFIED ENERGIES INC	900730	665	46.0%	4	18.3%	3	4
DIVERSIFOODS INC	850521	388	17.95%	2	25.8%	1	4
DOME MINES LTD	870506	NA	NA	0	0.0%	0	2
DOME-PETE-LTD	870414	504	97.3%	1	33.5%	1	2
EMHART CORP VA	890320	2479	74.9%	3	22.6%	3	5
ENTEX INC	871005	497	37.5%	0	0.0%	0	4
FIRESTONE INC	880307	2849	154.0%	0	0.0%	0	2
GCA CORP	880302	91	379.50%	1	8.8%	1	3
GELCO CORP	871005	247	55.6%	0	0.0%	0	3
GENERAL FOODS CORP	850925	5722	48.1%	0	0.0%	0	4
GIFFORD HILL & CO INC	860909	274	38.38%	1	22.2%	1	3
GRAPHIC SCANNING CORP	901231	168	33.68%	2	5.4%	2	6
GREAT NORTHERN NEKOOSA	891030	3596	64.4%	0	0.0%	0	4
GROLIER INC	880311	474	169.44%	3	11.0%	1	2
HAMMERMILL PAPER CO	860812	1000	56.4%	0	0.0%	0	5

Table VII (*continued*)

Target	Announced	Purchase Price	Premium	Divest	Min Val Divested	Selloffs w/ Value	Segn
HARCOURT BRACE JOVANOVICH	910808	55	20.0%	1	0.0%	0	3
HOLLY FARMS CORP	881011	1222	83.01%	4	40.9%	3	4
HOOVER UNIVERSAL	850304	489	61.33%	3	44.4%	1	3
HUGHES TOOL CO	861022	653	53.4%	4	0.0%	0	2
INEXCO OIL CO	860513	138	87.7%	0	0.0%	0	2
JP INDUSTRIES	900326	186	37.03%	0	0.0%	0	2
JEPSON CORP	890727	226	14.29%	2	24.8%	1	3
KAISERTECH LTD DEL	880524	868	63.1%	3	6.3%	1	3
KOPPERS CO	880302	1659	93.7%	10	40.1%	6	3
KRAFT INC NEW	881017	13905	95.8%	4	0.0%	0	3
LEAR SIEGLER INC	861217	1049	9.7%	2	48.3%	1	3
LEASEWAY TRANSPORTATION CO	861113	602	11.8%	3	0.0%	0	5
LIQUID AIR CORP NORTH AMER	880226	466	60.9%	0	0.0%	0	2
LOWENSTEIN M CORP	851008	263	32.63%	0	0.0%	0	3
LUCKY STORES INC	880323	2509	146.4%	1	0.0%	0	3
MCA INC	900924	4849	18.9%	0	0.0%	0	7
MACMILLAN INC	880721	2236	67.1%	7	24.1%	6	5
MAGIC CHEF INC	860324	723	40.52%	2	0.0%	0	3
MANPOWER INC NEW	870803	1329	67.51%	2	4.1%	2	2
MOHASCO CORP	880509	508	46.73%	2	54.5%	2	3
MOORE MC CORMACK RES INC	880223	356	141.2%	2	60.7%	2	7
NABISCO BRANDS INC	850530	4929	56.7%	4	4.1%	1	4
NATIONAL CAN CORP	850319	401	33.86%	0	0.0%	0	3
NEW WORLD ENTERTAINMENT LTD	890410	94	211.30%	1	0.0%	0	2
NORTH AMERN PHILIPS CORP	870818	1624	31.8%	4	0.0%	0	5
NORTON CO	900425	1883	66.3%	1	0.0%	0	2
PACIFIC LUMBER CO	851001	866	39.1%	1	34.6%	1	3
PACIFIC RESOURCES INC HI	890106	327	42.06%	0	0.0%	0	2
PENNWALT CORP	890320	1042	28.0%	1	0.0%	0	3
PHILIPS INDUSTRIES INC	900605	527	23.3%	0	0.0%	0	5
PILLSBURY CO	881003	5688	80.2%	11	16.7%	5	2
PULLMAN COMPANY DE NEW	880708	380	51.02%	7	33.7%	4	4
PUROLATOR COURIER CORP	870331	306	45.45%	3	94.9%	3	2
REICHHOLD CHEMICALS INC	870624	447	27.32%	1	0.0%	0	2
REVLON INC	850815	2214	43.2%	15	135.3%	9	5
RICHARDSON VICKS INC	851001	1611	89.0%	4	0.0%	0	2
ROLLINS COMMUNICATIONS INC	860513	599	50.46%	0	0.0%	0	3
SCM CORP	850822	738	55.8%	4	108.8%	4	6
SAGA CORP	860508	497	47.7%	2	60.3%	1	3
SANDERS ASSOC INC	860710	1175	90.5%	0	0.0%	0	2
SMITHKLINE BECKMAN CORP	890331	7818	30.9%	1	0.0%	0	4
SOUTHWEST FOREST INDS INC	870128	396	88.3%	1	56.8%	1	3
SQUARE D CO	910219	2067	85.3%	4	1.0%	1	2
STALEY CONTL INC	880407	1075	66.9%	0	0.0%	0	2
STAUFFER CHEM CO	850220	1218	69.7%	6	155.2%	5	5
STEVENS J P & CO INC	880301	1108	136.2%	6	75.3%	4	5
TW SVCS INC	881007	1651	82.6%	3	1.8%	1	3
TAFT BROADCASTING CO	870415	1446	36.5%	1	0.0%	0	3
TELEX CORP	871208	910	20.1%	1	0.0%	0	2
TEXAS EASTERN CORP	890217	2824	82.0%	4	67.3%	4	6
TIGER INTL INC	881219	740	54.6%	0	0.0%	0	2
TRANSWAY INTERNATIONAL CORP	851001	316	49.42%	0	0.0%	0	4
UNITED ARTISTS ENTRMT CO	910501	1206	26.3%	0	0.0%	0	3
WALKER HIRAM RES LTD	860319	2038	17.8%	3	152.6%	3	3
WESTBURNE INTERNATIONAL INDS L	870121	175	24.07%	1	0.0%	0	9
WHITE CONS INDS INC	860303	741	35.3%	2	1.6%	1	2
XIDEX CORP	880712	373	54.17%	1	0.0%	0	3

calculating both their acquisition prices and the proceeds from the disposition of divested units, whereas we exclude acquired debt from both calculations.

B. Who are the Buyers in Post-Takeover Breakups?

If breakup takeovers restore value by reorganizing segments of diversified firms as stand-alone entities, then the buyers of the divisions divested from a diversified firm after takeover will tend to be LBOs or other firms likely to operate the division as a stand-alone unit. To provide evidence on this issue, we examine the buyers of all of the divisions divested by the acquirers of the 100 large targets.

For the 227 divisions we know were divested by these acquirers, we classify the buyer's relation to the divested division based on the descriptions of their lines of business in the IDDMA file and/or the PR Newswire M&A file of Lexis/Nexis. We are unable to apply an SIC code algorithm because many of the buyers are either foreign or are not publicly traded. Buyers are categorized into the following types: LBOs, related focused, related diversified, unrelated focused, unrelated diversified, spinoffs/equity carve-outs, and unnamed.[9] All acquisition groups are classified as LBOs, the adjective related is applied instead of unrelated if the main line of business of the divested division is related horizontally or vertically to a line of business of the buyer, and the adjective focused is applied instead of diversified if the buyer has one main line of business only. The categorizations of buyers as related/unrelated and focused/diversified are thus a function of our interpretation of Lexis/Nexis information. We find that the number of buyers in each group is as follows: 67 LBOs, 80 related focused, 46 related diversified, five unrelated focused, one unrelated diversified, five spinoffs/equity carve-outs, and 23 unnamed. As expected, most of the identifiable buyers are either LBO groups or other firms likely to operate the divested division as a stand-alone operation. Not classifying related diversified buyers as part of this group results in 75 percent (152 of 204) of identifiable buyers being classified as "stand-alone operators," whereas including them increases the rate to 97 percent (198 of 204). The 75 percent to 97 percent rate is somewhat higher than that obtained by John and Ofek (1995) for a sample of buyers of divested divisions, using an analogous measure. They find that, during 1986–1988, 48 percent of bidders and targets with available information have a 4-digit SIC code in common among the top five main SIC codes of the buyer and the two main SIC codes of the divested segment. In addition, a further 21 percent of the buyers are LBOs. The somewhat lower proportion of "related" buyers they document may reflect a stricter definition of relatedness, as well as a lower likelihood of buyers of divisions sold in voluntary restructurings being related to the divested divisions.

[9] The seven Stauffer Chemical divisions later divested were also part of the nine Chesebrough Ponds divisions later divested. We therefore classified these divisions only once in our analysis of buyers.

IV. Conclusions

Previous literature has documented large and persistent value losses from diversification and the frequent use of breakups after takeovers. These two phenomena may be linked, with breakup takeovers of diversified firms undoing the value destruction created by combining business lines whose values are greater as stand-alone operations. We investigate the potential linkage in two steps. First, we see whether diversified firms in which more value is being destroyed are more likely to be taken over. In addition, we examine whether breakup takeovers are more likely than other takeovers to target value destroying diversification. The second step is taken both by exploiting LBO's greater propensity than other acquirers to breakup target divisions, and by following the breakup activity after takeover of a sample of large acquisitions.

Our measure of value destruction is the Berger and Ofek (1995) excess value measure, which compares the sum of the imputed stand-alone values of the segments of diversified firms to their actual values. The imputed stand-alone values are based on industry median multipliers of actual value to either assets or sales.

We show that the value loss from diversification is significantly related to the probability of subsequent takeover, with greater value losses associated with higher takeover probabilities. Conditional on takeover occurring, greater value losses are associated with higher probabilities that the acquirer is an LBO group. This result is consistent with LBOs being more likely than other acquirers to break-up the target.

For the sample of large acquisitions, we find that half of the large diversified targets are broken up, and that the mean value effect of diversification is −21 percent to −37 percent for these firms. In contrast, the large targets not broken up after takeover have a mean value effect from diversification of −5 percent. These results are consistent with the market for corporate control targeting and breaking-up combinations of business lines which have greater value when each line is operated on a stand-alone basis. If this is indeed what is going on, the buyers of the divisions from the broken-up target should tend to operate the divisions as stand-alone businesses. Based on an investigation of the buyers of the divested divisions from the sample of large targets, we find that 152 of 204 identifiable buyers are either LBOs or single-line firms that operate in a line of business related to that of the divested division.

Appendix

Multiplier estimation of imputed value and excess value: Equations (1) and (2) illustrate the approach:

$$\mathrm{I(V)} = \sum_{i=1}^{n} \mathrm{AI}_i * \left(\mathrm{Ind}_i \left(\frac{\mathrm{V}}{\mathrm{AI}} \right)_{mf} \right) \tag{1}$$

$$\mathrm{EXVAL} = \ln\left(\frac{\mathrm{V}}{\mathrm{I(V)}} \right) \tag{2}$$

where:

$I(V)$ = the imputed value of the sum of a firm's segments as stand-alone firms.

AI_i = segment i's value of the accounting item (sales or assets) used in the valuation multiple.

$Ind_i(V/AI)_{mf}$ = the multiple of total capital to an accounting item (sales, assets, or EBIT) for the median single-segment firm in segment i's industry.

EXVAL = the firm's excess value.

V = the firm's total capital (market value of common equity + book value of debt).

n = the total number of segments in segment i's firm.

Equation (1) shows that the firm's imputed value is the sum of segment-imputed values, which are obtained by multiplying an industry median multiplier of total capital to an accounting item by the segment's level of the accounting item. Equation (2) shows that the firm's excess value measure is the natural logarithm of the ratio of the firm's actual value to its imputed value.

To compute excess value using the sales multiplier, we multiply the industry median multiple of capital-to-sales for the stand-alone firms in the segment's industry by the segment's sales to obtain the imputed capital of the segment. We repeat this process for each of the firm's segments and then sum to obtain the firm's imputed value. Finally, we find the firm's excess value by taking the natural logarithm of the ratio of actual to imputed value. Extreme excess values are excluded from the analysis, with "extreme" defined for all three multipliers as natural logarithms of actual to imputed value above 1.386 or below −1.386 (i.e., actual values either more than four times imputed, or less than one-fourth imputed).

The asset multiple imputed values are found in an analogous manner. Another issue that arises is that it is much more common for the segment asset figures from the CIS tape to disagree with the COMPUSTAT firm totals than is the case with sales. The segment sum is usually less than the firm figure, indicating that the problem arises from unallocated assets. We deal with this problem in one of two ways: If the sum of the segment asset figures for a firm deviates from the firm's asset figure by more than 25 percent, we exclude the observation from all analyses using the asset multiples. If the deviation is within 25 percent, we adjust the firm's imputed value to reflect the fact that the multipliers have been multiplied by segment asset figures that are too small or too large. Specifically, the firm's imputed value is grossed up or down by the percentage deviation between the sum of its segments' assets and total firm assets. The excess value measure based on asset multiples is then found in the same way as the measure using sales multiples.

REFERENCES

Barber, B. M., D. A. Palmer, and J. Wallace, 1995, Determinants of conglomerate and predatory acquisitions: Evidence from the 1960s, *Journal of Corporate Finance* 1, 283–318.

Berger, P. G., and E. Ofek, 1995, Diversification's effect on firm value, *Journal of Financial Economics* 37, 39–65.

Bhagat, S., A. Shleifer, and R. W. Vishny, 1990, Hostile takeovers in the 1980s: The return to corporate specialization, Brookings Papers on Economic Activity: Microeconomics, 1–72.

Comment, R., and G. A. Jarrell, 1995, Corporate focus and stock returns, *Journal of Financial Economics* 37, 67–87.

Harris, M., and A. Raviv, 1991, The theory of capital structure, *Journal of Finance* 46, 297–355.

Hasbrouck, J., 1985, The characteristics of takeover targets: q and other measures, *Journal of Banking and Finance* 9, 351–362.

Healy, P., K. Palepu, and R. Ruback, 1992, Does corporate performance improve after mergers?, *Journal of Financial Economics* 31, 135–175.

Israel, R., 1991, Capital structure and the market for corporate control: The defensive role of debt financing, *Journal of Finance* 46, 1391–1409.

Jensen, M. C., 1986, Agency costs of free cash flow, corporate finance, and takeovers, *American Economic Review* 76, 323–329.

Jensen, M. C., 1989, Eclipse of the public corporation, *Harvard Business Review* 67, 61–74.

Jensen, M. C., 1991, Corporate control and the politics of finance, *Journal of Applied Corporate Finance* 4, 13–33.

Jensen, M. C., 1993, The modern industrial revolution, exit, and the failure of internal control systems, *Journal of Finance* 48, 831–880.

John, K., and E. Ofek, 1995, Asset sales and increase in focus, *Journal of Financial Economics* 37, 105–126.

Kaplan, S., 1989, The effects of management buyouts on operating performance and value, *Journal of Financial Economics* 24, 581–618.

Kaplan, S., and J. Stein, 1993, The evolution of buyout pricing and financial structure in the 1980s, *Journal of Economics* 108, 313–357.

Kaplan, S., and M. Weisbach, 1992, The success of acquisitions: evidence from divestitures, *Journal of Finance* 47, 107–138.

Lang, L. H. P., and R. E. Stulz, 1994, Tobin's q, corporate diversification and firm performance, *Journal of Political Economy* 102, 1248–1280.

Lang, L. H. P., R. E. Stulz, and R. A. Walking, 1989, Managerial performance, Tobin's q, and the gains from successful tender offers, *Journal of Financial Economics* 24, 137–154.

Manne, H. G., 1965, Mergers and the market for corporate control, *Journal of Political Economy* 73, 110–120.

Marris, R., 1963, A model of the 'managerial' enterprise, *Quarterly Journal of Economics* 77, 185–209.

Mitchell, M., and K. Lehn, 1990, Do bad bidders become good targets?, *Journal of Political Economy* 98, 372–398.

Morck, R., A. Shleifer, and R. W. Vishny, 1988, Characteristics of targets of hostile and friendly takeovers, in A. J. Auerbach, ed.: *Corporate takeovers: Causes and consequences* (University of Chicago Press, Chicago, IL).

Palepu, K., 1986, Predicting takeover targets: A methodological and empirical analysis, *Journal of Accounting and Economics* 8, 3–35.

Servaes, H., 1991, Tobin's q and the gains from takeovers, *Journal of Finance* 46, 409–419.

Servaes, H., 1996, The value of diversification during the conglomerate merger wave, *Journal of Finance* 51, 1201–1225.

Stulz, R. M., 1988, Managerial control of voting rights: Financing policies and the market for corporate control, *Journal of Financial Economics* 20, 25–54.

C
Joint Ventures

[18]

THE JOURNAL OF FINANCE • VOL. XL, NO. 2 • JUNE 1985

Corporate Combinations and Common Stock Returns: The Case of Joint Ventures

JOHN J. McCONNELL and TIMOTHY J. NANTELL*

ABSTRACT

The gain to stockholders from mergers is well documented. However, there is little evidence as to whether the source of the gain is due to synergy or management displacement. Merger is just one of an almost limitless variety of ways in which firms combine resources to accomplish some objective. A joint venture is another. In addition to being of interest as an independent phenomenon, because the original managements of the parent firms remain intact under a joint venture, investigation of wealth gains from joint ventures provides an opportunity to isolate the management displacement hypothesis from the synergy hypothesis as the source of gains in corporate combinations. Our results are 1) there are significant wealth gains from joint ventures, 2) the smaller partner earns a larger excess rate of return while the dollar gains are more equally divided, and 3) the gains, scaled by resources committed, yield "premiums" similar to those in mergers. We are inclined to interpret our results as supportive of the synergy hypothesis as the source of gain from corporate combinations.

THIS PAPER IS AN empirical investigation of the common stock returns of U.S. companies that enter into joint ventures with other U.S. companies. We consider joint ventures in the context of what is by now a burgeoning literature examining the security returns of companies involved in intercorporate mergers and tender offers.[1] In this context, our objective is to provide evidence as to the source of the well-documented gains to stockholders of firms involved in mergers and tender offers. In addition, joint ventures are an interesting economic phenomenon in their own right. They are undertaken by many of the largest U.S. companies, involve billions of dollars in capital expenditures annually, and are subject to considerable scrutiny in the popular press. In this regard, our analysis provides data on what is as yet a relatively unexplored area of economic activity.[2]

A corporate merger represents the joining together of all the resources of two companies under a single management to accomplish some set of objectives. Empirical studies have found that mergers generally result in significant increases in the total market values of the merging firms with the stockholders of the

* Purdue University and University of Minnesota, respectively.

[1] See, for example, Asquith [1], Asquith, Bruner, and Mullins [2], Bradley [9], Bradley, Desai and Kim [10, 11], Dodd [13], Eckbo [16], Kim and McConnell [24], Langetieg [25], Malatesta [28], Mandelker [30], and Schipper and Thompson [37].

[2] Previous economic studies of various aspects of U.S. domestic joint ventures include Berg and Friedman [3–7], Boyle [8], Duncan [15], Fusfeld [19], and Pfeffer and Nowack [35]. For the most part, these studies employ accounting and aggregate economic data. To our knowledge, ours is the first study to use stock market data to address questions regarding joint ventures.

acquired company receiving substantial "excess" returns and the stockholders of the acquiring company earning small or negligible "excess" returns.[3]

Two general hypotheses have been proposed to explain the large increases in wealth associated with mergers.[4] The first is that the pooling of the resources of the two merging companies gives rise to "synergies" which take the form of economies of scale, the combining of complementary resources, increased market power, improved production techniques, improved marketing and product distribution opportunities, the redeployment of assets to more profitable uses, and so on. The second is that the merger facilitates the replacement of the acquired company's inefficient, ineffective, or deliberately misintentioned management. Unfortunately, various studies of mergers have found it difficult (or impossible) to distinguish empirically between these hypotheses.

In contrast to a merger, a joint venture involves the joining together of a subset of the resources of two (or more) companies to accomplish some objective under the combined management of two (or more) parent companies. In this regard, the primary distinction between a corporate merger and a corporate joint venture is that, although the management of the resources involved in the joint venture differs from that of the management of the parent company, the original management of the parent firms remains intact under the joint venture. Indeed, in regards to the combining of resources, it can be argued that a merger is a special (limiting) case of a joint venture. Thus, if the "synergy" hypothesis of mergers is correct, the stock returns to companies involved in joint ventures should "look like" those of companies involved in mergers. That is, a study of joint ventures provides an opportunity to isolate the "management displacement" hypothesis of mergers from the "synergy" hypothesis.

There is yet another, still broader, perspective in which joint ventures and, by extension, corporate mergers can be considered. That is, that both types of activities merely represent two of a nearly limitless variety of ways in which firms can combine resources to accomplish some objective. Other methods include franchising and trademark agreements, long-term buy/sell agreements, and one-time-only buy/sell transactions. Perhaps the simplest form of intercorporate combination of resources is the classic capital budgeting or investment project in which one firm acquires a variety of resources from a variety of suppliers and combines them to accomplish some objective under its own management. From this perspective, then, intercorporate joint ventures and mergers are merely two special cases of capital investment projects.

As a test of the premise that the wealth increases that accompany corporate mergers reflect the types of gains (or synergies) that are presumed to accompany other instances in which corporations combine resources to accomplish some set of objectives, this paper reports the results of an event-time analysis of the stock returns of 210 U.S. companies that entered into 136 domestic joint ventures over the period 1972–1979. To establish the background for the analysis, Section I

[3] Until recently, the negligible "excess" returns to the acquiring company were somewhat of a puzzle. For appealing explanations of this phenomenon, see Asquith, Bruner, and Mullins [2], Bradley, Desai, and Kim [10], Schipper and Thompson [37], and Malatesta and Thompson [29].

[4] See, for example, Jensen and Ruback [23].

contains a brief discussion of joint venture prosecution under federal antitrust legislation and summarizes the motives for joint ventures as given by corporate managers. Both the history of antitrust proceedings and the managerial motives for joint ventures are shown to parallel those of corporate mergers. Section II describes the sample. Section III describes the data and statistical methodology employed in the analysis while Section IV presents the results. The final section contains a summary and some concluding remarks.

I. Perspectives on Corporate Joint Ventures

In addition to the argument that intercorporate joint ventures and mergers represent similar economic phenomena, parallels between mergers and joint ventures can be seen in the motives given by managers for participating in them and in the way in which both types of transactions have been prosecuted under federal antitrust legislation.

Melicher and Nielsen [32] surveyed managers and reviewed proxy statements describing mergers to compile a list of stated motives for mergers. Their list is contained in Table I along with a similar list of motives for joint ventures as compiled by Berg and Friedman [5] by means of a questionnaire survey. Examination of the two lists indicates a significant overlap in the apparent (or at least the stated) motives for corporate mergers and joint ventures. These can loosely be categorized as achievement of operating and production economies, achievement of marketing efficiencies, achievement of vertical integration, acquisition of enhanced financial resources, and exploitation of patent rights.

Similarities between corporate mergers and joint ventures are evident also in the way in which both have been prosecuted under the federal antitrust laws. Traditionally, the Justice Department has challenged the legality of mergers under Section 1 of the Sherman Act and under the "anticompetitive" provisions

Table I

Managerial Motives for Mergers and Joint Ventures

Motives for Mergers[a]	Motives for Joint Ventures[b]
1. Extension of Existing Markets	1. To Acquire Skills and Technical Know How
2. Improved Distribution Network	2. To Acquire Distribution Facilities
3. Extension of Product Lines	3. To Acquire Production Facilities
4. Improved Production Facilities	4. Joint Venture is a Customer of a Parent
5. Anticipation of Operating Economies	5. Joint Venture is a Supplier of a Parent
6. Improvement of Earnings Stability	6. To Research and Develop a New Product or Process
7. Achievement of Vertical Integration	7. To Acquire Capital
8. Acquisition of New Technologies	8. To Produce for Government Contract
9. Improvement of Research Facilities	9. To Purchase Government Owned Facility
10. Acquisition of Financial Resources	10. To Exploit a Product or a Licensed Process
11. Anticipation of Management Economies	
12. Acquisition of Government Contracts	
13. Acquisition of Timber or Patent Rights	

[a] Source: Melicher and Nielsen [32].

[b] Source: Berg and Friedman [5].

of Section 7 of the Clayton Act.[5] The Justice Department has challenged joint ventures under these same laws, and the courts have applied the same tests of unlawfulness. Additionally, when the courts have concluded that a joint venture represents a potential restraint of trade or that it will substantially lessen competition, remedies similar to those applied in antitrust judgments against potential mergers have been applied. Specifically, the courts have ordered that the joint venture either be dissolved or that the joint venture cease from acquiring further market share.[6] Given the parallels between intercorporate mergers and joint ventures as perceived by the courts and corporate managers, the premise for the empirical tests conducted in this paper—i.e., that the "synergy" gains in mergers and joint ventures should be "similar"—appears to be a reasonable one.[7]

II. Sample Selection

To conduct our investigation, an initial sample of joint ventures involving U.S. corporations was taken from the "Joint Venture Roster" published in *Mergers and Acquisitions* over the period beginning January 1972 and ending December 1979. Based on the description provided by *Mergers and Acquisitions* it is not clear whether the tabulation of joint ventures is exhaustive (although it most certainly is not) and it is not clear how the "Roster" is constructed. However, over the eight years considered, the periodical did report approximately 3500 joint ventures involving U.S. companies.

In order to be included in the final sample, the joint venture had to meet several additional criteria. First, both (or all) of the parent companies involved had to be U.S. corporations.[8] Second, an announcement of the joint venture had

[5] Eckbo [16], Stillman [38], and Wier [41] examine common stock returns around events associated with antitrust proceedings initated by the U.S. Justice Department against potential corporate mergers.

[6] Brodley [12] surveys judicial cases involving the legal status of joint ventures under the antitrust laws through 1976. Two other more recent cases involve: (1) the forced dissolution in 1981 of a joint venture, called Premiere, between four movie studios and Getty Oil (see [34, pp. 40–41]), and (2) the international joint venture between General Motors and Toyota (see [20, pp. 1+]).

[7] One perception is that intercorporate joint ventures and mergers are different economic phenomena because joint ventures are formed primarily to undertake new projects whereas mergers primarily involve the joining together of existing projects. This perception is not entirely accurate. On the one hand, in most instances joint ventures involve an expansion of activities in which one or both of the joint venture partners had been previously engaged. On the other hand, the result of many mergers is that one or both of the merging companies reorganizes its existing activities or redeploys assets in new ways. In many cases, the redeployment of assets and the reorganization of activities that comes about as a result of the merger can be viewed as a new project. Presumably, there are instances in which a joint venture is the most efficient form of organization to accomplish some set of objectives and there are other instances in which a merger is the most efficient form of organization to accomplish the objectives. A separate question is: What are the fundamental characteristics of the organizational forms that determine which is the most efficient form in the various cases? We do not explore that question in this paper. However, Fama and Jensen [17, 18] provide a framework for analyzing the comparative advantages of alternative organizational forms. Before addressing that question, we address the more basic question in this paper of whether joint ventures are value-creating activities.

[8] Our sample is limited to domestic joint ventures so as to avoid contaminating the results with any international "diversification" effects that may occur in international joint ventures. However,

Table II

Description of the Sample of Joint Ventures

A. Chronological Profile

Year of Initiation	Number
1972	25
1973	18
1974	12
1975	15
1976	15
1977	12
1978	22
1979	17
Total	136

B. Type of Joint Venture

Category	Number
Real Estate Development	18
TV Programming, Motion Pictures, Video Games, etc.	14
Develop Nuclear Power, Uranium Production, etc.	9
Coal Mining or Develop Coal Mine	8
Petrochemical Facility	7
Convert Waste to Energy	5
Develop Satellite Communications	4
All Others	71
Total	136

to be reported in the *Wall Street Journal* and to be referenced in the *Wall Street Journal Index*. Third, joint ventures in output price regulated industries were excluded.[9] Fourth, the common stock returns for at least one of the parent companies had to be available on the Investment Services Laboratory, Inc. (ISL) daily returns tape over a period beginning 180 days prior to the joint venture announcement and ending 180 days following the announcement. This last criterion means that all of the parent companies included in the stock returns analysis were listed on the New York Stock Exchange (NYSE) or the American Stock Exchange (ASE) around the date of the joint venture announcement.

This search and screening procedure yielded a sample of 210 companies involved in 136 joint ventures. Table II contains some statistics which describe the sample. Panel A tabulates the joint ventures by year of initiation. According to Panel A, the announcements of joint ventures in the sample were distributed approximately evenly over the time period examined.

Panel B tabulates the joint ventures by the type of undertaking involved. This panel contains eight categories: (1) real estate development; (2) television pro-

Lummer [27] has documented results for international joint ventures that are similar to those reported here for domestic joint ventures.

[9] Excluded from the sample on the basis of this criterion were three joint ventures among electric utilities for the construction of power generating units, six joint ventures among oil and gas pipeline companies for the construction of oil and gas pipelines, and eight joint ventures between oil and gas companies for drilling and exploration for oil and natural gas.

gramming, motion pictures, video games, etc.; (3) development of nuclear power, uranium production, etc.; (4) coal mining or development of coal mines; (5) construction or development of petrochemical facility; (6) conversion of waste to energy; (7) development of satellite communications; and (8) all others. To determine the category into which each joint venture should be placed, the *Wall Street Journal* article describing the venture was read. The sample is reasonably heterogeneous. By far, the category containing the largest number of joint ventures is "all others." This category contains joint ventures as disparate as catalogue showrooms, leasing services, microfiche systems, newsprint mills, and sporting goods importation. However, the real estate development category, with 18 joint ventures, does represent about 13 percent of the sample and the television programming, motion pictures, video games, etc., with 14 joint ventures, represents about 10 percent of the sample.

III. Statistical Methodology and Data

The primary methodology used to measure the magnitude of security price reactions to announcements of joint ventures is the by now standard residual analysis technique based upon the market model. Additionally, we repeated all of the tests reported here using the comparison period methodology developed by Masulis [31] and found the results to be qualitatively identical to those discussed below.

One of the requirements for the computation of the test statistics employed in most event studies—including this one—is that the events considered not be contemporaneous, otherwise the assumption of cross-sectional independence of returns is likely to be violated. That requirement is met for the sample used in this study. However, even though the joint venture announcements themselves are not contemporaneous, in 65 cases our sample includes the common stock of two or three firms involved in the same joint venture. In these instances the assumption of cross-sectional independence of returns is likely to be violated. To correct for this potential problem, the common stocks of firms in the same joint venture are formed into an equally-weighted portfolio and the portfolio is treated as a single "security" in conducting the statistical analysis that follows. This procedure, then, means that the full sample includes only 136 "securities," each of which represents a single joint venture, even though the common stocks of 210 firms are represented in the sample.

In the tests reported below, the day on which the initial article describing a joint venture appeared in the *Wall Street Journal* is numbered event day $t = 0$. The trading days prior to that day are numbered event days $t = -1$, $t = -2$, $t = -3$, and so on and subsequent trading days are numbered event days $t = +1$, $t = +2$, $t = +3$, and so on. In most cases, the first documented public announcement of a joint venture occurs on the trading day prior to publication of the announcement in the *Wall Street Journal*, i.e., event day $t = -1$. Since it is not possible to determine whether the public announcement came before or after the close of trading on day $t = -1$, the impact of the announcement on the security's price is measured over the two-day trading period consisting of day $t = -1$ and day $t = 0$. Henceforth, this two-day trading interval is referred to as the announcement period.

The test procedure is implemented by computing ex post excess security returns or security prediction errors (PE) as

$$\mathrm{PE}_{jt} = R_{jt} - (\hat{\alpha}_j + \hat{\beta}_j R_{mt}) \tag{1}$$

where R_{jt} and R_{mt} are the observed returns for security j and a market index, respectively, over the two-day event time period day $t - 1$ through day t. The coefficients $\hat{\alpha}_j$ and $\hat{\beta}_j$ are the ordinary least squares estimates of the intercept and slope, respectively, of the market model regression. To compute prediction errors prior to and including the announcement date, the security specific parameters $\hat{\alpha}_j$ and $\hat{\beta}_j$ were estimated with ordinary least squares regression using 60 two-day returns beginning with event day $t = -180$ and ending with event day $t = -61$. To compute prediction errors following the announcement date, the market model parameters were computed using 60 two-day returns beginning with event day $t = +61$ and ending with event day $t = +180$.

The sample cross-sectional average two-day prediction error is computed as

$$\overline{\mathrm{PE}}_t = \sum_{j=1}^{N} \frac{\mathrm{PE}_{jt}}{N} \tag{2}$$

where N is the number of observations (i.e., joint ventures) in the sample over the event period day $t - 1$ through day t. Thus, the announcement period average prediction error, $\overline{\mathrm{PE}}_0$, is the estimated "unexpected" change in stockholders' wealth associated with the public announcement of a joint venture. Cumulative average prediction errors (CPE) are also examined and are computed as

$$\mathrm{CPE}_t = \sum_{k=-60}^{t} \overline{\mathrm{PE}}_k \tag{3}$$

for $t = -61$ through $t = +60$. The daily stock returns data used in the tests were taken from ISL daily returns files. The daily market index used is the CRSP value-weighted index of NYSE and ASE securities.

The hypothesis that the average prediction error over any two-day interval or the hypothesis that the cumulative average prediction error over any given interval equals zero is tested using standardized prediction errors as described in the Appendix to Dodd and Warner [14] or in Linn and McConnell [26]. This test procedure yields a z-statistic which is distributed unit normal in the absence of abnormal prediction errors. Additionally, as a check on the possibility that the mean return is unduly influenced by outlier returns, a median test of the null hypothesis is also employed. The particular test used here is the median signed rank (Wilcoxon) test (see, e.g., Hollander and Wolfe [22, pp. 39–40]).

IV. Empirical Results

A. *Wealth Gains for the Entire Sample*

Estimated changes in stockholder wealth associated with joint venture announcements are presented in Table III for the full sample of 210 firms involved

Table III

Summary of Two-Day Average Prediction Errors and Cumulative Average Prediction Errors (in percent) Surrounding the Announcement of U.S. Domestic Joint Ventures: 1972–1979 (Full Sample, $N = 136$)

(1) Event Day	(2) Two-Day Average Prediction Error (percent)	(3) Percent Positive Two-Day Prediction Errors	(4) Cumulative Average Prediction Error (percent)
−60	−0.25%	45%	−0.25%
−50	−0.06	46	0.43
−40	−0.31	43	0.10
−30	0.32	53	0.92
−20	−0.58	38	0.52
−10	0.40	51	0.94
− 8	0.36	52	1.30
− 6	0.19	50	1.48
− 4	−0.01	51	1.47
− 2	−0.06	43	1.41
0	0.73%	67%	2.15%
+ 2	0.20	50	2.34
+ 4	0.11	48	2.45
+ 6	−0.22	44	2.23
+ 8	0.34	45	2.57
+10	0.32	50	2.89
+20	0.02	51	2.62
+30	−0.28	48	1.90
+40	−0.12	47	1.81
+50	0.29	52	1.73
+60	−0.26	47	2.15

in the 136 announcements. Column (1) identifies the event day relative to event day zero; Column (2) presents the average prediction error ($\overline{PE}_t$) over event day $t - 1$ through day t; Column (3) presents the percentage of two-day PEs that are positive over event day $t - 1$ through day t; and Column (4) contains the cumulative average prediction error (CPE_t) from event day $t = -61$ through event day t.

Table III shows that the two-day announcement period average prediction error is 0.73 percent. With a z-statistic of 4.10, the null hypothesis of no announcement effect can easily be rejected at the 0.01 level of significance. This result is not due to a few outlier observations as 91 (i.e., 67 percent) of the announcement period PEs are positive. Additionally, the null hypothesis of no announcement effect can be rejected at the 0.01 level of significance according to the median signed rank (Wilcoxon) test.

Examination of Column (4) shows that over the 62-day period beginning with event day −61 and ending on event day 0 the CPE accumulates to 2.15 percent. The z-statistic for this CPE is 1.54 which allows rejection of the null hypothesis at the 0.10 level of significance. Finally, on event day +60 the CPE is at the same level (i.e., 2.15 percent) as it was on event day 0. Thus, there appears to be no further systematic valuation effect following the initial announcement.

The results indicate that the stockholders of companies involved in joint ventures earn statistically significant excess returns around the time at which intercorporate joint ventures are announced. While the announcement period return of 0.73 percent appears to be "small" it is larger (in absolute value) than any other two-day average prediction error over the 122-day interval surrounding the announcement of the joint ventures. Additionally, the percentage of positive PEs during the two-day event period is greater than the percentage of positive PEs over any other two-day period in the same 122-day interval.

Another way in which to assess the impact of joint venture announcements on shareholder wealth is to convert the average prediction error to a dollar value. To do this, for each of the 210 securities in the sample, the two-day announcement period prediction error was estimated and multiplied by the security's total market value as of event day $t = -61$. The cross-sectional average of these dollar values is $4,837,893. The degree to which this amount is impressive, of course, lies to a large extent in the eye of the beholder, but it is useful to note that this average "unexpected" wealth increase is greater than the total market values of the equity of a significant fraction of all companies listed on the ASE and NYSE. This relatively large dollar amount associated with a relatively small percentage excess return comes about because the sample includes many of the largest companies listed on the two major exchanges, including International Business Machines, General Electric, Gulf and Western Industries, and Goodyear Tire and Rubber.

The excess returns documented here can be interpreted as being "similar" to those earned by companies involved in mergers. As an example, Asquith [1] finds that the combined excess returns over days −1 and 0 for target (i.e., acquired) firms involved in mergers is approximately 6.5 percent, whereas the combined excess return for bidding (i.e., acquiring) companies over the same interval is approximatley 0.3 percent.[10] Because it is not possible to identify acquired and acquiring firms in joint ventures, it seems reasonable that the estimated average wealth increase for *all* firms involved in joint ventures should lie somewhere between those for acquired and acquiring companies in mergers, which it does.

Additionally, Asquith documents that over a 60-day period prior to the merger announcement the CPE increases by approximately 11.0 percent for acquired companies, whereas the CPE is approximately unchanged over the same interval for acquiring companies. Asquith attributes the increase in acquired companies' CPE prior to the event to leakage of information regarding the impending merger announcement. If we attribute the pre-announcement increase in the CPE associated with joint ventures to the same phenomenon, the change in the CPE for all joint ventures again lies somewhere between that for acquiring and acquired companies in mergers.

[10] We compare our results with those of Asquith [1] primarily for convenience. Asquith's results appear to be representative of those found by others. Jensen and Ruback [23] provide a comprehensive review of studies of the stock returns of firms involved in mergers and tender offers. For other references see footnote 1.

Given the description of the sample in Section II, a question that may come to mind is whether the results reported in Table III contain an industry bias due to the apparent "overrepresentation" of joint ventures categorized as real estate or television programming, motion pictures, video games, etc. To check for this possibility the test statistics were reestimated for the sample after deleting companies involved in these two categories of joint ventures. The results are reported in Table IV, Columns (2)–(4).

As the table indicates, the results for this subsample of joint ventures are nearly identical to those for the full sample. The two-day announcement period average prediction error is 0.74 percent ($z = 3.46$); over the period $t = -61$ to $t = 0$ the CPE increases to 3.39 percent ($z = 1.62$); and over the period $t = +1$ to $t = +60$ the CPE declines by 0.61 percent ($z = 1.26$). The number of positive PEs during the two-day announcement period is 70 out of a total of 104 (i.e., 67 percent of the PEs are positive), and the median signed rank (Wilcoxon) test permits rejection of the null hypothesis at the 0.01 level of significance. Finally, the dollar value of the two-day announcement period excess return per firm is $6,858,933. Given that the remaining joint ventures are approximately evenly spread over a variety of industries, there does not appear to be any significant industry bias in the results.

Another possible factor which may be influencing the test results is the release of other firm-specific information simultaneously with the announcement of the joint venture. To determine the extent of "contaminated" announcements, the *Wall Street Journal Index* was searched for other announcements by firms in the sample over the two-day joint venture announcement period. Thirty companies were identified which made announcements regarding earnings, dividends, financing decisions, capital expenditures, or mergers during the joint venture announcement period. Joint ventures involving these firms were deleted from the sample and the statistical tests were conducted on a "noncontaminated" sample of 108 joint ventures remaining. The results for this smaller sample are reported in Table IV, Columns (5)–(7).

As Table IV indicates, the results of the noncontaminated sample are very similar to those for the full sample. The two-day announcement period $\overline{\text{PE}}$ is 0.85 percent ($z = 3.45$); over the period $t = -61$ through $t = 0$ the CPE increases to 2.98 percent ($z = 2.11$); and over the period $t = +1$ through $t = +60$ the CPE declines by 0.23 percent ($z = 0.36$). The number of positive PEs during the announcement period is 74 out of 108 (i.e., 69 percent of the PEs are positive) and the median signed rank test permits rejection of the null hypothesis at the 0.01 level of significance. Thus, the results do not appear to be driven by other firm-specific information released at the same time as the joint venture announcement.

Two other caveats should be mentioned at this point. First, because of the manner in which our sample was compiled, in most cases our results measure the effect of the announcement of the successful completion of joint venture negotiations. Because most of the uncertainty regarding joint venture negotiations has been resolved by the announcement date, our statistical procedure is likely to overestimate the announcement effect of the initiation of joint venture negotiations.

Table IV

Summary of Two-Day Average and Cumulative Average Prediction Errors (in percent) Surrounding the Announcement of U.S. Domestic Joint Ventures: 1972–1979 (Full Sample Excluding Joint Ventures, Categorized as Real Estate or TV Programming, Motion Pictures, Video Games, etc., $N = 104$, and Noncontaminated Sample, $N = 108$)

	Full Sample Excluding Joint Ventures Categorized as Real Estate or TV Programming, Motion Pictures, Video Games, etc., ($N = 104$)			Noncontaminated Sample ($N = 108$)		
(1) Event Day	(2) Two-Day Average Prediction Error (percent)	(3) Percent Positive Two-Day Prediction Errors	(4) Cumulative Average Prediction Error (percent)	(5) Two-Day Average Prediction Error (percent)	(6) Percent Positive Two-Day Prediction Errors	(7) Cumulative Average Prediction Error (percent)
−60	−0.29%	45%	−0.29%	−0.35%	42%	−0.35%
−50	−0.15	47	0.77	−0.13	44	0.44
−40	−0.40	42	0.46	−0.35	41	0.16
−30	0.26	52	1.46	0.17	50	1.16
−20	−0.21	42	1.64	−0.60	38	0.83
−10	0.50	51	1.88	0.58	56	1.58
− 8	0.51	55	2.39	0.42	55	2.01
− 6	0.35	50	2.73	0.23	50	2.24
− 4	0.14	54	2.88	0.06	51	2.29
− 2	−0.24	42	2.64	−0.17	44	2.13
0	0.74%	67%	3.39%	0.85%	69%	2.98%
+ 2	0.14	52	3.52	0.10	53	3.08
+ 4	0.15	46	3.68	0.16	50	3.24
+ 6	−0.29	40	3.39	−0.45	41	2.78
+ 8	0.20	41	3.59	0.38	41	3.17
+10	0.30	51	3.89	0.51	52	3.68
+20	0.17	52	3.78	−0.11	50	3.35
+30	−0.25	50	3.48	−0.43	48	2.68
+40	−0.20	45	3.57	−0.07	48	2.92
+50	0.25	50	2.65	0.18	52	2.73
+60	−0.14	50	2.78	−0.37	44	2.75

Second, we have attributed the entire market reaction to joint venture announcements to the joint venture, per se. It is possible that joint venture announcements convey additional implicit information to the market about the firm's past or future earnings or investment opportunities. Thus, the wealth increases that we have observed may be a reflection of this other implicit information. However, when we omitted instances in which a firm released other explicit information contemporaneously with the joint venture announcement, the results were very similar to those for the overall sample. Thus, although we cannot rule out an "information" argument as the source of the documented wealth increases, the tests conducted appear to reduce the likelihood of that explanation.

B. Division of Wealth Gains Between Participating Firms

With these caveats in mind, the excess returns and wealth gains reported so far for joint ventures are analogous to those reported for corporate mergers. To push the analogy between mergers and joint ventures a bit further, it can be argued that relative size serves as a proxy for the acquiring and acquired firms in mergers. That is, the acquiring firm is typically the larger of the two firms in a corporate merger. Indeed, Asquith, Bruner, and Mullins [2] have argued that the failure of most studies of mergers to detect any effect of the merger on the acquiring company's shares is due to the fact that the acquiring company is significantly larger than the acquired company. Thus, if the dollar value of the gain in a merger is typically divided approximately evenly between the acquired and acquiring companies and if the acquiring company's market value is 20 times that of the acquired company, then a 10 percent increase in the value of the stock of the acquired company will translate into a 0.5 percent increase in the value of the stock of the acquiring company. Bradley, Desai, and Kim [10] present a similar argument as part of their explanation for the division of gains in tender offers between the bidder and target firms. Asquith, Bruner, and Mullins [2] present evidence to support this argument for mergers, but the evidence of Bradley, Desai, and Kim does not appear to support the argument for tender offers.

To determine the validity of the relative size hypothesis in joint ventures, a subsample of joint ventures in which both (or all) parent companies were included in the full sample was identified. The firms in this sample were then categorized as either the "small" or "large" firm in the joint venture according to the total market value of their common stock 61 trading days before the initial announcement of the joint venture. Both the large firm and the small firm samples contain 65 securities. The remaining 80 companies in the full sample were placed into a third, "all other," category. This sample primarily contains firms for which the joint venture partner's common stock was not listed on either the NYSE or ASE during the period of the study. Presumably, in comparison with their partners, the companies in this sample are relatively even larger than those in the "large" firm sample are in comparison with their "small" joint venture partners. The statistical tests reported above for the full sample were then repeated for each of the three subsamples.[11] The results are reported in Table V. Columns (2)–(4) contain results for the small firm sample; Columns (5)–(7) contain results for the large firm sample; and Columns (8)–(10) contain results for the all other firm sample. To give some indication of the relative sizes of the firms in the three samples, the average market values of the common equity of the companies in the small, large, and all other firm samples are $625 million, $3,413 million, and $1,008 million, respectively.

According to the relative size hypothesis, the excess return of the small partner in a joint venture should be larger than that of the larger partner, but the dollar value of their gains should be approximately equal. Consistent with this hypothesis, the two-day announcement period excess return for the small firm sample is 1.10 percent ($z = 2.77$). For the large firm sample the two-day announcement period excess return is 0.63 percent ($z = 2.30$), and for the all other sample the excess return is 0.57 percent ($z = 1.98$). For all three samples the announcement period average prediction error is different from zero at the 0.05 level of significance according to their z-statistics. For the three samples the percentage of positive announcement period PEs are 57 percent, 57 percent, and 65 percent, respectively, and the median signed rank (Wilcoxon) test permits rejection of the null hypothesis for the three samples at the 0.10 level of significance, the 0.05 level of significance, and the 0.02 level of significance, respectively. Based on these results, then, shareholders appear to gain when companies enter into joint ventures regardless of the relative size of their partner. However, the shareholders of the smaller firm involved in the joint venture appear to earn larger percentage excess returns than the shareholders of the larger firm.

As a final step in this analysis, the cross-sectional average of the dollar values of the announcement period returns was computed for the large firm and small firm subsamples. Again, consistent with the relative size hypothesis, these amounts were $4,537,522 and $6,650,544, for the small firm and the large firm sample, respectively. In short, in joint ventures the shareholders of the smaller partner, on average, receive a larger announcement period excess return, but a smaller dollar value gain than the shareholders of the larger partner.[12]

C. *Wealth Gains Scaled by Amounts Invested*

While the pattern of excess returns to stockholders of companies engaged in joint ventures bears a striking resemblance to that of returns to stockholders of merging firms, it can be argued that for even the small firm sample the announcement period excess return is only slightly greater than 1 percent and this bears little resemblance to the 10 percent to 30 percent excess returns generated for

[11] Each of the samples contains only one firm from each joint venture. Thus, in these samples each security represents a single firm.

[12] A similar "size" effect appears to be at work in corporate spin-offs. Both Hite and Owens [21] and Schipper and Smith [36] note that corporate spin-offs can be thought of as reverse mergers. Both studies examine stock price reactions around announcements of corporate spin-offs and both find that relatively large spin-offs generate larger stock price reactions than relatively small spin-offs. Thus, the "size" effect in corporate combinations (or their mirror image) appears to be pervasive.

Table V

Two-Day Average and Cumulative Average Prediction Errors (in percent) Surrounding the Announcement of U.S. Domestic Joint Ventures: 1972–1979

	Small firm Sample ($N = 65$)			Large Firm Sample ($N = 65$)			All Other Firm Sample ($N = 80$)		
(1) Event Day	(2) Two-Day Average Prediction Error (percent)	(3) Percent Positive Two-Day Prediction Errors	(4) Cumulative Average Prediction Error (percent)	(5) Two-Day Average Prediction Error (percent)	(6) Percent Positive Two-Day Prediction Errors	(7) Cumulative Average Prediction Error (percent)	(8) Two-Day Average Prediction Error (percent)	(9) Percent Positive Two-Day Prediction Errors	(10) Cumulative Average Prediction Error (percent)
−60	−0.13%	45%	−0.13%	0.58%	56%	0.58%	−0.65%	46%	−0.65%
−50	−0.12	45	0.74	−0.15	51	0.77	0.02	46	1.17
−40	0.04	51	0.81	0.43	65	1.82	−0.87	39	−1.11
−30	0.43	57	1.07	0.12	51	2.53	0.38	55	0.21
−20	−0.56	38	1.36	0.20	48	2.38	−0.84	33	−0.60
−10	−0.40	43	1.56	0.43	59	2.95	0.54	50	−0.31
− 8	0.40	54	1.96	−0.44	37	2.51	0.64	53	0.33
− 6	0.26	45	2.22	0.49	65	3.00	0.02	49	0.35
− 4	−0.09	51	2.13	−0.40	52	2.60	0.12	49	0.47
− 2	−0.78	45	1.35	−0.30	39	2.30	0.41	49	0.88
0	1.10%	57%	2.45%	0.63%	57%	2.93%	0.57%	65%	1.45%
+ 2	0.57	40	3.03	−0.05	52	2.88	0.17	52	1.62
+ 4	0.21	55	3.24	0.20	48	3.08	−0.02	51	1.60
+ 6	−0.76	49	2.87	0.01	37	3.09	−0.04	47	1.56
+ 8	−0.02	52	2.85	0.04	45	3.13	0.57	44	2.13
+10	0.18	58	2.20	0.20	41	3.17	0.58	49	2.71
+20	0.69	57	3.36	0.41	52	3.19	−0.33	49	1.97
+30	0.00	51	2.83	0.12	54	3.05	−0.57	44	1.01
+40	0.14	51	3.31	0.22	52	3.57	−0.35	39	0.56
+50	0.09	49	2.93	0.21	52	3.35	0.44	55	0.91
+60	0.15	48	3.47	−0.10	52	3.03	−0.33	43	1.72

the target firms involved in mergers and tender offers. Thus, it seems unrealistic to argue that these episodic events are "merely" another example of a standard capital budgeting project. However, to put this in perspective, recall, as we noted above, that a merger involves the pooling of all the assets of the merging firms, whereas a joint venture involves a combining of only a subset of the involved companies' assets. Presumably the amount of the net present value generated by a project bears some relationship to the initial outlay required. Thus, to compare the total gains in joint ventures with those generated by mergers, it seems reasonable to scale the gains by the amount of resources involved. To do this, each *Wall Street Journal* article describing a joint venture was carefully read to determine whether the outlay required for the project was identified for each partner. In some cases the article reported only the total amount involved. In those cases we assumed an equal contribution by each of the partners. By following this procedure, we identified the dollar amount of the initial outlay for 88 of the 210 companies in the full sample.[13] The smallest estimated outlay was \$0.9 million, the largest was \$1.37 billion, and the median amount was \$35.0 million.

An estimate of the "premium" (or scaled gain) generated by each firm in the sample was computed as

$$Q_j = \frac{\mathrm{PE}_j \cdot \mathrm{MV}_j}{I_j} \tag{4}$$

and the average premium for the sample was computed as

$$\bar{Q} = \frac{1}{N} \Sigma_{j=1}^{N} Q_j \tag{5}$$

where PE_j is the two-day announcement period prediction error for company j, I_j is the dollar amount of resources committed to the project by company j, and MV_j is the total market value of the common stock of company j 61 days prior to the announcement date of the joint venture.

For this sample the estimated value of $\bar{Q}$ is 0.541 with a standard deviation of 3.88. This number lies substantially above the range of "typical" premiums estimated for mergers and tender offers. However, this estimate was substantially affected by one significant outlier observation. For one company, Q_j was estimated to be 27.0. That is, for one company the wealth gain in the joint venture was estimated to be 27 times the amount of funds committed to the project. When this observation is omitted from the sample, the average premium becomes 0.230 with a standard deviation of 2.60.[14] The average joint venture premium, then,

[13] For 66 of the 88 companies, the actual dollar outlay for each company could be determined from the *WSJ* article. For the remaining 22 companies, which were involved in nine joint ventures, only the combined total dollar outlay for the entire joint venture could be determined. For these 22 cases, we assumed that the total outlay was funded by equal contributions of the joint venture partners. This assumption seems reasonable given that equal contributions were, in fact, reported for 48 of the 66 firms in which the individual dollar contribution could be identified.

[14] Predictably the median premium of 0.06 lies below the mean. It is difficult to compare this number with those calculated in mergers and tender offers because few studies report the median wealth gain.

lies comfortably within the range of premiums that have been documented in studies of intercorporate mergers and tender offers.[15]

There is, however, one potentially important difference between the mean scaled wealth gain computed for firms involved in joint ventures and those computed for firms involved in intercorporate acquisitions. In a merger the premium is computed by dividing the change in stockholders' wealth by the total capitalized value of the common stock of the participating company. In computing the joint venture premiums, we have divided the change in stockholders' wealth by the stated dollar contribution of the joint venture partner. It is possible that the stated dollar value of the contribution understates the total capitalized value of each partner's contribution if nonfinancial resource commitments like patent rights, access to new technology, and specialized labor have not been included. The extent to which this factor might bias the results is impossible to determine. It is still the case, however, that even if nonfinancial resource commitments were equal in size to reported financial commitments, the scaled wealth gain in joint ventures would lie within the range of premiums documented for intercorporate acquisitions—albeit at the lower end of the range.[16]

V. Summary and Conclusion

U.S. domestic joint ventures are wealth-creating intercorporate transactions for the shareholders of the participating companies. For the 210 companies examined in this study, the average estimated increase in shareholder wealth associated with the joint venture is approximately $5.0 million. *Mergers and Acquisitions* has reported that over the period 1972–1979 approximately 7,000 U.S. corporations initiated intercorporate joint ventures. The companies included in our sample are among the largest corporations in the U.S. As a consequence, the resources involved and the wealth created by this sample of joint ventures may overstate those for the "average" joint venture. Nevertheless, because of the number of companies involved, because of the dollar amount of resources committed, and because of the dollar amount of wealth created, the evidence indicates that intercorporate joint ventures play a significant role in U.S. economic and commercial activity and probably deserve somewhat greater attention from financial economists than they have heretofore received.

Additionally, and more importantly for the purposes of this paper, the stockholder returns reported here bear a striking resemblance to those earned by the stockholders of firms involved in other types of corporate combinations. The stockholders of the smaller partner in the joint venture earned a larger "excess" return than the stockholders of the larger partner. However, the average dollar value of the gains tends to be more equally divided. A similar result appears to be at work in mergers. Furthermore, when the dollar value of the gain in the joint venture is scaled by the amount of resources committed to the project, the

[15] In their study of corporate spin-offs, Hite and Owers [21] also compute a measure of the "scaled" wealth increase due to spin-off announcements. To do so, they divide the dollar value of the wealth increase by the capitalized value of the assets which are spun-off. Their average scaled wealth gain is also quite large—on the order of 100 percent of the value of the assets spun-off for the total sample and approximately 50 percent of the value of the assets spun-off for the "small" spin-off sample.

[16] We wish to thank the referee for suggesting this (and many other) valuable point(s) to us.

average "premium" generated lies in the range of premiums generated in intercorporate mergers and tender offers.

The similarity in results for studies of mergers and joint ventures is interesting because of the one major factor that distinguishes them: In mergers, companies pool all of their resources under the ultimate direction of the management of the acquiring company. Thus, it is difficult to distinguish between the synergy hypothesis and the management displacement hypothesis as explanations for the large wealth increases that typically accompany intercorporate mergers and tender offers. In joint ventures, companies combine a subset of their resources to accomplish some objective and, although a primary responsibility for managing the joint venture may reside with the managers of one of the involved parent companies, the original managements of the parent companies are unchanged.

Given the similarities between results reported in various studies of mergers and those reported here for joint ventures, we are inclined to interpret our results as supportive of the synergy hypothesis as the source of gains in other types of corporate combinations. Of course, in no way do our results tell us what the fundamental economic factors are that generate the substantial wealth increases associated with mergers and joint ventures—labelling a phenomenon is not the same as explaining it. Our results do, however, suggest that other types of intercorporate transactions may also generate significant wealth increases for the participating companies' shareholders. If so, then a more careful analysis of these other types of transactions may yield insights into what the fundamental factors are that determine security values. Such information would undoubtedly be of interest to scholars, policy makers, investors, and managers.

REFERENCES

1. P. Asquith. "Merger Bids, Market Uncertainty, and Stockholder Returns." *Journal of Financial Economics* 11 (April 1983), 51–84.
2. ———, R. F. Bruner, and D. W. Mullins. "The Gains to Bidding Firms from Merger." *Journal of Financial Economics* 11 (April 1983), 121–140.
3. S. V. Berg and P. Friedman. "Joint Ventures, Competition and Technological Complementarities: Evidence from Chemicals." *Southern Economic Journal* 43 (January 1977), 1330–37.
4. ———. "Technological Complementarities and Industrial Patterns of Joint Venture Activity." *Industrial Organization Review* 6 (1978), 110–16.
5. ———. "Joint Ventures in American Industry Part II: Case Studies of Managerial Policy." *Mergers and Acquisitions* 13 (Fall 1978) 9–17.
6. ———. "Causes and Effects of Joint Venture Activity: Knowledge Acquisition vs. Parent Horizontality." *Antitrust Bulletin* 25 (Spring 1980), 143–68.
7. ———. "Impacts of Domestic Joint Ventures on Industrial Rates of Return: A Pooled Cross-Section Analysis: 1967–1975." *Review of Economics and Statistics* 63 (May 1981), 293–98.
8. S. Boyle. "An Estimate of the Number and Size Distribution of Domestic Joint Subsidiaries." *Antitrust Law and Economic Review* 1 (Spring 1968), 81–92.
9. M. Bradley. "Interfirm Tender Offers and the Market for Corporate Control." *Journal of Business* 53 (October 1980), 345–76.
10. ———, A. Desai, and E. H. Kim. "Specialized Resources and Competition in the Market for Corporate Control." Unpublished working paper, University of Michigan, 1983.
11. ———. "The Rational Behind Interfirm Tender Offers: Information or Synergy?" *Journal of Financial Economics* 11 (April 1983), 183–206.
12. J. F. Brodley. "The Legal Status of Joint Ventures Under the Antitrust Laws: A Summary Assessment." *Antitrust Bulletin* 21 (Fall 1976), 453–83.

13. P. Dodd. "Merger Proposals, Management Discretion and Stockholder Wealth." *Journal of Financial Economics* 8 (June 1980), 105–38.
14. ——— and J. Warner. "On Corporate Governance: A Study of Proxy Contests." *Journal of Financial Economics* 11 (April 1983), 401–38.
15. J. L. Duncan. "Impacts of New Entry and Horizontal Joint Ventures on Industrial Rates of Return." *Review of Economics and Statistics* 64 (May 1982), 339–43.
16. E. B. Eckbo. "Horizontal Mergers, Collusion and Stockholder Wealth." *Journal of Financial Economics* 11 (April 1983), 241–76.
17. E. Fama and M. J. Jensen. "Agency Problems and Residual Claims." *Journal of Law and Economics* 27 (June 1983), 327–49.
18. ———. "Separation of Ownership and Control." *Journal of Law and Economics* 27 (June 1983), 301–25.
19. D. R. Fusfeld. "Joint Subsidiaries in the Iron and Steel Industry." *American Economic Review* 48 (May 1958), 578–87.
20. "GM-Toyota Venture Stirs Major Antitrust and Labor Problem." *Wall Street Journal* (June 10, 1983), p. 1+.
21. G. L. Hite and J. Owers. "Security Price Reactions Around Corporate Spin-off Announcements." *Journal of Financial Economics* 12 (December 1983), 409–36.
22. M. Hollander and D. A. Wolfe. *Nonparametric Statistical Methods*. New York: Wiley, Inc., 1973.
23. M. J. Jensen and R. Ruback. "The Market for Corporate Control: The Scientific Evidence." *Journal of Financial Economics* 11 (April 1983), 5–50.
24. E. H. Kim and J. J. McConnell. "Corporate Merger and the Co-Insurance of Corporate Debt." *Journal of Finance* 32 (May 1977), 789–810.
25. T. C. Langetieg. "An Application of a Three-factor Performance Index to Measure Stockholder Gains from Merger." *Journal of Financial Economics* 6 (December 1978), 365–84.
26. S. C. Linn and J. J. McConnell. "An Empirical Investigation of the Impact of Antitakeover Amendments on Common Stock Prices." *Journal of Financial Economics* 11 (April 1983), 361–99.
27. S. L. Lummer. "International Joint Ventures: Valuation Effects and Diversification Effects." Unpublished Ph.D. dissertation, Purdue University, 1983.
28. P. H. Malatesta. "The Wealth Effect of Merger Activity and the Objective Function of Merging Firms." *Journal of Financial Economics* 11 (April 1983), 155–82.
29. ——— and R. Thompson. "Partially Anticipated Events: A Model of Stock Price Reactions with an Application to Corporate Acquisitions." Unpublished manuscript presented at Western Finance Association meeting, June 1983.
30. G. Mandelker. "Risk and Return: The Case of Merging Firms." *Journal of Financial Economics* 1 (December 1974), 303–36.
31. R. Masulis. "The Effects of Capital Structure Change on Security Prices: A Study of Exchange Offers." *Journal of Financial Economics* 8 (June 1980), 139–77.
32. R. W. Melicher and J. F. Nielsen. "Financial Factors that Affect Acquisition Prices." *Review of Business & Economic Research* 13–14 (Winter 1977/78), 94–106.
33. Mergers and Acquisitions. McLean, VA: Information for Industry, 1971–1979.
34. "No, No, Nova." *Forbes* (May 23, 1983), 40–41.
35. J. Pfeffer and P. Nowack. "Joint Ventures and Interorganizational Interdependence." *Administrative Science Quarterly* 21 (September 1976), 398–418.
36. K. Schipper and A. Smith. "Effects of Recontracting on Shareholder Wealth: The Case of Voluntary Spin-offs." *Journal of Financial Economics* 12 (December 1983), 436–68.
37. K. Schipper and R. Thompson. "Evidence on the Capitalized Value of Merger Activity for Acquiring Firms." *Journal of Financial Economics* 11 (April 1983), 85–120.
38. R. Stillman. "Examining Antitrust Policy Towards Horizontal Mergers." *Journal of Financial Economics* 11 (April 1983), 225–40.
39. *Wall Street Journal Index*. New York: Dow-Jones, Inc., 1962–1980.
40. *Wall Street Journal*. New York: Dow-Jones, Inc., 1962–1980.
41. P. Wier. "The Costs of Antimerger Lawsuits: Evidence from the Stock Market." *Journal of Financial Economics* 11 (April 1983), 207–24.

[19]

ELSEVIER Journal of Financial Economics 49 (1998) 255–279

JOURNAL OF Financial ECONOMICS

The economics of parent-subsidiary mergers: an empirical analysis[1]

Myron B. Slovin[a], Marie E. Sushka[b,*]

[a] *Louisiana State University, Baton Rouge, LA 70803, USA*
[b] *College of Business, Arizona State University, Tempe, AZ 85287, USA*

Received 27 April 1995; received in revised form 2 October 1997

Abstract

We examine parent-subsidiary mergers, transactions that do not entail arm's length bargaining or a change in control. These mergers are typically followed by considerable restructuring of subsidiaries. Minority and parent returns are not significantly different from returns at third party buyouts of parent-controlled subsidiaries, transactions that entail arm's length negotiations and a change in control. Buyer returns are negative, consistent with overbidding. We conclude that parent-subsidiary mergers facilitate corporate restructuring, foster the reallocation of resources toward higher valued uses, and increase value for both parent and subsidiary. © 1998 Elsevier Science S.A. All rights reserved.

JEL classification: G32; G34

Keywords: Parent-subsidiary mergers; Majority control; Minority shareholders

1. Introduction

It is well documented that conventional corporate mergers and acquisitions generate substantial gains in shareholder wealth for target firms. Two salient

---

* Correspondence author. Tel.: 602/965-6581; fax: 602/965-8539; e-mail: marie.sushka@asu.edu.

[1] We acknowledge the valuable comments and suggestions of the anonymous referee and of the editor G. William Schwert. We thank Wan L. Lai for his research assistance. This research was partially supported by a grant from the Dean's Council of 100 summer research program at Arizona State University, College of Business.

0304-405X/98/$19.00
PII S0304-405X(98)00024-5

aspects of these events are a contest for the control of the target and the presence of voluntary arm's length bargaining between buyer and seller, characteristics that enhance the prospect that each party's interests are satisfied and resources are reallocated toward higher valued uses. We investigate the effects of mergers between two publicly traded and legally distinct, but affiliated, operating firms, one with longstanding majority control and a fiduciary responsibility over the other. Such transactions eliminate minority shareholders so the unit becomes a wholly-owned subsidiary of the parent. Parent-subsidiary mergers, not previously examined in the finance literature, have implications for economic aspects of corporate governance and provide perspective about the value of having a publicly traded, minority interest in a subsidiary. Unlike conventional mergers or tender offers, parent-subsidiary mergers are conducted without arm's length bargaining or a change in control. Parent managers initiate the merger, set the terms, and control approval, a process that suggests the potential for parent self-dealing. At the same time, however, as majority blockholder, a parent has a fiduciary responsibility and a legal obligation for fair treatment of minority shareholders of the subsidiary.

We discuss motivations for parent-subsidiary mergers and document that they are not rare events. We assess whether these transactions are economically efficient (i.e., move resources to higher valued uses) and examine how they affect minority and parent shareholder wealth. One benchmark for our analysis is the wealth effects on parties involved in conventional mergers, about which there is extensive evidence. We provide an additional benchmark by evaluating third party buyouts in which a parent's majority ownership of a subsidiary is sold to an unaffiliated buyer who purchases all shares on the same terms, thereby eliminating minority shareholders. Unlike parent-subsidiary mergers, third party buyouts entail a transfer of control and take place in a contestable market with arm's length negotiations between the buyer and selling parent. Since the same price is paid for minority and parent-held subsidiary shares, third party buyouts eliminate the potential for parent self-dealing at the expense of minority shareholders. We also assess how wealth effects of parent-subsidiary mergers are influenced by a corporate charter requirement that the transaction be approved by a majority vote of minority shareholders, a landmark Delaware Supreme Court decision (Weinberger v UOP, 1983) that narrowed the legal options available to dissenting minority shareholders, and the choice of cash or parent equity as the means of payment.

Our results indicate that parent-subsidiary mergers enhance the wealth of minority shareholders, and that their share of the overall gains in value exceeds their proportional ownership of the subsidiary. Announcements of parent-subsidiary mergers generate a statistically significant two-day average (and median) excess return to subsidiary shareholders of 18.53% (14.18%). This exceeds the two-day average returns ranging from 6.2% to 13.4% reported by Jensen and Ruback (1983) for targets of conventional mergers. Parent excess returns are also significantly positive, with a two-day average (and median) return of 2.13% (0.70%). Post-announcement values of the combined entities significantly exceed the sum of the separate, pre-announcement values of the affiliated units, an indication that parent-subsidiary mergers generate productive gains. Post-merger restructurings of these subsidiaries are common, which suggests parent-subsidiary mergers facilitate corporate refocusing and foster the reallocation of resources to higher valued uses. For third party buyouts, there are significantly positive two-day average (and median) excess returns of 20.92% (12.87%) to subsidiary shareholders and 2.78% (1.94%) to parent shareholders. Buyers sustain negative average (median) excess returns of −0.81% (−0.65%) in these transactions. Excess returns to minority shareholders from third party buyouts are not statistically different from excess returns they earn from parent-subsidiary mergers.

A corporate charter requirement for super-majority rather than simple majority voting in a parent-subsidiary merger reduces gains to parents, but does not affect gains to minority shareholders. We attribute the reduction in parent gains to the substantive compliance and transactions costs incurred in meeting legal mandates that are automatically triggered by a super-majority vote, but are not applicable when approval is controlled by the parent through a simple majority vote. Subsequent to a 1983 court decision (Weinberger v UOP) which limited minority shareholders' access to injunctive relief in parent-subsidiary mergers, we find reduced gains to subsidiaries and increased gains to parents, evidence that changes in legal standards influence parent decisions about terms offered to minority shareholders. Gains to minority shareholders are greater for cash than equity transactions, suggesting that tax effects are associated with the means of payment, while parent returns are not affected by the means of payment.

Prior studies demonstrate wealth gains when parents create publicly traded minority interests in subsidiaries. These gains have been attributed to benefits from restructuring and external monitoring (Schipper and Smith, 1986), agency considerations (Allen et al., 1995), and avoidance of parent equity issuance (Nanda, 1991). Our study indicates that there are also wealth gains when a parent eliminates a publicly traded minority interest through a parent-subsidiary merger and that the transaction typically precedes a restructuring of subsidiary and/or parent operations. Our results are consistent with Easterbrook and Fischel's (1982) contention that legal standards pertaining to conflicts of interest are a costly factor for a parent that wants to undertake major investment and restructuring activities, a hindrance that is eliminated when the subsidiary is wholly-owned. As a result, a parent-subsidiary merger facilitates the reallocation of resources toward higher valued uses, generating market expectations that the merged entity will be more profitable than the separate affiliated entities. We find that excess returns to minority shareholders in parent-subsidiary mergers are similar to returns they receive in arm's length third party buyouts of subsidiaries. We conclude that parent-subsidiary mergers enhance corporate flexibility without harming minority shareholder interests.

The remainder of the paper is organized as follows. In Section 2, we discuss parent-subsidiary mergers and compare these transactions to third party buyouts of publicly traded subsidiaries. Section 3 details data and methodology, and empirical results are reported in Section 4. Section 5 contains conclusions.

2. Implications of eliminating minority shareholders in publicly traded subsidiaries

2.1. Parent-subsidiary mergers

Our work assesses the economic issue of whether parent-subsidiary mergers are productive transactions that enhance shareholder value or a mechanism to redistribute wealth from minority shareholders of the subsidiary to the parent. We also examine motivations for these mergers since parents already have pre-existing control of the subsidiary. Majority-controlled, publicly traded subsidiaries originate from partial acquisitions, equity carve-outs, and partial spin-offs. Regardless of origin, a majority-controlled subsidiary is operated by the parent through a board of directors composed of parent nominees. This governance structure is typically maintained for a considerable period.

There are several differences between the merger of a subsidiary into its parent and a conventional corporate control transaction. In a merger or acquisition between unaffiliated companies, each side bargains for its own interests through arm's length negotiations, and approval typically requires a simple majority shareholder vote. In a tender offer, an acquirer deals directly with shareholders who individually decide whether to accept or reject the offer. By comparison, a parent can force a parent-subsidiary merger and impose transaction terms on minority shareholders by voting its majority shareholding in the subsidiary. If parent ownership is sufficiently great (usually 90%), a shareholder vote is not required. Parent-subsidiary mergers have economic implications because of their impact on corporate decision making, and legal ramifications because of the potential for parents to harm minority interests. Minority shareholders typically accept the parent's offer in these transactions rather than confront the procedural impediments and expense of litigation. In some cases, corporate charters require that these mergers be approved by a majority vote of minority shareholders, a procedure that gives the minority veto power over the transaction and creates uncertainty for the parent. Regardless of the type of vote required, dissenting subsidiary shareholders have legal recourse via a judicial appraisal proceeding, which determines the fair cash value of their shares. The Delaware appraisal statute provides that fair cash value excludes any gain generated by a parent-subsidiary merger.

The merger of a controlled subsidiary into its parent can enhance the value of the combined entity by reducing proprietary costs that arise from disclosure, conflicts of interest, and potential legal costs, and/or by generating gains in productive efficiency. Dye (1986), Darrough and Stoughton (1990), Wagenhofer (1990), and Verrecchia (1990) develop theoretical models demonstrating that disclosure can reduce shareholder value by revealing information to competitors or increasing legal costs. In these models, proprietary costs of disclosure take the form of increased entry, increased production by other firms in the industry, and regulatory actions. Merging the subsidiary eliminates the parent's risk of legal liability that arises from disclosure obligations to minority shareholders. From this perspective, a parent-subsidiary merger replaces the subsidiary's diffuse public capital with parent capital and reduces proprietary costs. There is little previous evidence on the costs and benefits of such disclosure.

Productive gains to a combined entity may arise from economies of scale or scope, centralized planning or control, and elimination of duplication or administrative services required of affiliated public companies. Moreover, a unified governance structure avoids conflicts of interest in the allocation between a public subsidiary and its parent of gains that arise from restructuring activities or corporate investment opportunities. Although restructuring or new investment may be feasible without the merger since the parent already has a controlling interest, Easterbrook and Fischel (1982) argue that parent fiduciary responsibility to minority shareholders in a public subsidiary can hinder such corporate actions by raising conflict of interest questions. For example, court decisions have disallowed certain intercorporate transactions as unfair to subsidiary minority shareholders, including unfair pricing of goods and services between parents and subsidiaries (Grimes v Donaldson, Lufkin, and Jenrette, Inc. (392 F. Supp. 1393 N.D. Fla. 1974)), and unfair treatment of subsidiary investment opportunities (Summa Corp. v TWA, Inc. (540 A. 2nd 403 Del 1985)). In terms of conflict of interest concerns, it may be difficult to structure inter-company transactions or allocate overhead costs, tax benefits, and corporate opportunities between a parent and its majority-controlled public subsidiary. This difficulty is reinforced by court rulings determining that the parent has the burden of proving the overall fairness of transactions in which there is a potential for self-dealing (Sterling v Mayflower Hotel Corp. 93 A. 2nd 107 (Del. 1952)), and that the parent is subject to discovery which can force disclosure of internal documents. Thus, elimination of minority shareholders through a parent-subsidiary merger can enhance firm value by enabling the parent to make investments it might not otherwise undertake because of these concerns.

There may, however, be costs associated with ending public trading in subsidiary shares that can be viewed as the converse of the gains generated when a parent takes a wholly-owned subsidiary public through an initial public offering, as developed in Schipper and Smith (1986). These costs include loss of access to market-based managerial compensation schemes and costs of capital, and reduced external monitoring. Moreover, Nanda (1991) argues that a governance structure composed of a parent and a publicly traded subsidiary reduces underinvestment problems by enhancing corporate financing flexibility. Consistent with Nanda's contention, Slovin and Sushka (1997) show that issuing seasoned equity through a majority-controlled public subsidiary enhances parent value.

Share prices convey market-based information about whether parent-subsidiary mergers are value increasing or decreasing for affiliated units and for the combined entity. We use event study methodology to assess alternative views about these mergers. If a parent-subsidiary merger is economically neutral (i.e., there is no overall gain to the transaction), and only redistributes wealth from the minority to the parent, then the value of subsidiary shares should fall and parent share value should increase by an amount equivalent to the loss sustained by minority shareholders of the subsidiary. If the merger is economically inefficient, the value of the combined enterprise should fall, and wealth redistribution becomes a plausible explanation for the transaction. If the merger is expected to be value enhancing, the announcement should increase the combined value of parent and subsidiary. However, alternative distributional outcomes are possible. If the price paid to minority shareholders is equivalent only to the pre-announcement value of their shares, that is, the price to which dissenting shareholders are entitled in an appraisal hearing, there should be no increase in subsidiary value and gains should accrue to parent shareholders. If the parent pays minority shareholders a premium over the pre-bid share price, there should be positive returns to subsidiaries. If the parent overpays relative to the expected gains from the transaction, parent value should fall. If all gains accrue to the subsidiary, as is typical for mergers and tender offers between unaffiliated firms, the value of minority shares should rise at news of a parent-subsidiary merger while parent value should remain unchanged or may fall if the parent overpays.

We assess additional factors which may affect the size and distribution of the wealth effects of parent-subsidiary mergers. One such factor is the effect of super-majority voting procedures that strengthen minority shareholder interests in parent-subsidiary mergers by giving minority shareholders a veto power over the transaction. Such a provision creates uncertainty for the parent about approval of the merger and may enhance the terms parents offer minority shareholders. Berger and Allingham (1983) indicate that a super-majority vote, unlike a simple majority vote, increases the amount and type of parent disclosures and other compliance activities that include the release of information about almost all aspects of the corporation's operations, management, and plans. Such required disclosures are a form of proprietary costs, which increase transactions costs and the probability that the parent may be sued for failure to disclose germane information. A second factor is the Delaware Supreme Court's decision in Weinberger v UOP, Inc. [457 A. 2nd. 701 (Del 1983)], which limited the right of dissenting minority shareholders to bring class actions suits to stop a parent-subsidiary merger, relegating them instead to appraisal. This decision raises the question of whether parents subsequently offered less favorable terms to minority shareholders of subsidiaries relative to the pre-Weinberger period, and addresses the broader issue of whether parent decisions about offer terms are influenced by a change in legal standards. We also assess the valuation effects of litigation in parent-subsidiary mergers. Finally, we examine how means of payment influences returns to minority shareholders and parents in parent-subsidiary mergers.

2.2. Third party buyouts of parent-controlled subsidiaries

Elimination of minority shareholders also occurs when a parent sells its majority holding in a subsidiary to a third party (unaffiliated) buyer who agrees to purchase the subsidiary's majority and minority shares at the same price. The buyer negotiates with parent managers to acquire the majority blockholding and makes a tender offer on the same terms to minority shareholders. Parent managers negotiate on behalf of all shareholders and seek to maximize the transaction price received by parent and minority shareholders. The buyer votes all acquired shares to approve the merger, and buys out any remaining shareholders at the transaction price. Unlike parent-subsidiary mergers, third party buyouts entail arm's length negotiations within a contestable environment and generate a change in control. These characteristics suggest that minority shareholders may obtain a greater increase in wealth in third party buyouts than in parent-subsidiary mergers. However, if managerial reputation, external monitoring, and appraisal standards induce market pricing in parent-subsidiary mergers, returns to minority shareholders should be similar for both types of transactions given similar gains in productivity.

Aside from the issue of bargaining environment, other characteristics of these transactions suggest the potential for greater gains to minority shareholders in third party buyouts than parent-subsidiary mergers. In a buyout, an unaffiliated third party acquires a combination of control (parent) and noncontrol (minority) shares, whereas a parent purchases only noncontrol (minority) shares in a parent-subsidiary merger. Studies by Lease et al. (1983, 1984) and DeAngelo and DeAngelo (1985), find that control shares are more valuable than noncontrol shares. From this perspective, a parent purchases less valuable noncontrol shares, so the offer terms to minority shareholders should be higher in third party buyouts than subsidiary mergers. Gains may also be higher to minority shareholders in a buyout when a third party has access to synergies from combining operations with the subsidiary that are not available to the parent. These synergies may arise if the subsidiary and buyer, but not the parent, are in the same or related industries. In addition, Roll (1986) suggests that because of hubris, the buyer is likely to offer an inappropriately high price for a target, a form of winner's curse. From this perspective, overbidding by third party buyers should generate a more favorable share price response for subsidiary and/or parent shareholders than a parent-subsidiary merger. Roll's hypothesis also implies that a parent might rationally acquire the minority shareholdings of its subsidiary, restructure the subsidiary, and subsequently sell it to a third party at a higher price than the parent originally paid to merge with the subsidiary.

3. Sample and methodology

To construct samples of parent-subsidiary mergers and third party buyouts, we examine the ownership structure of every firm included in Standard and Poor's Stock Reports for NYSE, Amex, and Nasdaq for each year from 1970 through 1993 to identify the set of publicly traded corporations for which a majority of shares (50% or more) are owned by another publicly traded firm. Parent-subsidiary mergers and third party buyouts of parent-controlled public subsidiaries are retained if both the controlled subsidiary and its parent have sufficient daily stock price returns on the CRSP file to conduct an event study analysis. Announcement dates are obtained from the *Wall Street Journal* and Dow Jones News Wire. Data about the terms of the transactions and characteristics of the firms are obtained from the National Stock Summary, the *Wall Street Journal*, the Directory of Obsolete Securities, Moody's Industrial Manuals, proxy statements, and Standard and Poor's Stock Reports.

We ensure that the parent's fiduciary responsibility to the subsidiary is unambiguous by requiring that the subsidiary is a majority-controlled, public company for at least six months prior to the merger or buyout announcement. Events are excluded if the intent to subsequently merge or sell the subsidiary is announced around the time that the unit is partially divested or majority control is established. These filters exclude two-step acquisitions from the sample. The final parent-subsidiary merger sample consists of 105 subsidiaries and 101 parents since in four cases parents announce an intent to merge with two public subsidiaries. In the third party buyout sample there are 38 parents and 38 subsidiaries, and in 19 events the buyer is a public company. Examination of information subsequent to announcements of parent-subsidiary mergers and third party buyouts indicates that all transactions in the samples are completed.

Descriptive statistics for parent-subsidiary mergers are reported in Panel A of Table 1. Subsidiaries operate as public companies for an average of 72 months (median of 60), from time of origin as a majority-controlled unit to merger announcement, although 30% are publicly traded subsidiaries of more than ten years. The mean (median) market value of subsidiaries is \$506 million (\$85 million), where market value is the number of shares outstanding multiplied by share price one week before the initial announcement. Parents are large firms

Table 1
Descriptive statistics for 105 parent-subsidiary mergers and 38 third party buyouts over the sample period 1970–1993 involving subsidiaries, parents, and buyers traded on NYSE, Amex, and Nasdaq

	Panel A Parent-subsidiary mergers		Panel B Third party buyouts	
	Mean (1)	Median (2)	Mean (3)	Median (4)
Market value[a] ($ millions):				
Parent[b]	3470.8	328.4	2304.0	787.8
Subsidiary	506.0	85.2	319.4	107.9
Buyer[c]	–	–	4516.0	846.1
Parent ownership of subsidiary	375.6	61.2	212.9	67.5
Parent ownership (%)[d]	71.1	73.0	69.2	71.5
Time from origin (months)	72	60	73	43

[a] Market value is calculated as the number of shares outstanding times the stock price one week prior to the event announcement.
[b] There are 101 firms in the parent sample as four parents announce the intent to merge with two subsidiaries.
[c] There are 19 publicly traded buyers for the sample of third party buyouts.
[d] Proportion of total subsidiary shares owned by the parent obtained from the proxy statement prior to the announcement.

with a mean (median) market value of $3,471 million ($328 million). The mean (median) proportion of subsidiary shares owned by parents is 71% (73%) based on data obtained from proxy statements just prior to the announcement. When the parent's stake in each subsidiary is valued at pre-announcement market prices, on average, subsidiaries account for 11% of parent market value (median is 19%).

In 54 cases, subsidiaries originate as partial acquisitions, and 51 subsidiaries originate as partial divestitures (48 equity carve-outs and three partial spin-offs). Subsidiary activities are typically in a different industry from the parent, since the entities share the same three-digit SIC code in only 19 cases (18%). Parent stock is the means of payment in 58 mergers (55%), while cash is used in 47 mergers (45%). Sixty-six events (63%) occur prior to, and 39 (37%) after, the Weinberger decision on February 7, 1983. Parent-subsidiary mergers are consummated expeditiously with a mean (median) period from initial announcement to completion of five (four) months. In 21 cases (20%), a majority vote by minority shareholders is required for approval; in 84 cases (80%) only a simple majority vote is necessary.

Descriptive statistics about third party buyouts, reported in Panel B, are similar in most categories to statistics for parent-subsidiary mergers. The mean (median) length of time from origination of public trading in a subsidiary to the buyout announcement is 73 (43) months. The mean (median) market value (one week prior to announcement) of subsidiaries is $319 million ($108 million) and parents have a mean (median) market value of $2,304 million ($788 million). The mean (median) proportion of subsidiary shares owned by parents is 69% (72%). When the parent's stake in the subsidiary is valued at market prices, subsidiaries account for 10% (mean and median) of parent market value. Subsidiaries originate as partial acquisitions in 13 cases (34%) and as equity carve-outs in 25 cases (66%). Based on Standard and Poor's Stock Reports and proxy statements, there is no evidence that a third party buyer held 5% or more of the targeted subsidiary's stock prior to the buyout announcement. Parents and subsidiaries typically operate in different industries, sharing the same three-digit SIC code in only five cases (13%). The 19 publicly traded buyers are large entities with a mean (median) market value of $4,516 million ($846 million) and share the same three-digit SIC code in eight of the 19 events (42%). This suggests there may be synergy gains to these transactions that are not available to the parent. Unlike parent-subsidiary mergers, cash is the typical means of payment in buyouts and only five events (13%) involve buyer equity. Third party buyouts conclude quickly, on average within four months (median is three months) of the initial announcement.

Stock price reactions are measured by estimating prediction errors using the market model method. We focus on the two-day event window defined as -1 and 0, where 0 is the date of the first public report of the event. Adjusted returns are the difference between the arithmetic return and the conditional expected return derived as the prediction value obtained from a least squares regression estimated over a pre-event period, -160 to -40, where the return on the CRSP equally-weighted index is the explanatory variable. As in Brown and Warner (1985), residuals are standardized to adjust for heteroskedasticity. In testing for statistical significance, the null hypothesis is that the mean standardized prediction error equals zero for each event subperiod. Under the null hypothesis, the standardized prediction error is approximately unit normal, so the z-statistic is the sum of the standardized prediction errors divided by the square root of the number of sample firms. Qualitatively similar results for significance are obtained (not reported in the tables) by using the traditional t test (Brown and Warner, 1980) and the standardized cross-sectional test (Boehmer et al., 1991). Statistical significance of median returns is assessed by using the sign test.

4. Empirical results

4.1. Parent-subsidiary mergers

In Panel A of Table 2, we report excess returns, percentage of excess returns positive, and the distribution of excess returns by quartile for the two-day announcement window, −1 and 0, where 0 is the day of the initial public report of a parent-subsidiary merger. In column (1), the two-day average excess return to subsidiaries is 18.53% with a z-statistic of 64.50, statistically significant at the 1% level; 96% of excess returns are positive. The distribution of excess returns indicates that the two-day return is not the result of outliers; the median return, 14.18%, is statistically significant. Daily excess returns are reported in Panel B and there is evidence of only modest market anticipation or information leakage. Subsidiaries earn post-event period excess returns that are not statistically different from zero. For a one-month interval around the announcement (not reported in the table), the excess return is 20.70% with a z-statistic of 16.05, indicating that 90% of the gains occur at the public announcement of the merger.

These results indicate that the value of the parent's offer to minority shareholders substantially exceeds the pre-announcement value of subsidiary shares. The median dollar gain in wealth to minority shareholders is $10.7 million and the aggregate gain is $2.1 billion, which is calculated using the two-day excess return to each subsidiary multiplied by the pre-merger market value of the subsidiary and the proportion of shares not held by the parent. The magnitude of the dollar value of these gains, together with the high percentage of events with positive two-day excess returns (96%), rejects the hypothesis that parent-subsidiary mergers redistribute pre-merger minority shareholder wealth to parents.

Despite appraisal statutes which entitle minority shareholders only to the worth of their shares prior to the merger, our evidence implies that, on average, minority shareholders obtain a significant increase in wealth that is at least as large as the average gain for targets of conventional mergers. Jensen and Ruback's (1983) summary of studies of targets in conventional mergers reports two-day average excess returns in the range of 6.2 to 13.4%, with a weighted average excess return of 7.7%. For the one-month period encompassing conventional merger announcements, Jensen and Ruback report target returns of 15.9%, suggesting considerable leakage of information. Our findings indicate that returns to subsidiary targets are concentrated at the announcement date, reflecting that a parent-subsidiary merger is largely a unilateral, internal decision made by parent managers, whereas conventional merger negotiations are bilateral and involve investment bankers, lawyers, and other outside agents. The absence of rising subsidiary stock prices prior to news of parent-subsidiary mergers suggests that the pre-announcement price of subsidiary stock excludes the value of post-merger benefits and thus is an appropriate measure of appraisal value.

In column (4) of Panel A, the two-day average excess return to parents is also positive, 2.13%, and significant at the 1% level, with a z-statistic of 7.19; 61% of excess returns are positive. The distribution of excess returns indicates that the two-day return is not the result of outliers; the median return, 0.70%, is

Table 2
Excess returns[a] (in percent) at announcements of 105 parent-subsidiary mergers, involving firms listed on NYSE, Amex, or Nasdaq, over the sample period 1970–1993; *z*-statistics[b] are in parentheses, the percentage of positive returns is in brackets, and *N* is the sample size

Event period	Subsidiary			Parent		
	Excess return	Distribution of returns		Excess return	Distribution of returns	
		Quartile	Return		Quartile	Return
	(1)	(2)	(3)	(4)	(5)	(6)
Panel A: Two-day announcement period returns (− 1 to 0)						
Merger announcement date	**18.53%**	25%	23.46	**2.13%**	25%	2.95
	(64.50)**	50%	14.18	(7.19)**	50%	0.70
	[0.96]	75%	5.84	[0.61]	75%	− 0.68
	$N = 105$			$N = 101$		
Lawsuit filing date	**0.88%**	25%	0.95	**−1.16%**	25%	0.09
	(1.93)	50%	− 0.24	(− 2.06)*	50%	− 0.66
	[0.48]	75%	− 0.89	[0.31]	75%	− 1.64
	$N = 27$			$N = 26$		

Panel B: Daily excess returns for the merger announcement

Event day	Excess return	z-statistic	Excess return	z-statistic
− 4	0.04	0.29	− 0.17	− 0.19
− 3	0.40	1.74	− 0.06	− 0.03
− 2	0.73	2.94**	− 0.44	− 2.31*
− 1	**12.19****	**57.70****	**0.97**	**5.36****
0	**6.34****	**30.22****	**1.16**	**4.83****
1	0.25	1.26	0.16	1.27
2	− 0.00	− 0.00	− 0.09	− 0.10
3	0.15	1.37	− 0.13	− 0.43
4	0.00	0.01	0.15	0.83

[a] The two-day excess return is estimated using the market model where the adjusted return is the difference between the arithmetic return and the conditional expected return derived as the prediction value obtained from a least squares regression estimated over the pre-event period, − 160 to − 40. Day 0 is the date of the initial report in the *Wall Street Journal*. The test statistic is based on standardized residuals as described in Brown and Warner (1985).

[b] Level of statistical significance is indicated by: * Significant at the 5% level; ** Significant at the 1% level.

statistically significant. The positive return to parents in subsidiary mergers is contrary to the negative returns to buyers documented for conventional mergers and acquisitions that suggest overbidding (Byrd and Hickman, 1992, −1.20%; Bradley et al., 1988, −2.90%; Jennings and Mazzeo, 1991, −0.80%; Servaes, 1991, −3.30%). The median dollar gain in parent shareholder wealth at parent-subsidiary mergers is $2.1 million and the aggregate gain is $2.8 billion, which is calculated using the two-day excess return for each parent multiplied by the pre-merger market value of its equity. This aggregate gain is only modestly larger than the $2.1 billion increase in minority shareholder wealth despite the parents' disproportionately large ownership stake in the subsidiary (mean of 71%). The sum of the aggregate dollar gains to both minority and parent shareholders from parent-subsidiary mergers is $4.9 billion. This is a substantial gain and is equal to 9.2% of the aggregate pre-announcement subsidiary value ($53.1 billion).

Our results for parent-subsidiary mergers are consistent with findings reported by Dodd and Ruback (1977) for a sample of 19 tender offers in which the bidder has prior control of the target. Our evidence indicates that the market expects the post-merger entity to be significantly more profitable than the existing separate, but affiliated, units. The substantial premium paid to minority shareholders of subsidiaries in parent-subsidiary mergers implies that minority shareholders receive a disproportionately large share of the gains. Minority shareholders receive 44% of the total increase in wealth generated by the mergers even though they own, on average, only 29% of the subsidiary. In 64% of the cases, the proportion of the gains sustained by minority shareholders exceeds their ownership proportion. Viewing the ratios of the gains and the ownership proportions as a sample of 105 matched pairs, the difference between the two variables is statistically significant (p-value of 0.002), based on the sign test; that is, we reject the null hypothesis that the probability of the gains ratio exceeding the ownership proportion is one-half in favor of the alternative hypothesis that the probability exceeds one-half. Thus, parent-subsidiary mergers generate increases in wealth for minority shareholders that are greater than the gains implied by pre-merger ownership proportions.

To assess the role of post-merger restructuring activities as the source of these gains, we obtain information about subsequent developments involving these subsidiaries for five years following completion of parent-subsidiary mergers. We examine numerous sources of public data, including the *Wall Street Journal*, Dow Jones News Wire, the Predicast F and S Index, Moody's Industrial Manuals, and annual reports. In Table 3, we delineate post-merger developments into two primary categories. One category is subsidiaries that are restructured and consists of 73 events (70% of the full sample). The other category contains events with no evidence of restructuring and consists of 32 (30%) events. Thus, in over two-thirds of the sample, there is evidence of restructuring of the unit in the post-merger period. Among the set of 73 events involving

Table 3
Restructuring developments involving wholly-owned units following completion of parent-subsidiary mergers

	Events	
	N (1)	% (2)
A. Subsidiary restructured after parent-subsidiary merger	**73**	**70%**
1. Parent restructures unit, then divests unit	33	32%
a. Sells unit to third party buyer	*27*	*82%*
b. Sells unit as a takeover defense	*2*	*6%*
c. Spins off unit	*4*	*12%*
2. Parent restructures unit and retains ownership	27	26%
a. Major contraction of unit operations	*7*	*26%*
b. Major expansion of unit operations	*18*	*67%*
c. Forms major joint venture through unit	*2*	*7%*
3. Parent restructures with unit as core business	13	12%
B. No evidence of restructuring	**32**	**30%**
1. Parent retains ownership	26	25%
2. No post-merger information about retained unit	6	6%

subsidiary restructuring, in 33 cases the parent restructures the unit and then divests it. The parent sells the unit to a third party in 27 cases, sells the unit as a takeover defense in two cases, and spins off the unit to parent shareholders in four cases. There are 27 events in which the parent carries out a restructuring of the subsidiary and retains ownership. In seven cases, the parent reduces the subsidiary's operations through layoffs, termination of product lines, plant closings, or the sale of some of the unit's operations. In 18 cases, the parent undertakes a major expansion of the subsidiary's activities via acquisitions, the receipt of new contracts, or the undertaking of major new investment projects. In two cases, the parent uses the subsidiary as a vehicle to form a major joint venture with an unaffiliated company. We find 13 cases in which the parent undertakes a major restructuring in which the subsidiary becomes the core business and most of the parent's other operations are divested. In most of these 13 cases, the name of the parent firm is changed to that of the subsidiary. For 32 (30%) events there is no evidence of restructuring. In 26 of these 32 cases, the parent retains the subsidiary as a wholly-owned unit, and there is ongoing news about the unit which suggests its post-merger activities remain similar to its pre-merger activities. In 6 cases, there is no specific information about the unit's activities, except that the unit continues to be part of the parent's operations.

The extent and character of subsequent corporate restructuring actions, and changes in operational activities, suggest that gains in wealth at parent-subsidiary merger announcements reflect the market's anticipation of enhanced productivity as some operations are terminated or divested, new activities are initiated, or continuing operations are conducted more efficiently within the new constituency structure. We estimate cross-sectional regressions (not reported in the tables) in which the two-day excess returns to subsidiaries and parents are each specified as a function of qualitative variables that reflect categories of subsequent restructuring activities. None of these variables is statistically significant, which implies that the market has little ability to predict specific future outcomes for specific firms. Nevertheless, our evidence is consistent with the view that a parent-subsidiary merger eliminates the cost of potential conflicts of interest with minority shareholders and permits the parent to undertake investments it might otherwise defer or forego.

4.2. Third party buyouts

In column (1) of Panel A in Table 4, the two-day average excess return to subsidiaries in third party buyouts is 20.92% with a z-statistic of 45.35, which is statistically significant at the 1% level; 95% of the returns are positive. A difference in means test between excess returns to minority shareholders in parent-subsidiary mergers versus third party buyouts generates a calculated t-value of 0.66, which is not statistically significant. Moreover, the median excess return to subsidiaries in third party buyouts is 12.87%, and statistically significant, but is lower than the median return of 14.18% in parent-subsidiary mergers. Applying a Mann–Whitney test, we find a calculated value of only 0.1, which indicates that the difference in median subsidiary returns for the two groups is not statistically significant. These results suggest that the typical parent-subsidiary merger generates returns to minority shareholders that are similar to the returns generated by third party buyouts. Thus, despite the difference in bargaining environment between parent-determined terms and arm's length negotiations, there are similar increases in the wealth of minority shareholders of subsidiaries in each type of acquisition.

In column (4), the two-day average excess return to parents in third party buyouts is 2.78% with a z-statistic of 5.08, significant at the 1% level; 71% of the returns are positive. This figure is about 50% larger than the two-day excess return of 1.8% reported by Hite et al. (1987) for parents that sell off wholly-owned divisions or subsidiaries to third party buyers. It is also greater than the return to parents in parent-subsidiary mergers, although a difference in means test is not statistically significant (the calculated t-value is 1.50).

The aggregate dollar gain in wealth to minority shareholders of subsidiaries from third party buyouts is \$1.1 billion. The aggregate dollar gain in parent shareholder wealth is \$2.3 billion. The ratio of the gains to minority

Table 4
Excess returns[a] (in percent) at announcements of 38 buyouts by unaffiliated third parties of parent majority-controlled public subsidiaries, where parent and subsidiary firms are traded on NYSE, Amex, or Nasdaq, over the sample period 1970 through 1993; *z*-statistics[b] are in parentheses, the percentage of positive returns is in brackets, and N is the sample size

Panel A: Two-day announcement returns

Event period	Subsidiary, $N = 38$			Parent, $N = 38$			Buyer, $N = 19$		
	Excess return	Distribution of returns		Excess return	Distribution of returns		Excess return	Distribution of returns	
		Quartile	Return		Quartile	Return		Quartile	Return
	(1)	(2)	(3)	(4)	(5)	(6)	(7)	(8)	(9)
− 1 to 0	**20.92%**	25%	26.29	**2.78%**	25%	6.16	**−0.81%**	25%	3.11
	(45.35)**	50%	12.87	(5.08)**	50%	1.94	(− 2.20)*	50%	− 0.65
	[0.95]	75%	4.95	[0.71]	75%	− 1.62	[0.42]	75%	− 3.23

Panel B: Daily excess returns at buyout announcement

Event day	Excess return	*z*-statistic	Excess return	*z*-statistic	Excess return	*z*-statistic
− 4	1.66	6.05**	0.81	2.12*	0.05	0.03
− 3	0.55	3.38**	0.24	0.45	1.24	1.86
− 2	2.21	3.74**	− 0.13	− 0.50	0.89	1.71
− 1	**11.05**	**25.60****	**1.58**	**2.53***	**0.29**	**0.75**
0	**9.86**	**36.27****	**1.20**	**4.65****	**−1.11**	**−3.86****
1	− 0.29	− 0.63	− 0.10	− 0.29	0.53	0.16
2	0.29	1.41	− 0.93	− 2.53*	− 0.44	− 0.77
3	0.84	2.92**	− 0.85	2.64**	− 0.49	− 1.55
4	0.49	0.90	0.37	0.61	− 0.38	− 1.09

[a] The two-day excess return is estimated using the market model where the adjusted return is the difference between the arithmetic return and the conditional expected return derived as the prediction value obtained from a least squares regression estimated over the pre-event period, − 160 to − 40. Day 0 is the date of the initial report in the *Wall Street Journal*. The test statistic is based on standardized residuals as described in Brown and Warner (1985).
[b] Level of statistical significance is indicated by: * Significant at the 5% level; ** Significant at the 1% level.

shareholders to the combined gains to parents and minority shareholders is 68%, which closely matches the mean proportion of subsidiary shares owned by parents, 69%. This result is expected since the buyer pays the same price for all subsidiary shares. When the ratios of the gains and the ownership proportions are treated as a sample of 38 matched pairs, the difference between the two variables is not statistically significant, based on the sign test. The total gain in subsidiary value for parent plus minority shareholders from third party buyouts is $3.4 billion, which is 28% of the pre-announcement value of the subsidiaries ($12.1 billion) and exceeds the comparable figure of 9.2% for parent-subsidiary mergers.

Since minority shareholders earn similar two-day excess returns in each type of transaction, it is parents that earn the additional gains from third party buyouts. Our evidence suggests that the greater increase in parent value at announcements of buyouts compared to parent-subsidiary mergers is the result of overbidding by third party buyers. In column (7), for the set of 19 publicly traded buyers, the two-day average excess return is −0.81%, which is statistically significant at the 5% level, given a z-statistic of −2.20; 58% of the returns are negative. Given the large market values of third party buyers, this result implies that the greater gains to parents reflect a transfer of wealth from buyers to parents as a result of overbidding, a phenomenon documented for buyers in conventional mergers. For the subset of 19 events in which the buyer, the parent, and the subsidiary each publicly trade, the aggregate gain in value (including the losses to buyers) is 9.7% of the pre-announcement value of the subsidiaries, which is similar to the figure for parent-subsidiary mergers.

4.3. Share price effects of characteristics of parent-subsidiary mergers

We examine several aspects of parent-subsidiary mergers that potentially affect gains to parents and subsidiaries. First, we disaggregate the sample on the basis of the type of voting requirement. When a super-majority vote is required, the two-day excess return to subsidiaries is 18.53% (z-statistic of 25.08). For events that require a simple majority vote, the two-day return to subsidiaries is identical, 18.53% (z-statistic of 56.21). Thus, a voting requirement that limits the power of the controlling parent by giving minority shareholders veto over the transaction does not generate greater returns for minority shareholders relative to events in which parents have unilateral authority to control the transaction. The two-day excess return to parents when super-majority voting is required is 0.33%, not statistically significant, given a z-statistic of 1.41, and 35% of the returns are positive. For transactions requiring a simple majority vote, the parent return is 2.57%, significant at the 1% level, given a z-statistic of 7.28, and 67% of the returns are positive. A difference in means test between these parent returns generates a calculated t-value of 1.74, significant at the 10% level. To determine whether the difference in voting requirement affects the total rate of return to the transaction, we weight the parent and minority shareholders' returns by their relevant market values. The results are 2.04% for the super-majority voting transactions and 3.45% for the simple majority voting transactions. A difference in means test generates a calculated *t*-value of 1.35. Thus, there is some evidence to suggest greater overall gains in value for mergers in which parents have unrestricted control relative to transactions in which parents must obtain a super-majority vote. Since super-majority voting necessarily increases compliance and other transactions costs of a parent-subsidiary merger, lower net gains can be expected from such transactions, and our results suggest that parents, rather than minority shareholders, bear these costs.

Second, we evaluate the effects of litigation on returns to parent-subsidiary mergers. We determine the frequency of litigation by examining the *Wall Street Journal* for evidence of shareholder lawsuits during the transaction period. We find 32 lawsuits (30%) among the 105 parent-subsidiary mergers, indicating that the typical parent-subsidiary merger does not induce litigation. There are two lawsuits (5%) among the 38 third party buyouts, an indication that buyouts are less litigious than parent-subsidiary mergers. In no case did a lawsuit prevent consummation of a parent-subsidiary merger. Only four of the 32 lawsuits in parent-subsidiary transactions were followed by an upward revision in the parent's offer to minority shareholders. At news of the revised offers, the two-day average excess returns for the four events are 8.82% (*z*-statistic of 4.71) to subsidiaries and 1.29% (*z*-statistic of 1.14) to parents (not reported in the table). To assess whether lawsuits increase transactions costs to parent-subsidiary mergers, slow the merger process, and harm parent and/or subsidiary value, we evaluate share price responses to announcements of 27 lawsuit filings. In Panel A of Table 2, the two-day average excess return to subsidiaries is 0.88% (*z*-statistic of 1.93), and the return to parents is −1.16% (*z*-statistic of −2.06). These results provide modest evidence that lawsuit filings generate an increase in wealth for minority shareholders and a loss in parent wealth.

Next, we assess the valuation effects of the Delaware Supreme Court's landmark decision in the Weinberger v UOP case. Sixty majority-controlled subsidiaries and their parents were publicly traded at the time the decision was reported on February 7, 1983 in the *New York Times* and the *Legal Times*. The two-day average excess returns at the announcement are 0.04% (*z*-statistic of 0.06) for subsidiaries and 0.32% (*z*-statistic of 0.47) for parents (not reported in the table). These results indicate that news of the Weinberger decision did not significantly alter parent or subsidiary wealth. As reported in Table 5, we find two-day excess returns to subsidiaries are 20.85% (*z*-statistic of 55.15) in the pre-Weinberger period and 14.65% (*z*-statistic of 29.32) in the post-Weinberger period based on our sample of 105 parent-subsidiary mergers. A difference in means test generates a calculated *t*-value of 2.03, significant at the 5% level. For parents, the two-day excess returns are 1.79% (*z*-statistic of 5.40) for the pre-Weinberger period and 2.68% (*z*-statistic of 4.70) for the post-Weinberger

Table 5
Two-day excess returns[a] (in percent) at announcements of 105 parent-subsidiary mergers, involving firms listed on NYSE, Amex, or Nasdaq, over the sample period 1970–1993, disaggregated by merger approval status, the Weinberger decision, means of payment, and origin of subsidiary. The z-statistics are in parentheses[b], the percentage of positive returns is in brackets, and N is the sample size.

Subsidiary (1)	Parent (2)	Subsidiary (3)	Parent (4)
(1) Merger approval status			
Majority of minority required		*Simple majority*	
18.53%	**0.33%**	**18.53%**	**2.57%**
(25.08)**	(1.41)	(56.21)**	(7.28)**
[1.00]	[0.35]	[0.95]	[0.67]
$N = 21$	$N = 20$	$N = 84$	$N = 81$
(2) Weinberger v UOP decision			
Before Weinberger		*After Weinberger*	
20.85%	**1.79%**	**14.65%**	**2.68%**
(55.15)**	(5.40)**	(29.32)**	(4.70)**
[0.98]	[0.59]	[0.92]	[0.63]
$N = 66$	$N = 63$	$N = 39$	$N = 38$
(3) Means of payment			
Equity		*Cash*	
12.14%	**2.29%**	**26.92%**	**1.93%**
(31.78%)**	(5.74)**	(57.68)**	(4.31)**
[0.95]	[0.59]	[0.96]	[0.62]
$N = 58$	$N = 56$	$N = 47$	$N = 45$
(4) Origin of subsidiary			
Partial acquisition		*Partial divestiture*	
18.23%	**2.03%**	**18.74%**	**2.21%**
(42.90)**	(5.69)**	(42.60)**	(4.48)**
[0.96]	[0.56]	[0.96]	[0.67]
$N = 54$	$N = 54$	$N = 51$	$N = 48$

[a] The two-day excess return is estimated using the market model where the adjusted return is the difference between the arithmetic return and the conditional expected return derived as the prediction value obtained from a least squares regression estimated over the pre-event period, − 160 to − 40. Day 0 is the date of the initial report in the *Wall Street Journal*. The test statistic is based on standardized residuals as described in Brown and Warner (1985).

[b] Level of statistical significance is indicated by: * Significant at the 5% level; ** Significant at the 1% level.

period, but a difference in means test generates a calculated t-value of −0.55, not significant at the 5% level. These results suggest that the Weinberger decision is associated with a subsequent reduction in wealth gains for subsidiaries in parent-subsidiary mergers and increased returns to parents, although the latter effect is not statistically significant. This decrease in gains to subsidiaries runs counter to the trend of increasing gains to targets of conventional mergers and acquisitions for a similar time period reported by Nathan and O'Keefe (1989). Thus, our results suggest that, subsequent to the Weinberger decision, parents make lower offers to minority shareholders than in the period prior to the decision. We conclude that legal standards applicable to parent-subsidiary mergers influence parent decisions about offer terms to minority shareholders.

Third, we examine the implications of the means of payment in parent-subsidiary mergers by disaggregating the sample into cash and equity events. Travlos (1987) reports that the use of equity in corporate control transactions has a negative effect on buyer returns, a result consistent with findings that equity issuance is a negative signal of firm value (Mikkelson and Partch, 1986; Asquith and Mullins, 1986; Masulis and Korwar, 1986). Theoretical models by Fishman (1988), Hansen (1987) Berkovitch and Narayanan (1990) predict a relationship between means of payment in corporate control contests and the probability of competitive bidding. Berkovitch and Narayanan demonstrate that a bidder's use of cash should vary directly with the probability of another bidder entering the auction. Since there is little or no probability that agents other than the parent will bid for minority shares of a controlled subsidiary, cash offers in parent-subsidiary mergers should be relatively rare. Nevertheless, we find that cash offers (47) are almost as common as equity offers (58), so the absence of competition does not explain the choice of means of payment. As a result, we consider the tax implications of the means of payment.

When a transaction is structured as a tax-free exchange of stock, no tax liabilities are generated for minority shareholders. However, as a cash sale is a taxable event, minority shareholders recognize a capital gain or loss depending on the transaction price and their basis in the property. Typically, a cash transaction generates a tax liability for minority shareholders which reduces their overall gains from the transaction. If the parent undertakes a cash transaction and compensates subsidiary shareholders for the recognition of these liabilities, the value of this tax consideration could be reflected in a more favorable share price reaction for the subsidiary and a less favorable reaction for the parent, relative to results in equity transactions. For equity transactions, the two-day average excess returns are 12.14% (z-statistic of 31.78) to subsidiaries, and 2.29% (z-statistic of 5.74) to parents. For cash transactions, the returns are 26.92% (z-statistic of 57.68) to subsidiaries, and 1.93% (z-statistic of 4.31) to parents. Differences in means tests for equity versus cash transactions generate calculated t-values of 4.71 for subsidiaries and -0.32 for parents, the former significant at the 1% level. The greater returns to subsidiary shareholders in cash transactions support the view that minority shareholders receive greater premiums to compensate for the tax effects of cash transactions.

We estimate a weighted least squares regression in which the two-day return to subsidiaries at 105 parent-subsidiary merger announcements, $SUBR$, is a function of qualitative variables that control for the means of payment and for the Weinberger decision. To correct for heteroskedasticity, the dependent and independent variables are divided by the standard deviation of the estimation period residuals. The variable *CASH* equals one for cash offers and zero for equity offers, while the variable *POST* equals one for post-Weinberger and zero for pre-Weinberger events. The estimated coefficients are reported below,

$$\underset{}{SUBR} = \underset{(7.04)^{**}}{13.58} + \underset{(5.78)^{**}}{16.01}\,CASH - \underset{(-\,2.88)^{**}}{8.10}\,POST, \quad R^2 = 0.27, F = 18.57^{**} \tag{1}$$

with z-statistics in parentheses. Both coefficients are statistically significant and the R^2 and F statistics are relatively high. The results indicate that subsidiary gains are lower for merger announcements in the post-Weinberger period than in the pre-Weinberger period, independent of the effect of the means of payment.

Finally, we assess whether the mechanism by which a publicly traded subsidiary originates affects the pattern of returns at parent-subsidiary mergers. Allen et al. (1995) find evidence that positive returns at spin-off announcements represent in part the regeneration of wealth lost at the announcement of the original acquisition and argue that this supports a correction-of-a-mistake hypothesis for spin-offs. They also find that spin-off returns are related to returns at acquisition announcements. We assess whether gains at parent-subsidiary mergers recapture wealth lost from earlier partial divestitures by disaggregating our sample on the basis of origin status. For units that originate by partial acquisition, the two-day excess returns at parent-subsidiary merger announcements are 18.23% (z-statistic of 42.90) for subsidiaries, and 2.03% (z-statistic of 5.69) for parents. For units that originate by partial divestiture, the returns are 18.74% (z-statistic of 42.60) for subsidiaries, and 2.21% (z-statistic of 4.48) for parents. The differences in these sets of returns are small and not statistically significant, so gains from parent-subsidiary mergers in which a minority stake was previously divested are no greater than for parent-subsidiary mergers that complete a partial acquisition.

To further test this hypothesis, we analyze parent stock price reactions at announcements of the original partial divestiture. Among 48 parents that reacquire full ownership of a subsidiary, we find origin announcement dates reported in the *Wall Street Journal* for 28 partial divestitures for which parent data are available on the CRSP daily return file. The following results are not reported in the table. The two-day average excess return to parents is 1.31%, significant at the 5% level (z-statistic of 2.20), and 75% of the returns are positive. These positive returns are not consistent with the hypothesis that shareholder gains from parent-subsidiary mergers represent the re-creation of value lost at the original partial divestiture. We further disaggregate the 28 events into subsamples of 21 events for which the parent's return at the original divestiture announcement is positive and seven events for which the return is negative, and compare the share price responses at the parent-subsidiary merger announcement. If the correction-of-a-mistake hypothesis is applicable, merger returns should be significantly greater for events in which the original divestiture has a negative valuation effect. At merger announcements, the two-day excess returns are 1.67% (z-statistic of 1.65) for parents with negative divestiture returns and 2.45% (z-statistic of 3.07) for parents with positive divestiture returns. As the difference in these returns is not significant, we conclude that gains to parent-subsidiary mergers are not the result of the re-creation of wealth lost at the partial divestiture.

5. Conclusions

In this paper we provide evidence about parent-subsidiary mergers, a type of corporate acquisition that does not entail arm's length bargaining and does not occur within a competitive environment since parents control a majority of the stock of their publicly traded subsidiaries. We analyze share price responses of subsidiaries and parents at announcements of parent-subsidiary mergers, and compare the results to conventional mergers as well as to third party buyouts of majority-controlled subsidiaries, transactions characterized by arm's length bargaining and a change in control. There are positive gains to subsidiaries in parent-subsidiary mergers that are at least as large as returns to targets in conventional mergers. We find that parents also earn positive returns. Thus, parent-subsidiary mergers are value enhancing for both subsidiary and parent shareholders, and the value of the combined enterprise is greater than the sum of the pre-announcement values of the separate entities. We find evidence of extensive restructurings and divestitures of subsidiaries following parent-subsidiary mergers. Our results are consistent with Easterbrook and Fischel's (1982) contention that the elimination of publicly traded minority shareholdings in a subsidiary increases corporate flexibility and enhances value by allowing the combined entity to make investments and conduct restructuring activities that might not otherwise be undertaken. In particular, a parent that wishes to restructure the activities of its publicly traded subsidiary can face charges of conflicts of interest and self-dealing because of legal standards that protect publicly traded minority interests.

We find that buyouts of subsidiaries by third parties generate positive returns for minority shareholders that are not significantly different from minority returns in parent-subsidiary mergers. There are greater gains to parents from third party buyouts compared to parent-subsidiary mergers, and negative returns to buyers that parallel evidence of overbidding in studies of buyer returns in conventional mergers and acquisitions. This evidence suggests that greater gains to parents in buyouts are due to a transfer of wealth from third party buyers to parents and are not due to a greater increase in subsidiary value from these transactions. We conclude that, despite the absence of arm's length bargaining, parent-subsidiary mergers are value enhancing for both parties and foster an efficient reallocation of resources toward higher valued uses. As such, these transactions enhance corporate flexibility without harming the interests of minority shareholders. Our work provides evidence that value is created when a publicly traded subsidiary becomes a wholly-owned unit of its parent.

References

Allen, J., Lummer, S., McConnell, J., Reed, D., 1995. Can takeover losses explain spin-off gains. Journal of Financial and Quantitative Analysis 30, 465–485.

Asquith, P., Mullins, D., 1986. Equity issues and offering dilution. Journal of Financial Economics 15, 61–89.

Berger, C., Allingham, T., 1983. A new light on cash-out mergers: Weinberger eclipses Singer. Business Lawyer 39, 1–24.

Berkovitch, E., Narayanan, M.P., 1990. Competition and the medium of exchange in takeovers. Review of Financial Studies 3, 153–174.

Boehmer, E., Musumeci, J., Poulsen, A., 1991. Event-study methodology under conditions of event-induced variance. Journal of Financial Economics 30, 253–272.

Bradley, M., Desai, A., Kim, E.H., 1988. Synergistic gains from corporate acquisitions and their division between the stockholders of target and acquiring firms. Journal of Financial Economics 21, 3–40.

Brown, S., Warner, J., 1980. Measuring security price performance. Journal of Financial Economics 8, 205–258.

Brown, S., Warner, J., 1985. Using daily stock returns. Journal of Financial Economics 14, 3–22.

Byrd, J., Hickman, K., 1992. Do outside directors monitor managers? Evidence from tender offer bids. Journal of Financial Economics 32, 195–222.

Darrough, M., Stoughton, N., 1990. Financial disclosure in an entry game. Journal of Accounting and Economics 12, 219–243.

DeAngelo, H., DeAngelo, L., 1985. Managerial ownership of voting rights: a study of public corporations with dual classes of stock. Journal of Financial Economics 14, 33–69.

Dodd, P., Ruback, R., 1977. Tender offers and stockholder returns: an empirical analysis. Journal of Financial Economics 5, 351–373.

Dye, R., 1986. Proprietary and nonproprietary disclosures. Journal of Business 59, 331–366.

Easterbrook, F., Fischel, D., 1982. Corporate control transactions. Yale Law Journal 91, 698–737.

Fishman, M., 1988. A theory of preemptive takeover bidding. Rand Journal of Economics 19, 88–101.

Hansen, R., 1987. A theory for the choice of exchange medium in mergers and acquisitions. Journal of Business 60, 75–95.

Hite, G., Owers, J., Rogers, R., 1987. The market for interfirm asset sales: partial sell-offs and total liquidations. Journal of Financial Economics 18, 229–252.

Jensen, M., Ruback, R., 1983. The market for corporate control: the scientific evidence. Journal of Financial Economics 11, 5–50.

Jennings, R., Mazzeo, M., 1991. Stock price movements around acquisition announcements and management's response. Journal of Business 64, 139–164.

Lease, R., McConnell, J., Mikkelson, W., 1983. The market value of control in publicly traded corporations. Journal of Financial Economics 11, 439–471.

Lease, R., McConnell, J., Mikkelson, W., 1984. The market value of differential voting rights in closely held corporations. Journal of Business 57, 443–468.

Masulis, R., Korwar, K., 1986. Seasoned equity offerings: an empirical investigation. Journal of Financial Economics 15, 91–118.

Mikkelson, W., Partch, M., 1986. Valuation effects of security offerings and the issuance process. Journal of Financial Economics 15, 31–60.

Nanda, V., 1991. On the good news in equity carve-outs. Journal of Finance 46, 1717–1738.

Nathan, K., O'Keefe, T., 1989. The rise in takeover premiums: an exploratory study. Journal of Financial Economics 23, 101–120.

Roll, R., 1986. The hubris hypothesis of corporate takeovers. Journal of Business 59, 197–216.

Schipper, K., Smith, A., 1986. A comparison of equity carve-outs and seasoned equity offerings: share price effects and corporate restructuring. Journal of Financial Economics 15, 153–186.

Servaes, H., 1991. Tobin's Q and the gains from takeovers. Journal of Finance 46, 409–420.

Slovin, M., Sushka, M., 1997. The implications of equity issuance decisions within a parent-subsidiary governance structure. Journal of Finance 52, 841–857.

Travlos, N., 1987. Corporate takeover bids, methods of payment and bidding firms' stock returns. Journal of Finance 42, 943–963.

Verrecchia, R., 1990. Information quality and discretionary disclosure. Journal of Accounting and Economics 12, 365–380.

Wagenhofer, A., 1990. Voluntary disclosure with a strategic opponent. Journal of Accounting and Economics 12, 341–363.

Part II
Buyouts

[20]

GOING PRIVATE: MINORITY FREEZEOUTS AND STOCKHOLDER WEALTH*

HARRY DEANGELO and LINDA DEANGELO
University of Rochester

EDWARD M. RICE
University of Washington

I. Introduction

Going private restructures corporate ownership by replacing the entire public stock interest with full equity ownership by an incumbent management group. In many going-private transactions, or minority freezeouts as they are frequently called, current managers have majority control of the public corporation and obtain complete equity ownership of the surviving private corporation. In some cases, managers share subsequent equity ownership with outside private investors who help finance the acquisition of publicly held stock. The reorganization of corporate ownership is effected through a variety of legal vehicles, a common example of which is a cash-out merger of the public firm into a shell corporation created expressly for the transaction and wholly owned by the management group.

Managerial conflicts of interest in going-private transactions are widely believed to result in "unfair" treatment of public stockholders (hence the

* We acknowledge helpful suggestions from workshop participants at the Universities of Oregon, Rochester, and Washington and at Washington University (St. Louis). Special thanks are due Yoram Barzel, Robert Bowen, David Burgstahler, Larry Dann, Peter Dodd, Frank Easterbrook, Kenneth French, Gregg Jarrell, Michael Jensen, Peter Linneman, Paul Malatesta, Ronald Masulis, David Mayers, Wayne Mikkelson, Jay Ritter, Clifford Smith, Lee Wakeman, Jerold Warner, Ross Watts, J. Fred Weston, and Jerold Zimmerman. We also thank James Sington and several others for research assistance. Connie Muscato provided invaluable help in the preparation of this manuscript. Financial support was provided by the Managerial Economics Research Center of the University of Rochester and the University of Washington (Graduate School of Business, Rainier Bank, and the Pacific Coast Banking School).

[*Journal of Law & Economics*, vol. XXVII (October 1984)]

popular label, minority freezeout). Although management owes a fiduciary duty to the public stockholders to negotiate fair value for their shares, management as purchaser of those shares has a countervailing incentive to minimize compensation paid. The same absence of arms-length bargaining characterizes freezeout mergers of a subsidiary into a parent corporation and "cleanup" tender offers by a controlling parent for subsidiary stock.[1] These parent-subsidiary transactions combine two operating corporations and, in this sense, differ fundamentally from a going-private transaction, which simply restructures the ownership of a single operating unit.

The belief that managerial conflicts of interest induce unfair treatment of public stockholders has generated proposals for radical revisions in the law governing going-private transactions. For example, Brudney and Chirelstein would prohibit all going-private transactions because they involve only the rearrangement of ownership of a single operating entity and thus, they assert, provide no significant productive benefit to offset the threat of managerial self-dealing.[2] In contrast, Brudney and Chirelstein would permit parent-subsidiary transactions (effected at a "fair price") because such transactions involve the combination of two operating entities and thus admit the possibility of productive gain.[3]

While he was a commissioner of the Securities and Exchange Commission, A. A. Sommer, Jr., also advocated substantial restrictions on going-private transactions, asserting that "[W]hat is happening is, in my estimation, serious, unfair, and sometimes disgraceful, a perversion of the whole process of public financing, and a course that inevitably is going to make the individual shareholder even more hostile to American corporate mores and the securities markets than he already is."[4] Indeed, the SEC viewed the danger of minority stockholder exploitation as sufficiently great to enact a de facto, temporary prohibition against going-private transactions. According to the *Wall Street Journal,* as many as twenty going-private filings were held up for several months during 1974–75 while the SEC sought to develop a policy on these transactions.[5] Among the

[1] Peter Dodd & Richard Ruback, Tender Offers and Stockholder Returns: An Empirical Analysis, 5 J. Fin. Econ. 351 (1977), provide an examination of cleanup tender offers.

[2] Victor Brudney & Marvin A. Chirelstein, A Restatement of Corporate Freezeouts, 87 Yale L. J. 1354 (1978), at 1367.

[3] *Id.* at 1371.

[4] A. A. Sommer, Jr., Going Private: A Lesson in Corporate Responsibility, Law Advisory Council Lecture, Notre Dame Law School, reprinted in Fed. Sec. L. Rep. (CCH) ¶ 84,695 (November 20, 1974).

[5] SEC Aide Attacks Firm "Going Private," Hints Agency May Act to Restrict Practice, Wall Street Journal, November 15, 1974, at 4; SEC Moving to Protect Minority Holders

alternatives considered by the SEC during 1975–77 were a requirement that firms pay "fair value" to minority stockholders as determined by two independent appraisers, outright prohibition of those transactions not made for a "valid business purpose," and a ban on voting by managers seeking stockholder approval of a going-private proposal. Although such restrictions have not been imposed, in 1979 the SEC adopted a rule that requires extensive disclosure of the purpose and fairness of going-private transactions.[6]

An a priori case can be made, however, that pure ownership structure changes can generate significant productive gains. For example, a return to private ownership potentially yields material reductions in registration, listing, and other stockholder servicing costs. Such a change also can introduce improved incentives for corporate decision makers, for example, by enabling managerial compensation to be tied more closely to discretionary effort. Just as important, the "frozen out" public stockholders can be expected to share in these gains because, under the U.S. legal system, their cooperation is required to effect a return to private ownership.

This paper tests the gains-sharing proposition by examining the average effect on public stockholder wealth of going-private proposals made by seventy-two New York Stock Exchange (NYSE) and American Stock Exchange (Amex) firms over the period 1973–80 (and of proposal withdrawals for a subset of sample firms). Section II gives a brief description of the techniques for going private. Section III discusses the potential productive gains from going private and develops testable predictions of the view that minority stockholders share in these gains. The remainder of the paper presents empirical tests. Specifically, Section IV outlines our sample selection procedure and presents sample descriptive statistics. Section V describes our statistical methodology. Section VI provides detailed empirical results, and Section VII concludes the paper with a brief summary of findings.

When Firms Buy Up Shares, "Go Private," Wall Street Journal, February 5, 1973, at 12; and Standards for Concerns that "Go Private" to be Topic of SEC Hearing, Wall Street Journal, February 7, 1975, at 16.

[6] Securities Act Release No. 33-6100 of 1979, SEC Rule 13e-3. The disclosure requirements of rule 13e-3 include an expression of whether other alternatives were considered and, if so, the reason for their rejection; disclosure of firm offers by unaffiliated persons during the preceding eighteen months; detailed discussion of fairness of the transaction to public stockholders (including reasons and weights given to various factors, where possible); and, when an expert has been hired to give a fairness opinion, disclosure of any limitations on the scope of such opinion. This rule also requires disclosure of whether the transaction must be approved by at least a majority of the public stockholders and whether a majority of nonemployee directors approved the transaction.

II. Institutional Details: Techniques for Going Private[7]

The element common to all going-private proposals is that a small group of investors, including current managers, seeks to acquire all publicly owned shares. These proposals can be classified into (1) pure going-private transactions, in which incumbent management seeks complete equity ownership of the surviving corporation, and (2) leveraged buyouts, in which management proposes to share equity ownership in the subsequent private firm with third-party investors.[8] Pure going-private transactions may be effected through merger, asset sale, tender offer, reverse stock split, or some combination thereof. Leveraged buyouts are typically structured as either mergers or asset sales.

In a going-private *merger,* the public firm is usually combined with a shell corporation created expressly for the purpose of going private. Under the merger agreement, the stockholders of the shell corporation (the incumbent management group) become the sole equity owners of the surviving firm. The public stockholders must surrender their shares and usually receive cash in return (although they sometimes receive debt or preferred stock in the surviving corporation). Stockholders of the public firm must vote to approve the merger.

In *asset sales,* a shell corporation controlled by the managers typically purchases all of the firm's assets for cash, which is then distributed to public stockholders. (Noncash consideration is occasionally distributed to stockholders in addition to cash, for example, a royalty trust interest, limited partnership interest, or shares in a subsidiary corporation.) Finally, the firm may choose not to liquidate following the asset sale, but rather to remain in existence as a closed-end fund (subject to the Investment Company Act of 1940, should more than one hundred stockholders

[7] The discussion in this section is based on Martin Lipton & Erica H. Steinberger, Takeovers and Freezeouts (1979); Edward F. Greene, Corporate Freeze-out Mergers: A Proposed Analysis, 28 Stan. L. Rev. 487 (1976); Lawrence Lederman, Leveraged Buy-Outs, in Eleventh Annual Institute on Securities Regulation (Arthur Fleischer, Jr. & Martin Lipton, Chairmen), Corporate Law and Practice Course Handbook Series No. 319, at 405–26 (1979); Arthur M. Borden & Harold M. Messmer, Jr., Going Private: A Review of Relevant Considerations, in Eleventh Annual Institute on Securities Regulation (Arthur Fleischer, Jr. & Martin Lipton, Chairmen), Corporate Law and Practice Course Handbook Series No. 319, at 427–95 (1979); Arthur M. Borden, Going Private—Old Tort, New Tort or No Tort?, 49 N.Y.U. L. Rev. 987 (1974); and Securities Act Release No. 33-5884 (November 17, 1977).

[8] These third-party participants provide financing for the transaction in exchange for substantial equity and debt interests (hence the popular term, leveraged buyout). Management may either increase or decrease its equity interest, but usually receives some (not controlling) equity participation in the private firm as well as long term employment contracts. The term leveraged buyout is also used to describe the purchase of an operating division by divisional managers in conjunction with outside private investors. Such leveraged buyout divestitures are not considered here.

remain following the asset sale). The surviving fund typically makes a cash repurchase tender offer immediately following the asset sale. Managers may or may not tender, but in any case, acquire the public firm's assets through their ownership of the shell corporation. Going-private transactions structured as mergers or asset sales typically require approval by 50 percent or 66⅔ percent of the outstanding voting stock, where the required percentage depends on state law and any modifications specified in the corporate charter.[9]

In contrast to mergers and asset sales, going-private *tender offers* do not require a vote and do not require public stockholders to surrender their shares involuntarily.[10] Like tender offers in general, these offers may be for cash, or they may be exchange offers for nonconvertible debt or preferred stock. Typically, the firm itself makes a cash offer for all shares, and management waives any right to participate. In some cases, the offer is made directly by an insider-manager, or by a corporation wholly owned by the management group.

Finally, a firm can go private by declaring a *reverse stock split,* where, for example, one new share is issued for each 1,000 previously outstanding. In some cases, stockholders are given the choice of redeeming their resulting fractional shares for cash or of purchasing sufficient additional fractional interests (at the redemption price) to acquire a full postreverse split share. In other cases, redemption of fractional shares is mandatory. Depending on state law, reverse splits may require an amendment to the corporate charter (and thus stockholder approval). Reverse stock splits are only occasionally used by firms to go private. The relative frequency of this and the other transactional forms is set forth in Section IV, following the discussion in Section III of the potential productive gains from going private.

III. The Gains from Going Private

Going private potentially generates real resource gains through reductions in registration, listing, and other stockholder servicing costs and through the introduction of an ownership structure that improves incen-

[9] This condition is necessary but not sufficient for approval of the proposed transaction because, in most cases, management cedes veto power to public stockholders. On the other hand, with sufficiently high ownership percentages (for example, at least 90 percent in Delaware and 95 percent in New York), management can bypass stockholder vote entirely by effecting a "short-form" merger. All going-private mergers in our sample are "long-form" mergers requiring stockholder approval.

[10] A nontendering stockholder cannot maintain an equity interest if a sufficient number of public shares are tendered by others so that the firm qualifies for and effects a short-form merger, as described in note 9 *supra*.

tives for corporate decision makers.[11] The savings in stockholder servicing costs alone can be significant. For example, in its 1976 proxy statement, Barbara Lynn Stores, Inc., estimated the annual cost of public ownership to be $100,000, which implies a total cost saving of $1,000,000 when capitalized in perpetuity at a conservative 10 percent. This cost saving is substantial when measured against the $1,383,017 market value of the company's publicly held stock immediately prior to announcement of its going-private proposal. More generally, Schneider, Manko, and Kant advise firms considering going public to expect recurring direct costs of public ownership in the range of $30,000 to $100,000 per year (not including management time).[12] Borden claims that the annual expenditures of public ownership are "$75,000 to $200,000 annually for an average public company of Amex size and considerably more if special problems should arise" (again excluding management time and indirect costs such as additional audit fees).[13] These figures also indicate a substantial (capitalized) cost saving when compared with $2,838,000, the median value of the public stock interest for our sample of pure going-private proposals (see Section IV).

The magnitude of real resource gains from a more efficient (private) ownership structure are more difficult to estimate. Nevertheless, such benefits can be realized, for example, when management's increased equity ownership percentage reduces their incentive to shirk.[14] Management's equity ownership percentage necessarily increases in a pure going-private transaction where, by definition, management acquires 100 percent stock ownership in the private firm. Management's residual claim interest can also increase via leveraged buyout through increased stock ownership and, indirectly, through employment agreements that tie managerial income more closely to firm profitability.

As a general rule, productive gains from organizational structure change will be realized when (ex post) managerial rewards are more closely linked to (ex ante) discretionary effort. As Easterbrook and Fis-

[11] Frank H. Easterbrook & Daniel R. Fischel, Corporate Control Transactions, 91 Yale L. J. 698 (1982), also argue that going private can generate productive gains.

[12] Carl W. Schneider, Joseph M. Manko, & Robert S. Kant, Going Public: Practice, Procedure and Consequences, 27 Vill. L. Rev. 1 (1981).

[13] Borden, *supra* note 7, at 1007. Borden's figures may overstate the annual costs of public ownership for companies seeking to go private, since these firms are likely to have a smaller than average public stock interest. On the other hand, if stockholder servicing expenditures contain a significant fixed-cost component, the burden on smaller firms may not differ materially from that on larger firms. The nature of this cost function is ultimately an empirical issue.

[14] Michael C. Jensen & William H. Meckling, Theory of the Firm: Managerial Behavior, Agency Costs, and Ownership Structure, 3 J. Fin. Econ. 305 (1976).

chel have argued, some profitable investment projects require a disproportionate effort by management and will therefore be undertaken only if management can capture a corresponding (disproportionate) share of the gains.[15] In these cases, productive efficiency is enhanced by managerial compensation arrangements that deviate from strictly proportionate sharing of investment returns among all (public and management) stockholders. However, under public stock ownership, such compensation schemes are subject to legal challenge by outside stockholders as "overly generous" to management. This threat of litigation is reduced under private ownership, which should enable managerial reward to be tied more closely to managerial performance, so that fewer profitable projects are forgone.

A stronger link between managerial performance and reward also can be achieved through a leveraged buyout. These transactions introduce third-party investors who take a substantial equity position in the private firm and who therefore have a greater incentive to monitor management (and allocate rewards appropriately) than do dispersed stockholders in a public firm. These third-party participants apparently also have a comparative advantage in monitoring management, as evidenced by the observation that certain investor groups specialize in these transactions.[16] Thus, a potential benefit from going private via leveraged buyout is superior managerial performance brought about because leveraged buyout specialists are better monitors of managerial decisions than are dispersed public stockholders.

A complementary monitoring effect is that going private through a leveraged buyout can reduce the marginal agency costs of debt financing because third-party equity investors have long-term relationships with institutional lenders. Consequently, the new equity owners have reduced incentives to transfer wealth from lenders, which, of course, encourages additional borrowing and thus provides the indirect benefit of a greater corporate tax shield. Our data provide some support for this hypothesized leverage effect. Specifically, pro forma financial statements (that is, forecasted private ownership statements) were available for five leveraged buyout proposals. For these firms, the median debt-to-assets ratio increased radically from a pre-offer .11 to a forecasted value under private ownership of .86. (For thirteen pure going-private transactions for which

[15] Easterbrook & Fischel, *supra* note 11.

[16] For example, see Takeover Catalyst: Firm Fashions a Formula that Eases Way for Firms to "Go Private," Wall Street Journal, September 14, 1978, at 48, regarding Oppenheimer & Co.; and Kohlberg, Kravis Hones Its Takeover Technique, Wall Street Journal, September 25, 1980, at 35.

we could obtain the relevant data, the median debt-to-assets ratio increased slightly from .26 to a forecasted .30.)

Our discussion has focused on the benefits of private ownership or, more precisely, the costs of public ownership that are avoided by going private. There are, of course, benefits to public ownership, such as access to capital at terms that reflect the beneficial effects of diversification. Clearly, different firms will select either public or private ownership depending on the organizational structure costs particular to their circumstances. However, there is no reason to expect that a firm currently operating with a given (public or private) ownership structure will always find the current structure to be most efficient. And, more to the point, some publicly held firms will find it cost effective to go private, for example, because they experience a reduction in profitable growth opportunities which, in turn, decreases the demand for access to the public capital markets.

The Division of Gains from Going Private

Although the existence of real resource gains from going private does not by itself imply that public stockholders benefit from the transaction, there is reason to believe that public stockholders do share in these gains. For example, if there were perfect competition for corporate control, then any productive gains from going private would be shared by stockholders in the public firm.[17] On the other hand, the perfectly competitive conditions are not satisfied where, as in the typical going-private transaction, management already holds majority ownership in the public corporation. The blocking power held by incumbent management will deter outside teams from incurring the costs of bidding to take the firm private. In addition, the perfectly competitive conditions are not met when incumbent management has a strict advantage over outside management teams in operating the firm. Nevertheless, even when incumbent management possesses significant control or human capital advantages, minority stockholders can be expected to share in the productive gains from going private.

Gains should accrue to minority stockholders because they have certain rights that make their cooperation necessary to return the firm to private ownership. These rights, which we discuss in turn below, are (1) the right to block a transaction through minority stockholder veto (in merger or asset sale proposals), (2) the right to refuse to sell shares (in

[17] For an analysis of perfect competition in the market for corporate acquisitions, see Michael Bradley, Interfirm Tender Offers and the Market for Corporate Control, 53 J. Bus. 345 (1980).

tender offer proposals), and (3) the right to challenge a transaction through private litigation.[18] Our prediction-oriented discussion takes these minority stockholder rights as given and should not be interpreted as claiming that the current regulatory and legal system is either redundant or the best of all conceivable systems.

As an empirical proposition, minority stockholders as a group have veto power in almost every going-private transaction for which state law requires a stockholder vote. Indeed, even when managers own sufficient shares to ensure passage of a going-private proposal, they typically waive this right.[19] One apparent reason they do so is that, in assessing the fairness of a going-private proposal, some courts have placed significant weight on whether a transaction is conditioned on minority approval.[20] A complementary factor is that the SEC views minority stockholder veto power as an important determinant of the fairness of a going-private transaction.[21]

Minority veto power implies that management cannot mandate the transaction unilaterally even when it owns an otherwise controlling share of the voting stock and it is uniquely able to effect the productive gains from going private. Rather, management is placed in a bilateral monopoly with public stockholders who will, in effect, use their blocking power to bargain over going-private compensation. Furthermore, because minority veto power implies that fewer shares (and hence less wealth) are required to defeat a going-private proposal, the costs (to outside stockholders) of

[18] Dodd & Ruback, *supra* note 1, argue that the returns earned by minority stockholders in cleanup tender bids are, in effect, out of court settlements paid to minority stockholders.

[19] In our sample, we found only four transactions in which management owned sufficient votes to approve the transaction unilaterally and exercised this right. All four transactions occurred during the early years (1974–76) of our sample period (1973–80). One of these transactions was successfully enjoined in the courts in 1975, and the company remains public at this writing.

[20] See Borden & Messmer, *supra* note 7, at 474, who cite the Delaware case of Wayne v. Utilities and Industries Corp., Del. Ch. No. 5733 (June 6, 1979), where the court noted that "even if it were not personally convinced of the fairness of a merger, the proposal that stockholder approval . . . be made to depend on a majority of the votes cast . . . by the minority stockholders would appear to negative any contention that the majority shareholders are exercising their coercive power to effect a merger for their exclusive benefit . . ."

[21] Members of the SEC staff at one point suggested that the agency seek public comment on a policy rule that would prohibit corporate insiders from voting their shares on a going-private proposal. (See Wall Street Journal, February 5, 1975, at 12.) In at least one case, the SEC apparently forced management (who owned 40 percent of the voting stock) to cast their votes proportionately with those of the public stockholders. (See Spartek, Inc. Winding up Sale of Assets, Calls Its Effort to Go Private "Traumatic," Wall Street Journal, April 2, 1979, at 10.) Adopted rule 13e-3 requires "detailed discussion" of "whether the transaction is structured so that approval of at least a majority of unaffiliated security holders is required." Securities Act Release No. 33-6100 (1979).

cartelization in opposition to management are lower than in other corporate transactions requiring stockholder approval. Thus, one would expect stronger opposition in going private than in other control-related transactions. Our sample provides some evidence consistent with this prediction, namely that some proposals that get as far as a stockholder vote are, in fact, defeated.[22] Given an effective threat of veto, managers will be forced to share a portion of any productive gains from going private with minority stockholders.

This prediction also holds in cases where minority stockholders do not have the voting rights to veto a going-private proposal. For example, in going-private tender offers, minority stockholders can block the transaction by simply choosing not to tender their shares.[23] Consequently, if management attempts to price the offer to appropriate the full gains from going private, public stockholders have an incentive to hold back their shares in order to extract greater compensation from management. Ceteris paribus, the incentive to hold out is greater the larger is the productive gain from going private relative to any costs of not tendering, such as reduced marketability or disclosure because others tendered their shares.[24]

Finally, public stockholders can, through private litigation, impose costly delays on managers seeking to go private and, in some cases, have a credible threat of stopping the transaction outright. Minority stockholders can seek appraisal of their shares and can challenge the transaction in both state and federal courts.[25] Borden reports that "almost every going private transaction to date has been met by a suit," and the evidence for

[22] Of the forty-two transactions in our sample that reached a stockholder vote, two were defeated. This evidence contrasts with that of Peter Dodd, Merger Proposals, Management Discretion and Stockholder Wealth, 8 J. Fin. Econ. 105 (1980), who found that, of seventy-one merger proposals put to a vote, none was defeated.

[23] In some instances (four out of sixteen in our sample), managers cede veto power to minority stockholders by conditioning the going-private tender offer on minority stockholder approval. In these instances, the earlier text discussion of minority stockholder veto power also applies.

[24] Offering circulars for going-private tender offers generally warn stockholders that not tendering may be costly because of potential delisting of firm securities (with associated loss of liquidity) and because of possible avoidance of SEC filing requirements (with associated minimal disclosure), should sufficient shares be tendered by others.

[25] For example, during our sample period, minority stockholders in Delaware corporations could challenge a freezeout merger on a variety of grounds, including fraud or unfair compensation. A recent Delaware decision curtailed stockholders' rights to bring suit on grounds of inadequate compensation, but expanded the scope of admissible arguments in an appraisal proceeding. See Weinberger v. UOP, Inc. 457 A.2d 701 (Del. Supr. 1983). Minority stockholders can also challenge a going-private transaction under federal securities law by claiming that management has failed to disclose material facts or has engaged in fraud.

our sample is consistent with this observation.[26] The ability to delay or stop a going-private transaction in the courts, like the ability to block a proposal through minority stockholder veto or refusal to tender shares, should enable minority stockholders to extract some portion of the productive gains from going private.

Testable Predictions and Empirical Issues

Two tests of the gains-sharing hypothesis are presented in Section VI below. The first test examines the average effect on minority stockholder wealth (open-market share values) at the time of initial public announcement of going-private proposals. The second test examines the average wealth effect associated with the withdrawal of proposals. The gains-sharing hypothesis will be refuted if, on average, we observe (i) a negative or zero change in public stockholder wealth at initial proposal or (ii) a positive or zero wealth effect associated with proposal withdrawal. Either observation would contradict the gains-sharing view by indicating that minority stockholders are damaged (or at least not made better off) in the typical going-private transaction.

A limitation of the initial proposal test is that announcement of a going-private proposal may implicitly reveal information about a firm's profitability as a *public* company. In other words, the act of bidding may reveal information about the company which is not directly related to the value of going private, but which is simultaneously capitalized in the firm's stock price. In principle, such implicit information may represent either good or bad news about future profitability. For example, bad news is revealed by a going-private proposal when the bid indicates that management's motivation for taking the firm private is that a (previously unanticipated) reduction in profitable growth opportunities has decreased the value of access to public capital markets.

On the other hand, it is more likely that good rather than bad news is revealed by these proposals, since management has an incentive to buy shares when its (presumably superior) information indicates greater

[26] Borden, *supra* note 7, at 1017. For our sample, we found evidence of stockholder litigation in 86 percent (thirty-one of thirty-six) of the pure going-private proposals for which we had access to a relatively complete legal summary. This sample (and those noted below) excludes cases where the Wall Street Journal did not report litigation and we did not have access to a proxy or prospectus, if issued. The incidence of legal challenge was approximately equal for merger (86 percent) and tender offer (91 percent) proposals. We found evidence of stockholder litigation in substantially fewer leveraged buyout proposals (12.5 percent, or three of twenty-four). A possible explanation for the lower incidence of suit here is that third-party participation in leveraged buyouts reduces the appearance of managerial self-dealing and thus makes it more difficult to mount an effective legal challenge.

profitability than does extant public information. An analogous information effect potentially confounds the stock value impact of merger proposals, since target firms frequently supply bidders with confidential information about target firm profitability when negotiating transaction terms.[27] Our primary concern here is with positive implicit information revealed by a going-private proposal, since if such information is present systematically, it would bias the initial proposal test in favor of the gains-sharing hypothesis. In Section VI, we provide some evidence on the importance of any such information effect by comparing the going-private compensation to the "with-information" market price observed after proposal.

A limitation of the withdrawal test is that the surprise element of such events is likely to be smaller for withdrawals than for initial proposals, since arbitrageurs will monitor the firm more closely after a proposal is announced. Moreover, because withdrawn proposals can be (and sometimes are) revived, the absolute value of the decrease in the probability of going private signaled by a withdrawal announcement is likely to be smaller than the corresponding probability increase at initial proposal. Consequently, even absent confounding information effects, the expected stock price decrease at withdrawal is likely to be smaller in absolute value than the stock price increase at initial proposal. In other words, the withdrawal test is less powerful than the proposal test, in the sense that it is less likely to isolate any wealth effects associated with going private. This difficulty is exacerbated because only a limited sample of withdrawn proposals is available.

An advantage of the withdrawal test is that any negative (implicit) information about the firm's prospects is likely to be small (relative to any

[27] Such implicit information effects may actually help reconcile the anomalous findings that cash tender offers are associated with increases in bidders' stock prices, while merger proposals, which are frequently structured as stock swaps, are associated with a decline in such prices (compare Bradley, *supra* note 17, and Dodd, *supra* note 22). Suppose that bidder management has superior inside information about their own firm's profitability (unrelated to the acquisition), which is not fully reflected in its pre-offer stock price. From bidder management's perspective, a cash offer will dominate a stock swap when their (superior) valuation of their own firm's prospects exceeds the market's valuation. A stock swap will be preferred when the reverse is true. Public traders therefore interpret a cash offer as good news (and a stock swap as bad news) about the *bidder's* prospects, independent of the acquisition. If such information effects are important, the bidder stock-price change at proposal announcement will be a biased (upward or downward depending on the consideration offered) signal of the acquisition's value to bidder stockholders. See also Stewart C. Myers & Nicholas J. Majluf, Stock Issues and Investment Policy When Firms Have Information That Investors Do Not Have (September 1981) (unpublished manuscript, MIT), who argue that the target firm's decision to sell shares via merger can implicitly reveal negative information about *target* profitability. However, the large positive returns to target stockholders documented in prior studies indicate that any such negative information cannot be the dominant factor determining changes in target value in acquisitions.

positive information effect at initial proposal).[28] It is difficult to argue that management as purchaser has the incentive to suppress "bad news" about the firm's future profitability while a going-private proposal is outstanding. Rather, because the revelation of bad news will make public stockholders view a going-private proposal more favorably, management has an incentive to reveal negative information as it arrives. Furthermore, increased scrutiny of the firm by arbitrageurs while a proposal is outstanding reduces the likelihood that any news about the firm's profitability (bad or good) can be suppressed by management. Of course, these arguments do not preclude the possibility that managers withdraw an offer because they obtain negative information about the firm's profitability. Nevertheless, they suggest that the withdrawal test is less likely than the initial proposal test to exhibit an information bias in favor of the gains-sharing view.

IV. Sampling Procedure and Descriptive Statistics

Firms proposing a going-private transaction were initially identified by direct inspection of each issue of the *Wall Street Journal* for the eight-year period 1973–80. For each firm so identified, we inspected (i) the *Wall Street Journal Index* listings for the five years surrounding the proposal; (ii) each relevant article cited therein; (iii) relevant proxy statements, purchase offers, or prospectuses; and where necessary (iv) relevant press releases supplied by the firm. This sampling procedure yielded seventy-two firms (with security returns data available from the Center for Research on Security Prices),[29] which made eighty-one going-private proposals during 1973–80. Of these seventy-two firms, sixty-four made one going-private proposal, seven made two proposals, and one made three proposals (while listed on the CRSP tape) to go private during 1973–80.

The public announcement date of each proposal, and, when relevant, of proposal withdrawal, was obtained from the sources just described. In almost every case, the *Wall Street Journal* was the primary source of announcement dates. In a few instances, the *Wall Street Journal* did not report the first proposal announcement, but the relevant announcement date appeared in a proxy statement, purchase offer, prospectus, or press

[28] We are primarily concerned with negative implicit information at withdrawal, since negative information would bias the withdrawal test in favor of the gains-sharing hypothesis. As an empirical matter, our evidence suggests that withdrawal announcements are accompanied by positive information about the firm more often than by negative information (see note 31 *infra*). Moreover, as elaborated in Section VI, there are reasons other than negative information about a firm's prospects that would lead managers to withdraw a proposal.

[29] Center for Research on Security Prices (CRSP) (public use daily computer tapes, Univ. Chicago, 1981).

release. In every case where double-checking was possible, the firm's specification of the first announcement date in proxy statements, press releases, and so on, agreed with the *Wall Street Journal* announcement date. Of the seventy-two initial proposals, thirty-nine were successful. We were able to identify withdrawal announcement dates for twenty-two of the unsuccessful proposals.[30] Four of these withdrawal announcements were judged to be confounded by the simultaneous release of other information, leaving eighteen clean observations for the second empirical test.[31]

Table 1 classifies all eighty-one proposals (seventy-two initial and nine revived) according to the structure of the transaction and by year of event.[32] Of the eighty-one total observations, forty-seven are pure going-private proposals (that is, no third-party equity participation in the private firm), twenty-eight are leveraged buyouts, and six are of unidentifiable form because they were withdrawn before the specific structure was announced. Of the seventy-two *initial* proposals, forty-five are pure going privates, twenty-three are leveraged buyouts, and four are of unidentifiable form.

Approximately two-thirds of these sample proposals occurred during 1977–80. There is a fair amount of year-to-year variation in the incidence of alternative types of going-private transactions. For example, in 1974, nine out of fourteen pure going-private proposals took the form of exchange or cash repurchase tender offers, while in later years the incidence of this structural form declined considerably. On the other hand, the incidence of pure going-private mergers and leveraged buyouts increased during the later sample period. The early predominance of going-private tender offers is consistent with the findings of Dann, Masulis, and Ver-

[30] In addition to the thirty-nine successful and twenty-seven failed proposals, five proposals were pending at the time of data collection and one was only partially successful (a tender offer that increased management ownership substantially but did not result in delisting).

[31] The events considered as confounding were simultaneous announcement of (1) a competing bid or expression of interest by others (three cases), (2) a 20 percent decrease in earnings (one case), and (3) a significant increase in reported oil property valuation (one case). The sample of eighteen withdrawals includes the second (clean) withdrawal announcement by one firm whose first withdrawal was confounded by an expression of interest by others. We repeated the withdrawal test by examining the first withdrawal announcement we could identify for the twenty-two firms (with no deletions for confounding events) and found qualitatively identical stockholder wealth effects—see the discussion in Section VI. For two of the twenty-two firms in the withdrawal sample, we could identify the withdrawal date for the second proposal, but not the first. Only two of the seventy-two initial *proposals* were potentially confounded (by mention of an executive rift and oil well drilling difficulties) and thus we made no adjustment for these firms; see also the text discussion in Section VI.

[32] One firm made three proposals. A further breakdown of the seventy-two firms making initial proposals is provided in Table 2 *infra*.

TABLE 1

NUMBER OF GOING-PRIVATE PROPOSALS BY YEAR AND TYPE OF TRANSACTION FOR EIGHTY-ONE PROPOSALS IN THE PERIOD 1973–80

TRANSACTION TYPE	YEAR OF PROPOSAL 1973	1974	1975	1976	1977	1978	1979	1980	TOTAL OBSERVATIONS
Merger*	0	3	2	2	3	8	4	5	27
Sale of assets	0	1	1	0	1	0	0	0	3
Tender or exchange offer	0	9	1	0	1	2	2	1	16
Reverse stock split	0	0	0	1	0	0	0	0	1
Subtotal of pure going-private proposals (without third-party equity participation)	0	13	4	3	5	10	6	6	47
Leveraged buyout (with third-party participation)†	0	1	1	3	6	1	12	4	28
Unclassified acquisition‡	0	0	1	0	0	1	2	2	6
Total observations	0	14	6	6	11	12	20	12	81

NOTE.—The eighty-one proposals include seventy-two initial proposals plus nine subsequent (revived) proposals.

*Includes three merger proposals in which managers had a sufficient number of shares to ensure the outcome and voted these shares in favor of the merger (one occurred in 1974, and two occurred in 1975).

†Includes one 1976 leveraged buyout proposal in which managers had sufficient number of shares to ensure the outcome and voted these shares in favor of the transaction.

‡These proposed transactions were withdrawn without public announcement (in our sources) of the proposed transactional structure.

maelen,[33] whose repurchase and intrafirm exchange offer samples were heavily weighted toward 1973–74 events.

Table 2 reports managers' stock ownership in the public firm for the full sample and for the sample partitioned by type of transaction and by success of the proposal. The seventy-two sample firms are classified in Table 2 (and in subsequent tables) using only the initial proposal for the cases where multiple attempts were made to go private. Inspection of Table 2 reveals that, for the typical going-private transaction, managers control a majority (median 50.9 percent) of the stock in the public firm. Majority ownership also characterizes the typical merger and tender offer transactions. Asset sales and leveraged buyouts with third-party participation are characterized by smaller (although not inconsequential) management ownership. Fifty-four percent (thirty-nine of seventy-two) of our firms were successful in the initial going-private attempt.[34] Merger proposals succeeded 81 percent of the time, while the success rates for other transactional forms were substantially lower, ranging from 40 percent for tender offers to 43 percent for leveraged buyouts.

Table 3 contains various firm-size measures and the debt-to-total-assets ratio for the sample partitioned by all proposals versus successful proposals and by pure going-private proposals versus leveraged buyouts. All partitions are similar with respect to financial leverage, with the median firms characterized by debt-to-asset ratios in the neighborhood of .12. Firms proposing leveraged buyouts appear to be slightly larger in terms of gross revenues, but there is no apparent difference in terms of total assets. On the other hand, the leveraged buyout subsample is characterized by a median market value of publicly held shares considerably greater than that of the pure going-private subsample.

Perhaps the most interesting fact revealed in Table 3 is that the market value of publicly held stock is quite small. For example, in the pure going-private sample, the median value of public stock is $2,838,000. The corresponding median values of total equity (including shares owned by management) are also relatively small. The median market value of total equity is $5,966,000 for the pure going-private sample and $15,381,000 for

[33] Larry Y. Dann, Common Stock Repurchases: An Analysis of Returns to Stockholders and Bondholders, 9 J. Fin. Econ. 113 (1981); Ronald W. Masulis, The Effects of Capital Structure Change on Security Prices: A Study of Exchange Offers, 8 J. Fin. Econ. 139 (1980); Ronald W. Masulis, Stock Repurchase by Tender Offer: An Analysis of the Causes of Common Stock Price Changes, 35 J. Fin. 305 (1980); Theo Vermaelen, Common Stock Repurchases and Market Signalling: An Empirical Study, 9 J. Fin. Econ. 139 (1981).

[34] This percentage understates the success rate because five proposals were pending at the time we collected our data and one tender offer proposal was partially successful. See note 30 *supra*.

TABLE 2

MANAGEMENT PRE-OFFER OWNERSHIP FRACTIONS IN SEVENTY-TWO SAMPLE FIRMS SEEKING TO GO PRIVATE IN THE PERIOD 1973–80

Type of Transaction in Initial Proposal	Number of Observations	Management's Mean (Median) Pre-Offer Ownership Fraction of Common Stock*	Number of Successful Initial Proposals	Management's Mean (Median) Pre-Offer Ownership Fraction in Successful Proposals
All going-private proposals	72	.452 (.509)	39	.463 (.480)
Merger proposals†	26	.529 (.530)	21	.546 (.600)
Asset sales†	3	.277 (.290)	1	.290
Tender or exchange offers†	15	.544 (.540)	6	.566 (.565)
Reverse stock split†	1	.570	1	.570
All leveraged buyouts with third party participation	23	.321 (.330)	10	.232 (.173)
Unclassified proposals	4	.404 (.322)	0	n.a.

*Management's pre-offer ownership percentages were taken without adjustment directly from proxy statements, prospectuses, articles in the *Wall Street Journal*, and *Moody's Industrial Manual*.

†There were no third-party participants in these pure going-private proposals.

TABLE 3
SIZE AND LEVERAGE MEASURES FOR SEVENTY-TWO SAMPLE FIRMS PROPOSING TO GO PRIVATE IN THE PERIOD 1973–80

	All Seventy-two Firms Making Proposals*	All Forty-five Pure Going-Private Proposals (no third-party participation)	Twenty-nine Successful Pure Going-Private Proposals (no third-party participation)	All Twenty-three Leveraged Buyout Proposals (with third-party participation)	Ten Successful Leveraged Buyouts (with third-party participation)
Book value of total assets (1000s)†	141,976 (53,388)	129,097 (41,153)	146,868 (52,052)	156,538 (48,244)	104,652 (51,681)
Book value of long term debt as a proportion of total book assets†	.169 (.126)	.187 (.129)	.194 (.122)	.139 (.125)	.144 (.121)
Annual revenue (1000s)†	183,873 (70,899)	159,140 (60,946)	190,278 (61,836)	203,143 (83,863)	187,502 (82,625)
Market value of all outstanding common shares forty trading days before initial proposal (1000s)‡	46,759 (13,075)	24,534 (5,966)	26,392 (7,009)	83,270 (15,381)	59,562 (15,812)
Market value of publicly held common shares forty trading days before initial proposal (1000s)‡	33,251 (6,274)	12,092 (2,838)	11,408 (3,865)	69,748 (11,198)	56,567 (12,953)
Number of stockholders†	4,819 (1,890)	3,324 (1,789)	3,982 (1,493)	6,432 (2,848)	6,623 (3,472)
Number of firms listed on American, New York Stock Exchanges*	49, 23	36, 9	25, 4	13, 10	5, 5

*Includes four NYSE-listed companies making initial proposals, which were withdrawn before transactional structure could be identified.

†Based on statistics reported in *Moody's Manuals* for the time period closest to the date of initial proposal.

‡Market value size measures were calculated from closing share prices reported in *Standard & Poor's Daily Stock Price Guide* and share ownership statistics reported in the sources cited in Table 2.

leveraged buyouts. The majority of sample firms (68 percent) are listed on the American Stock Exchange, with the remainder (32 percent) listed on the New York Stock Exchange. (Our sampling criterion that stock returns be available on the CRSP daily tape limits our sample to firms listed on these two exchanges.) The median firm was exchange listed for 7.95 years before it proposed to go private (7.37 years for the pure going-private subsample and 9.33 years for leveraged buyouts).

V. Statistical Methodology

We estimate the wealth effects of going-private proposal and withdrawal announcements on minority stockholders using standard event-time methodology.[35] The results reported below measure wealth effects relative to a benchmark given by the single factor market model with equal-weighted market index. We repeated all tests using (i) the single factor market model with the *Standard & Poor's Index,* (ii) the comparison period approach outlined by Masulis,[36] and (iii) the market factor approach of Dimson,[37] with one lead and one lagged factor and for both the equal-weighted and *Standard & Poor's* indexes. The results under these alternate methodologies (not reported here) are qualitatively identical to the equal-weighted market model results.

Let $j = 1, \ldots, N$ index a sample of N observations (firms). For each observation, calendar time is translated to event time using the following conventions. Event day $t = 0$ represents the trading day on which the *Wall Street Journal* first published a report of the transaction under study (either initial going-private proposals or withdrawal announcements). In most cases, the first public announcement of a proposal or withdrawal occurred on the immediately prior trading day, event day $t = -1$. Because we cannot tell whether public announcement came before or after the close of trading on $t = -1$, we measure the announcement price effect over the two-trading-day period consisting of days $t = -1$ and $t = 0$ (hereafter designated the announcement period). The postannouncement period consists of trading days $t \geq +1$ where, for example, $t = +10$ represents the tenth trading day following the first published report of the event under study. Similarly, the preannouncement period consists of event days $t \leq -2$, where, for example, $t = -10$ represents the tenth trading day prior to the first publication of announcement.

[35] For example, Eugene F. Fama, Foundations of Finance (1976); G. William Schwert, Using Financial Data to Measure Effects of Regulation, 24 J. Law & Econ. 121 (1981).

[36] Masulis, The Effects of Capital Structure Change on Security Prices, *supra* note 33.

[37] Elroy Dimson, Risk Measurement When Shares are Subject to Infrequent Trading, 7 J. Fin. Econ. 197 (1979).

Now define the following variables:

r_{jt} = single-day rate of return on sample stock j over event day t (dividend inclusive);

r_{mt} = single-day rate of return on equally weighted market portfolio over event day t (dividend inclusive);

R_{jt} = $(1 + r_{jt})\ (1 + r_{jt-1}) - 1$,
= two-day rate of return on sample stock j over event days t and $t - 1$ (dividend inclusive);

R_{mt} = $(1 + r_{mt})\ (1 + r_{mt-1}) - 1$,
= two-day rate of return on equally weighted market portfolio over event days t and $t - 1$ (dividend inclusive);

$\hat{\mu}_{jt}$ = $\hat{\alpha}_j + \hat{\beta}_j R_{mt}$,
= estimated normal two-day return on j at t (parameter estimates, $\hat{\alpha}_j$ and $\hat{\beta}_j$, were obtained using the standard approach of a time-series ordinary least squares regression of R_{jt} on a constant and R_{mt});[38] and

PE_{jt} = $R_{jt} - \hat{\mu}_{jt} = R_{jt} - \hat{\alpha}_j - \hat{\beta}_j R_{mt}$,
= two-day prediction error or estimated abnormal return on j at t.

The sample average two-day prediction error at event day t is given by

$$\overline{PE}_t = \left(\frac{1}{N}\right) \sum_{j=1}^{N} PE_{jt},$$

where N is the number of observations in the sample.[39] Thus, the an-

[38] The inputs to this regression consist of the eighty nonoverlapping, two-day (individual security and market) returns observed from 279 event days prior to the initial going-private proposal through 120 event days prior to initial proposal. Ten of the seventy-two sample firms had missing returns on the second day of at least one two-day interval during the parameter estimation period. (The maximum number of missing two-day returns for one firm was five out of a possible eighty.) To adjust for the resulting heterogeneity in return intervals, we estimated market model parameters for these companies using generalized least squares.

[39] In calculating $\overline{PE}_t$, N is reduced over event time as going-private proposals succeed and firms are delisted. When an individual security was still listed but its return was missing on a given event day, its prediction error was treated as zero in calculating $\overline{PE}_t$ for that day. The firm's prediction error for the next trading day, T, was then calculated as

$$PE_{jT} = R_{jc} - \hat{\alpha}_j (M + 1) - \hat{\beta}_j R_{mc}$$

where M = number of missing two-day periods prior to T; R_{jc} = security j's cumulative raw return over the $(M + 1)$ two-day periods from the last observed trade through T; and R_{mc} = the cumulative market return over the same period. This adjustment attributes the abnormal return for all $(M + 1)$ two-day periods to the final two days. It is consistent, except for heteroscedasticity weighting, with the generalized least squares procedure used to estimate $\hat{\alpha}$ and $\hat{\beta}$. See note 38 *supra* and note 42 *infra*.

nouncement period average prediction error, $\overline{PE}_0$, estimates the average unexpected percentage wealth change for public stockholders associated with announcement of the event under study.

If the gains-sharing hypothesis is descriptive, we should observe (1) a significantly positive $\overline{PE}_0$ when time 0 represents the initial proposal of the going-private transaction, and (2) a significantly negative $\overline{PE}_0$ when time 0 represents the withdrawal of a proposal. To assess the statistical significance of the announcement period average prediction error, we employ the t-statistic $t = \overline{PE}_0/\hat{\sigma}$ where $\hat{\sigma}$ is a time-series estimate of the dispersion in two-day average prediction errors.[40] The assumption of the null hypothesis here is that average prediction errors are drawn from a stationary and independent normal distribution.

We are also interested in the cumulative average prediction error (abnormal returns for public stockholders) over particular event-time intervals:

$$\overline{CPE}(a, b) = \sum_{\substack{t=a \\ t \text{ even}}}^{b} \overline{PE}_t.$$

Thus, for example, $\overline{CPE}(-40, 0)$ represents the sample average cumulative prediction error for the forty days prior to announcement through the announcement itself. The statistical significance of $\overline{CPE}(a, b)$ will be assessed by the t-statistic $t = \overline{CPE}/\hat{\sigma}_{CPE}$, where $\hat{\sigma}_{CPE}$ is the estimated dispersion in the cumulative prediction error.[41]

[40] Here, $\hat{\sigma}$ is calculated from the average prediction errors in a comparison period outside the regression estimation period. Specifically, the comparison period consists of the fifty-six (event) two-day periods in the set $C = \{t \text{ such that } t = -118, -116, \ldots, -8\}$, where $t = 0$ represents the day of initial proposal (for both the proposal and withdrawal tests). Thus, the standard deviation is calculated according to

$$\hat{\sigma} = \sqrt{\sum_{t \epsilon C} (\overline{PE}_t - X)^2/55}$$

where $X = \Sigma_{t \epsilon C} \overline{PE}_t/56$. We also ran all tests using the comparison period $C' = \{t \text{ such that } t = -118, -116, \ldots, -42\}$ and found qualitatively identical results (not reported here).

[41] $\hat{\sigma}_{CPE}$ is estimated as $\hat{\sigma}\sqrt{N}$, where N is the number of two-day periods between dates a and b (that is, $N = (b - a)/2 + 1$). The t-statistic is appropriate under the assumption of the null hypothesis that average prediction errors are normal, stationary, and independent over time. We also calculated t-statistics that correct for first-order serial correlation using the method suggested by Richard Ruback, The Effects of Discretionary Price Control Decisions on Equity Values, 10 J. Fin. Econ. 83 (1982). These adjusted t-statistics were qualitatively identical to those reported below; generally, they were higher in absolute value because of slightly negative first-order serial correlation. For example, in Section VI *infra*, the t-statistic for $\overline{CPE}(-40, 0)$ increases from 12.39 to 16.14.

TABLE 4

PERCENTAGE TWO-DAY AVERAGE ($\overline{PE}$) AND CUMULATIVE AVERAGE ($\overline{CPE}$) PREDICTION ERRORS FOR THE EIGHTY-DAY PERIOD CENTERED AROUND ANNOUNCEMENT OF AN INITIAL GOING-PRIVATE PROPOSAL FOR SEVENTY-TWO FIRMS IN THE PERIOD 1973–80

Trading Day	$\overline{PE}$(%)	$\overline{CPE}$(%)	Positive:Negative Two-Day Prediction Errors
−40	.41	.41	36:36
−30	−.13	−.13	30:42
−20	−.11	1.15	32:39
−18	.32	1.47	33:38
−16	.78	2.25	38:33
−14	−.63	1.62	25:46
−12	.58	2.20	43:28
−10	.78	2.98	40:31
−8	.43	3.41	35:36
−6	−.06	3.35	39:31
−4	1.80	5.15	39:28
−2	2.99	8.14	39:23
0	22.27	30.40	68:4
+2	.27	30.67	31:41
+4	−.90	29.77	31:41
+6	.08	29.85	36:35
+8	.40	30.25	41:30
+10	.79	31.03	39:32
+12	−1.45	29.58	24:47
+14	.37	29.96	37:34
+16	−.42	29.53	31:40
+18	−.03	29.50	33:37
+20	.24	29.74	33:37
+30	−.18	28.29	30:40
+40	.17	28.53	38:30

VI. EMPIRICAL RESULTS

Initial Proposal Test

For the full sample of seventy-two firms, Table 4 presents the average change in public stockholder wealth associated with the initial proposal to go private. The common stock returns (two-day prediction errors) indicate that public stockholders experience substantial wealth increases, on average, when incumbent management proposes a return to private ownership status. The average change in stockholder wealth at announcement is $\overline{PE}_0 = 22.27$ percent. The associated t-statistic is $t = 41.57$, which indicates a significantly positive average wealth change at any conventional level of statistical significance.[42]

Table 4 indicates also that, on average, public stockholders experienced substantial wealth increases immediately prior to formal proposal. Similar price patterns have been observed in previous acquisition studies[43] and have been interpreted as attributable to leakage of information about the proposal itself.[44] This pattern suggests that the two-day average prediction error $\overline{PE}_0$ underestimates the wealth effects associated with proposal. Consequently, the cumulative average prediction error beginning early enough to capture any prior leakage may be a better measure of the effect on public stockholders. We chose to measure cumulative returns beginning with event day $t = -40$ based on Bradley's study of interfirm tender offers, which concluded that two calendar months were sufficient to capture any significant price effects of leakage.[45] Under this cumulative measure, public stockholders experienced a wealth increase of $\overline{CPE}(-40, 0) = 30.40$ percent associated with proposals to go private, which, again, is significantly positive at any conventional level ($t = 12.39$). Public stockholder gains are even more substantial when measured as the 56.31 percent average premium above market (as of two

[42] For four sample firms, trading was suspended at the time the proposal was announced but resumed no later than day $t = +7$. For these firms, Table 4 (and each subsequent table) adjusts "event time" by defining $t = 0$ as the first trading day following public announcement of a going-private proposal. If the four firms with trading suspensions are treated as having zero prediction errors at $t = 0$, then the announcement return is $\overline{PE}_0 = 19.10$ with $t = 33.97$, which continues to indicate a significantly positive wealth effect for public stockholders. Six other firms did not trade on event day $t = -2$, which, together with the four day 0–suspended firms, accounts for the fact that only sixty-two firms' returns are contained in the day $t = -2$ average in Table 4. We also computed a t-statistic for the two-day announcement period prediction errors that corrects for heterogeneity in return intervals. This t-statistic deflates each firm's $t = 0$ prediction error (where time 0 is defined as in Tables 4 and 6) by the square root of the number of two-day periods over which the firm's prediction error was computed. The square root adjustment corrects for heteroscedasticity (in the ten firms for which $t = 0$ prediction errors represent returns over a period exceeding two days) in a manner consistent with the GLS procedure for estimating market model parameters (see notes 38 and 39 *supra*). For the full sample and all subsamples tested, the adjusted t-statistics for $\overline{PE}_0$ were slightly smaller in absolute value than those reported in the text, but qualitatively identical. For example, the adjusted t-statistic for $\overline{PE}_0$ is 37.78 for the full sample of seventy-two initial proposals.

[43] Bradley, *supra* note 17.

[44] Consistent with this leakage interpretation, Arthur J. Keown & John M. Pinkerton, Merger Announcements and Insider Trading Activity: An Empirical Investigation, 36 J. Fin. 863 (1981), report evidence of unusually large trading volume in target firms' shares in the three weeks prior to merger proposals.

[45] Bradley, *supra* note 17.

months before proposal) that managers initially offered in the fifty-seven sample proposals involving strictly cash compensation.

According to the initial proposal test outlined in Section III, the gains-sharing hypothesis would be refuted if, on average, we observed no change or a decrease in public stockholder wealth when management proposed to go private. The evidence reported above indicates statistically significant average wealth increases at proposal and thus is consistent with the gains-sharing view. As we discussed in Section III, this test potentially contains an information bias in favor of the gains-sharing hypothesis. Because management's proposal may implicitly reveal that the firm's prospects as a *public* company are better than previously thought, the equity value change at proposal can overstate the marginal value of going private to public stockholders.

One way to assess the importance of any implicit information effect is to exploit the rational expectations condition that the open market price following proposal capitalizes both the value of going private (weighted by the probability of going private) and the value of the firm as a public concern (weighted by the probability of remaining public and including the value of any new information revealed by the bid). Given that success is not assured, observation that the with-information market price is, on average, below the cash offer price would provide evidence that going private would make the public stockholders better off. On the other hand, observation that the postannouncement market price exceeds the initial offer price would not necessarily indicate that public stockholders are harmed by the transaction. Because the initial offer price is frequently increased (twenty-one of our fifty-seven cash bids were subsequently increased,[46] while only two bids were subsequently lowered), the open market price following initial proposal should be bid up, possibly above the initial offer price, to reflect this prospect.

Two other factors potentially affect the interpretation of the spread between the initial offer and the with-information open market price. First, the open market price should incorporate a discount for the delay in receipt of the going-private compensation. Second, the open market price should include a premium for any cash dividends over the interval between initial proposal and consummation of the transaction. In the test presented below, the first factor will make going private appear more attractive while the second factor should partially offset this effect. Given these potentially confounding factors, the test that follows should be interpreted with caution.

For our sample, fifty-seven (of the seventy-two) firms announced a cash offer price at the time of initial proposal. For the fifty-seven cash bids, the

[46] Five of the twenty-one offer-price increases came in the form of revived bids.

average abnormal change in market value (measured from the close of trading on day t = −40 through proposal) was $\overline{CPE}$ (−38, 0) = 33.02 percent, which is *below* the 56.31 percent mean premium (measured relative to the t = −40 closing market price) management offered as going-private compensation. The offer price exceeded the with-information open market price (measured five trading days after proposal) by an average of 13.86 percent.[47] This price difference is significant at all conventional levels under the test statistic employed by Bradley[48] to assess the same relative price relationship for interfirm cash tender bids.[49] We also note that the offer price exceeded the with-information market price for fifty-one of the fifty-seven firms in our cash sample. All of this evidence is consistent with the hypothesis that the large wealth increases observed at initial proposal are not caused solely by new information about the firm's value as a public concern.

A Closer Look at Stockholder Returns at Initial Proposal

The statistics reported in Table 4 provide evidence of significant *average* wealth increases for public stockholders at initial proposal of a going-private transaction. The table also indicates that, for almost every firm (sixty-eight of seventy-two), stockholder wealth increased at $t = 0$. Of the four firms with negative prediction errors at $t = 0$, three experienced time 0 returns of less than 3 percent in absolute value (specifically, PE_0 = −2.14 percent, −0.72 percent, and −0.39 percent) following a period of substantial price appreciation (*CPE* (−40, −2) = 38.51 percent, 38.29 percent, and 26.48 percent, respectively). The remaining firm experienced large negative returns both at $t = 0$ and during the immediately preceding period (PE_0 = −22.12 percent and *CPE* (−40, −2) = −19.74 percent). For this firm, the press release announcing the going-private proposal also announced drilling difficulties with two oil well prospects. This press release raises the possibility that the negative returns were caused by bad news unrelated to the going-private proposal.

Table 5 provides corroborating evidence that going-private proposals

[47] On average, there were 146 trading days (126 median) between announcement and delisting for successful initial proposals. Given approximately twenty trading days per month, the average delay in payment is about 7.3 months (6.3 median). Thus, ignoring future offer-price increases and intermediate cash dividends, it would take a riskless interest rate of more than 22 percent per year to explain the 13.86 percent average spread between offer and market solely on the basis of payment timing.

[48] Bradley, *supra* note 17, at 364.

[49] For a given firm, let x represent the ratio of (i) the initial cash offer price minus the market price as of five trading days after proposal to (ii) the dividend-adjusted market price forty trading days before proposal. Letting $\bar{x}$ and $\sigma_{\bar{x}}$ represent the cross-sectional mean and associated standard deviation, the test statistic is $\bar{x}/\sigma_{\bar{x}}$ = 18.25 percent/1.97 percent = 9.26.

TABLE 5
FREQUENCY DISTRIBUTION OF ESTIMATED PUBLIC STOCKHOLDER WEALTH CHANGES ASSOCIATED WITH INITIAL GOING-PRIVATE PROPOSALS IN THE PERIOD 1973–80

PERCENTAGE RATE OF RETURN, *R*, ACCRUING TO PUBLIC STOCKHOLDERS	FULL SAMPLE OF SEVENTY-TWO INITIAL PROPOSALS: Firms with Two-Day Announcement Period Prediction Error, PE_0, in Specified Returns Interval	FULL SAMPLE OF SEVENTY-TWO INITIAL PROPOSALS: Firms with (Leakage Inclusive) Cumulative Prediction Error, *CPE* (−40, 0), in Specified Returns Interval	SUBSAMPLE OF FIFTY-SEVEN CASH PROPOSALS:* FIRMS WITH CASH-OFFER PREMIUMS† IN SPECIFIED RETURNS INTERVAL
110 < R	0	1	5
100 < R ≤ 110	0	0	0
90 < R ≤ 100	0	0	0
80 < R ≤ 90	2	1	5
70 < R ≤ 80	0	4	4
60 < R ≤ 70	1	1	7
50 < R ≤ 60	4	4	7
40 < R ≤ 50	3	8	13
30 < R ≤ 40	8	15	4
20 < R ≤ 30	13	16	5
10 < R ≤ 20	21	9	2
0 < R ≤ 10	16	6	3
−10 < R ≤ 0	3	5	2
−20 < R ≤ −10	0	1	0
R ≤ −20	1	1	0
Maximum (%)	89.94	137.53	200.00
Mean (%)	22.27	30.40	56.31
Median (%)	18.89	28.62	50.00
Minimum (%)	−22.12	−41.87	−8.91

*Excludes fifteen initial proposals either withdrawn before specific compensation was disclosed (four cases) or where noncash compensation (for example, a royalty trust interest or notes) was offered (eleven cases).

†Offer premium is defined here as the percentage by which the cash price offered by management (at the time of initial proposal) exceeded the (dividend-adjusted) market closing price forty trading days prior to proposal.

are associated with substantial positive stockholder wealth effects. The two middle columns of the table summarize the cross-sectional distributions of announcement period two-day prediction errors (PE_0) and cumulative prediction errors ($CPE\,(-40, 0)$) for the full sample of seventy-two firms making initial proposals. Both distributions indicate that in almost all cases public stockholder wealth increased at proposal, and that in most cases stockholder wealth increased by a strikingly large amount. For example, thirty-six of the seventy-two sample firms had cumulative prediction errors over day $t = -40$ through proposal in excess of 28.62 percent (the median $CPE\,(-40, 0)$), and nineteen of these had cumulative returns of more than 40 percent.

The last column in Table 5 reports offer premiums for the fifty-seven sample proposals involving strictly cash compensation. These premiums are defined as the price offered at initial proposal measured relative to the market price as of forty trading days before proposal. Dramatically large premiums characterize most firms in the cash subsample. Premiums of 50 percent or more were offered in twenty-eight (of fifty-seven) cases, 80 percent or greater premiums were offered in ten cases, and 110 percent or greater premiums were offered in five cases. One possible benchmark for assessing these going-private offer premiums is provided by Bradley and Jarrell and Bradley,[50] who documented average offer premiums of the same order of magnitude (49–56 percent, depending on sample period) for successful interfirm cash tender offers.[51]

Finally, Table 6 indicates that public stockholders experienced large (statistically significant) average wealth increases at proposal of both pure going-private transactions and leveraged buyouts. The table also reveals that public stockholders earned large positive returns whether or not management held a majority of the stock in the public firm. These observations indicate that the earlier inference in support of the gains-sharing hypothesis (drawn from the average wealth effect for the full sample) is also appropriate for these subsamples characterized by different (planned and existing) managerial ownership structures.

For successful proposals, Table 6 reveals no significant additional ab-

[50] Bradley, *supra* note 17, at 364; Gregg A. Jarrell & Michael Bradley, The Economic Effects of Federal and State Regulations of Cash Tender Offers, 23 J. Law & Econ. 371 (1980).

[51] Several factors dictate that the two figures are not strictly comparable. For example, interfirm tender offers involve two operating entities and thus may differ significantly from going-private transactions in the source and magnitude of potential productive gains. Another factor is that many interfirm tender offers are subject to prorating (because the bidder does not seek all shares), whereas, in going-private transactions, all publicly held shares are eligible to receive the premium offered. Finally, there are differences across samples in success rates and and potentially in time lags until payments are received.

TABLE 6

ESTIMATED AVERAGE STOCKHOLDER WEALTH EFFECTS FOR SAMPLE OF SEVENTY-TWO INITIAL GOING-PRIVATE PROPOSALS IN THE PERIOD 1973–80, PARTITIONED BY OFFER OUTCOME, EXTENT OF THIRD-PARTY PARTICIPATION, AND MANAGEMENT'S PRE-OFFER EQUITY OWNERSHIP PERCENTAGE

Sample Partitioning (Firms in Subsample; Making Cash Offers)	Sample Average Prediction Error (%)			Mean Cash Premium Offered to Public Stockholders (Relative to Dividend-adjusted Market Price Forty Trading Days before Proposal)
	At Announcement of Initial Proposal $\overline{PE}_0$ (t-Statistic)	From Two Months Prior through Proposal $\overline{CPE}$ (−40, 0) (t-Statistic)	Over Two Months following Proposal $\overline{CPE}$ (2, 40) (t-Statistic)	
Pure going privates (45;35)*	25.17 (34.94)	32.80 (9.94)	−2.38 (−.74)	54.49
Leveraged buyouts (23;22)	16.99 (20.66)	27.03 (7.17)	−.15 (−.04)	59.21
Management % ≥ 50 (39;32)†	27.04 (35.36)	35.37 (10.09)	−4.97 (−1.45)	57.67
Management % < 50 (33;25)	16.62 (21.94)	24.54 (7.07)	1.62 (.48)	54.52

Successful proposals (39;33)	21.09 (25.07)	28.41 (7.37)	.83 (.22)	55.18
Unsuccessful proposals (27;19)‡	19.11 (19.87)	29.61 (6.72)	−4.20 (−.98)	55.19
Successful, management % ⩾ 50 (19;17)	22.94 (19.76)	28.81 (5.42)	−1.48 (−.29)	47.70
Unsuccessful, management % ⩾ 50 (14;11)	25.28 (17.23)	39.31 (5.85)	−8.06 (−1.23)	68.96
Successful, management % < 50 (20;16)	19.33 (17.89)	28.03 (5.66)	2.69 (.56)	63.13
Unsuccessful, management % < 50 (13;8)	12.46 (12.01)	19.17 (4.03)	−.04 (−.01)	36.36

*The pure versus leveraged buyout partitioning excludes four initial proposals withdrawn before the transactional structure could be identified.

†Management % = management's pre-offer equity ownership percentage.

‡The unsuccessful subsample excludes five pending and one partly successful proposals (a tender offer that increased management ownership substantially but did not result in delisting).

normal stock price appreciation in the postannouncement period (contrary to what one would expect as the probability of success increased over time). For this subsample, we also calculated cumulative average prediction errors through day $t = 130$ and found no evidence of significant abnormal value changes ($\overline{CPE}$ (2, 130) = −0.89 percent, $t = -0.13$).[52] For unsuccessful offers, there is weak evidence of postannouncement abnormal stock price decline (which one would expect as the probability of success declined). A shortcoming of these tests is that because we do not know the precise timing of probability revision, we necessarily average multiple periods of normal returns into $\overline{CPE}$. The effect of this averaging (with added noise) is to make it more difficult to detect any abnormal returns.[53] In the next section we provide a more powerful test (for unsuccessful offers) that examines stockholder wealth changes at the time of proposal withdrawal.

Withdrawal Test

According to the gains-sharing hypothesis, public stockholder wealth will decrease, on average, when going-private proposals are withdrawn. To test this prediction, we employ the sample of eighteen firms for which we were able to identify clean withdrawal announcement dates.[54] The firms in the withdrawal sample are representative of the full sample in terms of the average stockholder wealth increase at initial proposal, management's ownership in the public firm, and the relative incidence of pure going-private and leveraged buyout proposals.[55]

[52] One possible explanation for the essentially zero abnormal return is that the benchmark normal return (estimated from the preannouncement period) is "too high" for returns accruing over the postannouncement period. The reason is that a credible promise to buy all publicly held shares at a fixed price effectively converts a residual cash flow interest into a fixed claim. Even without adjusting for such a risk shift, we observe *normal* stock price appreciation in the postannouncement period for the bulk of the sample proposals. For the thirty-three successful cash proposals, the open market price converged upward to an average of 96.5 percent of the final offer price at delisting. Thus, for the successful proposal row in Table 6, the gap between $\overline{CPE}$ (−40, +40) = 29.24 percent and the 55.18 percent mean cash offer premium does not indicate a failure of market prices to adjust to the cash offer price. Rather, the gap can be explained by (1) the time lag between proposal and outcome (which is typically greater than forty days), (2) the difference between compounded raw returns and summed abnormal returns, and (3) differences across the cash and noncash subsamples.

[53] Stephen J. Brown & Jerold B. Warner, Measuring Security Price Performance, 8 J. Fin. Econ. 205, n.32 (1980).

[54] See Section IV and note 31 *supra*.

[55] For the full sample of seventy-two firms, the two-day average prediction error at initial proposal is $\overline{PE}_0$ = 22.27 percent, the cumulative prediction error over the forty days prior through proposal is $\overline{CPE}$ (−40, 0) = 30.40 percent, and the average cash offer premium (measured relative to the market price forty days before proposal) is 56.31 percent. The

Table 7 presents the data required to test the prediction of a negative wealth effect at withdrawal. In particular, Part A of the table reports two-day average ($\overline{PE}$) and cumulative average ($\overline{CPE}$) prediction errors for the eighty-trading-day period surrounding withdrawal for the eighteen sample firms with clean withdrawal announcements. The two-day average announcement period prediction error is $\overline{PE}_0 = -8.88$ percent, which is statistically significant at all conventional levels ($t = -7.20$) and which is therefore consistent with the gains-sharing hypothesis.

Two points should be noted about the cumulative prediction errors in Part A of Table 7. First, the large positive average returns prior to withdrawal announcement ($\overline{CPE}(-40, -2) = 12.89$ percent, $t = 2.34$) can be explained by the fact that seven of the eighteen sample firms made their initial going-private proposals during this period. When these seven firms (and their positive proposal-related returns) are dropped from the withdrawal sample, the preannouncement return becomes insignificantly different from zero ($\overline{CPE}(-40, -2) = 1.20$ percent, $t = 0.16$). Second, although the postannouncement return is positive ($\overline{CPE}(2, 40) = 3.43$ percent), it is insignificantly so ($t = 0.62$) and thus is consistent with semistrong form market efficiency.

Complementary evidence supporting the gains-sharing view appears in Part B of Table 7, which presents the frequency distribution of prediction errors at withdrawal announcement. The median public stockholder wealth decline at withdrawal is -7.33 percent, which represents a substantial change over a two-day interval. Moreover, a negative wealth effect characterizes almost all sample firms: sixteen of the eighteen had negative prediction errors at withdrawal and the other two are trivially positive (0.06 percent and 0.07 percent). The conclusions are unchanged when the sample includes the initial withdrawal announcement for all twenty-two sample firms, (including those experiencing potentially confounding events at withdrawal announcement).[56] For this latter sample of twenty-two firms, $\overline{PE}_0 = -6.24$ percent, which is statistically significant at all conventional levels ($t = -6.07$). Seventeen of the twenty-two firms had negative prediction errors at withdrawal announcement. All of this evidence is consistent with the gains-sharing hypothesis.

---

corresponding figures are 20.72 percent, 35.57 percent, and 63.89 percent for the sample of eighteen withdrawals and 17.90 percent, 31.45 percent, and 62.09 percent for the sample of twenty-two withdrawals, which includes events confounded by the simultaneous release of other information. Management's mean (median) pre-offer ownership percentage is 47.41 percent (52.50 percent) for the sample of eighteen withdrawals compared with 45.20 percent (50.90 percent) for the full sample. The withdrawal sample contains 38.9 percent leveraged buyouts versus 31.9 percent for the full sample.

[56] See note 31 *supra*.

TABLE 7

A. Percentage Two-Day Average ($\overline{PE}$) and Cumulative Average ($\overline{CPE}$) Prediction Errors for the Eighty-Day Period Centered around Announcement of a Going-Private Withdrawal: Eighteen Firms in the Period 1973–80

Trading Days	$\overline{PE}$(%)	$\overline{CPE}$(%)	Positive:Negative Two-Day Prediction Errors
−40	1.41	1.41	9:9
−30	−1.21	−.41	7:10
−20	−.22	8.80	8:10
−18	.48	9.28	8:10
−16	.05	9.32	8:10
−14	−.28	9.04	9:9
−12	2.15	11.20	9:9
−10	1.40	12.60	10:8
− 8	.24	12.84	9:8
− 6	−.46	12.38	8:8
− 4	2.47	14.86	8:9
− 2	−1.97	12.89	6:10
0	−8.88	4.00	2:16
+ 2	.39	4.39	13:5
+ 4	1.02	5.41	10:8
+ 6	−1.22	4.19	9:9
+ 8	.48	4.67	8:10
+10	.64	5.30	10:8
+12	−.33	4.98	7:11
+14	.25	5.23	9:9
+16	1.90	7.12	9:9
+18	−1.43	5.70	5:13
+20	−.46	5.24	9:9
+30	1.72	8.84	10:8
+40	−.84	7.43	8.10

B. Frequency Distribution of Two-Day Announcement Period Prediction Errors PE_0 (%) at Announcement of Proposal Withdrawal

		Number of Firms
$0 < PE_0$		2
$-5 < PE_0 \leq 0$		5
$-10 < PE_0 \leq -5$		4
$-15 < PE_0 \leq -10$		4
$-20 < PE_0 \leq -15$		2
$PE_0 \leq -20$		1
Maximum PE_0 (%)	.07	
Median PE_0 (%)	−7.33	
Minimum PE_0 (%)	−28.58	

In addition, seventeen of the twenty-two firms in the withdrawal sample had announced a cash offer price before the withdrawal announcement. Of these seventeen firms, thirteen had open market share prices below the cash offer price immediately before withdrawal. This price relationship suggests that going private would have made the outside stockholders in these firms better off than they would be under public ownership. Evidently, the management group believed that to pursue the proposal would not be in its best interests. Possible reasons for withdrawing a proposal are that (i) managers learned bad news about the firm's future prospects,[57] (ii) managers discovered that litigation would result in greater than expected legal fees, and/or (iii) disagreements arose within the management group over the private firm's planned ownership structure or the acceptability of available debt financing terms. Unfortunately, publicly available data do not allow us to distinguish among these potential explanations.

Of the four firms in the withdrawal sample for which the market price exceeded the cash offer price, one case stands out clearly. For this firm, the market price immediately before withdrawal was 217 percent above the offer price. The market price immediately following withdrawal also exceeded the offer price by a substantial amount. Management controlled 68 percent of the votes (more than the 66⅔ percent required by statute to approve the transaction) and had announced its intention to vote for the proposed merger. However, before withdrawal, the transaction was enjoined in the courts and the withdrawal announcement indicated that management did not intend to pursue the issue. In this case, at least, the legal system apparently deterred a going-private transaction at terms which were unattractive to public stockholders.

Finally, for each firm in the withdrawal sample, we calculated the cumulative prediction error, beginning forty trading days before initial proposal and ending at withdrawal. Net of the substantial decline at withdrawal, the average cumulative prediction error is 21.89 percent.[58] As Table 7 indicates, this net positive return is maintained through forty trading days after withdrawal. There are at least three potential (not mutually exclusive) explanations for the positive returns net of both proposal and withdrawal announcement effects. First, the return may include a permanent upward revaluation of the firm's prospects as a public company. Second, the return may incorporate a positive probability that man-

[57] But see Section III *supra*.

[58] As explained in note 31 *supra*, there were two firms for which we identified a withdrawal date on the second proposal, but not the first. The 21.89 percent average figure excludes these two firms and thus is based on the cumulative prediction errors surrounding the initial proposal and withdrawal for the remaining twenty firms.

agers will revive the proposal to go private at a premium over market. Third, the return may capitalize the prospect that another party will offer to acquire the firm because it is now apparent that substantial benefits can be realized by changing the firm's organizational structure. Whatever the explanation, the evidence indicates that although going private appeared to be the preferred alternative for public stockholders, the withdrawal left them wealthier on average than they were before the initial proposal.

VII. Summary

In a going-private transaction, the full equity interest in a public corporation is acquired by an incumbent management group. Going-private transactions are commonly labeled minority freezeouts, since in the typical case management already owns the majority of outstanding shares in the public corporation and the minority stockholders are "cashed out" of their investment in the firm. Because management is both purchaser of the public shares and agent for the sellers, going private frequently evokes charges of unfair treatment of minority stockholders. Indeed, some members of the legal community have called for a per se prohibition of these transactions based on the assertion that any productive gain from going private is small while the potential for exploitation of minority stockholders is large.

On the other hand, going private can generate significant productive gains through savings of registration and other public ownership expenses, and through improved incentives for corporate decision makers under private ownership. Moreover, the U.S. legal system provides minority stockholders with certain rights that should enable them to capture a positive share of the productive gains from going private. We tested this gains-sharing hypothesis by examining the effect on public stockholder wealth (open market share values) of (i) public announcement of going-private proposals by seventy-two Amex- and NYSE-listed firms during 1973–80 and (ii) withdrawal of going-private proposals by a subset of these firms. The gains-sharing hypothesis predicts positive wealth changes for public stockholders associated with i and negative wealth effects associated with ii.

The results of both tests are consistent with the gains-sharing hypothesis. In the two days surrounding the initial proposal to go private, the wealth of public stockholders increased by an average of 22.27 percent. Including the effects of preproposal leakage, public stockholder wealth increased an average of 30.40 percent at proposal. In contrast, stockholder wealth decreased an average of 8.88 percent at withdrawal of going-private proposals. All of these average wealth effects are significantly different from zero (at very high levels) under standard statistical tests for abnormal share price changes. Moreover, for almost every firm within each sample, the direction of change in stockholder wealth is the same as that of the average.

The principal criticism applied to going-private transactions is based on the absence of arms-length negotiation between management as purchaser of the public stock interest and management as agent for the selling public stockholders. In contrast, the typical interfirm merger or tender offer is characterized by arms-length bargaining between buyer and seller. Thus, it is worth noting that the 30 percent average stockholder wealth increase we have documented for going-private transactions is the same order of magnitude as the 24 percent average wealth increase experienced by target stockholders in merger transactions[59] and the 40 percent average wealth increase experienced by target stockholders in successful interfirm cash tender bids.[60] Moreover, the 56 percent average premium above market offered by management in cash going-private proposals compares favorably with the 49–56 percent average offer premiums reported in the interfirm cash tender offer studies by Bradley and Jarrell and Bradley.[61] Although we hesitate to push such cross-sectional comparisons too far, we believe that the similarity of stockholder gains observed in going-private and arms-length acquisitions suggests that, for our sample firms, going-private transactions did not result in the systematic exploitation of minority stockholders.

[59] Dodd, *supra* note 22, at 115.

[60] Bradley, *supra* note 17, at n.21; Jarrell & Bradley, *supra* note 50, at 389.

[61] Bradley, *supra* note 17; Jarrell & Bradley, *supra* note 50.

[21]

Journal of Financial Economics 24 (1989) 217–254. North-Holland

THE EFFECTS OF MANAGEMENT BUYOUTS ON OPERATING PERFORMANCE AND VALUE

Steven KAPLAN*

University of Chicago, Chicago, IL 60637, USA

Received October 1988, final version received August 1989

This paper presents evidence on changes in operating results for a sample of 76 large management buyouts of public companies completed between 1980 and 1986. In the three years after the buyout, these companies experience increases in operating income (before depreciation), decreases in capital expenditures, and increases in net cash flow. Consistent with the operating changes, the mean and median increases in market value (adjusted for market returns) are 96% and 77% from two months before the buyout announcement to the post-buyout sale. The evidence suggests the operating changes are due to improved incentives rather than layoffs or managerial exploitation of shareholders through inside information.

1. Introduction

Management buyouts (MBOs) have increased in both size and number in recent years. Before 1980, MBOs were infrequent and usually involved smaller companies. According to the Joint Committee on Taxation (1989), MBOs and third-party leveraged buyouts accounted for approximately 20% of all takeover activity in the United States between 1985 and 1987. In the typical MBO, buyout investors, including some of the firm's current managers, pay prebuyout shareholders a premium of more than 40% above the prevailing market price to take the company private [see DeAngelo, DeAngelo, and Rice (1984), Marais, Schipper, and Smith (1989), and my results which follow]. Several sources of wealth increases to shareholders and buyout investors are frequently mentioned: reduced agency costs and new incentives, wealth transfers

*I wish to thank Paul Asquith, Alan Auerbach, George Baker, Richard Caves, Eugene Fama, Robert Glauber, Paul Healy, Richard Leftwich, Krishna Palepu, Andrei Shleifer, Robert Vishny, Karen Wruck, and seminar participants at the Harvard Business School, Sloan School, University of Rochester, University of Chicago, University of Michigan, University of Southern California, and New York University for comments on earlier versions of this paper. Harry DeAngelo (the referee) and Richard Ruback (the editor) were particularly helpful in improving the paper. I especially would like to thank my dissertation chairman, Michael Jensen, for his generous support throughout. Financial support was provided by the Graduate School of Business, University of Chicago and by the Division of Research, Harvard Business School.

from employees and public bondholders to the investor group, information held by managers that is not known by public shareholders, and tax advantages.[1] The first three of these nonmutually exclusive explanations for buyout gains predict that operating cash flows increase after the buyout.

Jensen (1986, 1988) argues that buyouts combine several powerful incentives that increase efficiency and value. Large debt-service payments force managers to find ways to generate cash and prevent them from wasting resources. Larger equity stakes give managers an incentive to find ways to pay off the debt while increasing value. Finally, the buyout specialist, who structures the transaction, monitors and controls the management team. According to this reduced-agency-cost or new-incentive hypothesis, the new incentives lead to increases in operating income and operating margins as well as reductions in wasteful capital expenditures.

Shleifer and Summers (1988) suggest that buyouts and takeovers transfer wealth to investors by laying off employees or reducing their wages. This employee-wealth-transfer hypothesis argues that operating income increases after the buyout at the expense of employee layoffs and wage reductions.

Lowenstein (1985) argues that managers have information about the company that is not available to other bidders. For example, at the time of the buyout announcement, managers may know that cash flows will be higher than the market expects. Because they have private information, managers can buy the company for less than a similarly informed bidder would be willing to pay, and informed shareholders would be willing to accept. This information-advantage or underpricing hypothesis also predicts that operating income is unusually high after the buyout.

This paper analyzes a sample of 76 management buyouts completed between 1980 and 1986 for evidence on whether the operating changes predicted by these hypotheses occur. The distinguishing feature of the analysis is the use of post-buyout information in addition to the pre-buyout information used in previous studies.

The 48 buyout companies with post-buyout financial data experience increases in operating income (before depreciation) and net cash flow as well as reductions in capital expenditures. Operating income, measured net of industry changes, is essentially unchanged in the first two post-buyout years and 24% higher in the third year. The change in operating income, however, does not control for post-buyout divestitures, which may lead the measured change in operating income to underestimate the true change. I measure operating income in relation to both assets and sales to control for post-buyout asset divestitures and acquisitions. The increases in both ratios are significantly greater than the industry changes, by approximately 20%.

[1]DeAngelo and DeAngelo (1987) and Shleifer and Vishny (1988) provide detailed descriptions of these sources of wealth gains.

The median net cash flow (the difference between operating income and capital expenditures), net of industry changes, in the first three post-buyout years is 22.0%, 43.1%, and 80.5% larger than in the last pre-buyout year. Similarly, buyout company increases in net cash flow to assets and to sales are significantly greater than the industry changes by approximately 50%.

The results for post-buyout operating changes are qualitatively similar to those in Smith (1989), who finds the buyout firms realize increases in (pre-tax) operating cash flow to operating assets as well as decreases in capital expenditures to sales.

The paper then considers whether the accounting changes represent valuable economic changes. To do so, I estimate market-adjusted returns to pre-buyout public shareholders and to post-buyout investors in those companies that can be valued after the buyout. Consistent with the results for operating changes, pre-buyout and post-buyout investors earn a median total market-adjusted return of 77.0% (mean = 96.0%). Pre-buyout public shareholders earn a median market-adjusted return of 37.2% (mean = 37.9%) and investors in post-buyout capital earn a median market-adjusted return of 28.0% (mean = 41.9%).

The results for post-buyout operating changes and for the total returns to management buyouts suggest that management buyouts are associated with valuable operating improvements. The remainder of the paper considers three hypotheses about the causes of the operating changes and value increases.

Employee-wealth-transfer hypothesis: Although some turnover may occur, the median change in employment for the buyout companies is 0.9%. This measure treats decreases in the labor force caused by divestitures as decreases in employment. For a subsample of buyouts that do not make large post-buyout divestitures, employment increases, by a median of 4.9%. The industry-adjusted change for this subsample is negative, but not significant. These results are not consistent with the notion that large numbers of employees are fired after buyouts. Because I do not have wage data, I cannot test for wage reductions.

Information-advantage or underpricing hypothesis: Although I cannot test this hypothesis explicitly, I examine several indirect pieces of evidence. First, I consider the pre-buyout shareholdings of informed parties (nonparticipating officers and directors as well as hostile third parties) who sell their shares into the buyout and do not invest in the equity of the post-buyout company. The informed nonparticipants hold a median $16.97 million or 10% of the equity of the pre-buyout company. If the buyout is underpriced, these nonparticipants irrationally sell their shares if they have the same information as the participating management team. Second, during the sample period, 46 proposed management buyouts were not completed. In 34 of these cases, the company was taken over by a different bidder. This suggests that managers and investors who propose a buyout must contend with an active market for corporate control. Third, I compare the pre-buyout financial projections managers give to shareholders with the actual post-buyout realizations. There is no evidence that the projections are low; in fact, they tend to be higher than future realizations. Finally, management turnover at the time of the buyouts is unusually high. None of these results supports underpricing.

Reduced-agency-cost or new-incentive hypothesis: As I do for the underpricing hypothesis, I examine indirect evidence concerning the new-incentive hypothesis. The equity holdings of the management team increase from a median of 5.88% to 22.63%. The increase is larger for managers other than the two top officers than the increase for the two top officers. These findings are consistent with new incentives having an important role in management buyouts.

In general, the results in this paper favor the reduced-agency-cost or new-incentive hypothesis over the employee-wealth-transfer and information-advantage hypotheses as explanations for post-buyout operating changes and wealth increases.

This paper complements previous work on sources of wealth gains in management buyouts. Kaplan (1989) and Schipper and Smith (1988) examine the value of tax benefits in management buyouts. Kaplan estimates tax benefits to have a lower bound of 21% and an upper bound of 143% of the premium paid to pre-buyout shareholders. Both Kaplan and Schipper and Smith argue that tax benefits are unlikely to be the entire source of value in management buyouts. In fact, Jensen, Kaplan, and Stiglin (1989) estimate that management buyouts increase net tax revenues under 1989 tax law. Marais, Schipper, and Smith (1989) examine wealth transfers from bondholders in a sample of MBOs announced between 1974 and 1985 and find minimal transfers on average.

The paper proceeds as follows. Section 2 describes the sample. Section 3 presents evidence on post-buyout operating changes. Section 4 measures returns to pre-buyout shareholders and post-buyout investors. Section 5 presents evidence on post-buyout changes in employment. Section 6 presents evidence on the information and reduced-agency-cost hypothesis. Section 7 concludes with a summary and discussion of the results.

2. Sample description

2.1. MBO companies

The sample of management buyouts is taken from companies delisted from the New York or American Stock Exchange during the period 1980–1985 and from companies listed as acquisitions (completed and pending) in W.T.

Grimm's Mergerstat Review from 1980 to 1985. The final sample satisfies the following criteria:

(1) The *Wall Street Journal* (*WSJ*) contains an announcement that the company proposes to go private.
(2) The newly private firm is an independent entity, not a subsidiary of another private company.[2]
(3) The proxy statement or *WSJ* confirms that at least one member of the incumbent management team obtains an equity interest in the new private firm.
(4) The total transaction value exceeds $50 million.[3]

Seventy-six companies, in buyouts completed between 1980 and 1986, meet these criteria. All 76 buyouts were announced in the period 1979–1985. Several buyouts listed as pending in 1985 were completed in 1986. Panel A of table 1 summarizes the distribution of these buyout announcements over time.

2.2. Pre-buyout data

For each successful MBO, information describing the transactions is taken from proxy, 10-K, 13-E, and 14-D statements and from the *WSJ*.[4] Stock prices two months before the buyout is announced and at delisting are obtained from Standard & Poor's *Daily Stock Price Record*. Other financial data are obtained from the COMPUSTAT Tapes.

2.3. Post-buyout data

Post-buyout information is available for 48 of the 76 MBOs in the *WSJ*, the list of SEC filing companies available from *Disclosure*, and *Going Public: The IPO Reporter*. Twenty-eight of these companies filed 10-Ks with the SEC because they had publicly held debt or preferred stock outstanding; nine companies issued publicly traded equity and filed offering prospectuses; two companies filed initial public offering prospectuses, but choose not to issue public equity; five companies were purchased by other publicly traded compa-

[2] Most of the sample companies filed a detailed proxy statement describing the proposed buyout. Proxy statements for leveraged buyouts with third-party buyers generally do not provide as much detail.

[3] The intent of this size criterion is to restrict the sample to larger, more fully disclosed transactions. This criterion also lowers the likelihood that the reduction of regulatory costs is a major source of value. Savings on the costs of preparing documents for public shareholders and the SEC are likely to be small in relation to value in these transactions.

[4] One company did not have any of these statements. The information used for this paper was obtained from the *Wall Street Journal* article.

Table 1

Distribution of 76 management buyouts completed in the period 1980–1986 by year, availability of post-buyout information, and information source.[a]

Panel A: Announcement dates of successful MBO proposals greater than $50 MM by year

	1979	1980	1981	1982	1983	1984	1985	Total
All firms	1	3	4	13	16	21	18	76
Firms with post-buyout data	0	1	3	7	9	15	13	48

Panel B: MBOs by original and latest source of post-buyout information[b]

	10-K report[c]	IPO filing[d]	Sale[e]	Releveraging filing[f]	Total
Original source of data	28	11	5	4	48
Latest source of data	14	13	14	7	48

[a]Firms included in the sample meet the following criteria: (1) The *Wall Street Journal* contains an announcement that the company proposed to go private; (2) the newly private firm is an independent entity; (3) the proxy statement or the *Wall Street Journal* confirms that at least one member of incumbent management will obtain an equity interest in the newly private firm; (4) the total transaction value exceeds $50 million. Companies were identified by (1) examining all companies delisted from the New York and American Stock Exchanges from 1980 to 1985 and (2) examining W.T. Grimm's Mergerstat Review from 1980 to 1985.

[b]Original source of data refers to the initial source of post-buyout information for a buyout company. Latest source of data refers to the most recent source of data or information for a buyout company.

[c]Company is in sample because it has publicly traded debt and files 10-K reports with the SEC.

[d]Company is in sample because it filed an initial public offering (IPO) prospectus after the buyout. After IPO, these companies file annual and 10-K reports.

[e]Company is in sample because it was purchased by a public company. The purchaser must file an 8-K report with the SEC describing its purchase.

[f]Company is in sample because it filed a prospectus to borrow money in the public bond markets after the buyout (usually to releverage the buyout company). After the debt issue, the company must file 10-K reports with the SEC.

nies; and four companies issued new publicly held debt to finance a releveraging. In addition to these 48 companies, one company made an initial public offering, but did not provide usable financial information; one company privately releveraged (twice); three companies were sold, but did not file usable public financial information; and one company filed for bankruptcy, but did not provide public financial information. Finally, 22 of 76 companies did not file a 10-K, had not gone public or bankrupt, and, apparently, had not been sold. Panel B of table 1 summarizes this information. The evidence presented in this paper reflects operating results through the end of fiscal year 1987.

2.4. Summary information and statistics

Table 2 provides summary information on the 76 sample buyout companies. The companies have a median equity market value of $253.8 million at the

Table 2

Summary statistics for size, premium, and leverage for 76 management buyouts[a] completed in the period 1980–1986 (dollars in millions).

Variable	Median	Mean	Std. dev.	N
Book value of total assets	$284.00	$525.8	$1081.0	76
Total equity value[b]	$253.8	$523.8	$ 889.1	76
Premium[c]	42.3%	45.9%	23.7%	76
Market-adjusted premium[d]	34.2%	32.3%	21.6%	76
Fees (% of market value of equity two months before proposal)	4.65%	5.26%	2.47%	70
Pre-buyout book value of total debt as percentage of value of total capital at time of buyout[e]	18.8%	20.7%	14.8%	76
Post-buyout book value of total debt as percentage of value of total capital at time of buyout[e]	87.8%	85.6%	14.3%	75
Post-buyout book value of new buyout debt as percentage of market value of equity two months before proposal	115.5%	122.1%	35.4%	75

[a] Financial and ownership data were obtained from proxy, 13-E, and 14-D statements describing the management buyouts. Stock price data were obtained from Standard and Poor's *Daily Stock Price Record*.

[b] Equity value is the value of all outstanding equity at the price paid to complete the buyout.

[c] Premium is calculated as the percentage difference between the final buyout price paid to pre-buyout shareholders and the value of the equity two months before the proposal.

[d] Market-adjusted premium equals [(1 + Premium)/(1 + Market adjustment)] – 1, where the market adjustment is the return to a portfolio with the same systematic risk over the same period.

[e] Value of total capital at the buyout is calculated as the sum of (1) the final buyout equity value, (2) the pre-buyout book value of debt, and (3) the pre-buyout book value of preferred stock.

time of the buyout. Pre-buyout shareholders of MBOs earn a median premium of 42.3%, where the premium equals the difference between the final purchase price of the equity in the MBO and the market price two months before the initial announcement.[5] [An analysis of excess returns suggests that the stock price begins to rise two months prior to the bid, either in anticipation of an MBO or because of hostile pressure.] In those cases where an MBO proposal followed a hostile takeover bid, the date of the hostile bid is considered the announcement date. The results also show that the buyouts experience very large increases in debt. The median ratio of (the book value of) pre-buyout debt to total capital at the buyout[6] equals 18.8%. The median ratio of post-buyout debt to total capital increases to 88.4%.

[5] Event-study methodology, which is not presented here, is consistent with these results. The median abnormal return from 40 trading days before through 60 days after the proposal is approximately 26%.

[6] Total capital equals the market value of equity (based on the buyout price) plus the pre-buyout book values of total debt and preferred stock.

3. Evidence on post-buyout operating cash flows

This section examines operating cash flows during the first three years after the buyout for the 48 companies in the sample with post-buyout financial information.

3.1. Methodology

The analyses focus on changes in three cash-flow variables:

(1) *Operating income* (*before depreciation*), which equals net sales less cost of goods sold and selling, general, and administrative expenses before depreciation, depletion, and amortization are deducted. This is the definition for Compustat data item A13. Operating income measures the cash generated from buyout company operations before depreciation, interest, or taxes. My calculations as well as Compustat's do not include gains or losses from sales of divisions or assets. All three hypotheses described in the introduction suggest that buyout companies experience increases in operating income.

(2) *Capital expenditures* (including capitalized leases), which measures new investment by the buyout company. It does not include acquisitions or receipts from divestitures. This definition is the same as that for Compustat data item A128. The reduced-agency-cost hypothesis [presented as free-cash-flow theory in Jensen (1986, 1988)] argues that buyout companies previously were investing in negative net present value projects. According to this hypothesis, reductions in capital expenditures increase company profitability and value.

(3) *Net* (*operating*) *cash flow*, which equals operating income before depreciation minus capital expenditures. Net cash flow measures the net cash produced from a company's operations before depreciation, interest, and taxes.[7] Net cash flow would be the primary component of the numerator in a net present value analysis to value a buyout company. A permanent increase in net cash flow, therefore, should lead to an increase in value.

The three cash-flow variables are all measured before taxes. This is important because buyouts have large effects on the taxes paid by buyout companies [see Kaplan (1989)]. Managerial operating decisions, not taxes or financial decisions, affect the three cash-flow variables analyzed in this section.

The analyses measure the percentage differences or changes in the cash-flow variables in the first three full years after the buyout (years +1, +2, and +3) compared to the last fiscal year before the buyout (year −1).[8] Results for year 0, the fiscal year that includes both pre- and post-buyout operations, are not presented here because they are difficult to interpret as pre- or post-buyout

[7]This measure does not include changes in working capital. Working-capital changes are not available for several companies and are difficult to interpret in the presence of assets sales in other buyouts.

[8]This method is similar to that used by Healy and Palepu (1988) and DeAngelo (1988).

performance. [Furthermore, measured operating income in year 0 is biased downward because of buyout-related fees and inventory write-ups.] To control for economy-wide and industry effects, the analyses also present an industry-adjusted percentage change in the cash flows. The industry-adjusted change equals the percentage change in the cash-flow variable for the buyout company minus the median percentage change over the relevant period for all firms in the same industry.

The firms in the same industry as the buyout company are those that have (1) the same four-digit SIC code on *Standard and Poor's Compustat Industrial and Research* tapes (comparisons are made at the three-digit level and then at the two-digit level when fewer than three industry matches are found) and (2) a total capital value of at least $40 million at the end of the year before the buyout.[9]

I measure each cash-flow variable in three ways: (1) in levels, (2) as a fraction of end-of-period total assets, and (3) as a fraction of annual sales. Each of these measures is imperfect. If the post-buyout companies pursue the same growth, divestiture, and acquisition strategies as the control firms, the industry-adjusted change in levels would be the appropriate measure of abnormal performance. Post-buyout acquisition and divestiture activity, however, affects the measured changes in the levels. If the buyout companies divest more or grow more slowly than the control companies, changes in operating income and capital expenditures will be underestimated.

I partially control for divestitures by using restated financial information when post-buyout financial statements provide pre-buyout financial data restated for divestitures. Only 5 of 48 buyouts explicitly restate pre-buyout results to be comparable to post-buyout results, however. At the same time, at least 20 of the 48 buyouts divest operations valued at more than 5% of the value of the going-private transaction.[10] I use the caveat, at least, because it is not always possible to determine when and at what price a divestiture has occurred.

Dividing the annual cash-flow variables by year-end total assets (adjusted for buyout accounting changes) or by annual sales partially controls for divestitures and differences in growth. A year's cash-flow variables are based on the same continuing operations as year-end total assets and the year's sales. In a loose sense, these variables measure return on assets and return on sales. They can be interpreted as measuring the efficiency with which the buyout firms use a given amount of assets or sales.

[9]All of the buyout companies have a total capital value of at least $40 million at the end of year −1. This criterion places a similar size restriction on the control sample.

[10]The results that follow are similar for the subsample of buyouts that excludes the 20 firms with post-buyout divestitures valued at more than 5% of the value of the going-private transaction. They are not presented separately.

For most of the buyouts, buyout accounting leads to a change (usually an increase) in the book value of the assets, representing the difference between the market value of equity (the purchase price) and the book value. To make intertemporal comparisons meaningful, I adjust pre-buyout assets by the size of the buyout-induced accounting change in assets, which is usually provided in the proxy statement describing the buyout. When the change in book value of assets is not provided, it is estimated as the difference between the buyout purchase price of equity and the pre-buyout book value. It is not necessary to make any adjustment to pre-buyout sales.

Even measuring the variables as a fraction of total assets or annual sales, however, is subject to criticism. For example, if MBOs tend to sell unprofitable divisions, measured operating income and net cash flow divided by total assets or by sales may increase without any real change having taken place.

The results for medians (and Wilcoxon signed rank tests) are presented rather than for means (and Student *t*-tests) to control for outliers that dominate the means in some of the small samples analyzed. The results for means are similar, and usually larger in absolute value. All significance levels are based on two-tailed tests. This approach is conservative and implicitly assumes a null hypothesis that post-buyout cash flows equal pre-buyout cash flows. Obviously, the results would be more significant if one-tailed tests were applied.

3.2. *Operating income*

Table 3 summarizes the changes in operating income (before depreciation). Panel A shows that the median increases are 15.6%, 30.7%, and 42.0%, in years +1, +2, and +3 in comparison with year −1. Measured net of industry changes, operating income is essentially unchanged in the first two post-buyout years and 24.1% higher in the third year. However, as discussed above the change for many buyout companies will be downward biased because many observations are not restated to take account of post-buyout divestitures. Similarly, it is likely that the change in operating income for many control firms is upward biased because control company observations are not restated to take account of acquisitions. (This will be true if the operating income of control firm acquisitions exceeds that of control firm divestitures.) Consistent with this, I find (but do not present in the table) that the industry-adjusted percentage changes in sales of the buyout companies are −7.7%, −6.0%, and 2.7% in years +1, +2, and +3. The decreases in years +1 and +2 are significant at the 1% level. The buyout companies grow slower at first than the industry controls.

Changes in operating income as a percentage of assets and as a percentage of sales partially control for differences in divestitures and acquisitions for both the buyout and control companies. Panel B shows that industry-adjusted

Table 3

Effect of management buyouts on operating income.

Median percentage change and industry-adjusted change in operating income, in operating income as a percentage of assets, and in operating income as a percentage of sales for 48 management buyouts completed in 1980–1986. Operating income equals net sales less cost of goods sold and selling, general, and administrative expenses before deducting depreciation and amortization. Year −1 is the fiscal year ending prior to buyout completion. Year +1 is the first full fiscal year of post-buyout operations. Significance levels are based on two-tailed Wilcoxon signed rank tests.

	From year i to year j			
Cash-flow measure	−2 to −1	−1 to +1	−1 to +2	−1 to +3
A. Operating income[a]	$N=48$	$N=45$	$N=37$	$N=19$
Percentage change	11.4%[c]	15.6%[c]	30.7%[c]	42.0%[c]
Industry-adjusted percentage change[b]	−1.2	−2.70	0.7	24.1
B. Operating income/assets	$N=46$	$N=42$	$N=34$	$N=15$
Percentage change	5.9	13.7[c]	20.1[c]	14.6[d]
Industry-adjusted percentage change[b]	5.0	16.6[c]	36.1[c]	21.3[d]
Level (median) at year −1: 13.1%				
C. Operating income/sales	$N=48$	$N=45$	$N=37$	$N=19$
Percentage change	−1.7	7.1[c]	11.9[c]	19.3[c]
Industry-adjusted percentage change[b]	−1.9	12.4[c]	23.3[c]	34.8[c]
Level (median) at year −1: 10.9%				

[a] Data for year −1 are obtained from post-buyout financial statements when available and from proxy statements describing the buyouts otherwise. Panels B and C use data only from proxy statements.

[b] Industry-adjusted change for a given period equals the difference between the change for the buyout company and the median change for a sample of companies in the same industry during that period.

[c] Significant at 1% level.

[d] Significant at 5% level.

increases in operating income to assets are 16.6%, 36.1%, and 21.3% in years +1, +2, and +3 relative to year −1. Similarly, panel C shows that buyout company operating margins, the ratio of operating income to sales, increase after the buyout. The increases are significantly greater than those of their industry counterparts, by 12.4%, 23.3%, and 34.8% in the first three years after the buyout. The results in panels B and C suggest that the buyout companies have significantly better operating returns on assets and on sales than their industry counterparts.

In addition, the results in table 3 underestimate the true change in operating income in year +1 because most MBOs write up the book value of their inventories at the time of the buyout. This 'paper' inventory write-up is expensed in the partial and first full years after the buyout. As a result, cost of goods sold is artificially high and the measured change in operating income during these periods underestimates the true change.

For the 25 companies that report the inventory write-up, the median write-up equals 12.3% of inventory (at the end of the year before the buyout), which equals 10.9% of operating income in that year. Although not reported in a separate table, the buyout companies reduce their inventory to sales ratio by approximately 10% in the year after the buyout. The post-buyout reduction in inventory is consistent with both improved inventory management and the expensing of the 'paper' inventory write-up. This suggests that the actual change in operating income in year +1 is potentially greater than the measured change by up to 10.9% (the amount of the paper inventory write-up).

The results in table 3 are consistent with better post-buyout operating performance. The increases would also occur, however, if buyout company managers use accounting slack to reduce measured operating income before the buyout. According to this view, the managers can purchase the company for less than its true value, and benefit from a measured increase in operating income after the buyout. DeAngelo (1986) examines a sample of management buyouts and finds no evidence of unusually negative earnings in the year before the buyout. Similarly, table 3 shows that the buyout companies experience small and statistically insignificant changes in all three measures of industry-adjusted operating income from year −2 to year −1. This result is consistent with managerial reduction of measured operating income only if the buyout companies would have been above-average performers without accounting manipulations. With such manipulations, these companies are measured as average performers. Managerial manipulation is also consistent with the results if managers consciously begin to reduce operating income two years before the buyout. Section 6 presents evidence on changes in insider shareholdings at the buyout and on management turnover that is not consistent with this managerial manipulation view.

3.3. Capital expenditures

Table 4 reports changes in capital expenditures. Panel A finds that the buyout companies reduce their level of capital expenditures in years +1, +2, and +3 relative to year −1. None of these reductions, however, is significant. The industry-adjusted changes in capital expenditures, however, are very negative, equal to −35.9%, −32.6%, and −64.4% for years +1, +2, and +3 compared with year −1. These results are significant in years +1 and +2. As with operating income, the large decreases in capital expenditures may be caused by a failure to take divestitures and acquisitions fully into account.

The results in panels B and C for capital expenditures as a percentage of assets and sales are similar to those found in panel A although the industry-adjusted changes are smaller. Nevertheless, the percentage changes and the industry-adjusted changes in the two ratios are all negative.

Table 4

Effect of management buyouts on capital expenditures.

Median percentage change and industry-adjusted change in capital expenditures, in capital expenditures as a percentage of assets, and in capital expenditures as a percentage of sales for 48 management buyouts completed in 1980–1986. Year −1 is the fiscal year ending prior to buyout completion. Year +1 is the first full fiscal year of post-buyout operations. Significance levels are based on two-tailed Wilcoxon signed rank tests.

Cash-flow measure	From year i to year j			
	−2 to −1	−1 to +1	−1 to +2	−1 to +3
A. Capital expenditures[a]	$N = 48$	$N = 39$	$N = 32$	$N = 14$
Percentage change	−1.5%	−21.1%	−21.4%	−6.9%
Industry-adjusted percentage change[b]	−7.9[d]	−35.9[c]	−32.6[d]	−64.4
B. Capital expenditures/Assets	$N = 46$	$N = 40$	$N = 34$	$N = 13$
Percentage change	−8.5	−11.9[d]	−25.4[d]	−24.5
Industry-adjusted percentage change[b]	−3.5	−6.1	−5.7	−19.3
Level (median) at year −1: 4.1%				
C. Capital expenditures/Sales	$N = 48$	$N = 44$	$N = 37$	$N = 16$
Percentage change	−5.4	−23.2[d]	−31.6[e]	−28.1
Industry-adjusted percentage change[b]	−4.4[e]	−16.7[d]	−16.8[e]	−25.6
Level (median) at year −1: 3.0%				

[a] Data for year −1 are obtained from post-buyout financial statements when available and from proxy statements describing the buyouts otherwise. Panels B and C use data only from proxy statements.

[b] Industry-adjusted change for a given period equals the difference between the change for the buyout company and the median change for a sample of companies in the same industry during that period.

[c] Significant at 1% level.

[d] Significant at 5% level.

[e] Significant at 10% level.

Negative industry-adjusted capital expenditures are consistent with reduced agency costs and increased efficiency if the pre-buyout companies have large amounts of free cash flow and were investing in negative net present value projects.

Low capital expenditures are also consistent with the hypothesis that buyout companies are cash-constrained and underinvest after the buyout. Similarly, the measured increase in operating income might be a byproduct of postponed maintenance expenditures. Under this view, the buyout companies are so heavily burdened by debt that they fail to invest in positive net present value projects and activities. This would destroy rather than create value.

The accounting evidence presented here cannot determine whether reductions in capital expenditures are value-increasing or value-decreasing. Evidence presented in section 4 suggests, however, that value is created in these transactions.

Table 5

Effect of management buyouts on net cash flow.

Median percentage change and industry-adjusted change in net cash flow, in net cash flow as a percentage of assets, and in net cash flow as a percentage of sales for 48 management buyouts completed in 1980–1986. Net cash flow is the difference between operating income and capital expenditures. Observations are not included for one company with negative cash flow in year −1. Year −1 is the fiscal year ending prior to buyout completion. Year +1 is the first full fiscal year of post-buyout operations. Significance levels are based on two-tailed Wilcoxon signed rank tests.

	From year i to year j			
Cash-flow measure	−2 to −1	−1 to +1	−1 to +2	−1 to +3
A. Net cash flow[a]	$N = 47$	$N = 37$	$N = 30$	$N = 14$
Percentage change	11.2%	41.1%[c]	59.3%[c]	95.6%[c]
Industry-adjusted percentage change[b]	2.5	22.0[d]	43.1[c]	80.5[d]
B. Net cash flow/Assets	$N = 45$	$N = 39$	$N = 33$	$N = 13$
Percentage change	5.3	43.4[c]	66.3[c]	79.4[c]
Industry-adjusted percentage change[b]	4.3	50.5[c]	85.4[c]	64.3[c]
Level (median) at year −1: 7.8%				
C. Net cash flow/Sales	$N = 47$	$N = 43$	$N = 36$	$N = 16$
Percentage change	−1.3	29.2[c]	42.0[c]	43.2[c]
Industry-adjusted percentage change[b]	−8.4[e]	45.4[c]	72.5[c]	28.3[c]
Level (median) at year −1: 6.8%				

[a] Data for year −1 are obtained from post-buyout financial statements when available and from proxy statements describing the buyouts otherwise. Panels B and C use data only from proxy statements.

[b] Industry-adjusted change for a given period equals the difference between the change for the buyout company and the median change for a sample of companies in the same industry during that period.

[c] Significant at 1% level.

[d] Significant at 5% level.

[e] Significant at 10% level.

3.4. Net cash flow

The results for operating income and capital expenditures suggest that the buyout companies are successful in generating cash after the buyout. This section examines net cash flow, the difference between operating income and capital expenditures.

The industry-adjusted changes in net cash flow in panels A, B, and C of table 5 are all positive and significant. Panel A shows that the net cash flow of the buyout increases 22.0%, 43.1%, and 80.5% more than that of other companies in the same industry in years +1, +2, and +3 compared with year −1. Similarly, panel B shows that the increase in net cash flow to assets for the buyout companies in those three years are 50.5%, 85.4%, and 64.3%. Finally, panel C shows industry-adjusted increases of 45.4%, 72.5%, and 28.3% in net cash flow to sales in years +1, +2, and +3 for the buyout companies.

If the increases in net cash flow are permanent, then, in the absence of tax and financing effects, the value of the buyouts should rise by the same percentage. The large increases in net cash flow are consistent with large increases in values. In fact, the changes in net cash flow are of the same rough magnitude as the premiums or excess returns paid to pre-buyout shareholders to take the company private. Again, the accounting data cannot establish whether the large increases in net cash flows are permanent, but section 4 presents evidence bearing on their permanence by examining investor returns in the buyouts.

3.5. Potential selection bias

The sample analyzed here is subject to a selection bias if buyout specialists and managers in the more successful buyouts sell their shares in an initial public offering (IPO) or sell the company to another buyer. Such sales improve the reputation of the buyout specialists and reduce the non-diversifiable risk held by the managers. In less successful buyouts, the buyout investors may be unable or unwilling to sell their shares. If this bias is present, the sample includes atypically successful buyouts.

Alternatively, the most successful buyouts may not need to raise additional funds in the public capital markets and may remain private. Less successful buyouts may need to return to the public capital markets or obtain funds from corporate buyers. If this bias is present, the sample includes atypically unsuccessful buyouts.

Although I cannot examine those companies for which data are unavailable, I can divide the sample of companies with post-buyout data into those for which post-buyout filings are required and those for which such filings are voluntary, and, therefore, may be related to post-buyout performance.

The first group, the 10-K companies, consists of buyouts with publicly held debt outstanding immediately after the buyout. It includes companies that (a) do not retire previously issued debt, (b) issue new debt securities to the public to finance the buyout, or (c) pay pre-buyout public shareholders a combination of cash and debt securities for their pre-buyout common stock. As long as some of its debt is publicly and widely held, a buyout company must provide post-buyout data (in SEC 10-K filings) unconditional on post-buyout performance. The changes for the 10-K companies, therefore, should represent unbiased measures of post-buyout performance.

The second group, the IPO/sale companies, includes companies that subsequently (a) are sold, (b) are releveraged, or (c) file prospectuses describing an actual or anticipated initial public offering of equity. Because these companies do not have publicly traded debt outstanding at the time of the buyout, their subsequent release of post-buyout information is possibly conditional on

Table 6

Estimates of selection bias: Effect of management buyouts on operating income by post-buyout data source.

Median percentage change and industry-adjusted change in operating income, in operating income as a percentage of assets, and in operating income as a percentage of sales by post-buyout data source[a] for 48 management buyouts completed in 1980–1986. Operating income represents net sales less cost of goods sold and selling, general, and administrative expenses before deducting depreciation and amortization. Year −1 is the fiscal year ending prior to buyout completion. Year +1 is the first full fiscal year of post-buyout operations. Significance levels of differences in percentage changes and industry-adjusted percentage changes from 0 are based on two-tailed Wilcoxon signed rank tests. Significance levels of differences in industry-adjusted percentage changes of 10-K and IPO/sale companies are based on two-tailed Wilcoxon rank sum tests.

Cash-flow measure	From year *i* to year *j*			
	−2 to −1	−1 to +1	−1 to +2	−1 to +3
A. Operating income[b]				
A.1 10-K companies	$N = 28$	$N = 26$	$N = 18$	$N = 6$
Percentage change	11.0%	14.3%[e]	16.2%[e]	13.6%
Industry-adjusted percentage change[c]	−1.4	−10.1	−7.8	−40.8
A.2 IPO/Sale companies	$N = 20$	$N = 19$	$N = 19$	$N = 13$
Percentage change	9.3	25.3[d]	45.0[d]	65.6[d]
Industry-adjusted percentage change[c]	−2.0	15.6[e]	24.4	42.0[f]
Significance level of differences in industry-adjusted percentage changes of 10-K and IPO/sale companies	0.88	0.01	0.07	0.06
B. Operating income/Assets				
B.1 10-K companies	$N = 27$	$N = 26$	$N = 16$	$N = 5$
Percentage change	6.6	11.2	13.6	−2.6
Industry-adjusted percentage change[c]	6.0	12.7[e]	26.0[e]	8.9
Level (median) at year −1: 12.5%				
B.2. IPO/Sale companies	$N = 19$	$N = 16$	$N = 18$	$N = 10$
Percentage change	2.8	20.2[d]	38.7[d]	24.6[e]
Industry-adjusted percentage change[c]	4.0	37.4[d]	59.3[d]	32.2[e]
Level (median) at year −1: 14.6%				
Significance level of differences in industry-adjusted percentage changes of 10-K and IPO/sale companies	0.74	0.08	0.11	0.29

continued over

post-buyout performance. If there is a selection bias, the IPO/sale companies will perform differently than the 10-K companies.

Tables 6 and 7 present results for changes in operating income and in net cash flow for these two groups separately. Table 6 shows that the IPO/sale companies experience larger increases in operating income than the 10-K companies. In general, these differences are significant. The difference is particularly large for the change in levels. Here, the industry-adjusted decreases in operating income for the 10-K companies are associated with industry-adjusted decreases in sales.

Table 6 (continued)

Cash-flow measure	From year i to year j − 2 to − 1	− 1 to + 1	− 1 to + 2	− 1 to + 3
C. Operating income/Sales				
C.1. 10-K companies	$N = 28$	$N = 26$	$N = 18$	$N = 6$
Percentage change	− 1.0	1.7	− 1.0	15.9
Industry-adjusted percentage change[c]	− 1.7	5.8	17.5[f]	31.0
Level (median) at year − 1: 11.9%				
C.2. IPO/Sale companies	$N = 20$	$N = 19$	$N = 19$	$N = 13$
Percentage change	− 5.9	11.6[d]	21.2[d]	23.9[e]
Industry-adjusted percentage change[c]	− 5.1	22.1[d]	34.1[d]	34.8[c]
Level (median) at year − 1: 10.6%				
Significance level of differences in industry-adjusted percentage changes of 10-K and IPO/sale companies	0.84	0.01	0.06	0.50

[a]10-K companies are those management buyouts that have publicly held debt outstanding after the buyout and therefore still file 10-K statements with the SEC, IPO/sale companies are those management buyouts that subsequently issue public equity, releverage using publicly held debt, or are sold to publicly held companies.

[b]Data for year − 1 are obtained from post-buyout financial statements when available and from proxy statements describing the buyouts otherwise. Panels B and C use data only from proxy statements.

[c]Industry-adjusted change for a given period equals the difference between the change for the buyout company and the median change for a sample of companies in the same industry during that period.

[d]Significant at 1% level.

[e]Significant at 5% level.

[f]Significant at 10% level.

At the same time, however, the industry-adjusted changes in operating income to assets and to sales for the 10-K companies are all positive. Three of the six are significant at the 10% level or better. This is consistent with the hypothesis that the 10-K companies are using their assets more efficiently than the industry controls.

In table 7, the industry-adjusted changes in net cash flow for both groups are still large and, in most cases, still significant. The 10-K companies obtain industry-adjusted increases in net cash flow of 17.8%, 39.2%, and 99.5%, although only the result for year +2 is significant at the 5% level. The 10-K companies also obtain large and significant industry-adjusted increases in net cash flow to assets and to sales.

In all but one of nine cases, the industry-adjusted change for the IPO/sale companies is higher than the industry-adjusted change for the 10-K companies after the buyout. (In year +3, industry-adjusted change in net cash flow is 99.5% for the 10-K companies versus 80.5% for the IPO/sale companies.) None of these, however, is statistically significant.

Table 7

Estimates of selection bias: Effect of management buyouts on net cash flow by post-buyout data source.

Median percentage change and industry-adjusted change in net cash flow, in net cash flow as a percentage of assets, and in net cash flow as a percentage of sales by post-buyout data source[a] for 48 management buyouts completed in 1980–1986. Net cash flow is the difference between operating income and capital expenditures. Year −1 is the fiscal year ending prior to buyout completion. Year +1 is the first full fiscal year of post-buyout operations. Observations are not included for one company with negative net cash flow in year −1. Significance levels of difference in percentage changes and industry-adjusted percentage changes from 0 are based on two-tailed Wilcoxon signed rank tests. Significance levels of differences in industry-adjusted percentage changes of 10-K and IPO/sale companies are based on two-tailed Wilcoxon rank sum tests.

	From year i to year j			
Cash-flow measure	−2 to −1	−1 to +1	−1 to +2	−1 to +3
A. Net cash flow[b]				
A.1. 10-K companies	$N=28$	$N=25$	$N=17$	$N=4$
Percentage change	9.2%	41.1%[d]	57.1%[d]	54.2%
Industry-adjusted percentage change[c]	1.3	17.8	39.2[e]	99.5
A.2. IPO/Sale companies	$N=19$	$N=12$	$N=13$	$N=10$
Percentage change	17.0	49.1[f]	61.5[d]	112.5[d]
Industry-adjusted percentage change[c]	13.7	38.5[f]	57.5[d]	80.5[e]
Significance level of differences in industry-adjusted percentage changes of 10-K and IPO/sale companies	0.91	0.49	0.64	0.79
B. Net cash flow/Assets				
B.1. 10-K companies	$N=27$	$N=26$	$N=16$	$N=4$
Percentage change	5.3	40.4[d]	36.6[e]	30.6
Industry-adjusted percentage change[c]	4.3	43.8[d]	78.7[d]	52.1[f]
Level (median) at year −1: 7.5%				
B.2. IPO/Sale companies	$N=18$	$N=13$	$N=17$	$N=9$
Percentage change	6.8	52.5[e]	76.9[d]	98.6[e]
Industry-adjusted percentage change[c]	−14.0	79.1[e]	107.4[d]	69.2[e]
Level (median) at year −1: 8.2%				
Significance level of differences in industry-adjusted percentage changes of 10-K and IPO/sale companies	0.51	0.43	0.38	0.56

The results in tables 6 and 7 suggest that if a selection bias is present, it is small. The existence of any selection bias depends on whether changes in net cash flow or changes in operating income are the more appropriate determinants of value increases.

The results in this section support the existence of post-buyout operating changes in the first three years after the buyout. Over these years, buyouts experience industry-adjusted increases in operating income and net cash flow, and decreases in capital expenditures.

Table 7 (continued)

Cash-flow measure	From year i to year j −2 to −1	−1 to +1	−1 to +2	−1 to +3
C. Net cash flow/Sales				
C.1. 10-K companies	$N=28$	$N=27$	$N=18$	$N=4$
Percentage change	−1.2	26.0[d]	23.1[e]	23.2
Industry-adjusted percentage change[c]	−6.7	41.6[d]	51.6[d]	28.2
Level (median) at year −1: 7.6%				
C.2. IPO/Sale companies	$N=19$	$N=16$	$N=18$	$N=12$
Percentage change	−1.4	45.1[e]	59.9[d]	50.8[d]
Industry-adjusted percentage change[c]	−15.7	55.6[d]	82.1[d]	34.3[d]
Level (median) at year −1: 6.8%				
Significance level of differences in industry-adjusted percentage changes of 10-K and IPO/sale companies	0.57	0.24	0.37	0.73

[a]10-K companies are those management buyouts that have publicly held debt outstanding after the buyout and therefore still file 10-K statements with the SEC. IPO/sale companies are those management buyouts that subsequently issue public equity, releverage using publicly held debt, or are sold to publicly held companies.

[b]Data for year −1 are obtained from post-buyout financial statements when available and from proxy statements describing the buyouts otherwise. Panels B and C use data only from proxy statements.

[c]Industry-adjusted change for a given period equals the difference between the change for the buyout company and the median change for a sample of companies in the same industry during that period.

[d]Significant at 1% level.

[e]Significant at 5% level.

[f]Significant at 10% level.

4. Wealth increases to investors in management buyouts

This section considers whether the accounting changes identified in section 3 represent real, that is, valuable, economic changes. To do so, I estimate the total market-adjusted returns earned by investors in a subsample of the management buyouts. Positive market-adjusted returns would be consistent with the existence of valuable operating changes.[11] Furthermore, if the changes in operating cash flows are real and valuable, they will be positively correlated with the market-adjusted returns.

4.1. Returns to investors

I was able to find a market value for the post-buyout equity of 25 buyout companies at some date after the buyout. I refer to the date that a market value is first available as the post-buyout valuation date. Eleven of the 25

[11]Operating changes are not the only explanation for large measured increases in value. Others include tax benefits and incorrect valuation by the market.

companies sold equity to the public through an IPO; six companies borrowed money in the public debt markets to purchase post-buyout equity and relever-age themselves; and eight companies were sold to public companies or liquidated. The average time from the going-private date to the post-buyout valuation date was 2.68 years. For these 25 companies, I estimate the nominal and market-adjusted returns to pre-buyout shareholders, to post-buyout in-vestors, and to the two groups combined.

The market-adjusted returns adjust the nominal returns obtained by pre-buyout shareholders and post-buyout investors by the return on investments with the same systematic risk over the same period. With the large and changing leverage in these buyouts and the extensive use of stock options, it is difficult to measure the systematic risk or β of the new buyout equity investments, and subsequently, market-adjusted returns to that equity. The systematic risk of total capital of the buyout companies (the asset β), however, should be relatively unaffected by the leverage. Accordingly, I calculate and present the nominal and market-adjusted returns to total capital (equity, debt, preferred stock, and capitalized leases) invested in the company at the time of the buyout. The appendix provides a detailed description of the method used to calculate the market-adjusted returns.

I use systematic risk as the measure of risk under the assumption that most pre-buyout public shareholders and post-buyout investors hold diversified investment portfolios. This may not be accurate for managerial holdings of post-buyout equity. Such holdings, however, account for only a small portion of the total capital invested in the buyout. The 25 companies with a post-buyout valuation have a median pre-buyout equity β, or systematic risk, of 0.73.[12] This suggests that the pre-buyout equity of the buyout companies has less systematic risk than that of the average company.

Panel A of table 8 presents the total returns to pre-buyout shareholders and post-buyout investors from two months before the buyout announcement until the post-buyout valuation date. The median total nominal return (*RET TOT*) is 220.3% (average = 235.0%). During the same period, the value-weighted index increases by a median of only 83.2% (average = 95.9%). Consistent with management buyouts generating large value increases, the median market-adjusted return to pre-buyout shareholders and post-buyout investors is 77.0% (average = 96.0%). This measure is positive in all but one case.

Table 8 also reports that the going-private or buyout equity price of these 25 companies is a median of 42.3% (average = 46.7%) higher than the price two months before the buyout announcement (*RET PRE*). The market-adjusted or excess return (*XRET PRE*) over this period is a median 37.3% (average = 37.9%). The median values of *RET PRE* and *XRET PRE* for the entire

[12] This is the Sholes and Williams (1977) beta estimate for the buyout company's common stock estimated from 600 to 100 trading days before the buyout announcement.

Table 8

Nominal and market-adjusted returns to investors in management buyouts.

Nominal and market-adjusted returns earned by pre-buyout shareholders and post-buyout investors for 25 management buyouts completed in 1980–1986 that have a post-buyout valuation. The market-adjusted return equals the nominal return adjusted for the return to a portfolio with the same systematic risk over the relevant period.

	Median[a]	Mean[a]	% > 0	N
A. Total returns to pre-buyout shareholders and post-buyout investors				
Total nominal return to buyout from two months before buyout announcement to post-buyout valuation date[b] [$RET\ TOT = (1 + RET\ PRE) * (1 + RET\ POST) + 1$]	220.3%	235.0%	100.0%	25
Total market-adjusted return[c] to buyout from two months before buyout announcement to post-buyout valuation date[b] [$XRET\ TOT = ((1 + XRET\ POST) * (1 + XRET\ PRE)) - 1$]	77.0	96.0	96.0	25
B. Returns to pre-buyout shareholders				
Percentage increase in stock price for (or nominal return to) pre-buyout shareholders from two months before buyout announcement to going-private date [*RET PRE*]	42.3	46.7	100.0	25
Market-adjusted return[c] to pre-buyout shareholders from two months before buyout announcement to going-private date [*XRET PRE*]	37.2	37.9	100.0	25

sample of 76 companies, 42.3% and 34.2%, are similar to the values for these 25 companies.

The nominal return on capital (*RET POST*) earned by the post-buyout investors from the going-private date until the valuation date for the buyouts is a median 111.3% (average = 127.9%). The median market-adjusted or excess return earned by post-buyout investors (*XRET POST*) is 28.0% (average = 41.9%). Post-buyout investors in 22 of the 25 companies earn positive market-adjusted returns during this period.

The finding that the market-adjusted return to post-buyout investors is positive contradicts the claim that similarly leveraged equity investments in the value-weighted market index would have earned more than equity investments (including stock options) in management buyouts. In fact, the returns imply that equity investors in the 25 buyout firms earn a median compound annual return of approximately 130% which exceeds the 74% compound annual return on a leveraged market-index investment calculated in a Goldman Sachs study.[13]

[13]See the letter from Louis Lowenstein in the *Harvard Business Review*, November–December 1989, p. 182, referencing a study by Leon Cooperman of Goldman Sachs. Furthermore, the quoted return of 74% is surely biased upward. It is based on a leveraged position in the S&P 400 (which is itself leveraged) purchased in mid-1982 (near the bottom of the market) and sold in mid-1987 (near the pre-crash market peak).

Table 8 (continued)

	Median[a]	Mean[a]	% > 0	*N*
C. Returns to post-buyout investors				
Nominal return to post-buyout total capital[d] from going-private date to post-buyout valuation date[b] [*RET POST*]	111.3	127.9	100.0	25
Market-adjusted return[c] to post-buyout capital from going-private date to post-buyout valuation date[b] [*XRET POST*]	28.0	41.9	88.0	25
Nominal return to investors in post-buyout equity[e] from going-private date to post-buyout valuation date[b] [*EQRET POST*]	785.6	4,274.6	100.0	25
Length of time from going-private date to post-buyout valuation date [*TIME PRIVATE*]	2.60 years	2.68 years		25

[a]All means and medians are significantly different from 0 at the 1% level.

[b]Market-adjusted return equals [(1 + Nominal return)/(1 + Market adjustment)] − 1, where the market adjustment is the return to a portfolio with the same systematic risk over the same period. The median systematic risk [Scholes and Williams (1977) beta] for pre-buyout equity is 0.73. Betas and market-adjusted returns are calculated using the return on the value-weighted NYSE–AMEX index. The median return on the value-weighted index is 83.2% (average = 95.9%) from two months before the buyout announcement to the post-buyout valuation date.

[c]Post-buyout total capital is valued as the sum of total common stock, preferred stock, debt, and capitalized leases (book value) at the going private date. The return to total capital is calculated as the sum of (1) the market value of common stock on the post-buyout valuation date; (2) the book value of preferred stock, debt, and capitalized leases on the post-buyout valuation date; and (3) the value of interest, dividend, and principal payments during the period between going private and the post-buyout valuation date.

[d]Post-buyout valuation date is the date of sale, IPO, or releveraging on which post-buyout equity can first be valued.

[e]Nominal return to investors in post-buyout equity equals the market value of post-buyout common equity (and options) at the post-buyout valuation date divided by the total investment in post-buyout common equity (and options) at the going-private date.

More detailed variable definitions are given in the appendix.

The market-adjusted returns calculated above probably underestimate the true returns for three reasons. First, the returns are net of the fees paid to investment bankers, bankers, and lawyers for help in taking the company private. The median fee in these transactions is 4.92% of the market value of equity two months prior to the buyout proposal. If these fees are included, the median total market-adjusted return increases from 77.0% to 88.5%, the average from 96.0% to 103.0%.

Second, the total return to post-buyout investors is calculated using the book value of debt at the post-buyout valuation date. Most of this debt is bank debt or privately held and therefore difficult to value. Using book value in this case probably underestimates the market value of the debt because total debt outstanding tends to be lower and operating income tends to be higher at the valuation date than at the going-private date. As a result, the outstanding debt will be less risky at the valuation date than at the going-private date. Holding the level of interest rates constant, the market value of debt will exceed the book value of debt at the valuation date. The market value of fixed-rate debt further exceeds its book value because interest rates tended to decline between 1980 and 1988.

Third, in at least two cases, post-buyout investors retain equity interests in divisions of the buyout companies that are spun off. Because the value of these spun off divisions is unknown, those values are not included in the return calculations. As long as the divisions have a positive value, the calculations underestimate the market-adjusted returns to buyout investors.

The evidence in table 8 that the buyouts earned large and significant market-adjusted returns is consistent with the evidence from the accounting data on changes in operating cash flows. As with the operating changes, these valuation results will be biased upward if the buyouts that can be valued are the better performers. The differences in post-buyout operating changes between the 25 buyouts that can be valued and the 23 that cannot are similar to those in tables 6 and 7. The industry-adjusted changes in net cash flow are similar for the two groups, and the industry-adjusted changes in operating income are larger for those companies that can be valued. The differences are not identical to those in tables 6 and 7 because some of the 10-K companies have a post-buyout valuation.

4.2. Comparison of returns and operating changes

This section tests whether changes in industry-adjusted operating income and net cash flow are related to the total market-adjusted return generated by the buyout. The analysis uses the last industry-adjusted change available at the time the buyout company can be valued. The buyout company value at the valuation date is likely to reflect the most recently available information. Because of the potential influence of outliers in a small sample and the noisy nature of the variables, this section focuses on nonparametric Spearman rank correlations.

The rank correlation of the industry-adjusted percentage change in net cash flow with the total market-adjusted returns is 0.56 (significant at the 2% level). The rank correlation of the industry-adjusted percentage change in operating income with the total market-adjusted return is 0.22 (significant at the 32% level). The respective parametric correlations are 0.37 and 0.36 (significant at the 12% and 9% levels).[14] These correlations suggest that the post-buyout operating changes have real valuation effects. The rank correlations suggest a

[14]The correlations are based on 19 and 22 observations, respectively.

stronger role for changes in net cash flow than for changes in operating income; the parametric correlations suggest the two measures have similar explanatory power.

The correlations of the industry-adjusted percentage changes measured in relation to assets and sales with total market-adjusted returns provide a different result. The rank correlation of the industry-adjusted percentage change in net cash flow to assets with the total market-adjusted returns is −0.15. The rank correlation of the industry-adjusted percentage change in operating income to assets with the total market-adjusted return is −0.06. The rank correlations, when the operating changes are measured in relation to sales, are −0.23 and −0.13. None of these is significant at greater than the 31% level. The results for parametric correlations are similar. These small correlations are less supportive of the hypothesis that post-buyout operating changes have real valuation effects (than the correlations using changes in levels).

The overall correlation results, therefore, give mixed support for the value of the operating changes. This is not surprising in view of the noise in the measures of operating change and market-adjusted returns.

Although they are not conclusive, the results in section 3 for post-buyout changes in operating income and net cash flow and those in section 4 for total returns to investors in management buyouts suggest that valuable operating improvements occur after the buyout. These results are consistent with three hypotheses or explanations. The remainder of this paper examines their relative merit.

5. Evidence on changes in employment

Shleifer and Summers (1988) argue that hostile takeovers and other control transactions can transfer value to shareholders from employees by breaking implicit contracts with those employees. Implicit contracts are broken by firing workers and/or reducing their wages. This section considers whether post-buyout decreases in employment accompany the operating changes.

Forty-two of the 48 buyout companies with post-buyout financial data also have post-buyout employment data. Table 9 presents the percentage change in employees at the end of the first full post-buyout year, year 1, in which employment numbers are reported in relation to the number of employees in the year before the buyout. In some cases, year 1 is the third or fourth year after the buyout. Table 9 then compares these changes in employment with the median industry change over the same period to obtain a measure of unexpected change in employees.

Panel A shows that the median change in employment for the buyout companies is 0.90%. Employment increases in 50% of the companies. At the same time, employment has grown 12.0% less in these buyout companies than

Table 9

Effect of management buyouts on employment.

Median percentage change and industry-adjusted change in employment following the buyout for 42 management buyouts completed in 1980–1986. Year −1 is the fiscal year ending prior to buyout completion. Year +1* is the first post-buyout year in which employment numbers are available. Significance levels are based on two-tailed Wilcoxon signed rank tests.

From year *i* to year *j*	*N*	Percentage change		Industry-adjusted change[a]	
		Median	% > 0	Median	% > 0
Panel A: Total sample					
−1 to 1*	42	0.9%	50.0%	−12.0[c]	30.9%[d]
Panel B: Sample excluding companies with significant divestitures and acquisitions[b]					
−1 to 1*	26	4.9	61.5	−6.2	38.5

[a]Industry-adjusted change for a given period equals the difference between the change for the buyout company and the median change for a sample of companies in the same industry during that period.

[b]The sample in panel B excludes companies that subsequently divested or acquired assets worth more than 10% of the capital value of the buyout company at the time of the buyout.

[c]Significant at 1% level.

[d]Significant at 5% level.

in other companies in the same industry (which is significant at the 1% level). This industry-adjusted result is consistent with the industry-adjusted decreases in sales experienced by the buyout companies.

The results in panel A do not control for post-buyout divestitures (or acquisitions). If a buyout company sells a division, its measured employment drops by the number of employees in the division. Unless the purchaser fires all of the division's employees, the measured change in employment in panel A overstates the true reduction in employment. Panel B controls for this overstatement by restricting the sample to the 26 companies whose post-buyout acquisition and divestiture activity does not exceed 10% of the buyout capital value. More than three-fifths (61.5%) of these companies increase employment, with a median increase of 4.9%. The industry-adjusted change is again negative (−6.2%), but is not significant.

In interpreting these results, the reader should note that the Shleifer and Summers (1987) argument pertains to actual employment changes rather than industry-adjusted changes. The results here do not support the view that buyout gains come from firing a large number of employees.

Although the data show that buyouts do not lead to large employment cuts, the results fail to address two important issues. First, I do not have data for buyout company wages. If the buyout companies succeed in negotiating wages downward, they will have an incentive to hire more workers. Second, it is not possible to estimate changes in the composition of employment; new employees may be hired after old employees are fired.

6. Evidence on information advantages and incentive changes

The information-advantage or underpricing hypothesis suggests that buyout investors and managers have information about potential operating changes or value increases that public shareholders do not have. Because of this information advantage, buyout investors can purchase the company for less than public shareholders would accept if all information were known. According to this view, operating changes would have occurred without the buyouts and public shareholders would have obtained the post-buyout returns earned by post-buyout investors. It is only because of their information advantage that buyout investors can obtain positive post-buyout returns.

In contrast to the underpricing hypothesis, the reduced-agency-cost or improved-incentive view argues that the debt burden, the equity incentives, and the monitoring associated with the buyout significantly reduce agency costs within the company. These improved incentives lead to value-increasing decisions and post-buyout operating improvements. Under this hypothesis, the buyout investors can obtain positive post-buyout returns even if public shareholders have the same information. The gains will not occur unless the buyout is completed or similar incentive changes occur in the public corporation. In this situation, public shareholders (and other potential bidders) bargain over the total gains from the buyout with the buyout investors. The likely outcome of such bargaining is a sharing of the gains in the buyout.[15]

The primary issue in distinguishing between the underpricing and reduced-agency-cost hypotheses is whether public shareholders (and other potential bidders) have the same information as buyout investors and managers. This section considers indirect evidence concerning this issue.

6.1. Evidence from the redistribution of equity in buyouts

6.1.1. Pre-buyout equity ownership

This section examines the shareholdings of managers and directors of the buyout company as well as other informed players who do not invest in post-buyout equity (referred to collectively as informed nonparticipants). According to the underpricing view, these informed nonparticipants know that the true value of the buyout company (even without the buyout) exceeds the buyout price. In this case, it would be irrational for them to approve the

[15]See DeAngelo, DeAngelo, and Rice (1984) for a discussion of the gain-sharing hypothesis.

buyout by selling their shares and thus forego participating in the MBO. The reduced-agency-cost hypothesis, on the other hand, has no such implications.

For each company in the sample, I distinguish those members of the board of directors and management who invest in post-buyout equity from those who do not. Those who invest in post-buyout equity are classified as management MBO participants. Those who sell their shares into the buyout transaction and do not invest in equity of the post-buyout company are classified as management nonparticipants.[16]

Similarly, I calculate the pre-buyout shareholdings of hostile parties that do not invest in post-buyout equity. Hostile parties are considered because they may have private information that leads them to invest in the pre-buyout equity of the buyout company. Hostile parties are classified as hostile nonparticipants. To be included as a hostile party, an investor group must have purchased more than 5% of the buyout company's stock in the two years before the buyout proposal and been opposed by incumbent management (as measured by public statements of opposition or targeted share repurchases). All stakes held at the time of the buyout proxy statement are included. Stakes are also included if they are held within three months of the buyout proposal, but sold before the date of the buyout proxy statement. The use of 5% shareholdings to measure hostile pressure understates the actual amount of hostile activity because hostile investors can exert pressure on companies without obtaining 5% stakes.

Table 10 presents the shareholdings of informed management participants in the MBO and informed nonparticipants. The results document the existence of significant informed nonparticipants. Panel A shows that management nonparticipants control a median 5.50% (average 9.66%) of the buyout company. In addition, hostile nonparticipants have stakes in 20 of 76 companies. The average stake of hostile parties in these 20 companies is 9.78%. The holdings of all informed nonparticipants equal a median of 10.00% (average 12.92%). These holdings are large, exceeding those of the management participants. In 5 of the 16 cases in which informed nonparticipants hold small stakes (less than 1%), the buyout company receives a hostile bid. In those five cases, however, the hostile bidder does not have an ownership stake. A significant nonparticipant exists, therefore, in all but 11 of the 76 buyouts in the sample.

This evidence is not supportive of the underpricing hypothesis. It is consistent with underpricing only if the informed nonparticipants receive large side-payments or are somehow coerced into accepting the buyout price. Pecuniary side-payments are not present in the buyouts in this sample – the

[16]In four MBOs, a father sold his shares in the company and retired, but his son succeeded him. In what follows, fathers are considered to be management nonparticipants. The results are not sensitive to this choice.

Table 10

Pre-buyout percentage and dollar shareholdings of informed parties in management buyouts.

Median and mean percentage and dollar shareholdings in buyout firm before management buyout by managers and directors participating in the buyout, managers and directors not participating in the buyout, and hostile investors not participating in the buyout in 75 management buyouts in 1980–1986.[a]

	Panel A: Percentage of total shares held in pre-buyout company			Panel B: Total value of shares held in pre-buyout company ($MM)		
	Median	Mean	N	Median	Mean	N
Management–MBO participants	4.67%	12.05%	74	$12.15	$39.80	74
All nonparticipants	10.00%	12.92%	75	$16.97	$32.56	75
Management non-participants	5.50%	9.66%	75	$ 8.30	$22.46	75
Hostile non-participants	0.00%	3.26%	75	$ 0.00	$10.11	75

[a]Shareholdings are calculated from information in proxy statements describing the buyout transactions. Shareholdings for management are calculated as of the time of the buyout. For hostile nonparticipants, shareholdings are calculated as of two months before the buyout proposal.

Management–MBO participants include those members of management and the board of directors of the buyout company who invest in equity of the post-buyout company. Management nonparticipants include those members of management and the board of directors of the buyout company who sell their shares into the buyout transaction and do not invest in equity of the post-buyout company. Hostile nonparticipants are outside investors who (1) hold at least 5% of the pre-buyout shares of the buyout company and (2) are opposed in some way by management, including statements of opposition or targeted share repurchases. All nonparticipants equals the sum of the shareholdings of management and hostile nonparticipants.

informed nonparticipants sever formal ties with the MBO company. Coercion also is unlikely because nonparticipating top managers and directors typically make up the special committee of directors that must approve the buyout proposal. If the buyout price is low, the informed nonparticipants can reject the buyout proposal. Underpricing is rational in this sample only if management nonparticipants receive nonpecuniary side-benefits, possibly from selling the company to their friends, the current managers.

6.1.2. Post-buyout equity ownership

Both underpricing and incentive considerations predict that the percentage of equity held by management increases after a MBO. If managers are risk-neutral, the expected value of the firm is maximized when managers own 100% of the equity [see, for example, Jensen and Meckling (1976) and Shavell (1979)]. Alternatively, if managers know the company is undervalued, they will rationally try to obtain as large an ownership interest as possible in the new buyout company. A risk-neutral manager would want to own 100% of the post-buyout equity if it were possible to purchase the company for less than its expected value.

If the principals who determine the equity stake of the agents in a buyout know the purchase price is low, the principals will want a larger amount of equity the larger the underpricing. They will compensate the agents with salary rather than with equity known to be undervalued. In contrast, if efficiency and incentive considerations are important, the principals will offer equity stakes to these agents.

As with pre-buyout equity ownership, I determine post-buyout equity ownership by examining the proxy statements for each company in the sample. Table 11 presents the distribution of pre- and post-buyout equity ownership held by buyout company managers, both as a percentage of total equity and in dollars. Panel A gives the pre-buyout ownership of the pre-buyout managers. Panels B and C present the pre- and post-buyout equity ownership of the post-buyout managers. And panel D presents the difference between these managers' pre- and post-buyout equity ownership.

As expected for both underpricing and incentive reasons, equity owned by managers as a percentage of total equity increases after the buyout. The pre-buyout management team owns a median of 5.88% of the pre-buyout equity (panel A), whereas the post-buyout management team owns a median of 22.63% of post-buyout equity (panel C). Panel D shows that the post-buyout managers increase their equity stakes by a median of 16.03%.

Similarly, before the buyout, directors and managers own a median of 19.30% of pre-buyout equity (in panel A). After the buyout, managers alone own a median of 22.63% of the post-buyout equity. Managers and directors control much more than 22.63%. In transactions involving a buyout specialist, at least one member of the buyout specialist sits on the board of directors. These specialists both own post-buyout equity and manage limited partnerships that buy post-buyout equity. In 62 transactions for which data are available, managers, directors, and buyout specialists together own or control a median 99.00% (average 83.10%) of post-buyout equity.

The distribution of the equity ownership between the two top managers and all other managers (summarized in table 11), however, favors an efficiency or incentive interpretation over one of underpricing. Panel D shows that the percentage of equity owned by the two top managers increases by a median of 4.41%, whereas the percentage owned by all other managers increases by 9.96%. In fact, the median total post-buyout percentage holdings of the two top managers are lower than those of the other managers. This is a puzzling result if the buyout participants know that the buyout price is low. On the other hand, the results suggest that new incentives for junior managers play an important role in buyouts.

The smaller increase in percentage equity for the two top managers could be caused by a liquidity constraint, but the changes in the dollar amount of

Table 11

Percentage and total dollar shareholdings in buyout firm before and after buyout by managers in 76 management buyouts in 1980–1986.[a]

	Percentage of total shares			Value of shares ($MM)		
	Median	Mean	*N*	Median	Mean	*N*
Panel A: Pre-buyout equity ownership of pre-buyout managers						
Chief executive officer	1.40	7.13	75	2.80	18.17	73
Two top managers	3.90	10.23	76	6.18	25.74	75
All other managers	1.19	1.97	76	2.54	5.59	75
All pre-buyout managers	5.88	12.20	75	12.80	31.33	74
All pre-buyout managers and directors	19.30	22.89	75	31.85	64.52	74
Panel B: Pre-buyout equity ownership of post-buyout managers						
Chief executive officer	1.09	6.42	74	2.55	17.17	73
Two top managers	1.48	7.59	76	3.95	21.06	75
All other managers	1.19	1.70	76	2.50	4.36	75
All post-buyout managers	3.50	9.30	76	7.87	25.42	75
Panel C: Post-buyout equity ownership of post-buyout managers						
Chief executive officer	6.40	14.75	67	1.03	12.24	65
Two top managers	7.54	18.39	68	1.54	13.41	67
All other managers	10.88	12.60	68	1.83	3.18	67
All post-buyout managers	22.63	30.99	68	4.13	16.58	67
Panel D: Difference between pre- and post-buyout equity ownership by post-buyout managers						
Chief executive officer	3.57	8.11	65	−1.55	−6.27	65
Two top managers	4.41	10.23	68	−1.55	−9.22	67
All other managers	9.96	10.79	68	−0.43	−1.50	67
All post-buyout managers	16.03	21.02	68	−3.69	−10.71	67

[a]Shareholdings are calculated from information in proxy statements describing the buyout transactions. Pre-buyout management is the management team of the buyout company at the time of the buyout proposal. Post-buyout management is the proposed management team for the post-buyout company. The top managers refer to those individuals who hold the title of chairman and president. Some companies will have only one top manager. All other managers refers to those managers who are not top managers. All post-buyout managers consist of the two top managers and all other managers.

equity holdings do not support this argument. Panel D of table 11 shows that the two top post-buyout managers reduce the dollar amount of their equity holdings by a median $1.55 million.

6.2. Hostile or competing bids

Section 6.1 does not consider MBOs that were proposed, but not completed. During the sample period, 46 companies made unsuccessful MBO proposals valued at $50 million or more. Of these, 22 were taken over by a publicly traded firm, 12 were taken over by a privately held firm, and only 12 did not experience a material change in control. Management lost control, therefore, in 34 of the 46 unsuccessful MBO bids. Overall, management lost control in 34 of 122 (46 + 76), or 27.9%, of the MBO bids proposed during the sample period. This measure understates the degree of competitive pressure on the buyout price because it does not include the unobservable cases in which potential bidders examined the buyout company and decided not to bid.

Lowenstein (1985) suggests that buyout investors pay public shareholders a low price unless a third party actually appears. He finds that the premium to pre-buyout shareholders is higher in nine management buyouts with at least three actual or potential bidders than in 19 management buyouts with fewer actual or potential bidders. I compare the market-adjusted returns earned by pre-buyout shareholders in buyouts with and without active third-party participation. Third-party participation is defined as buyouts in which hostile nonparticipants hold at least a 5% stake or in which a formal third party makes a competing bid. I find that the median market-adjusted returns are 33.1% and 37.1% for the two groups of firms. The 4.0% difference is not statistically significant ($p = 0.41$).

The evidence in this section suggests that managers and investors who propose a buyout face an active market for corporate control that limits the degree of underpricing that can occur.

6.3. *Actual performance versus management projections*

In the majority of MBOs, the buyout company includes the financial projections given to prospective lenders in the proxy statement describing the transaction. These typically include projections of operating income, but not of capital expenditures. If buyout company managers purposely mislead public shareholders by understating the projections, buyout company performance will systematically exceed the projections. Alternatively, performance that does not exceed the projections is consistent with the hypothesis that buyout investors, public shareholders, and other potential buyers have access to the same information. In a recent paper on management forecasts in 'normal', nontakeover circumstances, McNichols (forthcoming) finds that management forecasts of earnings are essentially unbiased. The median management forecast error (actual earnings less the management forecast) in her sample is -0.00001 times the company stock price.

Thirty-two of the buyout companies provide usable projections in the proxy statements that describe the buyout. To be usable, the projections must provide an estimate of earnings before interest and taxes (*EBIT*) or operating income before depreciation for year 1 after the buyout. To obtain projected operating income when only *EBIT* is provided, I add the depreciation and

Table 12

Actual versus projected performance for management buyouts.[a]

Median difference between (1) actual and projected operating income and (2) actual and projected operating income to sales ratios of buyout companies in the two years following the buyout for 32 management buyouts completed in 1980–1986. Year −1 is the fiscal year ending prior to buyout completion. Operating income equals net sales less cost of goods sold and selling, general, and administrative expenses before deducting depreciation and amortization. Year +1 is the first full year of post-buyout operations. Significance levels are based on two-tailed Wilcoxon signed rank tests.

	(Actual–Projected) / Projected			
Performance measure	Year +1	% > 0	Year +2	% > 0
A. Total sample				
A.1. Operating income	$N = 32$		$N = 25$	
Percentage difference	−20.7%[c]	37.5%	−25.8%[c]	28.0[d]
A.2. Operating income/Sales	$N = 29$		$N = 20$	
Percentage difference	−6.4	37.9	−15.9[c]	20.0[c]
B. Limited acquisition and divestiture sample[b]				
B.1. Operating income	$N = 20$		$N = 14$	
Percentage difference	−19.4[c]	30.0	−20.7	35.7
B.2. Operating income/Sales	$N = 19$		$N = 12$	
Percentage difference	−7.1	36.8	−17.1[d]	25.0

[a]Projected operating income and projected sales are obtained from the proxy statements that describe the buyout transaction.

[b]The sample in panel B excludes companies that (1) subsequently divested or acquired assets worth more than 10% of the capital value of the buyout company at the time of the buyout.

[c]Significant at 1% level.

[d]Significant at 5% level.

amortization in the year before the buyout to projected *EBIT*. Because depreciation and amortization would have been expected to increase, this measure of projected operating income tends to understate actual projections.

Panel A.1 of table 12 shows that only 37.5% and 28.0% of the buyout companies meet the projections provided in the proxy statement in the first and second full years after the buyout. Actual operating income in those two years is 20.7% and 25.8% less than projected operating income. These shortfalls are significant at the 1% level. Panel A.2 presents a similar pattern for operating margins, with shortfalls of 6.4% and 15.9% in the first two post-buyout years. Restricting the sample to those buyouts with limited post-buyout divestiture and acquisition activity yields qualitatively similar results (panel B).

The finding that the MBOs underachieve their projections is not consistent with managers misleading public shareholders about company value by providing downward-biased estimates of operating income. The projection results suggest, but do not prove, that buyout investors and public shareholders have similar information sets. It is still possible that buyout investors have superior information, ex ante, about the distribution of future operating income. For example, buyout investors might know that the probability that operating income will fall below required debt service payments is much smaller than public shareholders believe.

6.4. Management turnover at the time of the buyout

The information-advantage hypothesis implies that the same managers run the company before and after the buyout. It would be irrational for a manager who knows the value of the company is higher than the buyout price to leave the company without investing in the new company. Alternatively, high management turnover would be consistent with the replacement of bad managers by good ones.

In 12 of 76 buyouts (15.8%), the CEO leaves the firm. In these 12 companies, the chairman also leaves the firm. (In most cases, the chairman and CEO are the same person.) In seven additional companies, the chairman, but not the CEO, leave. Therefore in 19 of 76 buyouts (25%), either the chairman, the CEO, or both do not join the new management team. In all of these cases, the departing executives approve the buyout either by tendering their shares or by voting for the buyout as members of the board of directors.

To put these numbers in perspective, Weisbach (1988) finds average annual CEO turnover to be 7.8% for a sample of 322 large firms. This turnover rate is not directly comparable to that for the buyout sample because it includes cases in which the CEO remains a manager of the company, usually as the chairman. The average annual frequency of a CEO leaving his company in Weisbach's sample is less than 7.8%. The 15.8% turnover rate of CEOs in the buyout sample exceeds Weisbach's average annual turnover of CEOs.

Warner, Watts, and Wruck (1988) find that the probability of a management change, defined as a change in the identity of the president, CEO, or chairman, in a given year is 18.3%. Again, this rate includes several cases in which the president, CEO, and chairman continue as managers of the company. Chairmen and CEOs leave the company in the Warner et al. sample less frequently on average. The 25% turnover for buyout-company chairmen or CEOs at the time of the buyout exceeds the average annual executive turnover in Warner et al. (1988). The unusually high top-executive turnover in buyout companies at the time of the buyout does not support a large role for superior managerial information.

If the findings on CEO turnover are combined with those on unsuccessful buyout proposals, the results are even more striking. In 34 of the 122 buyouts proposed, management loses control. In an additional 12, the CEO leaves the firm. Therefore, 46 of the 122 companies that propose buyouts, or 37.7%, effectively have new CEOs.

Overall, the results in section 6 on the distribution of pre-buyout and post-buyout equity, the number of unsuccessful bids, management projections, and management turnover do not support the hypothesis that superior managerial information is important in buyout transactions. Instead, the evidence supports the hypothesis that new buyout incentives play an important role in generating operating improvements and value increases.

7. Conclusion

This paper presents evidence on post-buyout operating changes in 48 large management buyouts completed between 1980 and 1986. These 48 companies experience increases in operating income (before depreciation) and net cash flow as well as reductions in capital expenditures. Operating income, measured net of industry changes, is essentially unchanged in the first two post-buyout years and 24% higher in the third year. The change in operating income, however, does not control for post-buyout divestitures, which may lead the measured change to underestimate the true change. Changes in the ratios of operating income to assets and to sales (which help control for divestitures and acquisitions) exceed the industry changes by approximately 20% in the first three post-buyout years.

The median net cash flow (the difference between operating income and capital expenditure), net of industry changes, in the first three post-buyout years is 22.0%, 43.1%, and 80.5% larger than in the last pre-buyout year. Similarly, buyout company increases in net cash flow to assets and to sales exceed the industry changes by approximately 50% during this period. The large magnitudes of the increases in net cash flow are driven both by increases in operating income and by decreases in capital expenditures.

Consistent with the evidence for operating changes, pre-buyout and post-buyout investors earn a combined median total market-adjusted return of 77.0% (mean = 96.0%). The changes in operating income and net cash flow are correlated (although not uniformly) with the market-adjusted returns.

I consider three explanations for the operating changes and value increases. First, I examine changes in employment after management buyouts. The median change for the buyout companies is 0.9%. For a subsample of buyouts that do not make large post-buyout divestitures, employment increases, by a median of 4.9%. The results do not support the view that investors benefit from large employment cuts.

I then present evidence that favors reduced agency costs rather than superior managerial information as an explanation for the operating changes. First, the holdings of informed parties who do not participate in the buyout (nonparticipating officers and directors as well as hostile third parties) are a median 10.0%, or $17 million. These nonparticipants irrationally sell their shares if the buyout is underpriced and they have the same information as the participating management team. Second, although the management team holds a much larger percentage of post-buyout equity than of pre-buyout equity, the increase is smaller for the two top managers than for all other managers. Third, post-buyout operating performance in the first two years after the buyout is below the projections provided by managers in the buyout proxy statement. Finally, management turnover at the time of the buyouts is unusually high.

Although not conclusive, the evidence presented here broadly supports the hypothesis that management buyouts experience post-buyout operating improvements and value increases. Moreover, the operating improvements and value increases appear to be generated by improved incentives rather than wealth transfers from employees or superior managerial information.

Appendix

Method for calculating excess returns to investors

This appendix describes the method used to calculate excess returns to pre-buyout shareholders and post-buyout investors.

In this analysis, time is measured as follows:

T1	*T2*	*T3*	*T4*
Two Months Before MBO Proposal	MBO Proposal	MBO Completed: Company Goes Private	IPO or Sale

The premium paid to pre-buyout shareholders (*RET PRE*) is calculated as the fractional difference between the buyout equity price (at *T3*) and the price of equity two months before the buyout proposal (*T1*):

$$RET\ PRE = [PRICE_{T3} - PRICE_{T1}] \div [PRICE_{T1}].$$

In general, the buyout price is the per-share cash payment received by pre-buyout shareholders. When the total payment includes a debt component, the buyout price is taken as the closing price per share on the day the buyout company stock is delisted. The excess or market-adjusted return to pre-buyout shareholders (*XRET PRE*) is obtained by adjusting *RET PRE* for the return to an investment with the same systematic risk over the same period:

$$XRET\ PRE = \big([1 + RET\ PRE] \div \left[1 + R_f + \beta^E * R_m \text{ over the same time period}\right]\big) - 1,$$

where R_f is the T-bill return, R_m is the Center for Research in Security Prices (CRSP) return on the value-weighted New York Stock Exchange–American Stock Exchange (NYSE–AMEX) index, and β^E is the Scholes and Williams (1977) β estimate for the firm's common stock estimated from 600 to 100 trading days prior to the buyout announcement. [The results for *XRET PRE* and *XRET POST* are qualitatively the same using an equal-weighted index and market-model estimates of β.] The total return to the investment of the same systematic risk is calculated by compounding monthly return data.

If the buyout company has issued equity (through an IPO), has borrowed debt from the public to repurchase private equity, or has been sold to a public company, the excess return earned by investors in the post-buyout company can be calculated. The calculations use the financial information provided in the initial public offering prospectuses, debt offering prospectuses, or 8-Ks describing the sales.

Because the buyouts are initially financed with a small amount of equity, it is difficult to estimate the beta that should be applied to that equity. Most equity betas would initially exceed five. Small percentage estimation errors could have large effects on measured expected returns. Instead, this paper measures post-buyout excess return as the excess return to total capital invested in the buyout company. With this method, it is not necessary to differentiate between debt and equity.

The total capital value of the buyout company at time T equals the sum of the values of equity, long-term debt, short-term debt, and capitalized leases when the buyout is completed:

$$TCAP_T = \text{Market value of equity}_T + \text{Book value of long-term and short-term debt}_T + \text{Book value of capitalized leases}_T.$$

At the time of the buyout (*T3*), the MBO is effectively a new company. The book value of new debt and new equity should equal their market values. Long-term debt issued by the company before the buyout, however, will typically have a book value different from its market value. Because such debt is typically a small part of total capital, *TCAP* will be a good measure of total value. At the time of the sale or IPO, *TCAP* will incorrectly estimate the true value of the company if the book value of the debt differs from its market value.

The total return to post-buyout investors is calculated as

$$RET\ POST = \frac{[TCAP_{T4} + \text{Interim payments to capital} - TCAP_{T3}]}{TCAP_{T3}}.$$

Interim payments to capital include the annual principal, interest, dividend and lease payments made between *T3* and *T4*. It is assumed that the interim payments are invested in a portfolio with the same systematic risk as the company as a whole. This adjustment will tend to underestimate the terminal value because such payments are made throughout the year, rather than at year-end.

The excess return earned by investors in the MBO company (*XRET POST*) is estimated as the difference between the total MBO return and the return on an investment of the same systematic risk over the same period:

$$XRET\ POST = \big([1 + RET\ POST] \big/ \big[1 + R_f + \beta^A * R_m \text{ over the same period}\big]\big) - 1,$$

where R_f is the T-bill return and R_m is the CRSP return on the value-weighted NYSE–AMEX index. β^A, the firm's asset β, is given by

$$\beta^A = \beta^E \div [1 + (1 - \tau) * D/E],$$

where β^E is the Scholes and Williams (1977) β estimate of the firm's common stock estimated from 600 to 100 trading days prior to the buyout announcement, τ is the marginal federal tax rate of 46% in effect during the estimation period, and D and E are, respectively, the book value of the firm's debt and the market value of the firm's equity at the end of the year before the buyout. This calculation (of the firm's asset β) assumes the firm's pre-buyout debt has a β equal to 0. Given the low level (and, therefore, risk) of pre-buyout debt, this assumption is reasonable. The calculation also assumes that the pre-buyout asset β equals the post-buyout asset β. This is conservative given the large increase in debt and accompanying interest deductions. The total return to the investment of the same systematic risk is calculated by compounding monthly return data.

References

DeAngelo, Harry and Linda DeAngelo, 1987, Management buyouts of publicly traded corporations, Financial Analysts Journal, May–June, 38–49.

DeAngelo, Harry, Linda DeAngelo, and Edward Rice, 1984, Going private: Minority freezeouts and stockholder wealth, Journal of Law and Economics 27, 367–401.

DeAngelo, Linda, 1986, Accounting numbers as market valuation substitutes: A study of management buyouts of public stockholders, The Accounting Review 61, 400–420.

DeAngelo, Linda, 1988, Managerial competition, information costs and corporate governance: The use of accounting performance measures in proxy contests, Journal of Accounting and Economics 10, 3–36.

Healy, Paul and Krishna Palepu, 1988, Earnings information conveyed by dividend initiations and omissions, Journal of Financial Economics 21, 149–176.

Jensen, Michael, 1986, Agency costs of free cash flow, corporate finance and takeovers, American Economic Review 76, 323–329.

Jensen, Michael, 1988, Takeovers: Their causes and consequences, Journal of Economic Perspectives 2, 21–48.

Jensen, Michael, Steven Kaplan, and Laura Stiglin, 1989, The effects of LBOs on tax revenues, Tax Notes 42, 727–733.

Jensen, Michael and William Meckling, 1976, Theory of the firm: Managerial behavior, agency costs and ownership structure, Journal of Financial Economics 3, 305–360.

Joint Committee on Taxation, 1989, Federal income tax aspects of corporate financial structures (U.S. Government Printing Office, Washington, DC).

Kaplan, Steven, 1988, Sources of value in management buyouts, Unpublished doctoral dissertation (Harvard University, Cambridge, MA).

Kaplan, Steven, 1989, Management buyouts: Evidence on taxes as a source of value, Journal of Finance 44, 611–632.

Lehn, Kenneth and Anette Poulsen, 1989, Free cash flow and stockholder gains in going private transactions, Journal of Finance 44, 771–788.

Lowenstein, Louis, 1985, Management buyouts, Columbia Law Review 85, 730–784.

Marais, Laurentius, Katherine Schipper, and Abbie Smith, 1989, Wealth effects of going private on senior securities, Journal of Financial Economics 23, 155–191.

McNichols, Maureen, forthcoming, Evidence on informational asymmetries from management earnings forecasts and stock returns, The Accounting Review.

Schipper, Katherine and Abbie Smith, 1988, Corporate income tax effects of management buyouts, Mimeo., June (University of Chicago, Chicago, IL).

Scholes, Myron and Joseph Williams, 1977, Estimating betas from nonsynchronous data, Journal of Financial Economics 5, 309–328.

Shavell, Steven, 1979, Risk sharing and incentives in the principal and agent relationship, Bell Journal of Economics 10, 55–73.

Shleifer, Andrei and Larry Summers, 1988, Breach of trust in hostile takeovers, in: Alan Auerbach, ed., Corporate takeovers: Causes and consequences (University of Chicago Press, Chicago, IL).

Shleifer, Andrei and Robert Vishny, 1988, Management buyouts as a response to market pressure, in: Alan Auerbach, ed., Mergers and acquisitions (University of Chicago Press, Chicago, IL).

Smith, Abbie, 1989, Corporate ownership structure and performance: The case of management buyouts, Mimeo., Jan. (University of Chicago, Chicago, IL).

Warner, Jerry, Ross Watts, and Karen Wruck, 1988, Stock prices, event prediction and event studies: An examination of top management restructurings, Journal of Financial Economics 20, 461–492.

Weisbach, Michael, 1988, Outside directors and CEO turnover, Journal of Financial Economics 20, 431–460.

[22]

THE JOURNAL OF FINANCE • VOL. XLVIII, NO. 5 • DECEMBER 1993

The Determinants of Leveraged Buyout Activity: Free Cash Flow vs. Financial Distress Costs

TIM OPLER and SHERIDAN TITMAN*

ABSTRACT

This paper investigates the determinants of leveraged buyout (LBO) activity by comparing firms that have implemented LBOs to those that have not. Consistent with the free cash flow theory, we find that firms that initiate LBOs can be characterized as having a combination of unfavorable investment opportunities (low Tobin's q) and relatively high cash flow. LBO firms also tend to be more diversified than firms which do not undertake LBOs. In addition, firms with high expected costs of financial distress (e.g., those with high research and development expenditures) are less likely to do LBOs.

THE AMERICAN CORPORATE SECTOR experienced a dramatic increase in leveraged buyout activity in the 1980s. Between 1979 and 1989 there were over 2,000 leveraged buyouts (LBOs) valued in excess of $250 billion.[1] These transactions have been the source of considerable controversy, perhaps because a number of individuals have become very wealthy as a result of LBOs while others have lost their jobs. Two central questions that have arisen in the debate about LBOs are:

1. Do LBOs create wealth, or do they merely redistribute wealth?
2. Does the debt taken on in LBOs cause problems in periods of economic distress?

Proponents of LBOs (e.g., Jensen (1986, 1989)) argue that the transactions create wealth by improving managerial incentives and forcing disgorgement of excess free cash flow that would otherwise be invested unwisely. Jensen also addresses the second question, and argues that the costs of financial distress in LBOs are not large. Critics of LBOs argue that most of the gains to equityholders arise because of tax savings (see Lowenstein (1985)) and the expropriation of nonequity stakeholders (e.g., employees and bondholders) and have expressed concern about the effect of financial distress on the ability of LBO firms to remain competitive in the event of an economic downturn.

* Cox School of Business, Southern Methodist University and Hong Kong University of Science and Technology, respectively. We thank seminar participants at UCLA, the 1992 AFA meetings, an anonymous referee, Jim Brandon, Larry Lang, Scott Lee, Julia Liebeskind, Jeffry Netter, Krishna Palepu, Gordon Phillips, Annette Poulsen, David Ravenscraft, Richard Ruback, Mike Vetsuypens, and Ivo Welch for helpful discussions and comments.

[1] Calculation based on statistics from W. T. Grimm (1990) and the ADP M & A Database.

Most academic studies (e.g., Kaplan (1989a) and Marais, Schipper, and Smith (1989)) agree that tax savings are a source of large gains, but conclude that wealth is also created in LBOs. For example, Kaplan (1989b), Muscarella and Vetsuypens (1990), and Smith (1990) find that cash flows improve after LBOs. However, recent financial problems incurred by firms that did LBOs in the late 1980s have generated renewed concerns about the potential financial distress costs created by these transactions.[2]

In an attempt to shed light on the above questions we examine the extent to which LBOs have been motivated by the benefits of incentive realignment and the extent to which they have been deterred by the possible financial distress costs of high leverage. We do this by comparing the characteristics of firms that have undertaken LBOs with those that have not. Evidence that LBOs are undertaken by firms with characteristics that indicate high incentive realignment potential would support the hypothesis that the transactions were motivated with the intention to create rather than just redistribute wealth. In addition, evidence that firms with high potential financial distress costs are deterred from undertaking LBOs would suggest that concerns about the impact of an economic distress on the viability of leveraged buyout firms are overstated.

Previous work by Lehn and Poulsen (1989) and Lehn, Netter, and Poulsen (1990) has also examined differences between LBO and non-LBO firms. These and other related papers mainly address the incentive gains of undertaking an LBO and devote much less attention to financial distress costs. Consequently, their tests are not structured in a way that allows them to assess the importance of incentive realignment in motivating LBOs relative to the role of financial distress costs in deterring these transactions. One could argue the Lehn and Poulsen's evidence in support of Jensen's free cash flow theory is also consistent with the hypothesis that firms initiate LBOs for other reasons, such as the tax benefits of debt, but may be deterred by the prospect of incurring high financial distress costs. This is because Lehn and Poulsen's proxy for free cash flow also measures the firm's growth options which lose value in the event of financial distress (e.g., Myers (1977)). A measure of the severity of agency conflict used in Lehn, Netter, and Poulsen (1990), the ratio of the firm's market value to the replacement value of its assets (Tobin's q), may also proxy for the cost of taking on debt since high q firms typically have less collateralizable assets and greater growth opportunities.

This paper analyzes variables that allow us to cross-sectionally distinguish the importance of the incentive realignment motive for LBOs from the importance of the financial distress cost deterrent to these transactions. In

[2] Academic studies of bankruptcy costs and bankruptcy cost reduction in highly levered transactions include Asquith, Gertner, and Scharfstein (1991), Kaplan and Stein (1991), and Opler (1993). A press account discussing apparent costs of the LBO wave is Faltermeyer (1991).

addition to examining Tobin's q and cash flow for LBO and non-LBO firms we examine a variable which interacts q and cash flow. A similar variable was used by Lang, Stulz, and Walkling (1991) to test the free cash theory of takeovers. While the financial distress cost theory suggests that q and cash flow are important determinants of the LBO choice it does not imply that the interaction between the two variables is important. In contrast, the free cash flow theory implies an important interaction effect between these variables. High q firms, being better managed, are likely to be less subject to the free cash flow problem.

Additional variables that distinguish the agency and financial distress cost theories are research and development (R & D) expenditures and selling expenses. R & D–intensive firms are likely to have greater agency problems since they are more difficult to monitor; however, they are also likely to have higher financial distress costs since they tend to be high-growth firms that produce relatively unique products (see Titman and Wessels (1988)). Similarly, since selling expenses proxy for product specialization and high overhead, the agency hypothesis and the financial distress hypothesis also provide conflicting predictions about the effect of this variable on the likelihood of a firm undertaking an LBO.

This paper separately analyzes earlier and later LBOs to assess whether the characteristics of LBO firms changed over time. One view put forth by journalists is that later deals were of poorer quality than earlier deals either because of the adverse incentives of fee-driven investment bankers, or because LBOs were being used as a takeover defense. A related paper by Kaplan and Stein (1991) finds that the later LBOs were priced higher and were financed to a much greater extent with publicly issued debt than were the earlier deals. Recent papers by Long and Ravenscraft (1992) and Opler (1993) report conflicting evidence about the improvement in cash flow following the later LBOs.

The plan of this paper is as follows. The next section discusses the rationale for high leverage in LBOs. Section II discusses firm characteristics that are related to the costs of debt financing and describes financial variables that are likely to be related to the incentive realignment potential from LBOs. Section III describes the sample. Section IV compares the characteristics of LBO firms and non-LBO firms, before and after industry adjustment using multinomial logit analysis. Section V concludes the paper.

I. Why Are Leveraged Buyout Firms so Highly Levered?

To understand why financial distress costs can deter LBOs, one must first understand why debt financing is an integral part of these transactions. Lowenstein (1985) argues that debt is used because of the tax savings. Although realizing the tax gain does not require an LBO, several organizational aspects of LBOs may allow firms to realize the gain while avoiding many of the associated costs of financial distress.[3] Even so, it is unlikely that LBO firms assume as much debt as they do for the tax benefit alone since many LBO firms took on much more debt than was necessary to eliminate their taxable earnings. For example, roughly 50 percent of the firms studied in Opler (1992) paid no income taxes after going private. This suggests that there must also be nontax-related motives for using debt in LBOs.

Grossman and Hart (1982) and Jensen (1986, 1989) argue that debt can induce management to act in the interests of investors in ways that cannot be duplicated with optimally designed compensation packages. This incentive effect is likely to be most important immediately following LBOs when tough restructuring decisions are made. In addition, the asymmetric information inherent in LBOs is likely to encourage the use of debt. Even a management team with little private information that is useful in valuing a firm given its current operating strategies will be likely to have an informational advantage in assessing the effects of the major changes that take place following an LBO. Signalling arguments made by Ross (1977), Leland and Pyle (1977), and others suggest that in the presence of substantial asymmetric information, managers with favorable information are likely to hold a large share of their firms' stock and obtain outside financing disproportionately with debt.

Although the LBO organizational form is designed to minimize the more direct costs of bankruptcy, many of the indirect financial distress costs discussed in the next section are still likely to accompany LBOs. A firm in a business where these financial distress costs are high will find it less attractive to take on the debt required to signal management's optimism, to align management incentives with those of investors, and to thus realize the gains from going private. Such firms may be able to realize large gains from incentive realignment but may find it too costly to take on the debt required by an LBO. Thus, the magnitude of financial distress costs as well as the gains from incentive realignment, may be important factors in determining whether a firm chooses to do an LBO.

II. Firm Characteristics and the Gains to Leveraged Buyouts

The previous discussion suggests that a tradeoff between incentive gains and potential financial distress costs determine which firms undertake LBOs. These costs and benefits are likely to differ across firms in ways that depend on their characteristics. Hence, their relative importance in determining which firms undertake LBOs can be indirectly assessed by comparing the characteristics of firms that implement LBOs with the characteristics of

[3] These features include (1) an institutionalized debt workout process (or the privatization of bankruptcy) that may lower bankruptcy costs, (2) strip financing where debt and equity are owned by the same investors which decreases conflict between different classes of securityholders, and (3) LBO sponsorship by specialist firms with reputational incentives to look out for debtholder interests (see DeAngelo and DeAngelo (1987), Jensen (1989), Opler (1993), and Wruck (1990)).

firms that remain public. The following subsections suggest a set of variables that serve as proxies for these characteristics.

A. Costs of Financial Distress

The variables used to identify financial distress costs include some of the those previously examined in Titman and Wessels's (1988) cross-sectional study of capital structure choice. These variables serve as proxies for the uniqueness and durability of a firm's products, the collateralizability of its assets, and the extent of its growth opportunities. As discussed in the next subsection, a number of these variables also proxy for the gains from incentive realignment.

Titman (1984) provides a model where a firm's customers, workers, and suppliers suffer when it goes out of business. As a result, these nonfinancial stakeholders are reluctant to do business with a firm in or near financial distress.[4] This cost of financial distress is likely to be highest among firms with relatively unique products that may require future service. Consistent with this prediction, Titman and Wessels (1988) find that several proxies for product uniqueness are negatively related to leverage ratios. Proxies for uniqueness include research and development divided by sales and selling expenses divided by sales. In addition, we examine a dummy variable for firms in the machinery and equipment industries (Standard Industrial Classification (SIC) codes between 3400 and 3999) since firms in these industries are likely to sell products requiring extensive future service and spare parts. Further support for our proxies is given in our related work (Opler and Titman (1992)) which shows that leveraged firms with relatively unique products suffer the greatest losses in periods of economic distress.

Galai and Masulis (1976) and Jensen and Meckling (1976) show that equityholders of levered firms have incentives to expropriate their debtholders. To the extent that debt can be collateralized, creditors are less vulnerable to expropriation because funds may only be used for a particular project. In addition, the risk of creditor expropriation is likely to be higher for firms with profitable growth options (Myers (1977)). Tobin's q, defined as the ratio of the market value of a firm's assets to the value of its gross capital stock adjusted for inflation, can serve as a proxy for the extent to which a firm's assets are collateralized and its growth. Another indicator of expected growth is the ratio of the firm's cash flow, measured as its operating income before interest, taxes and depreciation (EBITDA), to the market value of its assets. Since the market value of assets should equal the risk-adjusted sum of discounted cash flows, firms with relatively greater cash flow to market value today are expected to have relatively less cash flow growth in the future. For both of these variables the market value of the firm's assets is measured as the sum of the market value of its equity and the book value of its debt. The ratio of

[4] Financially distressed firms may also be unable to credibly commit to carrying out implicit agreements with their nonfinancial stakeholders (see Maksimovic and Titman (1991)).

research and development expense to sales which was previously mentioned as a proxy for product uniqueness is also likely to serve as a proxy for future growth opportunities.

B. Incentive Realignment

Jensen (1989) argues that LBOs improve management incentives by giving managers a greater equity stake, by bringing greater monitoring by outside LBO sponsors such as Kohlberg, Kravis, and Roberts, and by raising the threat of job loss in the event of poor performance (see Gilson (1989)). This realignment of incentives may lead managers to divest low-synergy assets and to cease spending cash on poor investment opportunities. The potential for incentive realignment is measured with the variables outlined below.

Most of the variables discussed in the last subsection also proxy for benefits associated with incentive realignment. For example, firms that do a lot of research and development are likely to be more difficult for outside shareholders to monitor and hence are likely to gain the most from improved managerial incentives. In addition, firms with high selling expenses may have inflated overhead and would similarly benefit from an LBO. In contrast to the financial distress hypothesis that suggests that these variables should be negatively associated with the incidence of LBOs, the preceding argument suggests that the relation should be positive.

The most direct measures of the gains associated with incentive realignment are Tobin's q and the cash flow variable described earlier. These are used by Lehn and Poulsen (1989) and Lehn, Netter, and Poulsen (1990) as proxies for Jensen's (1986) free cash flow problem and management quality. Unfortunately, these variables do not allow us to separate the effects of financial distress costs from the gains from incentive realignment since both hypotheses predict a positive relation between these variables and the likelihood of undertaking an LBO. In order to distinguish the free cash flow explanation for LBOs from the deterrence effect of financial distress costs we construct a dummy variable that identifies firms that simultaneously have low (lower than median) q and high (higher than median) cash flow. A similar approach is employed by Lang, Stulz, and Walkling (1991) to test the free cash flow explanation of takeovers. We interpret the free cash flow theory to imply that only those high cash flow firms with poor management quality are good LBO candidates. While the financial distress cost and the free cash flow theories both predict that low q and high cash flow firms are likely to go private, the theories are distinguishable since only the agency theory predicts that this interaction variable is important. Using similar logic, we investigate whether firms that are highly unlikely to have free cash flow problems, identified with a high q and low cash flow dummy, are less likely to undertake LBOs.

The gains from incentive realignment may also be related to the degree to which the LBO candidate is diversified. Indeed, several studies suggest that diversified firms are more likely to suffer from agency problems (e.g., Comment and Jarrell (1992) and Morck, Shleifer, and Vishny (1990)). For example, diversified firms may cross-subsidize poorly performing divisions with the proceeds of strongly performing divisions (see Bhide (1990) and Jensen (1989)). Muscarella and Vetsuypens (1990), Liebeskind and Opler (1992), and Liebeskind, Wiersema, and Hansen (1992) show that many firms divest assets and become more focused after going private. Consistent with this observation, Opler (1993) finds that nearly half of the firms that undertook LBOs in 1987 and 1988 precommited to sell off assets in their bank debt covenants. To investigate the possibility that LBOs are motivated by the gains from selling off assets we investigate whether firms that undertake LBOs are more diversified than others.

To empirically measure diversification we construct a Herfindahl index which accounts for the distribution of the firm's employees across SIC codes.[5] In addition, we include a dummy variable that identifies firms that are both more diversified than average and have low q. We hypothesize that highly diversified firms with low q's (i.e. firms that have failed to create value through diversification) are good candidates for LBOs. Given that the level of diversification is correlated with size, which is likely to affect the ability to finance an LBO, we include the log of assets as a proxy for size in subsequent logits. Size may also proxy for the costs of financial distress.

C. Summary

This section reviews the two principal hypotheses that we investigate in this study: (1) that LBOs are motivated by the gains from realigning incentive problems (particularly those associated with free cash flow), and (2) that LBOs are deterred by potential financial distress costs. We have operationalized these hypotheses by suggesting proxy variables for financial distress costs and incentive realignment potential. Table I summarizes the proxy variables and their expected relation to the incidence of leveraged buyout activity.

III. Data

Most of the variables discussed in the preceding section are obtained from the NBER Manufacturing Firm Panel (described in Hall (1990)) which covers more than 2,500 large companies in the 1959 to 1987 period. This file is drawn primarily from the Industrial COMPUSTAT tapes. The diversification index is constructed using establishment level data on employment taken from the 1981 and 1985 versions of the TRINET Large Establishment Data Base. We obtain a list of firms that were dropped from the *NBER Manufacturing Firm Panel* because of LBOs and acquisition by a private company

[5] The industry focus index is computed as an employee-weighted Herfindahl index over three-digit SIC codes. The Herfindahl index was computed as $\Sigma_{i=1} e^2(\surd(\Sigma_{i=1} e_i)^2$ where i indexes SIC industries and e is the number of the firm's employees in each industry. This index may range between 0 and 1.

from Bronwyn Hall. This list is supplemented and verified using the ADP M & A Database, the *Wall Street Journal Index*, the *Standard and Poors News*, and a list of restructurings in the 1980s from the Dow Jones Broad Tape.[6] In total, we obtain a sample of 180 firms that undertook LBOs in the 1980 to 1990 period. LBOs are defined as transactions where the equity of a publicly traded firm was delisted while the firm was not merged into another firm. Cases where delisted firms were merged into shell organizations established by LBO sponsors are also classified as LBOs.

Table II shows the number of firms in the sample by year and the mean book value of their assets. The sample is most heavily concentrated in 1986 to 1988 and is very thin in 1989 and 1990. The non-LBO control sample consists of all firms on the *Manufacturing Panel* that are not in our LBO sample for which the requisite data are available.

Because our dataset spans 11 years we report the subsequent analyses for two subsamples: 1980 to 1984 and 1985 to 1990. One advantage of breaking the sample in this way is that many theories of LBOs are developed with knowledge of transactions that took place before 1985 so the post-1985 sample offers a cleaner test. The later subsample also includes a greater proportion of defensive transactions and has more large buyouts. Many later transactions carry higher prices relative to cash flow and have management teams with smaller equity stakes (Kaplan and Stein (1991)). Thus, firms making these transactions may be subject to a much different risk of financial distress than those in transactions in the early 1980s. By comparing the characteristics of firms making early and later LBOs we hope to clarify this issue. In the earlier (or later) subsample the explanatory variables are measured using 1980 (or 1985) data.

IV. Empirical Results

Table III presents a matrix of the Pearson correlations between the explanatory variables as well as their correlations with a dummy variable which identifies firms that undertake LBOs. There is a significant positive relation in both subperiods between the LBO dummy variable and the cash flow variable and the high cash flow/low q variable. The correlation of the LBO dummy with Tobin's q is significant and negative in both time periods while the diversification index appears to be important in the second subperiod only. The machinery industry dummy variable is significantly negatively related to LBO incidence in both subperiods, as predicted by the financial distress costs hypothesis, while the R & D variable is a significant predictor of LBOs in the first but not the second subperiod. The size variable is not significant in either subperiod. These simple correlations suggest that financial distress costs were a less-important deterrent to LBOs in the second subperiod while the gains from breaking up highly diversified firms became a more-important determinant of LBO activity as the 1980s progressed.

[6] This list was kindly provided by Mark Mitchell.

Table I

Proxies for Determinants of the LBO Choice

Expected signs from the logit equations predicting LBOs are shown.

Variable	Proxying for (Theory)	Expected Sign
Operating income/assets	Free cash flow (incentive realignment theory)	positive
	Lack of growth options (financial distress theory)	positive
Cash & marketable securities	Free cash flow (incentive realignment theory)	positive
Tobin's q	Quality of investment opportunities (incentive realignment theory)	negative
	Low collateral, growth options (financial distress theory)	negative
Machinery industry dummy	Product uniqueness (financial distress theory)	negative
R & D expense	Product uniqueness, growth options (financial distress theory)	negative
Selling expenses	Product uniqueness (financial distress theory)	negative
Integration index	Direct financial distress costs (financial distress theory)	negative
Diversification index	Good asset utilization (incentive realignment theory)	negative
	Direct financial distress costs (financial distress theory)	negative
Log of assets	Low average financial distress costs (financial distress theory)	positive
High cash flow × low Tobin's q	High potential to waste resources and poor resource utilization (incentive realignment theory)	positive
Low cash flow × high Tobin's q	Low potential to waste resources and good resource utilization (incentive realignment theory)	negative
Diversified × low Tobin's q	High potential to waste through cross-subsidization and poor resource utilization (incentive realignment theory)	positive

Table II

Number of Going Private Transactions with Mean Book Value by Year

Year	Number	Mean Book Value ($000,000)
1980	4	95.0
1981	14	109.7
1982	17	80.3
1983	12	67.3
1984	30	162.2
1985	23	184.3
1986	29	228.0
1987	25	348.1
1988	19	208.3
1989	6	1047.5
1990	1	446.1

Our multivariate results are reported in Table IV. This table reports coefficients from multivariate logit regressions using all of the above-described variables as well as separate logits using variables representing deviations from industry means.[7] The results show that after controlling for other effects firms with high cash flow are more likely to do LBOs; however, the coefficients on our cash flow variable are not statistically significant in either subperiod. The coefficients of Tobin's q are not statistically significant. After industry adjustment, the coefficients on the cash flow variable remain statistically insignificant in both subperiods. On the other hand, the coefficient on Tobin's q is negative and statistically significant in the 1985 to 1990 period. As discussed earlier, this is consistent with both the free cash flow and the financial distress cost deterrence hypothesis hypotheses. The variable design to capture the prediction of the free cash flow theory, a dummy variable which identifies high cash flow and low q, is statistically significant in the first two logit regressions shown in Table IV, supporting the free cash flow theory in both periods.[8] Similarly, the dummy variable which identifies firms that are unlikely to have free cash flow problems (low cash flow and high q) has a significant negative coefficient in both subperiods. None of the

[7] Industry effects are adjusted out by subtracting the median values of a variable within the firm's primary three-digit SIC code. This adjustment will not be perfect for firms which conduct business in several different three-digit SIC codes.

[8] We also examined a variable which interacted three-year stock returns prior to an LBO with cash flow using the logic in Denis (1990) that firms with poor returns on investment are most likely to suffer from agency problems which can be reduced by an LBO. This variable was not an economically nor a statistically significant predictor of LBOs. While apparently inconsistent with the free cash flow theory, dummy variables based on past stock returns are likely to have low power because LBO firms may have established poor investment records prior to the time when we began measuring the stock return.

Table III

Pearson Correlation Matrices by Time Period

Coefficients which differ significantly from zero at less than the 0.05 level are marked with *one asterisk* while those significant at the 0.10 level are marked with *two asterisks*. "Operating income/assets" is earnings before interest, taxes, depreciation, and amortization divided by the sum of the book value of debt and the market value of quity. "Tobin's q" is defined as the ratio of the book value of debt plus the market value of equity divided by the book value of total assets. The "Machinery industry dummy" is equal to one when firms' primary four-digit SIC is between 3400 and 4000. "R & D/sales" is the ratio of research and development expenditures to net sales revenue. "Selling expenses/sales" is the ratio of selling, general, and adminitrative expenses to sales. "Log of assets" is the logarithm of the book value of total assets. The diversification index is a "Herfindahl focus index" defined over the firm's four-digit SIC business activities. This is computed as the sum of squared business shares in these activities. "High cash flow, low q" is a dummy variable which is equal to one for firms with above the sample median operating income/assets and below sample median Tobin's q. Diversified, low q is a dummy variable which is equal to one for firms with above the sample median Herfindahl ratio, and below sample median Tobin's q.

	(1)	(2)	(3)	(4)	(5)	(6)	(7)	(8)	(9)	(10)	(11)
Panel A. 1980–84 (N = 1863)											
(1) LBO dummy	1.00										
(2) Operating income/assets	0.05*	1.00									
(3) Tobin's q	−0.06	−0.08*	1.00								
(4) Machinery industry dummy	−0.11*	−0.08*	0.05*	1.00							
(5) R & D/sales	−0.09*	−0.06*	0.28*	0.31*	1.00						
(6) Selling expenses/sales	−0.04**	−0.04**	0.13*	0.16*	0.51*	1.00					
(7) Log of assets	−0.02	0.03	−0.08*	−0.16*	−0.06*	−0.20*	1.00				
(8) Herfindahl focus index	0.05*	0.02	−0.07*	−0.13*	−0.11*	−0.19*	0.69*	1.00			
(9) High cash flow, low q	0.14*	0.21*	−0.39*	−0.13*	−0.22*	−0.11*	−0.04*	−0.02*	1.00		
(10) Low cash flow, high q	−0.10*	−0.11*	0.53*	0.20*	0.33*	0.17*	−0.06*	−0.13*	−0.54*	1.00	
(11) Low focus, low q	0.02	0.08*	−0.22*	−0.04*	−0.05*	0.05*	−0.27*	−0.23*	0.37*	−0.28*	1.00
Panel B. 1985–90 (N = 1652)											
(1) LBO dummy	1.00										
(2) Operating income/assets	0.054**	1.00									
(3) Tobin's q	−0.08*	0.00	1.00								
(4) Machinery industry dummy	−0.08*	−0.01	−0.16*	1.00							
(5) R & D/sales	−0.02	−0.01	0.21*	0.05*	1.00						
(6) Selling expenses/sales	−0.04	−0.09*	0.10*	0.19*	0.01	1.00					
(7) Log of assets	0.02	0.05*	0.06*	−0.15*	−0.05*	−0.24*	1.00				
(8) Herfindahl focus index	−0.08*	−0.04**	0.05*	0.21*	0.07*	0.31*	−0.55*	1.00			
(9) High cash flow, low q	0.14*	0.18*	−0.36*	−0.00	−0.02	−0.14*	−0.06	−0.06*	1.00		
(10) Low cash flow, high q	−0.11*	−0.06**	0.52*	0.03	0.06**	0.25*	−0.05**	0.16*	−0.37*	1.00	
(11) Low focus, low q	0.09*	−0.02	−0.55*	0.11*	−0.03	−0.06**	−0.16*	0.04	0.66*	−0.56*	1.00

coefficient estimates for these variables differ significantly in the two subperiods.

The results in Table IV are also consistent with the theory that potential financial distress costs deter LBO activity. In both subperiods firms with high R & D expenditures as well as firms in the machinery and equipment industries were less likely to undertake LBOs. This evidence is especially strong in the earlier subperiod and supports the financial distress hypothesis. However, the coefficient of selling expenses is positive in both subperiods and significantly so in the 1985 to 1990 subperiod, supporting the incentive realignment hypothesis. The difference between the coefficients of the R & D variable is significantly different in the two subperiods while the difference between the coefficient of selling expenses in the two subperiods is not significant.

We also compare the level of diversification of LBO targets to nontargets. We find that firms which did LBOs in the early 1980s were not more diversified than other firms. On the other hand, firms which did LBOs in the 1985 to 1990 period were more diversified than others. The dummy variable that interacts q and diversification is not statistically significant in the later subperiod and is statistically significant in the earlier subperiod with a negative sign—opposite of that hypothesized (the industry-adjusted dummy is also significant with a negative sign in the 1985 to 1990 period). However, the correlation matrix of these variables shows that the low q, high cash flow dummy variable is highly correlated with the low q, high diversification dummy. In fact, in an unreported logit, we find that the low q, high diversification dummy variable has a statistically significant, positive sign when the low q, high cash flow variable is deleted. Therefore, because of a multicollinearity problem we are hesitant to rule out the theory that poorly diversified firms are good LBO candidates based on this finding. It may be that a good description of an LBO candidate is that it has low q and both high cash flow and a high level of diversity.

V. Conclusion

This paper investigates the motives for LBOs by comparing firms that undertook LBOs in the 1980s to those that did not. The results suggest that free cash flow problems as well as potential financial distress costs are important determinants of which firms undertake LBOs. Consistent with the free cash flow hypothesis we find that high cash flow firms that also have low Tobin's q are more likely to undertake an LBO. Consistent with the financial distress costs hypothesis we find that LBO firms have relatively low R & D expenditures and are unlikely to be manufacturers of machines and equipment. In the 1985 to 1990 time period we also find that firms undertaking LBOs are more diversified than other firms in the economy.

The fact that financial distress costs deter LBOs suggests that debt financing is crucial for realizing the gains from going private. If this were not the case, firms with high potential financial distress costs could still go private,

Table IV

Logit Regressions of the Probability of Going Private in the 1980 to 1984 and 1985 to 1990 Periods

Probability values associated with the asymptotic χ^2 statistic that a coefficient is statistically different from zero are also reported. Coefficients which differ significantly from zero at less than the 0.05 level are marked with *one asterisk* while those significant at the 0.10 level are marked with *two asterisks*. A χ^2 test for change in coefficients between 1980–84 and 1985–90 is also reported. "Operating income/assets" is earnings before interest, taxes, depreciation, and amortization divided by the sum of the book value of debt and the market value of equity. "Tobin's q" is defined as the ratio of the book value of debt plus the market value of equity divided by the book value of total assets. The "Machinery industry dummy" is equal to one when firms' primary four-digit SIC is between 3400 and 4000. "R & D/sales " is the ratio of research and development expenditures to net sales revnue. "Selling expenses/sales" is the ratio of selling, general, and administrative expenses to sales. "Log of assets" is the logarithm of the book value of total assets. The "Diversification index" is a Herfindahl index defined over the firm's four-digit SIC business activities. This is computed as the sum of squared market shares in these activities. "High cash flow, low q" us a dummy variable which is equal to one for firms with above the sample median operating income/assets and below sample median Tobin's q. "Diversified, low q" is a dummy variable which is equal to one for firms with above the sample median Herfindahl ratio, and below sample median Tobin's q.

Variable	1980–84		1985–90		Industry Adjusted 1980–84		Industry Adjusted 1985–90	
	Coefficient	p-Value	Coefficient	p-Value	Coefficient	p-Value	Coefficient	p-Value
Intercept	−3.06	0.001*	−2.25	0.001*	−1.79	0.001*	−2.46	0.001*
Operating income/assets	0.41	0.15	0.15	0.52	−0.02	0.91	0.06	0.79
Tobin's q	0.02	0.87	−0.14	0.31	−0.03	0.78	−0.27	0.09**
Machinery industry dummy	−0.69	0.02*	−0.36	0.13	—	—	—	—
R & D/sales	−51.6	0.002*	−21.8	0.001*	1.22	0.001*	0.52	0.01*
Selling expenses/sales	0.78	0.54	2.01	0.01*	−0.84	0.48	0.80	0.08**
Log of assets	−0.11	0.24	0.02	0.80	−0.14	0.12	0.02	0.80
Diversification index	−0.34	0.52	0.82	0.10**	−0.02	0.41	0.06	0.56
High cash flow, low q	1.03	0.003*	0.79	0.02*	0.34	0.23	0.83	0.02*
Low cash flow, high q	−0.38	0.46	−0.77	0.06**	−0.90	0.03*	−0.74	0.03*
Diversified, low q	−0.56	0.15	−0.18	0.65	−0.68	0.08*	−0.98	0.01*
Sample size–no LBO	1769		1551		1769		1551	
Sample size–LBO	69		101		69		101	
χ^2	70.8*		73.7*		35.6*		24.3*	
Cragg-Uhler R^2	0.14		0.12		0.09		0.04	

using less debt and more equity than the typical LBO firm. As we mentioned earlier, a large percentage of LBO firms use more debt than is needed to eliminate taxes so that this crucial role for debt is unlikely to be taxes. The results in this paper support the idea that the role for debt relates to the incentive problems associated with free cash flow. However, to fully understand the LBO phenomenon, additional empirical work examining the determinants of the financial structures of these transactions is needed.

REFERENCES

Asquith, Paul, Robert Gertner, and David Scharfstein, 1991, Anatomy of financial distress: An examination of junk-bond issuers, Manuscript, University of Chicago.

Bhide, Amar, 1990, Reversing corporate diversification, *Journal of Applied Corporate Finance* 3, 70–81.

Comment, Robert, and Gregg A. Jarrell, 1992, Corporate focus, stock returns and the market for corporate control, Working paper, MERC, University of Rochester.

DeAngelo, Harry, and Linda DeAngelo, 1987, Management buyouts of publicly traded corporations, *Financial Analysts Journal* 43, 38–49.

Denis, David, 1990, Corporate investment decisions and corporate control: Evidence from going private transactions, Manuscript, Virginia Polytechnic Institute and State University.

Galai, Dan, and Ronald Masulis, 1976, The option pricing model and the risk factor of stock, *Journal of Financial Economics* 3, 53–81.

Gilson, Stuart, 1989, Management turnover and financial distress, *Journal of Financial Economics* 25, 241–262.

Grimm, W. T., 1990, *Mergerstat Review* (W. T. Grimm and Co., Chicago).

Grossman, Sanford, and Oliver Hart, 1982, Corporate financial structure and managerial incentives, in J. McCall, ed.: *The Economics of Information and Uncertainty* (University of Chicago Press, Chicago).

Hall, Bronwyn, 1990, The manufacturing sector master file: 1959–1987, NBER Working Paper 3366.

Jensen, Michael, 1986, Agency costs of free cash flow, corporate finance and takeovers, *American Economic Review* 76, 323–329.

———, 1989, Eclipse of the public corporation, *Harvard Business Review* 67, 61–75.

——— and William H. Meckling, 1976, Theory of the firm: Managerial behavior, agency costs and ownership structure, *Journal of Financial Economics* 11, 5–50.

Kaplan, Steven, 1989a, Management buyouts: Evidence on taxes as a source of value, *Journal of Finance* 44, 611–632.

———, 1989b, The effects of management buyouts on operating performance and value, *Journal of Financial Economics* 25, 217–254.

——— and Jeremy Stein, 1991, The evolution of buyout pricing and financial structure in the 1980s, Working paper, University of Chicago.

Lang, Larry, René Stulz, and Ralph Walkling, 1991, A test of the free cash flow hypothesis: The case of bidder returns, *Journal of Financial Economics* 28, 315–335.

Lehn, Kenneth, and Annette Poulsen, 1989, Free cash flow and stockholder gains in going private transactions, *Journal of Finance* 44, 771–788.

Lehn, Kenneth, Jeffry Netter, and Annette Poulsen, 1990, Choice of organizational form: The case of leveraged recapitalizations and leveraged buyouts, *Journal of Financial Economics* 27, 315–354.

Leland, Hayne, and David Pyle, 1977, Information asymmetries, financial structure and financial intermediation, *Journal of Finance* 32, 371–387.

Liebeskind, Julia, and Tim C. Opler, 1992, The causes of corporate refocusing, Working paper 92-0702, Cox School of Business, Southern Methodist University.

Liebeskind, Julia, Margarethe Wiersema, and Gary Hansen, 1992, LBOs, corporate restructuring, and the incentive-intensity hypothesis, *Financial Management* 31, 73–88.

Long, William, and David Ravenscraft, 1992, The financial performance of whole company LBOs, Manuscript, University of North Carolina, Chapel Hill.

Lowenstein, Louis, 1985, Management buyouts, *Columbia Law Review* 85, 730–784.

Maksimovic, Vojislav, and Sheridan Titman, 1991, Financial policy and a firm's reputation for product quality, *Review of Financial Studies* 4, 175–200.

Marais, Laurentius, Katherine Schipper, and Abbie Smith, 1989, Wealth effects of going private for senior securities, *Journal of Financial Economics* 23, 155–191.

Morck, Randall, Andrei Shleifer, and Robert Vishny, 1990, Do managerial objectives drive bad acquisitions?, *Journal of Finance* 45, 31–48.

Muscarella, Chris J., and Michael R. Vetsuypens, 1990, Efficiency and organizational structure: A study of reverse LBOs, *Journal of Finance* 45, 1389–1413.

Myers, Stewart C., 1977, Determinants of corporate borrowing, *Journal of Financial Economics* 5, 147–175.

Opler, Tim C., 1992, Operating performance in leveraged buyouts: Evidence from 1985–1989, *Financial Management* 21, 37–41.

———, 1993, Controlling financial distress costs in leveraged buyouts with financial innovation, *Financial Management* 22, 79–90.

Ross, Steven, 1977, The determination of financial strucutre: The incentive-signalling approach, *Bell Journal of Economics* 8, 23–40.

Smith, Abbie, 1990, Capital ownership structure and performance: The case of management buyouts, *Journal of Financial Economics* 27, 143–165.

Titman, Sheridan, 1984, The effect of capital structure on a firm's liquidation decision, *Journal of Financial Economics* 13, 137–151.

——— and Roberto Wessels, 1988, The determinants of capital structure choice, *Journal of Finance* 43, 1–19.

Wruck, Karen, 1990, Financial distress, reorganization and organizational efficiency, *Journal of Financial Economics* 27, 419–444.

[23]

ELSEVIER Journal of Financial Economics 48 (1998) 283–332

JOURNAL OF Financial ECONOMICS

Employee buyouts: causes, structure, and consequences[1]

Susan Chaplinsky[a,*], Greg Niehaus[b], Linda Van de Gucht[c]

[a] *Colgate Darden Graduate School of Business Administration, University of Virginia, Charlottesville, VA 22906, USA*

[b] *The Darla Moore School of Business, The University of South Carolina, Columbia, SC 29208, USA*

[c] *Department of Applied Economics, Catholic University Leuven, 3000 Leuven, Belgium*

Received 7 December 1994; received in revised form 25 August 1997

Abstract

This paper investigates the motivations for and consequences of including a broad group of employees in leveraged buyouts by comparing employee buyouts (EBOs) to transactions where only top level managers participate, or management buyouts (MBOs). We examine the implications of including employees in a buyout from a labor contracting, financing, and management control point of view. A major finding is that employee participation helps to finance the buyout. The EBO allows firms to gain access to excess pension assets by converting employees' defined benefit pension capital into equity claims, thus freeing the excess assets in the pension plan to help fund the buyout. Also, employee participation substitutes equity claims for cash labor compensation costs and therefore allows the firm to borrow more than otherwise would be possible. There is also evidence consistent with managers including employees to maintain or enhance incumbent management's control.

JEL classification: G34

Keywords: ESOP; LBO; Employee ownership; Labor contracts

---

* Corresponding author: Tel.: 804/924-4810; fax: 804/243-7676; email: chaplinsky@virginia.edu.

[1] The authors appreciate the helpful comments received from Edward Rice (the referee), Clifford Smith (the editor), Tom George, N.R. Prahbala, Greg Roth, Anil Shivdasani, Neil Sicherman, Luigi Zingales, the seminar participants at Harvard University, Michigan State University, the Universities of Georgia, Pittsburgh, and South Carolina, the 1994 Financial Management Association Meeting, the 1994 Western Finance Association Meeting, the research assistance of Rohan Christie-David, Andy Saporoschenko, Tom Smythe, and Cynthia McDonald.

0304-405X/98/$19.00
PII S0304-405X(98)00013-0

1. Introduction

During the 1980s, a small number of U.S. corporations went private by selling a large part of the firm's equity to a broad group of employees through an employee stock ownership plan (ESOP). Because employee buyouts (EBOs) result in a large increase in employee ownership, these transactions present an opportunity to examine the implications of making employees residual claimants in their firm. Despite a number of studies examining going private transactions, systematic evidence on the factors that motivate employee participation in buyouts remains unexplored.[2] In this paper, we examine and provide evidence on a number of hypotheses concerning the costs and benefits of employee ownership. We focus, in particular, on the circumstances that lead employees to participate in a buyout, and on the consequences of their participation for the structure and decisions of the post-buyout firm.

One approach to investigating why a broad group of employees participate in a buyout is to examine the issue from the perspective of an optimal labor contract. Cash flow rights can improve employee incentives (see, Alchian and Demsetz, 1972). These rights can also mitigate asymmetric information problems when negotiating labor contracts (Ben-Ner and Jun, 1996; Kovenock and Sparks, 1990). In addition, employee control rights can help protect employees' firm-specific capital (see, e.g., Klein et al., 1978; Williamson, 1979). However, a related cost of employee ownership is inefficient risk-sharing.

An alternative, but not mutually exclusive perspective, from which to examine employee participation is that of corporate finance. For example, leveraged ESOPs can provide a tax-advantaged source of funds (Beatty, 1995). Another financing benefit of including employees in buyout transactions occurs if the shares received by employees substitute for ongoing cash compensation commitments to pay wages or retirement plan contributions. In this case, part of the firm's existing operating commitments to labor costs are reduced in the post-buyout firm, and these funds become available to service the interest payments on the buyout debt. This substitution lowers leverage-related costs and allows EBO firms to borrow more than otherwise would be possible (Stewart, 1991). A potential cost of raising funds through an ESOP, however, is the presence of a new claimant group – employees – whose interests can conflict with those of other capital providers (Jensen and Meckling, 1979).

A third perspective from which we examine employee participation is that of managerial control. In particular, we examine whether employees are included because the ESOP helps incumbent management to maintain or enhance their control (see, e.g., Stulz, 1988; Gordon and Pound, 1990; Chang, 1990; Chang and

[2] For literature on MBOs, see, DeAngelo et al. (1984), DeAngelo and DeAngelo (1987), Lehn and Poulsen (1989), Hite and Vetsuypens (1989), Kaplan (1989a,b), and Palepu (1990).

Mayers, 1992; and Chaplinsky and Niehaus, 1994). This motivation does not exclude other perspectives. Indeed, if there are financing or labor contract advantages to including employees in a buyout, then doing so will also help managers maintain control. On the other hand, due to potential wealth transfers, the inclusion of employees in the buyout transaction could enhance managerial control even when there are no net financing or labor contracting advantages.

We compare EBOs to buyout transactions in which the only employees participating are top-level managers, or management buyouts (MBOs). This approach controls for the other organizational changes that are associated with employee buyout transactions, such as the increase in leverage and management ownership, and the change to private ownership.

Our findings suggest that all three perspectives are relevant to understanding why employees participate in buyouts. Consistent with the optimal labor contract perspective, there is evidence suggesting that employee incentives, firm-specific capital, and risk-bearing are important considerations. For example, all of the consulting firms in our buyout sample include employees as equity participants, which is consistent with employee ownership being more likely when employee effort is difficult to monitor. EBO firms are more likely than MBO firms to have excess pension assets, which is consistent with employees of EBO firms having more firm-specific capital that is subject to appropriation. And consistent with risk-sharing considerations, employee participation is more likely in firms where the ownership can be spread more diffusely across employees, such as in firms with relatively low values of assets per employee.

Consistent with optimal financing policy, we find that tax avoidance is a strong motivation for including employees for a few firms, but not for the majority. Motivations related to financing considerations, nevertheless, appear important. As mentioned above, EBO firms are more likely to have excess pension assets in defined benefit pension plans than MBO firms. Almost always, EBO firms with excess pension assets undertake an excess asset reversion at the time of the buyout. The excess pension assets materially reduce the amount of outside debt financing that is needed for the buyout. The existing literature often associates the termination of pension plans with the appropriation of employees' firm-specific pension capital (see, e.g., Pontiff et al., 1990; Ippolito and James, 1992). An alternative interpretation, which is consistent with the structure of EBO transactions, is that the EBO converts employees' defined benefit pension capital into equity claims, which frees the excess cash assets in the pension plan to help finance the buyout.

Also consistent with the financing perspective is the evidence that EBO firms have significantly lower pre-buyout stock price performance, indicating lower future expected cash flows, and lower pre-buyout financial leverage, suggesting higher leverage-related costs, than MBO firms. These findings suggest that EBO firms are more likely to be constrained in their ability to raise outside capital. By substituting equity claims for cash compensation, EBO firms increase their ability to support the debt needed to fund the buyout. In addition, a number of EBOs take place in industries that are under competitive pressure to lower labor costs, such as the textile, steel, and automobile industries. Consistent with the asymmetric information argument, employee ownership appears to be beneficial in obtaining concessions from employees. These concessions, in turn, enhance the firm's ability to borrow.

Some of the above findings, as well as additional results, are also consistent with the hypothesis that EBOs are used by managers to maintain or enhance their control. Relative to MBO firms, EBO firms are more frequently under takeover pressure, and their poorer prior performance suggests managers of EBO firms would be concerned about losing their jobs. In addition, managers of EBO firms tend to have lower pre-buyout ownership than managers of MBO firms, suggesting that EBO managers have less ability to defend against a takeover bid. Finally, the evidence on post-buyout ownership indicates that EBO managers typically have greater control in the post-buyout firm than MBO managers, owing to the lack of third-party equity participation in EBOs and the failure of employees to gain significant control rights early in the buyout. Typically employees do not control the voting of unallocated ESOP shares, and they rarely receive board representation. While these findings are consistent with EBOs being used to enhance managerial control, the general lack of employee control rights and the low level of third-party equity participation are also consistent with EBOs being structured to minimize potential conflicts among the providers of the buyout capital.

The paper proceeds as follows. In the next Section, we describe our sample of EBOs and MBOs and describe the institutional features of employee buyouts. In Section 3, we discuss the hypotheses concerning the benefits and costs of employee participation in buyouts. The evidence presented in Section 4 is divided into three parts: (1) evidence on the pre-buyout characteristics of firms undertaking EBOs versus MBOs, (2) evidence on the financial and ownership structure of EBO firms, and (3) evidence on the post-buyout asset sales and employment growth. We end with a short summary and our interpretation of the evidence.

2. Design of the study and sample descriptions

Because of the large increase in employee ownership occurring at the time of the transaction, employee buyouts provide an opportunity to examine the costs and benefits of employee ownership. To control for the other organizational changes occurring simultaneously with the increase in employee ownership (the increase in managerial ownership and leverage associated with going-private transactions), we compare EBO transactions to management buyouts without broad employee participation or MBOs. Thus, the analysis focuses on the primary distinction between EBOs and MBOs, which is the breadth of employee ownership.

Generally speaking EBOs involve more broad based employee participation than MBOs, although the breadth of employee participation varies in both types of transactions. Some MBOs can involve a very large management buyout group. For example, the MBO of CS-First Boston included 290 managers in the buyout group. Conversely, employee participation in EBOs may be limited to a subset of employees, such as those EBOs that include only salaried workers as equity participants.

2.1. EBO sample

We search the Wall Street Journal Index, the NEXIS database, and a list of leveraged ESOP transactions supplied by the National Center for Employee Ownership (NCEO) to identify publicly held firms during 1980–1990 that either successfully go private while giving non-managerial employees equity stakes in the post-buyout firm through an ESOP, or divest assets to a newly formed private firm in which non-managerial employees have an equity stake through an ESOP. The former type of transaction is referred to as a full EBO and the latter as a spinoff EBO.

To be included in the sample, a transaction must satisfy each of the following conditions. First, the post-buyout firm must not be publicly traded. Second, the buyout announcement must appear in the Wall Street Journal Index or NEXIS. Third, we can obtain a Securities and Exchange Commission (SEC) filing describing the transaction, such as a proxy statement, a Schedule 13E-3, or 8-K filing.

We gather information on each EBO from SEC filings and collect pre- and post-transaction information from the Wall Street Journal, NEXIS, and publications included in ABI Proquest. Other financial data are taken from Compustat and the Center for Research in Security Prices (CRSP). There are 18 full EBOs and 14 spinoff EBOs satisfying these conditions. The name, transaction size, as measured by the market value of repurchased securities, and the general industry affiliation of each EBO is listed in Table 1. A brief case description of each full EBO appears in Appendix A.[3]

In all of the EBOs, employees receive their equity stakes through ESOPs, which are defined contribution pension plans with two unique features. First, at

[3] As a result of our focus on publicly held companies, the sample does not contain some well-known buyouts, including Avis, Inc., Simmons, Inc., and Burlington Industries. Buyouts were also attempted by employees but did not ensue in a number of cases, including Alaska Airlines, Eastern Airlines, Frontier Airlines, Pan American Airlines, Peoples Express, and Scott and Fetzer.

Table 1
Transaction size in value of securities repurchased, and industry of the sample of employee buyouts (EBOs) during 1980–1990.

EBOs are identified from a search of the Wall Street Journal Index, NEXIS databases, and a list of leveraged employee stock ownership plan (ESOP) transactions supplied by the National Center for Employee Ownership.

Year	Name	Transaction size (in $millions)	Industry
Panel A: Full EBOs are employee buyouts of entire companies			
1980	Pamida	36	Retail Stores
1982	Dentsply	139	Equipment
1982	Dan River	135	Textiles
1983	Cone Mills	385	Textiles
1983	Raymond Int'l	168	Engineering Services
1983	U.S. Sugar	245	Food
1984	American Sterilizer	230	Hospital Equipment
1984	Blue Bell	741	Textiles
1984	Lyon Metal	28	Steel Containers
1984	National Color Labs	5	Photo Finishing
1984	Parsons Corp	557	Eng. and Constr. Services
1986	Amsted	512	RR and Building Products
1987	Charter Medical	1900	Hospitals
1987	Dyncorp	235	Defense Contractor
1988	Arthur D. Little	46	Engineering Consulting
1988	American Standard	2300	Building Products
1988	Northwestern Steel and Wire	188	Steel
1989	Security American Finance	16	Insurance
Panel B: Spinoff EBOs are employee buyouts of subsidiaries or divisions (The parent company is given in parentheses)			
1981	Hyatt-Clark (GM)	53	Machinery
1981	Alco-Gravure (MacMillan)	25	Publishing
1982	Weirton Steel (National Steel)	181	Steel
1984	Otasco (Rapid American)	125	Motor Vehicle Parts
1984	Seymour Wire (National Dist.)	10	Metals
1985	Avondale Shipyard (Ogden Corp)	375	Shipbuilding
1985	Crusteel - CMC Holdings (Colt Ind.)	135	Steel
1986	Republic Storage Systems (LTV)	200	Furniture
1986	Mosler Safe (American Standard)	158	Metals
1986	American Blg and Polymer (Cronus Ind.)	108	Metals
1987	Health Trust (Hosp. Corp of Amer.)	2196	Hospitals
1988	Epic Healthcare (Am. Medical)	790	Hospitals
1989	Dynamic Eng. (Questech)	6	Engineering Consulting
1989	Republic Eng. Steels (LTV)	220	Steel

least 50% of an ESOP's assets must be invested in the equity securities of the sponsoring plan. Second, the ESOP can borrow funds for the purpose of purchasing the employer's securities. In our sample, all of the firms use leveraged ESOPs, with the exception of Cone Mills.

In a typical EBO, the ESOP trust borrows funds that are then transferred to the buyout firm in exchange for equity claims. The funds from the ESOP loan, along with other equity and debt funds, are then used to repurchase the firm's existing equity securities, converting all publicly held shares to privately held shares. Contrary to what the term 'employee buyout' may suggest, in most instances the ESOP does not become the sole equity holder. Managers typically obtain ownership claims outside of the ESOP and in some cases, investment banks, and other institutional investors receive equity stakes.

The firm usually guarantees the ESOP loan by committing to make the contributions to the ESOP necessary to service the loan. As the ESOP loan is paid off, shares are allocated to employees' individual accounts, usually in proportion to their compensation. Since the ESOP loan is nominally repaid from the firm's cash flows, it may appear that employees receive shares without contributing capital for the buyout. However, employees often contribute capital indirectly, by foregoing some other form of compensation (Chaplinsky and Niehaus, 1990). We document the types of compensation changes that occur in full EBOs in Appendix A, and the types of compensation changes that occur in spinoff EBOs in Appendix B. As noted there, compensation changes occurring at the time of the EBO range from work-rule changes to large reductions in cash wages. For most firms in our sample, however, employees contribute capital by accepting the elimination of, or reductions in, existing deferred compensation plans. From an economic perspective, employees pay a fair price for their ESOP shares if the present value of employee compensation concessions, which represents the capital contributed by employees, is equal to the value of the ESOP shares. The complex nature of the compensation exchanges and the lack of detailed reporting often prevents assessment of whether the price paid by employees is equal to the value of their ESOP shares.

Employees cannot remove the shares allocated to their ESOP accounts until their service with the firm ends. Private firms, like EBO firms, must offer to repurchase retirees' stock at a price determined by an independent valuation. In this way, retirees can cash out and diversify. In addition, employees who have reached the age of 55 or have achieved 10 years of service, whichever is later, can require that the assets in their ESOP account be diversified (Scholes and Wolfson, 1990). However, assuming the inability of employees to use ESOP shares as collateral, the illiquidity of ESOP shares can impose costs on employees without other resources or savings to cover expenses that may occur over time.

Conceivably, EBOs could take place without an ESOP. Employees could all agree individually to borrow on their personal accounts the funds needed to purchase a large stake in the firm. The leveraged ESOP, however, provides several advantages, one being tax benefits (see later sections and Beatty, 1995). In addition, the ESOP mechanism is likely to reduce transaction costs and expected default costs. Finally, assuming there is an advantage to having employees as a group own a large stake, an ESOP enhances cooperative behavior among employees by restricting their ability to sell shares to non-employee investors.

2.2. Comparison sample of MBOs

For comparison purposes, a sample of MBOs completed during the 1980s is collected from information obtained from Securities Data Corporation and the IDD Mergers and Acquisition database. To be included in the MBO sample, a buyout announcement must appear in the Wall Street Journal Index or NEXIS, and top level management must take a stake in the post-buyout equity. The full MBO and parent firms of spinoff MBOs must be included in CRSP. The MBO sample consists of 118 full MBO and 64 spinoff MBOs.

The industry concentration of EBOs (see Table 1) indicates that three of the 18 full EBO firms and one of the spinoff EBO firms are in the engineering consulting business, and have the Standard Industrial Classification (SIC) code of 87. However, none of the MBOs is in the consulting business. On the other hand, every two-digit SIC code with more than four full MBOs also has at least one EBO. Both EBOs and MBOs occur with some frequency in the steel and textile industries. Eight EBOs and seven full MBOs are in the steel industry (SIC codes = 33, 34), and three EBOs and seven full MBOs are in the textile industry (SIC codes = 22, 23, 24). The latter findings suggest that employee participation is not determined solely by industry factors.

Table 2 provides summary statistics on the size of EBO and MBO transactions as measured by the market value of repurchased securities. Full EBOs range in size from \$5 million to \$2.3 billion, and have a median value \$209 million. Full MBOs range in size from \$5 million to \$3.7 billion, and have a median value of \$172 million. Although smaller, the median size of MBO transactions is not statistically different from EBOs. Spinoff EBOs range from \$6 million to \$2.2 billion, with a median of \$147 million. The median spinoff MBO transaction is \$205 million, which is not statistically different from that of spinoff EBOs.

Table 3 investigates the market-adjusted returns surrounding the announcements of EBOs and MBOs. Market-adjusted returns are computed for each day t as the firm's stock return minus the return on the CRSP equal weighted index. The median three-day market-adjusted return from the day before the buyout announcement through day one following the announcement is 13.3% for full EBOs. This is similar to the 11.5% return that Chang (1990) reports for his

Table 2
Transaction size, in value of securities repurchased, in millions of dollars for employee buyouts (EBOs) and management buyouts (MBOs).

EBOs are buyouts where a broad group of employees receive equity stakes. EBOs are identified from a search of the Wall Street Journal Index, NEXIS databases, and a list of leveraged ESOP transactions supplied by the National Center for Employee Ownership from 1980–1990. Full buyouts are purchases of an entire company. Spinoffs are buyouts of divisions or specific assets. MBOs are buyouts where current management holds an equity stake in the post-buyout firm, but not a broad group of employees. MBOs are obtained from the Securities Data Corporation and the IDD Merger and Acquisition databases. The t-test for differences of means, and the rank sum test for differences of median values, indicates that the average and median values for the EBO and MBO samples are not statistically different.

	Transaction size (in $millions)	
	Employee buyouts	Management buyouts
Panel A: Full buyouts		
Median	209	172
Mean	437	391
Minimum	5	5
Maximum	2300	3700
N	18	116
Panel B: Spinoffs		
Median	147	205
Mean	327	350
Minimum	6	99
Maximum	2196	1700
N	14	64

sample of ESOP buyouts. The 13.3% return for full EBOs is not statistically different from the median return of 14.9% for full MBOs. Table 3 also reports the stock price reaction for the parent firms of spinoff EBOs and MBOs. For the parents of both spinoff EBOs and spinoff MBOs, the median market-adjusted returns are close to zero at − 0.6% for EBOs and 0.4% for MBOs, and are not statistically different from one another.

To assess the total gain to shareholders, we calculate market-adjusted returns from five days before the date of the first mention of takeover activity until the buyout is completed. For full buyouts, we cumulate returns until five days after the buyout is approved by shareholders or until the stock stops trading if shareholder approval is not reported in the Wall Street Journal. For spinoff buyouts, we cumulate returns until 50 days after the buyout announcement

Table 3

Cumulative market-adjusted returns (MAR) surrounding the announcement of employee buyouts (EBOs) and management buyouts (MBOs).

Market-adjusted returns returns for day t are calculated as the return on the stock, minus the return on the Center for Research on Security Prices (CRSP) equal-weighted market portfolio. Market-adjusted returns are compounded daily. For full buyouts, the ending date for the buyout period is the last day the stock trades, unless a prior Wall Street Journal announcement indicates the buyout was approved by shareholders, in which case the ending date is five days after the approval date. For spinoff buyouts, the ending date for the buyout period is 50 days after the buyout announcement, unless a Wall Street Journal announcement indicates the buyout was approved by shareholders, in which case the ending date is five days after the approval date. Using a t-test and the rank sum test, in no case do we reject that the mean or median value, respectively, for EBOs is the same as for MBOs.

Type of buyout	Market-adjusted returns (percent)				
	N	Median	Mean	Standard deviation	% Positive
Panel A: Cumulative MAR from 1 day prior to 1 day following buyout announcement					
Full EBO	18	13.3	15.8	15.3	88.9
Full MBO	94	14.9	18.8	17.2	91.4
Spinoff EBO (parent)	12	– 0.6	0.2	5.4	33.3
Spinoff MBO (parent)	56	0.4	2.7	14.3	60.7
Panel B: Cumulative MAR from 5 days prior to 1st mention of takeover activity to ending date of buyout period					
Full EBO	18	26.1	30.2	25.0	88.9
Full MBO	94	24.7	26.3	29.8	87.1
Spinoff EBO (parent)	12	– 7.5	– 9.1	12.7	33.3
Spinoff MBO (parent)	56	– 1.3	– 1.0	24.7	42.9

unless a Wall Street Journal announcement indicates shareholder approval, in which case, the ending date is five days following the approval date.

The median market-adjusted return for full EBOs over the entire contest is 26.1%, which is not statistically different from the median value of 24.7% for the full MBO sample. The median market-adjusted return for spinoff parents over the entire contest is – 7.5% for EBOs and – 1.3% for MBOs. The difference in medians, however, is not statistically significant.

In summary, the descriptive evidence in the first three tables indicates that EBOs and MBOs occur in the same industries, and have similar transaction sizes and stock price reactions. We now turn to the theoretical arguments and develop specific hypotheses for when employees are likely to be included in a buyout.

3. Benefits and costs of including employees in a buyout

In this section, we summarize the costs and benefits of employee ownership that have been proposed in the labor contracting and finance literatures. Traditionally, the role of employee ownership in labor contracts is studied without consideration of the financing and managerial control implications to the firm. Likewise, the finance literature often does not take into account the labor contract motivations for establishing a leveraged ESOP, but instead focuses on tax and managerial control issues. We argue, however, that labor contracting, financing, tax, and control considerations are important in determining whether employees participate in a buyout.

3.1. Labor contract restructuring

We first hold financing fixed and focus on the impact of employee ownership from an optimal labor contract perspective. The labor economics literature suggests that the desirability of employee ownership depends on four factors: employees' firm-specific capital, asymmetric information, incentives, and risk-sharing.

3.1.1. Protecting employees' firm-specific capital

Klein et al. (1978) and Williamson (1979) suggest that employee control rights can protect employees' firm-specific capital. Specialized skills (Becker, 1975), monitoring costs (Lazear, 1981), and information asymmetries (Salop and Salop, 1976) can result in employment contracts with the feature that the present value of an employee's expected future compensation from their current employment exceeds the employee's next best alternative. For example, contracts that pay less than the value of marginal product early in an employee's career, and more than the value of marginal product late in the employee's career, create a situation where older employees earn more than they can earn in their next best alternative. These contracts may be implicit. Informed employees will be concerned prior to entering such a contract that these quasi-rents will be appropriated by opportunistic owners. Employees can protect themselves from opportunism by obtaining control rights, either through board representation, also known as codetermination, or share ownership. Thus, employee ownership can be part of an efficient labor contract that induces employees to make firm-specific investments in the future (Furubotn, 1988; Chapman, 1993; Hyde, 1993).[4]

[4] While some authors suggest unions are an effective mechanism for protecting firm-specific capital from opportunism, Howse and Trebilcock (1993) argue that collective bargaining rules are generally insufficient for this purpose. Fruhan (1985) suggests that some EBOs occur because union contracts contain shutdown benefits that create a large liability that offsets the potential benefits of liquidation. However, we are aware of only one instance of shutdown benefits in our sample, and that involves Weirton Steel.

This argument implies that EBOs are more likely when other mechanisms for protecting employees' capital, such as implicit contracts, have become less effective and when firm-specific investments enhance productivity. Implicit contracts prevent opportunism when the one-time gain from opportunistic behavior is less than the present value of future rents foregone as a result of employees no longer trusting their employer (Klein and Leffler, 1981). Hence, implicit contracts are likely to become less effective when a firm is performing poorly, because the firm's expected life is shorter and future foregone rents will be lower.

The previous discussion raises the issue of whether EBOs can be used to protect employees' existing firm-specific capital that has accumulated from past investments as opposed to capital from future investments. In particular, suppose that as a result of past implicit contracts, employees have accumulated firm-specific capital, and that circumstances have changed so that the implicit contract is more likely to be broken and the capital appropriated. Can employees prevent the appropriation by purchasing control rights from existing shareholders? The problem this scenario presents to employees is that they have to compensate shareholders for foregoing the gains from appropriation. Thus, shareholders would seem to extract the value of employees' existing capital through the buyout price. However, if employees place a higher value on the right to control whether their capital is appropriated than shareholders do because of risk aversion or a higher perceived likelihood of appropriation, or if the dissipative costs associated with shareholder appropriation are high, then a mutually beneficial trade between employees and existing shareholders could take place. The likelihood that the protection of existing capital would motivate an EBO increases as employees' existing firm-specific capital increases, and as the immediate threat of appropriation increases.

The protection of employees' existing or future firm-specific capital ultimately is a concern about employees being compensated for the value of their marginal product. A related argument that does not rely on employees accruing firm-specific capital posits that because of asymmetric information employees are concerned about the negotiated level of compensation. As we now discuss, there is potentially a role for EBOs to improve labor contracting in this context, but employee cash flow rights play the key role in this argument, not control rights.

3.1.2. Labor contract restructuring under asymmetric information

If managers are better informed than employees about the value of the marginal product of labor, or about rents that the firm is earning, employees may doubt managers' claims when negotiating new labor contracts. Ben-Ner and Jun (1996) and Kovenock and Sparks (1990) present models where granting employees cash flow rights can reduce inefficiencies associated with this asymmetric information. To convey the intuition of these models, suppose that employees are less informed about product market conditions than management. Then employees will be concerned that managers, acting on behalf of owners, will seek a labor contract that gives employees less than the value of their marginal product. Employees, knowing that they have inferior information, interpret a fixed wage offer as indicating that the managers have good information about product market conditions. In contrast, an offer with equity shares suggests managers want to share the bad results with employees. An equilibrium is established where profitable firms pay fixed wages and poorly performing firms compensate employees with equity shares. The key prediction from these models is that poorly performing firms are more likely to engage in an EBO than an MBO.

Employees are more likely to distrust management's motives when wage concessions are sought or when employees' firm-specific capital is threatened. Thus, the firm-specific capital arguments discussed above, and the asymmetric information arguments are complementary in the sense that both are likely to be important under similar circumstances. The importance of credibility in negotiating wage concessions is emphasized in DeAngelo and DeAngelo's analysis of labor contract restructuring in the steel industry (DeAngelo and DeAngelo, 1991). They show that layoffs, reductions in management compensation and dividends, and lower reported earnings are often combined in a concerted effort to make credible the need for union concessions. Granting employees cash flow rights is a potential substitute for these actions. The relatively large number of EBO firms in industries, like steel and textiles, that faced increased competition during the 1980s from foreign firms with lower labor costs is consistent with the argument that employee ownership helps these firms negotiate compensation concessions.

3.1.3. Improved incentives

A potential benefit of employees sharing in the firm's residual cash flows is greater employee effort and improved monitoring of employees and managers (Alchian and Demsetz, 1972). Accordingly, a large number of EBO firms cite improved employee performance as a rationale for greater employee ownership. Free rider problems, however, are likely to reduce the magnitude of potential productivity gains, especially in firms with large workforces. Employee ownership is more likely to be used as an incentive mechanism when the productivity of a team member is difficult to assess, as in professional activities such as consulting and law (Alchian and Demsetz, 1972). The fact that all four buyout firms in the consulting business include employees is consistent with the incentive hypothesis.

3.1.4. Inefficient risk-sharing

Because of their relatively large equity stakes, managers in both EBOs and MBOs are likely to hold undiversified portfolios. With EBOs, however, general employees also are likely to hold undiversified portfolios. All things being equal, the resulting cost of employee risk-bearing increases with the proportion of each employee's wealth invested in the firm, and with the variability of cash flows.[5] Thus, the greater the number of employees over which a given aggregate employee ownership stake can be spread, the less risk that each individual employee must bear in an EBO. Holding firm size and managerial ownership fixed, risk-bearing costs for employees decline as the number of employees increases and as the variability of cash flows decreases, and thus we expect the likelihood of employee participation to vary with these factors. However, if the above ceteris paribus condition is not met, and managerial ownership in particular is not held constant, then the prediction about the variability of cash flows does not necessarily follow. As the variability of cash flows increases managers may be more likely to seek general employee participation in an effort to reduce their own risk-bearing costs without sacrificing control. This prediction is considered further in Section 3.4.

3.2. Tax advantages

One frequently cited motivation for EBOs is the tax benefits available to the sponsoring firm when employees participate in a buyout through an ESOP. These benefits include the following:

Interest exclusion. After 1984, financial institutions that make loans to ESOPs can exclude 50% of the interest received on the loans from taxable income. After July 1989, the interest exclusion only applies if the ESOP holds more than 50% of the sponsoring firm's equity.

Dividend deduction. Dividends paid on ESOP stock are deductible expenses at the corporate level if they are distributed directly to employees (effective post-1984) or used to pay off the ESOP loan (effective post-1986).

Avoid excise tax on excess pension assets. In 1986, Congress introduced an excise tax on reversions of excess assets from a defined benefit plan. However, if excess pension assets are placed in an ESOP, the excise tax is reduced.

Ability to use loss carryforwards. The Tax Reform Act of 1986 restricts the ability of corporations to carry losses forward following a change in control, unless an ESOP purchases at least 50% of the equity.

Owners of closely held firms can defer capital gains tax. After 1984, an owner of a closely held company can defer capital gains taxes arising from a buyout by selling at least 30% of the outstanding shares to an ESOP.

Beatty (1995) finds that the interest exclusion and dividend deduction incentives provide measurable tax benefits to public firms using leveraged ESOPs.

---

[5] There is some evidence that firms structure the plans to reduce risk-sharing costs. For example, Amsted established additional defined benefit plans with an offset provision tied to the ESOP's performance that provided a floor on retirement income. Also, ESOPs hold preferred stock in six of the 18 full EBOs in our sample.

However, since more than half of the EBOs occur prior to the enactment of these ESOP tax benefits, taxes cannot be the sole explanation for employee participation in buyouts. The tax benefits associated with ESOPs do not yield a uniform prediction about the circumstances in which EBOs would arise. The dividend deduction suggests that firms with a higher demand for tax shields would be more likely to include employees in the buyout. The pension tax benefit implies that EBOs after 1986 would be more likely than MBOs to have overfunded pension plans, and the tax loss carryforward benefit implies that EBOs would be more likely to have unused tax loss carryforwards.

3.3. *Financing implications*

We now discuss the effects of ESOP financing on leverage-related costs and incentive conflicts among capital providers.

3.3.1. *Lowering leverage-related costs*

Substituting equity claims for cash employee compensation costs, consisting of wages and contributions to pension plans, can lower the leverage-related costs arising from potential bankruptcy and agency costs for a given level of debt (Peterson, 1994; Stewart, 1991). To illustrate, suppose that fixed wages are reduced and employees receive equity claims of equal present value. Although the present value of expected cash flows to employees is unchanged by this substitution, the substitution creates flexibility for the firm because cash flows that would have been allocated to employees can now be used for other purposes, such as paying off debt. In addition, to the extent that bankruptcy courts treat employee equity claims like other equity claims, the substitution places creditor claims above part of employee compensation in the event of default, which also could lower leverage-related costs.

In essence, the substitution lowers the priority of at least part of employee compensation costs for an on-going firm. Further, if employee participation helps to elicit compensation concessions, as suggested by Ben-Ner and Jun (1996) and Kovenock and Sparks (1990), these savings are also available to service the buyout debt. The implication of these arguments is that employee participation facilitates financing for the buyout and, in the extreme, can relax a borrowing constraint that prevents a buyout from occurring. Accordingly, firms with higher leverage-related costs are more likely to include employees in the buyout.

The capital structure literature suggests that leverage-related costs depend on expected cash flows, the variability of cash flows, and the costs of redeploying assets. Myers (1977) and Williamson (1979) suggest that redeployment costs are higher for firm-specific assets. Further, Shleifer and Vishny (1992) point out that redeployment costs are likely to be high when secondary markets are illiquid, which might occur, for example, when there are few buyers for the assets because of depressed industry performance.

3.3.2. Conflicts among claimants

Making employees substantial equity holders can create additional conflicts among capital providers. For example, conflicts can arise between employees and outside investors over the level of wages and benefits, and over strategic decisions like plant closings and layoffs that are difficult to anticipate and resolve contractually. The costs of resolving conflicts are further likely to increase when employees are heterogeneous in their interests and skills (Hansmann, 1990, 1993).

One way to reduce conflicts between EBO debtholders and employees is to limit employees' control rights while the debt is outstanding. The institutional features of the ESOP loan are well suited for this purpose. ESOP shares are allocated to employees as the principal on the ESOP loan is repaid. While employees must receive control rights on allocated shares, the control rights on unallocated shares can rest with the ESOP trustee. Thus, conflicts between employees and ESOP lenders can be mitigated by having an ESOP trustee who controls unallocated shares and is appointed by non-employee capital providers.

Outside equity holders, on the other hand, cannot avoid potential conflicts with employees indefinitely because ESOP shares eventually are allocated to employees. At this point, outside equity holders must contend with another sizable blockholder group whose interests may conflict with their own. If agency costs associated with outside equity are higher in EBOs than in MBOs, then less outside equity should be observed in EBOs.[6]

3.4. Management control

Finally, we examine whether employee participation in a buyout is motivated by managers' desire to enhance or retain control. Stulz (1988), Gordon and Pound (1990), and Chang and Mayers (1992) argue that ESOPs can expand managers' control rights beyond their percentage ownership if managers directly control unallocated shares, or if the parties controlling ESOP shares, either the employees or the trustee, are more likely to be aligned with managers than outside investors. Accordingly, EBO managers can obtain greater control in the post-buyout firm than MBO managers, holding constant managers' percentage ownership and the firm's leverage. Moreover, to the extent that employee

[6] There are additional costs of resolving conflicts among EBO stakeholders because of the ill-defined nature of the laws concerning employee participation in buyouts. Both MBOs and EBOs are frequently subjected to lawsuits by pre-buyout shareholders. However, under the Employee Retirement Income Security Act (ERISA), the Department of Labor (DOL) has responsibility to ensure that employees are treated 'fairly' when an ESOP is used in a buyout (Chaplinsky et al., 1994; Seelig, 1986). In our sample of full EBOs, four firms are subject to challenge under ERISA and these suits take an average of four years to settle.

ownership replaces equity ownership by third party investors, such as more typically Kohlberg, Kravis, and Roberts, Inc. (KKR), who are likely to monitor management, managerial control can be further enhanced relative to MBOs.[7]

Managers would be more likely to include employees and enhance their control if they are concerned about being replaced if the alternative in our analysis, an MBO took place. Managers' concerns about being replaced are likely to be related to several observable factors. First, prior takeover pressure could suggest that at least some outsiders believe management should be replaced. Second, poor pre-buyout performance could foster the perception that incumbent management is part of the problem. Third, low pre-buyout managerial ownership suggests managers are more vulnerable to replacement. In addition, including employees in a buyout could help managers retain control if employees believed that an outsider is more likely to appropriate their firm-specific capital than incumbent management (Shleifer and Summers, 1988). In this case, employees could be willing to contribute part of their capital to help incumbent management maintain control.[8] Thus, the managerial control hypothesis predicts that managers are more likely to pursue an EBO when the firm is under takeover pressure, performs poorly, has low managerial ownership, or when employees have firm-specific capital that is subject to appropriation.

4. Evidence

The evidence compares EBOs and MBOs with respect to their: (1) pre-buyout characteristics, (2) post-buyout financial structure, and (3) decisions and experience after the buyout.

4.1. Pre-buyout characteristics

In this section we relate the pre-buyout characteristics of EBOs to the theoretical motivations developed in the previous section. The pre-buyout characteristics reviewed are financial performance, pension plans, takeover pressure, the ownership by directors and officers, firm-specific assets, leverage,

[7] Greater managerial control can be wealth increasing or decreasing. We therefore do not use the term 'entrenchment' which typically has a negative connotation. We do not attempt to estimate the wealth effects associated with greater management control in EBO transactions because it would require controlling for (1) all of the costs and benefits of employee ownership previously discussed, (2) all the determinants of value from going private transactions in general, and (3) all the potential wealth transfers from employees and other stakeholder groups.

[8] See Chapman (1993) for a critical evaluation of the Shleifer and Summers (1988) hypothesis. Whether the breaching of implicit contracts with employees is the motivation for leveraged buyouts is explored theoretically by Habib (1995) and empirically by Ippolito and James (1992).

and assets per employee. We begin with univariate comparisons of the pre-buyout characteristics of EBO and MBO firms in Table 4. For the most part, the hypotheses are stated as predictions about a particular variable holding other factors constant. Therefore, the univariate analysis should be viewed more as data description than hypothesis testing.

4.1.1. Univariate analysis

Pre-buyout performance bears on a number of the motivations for EBOs. In particular, the arguments about how employee ownership affects leverage-related costs, labor contracting under asymmetric information, the possible appropriation of employees' firm-specific capital, and managerial control all imply that employee participation is more likely when the firm is performing poorly. Only the tax motivation implies the opposite. Stock price performance evidence indicates that EBOs generally have poorer performance than MBOs prior to the buyout. For example, the median market-adjusted return from 550 days before the buyout through 50 days before the first indication of a change in control (MAR[– 550, – 50]) is – 23.3% for EBOs versus – 3.6% for MBOs, a difference that is significant at the 1% level. Moreover, 16 of the 18 full EBOs have negative market-adjusted returns over this pre-buyout period. The two firms with positive market-adjusted returns are consulting firms. To control for differences in risk, we also examine size-decile returns as calculated by Dimson and Marsh (1986). The median value of size-decile returns for EBOs is – 33.7%, significantly less than the 1.4% observed for MBOs.[9]

With respect to accounting-based performance measures, the median values of the pre-buyout return on assets (ROA) and sales growth (SALESGR) measures for EBOs are less than the medians for MBOs, but the differences are not statistically significant. We find the same result after controlling for industry factors by subtracting the industry averages from each firm's value.

Additionally, we examine the production costs of EBOs and MBOs using a variable that measures the average cost of goods sold, divided by sales (COGS). Cost of goods sold typically includes labor costs, raw materials, and operating expenses depending on whether the firm is in the manufacturing or service sector. The results indicate that the value of COGS is significantly higher, and therefore the gross profit margin is lower in EBOs than MBOs. However, we do not find significant differences after controlling for industry.

---

[9] Market model abnormal returns generally indicate that the median EBO underperforms relative to the median MBO, but the difference is not statistically significant. We place more emphasis on the market-adjusted returns because of concerns about cumulating estimation errors in market model parameters over long intervals and because the market model results are sensitive to the estimation period.

The presence of a defined benefit pension plan is one factor that previous research associates with whether employees either have or will accrue firm-specific capital (see, Ippolito and James, 1992; Pontiff et al., 1990). Defined benefit pension plans are typically structured so that legal pension liabilities to a particular employee increase at an increasing rate with the employee's service. To the extent that employees pay for their pension benefits uniformly over their career through foregone wages, employees overpay, relative to their legal benefits, early in their careers. The accumulated value of these overpayments is the value of employees' firm-specific pension capital. Since a plan termination can cause employees to lose their firm-specific pension capital, the willingness of employees to accumulate this firm-specific capital rests on an implicit agreement that the firm will not opportunistically terminate the pension plan. Plan terminations do not necessarily impose losses on employees. A new pension plan, or an adjustment in other compensation, can compensate employees for losses arising from a terminated plan.

While employee firm-specific capital exists in most defined benefit plans, it does not arise in defined contribution plans which is the other major type of employer-sponsored pension plan. Table 4 indicates that 77.8% of the EBO firms have a defined benefit plan prior to the buyout (DB PLAN), compared to 60.4% for MBO firms. However, a chi-square test of homogeneity fails to reject the hypothesis that the proportions are the same.

The amount of capital that employees have at stake in their defined benefit pension plans depends on a number of firm and labor force characteristics (Peterson, 1992). Ippolito and James (1992) and Pontiff et al. (1990) use the difference between the value of pension assets and the legal pension liability as a measure of the amount of employees' capital that can be appropriated through a plan termination. This measure is accurate if firms fund their pension plans so that the value of pension assets equals the accumulated payments made by employees.

Following the existing literature, we examine the extent to which pension assets differ from legal pension liabilities for those firms that have defined benefit plans using the variable PENSFUND, which equals the value of pension assets, minus vested pension liabilities, divided by corporate assets. Positive values for PENSFUND indicate that there are excess pension assets relative to legal liabilities and thus employees have capital that is subject to appropriation. The median value of PENSFUND for EBO firms is 4.7%, compared to 1.2% for MBO firms. The difference in medians is statistically significant at the 5% level. The higher value of excess pension assets is consistent with employees having more capital at stake in EBO firms. If, contrary to the assumption underlying this analysis, the amount of overfunding is unrelated to the amount of employee capital, the threat of opportunism related to plan termination still increases as overfunding increases, because termination allows the firm to remove the excess assets and use them for other purposes.

Table 4
Pre-buyout characteristics of employee buyouts (EBOs) and management buyouts (MBOs) of entire companies completed during 1980–1990.

Compustat variables are indicated in parentheses with the description of each analysis variable. The mean and median values for each variable are compared for the EBO sample and the MBO sample. Statistical significance at the 1%, 5%, and 10% levels are noted, respectively, with *, **, ***. Difference in means is based on a t-test, and difference in medians is based on a rank sum test. For two dichotomous variables, DB PLAN and TAKEOVER, a chi-square test is used to measure the difference in proportions. Unless otherwise noted, annual financial statement data are from Compustat, Moody's, or Securities and Exchange Commission disclosure documents, and stock return data are from the Center for Research on Security Prices (CRSP).

Variable	Description	Statistic	EBOs	MBOs
MAR[– 550, – 50]	Market adjusted holding period return from day – 550 to day – 50, where day 0 is the first indication of a possible change in control.	*N*	18	95
		Median	– 23.3%*	– 3.6%
		Mean	– 24.3%*	6.2%
Size-Decile Adjusted Return [– 550, – 50]	Holding period return net of size decile holding period return from day – 550 to day – 50, where day 0 is the first indication of a possible change in control.	*N*	18	95
		Median	– 33.7%***	1.4%
		Mean	– 32.4%**	12.2%
ROA	Return on assets (ROA), taken as average annual operating income (V13), divided by total assets (V6), for three years prior to the buyout.	*N*	17	89
		Median	– 14.4%***	16.0%
		Mean	– 11.8%	11.9%
ROA minus Industry Avg. ROA	Average difference between ROA and industry average value of ROA for three years prior to the buyout.	*N*	17	89
		Median	4.5%	6.8%
		Mean	6.8%	4.3%
SALESGR	Average annual growth in sales (V12) for the three years prior to the buyout.	*N*	17	86
		Median	8.3%	10.7%
		Mean	9.1%	13.3%
SALESGR minus Industry Avg. SALESGR	Average difference between SALESGR and the industry average value of SALESGR for the three years prior to buyout.	*N*	17	86
		Median	– 11.6%	– 8.2%
		Mean	– 30.4%	– 38.5%
COGS	Average value of cost of goods sold (COGS), (V41) divided by sales (V12), for the three years prior to buyout.	*N*	15	89
		Median	76.1%**	68.8%
		Mean	76.7%**	66.8%

COGS minus Industry Avg. COGS	Average difference between COGS and the industry average value of COGS for the three years prior to buyout.	*N*	15	89
		Median	– 2.4%	– 5.9%
		Mean	– 27.1%	– 14.9%
DB PLAN	Dichotomous variable equal to one if the firm has a defined benefit pension plan prior to the buyout.	*N*	18	91
		Median	1.0	1.0
		Mean	77.8%	60.4%
PENSFUND[a]	Average value of pension assets (V245), minus vested pension liabilities (V243), divided by assets (V6), for the year prior to the buyout.	*N*	14	55
		Median	4.7%**	1.2%
		Mean	6.4%**	1.7%
TAKEOVER	Dichotomous variable equal to one if the firm was subject to takeover pressure, according to the Wall Street Journal and Nexis sources, prior to the buyout, and equal to zero otherwise.	*N*	18	117
		Median	100.0%	0.0%
		Mean	61.1%**	34.2%
D&O_OWN	Pre-buyout ownership of directors and officers obtained from proxy statements.	*N*	18	92
		Median	5.8%*	16.4%
		Mean	20.0%	22.7%
MARKET/BOOK	Average value of the ratio of market value of equity (V24*V25) plus book value of assets (V6), minus the book value of equity (V60), divided by book value of assets (V6), for three years prior to the buyout.	*N*	15	89
		Median	0.98*	1.16
		Mean	1.04**	1.38
INTANG_ASSETS	Average value of intangible assets (V33), divided by assets (V6), for the three years prior to buyout.	*N*	12	82
		Median	0.6%	0.8%
		Mean	1.9%*	6.0%
R&D_SALES	Average value of research and development expenses (V46), divided by sales (V12), for three years prior to buyout.	*N*	8	41
		Median	0.5%	0.9%
		Mean	0.9%	1.8%
STD(ROA)	Standard deviation of first difference in rate of return on assets for the five years prior to the buyout.	*N*	17	84
		Median	4.1%	4.7%
		Mean	6.0%	8.2%

continued over

Table 4 (Continued)

Variable	Decription	Statistic	EBOs	MBOs
LTD_VALUE	Average value of long term debt (V9) over the market value of equity (V24*V25) plus long term debt (V9) for three years prior to the buyout.	*N*	17	89
		Median	12.0%*	27.0%
		Mean	15.8%*	29.5%
LTD_ASSETS	Average value of long term debt plus debt in current liability (V34) over assets (V6) for three years prior to the buyout.	*N*	17	89
		Median	9.5%*	30.4%
		Mean	14.9%*	39.4%
UNUSED LOSS CARRY-FORWARDS	Average value of unused loss carryforwards (V52) divided by total assets (V6) for three years prior to the buyout.	*N*	15	83
		Median	0.0%	0.0%
		Mean	2.3%	1.1%
EMPLOYEES	Average number of employees (in thousands) during the three years prior to the buyout.	*N*	17	89
		Median	7.6*	2.4
		Mean	10.3***	5.0
ASSETS_EMP	Average annual total assets (V6) per employee (V30) for the three years prior to the buyout.[b]	*N*	17	88
		Median	44.9*	60.5
		Mean	46.0	212.8

[a]Only firms with defined benefit plans are included.
[b]A few financial institutions with very large values of assets relative to employees increase the mean significantly. Excluding financial institutions does not change the conclusions of the analysis.

Nine of the 13 full EBOs with excess pension assets terminate a pension plan at the time of the EBO. In seven of the nine cases, it appears that the firm uses the excess assets to finance the buyout without necessarily imposing losses on employees. The mechanism by which this occurs is best illustrated with a simple example. Suppose that a firm with $50 million in excess pension assets establishes an ESOP that borrows $50 million. The proceeds of the ESOP loan are given to the sponsoring firm to repurchase outstanding shares. In exchange, the ESOP receives shares in the post-buyout firm, all of which are unallocated. Immediately following the buyout, the overfunded pension plan is terminated and the excess assets are used to pay off the ESOP loan, which allocates shares to employees. Provided employees do not pay for their ESOP shares by foregoing other compensation, the essential aspect of the transaction is that employees trade their defined benefit pension capital for equity capital. The ESOP loan serves simply as a bridge loan that gives the firm access to the cash in the overfunded pension plan until the plan is terminated. This scenario effectively describes seven of the nine terminations, where the excess assets were rolled into the ESOP to repay the ESOP loan immediately following the buyout.

Management's reluctance to impose losses on employees could suggest that they perceive the loss of future employee investments in the firm to be an important source of value. Alternatively, as Shleifer and Summers (1988) suggest, incumbent managers may be more reluctant to appropriate employees' firm-specific capital even though it is in shareholders' best interest to do so. Another potential interpretation is that the excess pension assets are rolled into the ESOP to reduce excise taxes on pension reversions. However, only three of the nine pension plan reversions take place after the excise tax becomes effective in 1986. Finally, the use of excess pension assets to reduce the level of debt could reflect creditors' desire to reduce quickly the post-buyout level of debt.

We also examine whether EBOs and MBOs are subject to prior takeover activity (TAKEOVER), which is defined as either a takeover bid or a Schedule 13D filing in the year prior to the buyout announcement. We find that 61.1% of the full EBOs experience takeover pressure prior to the buyout, compared to only 34.2% of the full MBOs, a difference which is statistically significant at the 5% level. The higher incidence of takeover pressure for EBOs is consistent with EBOs being motivated as a means to protect employees' firm-specific capital, and also with the managerial control hypothesis.

The ownership by directors and officers is examined to provide insight into how capable management is of fending off a takeover threat. Pre-buyout ownership by directors and officers (D&O_OWN), as reported in the firm's proxy statement during the year prior to the buyout, is 5.8% for the median EBO and 16.4% for the median MBO, and this difference is statistically significant. Among firms that are subject to takeover pressure, the median value of director and officer ownership also is lower for EBOs at 3.0%, than for MBOs at 7.4%, however, the difference is not statistically significant. These findings are consistent with the argument that managers with low ownership stakes are more likely to include employees in a buyout when they have limited means of defending against a takeover attempt.

Since EBOs are predicted to have greater leverage-related costs, we examine whether EBOs have assets with greater firm-specific value (Myers, 1977; Williamson, 1979). While measuring the extent to which assets have firm-specific value is difficult, we follow the existing literature and use the following proxies: (1) the market-to-book ratio (MARKET/BOOK) which equals the market value of equity, plus the book value of assets, minus the book value of equity, divided by the book value of assets (Smith and Watts, 1992), (2) the ratio of intangible assets to total assets (Titman and Wessels, 1988), and (3) the ratio of research and development expenses to sales (Long and Malitz, 1985).

Contrary to the prediction that EBO firms have a higher proportion of firm-specific assets, the median values of all three measures indicate that EBO firms typically have a lower proportion of firm-specific assets than MBO firms, although the difference is statistically significant only for the market-to-book ratio. One explanation for the lower market-to-book ratios observed for EBOs follows from the earlier evidence that EBO firms typically have poor performance prior to the buyout which, in turn, suggests a higher likelihood of distress. All else being equal, a higher likelihood of distress would reduce the market value of the firm and lower the market-to-book ratio.

Capital structure theory generally hypothesizes that leverage-related costs are positively related to the variability of cash flows. Accordingly, firms with higher variability of cash flows may be more likely to include employees in a buyout, because their leverage-related costs make it more costly to borrow the funds necessary for the buyout without a change in operating commitments to employees. The arguments concerning risk-bearing costs have conflicting predictions about the effect of cash flow variability on the likelihood of employee participation. The risk-bearing costs associated with employee ownership imply that employee participation would be less likely the higher the variability of the firm's cash flows, holding managerial ownership fixed. However, managers, in an effort to maintain control, while at the same time reducing their own risk-bearing costs, may be more inclined to include employees in a buyout, the greater the variability of cash flows. Consistent with conflicting effects, the standard deviation of the first difference in the ratio of operating income to assets, shown in Table 4 as the variable STD(ROA), does not differ significantly for EBO firms and MBO firms.

An alternative approach to assessing leverage-related costs is to examine the firm's pre-buyout financial leverage ratios. A large body of theory proposes that a firm's leverage ratio is endogenously chosen by management to take account of all of the costs and benefits of debt. Since many of the costs and benefits are admittedly hard to measure, the firm's pre-buyout leverage provides a 'reduced form' measure of a firm's leverage-related costs under the assumption that the benefits of debt are constant across firms. The leverage ratios reported in Table 4, LTD_VALUE and LTD_ASSETS, indicate that EBOs experience significantly lower median values of pre-buyout leverage than MBOs. These results are consistent with EBOs having higher leverage-related costs than MBOs prior to the buyout.

A tax based motivation for EBOs is explored with the variable unused loss carryforwards. EBOs could be motivated to preserve unused loss carryforwards if the transaction results in more than 50% of employee equity being placed in an ESOP. However, the median value of unused loss carryforwards is zero for both EBOs and MBOs, which is inconsistent with unused loss carryforwards motivating employee participation in most transactions.

The incentive alignment hypothesis suggests that employee participation is valuable because it increases the productivity of workers. However, the magnitude of potential productivity gains are likely to be reduced by free rider problems, which increase, all else being equal, with the number of employees. The median level of employment is significantly greater in EBOs than in MBOs, and thus this finding is inconsistent with the incentive alignment hypothesis.

The final variable explored in Table 4, assets per employee (ASSETS_EMP), examines whether the risk-sharing costs of general employees are higher in EBOs or MBOs. EBO firms have a lower median value of assets per employee than MBOs, and the difference is statistically significant at the 1% level. The lower the value of the firm's assets per employee, the less wealth that each individual employee must invest in order for employees as a group to obtain a given ownership stake. Since employee diversification opportunities increase as the wealth invested decreases, the finding of lower assets per employee is consistent with employees' risk-bearing costs being lower in EBOs.

4.1.2. Multivariate analysis

To examine whether the findings from the univariate analysis also are valid in a multivariate context, Table 5 summarizes the results of three logit models, where the dependent variable for each model is the probability that an EBO will occur, divided by the probability that an MBO will occur. Given the small number of observations and the potential for collinearity among variables, not all of the variables examined in the previous section are included in any single model. Instead, each specification includes one measure for each of the main factors that are hypothesized to affect the choice to include employees in the buyout. These hypothesized factors are firm performance, pension funding, leverage-related costs, takeover pressure, employee risk-bearing costs, and the level of ownership by officers and directors. To prevent omitting all firms without defined benefit plans from the models, the pension funding variable is assigned a zero value if the firm does not have a defined benefit plan. Since the choice of variables to include in the models is conditioned on the univariate results, the reported *p*-values should be interpreted with caution.

Table 5
Logit analysis of the probability of an employee buyout (EBO) relative to a management buyout (MBO) of entire companies.

The dependent variable equals the probability that an EBO will occur, divided by the probability that an MBO will occur. Coefficient estimates are reported with p-values below in parentheses. Independent variables are defined in Table 4.

Underlying factor	Independent variable	Model 1	Model 2	Model 3
Intercept	Intercept	− 0.34	− 0.03	0.77
		(0.74)	(0.98)	(0.43)
Firm performance	MAR[− 550, − 50]	− 2.59	− 2.62	− 2.18
		(0.06)	(0.05)	(0.08)
Pension funding	PENSFUND	11.64	16.85	15.17
		(0.14)	(0.07)	(0.06)
Leverage-related costs	LTD_VALUE	− 5.41	− 5.68	
		(0.02)	(0.02)	
Leverage-related costs	MARKET/BOOK			− 0.02
				(0.42)
Takeover pressure	TAKEOVER	1.46	1.28	0.66
		(0.05)	(0.11)	(0.40)
Employee risk-bearing costs	ASSETS_EMP	− 0.03	− 0.03	− 0.02
		(0.03)	(0.03)	(0.11)
Ownership of officers and directors	D&O_OWN		0.02	
			(0.41)	
Sample size	# of EBOs	17	17	15
	# of MBOs	73	63	69

The logit models indicate that, after controlling for other factors, the likelihood of an EBO is (1) negatively related to pre-buyout stock market performance, (2) positively related to pension funding, (3) negatively related to pre-buyout leverage, and (4) negatively related to the value of assets per employee. In the last specification, the coefficient on the market-to-book ratio is negative, but not statistically significant, which suggests that after controlling for other factors, EBO firms do not have lower market-to-book ratios.

Two important conclusions emerge from the evidence on the pre-buyout characteristics that help explain why employees participate in buyouts. First, EBO firms often have excess pension assets that can be used to help finance the buyout. By rolling over the excess assets into an ESOP and allocating shares to employees, managers gain access to the cash in the pension plan without necessarily imposing losses on employees. Further, EBOs' poorer performance and lower pre-buyout financial leverage suggest that EBO firms have higher leverage-related costs than MBO firms under their pre-buyout operating commitments. By substituting equity for part of ongoing cash labor compensation costs and perhaps even lowering these costs, the EBO firm increases its ability to cover interest payments, which helps the firm to obtain borrowing for the buyout. Second, there is evidence consistent with managers including employees in the buyout to enhance managerial control. This conclusion follows from the results indicating that, relative to MBOs, EBOs have poorer performance, greater takeover pressure, lower levels of pre-buyout management ownership, and greater risk of appropriation of employees' capital.

4.2. Structure of EBO transactions

4.2.1. Labor contract restructuring

Cash commitments for employee compensation will be reduced following the buyout to the extent that an ESOP replaces pre-buyout cash commitments for wages and pension plans. In addition, an EBO may also be accompanied by concessions that lower the level of post-buyout cash payments promised to employees. Since either of these changes can be instrumental in obtaining financing, we look for changes in non-management employee compensation occurring at the time of EBOs that are consistent with reductions in cash compensation costs. The case descriptions in Appendix A summarize the reported labor contract changes for the full EBOs and Appendix B summarizes the reported changes for five spinoff EBOs. For the 18 full EBOs, the evidence indicates that one firm reports wage reductions, eight firms terminate defined benefit plans, and one firm terminates a defined benefit plan and lowers wages. Thus, ten of the full EBOs, representing 56% of the sample, involve compensation changes that reduce the cash burden of labor costs relative to the pre-buyout period.

While the evidence indicates that EBOs frequently involve labor contract changes that enhance debt repayment, some MBOs involve similar changes (e.g., see Denis, 1995, for a discussion of Safeway's LBO). Therefore, we examine proxy, Schedule 13E-3, and 14D-1 statements describing MBO transactions for evidence of labor contract changes at the time of the buyout. These statements are obtained from the SEC Edgar On-line Proxy Service and from Disclosure, Inc. Because disclosure documents are not available for a number of the MBOs, the sample is reduced to 39 full MBOs. The average transaction size of these MBOs does not differ significantly from the average transaction size of the full EBOs. In contrast to the EBO firms, no MBO reduces wages and only one MBO terminates a pension plan. Four EBO firms and two MBO firms also terminate other compensation plans like profit sharing, stock option, or bonus plans, but it is not possible to discern the effects of these changes on cash compensation costs. Thus, one of 39, or 2.6%, of the MBO transactions shows evidence of labor contract changes that lower pre-buyout cash commitments for employee compensation costs versus 56% of the EBOs.[10] A chi-square test rejects the hypothesis that the proportions are the same at the 1% level. This evidence is consistent with EBOs being motivated in part by attempts to enhance the firm's ability to borrow funds for the buyout.

Additional evidence that employee participation influences the ability of firms to borrow to finance a buyout is the observation that four full EBOs are preceded by failed attempts at an MBO or leveraged buyout (LBO). In part, the failure is due to a lack of financing. In three of the four, we observe labor contract changes at the time of the EBO which reduce cash compensation costs. For example, the EBO at Lyon Metal, following two failed takeover attempts by outside bidders and a failed MBO, was not successful until the court approved the use of excess pension benefits to finance the buyout and the union agreed to concessions. The case studies for Amsted Industries, Blue Bell, and Dan River illustrate this point further.

4.2.2. Post-buyout financial structure

In Table 6, we report information on the financial structure of the full EBO firms and the subsample of 39 full MBOs for which we were able to obtain post-buyout financial information. Table 6 reports the leverage ratios, debt claims, and equity claims for these firms.

Leverage. In Table 6 we compare the post-buyout leverage ratios of EBO and MBO firms. Leverage is measured as the ratio of long term-debt inclusive of debt in current liabilities and capitalized leases, to total capitalization. Total capitalization is taken from the pro-forma statement of capitalization for the buyout transaction. When this information is unavailable, total capital is the sum of preexisting debt, less noted repayments, if any, plus acquisition-related long-term debt, preferred stock, and common stock. As previously noted, nine EBO firms and one MBO firm use excess pension assets to finance the buyout. Typically, firms use the excess assets to repay part of the buyout debt, and therefore we report a leverage ratio before and after the reversion of excess assets.

Using the pre-reversion measure of leverage, the median EBO has a post-buyout leverage ratio of 89.6%. By comparison, the median post-buyout leverage ratio for MBOs is 74.8%, which is significantly different at the 1% level from the EBO leverage ratio.[11] Factoring in the reversion of excess assets, the median

[10] We also searched the MAJPAP and PRNEWS files of NEXIS for evidence of labor contract changes in EBOs and MBOs in the buyout year and for the three years thereafter. We found few reports of labor contract changes, and no evidence that distinguished EBO firms from MBO firms. Therefore, SEC disclosure documents appear to be a better source for labor contract changes.

[11] The post-buyout leverage ratio for MBOs is lower than the 89.1% reported in Kaplan and Stein (1993). However, our sample includes smaller MBOs than Kaplan and Stein, who examine MBOs which exceed $100 million in size. The median MBO transaction size in Kaplan and Stein is $395 million, versus $256 million for our MBO subsample.

Table 6
Financial structure of employee buyouts (EBOs) compared to management buyouts (MBOs) of entire companies that were completed between 1980–1990.

Data are from SEC filings. Total capitalization is that reported on the pro-forma statement of capitalization for the transaction. If unavailable, total capitalization is the sum of pre-existing long-term debt, less any disclosed refundings, and acquisition-related long-term debt, preferred stock, and common stock. Equity claims are reported on a fully diluted basis, with ownership determined as a percentage of total votes. Statistical significance at the 1%, 5%, and 10% levels are noted, respectively, with *, **, ***. Difference in means is based on a *t*-test and difference in medians is based on a rank sum test.

Ratio	Statistic	EBOs	MBOs
Panel A: Post-buyout leverage			
Long term debt/total capitalization, prior to reversion of excess pension assets	*N*	18	37
	Median	89.6%*	74.8%
	Mean	85.1%	75.2%
Long term debt/total capitalization, after reversion of excess pension assets	*N*	18	37
	Median	79.5%*	74.8%
	Mean	81.5%	75.2%
Panel B: Post-buyout debt claims			
Bank debt/total capitalization after reversion of excess pension assets	*N*	18	35
	Median	62.3%*	48.8%
	Mean	61.5%*	46.3%
ESOP loan/total capitalization after reversion of excess pension assets	*N*	18	n.a
	Median	30.6%	n.a
	Mean	35.2%	n.a
Panel C: Post-buyout equity claims			
Percentage of equity held by third party and institutional investors	*N*	18	39
	Median	9.6%*	62.0%
	Mean	16.5%*	54.8%
Percentage of equity held by managers	*N*	18	39
	Median	24.0%*	38.8%
	Mean	24.4%*	45.2%
Percentage of equity held by employees and the ESOP	*N*	18	n.a.
	Median	56.9%	n.a.
	Mean	59.1%	n.a.

post-buyout leverage for EBOs falls from 89.6% to 79.5%. The ten percentage point drop in the median leverage ratio illustrates that the reversion of excess pension assets has an important moderating effect on the leverage of EBOs. After the reversion, the median EBO leverage ratio is still significantly higher than the leverage ratio for MBOs, but the magnitude of the difference is considerably smaller.

Debt claims. Jensen (1989) and James (1987) argue that the type of debt financing used, whether private or bank debt versus public debt, can have important implications for monitoring management. In particular, a bank's incentive to monitor firm performance will likely increase with the ratio of bank debt to total capital. Hence, we investigate the extent to which EBOs and MBOs differ in this ratio. For the median EBO, the ratio of bank debt to total capital is 62.3% versus 48.8% for MBOs, a difference that is significant at the 1% level. The reliance on bank debt by EBOs is further highlighted by the fact that in 12 of the 18 full EBOs, bank debt in conjunction with excess pension assets provides all of non-equity funding for the transaction.

Typically, the ESOP loan, which represents 30.6% of the total capital for the median EBO, is borrowed from a bank. The use of bank debt could be related to the tax benefits of the interest exclusion received on ESOP loans made by banks. However, the interest exclusion became applicable after 1984, and ten of the eleven EBOs conducted before 1985 were financed solely with bank debt.

Public debt, and in particular high-yield debt, become more prevalent as a source of LBO financing during the latter half of 1980s (Kaplan and Stein, 1993). To determine whether the greater use of bank debt in EBOs can be attributed to the timing of the transaction, we estimated the following regression:

$$(\text{Bank Debt})/(\text{Total Capitalization}) = \alpha + \beta_1 * \text{EBO} + \beta_2 * \text{Trend} + \varepsilon, \quad (1)$$

where EBO equals 1 if the transaction is an EBO, and 0 if it is an MBO, and Trend is a time trend. The results indicate that the estimate of β_1 is positive and significant at the 10% level, and the estimate of β_2 is not significant, suggesting that timing is not a major driver of bank debt.

The greater use of bank debt in EBOs is consistent with some of the earlier evidence presented on the factors that distinguish EBOs and MBOs. First, as mentioned above, James (1987) suggests that banks offer valuable monitoring services that help resolve informational asymmetries between management and outside creditors. The periodic reevaluation of credit at relatively short intervals, which would occur with bank loans or lines of credit, is likely to be especially valuable for EBO firms with high debt levels and a recent history of poor performance. Conversely, EBOs unwilling to submit to such scrutiny could find public market funding alternatives considerably more costly. The poor pre-buyout performance of EBOs is also consistent with Gilson et al. (1990) and Jensen's (1989) view that buyouts that are structured with concentrated holdings of private debt help to reduce the direct costs of financial distress.

Equity claims. The structure of equity claims provides information on the allocation of control, as well as additional information on monitoring performed in EBOs. In the typical MBO, institutional or third party investors hold majority equity stakes in the post-buyout firm. It is generally accepted that large ownership stakes by buyout specialists provide an important monitoring function (Jensen, 1989). However, similar equity holdings are not observed in EBOs.

For the full EBOs, third party and institutional investors obtain a median 9.6% of the post-buyout equity, compared to 62.0% for MBOs.

The relative absence of third party equity investors in EBOs is consistent with outside equity holders being reluctant to participate in EBOs given the potential for conflicts of interest with employee owners. An alternative explanation is that EBO managers pursue an EBO to enhance their control, replacing third party investors with the ESOP, whose shares are either controlled by management, by trustees appointed by management, or by employees. Regardless of the reason, monitoring by third party and institutional investors is limited in EBOs. Unless banks provide an alternative monitoring mechanism (see James, 1987), the evidence suggests that EBO managers operate with less outside monitoring than MBO managers.

Another factor affecting managerial control is the post-buyout ownership by managers. As reported in Table 6, the median level of managerial ownership is 24.0% for EBOs, and 38.8% for MBOs, and the difference in medians is significantly different from zero. By comparison, Kaplan (1989a) reports that MBOs with a minimum transaction size of $50 million have a median post-buyout management ownership of 22.6%. While this suggests that MBO managers have at least as much control as EBO managers, this interpretation ignores the possibility that EBO managers control unallocated ESOP shares, an issue we review below.

4.2.3. Employee control in EBOs

Table 6 indicates that for the sample of full EBOs, the median level of shares held by the ESOP and post-buyout employee ownership is 56.9%, on a fully diluted basis. This compares to a median level of pre-buyout employee ownership, which includes pre-existing ESOP shares and shares held by other pension plans, of 1.5%. Thus, when the ESOP loan is repaid, which occurs after nine years for the median firm, and the ESOP shares are fully allocated to employees' accounts, employees typically end up as majority shareholders in EBO firms. However, since most ESOP shares are unallocated immediately following the buyout, the ownership percentage reported for employees on a fully allocated basis overstates the actual control rights employees initially receive in an EBO. Employees must receive the cash flow and control rights on their allocated shares, but they do not necessarily receive the rights associated with unallocated shares.

Employees can control the voting of unallocated ESOP shares, if the trustee is directed by the plan document to vote the unallocated shares in the same proportion as the allocated shares are voted. Chaplinsky and Niehaus (1994) report that over 80% of ESOPs in publicly held firms require the trustee to vote unallocated shares as allocated shares are voted. Thus, in most public firms, employees effectively control the voting of all ESOP shares, regardless of whether the shares are actually allocated. In contrast to the experience of public firms, in only three of the full EBOs do employees control the unallocated shares. That is, trustees generally vote unallocated shares independently of how allocated shares are voted. The implication is that employees do not receive the control rights associated with unallocated ESOP shares. These rights usually rest with a trustee who is either appointed by the board or is a member of the board.

To examine employee control rights one year after the buyout, we assume that the ESOP loan is repaid uniformly over time, and that excess pension assets are used to increase allocated shares immediately following the buyout. Under these assumptions, employees control 15.7% of the shares one year after the buyout for the median firm, well below the 56.9% reported on a fully allocated basis.

Even though direct voting of shares by employees is limited, employees potentially can influence firm decision-making through board representation. However, in only three of the 18 full EBOs do we find employee representatives on the board and then only as minority members. Employee influence is more frequent in spinoff EBOs, as six of the 14 spinoff EBOs have employees represented on the board. In five of the six spinoff EBOs with employee representation, unions negotiate on behalf of employees in the buyout (see Appendix B). Employee representation also appears to be related to the level of employee ownership, as employee ownership is close to 100% in all but one of the transactions with employee representation. More importantly, even in the transactions with employee representation, employees typically do not obtain a majority of the board seats. Among the spinoff EBOs, only Seymour Wire's board has more employee members than managers and outsiders.

The general lack of initial employee voting rights and board representation is consistent with lenders providing funding only if the potential conflicts between employees and non-employee investors over corporate policy are mitigated. One way to mitigate such conflicts is to reduce employee control rights until the debt is repaid. A revealing example of this strategy is Weirton Steel (see Appendix B). Following the buyout, its board consisted of three union representatives, the CEO, and eight outside members. Outside members were added to the board at creditors' insistence so that the firm would be independent of employee control for the first six years after the buyout. Hence, the evidence suggests that EBOs are structured to reduce the costs of employee ownership.

The lack of employee control of unallocated ESOP shares is also consistent with the hypothesis that managers include employees to enhance managerial control. When ESOP shares are combined with the shares directly owned by management, EBO managers generally obtain greater control in the post-buyout period than MBO managers. The possibility that employees would compete with managers for control once the ESOP shares are allocated to employees suggests that the managers, at the time of the buyout, are willing to accept the possibility of less control in the future for additional control immediately following the buyout. Of course, control-seeking managers who anticipate leaving the firm after a few years might find this to be a desirable tradeoff.

4.3. Post-buyout record

Previous studies investigate whether the high debt service payments resulting from leveraged buyouts lead to asset sales, layoffs, and, ultimately, the failure of the enterprise (see, e.g., Kaplan, 1991; Muscarella and Vetsuypens, 1990; and Opler, 1993). As discussed earlier, a potential disadvantage of employee ownership is that it could lead to conflicts between employees and other investors, and inhibit managers' ability to restructure and, therefore, to survive. On the other hand, one would expect EBOs to be structured to minimize these conflicts, and indeed the evidence on employees' limited control rights is consistent with this view. To investigate whether employee participation affects a buyout firm's ability to restructure, we compare EBOs and MBOs with respect to asset sales, employment growth, and survivorship.

Using information from the Wall Street Journal Index, we compare the proportion of EBO firms that sell assets relative to the number of MBO firms that sell assets subsequent to the buyout, through 1993. Although our tests do not account for the size and quality of the assets sold, we find that 16.7% of the 18 full EBOs had asset sales, compared to 38.5% of the 118 full MBOs. A chi-square test of homogeneity rejects the hypothesis that the proportions are the same at the 10% level. It is not clear whether the reduced number of asset sales by EBO firms is indicative of a lack of assets valuable to others or whether employee ownership hampers managers' ability to restructure. In theory, one reason EBO firms could have fewer assets that have value to others is that their assets have more firm-specific value. However, our earlier presented measures of firm-specific assets do not support this explanation.

To examine whether employment growth differs between EBOs and MBOs in the post-buyout period, we gather firm-level employment data from Standard and Poors' Register of Corporations, Directors and Officers for the year prior to the buyout, and for the third and fifth year after the buyout. Table 7 summarizes the post-buyout employment changes for full EBOs and full MBOs. The median EBO firm reduces employment in the three years after the buyout by 3.8%, while the median MBO firm does not change employment. The difference in median values for EBOs and MBOs is not statistically significant at the 10% level. For the five-year period, the median percentage decline in employment is 7.7% for EBOs, and 0.0% for MBOs, but again the difference in median values is not statistically significant.

The last two rows of Table 7 present employment changes after adjusting for industry effects. Specifically, we calculate the difference between the percentage change in employment for each firm and subtract the percentage change in industry employment over the period, where industry employment is based on the figure reported in Employment and Earnings for the three-digit standard industrial classification (SIC) code. For this measure, if the three-digit data are unavailable, the two-digit code is used. Relative to their industry, both the

Table 7
Percentage change in employment, for employee buyouts (EBOs) and full management buyouts (MBOs) of entire companies completed during 1980–1990, from one year before the buyout through three and five years after the buyout.

Data are adjusted for industry by taking the buyout firm's percentage change in employment and subtracting the percentage change in employment for all firms in the same industry, as defined by the three-digit standard industrial classification (SIC) code. The two-digit SIC code is used if the three-digit code is unavailable. Industry data are reported by Employment and Earnings. In no case do we reject that the mean or median value for EBOs is the same as for MBOs. Difference in means is based on a *t*-test, and difference in medians is based on a rank sum test.

Post-buyout time period	Industry adjusted	Statistic	Employment growth	
			EBOs	MBOs
3 Years	No	*N*	18	94
		Median	– 3.8%	0.0%
		Mean	– 1.4%	19.3%
5 years	No	*N*	15	
		Median	– 7.7%	0.0%
		Mean	3.3%	22.6%
3 years	Yes	*N*	18	80
		Median	– 9.6%	– 1.8%
		Mean	– 1.6%	21.2%
5 years	Yes	*N*	15	81
		Median	– 10.8%	– 1.7%
		Mean	2.4%	26.4%

median EBO and MBO firms reduce employment after the buyout. While the decrease for EBO firms is larger than for MBO firms, the difference between the median values of EBO and MBO firms is not statistically different from zero. Thus, the results indicate that employee ownership does not prevent managers from reducing employment to the same extent as in MBOs. In addition, we find based on information obtained from the Wall Street Journal, NEXIS, and ABI Proquest, that at least seven of the 18 full EBO firms announce layoffs or plant closings, and three of the 14 spinoff EBOs announce layoffs or plant closings subsequent to the buyout, through 1993. This evidence is consistent with the finding that EBOs are structured to reduce the influence of employees and the potential conflicts posed by employee control.

The long-term outcomes for EBOs and MBOs as ongoing concerns are similar. By the end of 1993, 12.5% of 32 EBO firms undergo Chapter 11 reorganizations, 18.8% are acquired, and 18.8% go public. Thus, 50% of the EBO firms remain private with considerable employee ownership. The results for the MBO sample are similar: 14.8% go into bankruptcy proceedings, 16.2%

are acquired, and 23.2% go public.[12] Thus, the survival rate for MBO firms is 45.8%. Additional evidence on the longer term effects of employee ownership is provided in the epilogues for the full EBOs in Appendix A. This evidence, and the evidence on survivorship rates, suggests that EBOs are a viable organizational structure for certain firms.

5. Conclusions

This article is the first study to empirically examine the factors that motivate employee participation in a buyout. The analysis yields a number of important findings that help to explain why employees participate in buyouts. Prior to the buyout, we observe that, relative to MBOs:

- EBO firms usually have a lower value of assets per employee.
- EBO firms have poorer stock price performance, and lower leverage.
- EBO firms are more likely to have overfunded pension plans.
- EBO firms are more likely to be under takeover pressure.
- EBO firms usually have lower ownership by officers and directors.

Following the buyout, we observe that:

- Cash-reducing compensation changes are reported by only 2.6% of MBOs compared to 56% of EBOs.
- EBO firms are as highly leveraged as MBO firms, but use a higher proportion of bank debt.
- EBO firms have lower percentage ownership by third party and institutional investors.
- Employees fail to obtain substantial control rights early in EBOs.
- EBO firms do not appear to differ from MBO firms with regard to employment growth or long-term outcomes.

As the number and scope of the findings might suggest, the evidence does not point to a single force motivating employee participation in buyouts. This is not surprising given the large number of theoretical factors affecting the costs and benefits of employee ownership, and given that EBOs involve substantial financial and operating changes. Nevertheless, we find three general themes present in many of the findings.

The first theme concerns the role that employee participation plays in the restructuring of labor contracts, and how the resulting changes facilitate

---

[12] These results are consistent with the LBO studies by Kaplan (1991), Degeorge and Zeckhauser (1993), and Van de Gucht and Moore (1997).

financing of the buyout. By having employees trade their capital in defined pension benefit plans for stock in the post-buyout firm, the firm is able to gain access to excess pension assets, which reduces the amount of outside borrowing that is needed. Also, EBO firms restructure labor contracts in ways that lower the pre-buyout cash commitments of employee compensation costs, and, perhaps, in some instances, lower the level of employee compensation costs. These changes, in turn, help the firm obtain the financing needed for the buyout. The poor performance of EBO firms, and their low level of pre-buyout leverage, suggests that these firms would have a hard time borrowing the funds necessary for the buyout absent these changes in labor contracts.

The second theme is that EBOs have characteristics and are structured to mitigate the costs of employee ownership. EBOs tend to have lower employee risk-bearing costs, as indicated by lower asset-to-labor ratios. Conflicts of interest between employees and debtholders are attenuated by withholding substantial control rights from employees until most of the buyout debt is retired. Perhaps to avoid the potential conflicts with employees, third-party equity investors have limited participation in EBOs. Consistent with the conflicts being effectively mitigated, post-buyout employment growth and long-term outcomes for EBO and MBO firms are similar.

Finally, the circumstances in which EBOs tend to occur, including low pre-buyout ownership by officers and directors, poor performance, takeover pressure, and high risk of employee firm-specific capital appropriation, are also the circumstances in which managers might be motivated to use an EBO to maintain control. As noted above, the ownership structure that emerges in EBOs typically features a large degree of managerial control. Our evidence, however, cannot distinguish whether this high degree of managerial control occurs from managers' desire for greater control, or to reduce the potential for conflicts among the capital providers to the buyout.

Appendix A. Case studies of full employee buyouts

Information for the case studies is obtained from SEC disclosure documents for the buyouts and text searches of Nexis and ABI Proquest files. Unless otherwise noted, employment information gathered from Standard and Poors' Register of Corporations is for one year before and five years after the EBO. Financial performance is measured by the pre-buyout market-adjusted stock return from day -550 to day -50 (MAR[-550, -50]), relative to the first mention of takeover activity. The appendix is updated for events through December 1993.

1. *American Standard, Inc.*

American Standard is a leading manufacturer of plumbing supplies, air-conditioners, and auto-related products. Prior to the buyout in March 1988,

American Standard attempted to change its strategic focus, selling several of its divisions, including Mosler Safe, to a management group in an ESOP spinoff. The firm's pre-buyout market-adjusted return in the two years leading up to the EBO, MAR[− 550, − 50], was − 7.4%. In January 1988, Black and Decker made an unsolicited bid of $56 per share for American Standard. After inviting offers from other parties, management proposed a recapitalization plan that included an ESOP. Black and Decker withdrew a $77 per share offer in March subsequent to American Standard's acceptance of a $78 per share, or $2.5 billion, buyout offer from Kelso and Company, Inc. No other outside bidders competed for the company.

The firm terminated its existing pension plan, and used the excess assets of $50 million to repay part of the ESOP loan. Subsequent to the buyout, the firm has recovered from financial distress suffered in 1990 in part due to greatly improved operating efficiency. This improvement generated some $200 million that has been used to reduce the buyout debt. The number of employees decreased from 50,400 employed one year prior to the buyout to 33,300 employed five years later. The firm remains privately held.

2. *American Sterilizer Co.*

American Sterilizer is a manufacturer of hospital equipment and health care products. There is no evidence of takeover pressure prior to the buyout in February 1985. However, during the year prior to the buyout, the firm omitted a dividend, combined two divisions, sold a division, and closed a plant. The MAR[− 550, − 50] was − 31.7%. Bristol-Myers provided $30 million in financing for the buyout in exchange for an option to acquire the AMSCO-Hall Surgical division. An additional $25 million was provided by the termination of an over-funded pension plan.

Subsequent to the buyout, American Sterilizer was merged in 1987 into a new company with new management, Amsco International. By the end of 1990, sales had increased, net income had doubled, and long-term debt was significantly reduced. In March of 1991, Amsco International went public. In the year following the IPO, its stock traded at prices 60% above the IPO offer price. The number of employees decreased from 3500 prior to the buyout to 2500 five years later.

3. *Amsted Industries, Inc.*

Amsted Industries is a diversified manufacturer of products for the construction, building, and railroad industries. In April 1985, Maxxam Associates filed a Schedule 13D with the SEC, disclosing its ownership of 8.6% of the shares. In response, Amsted filed suit and took other defensive measures such as adopting a poison pill. The firm's MAR[− 550, − 50] was − 1.8%. After investigating a number of alternative transactions, including the use of an ESOP in a leveraged buyout, an ESOP was established. In October 1985, the defined benefit pension plans were terminated. A month later, management and the employees proposed an EBO for $550 million, or $50 per share, but did not obtain financing for the transaction. In early 1986, directors considered a revised buyout offer of $517 million by management and employees which, after further revision, was approved by shareholders in May 1986. The proposed ESOP included a feature that guaranteed employees a minimum retirement benefit. Excess assets from the termination of an over-funded pension plan covering salaried workers provided $75 million, which was used to repay part of the ESOP loan. Union pension plans continued as before the EBO. Other changes in compensation include the termination of a stock appreciation plan, and an employee capital accumulation plan.

Due to expenses for the ESOP, the firm reported losses in its first year, but income has improved since then. The firm has reopened several plants, acquired another firm, and its bond rating has improved. Preferred stock issued in connection with the EBO has been recalled. Employment increased over the five years following the EBO from 6900 to 8100. The firm remains privately held.

4. *Blue Bell Inc.*

Blue Bell manufactures apparel products under three major brands: Wrangler, Jantzen, and Red Kap. The pre-buyout market-adjusted return for Blue Bell in the two years leading up to the EBO in May 1984 was − 45.9%. In 1981, Bass Brothers Enterprises began accumulating Blue Bell stock, and had acquired 23% of the stock by 1984. When Blue Bell management and Bass could not come to terms, Blue Bell repurchased the shares from Bass in several transactions. Prior to the last repurchase, Blue Bell management approached Kohlberg, Kravis, and Roberts, Inc. (KKR) in April 1983, and Kelso and Company, Inc. in July 1983, about the possibility of a buyout, but no proposal materialized. In April 1984, Canada's Belzberg family made a Schedule 13D disclosure, and by June had requested U.S. government clearance to acquire half of Blue Bell's stock. In response, Blue Bell's management approached Forstmann, Little and Company about a possible buyout. No proposal materialized from that approach and Blue Bell's management again requested Kelso to develop a proposal for a buyout. In July, after encountering difficulties in obtaining financing at $51 per share, Blue Bell agreed to an EBO at $47.50 per share. There is no evidence that excess assets from terminated pension funds provided funds for the transaction. Five established pension plans covering general workers continued after the EBO.

Two years after the buyout, Blue Bell was acquired by VF Corporation, a rival firm and the maker of Lee jeans. VF Corporation's overall acquisition cost was $90 million above the buyout price. Analysts attribute some of the gain in value to the improved operating performance. The ESOP became the second-largest holder of VF stock. Employment fell from 34,000 prior to the EBO to 20,000 at the time of VF's purchase.

5. *Charter Medical Corporation*

Charter Medical operates a network of psychiatric hospitals, and is a major supplier of employee mental health care services. In the early to mid 1980s, the psychiatric hospital industry experienced rapid growth. Employee mental health-care coverage plans made up 70% of Charter's revenues, leaving the company vulnerable in the late 1980s when many firms reduced spending on these plans. In response, the firm laid off workers and closed some clinics. Prior to the EBO in September 1987, the MAR[– 550, – 50] was – 34.6%. In September 1987, senior managers proposed to take the firm private at $40 per share. No competing bids followed, largely because the Chief Executive Officer (CEO), William A. Fickling Jr., and his family controlled over 75% of the shares. The stock market crash in October 1987 changed the outlook for the company. For a time, it appeared that available financing would fail to produce an offer high enough to be deemed fair from the shareholders' point of view. In March 1988 the board approved a revised plan to take the firm private for $30.25 per share in cash, and $7.00 per share in pay-in-kind debentures.

The ESOP, which served as the sole pension plan for the 14,000 employees, acquired 68% of the equity at the time of the buyout. A year later, despite reported losses, the ESOP bought more shares from Fickling at a price 15% higher than at the time of the buyout, which was a price provided in the original buyout agreement, and employee ownership increased to 81%. Less than one month later, Charter executives revealed accounting errors that might have led to the overvaluation of the firm. By the end of 1990, Charter defaulted on $1.8 billion in debt. Charter filed for Chapter 11 in June 1992, and emerged a month later as a publicly held firm with bondholders owning 93% of the equity. The ESOP retained only 2.4% ownership, worth $16.8 million, in contrast to its original stake of $455 million. Because the value of the ESOP had been so diluted, the firm committed to a second pension plan. The Department of Labor successfully filed suit against the ESOP trustee and Fickling claiming that the valuation in the second ESOP transaction failed to properly account for the debt issued to finance the ESOP stake.

Since exiting from Chapter 11, Charter has achieved a modest comeback. Operating income has increased 21%, and its stock price rose from $7 per share, when the firm emerged from bankruptcy to $11 per share in July 1993. The seven-member board, controlled by four outside members, ousted Fickling, who held options to hold up to 13% of post-reorganization equity, from his position as CEO and chairman. Despite the firm's problems, employment grew from 6,200 prior to the EBO to 17,000 five years later.

6. *Cone Mills Corporation*

Cone Mills manufactures and markets textile products. In late October 1983, Western Pacific Industries announced both that it held 333,000 shares, and that it had acquired an option to purchase 600,000 more shares from Caesar Cone II, a director and member of the founding family. Cone Mills resisted Western Pacific's attempts to gain control, and searched for a friendly buyer. A buyout plan involving current managers, an ESOP, and institutional investors was proposed in November 1983. Prior to the formation of the buyout plan, the firm's MAR[– 550, – 50] was – 15.9%. Shareholders approved the $70 per share EBO in March 1984.

The firm terminated an existing pension plan at the time of the buyout, generating approximately $50 million in excess assets. Since employees received preferred shares with no voting rights in the ESOP, management and institutional investors held all of the post-EBO control, holding 83.3% and 16.7% of the voting shares, respectively. In 1991, the courts ruled that employees had been misled about their retirement benefits. When the firm went public in 1992, part of the IPO was earmarked to redeem 49% of the preferred stock held by employees. The union challenged the fairness of the IPO wherein common shareholders stood to gain 1,200% on their investment, while the value of the preferred shares held by employees had not increased. In response, the firm agreed to establish a 401(k) plan for employees. In 1993, the courts awarded $15 million to employees, thereby ending the five-year class action suit.

Shortly after the buyout, Cone Mills closed eight plants due to competition from high levels of imported goods, and reduced domestic demand for the company's goods. However, the firm has made acquisitions in the U.S. and internationally, and in recent years has experienced growing revenues from international sales. Within one year after the IPO, the stock price increased by 50%. At the end of 1993, Cone Mills was the world's largest producer of denim, with a market share of 25%. Employees, which numbered 14,000 before the buyout, numbered 10,100 five years later.

7. *Dan River, Inc.*

Dan River, Inc. manufactures and markets textile products. Prior to the EBO in December 1982, the firm embarked on a reorganization plan that resulted in layoffs at all levels of the firm. In 1982, Dan River halved its quarterly dividend, and salaried employees accepted a 6-month delay, and subsequent reduction, of ordinary merit increases. The MAR[– 550, – 50] was – 18.3%. In September 1982, Carl Icahn with firms controlled by him, acquired 6.9% of the common stock of Dan River, and expressed interest in acquiring Dan River at a price of approximately $16 per share. In response, Dan River's board of directors authorized a series of cumulative convertible voting preferred stock, and issued all shares to a stock bonus plan for salaried employees. The board maintained that the immediate issue of shares to the stock bonus plan was compensation for the earlier reduction in merit increases. Icahn filed suit to void the stock bonus plan, and commenced a tender offer of $18 per share in October 1982 with the intent of liquidating a portion of the firm after the takeover. The board of directors rejected Icahn's offer. Dan River explored several transactions to thwart the hostile tender offer, including a self-tender and a leveraged buyout, but no action was taken, in part due to uncertainties over financing. In late December 1982, Kelso and Company, Inc. presented a proposal to Dan River's management to acquire the firm in a leveraged buyout at $20 per share, or $135 million, with the intention of continuing operations. In April 1983, the board approved the EBO at $22.50 per share. The firm replaced its existing pension plans with the ESOP, and used $16 million in excess assets from the terminated plans to repay part of the ESOP loan. Employees also agreed to the termination of Dan River's profit sharing and stock bonus plans.

In 1985, Dan River sold five plants to Alchem Capital. In 1987, the firm considered raising capital by going public. However, the IPO did not materialize. In 1989, Dan River was acquired by a private investment group headed by Joseph Lanier. The ESOP trustee agreed to the acquisition because it provided the firm with the capital necessary to further modernize and expand facilities. Employees, numbering 17,000 before the buyout, numbered 7000 at the time of Lanier's purchase.

8. *Dentsply International, Inc.*

Dentsply International is the world's largest manufacturer and distributor of dental supplies and equipment. In late 1980, Cooper Laboratories took a small position in Dentsply, and began discussions with the firm about a possible takeover. In October 1981, Cooper increased this position to 7%, and stated in a Schedule 13D disclosure its intention to acquire more shares. Dentsply's board rejected Cooper's overtures, and developed an EBO proposal in response. The firm's MAR[– 550, – 50] was – 42.8%. Management claimed that its motivation for the proposal was eliminating Cooper's threat by gaining majority ownership through the ESOP. In May 1982, the board of directors approved the buyout, including the repurchase of Cooper's shares, at $25.50 per share, or $130 million. The buyout was partially funded by $10 million in excess assets from a terminated pension plan. The ESOP also resulted in the termination of the existing employee stock purchase plan.

Since the buyout, the firm has performed well. Sales in 1981 were $200 million compared to approximately $400 million in 1992. Employees, numbering 7100 before the buyout, numbered 3500 five years later. Ten years after the buyout, Dentsply merged with Gendex Corporation, a publicly held maker of dental X-ray equipment. Under the terms of the merger, all shares of Dentsply were exchanged for 13.8 million shares of Gendex common stock in a transaction worth $590 million, or over five times the original EBO stock valuation. Dentsply's ESOP received 56% of the post-merger shares.

9. *Dyncorp Inc.* (*formerly Dynalectron Corporation*)

Dyncorp is a professional service company that provides technical support for defense and commercial aviation. Prior to the EBO in October 1987, the MAR[– 550, – 50] was – 20.6%. The completion of the EBO in 1988 culminated an internal struggle for control between Dyncorp's chairman of the board, Jorge Carnicero and its president and chief executive officer, Daniel Bannister. Carnicero initiated the takeover battle by offering to purchase all of Dyncorp's shares in an MBO, to be known as CJM Holdings, for $24 per share in September 1987. A special committee assembled to consider the buyout announced its intention to solicit other offers. Two weeks later, Bannister had formed a group, consisting of two outside investors, Capricorn Investors, L.P. and Pittsfield Finance Company, and employees, known as DME holdings, that proposed to buy the firm for $24.25 per share, or $235 million. Ultimately Bannister's plan prevailed. Bannister noted that his plan differed from the rival Carnicero plan largely on the basis of the potential productivity gains under employee ownership. The company terminated an over-funded pension plan that generated $7.5 million in excess assets, which was used to repay part of the loan. At the same time, the firm instituted a new stock incentive plan for key employees.

The post-EBO performance of the company appears to be excellent. In 1993, the company announced the completion of its tenth acquisition since the buyout. Through these acquisitions, the company has successfully reduced its reliance on contracts sponsored by the Department of Defense. Despite the large growth in assets, the company is ahead of schedule on debt repayment, announcing an early redemption of some of its buyout debt in 1992. Prior to the buyout, the company had 9950 employees, who five years later numbered 18,000. The company remains privately held.

10. *Arthur D. Little, Inc.*

Arthur D. Little is a multinational professional services company whose primary business is technology and management consulting. Prior to the EBO in March 1988, the company performed well, as evidenced by a MAR[– 500, – 50] of 7.6%. At the time of the EBO, 70% of the company's equity was held by employees in the Memorial Drive Trust (MDT). In July 1987, Plenum Publishing Corporation made an unsolicited offer to buy the remaining 30% of publicly held equity. A.D. Little rejected Plenum's offer, and proposed to buy the public equity through an ESOP for $60 per share. Funding for the transaction did not involve excess pension assets. In addition to the ESOP, pension benefits continued to be paid from MDT and a 401(k) plan.

The post-EBO performance of the firm also appears to be strong. Annual revenues of A.D. Little reached a record $358 million in 1991, a 13% increase over 1990. Employment levels decreased slightly, from 2600 prior to the buyout to 2400 five years later. The company remains employee-owned and privately held.

11. *Lyon Metal Products*

Lyon Metal Products manufactures metal storage products and storage systems. The $28 million EBO announced in February 1985 followed an extended period of sub-par performance, and a two-year takeover battle for the firm. In the two years leading up to the EBO, the firm reported earnings losses, omitted a dividend, and initiated a cost-containment program that included the sale of a plant. The MAR[– 550, – 50] was – 60.0%. During the same period, the firm agreed to separate mergers with Minstar Inc. and Auron Corporation, but both offers failed. The proposed merger with Auron failed when a lawsuit over the ownership of excess pension assets prevented the timely use of the assets for financing. A management buyout of the firm also failed when compensation concessions required to finance the buyout were rejected by union employees in July 1984. In February 1985, management and salaried workers, with the use of an ESOP, offered to purchase the outstanding public equity at $20 per share. This offer was contingent on the use of the disputed $12 million in excess pension assets to finance the buyout. The excess assets were used to purchase ESOP shares. In connection with the offer, the EBO repurchased the 38% stake held by Jacobs, and terminated an existing stock option plan.

Subsequent to the EBO, the firm purchased Model Industries and AMD Industries, both steel storage manufacturers, in 1987. Before the buyout, employees numbered 1100, and three years later, the firm employed 628. The firm is the leading U.S. manufacturer of steel shelving and related storage products. The firm remains employee-owned and privately held.

12. *National Color Laboratories, Inc.*

National Color Laboratories (NCL) specializes in photographic imaging and film processing. Immediately prior to the buyout in August 1984, there is no evidence of takeover-related activity, which is not surprising given that four management shareholders collectively owned 72% of the shares. In August of 1982, two years before the EBO, Carnation Company discussed a possible purchase of NCL, but these talks terminated without further interest surfacing. Prior to the buyout, the MAR[– 550, – 50] was – 3.5%. An acquisition group of major shareholders and an ESOP completed a leveraged buyout for the firm, valued at $4.50 per share, or $5.2 million, in February 1985. While the major shareholders retained a 36% stake, terms were arranged for the firm to purchase the remaining shares in the future. Excess assets from terminated pension plans do not appear to have provided any of the buyout financing. However, an employee stock purchase plan and an employee stock award plan were terminated, and the firm ended contributions to the profit sharing plan.

Little is reported about the post buyout performance of the company except that the firm remains privately owned. Employment levels are unchanged since the time of the buyout, and remain at 175 employees.

13. *Northwestern Steel and Wire*

Northwestern Steel and Wire is a leading U.S. producer of structural steel products and fabricated wire products. Since May of 1986, Northwestern's management had been under pressure from a group of shareholders, who had collectively filed a Schedule 13D with the SEC, to increase shareholder value. The shareholder group consisted primarily of descendants of the founder, and held 54% of the equity. The company's MAR[– 550, – 50] was – 3.8%. In response to this pressure, management considered an MBO, as well as several bids made by the shareholder group, but none gained board approval. In response to a proposal by the United Steelworkers of America (USW), management explored and ultimately agreed to an EBO in February 1988. As part of the agreement, USW workers agreed to a 7% reduction in employment costs from existing levels, and to the termination of their profit sharing plan. Union workers would receive $10 million in cash from the plan as part of the termination. Salaried workers, except for management, agreed to a 7% cut in employment costs, and to the suspension of existing stock bonus and incentive plans.

Following the EBO, Northwestern has achieved substantial operating improvements, but has also struggled with a high debt load. In March 1992, Kohlberg and Co. purchased $35 million of newly issued shares, representing 52 percent of the common stock. In June 1993, the company completed an initial public offering, and issued senior notes. Together these issues reduced aggregate indebtedness, and lowered interest expense. After the sale, Kohlberg owned 36% of the outstanding common shares, management 44%, and the ESOP 20%. Before the buyout, employees numbered 2300, and five years later, the firm employed 2800.

14. *Pamida, Inc.*

Pamida is a general retailer that operates a chain of discount stores throughout the Midwest. Prior to the buyout in June 1980, there is no evidence of control-related activities, most likely because D.J. Witherspoon, the CEO and chairman of the board, owned 44% of the equity. Throughout the 1970s, the firm considered a variety of ways for Witherspoon to retire and transfer the company to new management. The firm had poor pre-buyout financial performance, as the MAR[− 550, − 50] was − 65.0%. The EBO finally proposed in 1980 was designed to provide for Witherspoon in retirement, to protect the value of investments to shareholders, and to preserve the jobs of employees. A revised offer of $6 per share was made and approved by shareholders in January 1981. Pre-buyout senior management and officials were retained, except for the chairman and the vice-chairman of the board. Excess assets from terminated pension plans do not appear to have provided any of the buyout financing.

In 1986, Pamida agreed to be acquired by management, Citicorp Capital Investors, and other institutional investors for $169.5 million. In this transaction, employees received $70.63 per share, compared to the $6 buyout price. In 1991, the firm went public again. In May 1993, Pamida operated 180 stores, compared to 200 prior to the buyout. Employment levels have remained steady at around 5000 employees since the buyout.

15. *Parsons Corporation*

Parsons is an engineering company specializing in heavy construction and building contracting. Parsons established its ESOP in 1975 through a wholly owned subsidiary RMP Inc., when it acquired a 30% stake from the trust of the late founder, Ralph M. Parsons. Prior to the EBO in September 1984, the firm performed exceptionally well, with a MAR[− 550, − 50] of 36.1%. Although not known at the time, in early 1984 the firm received an unsolicited inquiry proposing an LBO with management at $30 per share. The firm rejected the offer, and no further discussions ensued with the third party. The firm began to consider going private through an ESOP with Kelso and Company, Inc. early in 1984. In September 1984, the firm accepted a revised $32 per share offer for the 71% of shares not already owned by the ESOP. Pre-existing defined contribution plans were consolidated into the ESOP.

The firm has performed well in the post-buyout years. In 1993, Parsons ranked second in the industry in domestic contracts. Employment levels decreased from 14,000 prior to the buyout to 8800 five years later. The company remains privately owned.

16. *Raymond International, Inc.*

Raymond International is an international engineering and construction company. Prior to the EBO proposal in May 1983, the firm performed poorly, with a MAR(– 500, – 50) of – 67.7%. The EBO was preceded by the disclosure in January that Jacobs Engineering Group had acquired a 9.9% interest in the firm. In late April, Raymond entered a standstill agreement with Jacobs Engineering, and repurchased its shares at $20.25 per share. Shortly thereafter, the company publicly announced that it was considering an EBO in which management, salaried employees, and Kelso and Company, Inc would participate. In the original offer, common shareholders received $25.00 per share. This offer was later increased to $27.50 per share. The ESOP replaced Raymond's existing pension plan. Terminating the pension plan provided $20 million in excess assets, which was used to repay part of the ESOP loan.

Revenues dropped from $1.6 billion in 1982, shortly before the EBO, to $845 million in 1984, the first year post-EBO. Raymond defaulted on $30 million in loans in 1986. The chairman and CEO who led the buyout attempt resigned, and banks took control of the firm in 1986. Attempts to renegotiate loan agreements and reorganize the firm ultimately failed, and the firm filed for Chapter 11 in August 1989. At that time, the firm employed only 500 employees, compared to 6000 prior to the EBO.

17. *Securities American Financial Enterprises, Inc. (SAFE)*

Securities American Financial Enterprises (SAFE) is the parent company of Security Life Insurance Co. of America (SLICA), which writes individual and group life and health insurance for firms of 15 to 5000 employees. At the time of the buyout proposal in February 1989, there is no evidence that the firm was under takeover threat, although management subsequently admitted to being approached in prior months by outside buyers. The firm's MAR[– 550, – 50] was – 26.10%. The terms of the buyout called for the ESOP to repurchase the public, non-management, shares for $10.50 per share. As a result, SAFE's ESOP would increase its holding from 12% to 53%. The EBO was structured to allow for the eventual liquidation of shares by the Chairman and founder of the firm, without a change in control that might involve the loss of other key personnel.

The post-EBO performance has been satisfactory. Duff and Phelps Credit Rating Co. lowered its rating from AA − to A + in July 1993. Return on assets declined from 6.61% in 1988 to 0.37% in 1992. As of December 1992, SAFE had reduced its EBO debt to $11 million from the original $15 million. Employment has remained steady at 86 employees since the buyout. The firm remains privately held.

18. *United States Sugar, Inc.*

U.S. Sugar is one of the nation's leading agricultural products companies. Prior to the buyout in September 1983, the MAR[− 550, − 50] was − 35.4%. However, there is no evidence of prior takeover activity. The motivation for the buyout appears to have been the desire of the C. S. Mott Family Holdings to reduce its 70% equity stake in the company to pursue several charitable activities connected with its foundations. Following completion of the EBO, the Charles Stewart Mott Foundation, the Mott Children's Health Center, and members of the Mott family continued to own in excess of 50% of the common stock. Although the firm intended to go private in 1983, following the tender offer, 5% of the public shares remained outstanding. A follow-up repurchase by the ESOP in 1987 completed the transaction to create a privately held company, and increased employee ownership to 44.2%.

Since the buyout, the firm has expanded into the growing and processing of citrus, as the growth in demand for raw sugar has declined. The firm established new labor practices to reduce costs and increase efficiency. Employment increased from 2100 prior to the EBO to 2400 three years later. The company remains privately held.

Appendix B.

Description of changes in compensation at the time of buyout and the composition of Boards of Directors (BOD) for spinoff EBOs.

EBO	ESOP Stake	Employees	Changes in compensation	Members of BOD
Hyatt-Clark	100%		Wages were cut approximately 25% and benefits by 50%. Compensation under the new plan includes lowered base pay, a monthly productivity bonus, sharing of after-tax profits above $500,000, and payment of 15% of salary as stock.	Three management, 3 union representatives, and 7 independent members

EBO	ESOP Stake	Employees	Changes in compensation	Members of BOD
Republic Engineered Steel	76%	1000 Salaried, 3900 Union	Forty-two month agreement whereby union employees were credited with $16 million towards purchase price from concessions granted under prior contracts. Union employees got $0.40 per hour increase in wages, plus some additional benefits. Salaried employees agree to salary reductions equal to $4.3 million.	Four management, 4 union, and 5 independent members approved by USW and company
Republic Storage Systems	100%	250 Salaried, 350 Union	All employees accept $0.15 per hour cut in wages and benefits for undisclosed period of time. A portion of future profit sharing is directed to repay the ESOP loan.	Two management, 2 employee, and 3 independent members
Seymour Wire	100%	55 Salaried, 165 Union	Work rule changes affect scheduling, reduced workforce through attrition.	Company president, union president, 5 elected employees, and 2 independent members selected by other members
Weirton Steel	100%	1300 Salaried, 6700 Union	Independent Steel Workers (ISW) accept hourly wage reductions from $25 to $19.70. With additional reductions in benefits, total labor costs fall to $16.94 per hour. Agreement calls for a six-year wage freeze and no-strike agreement.	CEO, 2 management, ISW president, 2 union approved members, and 8 independent members.

References

Alchian, A., Demsetz, H., 1972. Production, information costs, and economic organization. American Economic Review 62, 777–795.

Beatty, A., 1995. The cash flow and informational effects of employee stock ownership plans. Journal of Financial Economics 38, 211–240.

Becker, G., 1975. Human Capital, 2nd edn., Columbia University Press, New York.

Ben-Ner, A., Jun, B., 1996. Buy-out in a bargaining game with asymmetric information. American Economic Review 86, 502–523.

Chang, S., 1990. Employee stock ownership plans and shareholder wealth: an empirical investigation. Financial Management 19, 48–58.

Chang, S., Mayers, D., 1992. Managerial vote ownership and shareholder wealth. Journal of Financial Economics 32, 103–131.

Chaplinsky, S., Niehaus, G., 1990. The tax and distribution effects of leveraged ESOPs. Financial Management 19, 29–38.

Chaplinsky, S., Niehaus, G., 1994. The role of ESOPs in takeover contests. Journal of Finance 49, 1451–1470.

Chaplinsky, S., Niehaus, G., Van de Gucht, L., 1994. Resolving the controversy over the valuation of employee claims in ESOP buyouts. Benefits Quarterly 10, 58–66.

Chapman, B., 1993. Trust, economic rationality, and the corporate fiduciary obligation. University of Toronto Law Journal 43, 547–588.

DeAngelo, H., DeAngelo, L., 1987. Management buyouts of publicly traded corporations. Financial Analysts Journal 43, 38–49.

DeAngelo, H., DeAngelo, L., 1991. Union negotiations and corporate policy: a study of labor concessions in the domestic steel industry during the 1980s. Journal of Financial Economics 30, 3–44.

DeAngelo, H., DeAngelo, L., Rice, E., 1984. Going private: minority freezeouts and stockholder wealth. Journal of Law and Economics 27, 367–401.

Degeorge, F., Zeckhauser, R., 1993. The reverse LBO decision and firm performance: theory and evidence. Journal of Finance 48, 1323–1348.

Denis, D., 1995. Organizational form and the consequences of highly leveraged transactions: Kroger's recapitalization and Safeway's LBO. Journal of Financial Economics 36, 193–224.

Dimson, E., Marsh, P., 1986. Event study methodologies and the size effect: the case of U.K. press recommendations. Journal of Financial Economics 17, 113–142.

Fruhan, W., 1985. Labor, management and the goose that laid the golden egg. Harvard Business Review 63, 131–141.

Furubotn, E., 1988. Codetermination and the modern theory of the firm: a property-rights analysis. Journal of Business 61, 165–181.

Gilson, S., John, K., Lang, L., 1990. Troubled debt restructuring: an empirical study of private reorganization of firms in default. Journal of Financial Economics 27, 315–353.

Gordon, L., Pound, J., 1990. ESOPs and corporate control. Journal of Financial Economics 27, 525–555.

Habib, M., 1995. Monitoring, implicit contracts and the lack of permanence in leveraged buyouts. IFA working paper 178–1996, London Business School.

Hansmann, H., 1990. When does worker ownership work? ESOPs, law firms, codetermination, and economic democracy. The Yale Law Journal 99, 1749–1816.

Hansmann, H., 1993. Worker participation and corporate governance. University of Toronto Law Review 43, 589–606.

Hite, G., Vetsuypens, M., 1989. Management buyouts of divisions and shareholder wealth. Journal of Finance 44, 953–970.

Howse, R., Trebilcock, M., 1993. Protecting the employment bargain. University of Toronto Law Review 43, 751–796.

Hyde, A., 1993. Ownership, contract, and politics in the protection of employees against risk. University of Toronto Law Journal 43, 721–749.

Ippolito, R., James, W., 1992. LBOs, reversions and implicit contracts. Journal of Finance 47, 139–167.

James, C., 1987. Some evidence on the uniqueness of bank loans. Journal of Financial Economics 19, 217–235.

Jensen, M., 1989. Capital markets, organizational innovation, and restructuring. Unpublished working paper 89–047, Harvard Business School.

Jensen, M., Meckling, W., 1979. Rights and production functions: an application to labor-managed firms and codetermination. Journal of Business 52, 469–506.

Kaplan, S., 1989a. The effects of management buyouts on operating performance and value. Journal of Financial Economics 28, 217–254.

Kaplan, S., 1989b. Management buyouts: Evidence on taxes as source of value. Journal of Finance 44, 611–632.

Kaplan, S., 1991. The staying power of leveraged buyouts. Journal of Financial Economics 29, 287–313.

Kaplan, S., Stein, J., 1993. The evolution of buyout pricing and financial structure in the 1980s. Quarterly Journal of Economics 108, 313–357.

Klein, B., Crawford, R., Alchian, A., 1978. Vertical integration, appropriable rents, and the competitive contracting process. Journal of Law and Economics 21, 297–326.

Klein, B., Leffler, K., 1981. The role of market forces in assuring contractual performance. Journal of Political Economy 89, 615–641.

Kovenock, D., Sparks, R., 1990. An implicit contract approach to employee stock ownership plans. Journal of Comparative Economics 14, 424–451.

Lazear, E., 1981. Agency, earnings profiles, productivity, and hours restrictions. American Economic Review 71, 606–620.

Lehn, K., Poulsen, A., 1989. Free cash flow and stockholder gains in going private transactions. Journal of Finance 44, 771–788.

Long, M., Malitz, I., 1985. Investment patterns and financial leverage. In: Friedman, B. (Ed.), Corporate Capital Structures in the United States. University of Chicago Press, Chicago.

Muscarella, C., Vetsuypens, M., 1990. Efficiency and organizational structure: a study of reverse LBOs. Journal of Finance 45, 1389–1413.

Myers, S., 1977. Determinants of corporate borrowing. Journal of Financial Economics 5, 147–175.

Opler, T., 1993. Controlling financial distress costs in leveraged buyouts with financial innovations. Financial Management 22, 50–57.

Palepu, K., 1990. Consequences of leveraged buyouts. Journal of Financial Economics 27, 247–262.

Peterson, M., 1992. Pension reversions and worker-stockholder wealth transfers. Quarterly Journal of Economics 107, 1033–1056.

Peterson, M., 1994. Cash flow variability and firm's pension choice: a role for operating leverage. Journal of Financial Economics 36, 361–384.

Pontiff, J., Shleifer, A., Weisbach, M., 1990. Reversions of excess pension assets after takeovers. RAND Journal of Economics 21, 600–613.

Salop, J., Salop, S., 1976. Self selection and turnover in the labor market Quarterly Journal of Economics 90, 620–627.

Scholes, M., Wolfson, M., 1990. Employee stock ownership plans and corporate restructuring: myths and realities. Financial Management 19, 12–28.

Seelig, S., 1986. Department of Labor puts hold on ESOP use in leveraged buyouts. Tax Notes 30, 922–924.

Shleifer, A., Summers, L., 1988. Breach of trust in hostile takeover. In: Auerbach, A. (Ed.), Corporate Takeovers: Causes and Consequences. University of Chicago Press, Chicago.

Shleifer, A., Vishny, R., 1992. Liquidation values and debt capacity: a market equilibrium approach. Journal of Finance 47, 1343–1366.
Smith, C., Watts, R., 1992. The investment opportunity set and corporate financing, dividend, and compensation policies. Journal of Financial Economics 32, 263–292.
Stewart, G.B., 1991. The Quest for Value: A Guide for Senior Managers. Harper Collins, New York.
Stulz, R., 1988. Managerial control of voting rights: financing policies and the market for corporate control. Journal of Financial Economics 20, 25–54.
Titman, S., Wessels, R., 1988. The determinants of capital structure choice. Journal of Finance 43, 1–19.
Van de Gucht, L., Moore, W., 1997. Predicting the duration and reversal probability of leveraged buyouts. Journal of Empirical Finance, forthcoming.
Williamson, O., 1979. Transaction-cost economics: the governance of contractual relations. Journal of Law and Economics 22, 233–261.

Name Index

The International Library of Critical Writings in Financial Economics

1. The Theory of Corporate Finance
(Volumes I and II)
Michael J. Brennan

2. Futures Markets
(Volumes I, II and III)
A.G. Malliaris

3. Market Efficiency: Stock Market Behaviour in Theory and Practice
(Volumes I and II)
Andrew W. Lo

4. Microstructure: The Organization of Trading and Short Term Price Behavior
(Volumes I and II)
Hans R. Stoll

5. The Debt Market
(Volumes I, II and III)
Stephen A. Ross

6. Options Markets
(Volumes I, II and III)
George M. Constantinides and A.G. Malliaris

7. Empirical Corporate Finance
(Volumes I, II, III and IV)
Michael J. Brennan

8. The Foundations of Continuous Time Finance
Stephen M. Schaefer

9. International Securities
(Volumes I and II)
George C. Philippatos and Gregory Koutmos

10. Behavioral Finance
(Volumes I, II and III)
Hersh Shefrin

11. Asset Pricing Theory and Tests
(Volumes I and II)
Robert R. Grauer

12. International Capital Markets
(Volumes I, II and III)
G. Andrew Karolyi and René M. Stulz

13. Financial Forecasting
(Volumes I and II)
Roy Batchelor and Pami Dua

14. Emerging Markets
Geert Bekaert and Campbell R. Harvey

15. Corporate Restructuring
(Volumes I and II)
John J. McConnell and David J. Denis

16. Recent Developments in Corporate Finance
(Volumes I and II)
Jay R. Ritter

Future titles will include:

Foreign Exchange Markets
Richard J. Sweeney

Financial Econometrics
Andrew W. Lo

Financial Markets and the Real Economy
John H. Cochrane

Corporate Restructuring
Volume II

The International Library of Critical Writings in Financial Economics

Series Editor: Richard Roll
Allstate Professor of Economics
The Anderson School at UCLA, USA

This major series presents by field outstanding selections of the most important articles across the entire spectrum of financial economics – one of the fastest growing areas in business schools and economics departments. Each collection has been prepared by a leading specialist who has written an authoritative introduction to the literature. A full list of published and future titles in this series is printed at the end of this volume.

Wherever possible, the articles in these volumes have been reproduced as originally published using facsimile reproduction, inclusive of footnotes and pagination to facilitate ease of reference.

Corporate Restructuring
Volume II

Edited by

John J. McConnell

Emanuel T. Weiler Distinguished Professor (Finance)
Purdue University, USA

and

David J. Denis

Burton D. Morgan Chair of Private Enterprise and Professor of Finance
Purdue University, USA

THE INTERNATIONAL LIBRARY OF CRITICAL WRITINGS IN FINANCIAL ECONOMICS

An Elgar Reference Collection
Cheltenham, UK • Northampton, MA, USA

Published by
Edward Elgar Publishing Limited
Glensanda House
Montpellier Parade
Cheltenham
Glos GL50 1UA
UK

Edward Elgar Publishing, Inc.
136 West Street
Suite 202
Northampton
Massachusetts 01060
USA

A catalogue record for this book is available from the British Library.

ISBN 1 84376 727 9 (2 volume set)

Printed and bound in Great Britin by MPG Books Ltd, Bodmin, Cornwall.

Contents

Acknowledgements

The editors and publishers wish to thank the authors and the following publishers who have kindly given permission for the use of copyright material.

Blackwell Publishing Ltd for articles: Vojislav Maksimovic and Gordon Phillips (1998), 'Asset Efficiency and Reallocation Decisions of Bankrupt Firms', *Journal of Finance*, **LIII** (5), October, 1495–532; Allan C. Eberhart, Edward I. Altman and Reena Aggarwal (1999), 'The Equity Performance of Firms Emerging from Bankruptcy', *Journal of Finance*, **LIV** (5), October, 1855–68; Vojislav Maksimovic and Gordon Phillips (2001), 'The Market for Corporate Assets: Who Engages in Mergers and Asset Sales and Are There Efficiency Gains?', *Journal of Finance*, **LVI** (6), December, 2019–65; Laura Casares Field and Jonathan M. Karpoff (2002), 'Takeover Defenses of IPO Firms', *Journal of Finance*, **LVII** (5), October, 1857–89; Robert Gertner, Eric Powers and David Scharfstein (2002), 'Learning about Internal Capital Markets from Corporate Spin-offs', *Journal of Finance*, **LVII** (6), December, 2479–506.

Elsevier for articles: L.Y. Dann and H. DeAngelo (1988), 'Corporate Financial Policy and Corporate Control: A Study of Defensive Adjustments in Asset and Ownership Structure', *Journal of Financial Economics*, **20**, 87–127; Stuart C. Gilson, Kose John and Larry H.P. Lang (1990), 'Troubled Debt Restructurings: An Empirical Study of Private Reorganization of Firms in Default', *Journal of Financial Economics*, **27** (2), October, 315–53; David J. Denis and Diane K. Denis (1993), 'Managerial Discretion, Organizational Structure, and Corporate Performance: A Study of Leveraged Recapitalizations', *Journal of Accounting and Economics*, **16**, 209–36; Robert Comment and Gregg A. Jarrell (1995), 'Corporate Focus and Stock Returns', *Journal of Financial Economics*, **37** (1), January, 67–87; Lane Daley, Vikas Mehrotra and Ranjini Sivakumar (1997), 'Corporate Focus and Value Creation: Evidence from Spinoffs', *Journal of Financial Economics*, **45**, 257–81; Jun-Koo Kang and Anil Shivdasani (1997), 'Corporate Restructuring During Performance Declines in Japan', *Journal of Financial Economics*, **46**, 29–65; Gayle R. Erwin and John J. McConnell (1997), 'To Live or Let Die? An Empirical Analysis of Piecemeal Voluntary Corporate Liquidations', *Journal of Corporate Finance*, **3** (4), December, 325–54; Todd C. Pulvino (1999), 'Effects of Bankruptcy Court Protection on Asset Sales', *Journal of Financial Economics*, **52**, 151–86; J. Harold Mulherin and Audra L. Boone (2000), 'Comparing Acquisitions and Divestitures', *Journal of Corporate Finance*, **6**, 117–39; David J. Denis and Timothy A. Kruse (2000), 'Managerial Discipline and Corporate Restructuring Following Performance Declines', *Journal of Financial Economics*, **55**, 391–424; Karin S. Thorburn (2000), 'Bankruptcy Auctions: Costs, Debt Recovery, and Firm Survival', *Journal of Financial Economics*, **58**, 337–68; Frederik P. Schlingemann, René M. Stulz and Ralph A. Walkling (2002), 'Divestitures and the Liquidity of the Market for Corporate Assets', *Journal of Financial Economics*, **64**, 117–44.

Journal of Financial and Quantitative Analysis for article: Jeffrey W. Allen, Scott L. Lummer, John J. McConnell and Debra K. Reed (1995), 'Can Takeover Losses Explain Spin-Off Gains?', *Journal of Financial and Quantitative Analysis*, **30** (4), December, 465–85.

Oxford University Press for article: Philip G. Berger and Eli Ofek (1999), 'Causes and Effects of Corporate Refocusing Programs', *Review of Financial Studies*, **12** (2), Summer, 311–45.

University of Chicago Press for article: Anand M. Vijh (2002), 'The Positive Announcement-Period Returns of Equity Carveouts: Asymmetric Information or Divestiture Gains?', *Journal of Business*, **75** (1), January, 153–90.

Every effort has been made to trace all the copyright holders but if any have been inadvertently overlooked the publishers will be pleased to make the necessary arrangement at the first opportunity.

In addition the publishers wish to thank the Library of Indiana University at Bloomington, USA for their assistance in obtaining these articles.

Part I
Asset Restructurings

A
Defensive Restructurings

[1]

Journal of Financial Economics 20 (1988) 87–127. North-Holland

CORPORATE FINANCIAL POLICY AND CORPORATE CONTROL*
A Study of Defensive Adjustments in Asset and Ownership Structure

Larry Y. DANN

University of Oregon, Eugene, OR 97403-1208, USA

Harry DeANGELO

University of Rochester, Rochester, NY 14627, USA

Received August 1986, final version received September 1987

This paper presents evidence that stockholder wealth declines on average when managers respond to attempted hostile takeovers with defensive changes in asset and ownership structure. The data also indicate that these corporate restructurings are typically quite large and that many are attempts by managers to create barriers specific to the hostile bidder and/or to consolidate a block of voting securities in the hands of management allies. The evidence suggests that defensive motives (whether beneficial or harmful) influence corporate asset and ownership structure.

1. Introduction

This paper investigates one aspect of the relation between managers' choice of corporate financial policy and the market for corporate control. We document the stockholder wealth effects and other attributes of four types of corporate asset and ownership structure changes – acquisitions, divestitures, and issuances and repurchases of voting securities – that target managers announced in response to hostile takeover attempts. For a sample of 39 defensive restructurings announced by managers of 33 exchange-listed target firms, we report the following principal empirical findings:

(1) Stockholder wealth declines on average by a statistically significant 2–3% at announcement of restructuring plans.

*We would like to acknowledge the helpful comments of Jim Brickley, Tom Copeland, Cliff Holderness, Chris James, Richard Leftwich, Ron Masulis, Wayne Mikkelson, Megan Partch, Ed Rice, Rick Ruback, Dennis Sheehan, Keith Smith, René Stulz, Jake Thomas, Ralph Walkling, Fred Weston, Peggy Wier, Jerry Zimmerman, and an anonymous referee. Special thanks are due Linda DeAngelo, Mike Jensen, and Jerry Warner. We have also benefited from the comments of participants in seminars at CRSP, Harvard, Iowa, Ohio State, Oregon, Southern California, UCLA, University of Washington, Utah, Washington University in St. Louis, and Yale. Gael Roberts provided invaluable help in the preparation of this manuscript. Partial financial support for this project was provided by the John B. Rogers Professorship of Banking and Finance of the University of Oregon, by the General Electric Foundation, by the Lynde and Harry Bradley Foundation, and by the Managerial Economics Research Center of the University of Rochester.

0304-405X/88/$3.50

(2) The median restructuring involves assets constituting 23% of the target's pre-offer equity value and represents a 17% change in the (absolute) number of board votes outstanding.
(3) Sample firms constitute 19% of exchange-listed targets of hostile tender bids during 1962–1983 and a full 36% of targets during 1980–1983.
(4) The typical sample firm is a large, older industrial concern in which incumbent managers own a small fraction of the common stock.
(5) Approximately 50% of sample restructurings represent attempts to create a consolidated block of voting securities or to enhance the proportionate voting power of a block already in place.
(5) At least 25% of sample restructurings represent attempts to create bidder-specific deterrents such as antitrust obstacles.
(7) Managers voluntarily put their planned restructurings to a stockholder vote in only one of 39 cases and sometimes went to great lengths to avoid doing so.
(8) There is little evidence that managers voluntarily sought purchasers on behalf of target stockholders.
(9) Contest outcomes are approximately evenly split among cases in which (i) the hostile bidder acquired control, (ii) another bidder acquired control, and (iii) the hostile bidder unilaterally withdrew in the face of managerial resistance.
(10) There is little evidence of a systematic relationship between the form of defensive restructuring and the eventual contest outcome.
(11) Hostile bidders rarely prevail in cases in which the planned restructurings were implemented by target managers.
(12) Target stockholders typically experience significant wealth gains over the period from contest initiation through outcome, but these gains are much smaller when incumbents retain control.
(13) Target stockholders typically lose large tender premiums and experience large share value declines when a sole bidder withdraws in the face of managerial resistance.

These findings provide evidence on whether the predominant effect of takeover defenses is to entrench managers at stockholders' expense or to benefit stockholders, e.g., by improving their takeover bargaining position. Our overall assessment is that the weight of the evidence best supports the entrenchment view. Our evidence is also potentially relevant to the empirical literature on the determinants of corporate financial policy. Prior research in this area has typically studied the stockholder wealth effects associated with a given transactional form, e.g., stock repurchase or divestiture. Our approach differs insofar as we group restructurings by common economic motivation (takeover defense) rather than by nominal transaction type. This approach provides evidence on the question of whether defensive considerations affect the choice of asset and ownership structure. It also yields several ideas for future research on the relation between the control market and investment/financing decisions undertaken outside the context of a takeover attempt. We discuss these issues in section 7 below.

Section 2 documents our sampling procedure and offers descriptive statistics to help place our sample in perspective. Sections 3 and 4 present and interpret the evidence on the stockholder wealth effects of defensive restructurings. Section 5 provides a descriptive synthesis of the attributes of sample restructurings. (An appendix provides case studies that serve as the basis for this summary.) Section 6 reports evidence on the wealth effects experienced by target stockholders over the entire control contest for the sample partitioned by contest outcome.

2. Sampling procedure and descriptive statistics

Our sampling procedure isolates asset and ownership structure changes announced by target managers in response to visible hostile takeover attempts. We focus on these so-called responsive restructurings because it is difficult to identify structural takeover barriers that might have been erected in anticipation of a control contest. Thus, our sampling procedure reflects the practical necessity of obtaining more reliable identification of structural takeover defenses at the cost of understating the incidence and variety of ways that managers may defensively adjust corporate structure. One consequence is that our findings probably reflect intermediate-strength structural defenses, rather than the full spectrum of such managerial decisions.[1] A related consequence is that our sample is of modest size – 39 announcements of defensive restructurings by managers of 33 New York (NYSE) or American Stock Exchange (ASE) listed firms.

We identified our 33 companies from a preliminary sample of 171 firms in the Austin (1983) and MERC (1983) data bases that faced hostile tender offers during 1962–1983 while exchange-listed. The preliminary sample consists of those cases classified as contested by Austin or MERC for which we could

[1]The reason is that we study cases in which *both* (i) bidder managers chose to initiate a hostile takeover attempt and (ii) target managers chose to respond by erecting structural barriers. Their relative strategic positions will influence whether the bidder attempts a hostile takeover and whether target managers resist. At one extreme, if the target's defensive position is weak, the bidder can effect a 'negotiated' control transfer by threatening to force a takeover despite any resistance. At the other extreme, a potential bidder will forego an otherwise attractive takeover if the target's defensive position is strong. Hostile takeover approaches by bidders – and defensive responses by targets – are observed in the 'marginal' cases in which both sides perceive that their strategic positions give them some chance of victory and that the approach and response are worth the risks.

verify in the *Wall Street Journal Index* (WSJI) or *Wall Street Journal* (WSJ) that both (i) a bidder announced a tender offer that was *not* conditional upon target board approval and (ii) target management publicly opposed the bidder. We inspected the WSJI for the three calendar years prior to and including each hostile tender offer announcement (and longer when necessary) to identify the earliest public report that the hostile bidder had purchased or planned to buy shares. In some cases, the WSJ reported disclosures by target or bidder that the parties had held earlier, private merger discussions. Because such discussions are not systematically disclosed, we took the date of the first WSJ report of the hostile bidder's stock purchase activity as an empirical proxy for initiation of the takeover attempt.

Since we expected to observe defensive restructurings in response to a (significant and exogenous) increase in the probability of a takeover attempt, we identified structural changes that target managers announced after contest initiation, but before the resolution of hostilities. We searched articles cited in the WSJI for announcements of planned acquisitions, divestitures, and issuances and repurchases of voting securities. Our analysis concentrates on these four transaction types because they represent discrete (and hence identifiable) shifts in corporate asset and ownership structure. The sample does not include asset sale or other lock-up provisions that were announced together with an agreement to support a white knight offer, based on our a priori judgment that these provisions are more properly viewed as part of a contract to transfer target control rather than as a structural takeover defense.

Our sample includes an announcement only if the WSJ reported that the hostile bidder filed suit or otherwise stated publicly that the restructuring was defensively motivated. This criterion is designed to isolate structural changes that represent takeover defenses. However, it does not provide absolute assurance of identifying only defensive actions since the hostile bidder has incentives to criticize policy shifts unrelated to the control contest if, by so doing, it can raise doubts about the integrity of target management. For our 39 sample restructurings, the specific indications of bidder opposition are: 32 engendered litigation by the hostile bidder, two were criticized as making the target less attractive as an acquisition candidate, one was labeled 'clearly defensive', one was simply reported to be 'opposed' by the bidder, and three were labeled 'not in stockholders' best interests'.

While our sample is small in absolute number, it nonetheless contains a significant fraction of the listed firms that faced hostile tender bids during 1962–1983. Specifically, table 1 reports that our 33 sample firms represent 19.3% of the exchange-listed targets of hostile bids according to the MERC and Austin data bases (which comprise the population from which we sampled). Moreover, our sample contains 35.8% of the targets of hostile bids during the 1980–1983 subperiod. These facts suggest that structural takeover defenses have become an important factor in the control market as it operates

Table 1

Time profile of announcements of target firms' adjustments in asset and/or ownership structure during a period of hostile takeover activity (33 New York and American Stock Exchange-listed firms).

Sample period	Number of firms that made initial announcement of structural change	Sample firms as a percent of listed targets of hostile tender bids[a]
1963–1969	1	2.9%
1970–1979	13	15.7%
1980–1983	19	35.8%
Total	33	19.3%

[a]This frequency is measured relative to the total number of exchange-listed targets (i) identified in the Austin and/or MERC data bases as having initial public announcement of a hostile tender bid during the specified period and (ii) confirmed as such by the *Wall Street Journal.*

today. Their increased importance may reflect major court decisions rendered in recent years – especially in the case of Panter v. Marshall Field & Co. – which adopted a broad interpretation of the business judgment rule and which therefore apparently expanded the set of feasible takeover defenses.[2]

The descriptive statistics in table 2 reveal that our sample consists primarily of sizable, older industrial concerns whose managers held a small fraction of the common stock. For example, the median target firm had a total equity value of $144 million two months before the hostile tender bid. The corresponding mean value is $362 million, and the substantial difference between mean and median reflects the inclusion of some very large firms that faced hostile bids in the 1980s. Incumbent directors and officers beneficially owned an average of only 5.0% (median 2.6%) of the outstanding stock. Our typical target firm had moderate amounts of long-term debt and liquid assets and relatively large employee and stockholder populations. The average company was incorporated more than 50 years before the takeover contest and, in many cases, had been in operation for even longer periods. The established nature of these target companies is also reflected in the fact that 30 firms (91%) were listed on the NYSE and only three were listed on the ASE at the time of the hostile bid.

[2]The appendix describes the takeover defenses that led Marshall Field stockholders to sue their board of directors for breach of fiduciary duty. This unsuccessful litigation worked through the courts during 1978–1981, a period which marks the increased incidence of structural takeover defenses documented here. The apparent protection afforded managers by the Marshall Field decision is underscored by Circuit Judge Cudahy's dissenting opinion which argued that '(T)he majority has adopted an approach which would virtually immunize a target company's board of directors against liability to shareholders...'.

Table 2

Mean and median company size measures and other descriptive attributes for 33 New York and American Stock Exchange-listed firms that announced defensive restructurings in response to an attempted hostile takeover in the period 1969–1983.

Target company attribute[a]	Mean	Median
1. Total market value of common stock as of two months before the hostile tender bid ($ millions)	362	144
2. Annual sales revenue ($ millions)	1,019	349
3. Book value of assets ($ millions)	843	390
4. Percentage ownership of common stock by officers and directors	5.0	2.6
5. Book value of long-term debt as a percentage of total assets	21.2	24.1
6. Book value of liquid assets (cash plus marketable securities) as a percentage of total assets	6.6	3.8
7. Number of employees	10,591	7,125
8. Number of stockholders	22,660	11,944
9. Corporate age at time of structural change (years)[b]	55	52

[a]Item 1 is drawn from *Standard and Poor's Security Owners' Stock Guide* and is based on the open market stock price and number of shares outstanding at the end of the calendar month that came at least two (but not more than three) months before the initial hostile tender offer announcement. Item 4 represents the beneficial share ownership by all directors and officers as given in the last proxy statement before the hostile bid. All other items are taken from the *Moody's Manual* that contains financial data for the latest available fiscal year before the bid. Items 2, 3, 5, and 6 exclude data for two financial institutions because their financial characteristics are clearly not representative of the remaining (industrial) firms in the sample.

[b]Corporate age is measured as the number of years between the initial date of incorporation (per *Moody's*) and the first restructuring announcement. This measure understates the actual business age of the typical firm since, in many cases, the target was initially incorporated to consolidate several ongoing corporations or was created as a legal entity to convert an operating partnership to corporate status.

The hostile bidders are a more heterogeneous group – 21 of the 33 takeover attempts were initiated by NYSE-listed companies, five involved ASE-listed bidders, and one involved a bidder with shares traded over-the-counter. The remaining six takeover attempts were made by a variety of individuals, private partnerships, closely-held corporations, and foreign firms whose shares were not traded on a domestic (U.S.) stock market. For the subsample of 27 bidders with domestically traded shares, the mean pre-offer market value of equity totals $529 million (median $403 million). The typical bidder in this subsample was only marginally larger than its target – on average, the target's pre-offer value represents a substantial 77.5% (median 77.1%) of the bidder's equity value. Interestingly, the hostile bidder group includes a significant number of alleged corporate 'raiders'. For example, 12 cases involved participation by nine individuals (such as Carl Icahn and Boone Pickens) who have initiated numerous takeover attempts and who are generally viewed as threatening to incumbent managers.

The typical restructuring we study here was undertaken by target managers during a protracted takeover contest that involved numerous actions and counteractions by both bidder and target. One indication of the extensive strategic interplay between target and bidder is the fact that, in the clear majority of our sample, the WSJ carried more than 20 different reports about the takeover attempt. The median elapsed time between contest initiation and outcome totals 90 trading days, or approximately four calendar months. There is substantial cross-sectional variation in contest duration – the shortest contest ended in 14 trading days, while the longest lasted a remarkable 647 trading days. The tender offer announcement represented contest initiation in only 16 of the 33 cases. In the remaining 17 cases, the tender offer was preceded by a period of publicly visible control-related activity that quite often involved open-market share accumulation by the eventual hostile bidder. These contests also commonly entailed considerable legal maneuvering by target and bidder, with both parties frequently bringing suits and countersuits on a variety of grounds and in various legal forums.

3. Wealth effects of defensive changes in corporate structure

We use standard event-study methods to assess the stockholder wealth consequences of managers' plans to erect structural takeover barriers.[3] We focus on the sample average prediction error (i.e., the abnormal share value change, denoted *pe*) for the period immediately surrounding announcement of the planned restructuring. For a given observation, the announcement period typically consists of the publication day of the first WSJ report of managers' plans and the immediately prior business day, on which the plans were actually disclosed. This period is the shortest identifiable time interval that should include the stock market's reaction to news of a given structural change (because disclosure may have come after trading ended). The assessment of stock returns over longer intervals is less reliable because such returns include

[3] For each firm, we calculated prediction errors based on continuously compounded returns and market model parameters estimated for the 200 trading days ending 101 trading days before initiation of the takeover attempt. We follow Dodd (1980) and others in calculating standardized prediction errors for the z-statistics reported in this and subsequent sections. An earlier draft provided details of the formulas used to calculate standardized prediction errors, cumulative prediction errors, and statistical significance tests. This documentation is available upon request. Readers interested in a general discussion of event-study methods are referred to Brown and Warner (1980,1985).

more noise, which makes it more difficult to isolate the value consequences of the policy shift. This issue is of particular concern here since the restructurings we study were announced during control contests which include numerous other disclosures (e.g., tender offer announcements) that usually affect target share prices.

We judge eight of the 39 restructuring announcements to be materially confounded by simultaneous arrival of other company-specific information. Specifically, three restructurings were announced within one day of revelation of the hostile tender offer, two were made within one day of a material judicial ruling that pertained to the takeover attempt, one was made within hours of expiration of an oversubscribed tender offer, and two, by the same company, could not be analyzed because they came three trading days apart in the midst of a six-day trading moratorium, during which the courts rendered an important decision pertaining to the takeover attempt and a white knight offered to acquire the target.[4] Because we know of no way to remove the influence of such contemporaneous confounding events on observed returns, we conduct our analysis of announcement-related stock returns on the remaining 31 uncontaminated restructuring announcements made by managers of 29 firms.

Table 3 summarizes our basic evidence on the wealth effects experienced by target stockholders when managers reveal plans to effect defensive adjustments in asset and ownership structure. The data indicate that, on average and in the majority of cases, announcements of these planned restructurings are associated with losses for target company stockholders. Specifically, panel A of the table reports that the sample mean prediction error is -2.33%, with a z-statistic of -4.01 which indicates a significant (at the 0.001 level) decline in stockholder wealth. The median prediction error of -2.73% similarly indicates a tendency toward losses for public stockholders as does the fact that 23 of the 31 announcements (74% of the sample) have negative prediction errors. The same general impression of stockholder losses is conveyed by the frequency distribution of announcement period prediction errors presented in panel B. The nonparametric binomial and Wilcoxon tests confirm at high levels of reliability that target share prices fall, on average, when managers announce plans for defensive restructurings.

[4] The three cases confounded by announcement of a hostile tender offer are Cities Service Co. (prediction error = 7.86%), Graniteville Co. ($pe = 2.85\%$), and Sparton Corp. ($pe = 14.86\%$). The two cases with simultaneous judicial rulings are Dan River Inc. ($pe = 1.93\%$) and Grumman Corp. ($pe = -3.76\%$). The case with simultaneous tender offer expiration is Ludlow Corp. ($pe = -8.91\%$). The trading suspension case is St. Joe Minerals Corp. ($pe = 15.23\%$ and 1.89% immediately before and after the trading halt). In fact, the first prediction error for St. Joe was observed on the single trading day that came between two trading suspensions. Also, it is confounded by a court decision in favor of the hostile bidder and by St. Joe's acknowledgment that its legal defenses had failed.

Table 3

Target firms' estimated abnormal equity value changes (prediction errors, *pe*) in the two-day period surrounding announcements of defensive adjustments in asset and/or ownership structure (sample of 31 uncontaminated announcements in the period 1969–1983).[a]

Panel A. Summary measures of estimated abnormal value changes

Mean prediction error	−2.33%
Median prediction error	−2.73%
Minimum prediction error	−8.99%
Maximum prediction error	12.63%
Number of negative : positive *pe*'s	23 : 8
Percentage of events with negative *pe*'s	74.2%
z-statistic to test hypothesis that expected value change is zero	−4.012
p-value under two-tailed *z*-test	< 0.001
p-value under binomial proportions test	0.007
p-value under Wilcoxon signed-ranks test	0.010

Panel B. Frequency distribution of estimated abnormal value changes

Magnitude of prediction error at announcement of structural change	Number of prediction errors in specified interval
$pe < -8\%$	4
$-8\% \leq pe < -6\%$	5
$-6\% \leq pe < -4\%$	4
$-4\% \leq pe < -2\%$	4
$-2\% \leq pe < 0\%$	6
$0\% \leq pe < 2\%$	1
$2\% \leq pe < 4\%$	3
$4\% \leq pe < 6\%$	3
$6\% \leq pe < 8\%$	0
$8\% \leq pe < 10\%$	0
$10\% \leq pe < 12\%$	0
$12\% \leq pe$	1

[a] For each company, a market model prediction error (*pe*) is calculated as the actual (dividend-inclusive) common stock return at announcement of the planned structural change net of the estimated normal return for the security. Normal returns were estimated using the standard one-factor market model with equal-weighted index over the 200-day period ending 101 days before contest initiation. In one case, the prediction error represents a three-day stock return because of a single missing return during the announcement period.

The 2–3% average share price decline probably underestimates the full stockholder wealth effect of the typical structural shift in our sample. The reason is that only the unanticipated component of the full wealth effect will be observed in the stock price change when target managers formally reveal plans for a particular structural adjustment. The issue of prior capitalization is of particular concern here since, before every announcement in our sample, arbitrageurs and other stock market traders had the opportunity to assess the vulnerabilities of a known bidder to various defensive actions that might be employed by target managers. Moreover, before almost every restructuring announcement, traders already had publicly available evidence that managers opposed (or were likely to resist) the bidder.[5] Although the attenuation problem suggests that the magnitude of the announcement return should be interpreted with caution, it does not affect inferences based on the observed direction of change in stockholder wealth.

4. Interpretation of the wealth effect evidence

One possible explanation for the average share price decline documented here is that the typical defensive restructuring represents managers' attempt to entrench themselves – i.e., the stockholder losses are directly attributable to target managers' decisions. In this view, the losses reflect a reduced likelihood of successful takeover as well as any reduction in profitability because the restructuring itself represents an inferior policy choice. Some indirect support for the entrenchment interpretation comes from the facts (documented in subsequent sections) that (i) target managers' planned restructurings sometimes led the hostile bidder to reduce the attractiveness of tender offer terms and that (ii) some restructuring plans were later dropped or modified as part of an agreement with the hostile bidder or with another firm that acquired control of the target.

Corroborative support for the entrenchment interpretation comes from the fact that managers of sample firms rarely put their plans to a stockholder vote. Because the courts view stockholder ratification as evidence that stockholders prefer a given policy, the practice of granting veto power to outside stockholders is quite common in other corporate transactions that involve visible managerial conflicts of interest (e.g., management buyouts or acquisitions by controlling parent corporations of minority holdings in a subsidiary). In the current context, a strategy available to managers would be to condition their restructuring plans upon eventual stockholder ratification. (If time pressure so

[5] For example, in 21 of the 31 announcements included in table 3, target managers had explicitly revealed their intention to oppose the bidder some time before they announced particular restructuring plans. In most of the remaining ten cases, other information previously reported in the financial press indicates that traders could have forecasted managerial opposition with reasonable confidence. Of these ten cases, four involve currently visible takeover attempts of the target firm by the eventual hostile bidders who had well-known 'raider' reputations, two involve prior reports of opposition by individual board members that did not yet represent the target's official position, one involves pre-emptive litigation brought by the bidder to prevent a defensive response, and one involves resignation of the hostile bidder's representative from the target board shortly before announcement of the tender offer.

dictated, managers could make final implementation of the restucturing subject to a stockholder vote to be held in a month or two.) This strategy would give managers better protection against charges of breach of fiduciary duty. However, managers voluntarily put their plans to a stockholder vote in only one sample case and, in some instances, went to great lengths to avoid doing so. A plausible explanation is that managers of these firms generally believed their plans would be vetoed because most stockholders viewed them as damaging entrenchment policies.

On the other hand, managerial self-protection is not the only possible explanation for the stockholder losses associated with the structural changes in our sample. For example, the average share price decline might be explained by a general implicit information effect of the type often hypothesized for corporate restructurings. In this view, the structural change announcement implicitly reveals that the target's expected profitability is lower than previously thought and hence that a lower share price is warranted, but not attributable to managerial entrenchment. This interpretation appears implausible here for several reasons. First, if managers and stockholders' interests are truly aligned, it is difficult to understand why managers would undercut their takeover bargaining position by revealing that the alternative-use value of the firm is lower than previously thought. Second, it is difficult to rationalize any takeover resistance under these circumstances, since stockholders would seem best served by a transaction which gave them a premium for their shares before the bidder discovered the impending profitability decline.

Finally, this explanation seems questionable given that, outside the context of a control contest, average share price *increases* characterize announcements of almost all of the nominal types of restructuring in our sample. Specifically, the negative average stock return we document cannot be explained simply as the typical effect for acquisitions, divestitures, and stock repurchases since these transactions are generally associated with share price increases (or perhaps zero price effect in the case of acquisitions). It is also unlikely that our findings could be explained by the negative share price effect usually found for public equity offerings. The reason is that the clear majority of equity issuances in our sample were private placements (rather than public offerings) and the available evidence indicates that announcements of common stock private placements are typically associated with share price increases [Wruck (1986)]. Section 5 provides more details on the stock returns for our sample partitioned by type of restructuring.

Another potential explanation for the observed share price decline is that the structural change announcement implicitly reveals that factors exogenous to managers have made it less likely they will be able to generate a multiple bidder auction for the target company. This explanation's credibility is reduced by ancillary evidence which suggests that most target firms' managers did not willingly promote an auction on behalf of stockholders. In 15 of the 33 sample contests, we find no evidence in WSJ reports that incumbents solicited or otherwise considered a white knight bidder. The hostile bidders unilaterally withdrew in 10 of these 15 cases – a regularity which suggests that incumbent managers did not consider a white knight because circumstances did not force them to do so. This interpretation seems reasonable given that we find no case in which incumbents sought to re-open negotiations with the hostile bidder, despite the fact (documented in section 6) that target stockholders typically experienced large wealth losses when bidders withdrew.

Further evidence of incumbents' reluctance to promote an auction is the fact that, for 13 of the remaining 18 contests, the first public indication that incumbents were considering a white knight occurred after other resistance efforts failed to deter the hostile bidder. We find evidence in only five contests that incumbents considered a white knight before the effectiveness of other resistance efforts became publicly known. Finally, financial press reports indicate that in eight of the ten cases in which target managers eventually capitulated to the hostile bidder, they did so only after (i) the bidder had acquired (or, with high probability, would soon own) close to a majority of target shares and/or after (ii) removal of important legal or regulatory barriers made it likely the takeover attempt would succeed. Of the remaining two capitulation cases, one came while a proxy fight vote outcome was in substantial doubt and the other came amid strong visible pressure by target stockholders to sell the company.

Viewed collectively, these facts suggest that incumbents generally preferred not to transfer target control to another management team and hence considered white knight offers desirable only when attempts to preserve their independence (i.e., to deflect the hostile bidder) proved ineffective. This interpretation in turn suggests that the average stockholder losses we observe at structural change announcements are not plausibly attributed to implicit information that incumbents were trying to generate an auction, but were having difficulties finding other bidders. Conversely, it offers somewhat greater assurance that the average stock price decline primarily reflects stockholder losses attributable to managers' attempts to resist takeover through defensive adjustments in corporate structure.

This interpretation of our evidence draws some ancillary support from recent studies which document that takeover resistance is often not in stockholders' interests and at best tends to be a break-even proposition. For example, public stockholders typically experience losses at announcement of 'greenmail' transactions in which a substantial share block is repurchased at a premium, often in exchange for the blockholder's promise not to seek control. Share values also fall on average (i) when target managers terminate merger negotiations, (ii) when managers reveal their opposition to an outsider's open market share accumulation, (iii) when managers seek to eliminate cumulative voting, and (iv) when managers create securities with so-called poison pill provisions. Share values are typically unaffected when managers bring litigation to stop or delay an extant tender offer and when they propose antitakeover charter amendments.[6] The fact that our stock price evidence fits the general pattern of prior studies lends additional credence to the interpretation that our sample restructurings typically served to protect incumbent managers at outside stockholders' expense.

An important caveat is that, even if one accepts the entrenchment interpretation of the evidence, it does not follow that stockholders will necessarily benefit from additional constraints on takeover defenses. For example, further limits on takeover resistance would undercut managers' ex ante incentives to invest in firm-specific human capital, and thus might harm stockholders on net through profits foregone because managers choose not to pursue some otherwise worthwhile projects that require such investments. At present, there is no evidence on the value consequences of these types of indirect effects on managerial behavior. And, of course, estimates of such indirect value consequences are clearly necessary to properly weigh the costs and benefits of proposed changes in the legal regime (and/or corporate charters) that would further limit takeover resistance.

5. Defensive restructurings: A closer look

Although our event-study analysis documents evidence necessary to assess the average stockholder wealth effect of defensive changes in corporate structure, it is also inherently limited insofar as it compresses into a single number information about managerial decisions that are often quite complex. This section seeks to provide a better understanding of these decisions by presenting a descriptive synthesis that (i) summarizes the principal nominal attributes of sample restructurings and that (ii) identifies four underlying economic motivations that appear to connect most sample cases. (The interested reader is referred to the appendix which contains detailed descriptions of each restructuring and which forms the basis for the summary presented here.) We also explore the relationship between restructuring type and eventual contest outcome.

[6]The stock returns evidence summarized in this paragraph is based on the following studies: greenmail – Dann and DeAngelo (1983), Bradley and Wakeman (1983), Mikkelson and Ruback (1985a, b), SEC (1984), and Holderness and Sheehan (1986); rejection of merger proposals – Dodd (1980); opposition to open market share accumulation – Mikkelson and Ruback (1985a); elimination of cumulative voting – Bhagat and Brickley (1984); poison pills – Malatesta and Walkling (1988) and Ryngaert (1988); litigation against an extant tender offer – Jarrell (1985, p. 165); antitakeover charter amendments – DeAngelo and Rice (1983), Linn and McConnell (1983), SEC (1985).

5.1. Attributes of defensive restructurings

The most striking property of our sample restructurings is that they tend to be large, both in terms of dollar values of the assets involved and in terms of the underlying change in corporate voting rights. In relative dollar value terms, the mean and median structural adjustments respectively represent 42.34% and 23.37% of the target's pre-offer equity value.[7] Twenty-eight of the 39 restructurings entail changes (through stock issuances or repurchases) in the number of outstanding votes in board elections. For this subsample, the planned structural changes involve a mean absolute percentage change in outstanding board votes of 27.62%, with a corresponding median of 17.15%. These figures clearly indicate that the typical target announcement in our sample represents plans for a major shift in corporate structure that could plausibly influence the outcome of the control contest.

Table 4 presents brief qualitative descriptions (as well as size and stock returns data) for our sample partitioned by nominal type of restructuring. The category descriptions in the first column represent our judgment of the principal attributes of the various planned structural changes. The remaining columns report estimates of gross size and stockholder wealth effects for the full sample (panel A) and for planned asset structure changes (20 acquisitions and divestitures in panel B), and planned ownership structure changes (31 stock issuances and repurchases in panel C). The total number of observations in panels B and C is 51 because 12 of the 39 cases involve changes in both asset and ownership structure, e.g., an asset purchase coupled with a private placement of voting securities. Consequently, the full sample averages are not simple weighted combinations of the averages for the panel B and C subsamples.

The subsamples of asset and ownership structure changes exhibit qualitatively similar average gross size and stockholder wealth effects. The 20 acquisitions and divestitures average 54.68% of the target's pre-offer equity value, compared to the 49.98% average size of the 31 issuances and repurchases. For both subsamples, the average share value decline is about 2%

[7] These size estimates were constructed from information reported in the financial press, corporate proxy statements, annual reports, *Moody's Manuals*, and *Standard and Poor's Security Owners' Stock Guide*. Dollar size figures represent the cash transaction values reported in the WSJ, or for issuances not involving cash, the number of shares to be issued times the pre-announcement market share price (except in two cases where stated value was the best available estimate). Vote percentage changes are the number of new votes issued divided by the number of current votes outstanding. In six cases involving issuance of a convertible security, vote changes are calculated as if conversion would occur immediately. In one case, our source documents contained insufficient data to construct a size estimate. In another three cases, it was not possible to construct an economically meaningful size estimate because the structural shifts themselves created unusual (contingent) voting rights and because they entailed stock dividends which, in part, simply divided stockholders' claims into two financial instruments.

and is significantly negative at the 0.052 and 0.001 levels, respectively, under a two-tailed z-test. Within the asset structure subsample, antitrust-related acquisitions tend to be smaller than other restructurings (probably because antitrust conflicts can be generated in relatively narrow markets). For almost all categories within a given subsample, we find negative average stock returns, and four exhibit losses that are significant at the 0.062 level or better (B.1, B.2, C.1, and C.4).[8] We are reluctant to place much emphasis on these tests because of the small number of observations in most categories and because, as we next discuss, table 4 groups the data by nominal restructuring type rather than by common economic motivation.

5.2. Common economic motivations for defensive restructurings

A close reading of table 4 (and the appendix) uncovers four common economic themes which link many sample restructurings. First, 11 of the 39 cases involve changes in target firm structure that were clearly connected to attributes of the hostile bidder. The restructurings that fit this pattern are those in categories B.1–B.3 and C.4 of the table and are comprised of target managers' plans to: (B.1) purchase assets that engender antitrust problems for the bidder, (B.2) purchase control of the bidder itself, (B.3) sell to a third party assets which overlap the bidder's line of business and which, according to the bidder, made the target an attractive acquisition candidate, and (C.4) issue new securities containing explicit contractual provisions conflicting with aspects of the hostile takeover attempt.[9] When viewed as a group, these cases suggest that one determinant of the chosen type of defensive restructuring is the ability to create barriers specific to the hostile bidder.

In comparison with the overall population of structural takeover barriers, our sample probably includes a disproportionately large number of bidder-specific defenses. The reason is that we study restructurings undertaken after managers had identified a threatening party and could therefore tailor their responses accordingly. Conversely, when it is difficult to identify possible

[8] The 12.63% return for category B.4 is a prominent exception. This figure is the prediction error for Signal Cos. (the only uncontaminated announcement in this category) whose structural adjustment was the sale of its major operating division for a price equal to 125% of the pre-announcement market value of the entire firm's equity. Interestingly, the hostile bidder sued to block the sale and, despite the large increase in target value, was able to obtain a court order that temporarily prohibited the divestiture.

[9] For more details on these cases, see the appendix entries for (B.1) Anaconda, Marshall Field, Royal Industries; (B.2) Cities Service, Martin Marietta, NLT; (B.3) Brunswick, Liggett; (C.4) El Paso, Lenox, Outdoor Sports. Less direct evidence that target managers tailor structural changes to create barriers specific to the hostile bidder can be found in the case descriptions for Continental Airlines, Diamond International, General Steel, Graniteville, Heli-Coil, Hi-Shear, Signal, and St. Joe Minerals, and for the second structural change by Cities Service.

Table 4

Size and other attributes of corporate structure changes announced by managers of 33 New York and American Stock Exchange-listed firms in response to an attempted hostile takeover in the period 1969–1983.

Description of the planned change in target firm structure	Number of cases[a]	Mean (median) value of structural change as a percentage of pre-offer target equity value[b]	Mean (median) absolute percentage change in the number of board votes outstanding[b]	Mean two-day prediction error at announcement of structural change[c] (z-statistic)
(A) Full sample	39	42.34% (23.37)	n.a.	−2.33% (−4.01)
(B) Acquisitions and divestitures	20	54.68 (27.00)	n.a.	−1.72 (−1.94)
1. Purchase of competitor of hostile bidder combined with private antitrust litigation	3	9.07 (9.07)	n.a.	−6.79 (−3.89)
2. Counteroffer for control of hostile bidder	3	110.05 (149.20)	n.a.	−4.81 (−1.95)
3. Sale to third party of assets in bidder's line of business	2	56.85 (56.85)	n.a.	−1.50 (−0.38)
4. Cash purchase or sale of assets with no connection to bidder's line of business	3	83.70 (82.73)	n.a.	12.63 (5.84)
5. Purchases of assets (for new voting securities) with no connection to bidder's business	9	36.22 (20.43)	n.a.	−0.91 (−1.27)

(C) Issuances and repurchases	31	49.98 (21.43)	27.62% (17.15)	−2.14 (−3.67)
1. Private block placement	14	41.53 (17.40)	20.00 (14.86)	−2.84 (−2.89)
2. Repurchase from current (public) stockholders	8	35.03 (30.47)	20.93 (16.85)	−1.18 (−0.93)
3. Issuance to dispersed group other than current holders	6	89.65 (97.06)	54.31 (39.06)	−1.47 (−1.37)
4. Issuance to current holders of securities with special voting rights that create barriers for extant bidder	3	n.a.	n.a.	−2.25 (−1.88)

[a] Twelve structural changes fall into categories listed under both (B) and (C). The overlap is largely explained by asset acquisitions that involved payment in the form of a private placement of voting securities. The overlapping cases break down as follows: B.5 together with C.1 (six cases), B.5 together with C.3 (three cases), B.2 together with C.3 (two cases), and B.3 together with C.2 (one case).

[b] These size figures exclude the three stock issuances in category C.4 because they created unusual (contingent) voting rights and because they were effected via stock dividends which, in part, divided stockholders' previously held claims into two separate financial instruments. These features make it difficult to construct a meaningful estimate of the magnitude of the net structural change engendered by each security issuance. Financial press reports provided sufficient detail to estimate the size of 35 of the remaining 36 planned changes in corporate structure. The size figures in (B) are based on 19 observations (2, 3, 2, 3, and 9 for B.1–B.5) while those in (C) are based on 28 observations (14, 8, and 6 for C.1–C.3).

[c] The prediction errors reported here are those for the uncontaminated sample of 31 announcements that appears in table 3. The subsamples contain the following numbers of announcements: (B) has 16 in total, with categories B.1–B.5 containing 3, 2, 2, 1, and 8, respectively; (C) has 26 in total, with categories C.1–C.4 containing 12, 5, 6, and 3, respectively.

acquirers, structural defenses undertaken in anticipation of a takeover attempt will more often create generalized defenses against a broad class of potential bidders. Thus, by excluding anticipatory defenses, our sample probably understates the relative importance of generalized defenses. For the same reason, it probably also understates the overall importance of structural takeover barriers in public corporations.

A second common theme connecting 19 restructurings is an attempt to create a consolidated vote block or to enhance the proportionate voting power of a block in place. The most obvious cases are the 14 private placements in category C.1.[10] The defensive nature of these private placements is corroborated by WSJ reports which indicate that most entail the issuance of new securities to parties friendly to management, to management-allied employee stock ownership plans, or to current management itself. Five of the repurchases in category C.2 also fit this general pattern since they were made by firms with a sizable management-allied block in place whose voting percentage would increase if publicly-held shares were repurchased.[11] Interestingly, managers of three sample firms announced plans during the control contest both to issue equity through a private placement and to repurchase shares from public holders. These cases offer especially clear evidence that vote consolidation per se is a significant consideration underlying a subset of stock repurchase activity.

Although the 19 cases of control consolidation typically involve a large shift in the number of outstanding board votes, only one would pro forma create a majority vote block. This finding suggests that these restructurings were motivated by (i) managers' belief that they could attract sufficient votes from public stockholders to form a majority coalition and/or by (ii) managers' attempt to generate potential veto power for a minority share block so that the bidder would find it more difficult to complete a subsequent merger or other major transaction with the target firm. Target managers' pursuit of substantial minority stakes also suggests they believe there is truth in the conventional wisdom that a minority share block can sometimes convey working control of a publicly-held corporation.

A third common economic motivation – dilution of the bidder's voting interest – characterizes eight sample restructurings. In these cases, financial

[10] We classified a transaction as a private placement if financial press descriptions indicated that securities would be issued to one or a few holders (rather than to a dispersed group). For more details, see the appendix entries for Continental Airlines, Dan River, General Steel, Graniteville, Hi-Shear (two transactions), Interstate Brands, Leeds & Northrup, Lightolier, Pogo, Rowan, Sparton, Sunshine Mining, and Union Commerce.

[11] See the appendix entries for Dan River, Grumman, General American Oil, Graniteville, and Pogo. Private placements were also announced during the control contests for Dan River, Graniteville, and Pogo.

press reports indicate that target managers planned to issue new equity claims to dilute the vote percentage held by a hostile bidder with apparent resource constraints.[12] For example, a private investor attempting a takeover of Hi-Shear had his stake diluted on two different occasions as he approached 50% ownership. In a similar vein, the chief executive officer of Heli-Coil announced plans for an acquisition that would almost triple the number of outstanding shares and claimed that the bidder (already smaller than Heli-Coil) 'can't print enough paper' to make its proposed stock-swap acquisition worthwhile. In the remaining cases, the hostile bidder either charged target managers with a dilution attempt or took other actions suggesting it would be vulnerable to such an attempt. The fact that some structural changes have dilution overtones while others appear motivated by vote consolidation suggests there is no single 'best' defense for all targets, but rather that each target's response depends on vulnerabilities of the particular hostile bidder.

A fourth theme connecting the restructurings announced by Brunswick and Liggett – and perhaps by Signal and St. Joe Minerals – is an attempt by target managers to accommodate bidders' pressure to reduce assets under their discretion. In all four cases, target managers announced plans to sell a major operating unit to a third party. The hostile bidder clearly sought the divested unit in the Brunswick and Liggett takeover attempts whereas the connection between the hostile bidder and target unit is less direct in the other cases. In three of the four cases, managers also planned a stock repurchase that would effectively distribute the divestiture proceeds to target stockholders. In essence, these transactions would transfer control of some target assets to a new management team, but would also potentially leave incumbents in control of a publicly-traded corporation. This fact suggests that some sample restructurings represent target managers' attempts to compromise by instituting a subset of the changes that the hostile bidder viewed as desirable.

Whatever the specific motivations, our sample restructurings are probably best viewed as strategic actions taken by target managers, given their forecast of the responses the hostile bidder would likely employ to circumvent a particular policy shift. Hostile bidders did, in fact, employ a variety of measures to counter incumbents' planned restructurings. For example, in eight cases, the bidder attempted to persuade target managers to drop their restructuring plans by explicitly linking implementation to reduced tender offer compensation or outright removal of the offer. In three cases, the restructuring required target stockholder approval and, in two of these instances, the bidder purchased shares quickly enough to block the proposal. In the remaining instance, the bidder waged (and narrowly lost) a proxy fight to prevent the

[12]See the appendix entries for Cities Service, Continental Airlines, Diamond International, General Steel, Graniteville, Heli-Coil, and Hi-Shear (two transactions).

restructuring. Finally, and most pervasively, hostile bidders commonly pressured managers to drop their plans in direct negotiations supplemented by litigation, and by statements to public stockholders that questioned the wisdom of those plans. This pressure evidently had some effect since roughly one quarter of the planned restructurings (10 of 39) were ultimately dropped or modified as part of a negotiated settlement with the hostile bidder or another party that acquired control.

5.3. Contest outcomes and restructuring type

An interesting empirical question is whether there is a systematic relation between the chosen form of defense and the eventual contest outcome. To assess this issue, we classified the outcomes of conflicts between hostile bidders and targets into three general categories. The first category contains the ten contests in which the hostile bidder acquired either a majority holding (eight cases) or a substantial minority stake and significant representation on the board of directors (two cases). The second category contains the 11 contests in which the hostile bidder dropped its takeover attempt in the face of a bid by another party (usually a so-called white knight). The third category contains the 12 contests in which the hostile bidder ended its takeover attempt with no third party bids outstanding. This relatively uniform distribution of contest outcomes is consistent with the view that hostilities over proposed control transfers tend to occur when both bidder and target rationally believe they have some chance to influence the outcome in their favor.

We find little evidence of a systematic relationship between control contest outcome and the type of defensive restructuring.[13] For most restructuring types, the profile of outcomes is roughly equivalent to that for the full sample. No group of acquisitions or divestitures has an outcome distribution that appears materially different from that of the full sample. The same conclusion applies to the group of 31 restructurings involving issuance or repurchase of voting securities. Within this category, however, we find that in all eight repurchase cases, the bidder did not acquire control of the target, and that in four of the six issuances to a dispersed group, the bidder did acquire a sizable stake and board representation. These facts offer some hint that stock repurchase served as a relatively strong deterrent and, conversely, that issuance to a dispersed group represented a relatively weak takeover defense in our sample contests.

[13] One plausible explanation is that bidders will rationally avoid hostile takeover attempts when the target can effect a strong defensive response (see footnote 1). Thus, if one particular form of restructuring represents an especially powerful defense, it should pre-empt hostile takeover attempts and hence will not be reflected in the defense versus outcome frequencies reported here.

6. Defensive restructurings: A broader view

6.1. Stock returns evidence

The stock returns reported earlier measure the wealth effects experienced by stockholders when managers announced defensive restructurings. As such, they represent appropriate data to assess whether these managerial actions typically served stockholders' best interests. Table 5 provides a broader perspective on our sample contests by documenting the net overall stockholder wealth effects associated with these hostile takeover attempts. The first four columns report sample sizes and target firm prediction errors at the dates of first public disclosure of (i) initiation of the takeover attempt by the hostile bidder, (ii) structural changes planned by incumbent managers, and (iii) outcome of the conflict between the hostile bidder and the target. The next two columns document cumulative prediction errors from 40 trading days before initiation through outcome and from structural change through outcome. The final column reports the average cash tender premium initially offered by the hostile bidders.[14] The rows present these figures for the full sample, and for subsamples partitioned by contest outcome.

The stock return data in table 5 reveal that the typical hostile takeover attempt generated substantial overall wealth gains for target stockholders. For example, in the two-day period surrounding public initiation of the contest, target share prices increased by an average of 15.34%. This figure probably understates the expected wealth effect of the typical takeover attempt since, over the 40 trading days prior to public initiation, share prices increased on average by an additional 10.40%.[15] A more complete measure of the wealth effects associated with these takeover contests is reported in the fifth column of the table. This measure indicates that, for the entire sample, stockholder wealth increased by an average of 37.71% over the period that spans 40 trading days prior to public initiation through the contest outcome.

This substantial wealth gain is primarily associated with the roughly two-thirds (21 of 33) of the contests in which the hostile bidder prevailed or withdrew in favor of an offer by a third party. For these two subsamples, stockholders experienced average wealth increases over the full period of

[14] Offer premiums are calculated as the percentage amount by which the cash tender price exceeds the (split and dividend adjusted) closing share price 41 trading days prior to contest initiation. This offer premium and the cumulative returns reported in table 5 are measured from a period roughly two calendar months prior to initiation because of the well-known empirical regularity (sometimes attributed to information leakage) that share prices tend to increase immediately before takeover proposals.

[15] This latter figure is statistically significant at the 0.01 level. For the three outcome partitions, the corresponding average returns are 8.75%, 2.60%, and 18.93%, respectively. The first figure is significant at the 0.05 level, the second is immaterially different from zero at conventional levels, and the third is significant at the 0.01 level.

Table 5

Target stockholder wealth effects associated with announcements of initiation of control contest, target's structural change, and contest outcome for 33 New York and American Stock Exchange-listed firms that faced hostile takeover attempts in the period 1969–1983.

		Mean, median, and fraction of positive observations of:[a]					
		Two-day prediction error at:[b]			Cumulative prediction error from:[b]		
Outcome of control contest	Number of contests	Initiation by hostile bidder	Planned structural change[c]	Outcome of control contest	40 days before initiation through outcome	Planned structural change through outcome	Mean and median cash premium offered in initial hostile tender bid[d]
Full sample	33	15.34%*	−2.33%*	−2.52%*	37.71%*	3.10%	56.51%
		11.48	−2.73	0.16	25.96	0.14	49.48
		(0.85)	(0.26)	(0.55)	(0.82)	(0.52)	
Hostile bidder successfully acquired	10	14.85*	−4.06*	−0.40*	42.97*	8.01	55.63
substantial stake and		10.41	−4.31	0.47	41.28	8.93	56.37
board representation		(0.90)	(0.10)	(0.70)	(0.90)	(0.60)	
Competing offer for control of target	11	15.63*	−2.57*	3.40*	57.58*	21.03*	58.09
engendered withdrawal		9.01	−3.94	1.14	36.18	25.05	49.25
by hostile bidder		(0.82)	(0.27)	(0.73)	(0.82)	(0.82)	
Incumbent managers retained control	12	15.49*	−0.34	−9.72*	15.12*	−17.42*	55.90
as hostile bid ended with		17.40	−1.75	−7.96	17.11	−14.46	46.72
no other offers outstanding		(0.83)	(0.40)	(0.25)	(0.75)	(0.17)	

[a]An asterisk indicates that the mean prediction error differs significantly from zero at the 0.01 level under a two-tailed z-test. In no case was an average prediction error significant at the 0.05, but not the 0.01 level.

[b]Contest initiation refers to the date of the first published report that the hostile bidder had bought or planned to buy target shares. Contest outcome refers to our judgment of the date at which the conflict between the hostile bidder and target was resolved.

[c]This column contains prediction errors for the uncontaminated sample of 31 announcements that appears in table 3. For the subsamples here, the number of uncontaminated announcements of structural changes is 10, 11, and 10, respectively.

[d]The offer premium represents the percentage by which the cash price per share initially offered by the bidder exceeds the target's share price as of the market close 41 trading days prior to contest initiation. These premium figures exclude four exchange offers and so the full sample contains 29 cash tender bids, of which 8, 9, and 12, respectively, fall in the subsamples.

42.97% and 57.58%, respectively. In contrast, the average overall wealth gain was 15.12% for stockholders of the remaining 12 firms for which the hostile bidder ended its takeover attempt with no third-party offers currently outstanding. For stockholders in these firms, the large average wealth increase they experienced early in the contest was substantially reversed – but not eliminated – as of the contest outcome.[16]

Several other figures in table 5 also suggest that target stockholders would have benefited from a successful takeover. Most obviously, stockholder wealth fell by a statistically significant average of 9.72% in the two days surrounding news that the hostile bidder planned to drop its takeover attempt even though no competing offers were outstanding. This outcome was probably anticipated to some degree since, for example, we observe an average decline in stockholder wealth of 17.42% when we cumulate stock returns over the period from the restructuring announcement through the contest outcome. Finally, according to figures reported in the WSJ, the hostile bidder's initially announced tender offer terms entailed a cash premium of some 56% above the market price that prevailed 41 trading days before contest initiation. Evidently, withdrawal of the hostile bidder's takeover proposal typically entailed a substantial opportunity loss for target stockholders.[17,18]

Despite the large stockholder losses associated with defeat of a takeover bid, the courts viewed almost all resistance in our sample as consistent with managers' fiduciary duty to stockholders. Specifically, financial press reports reveal only six cases in which the courts granted a temporary restraining order

[16]As a sensitivity check, we replicated this analysis using the market adjusted returns approach described by Brown and Warner (1985, p. 7). Under this alternative estimation procedure, the absolute magnitudes of abnormal returns are somewhat smaller, but the relative magnitudes across subsamples are essentially unchanged from table 5. For the full sample and the first two outcome partitions, we again find significant positive abnormal returns over the period from 40 days before contest initiation through contest outcome. For the cases in which hostile bidders unilaterally withdrew, we find positive but insignificant returns over this period. Importantly, both estimation procedures yield wealth effect estimates which suggest that target stockholders typically would have been better off had the hostile takeover attempt succeeded.

[17]The same qualitative picture emerges when we calculate a blended premium that weights the tender offer price by its nominal proration factor and that conservatively treats the offer's expected second-stage value as equal to the pre-offer market price. For this subsample, the blended premium averages 42.35%, a figure which also suggests that target stockholders typically experienced a substantial opportunity loss when bidders withdrew.

[18]This inference is also supported by the fact that we find no indication of statistically positive cumulative average returns for (i) the period from structural defense through one and two years after contest outcome and for (ii) the period from contest outcome through one and two years after outcome. Some readers have suggested that these returns should be significantly positive if managers' defensive actions were in the 'long-run' interests of stockholders, but were not recognized as such during the takeover contest. (This 'long-run' interests scenario presumes a semi-strong form inefficient stock market, a condition which would contradict the premise of our earlier tests.) A caveat here is that the insignificant returns we observe may be due to the small sample size and long cumulation intervals. On the other hand, for reasons discussed in section 6.2, the observation of statistically positive returns over these cumulation intervals would not be sufficient to conclude that managers' defensive actions served stockholders' best interests.

(or stronger prohibition) against managers' planned restructurings and no case in which defeat of a tender bid was judged counter to stockholders' interests.[19] One possible explanation is that the courts generally evaluate challenged takeover defenses according to the business judgment rule which presumes that corporate policies are acceptable unless litigants can establish that managers engaged in self-dealing transactions or otherwise acted in bad faith.[20] The apparent consequence is that managers can legally erect structural barriers against takeovers that would pay stockholders significant premiums for their shares.

6.2. The stock returns evidence in perspective

Some readers of earlier drafts have argued that the cumulative returns data show that target stockholders typically were not harmed by managers' defensive restructurings. One variant of this argument is based on the observation that average stockholder wealth increased over the entire contest even for the subsample in which hostile bidders withdrew unilaterally. There are two misconceptions with this view. First, this cumulative return measures the total wealth impact of (outsider-initiated) takeover attempts, so that one cannot plausibly attribute the overall value increase narrowly to incumbent managers' defensive actions. Second, it is incorrect to infer from the observed positive cumulative return alone that stockholders were better off ex post because of managerial resistance. This inference requires comparison of stockholders' realized return with their expected payoff had the bidder not withdrawn in the

[19]The six cases vary considerably in terms of the strength of judicial impediments to managers' planned structural changes. The Harsco repurchase plans were temporarily restrained, but this prohibition was evidently unimportant since the court order was dissolved almost immediately. The Signal divestiture was temporarily prohibited, but was ultimately completed after the hostile bidder failed to post the $25 million bond required by the courts. In the Hi-Shear case, the courts enjoined the voting of shares issued in a friendly hands placement, but the court order was effectively overturned in the negotiated settlement of the control contest. In the Royal Industries case, the courts stopped an antitrust-motivated acquisition that could have been, but was not, completed after a white knight acquired control of the target. The courts restrained St. Joe's repurchase offer, but St. Joe's appeal of this decision was not resolved because it dropped the repurchase offer as part of an agreement with a white knight. In the Outdoor Sports case, the courts prohibited a stock issuance on grounds that it represented an illegal attempt to modify the corporate charter without stockholder approval. Outdoor Sports was unable to convince the courts to reverse this ruling.

[20]The burden of proof shifts to managers only when the questioned policy involves acute managerial conflicts of interest. Paradoxically, the courts have not viewed control contests as inherently involving such conflicts, even though a successful takeover typically generates substantial wealth gains for public stockholders, and can simultaneously engender significant managerial welfare losses. Thus, managers can legally institute structural changes that have entrenchment overtones, unless litigants can convince the courts that entrenchment was the primary motive for the policy in question. For additional discussion of the business judgment rule and the role it plays in governing managerial resistance to takeovers, see Easterbrook and Fischel (1981a, b) and Lipton (1981).

face of resistance. (As noted earlier, stockholders typically realized returns less than the premium offered by the bidder prior to withdrawal.)

Another variant of the argument is based on the cumulative stock returns measured from just after the restructuring announcement through the contest outcome. Specifically, the cumulative losses for the subsample in which hostile bidders unilaterally withdrew are roughly offset on a frequency-weighted basis by the cumulative gains in the remaining cases. But rather than estimating the incremental wealth effect of defensive restructurings, this weighted-average figure simply measures the post-announcement cumulative stock return, conditional upon prior revelation of defensive action. The incremental value of managers' defensive restructurings is properly assessed by the difference between (i) stockholders' expected wealth conditional upon defensive action and (ii) their expected wealth conditional upon no defensive action. Cumulative stock returns – measured either over the entire contest or over the post-defense period – do not measure this difference. The stock return at restructuring announcement provides the best available evidence on which of the two conditional returns is larger and hence on whether stockholders were typically helped or harmed by the restructuring per se.

When compared to the large net wealth gains generated by the hostile bidder through its takeover attempt, the average share price decline observed at restructuring announcement – although statistically significant – constitutes a relatively small loss for target stockholders.[21] This comparison suggests that the typical sample restructuring is most appropriately viewed as marginally increasing the chance of deflecting a takeover, and not as a policy shift that by itself effectively defeated the hostile bidder. This interpretation is further supported by the fact that, for the subsample in which the hostile bidder eventually ended its takeover attempt with no extant third party offers, the 9.72% average share value decline at contest outcome is much more pronounced than that observed at restructuring announcement, both for the full sample and for this particular outcome subsample.[22] These comparisons raise a question about the extent to which target managers' restructurings actually influenced contest outcomes.

At least a partial answer to this question is provided by table 6 which reports data on the relationship between implementation of managers' planned restructurings and eventual contest outcomes. We find that, of the 39 an-

[21] Strictly speaking, this statement assumes that the attenuation problem discussed in section 3 does not materially diminish the stock returns observed at restructuring announcement.

[22] For this subsample, the statistically immaterial −0.34% mean prediction error at structural change announcement can be partially explained by one sample point (the Signal Cos. case discussed in footnote 8) with a positive 12.63% return. When this return is dropped, the subsample mean prediction error becomes −1.78% which is significant at the 0.054 level under a two-tailed z-test, but which is still small relative to the −9.72% average share price impact at contest outcome.

Table 6

Resolution of target managers' announced plans to effect defensive adjustments in corporate asset and ownership structure in response to a hostile takeover attempt in the period 1969–1983 (39 announcements by managers of 33 New York and American Stock Exchange-listed firms).

		Number of cases and percentage of subsample in which:		
Outcome of control contest	Number of cases[a]	Plans actually implemented by target managers	Plans dropped or modified in negotiated settlement with hostile bidder or eventual acquirer	Plans dropped but not as part of negotiated settlement with hostile bidder or eventual acquirer[b]
Full sample	39	25 (64%)	10 (26%)	4 (10%)
Hostile bidder successfully acquired substantial stake and board representation	10	3 (30%)	5 (50%)	2 (20%)
Competing offer for control of target engendered withdrawal by hostile bidder	16	11 (69%)	4 (25%)	1 (6%)
Incumbent managers retained control as hostile bid ended with no other offers outstanding	13	11 (84%)	1 (8%)	1 (8%)

[a]The figures in this column refer to the total number of distinct announcements of structural changes made by target managers. The number of firms represented in the full sample is 33, while the three subsamples contain 10, 11, and 12 firms, respectively.

[b]The four structural changes in this column were not implemented because: bankers withdrew the buyer's financing for a private placement (1 case), target managers and the buyer in a planned private placement did not agree on terms (2 cases), and target managers were unable to complete the transaction after the hostile bidder obtained a preliminary injunction to prevent its implementation (1 case).

nounced structural changes, 25 were actually implemented by target managers, 10 were dropped or modified in a negotiated settlement with the hostile bidder or eventual acquirer, and 4 were not implemented because of other impediments to their completion. When target managers actually implemented their plans, the hostile bidder was rarely successful in its takeover attempt. Specifically, only three of the 25 implemented structural changes were followed by a transfer of control to the hostile bidder. In contrast, the hostile bidder succeeded in seven of the 14 cases in which the announced policy shift was not implemented. These observations suggest that structural changes – perhaps in combination with other defenses employed by incumbent managers – often served as important deterrents to hostile bidders.

Table 6 further indicates that the announced restructurings were actually implemented considerably more frequently when incumbents retained control than when the hostile bidder prevailed (11 of 13 versus 3 of 10 cases). The data also show that managers' plans were implemented in a reasonably high proportion of instances in which the hostile bidder withdrew in favor of a third-party offer (11 of 16 cases). This observation is consistent with our earlier evidence that some restructurings appear tailored to create barriers specific to the hostile bidder. Finally, an indication that potential acquirers found incumbents' plans undesirable is the fact that ten of these plans were dropped or modified through agreements with the hostile bidder or another party that eventually acquired target control. Viewed collectively, the table 6 data provide additional evidence that announced restructurings likely had some influence on the outcomes of sample contests.

7. Summary and implications for future research

The evidence in this study indicates that target stockholders experience statistically significant average wealth losses at announcement of defensive corporate restructurings. These restructurings are typically quite large, and many involve consolidation of a block of voting securities in the hands of friendly parties and/or creation of barriers specific to the hostile bidder. The hostile takeover attempts typically generate large overall wealth gains for target stockholders, but the evidence indicates that these gains arise in spite of, not due to, target managers' actions. We find that stockholders' gains are primarily associated with the roughly two-thirds of the contests in which the hostile bidder or a competing bidder prevails. In the remaining cases, stockholders typically lose large tender premiums and experience large share value declines when a sole bidder withdraws in the face of resistance by incumbent managers. We find little evidence in financial press reports that incumbents voluntarily sought purchasers on behalf of target stockholders. Finally, while the data do not establish that defensive restructurings determined contest outcomes, we find that hostile bidders rarely prevail when incumbents implement their planned structural changes.

Our overall reading of the evidence is that the typical sample restructuring is best explained as an attempt by target managers to entrench themselves at stockholders' expense. While the entrenchment interpretation is a matter of judgment, the data clearly establish that defensive motives – whether beneficial or harmful – influence managers' choice of asset and ownership structure during a contest for corporate control. The extent to which defensive considerations motivate managerial policies outside this particular setting remains an open empirical issue. The findings reported here indicate that the relationship between the control market and investment/financial policy is an issue worthy of further examination. Specifically, the findings suggest a number of potentially fruitful areas for future empirical study.

For example, the finance literature documents that stock repurchase announcements are associated with large share price increases but does not consider the possibility that control consolidation may help explain this empirical regularity.[23] Our findings suggest that stock repurchases may be motivated in part by managers' attempts to increase their vote ownership percentage and that the observed share value increases may reflect the market's perception that managers undertake repurchases when they foresee a higher probability of takeover. The vote consolidation explanation for stock repurchase is also an implication of recent capital structure models formulated by Harris and Raviv (1988) and Stulz (1988). Thus, it seems worthwhile to re-examine broader samples of stock repurchases, intrafirm exchange offers, recapitalizations, etc. to assess whether control consolidation (and an ancillary takeover-related positive information effect on share prices) is an important factor underlying these restructurings.

Our data also suggest that the general decision to expand company operations represents a promising area for investigation of the link between the control market and corporate investment policy. Prior studies document stockholder losses for some companies announcing additional capital expenditures and for the typical firm announcing plans to raise additional equity capital to undertake new investments. There is also evidence that stockholders of some firms experience losses when managers reveal plans to expand via acquisition.[24] We find that acquisitions by target firms sometimes involve changes in the company's asset mix or voting rights distribution that apparently make a hostile takeover more difficult. In our view, it seems implausible that defensive motives could be the dominant factor that explains

[23] See Dann (1981), Masulis (1980), Vermaelen (1981), and Rosenfeld (1982).

[24] For documentation of the average share price declines cited here, see McConnell and Muscarella (1985) on the effects of additional capital expenditures in the oil industry; Dann and Mikkelson (1984), Asquith and Mullins (1986), and Masulis and Korwar (1986) on the effects of primary equity offerings; and Dodd (1980) on the effects of mergers.

corporate investment decisions. Nevertheless, it seems possible – and worthy of closer examination – that such motives may partially explain the stockholder losses documented in some previous studies of investment policy.

Our sampling algorithm isolates (a subset of) firms whose managers had sufficient flexibility to effect a defensive restructuring in response to a hostile takeover attempt. This fact suggests that the ex ante choice of a capital structure that preserves financial flexibility (in the form of unused borrowing capacity, ability to issue securities with specialized defensive covenants, etc.) can itself represent a takeover defense. This observation, in turn, suggests that the preservation of flexibility potentially entails costs (e.g., by facilitating damaging defensive restructurings) as well as benefits [Myers and Majluf (1984)]. At present, it is an open empirical question whether these particular costs and benefits represent important determinants of the optimal amount of financial flexibility in a given firm's capital structure.

By construction, our sample does not include defensive adjustments in operating and financial policy undertaken in anticipation of a takeover attempt. For example, our sample excludes cases in which managers have deliberately developed organizational structures or lines of business that are technically complex and hence that would be difficult for many potential bidders to operate profitably without incumbents' cooperation. A systematic study of anticipatory takeover defenses would be particularly worthwhile because it would help clarify how managers exercise their discretion over corporate policy to create unique (i.e., incumbent-specific) advantages over alternative management teams. However, because evaluating the effects of particular policy decisions requires knowledge of much firm-specific detail, the systematic study of anticipatory structural defenses will surely prove to be a difficult empirical task.

Our analysis uncovers several restructurings in which incumbents apparently sought to retain control of the surviving publicly-traded firm by effecting some, but not all, of the hostile bidder's objectives. These compromise restructurings largely involve divestitures and stock repurchases, and share the common element of removing a portion of the target's assets from incumbent managers' control. In short, they seem to be cases in which target managers sought to accommodate control market pressures to limit the assets under their discretion. This observation in turn suggests it would be useful to investigate further how the control market per se constrains the magnitude and mix of resources subject to managerial discretion. As elaborated by Jensen (1987), the range of such control market/corporate finance interactions is potentially quite large and extends from divestitures, spinoffs, stock repurchases, and liquidations to the general questions of optimal debt and dividend policies.

Finally, our findings suggest that detailed study of the application and evolution of the business judgment rule would help clarify how managers' decisions are disciplined by external monitoring mechanisms. Several questions come to mind. First, given that judges have insufficient expertise to readily identify optimal corporate policies, what practical guidelines do they apply to assess whether particular decisions best served stockholders' interests? What common elements link the evidence outside stockholders use to argue that managers' decisions constituted a breach of fiduciary duty? What common attributes underlie the evidence that managers cite to establish that allegedly self-interested decisions actually enhanced stockholders' welfare? A systematic analysis of these issues would not only clarify how the courts discipline managerial behavior, but would also provide evidence on the difficulties that monitoring agents generally face when evaluating managers' decisions. Such evidence would provide a valuable assessment of the extent to which managerial self-interest can influence corporate asset and ownership structure.

Appendix

Descriptions of defensive restructurings and the control contests in which they were undertaken

This appendix provides details of the defensive restructurings announced by managers of sample firms. Each case begins with a description of the planned structural change and then attempts to place this decision in perspective by describing the nature and sequence of other events in the takeover contest that we judged to be relevant. The target and hostile bidder are identified on the left and right respectively above the case description. The case write-up identifies other bidders and provides details such as their relationship to the target, when they entered the contest, etc. For each structural defense, we report (i) the target firm's two-day abnormal stock return at announcement (labelled prediction error, *pe*), (ii) the relevant announcement date (i.e., the final trading day in the announcement period), and (iii) the alpha-numeric classification of the defense type (see table 4 in the text above for class definitions). We also identify those restructuring announcements we judged to be confounded by the simultaneous release of other information.

Anaconda Co. **Crane Co.**

Anaconda acquired Walworth Co. which, like Crane, was a large producer of industrial valves and brought private antitrust litigation that challenged Crane's share purchase plans (*pe* = −4.51%; 10/30/75; B.1). Crane lowered its offer price in response and sought an injunction against the Walworth transaction. After the courts refused to stop the Walworth acquisition, Crane agreed not to seek representation on Anaconda's board. Approximately two months later, Anaconda agreed to be acquired by Tenneco which subsequently withdrew in the face of an offer by ARCO. Anaconda did not oppose the ARCO offer and the two companies eventually merged.

Brunswick Corp. **Whittaker Corp.**

Brunswick agreed to sell its Sherwood Medical unit to American Home Products Corp. (*pe* = 5.86%; 2/12/82; B.3/C.2). Whittaker sought Brunswick primarily to combine the Sherwood unit with its own medical operations. Before AHP's interest in Sherwood was publicly known, Whittaker (unsuccessfully) sought a court order preventing a sale of the unit. AHP's interest in Sherwood apparently strengthened Brunswick's bargaining position since, on the day before the divestiture announcement, Whittaker sweetened its bid for Brunswick. Whittaker subsequently lost a series of legal challenges to the Sherwood sale and withdrew its bid. (Brunswick's investment bankers testified that the overall value to stockholders was somewhat greater under Whittaker's offer than under AHP's offer, but that the choice ultimately rested on business judgment.) AHP acquired a substantial number of Brunswick shares in a heavily oversubscribed tender offer and, as previously agreed, Brunswick repurchased those shares in exchange for the Sherwood unit.

Cities Service Co. **Mesa Petroleum Co.**

Cities announced a pre-emptive offer for control of Mesa because it alleged that Mesa was planning a takeover bid (*pe* = 7.86%, confounded; 6/1/82; B.2). This announcement came after a period of open-market purchases by Mesa and immediately before Mesa's bid for Cities shares. It followed by about one week a Cities' stock issuance that Mesa charged was designed to dilute its equity interest (*pe* = 3.41%; 5/20/82; C.3). At their respective proration deadlines, Cities' offer for Mesa was undersubscribed while Mesa's bid was oversubscribed by an amount that would give it a near-majority stake. Cities then agreed to be acquired by Gulf Oil Corp., which represented a significant policy shift since Cities' CEO had previously stated that 'we're telling anyone who comes along with an offer to buzz off'. This agreement came after Mesa revealed it had been tendered a substantial stake, but before the deadline that would prevent Cities holders from withdrawing their shares and tendering them to another bidder. Shortly thereafter, Mesa agreed not to pursue Cities in exchange for a reciprocal promise from Cities. Gulf's share price fell substantially at announcement of the white knight deal and Gulf later withdrew its offer, citing FTC objections. Cities immediately sought another buyer and eventually was acquired by Occidental Petroleum Corp.

Continental Airlines, Inc. **Texas International Airlines Inc.**

Continental agreed to sell a majority share block to an employee stock ownership plan (*pe* = −6.20%; 4/9/81; C.1). At this time, Texas Air held a near-majority of Continental stock acquired through open market purchases and a recently completed tender offer. The ESOP issuance would substantially dilute Texas Air's stake and would give majority voting power to a management-allied group. The issuance was conditioned upon availability of bank financing, but not upon stockholder approval. Texas Air (and other stockholders) tried to block the sale in numerous legal and regulatory forums. The courts and the Civil Aeronautics Board refused to block the sale. The NYSE announced that Continental's listing depended on stockholder approval of the issuance. Continental indicated it would explore listing elsewhere. The California Commissioner of Corporations also ruled that the issuance required stockholder approval. Two weeks later, the U.S. Senate approved legislation pre-empting this ruling. One week later, the CAB removed some important obstacles to Texas Air's takeover attempt and Continental's bankers immediately withdrew financing for the ESOP transaction. (Continental's chairman committed suicide the next day.) Hostilities continued. Texas Air purchased additional shares to attain a majority stake and received final regulatory approval to take control of Continental. The firms then negotiated a settlement which gave control to Texas Air.

Dan River Inc. **Carl Icahn (group of affiliated companies)**

Dan River issued a block of convertible voting preferred stock to a newly created bonus plan for salaried employees (*pe* = −5.50%; 10/6/82; C.1). The new shares represented a substantial minority of board votes and could veto a merger proposal if one-third of the class objected. Icahn immediately sued over the issuance (as did other stockholders who claimed it imposed a 'chilling effect on nascent tender offers'). Icahn also announced a tender offer promising stockholders substantially higher compensation if the board refrained from defensive transactions. Several hours before Icahn's bid was to expire, Dan River announced a repurchase 'for the purpose of ... oppos(ing) the Icahn offer' (*pe* = 1.93%, confounded; 11/23/82; C.2). Dan River also announced accelerated discussions with an unidentified company concerning a possible purchase of some or all shares. Icahn's bid was apparently undersubscribed, since he immediately extended the offer and sued over the repurchase. Three weeks later, Dan River sold a share block to Hanson Trust PLC and said the firms were exploring merger possibilities. However, two weeks later, Dan River announced an (eventually completed) management buyout at a price substantially above Icahn's bid. Icahn and Dan River agreed that, while the buyout was in process, Icahn would not pursue control and Dan River would refrain from a long list of structural changes, including the issuance of equity.

Diamond International Corp. **Cavenham Holdings Inc.**

Diamond agreed to acquire Brooks-Scanlon Inc. for a combination of newly issued shares and cash (*pe* = −1.29%; 12/21/79; B.5/C.3). The Brooks transaction was announced while Cavenham – a firm controlled by Sir James Goldsmith – was accumulating Diamond shares in the open market. (The transaction has overtones of a dilution attempt since it would materially increase the number of outstanding Diamond shares and since Goldsmith was simultaneously selling off other assets, ostensibly to finance the purchase of Diamond stock.) Goldsmith responded with a proxy fight to block the Brooks acquisition and with a tender offer for a substantial minority of Diamond shares in which he promised a higher price if Diamond stockholders vetoed the acquisition. Diamond stockholders ultimately approved the Brooks acquisition by a slim margin. However, numerous proxies were challenged by both sides and one month elapsed until the final vote count was announced. During this period, Diamond and Goldsmith negotiated a truce in which the latter obtained board representation in exchange for increased tender offer compensation and a standstill promise limiting his ownership to a substantial minority stake. One and a half years later, Diamond agreed to be (and was eventually) merged into one of Goldsmith's companies. Following this agreement, Diamond began a major divestiture program in which many units were sold to various buyers.

El Paso Co. **Burlington Northern Inc.**

El Paso authorized a dividend of a new class of preferred shares payable to common stockholders (*pe* = −8.99%; 12/27/82; C.4). The preferred would elect one-third of the board if an outside party acquired 25% of El Paso's common and did not immediately offer to buy the remaining shares at the highest price it had previously paid. (Burlington had offered to buy just over 50% of El Paso's common.) Burlington reported that roughly 50% of El Paso's common had been tendered. El Paso revealed it was discussing with other companies the sale of its exploration properties, acquisition of which represented Burlington's principal objective. El Paso rejected Burlington's request for the chance to outbid third parties and said that Burlington bids would be considered only if its tender offer were withdrawn. El Paso had also tried to block Burlington's takeover on antitrust grounds but, in an apparent shift in policy, the Justice Department gave Burlington expedited approval to pursue El Paso. The firms then negotiated a settlement which included agreement that (i) El Paso would rescind the preferred stock dividend and defensive bylaw changes it had instituted, (ii) Burlington would proceed with a tender offer under substantially the same terms (except the proration pool would be reopened to allow inclusion of shares owned by holders who had followed management's earlier recommendation not to tender), and (iii) Burlington would not be obligated to buy the minority shares outstanding after the tender offer (although six months later it offered to do so).

General American Oil Co. of Texas **Mesa Petroleum Co.**

GAO announced a repurchase offer for a substantial minority stake and reserved the right to buy a majority if tendered (*pe* = −0.15%; 12/23/82; C.2). The repurchase would increase the voting power of a substantial minority block held by foundation/trusts for which GAO's managers served as directors/trustees. The repurchase offer came several days after Mesa announced its bid for GAO shares and one day before GAO initiated a search for a white knight. Mesa's bid attracted a substantial majority of GAO shares, including those held by the management-run foundation. (The foundation directors said the Mesa bid was inadequate and that they had tentatively tendered the share block only to protect its proration position.) Immediately before the withdrawal deadline for Mesa's bid, the parties announced an (eventually completed) agreement in which Phillips Petroleum Co. would acquire GAO and Mesa would receive expense reimbursement. In the process, Mesa reduced its debt substantially since it had previously issued bonds convertible into shares of GAO acquired earlier.

General Steel Industries Inc. **Walco National Corp.**

General Steel agreed to acquire Gruendler Crusher and Pulverizer Co. for a minority share block and cash (*pe* = −1.30%; 6/25/81; B.5/C.1). This transaction came two months after Walco purchased a significant minority position in General Steel and four months before Walco's tender offer. Walco said it was making the offer because it believed that General Steel was seeking acquisitions to dilute Walco's holding. Shortly after the tender announcement, General Steel authorized a search for a white knight. General Steel sued Walco because it sought just over a 50% stake and because its controlling stockholder (a member of Congress) allegedly led a lavish lifestyle and furthered his political interests at Walco stockholders' expense. Walco countersued and charged that General Steel had issued stock in its earlier acquisition as a means of diluting Walco's stake. A federal judge sided with General Steel and forced Walco's controlling stockholder to make some (potentially) politically embarrassing disclosures about his Walco-funded perquisites and required Walco to dispose of some recently acquired General Steel shares. Shortly thereafter, the firms negotiated a settlement in which all litigation was dropped and Walco agreed to support a merger between General Steel and Lukens Steel Co.

Graniteville Co. **Southeastern Public Service Co.**

Graniteville agreed to issue a block of common stock to a newly created employee stock ownership plan (*pe* = 2.85%, confounded; 4/26/83; C.1). This issuance was announced after a period of open-market share accumulation by Southeastern – one of Victor Posner's companies – and preceded by three days a scheduled stockholder vote over the addition of Posner and two associates to Graniteville's board. Posner immediately announced a tender offer for control and brought litigation which claimed, among other things, that the issuance represented a dilution attempt. The courts refused to block the ESOP issuance, but Posner continued to pursue control. Graniteville then announced a repurchase tender offer (*pe* = −7.95%; 5/16/83; C.2). Shortly after the courts refused to enjoin the repurchase, the control contest ended with a negotiated truce in which Posner agreed to sell his share block to a company (headed by a Graniteville director) which would acquire the remaining Graniteville shares at a price substantially below that paid to Posner. Sometime later, this plan was dropped because the director's company could not arrange financing. Graniteville then supported a new and eventually successful acquisition proposal from Posner.

Grumman Corp. **LTV Corp.**

Grumman announced plans to repurchase a significant number of shares in the open market (*pe* = −3.76%, confounded; 10/14/81; C.2). Grumman's pension and employee investment plans already held a substantial minority stake and top Grumman officials served as plan trustees. On the day prior, the pension plan undertook a sizable open-market share purchase. Grumman had also filed a private antitrust suit against LTV and, on the day after the repurchase announcement, a federal judge granted a preliminary injunction against LTV's takeover attempt. Two weeks later, the FTC also sued on antitrust grounds. An appellate court upheld the earlier injunction and LTV dropped its bid rather than face the prospect of a 'long and costly' court battle. (LTV tried unsuccessfully to have the courts declare that Grumman's repurchase program and pension plan stock purchases were illegal. The Labor Department also brought suit against the pension plan trustees and, after LTV withdrew its bid, obtained a judgment that the trustees *had* breached their fiduciary duty.)

Harsco Corp. **Crane Co.**

Harsco announced the repurchase of a small number of shares held by four professional traders and said it might buy more shares (*pe* = −0.95%; 2/27/81; C.2). This announcement followed revelation of Crane's tender bid by about five weeks. Crane obtained a temporary court order against the repurchases, but this order was dissolved almost immediately. Harsco then announced plans for a modest dividend increase. Crane allowed its bid to expire after attracting only a small number of shares. No hostilities were observed for one and a half years, at which time Harsco repurchased Crane's stake.

Heli-Coil Corp. **Mite Corp.**

Heli-Coil agreed to acquire Garlock, Inc. for common and convertible preferred stock (*pe* = 2.51%; 11/6/69; B.5/C.3). The transaction would almost triple the Heli-Coil shares outstanding (assuming full conversion of preferred) and would materially dilute Mite's 36% stake. Mite had acquired its stake in an exchange offer completed about two weeks before the Garlock announcement. Mite said it would vote against the acquisition (if put to a vote) and made another bid for Heli-Coil. This bid was heavily oversubscribed and Mite attained a majority stake. Heli-Coil's board then agreed to merge with Mite and to drop the Garlock transaction. [The board's cooperation was apparently necessary because stockholders had amended the bylaws (i) to require supermajority approval to acquire Heli-Coil and (ii) to provide staggered terms for directors. Amendment ratification came while Mite held about one-quarter of Heli-Coil's shares and while its bid was outstanding.]

Hi-Shear Corp. **Frank Klaus**

Hi-Shear agreed to acquire Western Methods Corp. for a newly issued minority share block (*pe* = 1.03%; 11/4/74; B.5/C.1). This transaction closely followed two other stock issuances by Hi-Shear – one to acquire Southern California Signal Industries Inc. and one to Hi-Shear's employee stock ownership plan (precise announcement dates unknown). All three issuances came during the month after Klaus announced he had acquired 50.4% of Hi-Shear's stock and intended to call a stockholders' meeting to take control. Klaus sued over the stock issuances, but could only prevent voting of the ESOP shares. Klaus lost the vote to oust management by a slim margin in which the remaining newly issued shares apparently were pivotal. Klaus then made another tender offer and Hi-Shear responded with another stock sale, this time to Midwood Industries, Inc. (*pe* = −3.94%; 2/3/75; C.1). Klaus narrowly lost another stockholder vote over board control (despite a court order that enjoined voting of Midwood's shares). Hostilities continued for another six months, at which time all litigation was settled. Klaus signed a standstill agreement and sold his shares to Midwood (which thereby attained a majority stake).

Interstate Brands Corp. **DPF Inc.**

Interstate agreed to issue a minority share block to IU International Corp. in exchange for IU's Farmbest Foods subsidiary (*pe* = −0.09%; 6/25/75; B.5/C.1). Interstate gave IU a two-year option to sell back the block at a price above that offered in DPF's tender bid. DPF sued both Interstate and IU and, two weeks later, the Farmbest transaction was called off. During this two-week period, it became clear that Interstate stockholders would tender a substantial minority stake to DPF. Shortly after acquiring this stake, DPF obtained written consents from other Interstate stockholders to restrict directors' powers, including their ability to issue stock. Two board members – one with a significant share interest – voted to approve the new constraints and were sued by the remaining board members for failing to disclose their role in an alleged conspiracy to seize control. DPF then acquired a near-majority stake by purchasing the shares held by the (now out-of-favor) board member. Shortly thereafter, Interstate and DPF negotiated a settlement which gave DPF 5 of 11 board seats. About one year later, Interstate's stock was delisted following a 'clean up' tender offer by DPF.

Leeds & Northrup Co. **Tyco Laboratories Inc.**

Leeds agreed to sell a block of convertible voting preferred stock to Cutler-Hammer Inc. ($pe = 4.48\%$; 1/7/77; C.1). This announcement followed a period of share accumulation by Tyco, against which Leeds brought litigation charging securities law violations. This litigation was temporarily settled when Tyco signed a standstill agreement limiting its Leeds holdings to a minority stake. Leeds then immediately announced the Cutler stock sale. Tyco was unable to force Leeds to rescind the issuance, but did acquire a somewhat larger minority stake via a tender offer. There was no sign of hostilities for about one and one-half years. During this period, Tyco sold its Leeds stock to Cutler and both Tyco and Cutler signed new standstill agreements.

Later, a second control contest erupted when Tyco began accumulating shares in Cutler (which then had a substantial minority stake and board representation at Leeds). Tyco sold its Cutler share block to Eaton Corp. In return, Eaton promised Tyco the Leeds share block currently held by Cutler after Eaton acquired control of Cutler. Shortly after the Tyco–Eaton pact was announced, Leeds gave Cutler permission (necessary because of their standstill agreement) to sell its Leeds shares to General Signal Corp. which acquired the remaining Leeds shares via merger.

Lenox Inc. **Brown-Forman Distillers Corp.**

Lenox declared a dividend of a new class of preferred shares payable to common stockholders ($pe = -1.95\%$; 6/16/83; C.4). The preferred gave holders the option to convert their securities into the voting shares of a corporation that acquired control of Lenox. This provision was evidently designed to threaten the Brown family's control of Brown-Forman. (The family owned a majority of Brown-Forman's voting stock which could have been transformed into a minority interest through conversion of Lenox preferred.) Lenox also authorized a large number of additional preferred shares that could be placed privately at the board's discretion. Nevertheless, Lenox strategists acknowledged that they expected stockholders to tender a substantial majority to Brown-Forman. Also, there was substantial uncertainty whether Lenox could legally issue securities convertible into another firm's stock. Before this question was resolved, Lenox dropped the preferred stock plan in exchange for a sweetened offer from Brown-Forman.

Liggett Group Inc. **Grand Metropolitan Ltd.**

Liggett agreed to sell its Austin Nichols division to Pernod Ricard S.A. ($pe = -8.85\%$; 4/23/80; B.3). Much of Liggett's business involved liquor distribution for Grand Met and Pernod Ricard. Before its takeover attempt, Grand Met had tried (unsuccessfully) to purchase Austin Nichols from Liggett. During the takeover attempt, Liggett held a confidential auction of Austin Nichols which Pernod Ricard won and in which Grand Met did not bid, although it had been notified of the auction. Grand Met made numerous attempts to have the courts block the divestiture, but the transaction was judged acceptable partly because Liggett had conducted the auction. Liggett completed the sale of Austin Nichols to Pernod Ricard, but Grand Met continued its takeover attempt. Standard Brands, Inc. then made an offer endorsed by Liggett's management. Grand Met substantially topped this offer, Standard Brands immediately withdrew, and Liggett agreed to support Grand Met's offer.

Lightolier Inc. **Criton Corp.**

Lightolier issued a minority share block to an employee stock ownership plan in exchange for a long-term promissory note (*pe* = −5.27%; 7/6/81; C.1). The issuance was announced one week after Criton revealed it might seek control of Lightolier. After the issuance, Criton announced a tender offer which Lightolier challenged on grounds of inadequate disclosure. Lightolier dropped its suit after Criton disclosed additional financial data. One week later, Bairnco Corp. announced a tender offer (at a price substantially above Criton's bid) that was supported by Lightolier's board. Criton did not increase its bid and Bairnco acquired control of Lightolier.

Ludlow Corp. **Tyco Laboratories Inc.**

Ludlow agreed to pay $25 million (cash on hand) to acquire the flexible packaging division of Continental Group, Inc. (*pe* = −8.91%, confounded; 3/13/79; B.4). The attractiveness of the packaging operation per se is unclear, but $25 million cash represented a significant fraction of Ludlow's assets and of the $67 million Tyco initially proposed to pay for all Ludlow shares. Ludlow used Massachusetts' takeover law to delay Tyco's bid and to limit its stock purchases. Tyco continued to challenge the Massachusetts law in court. The contest ended when Tyco unilaterally withdrew after Ludlow completed the packaging division acquisition. (Tyco said it decided to withdraw after further consideration of the effects of the acquisition.) There was no sign of hostilities for two years, at which time Tyco began accumulating additional Ludlow shares. After protracted litigation between Ludlow and Tyco, Ludlow agreed to be acquired by Bairnco Corp. However, Tyco substantially topped Bairnco's bid, Bairnco did not increase its offer, and Ludlow agreed to be (and was eventually) acquired by Tyco.

Marshall Field & Co. **Carter Hawley Hale Stores Inc.**

Marshall Field agreed to acquire five department stores in the Pacific Northwest (*pe* = −7.60%; 1/23/78; B.1). Marshall Field challenged Carter Hawley Hale on grounds that a merger would unlawfully reduce competition and cited antitrust problems in the Seattle market. Shortly thereafter, Marshall Field announced plans to expand in other markets in which CHH was an established competitor. The contest ended when CHH withdrew its offer, questioning the wisdom of Marshall Field's planned expansion. Marshall Field stockholders brought litigation that charged the board with breach of fiduciary duty in resisting CHH. This litigation lasted for several years and, shortly after the final court decision in favor of the board, Carl Icahn began accumulating Marshall Field stock. Marshall Field opposed Icahn and agreed to support an (ultimately successful) offer from Batus Inc.

Martin Marietta Corp. **Bendix Corp.**

Martin Marietta announced a counterbid for Bendix (*pe* = −2.54%; 8/31/82; B.2/C.3). The counterbid came several days after Bendix's offer for Martin Marietta and was rejected by Bendix. Early in the contest, Bendix's offer was oversubscribed and was set to expire before Martin Marietta's. Immediately after Bendix revealed that its offer was oversubscribed, United Technologies Corp. joined Martin Marietta's attempt to acquire Bendix. To induce UT's participation, Martin Marietta agreed not to solicit a white knight. Martin Marietta also enhanced the credibility of its counterbid by unilaterally waiving its right to withdraw in almost all circumstances (including any settlement in which Bendix might acquire Martin Marietta).

Bendix acquired a 70% stake in Martin Marietta but, because of a delay required by state law, could not take immediate control of Martin Marietta. Because Bendix and Martin Marietta were incorporated under different state laws, there was substantial legal uncertainty about which company would be the first to take control of the other. Faced with the prospect that Martin Marietta might be able to buy enough shares to take immediate control, Bendix agreed to be acquired by Allied Corp. Simultaneously, Allied announced plans to acquire Martin Marietta. However, Martin Marietta quickly purchased a (previously tendered) near-majority stake in Bendix which gave it a stronger bargaining position to deflect Allied's takeover attempt. The parties then negotiated an agreement in which Allied acquired Martin Marietta's stake in Bendix in exchange for a promise not to seek control of Martin Marietta.

NLT Corp. **American General Corp.**

NLT announced a counteroffer for American General which followed by about five weeks revelation of American General's exchange offer for NLT ($pe = -7.07\%$; 5/20/82; B.2/C.3). NLT's counteroffer included special 'early pay' provisions to acquire some American General preferred stock which would apparently enable NLT to veto American General's bid. (Paradoxically, NLT had previously brought private antitrust litigation which charged that a combination of the two firms would unlawfully reduce competition in the home service life insurance industry. NLT dropped its antitrust suit when it announced its counteroffer.) American General tried unsuccessfully to block the counteroffer in court and NLT bought the preferred stock. American General responded by offering NLT stockholders a substantially higher price only if the NLT board dropped its counterbid and supported the new offer. American General said it would leave its offer open for three months to give NLT's board the opportunity to prove it could do better for stockholders (who strongly pressured management to sell the company). NLT's board agreed to the new proposal and the two firms eventually merged.

Outdoor Sports Industries Inc. **Telvest Inc.**

OSI declared a dividend of a new class of preferred payable to common stockholders ($pe = 4.19\%$; 2/2/79; C.4). The preferred gave holders the right to veto any merger or similar transaction with a party owning 20% or more of OSI. Telvest held a 19.8% stake at the time and had previously advanced a plan to liquidate OSI. Telvest charged that the preferred stock dividend unlawfully amended the corporate charter without stockholder approval, and obtained a preliminary injunction to block distribution of the preferred. Telvest then announced an offer to increase its equity interest to 42%. OSI responded by retaining an investment banking firm to search for a superior offer. It also announced plans to hold a stockholder vote on charter amendments similar to the vote provisions of the preferred stock whose issuance had been blocked. Telvest dropped its offer when the SEC expressed concerns about Telvest's ability to exercise voting rights on tendered shares. Arctic Enterprises Inc. immediately disclosed an offer for OSI. One day later, OSI agreed to be (and was eventually) acquired by Brown Group Inc.

Pogo Producing Co. **Northwest Industries Inc. and Sedco Inc.**

Pogo announced a repurchase tender offer which matched the per-share bid price and quantity of shares sought by N-S in their bid revealed one week earlier ($pe = -2.73\%$; 4/28/83; C.2). Pogo's repurchase offer came within two days after its stockholders defeated a management-sponsored 'fair price' charter amendment that would have set a floor on acceptable acquisition prices. One week later, Pogo sold a block of new convertible preferred to a small group of firms that included Pennzoil Co. ($pe = -8.29\%$; 5/5/83; C.1). (Pogo had been split off from Pennzoil several years earlier and the chairmen of the two companies were brothers.) Pogo's repurchase offer was almost fully subscribed, while N-S's bid attracted approximately one-third of the amount sought. As a result, N-S attained a substantial minority interest in Pogo, as did the companies aligned with Pogo. Notwithstanding their large block position N-S did not pursue representation on Pogo's board.

Raybestos-Manhattan Inc. **Hi-Shear Industries Inc.**

Raybestos agreed to acquire AVC Corp. for newly issued shares and cash (*pe* = −3.85%; 10/14/80; B.5/C.3). At the time, AVC held a minority interest in Raybestos and had agreed to be acquired by Hi-Shear. Raybestos feared that acquisition of AVC by Hi-Shear would enable the latter firm to take over Raybestos. Thus, before making its own proposal to acquire AVC, Raybestos tried (unsuccessfully) to induce Hi-Shear to sign a standstill agreement limiting its Raybestos stake. Following announcement of the Raybestos–AVC transaction, Hi-Shear announced a tender offer for Raybestos stock which ultimately gave Hi-Shear a substantial minority position. Hi-Shear announced it would vote against the AVC acquisition and, shortly thereafter, the parties agreed that Raybestos would acquire AVC for a significantly lower price. Raybestos also agreed to give minority board representation to Hi-Shear.

Rowan Cos. Inc. **Chicago Bridge & Iron Co.**

Rowan agreed to issue a block of convertible preferred stock to a business partner, Armco, Inc., in exchange for ownership in two oil drilling ventures (*pe* = −6.98%; 6/26/78; B.5/C.1). (CBI was interested in Rowan as a means of converting over from serving the oil industry into exploration/production.) CBI responded to the Armco transaction by lowering its offer price and by bringing suit. Schlumberger Ltd., a major provider of oil field services, then acquired a minority interest in Rowan in the open market. (Rowan management said it had no connection with Schlumberger.) Shortly thereafter, CBI withdrew and cited the Armco and Schlumberger purchases as jeopardizing its ability to acquire control of Rowan.

Royal Industries Inc. **Monogram Industries Inc.**

Royal agreed to acquire Sar Industries Inc., a competitor of Monogram in the sanitation equipment business (*pe* = −8.26%; 10/28/76; B.1). Sar had previously filed a private antitrust suit against Monogram in which a judge had issued an injunction against Monogram and had said that Sar would most likely be able to prove some of its charges. Royal also brought private antitrust litigation against Monogram on grounds that a takeover of Royal (and hence of Sar) would extend Monogram's alleged monopoly power. Monogram obtained a temporary restraining order against the Sar acquisition. Royal then announced plans to call a special stockholders' meeting to amend its bylaws to require a supermajority vote to approve a merger. Monogram obtained a temporary restraining order against the special meeting and, one week later, Royal agreed to be (and was eventually) acquired by Lear Siegler Inc.

Signal Cos. **Cemp Investments Ltd.**

Signal agreed to sell its oil and gas subsidiary to Burmah Oil Co. (*pe* = 12.63%; 12/24/73; B.4). The subsidiary's operations were tangentially related to the business interests of Cemp insofar as Cemp was owned by the Bronfman family which held a substantial stake in Distillers Corp.–Seagram's Ltd., which itself owned Texas Pacific Oil Co. One month before announcement of Cemp's interest in purchasing Signal shares, Signal had agreed to be acquired by United Aircraft Corp. Two weeks after Cemp's announcement, Signal reported a large oil discovery. Shortly thereafter, the Signal–United Aircraft merger was called off because of disagreements over the value of Signal's oil reserves. Cemp's tender offer gave it a somewhat larger minority stake in Signal which continued litigation to force Cemp to divest its shares. Signal then announced the sale of its oil and gas subsidiary. Cemp immediately brought suit and obtained a court order against the transaction. The court order was dissolved when Cemp failed to post a $25 million 'good faith' bond. Signal then completed the sale of its oil and gas unit to Burmah. Five months later, Signal and Cemp settled their litigation with an agreement in which Signal repurchased most of Cemp's interest at a price simultaneously offered to public stockholders in a repurchase tender bid.

Sparton Corp. **Servotronics Inc.**

Sparton's board agreed to issue a minority share block to Sparton's president and his brother in exchange for Lake Odessa Machine Co. (*pe* = 14.82%, confounded; 12/16/70; B.5/C.1). This transaction was announced on the same day as Servotronics' tender bid. (Sparton simultaneously said it might make a repurchase offer.) Sparton completed the Lake Odessa transaction, but Servotronics continued its takeover attempt. Sparton's president and his brother then made a tender offer to obtain a larger minority position. They purchased a substantial number of shares in a heavily oversubscribed bid and Servotronics withdrew its undersubscribed offer. Servotronics nevertheless pursued litigation alleging waste of corporate assets and disclosure law violations by Sparton's board. This litigation was settled one and one-half years later with an agreement that (i) required the Lake Odessa transaction to be submitted to a stockholder vote and (ii) gave cash payments to Servotronics and another stockholder who had also sued Sparton.

St. Joe Minerals Corp. **Seagram Co.**

St. Joe announced a repurchase tender offer and that it was putting its 92% interest in CanDel Oil Ltd. up for sale (*pe* trading suspension, see below; C.2). St. Joe simultaneously revealed it would seek a white knight, but also threatened liquidation if a satisfactory takeover were not achieved promptly. Earlier in the contest, St. Joe's management had said the company was not for sale. The shift in policy came amid signs that St. Joe's defenses were failing. For example, before the repurchase announcement, St. Joe agreed to drop its attempt to block Seagram's offer on grounds of state takeover law violations. A federal judge subsequently restrained St. Joe from proceeding with its repurchase, but allowed it to seek buyers for CanDel and to negotiate with potential white knights. Four days later, St. Joe agreed to sell CanDel to a Canadian firm, which would facilitate non-Canadian white knight bids for St. Joe (*pe* trading suspension, see below; B.4). The next day, an appellate court upheld the earlier decision restraining St. Joe's repurchase and St. Joe then immediately agreed to be acquired by Fluor Corp. Seagram withdrew its offer and Fluor acquired St. Joe. (We have incomplete stock returns to analyze the restructuring announcements because of a six-day trading suspension that ended 4/2/81. The returns immediately before and after the suspension were *pe* = 15.23% and *pe* = 1.89%. The first return was observed on the single trading day between two suspensions that lasted one and six exchange trading days (three and eight calendar days). This return is also confounded by a court decision in favor of the hostile bidder and by St. Joe's concession that its legal defenses had failed.)

Sunshine Mining Co. **Hunt International Resources Corp.**

Sunshine agreed to issue an undisclosed number of shares to Silver Surprize, Inc. in exchange for SSI's assets (*pe* = 2.72%; 4/30/79; B.5/C.1). SSI owned mining claims adjacent to Sunshine property and had been involved in litigation with Sunshine over the rights to an ore body overlapping both firms' land. The proposed issuance appears to be part of a settlement between Sunshine and SSI. Hunt nevertheless brought litigation charging that the issuance violated stockholders' pre-emptive rights. The SSI transaction was announced two weeks after Hunt rejected Sunshine's offer to repurchase Hunt's stake at a substantial premium. It came four weeks after termination of a tender bid by Hunt against which Sunshine stockholders had brought substantial litigation. (Immediately after bid termination, Sunshine's board announced it had retained an investment banker to help find other buyers.) Five weeks after announcement of the SSI transaction, Sunshine and Hunt settled their conflicts with an agreement in which Hunt sold its shares to Sunshine and to a company owned by Sunshine directors.

Union Commerce Corp. **Huntington Bancshares Inc.**

Union Commerce sold a minority block of voting preferred stock to a small group of firms that, like UC, were based in Ohio (*pe* = −4.76%; 10/7/82; C.1). This sale followed by five months a friendly bid for UC by Central Bancorp. The preferred issuance was apparently designed to placate regulators' concerns about Central's offer by increasing the equity capital base available to a combined UC–Central corporate entity. (Central had earlier issued additional stock with the same objective.) The capital infusions were evidently insufficient since, five weeks later, the Federal Reserve Board denied Central permission to acquire UC, in part because of insufficient equity capital. Three days after the FRB's decision, Huntington acquired control of UC and the two firms eventually merged.

References

Asquith, P. and D. Mullins, Jr., 1986, Equity issues and offering dilution, Journal of Financial Economics 15, 61–89.

Austin, D., 1983, Tender offer data base (D. Austin & Associates, Toledo, OH).

Bhagat, S. and J. Brickley, 1984, Cumulative voting: The value of minority shareholder voting rights, Journal of Law and Economics 27, 339–365.

Bradley, M. and L. Wakeman, 1983, The wealth effects of targeted share repurchases, Journal of Financial Economics 11, 301–328.

Brown, S. and J. Warner, 1980, Measuring security price performance, Journal of Financial Economics 8, 205–258.

Brown, S. and J. Warner, 1985, Using daily stock returns: The case of event studies, Journal of Financial Economics 14, 3–31.

Daniel, W., 1978, Applied nonparametric statistics (Houghton-Mifflin, Boston, MA).

Dann, L., 1981, Common stock repurchases: An analysis of returns to bondholders and stockholders, Journal of Financial Economics 9, 113–138.

Dann, L. and H. DeAngelo, 1983, Standstill agreements, privately negotiated stock repurchases, and the market for corporate control, Journal of Financial Economics 11, 275–300.

Dann, L. and W. Mikkelson, 1984, Convertible debt issuance, capital structure change and financing related information, Journal of Financial Economics 13, 157–186.

DeAngelo, H. and E. Rice, 1983, Antitakeover charter amendments and stockholder wealth, Journal of Financial Economics 11, 329–359.

Dodd, P., 1980, Merger proposals, management discretion and stockholder wealth, Journal of Financial Economics 8, 105–138.

Easterbrook, F. and D. Fischel, 1981a, The proper role of a target's management in responding to a tender offer, Harvard Law Review 94, 1161–1204.

Easterbrook, F. and D. Fischel, 1981b, Takeover bids, defensive tactics, and shareholders' welfare, Business Lawyer 36, 1733–1750.

Harris, M. and A. Raviv, 1988, Corporate control contests and capital structure, Journal of Financial Economics, this issue.

Holderness, C. and D. Sheehan, 1985, Raiders or saviors? The evidence on six controversial investors, Journal of Financial Economics 14, 555–579.

Jarrell, G., 1985, The wealth effects of litigation by targets: Do interests diverge in a merge?, Journal of Law and Economics 28, 151–177.

Jensen, M., 1987, The takeover controversy: Analysis and evidence, forthcoming in: J. Coffee, L. Lowenstein, and S. Rose-Ackerman, eds., Knights, raiders and targets (Oxford University Press, Oxford). Also in: 1986, Midland Corporate Finance Journal 4, 6–32.

Linn, S. and J. McConnell, 1983, An empirical investigation of the impact of 'antitakeover' amendments on common stock prices, Journal of Financial Economics 11, 361–399.

Lipton, M., 1981, Takeover bids in the target's boardroom: An update after one year, Business Lawyer 36, 1017–1028.

Malatesta, P. and R. Walkling, 1988, The impact of poison pill securities on stockholder wealth, Journal of Financial Economics, this issue.

Masulis, R., 1980, Stock repurchase by tender offer: An analysis of the causes of common stock price changes, Journal of Finance 35, 305–319.

Masulis, R. and A. Korwar, 1986, Seasoned equity offerings: An empirical investigation, Journal of Financial Economics 15, 91–118.

McConnell, J. and C. Muscarella, 1985, Corporate capital expenditure decisions and the market value of the firm, Journal of Financial Economics 14, 399–422.

MERC, 1983, Tender offer data base (Managerial Economics Research Center, Graduate School of Management, University of Rochester, Rochester, NY).

Mikkelson, W. and R. Ruback, 1985a, An empirical analysis of the interfirm equity investment process, Journal of Financial Economics 14, 523–553.

Mikkelson, W. and R. Ruback, 1985b, Targeted repurchases and common stock returns, Working paper (University of Oregon, Eugene, OR).

Myers, S. and N. Majluf, 1984, Stock issues and investment policy when firms have information that investors do not have, Journal of Financial Economics 13, 187–221.

Rosenfeld, A., 1982, Repurchase offers: Information adjusted premiums and shareholders' response, Working paper (Purdue University, West Lafayette, IN).

Ryngaert, M., 1988, The effect of poison pill securities on shareholder wealth, Journal of Financial Economics, this issue.

Securities and Exchange Commission, 1984, The impact of targeted share repurchases (greenmail) on stock prices, Report of the office of the chief economist (SEC, Washington, DC).

Securities and Exchange Commission, 1985, Shark repellents and stock prices: The effects of antitakeover amendments since 1980, Report of the office of the chief economist (SEC, Washington, DC).

Stulz, R., 1988, Managerial control of voting rights: Financing policies and the market for corporate control, Journal of Financial Economics, this issue.

Vermaelen, T., 1981, Common stock repurchases and market signalling: An empirical study, Journal of Financial Economics 9, 139–183.

Wruck, K., 1986, Management financing decisions and firm value: An examination of private sales of common stock, Dissertation proposal (Graduate School of Management, University of Rochester, Rochester, NY).

[2]

Journal of Accounting and Economics 16 (1993) 209–236. North-Holland

Managerial discretion, organizational structure, and corporate performance

A study of leveraged recapitalizations

David J. Denis and Diane K. Denis*
Virginia Polytechnic Institute and State University, Blacksburg, VA 24061, USA

Received May 1991, final version received July 1992

We examine the impact of highly leveraged transactions on managerial discretion over investment policy using a sample of 39 proposed leveraged recapitalizations. We find significant decreases in undistributed cash flow, capital expenditures, and total assets following completed recapitalizations. The reductions in investment are significantly correlated with the cumulative abnormal returns earned by the shareholders of the recapitalizing firms. Moreover, we find evidence of poor investment decisions on the part of the sample firms in the years leading up to the recapitalizations. The overall results are consistent with the hypothesis that increased debt plays a valuable role in limiting managerial discretion.

1. Introduction

During the 1980's the number and magnitude of leveraged buyouts and leveraged recapitalizations grew dramatically. Proponents of these highly leveraged transactions (HLTs) claim that they lead managements to make better operating and investment decisions. Critics argue that the resulting high levels of debt force a short-term orientation on firms, thereby reducing their competitiveness. Such controversy is claimed to have contributed to the collapse of the high-yield debt market and increased restrictions on bank lending and has led to

Correspondence to: David J. Denis, Department of Finance, R.B. Pamplin College of Business, Virginia Polytechnic Institute and State University, Blacksburg, VA 24061, USA.

*We are grateful to Jeff Coles, Larry Dann (the discussant and referee), Rob Hansen, Dana Johnson, Jeff Netter, Dilip Shome, participants of the KPMG Peat Marwick/John M. Olin Conference on Managerial Incentives and Corporate Performance, and Ross Watts (the editor) for their comments and suggestions, and to Keith Ingels and Michelle Rachmaninoff for valuable research assistance. This research has been partially funded by summer research grants to both authors from the R.B. Pamplin College of Business, Virginia Polytechnic Institute and State University.

several congressional proposals designed to limit the extent of these transactions. [See Waite (1991).]

This paper offers further insights into the economic consequences of highly leveraged transactions by examining their effects on managerial discretion over investment policy. Jensen (1986) and Stulz (1990) argue that the extreme amounts of debt taken on in an HLT reduce the level of investment undertaken by the firm. This constraint is valuable if the firm's management group has incentives to invest in projects that reduce shareholder wealth.[1] Alternatively, such a constraint is value-decreasing for the firm if management is forced to inefficiently conserve cash by bypassing valuable investment opportunities.

Recent studies provide evidence consistent with the hypothesis that controlling managerial discretion over investment decisions may be valuable to the shareholders of some firms.[2] However, there is little direct evidence on whether HLTs do in fact reduce the amount of internally-generated funds available for investment. Ceteris paribus, large increases in debt will reduce discretionary cash flow. Recent studies have documented, however, that leveraged buyouts are followed by significant improvements in operating performance [Kaplan (1989b), Muscarella and Vetsuypens (1990), and Smith (1990)] and significant reductions in tax payments [Kaplan (1989a)]. Thus, it is not clear that cash flows are reduced, on net, by these transactions. Furthermore, as noted above, cash flow reductions are not necessarily value-increasing. Managers may be constrained from investing in projects that would increase shareholder wealth.

We address these issues by studying a sample of 39 leveraged recapitalizations proposed between 1984 and 1988. Leveraged recapitalizations are similar to leveraged buyouts in that they also result in increased leverage and managerial share ownership. Leveraged recapitalizations differ in three important respects, however, allowing for a much cleaner examination of the effect of increased debt on managerial discretion. First, firms undergoing leveraged recapitalizations remain publicly traded firms. This provides us with more complete access to post-transaction data than is typical in LBO studies and ensures that we are not measuring changes in value that are attributable to becoming a private entity.

[1] For example, Murphy (1985) presents evidence that CEOs can increase their compensation by increasing firm size, regardless of the valuation consequences of the increase. Shleifer and Vishny (1989) suggest that management teams may seek to entrench themselves by investing in assets which are more profitable under their management than under the management of their closest competitors, whether or not such investments are value-increasing.

[2] A number of studies document significant negative wealth effects for acquiring firms in acquisitions completed after 1980. See Jarrell and Poulsen (1989) and Loderer and Martin (1990) for comprehensive studies of the returns to acquiring firms in corporate acquisitions. Evidence in Morck, Shleifer, and Vishny (1990) suggests that managerial objectives often explain the decision to make value-reducing acquisitions. Lehn and Poulsen (1989) find that the returns to firms which go private are positively related to a measure of discretionary cash flow. Baker and Wruck (1990) present clinical evidence consistent with the hypothesis that changes in organizational structure surrounding leveraged buyouts promote efficient investment behavior.

Second, Lowenstein (1985) argues that managers possessing private information may be able to purchase their firm in a leveraged buyout for less than its true value.[3] Because management does not buy out the remaining shareholders in recapitalizations, undervaluation of the firm is likely to be a less important motivation for the sample transactions than for LBOs. Third, LBO specialists such as Kohlberg, Kravis, and Roberts (KKR) do not play a role in the governance of firms that undergo leveraged recapitalizations, enabling us to control for the improved monitoring typically ascribed to the LBO specialist [see Jensen (1989)].

Our results show that leveraged recapitalizations do reduce managerial discretion over investment decisions, on average. Undistributed cash flow relative to total assets, where undistributed cash flow is measured as operating income less tax, interest, and dividend payments, decreases a median 31.1% from the year prior to, through the year following, completion of the recapitalization, despite the fact that the sample firms exhibit improvements in operating income similar to those documented in the LBO literature. On average, post-recapitalization undistributed cash flow would fund, at most, 63.4% of the capital expenditure level that may have been expected in the absence of the recapitalization. The effect of the cash flow reduction is evident in significant reductions in both capital expenditures and total assets over the same time period. Capital expenditures are reduced a median of 35.5%, while total assets decline a median of 6.1%. Adjusted for changes in a control set of firms, the reductions in investment are even larger, with medians of 45.6% for capital expenditures and 42.3% for total assets.

We find that the sample recapitalizations are associated with significant increases in the wealth of the recapitalizing firms' shareholders. These wealth increases are correlated with the reduction in capital expenditures and the reduction in total assets following the recapitalization at the 0.11 and 0.10 significance levels, respectively. Furthermore, announcements of investment decisions in the five-year period preceding the recapitalizations are associated with significantly negative abnormal returns, on average. These firms were misallocating resources in the years leading up to the recapitalization, suggesting that it is more likely value-decreasing investments that are being precluded. Following the recapitalization, the sample firms announce significantly fewer investment decisions, and the wealth effects of the announced investments are not significantly different from zero. However, we cannot reject the hypothesis that the abnormal returns associated with pre- and post-recapitalization investments are equal.

The paper is organized as follows. Section 2 describes the sample selection process and documents both the changes in financial and ownership structure

[3] Kaplan (1989b) and Smith (1990) provide indirect evidence that suggests that superior managerial information is unlikely to account for the observed gains from management buyouts.

and the cumulative abnormal returns around the sample recapitalizations. Section 3 documents the post-recapitalization changes in operating results. Section 4 presents evidence that the changes in operating results are valuable and section 5 concludes.

2. Sample selection and description of leveraged recapitalizations

2.1. Sample selection process

We initially identify our sample by searching the *Dow Jones News Retrieval Service* for any form of the word 'recapitalize' over the period 1984–1988. We then select those cases in which firms proposed leveraged recapitalizations (recaps) consisting of some payout to common shareholders that is financed by new borrowings. This results in an initial sample of 40 proposed recapitalizations. One transaction is excluded because the recap proposal would create a new class of shares with limited voting rights, leaving a final sample of 39 proposed recaps. While this sample size is relatively small we believe it is comprehensive. Using a similar sampling procedure, Gupta and Rosenthal (1991) identify 27 completed recaps over the same time period, while Kaplan and Stein (1990) report that databases compiled by Securities Data Company and Salomon Brothers identify 31 completed recapitalizations as of July 1989.

The sample firms are generally larger, more well-established firms. The companies have median total assets of over $2.2 billion and have been incorporated for a median of 66 years. Thus the sample firms more closely resemble those studied in Dann and DeAngelo's (1988) and Denis' (1990) studies of defensive restructurings than those examined in studies of going private transactions.

Table 1 summarizes the events preceding the proposed recapitalizations. Thirty-five of the 39 sample recaps are associated with events in the corporate control market which pose some threat to the incumbent management team.[4] In 24 of these cases a formal offer for the sample firm precedes the recap proposal. Thus, although they are technically voluntary actions taken by managements, leveraged recapitalizations are seldom undertaken without pressure. This may explain why managers would propose a transaction that could severely limit their discretion over their firms' operating policies. The appendix describes in more detail the relevant events surrounding each transaction.

Table 1 also documents the outcome of each proposal. In 29 cases the sample recapitalization is completed and there is no subsequent transfer of control to another firm. The remaining 10 proposed recaps are not completed; nine firms

[4] In several firms more than one of the precipitating events listed occurred. In such cases the firm was labeled according to the event which represented the strongest control threat.

Table 1

Frequency distribution of corporate control events and eventual outcomes associated with the sample of 39 leveraged recapitalizations proposed over the period 1984–1988. Relevant events are identified by examining the *Wall Street Journal Index* during the period surrounding the proposed recapitalizations.

Panel A. Precipitating events	
Takeover offer for sample firm	24
Acquisition of stake in sample firm	2
Attempted leveraged buyout of sample firm	2
Published rumors of takeover bid for sample firm	6
Proposed proxy contest for sample firm board seats	1
None	4
Total	39
Panel B. Outcome of proposed recapitalizations	
Recapitalizations completed	29
Sample firm acquired by another firm	9
Recapitalization proposal withdrawn	1
Total	39

are acquired by other firms and one firm remains an independent entity. The majority of our analysis focuses on the 29 completed recapitalizations.

The sample recapitalizations are effected in a variety of ways, as documented in the appendix. The common characteristics they share are a large increase in leverage and a large payout of some type to common shareholders. The payouts are made via special dividends, share repurchases, and exchange offers made up of some combination of cash, debt securities, and/or new common shares for existing shares. Management and employee stock ownership plans often do not participate in the cash portion of the distribution, resulting in increased percentage ownership stakes for these two groups.

2.2. Changes in financial and ownership structure

Table 2 documents changes in ownership structure and leverage surrounding the 29 completed recapitalizations.[5] We define managerial ownership as the beneficial ownership of all officers and directors. The results indicate that the increases in managerial ownership of shares are smaller than those documented in the LBO literature. Prior to the proposed recap the median beneficial

[5] Our ownership data is obtained primarily from corporate proxy statements immediately prior to and immediately following the sample recapitalizations. Where proxies are unavailable, the data is obtained from either *Value Line* or *Spectrum 6*. Changes in leverage are computed using data from Compustat for the years immediately prior to and immediately following the sample recaps.

Table 2

Changes in ownership structure and capital structure associated with the sample of 29 completed leveraged recapitalizations over the period 1984–1988. Means are presented above medians. *P*-values measure the significance of pairwise changes in the variables and are computed using a standard *t*-test for differences in means and the Wilcoxon signed-rank test for differences in medians.

Variable	Pre-recap	Post-recap	*P*-value
Beneficial ownership of	5.2%	7.7%	0.003
officers and directors[a]	1.7%	3.6%	0.001
Ownership of officers, directors,	9.4%	18.6%	0.000
and employees[a]	5.9%	14.7%	0.000
Total debt/	41.3%	102.9%	0.000
Total assets[b]	44.6%	86.1%	0.000
Long-term debt/	18.1%	69.2%	0.000
Total assets[b]	15.1%	49.9%	0.000

[a] Beneficial ownership of officers, directors, and employees is obtained primarily from corporate proxy statements. Where proxy statements are unavailable, ownership information is obtained from *Value Line* and *Spectrum 6*. Changes in ownership structure are measured from the last reported ownership prior to the recapitalization to the first report of ownership following the recapitalization.

[b] The change in total and long-term debt to total assets is computed from Compustat data and is measured from the last fiscal year prior to the recapitalization to the first full year following the recapitalization.

ownership of officers and directors is 1.7% (mean = 5.2%). Following the recapitalization median managerial ownership increases to 3.6% (mean = 7.7%).[6] These differences are significant at the 0.01 level. By way of comparison, Kaplan (1989b) finds that the median management team owns an additional 16% of the total shares of its firm following management buyouts. In addition, buyout specialists generally own large portions of post-LBO firms; we find no evidence of increased third-party block ownership following the sample recapitalizations.

The above evidence suggests that arguments for improved managerial incentives through increased ownership and improved monitoring are weaker for leveraged recapitalizations than for leveraged buyouts. Nonetheless, managerial ownership does increase significantly and this may have positive effects on the recapitalizing firms. Jensen and Murphy (1990) emphasize the role of managerial ownership of shares in strengthening the link between managerial compensation and corporate performance. Baker and Wruck (1990) argue that increased

[6] Mikkelson and Partch (1989) provide a useful benchmark for comparing the ownership of the sample firms with a random sample of firms of similar size. The mean (median) managerial ownership of firms of similar size (in 1983 dollars) in Mikkelson and Partch's study is 6.4% (3.2%). Thus the sample firms move from slightly below to slightly above normal managerial ownership as a result of the recapitalizations.

managerial ownership can counterbalance incentives to conserve cash at the expense of value maximization in highly leveraged transactions.

Table 2 also documents changes in the combined ownership of managers and employees. These increases are much larger than the increases in the ownership of managers alone.[7] Combined manager/employee ownership of shares increases from a median of 5.9% (mean = 9.4%) prior to the recap to a median of 14.7% (mean = 18.6%) following the recap. These differences are significant at the 0.01 level. Thus, while there are relatively small changes in managerial ownership of cash flow rights following the sample transactions, there may be more substantial changes in managements' control of voting rights. If managers and employees vote as a block, then the results in table 2 indicate a substantial consolidation of voting power in the hands of the incumbent management team following recapitalizations. Stulz (1988) suggests that this can be either value-increasing or value-decreasing for the recapitalizing firm.

Table 2 indicates that leverage increases following recaps are similar to those observed following leveraged buyouts. The median ratio of the book value of total debt to total assets increases from 44.6% (mean = 41.3%) to 86.1% (mean = 102.9%). The change is significant at the 0.01 level. As a rough comparison, Kaplan (1989b) finds that the median ratio of total debt to total capital increases from 18.8% to 87.8% for his sample of management buyouts. Similarly, the sample firms' median ratio of long-term debt to total assets increases from 15.1% (mean = 18.1%) to 49.9% (mean = 69.2%), significant at the 0.01 level.[8]

2.3. Cumulative abnormal returns around recapitalizations

Table 3 documents cumulative abnormal returns (*CARs*) for the period surrounding the 39 proposed recapitalizations and the subset of 29 completed recaps. We are interested in measuring the change in firm value associated with the recapitalizations. Measuring the abnormal returns only over the two days surrounding the recap announcement is inappropriate because it measures only the marginal value of the recap proposal relative to the expected value of the control threat. For this reason, we define the initiation date to be the date of the first indication of any corporate control activity or the date of the recap

[7] These increases reflect the nine firms that increase employee stock ownership as part of the recapitalization. For example, Kroger's stock option plan was altered so that all employees, rather than just top management, could increase their fractional ownership. Kroger's employee ownership increased from 6% to 25% while its management ownership increased from 2.9% to 3.2%. For the sample as a whole the changes in ownership are not correlated with any of the changes in operating variables documented in section 3.

[8] The increases in debt ratios are due primarily to an increase in debt, rather than to a decrease in total assets. For example, average long-term debt increases from $640 million to $1,573 million.

Table 3

Cumulative abnormal returns (*CARs*) from 40 days prior to initiation through completion. Initiation is defined as the date of the first indication of any corporate control activity or the date of the recap announcement, whichever is earlier. Completion is the date upon which all uncertainty as to the outcome of the recap proposal is resolved. The sample includes 39 leveraged recapitalization proposals over the period 1984–1988.[a, b]

	Full sample ($N = 38$)[c]	Completed recaps ($N = 28$)	Recaps not completed ($N = 10$)
Mean *CAR*	35.8%	32.0%	46.4%
Median *CAR*	29.4%	26.2%	42.1%
Minimum *CAR*	– 12.5%	– 12.5%	– 10.0%
Maximum *CAR*	125.0%	125.0%	84.3%
t-statistic	6.91***	5.23***	4.96***
Percent positive *CARs*	89.5	89.3	90.0

***denotes significance at the 0.01 level.

[a] *CARs* are computed using the standard market model technique where parameters are estimated over the 250-trading-day period beginning 290 days before the initiation date.

[b] The median number of trading days between initiation and completion is 46 for the full sample, 31 for completed recapitalizations, and 65 for recaps not completed.

[c] The sample size is reduced from 39 to 38 because we do not have stock returns data for one of the sample firms (Multimedia).

proposal, whichever is sooner, and the completion date as our estimate of the date upon which all uncertainty as to the outcome of the recap proposal is resolved.[9] We then cumulate abnormal returns over the interval extending from 40 days prior to initiation through the completion date. Abnormal returns are computed using the standard market model technique; parameters are estimated over the 250-day period beginning 290 days prior to the initiation date.

The table 3 results indicate that firms proposing leveraged recapitalizations experience substantial increases in shareholder wealth. The sample as a whole displays a median *CAR* of 29.4% (mean = 35.8%). The *CAR* for the sample of completed recaps is 26.2% (mean = 32.0%)[10] and 89.3% of the completed

[9] Nine proposed recapitalizations are deemed resolved when it is announced that the firm has agreed to be acquired or taken private and one when the abandonment of the recap proposal is announced. Twelve firms announce that the hostile bidder has withdrawn or that the bidder's shares have been repurchased by the firm. In seven cases there is an announcement that the recap proposal has been either approved or implemented. There are ten firms for which we found published references to the recap having been previously completed but did not find specific announcements of the approval or completion of the recap. The original announcement date is used as the completion date in these ten cases.

[10] As documented in table 1, nine of the ten recapitalizations that are not completed result in a change in control of the sample firm. The results in table 3 suggest that changes in control result in higher *CARs* than are obtained when the firm remains independent through a leveraged recapitalization. However, the differences in *CARs* are not statistically significant at conventional levels. For an analysis of defensive restructurings involving payouts to shareholders, see Dann and DeAngelo (1988) and Denis (1990).

recapitalizations are characterized by positive *CAR*s.[11] These *CAR*s are very similar to those observed in LBOs. Kaplan (1989b) reports a median abnormal return of approximately 26% for the period from 40 days prior to through 60 days after proposed management buyouts.[12]

One interpretation of the *CAR* evidence is that the leveraged recapitalizations generate significant increases in shareholder wealth. We present evidence in subsequent sections that provides some support for this interpretation. However, this interpretation should be made with caution since the recapitalization is often just one of several managerial actions taken during the course of a corporate control contest.[13] An alternative interpretation is that, although the current control contest is resolved, the sample firm may still remain 'in play'. Consequently, the positive *CAR*s will reflect expected future takeover benefits. We find this interpretation less plausible given the fact that only one of the 29 firms completing recapitalizations was acquired over the subsequent three-year period. Such a low takeover rate seems inconsistent with the magnitude of the *CAR*s documented in table 3.

3. Post-recapitalization changes in operating results

In this section we examine changes in operating results following the 29 completed recapitalizations and report the extent to which the financial and ownership structure changes documented in section 2.2 affect operating cash flows and managerial discretion over the firm's investment decisions.

3.1. Methodology

Our analysis focuses on percentage changes in selected operating variables over the period extending from the last fiscal year prior to the recapitalization (year −1) to the first two full years after the recapitalization is completed (years

[11] Our results are not sensitive to the method used to compute abnormal returns. We replicate the analysis using the market-adjusted return approach and the market model procedure with parameters estimated over the 250-day period beginning 41 days after completion date. Median market-adjusted returns are 35.7% for the full sample, 31.6% for completed recaps, and 42.2% for recaps not completed. Using the post-completion estimation period for completed recaps, median abnormal returns are 28.0%

[12] We calculate two-day recap announcement *CAR*s as a measure of the marginal value of the recap proposal relative to the expected value of the control threat. Median two-day *CAR*s are 3.35% (mean = 4.57%) for the total sample and 2.78% (mean = 4.55%) for the 29 completed recaps, all significant at at least the 0.05 level.

[13] An interesting comparison is to examine the valuation effects of the four sample recaps not associated with any corporate control threat. For these firms, the median *CAR* is 14.52% during the two days surrounding the announcement of the recap proposal. This provides additional suggestive evidence that the recaps generate significant wealth increases.

+1 and +2). Year 0 is defined as the fiscal year during which the recap is completed. All variables are obtained from the Compustat tapes.

We begin by analyzing changes in operating income and undistributed cash flow. Operating income is measured before depreciation (Compustat #13) and provides an estimate of the cash generated from current operations. Kaplan (1989b), Muscarella and Vetsuypens (1990), and Smith (1990) document significant increases in operating income following buyouts. Because Kaplan (1989b) observes that changes in the level of operating income will be underestimated if the sample firms engage in post-recap divestiture activity, we scale each year's operating income by the corresponding level of total assets (Compustat #6).

We use Lehn and Poulsen's (1989) measure of undistributed cash flow. This variable is defined as operating income (Compustat #13) minus the sum of taxes paid (Compustat #16), interest payments (Compustat #15), preferred stock dividends (Compustat #19), and common stock dividends (Compustat #21). Thus it measures after-tax cash flows that are not distributed to security holders. We scale each firm's undistributed cash flow by its total assets. This measure provides a direct estimate of the extent to which discretionary cash flows are reduced in the post-recapitalization period.

We also report percentage changes in the above variables relative to a sample of control firms to account for possible industry or economy-wide factors. For each sample firm, a control firm is identified as the firm listed on Compustat that has the same four-digit SIC code and is nearest in market value of equity to the sample firm prior to the recapitalization. A control-firm-adjusted change equals the percentage change in the operating variable for the sample firm minus the percentage change for its control firm over the same period.

We present median rather than mean changes in the operating variables due to the small sample size. Results using means are generally larger and more significant, but are often driven by outliers. We measure the significance of median changes conservatively by reporting two-tailed tests of significance using the Wilcoxon signed ranks test.

3.2. Changes in operating variables

Table 4 documents year −1 levels of the operating variables and percentage changes in these variables in the years following the completed recapitalizations. Consistent with the findings of Kaplan (1989b), Muscarella and Vetsuypens (1990), and Smith (1990) for LBOs, the sample firms display substantial improvements in operating performance. The median change in the ratio of operating income to total assets is 21.5% from year −1 to year +1. The control-firm-adjusted change is 21.8% over the same time period. The ratio of operating income to total assets increases for the sample firm relative to its

Table 4

Median year −1 level, percentage change, and control-firm-adjusted percentage change in operating income, undistributed cash flow, capital expenditures, and total assets for the 29 completed recapitalizations over the period 1984–1988. Year 0 is defined as the fiscal year during which the recap is completed. A control firm is defined as that firm with the same four-digit SIC code that is nearest in market value of equity to the sample firm. Significance of median percentage changes are measured using two-tailed Wilcoxon signed-rank tests. Percent positive changes are listed in parentheses.[a]

Operating variable	Level year −1	Changes between years −1 and +1 ($N = 29$)	Changes between years −1 and +2 ($N = 17$)
A. Percentage change			
Operating income/ Total assets	0.152	21.5%** (62.1)	14.9% (58.8)
Undistributed cash flow/ Total assets	0.076	−31.1%** (37.9)	−14.5% (37.5)
Capital expenditures	$153.1m	−35.5% (27.6)	−41.5%** (23.5)
Total assets	$2,234.8m	−6.1%** (31.0)	−5.7% (41.2)
B. Control-firm-adjusted percentage change[b]			
Operating income/ Total assets		21.8%*** (79.3)	17.7%* (64.7)
Undistributed cash flow/ Total assets		−17.6% (41.3)	−8.4% (47.1)
Capital expenditures		−45.6%** (32.1)	−65.3%*** (18.8)
Total assets		−42.3%*** (24.1)	−56.6%*** (17.6)

***, **, and * denote significance at the 0.01, 0.05, and 0.10 levels, respectively.

[a]Operating income is measured before depreciation and is scaled by the book value of total assets. Undistributed cash flow is defined as operating income minus the sum of interest expenses, tax expense, preferred stock dividends, and common stock dividends and is also scaled by total assets.

[b]Control-firm-adjusted change is defined as the percentage change of the sample firm minus the percentage change of the control firm over the same interval.

control firm in 79.3% of the sample cases. These changes are significant at at least the 0.05 level.[14]

The undistributed cash flow results suggest that cash flow is substantially reduced following the completed recapitalizations, despite the significant

[14]Smith (1990), in her study of management buyouts, develops an alternative measure of operating cash flows that mitigates the potential influence of accruals on the operating income measure. She defines operating cash flow as the net increase in cash and marketable securities from

operating improvements. The median change in the ratio of undistributed cash flow to total assets is −31.1% over the −1 to +1 period. This change is significant at the 0.05 level. The control-firm-adjusted change is −17.6% over the same interval, but is not significantly different from zero.

The above measure of undistributed cash flow does not take into account cash that might be generated by selling assets of the firms following the recapitalizations. If cash flows are truly reduced, there should be changes in the levels of investment undertaken by the sample firms. To examine this issue, table 4 also reports percentage changes in capital expenditures and total assets in the years immediately following the sample recapitalizations. Capital expenditures (Compustat #128) measure new investment by the recapitalizing firm, exclusive of acquisitions. If leveraged recapitalizations limit new investment, we would expect reductions in capital expenditures. Changes in total assets (Compustat #6) provide a measure of the firms' net investment.

For the sample firms, the median percentage change in the level of capital expenditures is −35.5% over the −1 to +1 period; this change is not statistically significant. However, 72.4% of the firms experience reductions in capital expenditures; this is significantly different from 50% at the 0.05 level. The median level of capital expenditure is $28.5 million less in year 1 than in year −1. The aggregate reduction in annual capital expenditures by the 29 sample firms is over $3 billion. The results are much stronger when changes in capital expenditures for the sample firms are compared to those of the control firms. The median adjusted change in capital expenditures from year −1 to year +1 is −45.6%, significant at the 0.05 level. The adjusted change is −65.3% over the −1 to +2 period, significant at the 0.01 level. These findings suggest that the sample firms significantly reduce their new investment relative to their industry peers following the sample recapitalizations.

The changes in total assets documented in table 4 indicate that the sample firms actually disinvest, on net, in the years following the recapitalizations. The median percentage change in total assets over the −1 to +1 period is −6.1%, significant at the 0.05 level. The median reduction in the level of total assets is $69.7 million. In aggregate, the sample firms reduce the assets under their control by $13.5 billion from year −1 to year +1. The control-firm-adjusted changes in total assets are −42.3% and −56.6% for the −1 to +1 and −1 to +2 periods, respectively, both significant at the 0.01 level. Relative to their

normal operations and operating assets as the average book value of current assets plus net property, plant, and equipment. (She adjusts these figures for post-MBO writeups of assets; such writeups do not occur following recaps.) Using Smith's measure, year −1 operating cash flow/operating assets is 17.8% and it increases by a median 18.8% from year −1 to year +1; 65.5% of the firms experience an increase. The median control-firm-adjusted change is 49.1%. Thus, accounting accruals are not a principal cause of the operating improvements reported by the firms in our sample.

industry peers, the recapitalizing firms appear to take steps that substantially reduce the assets under their control.[15]

In order to conclude that leveraged recaps reduce managerial discretion over cash flow we need to establish a link between the reductions in internally generated cash flow and the reductions in capital expenditures. For example, if the reduced year +1 cash flow would still cover expected year +1 capital expenditures in the absence of the recap, then the link is weak, at best. Accordingly, panel A of table 5 presents the ratio of year +1 undistributed cash flow to three alternative estimates of what year +1 capital expenditures by the sample firms would have been if the recapitalization had not occurred. The first measure assumes that year +1 capital expenditures would have been the same as year −1 capital expenditures. The second measure assumes that capital expenditure growth between years −1 and +1 would have been the same as over the previous two-year period, years −3 to −1. The third measure assumes that the sample firms' capital expenditures would have grown at the same rate as did the control firms' capital expenditures between years −1 and +1.

The panel A results clearly indicate that management is constrained in its investment. The median ratio of year +1 undistributed cash flow to year −1 capital expenditure is 0.634. The ratio is less than 1.0 for 22 (75.9%) of the 29 firms; it is less than 0.8 for 21 (72.4%) of the firms. The median ratio falls to 0.464 and 0.343 when adjustments are made for the sample firms' previous two-year growth rate and the control firms' concurrent growth rate, respectively.

Panel B of table 5 presents median year −1 to +1 percentage changes in the individual components of the undistributed cash flow variable. These results indicate that the median 256.6% increase in interest payments brought on by the recap is solely responsible for the observed reduction in discretionary cash flow. The observed increase in operating income and decreases in taxes and dividends would increase undistributed cash flow.[16]

[15] The median percentage change in the total assets of the control firms from year −1 to year +1 is 17.7%. Thirteen of the 29 control firms experience increases of at least 20% in total assets. In six of these firms the large increase in assets primarily reflects capital expenditures and an accompanying increase in the level of current assets. Three firms increase assets primarily through acquisitions. The remaining four firms increase assets through some combination of capital expenditures and acquisitions.

[16] The large and significant percentage decrease in taxes raises a question as to the extent that interest-related tax decreases are responsible for the *CAR*s generated by the recap. While tax savings and reduced managerial discretion over investment are not mutually exclusive explanations for recap premiums, if tax savings explain virtually the entire *CAR*, the role of managerial discretion may be relatively unimportant. The present values of future interest-related tax savings were estimated using actual changes in tax payments in years 0, 1, and 2 and assuming that the year 2 savings would continue forever. Alternative discount rates of 10% and 15% were used. The resulting estimate of the present value of tax savings was then compared to the dollar value of the *CAR* for each firm. At most, the median ratio of tax savings to *CAR* is 0.225. Spearman rank correlations indicate that the present value of tax savings and the dollar *CAR* are not significantly correlated. The measure used implicitly assumes that the entire *CAR* is attributable to the leveraged

Table 5

Panel A presents median ratios of year +1 undistributed cash flows to three alternative measures of predicted year +1 capital expenditures in the absence of a recapitalization for 29 recaps completed over 1984–1988. The percentage of firms with ratios less than 1.0 and less than 0.8 are also presented. Panel B presents median percentage changes in the individual components of the firms' undistributed cash flow ratios between year −1 and year +1. Year 0 is defined as the fiscal year during which the recap is completed.

A. Undistributed cash flow / Predicted capital expenditure

	Capital expenditure measure		
	Year −1[a]	Two-year growth-adjusted[b]	Control-firm growth-adjusted[c]
Median ratio	0.634	0.464	0.343
Percentage < 1.0	75.9	75.9	72.4
Percentage < 0.8	72.4	69.0	69.0

B. Percentage changes in individual components of undistributed cash flow

Variable	Median percentage change year −1 to year +1
Operating income	12.7
Tax	−73.4***
Interest	256.6***
Dividends on preferred	−57.8
Dividends on common	−75.2***

*** denotes significance at the 0.01 level.

[a]Predicted year +1 capital expenditure equals year −1 capital expenditure.
[b]Predicted year +1 capital expenditure equals year −1 capital expenditure times one plus the sample firm's percentage growth in capital expenditure between year −3 and year −1.
[c]Predicted year +1 capital expenditure equals year −1 capital expenditure times one plus the control firm's percentage growth in capital expenditure between year −1 and year +1.

Overall, the changes in operating variables documented in this section indicate that the increased debt taken on in the sample recaps reduces managerial discretion over cash flow. Operating income relative to assets increases but undistributed operating income falls. While additional cash may be generated via the sale of assets, the reductions in capital expenditures and in total assets suggest that the cash is generally being used to meet the firms' existing cash flow needs rather than to invest in additional projects or businesses.

recapitalization, rather than to expectations of future control threats. We feel this is an appropriate assumption for the reasons discussed previously. We also, however, measure the correlation between the present value of the tax savings and the two-day abnormal returns associated with the recap announcement; there is no significant correlation.

4. The value of reducing managerial discretion

The results in the previous section suggest that managerial discretion over a firm's investment policy is reduced considerably by a recapitalization. Stulz (1990) shows that this can either increase or decrease the value of the firm. Reductions in capital expenditures and in total assets can be value-increasing if the sample firms are characterized by agency problems that would lead management to invest in negative net present value projects. However, the observed reductions in capital expenditures and total assets are also consistent with the hypothesis that the cash flow limitations imposed by increased debt lead the sample firms to underinvest following the recapitalizations.

In this section we attempt to identify the extent to which the operating changes documented in section 3 enhance the value of the recapitalizing firms. We do this by examining the investment decisions of the recapitalizing firms in the years prior and subsequent to the recap and by correlating the post-recap changes in capital expenditures and total assets with the wealth effects of the recapitalizations documented in section 2.3.

4.1. Wealth effects of investment decisions

Reducing investment expenditures increases shareholder wealth if it is negative net present value projects that are being precluded. We do not know what future investments would have been made by the sample firms in the absence of the recapitalization. We expect, however, that firms that have made value-reducing investments in the recent past would be more likely to do so in the future, ceteris paribus.

To examine pre-recap investment decisions, we search the *Wall Street Journal Index* for the five years preceding each of the 29 completed recapitalizations. We identify all announcements for which there was an expenditure of corporate resources for a purpose other than a disbursement to the claimholders of the firm. This process results in a total of 167 announced investment decisions; 79 are acquisitions of some type and 88 are nonacquisitions. Acquisitions include the purchase of assets from other firms and the purchase of any fractional stake in other firms. Nonacquisitions include general capital expenditures, plant expansions, joint ventures, research and development expenditures, and marketing/advertising expenditures. The number of announcements made by each firm ranges from 0 (five firms) to 29 (one firm) with a median of 5. We also examine the investment decisions of the control firms over the same period. For these firms we find 107 investment decisions announced in the *Wall Street Journal Index*, 63 acquisitions and 44 nonacquisitions.

Using the market technique outlined in section 2.3 we compute abnormal returns on the announcement of each investment decision. We report *CAR*s for the event windows from one day before the event date through one day following the event date [−1, 1] and from five days prior to the event date through one day after the event date [−5, 1].[17] Panel A of table 6 reports the *CAR*s associated with the pre-recapitalization investment decisions of the sample firms and of their control firms. The average *CAR* associated with the announced investment decisions of the sample firms is −0.90% for the [−1, 1] window and −0.88% for the [−5, 1] window. These *CAR*s are significantly negative at the 0.01 level. This provides evidence that the sample firms were characterized by unprofitable investments in the years preceding the sample recapitalizations.

Table 6 also reports *CAR*s for acquisition and nonacquisition investments separately. Acquisition *CAR*s are −0.89% for the [−1, 1] window and −0.82% for the [−5, 1] window. They are significant at the 0.01 level for the [−1, 1] window and at the 0.10 level for the [−5, 1] window. These results are similar to those in Mitchell and Lehn (1990) who find that firms making unprofitable acquisitions are more likely to become takeover targets themselves. The majority of our sample firms appear to be takeover targets and are also characterized by unprofitable acquisitions prior to becoming a target. This supports the hypothesis that the correction of poor acquisition strategies is both a motivation for the attempted acquisitions of the sample firms and a benefit of reducing managerial discretion over investment decisions.

The *CAR*s for nonacquisitions are −0.91% for the [−1, 1] window and −0.92% for the [−5, 1] window, significantly different from zero at the 0.01 and 0.05 levels, respectively. These findings are in striking contrast to those typically found for nonacquisition investments.[18] For example, McConnell and Muscarella (1985) find that investing firms' shareholders typically benefit from the announcement of a planned increase in capital expenditures.[19] Similarly, McConnell and Nantell (1985) find increases in the share prices of firms announcing the formation of joint ventures.

The control firms are not characterized by the same tendency to have invested unprofitably. Control firm acquisition *CAR*s are negative, on average, but do not differ significantly from zero. Average control firm nonacquisition *CAR*s are insignificantly positive. Differences between the average *CAR*s of the sample and

[17]To control for the possibility of information leakage prior to announcements as well as additional information released about particular investments after the initial announcements, we also computed *CAR*s over the [−40, 1] and [−40, 40] event windows. Since extending the event windows did not alter any results, we report only the *CAR*s for the [−5, 1] and [−1, 1] windows.

[18]An exception to this general statement can be found in Denis (1992). He finds evidence of negative abnormal returns associated with nonacquisition investments announced by a sample of going private candidates.

[19]Note, however, that our results are not directly comparable with those of McConnell and Muscarella. They examine unexpected changes in the *level* of capital expenditures, while our announcements are for the most part specific expenditures such as a plant expansion, research and development expenditure, etc.

Table 6

Cumulative abnormal returns (*CARs*) associated with announcements of investment decisions by the sample of 29 firms undergoing leveraged recapitalizations over the period 1984–1988 and by their control firms.[a] Investment decisions are identified by searching the *Wall Street Journal Index* for the five-year period ending with the sample recapitalization. In panel A, mean *CARs* are reported with *t*-statistics in parentheses and sample size in brackets below for all announced investment decisions and for acquisition and nonacquisition subsamples.[b,c] Panel B reports pairwise differences in average abnormal returns of announced investment decisions between the sample and control firms.

A. Abnormal returns

	Sample firms		Control firms	
Type of investment	[− 1, 1]	[− 5, 1]	[− 1, 1]	[− 5, 1]
All investments	−0.90%	−0.88%	−0.17%	−0.46%
	(−4.09)***	(−2.84)***	(−0.63)	(− 1.21)
	[N = 167]	[N = 167]	[N = 107]	[N = 107]
Acquisitions	− 0.89%	− 0.82%	− 0.41%	− 0.81%
	(−2.62)***	(− 1.71)*	(− 1.11)	(− 1.53)
	[N = 79]	[N = 79]	[N = 63]	[N = 63]
Nonacquisitions	−0.91%	−0.92%	0.17%	0.02%
	(− 3.14)***	(−2.24)**	(0.38)	(0.03)
	[N = 88]	[N = 88]	[N = 44]	[N = 44]

B. Pairwise differences in average abnormal returns per firm [− 1, 1]

	Sample	Control	Difference
Mean	− 0.56%	0.05%	− 0.61%
t-statistic	− 2.95***	0.16	− 1.64*
Fraction negative	0.71**	0.56	0.64*
Number of firms	28	28	28

***, **, and * denote significance at the 0.01, 0.05, and 0.10 levels, respectively.

[a]A control firm is defined as that firm with the same four-digit SIC code that is nearest in market value of equity to the sample firm.

[b]Abnormal returns are computed using the standard event-study technique where parameters are estimated over the 250-day period beginning 290 days prior to each announcement date.

[c]Event day 0 is defined as the date of *Wall Street Journal* publication.

control firms over the [−1, 1] window are significant at the 1% level for all investments and for the acquisition and nonacquisition subsamples. The difference over the [−5, 1] window is significant at the 5% level for nonacquisition investments.[20]

[20]It is well-documented that acquisitions financed with new equity result in lower abnormal returns for the acquiring firm than those financed with cash or debt. [See, for example, Asquith, Bruner, and Mullins (1986) and Travlos (1987).] The *Wall Street Journal Index* entries indicate that 9 of 79 acquisitions by the sample firms and 10 of 63 acquisitions by the control firms involved new equity financing. Thus, the more negative *CARs* associated with sample firm acquisitions cannot be accounted for by a higher incidence of equity financing by sample firms than by control firms.

The samples of recapitalizing firm and control firm announcement effects are not necessarily random samples. For this reason, panel B provides pairwise comparisons of the average announcement effects for each sample and control firm. For each firm, we average the three-day [−1, 1] *CAR*s associated with each announced investment decision. We then compare the average effects of the sample firm's announcements with those of its control firm. The results confirm the general pattern documented in panel A. The sample firms are characterized by investment decisions which significantly reduce shareholder wealth, while the announcements of the control firms have no significant impact on shareholder wealth. The difference in average investment decision announcement effects between the sample and control firms is significant at the 0.10 level.

The results in table 6 indicate that the sample firms systematically invested in value-reducing projects in the years leading up to the proposed recapitalizations and that these poor investment decisions cannot be attributed to factors which affect other similar firms. This evidence is consistent with the hypothesis that reducing managerial discretion over investment policy should be valuable for these firms.[21]

We also examine the wealth effects of announced investment decisions in the post-recapitalization period for evidence regarding the extent to which the pattern of value-reducing investment is reversed following the recap. We search the *Wall Street Journal* for investment decision announcements over the three years following each of the 29 completed recapitalizations. This process results in a total of 36 announcements. Consistent with increased constraints on discretionary expenditures, there is a dramatic reduction in announced investment decisions following the completed recaps. Prior to the recapitalizations the sample firms announce a median of 1.2 (mean = 1.7) investment decisions each year. Following the recap, the sample firms announce a median of 0.3 (mean = 0.7) investment decisions per year. The differences in median and mean number of announcements per year are significant at the 0.01 level using paired comparisons tests.

Panel A of table 7 presents a comparison of the average three-day [−1, 1] *CAR*s associated with the pre-recapitalization and post-recapitalization investment decisions. Unlike the pre-recap announcements, post-recap investment decisions are not associated with significant *CAR*s. The average *CAR* associated with the post-recap investment decisions is −0.26%. Moreover, only 56% of the post-recap announcements are associated with negative *CAR*s. However, the difference in average announcement effects between the pre-recap and post-recap samples, −0.64%, is not significantly different from zero using a standard two-sample *t*-test.

[21] We also replicate the analysis in this section using the 219 investment decisions announced by the full sample of 39 firms proposing leveraged recapitalizations. The results are qualitatively identical. For example, the mean *CAR*s are −0.56% for the [−1, 1] window and are significantly negative at the 0.05 level.

Table 7

The wealth effects of pre- and post-recap investment decisions for the sample of 29 firms undergoing leveraged recapitalizations over the period 1984–1988. Investment decisions are identified by searching the *Wall Street Journal Index* for the five years preceding and the three years following each recapitalization. Panel A reports three-day [− 1, 1] *CAR*s associated with announced investment decisions. Panel B presents a pairwise comparison of the average pre- and post-recap average announcement effects for each firm.

	Pre-recap	Post-recap	Difference
A. Abnormal returns			
Mean	− 0.90%	− 0.26%	− 0.64%
t-statistic	− 2.84***	− 0.47	− 1.16
Fraction negative	0.66***	0.56	
Number of firms	167	36	
B. Pairwise differences in average announcement effects per firm			
Mean	− 0.56%	− 0.28%	− 0.28%
t-statistic	− 2.95***	− 0.70	− 0.82
Fraction negative	0.71*	0.53	0.57

*** and * denote significance at the 0.01 and 0.10 levels, respectively.

[a]Abnormal returns are computed using the standard event-study technique where parameters are estimated over the 250-day period beginning 290 days prior to each announcement date. Event day 0 is defined as the date of *Wall Street Journal* publication.

In panel B, we present a pairwise comparison of the average announcement effects for each firm in the pre-recap and post-recap periods. Prior to the recapitalization, the average *CAR* associated with each firm's announced investment decisions is − 0.56% and is significant at the 0.01 level. Following the recap, the average announcement effect for each firm is − 0.28% and is not significantly different from zero. Again the difference between pre-recap and post-recap average announcement effect is not significantly different from zero. Thus, there is no evidence that managers make better investments following recaps, only that they make fewer investments. However, the small sample size reduces the power of the paired comparisons test, so some caution should be exercised in interpreting the statistical significance of the results in panel B.

We measure the economic significance of the reduction in number of investments following the sample recapitalizations by computing a measure of the aggregate dollar change in shareholder wealth associated with announced investment decisions in the pre- and post-recap years. Specifically, for each announced investment decision, we multiply percentage three-day abnormal returns by the market value of the firm's equity at the time of the announcement. Prior to the recap, announced investment decisions reduce shareholder wealth by a median of $6.6 million (mean = $14.9 million) per firm per year. As a group, then, the sample firms' investment decisions reduce aggregate shareholder wealth by $477.3 million annually over the five years prior to their recapitalizations. In contrast, investment decisions announced following the recap reduce shareholder wealth by a median of $1.2 million (mean = $0.9 million) per firm per year, an aggregate shareholder wealth reduction of only $16.0 million annually. The differences between the pre- and post-recap periods are significant at the 0.05 level using paired comparisons tests. Thus, the decrease in investment associated with the sample recapitalizations appears to have led to economically significant reductions in shareholder wealth loss.

4.2. Correlations between CARs and operating changes

If the operating changes documented in table 4 are valuable they should be correlated with the cumulative abnormal returns earned by the shareholders of the recapitalizing firms. In this section we test for a relation between the cumulative abnormal returns documented in section 2.3 and the changes in operating variables over the period from one year prior to through one full year following the sample recaps.[22] We focus on nonparametric Spearman rank correlations due to potential problems with outliers in the small samples we study. Given the small sample sizes and the noise inherent in the variables, these tests are not very powerful and are thus biased somewhat against finding any significant correlations.

The rank correlations of operating changes with *CAR*s and the associated *p*-values are presented in panel A of table 8. The results indicate that reductions in the levels of capital expenditures and total assets are correlated with the wealth increases from the sample recapitalizations at the 0.11 and 0.10 significance levels, respectively. The rank correlations of percentage changes in capital expenditures and total assets with cumulative abnormal returns are −0.30 and −0.32, respectively. The correlations are weaker, however, when changes in capital expenditures and total assets are measured relative to the control firms. These rank correlations are −0.18 and −0.17 and are not significantly different from zero at conventional levels.

We do not find any significant correlations between changes in operating income and *CAR*s or between changes in undistributed cash flow and *CAR*s. The former result appears to contrast with Kaplan's (1989b) findings of a significant positive correlation between changes in operating income and the total returns for his sample of management buyouts. However, we measure operating income relative to total assets for reasons discussed in section 3.1. Using this relative measure of operating income, Kaplan's correlations are also insignificant.

[22] We also perform similar correlation tests of changes in ownership structure with cumulative abnormal returns earned by the shareholders of the recapitalizing firms. Neither the change in managerial ownership nor the change in managerial + employee ownership is significantly related to the *CAR*s or the two-day abnormal returns around the announcement of the recaps.

Table 8

Spearman rank correlations and cross-sectional regressions relating the cumulative abnormal returns (*CARs*) around recapitalizations and operating changes for the sample of 29 completed leveraged recapitalizations over the period 1984–1988. *CARs* are measured from 40 days prior to the initiation date through the completion date of the recap proposal.[a] Initiation is defined as the date of the first indication of any corporate control activity or the date of the recap announcement, whichever is earlier. The completion date is that date on which all uncertainty as to the outcome of the recapitalization proposal is resolved. Operating changes are measured as percentage changes from the last full fiscal year prior to the recapitalization to the first full fiscal year following the recapitalization. Results are reported for unadjusted percentage changes and control-firm-adjusted percentage changes. Two-tailed *p*-values are reported in parentheses below.

A. Spearman rank correlations

	Capital expenditures/ Total assets	Total assets	Operating income/ Total assets	Undistributed cash flow
Unadjusted percentage changes	– 0.30 (0.11)	– 0.32 (0.10)	0.09 (0.63)	0.08 (0.71)
Control-firm-adjusted percentage changes[b]	– 0.18 (0.36)	– 0.17 (0.40)	0.06 (0.76)	0.00 (0.99)

B. Cross-sectional regressions

Model[c]	Intercept	Capital expenditures/ Total assets	Total assets	Operating income/ Total assets	Undistributed cash flow	Adj. R^2
(1)	0.29 (0.00)	– 0.13 (0.06)	– 0.03 (0.91)	0.08 (0.67)	– 0.03 (0.62)	0.03
(2)	0.33 (0.00)	– 0.02 (0.74)	– 0.03 (0.78)	0.01 (0.51)	0.05 (0.31)	– 0.10

[a]Cumulative abnormal returns are estimated using standard event-study techniques where market-model parameters are estimated over the 250-day period beginning 290 days prior to the initiation date.

[b]A control firm is defined as that firm with the same four-digit SIC code that is nearest in market value of equity to the sample firm.

[c]Independent variables are unadjusted percentage changes in model (1) and control-firm-adjusted percentage changes in model (2).

The correlation results thus provide some mixed support for the hypothesis that the operating changes documented in table 4 represent changes which are valuable to the recapitalizing firms' shareholders. Panel B of table 8 presents estimates of multivariate regressions of *CARs* on the observed changes in operating variables. While our small samples and the potential for influential outlier observations may result in misleading coefficients, the regression approach provides estimates of the partial effects of each operating change on the *CARs*.

Model (1) relates *CARs* to unadjusted percentage changes in the operating variables and model (2) uses control-firm-adjusted percentage changes in operating variables. The results presented in panel B indicate that the percentage change in capital expenditures remains a significant explanator, with a coefficient of −0.13, significant at the 0.06 level. None of the other variables has a significant coefficient.

5. Conclusions

In this paper we explore the impact of highly leveraged transactions on managerial discretion over investment policy using a sample of 29 completed leveraged recapitalizations. Unlike leveraged buyouts, these transactions do not result in the sample firms going private or being monitored by LBO specialists. This allows for a much cleaner examination of the role of increased debt in limiting managerial discretion. Our results suggest that leveraged recaps play a significant role in limiting the amount of investment undertaken by the sample firms following the recapitalizations. These limits on investment appear to be valuable to the shareholders of the recapitalizing firms. The sample recaps are associated with significant increases in shareholder wealth, and these increases are significantly correlated with the reductions in investment observed following the recaps. Furthermore, our evidence indicates that the sample firms systematically misallocated resources through poor investment decisions in the years leading up to the sample transactions.

These findings are broadly consistent with the notion that increased debt plays a valuable role in limiting managerial discretion. Thus our results support the predictions of Jensen (1986) and Stulz (1990). The results also provide additional insight for the public policy debate surrounding highly leveraged transactions. A frequent criticism of HLTs is that they force cut-backs in investment, thereby damaging the long-run competitiveness of the levered firms. Our results do support the hypothesis that investment is reduced following increases in leverage, but there is no evidence that these reductions are damaging to the levered firm. Rather, highly leveraged transactions play an important role in reallocating corporate resources to more profitable uses.

A remaining question is the extent to which our results for leveraged recapitalizations generalize to other highly leveraged transactions. As noted previously, the sample firms appear to be much larger, older firms than those examined in previous studies of LBOs. However, there is evidence that suggests that at least a portion of the gains from LBOs comes from reductions in managerial discretion such as those documented here. For example, Lehn and Poulsen (1989) find that going-private candidates are characterized by significantly more undistributed cash flow than a set of control firms. Denis (1992) finds that going-private candidates, particularly those whose buyout attempts are associated with external attempts to transfer control of the firm, are characterized by poor investment decisions in the years preceding the buyouts. Baker and

Wruck's (1989) study of the buyout of O. M. Scott suggests that investment policy limits are an important feature of the post-buyout organizational structure.

Appendix

This appendix contains a brief description of the recapitalizations in the sample. Each description contains the name of the firm and its CUSIP number followed by a synopsis of the relevant events surrounding the recapitalization transaction. When available, the announcement date of the recapitalization is included.

American Standard 02971710
American Standard announced a cash-and-debt recapitalization plan valued at $68–$70 a share (2/19/88). The move was in response to Black and Decker's $65-per-share hostile cash tender offer (1/27/88). The contest ended when Black and Decker withdrew and the firm was taken private by white knight Kelso and Co. (3/23/88).

Anderson, Clayton, and Co. 03360920
Anderson Clayton announced a recapitalization (2/9/86). Later, a share repurchase at $60 per share for 66% of its shares was announced (8/25/86). The move was in response to a hostile takeover bid (5/30/86). The contest ended with Quaker Oats winning its bid for control (9/29/86).

Burlington Industries Inc. 12169110
Burlington announced its intention to purchase as much as 30% of its shares as the first step in a proposed restructuring (5/12/87). The move was the firm's latest defense against a tender offer by Asher Edelman and Dominion Textile. The contest began with the disclosure of a 4.9% stake held by Edelman (4/9/87) and ended with a friendly buyout by a Morgan Stanley-led group (9/4/87).

CBS Inc. 12484510
CBS offered to repurchase 21% of its common stock (7/5/85). The move was in response to a takeover bid by Ted Turner. The contest began with a proposed proxy contest by a politically conservative group (2/8/85) and ended with management retaining control after executing the repurchase (8/2/85).

Caesars World Inc. 12769510
Caesars World announced plans to pay a $26.25 special dividend and add $1 billion of new debt (4/6/87). The move was designed to defeat a hostile takeover bid. Caesars World later dropped its recapitalization plan and instead launched a plan to repurchase 31% of its shares (9/8/87). The contest began with a hostile bid by Sosnoff (3/9/87) and ended with Sosnoff dropping its bid (6/16/87) and managers retaining control.

Carter Hawley Hale 14622710
Carter Hawley Hale announced plans to spin off a division to shareholders and make a special payout of $325 million (12/9/86). The contest began with a hostile bid from Limited (11/26/86) and ended with the announced restructuring.

Colt Industries Inc. 19686470
Colt proposed a recapitalization that would give shareholders a special dividend of $85 and one new share in exchange for each share (7/21/86). The move was financed through $1 billion in bank borrowing and $500 million in new debentures.

FMC 30249130
FMC announced plans for a recapitalization that would give shareholders a special dividend of $80 per share and one share in the recapitalized firm in exchange for each share (2/24/86). The plan would increase insider ownership from 19% to 41%. The board acknowledged concern about the possible emergence of an unfriendly suitor.

GenCorp 36868210
GenCorp announced plans to buy back 54% of its stock for $1.6 billion (4/7/87). The move was designed to fight a hostile takeover bid by a partnership consisting of AFG Industries and Wagner & Brown. The contest began with the hostile bid (3/18/87) and ended when W&B dropped its bid in the face of the repurchase tender offer (4/8/87).

Gillette Co. 37576610
Gillette blocked a takeover attempt by Revlon by agreeing to buy Revlon's 13.9% interest. The firm also announced plans to buy as many as seven million of its shares in the open market or through private transactions (11/25/86). The contest began with a hostile bid by Revlon (11/14/86) and ended with the targeted repurchase and announcement of the open market repurchases.

Goodyear Tire and Rubber Co. 38255010
Goodyear announced a plan to repurchase as many as 20 million of its shares and sell as many as three major units (11/7/86). The contest began with the disclosure of a large stake held by Sir James Goldsmith (10/29/86) and ended with the firm buying back Goldsmith's stake and announcing a tender offer for a further 36.5% of the firm's shares (11/21/86).

HBO & Co. 40410010
HBO proposed a recapitalization, citing the need to maintain shareholder value and defend against a possible hostile takeover (5/29/86). The firm later withdrew the recapitalization plan and proposed to purchase as much as 26% of its shares in the open market (8/7/87).

Harcourt Brace Jovanovich 41163110
Harcourt announced plans to recapitalize by increasing debt and paying a large special dividend (5/27/87). The move was designed to defeat a hostile bid by British Printing & Communications. The contest began with the hostile bid (5/19/87) and ended with the implementation of the recapitalization plan (7/27/87).

Holiday Corp. 43507110
Holiday proposed a special dividend of $65 per share (11/13/86). The contest began with a rumored hostile takeover by Donald Trump (9/29/86) and ended with the approval of the recapitalization plan (3/2/87).

I.U. International 45069410
I.U. proposed a restructuring plan which included a $14-per-share cash payment (1/29/88). The move was in response to a hostile $17.50-per-share tender offer from NX Acquisition Corp. (1/6/87). The firm eventually agreed to a sweetened bid of $22.25 a share from NX (3/7/88).

Inco Ltd. 45325840
Inco planned to distribute more than $1 billion to shareholders in a special dividend intended to thwart any takeover attempts (10/4/88).

Interco 45850610
Interco's board approved a $2.8 billion restructuring program consisting of a special dividend of $14 cash and $11 in senior subordinated debentures per share (9/21/88). The move was aimed at thwarting a hostile takeover bid from a group led by the Rales brothers (7/29/88). The firm retained control after amending its recapitalization plan to consist of cash and securities valued at $71 a share (11/23/88).

Kraft Inc. 50090210
Kraft announced it was developing a cash-and-securities swap plan valued at at least $110 per share (10/24/88). The move was in response to a hostile tender offer bid from Philip Morris Cos. (10/18/88). The contest ended when Kraft accepted a sweetened offer from Philip Morris (10/31/88).

Kroger 50104410
Kroger announced a restructuring proposal which would possibly include a special dividend (9/14/88). The move was in response to the Haft family's receipt of federal clearance to accumulate an unspecified stake in Kroger (9/13/88). Kohlberg, Kravis, Roberts and Co. (KKR) made a subsequent unsolicited bid. The contest ended when KKR ended its bid and left Kroger to pursue its special dividend and restructuring plan (10/12/88).

Moore McCormack 61579810
Moore McCormack proposed to pay a special dividend of $24.60 cash and $6.62 in debentures per share (3/24/88). The move was in response to a hostile tender offer by Southdown (2/23/88). The contest ended when Southdown agreed to acquire Moore McCormack at an increased price (4/7/88).

Multimedia
Multimedia's board approved a cash-and-debt recapitalization plan which included an option to take a reduced amount of cash and retain some equity interest (4/9/88). The contest began with an LBO proposal by a management-led group of investors (2/4/85) and became a recapitalization proposal when the option to retain equity was added. The contest ended when shareholders approved the recapitalization (9/27/85) after purchasing the 10% stake of a competing bidder.

Newmont Mining Corp. 65163910
Newmont announced plans for a major restructuring that included a $33-per-share dividend (9/22/87). The move was designed to defeat a bid from Ivanhoe Partners. The restructuring would grant minority owner Consolidated Gold Fields a bigger stake in the firm. The contest began with the disclosure of a 9.1% stake held by Ivanhoe (8/14/87) and ended with Ivanhoe withdrawing its bid (11/19/87).

Optical Coating Laboratories 68382910
Optical Coating's board approved a recapitalization plan which involved a $13-per-share cash payout (1/6/88).

Owens Corning 69073420
Owens Corning announced a recapitalization plan which would give shareholders $52 plus $35 face amount of new junior debt in exchange for each share (8/29/86). The contest began with a hostile bid from Wickes (8/6/86) and ended with Wickes dropping its bid (9/2/86).

Phillips Petroleum Co. 71850710
Phillips announced plans to recapitalize the company by more than doubling the firm's debt while reducing public ownership of the firm (12/24/84). The contest began with a takeover bid from T. Boone Pickens (11/8/84) and ended with Pickens dropping his bid and accepting the recapitalization (12/24/84).

Phillips-Van Heusen 71859210
Phillips-Van Heusen announced an acquisition program and a stock buyback of 5.2 million shares at $28 each (7/31/87). The move may have been designed to make the company less attractive as a takeover target. The contest began with a hostile bid by Rosewood Financial (7/13/87) and ended with Rosewood dropping its bid in light of the repurchase tender offer (8/4/87).

Quantum Chemical 74763310
Quantum announced a recapitalization plan involving a $50-per-share special dividend (12/29/88).

Rexnord 76168810
Rexnord approved a restructuring plan in order to maintain its independence (11/24/86). The plan was subsequently abandoned when Banner Industries agreed to acquire the firm (1/27/87).

Santa Fe Southern Pacific 80218310
Santa Fe announced that it would pay shareholders at least $4 billion in a restructuring of the firm (12/14/87). The contest began with the announcement that Henley Group held a 5.03% stake in Santa Fe (3/31/87) and ended with the announced restructuring.

Shoney's 82503910
Shoney's board approved a recapitalization plan involving a cash-and-debt special dividend (3/8/88).

Standard Brands Paint Co. 85315610
Standard Brands offered to buy as much as 53% of its common stock in a recapitalization plan (11/11/87). The contest began with a hostile offer from Entregrowth (7/22/87) and ended with the successful repurchase tender offer (1/5/88).

Sterling Software 85954710
Sterling announced its intention to proceed with a recapitalization plan (2/22/88). The firm had previously explored a management-led buyout (1/22/88). The recapitalization plan was abandoned after debtholders failed to tender enough debt to make the transaction work (5/31/88).

Swank Inc. 86971620
Swank announced a recapitalization plan that included a share repurchase in which most shareholders would receive $17 in cash and a share of new common stock (9/30/87). The firm also declared a distribution of a preferred stock purchase right. The measures were designed to fend off a hostile takeover.

Telex Corp. 87957310
Telex announced its plan to offer $45 in cash and $15 of 15-year debentures for each of its shares (11/6/87). The contest began with a $65-per-share bid from Asher Edelman (10/9/87) and ended with Telex accepting an offer from Memorex (12/15/87).

UAL Corp. (Allegis) 90254910
Allegis announced a plan to pay a dividend of $60 per share that would be financed primarily through additional borrowing (5/29/87). The action came after the disclosure that Coniston Partners held a large stake in the firm. The contest began with an offer from the pilots union to buy Allegis (4/6/87) and ended with the resignation of the chairman (6/11/87) and a repurchase tender offer for 63% of its shares (2/1/88).

USG Corp. 90329330
USG announced a recapitalization and restructuring plan that offered holders $37 a share in cash, debt, and stock (5/3/88). The contest began with the acquisition of a 9.8% stake by Desert Partners (10/6/87) and ended with shareholders approving the recapitalization plan (7/11/88).

Union Carbide Corp. 90558110
Union Carbide announced an offer to exchange cash and debt securities for 35% of its shares (12/16/85). The firm was seeking to fend off a hostile takeover attempt by GAF Corp. The contest began with rumors of a GAF bid (8/30/85) and ended with GAF abandoning its bid in the face of the buyback offer (1/9/86).

Unocal Corp. 91528910
Unocal announced a plan to repurchase 49% of its shares using $6.28 billion face value of notes (4/17/85). The $72-per-share offer would be made only if a T. Boone Pickens group succeeded in acquiring a majority of Unocal shares in its $54-per-share bid. The contest began when the Pickens group acquired a 7.9% stake (2/15/85) and ended with management retaining control by defeating a Pickens-led proxy bid and completing the repurchase (5/30/85).

Warnaco 93439110
Warnaco announced a recapitalization plan (3/24/86). The contest began with a management buyout proposal (11/1/85) and ended with the board approving a takeover by W Acquisition (4/28/86).

References

Asquith, Paul, Robert F. Bruner and David W. Mullins, 1986, Merger returns and the form of financing, Working paper (Harvard Business School, Boston, MA).

Baker, George P. and Karen H. Wruck, 1989, Organizational changes and value creation in leveraged buyouts: The case of O. M. Scott & Sons Company, Journal of Financial Economics 25, 163–190.

Dann, Larry Y. and Harry DeAngelo, 1988, Corporate financial policy and corporate control: A study of defensive adjustments in asset and ownership structure, Journal of Financial Economics 20, 87–128.

Denis, David J., 1990, Defensive changes in corporate payout policy: Share repurchases and special dividends, Journal of Finance 45, 1433–1456.

Denis, David J., 1992, Corporate investment decisions and corporate control: Evidence from going private transactions, Financial Management, forthcoming.

Gupta, Atul and Leonard Rosenthal, 1991, Ownership structure, leverage, and firm value: The case of leveraged recapitalizations, Financial Management 20, 69–83.

Jarrell, Gregg A. and Annette B. Poulsen, 1989, The returns to acquiring firms in tender offers: Evidence from three decades, Financial Management 18, 12–19.

Jensen, Michael C., 1986, Agency costs of free cash flow, corporate finance, and takeovers, American Economic Review 76, 323–329.

Jensen, Michael C., 1989, Active investors, LBOs, and the privatization of bankruptcy, Journal of Applied Corporate Finance 2, 35–44.

Jensen, Michael C. and Kevin J. Murphy, 1990, Performance pay and top-management incentives, Journal of Political Economy 98, 225–264.

Kaplan, Steven, 1989a, Management buyouts: Evidence of taxes as a source of value, Journal of Finance 44, 611–632.

Kaplan, Steven, 1989b, The effects of management buyouts on operating performance and value, Journal of Financial Economics 24, 217–254.

Kaplan, Steven N. and Jeremy C. Stein, 1990, How risky is the debt in highly leveraged transactions? Evidence from public recapitalizations, Journal of Financial Economics 27, 215–247.

Lang, Larry, Rene M. Stulz, and Ralph Walking, 1991, A test of the free cash flow hypothesis: The case of bidder returns, Journal of Financial Economics 29, 315–336.

Lehn, Kenneth and Annette Poulsen, 1989, Free cash flow and stockholder gains in going private transactions, Journal of Finance 44, 771–788.

Loderer, Claudio and Kenneth Martin, 1990, Corporate acquisitions by listed firms: The experience of a comprehensive sample, Financial Management 19, 17–33.

Lowenstein, Louis, 1985, Management buyouts, Columbia Law Review 85, 730–784.

McConnell, John J. and Chris J. Muscarella, 1985, Corporate capital expenditure decisions and the market value of the firm, Journal of Financial Economics 14, 399–422.

McConnell, John J. and Timothy J. Nantell, 1985, Corporate combinations and common stock returns: The case of joint ventures, Journal of Finance 40, 519–536.

Mikkelson, Wayne H. and M. Megan Partch, 1989, Manager's voting rights and corporate control, Journal of Financial Economics 25, 263–290.

Mitchell, Mark and Kenneth Lehn, 1990, Do bad bidders become good targets ?, Journal of Political Economy 98, 372–398.

Morck, Randall, Andrei Shleifer and Robert W. Vishny, 1990, Do managerial objectives drive bad acquisitions?, Journal of Finance 45, 31–48.

Murphy, Kevin J., 1985, Corporate performance and managerial remuneration: An empirical analysis, Journal of Accounting and Economics 7, 11–42.

Muscarella, Chris, J. and Michael R. Vetsuypens, 1990, Efficiency and organizational structure: A study of reverse LBOs, Journal of Finance 45, 1389–1413.
Shleifer, Andrei and Robert W. Vishny, 1989, Managerial entrenchment. The case of manager-specific investments, Journal of Financial Economics 25, 123–139.
Smith, Abbie, 1990, Corporate ownership structure and performance: The case of management buyouts, Journal of Financial Economics 27, 143–164.
Stulz, Rene M., 1988, Managerial control of voting rights: Financing policies and the market for corporate control, Journal of Financial Economics 20, 25–54.
Stulz, Rene M., 1990, Managerial discretion and optimal financing policies, Journal of Financial Economics 26, 3–28.
Travlos, Nickolaos G., 1987, Corporate takeover bids, method of payment, and bidding firms' stock returns, Journal of Finance 42, 943–964.
Waite, Stephen R., 1991, The eclipse of growth capital, Journal of Applied Corporate Finance 4, 77–85.

[3]

THE JOURNAL OF FINANCE • VOL. LVII, NO. 5 • OCTOBER 2002

Takeover Defenses of IPO Firms

LAURA CASARES FIELD and JONATHAN M. KARPOFF*

ABSTRACT

Many firms deploy takeover defenses when they go public. IPO managers tend to deploy defenses when their compensation is high, shareholdings are small, and oversight from nonmanagerial shareholders is weak. The presence of a defense is negatively related to subsequent acquisition likelihood, yet has no impact on takeover premiums for firms that are acquired. These results do not support arguments that takeover defenses facilitate the eventual sale of IPO firms at high takeover premiums. Rather, they suggest that managers shift the cost of takeover protection onto nonmanagerial shareholders. Thus, agency problems are important even for firms at the IPO stage.

DESPITE 20 YEARS OF RESEARCH on the topic, there still is little consensus about the effects of corporate takeover defenses. In this paper, we use information from an unusual natural experiment—the use of takeover defenses by firms as they go public—to examine the motives for and consequences of such defenses.

The traditional view is that IPO firms should have—and in fact do have—few if any takeover defenses. For example, Frank Easterbrook and Daniel Fischel (1991, pp. 204–205) argue that "Firms go public in easy to acquire form: no poison pill securities, no supermajority rules or staggered boards. Defensive measures are added later, a sequence that reveals much." This view reflects two assumptions. The first is that takeover defenses lower firm values because they insulate managers from the discipline of the market for corporate control. The second assumption is that agency conflicts between managers and nonmanagerial shareholders are negligible at IPO firms. This is because the proceeds from an IPO accrue to a relatively small number of firm principals who internalize most of the costs and benefits. If a takeover defense lowers the firm value, these principals would have incentive to avoid its use at the time of the IPO.

* Field is from Penn State University and Karpoff is from the University of Washington. We thank Morris Danielson; Rob Daines; Larry Dann; Rick Green; Gordon Hanka; Jarrad Harford; Robert Kieschnick; Michael Klausner; Michelle Lowry; Ron Masulis; Chris Muscarella; Scott Lee; John Lott; Paul Malatesta; Todd Perry; Dennis Sheehan; René Stulz; and an anonymous referee for helpful comments; as well as seminar participants at the University of Arizona, California State University, Northridge, the University of Connecticut, the Dartmouth-JFE Conference on Corporate Governance, the University of Delaware, Emory University, the 2000 FMA meetings, the University of Oregon, Penn State University, the University of Texas at Dallas, the University of Utah, Vanderbilt University, and especially Harold Mulherin. We also thank Vera Allain, Christopher Reed, and Lloyd Taliaferro for research assistance, and The Institute for Quantitative Research in Finance for financial support.

More recent theories, however, suggest that takeover defenses might be important for IPO firms. Brennan and Franks (1997) argue that firm insiders opportunistically take steps at the IPO to ensure that they will maintain their private benefits of control after the firm's stock is publicly traded. This suggests that they could use takeover defenses to help insulate themselves from the market for control. An alternative view is that takeover protection is an implicit portion of IPO managers' compensation, implying that the managers sacrifice some pecuniary compensation to achieve greater job security. A third view is suggested by Zingales (1995) and Mello and Parsons (1998), who argue that the IPO is the first stage in the eventual sale of the firm. This suggests that takeover defenses can be used to facilitate the future sale of the firm and increase its expected takeover premium.

In this paper, we examine the traditional and more recent theories empirically. We find that many firms deploy takeover defenses when they go public. In our sample of 1,019 industrial firms going public from 1988 to 1992, 53 percent have at least one takeover defense at the time of their IPO, including classified boards, supermajority voting provisions, fair price charter amendments, and even poison pills. Firms also tend to select their longer term defensive postures at the time of their IPOs. Although the average firm has 1.71 takeover defenses at its IPO, it acquires only 0.19 additional defenses during the five-year period after its IPO.[1] These results reject the traditional view that IPO managers avoid using takeover defenses. In contrast, they indicate that control issues are important even at the IPO stage.

We also conduct tests to better understand the reasons IPO firms implement defenses. On this matter, most of our results support Brennan and Franks' (1997) argument that IPO managers seek to maintain their private benefits of control after taking the firm public. For example, we find that managers deploy takeover defenses particularly when they own few shares, enjoy high compensation, and are relatively free from monitoring by nonmanagerial shareholders. This suggests that IPO managers are likely to deploy defenses when their personal benefits are high and they bear few of the costs. Also consistent with Brennan and Franks' argument, we find that takeover defenses at the time of the IPO are associated with longer term firm independence. In contrast, we do not find support for arguments that takeover defenses are an implicit portion of managers' compensation or that defenses help in the eventual sale of the firm by increasing expected takeover premiums.

This paper is organized as follows. Section I describes our sample of 1,019 firms that went public during the 1988 to 1992 period. Section II reports on the uses of various types of takeover defenses in the IPO firms, and, in Section III, we compare the uses to those in seasoned corporations. In Sec-

[1] The 1.71 figure excludes blank check preferred stock, but includes the nine other types of defense summarized in Table II. Rydqvist and Högholm (1995), Field (1998), Coates (2000), and Daines and Klausner (2001) also provide evidence about the use of takeover defenses at IPO firms.

tion IV, we examine the determinants of the likelihood that an IPO firm will deploy a takeover defense. Section V reports on how takeover defenses at the time of the IPO affect both the probability the firm subsequently will be acquired and the acquisition premium for those firms that are acquired. In Section VI, we examine the relation between the use of a takeover defense and the firm's operating performance in the years following its IPO. Section VII summarizes and concludes the paper.

I. Description of the IPO Sample

We use information from the Securities Data Corporation to identify all industrial firms that went public from 1988 through 1992. To be included in the sample, the IPO must involve common stock offered at a minimum price of $1.00 per share and issued through a firm commitment underwriting agreement. In addition, the firm must be incorporated in the United States at the offer date and be identified on the 1996 CRSP daily tape as having been listed within three months of the offer date. These criteria yield a sample of 1,019 IPOs, which explicitly excludes IPOs by financial institutions, real estate investment trusts, and closed-end mutual funds.

Panel A of Table I reports on the characteristics of the 1,019 sample firms. The mean company age at the time of the IPO is 18.1 years. This is higher than the mean of 12.7 years reported by Ritter (1991), although as indicated by the median of 8.0 years, the distribution is skewed toward older firms. Total assets before the IPO average $243.1 million, with a median of $27.7 million. The mean ratio of long-term debt to total assets is 31.1 percent (median = 22.0 percent).

As reported in Panel B of Table I, the gross proceeds from the issues average $33.6 million, with a median of $16.5 million. Thus, the gross proceeds are smaller, on average, than the firms' book value of assets. Mikkelson, Partch, and Shah (1997), in contrast, report that mean proceeds exceed mean assets for a sample of 283 IPOs from 1980 to 1983. An average of 33 percent of the post-IPO outstanding shares are offered at the IPO (median = 31 percent). Sixteen percent of these shares are sold by pre-IPO shareholders. The average one-day initial return of 10.9 percent falls between the 14.06 percent documented by Ritter (1991) for IPOs from 1975 to 1984, and the 8.5 percent documented by Michaely and Shaw (1994) for the 1984 to 1988 period.

II. On the Uses of Takeover Defenses by IPO Firms

Table II reports on the presence of each of 10 types of takeover defenses disclosed in the by-laws or prospectuses of the 1,019 IPO firms in the sample. The features of each defense are described in the Appendix. One striking fact is that many defenses are in place at the time of the IPO. Classified boards, supermajority vote requirements, and shareholder meet-

Table I

Characteristics of Firms Issuing IPOs during the Period 1988 to 1992

The sample consists of 1,019 firm commitment initial public offerings of stock (no unit offerings) by U.S. companies with an offer price of at least $1.00. Information is obtained from offering prospectuses and (for the initial return) the 1998 CRSP daily return files. *Company age* is the age of the company at the time of the IPO. *Total assets* and *long-term liabilities* are measured in the year prior to the IPO, as reported in the IPO prospectus. *Total gross proceeds from the offering* are the gross proceeds earned by the company from the IPO. *Shares offered as a fraction of the total shares outstanding* is the shares offered divided by the shares outstanding after the IPO. *The initial return* is the percentage difference between the offer price and the first-day closing price reported on the CRSP file, less the contemporaneous daily return on the value-weighed CRSP index.

	Mean	Median
Panel A: Firm Characteristics		
Company age (years)	18.1	8.0
Total assets before IPO ($ million)	243.1	27.7
Long-term liabilities/Total assets	31.1%	22.0%
Panel B: Offering Characteristics		
Total gross proceeds to the company from the offering ($ million)	33.6	16.5
Shares offered as a fraction of total shares outstanding	32.5%	31.1%
Shares offered by pre-IPO shareholders as a fraction of total shares offered	15.5%	0.0%
Initial return	10.9%	5.2%

ing restrictions, for example, all are deployed by substantial minorities of the firms. In addition, 5.4 percent of the firms have unequal voting rights (typically through dual class shares), and 4 percent have stakeholder provisions that allow directors to consider the interests of constituencies other than shareholders in making business and control decisions. Even poison pills appear in some (2.3 percent) IPO firms' governance structures.

The assertion at the beginning of this paper by Easterbrook and Fischel (1991, pp. 204–205) claims that managers wait until after the IPO to acquire most of their takeover defenses. Such a view seems particularly appealing if one thinks of defenses as lowering firm values. We would expect managers to wait until after share ownership is somewhat diffuse, at which time they would bear little of the cost of any new defenses that are adopted.

The evidence, however, contradicts this view. We collected data on defenses acquired during the five years after the IPO by examining proxy statements and news reports on Lexis/Nexis and the Dow Jones News Retrieval Service. A total of 142 of our 1,019 firms acquired poison pills during this five-year period, and 50 firms acquired classified boards. Virtually no other types of defenses were adopted by any of the 1,019 firms during the

Table II

Frequencies of Takeover Defenses in IPO and Seasoned Firm Samples

Frequencies of 10 types of takeover defenses deployed at 1,019 firms that went public between 1988 and 1992 and at 524 seasoned firms with publicly traded stock. The seasoned firm frequencies are weighted averages of the seasoned firms' use of each provision, where the weights are the fractions of the IPO firms that went public in each year from 1988 through 1992. See the Appendix for a description of each type of takeover defense. "na" indicates that the data are not available.

Takeover Defense	Proportion of Firms with Takeover Defense (%): IPO Firms	Proportion of Firms with Takeover Defense (%): Seasoned Firms	t-Statistic for Difference in Proportions
1. Antigreenmail provision	1.9	10.1	−5.95***
2. Blank check preferred stock	85.1	84.1	0.49
3. Classified board	36.2	55.4	−7.27***
4. Fair price provision	9.7	40.6	−13.23***
5. Poison pill	2.3	62.1	−27.57***
6. Stakeholder clause	4.0	5.7	−1.39
7. Shareholder meeting restrictions	30.4	41.3	−4.22***
Meetings called only by directors or executives	15.4	na	na
Supermajority required to call special meeting	2.6	na	na
Advance notice requirement	19.1	na	na
Restrictions on action by written consent	23.0	na	na
8. Supermajority vote requirements	28.9	26.5	0.97
Supermajority required to approve mergers	9.2	na	na
Supermajority required to replace directors	27.3	na	na
9. Unequal voting rights	5.4	10.4	−3.34***
10. Miscellaneous antitakeover provisions	13.7	na	na
Board can be removed only for cause	12.8		
Merger must be approved by an inside director	0.2		
Restrictions on transfer of common stock	0.1		
Merger must be approved by separate class of stock	0.3		
Restrictions on how many IPO shares may be purchased	0.2		
Restrictions on votes each shareholder may cast	0.4		

*** Statistical significance at the one percent level, based on a two-tailed test.

five years after their IPOs. (Several firms eliminated takeover defenses, including seven firms that changed from classified to annually elected boards.) We therefore include data only on the subsequent adoptions of poison pills and classified boards.

The adoption rate for new defenses is very small compared to the defenses deployed at the time of the IPO. The average number of defenses at the time of the IPO is 1.71 (excluding blank check preferred stock).[2] In contrast, only an average of 0.19 new poison pills or classified boards are adopted during the five years after the IPO, or 0.04 per year. Therefore, in any one of the five years after the IPO, the unconditional expected rate of change in the number of defenses is approximately 0.04/1.71 = 2.2 percent.

Thus, the evidence indicates that many firms deploy takeover defenses at the time of their IPOs, and firms do not substantially change their defensive postures during the five years after their IPOs. This is inconsistent with the view that IPO firms do not have takeover defenses. Rather, it indicates that managers take efforts to increase their authority over unsolicited takeover offers even at the IPO stage.

III. Comparisons to the Uses of Takeover Defenses at Seasoned Corporations

A. Firm-Level Defenses

As a basis for comparison, Table II also reports on the contemporaneous use of takeover defenses in a sample of 524 seasoned corporations. Data on the defenses deployed by these firms were hand-collected from files maintained by Institutional Shareholders Services, Inc. (ISS), supplemented by additional data provided by Rosenbaum (1989, 1995).[3]

The use of most takeover defenses among the seasoned firms increased during the 1988 to 1992 period of our IPO sample. To make a time-weighted comparison with the IPO firms, we compute a weighted average of the seasoned firms' use of each type of takeover defense. The weights are the fractions of the IPO firms that went public in each year from 1988 through 1992. So, for example, the fraction of the seasoned firms using classified boards that is reported in Table II (55.4 percent) is a weighted average of the

[2] As discussed by Rosenbaum (1995, p. xiii), blank check preferred stock can be used as a takeover defense because it can facilitate the adoption of a poison pill. It also can have a purpose unrelated to takeover defense, namely, raising outside capital. That most IPO firms have blank check preferred stock suggests that it does not impose substantial costs on the firms' principals. Because it appears to be a boilerplate item that is included in most IPO governance packages, we exclude blank check preferred stock from most of the summary totals reported in this paper.

[3] The seasoned firms do not constitute a matched control sample for the IPO firms because they are not matched by size, industry, or other firm characteristics. It is difficult to obtain comprehensive data on firms' takeover defenses. To our knowledge, the Rosenbaum data are the only such summary data on seasoned companies that are available to the public. The ISS data are not publicly available. Where the two data sources overlap, we find discrepancies in nearly 20 percent of the covered firms. Most discrepancies were resolved by examining proxy materials during the 1988 through 1992 period, but unresolved discrepancies remain for seven percent of the comparison firms. In the tests reported, we use ISS data when discrepancies exist. The results are not materially affected, however, when we instead use Rosenbaum's data as the default.

fraction of these firms that had classified boards in each year from 1988 to 1992. The actual percentage of seasoned firms that had classified boards was slightly smaller than 55.4 percent in 1988, and slightly larger than 55.4 percent in 1992.

The data indicate that IPO firms deploy antigreenmail provisions, classified boards, fair price provisions, poison pills, shareholder meeting restrictions, and unequal voting rights less frequently than do the seasoned firms, and, in each case, the difference is statistically significant. Use rates are not significantly different for stakeholder clauses, blank check preferred stock, and supermajority vote requirements.[4]

The difference in use rates for poison pills is particularly large, as 62 percent of seasoned corporations and only 2 percent of the IPO firms have them. We can make two conjectures about the reason for such a large discrepancy. One possibility is that pills are particularly costly for IPO managers, perhaps because pills decrease share values and IPO managers tend to hold relatively large equity stakes in their companies. Another possibility is that the actual presence of a poison pill is not important because, unlike other defenses, pills can be deployed at virtually any time without shareholder approval or amending the corporate charter. Daines (2001) goes so far as to argue that the actual deployment of a poison pill has become *meaningless* because managers can adopt one whenever they desire: "[E]very firm has a poison pill—either actual or latent . . . and there is no variation between firms with respect to the degree they are protected by a poison pill" (p. 4). Consistent with this view, most recent research indicates that the adoption of a poison pill has a statistically insignificant effect on firm value.[5]

Only 1.9 percent of IPO firms have antigreenmail provisions, compared to 10.1 percent for the comparison firms. By eliminating one way a bidder can profit from making an unsolicited takeover bid, antigreenmail provisions may deter such bids. But they also prevent incumbent managers from paying greenmail to deter an unwanted bid. Thus, the net effect of an anti-

[4] Note that the shareholder meeting restrictions and supermajority vote restrictions categories are further partitioned for the IPO firms. For example, shareholder meeting requirements refer to any of four subprovisions that affect shareholders' abilities to call special meetings or act outside of a regular shareholder meeting. At 15.4 percent of the IPO firms, special shareholder meetings can be called only by directors or executives. At 2.6 percent of the firms, a supermajority of shareholders is required to call a special meeting. Advance notice of stockholder proposals and/or nominations of directors is required for 19.1 percent of the firms, and 23.0 percent of the IPO firms have restrictions on action by written consent. A total of 30.4 percent of the IPO firms have at least one of these shareholder meeting restrictions. We do not have a breakdown by subcategory for the seasoned firms, but 41.3 percent of these firms have at least one shareholder meeting restriction.

[5] Early poison pill studies (Malatesta and Walkling (1988), Ryngaert (1988)) conclude that pills reduce share value, and Bizjak and Marquette (1998) find a positive mean stock return when firms revise poison pills in response to shareholder pressure. Later studies, however, by Brickley, Coles, and Terry (1994), Comment and Schwert (1995), and Danielson and Karpoff (2001) find insignificant average stock price reactions to poison pill adoptions.

Table III
Average Number of Takeover Defenses in IPO and Seasoned-Firm Samples

The average number of up to 10 types of takeover defenses deployed at 1,019 firms that went public between 1988 and 1992 and at 524 seasoned firms with publicly traded stock. The seasoned firm frequencies are weighted averages of the seasoned firms' use of each provision, where the weights are the fractions of the IPO firms that went public in each year from 1988 through 1992. See the Appendix for a description of each type of takeover defense. "na" indicates that the data are not available.

	IPO Firms	Seasoned Firms	*t*-Statistic for Difference in Means
Mean number of all categories of takeover defense, including miscellaneous defenses	2.56	na	na
Mean number of takeover defenses 1–9 identified in Table II	2.04	3.36	−8.17***
Mean number of takeover defenses 1–9 identified in Table II, excluding blank check preferred stock	1.19	2.52	−11.35***

*** Statistical significance at the one percent level, based on a two-tailed test.

greenmail provision on takeover deterrence is ambiguous.[6] We include antigreenmail provisions in our analyses of takeover defenses. All of our empirical results are qualitatively unaffected, however, if antigreenmail provisions are excluded.

Table III reports summary statistics on the uses of takeover defenses. The IPO firms deploy an average of 2.56 of the 10 defenses listed in Table II. Excluding the provisions in the miscellaneous category, for which we lack data from the seasoned firms, IPO firms deploy an average of 2.04 per firm. The seasoned firms, in contrast, have an average of 3.36 defenses. Excluding blank check preferred stock, IPO firms deploy an average of 1.19 defenses, compared to 2.52 for the seasoned firms. The *t*-statistic for the difference in means is −11.35 and is statistically significant at the one percent level. Table IV reports a frequency table of the total number of defenses deployed for each group. A total of 53 percent of the IPO firms deploy at least one of the nonmiscellaneous takeover defenses. Thirty-four percent deploy two or more defenses, and 22 percent have three or more. By comparison, 90 percent of the seasoned corporations have at least one defense, 71 percent have two or more, and 51 percent have three or more.

Thus, while IPO firms deploy defenses, they do so at a lower rate than large seasoned corporations. Seasoned corporations may have more takeover defenses simply because they have had more time to acquire them or because a greater use of defenses is optimal for large firms. An alternative

[6] Consistent with this ambiguous effect on takeover deterrence, Eckbo (1990) reports that the empirical evidence on the valuation effect of greenmail prohibition also is mixed.

Table IV

Frequency Distribution of the Total Number of Takeover Defenses in IPO and Seasoned Firm Samples

The total number of eight types of takeover defenses (those numbered 1–9 in Table II, less blank check preferred stock) deployed at 1,019 firms that went public between 1988 and 1992 and at 524 seasoned firms with publicly traded stock. The seasoned firm frequencies are weighted averages of the seasoned firms' use of each provision, where the weights are the fractions of the IPO firms that went public in each year from 1988 through 1992.

Number of Defenses	% IPO Firms	% Seasoned Firms
0	46.7	10.5
≥1	53.3	89.5
≥2	33.7	70.9
≥3	22.0	50.7
≥4	7.7	29.9
≥5	1.8	11.8
≥6	0.4	2.3

possibility is that agency costs are lower at IPO firms than at seasoned corporations and that IPO managers have relatively strong incentives to adopt value-maximizing defenses. According to this view, the difference in use rates implies that takeover defenses impose net costs on nonmanagerial shareholders. Otherwise, IPO managers would deploy defenses at a rate similar to that observed at seasoned firms.

B. Coverage by State Antitakeover Laws

State antitakeover laws constitute an important component of any U.S. corporation's total defensive posture. Consistent with the notion that the state of incorporation matters to at least some IPO managers, 23 percent of our IPO firms reincorporated into new states within two years before going public. The majority of firms reincorporate from states with relatively unrestrictive takeover laws to states with more restrictive takeover laws. For example, 32 percent of the reincorporations involved firms moving from California or Texas—which have no significant antitakeover laws—to Delaware, which has a freeze-out law (otherwise known as a business combination law).

Table V reports on coverage by each of five common types of state antitakeover laws. (The Appendix contains descriptions of these laws.) Fewer IPO firms than seasoned firms are covered by each of these laws, and in all cases, the differences are statistically significant. For example, 20 percent of the IPO firms are covered by control share acquisition laws, compared to a weighted average coverage rate of 25 percent for the seasoned firms. The differences are similar for fair price laws (11 percent versus 14 percent), cash-out laws (1.5 percent versus 3.6 percent), and poison pill endorsement laws (18 percent versus 32 percent). A total of 80 percent of the IPO firms are incorporated in states that have freeze-out laws, compared to 88 percent

Table V

Coverage by State Antitakeover Laws

Proportion of 1,019 IPO firms incorporated in states with each of five types of state antitakeover laws at the time of the initial public offering, 1988 through 1992. Also reported is a weighted average of the proportions of 524 publicly traded seasoned firms that were covered by each type of law from 1988 through 1992. The weights are determined by the proportions of the IPO firms that went public in each of the years from 1988 through 1992. See the Appendix for descriptions of the state antitakeover laws.

	Proportion of Firms with Stated Characteristic (%)		
	IPO Firms	Seasoned Firms	t-Statistic for Difference in Proportions
Type of state antitakeover law			
Freeze-out law	79.8	88.2	−4.43***
Control share acquisition law	19.7	25.1	−2.35**
Fair price law	10.7	13.8	−1.72*
Cash-out law	1.5	3.6	−2.37**
Poison pill endorsement law	18.3	32.5	−5.93***
Proportion of firms incorporated in Delaware	58.8	51.7	2.63***
Proportion of firms opting out of coverage by a state antitakeover law	7.9	3.1	4.26***

***, **, and * Significant at the 0.01, 0.05, and 0.10 levels, respectively, based on a two-tailed test.

for the seasoned firms. The high rate of coverage by this type of law reflects the fact that Delaware has a freeze-out law. As reported in Table V, 59 percent of the IPO firms and 52 percent of the seasoned firms are incorporated in Delaware.

Most states permit individual firms to opt out of coverage by some or all of an antitakeover law's provisions. A total of eight percent of the IPO firms that are incorporated with states having antitakeover laws (69 out of 868) have language in their corporate charters or prospectuses that indicate that they opted out of such coverage at the time they went public. The weighted mean opt-out rate for the seasoned firms is three percent. The difference is statistically significant at the one percent level, indicating that the IPO firms took actions to avoid coverage by antitakeover defenses at a greater rate than the seasoned firms.

In summary, IPO firms are covered by fewer antitakeover laws than seasoned firms, and the differences in coverage rates are statistically significant for all five of the common antitakeover laws examined. This holds despite the fact that a relatively high percentage of IPO firms incorporate in Delaware, a state that has an antitakeover law. IPO firms also opt out of coverage by antitakeover laws at a significantly higher rate than seasoned firms. Thus, IPO firms deploy takeover defenses at both the firm and state law levels, but at lower rates than large, seasoned corporations.

IV. The Determinants of IPO Firms' Use of Takeover Defenses

A. The Effects of Managerial Characteristics, Ownership, and Board Structure

IPO managers' use of takeover defenses implies that control issues are important to them. This and the following sections explore the reasons why. One reason is suggested by Brennan and Franks' (1997) argument that insiders value control and take steps at the time of the IPO to protect their control benefits. This argument implies that managers use takeover defenses to protect their personal benefits of control. Brennan and Franks presume that managers opportunistically shift much of the cost of takeover protection onto nonmanagerial shareholders.[7] If so, we should observe the defenses primarily where managers own few shares—thus bearing little of the cost of lower share values—and are not closely monitored by nonmanagerial pre-IPO shareholders. We call this view the control benefits hypothesis.

An alternative possibility is that managers' extra takeover protection does not reflect opportunism, but rather, an implicit part of their compensation. According to this view, managers pay for any emoluments that arise from greater takeover protection through lower pay or lower values in their personal holdings of the company's stock. We call this the implicit compensation hypothesis.

To test these propositions, we examine the characteristics of IPO firms that use takeover defenses. Our first empirical model is a logistic regression in which the (untransformed) dependent variable equals one if the firm has any of the provisions listed in Table II other than blank check preferred stock, and zero otherwise.[8] We examine three groups of explanatory variables. The first group includes three measures of managers' personal benefits of control.

1. *Compensation* is the natural logarithm of the total amount of executives' cash compensation for the fiscal year before the IPO, as reported in the IPO prospectus. The control benefits hypothesis implies that the likelihood of a takeover defense increases with *Compensation*, since managers' pay most likely is correlated with their benefits of control. The implicit compensation hypothesis, in contrast, implies that the takeover protection substitutes for pecuniary compensation and suggests that the likelihood of a defense should be negatively related to managers' pecuniary compensation.

[7] In Brennan and Franks' model, the takeover protection arises from dispersed ownership, which is facilitated by underpricing at the IPO. They find that ". . . for the median issue, over 75 percent of underpricing costs are borne by nondirectors . . ." (Brennan and Franks 1997, p. 392).

[8] We exclude blank check preferred stock because, as reported in Table II, it appears to be a boilerplate item that is included by most firms. Its use by IPO firms is not significantly related to any of the explanatory variables discussed below. Some of the results become statistically insignificant when blank check preferred stock is included as a takeover defense. But the results are not sensitive to other modest changes in the definition of the dependent variable. For example, the results are qualitatively the same as those in Table VI when antigreenmail or miscellaneous provisions are excluded.

2. *CEO Tenure* is the number of years the CEO has been with the firm. We conjecture that any managerial rents, including any nonpecuniary benefits the CEO derives from the job, are positively related to how long he or she has had the job. Hence, top managers' desire for takeover protection should be positively related to *CEO Tenure*.
3. *CEO Age* is the age of the company's Chief Executive Officer. We conjecture that the present value of any personal pecuniary or nonpecuniary benefits of continued control over corporate resources is negatively related to the CEO's age, because older CEOs generally have fewer working years over which to enjoy such benefits. Under this conjecture, older managers will lobby less for the inclusion of takeover defenses, and the use of takeover defenses should be negatively related to *CEO Age*.

The second group of explanatory variables consists of six variables that reflect the monitoring and control of the firm's managers.

4. *Inside Ownership* is the percent of the firm's common stock owned by directors and officers before the initial public offering. The control benefits hypothesis implies that managers adopt value-decreasing defenses when they do not bear much of the cost personally in terms of lower share values. A second effect is that managerial share ownership in and of itself can substitute for takeover defenses in deterring undesired takeover bids. Both effects predict a negative relationship between the likelihood of a takeover defense and *Inside Ownership*.[9]
5. *Venture* is a dummy variable set equal to one if the IPO firm is financed with venture capital.
6. *Develop* is a dummy variable set equal to one if the IPO firm is a development-stage company. A development-stage company is defined (by FASB statement number 7) as one in which planned principal operations have not commenced or no significant revenue has yet been earned.

   Since venture capitalists specialize in small firm investments, we conjecture that they will be skilled in monitoring managers. Barry and Turki (1997) report that development-stage IPO firms tend to be younger and smaller than other IPO firms, suggesting that they have relatively few nonmanagerial shareholders and fewer potential conflicts between managers and other pre-IPO investors. If takeover defenses are costly to nonmanagerial shareholders, as implied by the control benefits hypothesis, both venture-backed and development-stage IPO firms should be less likely than other firms to deploy them.

[9] The control benefits hypothesis is similar to an argument regarding inside ownership made by Malatesta and Walkling (1988) for seasoned corporations. We use insiders' shareholdings *before* the IPO because this reflects the share of any costs or benefits of a takeover defense that are borne by the insiders. In later tests of acquisition likelihood after the IPO, we use insiders' shareholdings *after* the IPO.

7. *Board Independence* is the fraction of the firm's board members that are neither officers of the firm nor officers of firms with which the firm has significant business connections. Previous research (e.g., Rosenstein and Wyatt (1990), Byrd and Hickman (1992)) indicates that independent directors increase the quality of the board's oversight of managers. If takeover defenses impose costs on nonmanagerial shareholders, they would be less likely to be used when managers are closely monitored by such shareholders.
8. *Board Size* is the number of people on the firm's board of directors.
9. *Boss* is a dummy variable set equal to one if the firm's CEO is also its board chairman. Jensen (1993) and Yermack (1996) argue that the board's ability to monitor managers and protect nonmanagement shareholders' interests decreases with its size. Jensen also argues that directors are more likely to acquiesce to the CEO's desires when he or she also is the board chairman. The control benefits hypothesis therefore implies that the likelihood of a takeover defense should be positively related to both *Board Size* and *Boss*.

The third group of explanatory variables includes control variables that may affect the use of a takeover defense.

10. *Assets* is the natural logarithm of the book value of firm assets, as reported in the IPO prospectus. Takeover vulnerability, and hence the potential value of a defense, may be related to the firm's size.
11. *Leverage* is the ratio of the book value of total debt to the book value of assets, as reported in the IPO prospectus. The firm's leverage, like its size, may affect the firm's vulnerability to takeover and the value of a takeover defense.
12. *State Law* is a dummy variable set equal to one if the state in which the IPO firm is incorporated has any one of the five state antitakeover laws discussed in Table V. We include it because some prior evidence indicates that firm-level defenses and state antitakeover laws are substitutes (e.g., see Karpoff and Malatesta (1989)).
13. *Delaware* is a dummy variable set equal to one if the IPO firm is incorporated in Delaware. We include this variable to measure whether defense likelihood is significantly different for the 59 percent of firms in the sample that incorporate in Delaware. By including a separate dummy for Delaware, *State Law* measures the incremental influence of being covered by a state law other than Delaware's freeze-out law.
14. Finally, we include dummy variables to control for the year in which the firm goes public.

The results from the logistic regression using these variables are reported as Model 1 in Table VI. The *Compensation* coefficient is positive, while that for *CEO Age* is negative. Both are significant at the one percent level. To the extent that these variables are correlated with managers' personal (pecuniary and nonpecuniary) benefits of continued control of the corporation, the

Table VI

The Determinants of IPO Firms' Use of Takeover Defenses

Models 1 and 2 are logistic regressions in which the dependent variable equals one if the firm had at least one takeover defense in place before going public. Model 3 is a Poisson maximum-likelihood model in which the dependent variable equals the number of takeover defenses in place before going public. The sample consists of 895 initial public offerings issued between 1988 and 1992 (576 in Model 2 and 888 in Model 3). The t-statistics are given in brackets. Each regression includes fixed year effect dummy variables. *Compensation* is the natural logarithm of the total amount of executives' cash compensation for the fiscal year before the IPO. *CEO Tenure* is the number of years the CEO has been with the firm. *CEO Age* is the age of the company's Chief Executive Officer. *Inside Ownership* is the percent of the firm's common stock owned by directors and officers before the IPO. *Venture* is a dummy variable set equal to one if the IPO firm is financed with venture capital. *Develop* is a dummy variable set equal to one if the IPO firm is a development-stage company. *Board Independence* is the fraction of the firm's board members that are neither officers of the firm nor persons with significant business connections to the firm. *Board Size* is the number of people on the firm's board of directors. *Boss* is a dummy variable set equal to one if the firm's CEO is also its board chairman. *Assets* is the natural logarithm of the book value of firm assets. *Leverage* is the ratio of the book value of total debt to the book value of assets. *State Law* is a dummy variable set equal to one if the state in which the IPO firm is incorporated has any one of the five state antitakeover laws discussed in Table V. *Delaware* is a dummy equal to one if the IPO firm is incorporated in Delaware.

Variable	Model 1: Overall Sample	Model 2: Omitting Reverse-LBOs, Carve-outs, and Dual-class IPOs	Model 3: Determinants of Number of Defenses
Compensation	0.432***	0.259*	0.309***
	[3.05]	[1.65]	[6.06]
CEO Tenure	0.013	0.021	0.006
	[1.01]	[1.13]	[1.32]
CEO Age	−0.028***	−0.033***	−0.006
	[−2.60]	[−2.67]	[−1.58]
Inside Ownership	−1.254***	−1.168**	−0.351***
	[−3.31]	[−2.47]	[−2.92]
Venture	−0.066	0.103	−0.023
	[−0.37]	[0.47]	[−0.38]
Develop	−0.889**	−0.945**	−0.709***
	[−2.46]	[−2.46]	[−4.21]
Board Independence	−0.586	−0.956*	0.141
	[−1.39]	[−1.87]	[0.98]
Board Size	0.177***	0.261***	0.040***
	[3.68]	[4.34]	[2.81]
Boss	0.339**	0.308	0.048
	[2.08]	[1.59]	[0.84]
Assets	0.098	0.146	−0.021
	[1.27]	[1.43]	[−0.84]
Leverage	0.035	0.009	−0.038
	[0.26]	[0.06]	[−0.75]
State Law	1.553***	1.257***	1.377***
	[5.47]	[4.09]	[8.81]
Delaware	0.266	0.478**	0.181***
	[1.39]	[2.18]	[2.71]
Constant	−7.887***	−6.760***	−4.790***
	[−5.13]	[−3.47]	[−8.71]
Likelihood ratio test statistic	172.74***	127.15***	380.79***
Pseudo R^2	0.16	0.16	0.11

***, **, and * Significant at the 0.01, 0.05, and 0.10 levels, respectively, based on a two-tailed test.

results indicate that managers' willingness to implement takeover protection increases with their control benefits. This result is consistent with the hypothesis that IPO managers take steps to preserve their control benefits. It is inconsistent with the view that takeover defenses are an implicit portion of managers' compensation. The positive coefficient for *CEO Tenure* also is consistent with the control benefits hypothesis, although it is not statistically significant at the 10 percent level.

The coefficient for *Inside Ownership* is negative and statistically significant at the one percent level. This result is consistent with the notion that managerial share ownership substitutes for takeover defenses to deter unwanted takeover bids. It also is consistent with the control benefits hypothesis, which implies that managers with large stockholdings are unlikely to adopt antitakeover protection because the subsequent loss in share values is personally costly to them.[10]

The likelihood of having a takeover defense is not significantly related to *Board Independence* or *Venture*. It is negatively related to *Develop*, indicating that defenses are unlikely where there are relatively few nonmanagerial shareholders on whom to shift the costs. The likelihood also is positively and significantly related to both *Board Size* and *Boss*. These findings suggest that takeover defenses are more likely to be used by IPO firms with relatively weak controls over senior management.

The likelihood that an IPO firm will use a takeover defense is positively and significantly related to whether the firm is incorporated in a state (other than Delaware) with at least one antitakeover law. This indicates that, among IPO firms, the uses of firm-level and state-level takeover defenses are complementary. The likelihood that a firm will deploy takeover defenses is not significantly related to firm size, leverage, or the Delaware dummy variable. Also, none of the year dummy variables is significantly different from zero, indicating that the probability of using at least one takeover defense did not change significantly during the sample period.

B. Results Excluding Reverse-LBOs, Equity Carve-outs, and Firms with Dual Class Stock

The sample of 1,019 IPOs includes several types of firms. In Model 2 of Table VI we exclude equity carve-outs, firms that previously were taken private in leveraged buyouts, and firms that went public with dual class stock. This reduces the sample to 579 normal IPOs. The results are qualitatively similar to those in Model 1. A primary difference is that the coefficient on managers' compensation is reduced in Model 2 (due primarily to the

[10] In tests not reported in the table, we included the square of *Inside Ownership* as an additional regressor. We also included interaction terms involving a dummy variable for firms in which managers' post-IPO ownership exceeds 50 percent. Our reasoning was that the relation between the likelihood of a takeover defense and managerial ownership may not be linear, or even monotonic. The coefficients for these variables, however, are statistically insignificant.

exclusion of the reverse-LBO firms). Also, the coefficients for the board independence and Delaware variables become statistically significant in Model 2. The signs and magnitudes of the other variables are similar to those in Model 1, indicating that the overall results are not driven by the inclusion of reverse-LBOs, equity carve-outs, and firms with dual-class stock.

C. *Determinants of the Number of Takeover Defenses at IPO Firms*

Model 3 in Table VI reports on a test in which the dependent variable is the *number* of takeover defenses used by each IPO firm. Data on all types of IPOs are included, although the results are roughly similar when reverse-LBOs, equity carve-outs, and dual-class firms are excluded. Because the dependent variable is a count variable, we use a Poisson maximum-likelihood model. (The results are qualitatively identical using a Tobit censored regression model, censoring the dependent variable at zero.)

The results are similar to those reported in Models 1 and 2. The number of takeover defenses deployed is positively and significantly related to executives' compensation (*Compensation*) and board size (*Board Size*), as well as the dummy variable indicating that the firm is located in a state other than Delaware with an antitakeover law (*State Law*). The number of provisions is negatively and significantly related to directors' and officers' stock ownership (*Inside Ownership*) and a dummy variable indicating that the firm is a development-stage company (*Develop*). Unlike the results in Model 1, *CEO Age* and the dummy variable indicating that the CEO is also the board chairman (*Boss*) are not statistically significant. In addition, the coefficient for the dummy variable for firms incorporated in Delaware is positive and significant at the one percent level.

D. *Sensitivity Tests*

We examined the effects on our results of several alternate characteristics of the IPO firms, including whether the IPO is an equity carve-out or reverse LBO. These characteristics, however, are unrelated to the likelihood of a takeover defense, and their inclusion in the tests does not materially affect the results reported in Table VI. The likelihood of using a takeover defense also is unrelated to measures of the IPO risk, including the initial one-day stock return and the number of risk factors listed in the prospectus. The likelihood is not significantly related to the number of the firm's employees or whether the firm is owned by members of the same family. It is positively related to the probability of acquisition, as estimated from models similar to those discussed below in Section V, but the coefficients are not statistically significant. The results are unaffected when we include board members with affiliations to the firm in the definition of *Board Independence*. The results also are qualitatively unaffected using probit models instead of logistic models. We conclude that the results reported in Table VI are not sensitive to changes in model specification.

We also examined the decision to deploy each of the takeover defenses listed in Table II separately, by estimating separate logistic regressions for each type of defense. The rationale for such tests is that managers' motives and their firms' characteristics may differ for different types of defenses. Most of the coefficients from these tests are similar in sign to those reported in Table VI, but the test statistics typically are smaller.

Two provisions—fair price provisions and supermajority vote requirements—can protect minority shareholders' interests if the firm is acquired or subject to a takeover bid. A fair price provision protects minority interests from being frozen out of a high takeover premium for their shares, and supermajority vote requirements increase minority shareholders' abilities to block self-dealing actions by majority shareholders. Such provisions may be valuable especially for small shareholders in firms that have large, controlling blockholders. As noted in Section III, supermajority vote requirements are deployed in IPO firms at roughly the same frequency as at seasoned corporations, indicating that they are popular even where the degree of separation between managers and owners is small.

In many model specifications, the use of a fair price provision or supermajority vote requirement is positively related to the number of five percent blockholders before the IPO. In most tests, however, the relationship is not statistically significant. Furthermore, the likelihood of one of these defenses is not significantly related to the fraction of shares controlled by blockholders. These results do not lend much support to the view that voting-related takeover defenses are adopted to protect minority shareholders' interests.

E. Summary: Control Benefits

The evidence reported in this section indicates that takeover defenses are more likely in firms with high managerial compensation, when managers' shareholdings are small, and when the direct oversight from nonmanagerial shareholders is relatively weak. That is, defenses are used when managers' benefits from takeover protection are large, their personal costs low, and they can act relatively independently of the oversight from other shareholders. These results are consistent with the control benefits hypothesis, which holds that IPO managers use takeover defenses to protect their control benefits and shift some of the cost onto nonmanagerial shareholders. The results are not consistent with the implicit compensation hypothesis, which implies that managers contract for extra takeover protection ex ante as part of their compensation.

V. Takeover Defenses, Acquisition Likelihood, and Takeover Premiums

A. Effects on Acquisition Likelihood

An additional motive for takeover defenses at IPO firms is suggested by Zingales' (1995) and Mello and Parsons' (1998) models, in which the IPO is the first stage in the eventual sale of the firm. According to this view, defenses can be used to facilitate control transfers at high share prices. As discussed by DeAngelo and Rice (1983), takeover defenses can encourage high takeover premiums because they help solve a rush-to-tender problem among shareholders and force bidders to negotiate directly with the firm's managers.

In this section, we test whether takeover defenses do, in fact, help increase expected takeover premiums for IPO firms. We first examine acquisition likelihood and then measure the effects of a defense on the premiums for those firms that were acquired. A total of 168 (16.5 percent) of our sample firms were acquired within five years of their IPOs. We have sufficient data to estimate the determinants of acquisition likelihood for 163 of these firms. Table VII reports on logistic regressions in which the (untransformed) dependent variable is one for these 163 firms, and zero otherwise. In addition to the five acquired firms with insufficient data, the tests omit 99 firms that were delisted for other reasons such as bankruptcies or failure to meet exchange listing requirements, plus 31 (for Model 1) or 36 (for Model 2) additional firms that have insufficient data for one or more variable used in the tests.[11]

We first model acquisition likelihood using control variables that are examined by previous researchers, including Palepu (1986), Ambrose and Megginson (1992), and Song and Walkling (1993). The purpose of this test is to provide a benchmark with which to compare our expanded model (Model 2) that includes governance variables. The control variables include *Assets* and *Leverage*, plus the following measures of the firm's asset structure and performance.

- *Market to Book Ratio* is the ratio of the market value of the firm's stock plus the book value of debt, divided by the book value of assets, measured at year-end following the IPO.
- *Property* is the ratio of the firm's property, plant, and equipment to total assets in the year of the IPO.
- *Liquidity* is the average ratio of net liquid assets (current assets minus current liabilities) to total assets for the three years before acquisition for those firms that were acquired and for years +3 through +5 relative to the IPO for firms that were not acquired.
- *Growth* is the average annual growth in sales for the three years before acquisition for those firms that were acquired and for years +3 through +5 relative to the IPO for firms that were not acquired.
- *Stock Return* is the firm's cumulative stock return for the three years after the IPO or up to two months before the acquisition announcement for those firms that were acquired within three years minus the contemporaneous cumulative return of the Nasdaq equal-weighted index.

[11] Sixteen of the sample firms were the targets of unsuccessful takeover attempts. The likelihood of receiving an unsuccessful bid is not significantly related to the presence of a takeover defense. The results reported below and in Table VII are not materially affected when unsuccessful acquisition bids are included in the definition of the dependent variable.

Table VII

Antitakeover Provisions and Acquisition Likelihood

Logistic regressions in which the dependent variable equals one if the firm is acquired within five years of its IPO. Model 1 includes variables examined in previous attempts to model acquisition likelihood. Model 2 includes additional governance variables. The sample consists of 885 initial public offerings issued between 1988 and 1992 for Model 1 and 880 IPOs for Model 2. *t*-statistics are given in brackets. Each regression includes fixed year effect dummy variables. *Assets* is the natural logarithm of the book value of firm assets as of the IPO. *Leverage* is the ratio of the book value of total debt to the book value of assets as of the IPO. *Market to Book Ratio* is the ratio of the market value of the firm's stock plus the book value of debt, divided by the book value of assets, measured in the year of the IPO. *Property* is the ratio of the firm's property, plant, and equipment to total assets in the year of the IPO. *Liquidity* is the average ratio of net liquid assets to total assets for the three years before acquisition for those firms that were acquired and for years +3 through +5 relative to the IPO for firms that were not acquired. *Growth* is the average annual growth in sales for the three years before acquisition for those firms that were acquired and for years +3 through +5 relative to the IPO for firms that were not acquired. *Stock Return* is the firm's cumulative stock return for the three-year period after the IPO, or up to two months before the acquisition announcement for those firms that were acquired within three years, minus the equal-weighted Nasdaq index measured over the same period. *Post-IPO Inside Ownership* is the percent of the firm's common stock owned by directors and officers immediately after the IPO. *Venture* is a dummy variable set equal to one if the IPO firm is financed with venture capital. *Develop* is a dummy variable set equal to one if the IPO firm is a development-stage company. *Board Independence* is the fraction of the firm's board members that are not officers of the firm or persons with significant business connections to the firm. *Board Size* is the number of people on the firm's board of directors. *Boss* is a dummy variable set equal to one if the firm's CEO is also its board chairman. *State Law* is a dummy variable set equal to one if the state in which the IPO firm is incorporated has any one of the five state antitakeover laws discussed in Table V. *Delaware* is a dummy variable set equal to one if the IPO firm is incorporated in Delaware. *Takeover Defense at IPO* is a dummy variable that equals one for firms that have at least one of the defenses listed in Table II (other than blank check preferred stock). *Takeover Defense after IPO* is a dummy variable that equals one for firms that acquire at least one new defense after the IPO.

Variable	Model 1: Using Standard Variables		Model 2: Introducing Governance Variables	
Assets	0.186***	[3.08]	0.173**	[2.492]
Leverage	0.023	[0.14]	−0.003	[−0.016]
Market to Book Ratio	−0.070**	[−2.11]	−0.060*	[−1.861]
Property	0.022	[0.06]	0.036	[0.101]
Liquidity	1.463***	[2.92]	1.805***	[3.368]
Growth	0.050	[1.24]	0.096*	[1.946]
Stock Return	−0.097	[−1.40]	−0.114	[−1.556]
Post-IPO Inside Ownership			0.129	[0.256]
Venture			−0.241	[−1.117]
Develop			−1.698***	[−2.613]
Board Independence			1.848***	[3.496]
Board Size			−0.072	[−1.375]
Boss			−0.024	[−0.122]
State Law			0.148	[0.437]
Delaware			0.245	[1.043]
Takeover Defense at IPO			−0.454**	[−2.230]
Takeover Defense after IPO			**−0.648*** **	**[−2.580]**
Constant	−5.450***	[−4.47]	−5.838***	[−4.493]
Likelihood ratio test statistic	33.16***		70.44***	
Pseudo R^2	0.04		0.09	

***, **, and * Significant at the 0.01, 0.05, and 0.10 levels, respectively, based on a two-tailed test.

The results from this logistic regression are reported as Model 1 in Table VII. In general, we find a greater degree of predictability in acquisition likelihood than do other researchers who examine seasoned firms. The coefficient for *Assets* is positive and statistically significant at the one percent level. This result differs from that found by Mikkelson and Partch (1989), Song and Walkling (1993), and Comment and Schwert (1995), who find that acquisition likelihood for seasoned companies is negatively related to firm size. While size appears to deter takeovers among larger, seasoned corporations, such is not the case among IPO firms. Some firms (e.g., Berkshire Hathway) are known to have minimum size requirements on their acquisitions. It is possible that some newly public firms are not acquired simply because they are too small to attract the attention of potential acquirers.

The *Liquidity* coefficient also is positive and significant. Again, this differs from some prior findings for large firms. Ambrose and Megginson (1992), Song and Walkling (1993), and Comment and Schwert (1995), for example, all report that acquisition likelihood for seasoned corporations is not significantly related to the fraction of a firm's assets that are liquid. The coefficient for *Market to Book Ratio* is negative and statistically significant at the 10 percent level, suggesting that IPO firms that go public with high market values are relatively unlikely to be acquired. *Stock Return* also is negatively related to acquisition likelihood, but its coefficient is statistically insignificant at the 10 percent level.

In Model 2, we include several aspects of the firm's governance structure, including *Venture*, *Develop*, *Board Independence*, *Board Size*, *Boss*, *State Law*, and *Delaware*. (Variable definitions are provided in Section IV and in Table VII.) *Post-IPO Inside Ownership* measures officer and director stock ownership immediately after the IPO.

We include two variables representing the firm's defensive posture. *Takeover Defense at IPO* is a dummy variable that equals one for firms that have at least one of the defenses listed in Table II at the time of the IPO (other than blank check preferred stock). Because acquisition likelihood might also depend on defenses acquired after the IPO, we also include a variable, *New Takeover Defense after IPO*, which equals one for firms that acquire at least one new defense after the IPO. As reported in Section II, relatively few defenses are acquired after the IPO.

The inclusion of these governance variables permits us to explain a greater portion of the variation in acquisition likelihood. The chi-squared test statistic for Model 2 is 70.4, and its pseudo R-squared is 0.09—double the levels in Model 1. Among the variables that reflect the firm's ownership and governance structure, the coefficient for *Board Independence* is positive and statistically significant at the one percent level, indicating that strong outside board representation tends to facilitate the acquisition of IPO firms. The coefficient for *Develop* is negative and significant, indicating that firms that are in their development stage at the time of their IPO are less likely than other IPO firms to be acquired within five years. Acquisition likelihood is not significantly related to *Post-IPO Inside Ownership*, *Venture*, *Board*

Size, *Boss*, *State Law*, or *Delaware*. Acquisition likelihood is negatively and significantly related to *New Takeover Defense after IPO*, suggesting that defenses acquired after the IPO help firms remain independent. Most important for our inquiry, however, is that the coefficient for *Takeover Defense at IPO* is negative and statistically significant at the five percent level (z-statistic = −2.23). Thus, the presence of a takeover defense at the time of the firm's IPO is negatively related to the probability of acquisition within five years. When all other regressors are set equal to their mean values, the implied probability of takeover is 16.8 percent for firms without takeover defenses and 11.4 percent for those with at least one defense, a difference of 5.4 percent. This result indicates that takeover defenses are associated with longer-run firm independence.

We conducted several tests to examine the sensitivity of this result to changes in model specification. For example, we included the measures of managers' personal benefits that are discussed in Section IV. We substituted slightly different measures for the regressors reported in the table (for example, using different benchmarks to measure abnormal stock returns, or measuring the market-to-book ratio other than at the time of the IPO). Few of the empirical results are affected qualitatively by such changes in model specification. In all tests, the coefficient for *Takeover Defense at IPO* remains negative and statistically significant, although in some cases at the 10 percent level.

B. Effects on Takeover Premiums

Among the 163 firms in our sample that were acquired within five years of their IPOs and that have sufficient data, 83 had takeover defenses at the time of their IPOs. As reported in Table VIII, the mean market-adjusted stock return during the 42 trading days before the acquisition announcement for these 83 firms is 6.0 percent, compared to 9.6 percent for the 80 acquired firms without takeover defenses. The mean two-day market-adjusted stock return upon the announcement is 18.5 percent for the firms with takeover defenses, compared to 14.8 percent for firms without defenses. For the period dating from the day after announcement until the earlier of delisting or six months following announcement (resolution), the mean market-adjusted returns are 8.9 percent for firms with defenses and 14.2 percent for those without defenses. Cumulated over the complete period from 42 trading days before the acquisition announcement until resolution, those with takeover defenses earn an average market-adjusted return of 33.3 percent, compared to 38.4 percent for those without defenses. None of these differences, however, are significantly different from zero at normal significance levels.

Table IX reports the results of multivariate tests of the takeover premiums among IPO firms. Our tests are structured to mimic those reported by Comment and Schwert (1995, Table 4). Model 1 reports estimates based on the full sample of 885 IPOs in our sample that have sufficient data on all

Table VIII

Announcement Period Returns for IPO Firms Acquired within Five Years

Announcement period returns for the 163 IPO firms which are acquired within five years of the IPO and have CRSP data available with which to calculate announcement period returns. Of these firms, 83 have takeover defenses in place before going public, while 80 did not. *Run-up* is the preannouncement cumulative abnormal return (CAR), measured from [−42,−2] days before the announcement (day 0 is announcement date). *Announcement return* is the CAR measured for the day of the announcement and the day before the announcement [−1,0]. *Resolution* is the CAR measured from the day after announcement through resolution, which is the earlier of delisting and six months [+1, Resolution]. *Total Period* is the CAR measured from two months before announcement through the earlier of six months after announcement or delisting [−42, Resolution]. All returns are measured net of market model returns. Market model parameters are estimated from day −295 (or first day CRSP, if later) through day −43.

Days over Which CARs Measured	Firms without Defenses before IPO	Firms with Defenses before IPO	*t*-Statistic for Difference in Means
Run-up [−42,−2]	9.6%***	6.0%**	0.93
Announcement Period [−1,0]	14.8%***	18.5%***	−1.35
Resolution [+1,min(delisting,126)]	14.2%***	8.9%***	0.91
Total Period [−42,min(delisting,126)]	38.4%***	33.3%***	0.69

*** and ** Significant at the 0.01 and 0.05 levels, respectively.

regressors. The takeover premium is measured as the cumulative market-adjusted abnormal stock return from 42 days before the announcement through the earlier of the date of delisting or six months after announcement. For firms that were not acquired, the abnormal return is set equal to zero.[12] Model 2 reports estimates based on the firms that were acquired within five years of their IPOs. Although 163 firms were acquired, we have sufficient data to estimate the regression for only 148 of these firms.

The results indicate that the presence of a takeover defense is not significantly related to takeover premiums in either Model 1 or Model 2. Takeover premiums also are not significantly related to whether the firm is incorporated in a state with an antitakeover law. The one variable that is significantly related to takeover premiums in both models is the prior three-year stock return. The negative coefficients indicate that firms with strong stock performance, when acquired, earn smaller takeover premiums than firms with poorer prior stock price performance.

Table X reports on tests in which the dependent variable is the actual takeover proceeds to target shareholders (expressed as a percentage of equity value 42 days before the takeover announcement), instead of cumula-

[12] Because most takeover premiums are positive, one might consider using a censored regression model to estimate Model 1. However, in our sample, 22 of the takeover premiums are negative. Even when we ignore these 22 observations and estimate Model 1 using a Tobit model and censor the dependent variable at zero, the results are qualitatively identical to those reported

Table IX

Firm Characteristics and Takeover Premiums

Ordinary least squares regressions in which the dependent variable is the takeover premium measured as the cumulative market-adjusted abnormal return from 42 days before announcement through the earlier of the date of delisting or six months after announcement. Model 1 includes all IPOs with available data [$N = 885$], where the takeover premium is set to zero for those firms not acquired. Model 2 includes only firms acquired within five years of the IPO and with available data [$N = 148$]. t-statistics are given in brackets. Each regression includes fixed year effect dummy variables. *Takeover Defense* is a dummy variable that equals one for firms that have at least one of the defenses listed in Table II (other than blank check preferred stock). *Assets* is the natural logarithm of the book value of firm assets as of the IPO. *Leverage* is the ratio of the book value of total debt to the book value of assets as of the IPO. *Market to Book Ratio* is the ratio of the market value of the firm's stock plus the book value of debt, divided by the book value of assets, measured in the year of the IPO. *Property* is the ratio of the firm's property, plant, and equipment to total assets in the year of the IPO. *Liquidity* is the average ratio of net liquid assets to total assets for the three years before acquisition for those firms that were acquired and for years +3 through +5 relative to the IPO for firms that were not acquired. *Growth* is the average annual growth in sales for the three years before acquisition for those firms that were acquired and for years +3 through +5 relative to the IPO for firms that were not acquired. *Stock Return* is the firm's cumulative stock return for the three-year period after the IPO, or up to two months before the acquisition announcement for those firms that were acquired within three years, minus the equal-weighted Nasdaq index measured over the same period.

Variable	Model 1: Including All Firms	Model 2: Firms Acquired within 5 Years of the IPO
Takeover Defense at IPO	**−0.017**	**0.044**
	[−1.018]	**[0.587]**
Takeover Defense after IPO	−0.023	0.110
	[−1.254]	[1.077]
State Law	−0.005	−0.035
	[−0.236]	[−0.316]
Assets	0.006	−0.046*
	[1.230]	[−1.749]
Leverage	−0.003	0.086
	[−0.203]	[0.657]
Market to Book Ratio	−0.001	0.013
	[−1.055]	[1.018]
Property	0.017	0.077
	[0.632]	[0.612]
Liquidity	0.084**	−0.070
	[2.015]	[−0.325]
Growth	0.004	0.001
	[0.921]	[0.084]
Stock Return	−0.012***	−0.035**
	[−2.636]	[−1.975]
Auction		−0.165
		[−1.043]
Constant	−0.038	1.341**
	[−0.396]	[2.467]
Adjusted R^2	0.006	0.036

***, **, and * Significant at the 0.01, 0.05, and 0.10 levels, respectively, based on a two-tailed test.

Table X

Firm Characteristics and Actual Takeover Proceeds

Ordinary least squares regressions in which the dependent variable is the actual takeover proceeds expressed as a percentage of equity value 42 days before the takeover announcement. Model 1 includes all IPOs with available data [N = 885], where takeover proceeds are set to zero for those firms not acquired. Model 2 includes only firms acquired within five years of the IPO and with available data [N = 148]. t-statistics are given in brackets. Each regression includes fixed year effect dummy variables. *Takeover Defense* is a dummy variable that equals one for firms that have at least one of the defenses listed in Panel A of Table V (other than blank check preferred stock). *Assets* is the natural logarithm of the book value of firm assets as of the IPO. *Leverage* is the ratio of the book value of total debt to the book value of assets as of the IPO. *Market to Book Ratio* is the ratio of the market value of the firm's stock plus the book value of debt, divided by the book value of assets, measured in the year of the IPO. *Property* is the ratio of the firm's property, plant, and equipment to total assets in the year of the IPO. *Liquidity* is the average ratio of net liquid assets to total assets for the three years before acquisition for those firms that were acquired and for years +3 through +5 relative to the IPO for firms that were not acquired. *Growth* is the average annual growth in sales for the three years before acquisition for those firms that were acquired and for years +3 through +5 relative to the IPO for firms that were not acquired. *Stock Return* is the firm's cumulative stock return for the three year period after the IPO, or up to two months before the acquisition announcement for those firms that were acquired within three years, minus the equal-weighted Nasdaq index measured over the same period.

Variable	Model 1: Including All Firms	Model 2: Firms Acquired within 5 Years of the IPO
Takeover Defense at IPO	**−0.022**	**0.040**
	[−0.911]	**[0.354]**
Takeover Defense after IPO	−0.036	0.127
	[−1.384]	[0.811]
State Law	0.001	−0.055
	[0.017]	[−0.333]
Assets	0.007	−0.085**
	[0.888]	[−2.155]
Leverage	0.005	0.371*
	[0.245]	[1.880]
Market to Book Ratio	−0.001	0.006
	[−0.983]	[0.329]
Property	0.009	0.019
	[0.216]	[0.101]
Liquidity	0.073	−0.329
	[1.198]	[−1.025]
Growth	0.002	−0.007
	[0.364]	[−0.314]
Stock Return	−0.008	−0.010
	[−1.265]	[−0.384]
Auction		−0.110
		[−0.468]
Constant	0.010	2.411***
	[0.072]	[2.975]
Adjusted R^2	−0.003	0.051

***, **, and * Significant at the 0.01, 0.05, and 0.10 levels, respectively, based on a two-tailed test.

tive stock returns over the takeover period. Actual proceeds are positively and significantly related to assets and leverage. They are not, however, significantly related to the presence of a takeover defense.

We also investigated several variations of Models 1 and 2 in Tables IX and X. We examined whether takeover premiums are related to the number of defenses deployed, or to the deployment of each of the 10 defenses listed in Table II considered individually, or to whether the IPO is an equity carve-out or reverse LBO. In none of these tests do we find evidence of a statistically significant relation between takeover premiums and either firm-level or state-level takeover defenses, considered individually or in total, at the time of the IPO.[13]

Zingales (1995) suggests that equity carve-outs are the most likely of all IPOs to be completed as a first stage in the sale of the firm. This suggests that any positive effect of a takeover defense on the expected takeover premium will be most evident in equity carve-out IPOs. However, we can uncover no evidence to support this conjecture either. In tests not reported in a table, we find that the effects of a takeover defense on acquisition likelihood and the realized takeover premium are not significantly different for equity carve-out IPOs than for other IPOs.

Thus, takeover defenses are associated with a lower takeover probability but not with an increase in premium for those firms that are acquired. These results are consistent with the hypothesis that IPO managers seek to maintain their control benefits even after taking their firms public. The results are inconsistent with the notion that takeover defenses are deployed to increase expected takeover premiums.[14]

VI. Post-IPO Operating Performance

If managers use defenses to protect their personal control benefits, they may extract those benefits at the expense of firm performance. Similarly, it appears that the defenses deter some acquisitions without any compensating increase in takeover premiums for firms that are acquired. These results suggest that takeover defenses may entrench managers and contribute to poor firm performance.

[13] In a separate test, we examined *expected* takeover premiums, where expectations are based on predicted values for acquisition likelihood and takeover premiums. We find no significant difference between firms with and without takeover defenses.

[14] Our results differ from those in Comment and Schwert (1995), who find that the presence of a poison pill increases the takeover premium while not affecting the acquisition likelihood. Our tests differ from theirs in several ways. We examine small, newly public companies and record the presence of takeover defenses at the time of the IPO, whereas Comment and Schwert examine NYSE- and AMEX-listed companies and record the presence of a takeover defense in the year before actual or potential acquisition. We consider a broad range of takeover defenses, whereas Comment and Schwert examine only poison pills and two types of state antitakeover laws. Other evidence on these issues is mixed. Ambrose and Megginson (1992), for example, find that classified boards are associated with a decrease in the likelihood a firm will be acquired, but that other takeover defenses have no significant effect on acquisition likelihood.

To examine this hypothesis, we investigate whether post-IPO operating performance is related to the presence of a takeover defense at the time of the IPO. We measure operating performance as operating return on assets (ROA), which is equal to operating income (Compustat item #13) divided by the book value of assets (Compustat item #6). Using the procedure proposed by Barber and Lyon (1996), we match each IPO firm in our sample with a matched control firm selected from the 1999 Compustat (annual and research) files. The control is the median firm within the same four-digit SIC code and ROA within 10 percent of the sample firm in the year of the IPO. If no matches are made at the four-digit level, we select from firms within the same three-digit SIC and, if necessary, two-digit SIC code. The raw change in ROA for IPO firm i from the year of the IPO to year t is

$$\Delta ROA_{i,(0,t)} = ROA_{i,t} - ROA_{i,0}.$$

The adjusted change in ROA, which controls for the contemporaneous change in firm i's matched control firm, is

$$\begin{aligned} Adjusted\ \Delta ROA_{i,(0,t)} &= (ROA_{i,t} - ROA_{i,0}) \\ &\quad - (Matched\ ROA_{i,t} - Matched\ ROA_{i,0}). \end{aligned}$$

Data to compute $\Delta ROA_{i,(0,1)}$ are available for 910 of the IPO firms, declining to 666 firms for the five-year ROA change ($\Delta ROA_{i,(0,5)}$). Data to compute *Adjusted* $\Delta ROA_{i,(0,1)}$ are available for 638 matched pairs of IPO and control firms, declining to 438 matched pairs for the five-year change (*Adjusted* $\Delta ROA_{i,(0,5)}$).

Table XI reports the raw and adjusted changes in ROA measured through each of the five years following the IPO. Consistent with the findings of previous researchers, the mean raw change for all firms is negative over all intervals examined.[15] The mean change from the year of the IPO to the following year, for example, is −0.054, with a t-statistic of −7.92. The mean change from the IPO year to year 2 is −0.075 with a t-statistic of −8.70. Operating ROA levels off after year 2, as the mean changes measured through years 3, 4, and 5 are similar to that for year 2.

The mean *adjusted change in operating ROA*, reported in Panel B, also is significantly negative for the first two years after the IPO. From the year of the IPO to the following year it is −0.022 with a t-statistic of −3.89. From the IPO year to year 2 it is −0.036 with a t-statistic of −4.71. The mean *adjusted change in operating ROA* reverses somewhat in subsequent years, however, and is insignificantly different from zero over the (0, 5) interval.

[15] Friedlan (1994), Jain and Kini (1994), Mikkelson, Partch, and Shah (1997), and Teoh, Welch, and Wong (1998) all show that operating performance tends to decline in the one to five years after a firm's IPO.

Table XI

Changes in Operating Performance after the IPO

Average changes in operating return on assets (ROA) for firms going public from 1988 through 1992, measured for each of five years after the IPO. Panel A reports the mean *raw change in operating ROA* dated from the year of the IPO. Panel B reports the mean *adjusted change in operating ROA*, where the adjusted change is the raw change minus the contemporaneous change in ROA for a control firm matched by industry and ROA performance in the year of the IPO (year 0). In Panel A, the number of firms for which ROA data are available range from 910 (for year 1 results) to 666 (for year 5 results). In Panel B, the number of matched pairs of firms range from 638 (for year 1 results) to 438 (for year 5 results). *t*-statistics are in parentheses.

	Change in Operating ROA Measured through				
	Year 1	Year 2	Year 3	Year 4	Year 5
Panel A: Raw Change in Operating ROA					
All firms	−0.054	−0.075	−0.072	−0.057	−0.067
	(−7.92)[a]	(−8.70)[a]	(−9.29)[a]	(−7.15)[a]	(−6.44)[a]
Firms without takeover defenses	−0.074	−0.105	−0.082	−0.054	−0.065
	(−6.35)[a]	(−6.08)[a]	(−5.74)[a]	(−3.87)[a]	(−3.36)[a]
Firms with takeover defenses	−0.037	−0.050	−0.064	−0.059	−0.069
	(−4.78)[a]	(−7.69)[a]	(−8.13)[a]	(−6.54)[a]	(−6.69)[a]
Difference in means	−0.037	−0.055	−0.019	0.006	0.004
	(−2.67)[a]	(−3.18)[a]	(−1.20)	(0.34)	(0.21)
Panel B: Adjusted Change in Operating ROA					
All firms	−0.022	−0.036	−0.033	−0.029	−0.002
	(−3.89)[a]	(−4.71)[a]	(−3.75)[a]	(−2.95)[a]	(−0.09)
Firms without takeover defenses	−0.034	−0.055	−0.054	−0.034	0.027
	(−3.95)[a]	(−4.00)[a]	(−3.14)[a]	(−1.85)[c]	(0.54)
Firms with takeover defenses	−0.014	−0.023	−0.019	−0.025	−0.021
	(−1.83)[c]	(−2.63)[a]	(−2.10)[b]	(−2.36)[b]	(−1.78)[c]
Difference in means	−0.020	−0.032	−0.035	−0.009	0.048
	(−1.71)[c]	(−2.10)[b]	(−1.91)[b]	(−0.46)	(1.11)

[a,b,c] Statistical significance at the 0.01, 0.05, and 0.10 levels, respectively, based on a two-tailed test.

The differences in means for both *raw ROA* and *adjusted ROA* are statistically insignificant for firms with and without takeover defenses over the (0, 4) and (0, 5) intervals, suggesting that longer term changes in operating performance are not related to the presence of a takeover defense at the time of the IPO. However, the results for years 1 and 2 indicate that, for periods shortly after the IPO, changes in operating performance tend to be more negative for firms without takeover defenses than for firms with defenses. Over the (0, 1) interval, for example, the mean *adjusted change in operating ROA* is −0.034 for firms without defenses, compared to −0.014 for firms with defenses. This difference is significantly different from zero at the 10 percent level.

This result is inconsistent with the notion that takeover defenses at the time of the IPO contribute to poor operating performance. Thus, while takeover defenses deter some acquisitions and appear to be used to protect managers' control benefits, there is no evidence that they degrade operating performance or are used to protect managers of firms that are expected to perform badly.[16]

VII. Conclusions

Many firms deploy takeover defenses when they go public. Among our sample of 1,019 industrial firms going public from 1988 through 1992, 53 percent have at least one takeover defense at the time of their IPOs. On average, a firm goes public with 1.71 defenses and adopts only 0.19 additional defenses during the five years after its IPO. Thus, the managers of a typical IPO firm seem to care about control issues, and they determine their firm's longer term defensive posture at the time of the IPO.

Zingales (1995) and Mello and Parsons (1998) argue that an IPO is the first stage in the eventual sale of the firm. This suggests that a takeover defense can be used to increase the expected takeover premium when the firm eventually is acquired. Our data, however, do not support this argument. We find that the presence of a takeover defense when a firm goes public is negatively related to the subsequent acquisition likelihood and is unrelated to the takeover premium for those firms that are acquired. Thus, it appears unlikely that takeover defenses systematically help in the eventual sale of the firm by increasing expected takeover premiums.

Instead, most of our findings support an explanation for takeover defenses that is suggested by Brennan and Franks (1997). According to this view, managers take steps at the time of the IPO to ensure the continuation of their personal benefits of control. This view is consistent with our finding that takeover defenses help firms remain independent after the IPO. It also is consistent with evidence that the probability that an IPO firm has a takeover defense is positively related to managers' compensation and is negatively related to managerial ownership and measures of how closely the managers are monitored by nonmanagerial shareholders. Thus, defenses are more likely when managers benefit personally from their positions, bear little of the effects on share value, and can act independently of nonmanagerial oversight. When they can, IPO managers appear to shift the cost of takeover protection onto nonmanagerial shareholders.

These findings indicate that there frequently exists some degree of agency conflict between managers and nonmanagerial shareholders *even at the IPO stage*. That is, the separation of ownership from management does not begin once the IPO occurs. Rather, it is a characteristic of any organizational form in which some of the equity capital is provided by people who do not also

[16] These results loosely are consistent with those in Danielson and Karpoff (2001), who find that the adoption of a poison pill among seasoned firms is associated with subsequent improvements in operating performance, relative to control firms matched by industry and prior performance.

manage the firm's operations. Since most firms raise equity capital from nonmanagerial institutions and individuals before the IPO stage, their equity agency problems are different from those of seasoned corporations only in degree, not in kind.

The existence of agency costs at the IPO stage does not necessarily represent an inefficiency. We would expect pre-IPO investors to pay prices for shares that reflect the expected costs of agency, just as they reflect such other costs as labor and capital. As Demsetz (1983) and others argue, the existence of agency costs does not make the diffusely held corporation inefficient. There are offsetting benefits (e.g., pooling of capital and risk sharing among owners) that make the diffusely held corporation efficient for some productive activities. The outcome may be inefficient only when compared to a Nirvana benchmark in which firms can realize the benefits from risk sharing *and* avoid the costs that arise when managers act as agents for shareholders.

Appendix

Table A.1 gives descriptions of the takeover defenses examined in this study.

Table A.1
Takeover Defenses Examined in this Study

Defense	Explanation
	Panel A: Firm-Level Takeover Defenses
1. Antigreenmail provision	Greenmail refers to an arrangement in which a company repurchases the stock held by a large shareholder, usually at an above-market price, in exchange for the shareholder's agreement not to launch a contest for control of the company for a specified period of time. An antigreenmail provision prohibits a company's managers from entering such an agreement unless the repurchase offer is made to all shareholders on a pro-rata basis, or shareholders approve the transaction.
2. Blank check preferred stock	This is authorized but unissued preferred stock for which the board of directors has broad discretion to establish voting, dividend, conversion, and other rights. Blank check preferred stock can be issued to parties friendly to management to block unwanted hostile bids. It also can be used as a vehicle to implement a poison pill.
3. Classified (or staggered) board	In a classified board, directors are divided into separate classes and elected to overlapping terms. For example, a firm with a three-class classified board would hold elections each year for one-third of the board seats, each with a three-year term. Because only one-third of the board can be replaced each year, a hostile bidder with voting control of the corporation may be unable to control the board for up to two years. Classifying the board also can deter proxy contests for control, because only one-third of the directors stand for elections in any one year.

Table A1—*Continued*

Defense	Explanation
	Panel A: Firm-Level Takeover Defenses (*continued*)
4. Fair price provision	This provision requires a large shareholder to pay a price set by formula for all shares acquired in the back end of a two-tier acquisition. Typically, the price to be paid is the highest price the shareholder paid for any shares acquired during the first stage of the acquisition. Most fair price provisions do not apply if the large shareholder's offer is approved by the target company's board or if the bidder obtains a specified supermajority level of approval from the target's shareholders.
5. Poison pills	Poison pills are securities that entitle their holders to special rights if the issuing firm becomes the subject of a takeover bid. In a typical case, the poison pill is established by issuing a special dividend in the form of a right to purchase additional shares of the issuing firm's common stock. The rights trade with the common shares until a triggering event such as an unsolicited takeover bid. When such an event occurs, the rights detach and may be exercised at a low price by shareholders other than the bidder. In most poison pills, rights-holders can purchase shares in the bidding company at low prices if the bidder acquires control of the issuing company. Poison pills are also called shareholders rights plans.
6. Stakeholder clause	This refers to charter language that permits directors to consider the effects of their decisions on constituencies other than stockholders. For example, directors may, or may be required to, evaluate the impact of a proposed change in control on employees, host communities, or suppliers. The clause provides a target company's board members with an explicit legal basis to reject takeover bids that are attractive to shareholders.
7. Shareholder meeting requirements	This is a category of antitakeover provisions that inhibit attempts to circumvent the normal corporate decision-making process. These provisions include rules that prohibit shareholders other than directors or executives from calling a shareholder meeting, that require a supermajority of shareholders to call a special meeting, that impose minimum advance notice of stockholder proposals and/or nominations of directors, or that prohibit shareholders from voting to take actions that otherwise would have to await a special or annual shareholder meeting. These restrictions override default provisions in most states' incorporation statutes that permit special meetings or action by written consent.
8. Supermajority vote requirement	These provisions establish approval levels (say of 75 or 85 percent of outstanding votes) for actions that otherwise would require simple majority approval. These requirements often exceed the level of shareholder participation at a meeting, making action that requires supermajority approval very costly. Supermajority requirements can apply to attempts to replace directors, or to significant transactions such as mergers or asset sales. Those that apply to the amendment of bylaws or corporate charters often are referred to as lock-in provisions.
9. Unequal voting rights	Unequal voting rights occur when common shares do not all have the same voting rights. Under one typical plan called a dual class capitalization, two classes of stock exist, one with voting rights superior to the other. A second type of plan grants long-term stockholders super voting rights.

Table A1—*Continued*

Defense	Explanation
	Panel A: Firm-Level Takeover Defenses (*continued*)
10. Miscellaneous antitakeover provisions	This category refers to any of several provisions that can impede an outside bid for control. The most common among the miscellaneous provisions in our sample of IPO firms is language that states that board members can be removed "only for cause," thus making more difficult any attempt to remove directors that seek to impede a takeover attempt.
	Panel B: State Antitakeover Laws
11. Freeze-out law	Also called a business combination statute, this type of law prohibits a large shareholder from engaging in any business combination with the covered firm for a specified number of years unless approval is obtained from the firm's directors before the large shareholder acquires more than a specified fraction of shares. Even after the mandatory waiting period, most freeze-out laws allow the business combination to proceed only if the transaction satisfies fair price provisions. Thus, the typical freeze-out law is like a fair price law with a forced delay. The Delaware freeze-out law, adopted in 1988, covers a large number of corporations. It requires a three-year waiting period, although it permits business combinations during the freeze-out period that are approved by two-thirds of the voting stock not held by the interested shareholder. It also permits some business combinations with third parties, such as a sale of assets, during the freeze-out period.
12. Control share acquisition law	First adopted by Ohio in 1982, this type of law requires shareholder approval before a large shareholder may vote shares obtained in a control share acquisition. A control share acquisition refers to an accumulation of shares to above a threshold level, for example, to one-fifth the outstanding shares of a covered corporation.
13. Fair price law	This type of law imposes restrictions that are similar to fair price provisions adopted by many firms. The law regulates the back-end price in a two-tiered takeover bid or other significant business combination involving a large shareholder. The typical fair price law prohibits business combinations between the firm and a large stockholder unless one of two conditions is met. Either (1) prior approval is granted by a supermajority (e.g., 80 percent) of all outstanding voting stock and by a supermajority (e.g., two-thirds) of the outstanding stock not held by the interested stockholder, or (2) stockholders receive a stipulated price for the stock acquired by the large stockholder as part of the business combination. The stipulated price is set by a formula that guarantees the price paid will be very high.
14. Cash-out law	This type of law requires any person who acquires a large stake (e.g., 20 percent) in a firm to notify all other shareholders of the acquisition. All other shareholders are then entitled to sell their shares to the acquirer at a price at least as high as the highest price the acquirer paid in the period over which the large shareholder acquired its shares. This law has been adopted by only three states and was rescinded by one of these states.
15. Poison pill endorsement law	This type of law grants firms the right to adopt poison pill takeover defenses. Poison pill laws can be important because the right to use a poison pill defense is more secure when explicitly authorized by statute and is less likely to be limited by court action.

REFERENCES

Ambrose, Brent, and William Megginson, 1992, The role of asset structure, ownership structure, and takeover defenses in determining acquisition likelihood, *Journal of Financial & Quantitative Analysis* 27, 575–589.

Barber, Brad, and John Lyon, 1996, Detecting abnormal operating performance: The empirical power and specification of test-statistics, *Journal of Financial Economics* 41, 359–400.

Barry, Christopher B., and L. Adel Turki, 1997, Development stage IPOs as a vehicle for financing innovation, Working paper, Texas Christian University.

Bizjak, John, and Christopher Marquette, 1998, Are shareholder proposals all bark and no bite? Evidence from shareholder resolutions to rescind poison pills, *Journal of Financial and Quantitative Analysis* 33, 499–521.

Brennan, Michael, and Julian Franks, 1997, Underpricing, ownership and control in initial public offerings of equity securities in the U.K., *Journal of Financial Economics* 45, 391–4_4.

Brickley, James, Jeffrey Coles, and Rory Terry, 1994, Outside directors and the adoption of poison pills, *Journal of Financial Economics* 35, 371–390.

Byrd, John W., and Kent A. Hickman, 1992, Do outside directors monitor managers? Evidence from tender offer bids, *Journal of Financial Economics* 32, 195–221.

Coates, John, 2000, Explaining variation in takeover defenses: Failure in the corporate law market, Working paper, Harvard Law School.

Comment, Robert, and William Schwert, 1995, Poison or placebo? Evidence on the deterrence and wealth effects of modern antitakeover measures, *Journal of Financial Economics* 39, 3–43.

Daines, Robert, 2001, Classified boards and corporate control: Takeover defenses after the pill, Working paper, New York University.

Daines, Robert, and Michael Klausner, 2001, Do IPO charters maximize firm value? Antitakeover protection in IPOs, *Journal of Law, Economics, and Organization* 17, 83–120.

Danielson, Morris, and Jonathan Karpoff, 2001, Do pills poison operating performance? Working Paper, Temple University and Emory University.

DeAngelo, Harry, and Edward Rice, 1983, Antitakeover charter amendments and stockholder wealth, *Journal of Financial Economics* 11, 329–360.

Demsetz, H., 1983, The structure of ownership and the theory of the firm, *Journal of Law and Economics* 26, 375–393.

Easterbrook, Frank H., and Daniel R. Fischel, 1991, *The Economic Structure of Corporate Law* (Harvard University Press, Cambridge, Mass).

Eckbo, B. Espen, 1990, Valuation effects of greenmail prohibition, *Journal of Financial and Quantitative Analysis* 25, 491–505.

Field, Laura Casares, 1998, The IPO as the first stage in the sale of the firm, Working paper, Pennsylvania State University.

Friedlan, John M., 1994, Accounting choices of issuers of initial public offerings, *Contemporary Accounting Research* 11 (Summer), 1–23.

Jain, Bharat, and Omesh Kini, 1994, The post-issue operating performance of IPO firms, *Journal of Finance* 49, 1699–1726.

Jensen, Michael, 1993, The modern industrial revolution, exit, and the failure of internal control systems, *Journal of Finance* 48, 831–880.

Karpoff, Jonathan M., and Paul H. Malatesta, 1989, The wealth effects of second generation state takeover legislation, *Journal of Financial Economics* 25, 291–322.

Malatesta, Paul H., and Ralph A. Walkling, 1988, Poison pill securities: Stockholder wealth, profitability, and ownership structure, *Journal of Financial Economics* 20, 347–376.

Mello, Antonio, and John Parsons, 1998, Going public and the ownership structure of the firm, *Journal of Financial Economics* 49, 79–109.

Michaely, Roni, and Wayne Shaw, 1994, The pricing of initial public offerings: Tests of adverse-selection and signaling theories, *Review of Financial Studies* 7, 279–319.

Mikkelson, Wayne, and Megan Partch, 1989, Managers voting rights and corporate control, *Journal of Financial Economics* 25, 263–290.

Mikkelson, Wayne, Megan Partch, and Kshitij Shah, 1997, Ownership and operating performance of companies that go public, *Journal of Financial Economics* 44, 281–307.

Palepu, Krishna, 1986, Predicting takeover targets, *Journal of Accounting and Economics* 8, 3–35.

Ritter, Jay, 1991, The long-run performance of initial public offerings, *The Journal of Finance* 46, 3–27.

Rosenbaum, Virginia K., 1989, *Corporate Takeover Defenses* (Investor Responsibility Research Center, Inc., Washington, D.C.).

Rosenbaum, Virginia K., 1995, *Corporate Takeover Defenses* (Investor Responsibility Research Center, Inc., Washington, D.C.).

Rosenstein, Stuart, and Jeffrey G. Wyatt, 1990, Outside directors, board independence, and shareholder wealth, *Journal of Financial Economics* 26, 175–191.

Rydqvist, Kristian, and Kenneth Högholm, 1995, Going public in the 1980s: Evidence from Sweden, *European Financial Management* 1, 287–315.

Ryngaert, Michael, 1988, The effect of poison pill securities on shareholder wealth, *Journal of Financial Economics* 20, 377–417.

Song, Moon, and Ralph Walkling, 1993, The impact of managerial ownership on acquisition attempts and target shareholder wealth, *Journal of Financial & Quantitative Analysis* 28, 439–457.

Teoh, Siew-Hong, Ivo Welch, and T.J. Wong, 1998, Earnings management and the long-run market performance of initial public offerings, *Journal of Finance* 53, 1935–1974.

Yermack, David, 1996, Higher market valuation of companies with a small board of directors, *Journal of Financial Economics* 40, 185–211.

Zingales, Luigi, 1995, Insider ownership and the decision to go public, *Review of Economic Studies* 62, 425–448.

B
Internal Asset Restructurings

[4]

JOURNAL OF FINANCIAL AND QUANTITATIVE ANALYSIS VOL 30 NO 4, DECEMBER 1995

Can Takeover Losses Explain Spin-Off Gains?

Jeffrey W. Allen, Scott L. Lummer, John J. McConnell, and Debra K. Reed*

Abstract

This paper evaluates the conjecture that excess stock returns that have been documented around the announcement of corporate spin-offs represent, at least in part, the re-creation of value destroyed at the time of an earlier acquisition. We evaluate this question with a sample of spin-offs that originated as earlier acquisitions. At the time of the original acquisition, on average, announcement period returns to the bidder and the combined bidder and target firm are negative and significant. Additionally, announcement period returns at the time of the spin-off are negatively and significantly correlated with acquisition announcement period returns.

I. Introduction

Hite and Owers (1983), Miles and Rosenfeld (1983), and Schipper and Smith (1983) document significant positive excess stock returns of approximately 2 percent to 3 percent during the two-day interval surrounding announcements of corporate spin-offs. These authors investigate a number of hypotheses to explain the increases in shareholder wealth that accompany spin-offs. Among these are the hypothesis that shareholder gains represent wealth transfers from senior claimholders (Hite and Owers (1983); Schipper and Smith (1983)), that gains derive from the relaxation of regulatory or tax constraints (Schipper and Smith (1983)), that gains result from enhanced contracting efficiency between the parent and the subsidiary and between the parent, the subsidiary, and other third-party entities (Hite and Owers (1983)), and that gains come about because the spin-off reorganizes and streamlines an unwieldy managerial structure (Schipper and Smith (1983)).

The wealth expropriation hypothesis is rejected by the data. The other hypotheses receive some support, but do not appear to explain fully the shareholder wealth gains associated with corporate spin-offs. This paper investigates an alternative explanation—that the wealth gains associated with corporate spin-offs result from the correction of a prior mistake. The mistake was an unprofitable earlier

*Allen, Cox School of Business, Southern Methodist University, Dallas, TX 75272, Lummer, Ibbotson Associates, Chicago, IL 60601, McConnell, Krannert Graduate School of Management, Purdue University, West Lafayette, IN 47907-1310; and Reed, College of Business Administration, University of Oklahoma, Norman, OK 73019. The authors thank JFQA Referee David Ravenscraft for helpful comments.

acquisition and the spin-off represents the undoing of that unwise takeover. The roots of this explanation can be found in Porter (1987), Ravenscraft and Scherer (1987), Scherer (1988), and Kaplan and Weisbach (1992).

In particular, Porter studies 33 major U.S. corporations over the period 1950 through 1986 and finds that more than half of their acquisitions were subsequently divested. He states:

> Recognizing past diversification mistakes, some companies have initiated large-scale restructuring programs (Porter (1987), p. 43).

In a detailed analysis of acquisitions that occurred between 1971 and 1982, Kaplan and Weisbach (1992) classify acquisitions that are later divested as being either successful or unsuccessful. Among other things, they compare the announcement period stock returns of the acquirer and the combined returns of the acquirer and the acquired firms for those acquisitions in the unsuccessful group with those in the successful group. They find that average announcement period returns to the acquirer are significantly lower for the unsuccessful than for the successful set of acquisitions. They interpret these results to indicate that when an unwise acquisition is undertaken, investors revise their expectations downward for the performance of the combined entity and the stock price of the acquirer declines appropriately. They do not distinguish between spin-offs and divestitures by other means in their analysis.

In a related study, Mitchell and Lehn (1990) examine the announcement period returns of the acquisitions of a large sample of firms, some of which later became acquisition targets themselves and some of which did not. They find that acquisition announcement period returns are more negative for subsequently divested acquisitions than are announcement period returns for acquisitions that are not divested regardless of whether the acquirer later became an acquisition target. In short, both targets and nontargets tend to divest unsuccessful takeovers. Mitchell and Lehn do not relate acquisition announcement period returns to subsequent divestiture announcement period returns nor do they distinguish their sample according to whether the divestitures were by means of a sell-off or a spin-off.

To motivate the investigation in this paper, suppose that the motive for some corporate spin-offs is to unwind an unsuccessful prior acquisition. Further, suppose that unsuccessful acquisitions are, on average, accompanied by a negative stock price reaction. Finally, suppose that when the spin-off is eventually announced, the market responds by rewarding the shareholders of the then combined firm. If so, the average positive stock price reaction that has been observed around the announcements of corporate spin-offs generally may merely represent the re-creation of wealth that was destroyed (or expected to be destroyed) as a result of the earlier (unwise) acquisition.

In this paper, we investigate the "correction-of-a-mistake" hypothesis as an alternative explanation for the positive excess returns that accompany corporate spin-off announcements generally. Support for this hypothesis does not mean, of course, that all spin-offs are undertaken to correct an unwise acquisition. It only means that the average positive stock price response across a large sample of spin-offs contains a component that represents the re-creation of wealth dissipated in the subset of unwise acquisitions and, as a consequence, provides an upward bias to the average stock price response around spin-off announcements.

We conduct the investigation with a sample of 94 spin-offs in which the spun-off entity had been previously acquired by the parent firm. The predictions of the hypothesis are threefold: first, the acquirer's stock price reaction around the announcement of a takeover that becomes spin-off is negative. A stronger version of this prediction is that not only are the stock returns to the acquiring firm negative, but that the loss in value to the shareholders of the acquiring firm is greater than the gain to the shareholders of the target such that the post-announcement value of the combined firm is actually less than the sum of the preannouncement values of the separate entities. That is, not only do the shareholders of the acquiring firm lose value, but there is a net loss in value to the shareholders of both firms at the time of the acquisition. Second, the average stock price reaction around spin-offs of prior acquisitions is more positive than the average stock price reaction around spin-offs generally. That is, if the value gain documented for spin-offs generally is attributable to the re-creation of value from the undoing of unwise acquisitions, then the spin-off announcement period returns for the spin-offs in this sample should be greater than those for a random sample of spin-offs—some of which represent the divestiture of an internally generated subsidiary and some of which represent the divestiture of a prior acquisition. Third, the stock price reaction around the announcement of spin-offs of prior acquisitions is positive, but is negatively correlated with the stock price reaction around the original acquisition. That is, the "bigger" the acquisition "mistake," the greater the rebound in price when the spin-off is announced.

Both the first and third of these predictions are supported by the data: over a two-day interval that encompasses the acquisition announcement date and the prior day, over a nine-day interval that surrounds the date of the initial acquisition announcement, and over the interval from 10 days prior to the date of the initial announcement through the date on which the acquisition agreement is announced, the average excess returns to the acquiring firm are negative and significantly different from zero. The magnitudes of the average excess returns over the three intervals are −0.68 percent, −1.06 percent, and −3.07 percent, respectively, with associated p-values of 0.05, 0.10, and 0.00. Furthermore, even the stronger variation of the first prediction is supported by the data: for a subsample of 40 cases in which stock price data are available for both the acquirer and the target firm, the *combined* average excess return is negative and significantly different from zero over the two-day interval that encompasses the initial announcement and the prior day, over the nine-day interval surrounding the acquisition announcement, and over the interval from 10 days before the initial announcement through the date of the acquisition agreement. The magnitudes of the combined bidder and target excess returns for these three intervals are −0.65 percent, −1.91 percent, and −2.14 percent, respectively, with p-values of 0.10, 0.04, and 0.06.

As regards the second prediction, both the two-day and the nine-day announcement period average excess returns surrounding the *spin-off* announcement are positive (+2.15 percent and +2.49 percent, respectively) and highly significant (p-value = 0.00 for both), but the average excess returns for this sample of spin-offs is not much different from that of spin-offs generally or from that of a matched sample of spin-offs that did not originate as takeovers. The average excess returns over the two-day and nine-day announcement periods for the matched sample of spin-offs are +1.85 percent and +2.94 percent, respectively.

Finally, as regards the third prediction, when a cross-sectional regression is estimated in which the dependent variable is the two-day (or nine-day) spin-off announcement period return and the independent variables include the acquirer's announcement period return, measured over the two-day or nine-day announcement interval or over the interval from 10 days before the initial announcement through the acquisition agreement date (and several control variables), the coefficient of the acquirer's announcement period excess return is always negative and typically significantly different from zero. Similarly, when the dependent variable is the spin-off announcement period return and the independent variable is the *combined* excess return of the bidder and target firms at the acquisition (and certain control variables), the coefficient of the combined bidder and target excess return is always negative and typically significantly different from zero (regardless of the interval over which acquisition excess returns are measured). In short, the bigger the acquisition mistake (i.e., the more negative the acquisition returns), the greater the wealth creation at the announcement of the spin-off.

We interpret the results to indicate that, at least in part, the positive stock price reaction around the announcement of corporate spin-offs that has been documented by Hite and Owers (1983), Miles and Rosenfeld (1983), and Schipper and Smith (1983) represents the recapturing of wealth that is lost (or expected to be lost) as the result of an unwise acquisition, rather than a wealth gain associated with the spin-offs, per se. In a recent analysis, Seward and Walsh (1992) focus on organizational change as the explanation of the gains in corporate spin-offs generally and meet with only limited success in their efforts. It is possible that their analyses (and those of others who seek to explain the stock price increases associated with the announcement of corporate spin-offs) would prove more powerful if they were to control for the increase in share price due to the re-creation of value lost in those spin-offs that began as acquisitions. The results do not indicate that all gains in corporate spin-offs are the result of undoing unwise acquisitions. Indeed, our failure to support the second prediction of the "correction-of-a-mistake" hypothesis points in the opposite direction. But, the results do indicate that studies that attempt to explain spin-off announcement period returns should control for this effect.

There are some managerial implications that follow from the results as well. First, the negative correlation between acquisition returns and spin-off returns suggests that managers who ignore negative stock market returns at the time of an acquisition can redeem themselves, at least partially, by divesting the same acquisition. Second, the results indicate that one potential source of gains in "bust-up" takeovers is the recapturing of stock market losses that were sustained earlier in value-reducing acquisitions undertaken by the firm that later becomes the target of the bust-up takeover.

In the next section, we provide further background discussion of spin-offs and acquisitions to motivate the empirical analysis that follows. Section III describes the sample and Section IV reports the empirical results. The final section summarizes and concludes the paper.

II. Background

In a corporate takeover—whether by means of a merger or an acquisition—two free-standing companies are joined to comprise one entity. In those cases in which the acquired firm is later spun-off, the combined enterprise once again becomes two free-standing companies.

In the typical corporate spin-off, a corporation (customarily called the "parent") forms a new, separate corporation and ownership to a subset of the assets of the parent is transferred to the newly created corporate entity. The shares in the new corporation are then distributed on a pro rata basis to the shareholders of the parent firm. When the spin-off involves the divestiture of a previous acquisition, it is often the case that the acquired firm had been operating as a wholly owned subsidiary of the parent firm. In these cases, the parent need not create a new corporate entity. Rather, the shares in the wholly owned subsidiary are distributed directly to shareholders of the parent firm—again on a pro rata basis.

Evidence from the stock market indicates that the shareholders of acquiring firms do not gain and, perhaps, lose a little at the time of the acquisition. Evidence to this effect is presented in Dennis and McConnell (1986), Bradley, Desai, and Kim (1988), Asquith, Bruner, and Mullins (1983), and Jarrell and Poulsen (1989), among others. However, with a comprehensive sample of mergers and acquisitions that took place over the period 1965 through 1988, Loderer and Martin (1990) report an apparent time dependency in the stock market reaction to corporate takeovers. Roughly speaking, during the 1960s, acquirers earned positive abnormal returns; during the 1970s, acquirer returns are not significantly different from zero; and during the 1980s, takeover announcements were accompanied by significantly negative announcement returns to acquiring firms.

Explanations that have been postulated to explain the lack of a positive valuation effect for acquirers include the inability of the acquirer's management to foresee the undesirable effects of the acquisition or managerial motives to undertake the acquisition despite the undesirable consequences for shareholders. These motives include hubris (Roll (1986)), growth-based compensation (Jensen (1986)), entrenchment (Shleifer and Vishny (1989)), and other forms of self-serving behavior (Morck, Shleifer, and Vishny (1990)). These explanations offer a corollary that is tempting to apply when interpreting the documented positive returns that accompany spin-off announcements—a correction-of-a-mistake hypothesis. According to this hypothesis, the negative effect of an acquisition is unwound by a spin-off, thereby "causing" a positive effect on stock price, when the spin-off of a previously acquired company is announced. In a large sample, of course, only a fraction of the spin-offs derive from prior acquisitions. Still, if the wealth gains associated with this subset are substantial enough, it could "cause" an average positive announcement period return for an entire sample of spin-offs even if the spin-off of subsidiaries that did not previously result from a prior acquisition generate a zero wealth effect. Specifically, it is possible that "generic" spin-offs do not create value, per se, rather it is the subset of spin-offs made up of prior acquisitions that is responsible for the average positive stock price reaction across a large sample of spin-offs. If so, then the average announcement period abnormal return for this subset of spin-offs would be larger than the average return across a random sample of spin-offs. More specifically, announcement period returns to a sample of spin-offs that originate with a takeover should be larger than those to a sample of spin-offs that arise from the spin-off of "home-grown" subsidiaries.

Additionally, if it is assumed that the re-creation of value at the spin-off is roughly proportional to the value lost at the announcement of the original takeover, the spin-off announcement period returns should be negatively correlated with the acquisition announcement period returns. That is, if bigger acquisition mistakes result in larger negative wealth effects at the announcement of the acquisition, then correction of these mistakes should give rise to larger positive wealth effects at the announcement of the spin-off.

Of course, acquirers can divest themselves of acquisition mistakes by means other than spin-offs. The most popular, but not the only alternative, is by sale of the subsidiary to another firm. For our purposes, though, that is not as clean an experiment because the positive abnormal returns that accrue to the seller in a "sell-off" may represent "overpayment" by the second acquirer.[1] More importantly, we are interested in whether the apparent inability of Hite and Owers (1983), Miles and Rosenfeld (1983), Schipper and Smith (1983), and Seward and Walsh (1992) to discover the "cause" of the positive abnormal returns around spin-off announcements is because they have not looked in the all the right places or, at least, have not controlled for all factors that contribute to spin-off announcement period returns.

III. Sample Selection

To conduct our investigation, an initial list of 1142 stock distributions that took place over the period 1962 through 1991 was identified from a search of the S&P Quarterly Dividend Record.[2] To be considered a spin-off, we require that the distribution be a pro rata distribution of the stock of a wholly owned subsidiary. Thus, this criterion excluded 451 distributions of stock in publicly-traded companies and 131 distributions that involved a voluntary self-liquidation. We also eliminated 92 distributions in which the spin-off could not be confirmed in CCH's Capital Changes Reporter and 38 nonvoluntary spin-offs. These criteria reduced the sample to 430 confirmed voluntary spin-offs. To be included in the sample for further analysis, we require that the spin-off be announced in the WSJ and that the parent firm's shares be traded on the NYSE, the AMEX, or the OTC/NASDAQ System at the time of the spin-off. These criteria reduced the sample to 342. Of these, eight were deleted because the spin-off announcement was accompanied by an earnings announcement (three), a change in dividend policy (two), or the spin-off was used as a takeover defense (three).[3] We further determined that 13 of these

[1] Analyses of the wealth effects of corporate sell-off have been conducted by Alexander, Benson, and Kampmeyer (1984), Hite, Owers, and Rogers (1987), Jain (1986), Klein (1986), and Rosenfeld (1984), among others

[2] These sources identify many share distributions as spin-offs that do not qualify as spin-offs for our purposes To qualify as a spin-off for possible inclusion in our sample, we require that the spin-off be a tax-free pro rata distribution of a wholly owned subsidiary This criterion excludes partial distributions and the return of capital contributions

[3] We determined that the spin-off was used as a takeover defense if the WSJ article announcing the spin-off indicated that the spin-off was intended to thwart a hostile takeover (two) or if a hostile bidder discontinued a bid shortly after the spin-off announcement (one)

spin-offs were undertaken expressly for the purpose of facilitating the acquisition of the subsidiary by another company. Because our focus is on spin-offs that give rise to two free-standing entities, these 13 observations (both the spin-off and the acquisition) are deleted from the analysis. If the spin-off is undertaken to facilitate acquisition of the subsidiary by another company, the positive announcement period stock price returns may merely represent "overpayment" by the *new* acquirer of the spun-off subsidiary. Or, to put it another way, the second acquisition may be a mistake. We exclude these from the sample to avoid contaminating the results with such a possibility.[4]

For the 321 spin-offs that remain in the sample, three avenues of inquiry were pursued to determine whether the spun-off entity originated with an earlier acquisition. First, the WSJ article describing the spin-off was read to discover whether it contained any reference to an original acquisition.

The second avenue of inquiry was Moody's Manuals. The entry for each company in the Manuals includes a "corporate history" section that presents an abbreviated history of the company's origins, its acquisitions, and certain other significant events in the life of the corporation. The history also gives the year in which the acquisition was consummated. Because the corporate history is updated at regular intervals and because certain events, especially events that occurred a number of years earlier, are occasionally dropped from the most recent history, each parent company's history was read at three-year intervals retrogressively from the year of the spin-off through 1955 to identify whether a spun-off entity originated with an earlier acquisition.

The third, and most fruitful, source of such information is the "company history" section of the spun-off subsidiary's 10K filings following the spin-off. Of the 321 spin-offs with stock returns data and with an "uncontaminated" announcement in the WSJ, 94, or nearly 30 percent of the sample, were identified from the various sources as having originated with an acquisition.

To determine whether an announcement of the acquisition appeared in the WSJ, both the acquiring and the acquired firm's entry in the WSJ Index was searched for the year of and (if necessary) the two years prior to the takeover consummation date identified in the Moody's Manuals or the spun-off company's 10K. Because the Index begins in 1958, for the years 1955–1957, the WSJ itself was searched to identify acquisition announcement dates.

As is well known, the initial announcement date of some acquisitions is ambiguous because some acquisitions are first announced as "talks have begun" followed by subsequent progress reports on the status of negotiations until an "agreement in principle" is announced. In other cases, the first announcement is the announcement of an "agreement in principle." In some cases, the ambiguity regarding the initial "information" date is heightened because there appears to be "leakage" of information regarding the takeover prior to any public announcement. There is, thus, the question as to when the market first learns of the acquisition and the related question as to when the full valuation effect of the takeover is impounded in the stock price Because of this ambiguity, care must be taken in

[4]We concluded that a spin-off was undertaken to facilitate acquisition of the subsidiary if the WSJ article indicated that the purpose of the spin-off was to facilitate acquisition of the subsidiary by another firm or if the subsidiary was acquired by another company within 60 days of the spin-off

identification of acquisition announcement dates. For acquirers, we identify the initial announcement date as the first date that the bidder and target are mentioned in the same WSJ article. For targets, the initial announcement date is the first date that the target is mentioned as a takeover candidate prior to the takeover by the successful bidder firm. We follow this procedure because there are some instances in which the target is identified as an acquisition candidate prior to any identification of the bidder.

Finally, to enter the *acquisition* sample, we require that either the acquirer or the target firm have shares listed on the NYSE, the AMEX, or the OTC/NASDAQ System at the time of the acquisition and that there be no "contaminating" information about the firm in the WSJ over the three-day interval surrounding the initial acquisition announcement.[5]

Of the 94 spin-offs that could be identified as having originated with an acquisition, 78 have uncontaminated acquisition announcement dates in the WSJ and stock price data are available for 73 of the acquirers and for 40 of the acquired firms at the time of the initial acquisition announcement. For all 40 cases in which stock price data are available for the target, stock price data are also available for the acquirer. Thus, the acquisition sample includes 40 observations in which it is possible to calculate the combined announcement effect for the bidder and target firms.

In 52 of the 73 cases for which we have returns for the acquiring firm, the initial announcement is an announcement of an agreement in principle. These 52 include 19 of the 40 cases in which stock price data are available for both the bidder and the target firms. In 21 cases, the first article mentions that negotiations are underway, but an agreement on terms is not reached until a later date. We identify this later date as the "acquisition agreement" date.[6] In those cases in which the initial announcement is the announcement of an agreement in principle, we use the initial announcement date as the acquisition agreement date.

In 36 of the 40 cases for which we have returns for the target, both the bidder and target firm are identified in the same initial announcement. As noted above, in 19 of these, the initial announcement is an announcement that an agreement in principle has been reached by the two parties. In 17 other cases, the initial announcement indicates that talks have begun, but terms of the agreement are not announced until a later date—the acquisition agreement date. Finally, for four cases, only the target is identified in the initial article discussing the takeover and the bidder is not identified until a later date. In these four cases, the initial announcement date differs for the bidder and the target firms. For all the acquisitions in the sample, the time elapsed between the initial announcement date and the acquisition agreement date ranges from one day to 162 days with a mean of 60 days and a median of 43 days.

---

[5]Two observations were deleted because of concurrent announcements of dividend increases by the acquiring firm

[6]In all 33 acquisitions in which the target was not publicly-traded, the initial article in the WSJ states that the target "has been acquired" or "has agreed to be acquired" In 19 of the 40 cases in which the target is publicly traded and the initial announcement is an announcement of an agreement in principle, the WSJ article cites either "board approval by both firms," "an agreement in principle between both firms," the signing of a "definitive agreement," or "agreement on the terms of a proposed merger"

As might be expected, the mean and median market values of bidder firms ($804 million and $381 million, respectively) are substantially larger than those of target firms ($118 million and $60 million, respectively). One other interesting statistic is the time interval between acquisition and spin-off. The mean (median) time elapsed between acquisition and spin-off is 88 months, the maximum is 356 months, and the minimum is nine months.

IV. Statistical Analysis

To conduct the analysis of stock price reaction to the announcements of takeovers and spin-offs, the CRSP daily stock returns file is used in conjunction with the market model procedure as described, for example, in Brown and Warner (1985) or Linn and McConnell (1983). When sufficient data are available, market model parameters are estimated over the period from 160 days before through 61 days before the announcement. In two cases, stock data are not available for this entire time period. In those cases, all available data prior to 61 days before the event are used. In five cases, daily stock data are not available on the CRSP file. These are events that occurred prior to the beginning date of the NYSE/AMEX daily file (i.e., prior to 1962) for firms listed on the NYSE or the AMEX or prior to the beginning date of the OTC/NASDAQ daily file for firms listed on the OTC/NASDAQ System (i.e., prior to 1972). For these observations, daily stock price data were collected from the WSJ. For both spin-offs and acquisitions, announcement period excess returns are computed over a two-day interval (which includes the day in which the initial announcement appeared in the WSJ and the prior day) and over a nine-day interval centered on the initial WSJ publication date. For acquisition announcements, excess returns are also calculated over the interval, which begins 10 days before the initial announcement date and ends on the acquisition agreement date. This longer time interval is used to capture the "full" valuation effect of the takeover. By beginning 10 days prior to the initial announcement, the interval should capture any preannouncement leakage of information. By ending on the acquisition agreement date, this interval should account for the resolution of any residual uncertainty that may occur between the time the negotiations commence and the time at which they are completed.

A. Stock Valuation Effects for Acquiring Firms

As reported in Table 1, for the sample of acquiring firms for which stock price data are available, the average announcement period returns over the two-day and nine-day intervals surrounding the initial acquisition announcement and over the interval from 10 days before the initial announcement through the acquisition agreement date are −0.68 percent, −1.06 percent, and −3.07 percent, respectively, with p-values of 0.05, 0.10, and 0.00. Thus, the announcement period returns of takeovers that become spin-offs are negative and significantly different from zero regardless of the acquisition announcement interval considered. These results are consistent with the hypothesis that the documented shareholder gains surrounding corporate spin-offs *merely* represent the re-creation of value destroyed at the time of the acquisition.

TABLE 1

Announcement Period Excess Returns to Acquirers for Acquisitions during the Period 1955–1991 that Became Spin-Offs during the Period 1962–1991

(p-values in parentheses)

Sample	Sample Size	Day −1 through Day 0	Fraction Positive	Day −4 through Day +4	Fraction Positive	Day −10 through Agreement Date[a]	Fraction Positive
Full sample	73	−0.68% (0.05)	0.45	−1.06% (0.10)	0.44	−3.07% (0.00)	0.32
1955–1969	27	1.02% (0.24)	0.56	0.15% (0.56)	0.44	−0.67% (0.40)	0.30
1970–1979	29	−1.10% (0.16)	0.55	−0.21% (0.44)	0.55	−2.61% (0.11)	0.45
1980–1990	17	−2.14% (0.00)	0.12	−4.09% (0.00)	0.24	−6.89% (0.00)	0.12
Target firm's operations related to those of the acquiring firm[b]	24	0.12% (0.77)	0.50	−0.63% (0.31)	0.46	−2.55% (0.14)	0.33
Target firm's operations unrelated to those of the acquiring firm	49	−1.06% (0.02)	0.43	−1.27% (0.12)	0.43	−3.29% (0.00)	0.31
Acquisitions with stock data for both acquiring and target firms	40	−1.61% (0.00)	0.35	−2.72% (0.01)	0.35	−4.76% (0.00)	0.30

[a] Average cumulative excess return from 10 days before the first announcement in the WSJ through the date the merger or acquisition was approved by both firms

[b] The parent and target firms are considered to be related if any of the SIC codes of the four primary lines of business in each firm overlap at the two-digit level SIC information was obtained from Dun and Bradstreets' Million Dollar Directory for the year prior to the acquisition

There are, however, other ways to consider the stock price reaction for acquisitions that later become spin-offs. One is according to the time interval in which the takeover occurred. When the takeover sample is divided into three time periods—1955–1969, 1970–1979, and 1980–1989—the announcement period returns, also displayed in Table 1, can be compared to those documented by Loderer and Martin (1990) over roughly similar time periods. For example, using a two-day interval, for the period 1955–1969, the average announcement period return is +1.02 percent (p-value = 0.24); for the period 1970–1979, the announcement period return is −1.10 percent (p-value = 0.16); and for the period 1980–1989, it is −2.14 percent (p-value = 0.00). For the interval beginning 10 days prior to the initial announcement and ending with the acquisition agreement date, the returns are more negative, but display a similar time series pattern: for the period 1955–1969, the average announcement period return is −0.67 percent (p-value = 0.40); for the period 1970–1979, it is −2.51 percent (p-value = 0.11); and for the period 1980–1989, it is −6.89 percent (p-value = 0.00). Over roughly similar time periods, Loderer and Martin (1990) report higher announcement period returns for each "decade" for a large sample of various types of takeovers. For their three time intervals, the announcement period excess returns are +1.72 percent (t-statistic = 8.52), +0.57 percent (t-statistic = 5.49), and −0.07 percent (t-statistic = −0.34).[7] Thus, the market reaction to the takeovers in our sample is more negative than for the population of takeovers generally.

[7] Loderer and Martin employ a six-day announcement period to compute excess returns

Another way in which to consider acquisitions is whether the bidder and target come from the same industry. Porter (1987) argues that diversifying takeovers are more likely to result in failure than are those in which the bidder and target come from the same industry. Kaplan and Weisbach (1992) find scant support for this contention. They classify a sample of acquisitions into diversifying acquisitions and related acquisitions. A related acquisition is one in which the acquirer and target share a two-digit SIC code in any of their four primary lines of business. All others are classified as diversifying acquisitions. They report that the announcement period returns to the acquirer and target are not significantly different between the two samples. When we use the same classification scheme for our sample, we have 24 related and 49 diversifying acquisitions. As shown in Table 1, announcement period returns are mildly different between the two samples with the mean announcement period return being modestly lower for diversifying acquisitions than for related acquisitions, but the *p*-values for the differences between the mean returns of the two samples over the three time intervals considered are only 0.45, 0.81, and 0.78.

B. Stock Valuation Effects for Target Firms

A third way in which to consider takeovers is by analyzing returns to the shareholders of the target firm. Announcement period returns for target firms are reported in Table 2. These results are similar to those reported for target firms in prior studies.[8] Specifically, announcement period returns are significantly positive for every announcement period considered, for the full sample of target firms, for acquisitions during the 1960s, the 1970s, and the 1980s, and regardless of whether the acquisition is classified as related or diversifying. Additionally, the target's announcement period excess returns are much larger when measured over the interval from 10 days before the initial announcement through the acquisition agreement date than when measured over the announcement periods, suggesting that this interval more accurately gauges the full valuation effect of the takeover.

C. Stock Valuation Effects for Combined Acquirer and Target Firms

To this point, the analysis considers returns separately for bidder and target firms. As we noted at the outset, a stronger test of the "correction of a mistake" hypothesis is whether the combined value of the bidder and the target decline at the time of the acquisition. To consider this question, we compute a value-weighted excess return for the combined acquirer and target firms where the weights are the market values of the bidder and target firms measured five days prior to the takeover announcement. Equivalently, we have computed the market-adjusted change in the aggregate market values of the bidder and target firm during the acquisition announcement period and divided that by the sum of their market values five days prior to the takeover announcement. This value is computed for the 40 cases in which stock price data are available for both the bidder and the target firm. The results are reported in Table 3.

[8]See, for example, Bradley, Desai, and Kim (1988) and Dennis and McConnell (1986)

TABLE 2

Announcement Period Excess Returns to Targets in Acquisitions during the Period 1955–1991 that Became Spin-Offs during the Period 1962–1991

(*p*-values in parentheses)

Sample	Sample Size	Day −1 through Day 0	Fraction Positive	Day −4 through Day +4	Fraction Positive	Day −10 through Acquisition Agreement Date[a]	Fraction Positive
Full sample	40	6 44% (0 00)	0 70	9 04% (0 00)	0 72	16 21% (0 00)	0 85
1955–1969	9	5 11% (0 02)	0 67	7 75% (0 02)	0 78	15 43% (0 00)	0 89
1970–1979	16	4 84% (0 07)	0 63	8 29% (0 04)	0 63	15 08% (0 00)	0 81
1980–1990	15	8 93% (0 00)	0 80	10 60% (0 00)	0 80	18 84% (0 00)	0 87
Target firm's operations related to those of the acquiring firm[b]	12	5 24% (0 00)	0 50	8 86% (0 00)	0 75	13 65% (0 00)	0 83
Target firm's operations unrelated to those of the acquiring firm	28	6 95% (0 00)	0 79	9 11% (0 00)	0 71	17 40% (0 00)	0 86

[a]Average cumulative excess return from 10 days before the first announcement in the WSJ through the date the merger or acquisition was approved by both firms

[b]The parent and target firms are considered to be related if any of the SIC codes of the four primary lines of business in each firm overlap at the two-digit level SIC information was obtained from Dun and Bradstreets' Million Dollar Directory for the year prior to the acquisition

TABLE 3

Combined Value-Weighted Announcement Period Excess Returns to the Bidder and Target Firms for Acquisitions that Became Spin-Offs during the Period 1962–1991

(*p*-values in parentheses)

Sample	Sample Size	Day −1 through Day 0	Fraction Positive	Day −4 through Day +4	Fraction Positive	Day −10 through Acquisition Agreement Date[a]	Fraction Positive
Full sample	40	−0 65% (0 10)	0 48	−1 91% (0 04)	0 48	−2 14% (0 06)	0 45
1955–1969	9	1 69% (0 06)	0 67	1 07% (0 26)	0 67	4 28% (0 05)	0 67
1970–1979	16	−1 72% (0 02)	0 38	−3 42% (0 05)	0 38	−4 74% (0 02)	0 38
1980–1990	15	−0 91% (0 08)	0 47	−2 09% (0 10)	0 47	−3 18% (0 09)	0 40
Target firm's operations related to those of the acquiring firm[b]	12	0 00% (0 98)	0 50	−0 99% (0 25)	0 50	−2 92% (0 13)	0 42
Target firm's operations unrelated to those of the acquiring firm	28	−0 93% (0 08)	0 46	−2 30% (0 06)	0 46	−1 79% (0 17)	0 46

[a]Average cumulative excess return from 10 days before the first announcement in the WSJ through the date the merger or acquisition was approved by both firms

[b]The parent and target firms are considered to be related if any of the SIC codes of the four primary lines of business in each firm overlap at the two-digit level SIC information was obtained from Dun and Bradstreets' Million Dollar Directory for the year prior to the acquisition

Regardless of the announcement period considered, the average excess return is negative and statistically significantly different from zero. The average values of this statistic for the two-day announcement period, for the nine-day announcement period, and for the interval from 10 days before the initial announcement through the acquisition agreement date are −0.65 percent (p-value = 0.10), −1.91 percent (p-value = 0.04), and −2.14 percent (p-value = 0.06). On average, it appears that acquisitions that result in spin-offs actually destroy value in the combined firms—keeping in mind, of course, that this analysis is conducted with only the 40 observations for which data are available for both the bidder and the target firm.

We also separate this sample into those that occurred during the periods 1955–1969, 1970–1979, and 1980–1989 and according to whether the acquisitions are related or diversifying. As shown in Table 3, the combined average excess returns to acquirers and targets are negative and significantly different from zero during the 1970s and the 1980s and they are positive and (generally) significantly different from zero during the 1955–1960 period. Finally, Table 3 also shows combined average excess returns tend to be negative, although not always significantly different from zero, regardless of whether the acquisition is related or diversifying.

D. Stock Valuation Effects of Spin-Offs

The results to this point are generally consistent with the first prediction of the "correction of a mistake" hypothesis—on average, acquisitions that end up as spin-offs generate stock valuation losses at the time of the original acquisition. We now turn to the second prediction—that announcement returns are more positive for spin-offs that originated as a takeover than for spin-offs generally. To test this prediction, announcement period excess returns are calculated for our sample of spin-offs for the two-day and the nine-day announcement intervals surrounding the spin-off announcement. The results are presented in Table 4.

As shown, the average announcement period returns are +2.15 percent and +2 49 percent for the two-day and the nine-day intervals, respectively, with associated p-values of 0.00 and 0.00. Thus, the spin-off announcement period returns for takeovers that become spin-offs are comparable to those reported by Hite and Owers (1983), Miles and Rosenfeld (1983), and Schipper and Smith (1983) for a more comprehensive set of spin-offs that may include some spin-offs that began as acquisitions and some that are the result of a divestiture of an internally developed subsidiary.

For a more direct look at the question of concern here, we assemble a sample of spin-offs that did not originate as acquisitions and that occurred over the same time period and are of roughly the same relative size as those in the sample of spin-offs that did begin as takeovers. Specifically, we reviewed all spin-offs not identified as beginning with an acquisition for evidence that the subsidiary was internally developed. In those cases in which there is ambiguity, the spin-off was dropped from further consideration. Of the remaining set, a sample of 120 spin-offs was constructed such that the relative sizes of the spin-offs in this sample and the decades in which the spin-offs occurred match those of the spin-offs in the original sample of spin-offs that began as acquisitions. The two-day and the nine-day announcement period returns for the "nonacquisition" sample of spin-offs are

TABLE 4

Announcement Period Excess Returns to Parent Firms for Spin-Offs during the Period 1962–1991 of Acquisitions that Occurred during the Period 1951–1991

(p-values in parentheses)

Sample	Sample Size	Day −1 through Day 0	Fraction Positive	Day −4 through Day +4	Fraction Positive
Full sample (p-values)	94	2 15% (0 00)	0 73	2 49% (0 00)	0 71
1962–1969	7	2 31% (0 02)	0 86	5 05% (0 00)	0 71
1970–1979	16	1 04% (0 23)	0 50	1 54% (0 35)	0 56
1980–1991	71	2 38% (0 00)	0 77	2 48% (0 00)	0 75
Target firms' operations related to acquiring firm[b]	31	1 07% (0 00)	0 71	2 72% (0 00)	0 71
Target firms' operations unrelated to acquiring firm	63	2 68% (0 00)	0 75	2 38% (0 04)	0 71
Acquisitions with stock data for both acquiring and target firms	40	1 77% (0 00)	0 72	2 88% (0 02)	0 75
Two-day acquisition announcement period					
Positive excess returns to the parent at acquisition announcement	33	1 69% (0 00)	0 58	3 26% (0 00)	0 58
Negative excess returns to the parent at acquisition announcement	40	2 62% (0 00)	0 63	3 38% (0 00)	0 63
Value-increasing acquisitions[b]	19	1 02% (0 42)	0 63	3 08% (0 01)	0 68
Value-decreasing acquisitions[c]	21	2 39% (0 11)	0 81	3 33% (0 00)	0 81
Day − 10 through acquisition agreement date					
Positive excess returns to the parent at acquisition announcement	25	1 60% (0 02)	0 56	3 17% (0 01)	0 60
Negative excess returns to the parent at acquisition announcement	48	2 37% (0 00)	0 63	3 63% (0 00)	0 60
Value-increasing acquisitions[b]	18	0 25% (0 83)	0 56	1 67% (0 38)	0 61
Value-decreasing acquisitions[c]	22	3 02% (0 00)	0 86	4 44% (0 00)	0 86

[a]The parent and target firms are considered to be related if any of the SIC codes of the four primary lines of business in each firm overlap at the two-digit level SIC information was obtained from Dun and Bradstreets' Million Dollar Directory for the year prior to the acquisition

[b]For this sample, the combined weighted average excess return of the bidder and target firms was positive during the acquisition announcement period

[c]For this sample, the combined weighted average excess return of the bidder and target firms was negative during the acquisition announcement period

+1 85 percent and +2 94 percent, respectively, and neither is significantly different from the corresponding statistic for the sample of spin-offs that began with an acquisition. The p-values for the differences between the average announcement period returns for the two samples over the two-day and nine-day announcement periods are 0 84 and 0.71, respectively.

Given the apparent time dependency in announcement period returns to acquirers and the lack of any difference in returns for related and diversifying acquisitions, it is interesting to conduct a parallel analysis for spin-offs. These results are presented in Table 4. There does not appear to be any pronounced periodicity in the announcement period returns or, at least, not one that parallels that for acquisitions. For spin-offs, the average announcement period returns are lower during the 1970s than in either the 1960s or the 1980s, but all are positive and significantly different from zero. Similarly, the classification of spin-offs as related or unrelated to the parent does not reveal any strong pattern in returns. For the two-day announcement period, the average excess return to unrelated spin-offs (i.e., those that undo diversifying takeovers) is greater then the two-day return for related spin-offs (+2.68 percent vs. +1.07 percent), but this pattern is not sustained over the nine-day interval in which the excess return to unrelated spin-offs is slightly greater than the excess return to related spin-offs (+2.72 percent vs. +2.38 percent).

The primary concern of this study, however, is whether the observed wealth gains at spin-off announcements represent the re-creation of value destroyed (or expected to be destroyed) at the time of the acquisition. To this point, based on average announcement period returns, the data provide only modest support for that contention. We consider that issue further by separating the sample of spin-offs into those for which the acquirer's announcement period return at *acquisition* was positive and those for which it was negative and then examine the announcement period returns at *spin-off*. In so doing, we are conditioning spin-off announcement period returns on the market's reaction at the time of the acquisition. If the correction-of-a-mistake hypothesis is correct, spin-off announcement period returns should be significantly more positive for those spin-offs in which the acquisition return is negative than those for which the acquisition announcement period return is positive.

As shown in Table 4, spin-off announcement period returns are positive and significantly different from zero regardless of whether the acquisition announcement period return is positive or negative and regardless of the interval over which acquisition or spin-off returns are measured. Additionally, and consistent with the correction-of-a-mistake hypothesis, the average spin-off announcement period return is larger for acquirers that experienced a negative market response at the acquisition announcement than for acquirers that experienced a positive announcement period return at acquisition. For example, for the set of acquirers for which the two-day acquisition announcement period return is positive, the average two-day spin-off announcement period return is +1 69 percent (p-value = 0.00) and the average nine-day spin-off announcement period return is +3.26 percent (p-value = 0.00). For the sample of acquirers for which the two-day acquisition announcement period return is negative, the average two-day spin-off announcement period return is +2.62 percent (p-value = 0.00), and the average nine-day return is +3.38 percent (p-value = 0.00). However, the p-values for the differences between the spin-off announcement period returns for two samples are only 0.58 and 0.98. When acquirer returns are measured over the interval from 10 days before the initial announcement date through the acquisition agreement date and the sample is separated into those with positive and negative acquisition announcement period returns, the two-day spin-off announcement period return for the former set is +1.60 percent and the two-day spin-off announcement period return for the latter set is +2.37 percent, but the p-value for the difference between the two is only 0.54.

Similarly, when the spin-off announcement returns are measured over the nine-day interval, the average excess return is higher for the sample for which the acquirer experienced a negative excess return at the acquisition than for the sample that experienced a positive excess return at the acquisition, but the difference between the two has a p-value of only 0.89. Thus, while the average spin-off announcement period return is higher when the bidder experiences a negative excess return at acquisition than when the bidder experiences a positive excess return at the time of acquisition, the differences are not statistically significant.

The same experiment is conducted for the 40 takeovers in which stock returns are available for both the bidder and target firms at the acquisition date. That is, the 40 takeovers in this sample are separated according to whether the combined excess return of the bidder and target was positive or negative during the various acquisition announcement periods. As shown in Table 4, the spin-off announcement period returns are higher for the "value-decreasing" acquisitions than for the "value-increasing" acquisitions when acquisition announcement period returns are measured over the two-day interval around the acquisition announcement, but the differences between the spin-off announcement period returns (whether measured over two days or nine days) are often not significantly different from each other at the 0.10 level. The differences between the samples are larger at the spin-off announcement date when the acquisition returns are measured over the interval from 10 days before the initial announcement through the acquisition agreement date, but they are still not significantly different from each other at the 0.10 level. For the set with negative acquisition announcement period excess returns for this interval, the two-day average spin-off announcement period excess return is +3.02 percent; for the set with positive excess returns over this interval, the two-day average spin-off announcement period excess return is only +0.25 percent.[9] The p-value for the difference between the two is only 0.18. Similar results are obtained when the spin-off announcement period returns are measured over the nine-day interval surrounding the spin-off announcement. In this case, the p-value for the difference between the two samples is 0.26.[10]

E. Multivariate Tests

Although the differences are not statistically significant, the univariate tests suggest that value-decreasing takeovers are associated with larger spin-off returns than are value-increasing takeovers. However, there may be other phenomena at work in the data as well (for example, a periodicity effect) that may influence the apparent relation between acquisition announcement returns and spin-off announcement returns. To control for other factors that may influence returns, we estimate two sets of cross-sectional multivariate regressions using the maximum likelihood regression procedure of Eckbo, Maksimovic, and Williams (1990). In the first set of regressions (reported in Table 5), the dependent variable is the two-day spin-off announcement period excess return. In the second set of regressions

[9]For the set with negative acquisition announcement period returns, the average acquisition announcement period excess return is −8 99 percent For the set with positive acquisition announcement period excess returns, the average acquisition announcement period return is +5 24 percent

[10]Although not reported in the table, when the sample is split according to the acquirer's nine-day (or combined firm nine-day) announcement period return, the results are very similar to those in Table 4

(reported in Table 6), the dependent variable is the nine-day spin-off announcement period excess return. Parallel regressions are estimated for each of the two dependent variables. In the first regression in each set, the independent variables include dummy variables to indicate whether the spin-off occurred during the 1970s or the 1980s, the dollar market value of the spun-off subsidiary as a fraction of the dollar market value of the pre-spin-off parent firm (i.e., to control for differences in the relative sizes of the parent and the subsidiary), and a dummy variable to indicate whether the acquirer and the target are in the same industry according to their two-digit SIC code (i.e., to answer the question of whether the original acquisitions are diversifying or related). One other factor that may influence the relation between the spin-off and acquisition announcement period excess returns is the relative length of time between the original acquisition and the spin-off. For example, the effect may be stronger for acquisitions and spin-offs that occur relatively closer in time to each other. To control for this effect, two dummy variables are included in the regressions. The first indicates whether the number of months that elapsed between the acquisition and the spin-off is 0 to 44. The second indicates whether the number of months lies between 45 and 88. Recall that the median number of months between the acquisition and the spin-off is 88.

The independent variables in the second regression in both Tables 5 and 6 include all those in the first regression plus the acquirer's two-day acquisition announcement period excess return. The independent variables in the third regression in each table include all those in the second except that the acquirer's nine-day announcement period excess return replaces the acquirer's two-day announcement period excess return. In the fourth regression, the independent variables are the same as those in the second, except that the acquirer's excess return calculated over the interval from 10 days before the initial announcement through the acquisition agreement date replaces the acquirer's two-day excess return. The sample size for these four regressions is 73. The results are reported in columns (1) through (4) of Tables 5 and 6.

According to the tables, relative size is a significant explanatory variable in each regression (all p-values < 0.01). The time period of the spin-off and the dummy variable for whether the parent and the subsidiary are related is not statistically significant in any of the regressions. There is some modest evidence that the relative time that has elapsed between the takeover and the spin-off is important when the dependent variable is the two-day excess return (Table 5), but not when the dependent variable is the nine-day spin-off excess return (Table 6).[11] Most importantly for the question addressed in this paper, the coefficient of the acquisition announcement period return is negative in each of the relevant regressions, indicating that higher spin-off returns are associated with lower returns to the acquiring firm at the acquisition. The significance level of this relation differs across the regressions. The relation is most significant in the regressions in Table 6 in which the dependent variable is the nine-day spin-off announcement period excess return. The p-values here are 0.02, 0.04, and 0.06. In Table 5, the p-values are 0.37, 0.08, and 0.02.

[11] We also counted the number of months that elapsed between the takeover and the spin-off and included that as a measure of time between the two events That variable also does not show up as significant in the regressions

TABLE 5

Cross-Sectional Regression Analysis of Two-Day Announcement Period Excess Returns at the Spin-Off Announcement of Previously Acquired Subsidiaries, 1962–1991

Independent Variable	[1]	[2]	[3]	[4]	[5][a]	[6][a]	[7][a]
Intercept	0.0260 (0.27)	0.0262 (0.27)	0.0268 (0.25)	0.0285 (0.21)	0.0336 (0.56)	0.0387 (0.47)	0.0424 (0.45)
Spin-off in 1970s	−0.0220 (0.40)	−0.0222 (0.40)	−0.0195 (0.45)	−0.0238 (0.34)	−0.0213 (0.72)	−0.0289 (0.60)	−0.0365 (0.51)
Spin-off in 1980s	−0.0025 (0.91)	−0.0025 (0.91)	−0.0040 (0.85)	−0.0068 (0.76)	−0.0163 (0.76)	−0.0216 (0.66)	−0.0225 (0.68)
Relative size of spin-off[b]	0.1081 (0.00)	0.1080 (0.00)	0.1114 (0.00)	0.1065 (0.00)	0.0877 (0.21)	0.0954 (0.15)	0.0878 (0.12)
Related acquisition[c]	−0.0199 (0.12)	−0.0201 (0.12)	−0.0181 (0.15)	−0.0188 (0.13)	−0.0064 (0.73)	−0.0052 (0.76)	−0.0108 (0.55)
Interval from acquisition to spin-off 0–44 months	−0.0262 (0.06)	−0.0260 (0.07)	−0.0327 (0.02)	−0.0320 (0.02)	−0.0248 (0.20)	−0.0320 (0.08)	−0.0281 (0.14)
Interval from acquisition to spin-off 45–88 months	−0.0092 (0.53)	−0.0093 (0.52)	−0.0118 (0.41)	−0.0128 (0.36)	−0.0049 (0.80)	−0.0122 (0.52)	−0.0089 (0.66)
Acquirer's day 0 to day −1 excess return		−0.0310 (0.39)					
Acquirer's day −4 to day +4 excess return			−0.1485 (0.08)				
Acquirer's day −10 through agreement date excess return				−0.1317 (0.02)			
Acquirer and target combined day 0 to day −1 excess return					−0.1542 (0.52)		
Acquirer and target combined day −4 to day +4 excess return						−0.2398 (0.03)	
Acquirer and target combined day −10 through agreement date excess return							0.2412 (0.03)
Sample size	73	73	73	73	40	40	40
R^2	0.147	0.198	0.228	0.252	0.138	0.185	0.194

The dependent variable is the two-day spin-off announcement period excess return. Regressions are estimated using the maximum likelihood procedure of Eckbo, Maksimovic, and Williams (1990) (*p*-values are in parentheses).

[a] Includes the 40 observations where stock price data are available for the acquiring and target firms at the acquisition date.

[b] Calculated as the market value of the spun-off firm measured on the first day of trading following the spin-off divided by the market value of the parent firm on the day prior to the spin-off ex-date.

[c] The parent and target firms are considered to be related if any of the SIC codes of the four primary lines of business in each firm overlap at the two-digit level. SIC information was obtained from Dun and Bradstreets' Million Dollar Directory for the year prior to the acquisition.

The regressions in columns (5) through (7) of each table parallel those in columns (2) through (4), except that the acquirer's acquisition excess return is replaced as an independent variable by the *combined* excess return to the bidder and the target firm. As might have been anticipated from the univariate tests of Table 4, the relation between spin-off announcement period excess returns and takeover announcement period excess returns is slightly stronger when the independent variable is the combined change in value of the bidder and target firms. In Table 6, the *p*-values are 0.07, 0.01, and 0.05 and, in Table 5, they are 0.52, 0.03, and 0.03. The only regression in which the coefficient is not significant on at least the 0.10 level is the one in which both the spin-off and acquisition announcement period excess returns are measured over a two-day interval. The relation is much stronger when both the spin-off and the acquisition announcement period returns are measured over longer intervals. A plausible (although not airtight) argument could be made that, given the leakage that often surrounds corporate takeovers and

TABLE 6

Cross-Sectional Regression Analysis of Nine-Day Announcement Period Excess Returns at the Spin-Off Announcement of Previously Acquired Subsidiaries, 1962–1991

Independent Variable	[1]	[2]	[3]	[4]	[5][a]	[6][a]	[7][a]
Intercept	0.0182	0.0122	0.0183	0.0198	−0.0035	0.0027	0.0051
	(0.50)	(0.65)	(0.50)	(0.48)	(0.94)	(0.95)	(0.92)
Spin-off in 1970s	0.0058	0.0120	0.0075	0.0070	0.574	0.0486	0.0440
	(0.85)	(0.69)	(0.80)	(0.82)	(0.25)	(0.30)	(0.39)
Spin-off in 1980s	−0.0112	−0.0073	−0.0075	−0.0103	0.0074	0.0014	0.0013
	(0.65)	(0.77)	(0.76)	(0.68)	(0.87)	(0.97)	(0.97)
Size of spin-off[b]	0.1467	0.1417	0.1378	0.1335	0.0915	0.0980	0.0900
	(0.00)	(0.00)	(0.00)	(0.00)	(0.12)	(0.07)	(0.13)
Related acquisition[c]	−0.0083	0.0059	0.0004	0.0025	0.0255	0.0259	0.0213
	(0.57)	(0.69)	(0.98)	(0.89)	(0.10)	(0.07)	(0.18)
Interval from acquisition to spin-off 0–44 months	0.0074	0.0056	0.0054	0.0001	0.0023	−0.0040	0.0040
	(0.65)	(0.74)	(0.75)	(0.99)	(0.88)	(0.80)	(0.81)
Interval from acquisition to spin-off 45-88 months	−0.0021	−0.0014	−0.0076	−0.0074	0.0095	0.0022	0.0058
	(0.90)	(0.93)	(0.65)	(0.66)	(0.57)	(0.89)	(0.52)
Acquirer's day 0 to day −1 excess return		−0.4903					
		(0.02)					
Acquirer's day −4 to day +4 excess return			−0.2074				
			(0.04)				
Acquirer's day −10 through agreement date excess return				−0.1843			
				(0.06)			
Acquirer and target combined day 0 to day −1 excess return					−0.2272		
					(0.07)		
Acquirer and target combined day −4 to day +4 excess return						−0.2553	
						(0.01)	
Acquirer and target combined day −10 through agreement date excess return							−0.1940
							(0.05)
Sample size	73	73	73	73	40	40	40
R^2	0.121	0.185	0.197	0.191	0.211	0.322	0.218

The independent variable is the nine-day spin-off announcement period excess return. Regressions are estimated using the maximum likelihood procedure of Eckbo, Maksimovic, and Williams (1990) (*p*-values are in parentheses).

[a] Includes the 40 observations where stock price data are available for the acquiring and target firms at the acquisition date.

[b] Calculated as the market value of the spun-off firm measured on the first day of trading following the spin-off divided by the market value of the parent firm on the day prior to the spin-off ex-date.

[c] The parent and target firms are considered to be related if any of the SIC codes of the four primary lines of business in each firm overlap at the two-digit level. SIC information was obtained from Dun and Bradstreets' Million Dollar Directory for the year prior to the acquisition.

other major corporate events, the longer time intervals are the more appropriate ones to consider. We will not make that argument, but merely note that the overall picture that appears to emerge from the analysis is that there is a negative relationship between spin-off announcement period returns and acquisition announcement period returns and that the relationship is more significant for the analysis that uses the longer announcement period.[12]

V. Comments and Conclusion

Several prior studies document average positive excess returns of +2 percent to +3 percent around announcements of corporate spin-offs. While a number of

[12] Each of the regressions was checked for outlier observations. In each case where the residuals gave evidence of an outlier, those observations were dropped from the analysis and the regression was reestimated. In no case did the sign of any coefficient change and, in no case did a coefficient that was significant at the 0.05 level become insignificant at that level.

hypotheses have been explored to explain this effect, none is able to explain fully the shareholder gains associated with corporate spin-offs. This paper considers the conjecture that the gains associated with spin-offs generally come about because some spin-offs represent the undoing of an earlier unwise acquisition. According to this "correction-of-a-mistake" hypothesis, the average stock price increases surrounding spin-offs merely represent the re-creation of wealth lost at the time of the original acquisition. The primary predictions of this hypothesis are as follows: first, at the time of acquisitions, the announcement period excess returns to the bidding firm are negative for acquisitions that later result in spin-offs. A stronger version of this prediction is that the combined announcement period excess return to the bidder and the target at the time of the acquisition are negative for acquisitions that later become spin-offs. Second, the average spin-off announcement period excess return for a sample of acquisitions that subsequently became spin-offs is larger than for spin-offs generally and for a sample of spin-offs that did not begin as acquisitions. Third, the spin-off announcement period excess returns for spin-offs that began with an acquisition are negatively correlated with the original acquisition announcement period excess returns. That is, the greater the original mistake, the greater the rebound when the spin-off is announced.

We test the various predictions of the correction-of-a-mistake hypothesis with a sample of 94 spin-offs that occurred over the period 1962 through 1991. In general, the results are consistent with the first and third predictions of the hypothesis, but not the second.

There are both managerial implications and implications for researchers that follow from the results. For managers, the results suggest that managers who undertake poor acquisitions can redeem themselves, at least partially, by subsequently divesting the unwise acquisition. For researchers, the results suggest that future investigations of the source of gains associated with spin-offs may be more successful if the investigators control for whether the spun-off subsidiary was the target of a prior acquisition.

References

Alexander, G. J ; P. G. Benson, and J. M. Kampmeyer "Investigating the Valuation Effects of Announcements of Voluntary Corporate Sell-offs" *Journal of Finance,* 39 (June 1984), 503–517.

Asquith, P.; R. F Bruner; and D. W Mullins. "The Gains to Bidding Firms from Mergers" *Journal of Financial Economics,* 11 (April 1983), 121–139

Bradley, M , A Desai; and E H Kim. "Synergistic Gains from Corporate Acquisitions and Their Division between the Stockholders of Target and Acquiring Firms" *Journal of Financial Economics,* 21 (May 1988), 3–40

Brown, S. J., and J B. Warner "Using Daily Stock Returns The Case of Event Studies" *Journal of Financial Economics,* 14 (March 1985), 3–31.

Dennis, D. K , and J J McConnell "Corporate Mergers and Security Returns" *Journal of Financial Economics,* 16 (June 1986), 143–187

Eckbo, B E., V Maksimovic, and J Williams. "Consistent Estimation of Cross-Sectional Models in Event Studies" *Review of Financial Studies,* 3 (No 3, 1990), 343–365

Hite, G L., and J. E Owers. "Security Price Reactions around Corporate Spin-off Announcements." *Journal of Financial Economics,* 12 (Dec 1983), 409–436

Hite, G. L.; J E Owers, and R C Rogers "The Market for Interfirm Asset Sales. Partial Sell-offs and Total Liquidations." *Journal of Financial Economics,* 18 (June 1987), 229–252.

Jain, P. C. "The Effect of Voluntary Sell-off Announcements on Shareholder Wealth." *Journal of Finance,* 40 (March 1985), 209–224

Jarrell, G , and A Poulsen "Stock Trading before the Announcement of Tender Offers· Insider Trading or Market Anticipation?" *Journal of Law, Economics and Organization,* 5 (Fall 1989), 225–248.

Jensen, M C "Agency Costs of Free Cash Flow, Corporate Finance and Takeovers" *American Economic Review,* 76 (May 1986), 323–329

Kaplan, S N , and M S Weisbach "The Success of Acquisitions: Evidence from Divestitures" *Journal of Finance,* 47 (March 1992), 107–138.

Klein, A "The Timing and Substance of Divestiture Announcements· Individual Simultaneous and Cumulative Effects." *Journal of Finance,* 41 (July 1986), 685–696.

Linn, S. C , and J J McConnell "An Empirical Investigation of the Impact of Antitakeover Amendments on Common Stock Prices" *Journal of Financial Economics,* 22 (April 1983), 361–399

Loderer, C , and K Martin "Corporate Acquisition Announcements Time Series Patterns." Working Paper, Univ. of Iowa (1990).

Miles, J A , and J D Rosenfeld "The Effect of Voluntary Spin-off Announcements on Shareholder Wealth" *Journal of Finance,* 38 (Dec 1983), 1597–1606

Mitchell, M L , and K Lehn "Do Bad Bidders Become Good Targets?" *Journal of Political Economy,* 98 (April 1990), 372–398

Morck, R , A. Shleifer; and R W Vishny "Do Managerial Objectives Drive Bad Acquisitions?" *Journal of Finance,* 45 (March 1990), 31–48.

Porter, M. "From Competitive Advantage to Corporate Strategy" *Harvard Business Review,* 65 (May–June 1987), 43–59

Ravenscraft, D J , and F M Scherer *Mergers, Selloffs and Economic Efficiency* Washington, D C The Brookings Institute (1987)

Roll, R "The Hubris Hypothesis of Corporate Takeovers" *Journal of Business,* 59 (April 1986), 197–216

Rosenfeld, J D. "Additional Evidence on the Relation between Divestiture Announcements and Shareholder Wealth" *Journal of Finance,* 39 (Dec 1984), 1437–1448

Scherer, F M. "Corporate Takeovers The Efficiency Arguments" *Journal of Economic Perspectives,* 2 (Winter 1988), 69–82

Schipper, K , and A Smith "Effects of Recontracting on Shareholder Wealth The Case of Voluntary Spin-offs" *Journal of Financial Economics,* 12 (Dec 1983), 437–467

Seward, J , and J Walsh "The Governance and Control of Voluntary Corporate Spin-offs An Investigation of the Contracting Efficiency Hypothesis" Working Paper, Dartmouth College and Univ of Michigan (1992)

Shleifer, A , and R W Vishny "Management Entrenchment The Case of Manager-Specific Investments" *Journal of Financial Economics,* 25 (Nov 1989), 123–139

[5]

ELSEVIER

Journal of Financial Economics 37 (1995) 67–87

JOURNAL OF Financial ECONOMICS

Corporate focus and stock returns

Robert Comment*[,a,b], Gregg A. Jarrell[a]

[a] *University of Rochester, Rochester, NY 14627, USA*
[b] *Office of Economic Analysis, U.S. Securities and Exchange Commission, Washington, DC 20549, USA*

(Received May 1991; final version received December 1993)

Abstract

Greater corporate focus is consistent with shareholder wealth maximization. Diseconomies of scope in the 1980s are confirmed by a trend towards focus or specialization, a positive relation between stock returns and focus increases, and the failure of diversified firms to exploit financial economies of scope (coinsurance of debt or reliance on internal capital markets). Large focused firms were less likely to be subject to hostile takeover attempts than were other firms, but diversified firms were distinguished in the 1980s mostly by being relatively active participants, as both buyers and sellers, in the market for corporate control.

Key words: Diversification; Business segment; Leverage; Internal capital market; Takeover
JEL classifications: G32; G34

1. Introduction

Conventional wisdom holds that economies of scope have been reversed in the 1980s. Managers are now advised to eschew diversification and to shrink the

*Corresponding author.

The Bradley Policy Research Center, William E. Simon Graduate School of Business Administration, University of Rochester, provided support for this research. This research was presented at SUNY Buffalo, the University of Chicago, the University of Rochester, and the 1992 ASSA and WEA meetings. Special thanks to our discussants Steven Kaplan, Michael Rozeff, and Karen Wruck. Any opinions expressed are those of the authors, not those of the Securities and Exchange Commission or its staff.

SSDI 0304405X9400777 X

far-flung enterprises that resulted from past diversification strategies. In their public statements, managers are apt to say that they want to concentrate on a core business, and they are likely to rationalize mergers and growth strategies, as well as divestitures and restructuring, as reflecting a strategy of specialization. This view marks a change from the steady increase in diversification since the 1950s and from the several theoretical justifications for diversification that have been advanced, including (i) managerial economies of scale, (ii) economies of scope in production and marketing, and (iii) financial synergies such as earnings smoothing and the efficiencies that arise with an internal capital market. The new emphasis on specialization is consistent with Jensen (1988), who argues that corporate diversification programs exemplify the theory that managers of firms with unused borrowing power and large free cash flows are more likely to undertake low-benefit or even value-destroying investments. Similarly, Meyer, Milgrom, and Roberts (1992) argue that failing businesses can have too-ready access to cross-subsidies when they are part of a diversified firm.

Our findings show a steady trend toward greater focus during the 1980s. We find that 55.7% of exchange-listed firms had a single business segment in 1988, compared to 38.1% in 1979, with other measures showing smaller proportionate increases. Perhaps more important, the trend toward greater focus is associated with greater shareholder wealth. This relation is not trivial in economic magnitude. A change of 0.1 in the absolute value of a revenue-based Herfindahl index of focus is associated with a stock return of about 4%, and changes this large occur about one year in ten. Adding or subtracting one business segment is associated with a return of about 5%, and changes this large occur about one year in eight.

We show that diversified firms do not take advantage of some of the underlying efficiencies thought to motivate diversification. We consider whether diversification (1) permits a greater use of debt (because the coinsurance of debt reduces default rates), (2) permits a substitution of intersegment cash transfers for arms-length transactions (because transaction costs are lower in internal capital markets than in external capital markets), or (3) increases the likelihood of takeover because (conversely) these intersegment transfers accommodate a waste of free cash flow. We find that debt does not increase systematically with diversification and that diversified firms do not rely any less on external capital market transactions. There is some evidence that diversification does make firms more likely to be takeover targets.

We have several reservations about these results. First, much of the trend in focus stems from sample turnover rather than from same-firm changes. Turnover was unusually high in the 1980s and new firms had higher focus than departing firms, but we still observe increases in focus on a same-firm basis for old-line firms (in the sample at the start of the decade). Second, our regression estimates of the wealth effects of focus are only reliably positive when an accounting measure of performance is included in the regression. Their inclusion could impart an upward bias to the effect of focus even after controlling, as we do, for the wealth effects of acquisitions and divestitures. Third, our exclusion of part-year returns (following the last accounting disclosure) for delisted companies could impart a downward bias. We tend to exclude the stock returns of acquisition targets, which are typically positive, as well as post-takeover changes in focus, which Bhagat, Shleifer, and Vishny (1990) find to be positive. Finally, weakness in our proxy measures of focus could explain the apparent failure of diversified firms to exploit financial efficiencies. Our measures of focus are validated, however, by evidence that the effects of corporate diversification on risk parallel the well-known effects of portfolio diversification on risk. Moreover, our measures of focus correlate well with frequency of participation in the market for corporate control: 22.8% of the most diversified firms participated in large acquisitions or divestitures each year versus just 3.4% of pure-play firms.

We discuss our sample and focus measures in Section 2. In Section 3 we present empirical evidence on the trend toward focus over the 1980s, while Section 4 covers the relation between changes in focus and stock returns. Participation in the market for corporate control is covered in Section 5, reliance on external capital markets is covered in Section 6, and the effect of focus on leverage and risk is covered in Section 7. Our conclusions appear in Section 8.

2. Measuring focus

Business-segment data is available from Compustat as of fiscal years ending June 1978, and our data stop with years ending October 1989. We restrict our attention to NYSE- and ASE-listed firms (about two thousand per year) because most unlisted firms report just one line of business each year. Although not reported here, average focus also increased among unlisted firms. Focus can change as a company divests or acquires assets, or directs its capital spending into new businesses, and it can shift over time due to divergent growth rates for the industries in which a company participates. We measure the change in focus over one-year intervals, aggregating across underlying events. This is necessary because segment data is reported annually, but appropriate also if focus-changing events tend to be heterogeneous or unannounced. In addition, judging from their public statements, top managers have come to view focus as a policy objective in and of itself. Our analysis of the wealth effects of undifferentiated changes in focus fills a void on either score.

Our use of segment-reporting data means that we rely on managers to define what constitutes a distinct business at their firms, subject to accounting standards and the demands of Wall Street analysts. An alternative source of information on focus is the Census Bureau's data on employment at individual plants and establishments, which require the use of standard industry classification (SIC) codes to combine establishments into business segments. These data have the advantage of being available for privately-held firms. Liebeskind and Opler (1992) analyze an extension of these data maintained by TRINET Inc., and find that average focus increased during the 1980s for both public and private firms. The trend was identified by Lichtenberg (1991), also using Compustat data, although he attributes it to shifts in reporting tastes. Managerial discretion is limited by the Financial Accounting Standards Board, which requires separate accounting for any segment amounting to more than 10% of the consolidated firm's sales, operating profits, or assets. What discretion remains will affect some measures of focus more than others. Herfindahl indexes give disproportionately small weight to the smaller segments that may or may not be reported, and our results hold for these measures as well as for the number of segments.

We use Compustat business-segment data to calculate five different measures of focus: (1) the proportion of firms reporting just one segment, (2) the number of segments reported by management, (3) the number of four-digit SIC codes assigned by Compustat, (4) a revenue-based Herfindahl index, and (5) an asset-based Herfindahl index. Compustat assigns as many as two four-digit SIC codes to each segment. A revenue-based Herfindahl index, F_{jt}, reflects the degree to which revenues are concentrated in just a few of a company's business segments. It is calculated across N_{jt} segments for the jth firm in fiscal year t as the sum of the squares of each segment i's revenue as a proportion of total revenue:

$$F_{jt} = \sum_{i=1}^{N_{jt}} \left(X_{ijt} \Big/ \sum_{i=1}^{N_{jt}} X_{ijt} \right)^2,$$

where X_{ijt} is the revenue attributable to a segment. An asset-based index is calculated in the same way using the book value of the identifiable assets of the segment. Segment revenue is defined to exclude intercompany sales, interest, nonoperating income, equity in earnings of unconsolidated subsidiaries, other income, rental income, gain on sale of securities or fixed assets, discontinued operations, excise taxes, and royalty income. We calculate changes in focus as first differences in F_{jt}.

3. Trend in focus

There is evidence of a trend toward diversification in American companies over the period 1950–1970. Ravenscraft and Scherer (1987) report that the proportion of manufacturing industry acquisitions that the Federal Trade Commission (FTC) characterizes as purely conglomerate in nature rose from 5% of total assets acquired in 1950–55, to 18% in 1956–63, to 36% in 1964–72, and fell to 32% in 1973–77. Also, the 471 companies in the FTC's Line of

Business Survey increased their average number of lines from under three in 1950 to over seven in 1975, while the top 200 companies increased their average number of lines from 4.8 to 10.9. This trend suggests that meaningful economies of scope existed through the 1960s.

Another explanation for corporate diversification is that antitrust restraints could have channeled growth by domestic firms in the direction of diversification (see, for example, Baker, 1992; Matsusaka, 1992). In 1982, the U.S. Justice Department issued new lenient antitrust guidelines for mergers, essentially acknowledging a trend in court decisions, and this relaxation could have contributed to greater focus. Weighing against this story is the fact that corporate diversification is common in other jurisdictions, such as Japan and Korea, and White (1988) says that the relaxation did not result in any rush of mergers among competitors, as one would expect from the lifting of a binding constraint.

Table 1a documents the average level of focus each year from 1978 to 1989 for exchange-listed firms. All measures show an increase in focus during this period, with the largest proportionate increase seen in the proportion of firms with a single segment, which increased by one-half from 38.1% in 1979 to 55.7% in 1988. (We do not have data for all firms in 1978 or 1989.) The number of SIC codes assigned by Compustat turns out to average five-thirds of the number of

Table 1a
Average level of focus among exchange-listed firms covered by Compustat, by year, for focus measured by the percentage of firms reporting a single business segment, the number of segments reported, the number of four-digit SIC codes assigned by Compustat, and by asset-based and revenue-based Herfindahl indexes

Fiscal years ending in:	Number of firms	Percent with one segment	Number of segments reported	Number of SIC codes assigned	Asset-based Herfindahl index	Revenue-based Herfindahl index
1978[a]	1,703	36.2	2.59	4.17	0.684	0.683
1979	2,008	38.1	2.53	4.09	0.698	0.696
1980	2,000	38.8	2.50	4.08	0.703	0.701
1981	1,991	40.2	2.45	4.03	0.709	0.707
1982	1,959	40.9	2.42	3.98	0.713	0.715
1983	1,963	41.8	2.38	3.91	0.716	0.721
1984	1,934	43.4	2.30	3.78	0.730	0.731
1985	1,917	46.0	2.20	3.63	0.745	0.748
1986	1,938	50.3	2.08	3.46	0.768	0.769
1987	2,038	53.6	2.00	3.32	0.786	0.788
1988	2,085	55.7	1.94	3.23	0.797	0.800
1989[a]	557	63.9	1.72	2.95	0.832	0.840

[a]Our data cover fiscal years ending June 1978 through October 1989, so not all firms are included in years 1978 and 1989.

Table 1b
Comparison of average focus levels in 1979 and 1988 for all firms that were exchange-listed at any time during 1979–88 and covered by Compustat in either year, by whether firms are in the sample both years (constant composition) or just one of the years (varying composition), measuring focus by a revenue-based Herfindahl index

	Number		Mean			
	1979	1988	1979	1988	Change	*T*-stat.
Constant composition	1,272	1,272	0.691	0.744	0.052	8.21
Varying composition	777	638	0.717	0.915	0.198	15.70

Table 1c
Average same-firm change in focus over the sample period, by endpoints of the longest period over which the change can be measured, beginning with 1979 and ending with 1988, with focus measured by a revenue-based Herfindahl index, for all exchange-listed Compustat firms

First year of interval	Last year of measurement interval 1980	1981	1982	1983	1984	1985	1986	1987	1988
1979	0.009	0.024	0.024	0.029[a]	0.057[a]	0.051[a]	0.025	0.073[a]	0.045[a]
1980		−0.003	−0.021	−0.009	−0.002	−0.017	−0.043	−0.016	−0.018
1981			0.016	0.016	0.015	−0.029	−0.009	0.024	−0.014
1982				−0.029[a]	0.013	0.057	0.009	−0.044	−0.019
1983					−0.006	−0.000	−0.051[a]	0.009	−0.020[a]
1984						0.007	0.033	0.013	−0.014
1985							0.010	−0.017	0.006
1986								0.003	−0.006
1987									−0.005

[a]Reliably different from zero at 5% level for two-tail test.

segments reported by management, and both of these focus measures increased by about one-fifth. The two Herfindahl indexes increased by about one-seventh.

We find that the average level of focus in 1979 is reliably different from the average in 1988 using a revenue-based Herfindahl index (even though this measure shows the smallest proportionate increase of the five). The test is performed in Table 1b for two mutually-exclusive groups. The constant-composition group includes firms that had Compustat data for the entire period. For this group, average focus increased from 0.691 to 0.744 (t-statistic of 8.21). The varying-composition group includes firms that arrived or departed during the period, and here average focus increased from 0.717 to 0.915 (t-statistic of 15.7). While arriving firms had relatively high focus and departing firms exhibited typical focus levels, the contribution of sample turnover to a trend in focus was probably not attributable to this fact alone, as it is likely that arriving firms have always had high focus levels. In the 1980s, however, this tendency combined with an unusually high rate of turnover to yield a trend. Exchange-listed firms were delisted due to takeovers at an average annual rate of 4.6% per year from 1980–89 compared to 1.5% per year from 1940–79.[1]

More-desegregated tests are reported in Table 1c. Here, we measure the focus change for each firm using the longest interval possible within our sample period, and report averages for groups of firms with common starting and ending years. All the groups with reliably-positive focus changes had 1979 starting dates (firms in the sample from the start), and none of these groups had negative average changes. In contrast, none of the groups with post-1979 starting dates had average changes that were reliably positive. Consequently, the trend in focus holds for individual firms and is not entirely an artifact of a shift in sample composition.

4. Wealth effect of focus

The existing evidence on the relation between focus and economic performance is inconclusive. Copeland and Weston (1979) cite several studies that find that the stock-price performance of conglomerate firms dominated that of mutual funds in the 1960s and early 1970s. In contrast, event studies comparing buyer stock returns in related versus diversifying acquisitions generally attribute a small penalty to diversification (see, for example, Eckbo, 1985; Sicherman and Pettway, 1987; Mørck, Shleifer, and Vishny, 1990; Kaplan and Weisbach, 1992). There is also an extensive literature on the correlation between levels of focus and accounting-based measures of performance. Chatterjee and Wernerfelt (1991) review this literature and find no consensus conclusion.

A number of studies consider the effects of focus on Tobin's q, the ratio of a firm's market value to the cost of replacing its assets. Teece (1982) argues that firms diversify in order to exploit excess capacity in some input factor, particularly management skills. If an input is imperfectly marketable, rents can accrue to the firm that employs it. These rents are then capitalized in the firm's stock price, thereby increasing q. Wernerfelt and Montgomery (1988) and Lang and Stulz (1993) find a positive correlation between levels of focus and q. Our

[1] We calculate these annual takeover rates as the number of exchange-listed firms delisted each year with CRSP delisting codes in the range 200–399, divided by the total number of listed firms as of the start of the year. This overstates the takeover rate somewhat because some transactions coded as exchanges (300–399) are reorganizations, not acquisitions. We believe the true takeover rate for these firms in the 1980s was 4.2% per year (Table 4) based on our mergers and acquisitions database, which begins in 1975.

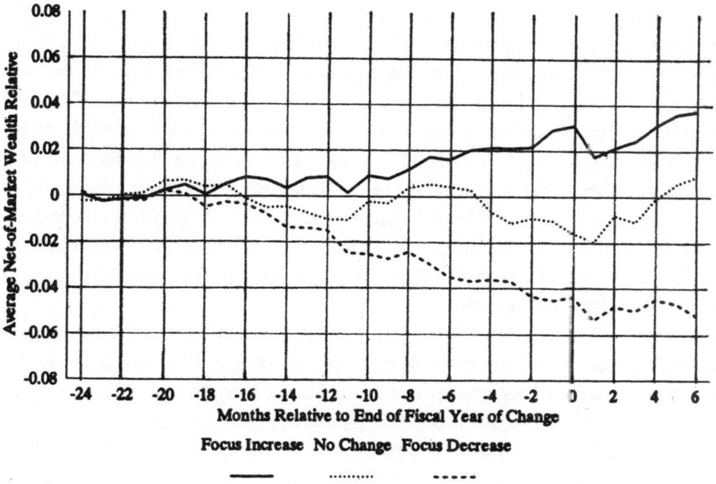

Fig. 1. Event-study showing the average wealth effect of focus changes for three groups of firms segmented by the direction of focus change. The sample consists of fiscal years in the period 1978–1989 for exchange-listed firms. Plotted points represent, for each group of firms, the average month-by-month value of a $1 initial investment in the firm less the corresponding month-by-month value of a $1 initial investment in the CRSP equally-weighted market portfolio. Month zero is defined as the last month of the fiscal year of the change in focus. Focus is measured by a Herfindahl index defined on revenue. There are 5,088 fiscal-years with increases in the Herfindahl index, 4,469 with decreases, and 7,056 with no change.

evidence (in Table 3) that asset turnover is higher at diversified firms suggests that book values will be marked to market more frequently at diversified firms, which could reduce q (as conventionally measured) and thus cause a positive correlation between focus and q.

Before turning to our regression tests of the relation between focus changes and stock returns, we use Fig. 1 to illustrate that our main conclusions hold on average. Fig. 1 is constructed by forming three groups according to the direction of the change in focus as measured by the revenue-based Herfindahl index, and shows cumulative net-of-market wealth relatives in event time, from 30 months before the last month of the year in which the focus change is measured (month zero of the bottom axis) to three months after. To get the running value of a $1 initial investment, we compute wealth relatives (one plus the monthly return) for each firm and cumulate these multiplicatively to reflect reinvestment. Each month, the corresponding wealth relative for the market portfolio is subtracted and the resulting net wealth relatives are then averaged and plotted. In effect, the only factor for which explicitly control is the general market return, with beta assumed equal to unity. The best average performance is seen among the firms experiencing increases in focus, and the worst performance occurs for firms that decreased their focus. The difference in net return over 34 months between the focus-increase and the focus-decrease groups is 7.4%. The statistical significance of the relation between focus and stock performance is established more reliably in the multivariate regression tests reported below, but a comparison of group means is possible with the data in Fig. 1. Based on wealth relatives as of month 3 (three months after the end of the fiscal year of the change in focus), the average for the focus-increase group (mean = 0.024, n = 5,088) is statistically significantly greater (t-statistic 4.11) than the average for the focus-decrease group (mean = − 0.050, n = 4,469).

Our formal analysis correlates fiscal-year changes in focus with both same-year stock returns and prior-year returns, using a multivariate, pooled, time-series cross-sectional regression covering about two thousand exchange-listed firms per year. We replicate our analysis using prior-year returns because focus changes could be announced or anticipated in the year before they take effect. Fiscal-year returns are compound CRSP monthly returns, including dividends. We get net-of-market estimates of wealth changes by including in our regressions the average return of (1) all exchange-listed firms in the market and (2) all other exchange-listed firms in the same industry, less the market average. The net-of-market industry return is set to zero if less than three other companies have the same SIC code. Industry classifications are based on the two-digit SIC code of a firm's primary business segment reported by CRSP.

We control for fiscal-year changes in total revenue, total assets, and earnings from continuing operations in the expectation that the wealth effects of changes in focus are secondary to the effects of operating performance. To render these accounting measures comparable across firms and time, we denominate annual dollar amounts as fractions of the beginning market value of common stock.

We control for the wealth effects of large acquisitions and divestitures by including dummy variables defined on (1) firm-years with acquisitions valued at $100 million or more and acquisitions of exchange-listed firms of any size, (2) divestitures valued at $100 million, and (3) firm-years with both types of events. The acquisition and divestiture data come from IDD Information Services and cover transactions announced in the period 1980–90. Information on acquisitions of exchange-listed firms comes from our proprietary mergers and acquisitions (M&A) database, which is derived from various keyword searches of the *Dow Jones News/Retrieval* database, as well as from inspection of the *Wall Street Journal* Index and Commerce Clearing House's *Capital Changes Reporter* (the original source for CRSP delisting codes).

Table 2 reports regression results for same-year returns and prior-year returns using four different measures of focus. Change in focus is reliably positively associated with same-year and prior-year stock returns for every measure of focus. Using the revenue-based Herfindahl index, the sum of the estimates for

Table 2

The dependence of fiscal year and prior fiscal-year stock return on fiscal-year change in focus for exchange-listed firms and fiscal years beginning in the period 1978–89, controlling for the CRSP equally-weighted market return and a net-of-market industry return, and for the fiscal-year change in total revenue, total assets, and earnings from continuing operations each denominated as fractions of beginning market value of equity

	Method of calculating focus and the time period over which the dependent variable, stock return, is calculated							
	Number of segments		Number of SIC codes		Asset Herfindahl		Revenue Herfindahl	
Explanatory variable	Prior-year return	Same-year return	Prior-year return	Same-year return	Prior-year return	Same-year return	Prior-year return	Same-year return
Constant	– 0.04 (– 7.12)	– 0.07 (– 15.3)	– 0.04 (– 7.07)	– 0.07 (– 15.4)	– 0.04 (– 7.08)	– 0.07 (– 15.4)	– 0.04 (– 7.18)	– 0.07 (– 15.4)
Equal-weighted market return	1.02 (59.3)	1.05 (65.2)	1.02 (59.3)	1.05 (65.2)	11.02 (59.3)	1.05 (65.2)	1.02 (59.4)	1.05 (65.2)
Net of market industry return	0.77 (39.0)	0.70 (37.4)	0.77 (39.0)	0.70 (37.3)	0.77 (39.0)	0.70 (37.4)	0.77 (39.0)	0.70 (37.3)
Change in focus	– 0.02 (– 2.52)	– 0.03 (– 5.29)	– 0.01 – 2.01)	– 0.02 5.75)	0.10 (2.33)	0.25 (6.57)	0.14 (3.43)	0.29 (7.30)

continued over

Change in total revenue	0.03	0.05	0.03	0.05	0.03	0.05	0.03	0.05
	(6.95)	(14.9)	(6.93)	(15.1)	(6.97)	(15.1)	(7.08)	(15.2)
Change in total assets	0.05	0.05	0.05	0.05	0.05	0.05	0.05	0.05
	(11.7)	(13.0)	(11.7)	(13.1)	(11.7)	(13.0)	(11.8)	(13.1)
Change in earnings	0.06	1.35	0.06	1.35	0.06	1.35	0.06	1.35
	(1.41)	(31.5)	(1.44)	(31.5)	(1.43)	(31.5)	(1.39)	(31.5)
Dummy for acquisitions (only)	0.02	0.01	0.02	0.01	0.02	0.01	0.02	0.01
	(1.01)	(0.64)	(0.98)	(0.64)	(1.00)	(0.68)	(1.00)	(0.64)
Dummy for divestitures (only)	0.02	0.13	0.02	0.13	0.02	0.13	0.02	0.13
	(0.75)	(5.49)	(0.78)	(5.39)	(0.80)	(5.46)	(0.73)	(5.44)
Dummy for both in same year	0.00	0.02	0.00	0.02	0.00	0.03	0.00	0.03
	(0.02)	(0.52)	(0.02)	(0.51)	(0.06)	(0.59)	(0.06)	(0.61)
R-square	0.267	0.330	0.267	0.330	0.267	0.330	0.267	0.331
N	16,565	17,135	16,562	17,132	16,565	17,135	16,565	17,135

Each of the four panels uses a different measure of focus (OLS estimates pooling firm-years, *t*-statistics in parenthesis). Dummy variables indicate years with large divestitures or acquisitions.

the two years indicates that an increase in focus of 0.1 is associated with an additional stock return of 4.3% (2.9% in the same year and 1.4% in the prior year). Similarly, an increase in the asset-based Herfindahl index of 0.1 yields a 3.5% increase in wealth over two years; a reduction of one in the number of SIC codes assigned by Compustat (indicating higher focus) yields a 3% increase, and a reduction of one in the number of segments yields a 5% increase. Divestitures (with no acquisition in the same year) are associated with an additional stock return of 13% in the same year and 15% over two years, while acquisitions are associated with average returns that are positive but not reliably greater than zero, whether or not they are accompanied by divestitures in the same year. These gains are larger than those reported in event studies, perhaps because our transactions are larger or because our return interval is longer.

These estimates of the wealth effects of focus could be biased upward by our inclusion of accounting-based measures of performance if measurement error in the accounting variables is negatively correlated with change in focus. In fact, our coefficient estimates for focus change are only reliably positive in regressions that include one or another of these accounting measures. In particular, divestitures have a tendency to generate both an increase in focus and a negative measurement error in the change in revenue (amounting to the revenue of the divested operation over the post-divestiture part of the fiscal year). Algebraically, this implies an upward bias in our estimated wealth effect of focus, as focus increases tend to be observed in those fiscal years (with divestitures) when the measured change in revenue underpredicts the stock return. Another way of stating this is that, based on a multitude of event studies, we know that sellers of corporate assets tend to capture the gains from trade. If these transactions incidentally increase focus for sellers (or reduce it for buyers) on average, then our wealth effect is preordained to some degree. This upward bias is mitigated by our inclusion of dummy variables for fiscal years with significant acquisitions and divestitures, and our reported estimate is otherwise robust, but this bias nevertheless implies that the wealth effects of focus changes might be smaller than we estimate.

Our estimates are essentially unchanged when we exclude firm-years with acquisitions or divestitures instead of introducing dummy variables for these events, and unchanged when we include these cases but allow the intercept and focus estimates to differ in fiscal years with these events. Our data on acquisitions and divestitures are limited to transactions exceeding $100 million in value, and smaller transactions could matter for small firms, but our estimate is more positive when we include just large firms (the one-quarter of our sample of firm-years for which a firm's market value of common stock exceeds $500 million), and remains reliably positive among large firms when we omit all three of the accounting-based measures of performance. In other unreported regressions, estimates of a positive relation between wealth changes and focus changes do not differ materially when regressions like those in Table 2 are replicated for various subsets of the sample (i.e., by survivorship, firm-size quartile, half-decade, by initial focus level, or by the direction of the change in focus).

Because stock returns are correlated with total revenue, another kind of spurious correlation could arise when we use a revenue-based Herfindahl index to measure focus. Both wealth and a revenue-based Herfindahl index of focus will tend to increase when the primary segment does surprisingly well, inflating our estimate of a (positive) causal relation between them. An offsetting negative bias arises when surprising performance occurs in ancillary segments instead, but the net effect could be positive. This problem also arises with a Herfindahl index based on assets (because assets change with earnings and earnings affect realized returns), but the number of segments and the number of SIC codes are less likely to change with surprising financial performance, and our conclusions do not depend on the measure of focus we use. Moreover, the problem only applies to same-year returns, not prior-year returns.

5. Focus and M&A activity

Table 3 reports frequency statistics to see whether diversified firms were relatively likely to participate in the market for corporate control in the 1980s as buyers or sellers of assets and subsidiaries. Our data on acquisitions and divestitures are described in Section 4. Large divestitures occurred during 2.8% of all firm-years, and large acquisitions during 4.9% of all firm-years, based on all exchange-listed firms for fiscal years beginning 1980–89. These frequencies exhibit a pattern when the sample is broken down by the level of diversification at the beginning of the year. Firms with just one segment divested in 0.8% of their years, those reporting five segments divested in 6.7%, and firms reporting six or more segments divested in 12.7% of their firm-years. Confirming this, the acquisition frequency exhibits the same pattern as the divestiture frequency: the corresponding values are 2.7%, 10.9%, and 13.5%. This is not just a size effect. Frequencies are uniformly higher for large firms, but association with focus persists. Large firms with just one segment divested in 2.6% of their firm-years, those reporting five segments divested in 11.5%, and those reporting six or more segments divested in 18.8% of their firm-years, with corresponding acquisition frequencies of 8.6%, 17.5%, and 20.5%. Table 3 also shows that both divestitures and acquisitions were more frequent during the second half of the 1980s than during the first half, approximately doubling for each category of focus.

If diversification is inefficient, diversified firms should have been likely takeover targets in the 1980s. Table 3 reports the frequency with which diversified and focused firms were the targets of unsolicited merger proposals or unnegotiated tender offers, and the frequency with which they were successfully acquired. We get this information from our M&A database (described earlier).

Table 3

Percentage of firms involved in the market for corporate control per year in the period 1980–1990, by the level of focus at the start of the year (measuring focus as the number of segments reported) for all exchange-listed firms, for those with market values of equity exceeding $500 million at the start of the year, and for two time periods

	All exchange-listed firms						Subgroup of firm-years where initial capitalization exceeds $500 million					
Number of segments	Firm-years	% sellers	% buyers	% either	% hostile offers	% bought	Firm-years	% sellers	% buyers	% either	% hostile offers	% bought
1	8,880	0.8	2.7	3.4	3.0	4.6	1,647	2.6	8.6	10.6	1.8	1.7
2	3,568	1.9	3.4	4.9	2.7	4.3	709	6.5	10.4	15.1	1.8	2.8
3	3,241	3.7	6.2	9.3	3.4	4.2	1,058	8.4	13.7	20.2	2.0	2.4
4	2,048	5.8	8.4	12.9	3.2	3.2	908	10.5	15.6	23.3	3.2	2.6
5	1,015	6.7	10.9	16.3	3.4	3.2	486	11.5	17.5	26.5	2.7	2.5
6–10	764	12.7	13.5	22.8	3.3	3.4	464	18.8	20.5	33.8	3.2	2.8
Total	19,516	2.8	4.9	7.1	3.1	4.2	5,272	7.9	12.9	39.1	2.3	2.3

Number of segments	Subgroup of fiscal years beginning 1/80–12/84						Subgroup of fiscal years beginning 1/85–11/89					
	Firm-years	% sellers	% buyers	% either	% hostile offers	% bought	Firm-years	% sellers	% buyers	% either	% hostile offers	% bought
1	3,956	0.3	1.9	2.1	1.9	4.1	4,924	1.3	3.4	4.4	3.8	4.9
2	1,819	0.6	2.1	2.6	1.8	4.2	1,749	3.3	4.7	7.3	3.7	4.4
3	1,743	1.4	3.7	5.0	2.2	3.9	1,498	6.3	9.1	14.2	4.7	4.6
4	1,189	2.5	5.9	8.1	2.1	3.0	859	10.2	11.9	19.7	4.8	3.5
5	623	3.2	8.8	11.2	2.7	2.9	392	12.2	14.3	24.2	4.6	3.6
6–10	491	9.2	11.0	17.3	3.1	3.5	273	19.0	17.9	32.6	3.7	3.3
Total	9,821	1.4	3.6	4.8	2.1	3.8	9,695	4.2	6.1	9.4	4.1	4.6

Sellers include firms with divestitures exceeding $100 million in value. *Buyers* had a purchase exceeding $100 million or acquired an exchange-listed firm of any size. *Either* is less than the sum of *buyers* and *sellers* because some firms are both buyers and sellers in the same fiscal year. *Hostile offers* are firms that received unsolicited merger proposals or unnegotiated tender offers, without regard to success. *Bought* firms are those that are successfully acquired or merged, without regard to friendliness.

We define targets without regard to outcome, so that not all targets are acquired. Announcements of merger agreements and negotiated tender offers do not qualify a firm as a target because we want the target category to include instances where public pressure (including share acquisition by arbitragers) is brought to bear on management prior to the conclusion of merger negotiations. Acquisitions are defined without regard to how the firm is put into play, so that not all acquisitions are classified as targets. In Table 3, the column for targets is labeled as '% hostile offers' and the column for successful acquisitions is labeled as '% bought'.

Exchange-listed firms were targeted at a rate of 3.1% per year and successfully acquired at a rate of 4.2% per year. Focused firms were more likely to be acquired (4.6% for single-segment firms compared to 3.4% for six or more segments). There was little difference, however, in the frequency in which firms were targeted (3.0% for pure-play firms compared to 3.3% for six or more segments). Among large firms, diversification increased the likelihood of receiving an unnegotiated takeover offer. Large, pure-play firms were targeted in 1.8% of all firm-years, while large firms reporting six or more segments were targeted in 3.2% of all firm-years. It seems that large, focused firms were relatively immune from hostile takeover attempts during the 1980s.

6. Focus and internal capital markets

Williamson (1986) argues that internal capital markets can dominate external capital markets by allowing a better allocation of capital across competing uses, better sharing of inside information, and better post-investment control. Managers can broaden their internal capital market and gain these economies by diversifying. Bhide (1990) suggests that improvements in the efficiency of external capital markets in the 1980s should then imply reductions in diversification, helping to explain the trend toward focus during the 1980s. These arguments imply that, by relying on inter-segment transfers of cash, diversified firms can limit their overall reliance upon and interaction with external capital markets.

We consider three measures of the degree of a firm's reliance on external capital markets. Two make use of data from flow-of-funds statements (from Compustat) detailing the amount of cash that passes annually between a firm and the capital market, both inflow and outflow. To make them comparable across firms, these amounts are denominated as percentages of the value of financial claims at the start of the year, calculated as the market value of equity plus the book values of long-term debt, short-term debt, and preferred stock. Cash inflow includes long-term borrowings and any proceeds from the sale of common or preferred stock, but not the proceeds of asset sales which would render this a proxy for asset transactions more than capital-market transactions.

Table 4
Average financial ratios by level of focus, including the average annual cash inflow or cash outflow between the firm and external capital markets as percentages of initial financial liabilities, debt as a percentage of financial liabilities, and short-term debt as a percentage of total debt, with focus measured as the number of reported segments and as a Herfindahl index defined on revenue, for exchange-listed firms in the period 1978–1989

Number of segments	Number of firm-years	Cash inflow	Cash outflow	Short-term debt as a % of debt	Debt as a % liabilities
1	8,930	10.1	8.9	26.8	33.5
2	3,697	9.8	9.2	23.6	34.3
3	3,369	9.5	9.0	22.1	34.3
4	2,230	8.6	9.3	21.9	33.9
5–10	1,963	9.5	10.2	20.5	38.2

Revenue Herfindahl	Number of firm-years	Cash inflow	Cash outflow	Short-term debt as a % of debt	Debt as a % liabilities
1	8,943	10.1	8.9	26.8	33.5
0.750–0.999	1,548	10.7	9.3	25.8	38.4
0.500–0.749	4,477	9.4	9.1	22.3	34.2
0.250–0.499	4,582	9.0	9.5	21.5	33.7
0.250	639	9.0	9.8	18.9	39.8

Cash outflow includes payments of interest and principal on debt, cash dividends on preferred and common, and security repurchases. The third measure of reliance on external capital markets, the percentage of debt that is due to be repaid within the next fiscal year, indicates proximity to renegotiation.

Table 4 shows that cash inflow does fall with diversification, but only from 10.1% for single-segment firms to 9.5% for firms reporting five or more segments. Meanwhile, cash outflow increases from 8.9% to 10.2% for these groups, so these two measures show small and contradictory effects. The third measure likewise shows little insulation from external capital markets, although the percentage of debt that is due in a year does decrease from an average of 26.8% for single-segment firms to 20.5% for firms reporting five or more segments. Elsewhere in Table 4, only small differences are observed when the subgrouping is based on a revenue-based Herfindahl index instead of the number of reported segments, and the patterns across groups are not generally uniform. On average, diversification does not appear to result in a meaningful substitution of in-house transactions for arms-length transactions. The economic benefits to a firm from having an internal capital market thus do not seem to include a reduction in its reliance on the external capital market, although there could be other benefits.

7. Focus, leverage, and risk

Combining businesses that have imperfectly-correlated earnings streams reduces the variability of earnings for the combination. Lower risk is probably not valuable *per se* to shareholders, who can diversify on personal account by holding portfolios of stocks. The ability of investors to diversify on personal account has probably increased in recent years due to reductions in transactions costs and growth in the mutual fund industry, and this could have reduced the rationale for corporate-level diversification. Levy (1991) argues that the ability of shareholders and financial intermediaries to construct portfolios of choice can be diminished by corporate-level diversification. For example, the combination of U.S. Steel and Marathon Oil as USX reduced the investment opportunities available to shareholders to just the shares of USX, while the recent split into two classes of stock, steel and oil, restored to shareholders a choice in how they apportion any investment between these two businesses, while preserving any financial or operating synergies at the corporate level.

Reduced variability of earnings can lead to planning and operating advantages for a firm, and can increase its debt capacity by reducing expected default rates. This claim, usually attributed to Lewellen (1971), predicts that diversified firms will use more debt by virtue of the reduction in default rates that comes with diversification (coinsurance of corporate debt). Amihud and Lev (1981) argue that managers benefit from the risk reduction associated with corporate diversification because they suffer less employment risk. By reducing volatility, corporate diversification can potentially increase firm value by cutting agency costs. Stulz (1990) argues that greater cash flow volatility increases the agency costs of managerial discretion, and hence reduces firm value. This reduction in value occurs because the more volatile or uncertain are future cash flows, the harder it is to identify and maintain an optimal capital structure that balances the costs of overinvestment due to too little debt [Jensen's (1986) free cash flow problem] and the costs of underinvestment due to too much debt, as described in Myers (1977).

As a rough test of whether diversification increases debt capacity or usage, Table 4 reports average leverage (the book value of debt denominated as a percentage of the sum of the market value of common stock and the book values of debt and preferred stock) by focus subgroups. The average leverage ratio lies in a range of 33–34% for all but three groups. It does rise to about 38–40% for the most-diversified group, based on either of the two measures of focus that we use here, but it also reaches this level for the (high-focus) group with revenue-based Herfindahl indexes in the range of 0.75 to 0.99. The economic significance of the difference is not large in any event. These results can be interpreted to mean either that diversification does not increase debt capacity or that managers of diversified firms do not choose to exploit their greater debt capacity.

Table 5
The dependence of risk on focus, leverage, size and industry, for exchange-listed firms in the period 1978–1988

	Dependent variable	
	Beta	Sigma
Constant	0.720 (30.3)	0.071 (82.1)
Focus level	− 0.027 (− 1.71)	0.005 (9.37)
Log of firm size	0.055 (21.5)	− 0.006 (− 60.7)
Debt ratio	0.063 (3.19)	0.017 (24.1)
R-square	0.113	0.320
N	19,952	19,953

Beta is the coefficient estimate from a market-model regression of the stock return on the return on the CRSP value-weighted market portfolio, and *sigma* is the standard deviation of the residuals from this regression, estimated using weekly returns during the fiscal year. A total of 26 industry dummy variables are included but their coefficients are not shown. *Focus level* is the revenue-based Herfindahl index, *debt ratio* is the book value of long-term debt and preferred stock divided by the same plus the market value of equity, and *log of firm size* is the market value of common stock (in $ millions), each defined as of the start of the fiscal year (OLS regressions, *t*-statistics in parentheses).

Finally, we document whether diversification affects systematic risk (beta) or firm-specific risk (sigma). Table 5 presents pooled time-series cross-sectional ordinary least squares regressions of risk levels on various explanatory variables measured as of the beginning of the risk-measurement period, including focus level, firm size (market value of equity), debt/equity ratio (the ratio of book value of long-term debt and preferred stock to the sum of the same plus the market value of equity), and industry factors (26 dummy variables for the most common two-digit SIC codes, the coefficients of which are not reported). Beta is computed using a single-factor market model based on a year's worth of weekly returns and sigma is the standard deviation of the residuals from this regression. We find that sigma increases with the level of focus as is expected from the effects of diversification, but that there is no reliable relation between equity beta and focus. A firm's overall beta should be a weighted average of the betas of its individual businesses, and thus unrelated to focus, so Table 5 holds no surprises.

8. Conclusion

The 1980s witnessed a reversal among American public firms of an earlier trend toward diversification. We find that the increase in focus measured across exchange-listed firms during the 1978–89 period is consistent with shareholder wealth maximization, implying that focus increased in the 1980s in part because economies of scope were negative on balance during the decade. This conclusion gains further support from our finding that some commonly-cited economies of scope go unrealized: corporate debt is not a meaningfully greater proportion of capital when debt payments are coinsured by diverse cash flows, and transactions in external capital markets are no less prevalent when internal capital markets are made available or enhanced through corporate diversification. While there is some evidence that large, focused firms were relatively immune from takeover attempts during the 1980s, consistent with economies of scope, focus had a much more pronounced effect on rates of participation in the market for corporate control in that diversified firms were much more active than focused firms as buyers and sellers of corporate assets.

References

Amihud, Yakov and Baruch Lev, 1981, Risk reduction as a managerial motive for conglomerate mergers, Bell Journal of Economics 12, 605–617.

Baker, George P., 1992, Beatrice: A study in the creation and destruction of value, Journal of Finance 47, 1081–1119.

Bhagat, Sanjai, Andrei Shleifer, and Robert W. Vishny, 1990, Hostile takeovers in the 1980s: The return to corporate specialization, Brookings Papers on Economic Activity: Microeconomics (Brookings Institution, Washington, DC).

Bhide, Amar, 1990, Reversing corporate diversification, Journal of Applied Corporate Finance 5, 70–81.

Chatterjee, Sayan and Birger Wernerfelt, 1991, The link between resources and type of diversification: Theory and evidence, Strategic Management Journal 12, 33–48.

Copeland, Thomas E. and J. Fred Weston, 1979, Financial theory and corporate policy (Addison-Wesley, Reading, MA).

Eckbo, B. Espen, 1985, Mergers and the market concentration doctrine: Evidence from the capital market, Journal of Business 58, 325–349.

Jensen, Michael C., 1986, Agency costs of free cash flow, corporate finance and takeovers, American Economic Review 76, 323–329.

Jensen, Michael, 1988, Takeovers: Their causes and consequences, Journal of Economic Perspectives 2, 21–48.

Kaplan, Steven N. and Michael S. Weisbach, 1992, The success of acquisitions: Evidence from divestitures, Journal of Finance 47, 107–138.

Lang, Larry H.P. and René M. Stulz, 1993, Does corporate diversification create value?, Working paper (New York University, New York, NY).

Levy, Hiam, 1991, Possible explanations of no-synergy mergers and small firm effect by the generalized capital asset pricing model, Review of Quantitative Finance and Accounting 1, 101–127.

Lewellen, Wilbur, 1971, A pure financial rationale for the conglomerate merger, Journal of Finance 26, 521–537.

Lichtenberg, Frank, 1991, The managerial response to regulation of financial reporting for segments of a business enterprise, Journal of Regulatory Economics 3, 241–249.

Liebeskind, Julia and Timothy C. Opler, 1992, The causes of corporate refocusing, Working paper (University of Southern California, Los Angeles, CA).

Matsusaka, John, 1992, Did tough antitrust enforcement cause the diversification of American corporation?, Working paper (University of Southern California, Los Angeles, CA).

Meyer, Michael., Paul Milgrom, and John Roberts, 1992, Organizational prospects, influence costs, and ownership changes, Journal of Economic & Management Strategy 1, 9–35.

Mørck, Randall, Andrei Shleifer, and Robert W. Vishny, 1990, Do managerial objectives drive bad acquisitions?, Journal of Finance 45, 31–48.

Myers, Stewart, 1977, The determinants of corporate borrowing, Journal of Financial Economics 5, 147–175.

Ravenscraft, David J. and Frederick M. Scherer, 1987, Mergers, sell-offs, & economic efficiency (Brookings Institution, Washington, DC).

Sicherman, Neil W. and Richard H. Pettway, 1987, Acquisition of divested assets and shareholder wealth, Journal of Finance 42, 1261–1273.

Stulz, René M., 1990, Managerial discretion and optimal financing policies, Journal of Financial Economics 26, 3–27.

Teece, David, 1982, An economic theory of multiproduct firms, Journal of Economic Behavior and Organization 3, 39–63.

Wernerfelt, Birger and Cynthia Montgomery, 1988, Tobin's q and the importance of focus in firm perfor-mance, American Economic Review 78, 246–250.

White, Lawrence, 1988, Panel discussion, in: A. Auerbach, ed., Corporate takeovers: Causes and consequences (University of Chicago Press, Chicago, IL).

Williamson, Oliver E., 1986, Economic organization: Firms, markets and policy control (New York University Press, New York, NY).

[6]

Causes and Effects of Corporate Refocusing Programs

Philip G. Berger
University of Pennsylvania and
Massachusetts Institute of Technology

Eli Ofek
New York University

We study the precursors and outcomes of refocusing episodes by 107 diversified firms that were not taken over between 1984 and 1993. These firms had more value-reducing diversification policies than diversified firms that did not refocus. However, major disciplinary or incentive-altering events (including management turnover, outside shareholder pressure, changes in management compensation, and financial distress) usually occurred before refocusing took place. The cumulative abnormal returns over a firm's refocusing-related announcements averaged 7.3% and were significantly related to the amount of value reduction associated with the refocuser's diversification policy.

Despite the weakening disciplinary role of the takeover market, there has been a rash of divestiture and split-up announcements by such prominent firms as AT&T, ITT, W. R. Grace, and others. These internal breakups are consistent with at least three explanations for the average value reduction of diversification during the 1980s and 1990s documented in Lang and Stulz (1994), Berger and Ofek (1995, 1996), and Comment and Jarrell (1995).

One possibility is that the refocusings were motivated by a gradual decrease over time in the benefits of creating an internal capital market [see Subrahmanyam and Titman (1999)]. Diversified firms create a larger internal capital market, which creates potential benefits by relaxing firmwide external funding constraints (Stulz 1990), and by giving headquarters control rights that enable it to actively shift funds toward more valuable projects (Stein 1997). These internalization benefits help to explain cross-sectional

We are grateful to Sunil Wahal for providing us with his data on activism by pension fund investors, and to David Yermack for providing his corporate governance data. We appreciate helpful comments from workshop participants at Columbia's Arden Homestead Conference, the joint Columbia–NYU Finance Conference, Harvard University, Hebrew University of Jerusalem, Ohio State University, Purdue University, University of Chicago, the 1997 AFA meetings, the Eighth Annual Conference on Financial Economics and Accounting, and, in particular, an anonymous referee, Dennis Caplan, John Core, Steve Kaplan, Nahum Melumad, Darius Palia, Krishna Palepu, Katherine Schipper, Abbie Smith, Jake Thomas, Sheridan Titman (the editor), Ralph Walking, and Mark Zmijewski. P. G. Berger acknowledges the financial support of Coopers & Lybrand. Address correspondence to Philip G. Berger, Sloan School of Management, MIT, 50 Memorial Dr., E52-325, Cambridge, MA 02142-1347, or e-mail: pberger@mit.edu.

The Review of Financial Studies Summer 1999 Vol. 12, No. 2, pp. 311–345

variation in the (generally positive) abnormal returns of bidding firms making diversifying acquisitions in the 1960s (Hubbard and Palia 1999). However, as public U.S. stock markets have become broader and more liquid, the advantage of internal capital markets relative to external markets has gradually decreased.

A second explanation for the increase in refocusing activity is that changes in regulatory and competitive conditions in the 1980s made focus more valuable. Shleifer and Vishny (1991) contend that less vigorous antitrust enforcement increased the ability of firms to achieve large scale in a single line of business. It has also been argued that effective management of organizations is reduced as they become more complex, so that increased focus could be motivated by the desire to enhance managerial efficiency. See, for example, Weston, Chung, and Hoag (1990, p. 236). As competitive pressures have intensified, the benefit of improved managerial efficiency has gradually increased.

Finally, the internal refocusing programs may be spurred by a reduction in agency conflicts between owners and managers. In contrast to the previous two explanations, one based on agency costs is inconsistent with the refocusing activity occurring voluntarily. Moreover, the agency explanation suggests that drastic changes in the firm's focus quickly follow events that reduce agency conflicts, in contrast to the more gradual shift toward focus suggested by the competing explanations.

To explore the antecedents and results of internal refocusing programs, we compare 107 diversified firms that underwent major refocusings during 1985 to 1993 without being taken over to a matched sample of 107 control firms. We find that corporate control events frequently precede the decrease in diversification. Twenty-two percent of refocusings are preceded by a change in CEO, 27% by a new outside blockholder, 19% by financial distress, 13% by an unsuccessful takeover bid, 12% by activism from pension fund investors, and 11% by a new compensation plan, each of which is significantly higher than the corresponding percentage for the matched control firms.

The finding on CEO turnover confirms evidence in Scherer (1988) and Ravenscraft and Scherer (1991), and supports Boot's (1992) argument that bad managers avoid the admission of past mistakes by not divesting, whereas new managers divest to gain from past managers' mistakes. The financial distress results augment Allen and McConnell's (1998) finding that carve-out subsidiaries exhibit poor operating performance and high leverage prior to the carve-out. Overall, 62% of our sample of divesting firms experienced at least one major corporate control event before restructuring. In contrast, just 18% of the matched firms had one of these events occur during the same time frame. The overall results on corporate control events confirm the evidence of Denis, Denis, and Sarin (1997), who show that 54% of firms decreasing diversification during 1985–1989 had at least one major corporate control event occur during the year prior to the diversification decrease, versus 27% for other firms.

We also show that the valuation consequences of diversification, estimated using Berger and Ofek's (1995) excess value measure, strongly affect the probability of divestiture. After controlling for other determinants of refocusing, we find that firms with the greatest value loss due to diversification are the most likely to have divestitures. Thus the firms that refocus are more likely to attract external pressure, and are more likely to be viewed negatively by the market.

We find that the characteristics of the diversification program affect refocusing likelihood. Firms are most likely to refocus when they have diversified into unrelated lines of business, when lines of business have experienced negative cash flow, and when the firm has a relatively high proportion of unallocated headquarters expenses. The first result is consistent with past findings that unrelated diversification is most damaging. The second result suggests that firms are quickest to refocus in response to immediate performance problems and, by implication, inefficient cross-subsidization. The last result is consistent with the view that internal capital markets supported by significant headquarters staff have proven to be inefficient. This evidence is exploratory and calls for more detailed research into the organizational economics of the diversified firm.

Finally, we examine the market reaction to restructuring-related announcements. The cumulative abnormal return (CAR) over a firm's refocusing-related announcements averages 7.3%. Moreover, cross-sectional variation in the magnitude of the CAR is positively related to the amount of value that was being destroyed by the refocuser's diversification policy. This result is consistent with divestitures reversing, at least in part, the value destruction from unsuccessful diversification strategies. Our finding complements those of John and Ofek (1995) and Allen et al. (1995). John and Ofek show that focus-increasing asset sales are associated with operating performance increases and that focus-increasing divestitures are associated with more positive seller stock returns at the divestiture announcement. Allen et al. examine spinoffs that originated as earlier acquisitions and find that announcement period returns at the time of the spinoff are significantly inversely related to the acquisition announcement period returns (of the bidder alone, and of the combined bidder and target).

Taken together, the results from our various tests are more consistent with the reduction of agency conflicts explaining the trend toward increased focus, rather than changes in the benefits from internal capital markets or changes in the regulatory or competitive environments. The finding that refocusing is more likely for firms with negative cash flow segments and greater headquarters expenses are consistent with both the agency and internal capital markets explanations. However, the evidence that most of the restructurings were preceded by events of external pressure, occurred at

The Review of Financial Studies / v 12 n 2 1999

firms with large diversification discounts, and were associated with large abnormal returns argues in favor of the agency cost explanation. These pieces of evidence indicate that managers usually had to be pressured into undertaking the restructuring and that the diversification policies being undone were destroying considerable value. If a gradual reduction in the benefits of internal capital markets motivated the refocusings, managers would not need to be strongly pressured and the value reduction from diversification would be more moderate.

As mentioned above, our findings on the relation between events of external pressure and refocusing are similar to those of Denis, Denis, and Sarin (1997). Our contribution differs from theirs mainly with respect to four dimensions of the refocusing decision that they do not examine. First, we explore the role of internal governance parameters and show that at least one (CEO option-based compensation) affects divestiture likelihood, and that several others (e.g., percentage of insiders on the board) do not. Second, we show that the characteristics of the diversification policy affect the probability of refocusing. Third, we test whether the market views the divestitures as reversing part of the value loss from diversification and find that it does. Finally, whereas the emphasis in Denis, Denis, and Sarin (1997) is on cross-sectional relations between managerial ownership and the level (and value effect) of diversification, our analysis emphasizes decreases in diversification and thus facilitates sharper tests of the motives for refocusing.

In Section 1 we present sample selection details and describe the sample. In Section 2 we examine the effect of market discipline on the decision to refocus. We present tests of the relation between value destruction from diversification and the probability of refocusing in Section 3. Section 4 examines the role of internal control mechanisms in motivating firms to refocus. Section 5 documents the market reaction to refocusing-related announcements and examines what factors explain the cross-sectional variation in market reaction. We summarize the results and offer our conclusions in Section 6. Appendix A provides additional details on our empirical approach and variable construction, and Appendix B provides details about the refocusing programs and the events of market discipline for our sample.

1. Sample Selection and Estimation of Segment Values

1.1 Sample Selection and Description

To identify our sample of refocusers, we obtain data for all firms that appeared on the Compustat Industry Segment (CIS) database during 1984–1993 that have total sales of at least \$100 million in 1984 (or their first year of existence), and no segments in the financial services industry (SIC codes between 6000 and 6999).[1] Firms with financial services segments are

[1] FASB no. 14 and SEC regulation S-K require firms to report audited segment information for segments whose sales, assets, or profits exceed 10% of consolidated totals.

removed from consideration because applying the valuation methods we use is problematic for such firms.

We use three levels of screening to identify the refocusing firms within the CIS observations. First, we gather information on the number of segments and the revenue-based Herfindahl index of each observation. The Herfindahl index, H, is calculated across n business segments as the sum of the squares of each segment i's sales, S_i, as a proportion of total sales:

$$H = \frac{\sum_{i=1}^{n} S_i^2}{\left(\sum_{i=1}^{n} S_i\right)^2}. \qquad (1)$$

Thus the closer H is to one, the more the firm's sales are concentrated within a few segments. Firms pass the first screen if they have at least one year during 1985–1993 in which they have both a decrease in the number of segments reported on the CIS database and an increase of at least 0.1 in their Herfindahl index.

The second screen eliminates firms without available Compustat data, firms for which we cannot calculate at least one of our three excess value measures, and firms in which the decrease in the number of segments is reversed within several years. The remaining 295 firms are examined in detail using Lexis/Nexis and the *Wall Street Journal* Index. We use this final screen because firms may decrease their number of reported segments without refocusing, due to such events as reconfigurations of existing lines of business or decreases to below 10% in the contribution of segment sales to firm sales. We also use the news stories to ascertain the time period over which each refocusing program occurs and to gather information on events that could reduce agency conflicts. Information on these events was gathered for the period from 12 months before the first divestiture announcement until 1 month after the announcement. Our procedures result in a sample of 107 refocusing observations.

Table 1 describes the sample of refocusing firms. Panel A shows that refocusings were more frequent during 1985–1988 than 1989–1993. Panel B demonstrates that the refocusing programs represent substantial restructurings. Both the drop in the number of reported segments and the increase in the revenue-based Herfindahl index from before to after the refocusing show that the extent of diversification was cut roughly in half. The divested businesses represented 49% (18%) of the parent's market value of equity (book value of assets) in the year prior to the start of the refocusing program. Finally, the last row of panel B portrays the short time frames of the restructurings, with a median of 2 years between the fiscal year prior to the first sale and the fiscal year of the last sale.

Appendix B provides details on the sample of 107 refocusing firms. The fourth column shows that just nine firms reported more than two segments by the end of their refocusing period. The value sold column reveals that the sum of all available prices paid for the equity of the divested divisions

The Review of Financial Studies / v 12 n 2 1999

Table 1
Description of refocus sample

A. Sample frequencies by first year of refocus program

Fiscal year 0	Number of firms	Frequence
1984	5	0.047
1985	11	0.103
1986	18	0.168
1987	14	0.131
1988	12	0.112
1989	9	0.084
1990	8	0.075
1991	13	0.121
1992	9	0.084
1993	8	0.075
Total	107	1.000

B. Descriptive statistics

Variable	Mean	Median	Std	Low	High
Number of segments before the refocus	3.514	3.000	1.239	2.000	7.000
Number of segments after the refocus	1.505	1.000	0.744	1.000	5.000
Change in the number of segments	−2.009	−2.000	1.042	−1.000	−6.000
Sales Herfindahl before the refocus	0.486	0.466	0.184	0.184	0.883
Sales Herfindahl after the refocus	0.837	1.000	0.214	0.362	1.000
Change in the sales Herfindahl	0.344	0.291	0.197	0.105	0.748
Number of divisions sold	3.617	3.000	2.887	1.000	15.000
Minimum value divested/market equity	1.185	0.489	2.392	0.025	15.730
Minimum value divested/total assets	0.238	0.176	0.286	0.013	1.369
Length of the refocusing program	1.887	2.000	1.030	1.000	5.000

The minimum value divested is the sum of all available sale prices of the divisions divested. Ratios using the minimum value divested are only included in the descriptive statistic calculations if the divestiture price is available for at least one divestiture. The length of the refocusing program is the number of years between the fiscal year prior to the first sale and the fiscal year of the last sale.

ranges, among firms with at least one available price, from a low of \$3 million for two divisions sold by North Star Universal to a high of \$5.1 billion for three divisions divested by Burlington Northern.

The return column reports the cumulative abnormal returns (CARs) from each firm's total set of divestiture-related announcements. For each divestiture we compute daily abnormal excess returns as the actual announcement returns minus the firm's expected daily return. Expected daily returns are computed using a market model estimated over the 250-trading-day period that ends prior to the firm's first refocusing announcement. The CAR for each divestiture cumulates the daily returns from the day before through the day after the announcement, and the total CAR reported in the return column of Appendix B cumulates the CARs for all of the firm's divestiture-related announcements. The largest negative reaction is Newmont Mining's CAR of −20.5%. Newmont announced a restructuring to fend off T. Boone Pickens' hostile takeover attempt, and subsequently sold or spun off six divisions. Arbitragers valued the restructuring at a lower amount than Pickens' offer, but the restructuring dissuaded the Pickens group from pursuing the takeover. In conjunction with the restructuring, Newmont also sanctioned employment contracts for 25 executives. Thus, although we later report that the refocusings are generally value enhancing, in some cases managers appear to remain strongly entrenched after refocusing. In such cases, the refocusing announced may fall short of market expectations, leading to the negative stock price reaction.

The last six columns of Appendix B detail the events of market discipline that occurred in the year preceding the start of each refocusing program. A perusal of these columns along with the individual CARs reveals that many of the most extreme market reactions were associated with refocusings in response to events of financial distress. The large market reactions in these cases are likely due in part to the fact that the expected return to equity holders from changing the firm's expected cash flows (because of refocusing) is larger when the amount of equity invested is smaller (i.e., when financial leverage is greater).

Our tests compare the refocusing firms to a nonrefocusing sample. In order to limit data collection costs for the non-refocusing sample, we use a matched control sample. The pool of potential matched firms includes those 1985–1993 observations of multisegment firms that did not enter the initial refocusing sample of 295 firms, had total sales of at least $100 million in 1984 (or their first year of existence), and had no financial services segments. To qualify as a matched control, the observation must be for the same year as the refocuser, have book value of assets within 20% of its matched refocuser, and have a revenue-based Herfindahl index within 0.2 of its matched refocuser. When these criteria resulted in multiple matches, we selected the match that minimized the sum of the size and Herfindahl index deviations. After selecting the matched firms, we followed the same procedures used for the refocusing firms to gather information on events that could reduce agency conflicts.

Table 2 compares the refocusing and matched control samples. For the refocusers, all variables are measured in the year prior to refocusing. The refocusers and controls have similar values for most of the variables reported. With respect to the matching variables, the deviations between the refocusers and their matched controls are, on average, within 3% for book value of assets and within .01 for the Herfindahl index. The only area in which the two samples appear to differ is in their performance prior to the refocusing year. Refocusers had somewhat slower growth (annual rate of change in sales) and a lower return on assets (EBITD/assets).

2. Refocusing and Market Discipline

2.1 The Effect of Market Discipline on Refocusing

Both Lang and Stulz (1994) and Berger and Ofek (1995) document large average value losses associated with diversification strategies in the 1980s. In addition, Comment and Jarrell (1995) and John and Ofek (1995) find

Table 2
Comparative statistics of diversified firms that do or do not refocus

Variable	No refocus	Mean refocus	Difference	No refocus	Median refocus	Difference
Total assets	1849	1806	43	749	760	−11
Leverage	0.308	0.325	−0.017	0.280	0.294	−0.013
Sales growth	0.084	0.067	0.017	0.068	0.048	0.021**
ROA (EBITD/assets)	0.152	0.114	0.038*	0.149	0.112	0.037*
Sales Herfindahl index	0.492	0.486	0.005	0.496	0.466	0.030
Number of segment	3.233	3.514	−0.281	3.000	3.000	0.000**

The sample includes 107 firms that refocused during the period 1985–1993. Each refocusing firm has a matched control firm of similar size and sales Herfindahl index at the end of year −1.
*,** denote significance at the 1% and 5% levels, respectively.

that stock prices increase significantly around increases in corporate focus. Although prominent examples like General Electric illustrate apparently successful diversification, the findings in these articles naturally raise the question of why so many unsuccessful diversification programs persist. Diversification may benefit managers because it brings growth which increases power and prestige [Jensen (1986) and Stulz (1990)], and compensation [Jensen and Murphy (1990)]. Moreover, diversification reduces the risk of the manager's undiversified personal wealth portfolio [Amihud and Lev (1981)] and increases the shareholders' dependence on her knowledge of the mix of businesses operated by the firm [Shleifer and Vishny (1989)]. As a result, managers may pursue diversification even if doing so reduces shareholder wealth.

If agency problems lead managers to pursue value-reducing diversification strategies, reductions in agency conflicts may need to occur before firms refocus. Agency conflicts can be reduced through several forms of market discipline. Dissatisfied stakeholders can press for the replacement of the CEO, consistent with Weisbach's (1995) finding that the likelihood of divesting "unsuccessful" acquisitions is positively correlated with CEO changes. Pension fund activism may reduce agency costs and lead to value-enhancing actions, although the evidence on this issue is mixed [see Opler and Sokobin (1996) and Wahal (1996)]. Product market competition can restrict managers' ability to continue to operate inefficiently [Hart (1983)], particularly if the resulting poor performance leads to financial distress [see John, Lang, and Netter (1992) and Ofek (1993)]. Finally, discipline imposed by the market for corporate control can temper agency problems at diversified firms [see Jensen and Ruback (1983), Bhagat, Shleifer, and Vishny (1990), and Berger and Ofek (1996)].

Table 3 shows the number of times various events occurred during the 13 month period examined for the 107 refocusers and their matched controls. The period extends from 12 months before the first sale or refocusing announcement until 1 month after that announcement. We examine four categories of events: management turnover, outside shareholder pressure, management compensation, and financial distress. Note that we do not construct the categories, nor the events within each category, to be mutually exclusive. The results indicate that corporate control events often precede refocusings. About 31% of the refocusers have a change in top management in the 13 month period we examine. A top management change is defined as any change in the set of individuals holding the titles CEO, president, or chairman of the board. The 31% management turnover rate is not significantly greater than the 22% rate for the matched controls. It is, however, much greater than the 11.5% rate reported by Warner, Watts, and Wruck (1988) from *Wall Street Journal* reports of the same definition of top management change for a random sample of 269 NYSE/AMEX firms during 1963–1978.[2] When we restrict attention to CEO turnover, the 22% rate for refocusers significantly exceeds the 7% rate for the controls and is much higher than the annual CEO turnover rates of 8% and 9% documented by Weisbach (1988) and Denis and Denis (1995). This result complements the finding of Denis, Denis, and Sarin (1997), who also find a significant difference in CEO turnover between refocusing firms and firms with no change in diversification.

We find that 27% of refocusers have a new outside blockholder, 13% are targets of unsuccessful takeover bids, 12% are targets of pension fund activism by one of nine major funds, and 33% have one of these events of outside shareholder pressure occur.[3] All four figures are significantly higher than the corresponding percentages for the controls, which experienced no unsuccessful takeover bids, had new outside blockholders (pension fund activism) in just 8% (3%) of the observations, and had at least one of the events of outside shareholder pressure with just 8% frequency.

A major change in the performance-based component of compensation (with respect to the mechanism used, the criteria, or the potential magnitude) can better align managers' interests with those of shareholders. For example, Dial and Murphy (1995) report that General Dynamics implemented a strategy that included downsizing, restructuring, and exit only after it engaged a new management team whose compensation was closely tied to shareholder wealth creation. We find that, in the year prior to restructuring, firms that refocused introduced new compensation plans with greater frequency than

[2] A different definition of top management turnover is reported by Mikkelson and Partch (1997) for our sample period. They find that complete turnover of the set of individuals holding the three top offices of CEO, president, and board chairman occurs at rates of 23.3% for the 5 year period 1984–1988, and 16.1% for 1989–1993. These rates are obviously not directly comparable to the annual rates of change in any of the individuals in this set, which is the definition used by Warner, Watts, and Wruck and by us.

[3] The data on pension fund activism are those used in Wahal (1996), and were kindly provided to us by the author. He examines all instances during 1987–1993 in which one of nine pension funds identified as "active" by Institutional Shareholder Services sent letters to investee firms targeting issues of performance, takeover defenses, or corporate governance. The nine funds had combined assets of $424 billion at the end of 1993. The 12% (3%) frequency of activism by pension fund investors for our refocusing (control) sample is based on the 1987–1993 period only, which includes 60 firms for each of the matched samples.

The Review of Financial Studies / v 12 n 2 1999

Table 3
Corporate control events in the year prior to refocusing

Group; action	Refocus Occurrences	Refocus Frequency	Control Occurrence	Control Frequency	Difference Frequency
Management turnover					
New CEO	23	0.215	7	0.065	0.150*
New top manager	33	0.308	23	0.215	0.093
Outside shareholder pressure					
Activism by pension fund investor	7	0.117	2	0.033	0.083***
New outside block holder	29	0.271	8	0.075	0.196*
Unsuccessful takeover bid	14	0.131	0	0.000	0.131*
Total — outside pressure	35	0.327	8	0.075	0.252*
Management compensation					
New compensation plan	10	0.106	1	0.012	0.095*
Financial Distress					
Dividend cut	7	0.065	4	0.037	0.028
Debt restructuring	12	0.112	0	0.000	0.112*
Chapter 11 filing	3	0.028	0	0.000	0.028***
Total — financial distress	20	0.187	4	0.037	0.150*
Summary					
New CEO, outside pressure, compensation plan, or financial distress	66	0.617	19	0.178	0.439*
At least one event	68	0.636	33	0.308	0.327*

The sample includes 107 firms that refocused during the 1985–1993 period. Each refocusing firm is matched with a control firm of similar size and sales Herfindahl index at the end of year −1. The table presents the total number and frequency of various events that occurred in a 13 month period for the refocus and matched control samples. The period extends from 12 months before the first sale or refocusing announcement until 1 month after that announcement. The frequency of activism by pension fund investors is calculated for the period 1987–1993 only, which includes 60 firms. The frequency of a new compensation plan is calculated for 179 firms with available proxy statement data for year −1.

*,*** denote significance at the 1% and 10% levels, respectively.

the matched control firms. We define a compensation plan as new only if a new form of compensation is used or a major adjustment in the extent to which compensation is performance-based occurs. The new plans we identify usually involve the introduction of stock option-based compensation. Eleven percent of the refocusing firms introduced a new compensation plan, versus just 1% for the controls. Thus, along with outside sources of discipline, internal changes in performance-based compensation are associated with the decision to refocus.

A number of the refocusers also experienced signs of financial distress in the period preceding the restructuring. Financial distress may reduce agency problems because when value-reducing behavior by the manager runs the risk of ending the firm's existence, the manager's desire to retain her job aligns her interests with those of the owners. Seven percent of the refocusers cut their dividend to common stockholders, 11% restructure debt agreements, 3% file for bankruptcy protection, and 19% exhibit at least one of these indications of financial distress. With the exception of the dividend cuts, the control firms do not exhibit any of these indications of financial distress during the 13 month period examined.

In total, 62% of the refocusers experience at least one of the incentive-aligning events in the period preceding the refocusing (excluding non-CEO management turnover). In contrast, just 18% of the controls experience one of these events. This evidence is thus consistent with the reduction of agency problems via external disciplinary events and new compensation arrangements playing an important part in corporate refocusing.[4]

3. Value Loss from Diversification and Subsequent Refocusing

3.1 Estimating Segment Values Using Comparable Firm Multiples

Whether or not a refocusing episode occurs is also likely to depend on the success of diversification. To measure diversification's value effect, we follow the procedures described in Berger and Ofek (1995). We measure the percentage difference between a firm's total value and the sum of imputed values for its segments as stand-alone entities (see Appendix A for additional details not described below). We calculate the imputed value of each segment by multiplying the median ratio, for single-segment firms in the same industry, of total capital to one of three accounting items (assets, sales, or EBITD) by the segment's level of the accounting item. The industry median ratios are based on the narrowest SIC grouping that includes at least five single-line businesses with at least $20 million of sales and sufficient data for computing the ratios.[5]

The sum of the imputed values of a company's segments estimates the value of the firm if all of its segments are operated as stand-alone businesses. The natural log of the ratio of a firm's actual value to its imputed value is our measure of excess value, or the gain or loss in value from diversification. Negative excess value indicates that diversification reduces the value of segments below that of their stand-alone counterparts.

3.2 Total Value Destruction and Subsequent Refocusings

To investigate whether value destruction drives refocusing, we compare the excess values of refocusers, measured in the year prior to the start of their refocusing, to those of all nonrefocusers. Table 4 shows that diversification is more value reducing among subsequent refocusers than among the matched

[4] Our concern is with whether external disciplinary events and new compensation arrangements affect diversified firms' decision on whether to divest businesses. A somewhat related issue (which we do not examine) is whether focused firms are also more likely to engage in asset sales when, for example, they are distressed or change CEOs. There are some indications in the prior literature that focused firms do respond to such pressures with asset sales [e.g., Brown, James, and Mooradian (1994) find that short-term lenders play a pivotal role in asset sales by a sample that includes both focused and diversified firms].

[5] The SIC code classifications are assigned by Compustat in its business segment file These business segment SIC codes are maintained on a historical basis so that, in contrast to the firm-level SIC codes on Compustat, industry membership will not be misclassified for past years in cases of industry changes. Therefore, the substantial disagreement between Compustat and CRSP classifications of firm-level SIC codes [Guenther and Rosman (1994); Kahle and Walkling (1996)] does not imply any measurement error in Compustat's assignment of business segment SIC codes.

The Review of Financial Studies / v 12 n 2 1999

Table 4
Value destruction in diversified firms that do or do not refocus

Variable	No refocus	Mean refocus	Difference	No refocus	Median refocus	Difference
Excess value, asset multiplier	−0.099	−0.273	0.174*	−0.184	−0.286	0.102***
Excess value, sales multiplier	−0.130	−0.305	0.175**	−0.172	−0.312	0.140**
Excess value, EBITD multiplier	−0.120	−0.238	0.119**	−0.123	−0.251	0.128***

The sample includes 107 firms that refocused during the period 1985–1993. Each refocusing firm has a matched control firm of similar size and sales Herfindahl index at the end of year −1. Excess value is the natural logarithm of actual value/imputed value where actual value is total book value of debt plus market value of equity, and imputed value is the sum of imputed values of the firm's segments. Each segment's imputed value is the segment's assets (sales, EBITD) multiplied by its industry median ratio of capital to the particular accounting item.

*,**,*** denote significance at the 1%, 5%, and 10% levels, respectively.

control firms. Using the asset (sales, EBITD) multiplier, the mean value loss among firms that begin refocusing the following year is 27% (31%, 24%), which is 17% (18%, 12%) more than the loss among the matched control firms. The differences in mean value destruction between the refocusers and the matched controls are significant at the .05 level. These results are consistent with restructuring occurring among multisegment firms whose diversification policies result in greater value losses. The inferences remain similar when the median value destruction of refocusers and nonrefocusers is compared. Restructuring firms destroy 10% more value based on the asset multiplier, 14% more using the sales multiplier, and 13% more using the EBITD multiplier, all significant at the .10 level or better.

The validity of the Table 4 results using the multiplier method depends on management disclosure policies. Theoretical models of managerial disclosure decisions suggest that managers may have incentives to misstate segment data to both providers of capital and product market competitors [see Darrough and Stoughton (1990), Wagenhofer (1990), Feltham, Gigler, and Hughes (1992), Feltham and Xie (1992), Newman and Sansing (1993), and Hayes and Lundholm (1996)]. In the setting we examine, managers have incentives to overstate value-relevant data on segments being divested. Reported earnings, sales, and assets of segments about to be divested could all be overstated by "borrowing" from the future (when new owners will control the segment). For example, earnings and assets could be overstated by extending more liberal credit terms without increasing bad debt expense and the corresponding allowance for doubtful accounts receivable. Earnings, however, are likely to be subject to the greatest incentives to overstate and are also easiest to overstate [see Givoly, Hayn, and D'Souza (1993) for an assessment of the quality of segment sales and earnings figures]. Such overstatements could potentially explain part of the excess value differences documented in Table 4, since they would artificially inflate the imputed values of segments about to be divested.[6] If managerial manipu-

[6] Noise is also introduced into the imputed segment values by the fact that some segments consist of diverse

lation of segment data does contribute to the reported results, however, it is surprising that the excess value differences between refocusing and non-refocusing firms are smallest using the EBITD multiplier.[7] Moreover, the earnings-management explanation is also inconsistent with the return on assets (ROA) and sales growth measures being smaller for refocusing firms than for the matched controls.[8]

The univariate tests in Tables 2 and 4 show that refocusers perform worse than the controls, have larger diversification discounts, but are otherwise similar. We examine the Pearson correlation coefficients for the set of variables used in Tables 2 and 4 in order to identify the relations among the firm characteristics. The results (which are not presented in a table) show that the pairwise correlations among the three excess value measures range between 43% and 68%. These relatively high correlations provide some assurance that the various excess value measures are measuring the same economic construct. The correlations are also generally consistent with excess value capturing an economic construct distinct from the other performance measures we use. Although the 50% correlation between the asset multiplier measure of excess value and return on assets ROA is high, the remaining excess value measures have correlations with ROA that are much lower, and of opposite sign to one another. Moreover, the correlations between the excess value measures and sales growth are also small.

Although the descriptive evidence from the univariate tests in Tables 2–4 is suggestive of refocusing firms being worse performers that have larger diversification discounts and more events of market discipline, we need to evaluate each explanatory variable after incorporating the effects of the other variables on divestiture likelihood. We therefore perform multivariate logit regressions in which a refocusing indicator is the dependent variable, and is set to 1 if the firm refocuses, 0 otherwise. The continuous independent variables are excess value, ROA, sales growth, and leverage. The three indicator explanatory variables, capturing events of market discipline, are set to 1 for the presence of a new CEO, one or more events of outside shareholder pressure, and one or more events of financial distress, 0 otherwise. These

---

industries [Benartzi (1995)]. No directional bias in imputed segment values results from cases where a segment consists of diverse industries rather than similar industries. In addition, management's ability to report multiple industries within one segment is limited by regulatory oversight from the SEC [see Benartzi (1995) for examples].

7 Examining past earnings patterns to reliably detect potential earnings management is subject to insurmountable difficulties for poorly performing firms [Dechow, Sloan, and Sweeney (1995)], let alone poorly performing segments.

8 One could also attempt to explain the univariate differences in excess value between refocusers and nonrefocusers on the basis of some type of selection bias. If segments of diversified firms are intrinsically worse than stand-alone firms, then imputing values based on the median pure play firm in the segment's industry overstates the value that the segment would have if divested. Such an explanation requires diversified firms to develop and acquire segments with intrinsically poor growth prospects, high risks, etc., relative to their industries.

The Review of Financial Studies / v 12 n 2 1999

variables are measured the same way as in Table 3. All explanatory variables are measured in the year prior to refocusing.

Panel A of Table 5 presents estimates from the following logit model of refocusing likelihood:[9]

$$\begin{aligned} \text{FOCUS}_{i,t} = \text{f}\,(&\text{EXVAL}_{i,t-1}, \text{ROA}_{i,t-1}, \text{GROWTH}_{i,t-1}, \text{LEV}_{i,t-1}, \\ &\text{NEWCEO}_{i,t-1}, \text{PRESSURE}_{i,t-1}, \text{DISTRESS}_{i,t-1}), \end{aligned} \quad (2)$$

where the variables are

$\text{FOCUS}_{i,t}$ = indicator of whether firm i begins a refocusing program in year t.

$\text{EXVAL}_{i,t-1}$ = firm i's excess value at the end of year $t-1$ (see Appendix A).

$\text{ROA}_{i,t-1}$ = firm i's year $t-1$ return (EBITD) on year $t-2$ assets.

$\text{GROWTH}_{i,t-1}$ = firm i's annual rate of change in sales from year $t-2$ to year $t-1$.

$\text{LEV}_{i,t-1}$ = leverage (book value of debt/total assets) of firm i at the end of year $t-1$.

$\text{NEWCEO}_{i,t-1}$ = indicator of whether firm i's CEO was replaced during the period extending from 12 months before the first sale or refocusing announcement until 1 month after that announcement.

$\text{PRESSURE}_{i,t-1}$ = an indicator of whether firm i experienced at least one event of outside shareholder pressure during the period extending from 12 months before the first sale or refocusing announcement until 1 month after that announcement. The events of outside shareholder pressure are activism by a pension fund investor, the addition of an outside blockholder, and an unsuccessful takeover bid.

[9] In order to conserve space, we do not report the coefficient estimates for the constant terms of the logit models.

$\text{DISTRESS}_{i,t-1}$ = an indicator of whether firm i experienced at least one event of financial distress during the period extending from 12 months before the first sale or refocusing announcement until 1 month after that announcement. The events of financial distress are a dividend cut, debt restructuring, and filing for protection from creditors under Chapter 11 of the U.S. bankruptcy code.

In addition to reporting the raw coefficient estimates from the logit estimation, we also provide a measure of the economic importance of the explanatory variables. This measure is the increase in the probability that the dependent variable takes the value of 1 for a change of 1 quartile from the median (a change from 0 to 1) in the value of each continuous (indicator) independent variable, holding all other continuous (indicator) independent variables constant at their medians (at 0).[10] We express all of the probability changes as increases by replacing the median of the continuous variable being evaluated with either its 25th or 75th percentile (whichever leads to a probability increase).[11]

The results in panel A of Table 5 show that excess value has a negative relation with refocusing probability, indicating that firms destroying more value with their diversification strategy are, all else being equal, more likely to refocus. For all three excess value measures, the coefficient estimate is negative. The significance of the estimates varies, with the asset multiplier measure of excess value of marginal significance, the sales multiplier measure significant at the .10 level, and the EBITD measure significant at the .01 level. The economic importance of the excess value measures is fairly high. Changing the asset (sales, EBITD) multiplier measure of excess value

[10] We adjust the inconsistent estimates of the intercept term to correct for choice-based sampling using the procedure outlined by Manski and Lerman (1977). Caudill and Jackson (1989) discuss the measurement of marginal effects in logit models with indicator explanatory variables. For the marginal effects of the continuous variables, note that the nonlinearity of the logit model could make inferences sensitive to the evaluation point chosen.

[11] Our logit models of refocusing likelihood do not attempt to incorporate the method of divestiture into the analysis. Firms divest business units either with asset sales to a third party or with spinoffs Spinoffs, which usually escape taxation at the parent level, are pro rata distributions of shares of a controlled subsidiary to the shareholders of the parent. Our 107 refocusing firms divested 385 business units using 363 asset sales and 22 spinoffs. Alford and Berger (1998) investigate the choice between sales and spinoffs, conditional on having already made the decision to divest. They note that whether versus how to divest can be thought of as separate nodes of a nested logit model in which an answer to the question of whether to divest may be affected by the answer to the question of how to divest. We do not attempt to use Alford and Berger's results to formally model the nested decision for the following reasons. First, just 6% of the divestitures in our sample are spinoffs. Moreover, the majority of firms in our sample that use spinoffs also use asset sales, so that our analysis would need to be done at the divested unit level rather than the parent firm level to incorporate the effects of divestiture method. Relatedly, we do not have many of the data items we would require to perform analysis at the divested unit level. Finally, the inferences of main concern in our logit models are the effects of excess value and the corporate control events, and the results on these variables are robust to the alternative specifications that we are able to employ.

The Review of Financial Studies / v 12 n 2 1999

Table 5
Refocus likelihood models

Independent variable	Coefficient estimate (p-value)	Change in probability	Coefficient estimate (p-value)	Change in probability	Coefficient estimate (p-value)	Change in probability
			Panel A. Matched sample			
Excess value, asset multiplier	−0.993 (0.104)	1.275%				
Excess value, sales multiplier			−0.570*** (0.068)	1.865%		
Excess value, EBITD multiplier					−1.738* (0.009)	4.870%
Return on assets	−5.322 (0.157)	2.301%	−7.634* (0.010)	2.161%	−15.775* (0.002)	9.481%
Sales growth	3.000** (0.024)	2.481%	2.359** (0.035)	2.204%	2.591** (0.064)	2.493%
Leverage	2.000 (0.141)	2.177%	0.528 (0.527)	0.623%	−0.363 (0.789)	0.313%
New CEO	1.056** (0.069)	14.160%	1.236** (0.018)	19.692%	0.556 (0.384)	7.254%
Outside shareholder pressure	1.933* (0.000)	33.350%	1.814* (0.000)	33.240%	2.056* (0.000)	39.700%
Financial distress	0.931 (0.236)	11.949%	1.066 (0.123)	16.138%		
$N = 0$ (no refocus)	80		106		69	
$N = 1$ (refocus)	79		105		69	
Model p-value	0.0004		0.0001		0.0007	
Pseudo-R^2	0.120		0.108		0.130	

Panel A reports logit regressions estimating the likelihood of refocusing. The dependent variable equals 1 if the firm refocused in the following year and 0 otherwise. The sample includes 107 firms that refocused during the period 1985–1993. Each refocusing firm has a matched control firm of similar size and sales Herfindahl index at the end of year −1. All independent variables are measured in the year prior to classifying the observation as refocusing or not refocusing. The change in probability is defined as the percentage increase in the probability of refocusing when the variable's median is replaced with either its 25th or 75th percentile (whichever leads to a probability increase), and all other variables are evaluated at their medians. When all of the explanatory variables have their median values, the probabilities of refocusing are 9.953% (asset multiplier regression), 11.765% (sales multiplier regression), and 12.084% (EBITD multiplier regression). Two-tailed p-values for the coefficient estimates are in parentheses. *,**,*** denote significance at the 1%, 5%, and 10% levels, respectively.

from its median to its 25th percentile increases the refocusing probability by 1.3% (1.9%, 4.9%) from its base level of about 10%. The marginal effect on refocusing likelihood of a 1 quartile change in the other performance-related variables, sales growth, and ROA tends to be slightly larger than that of excess value, and both ROA and sales growth generally have statistically significant effects on the decision to refocus.[12]

[12] We have also estimated all of the logit regressions reported in the article with additional performance

Causes and Effects of Corporate Refocusing Programs

Table 5
(continued)

Independent variable	Coefficient estimate (p-value)	Change in probability	Coefficient estimate (p-value)	Change in probability	Coefficient estimate (p-value)	Change in probability
	Panel B. Full sample, years assigned randomly to nonrefocusing firms					
Excess value, asset multiplier	−1.310* (0.002)	3.127%				
Excess value, sales multiplier			−0.854* (0.000)	3.331%		
Excess value, EBITD multiplier					−1.133* (0.007)	2.577%
Return on assets	−0.232 (0.905)	0.085%	−2.255 (0.111)	0.216%	−5.505* (0.010)	2.235%
Total assets	−0.298* (0.001)	4.259%	−0.143*** (0.059)	1.933%	−0.245** (0.016)	3.531%
Sales growth	−0.055 (0.862)	0.046%	−0.018 (0.949)	0.015%	−0.064 (0.883)	0.055%
Leverage	0.946 (0.165)	1.147%	0.888 (0.113)	1.093%	−0.251 (0.759)	0.285%
Sales Herfindahl	−2.264* (0.002)	3.932%	−2.037* (0.001)	3.555%	−3.001* (0.000)	5.601%
$N = 0$ (no refocus)	500		645		469	
$N = 1$ (refocus)	79		105		69	
Model p-value	0.0001		0.0001		0.0001	
Pseudo-R^2	0.058		0.051		0.061	

Panel B logit regressions estimating refocus likelihood models. The dependent variable equals 1 if the firm started refocusing during the year and 0 if it continued to report two ore more segments. To achieve consistency with the years of the refocusing observations, a year (1985–1993) is assigned randomly to each of the nonrefocusing firms with complete data. All independent variables are measured in the year prior to classifying the observation as refocusing or not refocusing. The change in probability is defined as the percentage increase in the probability of refocusing when the variable's median is replaced with either its 25th or 75th percentile (whichever leads to a probability increase), and all other variables are evaluated at their medians. When all of the explanatory variables have their median values, the probabilities of refocusing are 11.764% (asset multiplier regression), 12.013% (sales multiplier regression), and 12.263% (EBITD multiplier regression), respectively. Two-tailed p-values for the coefficient estimates are in parentheses.

*,**,*** denote significance at the 1%, 5%, and 10% levels, respectively.

The disciplinary events, especially outside shareholder pressure, are important determinants of refocusing. Experiencing one or more events of outside shareholder pressure in the previous year increases a firm's probability of refocusing by between 33.2% and 39.7% (significant at the .01 level). The replacement of the CEO during the previous year increases the

measures such as EBITDA/sales added to the explanatory variables. The additional performance measure is sometimes significantly related to refocusing likelihood, but its addition does not affect the inferences on the excess value measures.

chances of restructuring by between 7.3% and 19.7%, with the estimate on this variable significant in two of the three logit models. Events of financial distress do not have a significant effect on refocusing activity in our logit estimations.[13] Overall, the results in panel A of Table 5 show that firms that reduce market value through diversification, perform poorly, and attract disciplinary events (particularly outside shareholder pressure) are more likely to refocus.[14]

The matched sample used in panel A of Table 5, and throughout the article, lowers data collection costs by using only a subset of the nonrefocusing diversified firms. However, the matched-firm design does not allow testing of the effect of the matching variables on the likelihood of refocusing. As a sensitivity test of the matched sample design, we present tests in panel B of Table 5 that use the full set of nonrefocusing firms with available information. The independent variables in panel B exclude the three indicators of events of market discipline used in panel A, since we did not collect these data for the full set of nonrefocusing companies. On the other hand, in addition to the variables used in panel A, we add the two matching measures to the explanatory variables used in panel B. Thus size (log of total assets) and the extent of diversification (the revenue-based Herfindahl index) are included among the independent variables. In the logit regressions we report in panel B, we follow Zmijewski (1984) by assigning randomly a year (1985–1993) to each of the nonrefocusing firms to achieve consistency with the years of the refocusing observations. As in panel A, all explanatory variables are measured in the year prior to classifying the observation as refocusing or nonrefocusing.

The results reported in panel B provide some additional insights into the refocusing decision. Compared with panel A, the probability increases in panel B indicate that ROA is a less important input to the refocusing decision for the full sample than for the matched sample. In contrast, the size and Herfindahl index variables used in selecting the matched sample are shown to be statistically and economically important in the full sample. The magnitude and significance of the estimates on excess value are generally somewhat greater than they were in panel A (additional tests not reported in a table show that the panel A results on excess value are very similar

[13] Note that we excluded the financial distress indicator variable from the logit regression that uses the EBITD multiplier measure of excess value. Only 3.7% of the 107 nonrefocusing firms had an event of financial distress (see Table 3), and only 69 of these firms had available data for the EBITD excess value regression. Thus the inclusion of the financial distress variable in this regression resulted in quasicomplete separation in the sample points and questionable validity of the model fit from the logit estimation.

[14] Because the regressions estimated in Tables 5, 6, and 9 pool observations across years, we are assuming that the models estimated are stationary over the 1985–1993 period. In addition, some of the estimated models include up to two of the same firms within the refocusing sample because these two firms experienced separate refocusing episodes. Including the same firm in different years may violate the assumption that the observations are independent. Therefore we also estimated all regressions using only the first refocusing episode for each refocusing firm. All inferences remained identical to those reported in the tables.

Causes and Effects of Corporate Refocusing Programs

Table 6
Diversification characteristics and refocusing

Independent variable	Coefficient estimate (*p*-value)	Change in probability	Coefficient estimate (*p*-value)	Change in probability
Excess value, sales multiplier			−0.713** (0.033)	3.163%
Number of segments	0.282** (0.034)	3.941%	0.157 (0.303)	2.321%
Number of related segments	−0.299* (0.078)	4.207%	−0.110 (0.586)	1.600%
A segment with negative CF	0.802** (0.022)	13.200%	0.511 (0.213)	8.415%
Unallocated expenses	20.700** (0.030)	2.895%	18.025*** (0.088)	2.748%
Return on assets			−6.438** (0.035)	4.347%
Sales growth			2.483** (0.034)	3.111%
Leverage			0.455 (0.607)	0.722%
New CEO			1.173** (0.030)	22.739%
Outside shareholder pressure			1.687* (0.000)	35.424%
Financial distress			0.944 (0.170)	17.413%
$N = 0$ (no refocus)	107		105	
$N = 1$ (refocus)	107		106	
Model *p*-value	0.0010		0.0001	
Pseudo-R^2	0.149		0.139	

Logit regressions estimating refocus likelihood models. The dependent variable equals 1 if the firm started refocusing in the following year and 0 otherwise. The sample includes 107 firms that refocused during the period 1985–1993. Each refocusing firm has a matched control firm of similar size and sales Herfindahl index at the end of year −1. The change in probability is defined as the percentage increase in the probability of refocusing when the variable's median is replaced with either its 25th or 75th percentile (whichever leads to a probability increase), and all other variables are evaluated at their medians. For the indicator variable, the change in probability is based on changing the variable from a value of 0 to 1. When all of the explanatory variables have their median values, the probabilities of refocusing are 14.919% (first regression) and 16.877% (second regression), respectively. The number of related segments is the difference between the total number of segments reported by the firm and the number of segments with different main 2 digit SIC codes. The segment with negative CF variable is an indicator equal to 1 if the firm reported at least one segment with negative EBITD in year −1. The unallocated expenses variable is the maximum of the difference between the sum of segment EBITD and total firm EBITD scaled by sales, and 0. Two-tailed *p*-values for the coefficient estimates are in parentheses.

*,**,*** denote significance at the 1%, 5%, and 10% levels, respectively.

to those in panel B when the indicator variables for the events of market discipline are excluded from the panel A regressions). A diversified firm destroying more value than three quarters, rather than half, of the panel B sample is between 2.6% and 3.3% more likely to refocus. The probability changes resulting from changes in the excess value measures are generally larger than those resulting from changes in the other variables, with size and the extent of diversification (i.e., the matching variables for the other tables) being the only exceptions. Overall the panel B results show that diversified firms are more likely to refocus when their diversification programs are less valuable, the firm is small, and the extent of prerefocusing diversification is large. The results also provide much weaker evidence that the likelihood of refocusing is increased by poor performance (as measured by ROA) and high leverage.

3.3 Diversification Characteristics and Subsequent Refocusing

We have established that firms with greater value losses from diversification are more likely to refocus. We now examine how individual determinants of the value loss influence the probability of refocusing. We investigate the effects of three factors: the extent to which the diversified lines of business are related; the existence of unprofitable segments; and the proportion of firm expenses not allocated to specific lines of business (unallocated expenses).

Table 6 presents the results of logistic regressions of the sources of diversification's valuation effect on the decision to refocus. The first regression uses only the sources of diversification's value effect as independent variables, whereas the second regression also includes the sales multiplier measure of excess value and the control variables from panel A of Table 5. We omit the additional explanatory variables from the first regression because the sources of diversification's value effect contribute to the excess value and performance-related variables, and may affect whether events of market discipline occur. The sources of diversification's value effect that we test probably represent only a subset of all of the factors influencing diversification's success. Thus we expect that diversification's total value effect (and the general performance-related variables) will better explain the decision to refocus than will the individual diversification characteristics we examine. Our main interest, however, is in whether specific characteristics of the diversification program are associated with refocusing likelihood, rather than in whether these characteristics add incremental explanatory power beyond that provided by measures such as excess value and the disciplinary events. Thus we emphasize the results from the first regression.

The first regression's results show that each of the three diversification characteristics significantly affects the probability of restructuring. The significantly positive coefficient estimate on the number of segments indicates that firms with more segments are more likely to refocus. Relatedness among the segments, however, completely mitigates this tendency, with the significant coefficient of −0.299 on the related segments variable of approximately equal magnitude to the positive coefficient on the number of segments variable.[15] This result is consistent with the arguments of many authors, following Rumelt (1974), that related diversified firms perform better than conglomerates. Our finding is also consistent with Daley, Mehrotra, and Sivakumar's (1997) result that spinoffs of unrelated businesses create more value than spinoffs of related segments, and with Berger and Ofek's (1995) finding that relatedness mitigates the value loss from diversification.

The estimate on the negative cash flow indicator is significantly positive, consistent with the presence of negative cash flow segments increasing the likelihood of refocusing. This finding supports arguments by Meyer, Milgrom, and Roberts (1992), Rajan and Zingales (1996), and Scharfstein and Stein (1996), who all present models which point to the managers of subunits with the poorest prospects being the most inclined to engage in personal rent-seeking activities. The Meyer, Milgrom, and Roberts and Scharfstein and Stein articles also show that such behavior can result in excessive investment cross-subsidies from better- to worse-performing segments, and Berger and Ofek (1995), Lamont (1997), and Shin and Stulz (1996) provide support for this contention.

Finally, we use the difference, scaled by sales, between the sum of the segments' EBITD and the firm's EBITD, when nonnegative, to measure unallocated expenses.[16] Unallocated expenses represent either the expenses that are not associated with the activities of individual business lines, or the net losses of business segments too small to be reported separately. In either case, the unallocated expenses are expenditures that do not directly produce any profit, and empirically we observe that they appear to explain the profitability loss from diversification (i.e., we find that when these expenses are left unallocated, the profitability of segments from diversified firms is equal to that of stand-alone companies). The results in the first column of Table 6 show that the coefficient on the unallocated expense measure is significantly positive, consistent with diversified firms that allocate less of their expenses to separately reported business lines being more likely to refocus.

The second regression in Table 6 shows that, as expected, the significance of the coefficients on the diversification characteristics decreases in the second regression, which adds the excess value measure, the performance-related controls, and the corporate control events as explanatory variables. The coefficients on the related segments variable and on the negative cash flow indicator retain the same signs as in the first regression, but at de-

---

[15] To measure relatedness, we classify all segments within a firm that have different SIC codes at the two-digit level as unrelated. We then measure the difference between the total number of segments reported by a firm and its number of unrelated segments. This related-segments variable varies between 0, when no segments are related, and −1, when no segments differ.

[16] The measure actually captures the difference between unallocated revenues and unallocated expenses.

The Review of Financial Studies / v 12 n 2 1999

creased significance levels. Of interest, the coefficient on unallocated expenses remains similar in magnitude and retains significance at the .10 level. The Table 6 results provide exploratory evidence that specific diversification characteristics affect the likelihood of refocusing. However, with the exception of unallocated expenses, the incremental explanatory power of these characteristics is not statistically significant after incorporating the total excess value measure and the control variables into the analysis.[17]

4. Further Evidence on the Causes of Refocusing Programs

The preceding sections provide evidence that both value loss from diversification and events of market discipline affect diversified firms' decisions on whether to refocus. To examine how the interaction between corporate control events and value loss affects the likelihood of refocusing, we divide the matched sample into four groups and compare the proportion of refocusers across the groups. Table 7 shows that two dimensions determine the group that a firm is placed in. The columns of Table 7 separate value losers and nonlosers, with a firm defined as a loser if its sales multiplier measure of excess value falls below zero. The rows of the table separate firms that have been subject to events of market discipline from those firms not subject to such events. All events from Table 3, other than non-CEO management changes, are included as events of market discipline.

The Table 7 results show that value destruction and reduction of agency problems both affect the decision to divest. Firms with both negative excess value and one or more disciplinary events are most likely to refocus, with 82% of such firms divesting. In contrast, refocusing by nonlosers with no disciplinary events is strikingly lower (with the difference significant at the .01 level), with just 16% selling businesses. Moreover, the 40% refocusing frequency among losers not subject to disciplinary events is significantly lower (.01 level) than the 82% rate among losers that are subject to such events. This last comparison indicates that firms with negative excess value are significantly more likely to refocus if they also are subjected to events of market discipline.[18]

[17] The results for the second regression in Table 6 remain very similar when the asset and EBITD measures of excess value are used in place of the sales measure reported in the table. All coefficient estimates retain the same sign, and the only large change in significance levels is a drop to below the .10 level on unallocated expenses when the EBITD excess value measure is used. In addition, comparing these results to those reported in panel A of Table 5 shows that, for all three excess value measures, the coefficient estimate on excess value is only marginally changed by the addition of the three diversification characteristics to the refocusing likelihood regression. This is consistent with the three characteristics capturing only a portion of diversification's total value impact.

[18] To test the conjecture that events of market discipline are more likely at firms that had been destroying more value, we measure excess value in the fiscal year prior to the 13 month period that we examined for events of market discipline. We then compare the means and medians of these prior year excess values for firms that were or were not subject to various events of market discipline. The results show that, for all three measures of excess value and all three events of market discipline examined, the prior year excess

Table 7
Value loss, changes in agency costs, and the decision to refocus

		Loser	Nonloser
Agency reduction	Number of firms that refocus	49	17
	Number of firms that do not refocus	11	8
	Total number of firms	60	25
	Percent refocusers	0.82	0.68
	p-value vs. upper-left quadrant	(n/a)	(0.16)
No agency reduction	Number of firms that refocus	34	7
	Number of firms that do not refocus	50	38
	Total number of firms	84	45
	Percent refocusers	0.40	0.16
	p-value vs. upper-left quadrant	(0.01)	(0.01)

Counts and frequencies of refocusing categorized by whether the diversified firm was subject to events of market discipline that could reduce agency problems and whether the firm lost value by being diversified. The sample includes 107 firms that refocused during the period 1985–1993. Each refocusing firm has a matched control firm of similar size and sales Herfindahl index at the end of year −1. A firm is defined as a loser if its sales multiplier measure of excess value is below zero at the end of year −1. A firm is defined as having had agency reduction if it had a new CEO, outside pressure, or events of financial distress during year −1. The two-tailed p-values are from tests of the significance of the difference in sample proportions of refocusers between each quadrant and the upper-left quadrant.

It is of interest to consider further the bottom panel of Table 7, which contains the firms not subject to external pressure. Forty-one of these 129 firms refocus, indicating that even without market discipline nearly one-third of diversified firms choose to refocus. Moreover, comparing the top-left and bottom-left quadrants of Table 7 reveals that of the 83 losers that refocused, 34 of them did so without external threats. Thus internal control mechanisms alone appear to lead to divestitures within a sizable minority of the unsuccessful diversified firms that refocus.

We investigate this conjecture by including governance and compensation variables along with the explanatory variables from Table 5, panel B in a model of refocusing likelihood. The results (not reported in a table) show that CEO options granted (or, alternatively, CEO-vested option ownership) increase the likelihood of refocusing. In contrast, CEO stock ownership does not. The stock ownership result contrasts with the findings of Denis et al. (1997). Our results are, however, consistent with the managerial risk aversion motive for diversification suggested by Amihud and Lev (1981), and further supported by May (1995), and with Tufano's (1996) evidence that option ownership reduces hedging in the gold mining industry, whereas stock ownership increases it. We did not find that CEO tenure or the percentage of insiders on the board was associated with the probability of refocusing.

values are lower for firms subsequently subject to a disciplinary event. The differences in mean (median) excess value are significant in four (two) of the nine comparisons.

The Review of Financial Studies / v 12 n 2 1999

Table 8
Abnormal returns around the refocusing-related announcements

Variable	Obs	Mean	Median	% positive
Abnormal return day −1	404	0.002	0.000	51.98%
Abnormal return day 0	404	0.011*	0.041*	61.14%*
Abnormal return day 1	404	0.006*	0.000	50.99%
Cumulative abnormal return days −1 to 1	404	0.019*	0.007*	59.41%*
CAR restructuring announcement	29	0.030***	0.008	62.07%
CAR first announcement	105	0.036*	0.012*	63.81%*
CAR second or later announcement	299	0.013*	0.006*	57.86%*
CAR all sale-related announcements	105	0.073*	0.044*	73.33%*

Abnormal returns of 404 refocusing-related announcements made by 105 firms. The events include 339 asset sale (or spinoff) announcements and 65 announcements that sales are under consideration or that a general restructuring has been approved. Abnormal returns are calculated using a market model with β calculated over 250 days prior to the event, and the equally weighted market portfolio used as the proxy for the market return.

*,*** denote significance at the 1% and 10% levels, respectively.

5. The Market's Reaction to the Refocusing

We examine the market reaction to divestiture-related announcements of the refocusing firms by computing abnormal excess returns as the actual announcement day returns minus the firm's expected daily return. Expected daily returns are computed using a market model estimated over the 250-trading-day period that ends prior to the firm's first refocusing announcement. Table 8 reports the abnormal stock returns of the sellers for each of 404 refocusing-related announcements made by the 105 refocusing firms. The abnormal return to the seller on the day preceding, the day of, and the day following the announcement is reported, along with the CAR over the 3-day period. The top four rows of the table show that the mean and median abnormal returns (and the percentage of these returns that are positive) are significantly greater than zero (50%) at the .01 level for both day 0 and the cumulative 3-day period. The average CAR for the seller is 1.9%, consistent with previous research.[19]

The 404 refocusing-related announcements include 339 divestiture announcements, 29 announcements of planned restructuring programs, and 36 announcements of the amount of consideration received for previously announced sales.[20] The bottom four rows of Table 8 provide CARs for

[19] Using 2-day windows ending on day 0, Jain (1985) and Hite, Owers, and Rogers (1987) document CARs of 0.5% and 1.7%. Using 3-day windows ending on day 0, Klein (1986) and John and Ofek (1995) find CARs of 1.1% and 1.5%. For samples restricted to voluntary spinoffs, the CARs for 2-day windows ending on day 0 have been documented at 2.9% by Schipper and Smith (1983) and 3.3% by Miles and Rosenfeld (1983) and Hite and Owers (1983).

[20] The 339 divestitures consist of 320 asset sales and 19 spinoffs. We do not perform a separate analysis of the market reactions to the two types of divestiture because we have so few spinoff observations. In addition, previous research indicates a significantly positive reaction to both divestiture methods.

various subsets of the 404 refocusing-related announcements. The 29 announcements of planned restructuring programs result in an average cumulative return for the announcer of 3%, significant at the .10 level. Many of these 29 announcements are the first of a series of announcements made by the refocusing firm. For all 105 refocusing firms, the CAR for the first announcement made averages 3.6%, with 63.8% positive, both of which are significant at the .01 level. The resolution of uncertainty may be smaller for second and subsequent announcements by refocusing firms. Therefore it is perhaps unsurprising that the CAR for second or later announcements by these firms averages a considerably smaller 1.3%, still significant at the .01 level. Finally, it is of interest to document the CAR over all of the 3-day announcement windows for each refocusing firm. The last row of Table 8 shows that the market reacts very favorably to the total refocusing program of the sample firms. The CAR over all refocusing announcements is 7.3% on average, 4.4% at the median, and is positive for 73.3% of the refocusing firms.

The positive market reaction to the refocusing is consistent with the view that firms are reversing value-destroying policies. We investigate this possibility further in Table 9 by regressing the total CAR from all refocusing announcements on the firm's excess value measure and other variables. In addition to the variables used in Table 5, we include indicator variables for the events of market discipline reported in Table 3. These events generally precede all of the refocusing announcements. The occurrence of disciplinary events may reduce the market's surprise at the time of a divestiture, but may also induce more value-increasing divestitures than those that occur for firms not subject to such events. Finally, we include a control variable for the number of sale-related announcements reported by the firm.

The results show a negative relation between excess value and the cumulative abnormal returns, significant at the .01 level for all three excess value measures, and generally insignificant coefficient estimates on the remaining variables. Thus firms with more value-reducing diversification policies appear to realize greater value from refocusing.[21] These results are consistent with the value loss from operating diverse businesses within one corporation being reversed (at least in part) when the diverse businesses are split apart. If the diversification discount had resulted only from past, irreversible mistakes, we would not expect excess value to be inversely related to the CARs from divestiture-related announcements.[22]

[21] As Lanen and Thompson (1988) demonstrate, a caveat to this conclusion is that cross-sectional associations between stock price reactions and a firm characteristic do not necessarily suggest that the characteristic has the same cross-sectional association with cash flow effects. Lanen and Thompson show that this caveat applies to any analysis of firm-specific decisions where the prior probability of a firm making a specific choice is likely to differ across firms because of cross-sectional differences in firm characteristics.

[22] When we perform the Table 9 regression with the excess value measure excluded, the magnitudes and significance levels of the coefficient estimates on the agency variables are similar to those reported.

The Review of Financial Studies / v 12 n 2 1999

Table 9
Excess value and the announcement returns

Dependent variable		CAR refocusing	
Observations	78	103	67
Adjusted R^2	0.054	0.154	0.153
Intercept	0.052	0.139	0.116
	(0.636)	(0.162)	(0.291)
Excess value, asset multiplier	−0.135*		
	(0.006)		
Excess value, sales multiplier		−0.075*	
		(0.004)	
Excess value, EBITD multiplier			−0.099**
			(0.012)
Return on assets	0.001	−0.272	−0.731**
	(0.998)	(0.268)	(0.013)
Total assets	−0.016	−0.016	−0.011
	(0.188)	(0.129)	(0.343)
Sales growth	0.058	0.047	0.005
	(0.513)	(0.562)	(0.947)
Leverage	0.007	−0.055	0.087
	(0.938)	(0.504)	(0.388)
Sales Herfindahl	0.087	0.040	0.099
	(0.313)	(0.577)	(0.230)
New CEO dummy	−0.044	−0.059***	−0.071***
	(0.244)	(0.078)	(0.092)
Financial distress dummy	0.066	0.100**	−0.002
	(0.160)	(0.014)	(0.965)
Outside pressure dummy	0.050	0.038	0.050
	(0.158)	(0.202)	(0.147)
Number of sale-related events	0.002	0.006	0.007
	(0.721)	(0.210)	(0.212)

Linear regressions relating the total cumulative abnormal returns of all refocus-related announcements to excess value prior to the first announcement and other control variables. The excess value variables are defined in table 4. Two-tailed p-values are in parentheses.

*,**,*** denote significance at the 1%, 5%, and 10% levels, respectively.

6. Conclusions

We study the antecedents and consequences of corporate refocusing programs. Corporate reorganizations are complex events with causes and effects that likely differ across situations. We attempt to capture some of this complexity by examining the effect of several factors on the likelihood of refocusing. The measures we investigate are the value impact of the diversification program, the characteristics of the diversification program, various events of market discipline, and various corporate governance variables.

We find that one cause of refocusings is the desire to enhance shareholder value. Diversified firms that refocus have significantly greater value losses from their diversification policies than multisegment firms that do not refocus. Individual characteristics of the diversification program also affect whether companies restructure. Relatedness among the lines of business reduces the probability of refocusing, whereas the presence of unprofitable segments and larger central overhead expenses increase refocusing likelihood.

If agency problems play a role in creating suboptimal diversification policies, such problems may have to be reduced before managers will undertake a divestiture program. Consistent with this conjecture, we find that corporate control events often precede refocusings. About 31% of refocusers have a change in top management in the period before their restructuring, three times the rate reported by Warner, Watts, and Wruck (1988) for a random sample of firms during an earlier time period. Moreover, 62% of refocusers have at least one corporate control event (other than non-CEO turnover) in the year preceding their first divestiture, whereas only about 18% of a matched sample have one of these events. Our evidence is thus consistent with the view that reduction in agency problems via corporate control events plays a crucial role in corporate refocusing choices.

Events of market discipline increase the likelihood of divestiture, after controlling for diversification's valuation consequences. Firms for which the valuation effect of diversification is negative refocus twice as frequently if they have been the target of one or more events of market discipline. We do not find, however, that external pressure is pervasive among refocusing firms that had value-reducing diversification policies. The presence of some negative excess value firms that refocus without external forces being brought to bear suggests that internal control mechanisms alone may correct value-reducing diversification in some firms. We test this implication and find that the level of, and the change in, CEO option ownership provides an effective internal incentive mechanism to induce CEOs to restructure. Future research examining the internal motives for refocusing in more detail could shed additional light on the effectiveness of various corporate governance mechanisms.

Finally, we examine the market reaction to restructuring-related announcements and find that the cumulative abnormal returns over all of the refocusing-related announcements of a refocusing firm average 7.3%, and that these abnormal returns are significantly related to the amount of value that was being destroyed by the refocuser's diversification policy. These results are consistent with refocusing creating economically significant enhancements to shareholder wealth. The fact that the gain from refocusing is positively related to the amount of value that was being destroyed indicates that divesting divisions from a diversified firm can reverse (at least in part) the value reduction arising from operating multiple lines of business within one firm.

Several areas for future research are suggested by our findings. Events of external pressure are effective in inducing managers to undertake value-enhancing refocusing activity. Why then must such large value reductions occur before external pressure is brought to bear? This question can be attacked by exploring the costs faced by those who create external pressure, and how these costs vary across outside blockholders, creditors, pension funds, and others. Another interesting issue arises from our exploratory evidence that internal capital markets supported by significant headquarters staff are inefficient, on average. Because the creation of an internal capital market is a frequently cited motive for diversification, particularly within less developed external capital markets, it is of interest to examine how the internal market benefits of diversification vary across countries and time. Finally, a related issue is to examine what factors create the cross-sectional variation in diversification's value effect. We find that the compensation policy of the CEO (with respect to stock options) affects the likelihood of refocusing. It would be of interest to know whether the compensation policy for divisional managers helps to explain which firms have less value reduction from their diversification policies.

Appendix A

Multiplier Estimation of Imputed Value and Excess Value:
Equations A.1 and A.2 illustrate the approach:

$$\mathrm{I(V)} = \sum_{i=1}^{n} \mathrm{AI}_i * \left(\mathrm{Ind}_i \left(\frac{\mathrm{V}}{\mathrm{AI}}\right)_{mf}\right) \tag{A.1}$$

$$\mathrm{EXVAL} = \ln\left(\frac{\mathrm{V}}{\mathrm{I(V)}}\right) \tag{A.2}$$

where:

I(V)	=	the imputed value of the sum of a firm's segments as stand-alone firms.
AI_i	=	segment i's value of the accounting item (sales, assets, or EBITD) used in the valuation multiple.
$\mathrm{Ind}_i(\frac{\mathrm{V}}{\mathrm{AI}})_{mf}$	=	the multiple of total capital to an accounting item (sales, assets, or EBITD) for the median single-segment firm in segment i's industry.
EXVAL	=	the firm's excess value.
V	=	the firm's total capital (market value of common equity + book value of debt).
n	=	the total number of segments in segment i's firm.

Equation (A.1) shows that the firm's imputed value is the sum of segment-imputed values, which are obtained by multiplying an industry median multiplier of total capital to an accounting item by the segment's level of the accounting item. Equation (A.2) shows that the firm's excess value measure is the natural logarithm of the ratio of the firm's actual value to its imputed value.

To compute excess value using the sales multiplier, we multiply the industry median multiple of capital-to-sales for the stand-alone firms in the segment's industry by the segment's sales to obtain the imputed capital of the segment. We repeat this process for each of the firm's segments and then sum to obtain the firm's imputed value. Finally, we find the firm's excess value by taking the natural logarithm of the ratio of actual to imputed value. Extreme excess values are excluded from the analysis, with "extreme" defined for all three multipliers as natural logarithms of actual to imputed value above 1.386 or below −1.386 (i.e., actual values either more than four times imputed, or less than one-fourth imputed).

The asset multiple imputed values are found in an analogous manner. Another issue that arises is that it is much more common for the segment asset figures from the CIS tape to disagree with the Compustat firm totals than is the case with sales. The segment sum is usually less than the firm figure, indicating that the problem arises from unallocated assets. We deal with this problem in one of two ways: If the sum of the segment asset figures for a firm deviates from the firm's asset figure by more than 25%, we exclude the observation from all analyses using the asset multiples. If the deviation is within 25%, we adjust the firm's imputed value to reflect the fact that the multipliers have been multiplied by segment asset figures that are too small or too large. Specifically, the firm's imputed value is grossed up or down by the percentage deviation between the sum of its segments' assets and total firm assets. The excess value measure based on asset multiples is then found in the same way as the measure using sales multiples.

The earnings before interest, taxes, and depreciation (EBITD) multiple imputed values use the same adjustment procedures as the asset multiple imputed values. One additional issue is how to treat segments with negative EBITDs, since multiplier approaches do not typically assign negative values to firms with negative earnings. We address this issue by replacing the EBITD multiplier with the segment's sales multiplier imputed value.

Appendix B

Table B.1
Description of Firms that Refocused

Name	Start refocus	#Segmen Start	End	#Div sold	Value sold	with value	Return	Mgt	Ust	Par	Div	Deb	cl l
ABITIBI PRICE INC	9106	6	3	4	336	3	−0.019	1	0	0	0	0	0
ACME-CLEVELAND CORP	8606	3	2	1	0	0	0.012	0	0	0	0	0	0
ALLEGHENY INTERNATIONAL	8602	5	1	15	492	5	0.452	0	1	1	0	1	0
ALLIED PRODUCTS	9102	3	1	8	77	2	0.108	0	0	0	0	1	0
ALLIS-CHALMERS CORP	8502	4	1	13	700	7	0.478	0	0	0	0	1	0
AMDURA CORP	8901	4	1	6	134	3	0.345	1	0	1	0	0	1
AMERICAN CYANAMID CO	8812	4	2	8	465	1	0.050	0	0	1	0	0	0
AMERICAN MAIZE-PRODS	8809	3	2	2	25	1	−0.016	2	0	0	0	0	0
ANACOMP INC	8607	2	1	3	0	0	−0.076	0	0	0	0	0	0
APACHE CORP	8707	2	1	5	108	2	0.017	0	0	0	0	0	0
ARDEN GROUP INC	9309	3	1	2	40	2	0.086	0	0	0	0	0	0

The Review of Financial Studies / v 12 n 2 1999

Table B.1
(continued)

Name	Start refocus	#Segmen Start	End	#Div sold	Value sold	with value	Return	Mgt	Ust	Par	Div	Deb	c11
ARMCO INC	9111	5	2	5	150	3	−0.160	1	0	0	1	0	0
ASTROTECH INTL	8710	3	1	3	11	1	0.291	2	0	0	1	1	0
BAIRNCO CORP	9206	4	2	2	0	0	0.116	0	0	1	0	0	0
BAXTER INTERNATIONAL INC	9204	4	2	3	1024	2	0.133	2	0	0	0	0	0
BELL INDUSTRIES INC	9210	4	3	1	0	0	0.023	0	0	1	0	0	0
BERGEN BRUNSWIG CORP	8711	3	2	1	40	1	0.007	0	0	0	0	0	0
BERGEN BRUNSWIG CORP	9202	2	1	1	78	1	0.038	0	0	0	0	0	0
BURLINGTON NORTHERN INC	8712	4	1	3	5086	3	−0.048	0	0	1	0	0	0
BUSINESS RECORDS HLDG	8602	3	1	2	108	1	0.160	0	0	0	0	0	0
CARDINAL HEALTH INC	8803	2	1	1	27	1	0.086	0	0	0	0	0	0
COMMUNITY PSYCHIATRIC	8904	3	1	1	131	1	0.011	0	0	1	0	0	0
COOPER COMPANIES INC	8710	4	1	4	261	4	0.162	0	1	1	0	0	0
CPC INTERNATIONAL INC	8703	3	2	5	982	3	0.098	2	1	1	0	0	0
CROSS (A.T.) & CO	9303	2	1	1	8	1	0.044	1	0	0	0	0	0
CRSS INC	9107	7	2	2	64	2	−0.075	1	0	0	0	0	0
DEKALB ENERGY CO	8602	5	1	4	105	3	0.095	2	0	0	1	0	0
DI GIORGIO CORP	8606	4	1	3	70	2	0.187	0	0	1	0	0	0
DIGICON INC	8603	3	1	6	23	3	0.271	0	0	1	0	1	0
DRAVO CORP	8602	4	1	8	10	1	−0.167	2	0	1	0	0	0
DUCOMMUN INC	8709	2	1	1	120	1	0.126	2	0	0	0	0	0
ECOLAB INC	8701	4	2	7	615	2	0.037	0	0	0	0	0	0
EL PASO ELECTRIC CO	9001	5	1	2	0	0	0.026	1	0	0	1	0	0
ETHYL CORP	8905	5	2	4	3678	4	−0.031	0	0	0	0	0	0
FAIRFIELD COMUNITIES INC	9312	2	1	1	41	1	0.357	1	0	1	0	0	1
FEDERAL-MOGUL CORP	9110	3	1	1	150	1	0.004	0	0	0	0	1	0
FERRO CORP	8508	6	4	3	0	0	−0.056	0	0	0	0	0	0
FURON CO	9201	5	1	7	0	0	0.059	1	0	1	0	0	0
GENCORP INC	8702	5	3	8	1528	6	0.012	1	1	1	0	0	0
GENERAL DYNAMICS CORP	9109	6	3	9	2612	6	0.303	1	0	0	0	0	0
GENERAL HOST CORP	8605	4	1	4	355	3	0.139	0	0	0	0	0	0
GRACE (W.R.) & CO	9010	4	2	10	632	6	0.036	1	0	0	0	0	0
GRC INTL INC	8905	3	1	4	5	2	0.243	2	0	1	0	0	0
HANOVER DIRECT INC	8905	2	1	4	28	3	0.025	0	0	1	0	0	0
INTERCO INC	8812	4	2	9	953	7	−0.190	0	1	0	0	0	0
INTERLAKE CORP	8602	4	2	1	49	1	0.101	0	0	0	0	0	0
JOHNSON WORLDWIDE	9405	2	1	2	0	0	0.007	1	0	0	0	0	0
KYSOR INDUSTRIAL CORP	8510	4	2	1	0	0	0.023	0	0	0	0	0	0
LAC MINERALS LTD	8807	3	1	2	62	2	0.091	0	0	1	0	0	0
LONE STAR TECHNOLOGIES	9302	3	2	1	150	1	0.330	0	0	0	1	0	0
LUKENS INC	9307	5	2	2	0	0	−0.007	0	0	0	0	0	0
MAXUS ENERGY CORP	8605	4	1	5	1517	4	0.031	0	1	0	0	0	0
MCDERMOTT INTL INC	8712	4	2	1	68	1	0.030	0	0	1	0	0	0
MCKESSON CORP	8701	6	5	8	0	0	−0.003	1	0	0	0	0	0
MEDALIST INDS	9204	4	1	5	65	1	#N/A	0	0	1	0	0	0
MORRISON KNUDSEN CORP	8802	4	2	2	14	1	0.021	1	1	1	0	0	0
NATIONAL INTERGROUP INC	9001	4	1	4	278	3	0.560	2	0	1	0	0	0
NATIONAL SEMICONDUCTOR	8812	2	1	2	488	2	0.092	0	0	1	0	0	0
NATIONAL-STANDARD CO	9001	2	1	8	0	0	0.170	0	0	0	0	0	0
NAVISTAR INTERNATIONAL	8411	2	1	2	488	1	−0.122	0	0	0	0	1	0
NEWMOUNT MINING CORP	8609	3	1	6	1024	6	−0.205	0	1	1	0	0	0
NICOR INC	8602	5	3	5	0	0	0.091	1	0	0	1	0	0
NORTH STAR UNIVERSAL INC	9009	3	1	4	3	2	−0.043	0	0	0	0	0	0
NOVA CORP ALTA	8906	7	2	2	516	2	0.166	0	0	0	0	0	0
NUI CORP	8710	4	1	1	17	1	0.173	0	0	0	0	0	0
OFFSHORE LOGISTICS	9010	2	1	1	0	0	−0.038	0	0	0	0	0	0
OGDEN CORP	8507	4	2	3	728	3	0.078	0	0	0	0	0	0
OUTBOARD MARINE CORP	8908	4	1	2	235	2	0.035	0	1	1	0	0	0

Causes and Effects of Corporate Refocusing Programs

Table B.1
(continued)

Name	Start refocus	#Segmen Start	End	#Div sold	Value sold	with value	Return	Mgt	Ust	Par	Div	Deb	c11
OWENS & MINOR INC	9201	3	1	2	53	2	0.070	0	0	0	0	0	0
OWENS CORNING FIBERGLAS	8602	5	2	8	236	1	0.179	0	1	0	0	1	0
PACIFIC ENTERPRISES	9205	4	1	4	686	3	−0.153	1	0	0	0	1	0
PANHANDLE EASTERN CORP	8608	4	1	2	1161	1	−0.021	0	1	0	0	0	0
PARAMOUNT COMMUNICATIO	8409	7	2	5	1290	2	−0.012	0	0	0	0	0	0
PLACER DOME INC	8909	2	1	3	663	3	0.007	1	0	0	0	0	0
POPE EVANS & ROBBINS INC	8505	2	1	1	52	1	−0.116	0	0	0	0	0	0
READING & BATES CORP	8705	4	1	4	92	2	0.178	0	0	0	1	1	0
RITE AID CORP	9408	3	1	2	217	4	0.183	0	0	0	0	0	0
ROBBINS & MYERS INC	8412	3	2	2	14	1	−0.026	0	0	0	0	0	0
ROBBINS & MYERS INC	9103	2	1	2	19	1	−0.011	0	0	0	0	0	0
ROLLINS TRUCK LEASING	8806	3	1	2	44	2	0.110	0	0	0	0	0	0
RYDER SYSTEM INC	9307	3	2	1	280	1	0.016	0	0	0	0	0	0
SENECA FOODS CORP	8604	4	3	2	42	1	0.069	0	0	0	0	0	0
SHERWIN-WILLIAMS CO	8507	4	2	3	240	1	0.062	0	1	0	0	0	0
SIZZLER INTL INC	8612	4	1	2	0	0	0.008	1	0	0	0	0	0
SOUTHEASTERN PUBLIC SVC	9309	4	1	3	87	2	#N/A	0	0	0	0	0	0
SOUTHERN NEW ENG TELE	8604	2	1	2	0	0	−0.022	2	0	0	0	0	0
SUDBURY INC	9203	2	1	6	0	0	−0.079	1	0	0	0	0	1
SYNTEX CORP	8410	6	2	3	60	1	0.050	0	0	0	0	0	0
TASTY BAKING CO	9303	2	1	1	0	0	0.059	1	0	0	0	0	
TELE-COMMUNICATIONS	9103	2	1	2	1246	2	0.085	0	0	0	0	0	0
THIOKOL CP	8902	3	1	2	1920	1	0.067	0	0	0	0	0	0
TRANSTECHNOLOGY CORP	9201	3	2	1	38	1	0.241	1	0	1	0	1	0
TRIARC COS INC	9207	7	1	1	21	1	−0.026	1	0	1	0	0	0
TYLER CORP/DE	8803	3	1	3	677	3	0.255	0	0	0	0	0	0
UNC INC	8809	4	1	2	119	2	0.045	0	0	0	0	0	0
UNION CORP	8702	5	1	5	69	1	0.143	1	0	0	0	0	0
UNITED INNS INC	8812	3	1	2	11	1	−0.054	0	0	1	0	0	0
UNIVAR CORP	8512	4	1	1	82	1	0.031	0	0	0	0	0	0
UNIVERSAL CORP/VA	9109	4	3	1	44	1	0.148	0	0	0	0	0	0
UPJOHN CO	8412	3	2	2	257	1	0.049	0	0	0	0	0	0
USX-U S STEEL GROUP	9104	2	1	2	0	2	0.062	0	0	1	0	0	0
VARLEN CORP	8808	3	2	4	0	0	−0.046	0	0	0	0	0	0
VULCAN MATERIALS CO	8710	4	2	2	0	0	0.043	0	0	0	0	0	0
WHITTAKER CORP	8503	5	2	4	147	2	0.443	0	1	0	0	0	0
WHITTAKER CORP	8904	2	1	15	368	4	0.293	0	1	0	0	0	0
XEROX CORP	8504	3	1	5	693	6	0.020	0	0	0	0	0	0
ZAPATA CORP	8808	3	2	4	895	4	−0.080	0	0	0	0	1	0

with value — represent the number of divisions sold with available sale price.
Return — the cumulative abnormal return from all announcement related to the refocus.
Mgt — equals 1 if CEO change, 2 if only president or chairman change, and 0 otherwise.
Ust — equals 1 if unsuccessful takeover.
Par — equals 1 if partial acquisition.
Div — equals 1 if dividend cut.
Det — equals 1 if debt restructuring.
c11 — equals 1 if filed for chapter 11.

References

Alford, A., and P. G. Berger, 1998, "The Role of Taxes, Financial Reporting, and Other Market Imperfections in Structuring Divisive Reorganizations," working paper, University of Pennsylvania.

Allen, J. W., S. L. Lummer, J. J. McConnell, and D. K. Reed, 1995, "Can Takeover Losses Explain Spin-off Gains?," *Journal of Financial and Quantitative Analysis*, 30, 465–485.

Allen, J. W. and J. J. McConnell, 1998, "Equity Carve-outs and Managerial discretion," *Journal of Finance*, 53, 163–186.

Amihud, Y., and B. Lev, 1981, "Risk Reduction as Managerial Motive for Conglomerate Mergers," *Bell Journal of Economics*, 12, 605–617.

Benartzi, S., 1995, "The Information Content of Line-of-Business Segment Reporting," working paper, University of Southern California.

Berger, P. G., and E. Ofek, 1995, "Diversification's Effect on Firm Value," *Journal of Financial Economics*, 37, 39–65.

Berger, P. G. and E. Ofek, 1996, "Bustup Takeovers of Value-Destroying Diversified Firms," *Journal of Finance*, 51, 1175–1200.

Bhagat, S., A. Shleifer, and R. Vishny, 1990, "Hostile Takeovers in the 1980s: The Return to Corporate Specialization," Brookings Paper on Economic Activity: Microeconomics, p. 1–72.

Boot, A. W., 1992, "Why Hang on to Losers? Divestitures and Takeovers," *Journal of Finance*, 47, 1401–1423.

Brown, D. T., C. M. James, and R. M. Mooradian, 1994, "Asset Sales by Financially Distressed Firms," *Journal of Corporate Finance*, 1, 233–257.

Caudill, S. B. and J. D. Jackson, 1989, "Measuring Marginal Effects in Limited Dependent Variable Models," *Statistician*, 38, 203–206.

Comment, R. and G. A. Jarrell, 1995, "Corporate Focus and Stock Returns," *Journal of Financial Economics*, 37, 67–87.

Daley, L., V. Mehrotra, and R. Sivakumar, 1997, "Corporate Focus and Value Creation: Evidence from Spinoffs," *Journal of Financial Economics*, 45, 257–281.

Darrough, M. N. and N. M. Stoughton, 1990, "Financial Disclosure Policy in an Entry Game," *Journal of Accounting and Economics*, 12, 219–243.

Dechow, P. M., R. G. Sloan, and A. P. Sweeney, 1995, "Detecting Earnings Management," *Accounting Review*, 70, 193–225.

Denis, D. J., and D. K. Denis, 1995, "Performance Changes Following Top Management Dismissals," *Journal of Finance*, 50, 1029–1057.

Denis, D. J., D. K. Denis, and A. Sarin, 1997, "Agency Problems, Equity Ownership, and Corporate Diversification," *Journal of Finance*, 52, 135–160.

Dial, J. and K. J. Murphy, 1995, "Incentives, Downsizing, and Value Creation at General Dynamics," *Journal of Financial Economics*, 37, 261–314.

Feltham, G. A., F. B. Gigler, and J. S. Hughes, 1992, "The Effects of Line-of-Business Reporting on Competition in Oligopoly Settings," *Contemporary Accounting Research*, 9, 1–23.

Feltham, G. A. and J. Z. Xie, 1992, "Voluntary Financial Disclosure in an Entry Game with Continua of Types," *Contemporary Accounting Research*, 9, 46–80.

FASB (Financial Accounting Standards Board), 1975, "Statement of Financial Accounting Standards No. 14: Financial Reporting for Segments of a Business Enterprise," FASB, Norwalk, CT.

Givoly, D., C. Hayn, and J. D'Souza, 1993, "The Quality and Information Content of Segment Reporting," working paper, Northwestern University.

Guenther, D. A. and A. J. Rosman, 1994, "Differences between Compustat and CRSP SIC Codes and Related Effects on Research" *Journal of Accounting and Economics*, 18, 115–128.

Hart, O. D., 1983, "The Market Mechanism as an Incentive Scheme," *Bell Journal of Economics*, 14, 366–382.

Hayes, R. M., and R. Lundholm, 1996, "Segment Reporting to the Capital Market in the Presence of a Competitor," *Journal of Accounting Research*, 34, 261–279.

Hite, G. L., and J. E. Owers, 1983, "Security Price Reactions Around Corporate Spin-off Announcements," *Journal of Financial Economics*, 12, 409–436.

Hite, G. L., J. E. Owers, and R. C. Rogers, 1987, "The Market for Interfirm Asset Sales: Partial Sell-offs and Total Liquidations," *Journal of Financial Economics*, 18, 229–252.

Hubbard, R. G., and D. Palia, 1999, "A Re-examination of the Conglomerate Merger Wave in the 1960s: An Internal Capital Markets View," forthcoming in *Journal of Finance*.

Jain, P. C., 1985, "The Effect of Voluntary Sell-off Announcements on Shareholder Wealth," *Journal of Finance*, 40, 209–224.

Jensen, M. C., 1986, "Agency Costs of Free Cash Flow, Corporate Finance, and Takeovers," *American Economic Review*, 76, 323–329.

Jensen, M. C. and K. J. Murphy, 1990, "Performance Pay and Top Management Incentives," *Journal of Political Economy*, 98, 225–264.

Jensen, M. C. and R. Ruback, 1983, "The Market for Corporate Control: The Scientific Evidence," *Journal of Financial Economics*, 11, 5–50.

John, K., L. H. P. Lang, and J. Netter, 1992, "The Voluntary Restructuring of Large Firms in Response to Performance Decline," *Journal of Finance*, 47, 891–917.

John, K. and E. Ofek, 1995, "Asset Sales and Increase in Focus," *Journal of Financial Economics*, 37, 105–126.

Kahle, K. M. and R. A. Walkling, 1996, "The Impact of Industry Classifications on Financial Research," working paper, Ohio State University.

Klein, A., 1986, "The Timing and Substance of Divestiture Announcements: Individual, Simultaneous and Cumulative Effects," *Journal of Finance*, 41, 685–696.

Lamont, O., 1997, "Cash Flow and Investment: Evidence from Internal Capital Markets," *Journal of Finance*, 52, 83–109.

Lanen, W. N. and R. Thompson, 1988, "Stock Price Reactions as Surrogates for the Net Cash Flow Effects of Corporate Policy Decisions," *Journal of Accounting and Economics*, 10, 311–334.

Lang, L. H. P. and R. E. Stulz, 1994, "Tobin's q, Corporate Diversification and Firm Performance," *Journal of Political Economy*, 102, 1248–1280.

Manski, C. F. and S. R. Lerman, 1977, "The Estimation of Choice Probabilities from Choice Based Samples," *Econometrica*, 45, 1977–1988.

May, D., 1995, "Do Managerial Motives Influence Firm Risk Reduction Strategies?" *Journal of Finance*, 50, 1291–1308.

Meyer, M., P. Milgrom, and J. Roberts, 1992, "Organizational Prospects, Influence Costs, and Ownership Changes," *Journal of Economics and Management Strategy*, 1, 9–35.

Mikkelson, W. H. and M. M. Partch, 1997, "The Decline of Takeovers and Disciplinary Managerial Turnover," *Journal of Financial Economics*, 44, 205–228.

Miles, J., and J. Rosenfeld, 1983, "An Empirical Analysis of the Effects of Spin-off Announcements on Shareholder Wealth," *Journal of Finance*, 38, 1597–1606.

Newman, P., and R. Sansing, 1993, "Disclosure Policies with Multiple Users," *Journal of Accounting Research*, 31, 92–112.

Ofek, E., 1993, "Capital Structure and Firm Response to Poor Performance: An Empirical Analysis," *Journal of Financial Economics*, 34, 3–30.

Opler, T. C., and J. Sokobin, 1996, "Does Coordinated Institutional Activism Work? An Analysis of the Activities of the Council of Institutional Investors," working paper, Ohio State University.

Rajan, R. G., and L. Zingales, 1996, "The Tyranny of the Inefficient: An Enquiry into the Adverse Consequences of Power Struggles," working paper, University of Chicago.

Ravenscraft, D., and F. M. Scherer, 1991, "Divisional Sell-off: A Hazard Function Analysis," *Managerial & Decision Economics*, 12, 429–438.

Rumelt, R. P., 1974, "Strategy, Structure and Economic Performance," working paper, Harvard Business School.

Scharfstein, D. S., and J. C. Stein, 1996, "The Dark Side of Internal Capital Markets: Divisional Rent-Seeking and Inefficient Investment," working paper, MIT and NBER.

Scherer, F. M., 1988, "Corporate Takeovers: The Efficiency Arguments," *Journal of Economic Perspectives*, 2, 69–82.

Schipper, K., and A. Smith, 1983, "Effects of Recontracting on Shareholder Wealth: The Case of Voluntary Spin-offs," *Journal of Financial Economics*, 12, 437–467.

Shin, H. H., and R. M. Stulz, 1996, "An Analysis of Divisional Investment Policies," working paper, Ohio State University and NBER.

Shleifer, A., and R. W. Vishny, 1989, "Management Entrenchment: The Case of Manager-Specific Investments," *Journal of Financial Economics*, 25, 123–139.

Shleifer, A., and R. W. Vishny, 1991, "The Takeover Wave of the 1980s," *Journal of Applied Corporate Finance*, 4, 49–56.

Stein, J., 1997, "Internal Capital Markets and the Competition for Corporate Resources," *Journal of Finance*, 52, 111–133.

Stulz, R. M., 1990, "Managerial Discretion and Optimal Financing Policies," *Journal of Financial Economics*, 26, 3–27.

Subrahmanyam, A., and S. Titman, 1999, "The Going Public Decision and the Development of Financial Markets," forthcoming in *Journal of Finance*.

Tufano, P., 1996, "Who Manages Risk? An Empirical Examination of Risk Management Practices in the Gold Mining Industry," *Journal of Finance*, 51, 1097–1137.

Wagenhofer, A., 1990, "Voluntary Disclosure with a Strategic Opponent," *Journal of Accounting and Economics*, 12, 341–363.

Wahal, S., 1996, "Pension Fund Activism and Firm Performance," *Journal of Financial and Quantitative Analysis*, 31, 1–23.

Warner, J. B., R. L. Watts, and K. H. Wruck, 1988, "Stock Prices and Top Management Changes," *Journal of Financial Economics*, 20, 461–492.

Weisbach, M. S., 1988, "Outside Directors and CEO Turnover," *Journal of Financial Economics*, 20, 431–460.

Weisbach, M. S., 1995, "CEO Turnover and the Firm's Investment Decisions," *Journal of Financial Economics*, 37, 159–188.

Weston, F. J., K. S. Chung, and S. E. Hoag, 1990, "Mergers, Restructuring, and Corporate Control," Prentice-Hall, Englewood Cliffs, NJ.

Zmijewski, M. 1984, "Methodological Issues Related to the Estimation of Financial Distress Prediction Models," *Journal of Accounting Research*, 22(suppl), 59–82.

[7]

ELSEVIER

Journal of Financial Economics 64 (2002) 117–144

JOURNAL OF Financial ECONOMICS

www.elsevier.com/locate/econbase

Divestitures and the liquidity of the market for corporate assets☆

Frederik P. Schlingemann[a], René M. Stulz[b,c,*], Ralph A. Walkling[b]

[a] *Katz Graduate School of Business, University of Pittsburgh, Pittsburgh, PA 15260, USA*
[b] *Department of Finance, Fisher College of Business, The Ohio State University, Columbus, OH 43210 , USA*
[c] *National Bureau of Economic Research, Cambridge, MA, USA*

Received 15 August 2000; accepted 5 July 2001

Abstract

The liquidity of the market for corporate assets plays an important role in explaining whether a firm divests a business segment, which segment the firm divests, and whether it divests a core segment or an unrelated segment. Firms are more likely to divest segments from industries with a more liquid market for corporate assets, unrelated segments, poorly performing segments, and small segments. Strikingly, the segment with the least liquid market is less likely to be divested than the best-performing segment, while the worst-performing segment is less likely to be divested than the segment with the most liquid market. © 2002 Elsevier Science B.V. All rights reserved.

JEL classificaion: G30; G34

Keywords: Asset liquidity; Divestitures; Corporate focusing

☆This paper incorporates parts of an earlier draft circulated under the title "Corporate focusing and internal capital markets". We thank Bill Schwert, Harry DeAngelo, Diane Denis, Denis Gromb, Prem Jain, Kose John, Kathleen Kahle, Wayne Mikkelson, Todd Perry, Raghuram Rajan, Henri Servaes, Andrei Shleifer, Jeremy Stein, Janice Willett, Luigi Zingales, an anonymous referee, and participants at the 1997 Financial Management Association meeting, the 1998 Western Finance Association meetings, the 1998 CEPR Conference in Gerzensee, the 1998 NBER Summer Institute, the 1999 ASSA meetings, and seminars at Georgetown University, Ohio State University, University of Chicago, and Tilburg University for helpful comments and suggestions. Protiti Dastidar, Nont Dhiensiri, Craig Doidge, Natasha Burns, Jan Jindra, Gueorgui Slavov, and Whuei-Wen (Christine) Lai provided excellent research assistance.

*Corresponding author. Department of Finance, Fisher College of Business, The Ohio State University, Columbus, OH 43210 , USA. Tel.: +1-614-292-1970; fax: +1-614-292-2359.

E-mail address: stulz@cob.osu.edu (R.M. Stulz).

PII: S0304-405X(02)00073-9

1. Introduction

The finance literature has identified several reasons for corporate divestitures. Among these reasons, three are prominent: (1) to have specific assets operated by those who can operate them most efficiently (the efficiency explanation); (2) to make the firm more efficient by reducing its degree of diversification (the focusing explanation); and (3) to relax credit constraints (the financing explanation).[1] Given the need to restructure, however, not all firms actually divest assets. We find that about half of the firms that reduce their number of business segments do not appear to divest a segment; instead, most of these choose to reorganize segments internally. We argue that if a firm has fundamental reasons to restructure, asset liquidity plays an important role in the process. In particular, asset liquidity can explain (a) why some firms choose to divest a business segment while other similar firms choose to restructure it, and (b) which business segment is most likely to be divested.

The market for corporate assets is like other markets. That is, for a transaction to occur, there must be a buyer and a seller. Since there is no organized market where corporate assets are traded, a firm that wants to dispose of an asset has to search for a buyer. If the market for the asset is liquid, buyers are easy to find and, therefore, a firm can sell the asset at a price close to the present value of its cash flows. If the market for the asset is not liquid, however, the selling firm has to offer a liquidity discount to attract a buyer in order to sell the asset. Attempts to sell an asset in an illiquid market can thus yield a price below the firm's reservation price, so that no sale takes place (see Shleifer and Vishny, 1992).

Firms divest a segment to accomplish operating, funding, or strategic objectives, not because that segment is liquid. In this paper, we consider "focusing" firms, which we define broadly to be firms that reduce their number of reported segments, and explore how asset liquidity helps explain whether such firms divest assets and which assets they divest. Firms that divest segments can do so to improve performance and raise funds. Firms do not generally have to sell a specific asset: selling any asset unrelated to the main activity of the firm can make the firm more efficient if it is a poor diversifier, and selling any asset will raise funds.[2] Consequently, liquidity has the potential to be important for focusing firms that have a choice of which assets to sell. We therefore view firms that seek to become more focused as providing a good exploring ground for the role of asset liquidity. When firms seek to divest assets but have a choice of assets to sell, we expect that assets that are relatively more liquid assets are more likely to be divested (we call this the asset liquidity hypothesis). Further, not all firms that seek to divest assets succeed in doing so. Conditional on the need to divest, we expect firms with assets that are more liquid to be more likely to actually divest them (we call this the firm liquidity hypothesis).

---

[1] For papers that emphasize these reasons, see Hite et al. (1987) and Maksimovic and Phillips (2001) for the efficiency hypothesis, John and Ofek (1995) and Berger and Ofek (1999) for the focusing explanation, and Shleifer and Vishny (1992) and Lang et al. (1994) for the financing explanation.

[2] See Daley et al. (1997) provide evidence that focusing makes the firm's remaining segments more efficient.

To investigate our two hypotheses about the role of liquidity in divestitures, we require (1) a sample of focusing firms, (2) a set of comparison firms, (3) data on the firms' divested and retained assets, and (4) a measure of asset liquidity. The business segment disclosures of firms allow us to identify the firm's business segments and their characteristics. With the segment data, we can look at firms as portfolios of segments and measure the liquidity of the markets for these segments. We start with a sample of firms that have reduced their number of reported business segments. According to the literature, such a sample includes all focusing firms that have decided to divest or restructure.[3] Our analysis of this sample divides the firms into two categories: firms that divest segments and firms that stop reporting segments but do not divest them. We refer to the latter as discontinuing firms. Applied to business segments, the firm liquidity hypothesis predicts that a firm seeking to divest segments is more likely to succeed if it has segments that are more liquid, and the asset liquidity hypothesis predicts that selling firms are more likely to divest their more liquid segments.

The microstructure literature has investigated liquidity in financial markets extensively. This literature uses bid–ask spreads, market depth, and volume as proxies for liquidity. Unfortunately, the markets for corporate assets do not have market makers who hold an inventory of corporate business segments to facilitate transactions; bid–ask spreads and market depth cannot be measured. Shleifer and Vishny (1992) and others argue that a high volume of transactions in an industry is evidence of high liquidity; discounts that sellers must offer to attract buyers are smaller in more active markets. Consequently, we use the volume of transactions in an industry as a measure of the liquidity of that industry's corporate assets. We proxy the liquidity of the market for a segment by the liquidity of its industry. The liquidity of an industry (at the two-digit SIC code level) is measured by taking the ratio of the value of the industry's corporate transactions (excluding the divested segments analyzed in this study) to the value of the industry's total assets. The liquidity index of a firm is the asset-weighted average of the liquidity indexes of its segments.

To test the firm liquidity hypothesis, we have to investigate whether our divesting firms have segments that are more liquid than those of other firms with the same fundamental reasons to focus. We therefore compare our divesting firms to other focusing firms that do not divest. Using traditional accounting measures of financial condition and performance, we find that firms that reduce their number of segments but do not divest are statistically indistinguishable from those that divest segments. Firm characteristics emphasized by the focusing and financing explanations of divestitures cannot differentiate between these firms. In contrast, the firm liquidity hypothesis helps to explain why the actions of these firms differ. We show that focusing firms that divest a segment have higher liquidity indexes than focusing firms that do not divest a segment—evidence supportive of the firm liquidity hypothesis.

[3] Berger and Ofek (1999) use an increase in the Herfindahl index based on segment sales rather than the number of segments to identify focusing firms. However, firms that decrease their number of segments normally experience an increase in their Herfindahl index. In our sample, 159 divesting firms out of 168 experience an increase in the sales-based Herfindahl index of at least 5%.

And given that a firm divests a segment, a segment with a higher liquidity index has a higher probability of being divested even after controlling for the segment's performance and for other segment characteristics. This supports the asset liquidity hypothesis.

The paper proceeds as follows. We describe our sample in Section 2. In Section 3, we show that the financing and focusing explanations are useful for explaining why some diversified firms divest a segment while others do not. Nevertheless, these explanations cannot differentiate between focusing firms that divest and focusing firms that do not divest. In Section 4, however, we show that liquidity differentiates among these firms. In Section 5, we find that liquidity also helps explain which segment the selling firm divests. Section 6 concludes.

2. The sample

We expect the firm liquidity hypothesis to be most relevant when the focusing or financing explanations of divestitures apply. We therefore investigate divestiture decisions for a sample of focusing firms. We use the broadest definition of focusing in the literature (see, e.g., Comment and Jarrell, 1995; John and Ofek, 1995) in that we define a firm to be focusing if it reduces the number of segments it reports. To construct the sample, we therefore begin with firms that decrease the number of reported industry segments for the first time during the period 1979–1994. For fiscal years ending after December 15, 1977, SFAS No. 14 requires that firms report information for segments that represent 10% or more of consolidated sales. The Business Information File of Compustat contains this information. We use the Compustat Full-Coverage Industry Segment File (CISF) database, including the Research Tapes, to identify these firms. The Full-Coverage File consists of all companies that file 10-Ks with the Securities and Exchange Commission. We exclude firms that have either a Compustat SIC or an Industry Segment Identification (SID) code between 6000 and 6999 (financial services industry), or between 4900 and 4999 (regulated utilities). We also exclude American Depository Receipts and firms with assets below $100 million. This leaves us with a sample of 325 firms. Our sampling criteria are similar to the criteria used by Berger and Ofek (1999), except that they use the Herfindahl index instead of the number of segments as a measure of diversification. Like us, they only include firms with more than $100 million in assets. They also investigate press announcements to find out how firms focus, so that their final sample has only firms for which they can identify how the firm focused. To construct our sample of focusing firms that divest a segment, we investigate each firm using LEXIS NEXIS to identify firms for which the decrease in the number of segments coincides with an actual divesting transaction reported in the financial press. The following sources are used in LEXIS NEXIS: PR Newswire, The Financial Times, Reuters Financial Service, The New York Times, The Chicago Tribune, Business Wire, and The Wall Street Journal. These criteria result in an initial sample of 168 divesting firms, each with total assets in excess of $100 million.

The remaining 157 focusing firms have no divestiture; we call these discontinuing firms. An important concern with our approach is that the discontinuing firms might be firms that, unbeknownst to us, actually divested one or more segments. We check in the Securities Data Corporation Mergers and Acquisitions Files for transactions involving these firms and find none. We also searched annual reports to investigate what happened to the segments no longer reported by the discontinuing firms, which we call the discontinued segments. We have annual reports available for 93 firms. For these 93 firms, 38 annual reports are uninformative. Twelve firms indicate that they changed their reporting. Ten firms discuss a restructuring that involves the merging of one segment into another. Nineteen firms report discontinued operations and sales of some assets, while seven firms report sales of assets without discontinued operations. Finally, two firms report a spinoff. There is a possibility that some of the firms that report asset sales or a spinoff should be in our divesting sample. However, we do not find a reported transaction corresponding to a segment divestiture for any of these firms. In any case, the classification of these firms does not affect our results.

The distribution of segments no longer reported, classified by whether or not they belong to divesting firms, is shown by year in Panel A of Table 1. The year 1981 has with 38 cases, the highest number of segments no longer reported. Not surprisingly, since our sample includes only the first time that a firm decreases its number of segments, the number of observations per year falls over time.

Panel B of Table 1 reports the decrease in the number of segments for the divesting firms as well as for the discontinuing firms. It shows that 142 divesting firms divested one segment, 22 divested two segments, and four divested three segments. Firms that decrease their number of reported segments for the first time but have no divestitures stop reporting 382 segments, or 2.43 segments per firm. In contrast, firms that divest a segment stop reporting 207 segments, or 1.23 segments per firm. In a number of cases, firms that stop reporting a segment in year t stop reporting all their existing segments from year $t-1$. In these cases, they report either only one segment in year t or one segment fewer than they did at $t-1$ but all the segments have a new name. As a result, 27 firms that had more than two segments before the change in reporting do not report any preexisting segment after the change. Finally, Panel C of Table 1 shows that most of our divestitures are in manufacturing (two-digit SIC code 20-39).

3. Comparison of divesting firms to other diversified firms and to discontinuing firms

Asset liquidity per se does not give rise to divestitures. In testing the firm liquidity hypothesis, we therefore attempt to control for the fundamental factors that initiate the divestiture process by selecting focusing firms for our sample. To investigate whether our sample selection criterion achieves this objective, we compare our divesting firms to other diversified firms and to focusing firms that do not divest a segment.

3.1. Comparison firms

We want to evaluate whether our divesting firms have fundamental reasons to divest that are consistent with the existing explanations for divestitures, and whether

Table 1
Sample breakdown
Our sample consists of all firms identified by the Compustat Business Information file as reporting a decrease in the number of segments over the period 1979–94. We exclude firms smaller than $100 million in assets, American Depository Receipts, and firms that have either a Compustat SIC or an Industry Segment Identification Code (SID) between 6000 and 6999 (financial services industry) and between 4900 and 4999 (regulated industries). Firms for which we could not confirm a transaction through *Lexis-Nexis* coinciding with the decrease in segments are labeled discontinuing firms. Firms for which we could identify a corresponding transaction are labeled divesting firms. Panel A presents the yearly distribution of the sample of firms. Panel B presents a frequency distribution of the number of segments within each firm that disappeared during the event year. Panel C presents the industry distribution over the following industries: mining (10–14), construction (15–19), manufacturing (20–39), transportation, communication, electric, gas, and sanitary services (40–49), wholesale trade (50–51), retail trade (52–59), and services (70–89).

Panel A: Yearly distribution of sample firms

	Divesting firms		Discontinuing firms		Total	
Event year	Frequency	Percent	Frequency	Percent	Frequency	Percent
79	9	5.36	22	14.01	31	9.54
80	11	6.55	13	8.28	24	7.38
81	21	12.50	17	10.83	38	11.69
82	12	7.14	19	12.10	31	9.54
83	9	5.36	9	5.73	18	5.54
84	18	10.71	16	10.19	34	10.46
85	14	8.33	9	5.73	23	7.08
86	14	8.33	13	8.28	27	8.31
87	11	6.55	4	2.55	15	4.62
88	10	5.95	6	3.82	16	4.92
89	9	5.36	8	5.10	17	5.23
90	5	2.98	2	1.27	7	2.15
91	9	5.36	8	5.10	17	5.23
92	5	2.98	2	1.27	7	2.15
93	6	3.57	6	3.82	12	3.69
94	5	2.98	3	1.91	8	2.46
Total	168	100	157	100	325	100

Panel B: Decrease in reported segments

	Divesting firms		Discontinuing firms		Total	
Decrease in segments	Frequency	Percent	Frequency	Percent	Frequency	Percent
1	142	84.52	125	79.62	267	82.15
2	22	13.10	24	15.29	46	14.15
3	4	2.38	5	3.18	9	2.77
4			1	0.64	1	0.31
5			2	1.27	2	0.62
Total	168	100	157	100	325	100

Panel C: Two-digit major industry classification of sample firms

	Divesting firms		Discontinuing firms		Total	
Two-digit SIC range	Frequency	Percent	Frequency	Percent	Frequency	Percent
10–14	4	2.4	4	2.6	8	2.5
15–19	.	.	1	0.6	1	0.3
20–39	131	78.0	134	85.4	265	81.7
40–49	9	5.4	3	1.9	12	3.6
50–51	13	7.7	5	3.2	18	5.5
52–59	6	3.6	6	3.8	12	3.7
70–89	5	3.0	4	2.6	9	2.8
Total	168	100	157	100	325	100

the focusing firms that do not divest have the same fundamental reasons. To do that, we compare our divesting firms to similarly diversified firms that do not focus (i.e., do not stop reporting a segment) as well as focusing firms that do not divest.

The sample of non-focusing firms is defined as follows. For each year t in which a sample firm reduces its number of segments, we identify a set of comparison firms. These are firms in the same annual sales decile in year $t-1$ with the same number of segments as the divesting firm, but that do not reduce their number of reported segments in year t. Size deciles are based on the annual sales deciles of all firms listed on Compustat. For any variable that we consider, we compare a sample firm to the average of its comparison firms provided that there are at least five comparison firms. In some analyses, the number of firms is reduced because the relevant data are not available for comparison or sample firms. The sample of focusing firms that do not divest is our sample of 157 discontinuing firms discussed in Section 2.

3.2. *Size, growth, investment, and diversification efficiency*

Table 2 compares characteristics of divesting firms, comparison firms, and discontinuing firms. The financing explanation would help explain divestitures if divesting firms are financially constrained relative to comparison firms. The focusing explanation would help explain why firms divest if divesting firms are poor diversifiers relative to comparison firms. Our results support both explanations. We find that divesting firms are growing significantly more slowly than comparison firms. The growth rates in sales, assets, capital expenditures, and cash flow are all significantly lower for divesting firms. The ratio of capital expenditures to sales for divesting firms is barely half that for comparison firms. The fact that divesting firms invest so little relative to the comparison firms is consistent with divesting firms being financially more constrained or having poorer investment opportunities. Divesting firms have significantly lower market-to-book asset ratios. We also compute the excess value measure of Berger and Ofek (1995). Unfortunately, the sample size is cut sharply when we compute excess value, which is calculated as the percentage difference between a firm's total value and the sum of imputed values for its segments as stand-alone entities.[4] Based on the excess value measure, divesting firms have a

[4] We follow the methodology of Berger and Ofek (1995) to calculate the firm's excess value due to its multi-segment character. This measure is calculated as the percentage difference between a firm's total value and the sum of imputed values for its segments as stand-alone entities. From the Compustat Industry Segment (CIS) database, we collect all non-financial (SIC codes outside the 6000–6999 range) single-segment firms during the 1984–95 period that satisfy the following criteria. The firm's total sales, as reported by Compustat, must be within a $\pm 1\%$ range of the total of the firm's segment sales, as reported in the CIS database. The market value of common equity (Compustat data items 199×25), the book value of debt (Compustat data items $5+34$), the carrying value of preferred stock (Compustat item 130), and sales (Compustat data item 12) must be available from the Compustat database. Finally, firm total sales must be at least \$20 million. Excess values that are smaller (larger) than -1.386 ($+1.386$), are considered outliers (see Berger and Ofek, 1995) and hence eliminated from the sample. Industry medians necessary to calculate the imputed values are based on four-digit SIC codes and a minimum of five firms to define an industry. Whenever the number of firms within an industry is less than five, we use the broader three-digit SIC codes, and, finally, if necessary, two-digit SIC codes.

Table 2
Firm characteristics

Columns present (respectively) medians and differences in medians of firm performance variables for the divesting firms (1), comparison firms (2), and the discontinuing firms (3). Each comparison value is calculated as the mean value of the performance measure for a portfolio that consists of a minimum of five firms in the same year, with the same number of segments, and in the same annual sales decile as the sample firm. Comparison firms cannot reduce the number of segments during the event year. Excess value is calculated as in Berger and Ofek (1995). The firm's q is defined as the sum of the book value of assets and the market value of equity net of the book value of equity divided by the book value of assets. The coefficient of variation in q (see Rajan et al., 2000) is multiplied by one hundred. Debt divided by assets denotes the firm's total liabilities divided by assets. The coverage ratio is defined as EBIT plus depreciation divided by interest expense. Cash includes inventories and is normalized by assets. Cash flow is defined as operating income before depreciation. Dividend yield is defined as the ratio of dividends per share to the market price per share. Statistical significance of the median difference is based on a Wilcoxon signed-rank test and is denoted with ***, **, and * for 1%, 5%, and 10% rejection levels, respectively.

	Divesting firms					Discontinuing firms			
	n	Sample (1)	Benchmark (2)	Difference (1)−(2)	p-Value	n	Sample (3)	Difference (1)−(3)	p-Value
A. Size									
Market value of equity	153	12.736	12.876	−0.056	*0.294*	131	12.208	0.528*	*0.070*
Sales	155	6.686	6.649	−0.066*	*0.097*	125	6.316	0.369	*0.273*
B. Growth rates, investment, and growth opportunities									
$(\text{Sales}_{t-1}/\text{Sales}_{t-2})-1$	153	0.067	0.103	−0.032**	*0.021*	123	0.102	−0.036	*0.177*
$(\text{Assets}_{t-1}/\text{Assets}_{t-2})-1$	153	0.075	0.105	−0.046***	*0.004*	123	0.089	−0.014	*0.539*
Cap. $\text{Exp}_{t-1}/\text{Sales}_{t-2}$	152	0.050	0.084	−0.035***	*0.001*	122	0.046	0.004	*0.324*
(Cap. Exp_{t-1}/Cap. $\text{Exp}_{t-2})-1$	152	0.104	0.168	−0.053	*0.296*	120	0.066	0.039	*0.237*
Excess value	91	−0.246	−0.108	−0.140**	*0.016*	69	−0.104	−0.142	*0.128*
q	151	1.089	1.243	−0.127**	*0.023*	124	1.037	0.052	*0.355*
Coefficient of variation in q	119	81.147	86.775	−3.022	*0.419*	71	91.170	−10.023	*0.287*
C. Leverage									
$\text{Debt}_{t-1}/\text{Assets}_{t-1}$	144	0.540	0.611	−0.080***	*0.001*	123	0.535	0.005	*0.947*
Coverage ratio	144	5.140	5.133	0.120	*0.557*	119	5.103	0.082	*0.999*
D. Cash flow and dividends									
$\text{Cash}/\text{Assets}_{t-1}$	144	0.031	0.063	−0.030***	*0.001*	123	0.029	0.002	*0.947*
Net $\text{Income}_{t-1}/\text{Sales}_{t-2}$	153	0.038	0.046	−0.007**	*0.011*	123	0.043	−0.005	*0.713*
Cash $\text{Flow}_{t-1}/\text{Sales}_{t-2}$	153	0.111	0.150	−0.034***	*0.001*	123	0.121	−0.010	*0.713*
Dividend yield	142	0.033	0.042	−0.014***	*0.001*	112	0.035	0.002	*0.715*

substantially larger diversification discount than comparison firms, which is consistent with their being poor diversifiers. We also estimate the Rajan et al. (2000) diversity measure.[5] According to this measure, diversification is more costly when investment opportunities differ more across segments. We find that this measure does not differ between divesting firms and comparison firms.

Turning to the discontinuing firms, we find that they are not significantly different from the divesting firms. Strikingly, the discontinuing firms invest little relative to the comparison firms, and their capital expenditures grow much less than the comparison firms'. However, the excess value of the discontinuing firms is similar to the excess value of the comparison firms. Unfortunately, the excess value estimate is available for only 69 discontinuing firms. Tobin's q can also be used as a proxy for whether a firm is a good diversifier. We compute Tobin's q as the ratio of the book value of assets minus the book value of equity plus the market value of equity to the book value of assets. The median Tobin's q for discontinuing firms is insignificantly lower than the Tobin's q for divesting firms, but is significantly lower than the Tobin's q for the comparison firms.

3.3. Cash flow and financial condition

In the third panel of Table 2, we report measures of leverage and interest coverage. Perhaps surprisingly given that they appear financially constrained, divesting firms have a lower ratio of debt to assets than comparison firms. The coverage ratio of divesting firms is insignificantly lower than for comparison firms. We also present cash to assets, net income to sales, cash flow to sales, and dividend yield for divesting firms and comparison firms. Comparison firms are significantly more profitable than divesting firms based on net income to sales or cash flow to sales. In addition, the ratio of cash to assets of divesting firms is half that for comparison firms. Finally, divesting firms have a significantly lower dividend yield than comparison firms. This evidence indicates that divesting firms are more likely to be credit constrained than comparison firms. Thus, our divesting firms seem to be poor diversifiers that are likely to be credit constrained.

3.4. Logit regressions

Based on accounting ratios, divesting firms differ significantly from diversified firms that do not focus, but do not differ significantly from focusing firms that do not divest. Consequently, the focusing and financing explanations cannot explain why some focusing firms divest and others do not. We now check whether this conclusion holds in multiple regressions. Panel A of Table 3 presents logit regressions in which

[5] Rajan et al. (2000) use the coefficient of variation of the weighted segment's q, CVQ, which is calculated as $\mathrm{CVQ} = \sqrt{\sum_{i=1}^{n}(\mathrm{SALES}_i/\sum_{i=1}^{n}\mathrm{SALES}_i) \times (q_i - \bar{q})^2}/\bar{q}$, where subscript i refers to segment i of the diversified firm, n to the total number of segments in the diversified firm, SALES to the segment sales, q is the median level of q for all Compustat firms in the same two-digit SIC code as the segment's two-digit SIC code, and $\bar{q}$ is the sales-weighted average q across the n segments of the diversified firm.

Table 3
Firm-level logit regression results
Logit regressions with a binary dependent variable that takes on the value zero for a comparison firm and one for a divesting firm (Panel A) and takes on the value zero for a discontinuing firm and one for a divesting firm (Panel B). Cells present (respectively) the coefficient, p-value, and the slope (defined as $\partial E[y]/\partial \mathbf{x}$, for the binary model $y_{(0,1)} = \boldsymbol{\beta}'\mathbf{x} + \varepsilon$, evaluated at the mean of $\mathbf{x}$), the pseudo-R^2, and the value of −2 times the log likelihood. Cash flow (CF) is defined as operating income before depreciation. Capital expenditures (CPX) are the firm's net capital expenditures. Debt divided by assets denotes the firm's total liabilities divided by assets. Excess value is calculated as in Berger and Ofek (1995). The coefficient of variation in q (see Rajan et al., 2000) is multiplied by one hundred. Accounting numbers are based on the firm-level data. The numerator in the ratios is measured in year −1 and the denominator in year −2. Statistical significance is denoted with ***, **, and * for 1%, 5% and 10% percent rejection levels, respectively.

Model	Intercept	CF/sales	CPX/sales	Debt/assets	Excess value	CVQ
Panel A: Divesting versus comparison firms						
(1)	−2.670***	−3.366***	−0.401	−0.558		
	0.001	*0.006*	*0.795*	*0.342*		
		−0.788	−0.100	−0.139		
	Pseudo-R^2 = 1.30%		−2 log likelihood = 1,200.7			
(2)	−2.733***	−2.805*	−1.455	−0.105	−0.400*	
	0.001	*0.082*	*0.561*	*0.894*	*0.041*	
		−0.670	−0.362	−0.026	−0.100	
	Psuedo-R^2 = 1.94%		−2 log likelihood = 753.6			
(3)	−2.564***	−1.233	−3.112	0.005		0.005*
	0.001	*0.374*	*0.135*	*0.994*		*0.089*
		−0.306	−0.756	0.001		0.001
	Pseudo-R^2 = 0.75%		−2 log likelihood = 871.2			
Panel B: Divesting versus discontinuing firms						
(1)	0.128	−0.810	1.273	−0.144		
	0.668	*0.619*	*0.524*	*0.852*		
		−0.234	0.432	−0.042		
	Pseudo-R^2 = 0.12%		−2 log likelihood = 387.3			
(2)	−0.112	0.383	1.301	0.246	−0.387	
	0.804	*0.887*	*0.719*	*0.815*	*0.256*	
		0.092	0.245	0.062	−0.891	
	Psuedo-R^2 = 0.63%		−2 log likelihood = 242.9			
(3)	0.761	−0.979	0.769	0.114		−0.005
	0.153	*0.673*	*0.786*	*0.906*		*0.241*
		−0.283	0.146	0.023		−0.001
	Pseudo-R^2 = 0.63%		−2 log likelihood = 258.2			

the dependent variable takes a value of one if the firm divests and zero otherwise. The regressions are estimated using the combined sample of divesting and comparison firms. Regression (1) uses cash flow, capital expenditures, and leverage as independent variables. Firms with higher cash flow are less likely to divest, but the other variables are not significant. The coefficient on cash flow is consistent with the efficiency, focusing, and financing explanations; the lack of significance of the other coefficients is not supportive of the financing explanation. Regression (2) adds excess value to the regression, but data constraints reduce the number of divesting firms in the sample by more than one third. Firms with a higher excess value (or, equivalently, a lower diversification discount) are less likely to divest. Cash flow is again negative and significant in that regression. Regression (3) uses the Rajan et al. (2000) measure of diversity instead of excess value. Firms with a higher diversity measure are more likely to divest. Cash flow is not significant in that regression.

In Panel B of Table 3, we estimate logit regressions in which the dependent variable takes a value of one for divesting firms and zero for discontinuing firms. The explanatory variables in the first regression are cash flow, capital expenditures, and leverage. No variable is significant. As in Panel A, Regression (2) adds the excess value and Regression (3) adds the Rajan et al. (2000) measure of diversity. Still, no coefficients are significant. In other regressions not shown, we find that other firm characteristics are not helpful in distinguishing between divesting and discontinuing firms. Tobin's q has a significant positive coefficient in some specifications.

These regressions show that while the focusing and financing explanations for divestitures apply to our sample, they cannot help explain why some focusing firms divest a segment and others do not.

4. The liquidity of the market for corporate assets and the divestiture decision

With the focusing and financing explanations for divestitures, a firm is more likely to divest if the market for a segment is more liquid since it is more likely to get a price close to the segment's fundamental value. With the financing explanation, variation in the liquidity of the market for corporate assets across industries helps explain why, among firms facing similar financial pressures, some firms divest a segment and others do not. With the focusing explanation, a firm is more likely to divest non-core segments when the market for non-core segments is more liquid. Consequently, the liquidity of the market for corporate assets can help to explain why, among otherwise comparable firms, some divest assets and others do not. However, a firm with no other motivation to divest a segment will not do so simply because the liquidity of the market for that segment increases. Consequently, absent a motive for divestiture, there is no reason for liquidity to differentiate between divesting and comparison firms. We therefore have no predictions for how the liquidity of segments of comparison firms differs from the liquidity of segments of divesting firms.

An asset market is more liquid if assets can be sold quickly without a discount. If the market has more transactions taking place, it means that buyers and sellers are active in that market, so that a potential seller can find buyers without having to discount the price as much relative to its fundamental value as it would in a less liquid market. We therefore use the "intensity" of corporate asset transactions within an industry as our proxy for that industry's asset market liquidity. We construct our segment liquidity measure by estimating a liquidity index at the two-digit SIC code level each year. To construct this index, we first collect from the SDC Mergers and Acquisitions database all corporate transactions at the two-digit SIC code level for each sample year. Corporate control transactions include all disclosed and completed leveraged buyouts, tender offers, spinoffs, exchange offers, minority stake purchases, acquisitions of remaining interest, privatizations, and equity carve-outs.[6] Buybacks (e.g., repurchases and self-tenders) are excluded from the sample. We then take the ratio of the value of corporate control transactions in a year (excluding the divestitures in our sample) to the total book value of assets of firms in the two-digit SIC code for that year as the industry's liquidity index. We recognize that the SIC codes reported by Compustat will differ from those of SDC (see Kahle and Walkling, 1996). We do not believe this materially affects our results. It is important to remove the divestitures in our sample from the transactions used to compute the liquidity index, otherwise an industry would show increased liquidity because of the divestitures we are examining.

The numerator of the liquidity index uses market values of transactions. In contrast, the denominator uses book values of industry assets. This makes it possible for the liquidity index for an industry to exceed one. We only use the liquidity index if it is between zero and one and if the industry has at least ten firms. Because of these constraints, we are unable to obtain a liquidity index for 16 out of 753 segments. Our results are qualitatively similar if we use the market value of firms (defined as total assets minus the book value of equity plus the market value of equity) in the denominator of the index rather than the book value of assets of firms. The liquidity measure based on book value is more appropriate because market values incorporate anticipatory takeover premia.

Fig. 1 shows how the liquidity index varies across industries and across time. Note that the figure includes all industries, not just those of our sample. Liquidity could not explain much if it varied little through time or across industries. Fig. 1 shows that there is significant variation in the index. Some industries have a low index throughout the period. Other industries have a high index during part of the period. No industry has a consistently high index value. We have index values for 73 industries. All but five industries have at least one year in which the index value is zero, indicating the absence of any transactions. The grand average of the index values is 0.05. Ten industries have an average that exceeds 0.10. The highest industry average of the index is 0.23. Fig. 2 shows the average and the standard deviation of the index for each industry. We again see substantial variation in these statistics across industries.

[6] We are grateful to Jeff Allen for providing us the sample of carve-outs used in Allen and McConnell (1998). In the sample period we start with 218 equity carve-outs with the announcement year and two-digit SIC code. For 199 observations we are able to find the corresponding transaction value. We use two methods to find the transaction value. First, we match the observations through the SDC New Issues database and find a transaction value for 170 observations. For 29 observations we use CRSP to obtain a proxy for the transaction value by taking the share price times the number of outstanding shares on the first trading day for the carved-out entity. For 19 observations we are unable to find a transaction value using either methodology. Our results are unchanged by taking into account carve-outs.

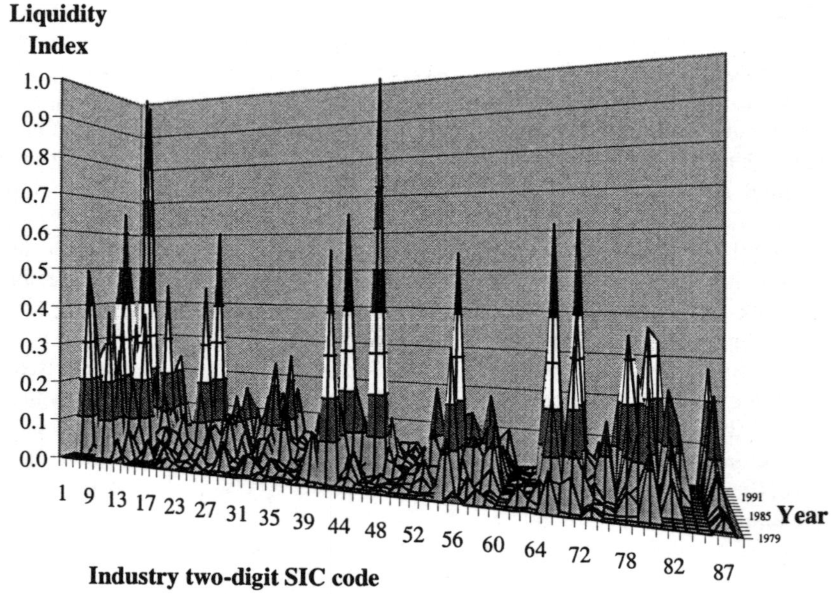

Fig. 1. Asset liquidity across time and industries. The graph plots average liquidity values for each of 73 industries defined at the two-digit SIC code level for each of the sample years 1979–1994. Liquidity is defined as the ratio of the value of all corporate control transactions in a year (excluding the sample observations) from SDC and the Allen and McConnell (1998) equity carve-out database divided by the total assets of firms in the same two-digit SIC code for that year.

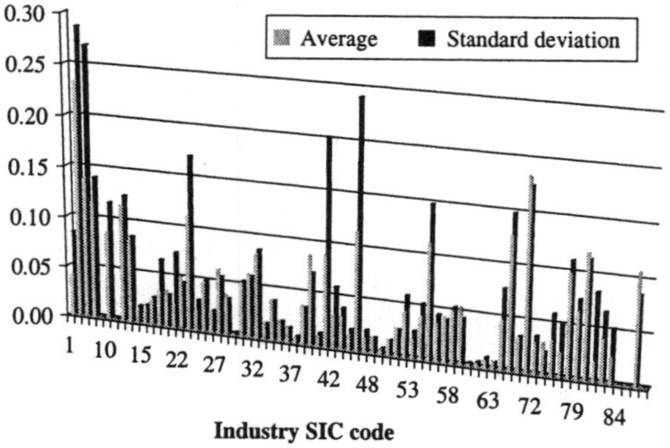

Fig. 2. Average and standard deviation of asset liquidity across industries. The graph plots the average and standard deviation of the liquidity values for each of 73 industries defined at the two-digit SIC code level for the sample years 1979–1994. Liquidity is defined as the ratio of the value of all corporate control transactions in a year (excluding the sample observations) from SDC and the Allen and McConnell (1998) equity carve-out database, divided by the total assets of firms in the same two-digit SIC code for that year.

Though the question of why one industry might have more corporate control transactions than another is important, we make no attempt to answer it in this study.[7] One reason for a high level of corporate transactions is that an industry has suffered a shock that makes it optimal for corporate assets to be rearranged within the industry. A situation in which many parties want to trade is one in which liquidity is high. Yet there is more to liquidity than industry clustering. In particular, we construct a liquidity index that attempts to measure whether divesting a segment would represent a large transaction relative to the volume of transactions in the industry. We therefore use as the liquidity index the assets of the segment divided by the sum of the value of the transactions in the industry as obtained from SDC. This index yields qualitatively similar but statistically weaker conclusions.

At the firm level, we define liquidity to be the asset-weighted average of the liquidity index corresponding to the industries of the firm's segments. In Panel A of Table 4, we report the asset-weighted average liquidity index for divesting firms, comparison firms, and discontinuing firms. We have no prediction for how the liquidity index of divesting firms should differ from the liquidity index of comparison firms, but we expect the liquidity index of divesting firms to be higher than the liquidity index of discontinuing firms. Panel A shows that there is no significant difference between the liquidity index of divesting firms and comparison firms. As expected, however, the liquidity index of divesting firms is significantly higher than the liquidity index of discontinuing firms. It is important to remember that in Table 2, none of the firm characteristics related to the focusing and financing explanations are significantly different between the divesting firms and the discontinuing firms. The liquidity index therefore has the potential to explain why, among otherwise comparable firms, some firms divest a segment and others do not.

If firms want to sell assets to raise funds, the weighted average of the liquidity indexes of all segments is not the relevant measure of liquidity. A firm might have mostly illiquid segments, but might also have one segment that is highly liquid. The financing explanation predicts that a firm considering selling assets to raise cash would be more likely to sell the segment that is highly liquid. Consequently, the liquidity index of the most liquid segment of the firm is another important liquidity measure to consider. We call this measure the firm's maximum liquidity index. Although we have no prediction for how the maximum liquidity index of divesting firms should compare to the maximum liquidity index of comparison firms, our univariate analysis shows that the maximum liquidity index is lower for the divesting firms than for the comparison firms. We expect the maximum liquidity index of divesting firms to be higher than the maximum liquidity index of discontinuing firms. Our univariate results indicate that it is insignificantly higher.

[7] Mitchell and Mulherin (1996) document that corporate acquisitions are clustered in industries. Mulherin and Boone (2000) confirm that this is true for the 1990s also, but surprisingly they show that there is an insignificant negative correlation between the rate of acquisitions and the rate of divestitures across industries. Industry shocks also play an important role in the model of Maksimovic and Phillips (2002). Andrade and Stafford (2000) document the role of industry expansions and contractions in mergers and acquisitions over the last three decades.

We now investigate whether adding liquidity to the multiple regressions of Table 3 helps explain why, among firms that have similar fundamental reasons to divest, some firms divest a segment while others do not. Since liquidity is not a sufficient motive for divestiture, it is not surprising that liquidity is not significant in differentiating between comparison firms and divesting firms. This is shown in Regressions (1) and (2) in Panel B of Table 4. It is also not significant in other specifications not shown here. But according to the firm liquidity hypothesis, liquidity should help differentiate between divesting and discontinuing firms. Section 3 shows that the focusing and financing explanations for divestitures apply equally well to divesting and discontinuing firms. Therefore, when comparing divesting firms to discontinuing firms, we are comparing firms that are similar in their fundamental reasons to divest, and we expect the firms with the more liquid segments to be more likely to divest a segment. We find that this is the case. In Regressions (1) and (2) in Panel C of Table 4, we find that the probability that a firm is a divesting firm increases significantly with both firm liquidity and maximum liquidity. In fact, the liquidity variable is the only significant variable in these regressions. The liquidity variable is also significant if we add it to regressions (2) and (3) in Panel B of Table 3. Thus, unlike firm characteristics such as cash flow, capital expenditures, excess value, and leverage, liquidity can explain why some firms stop reporting a segment without divesting it while others stop reporting a segment and divest it.

5. Which segments are divested?

In this section, we investigate the firm's choice of segment to divest. The focusing explanation predicts that unrelated segments are more likely to be divested to increase the firm's concentration on core assets. The efficiency explanation predicts that segments that perform poorly relative to their industry are more likely to be divested. The financing explanation predicts that segments with low cash flow and high capital expenditures are more likely to be divested because they drain the resources of credit-constrained firms. Our asset liquidity hypothesis builds on the focusing and financing explanations, asserting that a firm is more likely to divest a segment if the market for that segment is liquid.

We first compare performance and liquidity variables for divested and retained segments. Logit regressions are then used to evaluate the importance of these variables as determinants of the segment divestiture decision. We conclude the section by showing that segment liquidity is helpful in explaining whether a firm divests a core segment or an unrelated segment.

5.1. Divested segments versus retained segments

Table 5 provides information on how the SIC codes of the divested and retained segments relate to the main SIC code of the firm. Fewer than 9% of the divested segments have the same four-digit SIC code as the parent and only 30% of the divested segments have the same two-digit SIC code as the parent. Consequently,

Table 4
Firm liquidity

In Panel A, columns present (respectively) medians and differences in median of firm performance variables for the divesting firms (1), the comparison firms (2), and the discontinuing firms (3). Each comparison value is calculated as the mean value of the performance measure for a portfolio that consists of a minimum of five firms in the same year, with the same number of segments, and in the same annual sales decile as the sample firm. Comparison firms cannot reduce the number of segments during the event year. Logit regressions in Panel B and C have a binary dependent variable that takes on the value zero for a comparison firm and one for a divesting firm (Panel B) and takes on the value zero for a discontinuing firm and one for a divesting firm (Panel C). Cells present, respectively, the coefficient, p-value, and the slope (defined as $\partial E[y]/\partial \mathbf{x}$, for the binary model $y_{(0,1)} = \boldsymbol{\beta}'\mathbf{x} + \varepsilon$, evaluated at the mean of $\mathbf{x}$), the pseudo-R^2, and the value of -2 times the log likelihood. Cash flow (CF) is defined as operating income before depreciation. Capital expenditures (CPX) are the firm's net capital expenditures. Debt divided by assets denotes the firm's total liabilities divided by assets. The firm liquidity index is defined as the size-based weighted average of the firm's segment values for the liquidity index. Segment liquidity is calculated as the ratio of the value of corporate control transactions within a year and two-digit SIC class and to the assets of all firms on Compustat in the same year and two-digit SIC class. The maximum liquidity is the maximum value for the liquidity index within the firm for a divested/non-reported segment. Accounting numbers are based on the firm-level data. The numerator in the ratios is measured in year -1 and the denominator in year -2. Statistical significance of the median difference in Panel A is based on a Wilcoxon signed-rank test. Statistical significance is denoted with ***, **, and * for 1%, 5%, and 10% rejection levels, respectively.

Panel A: Univariate analysis

		Divesting firms				Discontinuing firms			
	n	Sample (1)	Benchmark (2)	Difference (1)–(2)	p-Value	n	Sample (3)	Difference (1)–(3)	p-Value
Liquidity index	145	0.019	0.029	−0.002	*0.160*	125	0.012	0.013*	*0.062*
Maximum liquidity index	145	0.035	0.063	−0.013***	*0.001*	125	0.025	0.012	*0.271*

continued over

Model	Intercept	CF/sales	CPX/sales	Debt/assets	Firm liquidity	Maximum liquidity
Panel B: Divesting versus comparison firms						
(1)	−2.696***	−3.381***	−0.410	−0.569	1.040	
	0.001	*0.006*	*0.790*	*0.332*	*0.614*	
		−0.791	−0.102	−0.141	0.260	
	Pseudo-R^2 = 1.32%		−2 log likelihood = 1,200.5			
(2)	−2.684***	−3.362***	−0.424	−0.564		0.277
	0.001	*0.006*	*0.785*	*0.337*		*0.793*
		−0.787	−0.106	−0.140		0.069
	Pseudo-R^2 = 1.30%		−2 log likelihood = 1,200.7			
Panel C: Divesting versus discontinuing firms						
(1)	−0.046	−1.118	1.471	−0.363	9.641**	
	0.883	*0.498*	*0.464*	*0.647*	*0.028*	
		−0.256	0.347	−0.086	2.456	
	Pseudo-R^2 = 1.44%		−2 log likelihood = 382.2			
(2)	−0.026	−0.833	1.093	−0.194		3.536*
	0.933	*0.610*	*0.586*	*0.803*		*0.075*
		−0.183	0.234	−0.458		0.919
	Pseudo-R^2 = 1.02%		−2 log likelihood = 383.9			

Table 5
Industry classification of divesting firms, discontinuing firms, divested segments, and discontinued segments
Cells present the frequency and percentage of segments with the same (different) SIC code as the firm, for the divestiture sample and the sample of discontinuing firms. Panel A is for segments that have disappeared and Panel B is for retained segments. SIC codes are measured at the four-digit, three-digit, and two-digit level.

SIC code level	Number of segments with same (different) SIC code as firm				Number of segments with same (different) SIC code as firm			
	Divesting firms				Discontinuing firms			
	Frequency		Percent		Frequency		Percent	
Panel A: Relatedness between firm and segments no longer reported								
4-digit	18	(191)	8.6	(91.4)	62	(320)	16.2	(83.8)
3-digit	24	(185)	11.5	(88.5)	94	(288)	24.6	(75.4)
2-digit	63	(146)	30.1	(69.9)	168	(214)	44.0	(56.0)
Panel B: Relatedness between firm and retained segments								
4-digit	110	(357)	23.6	(76.5)	49	(213)	18.7	(81.3)
3-digit	170	(297)	36.4	(63.6)	77	(185)	29.4	(70.6)
2-digit	254	(213)	54.4	(45.6)	112	(150)	42.8	(57.3)

whether we use the four-digit or the two-digit SIC code, almost 70% of the divested segments can be classified as belonging to an industry unrelated to the core activities of the parent. In contrast, more than 50% of the retained segments belong to the same two-digit SIC code as the firm. To capture the segments least likely to be related to the main activities of the firm, we classify segments that share their two-digit SIC code with the firm as core segments and the other segments as non-core segments. The typical divested segment is therefore a non-core segment, which is consistent with the focusing hypothesis.

Table 6 compares divested segments to retained segments. It is clear that the divested segments are smaller than the retained segments. Divested segments are less efficient, and they have poorer growth opportunities based on both sales growth and the median q of the two-digit SIC code of the segment.[8] Divested segments also are less profitable, and have lower capital expenditures.[9] Finally, as predicted by the

[8] Recent papers by Chevalier (2000) and Whited (2001) provide evidence that segments of conglomerates may differ systematically from their single-segment firm counterparts, making the median q of the two-SIC code industry of the segment a questionable estimate of the segment's growth opportunities. However, sales growth uses within-firm data rather than industry data to proxy for investment opportunities and leads to the same conclusion as the industry median q.

[9] Wysocki (1998) finds that segments no longer reported are less profitable. Based on the work of Francis et al. (1996), he raises the concern that firms write down assets of segments in preparation for selling them or liquidating them. If this were an important issue in our data, we would overstate the importance of profitability as a determinant of the divestiture decision.

Table 6

Univariate analysis for divested, discontinued, and retained segments

Cells represent median values of performance. Segment accounting data are taken from the Compustat CISF Full-Coverage Segment File. Cash flow (CF) is defined as operating profits plus depreciation. Tsales denotes the aggregated sales for the firm. Capital expenditures (CPX) are net capital expenditures (i.e., gross capital expenditures minus depreciation). Segment median industry q is calculated as the fraction of the book value of total assets minus the book value of equity plus the market value of equity and the book value of total assets of all Compustat firms with the same two-digit SIC code as the segment. Segment liquidity is calculated as the ratio of the value of corporate control transactions within a year and two-digit SIC class to the assets of all firms on Compustat in the same year and two-digit SIC class. The difference in q is between divested (non-reporting) non-core segments and all retained segments. The change in the coefficient of variation in Tobin's q (ΔCoefficient of Variation in q) is denoted in percent change. The t subscript refers to the year relative to the focusing year t. Ratios are truncated at minus and plus one, growth variables at −100% and +200%. Asset and sales numbers are in $ millions. Statistical significance of the difference in medians is denoted with ***, **, and * for 1%, 5%, and 10% rejection levels, respectively.

	Divesting firms				Discontinuing firms	Difference between divested and discontinued segments	
	Divested (1)	Retained (2)	Difference (1)−(2)	*p*-value	Discontinued (3)	Difference (1)−(3)	*p*-Value
Size							
ln $(Sales)_{t-1}$	4.621	5.452	−0.831***	*0.001*	4.817	−0.196	*0.436*
ln $(Assets)_{t-1}$	4.240	5.158	−0.918***	*0.001*	4.312	−0.072	*0.430*
Growth rates, investment, and growth opportunities							
$(Sales_{t-1}/Sales_{t-2})-1$	0.016	0.047	−0.031	*0.163*	0.021	−0.005	*0.911*
$(Sales_{t-1}/Tsales_{t-2})-1$	0.097	0.231	−0.134***	*0.001*	0.146	−0.049***	*0.003*
$(Sales_{t-2}/Tsales_{t-3})-1$	0.107	0.223	−0.116***	*0.001*	0.156	−0.049**	*0.016*
$((Sales/Tsales)_{t-1}/(Sales/Tsales)_{t-2})-1$	−0.030	0.003	−0.033**	*0.014*	−0.017	−0.013	*0.150*
$((Sales/Tsales)_{t-2}/(Sales/Tsales)_{t-3})-1$	−0.033	−0.007	−0.026	*0.198*	−0.015	−0.018	*0.284*
Net $CPX_{t-1}/Sales_{t-2}$	0.027	0.040	−0.013***	*0.006*	0.036	−0.009***	*0.008*
Net $CPX_{t-2}/Sales_{t-3}$	0.032	0.042	−0.010**	*0.022*	0.038	−0.006	*0.151*
$(CPX_{t-1}/CPX_{t-2})-1$	−0.150	−0.016	−0.134**	*0.022*	−0.003	−0.147*	*0.056*
$(CPX_{t-2}/CPX_{t-3})-1$	0.056	0.014	0.042	*0.658*	0.029	0.027	*0.618*
Segment Median Industry q	1.156	1.269	−0.113**	*0.024*	1.197	−0.041	*0.737*
ΔCoefficient of Variation in q (× 100%)	−0.151	−0.171	0.020	*0.709*	−0.186	0.035	*0.686*
Cash flow							
$CF_{t-1}/Sales_{t-2}$	0.071	0.122	−0.051***	*0.001*	0.100	−0.029**	*0.011*
$CF_{t-2}/Sales_{t-3}$	0.097	0.131	−0.034***	*0.001*	0.112	−0.015*	*0.082*
Liquidity measures							
Segment Liquidity	0.025	0.016	0.009**	*0.014*	0.020	0.004*	*0.067*
Segment Liquidity (Core Segments)	0.022	0.018	0.004	*0.623*	0.021	0.000	*0.999*
Segment Liquidity (Non-core Segments)	0.027	0.016	0.110**	*0.012*	0.020	0.006*	*0.086*

asset liquidity hypothesis, the liquidity index of divested segments is significantly higher than the liquidity index of retained segments.

In Section 3, we find that, among firms that stop reporting a segment, firms with a higher liquidity index are more likely to divest that segment. If the focusing firms that divest do so because they have segments that are more liquid, we should find that divested segments are more liquid than discontinued segments. We find that divested segments are more liquid than discontinued segments, but the difference in liquidity between divested and discontinued segments is only significant for non-core segments. There are few other significant differences between divested and discontinued segments. Discontinued segments are larger, more profitable, and have better investment opportunities than divested segments. The size difference between divested and discontinued segments could be interpreted as further evidence of the importance of liquidity, if one believes, as Shleifer and Vishny (1992) argue, that liquidity decreases with size.

A potentially confounding factor in this analysis is that firms are required to report segments with sales that exceed 10% of the firm's total sales. Thus, small segments might no longer be reported simply because their sales fall below the threshold. This could explain why firms stop reporting a segment without divesting it. They would still want to keep the segment, so that they would not divest it, but they would not be required to report it. We do not find that the 10% threshold explains our results. Instead, we find that divested segments are more likely to have sales below 10% of total sales than discontinued segments. For the firms that divest segments, 46.9% of the divested segments have sales of less than 10% of the firm's total sales. In contrast, only 19.9% of segments retained by these firms have sales of less than 10% of the firm's total sales. For the discontinuing firms, 36.4% of the discontinued segments have sales below 10%, and 22.5% of the segments still reported have sales below 10%.

5.2. Industry-adjusted comparisons

The efficiency explanation predicts that divested segments are inefficient relative to their industry. In Table 7, we provide industry-adjusted comparisons of divested segments relative to retained segments and discontinued segments. The table reveals that divested segments perform poorly relative to their industry. The fact that these segments invest less than their industry and have lower sales growth is consistent with divesting firms being financially constrained. The discontinued segments also have lower industry-adjusted sales growth and capital expenditures than their industry, which is consistent with the discontinuing firms having financial constraints. Since their level of cash flow to sales significantly exceeds that of their industry, however, the discontinued segments do not appear to be less efficient than their industry.

Segments retained by divesting firms have higher industry-adjusted cash flows. However, the retained segments invest less than their industry, which is again consistent with the hypothesis that divesting firms are financially constrained. Finally, retained segments have lower sales growth than their industry.

Table 7
Univariate analysis for industry-adjusted segment performance
Cells represent median values of industry-adjusted performance of divested segments, discontinued segments, and retained segments. Segment accounting data are taken from the Compustat CIS Full-Coverage Segment File. Cash flow (CF) is defined as operating profits plus depreciation. Tsales denotes the aggregated sales for the firm. Capital expenditures (CPX) are net capital expenditures (i.e., gross capital expenditures minus depreciation). Industry adjustments are based on the difference between the variable and the median value of all Compustat firms with the same two-digit SIC code in the fiscal year before the event. Ratios are truncated at minus and plus one and capital expenditures growth at minus and plus 200%. Asset and sales numbers are in $ millions. Statistical significance of the difference in medians is denoted with ***, **, and * for 1%, 5%, and 10% rejection levels respectively.

		Segments no longer reported (1)			Retained segments (2)			Difference (1)–(2)	
Variable	Event	*n*	Median	*p*-Value	*n*	Median	*p*-Value	Median	*p*-Value
CF/sales	Divestiture	120	−0.017***	*0.001*	290	0.024***	*0.001*	−0.042***	*0.001*
	Discontinued	231	0.013***	*0.009*					
	Difference		−0.030***	*0.008*					
CPX/sales	Divestiture	118	−0.024**	*0.030*	289	−0.016***	*0.001*	−0.008***	*0.005*
	Discontinued	230	−0.016***	*0.001*					
	Difference		−0.008**	*0.013*					
CPX growth	Divestiture	113	−0.228***	*0.001*	276	−0.082	*0.227*	−0.145**	*0.037*
	Discontinued	220	−0.102	*0.181*					
	Difference		−0.126*	*0.054*					
ln (Sales)	Divestiture	119	0.707***	*0.001*	290	1.219***	*0.001*	−0.512***	*0.002*
	Discontinued	231	0.739***	*0.001*					
	Difference		−0.032	*0.910*					
Sales growth	Divestiture	119	−0.060***	*0.001*	289	−0.022***	*0.003*	−0.037**	*0.012*
	Discontinued	231	−0.062***	*0.001*					
	Difference		0.002	*0.910*					

5.3. Relative ranking for divested segments

Stein (1997) argues that an advantage of internal capital markets is that they can better allocate resources by ranking performance across divisions. This suggests that firms might choose to divest segments that perform poorly relative to other segments within the firm. In Table 8, we examine how the relative ranking of the segments within the firm helps explain the divestiture decision. To construct the table, we rank segments according to various financial characteristics. We then compare these rankings to the likelihood of the segment being divested. Consider, for example, all firms with five segments with the segments ranked within each firm according to liquidity. If liquidity does not matter for the divestiture decision, we would expect 20% of the segment divestitures to occur in each of the five ranked segments. We use a Pearson chi-square statistic to test for an equal distribution of divestitures across the ranked segments. We then report in the table the number of segments no longer reported for each rank for each characteristic. The first characteristic we consider is the cash flow performance of the segment. We find that 49 out of 124 (40%) divested segments have the lowest cash flow performance in their firm. At the same time,

Table 8
Relative ranking of within firm performance of divested segments
Cells present the number of divested segments within a ranking for different variables. The number of divisions denotes the total number of segments within a firm and the rank denotes the relative magnitude, from low to high, of the variable. Cash flow (CF) is defined as operating profits plus depreciation. Capital expenditures (CPX) are net capital expenditures (i.e., gross capital expenditures minus depreciation). Segment q is calculated as the book value of total assets minus the book value of equity plus the market value of equity divided by the book value of total assets of all Compustat firms with the same two-digit SIC code as the segment. Segment liquidity is calculated as the ratio of the value of all corporate control transactions within a year and two-digit SIC class and the assets of all firms on Compustat in the same year and two-digit SIC class. The last row denotes the total number of divested segments, n, for each firm. Ties are assigned to the higher rank. The last column denotes the Pearson χ^2 test-statistic for a uniform distribution across ranks. Significance is denoted with ***, **, and * for 1%, 5%, and 10% rejection levels and indicates rejection of equality of the variation across the rankings.

		Number of segments within firm							Pearson χ^2 test-statistic
Variable	Rank	2	3	4	5	6	7	n (row)	
CF/sales	1 (low)	9	17	14	5	3	1	49	
	2	5	7	9	8	9	1	39	39.15*
	3		6	7	4	1	0	18	
	4			6	3	3	1	13	
	5				3	1	0	4	
	6					0	0	0	
	7 (high)						0	0	
ln(Sales)	1 (low)	13	21	20	6	6	0	66	
	2	1	7	10	8	4	2	32	72.65***
	3		2	5	4	2	0	13	
	4			1	4	1	1	7	
	5				1	2	0	2	
	6					2	0	2	
	7 (high)						0	0	
CPX/sales	1 (low)	11	11	10	5	4	2	43	
	2	3	8	10	6	4	1	32	22.15
	3		10	6	7	2	0	25	
	4			9	3	4	0	16	
	5				3	3	0	6	
	6					0	0	0	
	7 (high)						0	0	
	n	14	30	36	24	17	3		
CPX growth	1 (low)	8	13	13	3	4	0	41	
	2	6	5	6	7	5	2	31	28.10
	3		7	10	5	2	0	24	
	4			4	4	4	0	12	
	5				5	1	1	2	
	6					0	0	0	
	7 (high)						0	0	

Table 8 (*continued*)

Variable	Rank	Number of segments within firm							Pearson χ^2 test-statistic
		2	3	4	5	6	7	*n* (row)	
Segment *q*	1 (low)	5	12	8	6	2	0	33	
	2	9	8	7	7	1	0	32	23.09
	3		10	8	0	4	1	23	
	4			11	2	2	0	15	
	5				8	5	0	13	
	6					3	0	3	
	7 (high)						0	0	
Segment liquidity	1 (low)	1	5	4	2	1	0	13	
	2	11	4	6	3	1	0	25	66.73***
	3		18	14	1	1	0	34	
	4			9	7	0	0	16	
	5				9	3	0	12	
	6					8	1	9	
	7 (high)						2	2	
	n	14	30	36	24	17	3		

however, 20 divested segments have the best cash flow performance in their firm. Strikingly, 66 divested segments are the smallest in their firm, but only seven are the largest. A segment is more likely to be divested when it is small rather than when it performs poorly. Forty-one divested segments have the highest industry *q* among firm segments but 33 have the lowest *q*, suggesting that segment growth opportunities measured by the industry *q* of single-segment firms in the industry are not important to the divestiture decision. However, among divested segments, 51% have the highest liquidity index in the firm and only 12% have the lowest liquidity index.

From this analysis, it is clear that a segment's size, liquidity, cash flow, and relatedness to the firm's core activities affect its probability of divestiture. Using a Pearson chi-square test, we can reject at the 10% level or better the equality of the variation across ranks for cash flow over sales, sales, and liquidity for the divested segments. The largest segment and the most illiquid segment are highly unlikely to be divested. Table 8 provides an interesting perspective on the economic importance of segment performance versus liquidity: the least-liquid segment is less likely to be divested than the best-performing segment, while the worst-performing segment is less likely to be divested than the most-liquid segment.

5.4. Logit analysis predicting which segments are divested

Given that divested segments are smaller, are more liquid, and have lower cash flow than other segments in their firm, we investigate whether each one of these variables is important. In Table 9, we report logit regressions for the probability that a segment is divested rather than retained. We first use a segment's cash flow, size,

Table 9

Retained versus divested segments logit regression results

Logit regressions with a binary dependent variable that takes on the value one for divested segments and zero for retained segments. Models (1)–(3) are for the divesting firms and model (4) is for the discontinuing firms. Cells represent (respectively) the coefficient, *p*-Value, and the slope (defined as $\partial E[y]/\partial \mathbf{x}$, for the binary model $y_{(0,1)} = \boldsymbol{\beta}'\mathbf{x} + \varepsilon$, evaluated at the mean of $\mathbf{x}$), the pseudo-R^2, and the value of −2 times the log likelihood. Cash flow (CF) is defined as operating income before depreciation. Capital expenditures (CPX) are the firm's net capital expenditures. Industry median variables are calculated as the median value of all Compustat firms within the same two-digit SIC code as the segment during the same year. The non-core dummy takes on a value of one when the 2-digit segment SIC code is different from the two-digit firm SIC code. Segment liquidity is calculated as the ratio of the value of all corporate control transactions within a year and two-digit SIC class and the assets of all firms on Compustat in the same year and 2-digit SIC class. The size < 10% dummy is equal to one if the segment sales are less than 10% of the firm's total sales and zero otherwise. Accounting numbers are based on the firm-level data. The numerator in the ratios is measured in year −1 and the denominator in year −2. Statistical significance is denoted with ***, **, and * for 1%, 5%, and 10% rejection levels, respectively.

Model	Intercept	CF/sales	Ind. median CF/sales	CPX/sales	Ind. median CPX/sales	Segment sales/ firm sales	Non-core dummy	Segment q	Segment liquidity	Size < 10% dummy
(1)	−0.183	−2.269**		−0.567		−4.992***	0.512*	−0.044	6.653**	
	0.774	*0.043*		*0.721*		*0.001*	*0.071*	*0.912*	*0.011*	
		−0.384		−0.104		−0.833	0.086	−0.007	1.121	
	Pseudo-R^2 = 16.14%					−2 log likelihood = 393.8				
(2)	−0.382	−2.433**	0.115	−0.945	3.367	−4.943***	0.484*	−0.078	6.741***	
	0.572	*0.047*	*0.969*	*0.548*	*0.567*	*0.001*	*0.087*	*0.734*	*0.009*	
		−0.401	0.019	−0.161	0.467	−0.829	0.082	−0.015	1.112	
	Pseudo-R^2 = 16.76%					−2 log likelihood = 393.5				
(3)	−0.629	−2.377**	0.044	−1.071	3.861	−4.454***	0.516*	−0.022	6.321**	0.249
	0.412	0.049	*0.991*	*0.496*	*0.543*	0.001	*0.074*	*0.958*	0.016	*0.470*
		−0.403	0.007	−0.182	0.662	−0.747	0.086	−0.004	1.082	0.046
	Pseudo-R^2 = 16.91					−2 log likelihood = 383.8				
(4)	1.438**	0.634	−1.271	−1.586	−10.274	−0.071	−0.028	−0.152	0.493	0.987***
	0.043	*0.446*	*0.743*	*0.281*	*0.084*	*0.897*	*0.931*	*0.745*	*0.824*	*0.004*
		0.137	−0.279	−0.347	−2.233	−0.021	−0.007	−0.034	0.102	0.214
	Pseudo-R^2 = 5.28%					−2 log likelihood = 398.4				

capital expenditures, industry q, liquidity index, and whether it is a core segment as independent variables. The dependent variable is set to one for divested segments and zero for retained segments. In Regression (1), we find that a segment is more likely to be divested if its cash flow is low, if it is a small segment, if it is a non-core segment, and if its liquidity index is high. The significance for non-core segment dummy is consistent with the focusing explanation. The significance of the cash flow variable is consistent with the financing explanation.

A segment with low cash flow can be divested for two separate reasons. One reason, provided by the efficiency explanation, is that the firm is unsuccessful at operating the segment efficiently. A second reason, coming from the financing explanation, is that the segment is consuming excessive corporate resources because its cash flow is too low and, as a result, a financially constrained firm can be less constrained without the segment. The efficiency explanation implies that a segment is more likely to be divested when the industry median cash flow is higher, since this means that the performance of the segment is poor relative to its industry. In Regression (2), we test this explanation by adding the industry median cash flow to Regression (1) as well as industry median capital expenditures. We find that the industry medians have insignificant coefficients. As a result, performance relative to the industry does not appear to be an important determinant of the divestiture decision. Following the model of Maksimovic and Phillips (2002) in which industry shocks reduce the comparative advantage of small segments proportionately more than the comparative advantage of large segments within a firm, one could also interpret industry cash flow as a proxy for industry shocks. With this interpretation, the evidence suggests that industry shocks are unlikely to be a sufficient explanation for why firms are more likely to divest small segments since the size variable remains significant after controlling for industry cash flow.

To this point, the importance of segment size is surprising. As previously mentioned, it is possible that the effect of size is due to segments that are below 10% of sales, so that the firm would no longer have to report them. In Regression (3), we add an indicator variable for segments smaller than 10% of firm sales. This dummy variable is not significant. Regression (4) estimates the same regression for discontinued segments. In Regression (4), the indicator variable is significant, while the other segment characteristics, except for the industry median capital expenditures to sales, are not significant. A second possibility is that size matters for the divested segments because, as advanced by Shleifer and Vishny (1992), liquidity is inversely related to size. If we add the log of segment sales or segment assets to the regressions, it has a negative coefficient but is not significant. Recent models (see, in particular, Meyer et al., 1990; Scharfstein and Stein, 2000) are consistent with the hypothesis that small segments draw rents in diversified firms. These models provide an alternate explanation for the importance of segment size in the divestiture decision.

5.5. Core versus non-core segments

In the analysis of Shleifer and Vishny (1992), firms sell assets to raise funds. Their analysis predicts that the most liquid segments of firms that divest to raise funds are more likely to be non-core segments than core segments. If firms that divest segments are firms whose core business is performing poorly and if this poor performance is the result of an industry effect, the bidders who would be best equipped to operate a core segment are financially constrained as well and hence will not be the highest bidders. Pulvino (1998) finds evidence supportive of the prediction that buyers outside the industry pay less. We find that for divesting firms, the most liquid segment among non-core segments has a significantly higher liquidity index than the most liquid segment among core segments. The importance of liquidity is again apparent: among firms that divest segments, the greater liquidity of non-core segments raises the possibility that the firm divests a non-core segment not because it wants to focus but because that segment can be sold most advantageously.

To investigate further whether differences in liquidity explain why some firms divest core segments and others divest non-core segments, we estimate a logit regression that takes a value of one if the firm divests a core segment and zero otherwise. The focusing argument for why firms divest non-core segments is that they are inefficient diversifiers. We proxy for the extent to which a diversified firm is an efficient diversifier by its excess value measure. The efficiency explanation predicts that a firm is more likely to divest segments that underperform relative to their industry. We therefore include in the regression the difference between the weighted average of industry-adjusted cash flows for core segments and non-core segments. The greater that difference, the more likely it is that a firm will divest non-core segments. Finally, the liquidity argument implies that a firm is more likely to divest a non-core segment if the liquidity of the non-core segment is higher than the liquidity of the firm's core segments. We therefore use as independent variables the liquidity index of the core (non-core) segment with the highest liquidity index defined as Max Core (Max Non-Core).

The regression estimates are as follows (p-values in parentheses):

Divest core segment =		
−1.056	+24.186 Max Core	−59.565 Max Non-Core
(0.072)	*(0.043)*	*(0.030)*
+1.063 Excess value	+3.473 Industry-adjusted cash flow difference.	
(0.224)	*(0.484)*	

Segment liquidity is a significant determinant of whether a firm divests core or non-core segments. The higher the maximum core liquidity, the more likely it is that a core segment is divested. The higher the maximum non-core liquidity, the less likely it is that a core segment is divested. The excess value and segment cash flow performance measures have no explanatory power in explaining why a firm divests core or non-core segments. These results are inconsistent with the view that firms shed non-core segments because they are poor diversifiers or because the segments underperform their industry.

Our regression estimates provide limited support for explanations of divestitures that rely on firms discovering that diversification is costly for them. Moreover, the coefficient for excess value is positive, as one would expect with the focusing explanation. In the regressions of Table 9, firms are more likely to divest non-core segments, and the intercept of the regression has this same interpretation. However, specific measures of diversification costs cannot explain this result. We also include a variable to investigate whether a firm is more likely to divest segments that would reduce the Rajan et al. (2000) diversity measure the most. The coefficient of this variable is never significant.

6. Conclusion

In this paper, we examine why firms divest assets and which assets they divest. The literature has argued that firms divest because they are inefficient diversifiers, have segments that could be operated more efficiently elsewhere, and/or are financially constrained. Though we find empirical support for these reasons in our sample, we show that they are only part of the story. These reasons cannot distinguish between "focusing" firms that reduce their number of segments through divestitures and those that do not. We show that differences across firms in asset liquidity can help explain why, among apparently similar firms, some firms divest a segment and others do not. We measure an industry's asset liquidity by the volume of corporate transactions relative to total industry assets. We show that firms with segments in industries that are more liquid are more likely to divest segments and we provide evidence that segment liquidity helps explain which segment is retained or divested by a divesting firm. Consistent with the arguments of Shleifer and Vishny (1992), part of the reason for why firms divest unrelated segments is that they tend to be in more liquid industries. These results are supportive of the hypothesis that segment liquidity plays an important role in explaining the divestiture decision.

References

Allen, J.W., McConnell, J.J., 1998. Equity carve-outs and managerial discretion. Journal of Finance 53, 163–186.

Andrade, G., Stafford, E., 2000. Investigating the economic role of mergers. Unpublished working paper, Harvard Business School, Boston.

Berger, P.G., Ofek, E., 1995. Diversification's effect on firm value. Journal of Financial Economics 37, 39–65.

Berger, P.G., Ofek, E., 1999. Causes and consequences of corporate refocusing programs. Review of Financial Studies 12, 311–345.

Chevalier, J., 2000. What do we know about cross-subsidization? Evidence from the investment policies of merging firms. Unpublished working paper, University of Chicago, Chicago.

Comment, R., Jarrell, G.A., 1995. Corporate focus and stock returns. Journal of Financial Economics 37, 67–87.

Daley, L., Mehrotra, V., Sivakumar, R., 1997. Corporate focus and value creation: evidence from spin-offs. Journal of Financial Economics 45, 257–281.

Francis, J., Hanna, J., Vincent, L., 1996. Causes and effects of discretionary write-offs. Journal of Accounting Research 34, 117–134.

Hite, G.L., Owers, J.E., Rogers, R.C., 1987. The market for interfirm asset sales: partial sell-offs and total liquidations. Journal of Financial Economics 18, 229–252.

John, K., Ofek, E., 1995. Asset sales and increase in focus. Journal of Financial Economics 37, 105–126.

Kahle, K.M., Walkling, R.A., 1996. The impact of industry classifications on financial research. Journal of Financial and Quantitative Analysis 31, 309–335.

Lang, L.H.P., Poulsen, A., Stulz, R.M., 1994. Asset sales, firm performance, and the agency costs of managerial discretion. Journal of Financial Economics 37, 3–37.

Maksimovic, V., Phillips, G., 2001. The market for corporate assets: who engages in mergers and corporate sales and are there gains. Journal of Finance 56, 2019–2065.

Maksimovic, V., Phillips, G., 2002. Do conglomerates allocate resources efficiently? Journal of Finance 57, forthcoming.

Meyer, M., Milgrom, P., Roberts, J., 1990. Organization prospects, influence costs, and ownership changes. Journal of Economics and Management Strategy 1, 9–35.

Mitchell, M., Mulherin, J.H., 1996. The impact of industry shocks on takeover and restructuring activity. Journal of Financial Economics 41, 193–229.

Mulherin, J.H., Boone, A.L., 2000. Comparing acquisitions and divestitures. Unpublished working paper, Pennsylvania State University, University Park.

Pulvino, T., 1998. Do asset fire sales exist? An empirical investigation of commercial aircraft transactions. Journal of Finance 53, 939–978.

Rajan, R., Servaes, H., Zingales, L., 2000. The diversification discount and inefficient investment. Journal of Finance 55, 35–80.

Scharfstein, D.S., Stein, J.C., 2000. The dark side of internal capital markets: divisional rent-seeking and inefficient investment. Journal of Finance 55, 2537–2564.

Shleifer, A., Vishny, R.W., 1992. Liquidation values and debt capacity: a market equilibrium approach. Journal of Finance 47, 1343–1366.

Stein, J.C., 1997. Internal capital markets and the competition for corporate resources. Journal of Finance 52, 111–133.

Whited, T., 2001. Is inefficient investment the cause of the conglomerate discount? Journal of Finance 56, 1667–1691.

Wysocki, P.D., 1998. Real options and the informativeness of segment disclosures. Unpublished working paper, University of Michigan, Ann Arbor.

[8]

ELSEVIER Journal of Financial Economics 45 (1997) 257–281

JOURNAL OF Financial ECONOMICS

Corporate focus and value creation Evidence from spinoffs

Lane Daley, Vikas Mehrotra*, Ranjini Sivakumar

University of Alberta, Edmonton, AB, Canada T6G 2R6

Received March 1996; received in revised form October 1996

Abstract

We test a prediction from the corporate focus literature that cross-industry spinoff distributions, where the continuing and spunoff units belong to different two-digit Standard Industry Classification codes, create more value than own-industry spinoffs. Our results indicate significant value creation around the announcement of cross-industry spinoffs only. We then provide evidence on whether the value creation comes from operating performance improvements, or bonding benefits, or both, where bonding refers to a pre-commitment by managers to avoid cross-subsidizing relatively poor performing units within the firm. We find a significant improvement in operating performance for cross-industry spinoffs, and none for own-industry cases. We do not find strong evidence of bonding to explain spinoff-related value creation. Further, the operating performance improvement is associated with the continuing rather than the spunoff entity, consistent with the hypothesis that spinoffs create value by removing unrelated businesses and allowing managers to focus attention on the core operations they are best suited to manage.

Keywords: Spinoff; Divestiture; Focus; Cross-subsidization

JEL classification: G34; G35

---

*Corresponding author.

We thank Mark Huson, Gregg Jarrell (the referee), Eizabeth Maynes, Wyne Mikkelson, Randall Morck, Bill Schwert (the editor), and seminar participants at the Northern Finance Association meetings in Quebec City and the Universities of Oregon, Waterloo, Wisconsin-Madison, and Alberta for helpful comments. Vikas Mehrotra also gratefully acknowledges funding from the Southam Edmonton Journal Faculty Fellowship.

PII S0304-405X(97)00018-4

1. Introduction

Recent research on asset sales has documented that dispositions involving assets outside of the core business of a firm are viewed by the market as increasing value while disposition of core assets is not. (See the Journal of Financial Economics, 1995, special issue on corporate focus; in particular, see Comment and Jarrell, 1995; John and Ofek, 1995; Berger and Ofek, 1995. These studies generally conclude a positive relation between corporate focus and firm value.) The shedding of these non-core assets is referred to as 'increasing corporate focus'. While corporate restructuring that increases focus appears to increase value, there is little evidence on what the source of this value creation is. In this study we employ a sample of asset dispositions referred to as corporate spinoffs to investigate several issues relating to the value of increased corporate focus.

Spinoffs differ from other modes of asset divestitures in that they do not involve any cash. A spinoff occurs when a firm creates a subsidiary to hold a portion of its assets, and then distributes the shares of the subsidiary to its shareholders to create an independent company. We refer to the pre-spinoff and continuing entity as the parent, and the spunoff unit as the subsidiary, even though there is no parent/subsidiary relation following the spinoff. We exploit the fact that spinoffs are unique among divestiture modes in that they allow us to observe the post-spinoff performance of both the retained and divested assets, permitting a direct comparison with the performance of the pre-spinoff firm. A similar observation cannot be made for asset sales. Thus it is not possible to examine performance changes around asset sales because there is no observable post-sale performance benchmark for the sold assets.

First, we test the prediction arising from the corporate focus literature that spinoffs that increase corporate focus should create more value than spinoffs that do not materially change corporate focus. While there is considerable evidence that spinoffs create value, (see, e.g., Miles and Rosenfield, 1983, Kudla and McInish, 1983; Hite and Owers, 1983; Schipper and Smith, 1983) there has been no attempt to relate the value creation to corporate focus. Schipper and Smith (1983) and Davidson and McDonald (1987) examine samples of spinoffs where explicit tax benefits lay behind the spinoff. Schipper and Smith (1983) and Hite and Owers (1983) examine spinoffs involving regulated firms. Schipper and Smith (1983) and Hite and Owers (1983) examine the importance of the bond holder to equity holder wealth transfer and conclude that it is not significant. Parrino (1997), however, finds a significant decline in the value of Marriott's bonds following Marriott's spinoff announcement. He concludes that the initial wealth transfer to Marriott's shareholders was largely dissipated in litigation and other transaction costs. Hite and Owers (1983) and Cusatis et al. (1993) examine the cases where one of the spunoff entities becomes a takeover target after the spinoff.

We define an increase in corporate focus as occurring when the business that is spunoff operates in a different two-digit Standard Industry Classification code from the core line of business for the pre-spinoff entity. We refer to these cases as cross-industry spinoffs. When the spunoff unit operates in the same industry, we classify the spinoff as not increasing corporate focus and refer to these as own-industry spinoffs. Our results indicate that only the cross-industry spinoffs are associated with positive and significant excess returns around spinoff announcements, consistent with the broader results from asset sale studies.

We also seek to provide evidence on whether the value increase we document for cross-industry spinoffs arises from performance improvements, or bonding benefits, or both. Performance improvement may follow focus-increasing events such as cross-industry spinoffs for several reasons. First, managerial skills may be well-suited to the management of core business, but not to the management of non-core assets. Consequently, freeing the managers from operations unrelated to the core business should improve corporate performance. We refer to this possibility as the Corporate Focus Hypothesis. John and Ofek (1995) refer to this condition as removal of 'negative synergies' between the retained and divested assets. Second, performance improvement may arise due to improvements in the alignment of incentives between managers and shareholders. The creation of a free-standing subsidiary allows for the writing of a variety of incentive plans for the subsidiary managers that may not have been optimal or feasible when the subsidiary was not publicly traded. In turn, the potential to write improved incentive contracts could improve the performance of the spunoff assets. We refer to this as the Incentive Alignment Hypothesis.

We capture performance by examining the change in return on assets (henceforth ROA, defined as the ratio of operating income to total assets) around the time of the spinoff. First, we compare the ROA measures for the pre-spinoff firm to that for the combined parent and subsidiary in the post-spinoff period. Accounting rules require that the assets transferred to the subsidiary be valued at carryover basis from the parent, implying that the total assets of the pre-spinoff firm are identical to the sum of the total assets held by the parent and the subsidiary immediately after the spinoff. This unique set of circumstances allows us to use accounting-based measures of performance to compare the pre-spinoff performance of the entity to the post-spinoff performance of the parent/subsidiary combined entity, without introducing measurement errors due to asset revaluations. In Healy et al. (1992), the authors provide a discussion of the problems they encountered in developing comparative accounting performance numbers for cases involving acquisitions, where accounting rules require revaluation of all assets and liabilities to market for the acquired entity. This results in non-comparable accounting ratios such as return-on-assets, return-on-sales, etc., because of the valuation changes booked at the time of the acquisition. Healy et al. were forced to make approximations of these effects that could introduce bias and measurement error into the comparative data. Since the accounting rules for spinoffs do not allow such revaluations, we need not make any adjustments to the reported results and thereby eliminate this source of measurement error in the accounting performance measures we employ.

We document significant improvements in ROA at the raw level, and after controlling for size, industry, and pre-spinoff performance, for cross-industry parent/subsidiary portfolios, but no significant changes for own-industry cases. We interpret these results as indicating that performance improvements provide at least a partial explanation for the value increase surrounding cross-industry spinoff announcements, and that this is an advantage of increasing corporate focus.

Focus-related value increase can also arise from bonding benefits, where bonding refers to a pre-commitment by managers to avoid cross-subsidization of poorly performing units by using free cash flow from more profitable units. Cross-subsidies may be directed either from the parent firm to poorly performing subsidiaries, or from subsidiaries (e.g. after raising capital ostensibly for use in the subsidiary's operations) to the parent's operations. Capital market participants understand these incentives, and respond positively when managers post bonds to restrict their ability to cross-subsidize poorly performing units. The ultimate bond in these situations is to separate the two units into independent organizations which are both subject to direct market discipline when raising new capital.

To investigate whether bonding benefits can explain part of the value creation around spinoff announcements, we argue that bonding is especially valuable when a firm needs to raise new capital since efficient capital markets are likely to incorporate the benefits of bonding in pricing the offering. We examine the frequency of debt and equity issues made by firms engaged in cross-industry spinoffs immediately before and after the spinoff, and find no evidence of an increase. Furthermore, the frequency of capital issuance is no different for cross- and own-industry spinoffs.

We also examine other indicators of bonding, such as an increase in leverage (as suggested by Jensen, 1986), and cash dividends (as suggested by Easterbrook, 1984), that might be used in conjunction with the spinoff to increase the benefits of the spinoff event. We find weak evidence of an increase in dividends in the cross-industry group, although this occurs in the year after the performance improvements have been realized. Thus, it seems more likely that the dividend increase is related to increased profitability rather than bonding. We do not find evidence of a significant change in financial leverage in either group. Overall, the evidence suggests that firms engaging in spinoffs do not engage in other means of bonding around the time of the spinoff.

Given that we document significant performance increases for cross-industry parent and subsidiary portfolios, we also seek to determine whether the improvement comes from the parent's operations, the subsidiary's operations, or both. Most corporate spinoffs are accounted for as discontinued operations, implying that the results of the subsidiary's operations are segregated from the parent in the financial statements of the pre-spinoff entity in the year the spinoff decision is made. We use this segregated information to obtain baseline estimates of the pre-spinoff performance levels of the parent and subsidiary units individually to examine whether the performance improvement lies in either or both of these operating units. Our results indicate that the performance increase is found in the parents alone. This is not consistent with the Incentive Alignment Hypothesis, which suggests that the performance improvement should arise in the subsidiary, as it is the incentive plans for the subsidiary managers which have the most potential to improve from the spinoff. The results are, however, consistent with the Corporate Focus Hypothesis, in which the removal of non-core businesses allows parent managers to focus attention on the core operations they are best suited to manage.

The remainder of the paper is organized as follows. Section 2 explains the sample selection criteria used to identify our sample of spinoffs. Section 3 defines our measure of announcement period excess returns and reports the results of tests for differences between own- and cross-industry spinoffs. Section 4 describes the construction of our performance measure and the statistical measures we utilize to detect performance changes, and the results of our analyses at the combined parent and subsidiary level. Section 5 describes the data used to examine the potential effects of bonding and discusses the results of our analysis. Section 6 re-examines the data on performance increases at the level of individual parents and subsidiaries. Our conclusions are presented in Section 7.

2. Sample selection

Our goal is to gain insight into the way focus-related value creation at the announcement of spinoffs is revealed in subsequent performance changes. However, we are not interested in cases where performance improvements lie in obvious candidate explanations such as tax savings, or the removal of regulatory constraints. We are also not interested in those cases where the spinoff was motivated by an ensuing acquisition. While these examples are part of the motivation for spinoffs, they represent only a part of the population of spinoffs and have been studied elsewhere. Moreover, value increases exist in spinoffs that are not motivated by these other factors. Our interest is in the source of this value creation.

We examine the performance of spinoff firms in a five-year window starting two years prior to, and ending two years following, the spinoff year. While it is possible that spinoffs may lead to changes in performance that are not in evidence in the first two years, and only appear in the more distant future, we believe that, at the announcement of spinoffs, such distant changes would be harder to anticipate. Second, performance changes beyond the second year would have to be larger to create the same announcement-date excess returns due to the effect of discounting. As it is, our results indicate that performance changes, if any, occur in the first year after the spinoff.

Our sample of spinoffs was identified by pooling information from several sources. We began by obtaining the identity of the pre-spinoff firms examined by Schipper and Smith (1983).[1] Their sample ended in 1981 and includes 93 firms. We then identified additional spinoffs by searching the Wall Street Journal index for news stories regarding spinoffs after 1981. We further supplemented this list with spinoff cases discussed in Kudla and McInish (1988) and Vijh (1994). We identified a total of 212 spinoffs using these procedures.

We then imposed the following data requirements in order for a spinoff to remain in our sample:

(1) For any year in a five-year window centered on the spinoff year, both the parent and the subsidiary had to be listed for at least one year on the Compustat annual industrial files spanning 1975–1994. If Compustat had data for some years, but not others, and the entity was still in existence, it was necessary that annual report data be available in our library to fill in the missing years. Imposing the Compustat availability criterion reduced the total sample to 151 spinoffs (a reduction of 61 spinoffs).

(2) Five firms were lost because the parent was not available on the Center for Research in Security Prices (CRSP) files to estimate announcement period returns.

(3) A precise announcement date and ex-dividend date for the spinoff must have been available from either the Wall Street Journal, the CRSP files, or prior research. Six firms were lost due to lack of an announcement date or ex-dividend date or both.

(4) Spinoffs involving a royalty trust, a Real Estate Investment Trust, or a firm with operations in a regulated industry, were dropped, resulting in a loss of 19 spinoffs.

(5) Another 32 firms were dropped because the subsidiary or the parent firm was acquired within two years of the spinoff since we require two years of accounting data for calculating performance changes. A little over half of these cases (18 out of 32) are own-industry spinoffs. There is some concern that dropping the acquired firms from our sample may impart a bias to our announcement date excess returns. Cusatis et al. (1993) document that takeover activity subsequent to a spinoff is higher than in the average population of firms, though still low in absolute terms. They demonstrate that takeover premiums

[1] We thank Katherine Schipper and Abbie Smith for making their sample available to us. We only received the list of firms actually used in Schipper and Smith (93 firms). In their paper they report having identified 177 spinoffs, of which only 93 survive a number of sample selection criteria having to do with identifiable event dates and return data.

explain a significant portion of the cross-sectional variation in excess returns at the time of the spinoff announcement. To the extent these acquisitions were anticipated at the time of the spinoff announcement, and since a majority of the dropped firms are from the own-industry category, dropping them from our sample would impart a downward bias to the estimation of excess returns around own-industry spinoff announcements.[2] To address these concerns, we re-calculated our announcement-period excess returns together with these 32 firms and find that the announcement-date excess return results for cross-versus own-industry spinoffs are not affected by including the acquired firms in our sample.

(6) Finally, four spinoffs were lost because they represented cases in which one firm engaged in multiple spinoffs within the five-year window centered on the ex-dividend year.

Imposing these criteria reduced the sample to 85 firms engaged in spinoffs. Of these, 60 relate to spinoffs where the operations of the parent and the subsidiary differ at the two-digit SIC code level and 25 arise where the parent and the subsidiary have the same two-digit SIC code. Schipper and Smith (1983) find that 72 of their sample of 93 are cross-industry spinoffs. They do not condition their announcement-date returns on cross- versus own-industry spinoffs.

We determine the SIC codes using the first two Dun and Bradstreet industry listings for the parent and subsidiary entities in the year following the spinoff. Compustat lists only one SIC code per firm, and will tend to overstate the number of cross-industry spinoffs. Repeating our analysis using Compustat SIC codes has no material effect on our results. Table 1 reports the frequency of spinoffs by ex-dividend year.

The median book value of total assets of the pre-spinoff entity is $657 million and $442 million for cross- and own-industry spinoffs, respectively. The median asset value for cross- and own-industry subsidiaries (the spunoff assets) is $119 million and $148 million, representing a median fractional value equal to 0.25 and 0.29 of the asset value of the pre-spinoff entity.

3. Announcement date excess returns for cross- and own-industry spinoffs

The emerging literature on corporate focus suggests that decisions to terminate non-core business operations by diversified companies are met with significant share price improvements. Comment and Jarrell (1995) document a positive relation between changes in corporate focus and stock returns. John and Ofek (1995) show that performance improvements following asset sales are limited to focus increasing sales. Berger and Ofek (1995) provide a measure of

[2]We are grateful to the referee for bringing this to our attention.

Table 1
Distribution of 85 spinoffs executed in the period 1975–1991 by year of spinoff distribution. The sample excludes cases where the spinoff was tax driven, involved a firm in a regulated industry, or where one of the spinoff entities was acquired in a subsequent two-year period. Cross-industry spinoffs involve the creation of two entities operating in different two-digit SIC codes and own-industry spinoffs involve the creation of two entities operating in the same two-digit SIC code. Years refer to the spinoff distribution (ex-dividend) dates

Year	Cross-industry spinoffs	Own-industry spinoffs	Total
1975	3	0	3
1976	1	1	2
1977	4	0	4
1978	1	0	1
1979	5	1	6
1980	4	1	5
1981	2	1	3
1982	5	0	5
1983	1	1	2
1984	5	4	9
1985	3	2	5
1986	2	2	4
1987	2	1	3
1988	6	2	8
1989	9	2	11
1990	2	5	7
1991	5	2	7
Grand Total	60	25	85

the discount associated with conglomerates. We test the prediction from this literature that announcement-date excess returns for cross-industry spinoffs are greater than those for own-industry spinoffs. (Table 2).

We compute announcement-period excess returns for each spinoff firm in the two-day interval (− 1,0) including the day preceding and the day of the announcement of a spinoff in the Wall Street Journal, using the value-weighted market return available on the CRSP tapes. We also compute excess returns using the equally weighted market index. The pattern of significance is unaffected, and we report only the value-weighted results.

For the entire sample, the mean announcement period excess return is 3.4% (significant at the 1% level). This is very similar to the announcement date excess returns reported in earlier studies. Schipper and Smith (1983) report a two-day announcement return of 2.8% while Hite and Owers (1983) report 3.3%. Thus it does not appear that our sample selection procedures, in particular our elimination of spinoffs where either the parent or subsidiary was acquired within two years of the spinoff, have produced a particularly unusual set of spinoffs. The

Table 2

Announcement date returns for 85 spinoffs identified for the period 1975–1991. Sample excludes cases where the spinoff was tax driven, involved a firm in a regulated industry, or where one of the spinoff entities was acquired in a subsequent two-year period. Cross-industry spinoffs involve the creation of two entities operating in different two-digit SIC codes and own-industry spinoffs involve the creation of two entities operating in the same two-digit SIC code. All announcement date excess returns are computed by comparing the 2-day announcement date return (day −1 and 0) for the spinoff firm to the 2-day return for the Center for Research in Security Prices (CRSP) value-weighted market index. The announcement date excess returns are then averaged across all entities in each classification and the mean and median values are reported. Days are measured relative to the Wall Street Journal announcement date, which is defined as day 0. The first number reported is the mean value; medians are reported in brackets. Means and medians are tested against zero by the appropriate t-statistic and the Wilcoxon sign rank test statistic. Asterisks indicate significance at the 5%(**) and 1%(***) level

Spinoff classification	Sample size	Announcement date return	Excess return
Own-industry	25	1.6%	1.4%
		[0.0%]	[− 0.1%]
Cross-industry	60	4.5%***	4.3%***
		[3.1%***]	[3.0%***]
Overall	85	3.6%***	3.4%***
		[2.2%***]	[1.4%***]

median spinoff firm produces an announcement period excess return of 1.4% (p-value from the Wilcoxon sign rank test is less than 0.01).

What is remarkable about these announcement-date excess returns is the difference between the own-industry and cross-industry sub-samples. The positive excess return in the full sample is driven solely by the cross-industry spinoffs. The mean announcement-period excess return in the cross-industry sample is 4.3% (significant at the 1% level), while it is 1.4% (insignificant at the 10% level) for the own-industry sample. A t-test for the equality of means across the two sub-samples is rejected at the 1% level. The median excess return is 3.0% (significant at the 1% level) for cross-industry spinoffs and − 0.1% for own industry spinoffs (insignificant at the 10% level). A Wilcoxon two-sample median test (based on normal approximation) rejects the null hypothesis that the medians across the two sub-samples are equal at the 5% level.

These results are consistent with our prediction that the resolution of internal problems of corporate focus is associated with value creation in spinoffs. We also measure the ex-dividend-date (days − 1 and 0) excess return to replicate the results obtained in Vijh (1994). For the whole sample, the mean (median) two-day excess return based on the value weighted CRSP index is + 3.6% (+ 2.1%), very similar to what is documented in Vijh (1994). The mean (median) excess return for cross-industry firms is + 3.9% (+ 2.1%), and for own-industry firms is + 2.8% (+ 1.1%). Both the means and medians are significant at the 5% level, although they are not statistically different across the two subsamples. Ex-dividend-date excess returns based on the equally weighted CRSP index provide similar results. These results provide additional confirmation that our sample is similar to the broader sample of spinoffs examined in previous research. In the next two sections we investigate whether the value creation around spinoff announcements is followed by performance improvements, or arises from bonding benefits.

4. Accounting performance changes following spinoffs

We examine the accounting performance for spinoff firms in each of the five years centered around the ex-dividend year. The performance measure we employ is the ratio of operating earnings-to-assets, calculated using the Compustat annual data item #13 divided by annual data item #6, which we label return on assets (ROA). There are several reasons for selecting ROA as our performance measure. First, we wish to document operating performance changes that are separate from the effects of taxes and bonding. Since bonding benefits could partially appear in the interest expense, and, through the deductibility of interest expense in tax expense, these components of net income are excluded to isolate the performance effects we wish to examine. Second, the ROA measure also removes the effect of any special one-time charges to net income. Third, ROA is preferred to such measures as profit margin (operating income/sales) or asset turnover (sales/assets) because we have no a priori basis to suggest where the source of performance improvements may lie. Since ROA is the product of profit margin and turnover (ROA = profit margin × asset turnover), it may increase significantly due to small, non-significant increases in both profit margin and asset turnover. Our theory of corporate focus is insufficient to provide precise predictions as to whether it is profit margin or asset turnover that is the main source of value creation in spinoffs. ROA measures the performance change from both sources and therefore represents a better measure of performance for our purposes.

Ultimately, we do document improvements in ROA for cross-industry spinoffs. Once this has been documented, an examination of profit margins and asset turnovers can provide additional insight into how the performance improvement is obtained. We provide information on profit margins and asset turnovers in Section 4.1.

As a complement to our examination of ROA, we also examine changes in the level of net capital expenditures. Even if there were no changes in ROA, value could be created by an expansion of the scale of operations following the spinoff. Changes in the level of net capital expenditures capture changes in the scale of operations due to new investment. In addition, John (1993) provides a model in which the ability to overcome the under-investment problem associated with debt use is the motivation underlying spinoffs. Our examination of changes in net capital expenditures should shed light on this possible source of value from spinoffs. We define net capital expenditure (CAP) as the ratio of capital expenditure to sales, using Compustat annual data item #128 divided by annual data item #12. We also computed CAP as the ratio of capital expenditures to assets. The results are identical to those reported in the paper and therefore not reproduced in the tables.

We examine the change in, rather than the level of, performance because changes incorporate a firm's past performance in its earnings expectations model. Barber and Lyon (1996) show that tests involving changes provide more power to detect abnormal performance than those based on levels.

We compute ROA and CAP during the post-spinoff period for each parent/subsidiary portfolio. We perform the analysis at the portfolio level to ascertain if performance improvements contribute to the value creation that occurs around spinoff announcements. Comparing the parent alone to the pre-spinoff entity may show performance improvement in cases where the poorly performing subsidiary unit was spun off even when there is no change in the performance of the parent's share of pre-spinoff assets, since the pre-spinoff entity's performance will be weighted by the retained and spunoff assets. Thus, comparing the parent alone to the pre-spinoff entity cannot address questions regarding net value creation at the portfolio level. Earlier studies (see, e.g., John and Ofek, 1995) that examine focus-increasing asset sales suffer from this shortcoming. It is not clear whether the increase in corporate focus brought about by the sale of unrelated assets results in overall performance gains since the performance of sold assets cannot be independently measured.

Combining performance data from the post-spinoff entities into a single portfolio is not difficult. Spinoffs are recorded at book value. This means that the reported value of total assets held by the parent and subsidiary immediately following the spinoff is identical to the total book value of assets recorded by the parent immediately before the spinoff. With the exception of per-share amounts, computing the value of combined financial statement amounts can be accomplished by simply adding up the reported values of the parent and subsidiary. For example, combined assets or operating income are just the sum of parent assets or operating income and the subsidiary assets or operating income. This approach ignores inter-corporate transactions. When the parent and subsidiary were a single financial reporting entity, consolidated financial reporting requirements would eliminate the effects of any inter-corporate exchanges from sales and costs. Profits on such exchanges would ultimately be recognized over time, but not necessarily in the period of the exchange. This may create an upward bias in measures such as sales, but should not create significant problems for measures such as return on assets.

We compare the change in the portfolio's ROA and CAP from the fiscal year preceding the spinoff distribution (the ex-dividend year) to the fiscal year following the spinoff distribution, that is, from year − 1 to year + 1 centered on the spinoff distribution year. We also report ROA and CAP changes for other intervals, in particular from year + 1 to year + 2 following the spinoff distribution, to check whether these changes are reversed in the second year.

An important issue in measuring abnormal performance is defining the appropriate benchmark. For the ROA and CAP measures, we produce both raw and three separate benchmark adjusted measures. Our analysis and tests closely follow the procedure outlined in Barber and Lyon (1996). We describe below our procedure for estimating abnormal performance using the ROA measure. Raw and adjusted changes in CAP are estimated similarly using Eqs (1)–(3) below.

Our first benchmark is the median return on assets ($IROA_{j,t}$) for all firms, excluding the spinoff firm, that share the same two-digit SIC code with the spinoff firm. We use

$$AROA_{j,t} = ROA_{j,t} - IROA_{j,t} \tag{1}$$

to compute the adjusted ROA by subtracting the benchmark return on assets from the return on assets of the spinoff firm. We call this industry-adjusted ROA. We then compute the change in the industry-adjusted ROA

$$\Delta AROA_j = AROA_{j,\mathrm{post}} - AROA_{j,\mathrm{pre}} \tag{2}$$

for each spinoff firm and report the median change

$$\overline{\Delta AROA} = \text{Median}\ (\Delta AROA_j) \tag{3}$$

across all spinoffs. We do not report mean changes since they are affected by extreme observations, and provide less powerful tests to detect changes in performance than tests based on medians. We also report the Wilcoxon sign rank test statistics associated with the median change in the industry-adjusted ROA.

Our second benchmark is defined as the median ROA for all firms, excluding the spinoff firm, that are in the same two-digit SIC code as the spinoff firm and with asset values within 20% of the asset value of the spinoff firm in the same fiscal year. We were unable to find three or more matches for 22 of the 85 firms in our sample. For these cases we relaxed the size criterion to within 50% of the spinoff firm's assets to obtain at least three matches for each spinoff firm. We re-estimate Eqs (1)–(3) to obtain the median change in size-adjusted ROA. We perform the size adjustment to address concerns expressed by Fama and French (1995), among others, that small firms have lower earnings-to-book-equity ratios.

Our third and last benchmark is the median ROA for all firms, excluding the spinoff firm, that are in the same two-digit SIC code as the spinoff firm, and whose ROA performance measure in the year prior to the ex-dividend year is within 20% of the ROA measure of the spinoff firm in the same year. Again, we use Eq. (1)–(3) to obtain median change in performance-adjusted ROA measures for the spinoff firms. Performance adjustment is necessary where the time series properties of accounting measures are characterized by a reversion to the mean. Comparing the performance measure of spinoff firms with an out-of-phase control group performance measure reduces the power of tests designed to detect abnormal performance. Barber and Lyon (1996) show that in cases where the sample firms have even slight differences in performance from population firms, test statistics that are not based on performance adjustment are poorly specified in the sense that the empirical rejection rates in their tests differ from the theoretical rejection rates.

4.1. Changes in return on assets

Table 3 presents portfolio level results for changes in ROA from year − 1 to year + 1, with the ex-dividend year defined as year 0. We also report ROA changes from year + 1 to year + 2 to check whether the spinoff related performance changes are reversed in the second year. The portfolio ROA measure in the post-spinoff period is computed by adding the operating income of the parent and subsidiary units in the fiscal year following the ex-dividend year and dividing the sum by the combined parent and subsidiary asset value at the beginning of the fiscal year. Pre-spinoff ROA is measured directly as the ratio of the parent's operating income to total assets in year − 1.

For cross-industry spinoffs, the median change in ROA from year − 1 to year + 1 is 3.0% (significant at the 5% level). The industry, size, and performance-adjusted change in ROA are 3.0% (significant at the 1% level), 2.8% (significant at the 10% level), and 3.1% (significant at the 5% level). For own-industry spinoffs, the median change in ROA is 0.0%. Neither the raw nor any of the adjusted measures of ROA change around the spinoff year (year − 1 to year + 1) are significant at the 10% level for own-industry spinoffs. A Wilcoxon two-sample median test based on normal approximation rejects the equality of median ROA changes across own- and cross-industry sub-samples at the 10%, 5%, and 10% levels for raw differences, and for the industry- and size-adjusted median changes, respectively. The test fails to reject equality of median ROA changes, for the cross- and own-industry sub samples at the 10% level for the performance-adjusted median changes.

We check the persistence of ROA changes by examining the ROA change in the second year following the spinoff (from year + 1 to year + 2). The raw differences, and the industry-, size-, and performance-adjusted ROA changes from year + 1 to + 2 are − 0.4%, + 0.1%, + 1.8%, and − 0.1% for cross-industry spinoffs. None are significant at the 10% level, indicating that ROA changes surrounding the spinoff distribution are not reversed in the second year following the spinoff. For own-industry spinoffs, we find weak evidence of ROA improvement during the second year after the spinoff distribution. The raw

Table 3
Median change in operating earnings-to-asset ratio (ROA) and capital expenditure-to-sales ratio (CAP) for parent/subsidiary portfolios for 85 spinoffs identified for the period 1975–1991. The sample excludes cases where the spinoff was tax driven, involved a firm in a regulated industry, or where one of the spinoff entities was acquired in a subsequent two year period. Cross-industry spinoffs involve the creation of two entities operating in different two-digit SIC codes and own-industry spinoffs involve the creation of two entities operating in the same two-digit SIC code. The term parent refers to the continuing entity that existed both before and after the spinoff. The term subsidiary refers to the independent newly created entity subsequent to the spinoff. The post-spinoff portfolio ROA is computed by adding the operating income of the parent and subsidiary units in the fiscal year following the ex-dividend year and dividing the sum by the combined parent and subsidiary beginning-of-fiscal-year asset value. CAP in the post-spinoff period is computed by dividing the combined capital expenditure by the combined sales figure for the parent and subsidiary units from the same fiscal year. Pre-spinoff variables are defined in the same way and measured directly in the fiscal year preceding the spinoff distribution. Industry-adjusted medians are computed by subtracting the median value for all firms in the same two-digit SIC code from the corresponding spinoff firm variable. Size-adjusted medians are computed by subtracting the median value for all firms in the same two-digit SIC code, whose asset value is within 20% of the asset value of the parent. Performance-adjusted medians are computed by subtracting the median value for all firms in the same two-digit SIC code, whose operating ROA in the year prior to the spinoff is within 20% of the operating ROA of the spinoff firm. Only changes in ROA and CAP (with the spinoff distribution year defined as year 0) are reported. Median changes (denoted by Δ followed by the variable name) are tested against zero using the Wilcoxon sign rank test statistic. Asterisks indicate significance at the 10%(*), 5%(**) and 1%(***) level

	Relative year (from, to)	Median change			
		Unadjusted	Industry-adjusted	Size-adjusted	Performance-adjusted
Cross-industry spinoffs (N = 60):					
ΔROA	(− 1, + 1)	3.0%**	3.0%***	2.8%*	3.1%**
	(− 1, 0)	0.8%	1.6%	0.8%	0.6%
	(0, + 1)	2.0%**	1.2%**	2.0%**	2.1%**
	(+ 1, + 2)	− 0.4%	0.1%	1.8%	− 0.1%
ΔCAP	(− 1, + 1)	0.1%	− 0.1%	− 0.3%	− 0.4%
	(+ 1, + 2)	0.0%	0.2%	− 0.1%	− 0.2%
Own-industry spinoffs (N = 25):					
ΔROA	(− 1, + 1)	0.0%	− 1.3%	− 2.4%	− 0.2%
	(− 1, 0)	− 2.5%**	− 2.3%*	− 1.5%	− 1.6%
	(0, + 1)	0.6%	1.3%	− 0.4%	0.7%
	(+ 1, + 2)	0.9%*	0.8%	0.8%	0.9%*
ΔCAP	(− 1, + 1)	− 0.2%	− 0.4%	− 1.2%	0.1%
	(+ 1, + 2)	0.2%	0.4%	0.8%	0.6%

ROA change from year + 1 to + 2 is 0.9% (significant at the 10% level). The changes in ROA adjusted for industry, size, and performance are 0.8%, 0.8%, and 0.9%, respectively, with only the performance-adjusted ROA change being significant at the 10% level.

While we concentrate on the ROA change from year − 1 to year + 1, we also examine performance changes from year − 1 to year 0, and from year 0 to year + 1 to isolate more precisely the timing of such changes. Our results show that for cross-industry spinoffs, the performance change is significant in year 0 to year + 1. For own-industry spinoffs, the ROA change is not significant over this period, although the point estimate is negative in the period − 1 to 0.

We also examined changes in profit margin (ROS), defined as the ratio of operating income to sales, and asset turnover, defined as the ratio of sales to total assets. For portfolios of cross-industry parents and subsidiaries, changes in ROS from year − 1 to year + 1, at the raw level, and for the industry-, size-, and performance-adjusted basis are 4.2%, 5.2%, 4.9%, and 5.0%. All are significant at the 1% level. The corresponding own-industry changes are 1.2%, − 0.2%, − 0.4%, and − 1.8%, with none being significant at conventional levels. In both cross- and own-industry spinoffs, the change in asset turnover is negative at the raw level and positive at the industry-, size-, and performance-adjusted levels, but never statistically significant. These results suggest that on average the source of the ROA improvement lies in cost savings which increases the ROS, but not in significant turnover increases.

4.2. Changes in capital expenditure

Table 3 also reports portfolio level results on changes in the ratio of capital expenditure to sales (CAP). For the cross-industry spinoffs, the change in CAP from year − 1 to year + 1 is 0.1% and is statistically not significant. The changes adjusted for industry, size, and performance are also statistically insignificant at the 10% level. Changes in CAP from year + 1 to year + 2 are also insignificant. For own-industry spinoffs too, the raw difference and adjusted changes in CAP from year − 1 to year + 1 are statistically insignificant at conventional levels. Changes from year + 1 to year + 2 are mostly positive, but statistically insignificant.

Overall, our portfolio-level results show significant positive changes in operating performance for cross-industry spinoffs only. Own-industry spinoffs do not seem to exhibit operating performance improvement immediately following the spinoff, although there is weak evidence supporting an ROA increase from year + 1 to year + 2. There is no evidence to support increases in capital investment subsequent to spinoffs for either cross- or own-industry spinoffs, inconsistent with the predictions of John's (1993) model. Rather, these results suggest that operating performance improvements, especially in the area of cost controls, lie behind at least part of the excess returns associated with cross-industry spinoff announcements. Moreover, the lack of operating performance changes for own-industry spinoffs is consistent with the lack of significant price effects at the announcement of own-industry spinoffs.

5. Spinoff's as a bonding mechanism

If equity markets discount the value of the pre-spinoff entity due to a potential for cross-divisional subsidies within the corporate whole, the spinoff may have been necessary as a mechanism to bond management against future subsidies to unprofitable divisions. The literature on assets sales suggests that part of the value from increased corporate focus comes from bonding against cross-subsidization of poorly performing units (bonding against the free cash flow problem identified in Jensen, 1986). Lang et al. (1995) provide evidence that the equity price revision around announcements of asset sales depends on how the proceeds from the asset sales are used. The price effect is significantly larger when the proceeds are used to increase dividends and repay debt than when the proceeds are retained. This is consistent with the managers having to bond by both disposing of the assets that could be cross-subsidized, and committing to use the proceeds in a manner that does not worsen the free cash flow problem. Since spinoffs do not involve any cash proceeds, we ask the following questions to examine whether bonding considerations play a role in spinoffs. First, when is bonding likely to be particularly valuable? Second, do we see increased use of alternative bonding mechanisms around the time of the spinoff?

From management's perspective, a pre-commitment to avoid future cross-subsidization makes particular sense if they need to raise capital, since the capital markets are likely to incorporate the benefits of such bonding in pricing the new issue. Bonding benefits may lie with the parent, if cross-subsidization of the subsidiary is a problem, or with the subsidiary, if the problem is that capital raised by the subsidiary would be sent upstream to the parent for other uses. In Section 5.1 we investigate whether the frequency of capital sourcing by spinoff firms increases after the spinoff.

We are also interested in whether spinoff firms use other methods for bonding against problems involving free cash flow around the time of the spinoff. Healy and Palepu (1993) discuss how a firm may engage in a variety of mechanisms to convey a commitment against misuse of free cash flows. We wish to examine if the execution of the spinoff occurs in concert with or without these other mechanisms. The mechanisms we examine are increases in the debt-to-equity ratio of the firm, indicating increased use of leverage (suggested by Jensen, 1986), and increases in cash dividends (suggested by Easterbrook, 1984). Both financial leverage and cash dividends bond managers to distribute corporate cash flows to capital providers and prevent re-direction of free cash flow to projects with negative net present values.

5.1. Frequency of external capital issuance

We collected data on the number of new equity and debt issues placed in public markets and reported in the Wall Street Journal over a 24-month span preceding the announcement date of the spinoff, and a second 24-month span following the ex-dividend date. Thus, pre-spinoff relative years are defined as

Table 4
Frequency of capital sourcing by relative year of issue for 85 spinoffs executed during 1975–1991 and reported in the Wall Street Journal. Panels A and B provide the frequency of capital issues for parent firms in years − 2 and − 1, the two years preceding the spinoff, and for the combination of parents and subsidiaries in years + 1 and + 2, the two years following the spinoff. Panels C and D provide the same information for subsidiaries alone. Pre-spinoff relative years are defined as 12-month periods with reference to the announcement month of the spinoff distribution. Post-spinoff relative years are defined as 12-month periods with reference to the ex-dividend month of the spinoff distribution. A one-tailed binomial test (or a normal approximation to a binomial test where appropriate) is used to test the statistical significance of the increase in frequency of capital issues following spinoffs. None of the test statistics reported here are significant at the ten-percent level.

Relative year	All issues	Debt issues	Equity issues
Panel A: Cross-industry parents and subsidiaries ($N = 60$)			
Year − 2	13	5	8
Year − 1	18	13	5
Year 1	17	9	8
Year 2	18	12	6
Year 1 − Year − 1	− 1	− 4	3
Year 2 − Year − 1	0	− 1	1
(Year 1 + Year 2)-(Year − 2 + Year − 1)	4	3	1
Panel B: Own-industry parents and subsidiaries ($N = 25$)			
Year − 2	5	3	2
Year − 1	2	1	1
Year 1	3	3	0
Year 2	4	3	1
Year 1 − Year − 1	1	2	− 1
Year 2 − Year − 1	2	2	0
(Year 1 + Year 2)-(Year − 2 + Year − 1)	0	2	− 2
Panel C: Cross-industry subsidiaries ($N = 60$)			
Year 1	6	2	4
Year 2	7	4	3
Panel D: Own-industry subsidiaries ($N = 25$)			
Year 1	0	0	0
Year 2	0	0	0

12-month intervals preceding the announcement date of the spinoff, and post-spinoff relative years are defined as 12-month intervals following the ex-dividend date. We ignore the offerings made between the announcement and ex-dividend dates of the spinoffs since it is not clear whether the spinoff announcement influences the market's perception of the potential for cross-subsidization within the pre-spinoff entity.

The combined frequency of issues by parents and subsidiaries is reported in Panels A and B of Table 4. Panels C and D provide similar results for subsidiaries alone, and, in conjunction with Panels A and B, can be used to obtain the results for parents alone. Cross-industry spinoffs engaged in a total of 31 offerings (18 debt and 13 equity issues) in the 24-month period prior to the spinoff announcement, and a total of 35 offerings (21 debt and 14 equity issues) in the 24-months following the ex-dividend date. The increase in the frequency of total, debt, or equity issues over this interval is not significant using a one-tailed test based on a binomial frequency distribution (or a normal approximation to the binomial distribution where appropriate). The increase in the frequency of issues from year − 1 to year + 1, and from year − 1 to year + 2, is also insignificant at the ten-percent level.

By comparison, own-industry spinoff firms engaged in a total of seven offerings both in the 24-months prior to the spinoff announcement and in the 24-months following the ex-dividend date. The increase in the frequency of issues from year − 1 to years + 1 and + 2 is not significant at the ten-percent level. Furthermore, given the relative sizes of the own- and cross-industry sub-samples (25 versus 60), the frequencies of total offerings are not significantly different for the two sub-samples. However, cross-industry subsidiaries are more active in issuing debt and equity (six debt and seven equity offerings) than own-industry subsidiaries (no offerings) in the 24-months following the ex-dividend date of the spinoff.

Overall, we view the evidence on the frequency of capital issues as failing to support a significant role for bonding in explaining value creation around spinoffs.

5.2. Changes in book leverage and dividends per share

The book value of the debt-to-assets ratio (book leverage or LEV) is computed by dividing the combined debt by the combined book-value of assets of the parent and subsidiary units from the same fiscal year. Pre-spinoff leverage is defined in the same way and is measured directly. Results are reported in Table 5.

We find that the median change in LEV for cross-industry spinoffs from year − 1 to year + 1 is − 1.5%, although it is not significant at the 10% level. Industry-, size-, and performance-adjusted median LEV changes are − 2.9%, − 1.8%, and − 3.1%, respectively. Only the performance-adjusted median

Table 5

Median change in accounting ratios for parent/subsidiary portfolios for 85 spinoffs identified for the period 1975–1991. The sample excludes cases where the spinoff was tax driven, involved a firm in a regulated industry, or where one of the spinoff entities was acquired in a subsequent two-year period. Cross-industry spinoffs involve the creation of two entities operating in different two-digit SIC codes, and own-industry spinoffs involve the creation of two entities operating in the same two-digit SIC code. The term parent refers to the continuing entity that existed both before and after the spinoff. The term subsidiary refers to the independent entity newly created subsequent to the spinoff. The book value of the debt-to-assets ratio (book leverage or LEV) is computed by dividing the combined debt by the combined book value of the assets of the parent and subsidiary units from the same fiscal year. Dividend per share (DIV) in the post-spinoff period is computed by adding the total dividends for the parent and subsidiary and dividing the sum by the number of shares for the parent company. Pre-spinoff variables are defined in the same way and are measured directly in the fiscal year preceding the spinoff distribution. Industry-adjusted medians are computed by subtracting the median value for all firms in the same two-digit SIC code from the corresponding spinoff firm variable. Size-adjusted medians are computed by subtracting the median value for all firms in the same two-digit SIC code, whose asset value is within 20% of the asset value of the parent. Performance-adjusted medians are computed by subtracting the median value for all firms in the same two-digit SIC code, whose ratio of operating earnings to assets in the year prior to the spinoff is within 20% of the operating earnings to asset ratio of the spinoff firm. Only changes in the above measures (with the spinoff distribution year defined as year 0) are reported. Median changes (denoted by Δ followed by the variable name) are tested against zero using the Wilcoxon sign rank test statistic. Asterisks indicate significance at the 10%(*), 5%(**) and 1%(***) level

	Relative year (from, to)	Median change			
		Unadjusted	Industry-adjusted	Size-adjusted	Performance-adjusted
Cross-industry spinoffs (N = 60):					
ΔLEV	(− 1, + 1)	− 1.5%	− 2.9%	− 1.8%	− 3.1% *
	(+ 1, + 2)	− 0.7%	− 1.1%	− 0.7%	0.1%
ΔDIV	(− 1, + 1)	0.0 c	1.1 c	− 2.8 c	− 3.0 c
	(+ 1, + 2)	0.0 c	3.8 c ***	2.5 c	1.0 c
Own-industry spinoffs (N = 25):					
ΔLEV	(− 1, + 1)	0.3%	− 1.0%	2.2%	2.4%
	(+ 1, + 2)	− 1.7% *	− 0.6%	− 0.5%	− 0.1%
ΔDIV	(− 1, + 1)	− 0.1 c	1.6 c	0.0 c	− 4.1 c
	(+ 1, + 2)	1.0 c	5.1 c	5.1 c	− 1.2 c

change is significant at the 10% level. For own-industry spinoffs, the raw change in LEV from year − 1 to year + 1 is + 0.3% (insignificant at the 10% level). The industry-, size-, and performance-adjusted median changes in LEV are also statistically not significant at the 10% level.

It is possible that spinoff firms take more than one year to increase their leverage. We examine leverage changes for both cross- and own-industry spinoffs from year + 1 to + 2. We do not find any evidence of an increase in LEV for either group of spinoffs in the two years following the ex-dividend date, although there is weak evidence that the unadjusted change in LEV for the own-industry spinoffs is negative.

Dividends per share (DIV) in the post-spinoff period is computed by adding the total dividends for the parent and subsidiary, and dividing this sum by the number of shares for the parent company. A potential problem with our dividend measure is that equity issues in the year following the spinoff make dividend comparisons difficult to interpret. As a practical matter, only two parents and five subsidiaries in our sample sold equity shares in the year following the spinoff; these companies are all from the cross-industry subsample. Removing them from the sample makes no material difference to our results.

For cross-industry spinoffs, we do not find any significant change in either raw or adjusted DIV from year − 1 to year + 1, although there is some weak evidence that the industry-adjusted DIV change from year + 1 to year + 2 is positive ($0.038, significant at the 1% level). We believe that this increase can be attributed to the increase in profitability for cross-industry spinoffs in the prior period. For own-industry spinoffs, the median change in unadjusted DIV from year − 1 to year + 1 is − $0.001, although this result is not significant at the 10% level. The industry-, size-, and performance-adjusted median changes in DIV are also not significant at the 10% level. DIV changes from year + 1 to year + 2 are also insignificant for own-industry spinoffs.

Because dividends per share are difficult to compare across firms, we also look at the number of cases where dividends are increased, decreased, or remain constant from year − 1 to year + 1. As many cross-industry firms increase their per-share dividends as those that decrease their per-share dividends. Seven own-industry firms increase per-share dividends, ten decrease per-share dividends, and eight leave them unchanged following spinoffs.

Overall, we fail to find evidence of an increase in leverage or dividends per share at the portfolio level for either group of spinoffs. We also estimate, but do not report, leverage and dividend changes for parents and subsidiaries individually. For cross-industry spinoffs, we find small declines in book leverage for both parents and subsidiaries in the year after the spinoff. Own-industry parents and subsidiaries do not show any significant change in book leverage following the spinoff year. The median change in dividends per share for own-industry parents alone is two cents (significant at the 5% level). There is no change in dividends per share for cross-industry parents. The median change in dividends for both cross- and own-industry subsidiaries is 0 cents. The median subsidiary does not pay dividends in the year of or the year following the spinoff. We view the evidence as failing to support the hypothesis that spinoffs are engineered to bond management against cross-subsidization of weak units within the corporate whole.

6. Tracing performance improvements to individual parent and subsidiary units

In Section 4, we documented a significant increase in return on assets (ROA) for the cross-industry spinoffs, but no significant improvement for own-industry spinoffs at the portfolio level. While operating performance improvement at the portfolio level for cross-industry spinoffs is consistent with corporate focus creating value in spinoffs, alternative explanations exist concerning which part of the portfolio, that is, either the parent or the subsidiary, might drive the observed operating performance improvement. By examining changes in the operating performance of the parents and subsidiaries individually, we provide evidence on which explanation of the two, or both, appear to be at work.

Schipper and Smith (1986), in their study of equity carve-outs, argue that carve-outs create value by creating a publicly traded subsidiary where market-based incentives can be applied. The implication is that value creation around equity carve-out announcements comes principally from performance improvements in the subsidiary rather than the parent. If the Incentive Alignment Hypothesis applies to value creation in spinoffs too, we should see performance improvements in the subsidiary following spinoffs. Alternatively, if getting back to core business is the source of gains behind spinoffs, we should see performance improvements to arise mainly from the parent companies. John and Ofek (1995) show that performance improvement for selling firms is limited only to those firms where they sell off unrelated assets, consistent with the hypothesis that getting back to core business leads to improved performance for selling firms. While managers of the subsidiary do not see a decrease in their span of operations following the spinoff, managers of the parent firm do. Thus, under the Corporate Focus Hypothesis, performance improvements should come mainly from the parent firms. We note that the above hypotheses are not mutually exclusive. Thus, we may see performance improvements in both the parent and the subsidiary.

We examine parents and subsidiaries separately by measuring the performance change from the fiscal year containing the spinoff distribution date to the following fiscal year (year 0 to year + 1). Accounting data for the subsidiaries are not available prior to the spinoff distribution, and data for the parent firms are available only as part of the combined pre-spinoff entity prior to the ex-dividend year. While accounting rules require retroactive segregation of net income of the subsidiary from that of the parent for financial reporting purposes, there is no such segregation for assets and no detail is provided in financial reports concerning individual revenues and expenses. Therefore, it is not possible to compute our ROA numbers for the years prior to year 0. Year 0 data are available from financial statements of the subsidiary produced after the year of the spinoff. Thus, our base year for measuring parent- and subsidiary-level performance changes is the year of the spinoff distribution itself. We report median changes in ROA from the year of the spinoff to the first fiscal year following it (year 0 to year + 1), and for an additional second year (year + 1 to year + 2) for parent and subsidiary entities in Table 6.

For cross-industry parents, the median change in ROA from year 0 to year + 1 is 2.4% (significant at the 5% level). The industry-, size-, and performance-adjusted median changes in ROA are 2.2% (significant at the 5% level), 2.3% (significant at the 1% level), and 1.1% (significant at the 5% level). The median ROA change from year + 1 to year + 2 is positive, albeit insignificant, indicating that it is not reversed in the second year after the spinoff.

For own-industry parents, the median change in ROA from year 0 to year + 1 is 1.8% (not significant at the 10% level). The industry-, size-, and performance-adjusted median ROA changes for own-industry parents are 0.7%, -1.3%, and 1.1%. None are significant at the 10% level. A Wilcoxon two-sample test for equality of median ROA changes for the cross- and own-industry sub-samples is rejected at the 10% level for unadjusted change in ROA, and rejected at the 5% level for industry- and size-adjusted change in ROA. The test is unable to reject the equality of medians for the performance-adjusted change in ROA. For own-industry parents, there is weak evidence that the unadjusted change in ROA in the second year (year + 1 to year + 2) is positive (+ 1.3%) and significant at the 10% level, whereas the industry, size, and performance adjusted ROA changes are positive, but not significant at the 10% level.

For subsidiaries, we do not report performance-adjusted measures since the performance match is done in year − 1, prior to the creation of the subsidiary. Thus, for subsidiaries we report only industry- and size-adjusted measures. For both own- and cross-industry subsidiaries, we do not see any significant change in any measure of ROA for the two intervals examined here (year 0 to year + 1, and year + 1 to year + 2).

Overall, our evidence suggests that the basis for portfolio-level operating performance improvement lies with the cross-industry parents, consistent with the Corporate Focus Hypothesis that managers become more effective at managing core assets when they eliminate unrelated assets. We fail to find evidence supporting the incentive alignment explanation as a source of operating performance gains from spinoffs.

Table 6

Median change in operating earnings-to-asset ratios for parents and subsidiaries for 85 spinoffs identified for the period 1975–1991. The sample excludes cases where the spinoff was tax driven, involved a firm in a regulated industry, or where one of the spinoff entities was acquired in a subsequent two-year period. Cross-industry spinoffs involve the creation of two entities operating in different two-digit SIC codes and own-industry spinoffs involve the creation of two entities operating in the same two-digit SIC code. The term parent refers to the continuing entity that existed both before and after the spinoff. The term subsidiary refers to the independent entity newly created subsequent to the spinoff. The return on assets (ROA) measure is computed by dividing operating income by the end-of-fiscal-year asset value. Industry-adjusted medians are computed by subtracting the median value for all firms in the same two-digit SIC code from the corresponding spinoff firm variable. Size-adjusted medians are computed by subtracting the median value for all firms in the same two-digit SIC code, whose asset value is within 20% of the asset value of the parent. Performance-adjusted medians are reported only for the parent units and computed by subtracting the median value for all firms in the same two-digit SIC code, whose operating ROA in the year prior to the spinoff is within 20% of the operating ROA of the spinoff firm. Only changes in the above measures from the spinoff distribution year to the following year are reported. Median changes (denoted by followed by the variable name) are tested against zero using the Wilcoxon sign rank test statistic. Asterisks indicate significance at the 10%(*), 5%(**) and 1%(***) level.

	Relative year (from, to)	Median change			
		Unadjusted	Industry-adjusted	Size-adjusted	Performance-adjusted
Panel A: *Cross-industry parents* (*N* = 60)					
ROA	(0, + 1)	2.1%***	2.3%***	2.3%***	1.1%**
	(+ 1, + 2)	0.3%	0.6%	1.5%	0.5%
Panel B: *Own-industry parents* (*N* = 25)					
ROA	(0, + 1)	1.8%	0.7%	− 1.3%	1.1%
	(+ 1, + 2)	1.3%*	1.0%	0.8%	1.1%
Panel C: *Cross-industry subsidiaries* (*N* = 60)					
ROA	(0, + 1)	− 0.2%	0.2%	0.1%	a
	(+ 1, + 2)	0.3%	− 0.2%	0.8%	
Panel D: *Own-industry subsidiaries* (*N* = 25)					
ROA	(0, + 1)	− 0.9%	− 0.1%	− 0.7%	a
	(+ 1, + 2)	− 0.8%	− 0.7%	− 0.1%	

[a]Performance adjusted measures are not reported in Panels C and D since subsidiaries do not exist in year − 1, the base year for the performance benchmark.

7. Conclusion

We test a prediction from the corporate focus literature that cross-industry spinoff distributions, where the continuing and spunoff units belong to different two-digit Standard Industry Classification codes, create more value than own-industry spinoffs. Our results indicate significant excess returns around the announcement of cross-industry spinoffs only. We interpret these findings as supporting the hypothesis that spinoffs create value only when they increase corporate focus, consistent with the broader results from asset sale studies. We then seek to determine whether the value increase in cross-industry spinoffs is empirically related to operating performance improvements, or bonding benefits, or both, where bonding refers to a pre-commitment by managers to avoid cross-subsidizing relatively poorly performing units within the firm.

We find significant increases in the operating-return-on-assets ratio (operating income/assets), which we refer to as ROA, for the cross-industry spinoffs using unadjusted numbers and numbers adjusted for firm size, industry, and performance, from the fiscal year preceding to the fiscal year following the spinoff distribution. ROA changes for the own-industry spinoffs are smaller in magnitude and insignificant over the same time period. We interpret these results as indicating that performance improvements provide at least a partial explanation for the value increase surrounding spinoff announcements, and that this is associated with increasing corporate focus.

Spinoffs may also create value by bonding management against future cross-subsidies to relatively poorly performing units within the firm. We argue that bonding is especially valuable when a firm needs to raise new capital, since efficient capital markets are likely to incorporate the benefits of bonding in pricing new issues. We examine the frequency with which firms involved in spinoffs make debt and equity offerings immediately before and after the spinoff, and find no evidence that firms engaged in cross-industry spinoffs increase their frequency of capital issuance, or have a greater frequency of capital issuance than firms engaged in own-industry spinoffs. We also examine changes in financial leverage and dividends around spinoff distributions to determine whether firms employ additional bonding means at the time they execute a spinoff. We do not find evidence of a significant change in leverage or dividends following spinoffs.

In summary, our evidence supports the theory that increased corporate focus through spinoffs creates value. We believe that this value creation arises primarily from performance improvements following the spinoff. Further, we find that the operating performance improvement is associated with the continuing rather than the spunoff entity, consistent with the hypothesis that spinoffs create value by removing unrelated businesses and allowing managers to focus attention on the core operations they are best suited to manage.

References

Barber, B.M., Lyon, J.D., 1996. Detecting abnormal operating performance: the empirical power and specification of test-statistics. Journal of Financial Economics 41, 359–399.

Berger, P.G., Ofek, E., 1995. Diversification's effect on firm value. Journal of Financial Economics 37, 39–65.

Comment, R., Jarrell, G.A., 1995. Corporate focus and stock returns. Journal of Financial Economics 37, 67–87.

Cusatis, P.J., Miles, J.A., Woolridge, J.R., 1993. Restructuring through spinoffs: the stock market evidence. Journal of Financial Economics 33, 293–311.

Davidson, W.N., III McDonald, J.L., 1987. Evidence of the effect on shareholder wealth of corporate spinoffs: the creation of royalty trusts. The Journal of Financial Research 10, 321–327.

Easterbrook, F.H., 1984. Two agency-cost explanations of dividends. The American Economic Review 74, 650–659.

Fama, E.F., French, K., 1995. Size and book-to-market factors in earnings and returns. Journal of Finance 50, 131–155.

Healy, P.M., Palepu, K.G., 1993. The effect of firms' financial disclosure strategies on stock prices. Accounting Horizons 7, 1–11.

Healy, P.M., Palepu, K.G., Ruback, R.S., 1992. Does corporate performance improve after mergers. Journal of Financial Economics 31, 135–175.

Hite, G.L., Owers, J.E., 1983. Security price reactions around corporate spinoff announcements. Journal of Financial Economics 12, 409–436.

Jensen, M.C., 1986. Agency costs of free cash flow, corporate finance, and takeovers. American Economic Review 76, 323–329.

John, K., Ofek, E., 1995. Asset sales and increases in focus. Journal of Financial Economics 37, 105–126.

John, T., 1993. Optimality of spinoffs and allocation of debt. Journal of Financial and Quantitative Analysis 28, 139–160.

Kudla, R.J., McInish, T.H., 1983. Valuation consequences of corporate spinoffs. Review of Business and Economic Research 18, 71–77.

Kudla, R.J., McInish, T.H., 1988. Divergence of opinion and corporate spinoffs. Quarterly Review of Economics and Business 28, 20–29.

Lang, L., Poulsen, A., Stultz., R., 1995. Asset sales, firm performance, and the agency costs of managerial discretion. Journal of Financial Economics 37, 3–37.

Miles, J.A., Rosenfeld, J.D., 1983. An empirical analysis of the effects of spinoff announcements on shareholder wealth. Journal of Finance 38, 1597–1606.

Parrino, R., 1997. Spinoffs and wealth transfers: the Marriott case. Journal of Financial Economics 43, 241–274.

Schipper, K., Smith, A., 1983. Effects of recontracting on shareholder wealth: the case of voluntary spinoffs. Journal of Financial Economics 12, 437–467.

Schipper, K., Smith, A., 1986. A comparison of equity carve-outs and seasoned equity offerings: share price effects and corporate restructuring. Journal of Financial Economics 15, 153–186.

Vijh, A.M., 1994. The spinoff and merger ex-date effects. Journal of Finance 69, 581–609.

[9]

THE JOURNAL OF FINANCE • VOL. LVII, NO. 6 • DECEMBER 2002

Learning about Internal Capital Markets from Corporate Spin-offs

ROBERT GERTNER, ERIC POWERS, and DAVID SCHARFSTEIN*

ABSTRACT

We examine the investment behavior of firms before and after being spun off from their parent companies. Their investment after the spin-off is significantly more sensitive to measures of investment opportunities (e.g., industry Tobin's Q or industry investment) than it is before the spin-off. Spin-offs tend to cut investment in low Q industries and increase investment in high Q industries. These changes are observed primarily in spin-offs of firms in industries unrelated to the parents' industries and in spin-offs where the stock market reacts favorably to the spin-off announcement. Our findings suggest that spin-offs may improve the allocation of capital.

THE PREVAILING MODEL OF THE FIRM in corporate finance envisions money flowing in from the capital and product markets and flowing out as investment spending, dividends, and debt payments. A recent line of research has been examining what actually happens when the money is inside the firm (Lamont (1997), Shin and Stulz (1998), Scharfstein (1998), Rajan et al. (2000)). How, for example, does corporate headquarters allocate funds across business and geographic units? If information and agency problems exist between headquarters and the external capital market—a theme that runs through a good deal of the corporate finance literature—does it also exist between headquarters and business units in the internal capital market? If so, do such problems distort investment allocations within the firm?

Understanding how internal capital markets work is important for two reasons. First, the relative efficiency of internal and external capital market transactions is a critical element in defining the boundaries of the firm, much in the same way that the relative efficiency of internal and external product-market transactions is important (Coase (1937)). Second, internal capital markets are an empirically important mechanism by which capital is

* Gertner is with the University of Chicago and NBER. Powers is with the University of South Carolina. Scharfstein is with the Massachusetts Institute of Technology and NBER. The authors thank seminar participants at the 1999 NBER Summer Institute, 2000 Eastern Finance Association Convention, Columbia University, London Business School, University of Chicago and University of South Carolina as well as Amy Dittmar, Jan Mahrt-Smith, Vikas Mehrotra, Ted Moore, Greg Niehaus, Henri Servaes, Anil Shivdasani, Jeremy Stein, René Stulz, and two anonymous referees for helpful comments.

allocated across and within lines of business. Indeed, most corporate investment is financed with internally generated cash flow over which the external capital market has limited control (MacKie-Mason (1990)).

There are mixed views on how well internal capital markets function. Alchian (1969) and Williamson (1970) argue that internal capital markets are more efficient than external markets because corporate headquarters is likely to be better informed than external suppliers of capital about investment opportunities.[1] By contrast, Meyer, Milgrom, and Roberts (1992), Wulf (1997), Rajan et al. (2000), and Scharfstein and Stein (2000) argue that rent seeking by divisional managers can distort the functioning of internal capital markets, inducing corporate headquarters to allocate excessive capital to divisions with poor investment opportunities where rent-seeking incentives are strongest.[2]

A growing empirical literature analyzes the workings of internal capital markets. Lamont (1997), for example, shows that when oil prices fell dramatically in 1986, diversified oil companies with businesses unrelated to oil made across-the-board cuts in capital expenditures, even though investment prospects in the non-oil businesses seem not to have changed as a result of the oil-price decline. While this study shows that companies use the cash flow generated by one division to cross-subsidize the others—essentially that an internal capital market exists—it does not tell us whether cross-subsidization is efficient or not.

The subsequent literature, by contrast, attempts to address this issue. Shin and Stulz (1998) present evidence that when capital is reallocated across divisions, it does not seem to go in any systematic way to the divisions with the better investment opportunities. Scharfstein (1998) shows that investment by conglomerate divisions tends to be less sensitive to Tobin's Q than investment by more focused firms. In addition, divisions tend to invest more than focused firms in low Q industries and less than focused firms in high Q industries. This problem is more pronounced in firms where management has small ownership stakes, with correspondingly weak incentives to make efficient investment allocations. Similarly, Rajan et al. (2000) show that conglomerates invest more than stand-alone firms in industries with poor investment opportunities, and that this effect is more pronounced in conglomerates that operate in businesses with very different investment opportunities.

[1] Both papers simply assume that headquarters is more informed and will monitor more because the external capital market is comprised of many small investors, none of whom have an incentive to become informed. But, if the external capital is supplied by a large investor such as a bank, will they not have the incentive to become informed and to monitor? Gertner, Scharfstein, and Stein (1994) and Stein (1997) present models in which corporate headquarters has more incentive to become informed than outside investors and, as a result, capital allocation is more efficient.

[2] Matsusaka and Nanda (1997) present a model analyzing the costs and benefits of internal capital markets that incorporates some of the benefits outlined by Alchian and Williamson and some of the costs associated with excessive investment.

This paper takes a different approach to these issues by examining spin-offs of multidivisional companies. In a spin-off, the parent company establishes one of its divisions as a new publicly traded company and distributes the shares of this company to the parent's existing shareholders. It is almost always structured as a tax-free transaction with no cash flow implications to the parent, spin-off, or shareholders.[3] The goal of this paper is to understand how the allocation of capital changes when a division is spun off.

There are several advantages of this approach. The main advantage is that we can compare the investment behavior of the same business in two different regimes for allocating capital—an internal capital market and an external capital market.[4] This addresses one criticism of previous work—that segments of conglomerates are somehow different than stand-alone firms in some unobservable way and thus should exhibit different investment behavior. We examine spin-offs rather than other kinds of divestitures such as equity carve-outs or asset sales, because spin-offs do not generate cash for either party. In this respect, we believe spin-offs are a well-structured "natural experiment" for our analysis, since there is no real change in financial resources. Thus, one is less likely to argue that a spin-off changes investment behavior because it changes the firm's financial resources, rather than changing underlying investment decisions.[5]

The second reason to look at spin-offs is that we do not have to rely as heavily on COMPUSTAT business segment data, as have previous studies of internal capital markets. Beginning in December 1977, firms were required to report key operating information (e.g., sales, assets, capital expenditures) for particular industries if they accounted for more than 10 percent of a company's consolidated sales, assets, or profits. Unfortunately, the reported segments may not correspond to an actual business unit and may also lump together business units in different industries. In a spin-off, however, the first annual report includes pro forma financial statements for two or more

[3] To be considered a tax-free event, the spin-off must meet the following five criteria as outlined in IRS Code Section 355: (1) The parent must possess control (>80 percent ownership of common stock voting power and >80 percent ownership of each class of nonvoting shares) of the subsidiary prior to the spin-off; (2) after the spin-off occurs, both the parent and the subsidiary must still be engaged in lines of business in which each has been active for at least five years; (3) the transaction must not be used as a means of avoiding dividend taxation; (4) shareholders of the parent must maintain a significant ownership interest in both the parent and the spin-off; and (5) the spin-off must have a substantial business purpose, separate from simply saving on income taxes.

[4] The requirement that there must be continuity between pre- and post-spin-off business lines in order for the spin-off to be considered a tax-free event helps ensure that pre- and post-spin-off data reflect the operating results of a similar collection of assets.

[5] Note that it is possible for a parent to strip the spin-off of financial resources such as cash prior to the spin-off. Alternatively, the parent could load the spin-off with an excess amount of debt in an effort to rid the parent of financial constraints (see, e.g., Parrino (1997)). Our analysis, however, indicates that these types of actions are not generally occurring. Spin-off firms are spun off with cash levels that are comparable to pre-spin-off years. In addition, spin-off firms begin life with debt-to-equity levels that are similar to the parent.

years, while the spin-off was part of the parent company. These data are more comprehensive than the limited information provided in the segment data and are more likely to correspond to an actual business unit in the firm.

As a caveat, it is important to keep in mind that companies choosing to spin off divisions are not a random subsample of public companies. If undertaking a spin-off is motivated by the desire to eliminate internal capital misallocation, then our sample is biased towards companies where investment misallocation is particularly severe. Thus, one must be careful when drawing conclusions about the overall efficiency of internal capital markets based on what we observe in spin-offs. Nevertheless, if an inefficient internal capital market is indeed one of the rationales behind a spin-off, then a spin-off is probably a good place to look for signs of such inefficiencies.

The evidence that we present is generally consistent with the view that investment is distorted in the internal capital markets of firms that subsequently spin off divisions. Basic investment theory predicts that firms should invest more when they have better investment opportunities; empirically, this usually takes the form of the Q theory, in which investment opportunities are measured by the ratio of the market value of the firm to the replacement cost of its assets. According to the Q theory, firms should invest more as Q rises. We examine the extent to which this is true before and after the spin-off. In particular, we estimate the sensitivity of the spin-off firm's investment to industry Q, while the spin-off is a subsidiary of the parent and afterwards when the spin-off is an independent firm.

Overall, we find an increased sensitivity of investment to Q after the spin-off. This increased sensitivity is more pronounced when the spin-off operates in industries that are unrelated to the parent's industry, and when the stock market responds favorably to the announcement of the spin-off. We also find that firms in low Q industries tend to cut investment relative to their industry peers after the spin-off, while firms in high Q industries tend to increase their investment relative to industry peers. Spin-off firms' investment also moves more closely in tandem with the investment of stand-alone firms after the spin-off. This effect is also more pronounced for unrelated spin-offs and for spin-offs in which the parent's stock price rises considerably in response to the announcement.

There is a large body of prior research on spin-offs. Researchers have documented that parent companies experience positive cumulative abnormal excess returns (CARs) at the announcement of a spin-off (Hite and Owers (1983), Miles and Rosenfeld (1983), Schipper and Smith (1983)). Spin-offs themselves experience positive long-term excess stock returns (Cusatis, Miles, and Woolridge (1993)) and improvements in operating performance (Woo, Willard, and Daellenbach (1992), Daley, Mehrotra, and Sivakumar (1997)). There is also increased analyst coverage and greater accuracy in analyst forecasts following spin-offs (Krishnaswami and Subramanian (1999), Gilson et al. (2001)). Dittmar and Shivdasani (2001) look at the change in investment behavior of *parent* companies after they *divest* businesses. They find that these firms seem to improve the internal allocation of capital and that they tend to increase their rate of investment, using the proceeds of the divestiture for funding. As far as we know, we are the first authors to explore actual changes in investment behavior of spin-off firms.

The remainder of the paper is organized as follows. Section I describes the data sources and the construction of the sample. Section II summarizes some of the key elements of the data. Section III analyzes the change in investment behavior before and after the spin-off. Section IV considers alternative interpretations of our findings. Section V concludes the paper.

I. Data and Construction of the Sample

We start with a list of 324 spin-offs from Securities Data Corporation's Mergers and Acquisitions Database, occurring between 1981 and 1996. To be included in our sample, a spin-off must satisfy the following criteria: (1) COMPUSTAT and CRSP data are available for at least one year after the spin-off transaction; (2) a copy of the spin-off's first annual report is available; (3) COMPUSTAT and CRSP data are available for the parent before the spin-off; (4) the spin-off is not a bank, financial services company, insurance firm, or financial holding company; (5) we can verify that the transaction is actually a spin-off by checking the annual report or a Lexis–Nexis news report; and (6) the spin-off is a "clean" transaction in which the parent company goes from 100 percent ownership to 0 percent ownership through a pro rata distribution of shares.

We eliminate 31 spin-offs because they are not included in the COMPUSTAT or CRSP databases. We drop 8 spin-offs because COMPUSTAT or CRSP data are not available for the parent, 5 spin-offs because we are unable to find annual reports on the spin-offs, and 51 spin-offs with SIC codes between 6000 and 6500 (financial service and insurance firms). We are unable to verify that a spin-off actually occurred in 12 instances and drop these firms as well.

Finally, we eliminate 65 spin-offs from the sample because they are not "clean" transactions. In several instances, the company was a spin-off of a prior equity carve-out where the parent had previously sold a portion of its ownership in the spin-off division in a public offering. Others are actually rights offerings rather than simple pro rata distributions of shares. Still others are, in fact, joint ventures with one parent deciding to relinquish its ownership interest in the venture by spinning off its share. The remaining 26 spin-offs are part of much more complex restructurings such as Morris Trust transactions, in which the spin-off occurs immediately prior to the merger of the parent with another firm. The complexity of these remaining transactions renders them unsuitable for our purposes. The final sample then consists of 160 corporate spin-offs.

Spin-off financial data are generally available on COMPUSTAT for the first year in which the spin-off operates as an independent entity. In about half the spin-offs, COMPUSTAT reports one year of pre-spin-off data. For the other half of the sample and for earlier years, we obtain pre-spin-off financial data from the pro forma data in the first annual report. The annual report includes income and cash flow statement data for up to three years before the spin-off and balance sheet data for up to two years before the spin-off. In addition, annual reports typically include a table of summary financial data with five years of the most important balance sheet and income statement data such as net income and total assets. Combining all of the available data generally provides two to three years of usable pre-spin-off operating profit and capital expenditure data for the spin-off. Parent company financial data comes exclusively from COMPUSTAT. Data for both spin-offs and parents run through 1998.

The combined pro forma and COMPUSTAT data are aligned into an event time panel of years -5 to $+5$, where year 0 is the fiscal year during which the spin-off occurs. Thus, year $+1$ constitutes the first full year of independent operations for the spin-off, while year -1 is the last full year of operations inside the parent. We have full data on most spin-offs beginning in year -2 (145 out of 160) running through year $+3$ (135 out of 160). Spin-offs drop out of the sample over time principally because they are acquired or merge. It is important to note that the assets of the spin-off remain on the books at their historical book value. Because no sale occurs, assets are not revalued to market values. This allows us to make meaningful comparisons of accounting data before and after the spin-off.

In the analysis, we use data from firms that operate in the same industries as the spin-offs to provide various benchmarks. Because many firms operate in multiple industries, we confine our comparison firms to "stand-alones," by which we mean firms that operate in only one industry. To identify stand-alones, we use COMPUSTAT segment data, which breaks out key operating data (sales, assets, operating income, capital expenditures, and depreciation) by principal lines of business. Firms are considered to operate in only one industry if, in their COMPUSTAT segment data, they report 100 percent of their sales in a single industry. After stand-alone firms are identified, we calculate industry median values (using COMPUSTAT data for the entire stand-alone firm) for items such as capital expenditures normalized by assets and Q. Spin-off and parent firms are excluded from all industry median calculations.

Our baseline definition of an industry is at the four-digit SIC-code level. A median for an industry is calculated if there are five or more stand-alone firms available for that particular industry. Median values are also calculated for all three-, two-, and one-digit industries in the same manner. Matching is then done at the most disaggregated level having at least five stand-alone firms.

Parents and spin-offs themselves are often comprised of multiple segments in different industries. In comparing these firms to an industry median, we need to take a weighted average of the various industries in which the firm operates. We weight by segment assets and calculate a "chop-shop" median.[6] For example, in the Kenner Parker Toys spin-off from General Mills in 1985, Kenner Parker Toys reports a Toys and Games segment (SIC 3944) with $419.2 in assets (all dollar values reported in millions unless otherwise specified.) General Mills reports three segments: Consumer Foods (SIC 2043), Restaurants (SIC 5812), and Specialty Retailing (SIC 5621) with assets of $1,091.8, $467.8, and $195.5, respectively. Thus, the industry, or "chop-shop" ratio of capital expenditures to assets for Kenner Parker Toys is simply the industry median for SIC 3944. For General Mills, the industry ratio is the asset-weighted average of 62 percent SIC 2043, 27 percent SIC 5812, and 11 percent SIC 5621.

Because spin-off segment data is unavailable prior to year −1, we use segment weights from the earliest available year when calculating chop-shop industry values for pre-spin-off years. For example, to calculate a chop-shop value for year −2 or −3, we use the segment data from year −1 (50 percent of sample) or year 0 if year −1 is not available. Note that while the weights might be from a later year, the industry median values are always from the appropriate year. In Section IV, we explore whether this approach introduces any biases that may drive our results.

Two key variables in the analysis are our measures of investment and investment opportunities. Since R&D data are not widely available for the spin-off firms (and certainly not before the spin-off), we focus on capital expenditures as our measure of investment. Capital expenditures are normalized by assets. We use end-of-year assets rather than start-of-year assets in this normalization because using end-of-year assets allows us to analyze more years of pre-spin-off data, and, if there are acquisitions or asset sales during the year, it normalizes by a more appropriate number.

Our primary measure of investment opportunities is the market value of the firm divided by the book value of assets, a proxy for Tobin's Q.[7] We calculate the market value of the firm as the book value of assets, plus the market value of common equity, less the sum of the book value of common equity and balance sheet deferred taxes.[8]

At times, we break out the analysis into two subsamples of spin-offs, those in industries related to the parents' industries and those in industries unrelated to the parents' industries. Coming up with a measure of relatedness is not straightforward. It is standard in the literature to define two businesses as unrelated if they operate in different two-digit SIC codes. This approach, however, is problematic, as the example of Maxus Energy's spin-off of Diamond Shamrock makes clear. Although the two companies are in

[6] The qualitative results do not depend on whether we weight by segment assets or segment sales.

[7] This is not exactly Tobin's Q because we do not attempt to adjust assets to measure the replacement cost of assets. Perfect and Wiles (1994) argue that this adjustment is of little consequence.

[8] See Smith and Watts (1992), Lang and Stulz (1994), Scharfstein (1998), and Rajan et al. (2000), among others, for examples of research using this particular proxy for Q.

different two-digit industries, they are certainly in related businesses: Maxus Energy is in petroleum exploration (SIC 1311), while Diamond Shamrock is in petroleum refining and marketing (SIC 2911).

Instead of using the two-digit approach, we use our own subjective assessment of whether the parent and spin-off are in related lines of business. This requires us to analyze the reported segments of both the spin-off and the parent as of year 0. In addition, we read annual reports, prospectuses, and news articles to get a full understanding of the businesses of the spin-off and parent and to discern whether these businesses are related or unrelated. Using this procedure, we classify 90 spin-offs as unrelated to the parent and 70 as related. After presenting a series of results using this measure of relatedness, we analyze the robustness of our results to using the standard two-digit method.

II. Characteristics of the Sample

Table I lists the number of spin-offs in each year and the total market value of equity spun off in that year. Table II, Panels A through C, provides summary statistics on some of the key variables for the spin-offs and parents in years −1, 0, +1. In year 0, a year that straddles both the pre- and post-spin-off periods, spin-offs have mean (median) total sales of \$601.3 (\$253.1) and total assets of \$569.7 (\$211.5), denominated in millions of 1997 dollars. Mean earnings before interest, taxes, depreciation, and amortization normalized by end-of-year assets (operating profit ratio) is 0.051. This is considerably less than the median of 0.117 because of a subset of companies with large operating losses. After subtracting the industry median, the industry adjusted operating income ratio is −0.066 (significant at the 1 percent level), while the median is −0.009 (significant at the 10 percent level).

Despite the fact that spin-offs have lower operating profit ratios than their industry peers, their Q at year 0 is not substantially different. The mean is a bit higher than the industry value, the median is a bit lower, but neither difference is statistically significant. While Q is not significantly different, spin-offs do have higher leverage than the median firm in the industry. Mean (median) leverage (defined as book value of long-term debt divided by book value of long-term debt plus the market value of equity) for spin-offs in year 0 is 0.295 (0.255), which is 0.049 (0.029) greater than the industry median; both differences are statistically significant.[9]

The average ratio of capital expenditures to assets—our measure of spin-off investment—is 0.086, while the median is 0.057. The mean difference between spin-off investment and the median industry investment is 0.014, which is statistically significant, while the median is 0.004, which is not. The latter comparison is probably more meaningful, given that the mean

[9] Dittmar (2002) also finds that spin-off leverage is higher than the leverage of firms in the same industry. However, after controlling for differences in firm characteristics such as R&D, taxes, and so forth, she finds no statistically significant difference.

Table I

Number of Spin-offs and Total Market Value per Year

This table lists the number of spin-offs in each year in our sample and the market value of the spin-off on the first day of trading denominated in millions of 1997 dollars. See Section II of the paper for details on the criteria for inclusion in the spin-off sample.

Year	Number	Market Value (Million 1997 $)
1982	1	66
1983	3	1,714
1984	7	2,920
1985	12	3,681
1986	10	9,200
1987	13	6,124
1988	17	9,045
1989	18	7,308
1990	10	4,654
1991	8	4,375
1992	12	7,568
1993	19	21,774
1994	16	14,284
1995	10	7,935
1996	4	1,605
All years	160	102,260

has some outliers. The bottom line from Table II, Panel A, is that in the year of the transaction, spin-offs generate lower operating profit and have higher leverage than their industry peers, but their Q and capital expenditure rates are about the same.

Table II, Panel B, summarizes the data on parent companies. They are considerably larger than the spin-offs with mean (median) sales of $2,846.1 ($1,115.2) and mean (median) assets of $3,817.9 ($978.9). In contrast to spin-offs, parents generate slightly higher operating profit than their industry peers, but the difference is not statistically significant. Parent companies have higher Q than the industry median; the mean difference is 0.329, while the median difference is 0.119, both of which are statistically significant.[10] Parents also have significantly higher leverage than the industry median. Despite higher Q ratios, parent investment rates are not significantly dif-

[10] A growing body of literature documents that diversified firms generally have lower valuations than a comparable portfolio of pure-play firms, a result known as the diversification discount (Lang and Stulz (1994), Berger and Ofek (1995), Comment and Jarrell (1995), Denis and Thothadri (1999)). On average, parents do not show evidence of the diversification discount; however, regression of Industry Adjusted Q on an asset-based Herfindahl index (not reported in tables) indicates that the more diversified the parent is, the larger is the diversification discount.

Table II

Characteristics of Spin-off Firms, Parent Firms, and a Comparison of Spin-off and Parent Firms in Years –1, 0, and +1

Panel A provides summary statistics on the sample of 160 spin-offs. Year 0 is the fiscal year during which the spin-off occurred. Operating profit ratio is earnings before interest, taxes, and depreciation divided by total assets. The variable Q represents the spin-off's (market value of common equity − book value of equity + total assets − deferred taxes)/total assets. Investment ratio is capital expenditures/total assets. Leverage is (long term debt + current portion of long term debt)/(long term debt + current portion of long term debt + market value of common equity + liquidation value of preferred). Median industry values are subtracted from operating profit ratio, Q, and investment ratio to generate the respective industry-adjusted variables. Panel B provides summary statistics on the sample of spin-off parents, with variables defined as in Panel A. Panel C compares parents and spin-offs, with the definitions of the variables as in Panel A. The upper value in each cell is the mean; the lower value in parentheses is the median. Significance of industry-adjusted differences is measured using both a t-statistic and a sign test. Asterisks next to mean and median values denote the significance level of each test.

	Year −1	Year 0	Year +1
Panel A: Spin-off Characteristics			
Sales (1997 millions of dollars)	590.5	601.3	630.4
	(239.7)	(253.1)	(263.5)
Assets (1997 millions of dollars)	568.4	569.7	589.0
	(189.6)	(211.5)	(197.5)
Operating profit ratio	0.061	0.051	0.073
	(0.115)	(0.117)	(0.121)
Industry-adjusted operating profit ratio	−0.059***	−0.066***	−0.041**
	(−0.014)	(−0.009)*	(−0.008)
Q		1.584	1.643
		(1.291)	(1.285)
Industry-adjusted Q		0.150	0.232**
		(−0.041)	(−0.011)
Leverage		0.295	0.301
		(0.255)	(0.267)
Industry-adjusted leverage		0.049**	0.039**
		(0.029)*	(−0.001)
Investment ratio	0.086	0.086	0.076
	(0.052)	(0.057)	(0.058)
Industry-adjusted investment ratio	0.013	0.014**	0.011
	(−0.004)	(0.004)	(0.002)
Number of obs. for investment ratio	158	156	156
Panel B: Parent Characteristics			
Sales (1997 millions of dollars)	3,054.8	2,846.1	2,855.1
	(1,259.0)	(1,115.2)	(1,134.8)
Assets (1997 millions of dollars)	4,290.0	3,817.9	3,853.5
	(1,330.2)	(978.9)	(1,144.0)
Operating profit ratio	0.135	0.136	0.144
	(0.140)	(0.145)	(0.142)
Industry-adjusted operating profit ratio	0.015*	0.015	0.029***
	(0.004)	(0.004)	(0.021)**
Q	1.573	1.756	1.751
	(1.347)	(1.471)	(1.480)
Industry-adjusted Q	0.147***	0.329***	0.344***
	(0.037)***	(0.119)**	(0.136)***

Table II—*Continued*

	Year −1	Year 0	Year +1
Panel B: Parent Characteristics (*continued*)			
Leverage	0.321 (0.282)	0.323 (0.252)	0.323 (0.257)
Industry-adjusted leverage	0.050*** (0.046)***	0.059*** (0.054)***	0.044** (0.025)*
Investment ratio	0.068 (0.052)	0.067 (0.053)	0.064 (0.048)
Industry-adjusted investment ratio	0.005 (0.002)	0.003 (0.000)	0.006 (−0.001)
Number of obs. for investment ratio	157	149	139
Panel C: Spin-off versus Parent in Year 0			
Spin-off sales/(spin-off sales + parent sales)	0.267 (0.211)	0.258 (0.214)	0.216 (0.256)
Spin-off assets/(spin-off assets + parent assets)	0.225 (0.193)	0.238 (0.195)	0.232 (0.192)
Spin-off operating profit ratio − parent operating profit ratio	−0.071*** (−0.021)	−0.078*** (−0.045)**	−0.065*** (−0.023)
Spin-off industry operating profit ratio − parent industry operating profit ratio	0.000 (0.000)	−0.001 (0.000)	0.005 (0.003)
Spin-off Q − parent Q		−0.199 (−0.224)***	−0.070 (−0.200)*
Spin-off industry Q − parent industry Q	−0.028 (0.000)	0.006 (0.000)	0.001 (0.000)
Spin-off leverage − parent leverage		−0.036 (−0.016)	−0.032 (−0.014)
Spin-off industry leverage − parent industry leverage	−0.001 (0.000)	−0.007 (0.000)	−0.011 (0.000)
Spin-off investment ratio − parent investment ratio	0.018** (0.007)*	0.021** (0.009)	0.012 (0.002)
Spin-off industry investment ratio − parent industry investment ratio	−0.002 (0.000)	−0.003 (0.000)	0.000 (0.000)

***Significance at the 1 percent level; **significance at the 5 percent level; *significance at the 10 percent level.

ferent than their industry peers. Thus, in the year of the transaction, parent companies seem to have somewhat higher operating profits, Q, and leverage than the industry, but they do not invest at a higher rate.[11]

[11] Schlingemann, Stulz, and Walkling (2001) find that diversified conglomerates are more likely to divest segments in industries with high capital expenditures and to invest less themselves. In contrast, we find no real differences in the industry investment rates of parents and spin-offs, and we find little difference in their own investment rates. What may explain the differing results is that their sample includes asset sales, which raise cash for the parent. This may, in fact, be their motive and may explain why they invest less and want to get rid of segments that need more capital investment. Powers (2001) shows that there are systematic differences in companies that engage in asset sales, carve-outs, and spin-offs.

Finally, Panel C of Table II compares spin-offs and parents. In year 0, the median spin-off is about 25 percent of the hypothetical combined entity (spin-off and parent together). Spin-offs also have lower operating profit and Q than their parents by a statistically and economically significant amount. Spin-off leverage is moderately less than parent leverage. Spin-off mean investment rates are significantly higher than they are for parents; however, the median difference is not statistically significant. There are no significant differences in operating profit, investment, and Q of the industries in which parents and spin-offs operate.

A number of earlier studies have found positive excess returns in the period during which the spin-off is announced, ranging from 2.8 percent to 5.6 percent (Hite and Owers (1983), Schipper and Smith (1983), Rosenfeld (1984), Slovin, Sushka, and Ferraro (1995), Daley et al. (1997)). In our sample, we find mean positive excess returns of 3.9 percent for the two-day period around the announcement. The median excess return is 2.23 percent, and 68.9 percent of the observations are positive. Both excess returns are statistically significant. Daley et al. and Desai and Jain (1999) show that announcement period returns are larger for unrelated spin-offs. In our sample, the mean announcement period return for unrelated spin-offs is 4.2 percent and the median is 2.3 percent, while, for related spin-offs, the mean is 3.3 percent and the median is 2.6 percent. These findings are similar in magnitude to the above studies, though the differences reported here are not statistically significant.

III. Investment Behavior before and after the Spin-off

A. Baseline Results

One of the most basic predictions of investment theory is that firms with better investment opportunities should invest more. Empirically, this prediction usually takes the form of a Q-based model of investment in which normalized capital expenditures are regressed on Q. Thus, one way to determine whether spin-offs change investment behavior is to examine whether there are changes in the sensitivity of investment to Q for spin-off firms before and after the spin-off. We estimate the following model for years -3, -2, -1, $+1$, $+2$, and $+3$, excluding the year of the spin-off, because it includes both pre- and post-spin-off periods:

$$I_{it} = \beta_{0i} + \beta_1 * Q_{it} + \beta_2 * Q_{it} * Before + \beta_3 * Before + \Sigma_t \gamma_t * Year_t + \varepsilon_{it}. \quad (1)$$

In equation (1), I_{it} is the ratio of capital expenditures to assets of firm i in period t. Firm fixed effects are captured in the firm-specific intercept term β_{0i}. *Before* is a dummy variable taking the value one in years -1, -2, and -3 and zero otherwise. Ideally, a firm-specific measure of Q should be used as a proxy for a firm's investment opportunities. However, because spin-offs are not publicly traded prior to year 0, we cannot observe the pre-spin-off market value of the firm, so a firm-specific measure of Q is unavailable. Instead, our measure of Q *for both the pre- and post-spin-off periods* is the median asset-weighted Q of stand-alone firms in the spin-off's industries. Although a firm-specific measure of Q *can* be calculated in the post-spin-off period, using it as our post-spin-off proxy for investment opportunities could bias our results if firm-specific Q is more (or less) informative about investment opportunities than is industry Q.[12] To minimize the effects of possible mid-year changes in business composition and investment opportunities, we take an average of Q in years t and $t-1$; none of the results depend critically on averaging in this way. $Year_t$ is a calendar year dummy.

Because other studies have found that cash flow, in addition to Q, explains capital expenditures (see, e.g., Fazzari, Hubbard and Petersen (1988)), we also estimate equation (1) in an augmented form:

$$\begin{aligned} I_{it} = \beta_{0i} + \beta_1 * Q + \beta_2 * Q * Before + \beta_3 * Before + \beta_4 * SOP_{it} \\ + \beta_5 * SOP_{it} * Before + \beta_6 * POP_{it} * Before + \Sigma_t \gamma_t * Year_t + \varepsilon_{it}, \end{aligned} \quad (2)$$

where SOP_{it} and POP_{it} are the asset-normalized operating profit of the spin-off and parent, respectively.

If investment spending in conglomerates is distorted in some way, then one would expect the spin-off's investment to be less sensitive to Q when it is part of the conglomerate than when it is an independent entity. That is, one would predict: $\beta_1 > 0$ and $\beta_2 < 0$ in equations (1) and (2). It is less clear how distortions in internal capital markets would change the relationship between investment and operating profit. However, if firms are financially constrained, one might expect a spin-off's operating profit to have a bigger effect on investment after it is spun off. When it is part of the conglomerate, the parent's operating profits should have a bigger effect on the spin-off's investment. Empirically, this implies $\beta_4 > 0$, $\beta_5 < 0$, and $\beta_6 > 0$.

The first column of Table III reports the results of estimating equation (1) for the entire sample. The estimate for the Q coefficient, β_1, is positive and statistically significant; after the spin-off, investment is positively related to industry Q. The coefficient estimate for the interaction term, β_2, is negative. These coefficient estimates suggest that the firm's pre-spin-off sensitivity of

[12] A potential concern is that industry Q might be a significantly worse proxy for investment opportunities than is firm-specific Q. We think this concern is of limited importance. Using COMPUSTAT data from 1980 to 1998 for all domestic firms having assets of at least \$100 million and primary SIC codes between 1000 and 4000 (2,556 firms, 19,335 observations), we estimate fixed-effects panel regressions with normalized capital expenditures as the dependent variable. We use normalized operating profit, year dummies, and either industry Q or firm-specific Q as regressors. Coefficient estimates for industry Q and firm-specific Q are 0.0236 (t-statistic = 18.40) and 0.0151 (t-statistic = 20.86), respectively. R-squared values for the two regressions are 0.0840 and 0.0891 as compared to an R-squared of 0.0655 without industry Q or firm-specific Q. These results demonstrate that, in this independent sample, the explanatory power of industry Q and firm-specific Q are quite similar.

Table III

The Sensitivity of Capital Expenditures to Industry Q and Profitability before and after Spin-off

This table reports the results of regression equations (1) and (2) as given in the text. The dependent variable is capital expenditures/assets. Industry Q is the asset-weighted industry median Q of the industries in which the spin-off operates. Operating profit ratio is earnings before interest, taxes, and depreciation divided by assets and is calculated for both the spin-off and the parent firm. Before takes the value 1 for years −3, −2, and −1 and takes the value 0 for years +1, +2, and +3. Year 0, the year of the spin-off, is excluded from the regression. The regressions include year dummy variables and firm fixed effects. The numbers in parentheses below the coefficient estimates are p-values.

	Full Sample	
Industry Q	0.024**	0.026**
	(0.020)	(0.015)
Industry Q * before	−0.012	−0.018**
	(0.150)	(0.038)
Before	0.026*	0.026
	(0.082)	(0.111)
Spin-off operating profit ratio		0.033**
		(0.032)
Before * spin-off operating profit ratio		−0.045***
		(0.006)
Before * parent operating profit ratio		0.073
		(0.110)
No. of firms	160	160
No. of observations	769	746
R^2	0.044	0.060

***Significance at the 1 percent level; **significance at the 5 percent level; *significance at the 10 percent level.

investment to Q is about half that of its post-spin-off level. However, the point estimate of the interaction coefficient is statistically insignificant with a p-value of 0.150.

The second column of Table III reports the results of estimating equation (2), the investment model including spin-off and parent operating profit. We observe the same pattern of Q coefficients, except that now the coefficient of the interaction term is statistically significant. The regression results also indicate that spin-off investment is sensitive to its own operating profit after the spin-off, but not before the spin-off. Instead, before the spin-off, *parent* operating profit is positively related to the division's investment. This finding is consistent with the view that, after the spin-off, firms are financially constrained by their own operating profit, but before the spin-off, they are constrained by the parent's operating profit. Despite the increased sensitivity of spin-off investment to own operating profit, the spin-off appears to be more responsive to investment opportunities after the spin-off has occurred. To the extent that operating profit proxies for investment opportunities, the increased sensitivity to the spin-off's own operating profit is also consistent with the firm's investment moving more in line with investment opportunities.

To get a sense of the magnitude of the difference in the sensitivity of investment to Q before and after the spin-off, consider the following calculations. The average of the industry Q values is 1.41. The within-firm, time-series standard deviation of industry Q is 0.215. Thus, using the estimates from the second column of Table III, before a spin-off, a one standard deviation increase in industry Q from its mean of 1.41 to 1.62 would be predicted to increase normalized investment by 0.0017. Evaluated at the mean investment rate of 0.082, the model predicts an increase to 0.084, a small effect. After the spin-off, the effects of an increase in Q are larger. A one standard deviation increase in industry Q increases normalized investment by .0056, which (at the mean investment level) amounts to an increase in the rate of investment to 0.088. In this case, a 14.9 percent increase in industry Q results in a 7.3 percent increase in the investment rate, an implied elasticity of almost 50 percent.

B. Related versus Unrelated Spin-offs

Table IV reports the result of estimating equations (1) and (2) after breaking out the sample into two subsamples based on whether the spin-off's industry is related to the parent's. There are two reasons to examine spin-offs of unrelated divisions separately. First, it has been argued that conglomerates comprised of unrelated businesses have been the least successful conglomerates (see, e.g., Lang and Stulz (1994) and Berger and Ofek (1995)). If distortions in investment spending contribute to the conglomerate discount, then it seems likely that we should find greater evidence of investment distortions in the unrelated subsample of spin-offs. Second, on a more practical level, industry Q—our proxy for divisional investment opportunities—may be a more appropriate measure of investment opportunities for unrelated divisions where there are no significant operating synergies with the rest of the company. For example, a paper manufacturer that is part of a conglomerate with a lumber division may have different investment opportunities than a stand-alone paper manufacturer. Since the stand-alone paper manufacturers that form the basis of our industry Q measure do not own lumber companies, there may be more measurement error in the Q estimates for the paper manufacturers operating alongside related divisions.

The results reported in the first and second columns indicate that when an unrelated firm is spun off, there is a statistically significant increase in the sensitivity of investment to industry Q. The same is not true for spin-offs of related businesses. As the third and fourth columns of Table IV indicate, investment is insensitive to industry Q after the spin-off. If anything, investment is more sensitive to Q *before* the spin-off for firms in industries related to the parent. We have no clear explanation of this finding.

Table IV

The Sensitivity of Capital Expenditures to Industry Q and Profitability Before and After Spin-off: Related Versus Unrelated Spin-offs

This table reports the results of regression equations (1) and (2) as given in the text. The sample is split according to whether the spin-off operates in industries that are related or unrelated to primary parent industries. This classification is based on the subjective assessment of the authors. The dependent variable is capital expenditures/assets. Industry Q is the asset-weighted industry median Q of the industries in which the spin-off operates. Operating profit ratio is earnings before interest, taxes, and depreciation divided by assets and is calculated for both the spin-off and the parent firm. Before takes the value 1 for years −3, −2, and −1, and takes the value 0 for years +1, +2, and +3. Year 0, the year of the spin-off, is excluded from the regression. The regressions include year dummy variables and firm fixed effects. The numbers in parentheses below the coefficient estimates are p-values.

	Unrelated Spin-offs		Related Spin-offs	
Industry Q	0.039***	0.043***	0.015	0.015
	(0.004)	(0.002)	(0.367)	(0.368)
Industry Q * before	−0.041***	−0.046***	0.030**	0.019
	(0.000)	(0.000)	(0.020)	(0.204)
Before	0.060***	0.051**	−0.026	−0.014
	(0.003)	(0.019)	(0.250)	(0.605)
Spin-off operating profit ratio		0.023		−0.012
		(0.265)		(0.632)
Before * spin-off operating profit ratio		−0.022		−0.042*
		(0.381)		(0.081)
Before * parent operating profit ratio		0.122*		0.026
		(0.051)		(0.723)
No. of firms	90	90	70	70
No. of observations	436	424	333	322
R^2	0.129	0.143	0.090	0.102

***Significance at the 1 percent level; **significance at the 5 percent level; *significance at the 10 percent level.

The estimated coefficients from the regressions for unrelated spin-offs suggest a larger effect of the spin-off on the investment–Q sensitivity. Using the regression estimates from the augmented specification (second column of Table IV), a one standard deviation increase in industry Q (using the mean industry Q value of 1.41 and the within-firm standard deviation of 0.228) implies a post-spin-off increase in the investment rate of 0.0098. Evaluated at the means for unrelated firms, investment would be predicted to increase from 0.087 to 0.097, an increase of 11.5 percent. This amounts to an implied elasticity of 71 percent. By contrast, the pre-spin-off sensitivity is essentially zero.

C. High versus Low Announcement Period Returns

Table V breaks out the sample based on the parent company's excess returns at the announcement of the spin-off. As discussed in Section II, mean

Table V

The Sensitivity of Capital Expenditures to Industry Q and Profitability Before and After Spin-off: Announcement Effects

This table reports the results of regression equations (1) and (2) as given in the text. High announcement effect spin-offs are those where two-day abnormal returns around the announcement are above the median of 0.0223. The dependent variable is capital expenditures/assets. Industry Q is the asset-weighted industry median Q of the industries in which the spin-off operates. Operating profit ratio is earnings before interest, taxes, and depreciation divided by assets and is calculated for both the spin-off and the parent firm. Before takes the value 1 for years −3, −2, and −1, and takes the value 0 for years +1, +2, and +3. Year 0, the year of the spin-off, is excluded from the regression. The regression includes year dummies and firm fixed effects. The numbers in parentheses below the coefficient estimates are p-values.

	High Announcement Effect		Low Announcement Effect	
Industry Q	0.058***	0.056***	0.010	0.013
	(0.000)	(0.000)	(0.514)	(0.422)
Industry Q * before	−0.034***	−0.033***	−0.002	−0.012
	(0.002)	(0.003)	(0.867)	(0.434)
Before	0.051***	0.051**	0.011	0.008
	(0.006)	(0.011)	(0.674)	(0.783)
Spin-off operating profit ratio		0.010		0.029
		(0.672)		(0.182)
Before * spin-off operating profit ratio		−0.001		−0.051**
		(0.979)		(0.017)
Before * parent operating profit ratio		−0.032		0.133**
		(0.635)		(0.043)
No. of firms	81	81	79	79
No. of observations	396	384	373	362
R^2	0.106	0.113	0.067	0.102

***Significance at the 1 percent level; **significance at the 5 percent level.

and median excess returns are positive, but there is considerable heterogeneity across firms. Announcement period returns reflect the cumulative response to many factors and are thus a noisy signal regarding the perceived benefits of the spin-off. However, if the stock market reacts favorably to the dismantling of an inefficient internal capital market, then we would expect spin-offs associated with large positive announcement effects to exhibit an increase in the post-spin-off sensitivity of investment to industry Q.

The first column of Table V shows that spin-offs with announcement effects above the median of 2.23 percent exhibit an increase in the sensitivity of investment to Q. Similar results hold for the estimation of equation (2). The third and fourth columns of Table V show that for firms with an announcement effect below the median, spin-off investment is insensitive to industry Q both before and after the spin-off.

It should be noted that the announcement effect sample split does not proxy for the relatedness sample split. Of the 90 unrelated spin-offs, 44 have announcement period returns greater than the median value, while of the 70 related spin-offs, 36 have announcement-period returns greater than the median.[13] Our findings (not reported in tables) indicate that within both the related and unrelated subsamples, the spin-offs with larger announcement effects exhibit greater increases in the sensitivity of investment to Q, both in terms of the magnitude and the significance of the estimated post-spin-off Q coefficients.

D. Changes in the Rate of Investment

If, as some theories predict, conglomerate divisions overinvest in low Q industries and underinvest in high Q industries, we would expect to see a drop in investment for spin-offs in low Q industries and an increase in investment for spin-offs in high Q industries following the separation. To address this implication, we start by calculating the average industry-adjusted investment rate in the three years before the spin-off and the average for the three years after the spin-off.[14] The change is a measure of whether firms increase investment relative to industry peers or cut investment relative to industry peers. The mean change, −0.0004, is close to zero and statistically insignificant. The average change in industry-adjusted investment, however, masks considerable variation across firms in their response to the spin-off.

The first column of Table VI, Panel A, presents the results of a regression of the change in average industry-adjusted investment on industry Q. Because we do not want to use information in Q that evolves during the period to explain changes in investment during the period, we use industry Q three years before the spin-off as our proxy for whether the firm is in a low Q or high Q industry. The coefficient of Q is positive and the intercept is negative, indicating that spin-off firms tend to increase investment in high Q industries and cut investment in low Q industries. Neither point estimate is statistically significant, however.

The first column of Table VI, Panel B, takes a nonparametric approach to the same question. Of the 100 firms in industries with Q below the mean (1.37) three years before the spin-off, 53 experience a reduction in average industry-adjusted investment rates, statistically indistinguishable from a coin

[13] The means tell a slightly different story. The mean announcement effect for unrelated spin-offs is 4.79 percent versus 2.96 percent for related spin-offs. Differences are not statistically significant at conventional levels.

[14] Industry-adjusted investment is calculated by subtracting industry investment/assets from spin-off investment/assets. The industry value is calculated using the same "chop-shop" methodology used for calculating industry Q. Where we have fewer than three years of data in either the pre- or post-spin-off periods, averages are calculated using the one year or two years of data that are available.

Table VI

Changes in the Industry-Adjusted Rate of Investment before and after Spin-off

Panel A: Regression results. The dependent variable in the regressions reported below is the change in the average industry-adjusted investment rate before (years −3, −2, −1) and after the spin-off (years +1, +2, +3). The industry-adjusted investment rate is the spin-off firm's capital expenditures/assets less the median capital expenditure/assets ratio for the industry in which the firm operates. Industry Q in year −3 is the independent variable. Unrelated spin-offs are those that operate in industries that are unrelated to primary parent industries. This classification is based on the subjective assessment of the authors. High announcement effect spin-offs are those where the two-day abnormal returns around the announcement are above the median of 0.0223. The numbers in parentheses below the coefficient estimates are p-values. Panel B: Nonparametric results. The cells in this panel report the number of instances in which the average industry adjusted investment rate rises or falls after the spin-off relative to before the spin-off. The industry-adjusted investment rate is the spin-off firm's capital expenditures/assets less the median capital expenditure/assets ratio for the industry in which the firm operates. Low Q industries are those with industry Q less than 1.37 in year −3. Unrelated spin-offs are those in industries unrelated to the parent based on the authors' subjective assessments. High announcement effect spin-offs are those where the two-day abnormal returns around the announcement are above the median of 0.0223. The numbers in parentheses indicate the confidence levels of a Wilcoxon signed rank test.

	Full Sample	Unrelated Spin-offs	Related Spin-offs	High Announcement Effect	Low Announcement Effect
		Panel A: Regression Results			
Industry Q in year −3	0.018	0.039**	−0.015	0.038***	−0.004
	(0.144)	(0.014)	(0.298)	(0.000)	(0.196)
Constant	−0.025	−0.063**	0.032	−0.041**	−0.111
	(0.177)	(0.010)	(0.115)	(0.011)	(0.290)
No. of firms/obs.	155	86	69	83	72
R^2	0.011	0.146	0.007	0.106	0.003
		Panel B: Nonparametric Results			
Low Q firms reducing industry-adjusted investment/ all Low Q firms	53/100	34/54***	19/46	18/37	36/63
	(0.324)	(0.009)	(0.164)	(0.512)	(0.494)
High Q firms reducing industry-adjusted investment/ all High Q firms	37/54**	24/31**	13/23	19/25***	18/29
	(0.014)	(0.019)	(0.260)	(0.002)	(0.552)

***Significance at the 1 percent level; **significance at the 5 percent level.

flip. By contrast, of the 55 firms with industry Q above the mean, 37 experience an increase in their industry-adjusted investment rates, which, using a one-sided sign test, is statistically significant.

The next columns split the sample by whether the spin-off is in an industry related to the parent. Here the results are stronger both in the regression framework and the nonparametric approach. The second column of the table reports the results for the spin-offs that are unrelated to the parent. The coefficient of industry Q is positive and statistically significant. The estimates imply that for industry Q greater than 1.64, industry-adjusted investment rises and for industry Q below this point, it falls. Likewise, in the nonparametric analysis, 34 of the 54 firms with industry Q below the mean experience a reduction in their industry-adjusted investment, and 24 out of 32 firms in high Q industries experience an increase in their industry-adjusted investment. As the third column of Table VI indicates, there are no statistically significant relationships between Q and investment changes for the subsample of related spin-offs. These findings are consistent with our fixed effects model in which we found that the increase in the sensitivity of investment to industry Q was restricted to the sample of unrelated spin-offs.

Finally, the last two columns of Table VI report the results for the sample based on whether the announcement period returns are above or below the median. The regression results in Panel A show there is a positive and statistically significant relationship between the change in industry-adjusted investment and industry Q for high announcement effect spin-offs. Thirty-one of the 55 firms in low Q industries experience a reduction in their industry-adjusted investment rates; however, this is insignificantly different from a coin toss. By contrast, 21 of the 28 firms in high Q industries increase their industry-adjusted investment rates; this is statistically significant. In the subsample of firms with low announcement-period returns, the change in investment rates is hard to distinguish from zero and bears no relation to Q. These results are all consistent with our earlier finding in Table V that firms with high announcement-period returns exhibit an increased sensitivity of investment to industry Q.

E. Alternative Measures of Investment Opportunities

Thus far, we have relied on industry median Q as a measure of investment opportunities, because we cannot measure actual firm Q prior to the spin-off. While this clearly measures investment opportunities with error, we argued that as long as this measurement error is the same before and after the spin-off, it is unlikely to be what is driving our results. Nevertheless, it is useful to see whether our results are robust to using other proxies for investment opportunities. One alternative is to use the investment rates of other stand-alone firms in the industry as a proxy for investment opportunities on the view that if other firms are making significant investments, it is arguably because investment opportunities are good in the industry. This would suggest estimating the following regression equation:

$$I_{it} = \delta_{0i} + \delta_1 * INDI_{it} + \delta_2 * INDI_{it} * Before + \delta_3 * Before + \Sigma_t \gamma_t * Year_t + \varepsilon_{it}, \qquad (3)$$

Table VII

The Sensitivity of Capital Expenditures to Industry Capital Expenditures before and after Spin-off

This table reports the results of regression equation (3) in which the dependent variable is capital expenditures/assets. Industry capital expenditures is the asset-weighted industry median capital expenditures of the industries in which the spin-off operates. Before takes the value 1 for years −3, −2, and −1, and takes the value 0 for years +1, +2, and +3. Year 0, the year of the spin-off, is excluded from the regression. High announcement effect spin-offs are those where the two-day abnormal returns around the announcement are above the median of 0.0223. Unrelated spin-offs are identified based on the subjective assessment of the authors. The regression includes year dummies and firm fixed effects. The numbers in parentheses below the coefficient estimates are *p*-values.

	Full Sample	Unrelated Spin-offs	Related Spin-offs	High Announcement Effect	Low Announcement Effect
Industry investment rate	0.312***	0.347***	0.392**	0.352**	0.258*
	(0.001)	(0.004)	(0.031)	(0.013)	(0.071)
Industry investment rate * before	−0.195*	−0.294**	−0.173	−0.284**	−0.111
	(0.052)	(0.029)	(0.293)	(0.031)	(0.507)
Before	0.022*	0.023	0.022	0.029*	0.013
	(0.058)	(0.140)	(0.208)	(0.058)	(0.464)
No. of firms	160	90	70	81	79
No. of observations	769	436	333	396	373

***Significance at the 1 percent level; **significance at the 5 percent level; *significance at the 10 percent level.

where I_{it} is again the spin-off's investment-to-assets ratio and $INDI_{it}$ is the weighted average (again using segment assets as weights) of median investment-to-assets ratios for stand-alone firms in the various industries of spin-off firm i at time t.

One drawback of this approach is that there may be other factors that drive stand-alone investment besides investment opportunities. For example, it is possible that stand-alone firms are more liquidity constrained than conglomerate divisions. Showing that spin-offs act more like liquidity constrained stand-alone firms does not prove that their investment is more sensitive to investment opportunities; it may only prove that they too are liquidity constrained once they are spun off.

The findings reported in Table VII are generally consistent with our previous results indicating that investment is less sensitive to investment opportunities before the spin-off. The first column shows the results of estimating this equation for the full sample. The estimated coefficient of industry investment is positive and statistically significant. More importantly, the coefficient of the interaction term is negative, with a *p*-value of 0.052. Thus, it appears that spin-off firm investment is more sensitive to industry investment after the spin-off than it is before the spin-off.

The second column shows the coefficient estimates for the sample of unrelated spin-offs. The results mirror those for the sample as a whole. Finally, the third column shows the results for related spin-offs, where we find the same pattern of coefficients. Here, however, the coefficient of the interaction term is statistically insignificant. Note that, when we used industry Q as the proxy for investment opportunities, we found that investment by related spin-offs was *more* sensitive to investment prior to the spin-off—a somewhat puzzling finding. These results suggest that this particular finding is not robust to alternative measures of investment opportunities.

The last two columns break out the results based on the magnitude of the announcement-period return. For high announcement-effect firms, the coefficients have the predicted sign and are statistically significant. For spin-offs with low announcement-period returns, the coefficients also indicate an increased sensitivity of investment to investment opportunities after the spin-off, but the coefficients are not statistically significant. Regressions not reported in the table indicate that unrelated spin-offs with high announcement-period returns exhibit the greatest increase in the sensitivity of spin-off investment to median industry investment. Including measures of spin-off and parent operating profit in the regressions has no appreciable impact on the estimated coefficients of δ_1 and δ_2.

IV. Robustness of the Results

In this section, we investigate whether our results reflect a genuine change in investment behavior or are simply the result of spurious correlation driven by various types of mismeasurement. In particular, we consider three issues: (1) the appropriateness of our industry benchmarks, particularly before the spin-off; (2) our measure of relatedness; and (3) whether spin-offs are becoming more like their industry benchmarks on all dimensions, not just on capital expenditures.

A. Pre-Spin-off Industry Benchmarks

While initial post-spin-off annual reports contain detailed financial information on the company before the spin-off, they often do not contain detailed segment data. Because spin-offs sometimes operate in multiple segments, we have made some assumptions about the pre-spin-off industry segments in order to construct our pre-spin-off industry Q and industry investment measures. Our approach has been to use the closest available segment data to determine pre-spin-off industry weights. To the extent that these weights are less accurate than the post-spin-off weights, our industry measures prior to the spin-off will be subject to more measurement error than the post-spin-off industry measures. This biases the estimated pre-spin-off sensitivity of investment to Q or industry investment towards zero. If this is the case, our results might be driven more by measurement error than by a change in investment behavior.

Table VIII

Single-Segment Firms and SIC-Code-Based Measure of Relatedness

This table reports the results of regression equation (1) in which the dependent variable is capital expenditures/assets. Industry Q is the asset-weighted industry median Q of the industries in which the spin-off operates. Before takes the value 1 for years −3, −2, and −1 and takes the value 0 for years +1, +2, and +3. Year 0, the year of the spin-off is excluded from the regression. Unrelated spin-offs are identified based on the subjective assessment of the authors. Single segment identifies those spin-offs that report data for only one segment in the years prior to the spin-off. Unrelated spin-offs based on the two-digit SIC code are those spin-offs where the spin-off and the parent segments in the year of the spin-off share no common two-digit SIC codes. The regression includes year dummies and firm-fixed effects. The numbers in parentheses below the coefficient estimates are p-values.

	Unrelated Spin-offs (Single Segment)	Unrelated Spin-offs Using Two-Digit SIC-Code Measure	Unrelated Spin-offs Using Both Measures
Industry Q	0.041**	0.023*	0.030**
	(0.016)	(0.079)	(0.037)
Before * industry Q	−0.043***	−0.025**	−0.038***
	(0.001)	(0.027)	(0.002)
Before	0.069**	0.030	0.049**
	(0.010)	(0.132)	(0.029)
No. of firms	57	101	76
No. of observations	264	494	372
R^2	0.148	0.075	0.120

***Significance at the 1 percent level; **significance at the 5 percent level; *significance at the 10 percent level.

To see whether this could explain our results, we separately analyze the spin-offs that report only one segment at the time of the spin-off. While it is possible that the firm operates in more than one segment prior to the spin-off, it seems unlikely that the pro forma data in the first annual report would reflect anything other than the single post-spin-off segment.

The first column of Table VIII repeats the estimation of equation (1) for unrelated spin-offs that operate in only one segment. There are 57 such firms. The coefficient estimates are essentially the same as the estimates for the full set of unrelated spin-offs. Therefore, it seems unlikely that our basic results are driven by inadequate segment information prior to the spin-off.

B. Measure of Relatedness

As discussed above, it is typical to say that two businesses are unrelated if they operate in different two-digit SIC codes. We have taken a different approach because businesses in different two-digit SIC codes can actually be related. The case of Maxus Energy mentioned previously is one example where the two-digit approach leads to a misleading conclusion about relatedness. Our approach has been to use a subjective assessment of whether two businesses are related. Because we focus much of our analysis on the unrelated spin-offs, it is natural to ask whether our classification scheme is appropriate. Are our results driven by our use of this scheme rather than the traditional two-digit method?

In an effort to address this question, we classify firms based on the two-digit method. The spin-off is considered to be related to the parent if, in year 0, the spin-off has a segment with the same two-digit SIC code as one of the parent's segments. This approach classifies 70 spin-offs as related and 90 spin-offs as unrelated. Of the 90 unrelated spin-offs according to the two-digit method, 67 (74 percent) are also classified as unrelated using our method. Of the 70 related spin-offs according to the two-digit method, 47 (67 percent) are classified as related according to our method.

As an example of where the two methods disagree, consider the spin-off of the Promus Companies, which created two independent firms, Promus Hotel Corp., which operates hotels, and Harrah's Entertainment, which operates casino hotels. The two-digit method classifies them as unrelated because they are in different two-digit SIC codes, while we classify them as related on the grounds that they both operate hotels (although admittedly, different types of hotels). On the flip side, we classify Earthgrains (which makes bread) as unrelated to its parent, Anheuser-Busch (which makes beer), while the two-digit method considers them related. It is possible to argue that these businesses are related in that they both supply retail grocers and use grain as an input, but we classify them as unrelated in our subjective scheme because the production technology and the final products are quite different. The important point that these examples illustrate is that all businesses are related in some way, but they differ in the extent to which they are related. Both classification schemes rely on implicit judgment about the extent to which businesses are related. Thus, it would be useful to know whether our results are driven by the judgments implicit in both schemes.

The second column of Table VIII reports the results for unrelated spin-offs based on the two-digit method. The results indicate that with this method, unrelated spin-offs also exhibit increased sensitivity of investment to industry Q after the spin-off. The third column shows the results for the 67 firms where the two methods agree in their classification of unrelated firms. The coefficient estimates are larger in absolute value and in significance than in the second column. We cannot say which classification method is better—both clearly have flaws—but we can say that our results are not driven by our particular classification scheme.

C. Are Spin-offs Changing on Other Dimensions as Well?

Another method of addressing the measurement error issue is to ask whether the spin-off firm becomes more like the median industry firm on other dimensions besides capital expenditures. If measurement error in the pre-spin-

Table IX

The Sensitivity of Spin-off Operating Profit Ratio to Industry Operating Profit Ratio before and after the Spin-off: Related and Unrelated Spin-offs

This table reports the results of regression equation (3) in which the dependent variable is now spin-off Operating profit ratio: (earnings before interest, taxes, and depreciation)/assets. Observations where spin-off operating profit ratio is less than the sample's 1st percentile or greater than the sample's 99th percentile are excluded. Industry operating profit ratio is the asset-weighted industry median for the industries in which the spin-off operates. Before takes the value 1 for years −3, −2, and −1, and takes the value 0 for years +1, +2, and +3. Year 0, the year of the spin-off, is excluded from the regression. To maintain comparability with the capital expenditure regressions, observations are included only when there is valid capital expenditure data. Unrelated spin-offs are identified based on the subjective assessment of the authors. The regression includes year dummies and firm fixed effects. The numbers in parentheses below the coefficient estimates are p-values.

	Full Sample	Unrelated	Related
Industry operating profit ratio	0.828***	0.929**	0.641*
	(0.004)	(0.033)	(0.078)
Before * industry operating profit ratio	−0.067	−0.274	0.206
	(0.766)	(0.472)	(0.434)
Before	−.006	0.035	−0.027
	(0.885)	(0.623)	(0.632)
No. of firms	160	90	70
No. of observations	737	420	317
R^2	0.065	0.117	0.075

***Significance at the 1 percent level; **significance at the 5 percent level; *significance at the 10 percent level.

off period is the source of our investment results, then we would expect this measurement error effect to carry over to other variables as well. Conversely, if measurement error is not significantly greater in the pre-spin-off period, then other characteristics of the spin-off firm will likely show the same relationship to median industry values in both the pre- and post-spin-off periods. Thus, we analyze changes in the sensitivity of spin-off operating profit to median industry operating profit before and after the spin-off.

Table IX presents regression results using equation (3), with the exception that investment has been replaced with operating profit for both the spin-off and the industry. To maintain comparability with the investment regressions, observations are included only if there is valid data for the investment regressions, that is, the observation was included in the prior investment analyses. In addition, observations where spin-off operating profit is greater than the 99th percentile for the sample or less than the 1st percentile are excluded to limit the impact of some large outliers.

For the full sample, we see that spin-off operating profit is positively related to industry operating profit for both the pre- and post-spin-off period. The coefficient for industry operating profit is 0.828 with a p-value of 0.004, while the coefficient of the interaction term is -0.067 with a statistically insignificant p-value of 0.766. These findings do not support the notion that there is greater measurement error prior to the spin-off than after the spin-off.

V. Conclusion

This paper documents the change in investment behavior that occurs after a spin-off. We find that spin-off investment moves more closely in line with median industry Tobin's Q and median industry investment after the spin-off. This effect is particularly pronounced in spin-offs of unrelated divisions and in spin-offs in which the stock market reacts favorably to the announcement of the spin-off. We also find that spin-offs of unrelated firms and those with high announcement-period returns tend to cut industry-adjusted investment after the spin-off in low Q industries and increase industry-adjusted investment in high Q industries.

The results indicate that one of the effects of spin-offs—or even one of the reasons they are undertaken in the first place—is to increase the efficiency of capital allocation. One cannot argue, however, that our findings indicate that internal capital markets are inefficient on average; the fact that a firm chooses to spin off a division in the first place is likely to bias our sample to firms with inefficient internal capital markets.

There are a number of questions left unanswered by our paper. First, why are spin-offs associated with an increased sensitivity of investment to investment opportunities? Is it because there is less cross-subsidization across business units? Is it because managers have higher-powered incentives in independent firms? Or is it because managers get more precise signals from the stock market about performance and investment opportunities? Second, why do some internal capital markets function poorly in some settings—as they presumably did in our sample of firms that chose to spin off divisions—but work well in other settings? Answering these questions is important, but will remain a challenge for future research.

REFERENCES

Alchian, Armen, 1969, Corporate management and property rights, in Henry Manne, ed.: *Economic Policy and the Regulation of Corporate Securities* (American Enterprise Institute, Washington, DC).

Berger, Philip G., and Eli Ofek, 1995, Diversification's effect on firm value, *Journal of Financial Economics* 37, 39–65.

Coase, Ronald, 1937, The nature of the firm, *Economica* 4, 386–405.

Comment, Robert, and Gregg Jarrell, 1995, Corporate focus and stock returns, *Journal of Financial Economics* 37, 67–87.

Cusatis, Patrick, James A. Miles, and J. Randall Woolridge, 1993, Value creation through spin-offs: The stock market evidence, *Journal of Financial Economics* 33, 293–311.

Daley, Lane, Vikas Mehrotra, and Ranjini Sivakumar, 1997, Corporate focus and value creation: Evidence from spin-offs, *Journal of Financial Economics* 45, 257–281.

Denis, David J., and Bharathram Thothadri, 1999, Internal capital markets, growth opportunities, and the valuation effects of corporate diversification, Working paper, Purdue University.

Desai, H., and P. C. Jain, 1999, Firm performance and focus: Long-run stock market performance following spin-offs, *Journal of Financial Economics* 54, 75–101.

Dittmar, Amy, 2002, Capital structure in corporate spin-offs, *Journal of Business*, forthcoming.

Dittmar, Amy, and Anil Shivdasani, 2001, Divestitures and divisional investment policies, Working paper, Indiana University.

Fazzari, Stephen M., R. Glenn Hubbard, and Bruce C. Petersen, 1988, Financing constraints and corporate investment, *Brookings Papers* 19, 141–195.

Gertner, Robert, David Scharfstein, and Jeremy Stein, 1994, Internal versus external capital markets, *Quarterly Journal of Economics* 109, 1211–1230.

Gilson, Stuart, Paul Healy, Christopher Noe, and Krishna Palepu, 2001, Analyst specialization and conglomerate stock break-ups, *Journal of Accounting Research* 39, 565–582.

Hite, Gailen L., and James E. Owers, 1983, Security price reactions around corporate spin-off announcements, *Journal of Financial Economics* 12, 409–436.

Krishnaswami, Sudha, and Venkat Subramanian, 1999, Information asymmetry, valuation, and the corporate spin-off decision, *Journal of Financial Economics* 53, 73–112.

Lamont, Owen, 1997, Cash flow and investment: Evidence from internal capital markets, *Journal of Finance* 52, 83–109.

Lang, Larry, and René Stulz, 1994, Tobin's *Q*, corporate diversification and firm performance, *Journal of Political Economy* 102, 1248–1280.

MacKie-Mason, Jeffrey, 1990, Do firms care who provides their financing? in R. Glenn Hubbard, ed.: *Asymmetric Information, Corporate Finance, and Investment* (University of Chicago: Chicago, IL).

Matsusaka, John G., and Vikram Nanda, 1997, Internal capital markets and corporate refocusing, *Journal of Financial Intermediation* 11, 176–211.

Meyer, Margaret, Paul Milgrom, and John Roberts, 1992, Organizational prospects, influence costs, and ownership changes, *Journal of Economics Management and Strategy* 1, 9–35.

Miles, James, and James Rosenfeld, 1983, An empirical analysis of the effects of spin-off announcements on shareholder wealth, *Journal of Finance* 38, 1597–1606.

Parrino, Robert, 1997, Spin-offs and wealth transfers: The Marriott case, *Journal of Financial Economics* 43, 241–274.

Perfect, Steven, and Kenneth Wiles, 1994, Alternative constructions of Tobin's *Q*: An empirical comparison, *Journal of Empirical Finance* 1, 313–341.

Powers, Eric, 2001, Spin-offs, sell-offs, and equity carve-outs: An analysis of divestiture method choice, Working paper, University of South Carolina.

Rajan, Raghuram, Henri Servaes, and Luigi Zingales, 2000, The cost of diversity: The diversification discount and inefficient investment, *Journal of Finance* 55, 35–80.

Rosenfeld, James J., 1984, Additional evidence on the relationship between divestiture announcements and shareholder wealth, *Journal of Finance* 39, 1437–1448.

Scharfstein, David, 1998, Evidence on the dark side of internal capital markets, NBER Working Paper No. 6352.

Scharfstein, David, and Jeremy Stein, 2000, The dark side of internal capital markets: Divisional rent-seeking and inefficient investment, *Journal of Finance* 55, 2537–2564.

Schipper, Katherine, and Abbie Smith, 1983, Effects of recontracting on shareholder wealth: The case of voluntary spin-offs, *Journal of Financial Economics* 12, 437–467.

Schlingemann, Frederick, René Stulz, and Ralph A. Walkling, 2001, Divestitures and the liquidity of the market for corporate assets, *Journal of Financial Economics* 64, 117–144.

Shin, Hyun Han, and René Stulz, 1998, Are internal capital markets efficient? *Quarterly Journal of Economics* 113, 531–552.

Slovin, Myron B., Marie E. Sushka, and Steven R. Ferraro, 1995, A comparison of the information conveyed by equity carve-outs, spin-offs, and asset sell-offs, *Journal of Financial Economics* 37, 89–104.

Smith, Clifford, and Ross Watts, 1992, The investment opportunity set and corporate financing, dividend and compensation policies, *Journal of Financial Economics* 32, 263–292.

Stein, Jeremy C., 1997, Internal capital markets and the competition for corporate resources, *Journal of Finance* 52, 111–133.

Williamson, Oliver, 1970, *Corporate control and business behavior*, (Prentice Hall, New Jersey).
Woo, Carolyn, Gary Willard, and Urs Daellenbach, 1992, Spin-off performance—A case of overstated expectations, *Strategic Management Journal* 13, 433–447.
Wulf, Julie, 1997, Influence and inefficiency in the internal capital market: Theory and evidence, Working paper, Columbia University.

[10]

Anand M. Vijh
University of Iowa

The Positive Announcement-Period Returns of Equity Carveouts: Asymmetric Information or Divestiture Gains?*

Using a sample of 336 carveouts that occurred in the period 1980–97, this article shows that the announcement-period returns increase with the ratio of subsidiary to nonsubsidiary assets. This finding contradicts the asymmetric information model proposed by Nanda. Additional tests relate the returns to the following divestiture-based explanations proposed by Schipper and Smith and others: refocusing of the parent and subsidiary operations, financing of new and existing projects, reducing the complexity of stock valuation, and enabling an eventual spinoff or third-party acquisition. The combined evidence rejects the asymmetric information hypothesis and supports the divestiture gains hypothesis of carveouts.

I. Introduction

Stock issues are important news. The market reaction depends on whether a firm sells more of its own stock in a seasoned equity offering (SEO) or the stock of a wholly owned subsidiary in an equity carveout. Masulis and Korwar (1986) examine a sample of 690 SEOs by industrial firms during the period 1963–80 and measure an average announcement-period excess return of –3.25%.[1] Schipper and Smith (1986) examine a sample of 76 carveouts during the period 1963–84 and measure an excess return of 1.83%.

The negative market reaction to SEOs is usually explained by asymmetric information. In the Myers and Majluf (1984) model, managers issue stock when they have private information that their stock is overvalued. Rational investors thus lower the stock price on the announcement of an SEO. The reasons behind

* I have benefited from comments of seminar participants at the American Finance Association meetings, Emory University, the Financial Association meetings, the University of Iowa, Oklahoma State University, Tulane University, and the University of Wisconsin. I wish to thank George Benston, Matt Billett, Arnie Cowan, Albert Madansky (the editor), and Vikram Nanda for specific comments. I also wish to thank Gonul Colak, Jennifer Westberg, and Sterling Yan for help with the data collection. I am especially obliged to a referee of the *Journal of Business* for many comments that improved this article substantially.

1. Asquith and Mullins (1986), Mikkelson and Partch (1986), and Schipper and Smith (1986) also document similar announcement-period returns for different samples of SEOs.

(*Journal of Business*, 2002, vol. 75, no. 1)

0021-9398/2002/7501-0006$10.00

the positive market reaction to carveouts are more varied. Schipper and Smith offer one set of reasons based on divestiture gains, such as obtaining separate financing for the subsidiary's investment projects, designing more efficient compensation contracts for the subsidiary's managers, and the creation of pure-play stocks. This list can be expanded to include other reasons associated with divestitures accomplished by spinoffs and asset sales, such as refocusing of the parent and subsidiary operations, and using proceeds to retire debt. Nanda (1991) offers another set of reasons based on asymmetric information. He argues that carveouts should be interpreted as not only issues of subsidiary stock but also as nonissues of parent stock. He extends the Myers and Majluf model to show that, on average, firms will issue subsidiary stock when the parent assets are undervalued and the subsidiary assets are overvalued. Rational investors raise the stock price as the positive information concerning larger parent assets dominates the negative information concerning smaller subsidiary assets.

Empirical verification of whether the positive announcement-period returns of carveouts reflect asymmetric information or divestiture gains, or both, has been scarce. Slovin, Sushka, and Ferraro (1995) provide some indirect evidence of asymmetric information. They show that rival firms in the subsidiary's industry earn an excess return of –1.1%, presumably because they share some of the subsidiary's overvaluation. However, their evidence of industry effects is based on a small sample of 36 carveouts, and it does not hold up for the rival firms in the parent's industry. Allen and McConnell (1998) provide some evidence of divestiture gains. They argue that the positive announcement-period returns arise when financially distressed firms use carveout proceeds to pay down on debt. Two other studies provide further evidence in support of divestiture gains, but they use issue-date returns or long-term returns after issue. Hand and Skantz (1997) find that the parent stocks earn negative returns during a 5-day period starting with the issue date, and they suggest that these returns reverse the earlier announcement-period returns. They question the rationality of positive announcement-period returns, but they also suggest that these may occur as investors confuse carveouts with spinoffs. Vijh (1999) examines 3-year returns of parent and subsidiary stocks after issue. He finds some evidence that the long-term returns are related to the number of business segments before carveout, which he uses as a proxy for divestiture gains arising from the refocusing of parent and subsidiary operations.

This article examines the announcement-period returns of a sample of 336 carveouts completed during the period 1980–97 to explore whether the returns are likely to be caused by asymmetric information or by the previously cited explanations of wealth gains from divestitures. I develop and test a prediction of Nanda's asymmetric information model, which states that the returns should decrease as the ratio of subsidiary assets to nonsubsidiary assets increases and should eventually become negative as this ratio exceeds one. My results are significant in the opposite direction of this prediction. On average, the announcement-period excess returns equal 4.92% when the precarveout subsidiary assets are greater than the nonsubsidiary assets, and they equal 1.19% when the subsidiary assets are smaller than the nonsubsidiary assets. The difference equals 3.73%, which is significant at the 1% level. The positive correlation between the excess returns and the ratio of subsidiary to nonsubsidiary assets is inconsistent with the asymmetric information hypothesis. It is simultaneously consistent with the divestiture gains hypothesis. Several studies of spinoffs and asset sales show that their wealth gains increase with such ratio.

Given the lack of support for the asymmetric information hypothesis, I turn my attention to a detailed analysis of the divestiture gains hypothesis. In particular, I subdivide the divestiture gains hypothesis into the following more specific components: the refocusing strategy hypothesis; the financing strategy hypothesis; the investment strategy hypothesis; the complexity, undervaluation, and pure play hypothesis; the managerial incentives hypothesis; and other miscellaneous hypotheses.

The refocusing strategy hypothesis is based on previous evidence by Comment and Jarrell (1995), John and Ofek (1995), Daley, Mehrotra, and Sivakumar (1997), and Desai and Jain (1999), who show that improving focus through spinoffs and asset sales leads to higher firm value. In support of this hypothesis, I first show that the parent and subsidiary firms in carveouts belong to different industry sectors just as often as in spinoffs and asset sales and that this difference is associated with higher announcement-period returns. Second, my methodology includes a detailed scrutiny of the *Wall Street Journal* reported motives for carveouts. I find that a majority of the *Wall Street Journal* reports mention lack of fit or focus and a desire to restructure operations by divesting subsidiary assets as a reason for carveout. Third, more than a third of all carveouts are followed by a complete spinoff or a third-party acquisition. The market reacts more positively to this last subset of cases on the announcement of carveout and on the subsequent announcement of spinoff or acquisition.

The financing strategy hypothesis and the investment strategy hypothesis both suggest that raising equity capital is a primary reason for carveouts. However, the financing strategy hypothesis suggests that capital is required to repay the parent's or the subsidiary's debt or for other financial contingencies, whereas the investment strategy hypothesis suggests that capital is required to finance the subsidiary's new projects or upgrade existing projects. The financing strategy hypothesis is based on Lang, Poulsen, and Stulz (1995) and Allen and McConnell (1998), who find that financially distressed parent firms raise capital by asset sales or equity carveouts and that the market reacts positively when this capital is used to repay debt. The investment strategy hypothesis is based on McConnell and Muscarella (1985), who find that the announcement of a capital expenditures plan results in a positive market reaction, and on Mikkelson and Partch (1986), who find that the announcement of an SEO leads to a less negative market reaction if proceeds are used to finance capital expenditures.

My evidence supports both the financing strategy and investment strategy hypotheses. The *Wall Street Journal* reports mention both reasons frequently, and cases where such reasons are mentioned result in more positive announcement-period returns. Stronger evidence in support of these two hypotheses is provided by the subsequent financing and investment activities of parent and subsidiary firms relative to industry- and size-matched control firms. The parent firms issue a greater number of SEOs than control firms over a 3-year period after carveout. This is surprising because parent firms receive nearly a third of the carveout proceeds represented by the sale of secondary shares and some part of the remaining proceeds that subsidiary firms use to repay debt owed to parent firms. One may imagine that, after raising substantial carveout capital, at least the subsidiary firms would stay away from equity markets for some time. However, the difference between the number of SEOs by subsidiary firms and control firms is even greater than between parent firms and control firms.

Investigation of capital expenditures provides more evidence on the financing strategy hypothesis and the investment strategy hypothesis. The parent firms have significantly lower capital expenditures than the control firms during the following 3 years, which suggests that the capital raised in carveouts and subsequent SEOs may be used to repay debt or meet other financial contingencies, as is suggested by the financing strategy hypothesis. The subsidiary firms have higher capital expenditures than the control firms, which, combined with the evidence on subsequent SEOs, supports the investment strategy hypothesis.

The evidence on subsequent SEOs by subsidiary firms reveals another similarity between spinoffs and carveouts. Aron (1991) has a model in which managers who receive stock-based compensation after spinoffs create firm value by exploiting investment opportunities. Her model predicts that new investment in spinoffs in the period immediately following spinoff will be higher than before spinoff and higher than in firms of similar characteristics that are not spun off. Krishnaswami and Subramaniam (1999) show that this prediction holds for spinoffs, and this article shows that it holds for carveouts. In many cases, it appears that spinoffs and carveouts differ only in whether financing is raised at birth or soon afterward.

The complexity, undervaluation, and pure play hypothesis is based on Schipper and Smith (1986), Vijh (1994), and Krishnaswami and Subramaniam (1999). The separation of unlike parent and subsidiary assets into independently traded units helps markets in understanding their combined value. It also attracts investors interested in only the subsidiary assets. Both factors increase the combined firm value. I find that many *Wall Street Journal* reports mention these reasons for carveouts and that such reasons are associated with higher than average announcement-period returns. The managerial incentives hypothesis is again based on the theoretical model by Aron (1991), who argues that improved managerial incentives created by stock-based compensation after spinoff lead to higher firm value. Surprisingly, I find that this motive is rarely mentioned in the *Wall Street Journal* reports. But that should not undermine its importance in wealth gains from divestitures. A recent paper by Larraza-Kintana et al. (2000) shows that stock-based compensation is used in nearly all firms after initial public offerings (IPOs). Finally, similar to the case of spinoffs, I find that carveouts are occasionally motivated by miscellaneous reasons, such as takeover defense, tax reduction, and regulatory compliance.

The overall evidence of this article is inconsistent with the asymmetric information hypothesis and consistent with the divestiture gains hypothesis. The positive announcement-period returns of equity carveouts arise because the combined firm value is expected to increase as a result of improved focus, new financing, reduced complexity, and improved managerial incentives. The remainder of the article is organized as follows. In Section II, I discuss the different hypotheses and their specific predictions. In Section III, I describe the data and methods. In Sections IV and V, the empirical predictions are tested, and in Section VI, I conclude.

II. The Asymmetric Information Hypothesis versus the Divestiture Gains Hypothesis

A. The Asymmetric Information Hypothesis (and the Contrast with the Divestiture Gains Hypothesis)

Nanda (1991) presents an asymmetric information model to explain when all-equity firms will forgo a positive net present value (NPV) project and when they will finance it with an SEO or an equity carveout. His model is briefly described as follows. Before the announcement of equity issue, the parent firm consists of nonsubsidiary and subsidiary assets in place. The value of nonsubsidiary assets is known to be either V_H^1 or V_L^1 with equal probability. The value of subsidiary assets is similarly known to be either V_H^2 or V_L^2 with equal probability. There is no correlation between the nonsubsidiary and subsidiary asset values. Thus, states HH, HL, LH, and LL are equally likely. State HL denotes that the nonsubsidiary assets are of high value and the subsidiary assets are of low value, and so on. The manager knows the true state, but the market knows only the probabilities. Thus, the nonsubsidiary assets have a market value of $(V_H^1 + V_L^1)/2$, and the subsidiary assets have a market value of $(V_H^2 + V_L^2)/2$.

In addition to the assets in place, the firm has a project under consideration. The project has a positive NPV, which is common knowledge. For simplicity, Nanda assumes that $V_H^1/V_L^1 = V_H^2/V_L^2 = \mu$, which means that there is equivalent information asymmetry concerning the nonsubsidiary and subsidiary asset values. He denotes $V_H^1/V_H^2 = V_L^1/V_L^2 = \gamma$, where γ is the ratio of the market value of the nonsubsidiary assets to subsidiary assets in both the high and low value states.

The manager has the choice of three actions: O, do not issue equity and forgo the project; S, sell subsidiary stock (i.e., do an equity carveout); and C, sell stock in the consolidated firm (i.e., do an SEO). Debt issues are not allowed. The manager's actions are guided by whether the equity issue will increase the value of existing equity. The possible equilibria are denoted by WXYZ, where W, X, Y, and Z are the actions taken by firms of type HH, HL, LH, and LL. At first, since W, X, Y, and Z may each take the values *O*, *S*, and *C*, a total of $3^4 = 81$ different equilibria appear possible. However, by using other criteria, Nanda shows that only the equilibria CSCC, SSCS, OSCC, OSOC, and OSOS are possible. In the first two cases, all firm types finance the project. This occurs when the project has a large NPV relative to the value of the assets in place. In the last three cases, the firm types HH, and possibly LH, forgo the project. This occurs when the project has a small NPV relative to the value of the assets in place.

Table 1 shows the revision in market values after the announcement of a carveout. Consider equilibrium SSCS to appreciate the calculations. After the announcement, the market knows that the firm type is HH, HL, or LL with equal probability. Thus, the ex post value of nonsubsidiary assets equals $(2V_H^1 + V_L^1)/3$. This exceeds their ex ante value by $[(2V_H^1 + V_L^1)/3] - [(V_H^1 + V_L^1)/2] = (V_H^1 - V_L^1)/6$. Similarly, the ex post value of subsidiary assets equals $(V_H^2 + 2V_L^2)/3$, which exceeds their ex ante value by $[(V_H^2 + 2V_L^2)/3] - [(V_H^2 + V_L^2)/2] = -(V_H^2 - V_L^2)/6$. Using the size ratio γ, the total revision in firm value equals $[(V_H^1 - V_L^1)/6] - [(V_H^2 - V_L^2)/6] = [(\gamma - 1)(V_H^2 - V_L^2)]/6$. The revision in firm value under each of equilibria CSCC, OSCC, and OSOC is similarly shown to be $[(\gamma - 1)(V_H^2 - V_L^2)]/2$. Under equilibrium OSOS the revision in firm value equals $-(V_H^2 - V_L^2)/2$, which is negative and unrelated to γ, because the announcement leads to downward revision in the value of subsidiary assets but no revision in the value of nonsubsidiary assets.

Nanda assumes that the nonsubsidiary assets are of greater value than the subsidiary assets, that is, that $\gamma > 1$. He does not offer any justification for this assumption, except that "we believe this is in line with the Schipper and Smith (1986) sample" (Nanda 1991, p. 1720, n. 9). Under this assumption, four of the five equilibria imply a positive return following the announcement of a carveout. In the fifth case, the return is negative. Nanda argues that this case is infrequent, occurring for very low NPV projects, as both firm types HH and LH forgo the project. Overall, announcing a carveout reveals negative information about the subsidiary assets and zero or positive information about the nonsubsidiary assets. If the nonsubsidiary assets are greater, then the net market reaction will be positive.

Within the range of γ values considered by Nanda, table 1 shows that the market reaction should be decreasing with decreasing γ. When $\gamma = 1$, the market reaction should equal zero. When $\gamma < 1$, the market reaction should be negative and decreasing, as the negative information concerning the sub-

TABLE 1 **Carveout Announcement-Period Revision in Market Value Predicted by the Asymmetric Information Model of Nanda (1991)**

	Nonsubsidiary Assets in Place		Subsidiary Assets in Place		
Equilibrium	Ex Post Market Value*	Revision in Market Value†	Ex Post Market Value‡	Revision in Market Value§	Total Firm Revision in Market Value
CSCC	V_H^1	$(V_H^1 - V_L^1)/2$	V_L^2	$-(V_H^2 - V_L^2)/2$	$(\gamma - 1)(V_H^2 - V_L^2)/2$
SSCS	$(2V_H^1 + V_L^1)/3$	$(V_H^1 - V_L^1)/6$	$(V_H^2 + 2V_L^2)/3$	$-(V_H^2 - V_L^2)/6$	$(\gamma - 1)(V_H^2 - V_L^2)/6$
OSCC	V_H^1	$(V_H^1 - V_L^1)/2$	V_L^2	$-(V_H^2 - V_L^2)/2$	$(\gamma - 1)(V_H^2 - V_L^2)/2$
OSOC	V_H^1	$(V_H^1 - V_L^1)/2$	V_L^2	$-(V_H^2 - V_L^2)/2$	$(\gamma - 1)(V_H^2 - V_L^2)/2$
OSOS	$(V_H^1 + V_L^1)/2$	0	V_L^2	$-(V_H^2 - V_L^2)/2$	$-(V_H^2 - V_L^2)/2$

NOTE.—The table summarizes the announcement-period returns predicted by Nanda's model. His model is described in Sec. II.A. In each equilibrium, the table shows the revision in the market value of the nonsubsidiary and subsidiary assets, and the total revision in the combined firm value following the announcement of carveout.

* The ex post market value is obtained by averaging the ex post value of nonsubsidiary assets in each of the states in which carveout occurs. This value equals V_H^1 in states HH and HL and V_L^1 in states LH and LL.

† The revision in market value is obtained by subtracting the ex ante market value of the nonsubsidiary assets, which equals $(V_H^1 + V_L^1)/2$.

‡ The ex post market value is obtained by averaging the ex post value of subsidiary assets in each of the states in which carveout occurs. This value equals V_H^2 in states HH and LH, and V_L^2 in states HL and LL.

§ The revision in market value is obtained by subtracting the ex ante market value of the subsidiary assets, which equals $(V_H^2 + V_L^2)/2$.

sidiary assets dominates the positive information concerning the nonsubsidiary assets.

The specific predictions of the divestiture gains hypothesis are described in the following section. But here I present a prediction common to all forms of the divestiture gains hypothesis that is the opposite of the main prediction of the asymmetric information hypothesis. It is reasonable to argue that the benefits of increased focus, new financing and investment opportunities, improved managerial incentives, and reduced complexity should increase with increasing size of the subsidiary assets relative to the combined assets. Hite and Owers (1983) and Krishnaswami and Subramaniam (1999) show that the market reaction to spinoffs is increasing with this relative size variable. Klein (1986) and Lang, Poulsen, and Stulz (1995) show that the market reaction to asset sales is also increasing with this variable. In the case of spinoffs, where no new shares are issued, this relative size variable equals $1/(1 + \gamma)$. It increases monotonically with decreasing value of γ, which shows the contrast with the asymmetric information hypothesis.

B. The Divestiture Gains Hypothesis

The *Oxford English Dictionary* defines a divestiture as the deprivation of a possession or a right. A carveout results in the partial loss of ownership and control of a subsidiary that was previously wholly owned and controlled by the parent. Strictly speaking, a carveout is only a partial divestiture whereas a spinoff or an asset sale are complete divestitures. In practical terms, all three forms of divestiture involve restructuring of operations and management. Carveouts invariably involve financing, asset sales usually involve financing (when the sale is for cash), but spinoffs do not involve financing. New investments often follow in each case, but this is not a requirement in any case. Below, I discuss several hypotheses related to the operations, management, ownership, financing, and investment aspects of carveouts.

The refocusing strategy hypothesis. An equity carveout replaces one legal firm with two firms of distinct boundaries. It is remarkable that the increase in carveout activity has coincided with a trend toward focus and specialization in recent years. Comment and Jarrell (1995) argue that the economies of scope have been reversed during the 1980s (and 1990s). They show that the average number of business segments and different standard industrial classification (SIC) codes used by firms included in the Compustat segment file decreased substantially from 1978 to 1989. They also show that focus-increasing firms earned superior long-term returns during this period, which may be partly the undoing of a 13%–15% diversification discount documented by Berger and Ofek (1995). The two separated firms after carveout are subject to the scrutiny of capital markets, which eliminates inefficient cross-subsidies and other wealth-decreasing activities invisible to shareholders of the combined firm. It also reduces any negative synergy between parent and subsidiary firms arising from the incompatibility of their businesses.

Previous research has shown the benefits of improving focus by spinoffs and asset sales. John and Ofek (1995) show that, in three-fourths of asset sales, the sold division has a different SIC code from the remaining divisions of the seller. They show that the announcement-period returns of asset sales are higher when the SIC code of the sold division is different from that of the seller and still higher when it is the same as that of the buyer. Daley, Mehrotra, and Sivakumar (1997) show that the announcement-period returns and the post-issue operating performance of spinoffs are higher when the parent and subsidiary have different SIC codes. Desai and Jain (1999) show that their long-term returns are also higher.

Vijh (1999) shows that the long-term returns of carveouts increase with the number of distinct business segments of the precarveout firm, which he uses as a proxy for the benefits of increased focus. I argue that some of the positive announcement-period returns of carveouts should also be attributed to the increased focus and the synergy gains from the separation of distinct businesses. The refocusing strategy hypothesis thus predicts the following. First, a careful analysis of the *Wall Street Journal* reports on carveouts will show frequent mention of refocusing and divestiture type of reasons given by the firm managers, the analysts, and the reporters. Second, firms proposing carveouts will be more diversified than the average firm. Third, the announcement-period returns will be higher in cases where the carveout leads to a greater increase in firm focus. Fourth, many carveouts will be followed by spinoffs or asset sales. This prediction follows from the observation that carveouts are only partial divestitures, as the parent firms often maintain a controlling stake in the subsidiary firms. A complete divestiture would require a spinoff or an asset sale. Fifth, if the market can rationally anticipate the second events, then the announcement-period returns will also be higher in cases where the carveout is followed by a spinoff or an asset sale.

The financing strategy hypothesis and the investment strategy hypothesis. Financing is an integral part of carveouts. This dimension distinguishes carveouts from spinoffs, which involve no immediate financing, and it relates them to asset sales, which are usually for cash and do involve immediate financing. The proceeds of carveout may belong to the subsidiary or the parent, depending on whether the issue involves primary or secondary shares, and it may be used to repay debt, meet other contingencies, or pay for the subsidiary's investment projects. Based on these considerations, I propose two separate hypotheses. The first hypothesis is termed the financing strategy hypothesis and is related to Lang, Poulsen, and Stulz (1995) and Allen and McConnell (1998). These studies view asset sales and carveouts as beneficial when the proceeds are used to repay debt. Allen and McConnell propose a managerial discretion hypothesis in which managers derive tangible or intangible compensation based on the size of assets under their control. They document that the carveout announcement-period returns are higher in cases where the proceeds are used to repay debt and are no longer subject to managerial discretion. They emphasize that their evidence does not explain why carveouts create value (i.e., why the average return is positive), only that due to agency costs the returns are higher if cash is removed from the firm. The financing strategy hypothesis proposed in this study is a little broader than Allen and McConnell's hypothesis. It includes the use of proceeds to repay debt and to meet other financial contingencies, such as build working capital or support cash flow needs of existing operations.

The second hypothesis is termed the investment strategy hypothesis. It emphasizes positive use of proceeds by retaining funds within the subsidiary firm to finance new projects or upgrade existing projects. Schipper and Smith (1986) suggest that this is an important motive for carveouts. Carveout announcements are often simultaneous announcements of the subsidiary's investment opportunities. Many studies have shown that the market reacts positively to the second set of announcements. For example, McConnell and Muscarella (1985) show that announcements of increases in planned capital expenditures are associated with significantly positive excess returns. Mikkelson and Partch (1986) show that the otherwise very negative excess returns of SEOs are only slightly negative and insignificantly different from zero when the stated purpose of the offering is to finance capital expenditures.

Both the financing strategy and the investment strategy hypotheses predict that the *Wall Street Journal* reports will mention the corresponding use of proceeds and that such reports will lead to more positive announcement-period returns. The financing strategy hypothesis also predicts that the issue will involve secondary shares and that such issue will result in a more positive reaction. In comparison, the investment strategy hypothesis predicts that the issue will involve primary shares and that such issue will result in a more positive reaction. The last prediction of the financing strategy and investment strategy hypotheses is as follows. The financing strategy hypothesis predicts that the financially constrained parent firms will raise more equity during the following years but that this equity may not result in greater capital expenditures. In comparison, the investment strategy hypothesis predicts that subsidiary firms will raise more equity and that this equity will result in greater capital expenditures.

The complexity, undervaluation, and pure play hypothesis. Schipper and Smith (1986) suggest that the initiation of public trading of subsidiary stock is an important reason for the market's enthusiasm. They argue that a carveout precommits the subsidiary to supply audited periodic financial reports, and they cite examples in which a resulting improvement in investor understanding of the subsidiary business is a major reason for carveout. In the case of spinoffs, Krishnaswami and Subramaniam (1999) use analyst forecast data to show that the earnings forecasts of the combined firm are less accurate than the earnings forecasts of the separated firms. Vijh (1994) shows that there are substantial ex date price and volume effects for spinoffs, which he relates to different investor clienteles for the two separated stocks. The attractiveness of pure-play stocks to such investors can also lead to positive announcement-period returns for carveouts, although the effect should be smaller (since only the subsidiary stock after carveout can be considered to be a pure-play stock).

The complexity, undervaluation, and pure play hypothesis predicts that the *Wall Street Journal* reports will mention this reason and that such reports will be associated with higher announcement-period returns. A second prediction follows from the observation that the complexity, undervaluation, and pure play effects all increase with the dissimilarity of parent and subsidiary assets. Empirically, this prediction coincides with a prediction of the refocusing strategy hypothesis, which says that the announcement-period returns will be higher when the parent and subsidiary firms belong to different industries.

The managerial incentives hypothesis and other miscellaneous hypotheses. Schipper and Smith (1986) argue that carveouts are associated with a restructuring of managers' responsibilities and incentives. Aron (1991) builds a model in which even the possibility of a future spinoff can create strong incentives for divisional managers. She argues that, after spinoff, the stock value of the subsidiary firm is a cleaner measure of managerial productivity than the stock value of the parent firm when the subsidiary was one of its many divisions. A stock-based compensation plan thus motivates the managers to work harder and exploit valuable investment opportunities. Since the value creation comes from exploiting investment opportunities, an important prediction of Aron's model is identical to a prediction of the investment strategy hypothesis. Both hypotheses predict that new financing and investment in subsidiary firms will be higher than in firms of similar characteristics that were not recently spun off. Finally, following Hite and Owers (1983) and Schipper and Smith (1983), I will also examine whether carveouts facilitate mergers, reduce taxes, or help with regulatory compliance.

C. Summary of Different Hypotheses and Possible Overlap

Table 2 summarizes the testable implications of the different hypotheses. Note that the hypotheses are neither independent nor mutually exclusive. The refocusing strategy and complexity, undervaluation, and pure play hypotheses both predict higher returns when the parent and subsidiary firms are in different industries; the investment strategy and managerial incentives hypotheses both predict that the subsidiary capital expenditures will be higher than matching firms; and the asymmetric information and complexity, undervaluation, and pure play hypotheses both assume that investors have incomplete information. Yet, every hypothesis has a distinct motivation and at least one distinct testable implication.

III. The Data and Methods

A. The Sample of Carveouts

The sample of carveouts used in this study starts with the sample used in Vijh (1999). My 1999 sample includes 300 cases during the period 1980–95

TABLE 2 Summary of the Asymmetric Information and Divestiture Gains Hypotheses of Carveouts

Hypothesis	Motivation	Testable implications
Asymmetric information	Carveouts occur when subsidiary assets are overvalued and nonsubsidiary assets are undervalued. Nonsubsidiary assets are usually bigger, so more positive information is released.	1. Excess returns will decrease with decreasing γ, the ratio of nonsubsidiary to subsidiary assets values.* 2. Excess returns will be positive when $\gamma > 1$, zero when $\gamma = 0$, and negative when $\gamma < 1$. 3. *Wall Street Journal* reports will mention asymmetric information types of reasons. Excess returns will be higher in such cases.
Divestiture gains:		
Refocusing strategy	Carveouts are a form of restructuring. Improved focus from separation of parent and subsidiary business increases the combined firm value.	1. *Wall Street Journal* reports will mention refocusing and divestiture types of reasons. Excess returns will be higher in such cases. 2. Parent firms before carveout will be more diversified than average. 3. Excess returns will be higher when parent and subsidiary are in different industries.† 4. Many carveouts will be followed by complete divestiture (spinoff or asset sale). 5. Excess returns will be higher when there is a subsequent complete divestiture.
Financing strategy	Carveouts are a financing mechanism. Proceeds are used to repay debt and meet other financial contingencies of parent (and possibly subsidiary).	1. *Wall Street Journal* reports will mention financing strategy types of reasons. Excess returns will be higher in such cases. 2. Issue will involve secondary shares. Excess returns will be higher for such issues.‡ 3. Parents will raise additional capital from SEOs during surrounding years. But parent capital expenditures will not be higher than matching firms.

Investment strategy	Carveouts are a financing mechanism. Proceeds are used to finance new projects or upgrade existing operations of subsidiary.	1. *Wall Street Journal* reports will mention investment strategy types of reasons. Excess returns will be higher in such cases. 2. Issue will involve primary shares. Excess returns will be higher for such issues.‡ 3. Subsidiaries will raise additional capital from SEOs during surrounding years. Subsidiary capital expenditures will be higher than matching firms.§
Complexity, undervaluation, and pure play	Carveouts result in greater information for a subsidiary that starts trading separately. Investors are attracted to such pure plays.	1. *Wall Street Journal* reports will mention complexity, undervaluation, and pure play types of reasons. Excess returns will be higher in such cases. 2. Excess returns will be higher when parent and subsidiary are in different industries.†
Managerial incentives	Carveouts enable firms to offer stock-based compensation to subsidiary's managers. This motivates them to work harder and exploit investment opportunities.	1. *Wall Street Journal* reports will mention managerial incentives types of reasons. Excess returns will be higher in such cases. 2. Subsidiary capital expenditures will be higher than matching firms.§

* "Excess return" is an abbreviation for carveout announcement-period excess return.
† Common to the refocusing strategy hypothesis and the complexity, undervaluation, and pure play hypothesis.
‡ Contrasts the financing strategy hypothesis and the investment strategy hypothesis.
§ Common to the investment strategy hypothesis and the managerial incentives hypothesis.

for which I could find information on both the parent and the subsidiary firms on the Center for Research in Security Prices (CRSP) tapes.[2] I here expand this sample to include carveouts completed during 1996 and 1997 from the Securities Data Company (SDC) database. I exclude cases where an announcement date cannot be found by using the procedure described below. I also exclude utility issues and penny stocks (i.e., cases where the parent stock price is less than one dollar on the announcement date). The net result is a sample of 336 carveouts completed during the period 1980-97.

I searched the *Wall Street Journal Index* during the period 1980–94 and its electronic *ProQuest* version during the period 1995–97 for the first publication date of a carveout announcement during the 2 years before the issue date. In cases when there is no *Wall Street Journal* report, I use the Securities and Exchange Commission (SEC) filing date in place of the publication date. A total of 311 carveouts in my sample are included in the SDC database. I can find the filing date in 300 of these 311 cases. In the remaining 25 cases that I collected from the *Mergers and Acquisitions* magazine, I can find the filing date in 24 cases by searching the Lexis/Nexis and the Compact Disclosure databases. Overall, I have the publication date in 185 cases, the filing date in 324 cases, both dates in 173 cases, and at least one date in all 336 cases.

B. Sample Distribution and Summary Statistics

Panel A of table 3 gives the sample distribution by the calendar year of announcement during the period 1980–97. The 336 carveouts issued new equity in the amount of $44.9 billion in the domestic market. The sample is more concentrated during the 1990s, with 204 of the 336 announcements occurring during the period 1990–97. The average offering value has also gone up, from $84 million during the period 1980–89 to $165 million during the period 1990–97.

Panel B of table 3 presents the summary statistics. Given the extreme skewness in variables, the medians and the first and third quartiles of distribution are reported. The median parent firm is valued at $720 million, and the median subsidiary firm is valued at $166 million. The median offering is worth 7.9% of the parent value and 27.5% of the subsidiary value on the listing date. The median dilution ratio, defined by the new primary shares offered to the total shares outstanding after issue, equals 0.203. The median book-to-market value equals 0.538 for parent firms and 0.431 for subsidiary firms. The subsidiary firms are more likely to be growth firms. Finally, in the

2. I (1999) collected my sample from two sources. First, I purchased a list of carveouts that occurred in the period 1980–95 from the Securities Data Company (SDC). Second, I collected from the *Mergers and Acquisitions* magazine a few carveouts for the period 1991–95 that were not included in the SDC data. My 1999 sample includes 328 cases for which I could find information on only the subsidiary firms. These cases are excluded in this study of the announcement-date returns of parent stocks.

TABLE 3 Sample Distribution over Time and Descriptive Statistics for Carveout Announcements, 1980–97

A. The Sample Distribution by the Year of Announcement

Year	Number of Announcements	Average Offering Value	Total Offering Value
1980	1	11	11
1981	11	13	143
1982	6	16	96
1983	15	47	705
1984	5	56	280
1985	20	69	1,380
1986	33	99	3,267
1987	19	128	2,432
1988	10	188	1,880
1989	12	78	936
1990	8	185	1,480
1991	28	63	1,764
1992	35	175	6,125
1993	40	173	6,920
1994	28	140	3,920
1995	26	196	5,096
1996	28	248	6,944
1997	11	137	1,507
1980–97	336	133	44,886

B. Other Descriptive Statistics

	Parent Firms			Subsidiary Firms		
Item Description	Q1	Median	Q3	Q1	Median	Q3
Firm value (million $)	138	720	2,793	58	166	457
Ratio of offering value to parent or subsidiary value	.035	.079	.186	.158	.275	.546
Dilution ratio				.116	.203	.357
Book-to-market value	.326	.538	.793	.254	.431	.646
Parent's fractional ownership of subsidiary after carveout	.500	.719	.828			

NOTE.—The sample of 336 carveout announcements during the period 1980–97 is obtained from the SDC and from the *Mergers and Acquisitions* magazine. It satisfies the following additional requirements: (1) The parent and subsidiary returns data are available on CRSP tapes, (2) the publication date can be found in the *Wall Street Journal Index* and/or the filing date can be found in the SDC, Lexis/Nexis, or Compact Disclosure databases (the earlier of the publication date and the filing date is chosen as the announcement date), (3) utility issues are excluded, (4) penny stocks (i.e., cases where the parent stock price is less than one dollar on announcement date) are excluded. The offering value is based on the offering price multiplied by the number of shares offered in the domestic market and is expressed in millions of dollars. The median offering value is 49. The firm value is measured by the market value of equity on the first trading day after carveout. The dilution ratio is measured by the number of primary shares offered, divided by the total outstanding shares after issue. The book-to-market value for parent firms is as of the last fiscal year ending before the carveout, and for subsidiary firms as of the first fiscal year ending after the carveout. Given the extreme skewness in all measures, only the first quartile, the median, and the third quartile values are reported.

median case, the parent firm continues to own 71.9% of the subsidiary's outstanding shares after carveout.

C. The Measurement of Announcement-Period Excess Returns

The measurement of announcement-period excess returns requires addressing questions related to the measure of excess returns and the length of the announcement period. I use two different measures of excess returns. First, for each day of the event period, I calculate the difference between the stock returns and the market returns. The mean market-adjusted excess returns and the *t*-statistics are calculated from the distribution of these return differences for all stocks included in the sample. Second, for each day of the event period, I also calculate the difference between the stock returns and the expected stock returns based on a market model. The mean market-model adjusted excess returns and the *t*-statistics are calculated from this latter distribution of return differences. The market returns used in both calculations are measured by the returns on the CRSP value-weighted portfolio of all stocks. To avoid biases arising from possible price runup before announcement, the market-model parameters are estimated over a 250-day period ending 250 days before the event period (which is shown to begin one day before the first announcement date).

Table 4 reports the market reaction on each day from AD − 5 to AD + 5, where AD denotes the first announcement date of the carveout and represents the last business day preceding the *Wall Street Journal* publication date in 79 cases, the SEC filing date in 202 cases, and a simultaneous day-before-publication date and filing date in 55 cases. Since the news may arrive before or after the end of trading on AD, one must include AD and AD + 1 in the announcement period. In addition, one should include AD − 1 if there is a significant market reaction on that day because of partial anticipation of news, leakage of news, or reporting delays.

Table 4 shows that the market reaction on each of AD − 1, AD, and AD + 1 is significantly positive, with *t*-statistics ranging between 2.30 and 3.56. I, therefore, measure the carveout announcement-period returns over a 3-day period spanning AD − 1 to AD + 1 in all subsequent tests. Table 4 also shows that, for all 336 carveouts, the 3-day mean market-adjusted excess return equals 1.94%, whereas the mean market-model adjusted excess return equals 1.93% (*t*-statistics = 5.68 and 5.64). The two alternate measures give nearly identical results. I use the market-adjusted excess returns in all subsequent calculations, but the inferences are unchanged by using the market-model excess returns. Finally, table 4 shows that parent stocks earn market-adjusted returns of 14.88% (*t*-statistic = 3.21) during a 250-day period ending on AD − 2, which could not have contributed to the undervaluation of parent stocks.

TABLE 4 Carveout Announcement-Period Excess Returns of Parent Stocks, 1980–97

Event Date	Market-Adjusted Excess Returns	Market-Model Adjusted Excess Returns
AD − 5	.03 (.24)	.05 (.31)
AD − 4	.14 (1.02)	.10 (.70)
AD − 3	.29 (1.72)*	.31 (1.83)*
AD − 2	.03 (.20)	.01 (.07)
AD − 1	.42 (2.30)**	.47 (2.48)**
AD	.67 (3.30)***	.63 (3.05)***
AD + 1	.87 (3.56)***	.84 (3.40)***
AD + 2	.19 (1.12)	.15 (.86)
AD + 3	.04 (.23)	.04 (.23)
AD + 4	−.19 (−1.29)	−.22 (−1.44)
AD + 5	−.23 (−1.58)	−.25 (−1.71)*
AD − 1 to AD + 1	1.94 (5.68)***	1.93 (5.64)***
AD − 251 to AD − 2	14.88 (3.21)***	
AD − 501 to AD − 252	4.59 (1.32)	

NOTE.—The sample of 336 carveout announcements during 1980–97 is obtained from the SDC and from the *Mergers and Acquisitions* magazine. It satisfies certain other restrictions discussed in table 3. AD denotes the first announcement date. It represents the day before the *Wall Street Journal* publication date in 79 cases, the SEC filing date in 202 cases, and a simultaneous day-before-publication date and filing date in 55 cases. Each day, the market-adjusted excess returns are computed by subtracting the value-weighted market returns from the stock returns, and the market-model adjusted excess returns are computed by using a market-model whose parameters are estimated over AD − 501 to AD − 252. The cumulative excess returns over the announcement period of AD − 1 to AD + 1 are obtained by the sum of daily returns for the market model, but not for the market-adjusted returns. In the latter case, the cumulative excess returns are obtained by subtracting the cumulative market returns from the cumulative stock returns over the 3-day period. The preannouncement excess returns, over AD − 501 to AD − 252 and AD − 251 to AD − 2, are similarly computed by subtracting the cumulative market returns from the cumulative stock returns. In six cases out of the total 336 cases, the returns data over AD − 501 to AD − 252 are inadequate to compute the market-model parameters. The reported market-model adjusted excess returns are calculated by averaging over the remaining observations. The *t*-statistics are reported in parentheses.

* Significant at the 10% level.
** Significant at the 5% level.
*** Significant at the 1% level.

IV. Cross-Sectional Tests of the Asymmetric Information Hypothesis

A. The Calculation of γ

The calculation of γ in Nanda's model requires the market values of the subsidiary and nonsubsidiary assets of a parent firm before the announcement date. The first problem concerns the definition of assets. Nanda assumes an all-equity firm, but real firms have varying amounts of debt. I, therefore, use two definitions of assets, one based on total assets, which gives the measure γ_1, and another based on net assets, which gives the measure γ_2.[3] The second problem concerns the inability to observe separate market values of subsidiary and nonsubsidiary assets on the announcement date. I overcome this limitation by using the market values on the listing date. This procedure will give the exact γ_1 and γ_2 if the unobserved changes in the market values of the subsidiary and nonsubsidiary assets between the announcement and the listing date are proportional. If the change in nonsubsidiary value is greater, perhaps because of the positive information conveyed by carveout, then the calculated values of γ_1 and γ_2 will be higher than the true values, but it will be so for all firms. The third problem arises because the market values of liabilities and preferred stock are almost never available. I overcome this problem by assuming that the market values of liabilities and preferred stock are equal to their book values.

I calculate the number of outstanding shares of the subsidiary before carveout (old shares) by subtracting the newly issued primary shares from all outstanding shares on the listing date. I have the data on total shares issued and the primary versus secondary shares issued in the large majority of carveouts that are included in the SDC database. However, in the 25 carveouts that originated from the *Mergers and Acquisitions* magazine, I do not have the data on primary versus secondary shares. In such cases, I assume that all new shares are primary shares. This approximation is justified by the observation that only primary shares are issued in 64% of all cases and that nearly 70% of the total issue volume consists of primary shares. I multiply the number of old shares of subsidiary firm by the stock price on the listing date to calculate the market value of the subsidiary stock in the combined firm. I then add the book value of assets other than common stock (Compustat item 6 minus item 60) in the year ending before carveout, if available, or the year of carveout, if not, to obtain the subsidiary total assets. I subtract the subsidiary total assets from the parent total assets calculated in a similar manner to obtain the nonsubsidiary total assets. The ratio of nonsubsidiary to subsidiary total assets equals γ_1. I obtain γ_2 by a similar procedure but by assuming that the debt, other liabilities, and preferred stock are absent.

The above procedure gives values of γ_1 and γ_2 in 279 and 292 cases,

3. "Total assets" refers to the bottom line on the assets or the liabilities side of the balance sheet. "Net assets" refers to the common stock; it equals the total assets minus debt, other liabilities, and preferred stock.

respectively. In the remaining cases, I cannot obtain a value because of data limitations, such as the Compustat data for the subsidiary or the parent firm is not available, the number of shares issued is not available, the calculated old shares of the subsidiary firm are negative, or the calculated market value of the nonsubsidiary assets is negative. To overcome the problem posed by the missing values of γ_1 and γ_2, I construct a third relative size measure. This measure equals the ratio of the market value of all outstanding equity of the subsidiary firm to the equity of the parent firm on the listing date. As a practical matter, the correlation between the decile ranks based on the three relative size measures is very high, ranging between 0.867 and 0.925. However, there is no obvious separation based on the third measure similar to $\gamma \leq 1$ versus $\gamma > 1$ for the first two measures.

B. The Relationship between the Excess Returns and γ

Panel A of table 5 shows the announcement-period returns across subsets formed by γ_1, the ratio of the market values of the nonsubsidiary and subsidiary total assets. The mean market-adjusted excess return equals 1.19% (*t*-statistic = 3.60) for the 232 cases for which the nonsubsidiary assets are greater than the subsidiary assets, or $\gamma_1 > 1$. The corresponding value equals 4.92% (*t*-statistic = 3.77) for the 47 cases for which the nonsubsidiary assets are smaller than the subsidiary assets, or $\gamma_1 \leq 1$. Recall that the asymmetric information model predicts a negative return for these cases. The difference between average returns for the $\gamma_1 > 1$ and the $\gamma_1 \leq 1$ cases equals 3.73% (*t*-statistic = 2.77), which is significant at the 1% level. The difference between median returns and the percent positive provides nonparametric confirmation of the results. Panel B of table 5 shows that the evidence with γ_2 is even stronger. All pieces of evidence in panels A and B are highly significant, but they are so in the opposite direction of the prediction of Nanda's asymmetric information model.

Panel C of table 5 shows the excess returns across 10 subsets formed by the decile ranks of $1/\gamma_1$, $1/\gamma_2$, and the third relative size measure. I prefer to use $1/\gamma$ instead of γ, as it is conventional in the divestitures literature to use the size of subsidiary assets divided by the total assets. The rank correlation between the decile ranks and the mean excess returns equals 0.84, 0.64, and 0.77 with the three measures (significant at the 1%, 10%, and 5% levels). These tests provide further evidence that the excess returns are increasing with the size of subsidiary assets relative to the nonsubsidiary assets.

My evidence is consistent with Allen and McConnell (1998), who find that the announcement-period returns are positively related to another relative size measure, formed by the ratio of the book value of assets of the carveout subsidiary to the book value of assets of the precarveout firm. However, they use this variable as one of the control variables in their paper and do not discuss its role in distinguishing between the asymmetric information and the divestiture gains hypothesis. I interpret my evidence as inconsistent with the

TABLE 5 **Tests of the Asymmetric Information Hypothesis Based on the Announcement-Period Excess Returns of Parent Stock Related to the Size of Subsidiary versus Nonsubsidiary Asset Value, 1980–97**

A. Announcement-Period Returns Related to Whether Subsidiary or Nonsubsidiary Total Assets Are Greater

			Market-Adjusted Excess Returns		
Description	Sample	Median $1/\gamma_1$	Mean (*t*-Statistic)	Median	Percent Positive
Nonsubsidiary total assets greater than subsidiary total assets ($\gamma_1 > 1$)	232	.127	1.19 (3.60)***	.70	57
Nonsubsidiary total assets smaller than subsidiary total assets ($\gamma_1 \leq 1$)	47	2.029	4.92 (3.77)***	2.35	72
Difference			3.73 (2.77)***	1.65	15
Ungrouped cases (γ_1 not available)	57		2.58 (2.61)***	.52	56
All cases	336	.184	1.94 (5.68)***	.95	59

B. Announcement-Period Returns Related to Whether Subsidiary or Nonsubsidiary Net Assets Are Greater

			Market-Adjusted Excess Returns		
Description	Sample	Median $1/\gamma_2$	Mean (*t*-Statistic)	Median	Percent Positive
Nonsubsidiary net assets greater than subsidiary net assets ($\gamma_2 > 1$)	230	.146	.63 (2.03)**	.51	53
Nonsubsidiary net assets smaller than subsidiary net assets ($\gamma_2 \leq 1$)	62	2.982	6.59 (6.63)***	5.45	84
Difference			5.96 (5.72)***	4.94	31
Ungrouped cases (γ_2 not available)	44		2.25 (1.93)*	.32	52
All cases	336	.234	1.94 (5.68)***	.95	59

C. Parent Announcement-Period Returns Related to Decile Ranks Formed by Different Relative Size Measures

	Ratio of Subsidiary Total Assets to Nonsubsidiary Total Assets ($1/\gamma_1$)			Ratio of Subsidiary Net Assets to Nonsubsidiary Net Assets $1/\gamma_2$)			Ratio of Subsidiary Stock Value to Parent Stock Value		
Decile Rank	Sample	Median $1/\gamma_1$	Excess Return[a]	Sample	Median $1/\gamma_2$	Excess Return[a]	Sample	Median Ratio	Excess Return[a]
Lowest	27	.012	.33	29	.011	.41	33	.022	.05
2	28	.033	1.10	29	.032	.47	34	.070	−.19
3	28	.063	−.17	29	.072	.37	33	.109	.83
4	28	.092	.71	30	.114	.22	34	.180	.83
5	28	.146	.40	29	.187	1.22	33	.254	1.58
6	28	.242	2.12	29	.300	1.76	34	.369	−.02
7	28	.359	1.83	30	.565	−.70	34	.543	.89
8	28	.664	1.79	29	.833	2.53	33	.763	5.86
9	28	1.100	3.85	29	1.807	5.32	34	1.087	5.49
Highest	28	2.607	6.13	29	6.403	7.54	33	1.724	4.30
Unranked	57		2.58	44		2.25	1		−1.08
Total	336	.184	1.94	336	.234	1.94	336	.313	1.94
Rank correlation			.84***			.64*			.77**

NOTE.—The sample of 336 carveout announcements during the period 1980–97 is obtained from the SDC and from the *Mergers and Acquisitions* magazine. It satisfies certain other restrictions discussed in table 3. The grouping procedure in panel A uses γ_1, the ratio of the market value of nonsubsidiary to subsidiary total assets. The grouping procedure in panel B uses γ_2, the ratio of the market value of nonsubsidiary to subsidiary net assets. The calculation of both γ_1 and γ_2 is discussed in Section IV.A. The three ranking procedures in panel C use $1/\gamma_1$, $1/\gamma_2$, and the ratio of subsidiary market value to parent market value on the listing date. Some observations in both panels cannot be grouped or ranked because of data limitations. Excess returns during the announcement period are calculated by subtracting the cumulative value-weighted market returns over AD − 1 to AD + 1 from the cumulative parent stock returns. The *t*-statistics in panels A and B are calculated by using the cross-sectional distribution of market-adjusted returns and are reported in parentheses. The Spearman rank correlations in panel C are calculated by the simple correlation between the decile ranking and the ranking of mean market-adjusted returns.

* Significant at the 10% level.

** Significant at the 5% level.

*** Significant at the 1% level.

[a] Mean market-adjusted excess return.

asymmetric information hypothesis, which suggests that a higher value of subsidiary assets relative to nonsubsidiary assets conveys more of the negative news and less of the positive news concerning asset values. My evidence is consistent with the divestiture gains hypothesis, which suggests that the divestiture of a larger subsidiary is associated with a higher increase in the market value of the parent firm.

V. Cross-Sectional Tests of the Divestiture Gains Hypothesis

A. Evidence Based on the Wall Street Journal *Reports*

I begin my investigation by analyzing statements made by the firm managers, the analysts, and the reporters to assess the motives behind carveouts. I examine every relevant statement from the first *Wall Street Journal* report that carries a story of the proposed carveout to calculate a zero-one (no-yes) code related to the components of the asymmetric information and divestiture gains hypotheses as shown in table 6. Multiple statements related to the same subset hypothesis for the same firm are counted only once.

The *Wall Street Journal* reports exist in 185 cases, but one or more relevant statements are available in 134 cases. These are the bigger carveouts, with an average offering value of $235 million, accounting for 70% of the total offering value of my sample. Their average announcement-period excess return equals 2.44% (t-statistic = 4.69), which is somewhat higher than the 1.62% (t-statistic = 3.57) return for the remaining carveouts. The difference equals 0.82% (t-statistic = 1.19) and can be attributed to statements related to divestiture gains that constitute the bulk of all statements.

Table 6 shows that only 11 out of 134 reports, or 8% of the sample, contain statements suggesting that the issuers may be offering overpriced subsidiary stock. Eight reports suggest that the subsidiary's industry may be overvalued, and three suggest that the subsidiary itself may be overvalued. Allstate Corporation, carved out by Sears, Roebuck & Company, provides an example of the former: "The offering comes at what seems an ideal time, given the soaring values of property and casualty stocks since last August's Hurricane Andrew" (*Wall Street Journal,* March 19, 1993). Sabre Group Holdings, Incorporated, carved out by AMR Corporation, provides an example of the latter: "But some airline industry experts aren't climbing on board. They note that AMR Chairman Robert Crandall is a take-no-prisoners competitor who rarely hands out gifts. 'Bob Crandall has always known when to sell off at the top,' says Ernest Arvai, a consultant to the reservation business based in Windham, N.H." (*Wall Street Journal,* October 7, 1996).

There is only one report suggesting that the nonsubsidiary assets may be overvalued. Surprisingly, there are 38 reports suggesting that the subsidiary, and possibly the parent, may be undervalued. These reports are not in the nature of overvalued-subsidiary–undervalued-parent, as suggested by Nanda's asymmetric information hypothesis, but rather in the nature of ignored and

TABLE 6 Analysis of the *Wall Street Journal* Reports for Evidence on the Asymmetric Information Hypothesis versus the Divestiture Gains Hypothesis, 1980–97

Description	Code	Number of Firms
Firms for which there is at least one statement suggesting asymmetric information:		12
Overvalued subsidiary assets	AA	11
Overvalued nonsubsidiary assets	AB	1
Undervalued subsidiary or nonsubsidiary assets (same as DU below)	DU	See below
Firms for which there is at least one statement suggesting divestiture gains:		133
Refocusing strategy hypothesis:		82
Direct statement of spinoff, split-off, asset sale, or other forms of divestiture	DS1	64
Lack of fit or focus, improve corporate strategy, restructure operations	DS2	42
Financing strategy hypothesis: repay debt, build working capital, finance existing operations, proceeds will be used for general corporate purposes	DF	76
Investment strategy hypothesis: invest in new projects or upgrade existing operations	DI	34
Complexity, undervaluation, and pure play hypothesis: unlock hidden values, create pure play stocks	DU	38
Managerial incentives hypothesis: creating incentive pay for managers, giving stock to managers	DM	3
Miscellaneous hypotheses:		16
Takeover defense	DT	8
Tax reduction	DX	4
Regulatory compliance	DR	6

NOTE.—This table includes 134 firms during the period 1980–97 for which the first *Wall Street Journal* report on carveout gives one or more reasons related to the asymmetric information hypothesis or the divestiture gains hypothesis. The table shows the frequency distribution of firms for which the firm managers, the analysts, or the reporters made one or more statements relating to the following broad categories.

unlocked values, as suggested by the complexity, undervaluation, and pure play hypothesis. Nabisco Holdings Corporation, carved out by RJR Nabisco Holdings Corporation, provides an example: "The planned Nabisco share offering is the culmination of a frustrating, two-year struggle by RJR management to increase the value of its tobacco-tainted stock by getting Wall Street to focus on the performance of red-hot Nabisco" (*Wall Street Journal*, October 31, 1994).

I find that 133 reports contain one or more statements related to the broad category of divestiture gains. Alternately, only one report does not mention such reasons. Statements related to the refocusing strategy hypothesis are the most numerous. There are 64 reports with statements of intended spinoff, split-off, asset sale, or other forms of divestiture, and 42 reports with statements that the carveout is part of a broader strategy to improve fit or focus, improve corporate strategy, or restructure operations. Lucent Technology, Incorporated, carved out by AT&T Corporation, provides an example of the former: "AT&T has set initial plans to spin off 15% to 20% of its equipment business in an initial public offering in March or April. The remaining 80% to 85% of the stock is expected to be distributed to AT&T shareholders as part of a planned three-way breakup of AT&T into separate, publicly held long-distance, computer, and equipment companies" (*Wall Street Journal,* February 6, 1996). ITT Educational Services, Incorporated, carved out by ITT Corporation, provides an example of the latter: "The announcement underscored ITT's recent efforts to revamp its collection of businesses" (*Wall Street Journal,* March 15, 1994).

Statements related to the financing strategy hypothesis are the second most numerous. Younkers, Incorporated, carved out by Equitable of Iowa Company, provides an example: "Equitable said it will use proceeds from the planned sale of its 4,703,555 Younkers shares for its life insurance and annuity business. Younkers itself plans to sell 1,466,445 new shares and use the proceeds to reduce debt" (*Wall Street Journal,* February 26, 1992).

Statements related to investment strategy are less numerous. Switchco, Incorporated, carved out by Graphics Scanning Corporation, provides an example: "Graphic Scanning, a data services communications concern, said the proceeds would help fund research and development and other operations. Switchco is starting up production of interactive packet switching products" (*Wall Street Journal,* August 11, 1981).

Surprisingly, there are only three statements related to the managerial incentives hypothesis. Also uncommon are statements related to takeover defense, tax reduction, and regulatory compliance. Still, reports containing these four types of reasons are twice as numerous as reports raising concerns about overvalued subsidiary or subsidiary's industry. The relative frequencies of different statements convey an unambiguous impression that carveouts are motivated by divestiture types of reasons.

B. Evidence on the Refocusing Strategy Hypothesis

Before carveout, the parent firms tend to be unfocused in their operations. The 184 firms for which I can find the Compustat segment data have an average of 2.94 business segments and 5.16 different SIC codes in the year before carveout. This compares with 1.53 business segments and 2.59 different SIC codes for all firms included in the segment file during the period 1983–97 (a total of 90,816 firm years). Desai and Jain (1999) document that even the 155 parent firms that spun off subsidiaries during the period 1975–91 have an average of 3.14 business segments. It is, therefore, not surprising that refocusing strategy types of reasons are more common than any other type of reasons in table 6.

Panel A of table 7 examines whether carveouts that mention refocusing strategy types of reasons earn higher announcement-period excess returns than the others. The difference equals 0.40% (t-statistic = 0.54), which is positive

TABLE 7 Tests of the Refocusing Strategy Hypothesis of Carveouts Based on the Announcement-Period Excess Returns of Parent Stocks, 1980–97

Description	Market-Adjusted Excess Returns			
	Number	Mean (t-Statistic)	Median	Percent Positive
Panel A. Based on the *Wall Street Journal* reports of refocusing strategy:				
Reports suggesting that carveout is a result of refocusing strategy, codes DS1 or DS2 from table 6	82	2.25 (3.65)***	1.30	65
No such reports	254	1.85 (4.53)***	.79	57
Difference of means—reports of refocusing strategy vs. no reports		.40 (.54)		
Panel B. Based on the relatedness of parent and subsidiary businesses:				
Different two-digit SIC code of parent and subsidiary	221	2.34 (5.27)***	1.14	63
Same two-digit SIC code of parent and subsidiary	100	.80 (1.44)	−.14	47
Incomplete SIC code data	15	3.84 (2.72)**	3.20	73
Difference of means—different vs. same two-digit SIC code		1.54 (2.17)**		
Panel C. Based on the second event after carveout:				
Spun off	43	3.86 (4.02)***	2.31	74
Acquired by third party	74	2.60 (3.39)***	.53	57
Acquired back by parent	28	2.01 (1.73)*	1.90	71
No second event	191	1.25 (2.83)***	.53	54
Difference of means—spun off vs. no second event		2.61 (2.47)**		
Acquired by third party vs. no second event		1.35 (1.53)		
Acquired back by parent vs. no second event		.76 (0.61)		

NOTE.—The sample of 336 carveout announcements during the period 1980–97 is obtained from the SDC and from the *Mergers and Acquisitions* magazine. It satisfies certain other restrictions discussed in table 3. Section II.B and table 6 provide a description of the refocusing strategy hypothesis. Excess returns during the announcement period are calculated by subtracting the cumulative value-weighted market returns over AD − 1 to AD + 1 from the cumulative parent stock returns. The t-statistics of sample means are calculated by using the cross-sectional distribution of market-adjusted returns and are reported in parentheses. The t-statistics in difference-of-means tests are calculated by assuming that the two samples may have unequal variances.

* Significant at the 10% level.

** Significant at the 5% level.

*** Significant at the 1% level.

but statistically insignificant.[4] Perhaps refocusing is such an essential part of carveouts that explicit statements do not result in a greater market reaction.

Panel B of table 7 examines whether the excess returns are higher when the refocusing benefits are greater, which occurs when the parent and subsidiary businesses are unrelated. I classify the parent and subsidiary businesses as unrelated if their two-digit SIC codes are different. The SIC codes are obtained from Compustat when available, and from CRSP otherwise.[5] Panel B shows that the SIC codes are different in 221 cases and the same in 100 cases. The excess returns average 2.34% in the first case and 0.80% in the second case (t-statistics = 5.27 and 1.44). The difference equals 1.54% (t-statistic = 2.17), which is significant at the 5% level.[6]

The final tests of the refocusing strategy hypothesis are based on the second event after carveout. Following Klein, Rosenfeld, and Beranek (1991), for every carveout, I examine whether there is a later complete spinoff, an acquisition by a third party, or an acquisition by the parent firm before the end of 1998. The first two actions result in a complete divestiture of the subsidiary firm. The third action can be interpreted as an admission that a spinoff or a third-party acquisition was intended but given up.

Panel C of table 7 shows that a second event occurs in 145 cases, or 43% of all cases. Third-party acquisitions are the most frequent second events (74 cases), followed by spinoffs (43 cases) and parent acquisitions (28 cases). If the market can rationally anticipate the second event on the announcement of the first event, then these cases should result in higher announcement-period excess returns. There is some evidence to support this conjecture. The carveouts that are followed by a complete spinoff earn announcement-period excess returns that are 2.61% higher than carveouts that are followed by no second event before the end of 1998 (t-statistic = 2.47). Corresponding differences for carveouts that are followed by a third-party acquisition are substantial but not statistically significant, while the differences for carveouts that are followed by a parent acquisition are small and insignificant.[7]

4. Relating announcement-period excess returns to the type of statements in the *Wall Street Journal* reports raises a potential concern. In 10 cases, the publication date is at least 2 days after the first announcement date, which is defined as the earlier of the day before publication date and the SEC filing date. The market may not have known the reasons given for these carveouts on the first announcement date. To correct for this problem, I repeated my tests after adding the 3-day excess returns around the publication date to the original announcement-period excess returns in these 10 cases. The results were nearly unchanged. I prefer to report results in this article with the original returns, because the cross-sectional variables other than the statement type are known on the first announcement date.

5. Kahle and Walkling (1996) show that the SIC codes from Compustat are generally more accurate.

6. As in my 1999 research, I also examined whether the announcement-period excess returns are higher when the precarveout firm has four or more segments. The results were insignificant and are not reported.

7. I also examined the second announcement-period excess returns. The subsidiary stocks that are spun off earn –0.60%, the stocks acquired by third parties earn 14.31%, and the stocks acquired back by parents earn 8.26% (t-statistics = 0.52, 5.95, and 1.96). The corresponding parent stocks earn 4.80%, 1.12%, and 2.50% (t-statistics = 3.60, 1.76, and 2.13).

TABLE 8 **Tests of the Financing Strategy Hypothesis and the Investment Strategy Hypothesis of Carveouts Based on the Announcement-Period Excess Returns of Parent Stocks, 1980–97**

		Market-Adjusted Excess Returns		
Description	*N*	Mean (*t*-Statistic)	Median	Percent Positive
Panel A. Based on the *Wall Street Journal* reports of financing strategy:				
Reports suggesting that carveout is a result of financing strategy, code DF from table 6	76	3.04 (4.06)***	1.42	70
No such reports	260	1.63 (4.24)***	.77	56
Difference of means—reports of financing strategy vs. no reports		1.41 (1.68)*		
Panel B. Based on the *Wall Street Journal* reports of investment strategy:				
Reports suggesting that carveout is a result of investment strategy, code DI from table 6	34	4.04 (2.83)***	1.70	74
No such reports	302	1.71 (4.97)***	.79	57
Difference of means—reports of investment strategy vs. no reports		2.33 (1.59)		
Panel C. Based on primary versus secondary stock issue:				
Only primary shares issued	186	1.62 (3.64)***	.86	59
Only secondary shares issued	47	1.02 (1.47)	1.01	57
Both primary and secondary shares issued	58	4.20 (4.49)***	1.66	66
Data on primary vs. secondary not available	45	1.33 (1.31)	.75	51
Difference of means—both primary and secondary vs. only primary		2.58 (2.49)**		
Difference of means—both primary and secondary vs. only secondary		3.18 (2.76)***		
Difference of means—only primary vs. only secondary		.58 (.72)		

NOTE.—The sample of 336 carveout announcements during the period 1980–97 is obtained from the SDC and from the *Mergers and Acquisitions* magazine. It satisfies certain other restrictions discussed in table 3. Section II.B and table 6 provide a description of the financing strategy hypothesis and the investment strategy hypothesis. Excess returns during the announcement period are calculated by subtracting the cumulative value-weighted market returns over AD − 1 to AD + 1 from the cumulative parent stock returns. The *t*-statistics of sample means are calculated by using the cross-sectional distribution of market-adjusted returns and are reported in parentheses. The t-statistics in difference-of-means tests are calculated by assuming that the two samples have possibly unequal variances.

* Significant at the 10% level.
** Significant at the 5% level.
*** Significant at the 1% level.

The combined evidence of tables 6 and 7 supports the refocusing strategy hypothesis. I point to the large frequency of related statements in the *Wall Street Journal* reports, the higher returns when the parent and subsidiary businesses are unrelated, the large frequency of subsequent complete divestitures, and the higher first announcement-period returns when there is a subsequent complete divestiture.

C. Evidence on the Financing Strategy and Investment Strategy Hypotheses

Panel A of table 8 shows that the 76 carveouts for which the *Wall Street Journal* reports mention financing strategy type of reasons (repay debt, build working capital, finance existing operations, general corporate purposes) earn

TABLE 9 **Additional Equity Offerings by Parent and Subsidiary Firms versus Industry and Size Matching Firms during 3 Years before to 3 Years after the Carveout Issue Date, 1980–97**

	Number of Equity Offerings				Capital Raised (Million $)		
Period	Parent or Subsidiary Firms	Matching Firms	Difference	χ^2-Statistic	Parent or Subsidiary Firms	Matching Firms	Difference
Panel A: Parent firms versus matching firms:							
Year −3	22	19	3	.23	2,024	1,049	975
Year −2	19	27	−8	1.49	5,550	3,140	2,410
Year −1	21	29	−8	1.38	6,353	4,376	1,977
Years −3, −2, and −1	62	75	−13	1.55	13,926	8,565	5,361
Carveout issue date							
Year +1	22	9	13	5.72**	4,776	1,265	3,511
Year +2	12	14	−2	.16	3,182	904	2,278
Year +3	18	9	9	3.13	5,090	2,093	2,997
Years +1, +2, and +3	52	32	20	5.44**	13,049	4,261	8,788
Years −3 to +3	114	107	7	.33	26,975	12,826	14,149

Panel B. Subsidiary firms vs. matching firms:							
Year −3		21				680	
Year −2		26				1,056	
Year −1		33				1,766	
Years −3, −2, and −1		80				3,502	
Carveout issue date	336				44,688		
Year +1	36	21	15	4.31*	5,785	1,571	4,214
Year +2	25	19	6	.88	2,813	1,433	1,380
Year +3	30	11	19	9.38***	3,369	1,735	1,634
Year +1, +2, and +3	91	51	40	14.29***	11,967	4,738	7,229
Years −3 to +3	427	131	296		56,655	8,240	48,415

NOTE.—The sample of 336 carveout announcements during the period 1980–97 is obtained from the Securities Data Company (SDC) and from the *Mergers and Acquisitions* magazine. It satisfies certain other restrictions discussed in table 3. For each parent and subsidiary firm, a matching firm is chosen, which is the closest in market value of all firms with the same 2-digit SIC code. The SIC code is obtained from Compustat when available, and from CRSP otherwise. If the SIC code is not available (as for a few subsidiary firms), then matching is done by market value alone. For each sample and matching firm, information on additional equity offerings is obtained by scanning the seasoned equity offerings data from SDC. A χ^2-statistic with one degree of freedom tests whether the difference between number of equity offerings by the sample and matching firms is statistically significant (Sachs 1982, pp. 467–72).

* Significant at the 10% level.

** Significant at the 5% level.

*** Significant at the 1% level.

TABLE 10 **Capital Expenditures by Parent and Subsidiary Firms versus Industry and Size Matching Firms during 1 Year before to 3 Years after the Carveout Issue Date, 1980–97**

	Capital Expenditures for Sample Firms		Capital Expenditures for Matching Firms		
Fiscal Year	Number	Median	Number	Median	Difference in Medians
Panel A. Parent firms vs. matching firms:					
Year −1	240	.0431	251	.0549	−.0118*
Year 0	238	.0528	243	.0557	−.0029
Year +1	222	.0528	222	.0529	−.0001
Year +2	198	.0507	200	.0527	−.0020*
Year +3	169	.0443	172	.0549	−.0106***
Panel B. Subsidiary firms vs. matching firms:					
Year −1	260	.0373	263	.0432	−.0059**
Year 0	288	.0443	244	.0416	.0027
Year +1	280	.0506	231	.0416	.0090
Year +2	238	.0513	203	.0396	.0117*
Year +3	200	.0446	181	.0443	.0003

NOTE.—The sample of 336 carveout announcements during 1980–97 is obtained from the SDC and from the *Mergers and Acquisitions* magazine. It satisfies certain other restrictions discussed in table 3. For each parent and subsidiary firm, a matching firm is chosen, which is the closest in market value of all firms with the same two-digit SIC code. The SIC code is obtained from Compustat, when available, and from CRSP otherwise. If the SIC code is not available (as for a few subsidiary firms), then matching is done by market value alone. Annual data on capital expenditures and sales are obtained from Compustat for a 5-year period beginning one fiscal year before the carveout year. Capital expenditures are normalized by sales and then compared across sample and matching firms. Due to extreme skewness in capital expenditures, the mean values are practically meaningless and are not reported. The Wilcoxon rank sum test is used to measure the statistical significance of the difference in capital expenditures for sample and matching firms (Sachs 1982, pp. 293–303).

* Significant at the 10% level.

** Significant at the 5% level.

*** Significant at the 1% level.

1.41% more than the remaining cases (t-statistic = 1.68). Panel B of table 8 shows that the 34 carveouts for which the *Wall Street Journal* reports mention investment strategy type of reasons (invest in new projects, upgrade existing operations) earn 2.33% more than the remaining cases (t-statistic = 1.59). The difference in excess returns is greater in the second case but, perhaps due to the smaller sample size and the assumption of unequal subsample variances in all difference of means tests reported in this article, the t-statistic is not significant at the 10% confidence level. I later show that the regression tests that implicitly assume equal subsample variances give significant t-statistics. I, therefore, interpret these results as an endorsement of the financing strategy and investment strategy hypotheses.

Panel C of table 8 relates the excess returns to whether the issue includes primary or secondary shares. I have the required data in 291 cases. Only primary shares are issued in 186 cases, only secondary shares are issued in 47 cases, and both primary and secondary shares are issued in the remaining 58 cases. The excess returns are substantially higher when both primary and secondary shares are issued than when only primary or only secondary shares are issued. The difference between only primary or only secondary issues is insignificant. I have no satisfactory explanation for these results.

Table 9 compares the equity financing activity of the parent and subsidiary firms with their matching firms. For each sample firm, I choose a matching firm that has the closest market value of all firms with the same two-digit SIC code. I then scan the SDC files for data on SEOs. Panel A shows that the parent firms raise $26,975 million from 114 SEOs over a period starting 3 years before the carveout issue date and ending 3 years after the carveout. In comparison, the matching firms raise $12,826 million from 107 SEOs. The parent firms raise 2.10 times as much equity as their size and industry matching firms. This ratio increases to 3.16 if I include the proceeds of secondary shares sold in carveout (which equal 30.15% of the total proceeds of $44,886 million in table 3).

Panel B of table 9 shows that even the subsidiary firms are heavy equity issuers despite the carveout. The subsidiary firms raise an additional $11,967 million from 91 SEOs over a 3-year period starting after the carveout issue date. In comparison, the matching firms raise $3,502 million from 80 SEOs before the issue date and $4,738 million from 51 SEOs after the issue date. Over the combined period, the subsidiary firms raise 1.45 times as much equity as their size and industry matching firms, a ratio that increases to 5.26 if I include the proceeds of primary shares sold in carveout.

The evidence of table 9 supports both the financing strategy and investment strategy hypotheses. To distinguish between them, I examine the capital expenditures data. Panel A of table 10 shows that the median capital expenditures normalized by sales for parent firms are less than for matching firms during each year of a 5-year period beginning one fiscal year before the carveout year. The difference is statistically significant during 3 of these 5 years. Panel B of table 10 shows that the median capital expenditures normalized by sales for subsidiary firms are less than for matching firms in the fiscal year before the carveout year but then increase to more than for matching firms during the following 4 years. The difference is statistically significant in years −1 and +2.

The combined evidence of tables 9 and 10 shows that the parent firms raise substantial amounts of equity, yet their capital expenditures are lower than for matching firms. This evidence is consistent with the financing strategy hypothesis. The parent firms may be using the proceeds to retire debt or meet other financial contingencies, as suggested by Allen and McConnell (1998). The subsidiary firms raise more equity than their matching firms, but they also spend more on capital expenditures. This evidence is consistent with the investment strategy hypothesis.

TABLE 11 Tests of the Complexity, Undervaluation, and Pure Play Hypothesis, Managerial Incentives Hypothesis, and Miscellaneous Hypotheses of Carveouts Based on the Announcement-Period Excess Returns of Parent Stocks, 1980–97

Description	Number	Market-Adjusted Excess Returns: Mean (*t*-Statistic)	Median	Percent Positive
Panel A. Based on the *Wall Street Journal* reports of complexity, undervaluation, and pure play stocks:				
Reports suggesting that carveout is a result of complexity and undervaluation of combined assets or creation of pure play stocks, code DU from table 6	38	4.02 (4.31)***	2.72	74
No such reports	298	1.68 (4.60)***	.81	57
Difference of means—reports of complexity, undervaluation, and pure play vs. no reports		2.34 (2.34)**		
Panel B. Based on the *Wall Street Journal* reports of managerial incentives:				
Reports suggesting that carveout is a result of managerial incentives, code DM from table 6	3	7.71 (1.64)	10.74	67
No such reports	333	1.89 (5.53)***	.93	59
Difference of means—reports of investment strategy vs. no reports		5.82 (1.23)		

Panel C: Based on the *Wall Street Journal* reports of miscellaneous reasons:				
Reports suggesting that carveout is part of a takeover defense, code DT from table 6	8	3.08 (1.26)	3.95	63
Reports suggesting that carveout is part of a tax reduction strategy, code DX from table 6	4	1.17 (.19)	−3.17	50
Reports suggesting that carveout is a result of regulatory reasons, code DR from table 6	6	.10 (.11)	1.05	66
No such reports	320	1.93 (5.53)***	.95	59
Since none of the miscellaneous factors are significant, the difference of means tests are not reported				

NOTE.—The sample of 336 carveout announcements during 1980–97 is obtained from the SDC and from the *Mergers and Acquisitions* magazine. It satisfies certain other restrictions discussed in table 3. Section II.B and table 6 provide a description of the complexity, undervaluation, and pure play hypothesis, managerial incentives hypothesis, and miscellaneous hypotheses. Excess returns during the announcement period are calculated by subtracting the cumulative value-weighted market returns over AD − 1 to AD + 1 from the cumulative parent stock returns. The *t*-statistics of sample means are calculated by using the cross-sectional distribution of market-adjusted returns and are reported in parentheses. The *t*-statistics in difference-of-means tests are calculated by assuming that the two samples may have unequal variances.

* Significant at the 10% level.

** Significant at the 5% level.

*** Significant at the 1% level.

TABLE 12 Multivariate Tests of the Carveout Announcement-Period Excess Returns, 1980–97

Variable	(1)	(2)	(3)	(4)	(5)	(6)	(7)	(8)	(9)	(10)
Intercept	−.82	2.34	1.63	1.71	1.68	1.50	1.66	−1.64	1.19	.90
	(−1.34)	(5.54)***	(4.19)***	(4.76)***	(4.65)***	(3.75)***	(4.56)***	(−2.32)**	(2.26)**	(1.66)*
REL_ SIZE_ RANK	.62							.69		
	(5.36)***							(5.64)***		
SAME_INDUSTRY		−1.54						−1.66	−1.30	−1.30
		(−2.04)**						(−2.20)**	(−1.64)*	(−1.65)*
DF			1.41					.33	.35	.36
			(1.73)*					(.38)	(.38)	(.39)
DI				2.33				1.68	2.29	2.26
				(2.06)**				(1.46)	(1.90)**	(1.89)*
DU					2.34			2.69	2.24	1.88
					(2.17)**			(2.43)**	(1.92)*	(1.61)
PS						2.69		2.42	2.84	2.93
						(3.00)***		(2.80)***	(3.13)***	(3.25)***
SPINOFF							2.20			2.25
							(2.16)**			(2.14)**
Sample	335	321	336	336	336	291	336	277	277	277
Adjusted R^2	.077	.010	.006	.010	.011	.027	.011	.155	.059	.071

NOTE.—The sample of 336 carveout announcements during 1980–97 is obtained from the SDC and from the *Mergers and Acquisitions* magazine. It satisfies certain other restrictions discussed in table 3. The dependent variable is the excess return calculated by subtracting the cumulative value-weighted market return over AD − 1 to AD + 1 from the cumulative parent stock returns. The independent variables are as follows: REL_SIZE_RANK: decile rank of the ratio of subsidiary market value to parent market value on listing date; SAME_INDUSTRY: A dummy that takes the value 1 if the parent and subsidiary have the same 2-digit SIC code, 0 otherwise; DF: a dummy that takes the value 1 if there is a *Wall Street Journal* report that mentions financing motives, 0 otherwise; DI: a dummy that takes the value 1 if there is a *Wall Street Journal* report that mentions investment motives, 0 otherwise; DU: a dummy that takes the value 1 if there is a *Wall Street Journal* report that mentions complexity, undervaluation, and pure play reasons, 0 otherwise; PS: a dummy that takes the value 1 if both primary and secondary shares are issued, 0 otherwise; SPINOFF: a dummy that takes the value 1 if the carveout is followed by spinoff of the subsidiary before 1998, 0 otherwise. Section V.A and table 6 provide a further description of the DF, DI, and DU variables. The *t*-statistics are reported in parentheses.

* Significant at the 10% level.
** Significant at the 5% level.
*** Significant at the 1% level.

D. Evidence on the Remaining Divestiture Gains Hypotheses

Panel A of table 11 shows that the 38 carveouts for which the *Wall Street Journal* reports mention complexity, undervaluation, and pure play type of reasons earn 2.34% more than the remaining cases (*t*-statistic = 2.34). This evidence simultaneously supports the divestiture gains hypothesis and contradicts Nanda's asymmetric information hypothesis. In many cases, the reports suggest that the subsidiary is hidden inside a complex organization and therefore undervalued by the market (recall the report on Nabisco Holdings Corporation, which refers to the subsidiary as "red-hot"). Although not shown in tables, the 11 firms for which the reports raise concerns of overvalued subsidiary or subsidiary's industry earn excess returns of 2.37%, insignificantly different from 1.93% for the remaining 325 firms. Further evidence on the complexity, undervaluation, and pure play hypothesis is provided by an earlier result from table 7, which shows that the excess returns are higher when the parent and subsidiary firms are in different industries.

Panels B and C of table 11 show the excess returns of firms that mention managerial incentives, takeover defense, tax reduction, and regulatory compliance type of reasons. The small sample sizes make these cases indistinguishable from the remaining cases. However, an earlier result from table 10 that shows that subsidiary firms undertake greater capital expenditures than matching firms provides some support for the managerial incentives hypothesis.

E. Regressions

Table 12 shows univariate and multivariate regressions of the carveout announcement-period excess returns. The regressions serve two purposes. First, the univariate regressions provide an alternative to the difference of means tests in tables 5, 7, 8, and 11 by assuming that the subsample variances are equal. Second, the multivariate regressions test whether the many cross-sectional determinants of excess returns remain significant in the presence of each other.

The cross-sectional determinants are as follows: REL_SIZE_RANK = decile rank of the ratio of subsidiary market value to parent market value on listing date; SAME_INDUSTRY = a dummy that takes the value 1 if the parent and subsidiary have the same two-digit SIC code, 0 otherwise; DF = a dummy that takes the value 1 if a *Wall Street Journal* report mentions financing motives, 0 otherwise; DI = a dummy that takes the value 1 if a *Wall Street Journal* report mentions investment motives, 0 otherwise; DU = a dummy that takes the value 1 if a *Wall Street Journal* report mentions complexity, undervaluation, and pure play reasons, 0 otherwise; PS = a dummy that takes the value 1 if both primary and secondary shares are issued, 0 otherwise; SPINOFF = a dummy that takes the value 1 if the carveout is followed by spinoff of the subsidiary before 1998, 0 otherwise.

Univariate regressions (1)–(7) show that each of the above seven variables is significant at the 10% confidence level, or better. The variable REL_SIZE_RANK is the dominant one, and it remains highly significant in the opposite direction of the asymmetric information hypothesis.

Multivariate regressions follow next. Regression (8) includes all variables except SPINOFF, which uses information available after the carveout. Regression (9) excludes both SPINOFF and REL_SIZE_RANK. The second variable is excluded because it is a proxy for wealth gains on account of all of the divestiture gains hypotheses, which are separately captured by SAME_INDUSTRY, DF, DI, and DU. Regression (10) includes SPINOFF, but it excludes REL_SIZE_RANK. Together, these regressions show the following results. First, DF becomes insignificant in the presence of other variables. Second, the remaining variables are quite stable. Their coefficients are statistically significant in at least two of the three multivariate regressions. Overall, the regression results uphold and even strengthen the evidence in favor of the different divestiture gains hypotheses.

VI. Conclusions

Using a sample of 336 carveouts that were done during the period 1980–97, this article examines whether the positive announcement-period returns of equity carveouts reflect the resolution of asymmetric information concerning the parent and subsidiary stock values, or the likely wealth gains from divestitures. The asymmetric information hypothesis is based on Nanda (1991), and it extends the Myers and Majluf (1984) framework to the case of parent and subsidiary stock issues. This framework has been used to explain the negative announcement-period returns of SEOs and the negative long-term excess returns of IPOs and SEOs. The divestiture gains hypothesis is based on Schipper and Smith (1986). It has long been used to explain the positive market reaction to spinoffs and asset sales.

The first part of this article shows that, unlike other security issues, asymmetric information does not explain the carveout decision. I reach this conclusion by deriving and testing a key prediction of the asymmetric information model, which states that the announcement-period returns should decrease with an increase in the ratio of overvalued subsidiary assets to the undervalued nonsubsidiary assets and eventually become negative as this ratio exceeds one. My results are significant in the opposite direction of this prediction.

The remainder of this article shows many results that support the divestiture gains hypothesis. First, I analyze the *Wall Street Journal* reports accompanying the carveout, and I find extensive evidence that the firm managers, the analysts, and the reporters treat carveouts like divestitures. Second, the parent firms before carveout are as diversified as the parent firms before spinoffs, and the market reaction is higher when they divest subsidiary business unrelated to the parent business. Third, many carveouts are followed by a complete spinoff or a third-party acquisition. I find some evidence that the market anticipates this second event on the announcement of carveout and reacts more enthusiastically in such cases. Fourth, the market also reacts positively when the *Wall Street Journal* reports mention that the carveout proceeds will be used to repay debt or meet other financial contingencies and to invest in new projects. I show that the parent and subsidiary firms issue more equity than size and industry matching firms despite the carveout. The additional equity appears to be used to meet the financial contingencies of parent firms and the investment needs of subsidiary firms. Fifth, I show that the market reacts more enthusiastically when the *Wall Street Journal* reports mention that carveout is intended to create pure plays and thereby unlock hidden values inside a complex firm structure. The combined evidence of this article thus shows that the market reacts positively to the announcement of carveouts because it thinks that carveouts create value by divesting unrelated businesses, enabling a complete spinoff or a third-party acquisition, providing new financing, undertaking new investments, and reducing stock complexity.

References

Allen, J. W., and McConnell, J. J. 1998. Equity carveouts and managerial discretion. *Journal of Finance* 53 (February): 163–86.

Aron, D. J. 1991. Using the capital market as a monitor: Corporate spinoffs in an agency framework. *Rand Journal of Economics* 22 (Winter): 505–18.

Asquith, P., and Mullins, D. W. 1986. Equity issues and offering dilution. *Journal of Financial Economics* 15 (January/February): 61–89.

Berger, P. G., and Ofek, E. 1995. Diversification's effect on firm value. *Journal of Financial Economics* 37 (January): 39–65.

Comment, R., and Jarrell, G. A. 1995. Corporate focus and stock returns. *Journal of Financial Economics* 37 (January): 67–87.

Daley, L.; Mehrotra, V.; and Sivakumar, R. 1997. Corporate focus and value creation: Evidence from spinoffs. *Journal of Financial Economics* 45 (August): 257–81.

Desai, H., and Jain, P. C. 1999. Firm performance and focus: Long-run stock market performance following spinoffs. *Journal of Financial Economics* 54 (October): 75–101.

Hand, J. R. M., and Skantz, T. R. 1997. The bad news in equity carveouts. Working paper. Chapel Hill: University of North Carolina.

Hite, G. L., and Owers, J. E. 1983. Security price reactions around corporate spinoff announcements. *Journal of Financial Economics* 12 (December): 409–36.

John, K., and Ofek, E. 1995. Asset sales and increase in focus. *Journal of Financial Economics* 37 (January): 105–26.

Kahle, K. M., and Walkling, R. A. 1996. The impact of industry classifications on finance research. *Journal of Financial and Quantitative Analysis* 31 (September): 309–35.

Klein, A. 1986. The timing and substance of divestiture announcements: Individual, simultaneous, and cumulative effects. *Journal of Finance* 41 (July): 685–95.

Klein, A.; Rosenfeld, J.; and Beranek, W. 1991. The two stages of an equity carveout and the price response of parent and subsidiary stock. *Managerial and Decision Economics* 12 (December): 449–60.

Krishnaswami, S., and Subramaniam, V. 1999. Information asymmetry, valuation, and the corporate spin-off decision. *Journal of Financial Economics* 53 (July): 73–112

Lang, L.; Poulsen, A.; and Stulz, R. 1995. Asset sales, firm performance, and the agency costs of managerial discretion. *Journal of Financial Economics* 37 (January): 3–37.

Larraza-Kintana, M.; Wiseman, R. M.; Gomez-Mejia, L. R.; and Welbourne, T. M. 2000. Framing, compensation, and employment risk influences on CEO risk taking behavior. Working paper. Tempe: Arizona State University.

Masulis, R. W., and Korwar, A. N. 1986. Seasoned equity offerings: An empirical investigation. *Journal of Financial Economics* 15 (January/February): 91–118.

McConnell, J. J., and Muscarella, C. J. 1985. Corporate capital expenditure decisions and the market value of the firm. *Journal of Financial Economics* 14 (September): 399–422.
Mikkelson, W. H., and Partch, M. M. 1986. Valuation effects of securities offerings and the issuance process. *Journal of Financial Economics* 15 (January/February): 31–60.
Myers, S. C., and Majluf, N. S. 1984. Corporate financing and investment decisions when firms have information that investors do not have. *Journal of Financial Economics* 13 (June): 187–221.
Nanda, V. 1991. On the good news in equity carveouts. *Journal of Finance* 46 (December): 1717–37.
Sachs, L. 1982. *Applied Statistics*. New York: Springer-Verlag.
Schipper, K., and Smith, A. 1983. Effects of recontracting on shareholder wealth: The case of voluntary spin-offs. *Journal of Financial Economics* 12 (December): 437–67.
Schipper, K., and Smith, A. 1986. A comparison of equity carveouts and seasoned equity offerings: Share price effects and corporate restructuring. *Journal of Financial Economics* 15 (January/February): 153–86.
Slovin, M. B.; Sushka, M. E.; and Ferraro, S. R. 1995. A comparison of the information conveyed by equity carveouts, spinoffs, and asset sell-offs. *Journal of Financial Economics* 37 (January): 89–104.
Vijh, A. M. 1994. The spinoff and merger ex-date effects. *Journal of Finance* 49 (June): 581–609.
Vijh, A. M. 1999. Long term returns from equity carveouts. *Journal of Financial Economics* 51 (February): 273–308.

[11]

ELSEVIER

Journal of Corporate Finance 3 (1997) 325–354

Journal of CORPORATE FINANCE

To live or let die? An empirical analysis of piecemeal voluntary corporate liquidations [1]

Gayle R. Erwin [a], John J. McConnell [b,*]

[a] McIntire School of Commerce, University of Virginia, Charlottesville, VA 22903, USA
[b] Krannert Graduate School of Management, Purdue University, IN 47907, USA

Received 1 March 1995; accepted 1 December 1996

Abstract

This paper is an in-depth investigation of 61 publicly-traded firms that chose to liquidate voluntarily on a piecemeal basis during the 1970s and 1980s. In comparison with their industry peers, these firms have lower Tobin's Q, a higher percentage of equity ownership by management and the board, a higher incidence of a member of the corporation's founding family in a key executive position or on the board, and a higher incidence of asset sales and prior attempts to transfer control of the firm. The average excess stock return of 20% around liquidation announcements is positively correlated with the fraction of stock owned by management and the board. These results suggest that firms that make the value enhancing decision to voluntarily liquidate confront low future growth opportunities, but the absence of future growth opportunities is not sufficient to bring about this decision. It is also necessary that decision makers have a vested interest in the outcome, either because of their ownership stake or because of their family affiliation with the business, and that the valuation consequences of the decision are greater, the more closely aligned are managerial and shareholder interests. © 1997 Elsevier Science B.V.

* Corresponding author. Tel.: +1-317-4945910; fax: +1-317-4949658; e-mail: mcconnel@mgmt.purdue.edu.

[1] We thank Ken Lehn (the editor), Gordon Phillips, Henri Servaes and Marc Zenner for many helpful conversations and suggestions. The first author gratefully acknowledges financial support from the McIntire School of Commerce Summer Research Grant. The second author acknowledges the support of the Center for International Business Education and Research at Purdue University.

PII S0929-1199(97)00003-5

JEL classification: G32; G33; G34

Keywords: Agency theory; Founders; Governance; Voluntary liquidations; Ownership structure

1. Introduction

This study is a detailed analysis of 61 publicly traded U.S. corporations that began and completed voluntary piecemeal liquidations during the period 1970–1991. Viewed from one perspective, a sample comprised of 61 observations over a 21-year span might relegate piecemeal voluntary liquidations to footnote material in the annals of corporate restructuring. Viewed from another perspective, on average, each year, three major U.S. firms voluntarily decide to discontinue operating as an integrated enterprise and to sell off all assets on a piecemeal basis. For many observers, this number may be surprisingly high.

The primary purpose of this study is to provide a detailed and comprehensive analysis of the characteristics and outcomes for publicly traded firms that choose to liquidate voluntarily. Along the way, however, the study also provides statistical and inferential evidence regarding larger themes in corporate finance and corporate governance. In particular, this study provides evidence concerning 'managerial theories' of the firm and the related debate as to whether corporate managers act in their own interests or in shareholders' interests when the two sets of interests are in conflict. [2] Unless they are compensated in some other way, for entrenched corporate executives, piecemeal liquidation of the firm represents a form of economic hara-kiri in which entrenched corporate executives voluntarily forfeit whatever rents or above market perquisites (if any) that accompany their positions for the (potential) benefit of shareholders. Prior studies by Kim and Schatzberg (1987), Hite et al. (1987), Skantz and Marchesini (1987) and Kudla (1987) document that share prices increase 10% to 12% in response to announcements of voluntary corporate liquidations. There is, thus, the appearance that managers altruistically throw themselves upon their economic swords for the sake of shareholders. This evidence appears to reject managerial theories of the firm. Our detailed analysis indicates that the story is not that simple.

The story appears to run as follows: First, for some companies, voluntary liquidation accompanies an idiosyncratic event in the life (or death) of the firm. For example, the Aguirre Company had operated in Puerto Rico as a producer of raw and semi-refined sugar, molasses, and related products since 1899. Actions brought by the Commonwealth of Puerto Rico in 1970 resulted in the transfer (or

[2] The theoretical and empirical literature on this subject is voluminous. Examples of the theoretical literature include Berle and Means (1932), Marris (1963), Manne (1965), Jensen and Meckling (1976) and Stulz (1988). Examples of the empirical literature include Holderness and Sheehan (1988), Morck et al. (1988a,b), McConnell and Servaes (1990) and Martin and McConnell (1991).

expropriation) of nearly all sugar-related assets away from the company. Following the expropriation, the primary assets remaining with the company included certain divisions engaged in the sale and distribution of construction materials and agricultural equipment. In 1977, after a lengthy court battle, the final judgment rendered on the expropriation claims awarded $36.5 million to the company from the Commonwealth of Puerto Rico. After reviewing available alternatives, including the expansion of the existing businesses and the sale or merger of the entire company — a process that involved preliminary talks through an investment banker with over 30 interested parties — the board of directors concluded that the action most beneficial to shareholders was liquidation of the company's assets on a piecemeal basis. The board approved the final plan of liquidation on March 7, 1978; the plan was approved by shareholders on December 15, 1978; and the final liquidating dividend was paid on December 1, 1981.

Second, even though idiosyncratic events play a role in the voluntary end of life for some companies, the sample is characterized by certain economic, organizational, and statistical regularities. Each of these regularities deserves separate enumeration and elaboration. First, firms that liquidate voluntarily have low Tobin's *Q*s relative to their industry peers (where *Q* is measured as the market value of equity plus the book value of debt divided by the book value of assets). Second, the current accounting rates-of-return-on-assets for the two sets of firms are about equal. On the presumption that the market-to-book ratio measures future growth opportunities, these data suggest that it is the absence of future growth opportunities rather than current profitability that is important in the decision by corporate officers to dissolve the firm.

Third, even after controlling for differences in growth opportunities, current profitability, and other financial characteristics of the firms, the fraction of shares owned by corporate officers and members of the board of directors is significantly higher in firms that choose to liquidate voluntarily than in their matched industry peer group. This evidence is consistent with various managerial theories of the firm which predict that managers are more likely to act in shareholders' interests, the higher is their personal ownership position in the firm's equity.

Fourth, firms that voluntarily choose to liquidate are characterized by a high incidence of the presence of the corporation's founder or members of the founder's family as key senior executives and/or members of the board. Even after controlling for share ownership and various financial characteristics of the firms, the presence of the founder or the founding family is significantly higher in firms that choose to liquidate than in their industry peer group. This result is consistent with theories and empirical studies that emphasize the role of influential investors as important forces in directing the firm toward value maximizing decisions. [3]

[3] See for example, Morck et al. (1988b) and Denis and Denis (1995).

Fifth, on a univariate basis, for firms that choose to liquidate voluntarily, the composition of the board of directors is such that the fraction of inside and/or affiliated board members is significantly greater for this sample than is the fraction of inside and/or affiliated board members of their industry peer group. However, on a multivariate basis, after controlling for the fraction of shares owned, the results indicate that it is not board composition, per se, but rather the board's ownership of the firm's shares that plays a significant role in the decision to liquidate.

Sixth, on neither a univariate nor a multivariate basis is the utilization of debt significantly different between firms that choose to liquidate and their industry counterparts. This result suggests that debt and the associated requirement that funds be paid out to service the debt is not an important factor in the decision of firms that choose to liquidate on a piecemeal basis.

Seventh, the fraction of firms that liquidate voluntarily that had asset sales over the three-year interval prior to the liquidation decision is significantly greater than the fraction of firms in the industry peer group that had asset sales over the same interval. Similarly, a significant fraction of firms in the sample actively sought acquirors for the whole firm in the three years preceding the liquidation decision, but these attempts at finding an acquiror for the whole firm failed, often because the price offered was deemed to be too low. Thus, the decision to liquidate the firm appears to be the culmination of a multistage effort to transfer assets to higher valued uses.

Eighth, the results of an event study centered on liquidation announcement events, including the initial announcement, board approval, and shareholder approval, are consistent with those of previous studies in that excess returns are positive and statistically significant, but at nearly 20%, they are much larger than reported in earlier studies. Cross-sectional regressions indicate that the value increase associated with liquidation announcements is positively related to the fraction of shares owned by corporate officers and members of the board and negatively related to current profitability. Thus, the wealth gain for shareholders is greater when management and the board own a larger stake in the firm and when assets are relatively less well utilized as measured by current profitability. One interpretation of this result is that, conditional on the decision to liquidate the firm, the market expects managers who have a larger ownership stake to redeploy assets more efficiently than managers who have a lower ownership stake.

Finally, we compare the discounted value of the stream of liquidating dividends paid with the stock price prior to the liquidation announcement. Corporate liquidations provide a laboratory to study whether standard capital budgeting techniques indicate that liquidation decisions are positive net present value (NPV) projects given ex post cash flows. On average, the discounted value of ex post cash flows is 16.6% greater than the firm's pre-announcement stock price. That is, assuming that actual cash flows are an unbiased estimate of expected cash flows, standard capital budgeting techniques indicate that, on average, corporate liquidations are positive NPV projects. Furthermore, the average of the announcement period event returns (i.e., 19.8%) is not significantly different from the calculated percentage NPV of the project. This result provides support for the use of traditional discounted cash flow analysis in capital budgeting.

The remainder of the paper reviews prior literature on voluntary liquidations (Section 2), describes the procedure used to identify the sample (Section 3), presents background information regarding events leading up to the liquidation decision and descriptive data on the financial characteristics of the firms in the sample (Section 4), presents the results of logistic regressions in which the firms in the liquidation sample are compared with their industry peers (Section 5), reports the results of an event study surrounding announcements of voluntary liquidations and cross-sectional regressions in which the announcement period excess return is the dependent variable (Section 6), describes the cash payoffs received by shareholders of the liquidating firms (Section 7), comments on the role of taxes in the decision to liquidate (Section 8), and summarizes the results (Section 9). Table 1 lists the firms in the sample as a resource for other scholars. Appendix A provides a narrative accounting of events leading up to and surrounding the decision to liquidate by eight of the firms in the sample. These narratives attempt to provide a description of the circumstances that surround a 'typical' firm that voluntarily liquidates.

2. Related studies

As regards prior studies of voluntary liquidations, our analysis can be viewed, at least in part, as updating results reported elsewhere and as providing a more comprehensive analysis of the questions at issue with a larger and more recent sample. For example, in their study, Kim and Schatzberg (1987) analyze a sample of 73 voluntary liquidations that were announced over the period 1963 through 1982 of which 30 were piecemeal liquidations; Hite et al. (1987) examine 49 piecemeal voluntary liquidations that were announced between 1962 and 1984; Skantz and Marchesini (1987, 1992) consider 37 piecemeal voluntary liquidations announced between 1970 and 1984; and Kudla (1987) examines 25 piecemeal voluntary liquidations announced between 1970 and 1982. These studies focus on the valuation effects of voluntary liquidations. Each reports that announcements to liquidate voluntarily are accompanied with significant stock price increases. For instance, Hite et al. report a two-day announcement period excess return of 12.24% at the initial announcement. Kim and Schatzberg report an average excess return of 11.44% around the initial announcement and 2.03% around the shareholder approval date. These authors do not, however, conduct cross-sectional regressions to determine whether the excess returns are correlated with the characteristics of the firms involved, although Hite et al. do report significantly larger announcement period excess returns for firms that have not been the target of a prior control attempt.

Table 1
List of firms in the sample of voluntary liquidations and dates of initial announcement and shareholder approval of the liquidating decision

Name of firm	Initial announcement date	Shareholder approval date	SIC code	Name of firm	Initial announcement date	Shareholder approval date	SIC code
Aguirre Co.	3/9/77	12/15/78	6500	Gulf Broadcast Co.	2/1/85	6/19/85	4833
American Controlled Industries	1/29/86	11/17/86	2670	Gulf United Corp.	6/30/82	1/4/84	6311
American Manufacturing Co., Inc.	6/28/79	9/28/79	2200	Handyman Corp.	9/26/86	12/18/86	5211
American Medical Affiliates, Inc.	10/30/81	5/28/82	8051	Heizer Corp.	12/1/83	2/28/84	6799
Amerifin Corp.	2/18/83	11/30/83	6799	Hines (Edward) Lumber Co.	7/5/85	10/23/85	5031
ANTA Corp.	1/20/84	4/26/84	3350	Hittman Corp.	10/12/82	11/22/82	3679
Apco Oil Corp.	3/2/76	10/27/77	2911	HS Group, Incorporated	7/13/84	8/30/84	100
Barber Oil Corp.	3/3/80	12/29/80	1220	Imark Industries, Inc.	10/14/87	2/11/88	5080
Bates Manufacturing Co.	3/1/79	5/24/79	1220	Kaiser Industries Corp.	5/6/76	4/20/77	3312
Bayuk Cigars, Inc.	10/6/81	12/21/81	2100	Kirby Industries	11/19/74	10/22/75	4400
Canal-Randolph Corp.	9/24/83	4/16/84	6512	Murray Mortgage Investors	11/19/80	4/29/81	6798
Cardiff Communications, Inc.	6/18/86	12/9/86	4841	OKC Corp.	7/26/79	5/13/80	2911
City Investing Co.	8/23/84	12/12/84	6799	Overseas National Airways, Inc.	4/2/76	9/7/78	4522
Columbia Corp.	2/11/76	5/28/76	2400	Panax Corp.	7/16/80	8/28/80	2711
Conroy, Inc.	8/17/83	12/30/83	2510	Pasco, Incorporated	5/22/75	12/30/75	2911

Cooper Laboratories, Inc.	10/1/82	6/28/84	2835	Procor, Incorporated	9/12/79	4/9/80	200
Cowles Communications, Inc.	3/30/82	11/5/82	4833	Reeves Telecom Corp.	1/19/79	5/17/79	4832
Dairy Queen Stores	12/19/77	2/27/78	5812	R.H. Medical Services, Inc.	1/14/80	8/27/80	3851
DCL Incorporated	2/21/79	1/14/80	7377	Rockower Brothers, Inc.	8/4/79	12/18/79	5600
Drewry Photocolor	5/2/88	5/2/88	7384	Rossmoor Corp.	1/25/80	6/17/81	6552
Electronic Tabulating Corp.	4/2/84	6/14/84	7374	Royal Castle System, Inc.	4/14/75	7/31/75	5812
Empire Financial Corp.	7/26/74	1/23/75	6036	San Juan Racing	7/7/77	10/13/81	7948
Financial Resource Corp.	4/1/82	6/15/82	6172	Telecor, Incorporated	8/17/78	4/3/79	7359
First Fidelity Investment Trust[a]	2/28/78	2/28/78	6798	Terrydale Realty Trust	2/9/81	1/28/82	6798
Gemtec Corp.	1/8/85	7/15/86	3842	Tishman Realty and Construction Co., Inc.	7/26/76	11/7/77	6500
Genway Corp.	11/24/86	12/22/86	6172	Trailerancho	6/17/77	7/3/78	6500
Glasrock Medical Services, Inc.	10/21/82	1/3/83	7350	U.S. Realty Investments[a]	2/18/81	1/6/82	6798
Global Gas	10/12/77	2/16/79	1311	Unity Buying Service Co., Inc.	9/15/83	4/27/84	5961
Gold Medallion Corp.	6/5/81	11/30/81	5122	Visual Sciences, Inc.	5/18/82	8/4/82	3661
Great Basins Petroleum Co.	11/11/80	8/26/81	1311	Western Development Corp.	1/2/84	4/20/84	200
Gross Telecasting, Inc.	3/21/84	5/31/84	4833				

[a]Trust only required Trustee Approval.

Ghosh et al. (1991) are interested in the operating and financial characteristics of firms that voluntarily liquidate. They consider a sample of 49 firms that announced voluntary piecemeal liquidations over the period 1962 through 1984. As do we, they conduct logistic regressions in which their sample of liquidating firms is compared with a control sample of non-liquidating firms in the same industries. They report that, in comparison with the non-liquidating sample, the liquidating firms are characterized by declining net sales, prior takeover attempts, and higher insider stock ownership (although the last variable is not always significant at the 0.05 level). They further report that P/E ratios and leverage are not different between the two samples. They interpret their evidence to indicate that ''...the concurrence of high insider ownership and prior takeover attempts possibly suggests that for self-interested managers, voluntary liquidation is a means to frustrate unfriendly suitors'' (p. 774).

In addition to the valuation effects and financial and operating characteristics of firms that undertake voluntary liquidations, we are interested in the events leading up to the decision to liquidate (including asset sales, takeover attempts, dividend cuts, loan defaults and so forth) and in the governance structure of these firms. Our motivation is twofold: First, because of the finality of the event, piecemeal voluntary liquidations are interesting events in their own right and, thus, merit comprehensive analysis. Second, voluntary liquidations are interesting because of what they can reveal about other prominent issues in corporate finance such as the role of stock ownership, the role and composition of the board of directors, the role and presence of founding families, the role of blockholders, and the role of leverage. These issues are particularly important when the firm confronts decisions in which value maximization potentially conflicts with managerial self interest. The decision to liquidate the firm clearly qualifies as such an event.

3. Sample selection

Our definition of a piecemeal voluntary liquidation requires that all of the assets of the firm be sold, that the assets be sold to at least two different buyers, that the firm cease to exist as a going concern, and that the firm had not previously filed for bankruptcy. We further require that the liquidation process be completed by year-end 1991. [4] We require that the liquidation be complete so as to be able to document the actual liquidating cash flows received by shareholders. To compile the sample of voluntary piecemeal liquidations, the Compustat research file and the CRSP NYSE, AMEX, and NASDAQ tapes were searched to identify all stocks

[4] A liquidation is considered complete during the year in which the final liquidating distribution is paid to shareholders as identified by the Prentice-Hall *Capital Adjustment Reporter* and/or the Commerce Clearing House *Capital Changes Reporter*.

delisted over the period 1970 through 1991 due to 'liquidation'. This search identified 365 possible piecemeal voluntary liquidations. To determine whether a firm satisfies our criteria, a search was conducted of the *Wall Street Journal*, Moody's *Industrial, Financial, and Transportation Manuals*, the Prentice Hall *Capital Adjustment Reporter*, Commerce Clearing House's *Capital Changes Reporter*, and corporate 10k's and proxy statements. This search indicated that 270 of the sample candidates were delisted due to merger, a chapter 7 liquidation, a chapter 11 bankruptcy filing, or a going private transaction. For 34 of the firms,

Table 2
Frequency distribution of voluntary corporate liquidation announcements and completions each year for 61 publicly traded firms that liquidated voluntarily on a piecemeal basis over the period 1970–1991. These firms both initiated and completed the liquidation between 1970 and 1991

A. Frequency distribution of liquidation announcements for the 61 firms in the sample

year of announcement	number of announcements for liquidations completed by 1991	year of announcement	number of announcements for liquidations completed by 1991
1970	—	1981	5
1971	—	1982	7
1972	—	1983	5
1973	—	1984	6
1974	2	1985	3
1975	2	1986	4
1976	5	1987	1
1977	5	1988	1
1978	2	1989	—
1979	7	1990	—
1980	6	1991	—

B. Frequency distribution of liquidation completions for the 61 firms in the sample

year of completion	number of completions of liquidations announced after 1970	year of completion	number of completions of liquidations announced after 1970
1970	—	1981	4
1971	—	1982	2
1972	—	1983	4
1973	—	1984	10
1974	—	1985	7
1975	—	1986	9
1976	1	1987	6
1977	1	1988	2
1978	1	1989	4
1979	3	1990	4
1980	2	1991	1

data are insufficient to determine precisely why the firm was delisted. The search definitively identified 61 firms delisted due to a voluntary piecemeal liquidation that was completed by the end of 1991.

Panel A of Table 2 presents a frequency distribution of the sample according to the calendar year in which the first announcement regarding the decision to liquidate appeared in the press and panel B gives a frequency distribution according to the year in which the liquidation was completed. Because the average (median) number of years from announcement to completion of a voluntary piecemeal liquidation is 4.04 (3.59) and because we require that the liquidation be completed by year-end 1991, the table gives the appearance that piecemeal liquidations dwindle to nothing in the latter half of the 1980's. In fact, our sample restrictions preclude the following announcements from entering the sample: three announcements in 1988, five in 1989, five in 1990 and four in 1991. The shortest time period elapsed from initial announcement to completion of the process is six months for Cardiff Communications. The longest time period elapsed is 13.5 years for San Juan Racing Association. On average, the first announcement in the press precedes the shareholder approval date by eight months (median = 6 months) and, on average, the time elapsed from shareholder approval to payment of the final dividend is 3.44 years (median = 3.09 years).

A review of Table 1 indicates some clustering of voluntary liquidations in the natural resources, real estate, and communications industries broadly defined. However, on a four-digit basis, the 61 voluntary piecemeal liquidations encompass 45 different SIC codes.

4. Background events and characteristics of firms that voluntarily liquidate

4.1. Background events

To identify events leading up to and surrounding the decision to voluntarily liquidate the firm, a search was conducted of the popular press including the *Wall Street Journal*, the *Dow Jones News Retrieval Service*, business periodicals, and such diverse trade publications as the *Oil and Gas Journal*, *Cable Television Business*, *Vending Times* and so on. For each firm, we also read annual reports, 10k's, and proxy statements. These sources were used to construct a narrative for each firm in the sample, eight of which are presented in Appendix A and the remainder of which are available from the authors. Major events that occurred in the three years preceding the liquidation decision include dividend omissions (5 firms), defaults on loan payments (6 firms), debt renegotiations (7 firms), operational restructuring other than the sale of assets (5 firms), turnover in top management (8 firms), solicitations of a buyer for the firm (9 firms), friendly merger attempts (15 firms), hostile takeover attempts (11 firms), leveraged buyout attempts (2 firms), proxy contests (1 firm), episodes of illegal insider trading (5 firms), and asset sales (39 firms). Thus, almost two-thirds of the firms in the sample discontinued the use of or divested certain assets in the three years prior to the decision to liquidate. Moreover, in 90% of these cases, the proceeds from asset sales were used to repay debt, rather than to expand the scale of the firm. [5]

Additionally, there are 46 incidents of an attempt to transfer control of the firm either by friendly or hostile means. These 46 control events (which include friendly merger attempts, proxy contests, leveraged buyouts, solicitation of a buyer for the firm, and hostile takeover attempts) encompass 23 different firms. Interestingly, more than half of these control events were friendly acquisition attempts and most were solicited by the liquidating firm. These findings suggest that the decision to voluntarily liquidate was more often proposed in the absence of any overt pressure from hostile suitors and was adopted after the board had pursued other alternatives for transferring control of the firm's assets — a finding that contrasts with the interpretation of events by Ghosh et al. (1991) who, as we noted, interpret similar findings to indicate that ''...voluntary liquidation is a means to frustrate unfriendly suitors''.

4.2. Ownership, governance, and operating data

Data on the composition of the board and equity ownership were gathered directly from corporate proxy statements for the three fiscal years prior to the year of the liquidation decision. Data collected include the number of shares held by members of the board, the number of shares held by the corporation's founding family, whether the corporate founder or a member of the founding family continued to play an active role in the management of the firm or as a member of the board, and whether each member of the board was also a member of corporate management or had some other affiliation with the firm, but was not a full-time employee. 'Affiliated' members include investment bankers who provided services to the firm, commercial bankers who have made loans to the firm, lawyers providing legal counsel to the firm, and accountants who have audited the firm. We categorize board members as 'insiders' if they are current or retired corporate officers or members of the founding family. All others are classified as 'outsiders'.

Data on operating performance, assets, liabilities, and the number of shares outstanding were collected from the Compustat research file. We also recorded the 'age' of the firm as the number of years between incorporation and the year of the liquidation decision.

Finally, to construct a control sample, Compustat was accessed to identify all firms with the same 4-digit SIC code as any of the firms in the liquidation sample. To enter the control sample, we require that the firm have market value of equity

---

[5] Lang et al. (1995) report that the average stock price reaction to asset sales is positive only when the proceeds are paid out.

within ±30% of the market value of equity of the liquidating firm and that the same financial and ownership data collected for the liquidation sample be available for the control firm. The net result is a control sample composed of 122 firms with at least one matching firm for every firm in the sample of liquidating firms.

5. Statistical analysis

5.1. Univariate statistical tests

Summary statistics for the two samples for the year prior to the liquidation decision are contained in Table 3. We also calculated these statistics for the second year and third year prior to the liquidation decision. Although we do not show these data here, we do comment on them and these statistics are available upon request. One reason we do not show the statistics here is that they exhibit relatively little year-to-year variation over the three years preceding the liquidation.

At the year-end prior to the liquidation decision, the mean (median) market value of equity for the liquidating firms is $77.49 million ($19.54 million) and it is $82.79 million ($21.09 million) for the control sample. On most of the financial characteristics considered, there is remarkably little difference in any year between the liquidation sample and the control sample.[6] For example, in year −1, the average (median) return on assets of the two samples are 0.11 (0.09) and 0.11 (0.10). Thus, it does not appear that liquidating firms are any more or less profitable than their nonliquidating industry counterparts. The one financial dimension on which the two samples differ is our proxy for Tobin's Q. For each of the three year-ends prior to the liquidation decision, the average of this ratio is 0.87, 0.82, 0.80 for the liquidation sample and it is 1.30, 1.32, 1.49 for the control sample. The differences between these averages are all statistically significant with p-values less than 0.01.

When the samples are compared according to the composition of their boards of directors and their equity ownership, the differences are striking. Regardless of the year considered, the average (median) percentage equity ownership by the board and the fraction of the board comprised of corporate insiders is significantly greater in the liquidation sample than in the control sample. For example, at the fiscal year-end preceding the liquidation announcement, mean (median) board equity ownership is 32.9% (27.0%) for firms that voluntarily choose to liquidate

[6] The sizes of the firms along with the fact that all were publicly-traded indicates that the companies are well-established enterprises. Further proof of that observation is the average age of the firms. On average, the liquidation announcement follows the date of incorporation by 23 years. Thus, the firms in the sample are not just 'trendy' fads that elect to go out of business after a brief moment in the sun.

Table 3
Characteristics of 61 publicly traded firms that liquidated voluntarily on a piecemeal basis over the period 1970–1991 and their size-matched industry counterparts one year prior to the initial liquidation announcement

Variable (year − 1)	Voluntary liquidations		Industry counterparts		Test statistic for difference in means[a]
	mean	median	mean	median	
Total debt + MV equity ($ millions)	199.47	39.42	142.32	49.85	0.70
Assets ($ millions)	402.43	49.45	272.21	36.59	0.67
Total debt ($ millions)	121.98	12.25	59.53	13.11	0.96
EBIDT/assets	0.11	0.09	0.11	0.10	−0.39
Tobin's Q	0.87	0.73	1.30	1.01	−2.87***
Total debt/assets	0.31	0.25	0.36	0.33	−0.96
LT debt/assets	0.23	0.15	0.24	0.17	−0.47
Total debt/(total debt + MV equity)	0.40	0.39	0.39	0.35	0.29
LT debt/(LT debt + MV equity)	0.33	0.29	0.32	0.26	0.15
(EBIDT − interest payments)/EBIDT	0.71	0.75	0.56	0.81	0.88
(Cash + MS)/assets	0.18	0.08	0.12	0.07	1.56
Asset sales (% of sample)	27.87	N.A.	4.10	N.A.	3.95***
Control event (% of sample)	22.95	N.A.	4.10	N.A.	3.32***
Price/EBIDT	7.12	3.71	6.84	4.91	0.18
Board stock ownership (%)	32.91	27.00	16.86	12.68	4.50***
Size of board	7.75	7.00	8.14	7.10	−0.62
Inside board members (%)	48.62	50.00	38.24	38.00	2.96***
Affiliated board members (%)	16.40	17.00	13.06	13.00	1.31
Outside board members (%)	34.98	33.00	48.46	50.00	−4.21***
Founder present (% of sample)	69.56	N.A.	31.82	N.A.	5.79***
Founding family present (% of sample)	75.41	N.A.	36.07	N.A.	5.57***
Founding family stock ownership (%)	27.52	22.98	21.58	16.42	1.47
Age of firm	23.67	18.50	23.06	16.04	0.21
Outside blockholder (% of sample)	32.79	N.A.	30.33	N.A.	−0.41

MV Equity: stock price at fiscal year-end times the number of shares outstanding; EBIDT: earnings before interest, depreciation and taxes; Total Debt: book value of short-term debt + long-term debt for fiscal year-end; MS: marketable securities; Price: price of common stock at fiscal year-end; Tobin's Q: (market value of equity + book value of debt)/book value of assets; Board stock ownership: percent of shares owned by board members; Founding family stock ownership: percent of shares owned by founding family board members; Age of firm: years from incorporation to liquidation announcement.
[a] t-statistic tests whether the mean of the liquidation sample is different from the mean of the matching sample. Similar results are obtained using a Wilcoxon rank sum test.
*** Statistically significant at the 1% level.
** Statistically significant at the 5% level.
* Statistically significant at the 10% level.

versus 16.9% (12.7%) for their nonliquidating industry counterparts. Similarly, for the sample of liquidating firms, corporate officers, on average, comprise 48.6% (50.0%) of the board versus 38.2% (38.0%) for the control sample. These ratios are statistically significantly different from each other with p-values less than 0.01.

Additionally, firms that choose to liquidate voluntarily have a significantly greater incidence of either the founder or a member of the founding family as a top corporate officer and/or a member of the board than do their industry peers, but the fraction of shares owned by the founding family is not significantly greater in the liquidation sample than in the control sample. The founder or a member of the founding family is present in 75.4% of the liquidation sample and in 36.1% of the control sample (p-value for difference < 0.01). Given the significant presence of the founding family, it could be that the liquidation decision is really a retirement decision. That is, it could be that, after a long and successful career, the founder has decided to retire and, in the absence of an obvious successor, the decision is made to liquidate the firm. To consider that possibility, we gathered data on the age of the founder in the 41 firms (67% of the sample) in which he/she held the position of chairman of the board, CEO, or president. The mean (median) age of this group is 60 (58) years. For the control sample, the founder held one of the top officer positions in 36% of the sample and the mean (median) age was 56 (56). The mean and median ages of the founders of the two groups are not significantly different from each other at the 0.10 level. We also gathered data on the ages of the CEO, chairman, and president of those firms in which the founder was not in an executive position. For the liquidation sample, the average ages of these three officers were 53, 53 and 54, respectively. For the control sample, the average ages were 51, 51 and 55. For none of the three sets of officers is the average age of the liquidation sample significantly different from the control sample. Additionally, a search of proxy statements and other background material did not reveal any cases in which retirement was cited as a motive for the decision to liquidate. Thus, these data do not appear to support the 'retirement story' of voluntary piecemeal liquidation.

Several other factors deserve mention because of their apparent absence as influential determinants of the decision to liquidate voluntarily. The first is debt. When leverage is measured by any one of four different ratios, the use of debt is not significantly different between the two samples for any of the three years prior to the decision to liquidate. The second is free cash flow. The difference between the two samples is not significant when free cash flow is measured as either (EBIDT-interest payments)/EBIDT or (cash + marketable securities)/assets. These statistics suggest that it is not leverage or the attendant requirement that cash flow be paid out to creditors that 'forces' firms to liquidate. This result appears to contradict the argument of Jensen (1986) regarding free cash flow and the role of debt in motivating managers to opt for difficult value enhancing choices. It could be, however, as proposed by McConnell and Servaes (1995), that equity ownership works in combination with debt and in the cases considered here, equity ownership is the more powerful determining factor. The third factor is outside blockholders. We define an outside blockholder as an institution, group, or individual who has no business or family ties to the firm or its inside or affiliated board members and who holds at least 5% of the firm's common stock. As shown in Table 3, outside blockholders are present in 32.8% of the liquidating firms and 30.3% of the control firms. These numbers are not significantly different from each other at the 0.10 level. There are, however, four cases in which an outside blockholder actively encouraged the firm to liquidate, but these are, to some extent, offset by two cases in which a blockholder actively sought (by means of a proxy fight) to prevent liquidation of the firm. [7] Fourth, the average ages of the firms in the two samples are nearly identical at about 23 years.

Finally, the tables indicate a significantly greater frequency of asset sales and control events during years immediately prior to the liquidation decision for the liquidation sample than for their industry peer group. These data suggest that the decision to liquidate the firm is the culmination of a multistage attempt to reallocate corporate assets to (presumably) higher valued uses.

As we noted earlier, results similar to ours have been reported for samples taken from earlier time periods. For example, Ghosh et al. report that relative to an industry-matched control group, liquidating firms were characterized by significantly higher inside ownership of stock and higher frequency of hostile takeover attempts, but no difference in leverage. They also report that liquidity is higher prior to liquidation decision. A result that we fail to confirm.

5.2. *Multivariate statistical tests*

We now estimate logistic regressions in which the dependent variable is one or zero depending on whether the firm is a member of the liquidating sample (1) or the industry peer sample (0) to determine which financial and organizational factors show up as significant determinants of the decision to liquidate on a multivariate basis. [8] A number of specifications of the regression are estimated with different sets of independent variables.

The first regression is reported in the second column of Table 4. The independent variables include current profitability (measured as EBIDT/total assets, hereafter ROA), Tobin's Q (measured as (market value of equity + book value of debt)/total assets)), total leverage (measured as total debt/total assets), free cash flow (measured as (EBIDT-interest payments)/EBIDT)), the fraction of shares owned by members of the board, an indicator variable equal to 1 when more than 50% of the board are corporate insiders, an indicator variable equal to 1 when a member of the founding family serves on the board of directors and/or holds a

[7] The four firms in which the blockholder encouraged liquidation are Amerifin Corp., Gemtec Corp., Hines (Edward) Lumber Co., and U.S. Realty Investments. The two firms in which the blockholder attempted to prevent the liquidation are City Investing and Gulf Broadcast Co.

[8] The results reported here use the choice based estimation procedure which weights the log–likelihood function by the true proportions of liquidating and nonliquidating firms in the population, as described in Palepu (1986).

340 G.R. Erwin, J.J. McConnell / Journal of Corporate Finance 3 (1997) 325–354

Table 4
Estimated coefficients from logistic regressions for 61 publicly traded firms that liquidated voluntarily on a piecemeal basis over the period 1970–1991 and their size-matched industry counterparts. The dependent variable in the regression is 1 for a voluntarily liquidating firm and 0 for a nonliquidating firm. (*t*-statistics are in parentheses)

Independent variable	(1)	(2)
Intercept	−2.77	−3.31
	−(1.24)	−(1.37)
Current profitability	−2.57	−3.13
	−(0.75)	−(0.92)
Tobin's *Q*	−0.89	−0.90
	−(1.85)*	−(1.96)*
Leverage	−0.42	−0.50
	−(0.31)	−(0.38)
Free cash flow	0.001	0.001
	(1.26)	(1.04)
Board stock ownership	3.23	
	(2.50)**	
Inside board stock ownership		2.73
		(1.66)*
Outside board stock ownership		8.45
		(2.31)**
Affiliated board stock ownership		−0.63
		−(0.07)
Inside board indicator	0.70	1.04
	(1.13)	(1.59)
Founding family indicator	1.53	1.84
	(2.01)**	(2.40)**
Blockholder indicator	0.18	0.17
	(0.29)	(0.26)
Age of chairman	−0.02	−0.01
	−(0.42)	−(0.26)
Age of CEO	0.04	0.04
	(0.29)	(0.31)
Age of president	−0.001	−0.001
	−(0.01)	−(0.01)
Age of firm	0.002	0.003
	(0.17)	(0.26)
Prior asset sales indicator	2.75	2.87
	(2.77)**	(2.82)**
Prior control event indicator	2.28	2.38
	(3.22)***	(3.43)***
Pseudo-R^2	0.38	0.39

*** Statistically significant at the 1% level.
** Statistically significant at the 5% level.
* Statistically significant at the 10% level.

top management position, an indicator variable equal to 1 when an outside blockholder is present, the age of the firm, an indicator variable equal to 1 when the firm experienced prior asset sales, an indicator variable equal to 1 when the firm experienced a control event during the three prior years, and the ages of the chairman, the president and the CEO. The statistically significant variables are Tobin's Q, the fraction of shares owned by members of the board, the presence of a member of the founding family on the board and/or in top management, and the indicator variables for prior asset sales and prior control events (all with p-values < 0.10).

To determine the sensitivity of the regression results to the specification of the model, we experimented with different sets of the independent variables and alternative measures of current profitability, leverage, and free cash flow. Regardless of the specification of the regression or the definitions of these variables, in no regression did any of them show up as statistically significant. We also experimented with various classifications of the board as being either insider or outsider dominated. In no case did the composition of the board show up as being statistically significant. Similarly, in no regression was the age of the firm, the ages of the top officers or the presence of an outside blockholder statistically significant. In contrast, regardless of the other variables included and the way in which the other variables are specified, Tobin's Q, fraction of the shares owned by the board, and presence of the founding family always show up as statistically significant as do the indicator variables for prior asset sales and prior control events.

The multivariate results indicate that after controlling for various operating and financial characteristics, firms that voluntarily choose to liquidate are characterized by significantly higher equity ownership by the board, significantly lower future growth opportunities (as proxied by Tobin's Q), and significantly higher presence of the firm's founding family than otherwise comparable nonliquidating firms. These results are consistent with managerial theories of the firm which predict that managers are more likely to act in shareholders' interests the higher the managers' equity ownership in the firm.

To explore further the role of equity ownership by the board, the fraction of shares owned by insiders, outsiders, and affiliated board members are entered separately into the regression. This regression is presented in the third column of Table 4. Both inside and outside share ownership are significantly higher in the liquidating sample than in the nonliquidating sample. This result indicates that it is not board composition, per se, but rather how much equity is owned by the board that plays a key role in the decision to voluntarily liquidate the firm.

The significance of the founding family's presence in firms that voluntarily liquidate, even after controlling for equity ownership, board composition, profitability, leverage, and so on, is consistent with the conjecture by Morck et al. (1988b) and Denis and Denis (1995) that certain individuals can have a disproportionate influence on the decision making process of the firm.

Thus, a story that is consistent with the data appears to be that it is low future growth opportunities that (appropriately) motivates management to voluntarily liquidate the firm, but the lack of future profitable investment opportunities is not a sufficient condition. It is also necessary that management have a significant equity position in the firm and/or that the founding family plays a major role in the decision making process. Finally, the high incidence of prior efforts to transfer control of the firm by other means and/or to restructure the firm, suggests that it is only after a significant search for a less 'final' solution that management, perhaps reluctantly, arrives at the decision to liquidate the firm. This story is also consistent with the individual case narratives in Appendix A.

6. Event study

6.1. Announcement period excess returns

We now investigate the wealth effects associated with our sample of piecemeal liquidations. In doing so, we examine common stock excess returns around three dates: (1) the date on which the firm first publicly announces its intention to liquidate; (2) the date on which the board of directors approves the plan of liquidation; and (3) the date on which the shareholders vote to approve the plan. We then conduct cross-sectional regressions in which the sum of excess returns around the three dates is the dependent variable.

Our analysis extends and complements earlier stock price studies in several ways. For example, Kim and Schatzberg (1987) include both piecemeal liquidations and whole firm acquisitions disguised as voluntary liquidations in their analysis and consider only the initial announcement and shareholder approval dates in their analysis. Hite et al., Skantz and Marchesini, and Kudla examine piecemeal liquidations, but consider only the initial announcement period excess returns. These differences in analyses between the earlier studies and ours turn out to be consequential.

To conduct the event study, stock returns are taken from the CRSP tape for NYSE, AMEX and NASDAQ firms. Sufficient stock returns data are available to conduct the event study for 55 firms. [9] The market model procedure as described in Kim and Schatzberg (1987) is used to estimate excess returns.

Table 5 presents two-day announcement period average excess returns around the initial announcement date, the board approval date, and the shareholder

[9] Two of the NASDAQ-listed stocks were delisted (i.e., closed their stock transfer books) prior to the initial announcement date; one of the NASDAQ firms was delisted after the initial announcement date, but stock price data are not available on the event dates; and stock price data are not available on CRSP for three of the firms on other exchanges.

Table 5
Average two-day announcement period excess returns for three dates: (1) the initial announcement date; (2) the board approval date; and (3) the shareholder approval date for 55 firms that voluntarily liquidated over the period 1970–1991[a]

Date	All firms	Firms with prior control event[b]	Firms without prior control event[b]	*t*-statistic for difference in means[c]
Initial announcement	13.71%*** (55;84%)	8.70%*** (23;83%)	17.50%*** (32;84%)	1.68*
Board approval	5.27%*** (34;70%)	9.10%*** (15;73%)	2.03%*** (19;67%)	2.20**
Shareholder approval	0.86%** (53;54%)	1.60%*** (23;70%)	0.25% (30;39%)	1.96*

[a] Sample size and % positive appear in parentheses.
[b] Control event occurs during the three years prior to the initial liquidation announcement. Control events include solicitation of buyers for the firm, friendly merger attempts, and hostile takeover attempts.
[c] Results from tests of differences in two-day average excess returns between firms with and without prior control events.
*** Statistically significant at the 1% level.
** Statistically significant at the 5% level.
* Statistically significant at the 10% level.

approval date. Each is positive and statistically significant (p-values < 0.05). These results indicate that the initial decision to liquidate the firm is good news for shareholders and that additional uncertainty is resolved about the decision at each approval date along the way. The sum of the excess returns over the three announcement dates is +19.8%. Given that the initial announcement date and the board approval date coincide for 21 firms, it is perhaps not surprising that the bulk of the wealth effect, 13.7%, occurs on the initial announcement date.

As suggested by Hite et al., because of prior control events, the liquidation decision may have been partially anticipated in those firms with such pre-liquidation activity. If so, as reported by Hite et al., the announcement period excess returns for these firms should be lower than for those firms with no prior control event. To investigate that issue, we split the sample into those with and without prior control events. Announcement period returns for the two samples are shown in the third and fourth columns of Table 5. Consistent with the idea that the liquidation announcement is less anticipated in the sample without prior control events, the excess return of +17.5% on the initial announcement date for this sample is more than twice the +8.7% for the sample with a prior control event. Note, however, that the relative sizes of the excess returns for the two samples is reversed on the board approval date — it is +9.10% for the sample with a prior control event and it is +2.03% for the sample with no prior control event. Additionally, examination of excess returns on the shareholder approval date indicates that the significant excess return on this date for the full sample is due entirely to the set with prior control events. When excess returns around the three dates are summed, the totals are nearly identical for the two samples — +19.4% and +19.8%.

Our results give rise to an alternative interpretation (than the one offered by Hite et al.) of the market's differential reaction to the initial announcements for the two samples. It goes as follows: Because prior attempts to transfer control of the firms in the sample with prior control events failed, the market gives less credibility to the initial announcement of an attempt to liquidate the firm for this sample than for the sample with no prior control event. As the market becomes less skeptical of the likelihood of a successful liquidation of the firm, the market attributes an equal valuation effect to that decision, regardless of prior attempts to transfer control of the firm by other means. On net then, these results reverse the conclusion of Hite et al. that the valuation effects of liquidation for firms with and without prior control events are significantly different from each other. The positive valuation consequences of the liquidation of the firm appear to be independent of prior takeover attempts.

6.2. Cross-sectional analysis

We now investigate the relation between the valuation effects and various financial, operating, and ownership characteristics of the sample by performing cross-sectional regressions. Care must be taken when interpreting the results of these regressions, however, because, at least in some cases, the event in question is likely to have been, at least partially, anticipated because of prior events in the life of the firm. To control for this effect, two indicator variables are included in each regression, one for a prior asset sale and one for a prior control event. The inclusion of the indicator for the prior control event allows us to test in a multivariate context, the conclusion by Hite et al. that excess returns differ between firms with and without prior control events.

Because we are interested in the total wealth effect associated with the decision to liquidate the firm, we use the sum of the two-day excess returns around the three events as the dependent variable in the regressions. In the first regression, the independent variables include ROA, Tobin's Q, total leverage, free cash flow, the fraction of shares owned by members of the board, an indicator variable equal to 1 when more than 50% of the board is comprised of corporate insiders, an indicator variable equal to 1 when a member of the founding family serves on the board of directors and/or in a key executive position, an indicator variable equal to 1 when an outside blockholder is present, an indicator variable equal to 1 when the firm experienced prior asset sales, and an indicator variable equal to 1 when the firm experienced a prior control event.

Table 6
Estimated coefficients from weighted least square regressions in which the dependent variable is the sum of two-day announcement period excess returns for 55 publicly traded firms that liquidated voluntarily on a piecemeal basis over the period 1970–1991. The two-day excess returns around three dates are summed. The three dates are: (1) the initial announcement date; (2) the board approval date; (3) the shareholder approval date. (*t*-statistics are in parentheses)

Independent variable	(1)	(2)
Intercept	0.13	0.10
	(1.02)	(0.75)
Current profitability	−1.03	
	−(3.73)***	
Tobin's *Q*	−0.01	−0.09
	−(0.09)	−(1.33)*
Leverage	−0.19	−0.24
	−(1.34)	−(1.56)
Free cash flow	0.0001	0.0001
	(0.72)	(0.40)
Board stock ownership	0.29	0.26
	(1.94)**	(1.73)*
Inside board indicator	0.05	0.05
	(0.87)	(0.84)
Founding family indicator	0.03	0.01
	(0.51)	(0.08)
Blockholder indicator	0.06	0.05
	(0.91)	(0.68)
Prior asset sales indicator	−0.09	−0.07
	−(1.63)*	−(1.25)
Prior control event indicator	−0.04	−0.07
	−(0.79)	−(1.20)
R^2	0.28	0.18

*** Statistically significant at the 1% level.
** Statistically significant at the 5% level.
* Statistically significant at the 10% level.

The results of the regression are presented in the second column of Table 6. Excess returns are negatively correlated with current profitability (p-value < 0.05), positively correlated with the fraction of shares owned by members of the board (p-value < 0.05), and negatively correlated with the presence of prior asset sales (p-value < 0.05). None of the other variables have p-values less than 0.10. As an experiment to determine whether it is only current, as opposed to future, profitability that matters, current profitability is omitted from the regression and the regression is reestimated with all other variables retained in the regression. The results, presented in the third column of Table 6, show that Q now enters the regression positively and significantly at the 0.10 level. The regression is then reestimated with alternative measures of leverage and free cash flow and other combinations of variables. In no case is the p-value of any of these variables less than 0.10. Importantly, in no case does the indicator variable for prior control events enter with a p-value less 0.10. The results indicate that market participants expect greater value to be created in the liquidation process by firms that have been performing relatively poorly on a current operating basis or have relatively poor prospects for the future (as measured by the ratio of market to book value of equity) and in which board members have a relatively large ownership stake in the firm. One interpretation of the results is that, given the decision to liquidate, market participants expect management to create greater value the greater is their ownership stake in the firm.

7. The discounted value of liquidating dividends

The decision to liquidate the firm is a capital (dis)investment decision such that voluntary corporate liquidations provide an opportunity to study whether standard capital budgeting techniques indicate that liquidation decisions are positive NPV projects given ex post cash flows. The traditional Sharpe–Lintner capital asset pricing model (CAPM) is used to estimate a risk-adjusted discount rate. That rate is then used to discount the actual dividends paid. The liquidating dividends are compiled from the Prentice-Hall *Capital Adjustment Reporter* and the Commerce Clearing House *Capital Changes Reporter*. To implement the CAPM, the yield on the 90-day treasury bill at the time of the initial liquidation announcement is used as the risk-free rate, the arithmetic average of the difference between the S&P 500 and the return on short-term treasury securities, as calculated by Ibbotson and Sinquefield, is used as the market risk premium, and betas are calculated as in Kim and Schatzberg (1987).

As shown in Table 7, the average stock price of the liquidating firms five days prior to the initial announcement is \$20.16 and the discounted value of the actual dividends paid is \$23.50. As a percentage of the pre-announcement stock price,

Table 7
Results of analysis of liquidating dividends paid out by 55 firms that liquidated voluntarily on a piecemeal basis over the period 1970–1991

	Mean	Median	Minimum	Maximum
Total dividends paid	\$ 29.92	\$ 20.86	\$ 2.20	\$ 101.50
Discounted value of dividends[a]	\$ 23.50	\$ 15.38	\$ 1.89	\$ 87.67
Pre-liquidation announcement price[b]	\$ 20.16	\$ 13.00	\$ 2.06	\$ 75.25
Post-liquidation announcement price[c]	\$ 22.71	\$ 14.56	\$ 2.53	\$ 86.63
Liquidation period (in years)[d]	3.48	3.21	0.08	9.25

[a] Discounted value of dividends is determined by discounting dividends paid with a risk-adjusted discount rate estimated with the traditional Sharp-Lintner CAPM.
[b] Measured five days before the initial liquidation announcement.
[c] Measured five days after the initial liquidation announcement.
[d] Defined as the period from shareholder confirmation of the liquidation decision through the date of the final liquidating dividend.

the difference between the two is +16.56%. That is, if the CAPM were the precise way in which market participants determined the value of future cash flows and if the actual cash flows are an unbiased reflection of market participants' expected cash flows, the announcement period average excess return would be +16.56%. This compares with the average initial announcement period excess return of +13.71% and the sum of the three announcement period returns of +19.84%. The average percentage NPV of the project is not significantly different from either the average initial announcement period return or the sum of the three announcement period average excess returns. For a sample of 37 firms that liquidate over the period 1970 through 1984, Skantz and Marchesini (1992) report a similar result. The similarity between the announcement period excess returns and the percentage NPV of the project provides at least some comfort for the straightforward application of the CAPM in capital budgeting analysis.

8. Taxes and the decision to liquidate

Under current tax law, when a corporation sells any of its assets, the corporation recognizes and is taxed on any gain realized upon the sale. The shareholders, in turn, are taxed on the amount by which the cash distributed to them exceeds the value of the adjusted basis for their common stock in the liquidating firm. However, prior to the Tax Reform Act of 1986, if the firm's assets were completely liquidated, gains on the sale of the assets were not taxed at the corporate level. Rather, the cash payouts to shareholders from the liquidation were taxed only at the personal level at which point they were treated as ordinary dividends and taxed accordingly. The only limitation was that the liquidation must be completed within one year following the decision to liquidate. However, that limitation was easily circumvented by simply transferring ownership of all non-liquidated assets to a liquidating trust within 12 months of the decision to liquidate. As a consequence, some transactions in which the entire firm was acquired were structured as voluntary liquidations rather than asset sales or acquisitions so as to capture the tax advantage of a voluntary liquidation relative to that of a merger or whole firm acquisition.

The Tax Reform Act of 1986 clearly removed the preferential tax treatment given to corporate liquidations, thereby eliminating the tax incentive to disguise acquisitions and asset sales as voluntary liquidations. Furthermore, the 1986 Act reduced the after-tax value of a voluntary piecemeal liquidation relative to the after-tax value that it would have had prior to the Act. However, for value maximizing firms, the Act has not changed the criterion for liquidation: If the 'bust-up' value of the firm exceeds its going concern value (or acquisition value), the firm should be liquidated. Consistent with that notion, announcements of voluntary piecemeal liquidations decline, but still occur after 1986. As we noted, we identified three in 1988, five in 1989, four in 1990 and four in 1991. Given our requirement that the liquidation be complete by year-end 1991 to enter our sample, these firms do not show up in our analysis. Nevertheless, voluntary piecemeal liquidations continue to be a mechanism for transferring control of resources to higher value uses.

9. Summary and conclusions

This paper presents the results of an analysis of a nearly comprehensive sample of publicly traded firms that initiated and completed voluntary liquidations over the period 1970 through 1991. We examine events leading up to the decision to liquidate, the ownership and governance structure of these firms, their financial characteristics, and their operating and financial performance prior to and at the time of their decisions to liquidate voluntarily. We also conduct an event study around three dates: (1) the date of initial announcement; (2) the date of approval of the plan of liquidation by the board of directors; and (3) the date of shareholder approval of the plan.

The results of the analyses indicate that, in comparison with a size-matched sample of their industry peers, firms that choose to liquidate voluntarily are characterized by low Tobin's Q, high percentage ownership of shares by management and members of the board of directors and a high incidence of the presence of the founding family on the board of directors and/or in a key management position, a high incidence of prior attempts to transfer control of the firm by other means, and a high incidence of prior asset sales. Contrarily, on the basis of current rate of return on assets, use of debt financing, free cash flow, composition of the board according to inside and outside directors, age of the firm, ages of the top corporate officers, and presence of an outside blockholder, these firms are not distinguishable from their industry peer group. The analysis of stock returns indicates that voluntary liquidations are, on average, associated with an increase in stock price of +20%.

One interpretation of the results is that it is not low current profitability or 'over-reliance' on debt financing that impels these firms to voluntarily undertake the value increasing decision to discontinue operating as a going concern. Rather, it is the absence of future growth opportunities, as evidenced by a low market-to-book ratio, that pushes the firm toward this decision. Furthermore, while the condition of low future growth opportunities is necessary, it is not sufficient. A further requirement is that the board of directors have a large stake in the firm's equity and/or that the founding family continues to play an important role in the decision making process of the firm. We interpret this latter result to be broadly consistent with managerial theories of the firm that argue that managers are more likely to act in shareholders interests when managers share in the equity ownership of the firm. Our cross-sectional regressions of stock returns indicate that market participants respond more favorably (i.e., the announcement period stock price reaction is higher) the poorer has been recent performance and the higher is the fraction of stock owned by the managers and the board of directors. Once shareholders have approved the decision to liquidate voluntarily, the board has significant discretion over the means by which assets are sold and the proceeds distributed. Thus, one interpretation of the positive correlation between the stock price reaction and board ownership is that market participants expect managers and the board to more efficiently dispose of assets, the more closely their interests are aligned with shareholders. This result, too, is then consistent with managerial theories of the firm.

Finally, as an experiment, we discount the liquidating cash flows (i.e., dividends) paid by the firm with a CAPM-determined risk-adjusted discount rate. We then compare the discounted value of these cash flows with the firm's pre-announcement stock price. The average percentage NPV of the (dis)investment decision is roughly the same as the average announcement returns. This result provides, at least some, reassurance for the practice of using discounted cash flows to evaluate capital budgeting alternatives.

Appendix A. Case histories of certain voluntary corporate liquidations

A.1. Barber Oil Corporation

Initial Announcement Date: 3/3/80; Total Assets (millions): $179.64; Tobin's *Q*: 0.56; Board Ownership: 11.2%; Founding Family on Board of Directors: No

After an unsuccessful attempt to voluntarily liquidate the firm in 1975, the board appointed a new management team. The intent of the new management was to expand the firm's operations in oil exploration, development, and distribution as well as to diversify into coal mining. However, the company experienced difficulty raising the required capital for this expansion and found itself as the target of a hostile takeover attempt by Hanson Industries in 1979. The board tried to block the takeover and solicited a friendly bid from Engelhard Minerals and Chemicals. Eventually, Hanson countered the Engelhard bid with a bid that could not be matched by Engelhard. Barber then attempted to negotiate a purchase agreement with Hanson but Hanson subsequently abandoned its takeover attempt. Early in 1980, after exploring the firm's alternatives, the board began a search for another potential buyer for the firm as a going concern. By year-end, after this search proved unsuccessful, the board adopted a plan of complete liquidation and dissolution of the firm.

A.2. City Investing

Initial Announcement Date: 8/23/84; Total Assets (millions): $8.361.0; Tobin's *Q*: 0.39; Board Ownership: 1.5%; Founding Family on Board of Directors: Yes

In 1980, after intense self-examination during a takeover battle with Tamco Industries, the board reviewed the range of values which might be realized for the assets of the firm if sold in an orderly and piecemeal fashion. Subsequently, the board adopted a partial divestiture program in which $800 million in assets were sold with intention of reducing its heavy debt burden of $1.5 billion. However, upon completion of the proposed asset sales, the firm still found itself in a vulnerable position and adopted a golden parachute plan for its officers. In May of 1984, the firm received two offers to acquire all the company's common stock. The first was made by an investor group led by Merrill Lynch (ML) for $50/share or $2.3 billion. The second offer, from corporate raider Victor Posner, proposed to acquire the firm for $52.50/share. However, the ML offer was revised and replaced by an offer from an investor group led by Kohlberg, Kravis, and Roberts (KKR) and ML to purchase three divisions for $1.25 billion. Upon careful consideration, the board accepted the KKR/ML offer. Posner subsequently countered with a $1.3 billion offer for the assets and filed suit against the proposed sale to KKR/ML.

In addition, Tamco Industries, a substantial shareholder from its previous takeover attempt, offered to buy two of City's remaining divisions for $560 million. In turn, Tamco's offer was countered at $565 million by KKR/ML. In September, the board voted in favor of the KKR/ML offers, rejected the Posner and Tamco bids, and proposed the piecemeal liquidation of the firm's remaining assets. During the following month, Tamco filed a suit against the board's proposed liquidation plan, stating that it was too costly. Joined by Posner, Tamco waged a proxy contest in an attempt to block the shareholder meeting scheduled to vote on adoption of the liquidation plan. However, these efforts were unsuccessful and a majority of shareholders ratified the board's plan for liquidation of the firm.

A.3. Glasrock Medical Services

Initial Announcement Date: 10/21/82; Total Assets (millions): $68.69; Tobin's *Q*: 1.42; Board Ownership: 13.0%; Founding Family on Board of Directors: No

During the mid-1970s, the firm adopted a major restructuring plan that focused its health care operations primarily in the medical services area. The operations of the firm were streamlined and there was a change in the top management of the firm. Late in the following year, a hostile takeover attempt emerged. In the course of the battle, Glasrock's chairman obtained a large enough ownership position to block the offer. The SEC began an investigation into these share purchases by the chairman and subsequently filed suit against the chairman for breaking disclosure laws. To discourage other unwanted takeover attempts, the board instituted a share repurchase program and financed it with $16 million in debt during 1980 and 1981.

However, early the next year, Airco, Inc. expressed an interest in obtaining all or some of the firm's assets. The board was open to negotiations and agreed to sell to Airco 14% of the firm's common shares for $20/share and elected two of Airco's officers as directors. Additionally, the board agreed to accept a tender offer in excess of $23/share. These negotiations continued for nearly a year, but eventually Airco determined that a tender offer for the firm as a going concern would not serve its shareholders' interests. Instead, Airco made an offer for 80% of the firm's operations. The board concluded that the offer was attractive, but that the remaining assets would not be profitable. Consequently, the board resolved that it would be in the best interests of Glasrock shareholders to sell certain assets of the firm to Airco and to sell its remaining subsidiaries to other buyers.

A.4. Handyman Corporation

Initial Announcement Date: 9/26/86; Total Assets (millions): $149.85; Tobin's *Q*: 0.59; Board Ownership: 58.7%; Founding Family on Board of Directors: Yes

Founded in 1962, Handyman consisted of subsidiaries engaged in the operation of 53 home improvement centers. In 1984, the board began a restructuring program that concentrated expansion efforts in its most profitable markets while closing and disposing of stores in less profitable markets. As a result, 21 stores were closed and sold by 1985. During the next two years, however, the home improvement industry experienced significant changes and increased competition which negatively affected the performance of Handyman's existing stores.

Despite increasing sales, profits from operations did not increase primarily because of the competitive pressure on prices and the substantial capital expenditures required to remodel and update the stores. During this period, the company also actively attempted to enlarge its market share and to achieve economies of scale by acquiring additional stores in its primary markets. This did not prove viable. After considering the adverse effects of increasing business competition, the relatively low return on its investments, and the value of its properties, the board determined that the liquidation of the firm's assets, in an orderly and piecemeal fashion, would result in distributions to shareholders in excess of what they would be able to realize in the foreseeable future by the sale of their common shares in the open market if the firm continued its operations.

A.5. Murray Mortgage Investors

Initial Announcement Date: 11/19/80; Total Assets (millions): $10.99; Tobin's *Q*: 0.75; Board Ownership: 11.4%; Founding Family on Board of Directors: Yes

Prior to its liquidation in 1981, Murray was organized as a business trust to invest in a diversified portfolio of real estate mortgage loans. However, due to unfavorable economic and financial conditions affecting the real estate industry, the trust did not institute any loans on new projects from September 1975 through June 1978 other than with respect to renewals, and increased or new loans relating to existing investments. The trust resumed its lending operations on a limited basis in July 1978 and these activities increased substantially during the next two years.

During 1980, in an attempt to make the trust a more profitable and attractive investment to its shareholders, the primary business goals of the trust were to increase its investment activity in first mortgage construction loans and to increase its capital base. The trust was able to increase its investment activity, but was unable to increase its capital base. Faced with its limited capital and the discount of the trust's market value relative to the book value of its assets, the board adopted a plan for the piecemeal sale of the firm's assets.

A.6. Overseas National Airways

Initial Announcement Date: 4/2/76; Total Assets (millions): $97.43; Tobin's *Q*: 0.80; Board Ownership: 5.1%, Founding Family on Board of Directors: No

As a supplemental air carrier, in a highly competitive industry, Overseas had suffered from increased operational costs and constraints from servicing its debt. As a result, the board initiated merger talks with another carrier in 1974. However, these negotiations did not prove to be fruitful. Throughout the following year, the firm's profits plunged and the firm defaulted on its debt obligation. Thus, when approached by Coca-Cola Bottling regarding the purchase of the firm, Overseas' board was receptive. However, after reviewing the net worth of the firm, the initial offer was reduced and eventually the buyout was canceled in May, 1976. The firm continued its dwindling operations and late in 1977 its chairman resigned. Due to substantial losses, the board sold two of the firm's DC-8 jet liners for $12 million, but did not believe that the firm's situation would improve in the foreseeable future. Since there did not seem to be any 'reasonable' interest in the carrier as a going concern, the board determined that the only remaining value-maximizing alternative for shareholders was voluntary liquidation of the firm.

A.7. RH Medical Services

Initial Announcement Date: 1/14/80; Total Assets (millions): $43.90; Tobin's *Q*: 0.95; Board Ownership: 60.4%; Founding Family on Board of Directors: Yes

Due to rising costs and competition in the health care industry, in 1977 the board planned to consolidate its operations into a health care group by merging with a large hospital. Eventually, these plans were canceled. However, in the course of these negotiations, the board assessed the negative impact that the rapid changes in the health care industry were having on the firm's operations. The board did not believe that this situation was likely to change and, furthermore, that the situation would continue to deteriorate. After reviewing the needed expansion and capital expenditures to earn an acceptable return for the shareholders, the board agreed that the complete piecemeal liquidation of the firm would be in the shareholder's best interests.

A.8. Unity Buying Service

Initial Announcement Date: 9/15/83; Total Assets (millions): $40.71; Tobin's *Q*: 0.50; Board Ownership: 69.4%; Founding Family on Board of Directors: Yes

Since its inception in 1971, the firm had principally been engaged in retail merchandising of a wide variety of products by direct response mail order activities. During the 1980s, the board adopted a major restructuring plan aimed at increasing working capital and reducing debt to help improve future earnings. However, these efforts did not substantially improve the financial situation of the firm. Furthermore, the company's operations had been adversely affected by inflationary increases in the cost of labor, merchandise, and services. The company had also experienced significant decreases in overall sales due to its increased merchandise costs during the past several years. Finally, the company's business had become highly competitive, of which many competitors had significantly greater financial resources available for expansion than was available to Unity. After reviewing these adverse developments and exploring its options, the board concluded that the situation was not likely to turn around in the foreseeable future. Accordingly, the board recommended that the firm be voluntarily liquidated.

References

Berle, A.A., Jr., Means, G.C., 1932. The modern corporation and private property, Macmillan, New York, NY.

Denis, D.J., Denis, D.K., 1995. Majority owner-managers and organizational efficiency. Journal of Corporate Finance 1, 91–118.

Ghosh, C., Owers, J.E., Rogers, R.C., 1991. The financial characteristics associated with voluntary liquidations. Journal of Business Finance and Accounting 18, 773–789.

Hite, G.L., Owers, J.E., Rogers, R.C., 1987. The market for interfirm asset sales: Partial selloffs and total liquidations. Journal of Financial Economics 20, 317–346.

Holderness, C.G., Sheehan, D.P., 1988. The role of majority shareholders in publicly held corporations. Journal of Financial Economics 20, 317–346.

Jensen, M.C., 1986. Agency costs of free cash flow, corporate finance, and takeovers. American Economic Review 76, 323–329.

Jensen, M.C., Meckling, W.H., 1976. Theory of the firm: Managerial behavior, agency costs, and ownership structure. Journal of Financial Economics 3, 305–360.

Kim, E.H., Schatzberg, J.D., 1987. Voluntary corporate liquidations. Journal of Financial Economics 19, 311–328.

Kudla, R.J., 1987. Corporate insiders and the voluntary liquidation decision, unpublished manuscript, University of Wisconsin – Eau Claire.

Lang, L., Poulsen, A., Stulz, R., 1995. Asset sales, firm performance, and the agency costs of managerial discretion. Journal of Financial Economics 37, 3–37.

Manne, H.G., 1965. Mergers and the market for corporate control. Journal of Political Economy 73, 110–120.

Marris, R., 1963. A model of managerial enterprise. Quarterly Journal of Economics 77, 185–209.

Martin, K., McConnell, J.J., 1991. Corporate performance, corporate takeovers, and management turnover. Journal of Finance 46, 671–688.

McConnell, J.J., Servaes, H., 1990. Additional evidence on equity ownership and market valuation: An empirical analysis. Journal of Financial Economics 27, 595–612.

McConnell, J.J., Servaes, H., 1995. Equity ownership and the two faces of debt. Journal of Financial Economics 39, 131–157.

Morck, R., Shleifer, A., Vishny, R.W., 1988a. Management ownership and market valuation: An empirical analysis. Journal of Financial Economics 20, 293–315.

Morck, R., Shleifer, A., Vishny, R.W., 1988b. Characteristics of targets of hostile and friendly takeovers, corporate takeovers: Causes and consequences, University of Chicago Press, Chicago, IL.

Palepu, K.G., 1986. Predicting takeover targets: A methodological and empirical analysis. Journal of Accounting and Economics 8, 3–35.

Skantz, T.R., Marchesini, R., 1987. The effect of voluntary corporate liquidation on shareholder wealth. Journal of Financial Research 11, 65–75.

Skantz, T.R., Marchesini, R., 1992. A test of a risk-adjusted dividend capitalization model: The case of liquidating firms. Journal of Financial Research 15, 11–26.

Stulz, R.M., 1988. Managerial control of voting rights, financing policies, and the market for corporate control. Journal of Financial Economics 20, 25–34.

[12]

ELSEVIER Journal of Corporate Finance 6 (2000) 117–139

Journal of CORPORATE FINANCE

www.elsevier.com/locate/econbase

Comparing acquisitions and divestitures

J. Harold Mulherin *, Audra L. Boone

Department of Finance, Smeal College of Business, Penn State University, University Park, PA 16802, USA

Abstract

We study the acquisition and divestiture activity of a sample of 1305 firms from 59 industries during the 1990–1999 period. Consistent with the importance of restructuring activity during the 1990s, we find that half of the sample firms are acquired or engage in a major divestiture. Consistent with the notion that economic change is a source of the observed restructuring activity, we find significant industry clustering in both acquisitions and divestitures. We also study the announcement effects of the two forms of restructuring and find that both acquisitions and divestitures in the 1990s increase shareholder wealth. Moreover, the wealth effects for both acquisitions and divestitures are directly related to the relative size of the event. The symmetric, positive wealth effects for acquisitions and divestitures are consistent with a synergistic explanation for both forms of restructuring and are inconsistent with nonsynergistic models based on entrenchment, empire building and hubris. © 2000 Elsevier Science B.V. All rights reserved.

JEL classification: G14; G34
Keywords: Acquisitions; Equity carve-outs; Spinoffs; Asset sales; Synergy

1. Introduction

In this paper, we study the causes and effects of acquisitions and divestitures during the 1990s. The general purpose of our analysis is to bring new evidence to bear on the contrasting views of corporate restructuring that have been presented

* Corresponding author. Tel.: +1-814-865-9201; fax: +1-814-865-3362.
E-mail address: jhm14@psu.edu (J.H. Mulherin).

PII: S0929-1199(00)00010-9

in research on earlier time periods.[1] We study whether corporate restructuring can best be typified as an efficient response to economic shocks or instead is better described as an imperfect reaction to management entrenchment and hubris.

Our initial analysis gauges the impact of economic shocks on corporate restructuring activity by studying whether there are industry patterns in acquisitions and divestitures. We follow the premise of recent studies of merger patterns by Mitchell and Mulherin (1996) and Andrade and Stafford (1999) that the clustering of restructuring activity in particular industries emanates from fundamental economic shocks. Our work can be distinguished from the other research by our emphasis on the 1990s and by our consideration of both acquisitions and divestitures. Consistent with the importance of economic shocks for restructuring activity, we find that both acquisitions and divestitures exhibit significant industry clustering.

To more directly determine the importance of economic shocks for acquisitions and divestitures, the main body of the paper uses event study analysis to empirically distinguish between two broad sets of theories of corporate restructuring: the nonsynergistic theory and the synergistic theory. The joint consideration of acquisitions and divestitures facilitates more refined tests of the two theories than can be attained by studying either acquisitions or divestitures in isolation. In particular, we study whether acquisitions and divestitures have an asymmetric or symmetric effect on shareholder wealth.

The first set of models that we test can collectively be labeled the nonsynergistic theory. These include models based on management entrenchment, empire building, and managerial hubris (see, e.g., Jensen, 1986; Roll, 1986; Shleifer and Vishny, 1989). Although differing in assumptions and emphasis, these theories generally predict an asymmetric relation between the wealth effects of acquisitions and divestitures. In the models, divestitures create wealth by increasing specialization and reducing agency costs, while acquisitions lower wealth by protecting management from market forces and by lessening corporate focus.

A second set of theories poses synergistic reasons for both acquisitions and divestitures. The origin of this line of thought is usually traced to Coase (1937) who theorizes that the size of the firm responds over time to factors that affect the relative costs of market pricing and internal management decisions. As an example, Coase (1937, Footnotes 31 and 32) argues that technological change will alter the efficient size of the firm and, by implication, affect the decision to engage in acquisitions or divestitures. Subsequent analysis has extended these insights. Klein et al. (1978) argue that acquisitions and divestitures represent reactions to changes in the transaction costs created by specialized assets. Bradley et al. (1988,

[1] Jensen and Ruback (1983) and Jarrell et al. (1988) provide the seminal surveys of acquisitions research. The Appendix to this paper highlights some of the more recent research on acquisitions as well as selected research on divestitures.

p. 4) posit that mergers occur when bidding firms attempt "to exploit a profit opportunity created by a change in economic conditions." Jensen (1993) more specifically relates the restructuring activity of the 1980s to changes in technology, input prices, and regulation. In contrast to the nonsynergistic theory, the synergistic models predict that both acquisitions and divestitures create wealth.

We test the predictions of the nonsynergistic and synergistic theories by studying the announcement effects of acquisitions and divestitures during the 1990s. We find that both acquisitions and divestitures create wealth. Moreover, the wealth effects for acquisitions and divestitures are directly related to the size of the restructuring event. The symmetric, positive wealth effects for both acquisitions and divestitures are consistent with a synergistic explanation for the two restructuring events and are inconsistent with nonsynergistic models based on management entrenchment, empire building, and hubris.

The sample used in our analysis is described in the following section. Section 3 characterizes the overall restructuring activity for the sample firms during the 1990s and Section 4 reports the industry patterns in acquisitions and divestitures. The fifth section presents the evidence on wealth effects. The final section summarizes the results and offers concluding comments.

2. The sample

The intent of our analysis is to study the causes and effects of acquisitions and divestitures during the 1990s. To implement our research design, we begin with a sample of firms covered by the Value Line Investment Survey and track their restructuring activity between 1990 and 1999. Our general procedure bears resemblance to recent research, such as Mitchell and Mulherin (1996) and Andrade and Stafford (1999), and allows us to estimate the rate of acquisitions and divestitures both in aggregate and at the industry level. The firms listed on Value Line are heavily followed in the media, allowing us to precisely pinpoint the incidence and nature of particular restructuring events. The use of Value Line also enables accurate assignment of firms to industries and avoids the ambiguity created from the reliance on SIC codes reported in CRSP and Compustat (see Kahle and Walkling, 1996).

The use of Value Line as the basis for our sample also facilitates comparisons of the wealth effects of acquisitions and divestitures. Rather than draw the two forms of restructuring from heterogeneous sets of firms, the acquisitions and divestitures are taken from a common universe. As reported below, this ensures that the relative size of the sample acquisitions and divestitures are of a comparable order of magnitude.

To form our sample, we begin with 1681 firms listed in the Value Line Investment Survey in the 1st quarter of 1990. We delete 376 firms for the following reasons: Value Line industries with fewer than nine US firms (110 deletions), particular Value Line categories, such as Diversified Company, Investment Company, REIT, and Unassigned (159 deletions), and non-US firms tracked by Value Line (107 deletions).

The resulting sample of 1305 firms is characterized in Table 1. The firms come from 59 industries spanning Aerospace/Defense to Trucking. By number of firms, the Electric Utility industry has the greatest representation with 102 firms. In terms

Table 1
The sample

Industry	Firms		Industry	Firms	
	Number	Value (US$ billions)		Number	Value (US$ billions)
Aerospace/defense	32	47	Medical services	9	10
Air transport	12	17	Medical supplies	37	58
Apparel	17	8	Metal fabricating	16	8
Auto parts	20	11	Metals and mining	12	21
Bank	50	97	Natural gas (dist)	28	14
Bank (Midwest)	23	28	Natural Gas (div)	22	45
Broadcasting/cable	10	28	Newspaper	13	30
Building materials	26	17	Office equipment	20	15
Chemical (basic)	10	68	Oilfield services	19	28
Chemical (diversified)	12	36	Packaging and contain	15	8
Chemical (specialty)	35	31	Paper	27	51
Computer and peripherals	37	105	Petroleum (integrate)	23	216
Computer software	17	21	Petroleum (produce)	18	22
Drug	19	153	Precision instrument	25	21
Electric utility	102	199	Publishing	17	30
Electrical equipment	20	98	Railroad	9	28
Electronics	38	15	Recreation	18	35
Environmental	11	32	Restaurant	17	18
Financial services	22	43	Retail store	27	85
Food processing	45	95	Retail (special lines)	49	34
Furniture	12	5	Securities brokerage	13	12
Grocery Store	19	20	Semiconductor	15	21
Homebuilding	11	2	Shoe	12	7
Hotel/gaming	14	13	Steel	25	19
Household products	10	42	Telecommunications	23	259
Industrial services	26	11	Textile	9	2
Insurance	47	105	Thrift	16	16
Machine tool	10	5	Toiletries/cosmetics	9	11
Machinery	32	16	Trucking	12	6
Machinery (constr.)	11	16	Full sample	1305	2514

This table reports the number and value of the sample firms by industry. The sample is formed from the firms covered by the Value Line Investment Survey in the 1st quarter of 1990. Industries with at least nine US firms are included in the analysis. The industries are reported in alphabetical order. Value (in US$ billions) is the sum of the equity value of the firms in an industry at year-end 1989 and is taken from the Daily Stock Price Record.

of equity value at year-end 1989, the Telecommunications industry is the largest at US$259 billion. The total value of the 1305 sample firms at year-end 1989 is US$2.5 trillion, which is 71% of the combined equity value of the listings on the NYSE, AMEX, and NASDAQ in 1989. The average firm in the sample has a value of US$1.9 billion at year-end 1989.

3. Overall acquisition and divestiture activity in the 1990s

For each of the sample firms, we track acquisition and divestiture activity during the 1990s. Relying on the Wall Street Journal Index, Lexis/Nexis, Mergers and Acquisitions, and other financial and news media, we determine whether and when a sample firm is acquired. Using the same sources, we also determine whether a sample firm engaged in any major divestitures, including corporate spinoffs, equity carve-outs and asset sales. The spinoffs and carve-outs in the sample are readily classifiable. By contrast, the choice of asset sales to include in the sample is somewhat more problematic, due to the substantial variation in the size of both the sample firms and their assets divested via direct sale. Our criterion in classifying an asset sale as ''major'' is that the sold assets were either worth at least US$100 million in absolute terms or represented at least 5% of the equity value of the divesting parent.

The results on overall acquisition and divestiture activity during the 1990s are reported in Table 2. A total of 335 firms (25.7% of the sample) are acquired but do not engage in a divestiture. In addition, 222 firms (17%) undertake a major

Table 2
Overall acquisition and divestiture activity

	# of Firms	Fraction of sample (%)	Average firm value (US$ billions)
Acquired	335	25.7	1.1
Divest	222	17.0	4.7
Both	46	3.5	2.9
Neither	702	53.8	1.4
Full sample	1305	100	1.9

This table reports the overall acquisition and divestiture activity for the sample firms in the 1990–1999 period. Acquisition and divestiture activity is determined by consulting the Wall Street Journal Index, Lexis/Nexis, Mergers and Acquisitions, and other financial and news media. Acquired reports — the firms that were acquired and did not engage in a major divestiture during the 1990–1999 period. Divest reports — the firms that engaged in at least one major divestiture (including spinoffs, equity carve-outs, and asset sales) but were not acquired. Both reports the firms that had at least one divestiture and were also acquired. Neither reports the firms that were not acquired and did not have a major divestiture. Average Firm Value reports the average equity value of the firms in a particular category as of year-end 1989.

divestiture but are not acquired. Finally, 46 firms (3.5%) engage in a divestiture and are later acquired.

As a whole, roughly half (46%) of the sample firms are acquired and/or engage in a major divestiture during the 1990s. These results indicate that the restructuring in the most recent decade has some comparability to the significant wave that occurred in the 1980s. As a comparison, Mitchell and Mulherin (1996) estimate that 48% of their sample firms were acquired or engaged in a defensive asset restructuring during the 1982–1989 period.

Table 2 also reports some characteristics of firms that turn out to be acquisition or divestiture candidates. Based on equity values at the time of the formation of the sample, firms that are acquired are smaller than average; the average value of the acquired firms as of year-end 1989 is US$1.1 billion. By contrast, the firms engaging in divestitures are much larger; the average value of a firm undertaking a major divestiture is US$4.7 billion. In results not reported in the table but available upon request, these relations hold at the industry level; acquired firms are generally smaller than their industry peers while divesting firms are larger than their industry counterparts. We report further data on the relative value of targets to bidders and divested subsidiaries to parents later in the text.

4. Acquisition and divestiture activity by industry

We next estimate whether there are industry patterns in the rate of acquisition and divestiture activity during the 1990s. Our analysis is motivated by the theory of the firm (e.g., Coase, 1937), which argues that firm size responds to changing economic conditions. Subsequent theory by Jensen (1993) more specifically relates corporate restructuring to changes in technology, input prices and regulation. Mitchell and Mulherin (1996) support the theory of the firm by finding significant patterns in acquisitions across industries in the 1980s. We provide further evidence by studying acquisitions in the 1990s and by extending the analysis to industry patterns in divestiture activity.

4.1. Industry patterns in acquisition activity

Table 3 reports the fraction of firms acquired for each of the 59 Value Line industries in the sample. In the median industry, 29% of the firms are acquired during the 1990s. But there is a notable variation in the rate of acquisitions across industries. Virtually every firm, 10 out of 11 or 91%, in the Environmental industry is acquired. By contrast, no firms in Homebuilding are acquired.

The variation in the rate of acquisitions is statistically significant. We compute the Pearson χ^2 that tests the null of no variation in the frequency of acquisition

Table 3
Acquisition activity by industry

Industry	% Acquired	Industry	% Acquired
Environmental	91	Recreation	28
Bank (Midwest)	57	Natural gas (div)	27
Bank	54	Industrial services	27
Broadcasting/cable	50	Paper	26
Petroleum (produce)	50	Auto Parts	25
Medical services	44	Machinery	25
Toiletries/cosmetics	44	Office equipment	25
Thrift	44	Financial services	23
Telecommunications	43	Food processing	22
Grocery store	42	Retail store	22
Electrical equipment	40	Textile	22
Electronics	39	Natural gas (dist)	21
Aerospace/defense	38	Oilfield services	21
Steel	36	Electric utility	20
Hotel/gaming	36	Metal fabricating	19
Publishing	35	Apparel	18
Computer and peripherals	35	Restaurant	18
Building materials	35	Petroleum (integrated)	17
Packaging and contain	33	Air Transport	17
Railroad	33	Chemical (diversified)	17
Trucking	33	Furniture	17
Precision instrument	32	Metals and mining	17
Insurance	32	Retail (special lines)	16
Drug	32	Household products	10
Securities brokerage	31	Machinery (constr.)	9
Chemical (basic)	30	Shoe	8
Machine tool	30	Newspaper	8
Medical supplies	30	Semiconductor	7
Computer software	29	Homebuilding	0
Chemical (specialty)	29	Full sample	29

This table reports the fraction of sample firms acquired in each industry in the 1990–1999 period. The data are sorted by the percent of industry members acquired. Acquisition activity is determined by consulting the Wall Street Journal Index, Lexis/Nexis, Mergers and Acquisitions, and other financial and news media.

activity across industries. The statistic is defined as Σ_i (Actual$_i$ − Expected$_i$)^2/Expected$_i$, where i represents the 59 industries in the sample and expected$_i$ equals the product of the average acquisition activity for the full sample, 29.2%, times the number of firms in the ith industry. The value of the statistic is 103 ($df = 58$, p-level = 0.001), indicating a rejection of the null.

A natural query is whether any of the sources of the inter-industry variation in acquisition activity can be identified. Jensen (1993) argues that the restructuring in the 1980s was induced by changes in regulation as well as a desire to eliminate industry overcapacity. In support of these conjectures, Mitchell and Mulherin (1996) find that the rate of takeover activity by industry is higher in deregulated industries and in low-tech industries with little or no research and development or other growth options.

We consider whether acquisition activity in the 1990s is driven by similar factors as the 1980s. We regress the rate of acquisition activity by industry on two variables. The first is a dummy variable equal to one for seven industries that underwent federal deregulation in the 1990s. The federal deregulation and the affected industries are: Riegle-Neal Act of 1994: Bank, Bank (Midwest) and Thrift, Telecommunications Act of 1996: Broadcasting/Cable TV and Telecommunications, Energy Policy Act of 1992: Electric Utility, and termination of the Interstate Commerce Commission: Railroad.

The second explanatory variable is the average R&D/Sales in a given industry in 1989 (obtained from Compustat). This variable tests whether the clustering of acquisitions in the 1990s is driven, in part, by the variation in underlying technology and growth options across industries.

The results of this regression are (t-statistic in parentheses):

$$\text{Acquisition activity} = 0.27(12.3) + 0.16\,(2.75)\,\text{Dereg Dummy} + 0.015(0.03)\,\text{R\&D/sales},$$

$N = 59$; F-value $= 3.89$ ($p = 0.03$); Adjusted $R^2 = 0.09$.

The positive and significant coefficient for the Deregulation Dummy indicates that, consistent with the 1980s, deregulation has a significant, positive effect on the acquisition activity in the 1990s. Of course, the affected industries differ over time. In the 1980s, deregulation induced significant merger activity in industries, such as air transport, natural gas and trucking. In the 1990s, deregulation was directed toward sectors including banking, electric utilities, and telecommunications. Indeed, past research has often excluded industries, such as banking, telecommunications and electric utilities due to heavy regulation. The removal of the regulatory burdens in these industries allows them to become part of mainstream merger analysis.

The coefficient for R&D/Sales is not significantly different from zero. In contrast to the 1980s, merger activity in the 1990s is not restricted to industries with low growth options. Indeed, some of the industries shown in Table 3 to have the highest rate of acquisition activity during the 1990s include Telecommunications, Electrical Equipment, and Electronics that are in high-tech, growing sectors. These results are consistent with related findings in Andrade and Stafford (1999) and indicate that mergers can facilitate both industry consolidation and industry expansion.

As a more direct analysis of acquisition activity in the 1980s and 1990s, we compare the rate of activity across industries in the two decades. Our sample has 42 industries that overlap those studied by Mitchell and Mulherin (1996, Table 3) for the 1980s. The simple correlation coefficient of the rate of acquisition activity between the two samples from the two decades is 0.25 ($p = 0.11$). This confirms that while there was significant restructuring activity in both the 1980s and 1990s, there was not a one-to-one relation in the affected industries.

4.2. *Industry patterns in divestiture activity*

We next analyze whether there are industry patterns in divestiture activity. Table 4 reports the results. For the median industry, 18% of the firms engaged in at least one major divestiture in the 1990–1999 period. Like acquisitions, however, there is a wide variation in divestiture activity across industries. In the Chemical (Diversified) industry, 67% of the firms undertook a major divestiture. By contrast, several industries, including Toiletries/Cosmetics, refrained from any measurable divestiture activity.

To determine whether the frequency of divestiture activity significantly differs across industries, we compute the Pearson χ^2 statistic. The value of the statistic is 110 ($df = 58$, p-level $= 0.001$), indicating a rejection of the null of no difference in divestiture activity across industries.

The estimates of acquisition and divestiture activity by industry in Table 3 and Table 4 allow us to do some analysis as to the nature of the shocks that induce the two forms of restructuring. If the underlying shocks are identical, then there will be a high, positive correlation between the rate of acquisitions and divestitures. Alternatively, if the underlying shocks are dissimilar, then there will be a strong, negative correlation between the relative occurrence of the two forms of restructuring at the industry level. The estimated correlation coefficient of the rate of acquisitions and divestitures is -0.08 (p-level $= 0.53$). Hence, acquisitions and divestitures are neither direct substitutes nor direct complements at the industry level. The estimate indicates, instead, that acquisitions and divestitures are induced by both common and dissimilar industry shocks. For example, exactly half of the 30 firms at the median or above in the ranking of acquisition activity in Table 3 are also at the median or above in the ranking of divestiture activity in Table 4. Dasgupta et al. (1999) report similar findings for a sample of mergers and divestitures in the 1986–1994 period.

The comparison of industry patterns in acquisitions and divestitures is somewhat crude as acquired firms, by the nature of our research design, cannot subsequently engage in a divestiture. To account for sample attrition due to acquisitions, we reestimated the rates of divestiture activity based on the available firm years for each industry. For example, in our sample, the Shoe industry has 12 firms, or a total of 120 firm years in the 1990–1999 period. But one firm in the industry was acquired in 1995, reducing the available firm years to 116. After accounting for sample attrition due to acquisitions, our estimates for the adjusted rate of divestiture by industry are also insignificantly related to the industry rate of acquisitions; the correlation coefficient is -0.03 (p-level $= 0.84$).

Table 4
Divestiture activity by industry

Industry	% Divesting	Industry	% Divesting
Chemical (diversified)	67	Restaurant	18
Chemical (basic)	50	Chemical (specialty)	17
Petroleum (integrate)	48	Air transport	17
Telecommunications	48	Petroleum (produce)	17
Medical services	44	Shoe	17
Natural gas (div)	41	Bank	16
Drug	37	Building materials	15
Electrical equipment	35	Office equipment	15
Paper	33	Retail store	15
Railroad	33	Natural gas (dist)	14
Trucking	33	Computer and peripherals	14
Financial services	32	Packaging and contain	13
Newspaper	31	Machinery	13
Insurance	30	Metal fabricating	13
Medical supplies	30	Computer software	12
Publishing	29	Electric utility	12
Electronics	26	Textile	11
Metals and mining	25	Machine tool	10
Food processing	24	Environmental	9
Retail (special lines)	22	Machinery (constr.)	9
Recreation	22	Furniture	8
Hotel/gaming	21	Semiconductor	7
Oilfield services	21	Thrift	6
Broadcasting/cable	20	Apparel	6
Household products	20	Auto parts	5
Precision instrument	20	Bank (Midwest)	0
Steel	20	Grocery store	0
Industrial services	19	Securities brokerage	0
Aerospace/defense	19	Toiletries/cosmetics	0
Homebuilding	18	Full sample	21

This table reports the fraction of the sample firms in each industry that engaged in at least one major divestiture (spinoff, equity carve-out, or asset sale) in the 1990–1999 period. The data are sorted by the percent of industry members performing at least one divestiture. Divestiture activity is determined by consulting the Wall Street Journal Index, Lexis/Nexis, Mergers and Acquisitions, and other financial and news media.

The similarity in results for both the unadjusted and adjusted rates of divestitures is due, in part, to the fact that a majority of the acquisitions in the sample occur in the second half of the 1990s. Table 5 reports that 33% of the acquisitions were completed in the 1990–1994 period, compared with 67% in the 1995–1999 period.

Overall, the analysis in this section finds significant industry clustering in both acquisitions and divestitures. These results are consistent with the theory of the firm, which predicts that corporate restructuring is a function of industry shocks

Table 5
Acquisition and divestiture activity by year

Year	Acquisitions		Divestitures	
	Number	Percentage (%)	Number	Percentage (%)
1990	38	10	22	6
1991	23	6	33	9
1992	21	6	36	10
1993	26	7	40	11
1994	19	5	47	13
1995	49	13	37	10
1996	41	11	53	14
1997	61	16	39	11
1998	61	16	36	10
1999	42	11	27	7
Total	381	100	370	100

This table reports the number and fraction of acquisitions and divestitures by year during the 1990–1999 period. Acquisitions and divestitures are assigned to the year of completion. Activity is determined by consulting the Wall Street Journal Index, Lexis/Nexis, Mergers and Acquisitions, and other financial media.

and changing economic conditions. In the next section, we estimate whether the reaction to changing economic conditions is wealth enhancing.

5. Wealth effects of acquisitions and divestitures

A large body of research has studied the wealth effects of acquisitions and divestitures. Much of the research on acquisitions is reviewed by Jensen and Ruback (1983) and Jarrell et al. (1988). The Appendix A to this paper notes some of the more recent research on acquisitions as well as selected research on divestitures.

In this section, we expand on the prior work by estimating the wealth effects of acquisitions and divestitures in the 1990s. Our joint consideration of acquisitions and divestitures allows us to distinguish between nonsynergistic and synergistic theories of corporate restructuring. In particular, we study whether acquisitions and divestitures have an asymmetric or symmetric effect on shareholder wealth.

5.1. Data used to estimate the wealth effects of acquisitions and divestitures

Our analysis of the wealth effects of acquisitions and divestitures employs standard event study techniques. As such, our only data requirement is stock price information around the announcement of the restructuring events. For acquisitions

Table 6
Data used to estimate wealth effects of acquisitions and divestitures

	No. of observations
Panel A. Data availability for acquisitions	
Total number of targets	381
Targets with stock price data	376
Acquisitions with available bidder data	281
Panel B. Data availability for divestitures	
Total Number of Divestitures	370
Spinoffs	106
Equity carve-outs	125
Asset sales	139

This table reports the data available for the estimation of the wealth effects of acquisitions and divestitures. Panel A reports data availability for acquisitions. Of the 381 target firms in the sample, 5 are delisted prior to being acquired, leaving 376 targets with available stock price data. Of these 376 targets, 63 are acquired by foreign bidders and 32 are acquired by private bidders, leaving 281 that are acquired by US publicly traded bidders, which have available stock price data. Panel B reports the number of observations in the full sample of divestitures as well as the subsamples for spinoffs, equity carve-outs and asset sales. For both acquisitions and divestitures, data from 1990–1998 are obtained from CRSP. Data from 1999 are obtained from the Daily Stock Price Record.

and divestitures in the 1990–1998 period, we obtain the data from CRSP. For events in 1999, we obtain the data from the Daily Stock Price Record.

Table 6 sketches the data available for the estimation of wealth effects. Panel A reports data availability for acquisitions. As reported previously in Table 2, a total of 381 sample firms are acquired in the 1990–1999 period. Five of these firms, however, are delisted prior to the announcement of their acquisition, leaving 376 target firms available for the analysis of wealth effects. Within this sample, 281 of the targets are acquired by US publicly traded firms having available stock price data to be used to estimate the wealth effects for the bidders as well as the combined target and bidder return.

Panel B of Table 6 reports the data availability for divestitures. As reported previously in Table 2, a total of 268 sample firms engaged in at least one major divestiture in the 1990–1999 period. Because some firms undertook more than one divestiture over the sample period, there are a total of 370 divestitures that can be used in the analysis of wealth effects. As noted in Table 6, within this divestiture sample, there are 106 corporate spinoffs, 125 equity carve-outs, and 139 asset sales.

5.2. *The relative value of acquisitions and divestitures*

Table 7 provides information on the relative size of the acquisitions and divestitures in the sample. Panel A reports the relative value of the acquisitions,

Table 7
Relative value of acquisitions and divestitures

Panel A. Relative value of acquisitions

Target value/bidder value	
Mean	42%
Median	27%
N	281

Panel B. Relative value of divestitures (subsidiary/parent)

	All	Spinoffs	Carve-outs	Asset sales
Mean	26%	22%	37%	18%
Median	13%	14%	17%	11%
N	370	106	125	139

This table reports information on the relative value of the sample acquisitions and divestitures. Panel A reports the relative value of the sample acquisitions, defined as the ratio of the equity value of the target divided by the equity value of the bidder, both measured 2 days prior to the initial announcement of the acquisition bid. Data are available for the 281 acquisitions where the bidding firm is a US publicly traded firm with available stock price data. Panel B reports the relative value of the sample divestitures. For spinoffs, the relative value is the equity value of the spinoff on the first day of trading divided by the equity value of the parent on the day before the spinoff. For equity carve-outs, the relative value is the equity value of the carve-out (offer price times total shares outstanding) divided by the equity value of the parent on the offer date. For asset sales, the relative value is the reported price of the asset sale divided by the asset value of the parent at the year-end prior to the announcement of the asset sale. For both acquisitions and divestitures, data from 1990–1998 are obtained from CRSP and Compustat. Data from 1999 are obtained from the Daily Stock Price Record and SEC filings.

defined as the equity value of the target divided by the equity value of the bidder, both measured two days prior to the initial announcement of the acquisition bid. Data are available for the 281 acquisitions with both target and bidder equity value. The average target firm is 42% as large as the average bidder. The median relative value is 27%. The median size of the target to the bidder is somewhat larger than that reported by Jarrell and Poulsen (1989, Exhibit 1) for acquisitions in the 1970s and 1980s (though not the 1960s), which is expected since we sampled the acquisition targets from firms covered by Value Line.

Panel B of Table 7 reports the relative value of the 370 sample divestitures. For spinoffs, the relative value is defined as the equity value of the spinoff on the first day of trading divided by the equity value of the parent on the day before the spinoff. The mean estimate for the relative value of spinoffs is 22% and the median is 14%.

To provide a comparable measure for equity carve-outs, the relative value is defined as the equity value of the carve-out (offer price times total shares outstanding) divided by the equity value of the parent on the offer date. The mean estimate for the relative value of carve-outs is 37% and the median is 17%. An alternative measure for the relative value of the sample carve-outs based on offer proceeds rather than total equity value of the subsidiary, not reported in the table, generates a mean of 16% and a median of 7%.

For asset sales, the relative value is defined as the reported price of the asset sale divided by the asset value of the parent at the year-end prior to the announcement of the asset sale. We choose to weight asset sales by parent asset value because using parent equity value can lead to relative values larger than 100%, especially for parents experiencing financial difficulty (see Brown et al., 1994). The mean estimate for the relative value of asset sales is 18% and the median is 11%.

Across all 370 observations, the average divestiture comprises 26% of the parent firm. The median relative value of the sample divestitures is 13%. Although there is some variation in the mean relative size across the three types of divestitures, the median relative values are comparable across divestiture types.

Overall, the data in Table 7 indicate that both the acquisition and divestiture samples entail important events. The relative value of target firms and divested firms are both more than 25% of the value of the bidding firm and the divesting parent, respectively. This facilitates a direct comparison of the wealth effects of the two forms of restructuring.

5.3. Wealth effects for the sample acquisitions and divestitures

In this section, we estimate the wealth effects of acquisitions and divestitures. Our primary objective is to test two contrasting theories of corporate restructuring: the nonsynergistic theory and the synergistic theory. Within the nonsynergistic theory, we group models based on management entrenchment, empire building, and managerial hubris. Within the synergistic theory, we include models such as Coase (1937), Klein et al. (1978), and Bradley et al. (1988). Our joint analysis of acquisitions and divestitures enables tests that directly distinguish between the two theories. In particular, the nonsynergistic theory predicts asymmetric wealth effects of acquisitions and divestitures (see, e.g., Shleifer and Vishny, 1989), while the synergistic theory predicts that both acquisitions and divestitures create wealth.

Table 8 sketches the specific analysis used to test the two competing theories. As noted in Panel A, both theories predict that the announcement effect of corporate divestitures will be positive. By contrast, the nonsynergistic theory predicts that the combined bidder–target return in acquisitions will be negative, while the synergistic theory predicts that the combined wealth effect in acquisitions will be positive.

As outlined in Panel B of Table 8, the two theories also make contrasting predictions regarding the relation between wealth effects and the relative size of the event. The nonsynergistic theory predicts that larger divestitures will have a more positive effect on shareholder wealth while larger acquisitions will be

Table 8
Predictions from models of corporate restructuring

	Nonsynergistic	Synergistic
A. Announcement effects		
Divestitures	positive	positive
Acquisitions (combined)	negative	positive
B. Relation between announcement effect and relative size of the event		
Divestitures	positive	positive
Acquisitions (combined)	negative	positive

This table compares and contrasts the predictions from two sets of theories offering nonsynergistic and synergistic models of corporate acquisitions and divestitures. Panel A reports the predictions of the two theories for the wealth effects at the announcement of acquisitions and divestitures. Panel B reports the predicted relation in regressions of announcement effects on the relative size of the corporate events.

relatively more detrimental to shareholders, as the acquisition of a larger target will induce greater management entrenchment. The synergistic theory predicts that larger acquisitions and divestitures will both have relatively more positive effects on shareholder wealth.

In our analysis of the wealth effects of acquisitions and divestitures, we estimate changes in equity value at the time of the announcement of the two restructuring events. Because we want to isolate on the specific market reaction to the two events, we focus on a narrow window of the (−1, +1) period around the events, where day 0 is the initial announcement as determined from Lexis/Nexis, the Wall Street Journal Index, and other financial and news media. Because of the employment of this narrow window, we simply rely on net-of-market estimates of the abnormal returns. In results available upon request, we also employ other estimation techniques, such as the market model and obtain findings comparable to those reported in the text. Similarly, the use of longer event windows does not alter the inferences drawn in the text. For events from the 1990–1998 period, the market index is the CRSP value-weighted index. For events in 1999, the market index is the S&P 500.

Table 9 reports the wealth effects for the sample acquisitions. Panel A reports the wealth effects for the entire sample of 376 targets with available stock price data. On average, the equity value of a target firm appreciates 21.2%, net-of-market, in the three days around the initial announcement of the acquisition. The median abnormal return in the (−1, +1) period is 18.4%. The significant, positive return for the sample targets is consistent with research from earlier time periods.

Panel B of Table 9 reports the wealth effects for the 281 acquisitions with available data for both targets and bidders. The results for the targets resemble the full sample of all acquisitions. On average, targets gain more than 20% at the announcement of an acquisition.

Table 9
Wealth effects for the sample acquisitions

Panel A. Wealth effects for the full sample of acquisitions

	Target
Mean	21.20%
(t-Stat.)	(16.8)
Median	18.40%
(p-Level)	(0.0001)
N	376

Panel B. Wealth effects for the acquisitions with available bidder data

	Target	Bidder	Combined
Mean	20.2%	−0.37%	3.56%
(t-Stat.)	(14.0)	(−0.69)	(6.23)
Median	17.4%	−0.87%	1.99%
(p-Level)	(0.0001)	(0.004)	(0.0001)
N	281	281	281

This table reports the wealth effects for the sample acquisitions. All estimates are net-of-market, cumulative abnormal returns for the (−1, +1) period, where day 0 is the date of the initial announcement of the acquisition bid, as determined from Lexis/Nexis, the Wall Street Journal Index, and other financial and news media. Panel A reports the wealth effects for the 376 targets with available stock price data. Panel B reports the wealth effects for the 281 acquisitions where the bidder is a US publicly traded firm with available stock price data. Note that bidder returns are based on the date of the first mention of the bidder in the financial press, which may be later than the initial announcement date for the target. The Combined Return is the value-weighted CAR, defined as: (target value × target CAR + bidder value × bidder CAR)/(target value + bidder value), where bidder and target values are the equity value 2 days prior to the initial acquisition announcement. Data from 1990–1998 are obtained from CRSP and the market index is the CRSP value-weighted index. Data from 1999 are obtained from the Daily Stock Price Record and the market index is the S&P 500. The t-statistic tests the null hypothesis that the mean CAR equals zero. The p-level is for the Wilcoxon sign rank test that the median differs from zero.

Bidders, on average, experience an insignificant mean change in wealth at the announcement of the acquisition. The median is also small in absolute terms, although the estimate is significantly negative. As in the prior research reviewed in the Appendix A, the bidder returns are somewhat sensitive to the event window. For example, in results not reported in the table, the net-of-market bidder return for the (−42, +1) period is positive but insignificant: 0.65% ($t = 0.91$). The small magnitude of the bidder returns is consistent with prior research and is generally interpreted as reflecting a competitive market for corporate control (see, e.g., Mitchell and Lehn, 1990).

To measure the total wealth effect of the acquisitions, we estimate the combined return, defined as the value-weighted CAR:

$$(\mathrm{TV}_i \times \mathrm{TCAR}_i + \mathrm{BV}_i \times \mathrm{BCAR}_i)/(\mathrm{TV}_i + \mathrm{BV}_i),$$

where $TCAR_i$ is the cumulative abnormal return for the ith target over the (−1, +1) period, $BCAR_i$ is the cumulative abnormal return for the ith bidder over the (−1, +1) period, and TV_i and BV_i are equity values for the ith target and bidder, respectively, 2 days prior to the initial acquisition announcement. The results indicate that the acquisitions in the sample create wealth. The combined return to targets and bidders averages 3.56%. This positive combined wealth effect for acquisitions is consistent with the synergistic theory.

Table 10 reports the wealth effects for the sample divestitures. On average, the divestitures create wealth. For the full sample of 370 divestitures, the average net-of-market return for the (−1, +1) period is 3.04%. The median abnormal return is 1.75%. The positive wealth effects hold for all three types of divestitures. The mean abnormal return is 4.51% for corporate spinoffs, is 2.27% for equity carve-outs, and is 2.60% for asset sales. These results are comparable in magnitude to research on divestitures from earlier time periods.

In results not reported in the table, we further study the subset of asset sales with data available for the buyers of the assets. Of the 139 asset sales in the sample, there are 56 cases where the buyer is either a foreign firm or a private US firm, leaving 83 cases where the buyer is a publicly traded US firm. In this subsample, the asset sales also create wealth. The mean CAR for the seller is 1.75% ($t = 2.57$) and for the buyer is 1.34%. The mean, value-weighted CAR for the buyer and the seller is 1.18% ($t = 2.88$).

Overall, the results on wealth effects indicate that both acquisitions and divestitures create wealth. These findings are consistent with the synergistic theory of corporate restructuring. The results indicate that corporate decisions to expand and to contract both benefit shareholders, on average, in the 1990s. These findings on wealth effects are consistent with the results in Maksimovic and Phillips (1999) that both mergers and asset sales improve total factor productivity.

Table 10
Wealth effects for the sample divestitures

	All	Spinoffs	Carve-outs	Asset sales
Mean	3.04%	4.51%	2.27%	2.60%
(t-Stat.)	(7.96)	(7.55)	(3.54)	(3.75)
Median	1.75%	3.64%	0.84%	1.53%
(p-Level)	(0.0001)	(0.0001)	(0.0002)	(0.0001)
N	370	106	125	139

This table reports the wealth effects for the sample divestitures. All estimates are net-of-market, cumulative abnormal returns for the (−1, +1) period, where day 0 is the date of the initial announcement of the divestiture, as determined from Lexis/Nexis, the Wall Street Journal Index, and other financial and news media. Data from 1990–1998 are obtained from CRSP and the market index is the CRSP value-weighted index. Data from 1999 are obtained from the Daily Stock Price Record and the market index is the S&P 500. The t-statistic tests the null hypothesis that the mean CAR equals zero. The p-level is for the Wilcoxon sign rank test that the median differs from zero.

5.4. Wealth effects and the relative value of acquisitions and divestitures

The basic results on wealth effects indicate that the average acquisition and the average divestiture in the 1990s create wealth. While consistent with the synergistic theory, the results do not indicate the sources of wealth gains from corporate restructuring. Moreover, the results do not conclusively reject the nonsynergistic theory, as the average returns do not account for the size of the particular restructuring events (see, e.g., Roll, 1986). To provide cross-sectional tests that distinguish between the synergistic and nonsynergistic theories, we estimate whether the wealth gains in the sample acquisitions and divestitures are related to the relative size of the restructuring events.

There is some prior analysis of this relation between wealth effects and the relative size of acquisitions and divestitures. Servaes (1991) finds that the combined return to targets and bidders is positively related to the relative size of the target. The papers on divestitures listed in the Appendix A generally report that the abnormal returns in corporate divestitures are directly related to the relative size of the divested entity. We extend this analysis by jointly studying acquisitions and divestitures in the 1990s.

Column (1) of Table 11 reports the results for the 281 acquisitions with available target and bidder data. The analysis entails an OLS regression that estimates the relation between the combined target and bidder return at acquisition

Table 11
Wealth effects and the relative value of acquisitions and divestitures

	(1)	(2)
	Acquisitions	Divestitures
Constant	0.022	0.022
(t-Stat.)	(3.11)	(4.79)
Relative value	0.033	0.031
(t-Stat.)	(3.45)	(3.01)
N	281	370
F-value	11.9	16.7
(p-Level)	(0.0007)	(0.0001)
Adjusted R^2	0.04	0.04

This table reports OLS regressions that estimate the relation between the relative value of acquisitions and divestitures and the wealth effects from the two events. Column (1) reports the results for acquisitions, where the dependent variable is the combined bidder and target net-of-market return at the announcement (days −1, +1) of the acquisition and the independent variable is the relative value of the acquisition (target value/bidder value), as defined in Panel A of Table 7. Column (2) reports the results for divestitures, where the dependent variable is the net-of-market return for the parent at the announcement (days −1, +1) of the divestiture and the independent variable is the relative value of the divestiture (divested entity/parent value), as defined in Panel B of Table 7. Data from 1990–1998 are obtained from CRSP and the market index is the CRSP value-weighted index. Data from 1999 are obtained from the Daily Stock Price Record and the market index is the S&P 500.

announcement and the relative value of the acquisition. The coefficient for Relative Value is positive and more than three standard errors different from zero. Hence, the combined target and bidder returns in the sample are directly related to the relative value of the acquisition.

Column (2) of Table 11 reports comparable analysis for the sample of 370 divestitures. Similar to the acquisition sample, the coefficient of Relative Value is positive and significant in the divestiture regression. Consistent with prior research, the wealth creation at the announcement of corporate divestitures is directly related to the relative size of the divestiture.

Interestingly, the estimated parameters in columns (1) and (2) of Table 11 are virtually identical. Hence, whether expanding or downsizing, the impact on shareholder wealth is comparably related to the relative size of the restructuring event. The results provide further support for the synergistic theory of acquisitions and divestitures and are not consistent with the nonsynergistic models.

6. Summary and concluding comments

In this paper, we compare the acquisition and divestiture activity of a sample of 1305 firms from 59 industries in the 1990–1999 period. We find a significant occurrence of these two forms of restructuring during the 1990s. Roughly half of the sample firms are acquired or engage in a major divestiture in the sample period.

We also find significant industry clustering in acquisition and divestiture activity during the 1990s. Consistent with results for the 1980s, we find that acquisition activity is greater in industries undergoing deregulation, although the specific industries affected by deregulation differ between the 1980s and 1990s. In contrast to the evidence for the 1980s, we find that acquisitions in the 1990s are not restricted to industries with low growth options.

We find that the acquisitions and divestitures in the 1990s create wealth. Indeed, the wealth creation from the two restructuring events is comparable in magnitude. The combined target and bidder return at the announcement of an acquisition averages 3.5%, while the announcement return for corporate divestitures averages 3.0%. Moreover, the wealth creation for both acquisitions and divestitures is directly related to the relative size of the restructuring event.

As a whole, these results are consistent with the predictions of the synergistic theory of the firm that changing economic conditions and industry shocks are at play in restructuring activity. Indeed, the results indicate that firms efficiently respond to economic change, whether such changes induce an expansion (via merger) or a reduction (via divestiture) in firm size. The symmetric relation for both acquisitions and divestitures is inconsistent with nonsynergistic models based on management entrenchment, empire building and managerial hubris, which argue that firms expand for reasons other than wealth creation. In the 1990s, the

Appendix A

A. Selected event studies of acquisitions that report target and bidder returns

Study	Time period	# Targets	# Bidders	Window	Target (%)	Bidder (%)	Combined
Bradley et al. (1988)	1963–1984	236	236	(− 5, + 5 last bid)	31.77	0.97	7.43%
Kaplan and Weisbach (1992)	1971–1982	209	271	(− 5, + 5 last bid)	26.90	− 1.49	3.74%
Asquith et al. (1990)	1973–1983	157	343	(− 1, 0)	18.04	− 0.85	not reported
Jarrell and Poulsen (1989)	1963–1986	526	462	(− 20, + 10)	28.99	1.29	not reported
Servaes (1991)	1972–1987	704	384	(− 1, resolve)	23.64	− 1.07	3.66%
Schwert (2000)	1975–1996	2,296	1,286	(− 63, 126)	22.00	− 1.00	not reported

B.1. Selected event studies of spinoffs that include analysis of CARs and relative size of the spinoff

Study	Source	Time period	# Obs	Window	CAR (%)	Relative size	Effect of relative size on CAR
Miles and Rosenfeld (1983)	Moody's Div Record	1963–1980	55	(0, + 1)	3.34	median = 10%	larger spinoffs have greater CAR
Hite and Owers (1983)	S&P Div Record	1963–1981	123	(− 1, 0)	3.30	median = 6.7%	positive regression coefficient
Schipper and Smith (1983)	CRSP Dist Codes	1963–1981	93	(− 1, 0)	2.84	mean = 19.7%	positive correlation
Krishnaswami and Subramaniam (1999)	CRSP Dist Codes	1979–1993	118	(− 1, + 1)	3.28	median = 13.8%	positive regression coefficient

B.2. Selected event studies of carve-outs that include analysis of CARs and relative size of the carve-out

Study	Source	Time Period	# Obs	Window	CAR (%)	Relative size	Effect of relative size on CAR
Schipper and Smith (1986)	SEC ROS tape	1965–1983	76	(− 4, 0)	1.83	median = 8%	positive correlation
Allen and McConnell (1998)	SEC, IDD, SDC	1978–1993	188	(− 1, + 1)	1.90	median = 14%	positive regression coefficient
Vijh (1999)	SDC, M and A	1980–1997	336	(− 3, + 1)	2.29	median = 7.9%	positive regression coefficient

B.3. Selected event studies of asset sales that include analysis of CARs and relative size of the asset sale

Study	Source	Time period	# Obs	Window	CAR (%)	Relative size	Effect of relative size on CAR
Klein (1986)	Mergers and Acquisitions	1970–1979	202	(− 2, 0)	1.12		positive regression coefficient
Lang et al. (1995)	SEC Form 8K	1984–1989	93	(− 1, 0)	1.41	median = 23%	positive regression coefficient

This appendix summarizes selected prior research on acquisitions and divestitures. Panel A reviews selected papers that study the announcement returns for targets and bidders in acquisitions. Panels B.1 to B.3 review selected papers on corporate spinoffs, equity carve-outs, and asset sales that include analysis of the effect of the relative size of the divestiture and wealth effects.

corporate restructuring decisions made by management, whether downsizing or expansion, on average benefit shareholders.

Our results on the incidence and wealth effects of corporate restructuring in the 1990s have important policy implications. Many have interpreted the abrupt reversal of corporate takeovers at the end of the 1980s as evidence that entrenched managers could rely on antitakeover provisions and state laws to inhibit the market for corporate control. Our results of an active corporate control market in the 1990s, however, support Comment and Schwert's (1995) forecast that the decline in takeovers in the late 1980s and early 1990s would prove to be driven by economic conditions rather than legal burdens.

Our results also have implications for corporate finance, which extend beyond the basic wealth effects emphasized in the paper. A growing body of research has presented evidence of systematic mispricing in long windows following corporate events, such as those studied in this paper (see Mitchell and Stafford, 1999 for a recent survey). Our evidence that both acquisitions and divestitures cluster in particular industries adds to the growing cautions being applied to the long-run performance studies. Such clustering indicates that the assumptions of independence that frame much of the statistical tests of long-run studies are misapplied.

Finally, there is clearly much to be gained from more detailed study of acquisitions and divestitures in the 1990s. One query raised by Klein and Murphy (1997) is the nature of gains from large vertical mergers, such as Merck's acquisition of Medco and Disney's acquisition of Capital Cities/ABC. A further line of study raised by our own findings of the industry clustering of acquisitions and divestitures is a comparison of the sources of gains from restructuring in industries with high growth options vis-à-vis low growth industries. More broadly, are the sources of gains from restructuring in the 1990s the same as in prior decades? Along these lines, Boone (1999) reports that the source of gains from corporate divestitures is sensitive to time period. Clearly, an ongoing comparison of acquisitions and divestitures will continue to enlighten us on the causes and effects of corporate restructuring.

Acknowledgements

We thank Ted Boone, Laura Field, Gordon Hanka, Kathy Kahle, Bill Kracaw, Jeff Netter, Kim Rodgers, Dennis Sheehan, and seminar participants at the University of South Florida for comments on prior drafts. We especially acknowledge the detailed comments and suggestions provided by Mike Ryngaert.

References

Allen, J.W., McConnell, J.J., 1998. Equity carve-outs and managerial discretion. Journal of Finance 53, 163–186.

Andrade, G., Stafford, E., 1999. Investigating the Economic Role of Mergers. Unpublished manuscript, Harvard Business School.

Asquith, P., Bruner, R.F., Mullins Jr., D.W., 1990. Merger Returns and the Form of Financing. Unpublished manuscript, Massachusetts Institute of Technology.

Boone, A.L., 1999. Can Focus Explain Carve-Out Gains? Unpublished manuscript, Penn State University.

Bradley, M., Desai, A., Kim, E.H., 1988. Synergistic gains from corporate acquisitions and their division between the stockholders of target and acquiring firms. Journal of Financial Economics 21, 3–40.

Brown, D.T., James, C.M., Mooradian, R.M., 1994. Asset sales by financially distressed firms. Journal of Corporate Finance 1, 233–257.

Coase, R.H., 1937. The nature of the firm. Economica 4, 386–405.

Comment, R., Schwert, G.W., 1995. Poison or placebo? Evidence on the deterrence and wealth effects of modern antitakeover measures. Journal of Financial Economics 39, 3–43.

Dasgupta, S., Goyal, V., Tan, G., 1999. Active Asset Markets, Divestitures and Divisional Cross-Subsidization. Unpublished manuscript, Hong Kong University of Science and Technology.

Hite, G.L., Owers, J.E., 1983. Security price reactions around corporate spin-off announcements. Journal of Financial Economics 12, 409–436.

Jarrell, G.A., Poulsen, A.B., 1989. The returns to acquiring firms in tender offers: evidence from three decades. Financial Management 18, 12–19.

Jarrell, G.A., Brickley, J.A., Netter, J.M., 1988. The market for corporate control: the empirical evidence since 1980. Journal of Economic Perspectives 2, 49–68.

Jensen, M.C., 1986. Agency costs of free cash flow, corporate finance, and takeovers. American Economic Review 76, 323–329.

Jensen, M.C., 1993. The modern industrial revolution: exit, and the failure of internal control systems. Journal of Finance 48, 831–880.

Jensen, M.C., Ruback, R.S., 1983. The market for corporate control: the scientific evidence. Journal of Financial Economics 11, 5–50.

Kahle, K.M., Walkling, R.A., 1996. The impact of industry classifications on financial research. Journal of Financial and Quantitative Analysis 31, 309–335.

Kaplan, S.N., Weisbach, M.S., 1992. The success of acquisitions: evidence from divestitures. Journal of Finance 47, 107–138.

Klein, A., 1986. The timing and substance of divestiture announcements: individual, simultaneous and cumulative effects. Journal of Finance 41, 685–696.

Klein, B., Murphy, K.M., 1997. Vertical integration as a self-enforcing contractual arrangement. American Economic Review 87, 415–420.

Klein, B., Crawford, R.G., Alchian, A.A., 1978. Vertical integration, appropriable rents, and the competitive contracting process. Journal of Law and Economics 21, 297–326.

Krishnaswami, S., Subramaniam, V., 1999. Information asymmetry, valuation, and the corporate spin-off decision. Journal of Financial Economics 53, 73–112.

Lang, L., Poulsen, A., Stulz, R., 1995. Asset sales, firm performance, and the agency costs of managerial discretion. Journal of Financial Economics 37, 3–37.

Maksimovic, V., Phillips, G., 1999. The Market for Corporate Assets: Who Engages in Mergers and Asset Sales and are there Efficiency Gains. Unpublished manuscript, University of Maryland.

Miles, J.A., Rosenfeld, J.D., 1983. The effect of voluntary spin-off announcements on shareholder wealth. Journal of Finance 38, 1597–1606.

Mitchell, M.L., Lehn, K., 1990. Do bad bidders become good targets? Journal of Political Economy 98, 372–398.

Mitchell, M.L., Mulherin, J.H., 1996. The impact of industry shocks on takeover and restructuring activity. Journal of Financial Economics 41, 193–229.

Mitchell, M.L., Stafford, E., 1999. Managerial decisions and long run stock price performance. Journal of Business, (forthcoming).

Roll, R., 1986. The Hubris theory of corporate takeovers. Journal of Business 59, 197–216.

Schipper, K., Smith, A., 1983. Effects of recontracting on shareholder wealth: the case of voluntary spin-offs. Journal of Financial Economics 12, 437–467.

Schipper, K., Smith, A., 1986. A comparison of equity carve-outs and seasoned equity offerings: share price effects and corporate restructuring. Journal of Financial Economics 15, 153–186.

Schwert, G.W., 2000. Hostility in takeovers: in the eyes of the beholder? Journal of Finance, (forthcoming).

Servaes, H., 1991. Tobin's Q and the gains from takeovers. Journal of Finance 46, 409–419.

Shleifer, A., Vishny, R.W., 1989. Managerial entrenchment: the case of manager-specific investments. Journal of Financial Economics 25, 123–139.

Vijh, A.M., 1999. The Positive Announcement-Period Returns of Equity Carveouts: Asymmetric Information or Divestiture Gains? Unpublished manuscript, University of Iowa.

[13]

THE JOURNAL OF FINANCE • VOL. LVI, NO. 6 • DEC. 2001

The Market for Corporate Assets: Who Engages in Mergers and Asset Sales and Are There Efficiency Gains?

VOJISLAV MAKSIMOVIC and GORDON PHILLIPS*

ABSTRACT

We analyze the market for corporate assets. There is an active market for corporate assets, with close to seven percent of plants changing ownership annually through mergers, acquisitions, and asset sales in peak expansion years. The probability of asset sales and whole-firm transactions is related to firm organization and ex ante efficiency of buyers and sellers. The timing of sales and the pattern of efficiency gains suggests that the transactions that occur, especially through asset sales of plants and divisions, tend to improve the allocation of resources and are consistent with a simple neoclassical model of profit maximizing by firms.

IN THE UNITED STATES there is a large and active market for corporate assets, from individual plants and divisions up to sales of entire corporations. Each year over the period 1974 to 1992, an average 3.89 percent of the large manufacturing plants in the country changed ownership.[1] This average masks substantial procyclical time variation, so that in expansion years, an average of 6.19 percent of manufacturing plants are involved in mergers and acquisitions and asset sales in each year. While the literature has succeeded in providing many insights about the gains and losses in mergers, mergers comprise only about one half of the total number of assets traded.[2] Much less is known about partial-firm asset sales.[3]

* Robert H. Smith School of Business, The University of Maryland. This research was supported by NSF Grant #SBR-9709427. We thank Judy Chevalier, John Graham, Peter MacKay, Steven Michael, Harold Mulherin, René Stulz, Michael Vetsuypens, an anonymous referee, and seminar participants at Duke, Illinois, NYU, The National Bureau of Economic Research, Stanford, University of Texas at Austin, University of Texas at Dallas, Virginia Tech, and the Western Finance Association meetings for helpful comments. We also thank Sang Nguyen and researchers at the Center for Economic Studies for their comments and help with the data used in this study. The research was conducted at the Center for Economic Studies, U.S. Bureau of the Census, Department of Commerce. The authors alone are responsible for the work and any errors or omissions.

[1] These statistics are described in detail below.

[2] For a comprehensive survey see Jensen and Ruback (1983) and also Ravenscraft and Scherer (1987).

[3] Early studies are Alexander, Benson, and Kampmeyer (1984), and Hite, Owers, and Rogers (1987). The number of transactions in these studies has been fairly small because the data is difficult to obtain. Schlingemann, Stulz, and Walkling (2002) also analyze segment sales.

In this study, we treat mergers, acquisitions, and asset sales as components of the overall market for firm assets in manufacturing industries. Using detailed plant-level data from the Longitudinal Research Database (LRD) compiled at the Census Bureau, we track sales of individual plants and benchmark their efficiency against that of other plants in the industry. We ask several questions: Does the market facilitate the reallocation of assets to more efficient uses? How big is the market for plants, and each of the segments (individual plants, divisions, and entire firms)? What are the factors that drive mergers and asset sales? We also ask whether firm organization affects how firms participate in the market for assets. Does the subsequent productivity of the transacted plants vary by the buying and selling firms' organizational characteristics?

An influential view in the literature is that major investment and takeover decisions of firms are influenced by conflicts of interest between managers and the owners of the firm.[4] This view suggests that many acquisitions are undertaken for empire building and managerial entrenchment by managers, and that they serve little economic purpose. Morck, Shleifer, and Vishny (1990) provide evidence that the stock market reacts negatively to diversifying acquisitions and to acquisitions where the bidder's managers perform poorly prior to the acquisitions. For asset sales, Jain (1985) finds that sell-off announcements are greeted positively by the market and that they proceed a period of negative returns for the sellers. Lang, Poulsen, and Stulz (1995) find asset sales follow poor firm-level performance. John and Ofek (1995) find that the remaining assets of the firm improve in performance after asset sales that subsequently leave the firm more focused. These studies suggest that transactions either follow inefficient investments by firms or act to unwind such investments.

An alternative view, modeled in Maksimovic and Phillips (2002), posits that firms grow and purchase assets efficiently across the industries in which they operate.[5] This model is also consistent with existing evidence.[6] The model makes specific testable predictions about the timing and the direction of sales. In our model, firms become focused when their prospects in their main industry significantly improve. They may optimally choose to remain unfocused if their prospects in their main industry are not as good as other firms that choose to become focused. Firms sell assets in their less productive divisions following positive demand shocks for these divisions.

[4] See Jensen (1986) and Hart and Moore (1995).

[5] The model is based on Lucas (1978). Lucas (1978) and Williamson (1985) stress the costs of managing a larger organization.

[6] We do not have transaction prices or stock price data. Thus, we cannot test whether one party gains or loses in the stock market as a result of the transaction. The advantage of our study is that we look at actual productivity changes while stock market data includes a response to the price paid and prior expectations, in addition to the value of any productivity changes.

The intuition for the Maksimovic and Phillips (2002) model is simple. Some firms are more productive and can produce more than other firms from a given number of plants. Firms adjust in size until the marginal benefit is equal to the marginal cost of production. As output prices increase, the more productive firms have a larger gain in value from the assets they control. As a result, they find it optimal to acquire plants from less productive firms in the industry, even when that entails some increase in the costs of management. By the same token, a positive shock in an industry increases the opportunity cost of operating as an inefficient producer in that industry. Thus, industry shocks alter the value of the assets and create incentives for transfers to more productive uses. Given the generally positive upward trend in GDP in the U.S. economy during the mid- and late 1980s, the model can explain the trend towards increased focus over this period.

Empirically we find that the pattern of transactions (procyclical sales and subsequent increases in productivity) is consistent with this model. Our empirical results show that assets are more likely to be sold (1) when the economy is undergoing positive demand shocks, (2) when the assets are less productive than their industry benchmarks, (3) when the selling division is less productive, and (4) when the selling firm has more productive divisions in other industries. For mergers and acquisitions, we find evidence that the less productive firms tend to sell at times of industry expansion. Firms are more likely to be buyers when they are efficient and are more likely to purchase additional assets in industries that experience an increase in demand.

Sellers *and* buyers of individual plants and divisions tend to be large conglomerates. A firm's internal organization has a significant effect on the probability that an asset is sold. Assets are significantly more likely to be sold by peripheral divisions than by main divisions of conglomerates. The sales of main divisions are much rarer events, perhaps because only divisions in which the firm has a core competency become main divisions. For conglomerates, we find that the probability of the whole firm being sold off is negatively correlated with firm size and with firm focus.

Our results show that most transactions in the market for assets result in productivity gains. The average productivity of the buyer's and seller's existing assets is an important determinant of the gain to trade, suggesting that firms have differing levels of ability to exploit assets, and that their comparative advantage is in their main industries. The subsequent observed increase in productivity of the transferred assets is consistent with these gains offsetting the increased costs to the purchasing firm of managing a larger organization.[7] Thus, the market for corporate assets facilitates the redeployment of assets from firms with a lower ability to exploit them to firms with a higher ability. There is less support for the hypothesis that

[7] Thus, the existence of measurable productivity gains following a transfer does not imply that the transfer's timing is not optimal. A full dynamic model would be necessary to address the question of the optimal timing of transfers.

empire building predominantly drives asset purchases. However, because measured gains are negative for a minority of transactions, we cannot reject the possibility that some transactions may be motivated by agency considerations.

Our evidence primarily relates to two literatures: the literature on asset sales and the literature on mergers. Our paper views and considers these two types of transactions as part of a larger market for assets. The literature on sales of plants and divisions is relatively small. Alexander et al. (1984), Jain (1985), and Hite et al. (1987) have found a positive stock market response to asset sales. Lang et al. (1995) have shown these asset sales follow poor firm-level performance and that the stock-market gains are positive for firms that pay out the proceeds instead of reinvesting within the firm.[8] John and Ofek (1995) show that the remaining assets of the firm improve in performance after asset sales that subsequently leave the firm more focused. Maksimovic and Phillips (1998) show that firms in Chapter 11 tend to sell their most efficient plants, whereas firms in a control sample tend to sell their least efficient plants.

Schlingemann, Stulz, and Walkling (2002) (SSW) examine sales of divisions. They compare firms that report the sale of one or more whole segments with a control sample of firms which do not divest. Working with accounting data, they predict how firms choose which segments to divest. SSW's principal finding is that the liquidity of the market for assets plays an important role in determining which asset is divested. The probability that a segment is divested is higher if the asset is in an industry with a liquid market for assets and if it performs poorly. The divested segments are on average smaller than segments that are retained.

There is a large literature on the gains from mergers that has examined the gains to the bidders and targets in the stock market. Lang, Stulz, and Walkling (1991) show that the total stock market gains in tender offers are highest when the bidder has a high Tobin's q and the target has a low q. This is consistent with the notion that gains are highest when well-managed firms take over badly managed firms. Less is known about the gains in partial firm sales. Several studies have examined the cash flow performance of firms before and after mergers. Matsusaka (1993) examines the ex ante financial performance of firms before they merge and Ravenscraft and Scherer (1987) examine the ex post financial performance of mergers using FTC line-of-business data. Other studies that have documented performance changes following mergers using the LRD include Lichtenberg and Siegel (1992) and McGuckin and Nguyen (1995, 1999). McGuckin and Nguyen (1999) show

[8] The advantage over using stock market data and event studies is that a stock market response reflects the price paid relative to anticipated gains. Gains in productivity can still occur if the excess stock market return equals zero if the seller captures the gains. Similarly a combined positive stock market response (for buyers and sellers) may reflect information being revealed about the assets' value in the future and may not represent any real productivity gains.

that whether a firm is multiplant or single plant affects observed productivity gains. Kaplan and Weisbach (1992) track firms after they merge and find that divestiture rates by purchasers of unrelated firms are higher than purchasers of related firms. Even the firms that were broken up, however, show positive combined stock market responses (buyer and seller) at the time of the acquisition and do not show declines in operating performance before they are broken up. Our theory predicts that firms will buy assets outside of their main areas of expertise during recessions and sell unrelated assets to firms expanding their core business units during booms. Fluck and Lynch (1999) also predict that conglomerate firms maximizing shareholder value will buy firms outside of their primary area of expertise during recessions.

Following Jensen (1986), several authors argue that firm investment and growth can be explained by managers' tendency to overinvest in projects that yield private gains. Using data on bidding firms, Lang et al. (1991) show that the shareholders do not benefit if acquisitions are made using free cash flows. Scharfstein (1997) and Rajan, Servaes, and Zingales (2000) argue that investment distortions are endemic within conglomerates. A similar logic might suggest that firms acquire plants and divisions that they cannot run efficiently. By contrast, our view of acquisitions is based on Maksimovic and Phillips (2002), who show that the growth by conglomerates' divisions is consistent with a simple profit-maximizing model with scarce managerial or organizational ability. Graham, Lemmon, and Wolf (2002) show that conglomerate firms purchase firms that have lower Tobin's q than the firms that remain single-segment firms. Chevalier (1999) also shows that conglomerate firms purchase firms that have a different sensitivity of cash flow to investment than firms that conglomerates choose not to purchase. These results are consistent with our model and evidence that conglomerate firms, given productivity differences, make selective acquisitions of certain types of firms.[9]

Two recent studies by Mitchell and Mulherin (1996) and Andrade and Stafford (1999) show that industry characteristics such as technological changes and capacity utilization are strongly associated with the incidence of mergers, takeovers, and investment. We are able to exploit plant-level data to obtain a more detailed picture of intraindustry firm-level determinants of asset transactions. Our evidence suggests that firm organization and efficiency drives most of the intraindustry trades.

The remainder of this paper is organized as follows. We discuss our analytical framework of analysis in Section I. The data is discussed in Section II. Section III presents the descriptive statistics of the market for assets. The firm's decisions to buy and sell and the gains from the transaction are analyzed in Sections IV and V, respectively. Section VI concludes.

[9] The evidence in Maksimovic and Phillips (2002) shows that conglomerates grow their more productive segments faster.

I. Framework for Analyzing Trades in Assets

The hypotheses that we examine are motivated by a neo-classical model of firm organization across multiple markets, advanced by Maksimovic and Phillips (2002). Firms sell some or all their assets when there is an expected gain in productivity if the assets are operated by another firm. These trades occur because firms differ in organizational ability and these differences determine their productivity in different industries. The model shows how a profit-maximizing firm chooses the quantity of capacity to employ in each industry and how demand shocks in one industry affect capacity decisions in other industries. It provides predictions on how firm organization affects who trades assets, and the magnitude of the gains from such activity. These predictions differ from the predictions of models that assume that firms acquire assets outside their main industry because managers engage in empire building behavior. Thus, the predictions of the model can be used to test the hypothesis that the trade in assets by multiindustry firms allocates assets to more productive uses. This section describes the model and sets out the hypotheses motivated by the model.

Consider first the market for assets when firms maximize profits and financial market imperfections are not material. Following Lucas (1978), Maksimovic and Phillips (2002) argue that management teams of firms or firm organizations differ in their ability to operate plants efficiently.[10] Management teams of all abilities find it more difficult to manage a large firm than a small firm. Thus, a high quality management team may operate a marginal plant in a large firm only as efficiently as a low quality management team operates a marginal plant in a small firm. Firm size and the scope of a firm's operations adjust until the profit from operating the marginal plant is equalized across all firms in the industry. As industry conditions change, a firm's comparative advantage in operating plants also changes. As a result, there are gains to trading assets, and trade occurs until the profit from operating the marginal plant is again equalized. In the equilibrium, firms with more skilled managers or organizations still have a higher average productivity than firms managed by less skilled managers.

The model focuses on how changes in industry demand affect the marginal value of plant production in single-segment and in multisegment firms, and thus the direction and the gains to trade in plants. As demand increases, output prices also increase, and the ability to produce more output per unit input becomes relatively more valuable. The increased value of output is now greater than the increased cost of operating the firm at a larger size. More productive firms can sell the output at a price that is high enough to compensate for the diseconomies of operating at a larger size. This raises the

[10] More generally, their model can be reinterpreted as positing the existence of a fixed firm-specific factor of production that induces diminishing returns to scale. Following Lucas (1978), they identify this factor with managerial, or more generally, organizational ability.

price of capacity in the market for physical assets and less productive managers will find it more advantageous to sell their plants to more productive managers instead of producing output themselves.

Thus the model predicts that assets flow from more productive to less productive firms when demand increases.[11] The divisions with more skilled management teams thus gain in size relative to divisions managed by less skilled managers in the same industry. The volume of sales is higher when the technology in the industry is such that productivity does not decrease steeply as a firm acquires more capacity in the industry. The magnitude of transactions in response to such demand shocks depends, in part, on whether or not there are significant diseconomies of scale.

When demand falls, the costs of managing a large firm outweigh the benefits of high productivity and at the margin firms may shed assets. However, if the overall trend in the economy exhibits positive growth, we would expect the magnitude of this flow to be lower empirically. Firms would expect such transactions to be reversed subsequently when economic growth resumes. In addition, the existence of transaction costs would reduce the incentive to engage in such transactions, as the opportunity cost of an asset being operated outside its best use is lower in a recession. Under these conditions, the incentives to engage in transactions will be larger after positive industry shocks, giving rise to more transactions when demand increases.

To summarize, the profit-maximizing model suggests tests of the following predictions.

HYPOTHESIS 1: *Sales of assets are more likely to occur when the industry receives a positive demand shock. The higher (lower) the productivity of a division (or a single-segment firm) the higher the probability that it buys (sells).*

Trade-offs between managerial ability and size also hold within multisegment firms. A firm grows its segments until the value of a marginal investment is equalized across industries in which it operates. Thus, the growth and efficiency of a segment may affect a firm's decision to buy or sell plants in another segment. The model predicts that a firm reduces its capacity in an industry by selling assets when the value of these assets to another firm is higher. The opportunity cost may be high either because other firms in the industry can better use the assets, or because the selling firm has better prospects in other industries. Thus, a multisegment firm sells plants in a segment when its other segments are growing fast and it is an efficient producer in these other segments. It may also sell a segment when the segment is not an efficient producer, but the industry is doing well and the plant is relatively more valuable to other, more efficient, producers. These predictions are summarized in the following hypothesis.

[11] The model allows buying of new capacity from an external market with an upward sloping supply curve. An upward sloping supply curve can be justified given adjustment costs for new capacity, or through time-to-build, or given increasing costs of needed inputs to build new capacity. Firms may also scrap assets if the demand in the industry is sufficiently low.

HYPOTHESIS 2: *Asset trades in multisegment firms follow a specific pattern: There is an increased probability that a segment is sold (purchased), when (1) the firm has lower (higher) productivity in an industry and this industry receives a positive demand shock, and (2) the firm's other segments have higher (lower) relative productivity and these other industries receive positive demand shocks.*

The asset purchase decision works similarly to the sale decision. Multisegment firms may purchase plants in an industry if their other segments are less productive producers in industries that receive a positive demand shock. In that case, these less productive segments optimally sell out to more productive producers in their respective industries, and the firm expands faster in its remaining segments. Firms may also purchase plants in an industry when their prospects elsewhere diminish. This occurs if they are more productive producers in other industries and these industries suffer negative demand shocks.

This prediction may also be used to distinguish the neoclassical model from several hypotheses about the acquisition decisions of multisegment firms when managers act opportunistically or when there are material financial market imperfections. Lamont (1997), for example, suggests that firms would be more likely to invest outside their main divisions when their main division receives a positive demand shock. Thus, if the main division of firms is more efficient than peripherals, this prediction on the effect of demand shocks on the purchase and sale decisions in other industries is opposite to that of our model.

Jensen's (1986) free cash flow theory suggests that when firms have excess cash flow, they tend to use it to acquire additional assets that they cannot operate efficiently. More recently Rajan et al. (2000) and Scharfstein and Stein (2000) have also argued that the organizational structure of conglomerates makes them likely to waste assets. Although we cannot identify the dissipation of shareholder wealth from managers overpaying for acquisitions or the appropriation of cash flows from assets, our empirical tests will detect the extent to which the dissipation of free cash flows in multisegment firms leads to acquisition patterns that differ from those predicted by efficient allocation across industries.

These predictions regarding the flow of assets between firms have implications for the analysis of firm organization and restructuring. Profit-maximizing firms grow more in industries in which they have a comparative advantage. Thus, on average, the larger divisions of multisegment firms are predicted to have a higher mean productivity than smaller, peripheral divisions.[12] As a result, in the long run, main divisions are more likely to be buyers and peripheral divisions are more likely to be sellers. For the same

[12] Maksimovic and Phillips (2002) examine this prediction and show it to be consistent with segment-level data constructed from underlying plant-level census data.

reason the expected gain in productivity is higher when the plant is sold by a peripheral division and purchased by a buyer's main division than if the purchase is of a plant in a buyer's peripheral division.

The differences in productivity between main and peripheral units of the same firm are also likely to create an association between organizational structure and trades following a demand shock. When the main division of a multisegment firm receives a positive demand shock, the firm will sell capacity in the peripheral divisions. When the main unit receives a negative demand shock, the firm will acquire assets in peripheral units.[13] We summarize these predictions in the following hypothesis.

HYPOTHESIS 3: *Multisegment firms increase their focus through acquisitions when demand is high in their main industries, and decrease their focus when demand is low. The probability that an asset is sold and the expected gain from the sale are higher for assets operated by peripheral divisions of firms.*

Our model does not make a distinct prediction for transactions involving the whole firm—such as mergers—and transactions involving only some plants or divisions. In fact, we expect the model to predict mergers less well than partial firm transactions: Mergers or acquisitions of multidivisional firms may involve the transfer of some divisions that do not fit under new ownership and that would not have occurred in isolation.[14]

II. Data

We use data from the Longitudinal Research Database (LRD), maintained by the Center for Economic Studies at the Bureau of the Census.[15] The LRD database contains detailed plant-level data for manufacturing plants (SIC codes 2000–3999) on the value of shipments produced by each plant, investments broken down by equipment and buildings, and the number of employees. The LRD tracks approximately 50,000 manufacturing plants every year in the Annual Survey of Manufactures (ASM). This database is only a survey for smaller plants. The ASM covers all plants with more than 250 employees. In addition, it also includes smaller plants that are randomly selected every fifth year to complete a rotating five-year panel. Once selected, plants

[13] We would also expect to see similar effects on other divisions when peripheral units receive demand shocks. However, because peripheral units are smaller than main units, these effects are less likely to be detectable.

[14] Another model that has implications for the timing of asset sales is Shleifer and Vishny (1992). Shleifer and Vishny stress the importance of asset sales that occur by firms with high debt when industries become temporarily distressed. We do not examine the predictions of this model in this paper given that this database does not have financial structure variables.

[15] For a more detailed description of the Longitudinal Research Database (LRD) see McGuckin and Pascoe (1988).

are required by U.S. law to answer the questions. Many data items used (e.g., the number of employees, employee compensation, total value of shipments) also represent items that are also reported to the IRS, increasing the accuracy of the data.

There are several advantages to this database. First, it covers both public and private firms in manufacturing industries. Second, coverage is at the plant level, and output is assigned by plants at the four-digit SIC code level. Thus, firms that produce under multiple SIC codes are not assigned to just one industry. Third, plant-level coverage means that we can track plants even as they change owners. In addition to a plant-level identifier, the database contains a code that identifies which assets change ownership. These two features are key to our study, as they allow us to identify assets that have changed hands from year to year. Thus, plants have to be part of an ASM panel for the plants to remain in our study.

We confine our analysis to the period 1974 through 1992. We use 1974 as the starting year of our analysis because it is the first year of a five-year panel; 1992 is the last year of data available to us. We aggregate plants into firm-level business segments at the three-digit SIC code level and exclude segments that are less than $1 million in real value of shipments in 1982 dollars. Our regressions contain observations beginning in 1979 given we use five years of lagged data in order to calculate productivity for each plant in each year.

III. The Basic Facts

Before preceding to test the hypotheses from the prior section, we first describe the data and present some basic facts about the market for assets.

A. The Number and Types of Transactions

We classify firms as single segment or multiple segment based on three-digit SIC codes. If a firm produces 97.5 percent of its sales or higher in one three-digit SIC code, we classify that firm as a single-segment firm and exclude the small peripheral segment. We classify all other firms as multiple-segment firms. For these firms, we also classify each segment as either a main segment or a peripheral segment. Main segments are segments whose real value of shipments (in 1982 dollars) is at least 25 percent of the firm's total shipments.

We classify transactions into three types: single-plant transactions by single-plant firms, multiplant transactions broken into full divisions and partial divisions (at the three-digit SIC code level), and full-firm transactions. We break transactions into these three categories as it seems plausible that transactions in which a single plant changes hands between multiplant firms in the same industry are marginal investment transactions that have the least implications for both future investment policy and corporate control.

Transactions in which a division is sold have greater implications for managerial control. Finally whole-firm transactions (mergers and acquisitions) include the purchase of a whole multisegment firm, and thus buyers may obtain extra assets outside of their area of expertise that they would not otherwise acquire. Gains may thus differ across transaction types.

Table I presents summary statistics for asset reallocations in our data set between 1974 and 1992. We break out the transactions into whole-firm dispositions (mergers and takeovers) and sales of assets by firms that remain in existence.[16]

Table I shows that from 1974 to 1992, the total number of plants reallocated in mergers and takeovers was approximately equal to the total number of plants reallocated in sales by ongoing firms. On average, 1.95 percent of plants are reallocated annually through takeovers and mergers, whereas 0.95 percent and 0.99 percent are reallocated through sales of entire and partial divisions, respectively. In each case, the plants reallocated tend to be below average in size (real value of shipments) for their industry. More plants than not are sold to buyers whose major focus is producing in the same industry, defined at the three-digit SIC code level.[17] The proportion of same industry buyers is lowest for whole-firm dispositions, and highest for partial-division sales. Table I also shows that more transactions occur in industries that are in expansion than in recession.

Table I also shows the two-digit SIC code industries with the highest and lowest rates of reallocations in our sample. The highest annual rate is 4.72 percent, for Rubber and Plastics, followed by Electronics, Primary Metal products, Optical Equipment, and Processed Food Products. The lowest annual reallocation rate is 2.77 percent, for Leather and Leather Products, followed by Clothes and Apparel, Printing and Publishing, Lumber and Wood products, and Oil Refining. Comparing the types of transactions across industries, it is evident that the rates of partial- and full-division sales in particular differ considerably within these industries. Thus, for example, the full-division sales rates for Rubber and Plastics and Leather and Leather Products are 1.33 percent and 0.68 percent, respectively. The corresponding rates for partial-division sales are 1.36 percent and 0.46 percent, respectively.

B. Who Are the Buyers and Sellers?

Table II shows the characteristics of the firms that sell and acquire assets, by transaction category. In the table, we also break out mergers and acquisitions into those that involve sellers with just one plant, sellers in just one industry, and sellers who operate in more than one industry. In all cases, the characteristics are measured in the year prior to the transaction. The acquiring firm in the case of partial and full divisional sales is the buying

[16] Thus, a firm that sells its only division is classified as a merger.

[17] More precisely, buyers for whom that industry is one of the top two industries in which they operate, and who produce at least 25 percent of their output in that industry.

Table I

Asset Reallocations: Summary Statistics

Sample characteristics for asset reallocations for the years 1974 to 1992. Reallocations include partial firm asset sales and sales through mergers and acquisitions in which the selling firm disposes of all its assets. Plant-level data is obtained from the Annual Survey of Manufactures from the Bureau of the Census, U.S. Department of Commerce. The average annual percentage of plants reallocated is the number of plants reallocated in a given year divided by the total plants, averaged over all years. The percentage sold to buyer inside industry excludes plant sales to buyers with no existing plants in manufacturing prior to the purchase. Average plant sizes are the total value of shipments in thousands of dollars for each plant deflated by three-digit SIC code deflators from the Bureau of Economic Analysis.

	Sample of Firms			
			Asset Sales	
	Total	Mergers and Acquisitions	Full Segment	Partial Segment
Panel A: Reallocation rates across and within industries				
Full period: 1974 to 1992				
Number of plants reallocated	35,291	17,720	8,556	9,015
Average annual % of plants reallocated	3.89%	1.95%[a,c]	0.95%	0.99%
% Plants sold to buyer inside industry				
Same three-digit SIC code	56.8%	54.1%[b,c]	55.5%	63.1%
Same four-digit SIC code	47.7%	44.9%[a,c]	47.9%	53.0%
Average plant size (Real $ in thousands, value of shipments)	$30,332	$28,435	$30,916	$33,506
Average industry plant size (Real $ in thousands, value of shipments)	$35,790	$34,569	$36,440	$37,574

continued over

	Sample of Firms			
			Asset Sales	
	Total	Mergers and Acquisitions	Full Segment	Partial Segment
Panel B: Reallocation rates by 2-digit SIC code				
Industry reallocations: Highest quartile				
SIC Code: 30, Rubber and plastic products Yearly percentage plant sales (number of sales)	4.72% (2167)	2.03% (974)	1.33% (577)	1.36% (616)
SIC Code: 36, Electronics/communications Yearly percentage plant sales (number of sales)	4.61% (3037)	2.12% (1397)	1.28% (840)	1.21% (800)
SIC Code: 33, Primary metal products Yearly percentage plant sales (number of sales)	4.49% (1663)	1.95% (732)	1.33% (487)	1.20% (444)
SIC Code: 38, Scientific/optical equipment Yearly percentage plant sales (number of sales)	4.38% (1113)	2.22% (570)	1.32% (332)	0.83% (211)
SIC Code: 20, Processed food products Yearly percentage plant sales (number of sales)	4.24% (2358)	2.23% (2358)	0.58% (603)	1.40% (1491)
Industry reallocations: Lowest quartile				
SIC Code: 29, Oil refining Yearly percentage plant sales (number of sales)	3.21% (307)	2.13% (307)	0.51% (71)	0.58% (82)
SIC Code: 24, Lumber and wood products Yearly percentage plant sales (number of sales)	3.04% (1436)	1.54% (743)	0.59% (273)	0.90% (420)
SIC Code: 27, Printing and publishing Yearly percentage plant sales (number of sales)	2.99% (1104)	1.84% (1104)	0.57% (331)	0.57% (344)
SIC Code: 23, Clothes and apparel Yearly percentage plant sales (number of sales)	2.95% (1495)	1.78% (893)	0.55% (275)	0.62% (327)
SIC Code: 31, Leather and leather products Yearly percentage plant sales (number of sales)	2.77% (253)	1.63% (143)	0.68% (63)	0.46% (47)

[a, b] Test of whether the proportion of mergers is significantly different from the proportion of full-segment sales at the 1 percent and 5 percent levels, respectively, using a two-tailed test.

[c] Test of whether the proportion of mergers is significantly different from the proportion of combined full- and partial-segment sales at the 1 percent level using a two-tailed test.

Table II

Asset reallocations: Summary Statistics

Sample characteristics for asset reallocations for the years 1974 to 1992. Reallocations include partial firm asset sales and sales through takeovers and mergers in which the selling firm disposes of all its assets. Plant-level data is obtained from the Annual Survey of Manufactures from the Bureau of the Census, U.S. Department of Commerce. Recession (expansion) years are the three years classified as having the largest decline (expansion) in the aggregate real value of industrial production. Industry capacity utilization quartiles are yearly quartiles based on the rates reported by the Department of the Census. Long-run industry growth/decline quartiles are calculated using growth rates for aggregate industry shipments over a 15-year period, with beginning and ending periods representing three-year averages for 1974 to 1976 and 1990 to 1992.

	Sample of Firms			
			Asset Sales	
	Total	Mergers and Takeovers	Full Division	Partial Division
Transactions by aggregate economy conditions				
Recession years (1981, 1982, 1991)				
Average % reallocated (total number)	3.57% (5,148)	2.16% (3,112)	0.70% (1,003)	0.72% (1,033)
Expansion years (1986, 1987, 1988)				
Average % reallocated (total number)	6.19% (8,989)	2.69% (3,904)	1.73% (2,509)	1.77% (2,576)
Indeterminate Years	3.21%	1.73%	0.70%	0.78%
Transactions by industry capacity utilization				
Low industry capacity utilization (bottom quartile)				
Average % reallocated (total number)	3.86% (8,618)	1.90% (4,244)	0.99% (2,210)	0.97% (2,164)
High industry capacity utilization (top quartile)				
Average % reallocated (total number)	3.69% (8,413)	1.92% (4,375)	0.87% (1,977)	0.90% (2,061)
Transactions by long-run industry growth/decline				
Quartile 1: Declining industry growth				
Average % reallocated (total number)	4.01% (6,290)	1.95% (3,058)	1.09% (1,707)	0.97% (1,525)
Quartile 2				
Average % reallocated (total number)	3.86% (5,250)	1.96% (2,666)	1.05% (1,425)	0.85% (1,160)
Quartile 3				
Average % reallocated (total number)	3.52% (10,008)	1.80% (5,131)	0.88% (2,505)	0.83% (2,372)
Quartile 4: High industry growth				
Average % reallocated (total number)	4.03% (15,746)	2.01% (7,870)	0.87% (3,405)	1.14% (4,471)

firm. In the case of mergers and acquisitions, these are the surviving firms. For mergers we also report the characteristics of buyers who operate in multiple three-digit SIC code industries.

Firms that sell full and partial divisions tend to be quite large (average revenues of $1.328 and $1.849 billion) and operate in an average of approximately eight three-digit industries. Sellers of partial divisions tend to operate a greater number of plants (an average of 31.48 in contrast to an average of 23.72 plants operated by sellers of entire divisions). Only approximately a quarter of the plants sold in the sales of entire divisions belong to one of the seller's main divisions, whereas approximately half of plants sold in partial division sales belong to one of the seller's main divisions.

Buyers of entire divisions are of similar size and operate a similar number of plants as the sellers, whereas the buyers of partial divisions are on average about two thirds as large as the sellers. Buyers in both categories tend to be slightly more focused than the sellers, operating in an average of approximately six three-digit SIC code industries. The buyers' main divisions acquired 53.8 percent and 63.1 percent of the plants purchased in entire and partial-division transactions, respectively. Thus, the market for asset sales is one in which both the buyers and sellers are conglomerate firms. The sellers sell peripheral divisions and marginal plants to the main divisions of the buyers. Although the buyers are somewhat smaller and more focused than the sellers, the differences between them are not large.

In contrast, the average seller in a merger operates 1.78 plants and has sales of $51 million. Approximately 80 percent of all full-firm sales (mergers and purchases) involve the sale of small, one-plant firms. About 10 percent of all mergers involve multiplant single-industry firms (average number of plants, 5.15) and approximately 10 percent involve multiple-industry firms. Even in this last category, the sellers have an average of only 7 plants, have sales of $239 million, and operate in an average of approximately three three-digit SIC code industries. Buyers of whole firms are larger than the sellers. On average, they operate 16.64 plants, produce in 4.66 three-digit SIC code industries, and have annual sales of $856 million. About a half of the acquired plants are operated by the buying firms' main divisions.

To summarize, we find several differences between the buyers in partial firm dispositions and mergers. On average, buyers of full or partial divisions tend to be larger than buyers in mergers, they operate more plants, and tend to operate in a larger number of industries. These differences arise because a larger proportion of buyers in mergers are single-industry firms. The subset of buyers in mergers who operate in multiple industries are slightly bigger in size and in the number of industries in which they operate.

C. Aggregate and Industry Demand and Asset Reallocations

We compare asset reallocations during economic expansions and recessions. We classify years as recession or expansion years by using aggregate and aggregate-detrended industrial production. Detrended industrial production is defined as the actual less predicted industrial production, where we calculate predicted industrial production from a regression of industrial production on a yearly time trend. Recession years are years in which both real and detrended industrial production decline relative to the previous year. We classify years as expansion years when both real and detrended industrial production increase relative to the previous year.

This procedure gives us results similar to the NBER recession dating procedure, which the NBER does quarterly. This procedure also allows us to classify a year such as 1980, which, according to the NBER, had a recession of less than six months. Using this procedure, we classify 1981, 1982, and 1991 as recession years. For comparability, we also take the top three expansion years—1986 through 1988. (Other expansion years were 1976 through 1978 and 1984 through 1985.) Given that actual and detrended industrial production did not move in the same direction, 1979, 1980, 1983, 1989, and 1992 are indeterminate years.

Table III shows that more assets are reallocated in expansions. The rates of reallocations during expansion years (the three years with the highest increases in the aggregate real value of industries production) and recession years (the three years with the largest decline in the aggregate real value of industries production) are 6.20 percent and 3.57 percent, respectively. The rates of full- and partial-division sales, in particular, are much higher in expansions (1.73 percent and 1.78 percent, respectively), than in recession years (0.70 percent and 0.72 percent, respectively). The reallocations rate due to mergers is somewhat higher in expansions than in recessions (2.69 percent compared to 2.16 percent). By contrast, the total reallocation rate in the remaining indeterminate years is 3.21 percent, the reallocation rate due to mergers is a low 1.73 percent, whereas the partial- and full-division sales rates are 0.78 percent and 0.70 percent, respectively. Thus, the partial- and full-division sales are sharply higher in expansion years.

We find that the number of transactions is sharply higher in expansions. The fact that transactions are lower in recessions is consistent with the overall positive growth trend in the economy causing firms to expect to need more capacity in the future, when growth resumes. In addition, transactions in recessions may result in gains that are less likely to offset transactions costs because the opportunity cost of an asset being operated outside its best use is lower in a recession.

We next explore differences in capacity utilization on the rate of transactions. We use industry-level capacity utilization data from the Bureau of the Census. For each year we use capacity utilization to classify into quartiles all the three-digit SIC industries. We report the average rate of transactions over the sample period for the top and bottom quartile. As Table II shows, the rates of reallocation do not differ materially across capacity utilization quartiles.

We also report the rates of reallocations by long-run industry growth. As Table III shows, more reallocations take place in the fastest growing industries—15,746 in the fastest growing quartile compared to 6,290 in the

Table III

Buyer and Seller Characteristics

Sample characteristics of purchasing firms prior to asset purchases for the years 1974 to 1992. Data is aggregated to firm-level from individual manufacturing plants. Plant-level data is from the Annual Survey of Manufactures from the Bureau of the Census, U.S. Department of Commerce. Buyers without any prior manufacturing plants (foreign buyers, outside manufacturing buyers) are excluded as prepurchase characteristics can not be calculated. Average buyer and seller size is the average value of total shipments deflated by industry price deflators from the Bureau of Economic Analysis. 1992 was the last year available at the time the study was conducted.

	Sample of Firms				
	Asset Sales		Mergers and Takovers		
	Full Division	Partial Division	Firms with Plants = 1	Firms with Plants > 1	Multiple Industry Firms (Three-digit SIC Code)
Seller characteristics prior to sale					
Full period: 1974 to 1992					
Number of selling firms	3,774	4,205	9,480	2,204	1,224
Average number of plants	23.72	31.48	1.00	5.15	7.0
Average seller size (millions $)	1,328	1,849	22	176	239
Average number of three-digit industries	7.56	7.77	1.00	2.21	3.17
Average number of four-digit industries	9.58	10.56	1.00	2.53	3.61
% of plants sold by seller in its primary line of business					
Seller's primary three-digit line(s)*	28.2%	50.8%	100.0%	70.6%	62.2%
Seller's primary four-digit line(s)*	25.6%	36.3%	100.0%	61.6%	54.9%
Buyer characteristics prior to purchase					
Full period: 1974 to 1992					
Number of buyers	2,267	2,755	1,648	4,530	3,627
Average number of plants	23.50	23.38	1.00	22.33	26.80
Average buyer size (millions $)	1,307	1,357	27.9	1,157	1,410
Average number of three-digit industries	6.24	5.75	1.00	6.00	7.24
Average number of four-digit industries	8.21	7.58	1.00	7.87	9.51
% of plants bought that are in buyer's home industry					
At the three-digit SIC code	53.8%	63.1%	59.1%	30.8%	26.3%
At the four-digit SIC code	47.9%	55.2%	49.9%	21.0%	17.4%

* If the seller (buyer) produces in multiple industries, the seller's (buyer's) home industries are those industries that have at least 20 percent of the firm's sales.

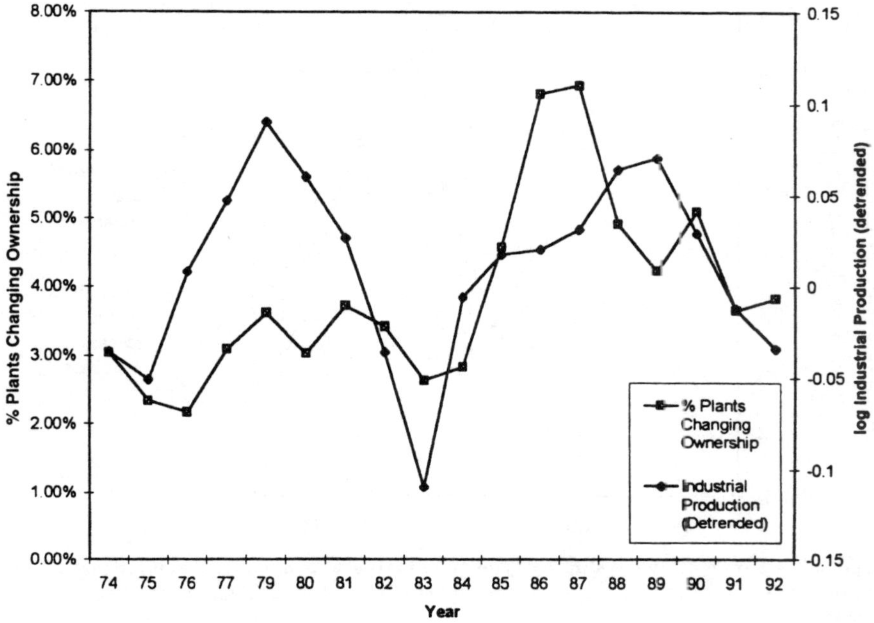

Figure 1. Left-hand scale is the total percentage of plants changing ownership by year. Right-hand scale is aggregate real industrial production detrended.

slowest growing quartile of industries. However, the overall rate of transactions is similar at approximately four percent. There is some limited evidence that industries which have more moderate growth rates have a somewhat lower rate of transactions, but the effect, if it exists, is relatively small.

We also subclassify the reallocations into those that occurred in years in which the industry (at the three-digit SIC level) was in expansion, and those that occurred in years in which the industry was in recession. For an industry to be classified as being in expansion, its real production in that year has to increase and its real level of output has to exceed its long-term trend level. For an industry to be classified as being in recession, the industry's real output has to decline in that year and the real level of output has to be below the long-term trend level.

Table III suggests that the average rate of reallocations, and in particular the rate of partial firm sales, is higher in periods of macroeconomic expansion. There is less evidence that differences in industry conditions have a material effect.

A similar pattern emerges when the time series of sales is plotted. Figure 1 shows both the annual rate of reallocations and detrended aggregate industrial production. Detrended industrial production is calculated as described earlier.

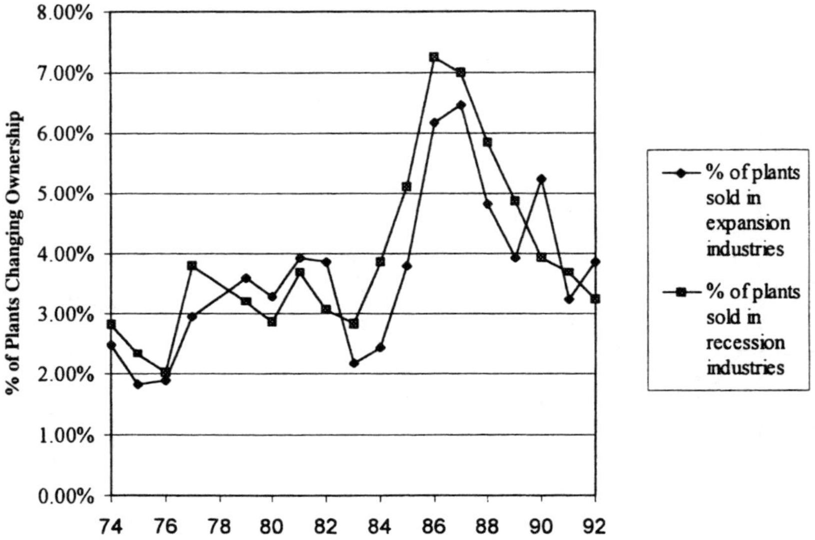

Figure 2. Change of ownership by type of industry. Expansion (recession) industries are the industries in which real and detrended value of shipments at the industry level increase (decline).

Figure 1 shows that, consistent with Table II, the annual percentage of plants that transferred ownership is high in expansions. It is highest in 1986 and in 1987, when nearly seven percent of the plants change ownership (adding up mergers and full- and partial-firm asset sales). The proportion of transactions that occur in industries that are in expansion also varies considerably, and is procyclical. In 1987 and 1988, when few industries are in recession, the number of plants transacted in these industries clearly declines.

However, when we plot the time series of the proportion of plants transacted in industries that were in recession and expansion in Figure 2, we find that the proportions are very similar. The reason for this result is that few industries are in recession when the overall economy is in expansion. Those that are in recession have a similar proportion of plants transacted. Thus, time series variation in the overall rate of asset reallocations is driven by economy-wide factors.

We next examine the time series variation in the percentage of plants broken down by mergers and acquisitions, division sales and partial-division sales. Figure 3 breaks the transactions into these categories. In particular, mergers are strongly procyclical, rising in the years before the 1982 recession to over three percent of plants, before falling to one percent of plants in 1984. The rate of mergers and acquisitions increased again to almost four percent of plants by 1987. Partial-firm asset sales vary less year by year; however they still hit a peak of over four percent (combining full and partial segment sales) in 1987.

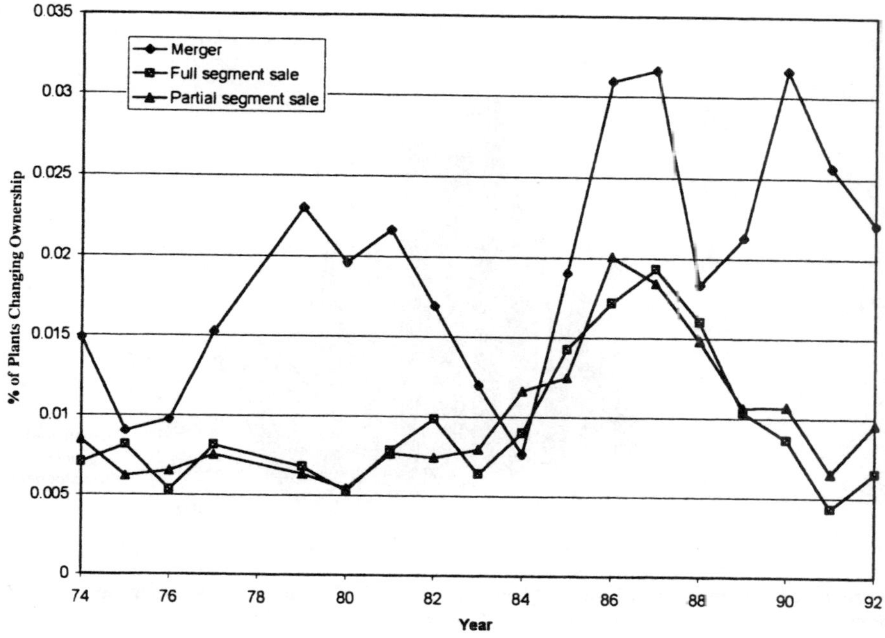

Figure 3. Percentage of plants reallocated through mergers, full-segment sales, and partial-segment sales by year.

The summary statistics suggest that the rate of asset sales, and in particular of full- and partial-divisions sales, is affected by economy-wide factors. There is less evidence that the average rate of transactions is affected by industry factors, such as capacity utilization and long-term growth. We next explore how within-industry and within-firm characteristics affect which firms sell plants and what plants firms choose to sell.

IV. The Probability of an Asset Sale

A. How Sales Vary with Firm Organization

In Figure 4, we show how the proportion of assets sold by division rank, where rank equals one for the largest segment by real value of shipments.

For firms with a given number of segments, as the segment rank of a particular segment increases, the proportion of its assets sold also increases sharply. The plants in the largest segment of a firm are the least likely to be sold. For example, the proportion of largest segment plants sold is less than one percent for firms with seven or more segments, whereas the proportion of plants that these firms sell in their smallest segments rises to three and four percent. Schlingemann et al. (2002) find using accounting data on whole

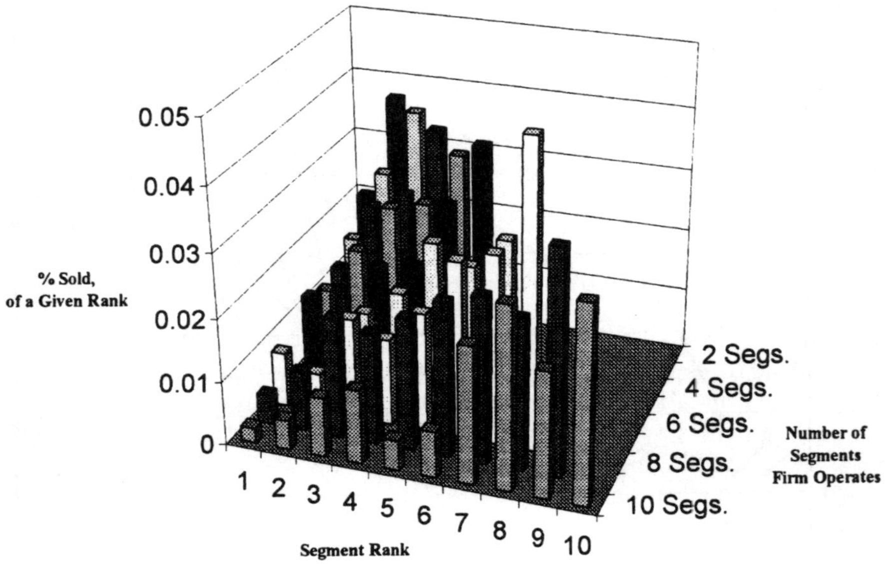

Figure 4. Percentage of plants sold via asset sale by segment rank as the number of segments the firm operates increases. Segment rank equals one for the largest segment a firm operates.

segments that a firm is more likely to sell small rather than large segments. Maksimovic and Phillips (2002) find that there is an inverse relation between the rank of a segment and its efficiency, and that the equally ranked segments of larger firms tend to be more efficient than those of smaller firms. Thus, Figure 4 accords well with the hypothesis that firms are more likely to sell their least efficient plants and also that, holding segment ranks constant across firms, the rate of plant sales is lower for more efficient segments.

There also exists an inverse relation between the number of segments a firm possesses and the probability that it will be acquired. Three percent of single-segment firms are bought out or merged, whereas only 1.5 percent of firms with six and seven segments are merged.

B. Measurement of Productivity and Demand in Business Segments

To analyze the relation between demand and firms' productivity on asset sales, we need measures of both these variables. We discuss our measures next.

B.1. Productivity of Business Segments

We calculate productivity for all firm segments at the plant level. Our primary measure of performance is total factor productivity (TFP). TFP takes the actual amount of output produced for a given amount of inputs and compares it to a predicted amount of output. "Predicted output" is what the plant should have produced, given the amount of inputs it used and the mean industry production technology in place. A plant that produces more than the predicted amount of output has a greater-than-average productivity. This measure is more flexible than a cash-flow measure of performance, and does not impose the restrictions of constant returns to scale and constant elasticity of scale that a "dollar in, dollar out" cash-flow measure requires.

In calculating the predicted output of each plant, we assume that for each industry there exists a production function that defines the relation between a plant's inputs and outputs. Then, for each industry, we estimate this production function using an unbalanced panel with plant-level fixed effects, using all plants in the industry within our 1974 to 1992 time frame. If a plant changes owners, we effectively treat the years under each owner as separate plants, allowing plant-level fixed effects to differ by each owner. For each industry, we calculate productivity using up to five years of lagged data. Thus we can calculate productivity for the 1979 to 1992 period. In addition, each plant has to have at least two years of productivity to be included. Finally, each input has to have a nonzero reported value.

In calculating productivity, we assume that the plants in each industry have a translog production function.[18] This functional form is a second-degree approximation to any arbitrary production function, and therefore takes into account interactions between inputs. To estimate predicted outputs, we take the translog production function and run a regression of log of the total value of shipments on the log of inputs, including cross-product and squared terms:

$$\ln Q_{it} = a_i + A + \sum_{j=1}^{N} a_j \ln L_{jit} + \sum_{j=1}^{N} \sum_{k=j}^{N} a_{jk} \ln L_{jit} \ln L_{kit}, \tag{1}$$

where Q_{it} represents output of plant i in year t, a_i is a plant-level fixed effect, and L_{jit} is the quantity of input j used in production for plant i for time period t. The parameter A is a technology shift parameter, assumed to be constant by industry, and $a_j = \sum_{i=1}^{N} a_{ji}$ indexes returns to scale. Plants that change ownership have a different fixed effect for each owner, allowing the plant-level fixed effect to differ by owner.

Our measure of TFP is the residual from equation (1) plus the plant-level fixed effect. We standardize plant-level TFP by dividing by the standard deviation of TFP for each industry. Thus, our comparisons of plants' TFP are not driven by differences in the dispersion of productivity within each industry. We discuss the details of the variables used and present some summary statistics from our estimation of TFP in the Appendix.

To check robustness of our regression results, we also use two alternative measures of productivity. First we use value added per worker. Value added per worker is defined as total sales less materials cost of goods sold, divided

[18] See Caves and Barton (1990) and especially Jorgenson (1986) for more details and extensive references on estimating firm production functions.

by the number of workers. This measure has been used in McGuckin and Nguyen (1995). Second, we use cash flow per dollar of sales. Cash flow is defined as sales less the sum of the materials cost of goods sold and the capital expenditures, all divided by the value of sales. Neither of these measures has the desirable theoretical properties of TFP. However, they have the advantage of being familiar, and since they are not computed from a regression, may have desirable statistical properties.

B.2. Demand in Business Segments

To examine the effect of demand on asset sales, we include measures of both aggregate and industry demand. For aggregate demand we use detrended aggregate industrial production, as described earlier.[19] We capture changes in demand for an industry's output using an indicator of economic activity in downstream industries. By using a downstream demand indicator we avoid potential endogeneity problems that may arise if we were to use changes in the value of an industry's own shipments to proxy for demand shocks. Our measure of downstream industry demand is based on a four-digit industry measure of downstream economic activity from Baily, Bartelsman, and Haltiwanger (1998). This measure is constructed by using the 1977 input–output matrix to construct a weighted average index of downstream economic activity, with weights equal to the share of total shipments from the industry in question.[20]

C. Probability of Asset Sales

We next analyze how seller characteristics and firm organization influence partial firm sales. We separately examine sellers who are single-segment firms, and those that are multiple-segment firms. To be included in the subsample of firms that might have a partial-firm sale, the single-segment firms must have at least two plants. The regressions in this table (and all subsequent tables) cover the years from 1978 to 1992.[21]

Hypothesis 2 above suggests that a multiple-segment firm's decision to sell plants or an entire segment is influenced by its performance in other segments. We test for this effect, and for the effect of industry- and economy-

[19] Results are similar using actual industrial production. We use detrended industrial production to capture the idea that reallocations take place in response to a shock to the marginal value of production.

[20] The measure was first used in Bartelsman, Caballero, and Lyons (1994) (BCL). The BCL measure is still subject to simultaneity bias if a demand shock to the upstream industry affects activity in the downstream industry. To avoid this problem, in constructing each upstream industry's index of downstream demand, we exclude all downstream industries from the index if they purchase a large share of their inputs from that upstream industry (see Shea (1993)). Our results are similar using either this series or the original one constructed by BCL. We would like to thank John Haltiwanger for kindly providing both of these data series to us.

[21] The beginning year for these regressions is 1978 as that is the first year the change in downstream industry demand is available. A previous version of the paper used the change in own industry shipments (beginning in 1975) and found similar results. We also included industry profitability in the regressions. This variable is insignificant when added to the existing variables.

wide conditions.[22] In each case, we run an unbalanced panel probit regression allowing for correlated residuals within panel units, and we report heteroskedasticity-consistent standard errors. We control for firm size, number of plants, and relative segment rank. Relative segment rank is defined as the segment rank, with the largest segment having rank equal to one, divided by the total number of segments.

The results in Table IV show that demand at the aggregate level affects the probability of a partial sale of plants. Plants and segments are more likely to be sold when aggregate industrial production is high. This effect is stronger for multiple-segment firms.

Productivity strongly affects the probability a plant is sold for multisegment firms. The probability of a sale declines as the plant productivity increases and as the plant's segment productivity increases. This is consistent with the firm selling its worst plants in its worst divisions.[23] Thus, the behavior of sellers is consistent with the hypothesis that they are selling plants for which they do not have superior expertise.

For multisegment firms, a firm's other segments' productivity affects the probability of a plant sale. The probability of sale is positively and significantly related to the segment's rank within the firm: The probability that a plant in a smaller segment is sold is higher, holding industry shocks and productivity constant. The probability of a plant sale is also higher if the firm's other segments are more productive. This effect is strongly significant. In addition, the probability that a plant is sold is higher when the firm's other segments are productive *and* the firm's other industries have a positive increase to demand. The estimated magnitude of this effect can be shown by varying the magnitude of the other segments' weighted TFP while holding all the remaining variables at their median values. The predicted probability that the segment is sold is 3.35 percent when the other segments' weighted TFP is relatively low (at the 10th percentile) and the other segment's relative demand is high. This probability increases to 4.16 percent when the other segments' weighted TFP is relatively high (at the 90th percentile), and relative demand is also high.

In Table V, we present robustness tests of our results using two alternative measures of efficiency: value added per worker and plant cash flow. The alternative measures of productivity yield similar results as those in Table IV.

In sum, the results in Tables IV and V confirm the importance of aggregate demand on the rate of transactions. They are also consistent with profit maximizing behavior by sellers. Plants are more likely to be sold when they

[22] In unreported regressions, we also analyze partial-segment and full-segment sales separately. We have also estimated the equation for main and peripheral divisions of multiple-segment firms separately. In all material respects, the results are qualitatively similar. In addition we analyzed alternative specifications in which the firm multiple segment variables were weighed by the size of each segment. The results do not differ in any material respect.

[23] In unreported regressions, we also examine the choice of which plant to sell within a segment. The probability that a plant is sold is negatively related to the difference between its productivity and that of the other plants in the segment.

Table IV

Partial Firm Sales

Regressions test the effects of plant-level productivity and industry-level demand on the decision to sell plants for single-segment and multiple-segment firms. The dependent variable is a binary variable that indicates that the firm sells a plant, while still remaining in operation the next year. Observations are at the plant level for all firms. Detrended aggregate industrial production is actual minus predicted U.S. aggregate industrial production where predicted industrial prediction is obtained by regressing industrial production on a yearly time trend. Productivity variables are industry and year adjusted. Segment variables are aggregated into three-digit SIC codes for industry segments from underlying plant-level data. We estimate the regressions using unbalanced panel probit regressions allowing for correlated residuals within panel units. Significance tests are conducted using heteroskedasticity consistent standard errors. Data are yearly from 1979 to 1992. (*p*-values are in parentheses.)

	Dependent Variable: Plant Sale		
Variable	Single segment firms (with >1 Plant)	Multiple segment firms	Test for Significant Diff.: Single vs. Conglomerate Firms (*p*-Value)[a]
Constant	−6.162	−1.774	
	(0.000)*	(0.000)*	(0.000)*
Aggregate industrial production	0.831	1.104	
(detrended)	(0.000)*	(0.000)*	(0.000)*
Industry sensitivity to aggregate	0.009	−0.006	
industrial production	(0.277)	(0.003)*	(0.056)***
Lagged productivity (TFP) of plant[b]	−0.021	−0.075	
	(0.797)	(0.001)*	(0.042)**
Lagged segment TFP	0.026	−0.338	
	(0.705)	(0.000)*	(0.000)*
Segment TFP * change in	−0.055	0.000	
downstream industry demand	(0.317)	(0.987)	(0.812)
Lagged firm size (coefficient * 10,000,000)	0.642	−0.038	
	(0.000)*	(0.000)*	(0.000)*
Average number of plants per	−0.002	−0.022	
industry segment	(0.378)	(0.000)*	(0.000)*
Firm multiple segment variables			
Segment rank/number of segments		0.080	
		(0.000)*	
Other segment's weighted TFP[c]		0.240	
		(0.000)*	
Relative demand * other segments		0.073	
weighted TFP[d]		(0.003)*	
Total plant years	45,959	259,065	
Chi-squared statistic	108.44	1940.91	
Significance level (*p*-value)	<1%	<1%	

*, **, *** Significantly different from zero at the 1 percent, 5 percent, and 10 percent levels, respectively, using a two-tailed test.

[a] Significance test for a multiple-segment dummy variable interacted with each independent variable in a regression with all firms with greater than one plant.

[b] Total Factor Productivity (TFP) is calculated using a translog production function.

[c] Other segments' productivity is weighted average of the firm's other segment(s) weighted by the segment(s) sales.

[d] Relative industry demand equals one (zero, minus one) when the segment's change in downstream industry demand is greater (equal, less) than the change in downstream demand of the firm's median segment. Relative industry demand is interacted with the firm's other segments' weighted TFP.

Table V

Robustness Tests: Alternative Measures of Efficiency

Regressions test the effects of plant-level efficiency measures and industry-level demand on the decision to buy out another firm for single-segment and multiple-segment firms. The dependent variable is a binary variable which indicates that the firm sells a plant, while still remaining in operation the next year. Observations are at the plant level for all firms. Efficiency variables are industry and year adjusted. Segment variables are aggregated into three-digit SIC codes. Detrended aggregate industrial production is actual minus predicted U.S. aggregate industrial production where predicted industrial prediction is obtained by regressing industrial production on a yearly time trend. Columns one and two use value added per worker as the measure of efficiency. Value added is sales less materials divided by the number of workers. Columns three and four use plant cash flow as the measure of efficiency. Cash flow is sales less materials cost of goods sold less capital expenditures divided by sales. We estimate the regressions using unbalanced panel probit regressions allowing for correlated residuals within panel units. Significance tests are conducted using heteroskedasticity consistent standard errors. Coefficients for the value added measure of efficiency are multiplied by one hundred. (*p*-values are in parentheses.)

	Dependent Variable: Plant Sale			
	Efficiency measure: Value added per worker		Efficiency measure: Plant cash flow	
Variable	Single-segment Firms (with >1 Plant)	Multiple-segment Firms	Single-segment Firms (with >1 Plant)	Multiple-segment Firms
Constant	−6.364	−6.236	−6.004	−1.799
	(0.000)*	(0.000)*	(0.000)*	(0.000)*
Aggregate industrial production (detrended)	0.880	0.980	0.802	1.100
	(0.000)*	(0.000)*	(0.000)*	(0.000)*
Lagged plant efficiency measure	−0.166	−0.184	−0.404	−0.363
	(0.000)*	(0.000)*	(0.003)*	(0.000)*
Lagged segment efficiency measure	−0.004	−0.001	0.345	−0.162
	(0.597)	(0.670)*	(0.040)**	(0.015)**
Lagged segment efficiency * change in downstream industry demand	0.061	0.046	−0.449	0.325
	(0.661)	(0.633)	(0.147)	(0.748)
Lagged firm size (coefficient * 10,000,000)	0.710	0.066	0.671	−0.037
	(0.000)*	(0.000)*	(0.000)*	(0.000)*
Average number of plants per industry segment	−0.003	−0.024	−0.003	−0.022
	(0.184)	(0.000)*	(0.224)	(0.000)*
Firm multiple segment variables				
Segment rank/number of segments		0.489		0.124
		(0.000)*		(0.000)*
Other segment's weighted efficiency[a]		0.006		0.109
		(0.792)		(0.097)***
Relative demand * other segments weighted efficiency[b]		0.129		−0.040
		(0.005)*		(0.450)
Total plant years	45,959	259,065	45,959	259,065
Chi-squared statistic	115.66	1561.24	95.39	623.74
Significance level (*p*-value)	<1%	<1%	<1%	<1%

*, **, *** Significantly different from zero at the 1 percent, 5 percent, and 10 percent levels, respectively, using a two-tailed test.

[a] Other segments' efficiency is weighted average of the firm's other segment(s) weighted by the segment(s) sales.

[b] Relative industry demand equals one (zero, minus one) when the segment's change in downstream industry demand is greater (equal, less) than the change in downstream demand of the firm's median segment. Relative industry demand is interacted with the firm's other segments' weighted TFP.

are not productive, when their segment is less productive, and when the firm has better performing assets elsewhere. This finding supports our Hypotheses 2 and 3.

In Table VI we analyze the economic significance of our regression results. Specifically, we analyze how the probability of a sale by a single-segment firm or a division of a conglomerate varies as the level of industrial production and the productivity of the asset vary, holding all other variables at their sample medians. The probability of a sale is derived using regression coefficients computed in Tables IV and V.

Panel A of Table VI shows how the probability that an asset is sold depends on the initial owner's corporate structure and the asset's productivity. In general, the probability that an asset is sold by a conglomerate firm rather than by a single-segment firm is higher by a factor of approximately four. Using our standard productivity measure, TFP, the probability that a median level asset is sold by a conglomerate firm in any year is 3.71 percent, whereas the corresponding probability for a single-segment firm is 0.85 percent. Assets operated by peripheral divisions of conglomerates are sold at a somewhat higher rate.[24] We also find that more efficient assets at the 90th percentile have a lower probability of being sold than less efficient assets (10th percentile). The results are not sensitive to the choice of productivity measure used. The table also shows that smaller peripheral divisions are more likely to be sold. The probability a division with segment rank equal to the 90th percentile is sold is 4.13 percent at the median productivity.

Panel B shows how variation in the real level of aggregate industrial production affects the probability of sale. We present results for the median level of detrended industrial production and for levels that correspond to the 90th and 10th percentiles, respectively. The rate of asset sales is very responsive to the variation in aggregate industrial production. Thus, for example, when the aggregate production is at the 90th percentile (the second highest year), the probability that an asset of a conglomerate firm is sold is 4.03 percent, whereas it is only 3.20 percent when the level of industrial production is at the 10th percentile (the second lowest year). The corresponding statistics for single-segment firms are 1.26 percent and 0.57 percent, again illustrating their lower participation in the market for partial-firm asset sales.

Panel C shows the combined effect of the variation in productivity and aggregate industrial production. A low productivity plant owned by a peripheral division of a conglomerate has a 4.82 percent probability of being sold when industrial production is high, whereas a high productivity plant at a time of low aggregate production has a probability of being sold of only 2.50 percent. The corresponding probabilities for single-segment firms are 1.46 percent and 0.48 percent, respectively.

[24] The difference between single-segment and conglomerate rates may arise in part because the exit from an industry is classified as a partial-firm sale for a multisegment firm, but a whole-firm sale in the case of a single-segment firm. We return to this point in our discussion of Table IX.

Table VI

Probability of an Asset Sale

Predicted probability of an asset sale varying performance measures and industrial production using the regression coefficients from Tables IV and V. Panel A presents results varying performance measures from the 10th to 90th percentiles. Panel B presents results varying detrended industrial production from its median value using yearly data from 1979 to 1992. Panel C varies both productivity and aggregate industrial production at their median values. We hold all other variables at their sample medians.

Panel A: Varying Initial Productivity/Performance

	10th Percentile	Median Level	90th Percentile
Single-segment firms			
Varying productivity (Table IV, column 1)	1.08%	0.85%	0.66%
Varying value added per worker (Table V, column 1)	1.02%	0.88%	0.72%
Varying cash flow (Table V, column 3)	0.99%	0.87%	0.77%
Conglomerate firms			
Varying productivity (Table IV, column 2)	4.32%	3.71%	2.86%
Also decreasing segment rank to 10% (main divisions)	4.11%	3.52%	2.71%
Also increasing segment rank to 90% (peripheral divisions)	4.80%	4.13%	3.20%
Varying value added per worker (Table V, column 2)	4.06%	3.66%	3.08%
Varying cash flow (Table V, column 4)	4.19%	3.59%	3.04%

Panel B: Varying Industrial Production

	10th Percentile	Median Level	90th Percentile
Single-segment firms			
(Table IV, column 1)	0.57%	0.85%	1.26%
Conglomerate firms			
All divisions (Table IV, column 2)	3.20%	3.71%	4.03%
Also decreasing segment rank to 10% (main divisions)	3.02%	3.52%	3.81%
Also increasing segment rank to 90% (peripheral divisions)	3.64%	4.13%	4.56%
All divisions (Table V, column 2)	3.21%	3.66%	4.09%
All divisions (Table V, column 4)	3.15%	3.59%	4.02%

Panel C: Varying Industrial Production and Productivity

	Productivity 10th and Industrial Production 90th percentile	Mean Level	Productivity 90th and Industrial Production 10th percentile
Single-segment firms			
Varying productivity (Table IV, column 1)	1.46%	0.85%	0.48%
Varying value added per worker (Table V, column 1)	1.39%	0.88%	0.51%
Varying cash flow (Table V, column 3)	1.32%	0.87%	0.56%
Conglomerate firms			
All divisions (Table IV, column 2)	4.82%	3.71%	2.50%
Also decreasing segment rank to 10% (main divisions)	4.59%	3.52%	2.36%
Also increasing segment rank to 90% (peripheral divisions)	5.34%	4.13%	2.80%
All divisions (Table V, column 2)	5.53%	3.66%	2.70%
All divisions (Table V, column 4)	4.67%	3.59%	2.66%

Taken together, the estimates in Table VI suggest that the probability that a plant is transferred is considerably higher if the plant belongs to a multisegment firm, particularly a small division of a multisegment firm. Inefficient plants are more likely to be sold than efficient plants, and there are considerably more sales in times of high production. These observations are consistent with the view that the market for plants facilitates the transfer of assets to productive uses, and that transfers occur at times when the marginal value of capital is high. There is no evidence that managers of conglomerate firms are less willing to sell assets than managers of single-segment firms.

D. Probability of Mergers and Acquisitions

In Table VII we analyze mergers and whole firm sell-offs. As before, we split the sample of selling firms into single-segment and multiple-segment firms. Because the majority of selling firms are small single-plant firms, we also analyze these separately.

The results in Table VII show that industry demand strongly influences mergers and acquisitions. The rate of mergers and firm sell-offs is higher when aggregate demand is high and in industries whose demand is sensitive to aggregate output shocks. In contrast to the case of partial firm sales, the role of productivity in predicting mergers is less clear-cut. The probability that a single-plant firm is sold decreases with its productivity. We find do not find similar significant effects with the sales of other firms. However, we do find that the probability that a multiple-segment firm is sold falls if the firm's productivity is high and when the industries in which it operates experience higher demand. This finding is consistent with the first hypothesis in this paper, that firms are more likely to sell in good times when they are less productive.

The significance of the relation between firm size and the probability of sale also differs across the categories in Table VII. There is a significant positive relation between firm size and the probability of sale for single-plant firms, no relation for multiple-plant single-segment firms, and a significant negative relation for multiple-segment firms. Controlling for size, focused firms are less likely to be sold then diversified firms.

E. Buyer Characteristics and the Probability of a Purchase

In Table VIII we examine the buyers of whole firms. We consider single-segment and multisegment firms separately. To investigate whether the motives for focus-increasing and diversifying purchases are the same, we classify multisegment buyers into those for whom the purchase increases firm focus and those for whom it decreases focus, as measured by the firm's herfindahl index across the segments it operates.

With only the exception of single-plant firms, we find that the probability that a firm is a buyer in a particular industry increases with the buying

Table VII

Mergers and Firm Selloffs: Selling Firm Characteristics

Regressions test the effects of plant-level productivity and industry-level demand on the decision to sell out or merge with another firm for single-segment and multiple-segment firms. The dependent variable is a binary variable that indicates that the firm sells to another firm. Productivity variables are industry and year adjusted. Firm-level variables are aggregated from plant-level data by weighting each plant by its real value of plant shipments. Industry-level variables are constructed for each firm using as weights the real value of that firm's industry production. We estimate the regressions using unbalanced panel probit regressions allowing for correlated residuals within panel units. Significance tests are conducted using heteroskedasticity-consistent standard errors following Huber–White. (p-values are in parentheses.)

	Dependent Variable: Firm Selloff			Test for Significant Diff.:
Variable	Single-segment Firms with 1 Plant	Single-segment Firms with >1 Plant	Multiple-segment Firms	Multiple-segment Interaction Variable (p-value)[a]
Constant	−1.833	−1.987	−1.808	
	(0.000)	(0.000)*	(0.000)*	(0.644)
Aggregate industrial production (detrended)	0.723	0.716	0.743	
	(0.000)*	(0.035)**	(0.006)*	(0.952)
Industry sensitivity to aggregate industrial production	0.012	0.013	0.018	
	(0.000)*	(0.054)***	(0.002)*	(0.519)
Lagged productivity of firm (TFP)[b]	−0.023	−0.018	−0.014	
	(0.041)**	(0.526)	(0.549)	(0.600)
Firm TFP * downstream industry shipments	0.181	0.070	−0.568	
	(0.191)	(0.864)	(0.028)**	(0.615)
Lagged firm size (coefficient * 10,000,000)	2.500	0.299	−0.145	
	(0.000)*	(0.186)	(0.042)**	(0.166)
Dispersion (herfandahl) across industries			−0.223	
			(0.000)*	
Total firm years	96,961	24,772	42,524	
Chi-squared statistic	56.12	11.62	39.36	
Significance level (p-value)	<1%	0.040	<1%	

*, **, *** Significantly different from zero at the 1 percent, 5 percent, and 10 percent levels, respectively, using a two-tailed test.

[a] Significance test for a multiple-segment dummy variable interacted with each independent variable in a regression with all firms with >1 plant.

[b] Total Factor Productivity (TFP) is calculated using a translog production function.

Table VIII

Mergers and Firm Selloffs: Buying Firm Characteristics

Regressions test the effects of plant-level productivity and industry-level demand on the decision to buy out another firm for single-segment and multiple-segment firms. The dependent variable is a binary variable that indicates that the firm buys another firm. Observations are at the firm level for all firms. Productivity variables are industry and year adjusted. Segment-level variables are aggregated from plant-level data by weighting each plant by its real value of plant shipments. Industry-level variables are constructed for each firm using as weights the real value of a firm's industry production. We estimate the regressions using unbalanced panel probit regressions allowing for correlated residuals within panel units. Focus-increasing (decreasing) purchases are transactions that result in the buying firm's sum of squared industry market shares (herfandahl) increasing (decreasing). Significance tests are conducted using heteroskedasticity-consistent standard errors following Huber–White. (p-values are in parentheses.)

	Dependent Variable: Firm Purchase			
	Single-segment Firms		Multiple-segment Firms	
Variable	With 1 Plant	With >1 Plant	Focus-increasing Purchase	Focus-decreasing Purchase
Constant	−2.381	−2.094	−2.122	−1.987
	(0.000)*	(0.000)*	(0.000)*	(0.000)*
Aggregate industrial production	0.551	0.450	0.914	0.817
(detrended)	(0.044)**	(0.206)	(0.001)*	(0.001)*
Industry sensitivity to aggregate	0.007	−0.008	−0.006	−0.004
industrial production	(0.216)	(0.318)	(0.371)	(0.512)
Lagged productivity of industry	−0.048	0.271	0.249	0.290
segment (TFP)[a]	(0.413)	(0.004)*	(0.100)***	(0.000)*
Firm TFP * downstream	0.618	0.884	0.062	−0.047
industry shipments	(0.580)	(0.643)	(0.549)	(0.412)
Lagged firm size	4.330	0.650	0.196	0.166
(coefficient * 10,000,000)	(0.000)*	(0.105)	(0.091)***	(0.051)**
Average number of plants per		0.027	0.090	0.075
industry segment		(0.000)*	(0.000)*	(0.000)*
Total plant years	77,713	24,774	40,152	40,498
Chi-squared statistic	21.33	99.85	141.37	144.31
Significance level (p-value)	<1%	<1%	<1%	<1%

*, **, *** Significantly different from zero at the 1 percent, 5 percent, and 10 percent levels, respectively, using a two-tailed test.

[a] Total Factor Productivity (TFP) is calculated using a translog production function.

firm's segment TFP, size, and with the number of plants the firm already owns. Acquisitions are more likely when aggregate industrial production is high. These results indicate that buying firms are growing in industries in which they are productive when demand is high.

Table IX calculates economic significance of the previous regressions in Tables VII and VIII. The table shows how the predicted probabilities of mergers or full firm purchases are affected by variation in firm productivity and

Table IX

Probability of Mergers

Predicted probability of a merger or full-firm purchase varying performance measures and industrial production using the regression coefficients from Tables VII and VIII. Panel A presents results varying performance measures from the 10th to 90th percentiles. Panel B presents results varying detrended industrial production from its median value over 1979 to 1992. Panel C varies both productivity and aggregate industrial production at their median values. We hold all other variables at their sample medians.

Panel A: Selling Firms

Varying productivity	10th Percentile	Median	90th Percentile
Single-segment selling firms	2.63%	2.55%	2.45%
Conglomerate selling firms	3.21%	3.01%	2.77%
Varying industrial production	**10th Percentile**	**Median**	**90th Percentile**
Single-segment selling firms	2.33%	2.55%	2.75%
Conglomerate selling firms	2.74%	3.01%	3.25%
Varying productivity & industrial production	**Productivity 10th, Industrial Production 90th Percentile**	**Median Level**	**Productivity 90th, Industrial Production 10th Percentile**
Single-segment selling firms	2.83%	2.55%	2.26%
Conglomerate selling firms	3.46%	3.01%	2.53%

Panel B: Buying Firms

Varying productivity	10th Percentile	Median	90th Percentile
Single-segment buying firms	1.85%	2.13%	2.56%
Conglomerate buying firms: Focus increasing	2.30%	2.47%	2.94%
Conglomerate buying firms: Focus decreasing	2.92%	3.27%	3.95%
Varying industrial production	**10th Percentile**	**Median**	**90th Percentile**
Single-segment buying firms	1.93%	2.13%	2.17%
Conglomerate buying firms: Focus increasing	2.03%	2.47%	2.56%
Conglomerate buying firms: Focus decreasing	2.76%	3.27%	3.37%
Varying productivity & industrial production	**Productivity 10th, Industrial Production 90th Percentile**	**Median Level**	**Productivity 90th, Industrial Production 10th Percentile**
Single-segment buying firms	1.78%	2.13%	2.60%
Conglomerate buying firms: Focus increasing	2.22%	2.47%	3.04%
Conglomerate buying firms: Focus decreasing	2.87%	3.27%	4.01%

demand conditions. For the case of buying firms, the explanatory variables and their variation parallel those discussed in the case of partial firm sales in Table VI.

Panel A shows the predicted probabilities of whole firms sales. As in the case of partial firm sales, whole single-segment firms are less likely to be sold than multisegment firms, at 2.55 percent and 3.01 percent, respectively. The difference between the two types of firms is less than the difference for asset sales. Taken together with the results on partial-firm sales in Table VII, our estimates predict that assets owned by conglomerate firms appear to be "in play" to a greater extent than assets owned by single-segment firms. Overall, predicted sales of multisegment firms are very sensitive to variations in both productivity and aggregate industrial demand.

Panel B shows predicted variation in the probability of purchase. Again, the predicted purchases by multisegment firms are higher than by single-segment firms. The predicted probability that a firm is a buyer varies with the firm's productivity. However, the predicted probability that a multisegment firm engages in a focus-decreasing purchase depends somewhat more on the buying firm's productivity. Both the probability of a purchase by a single-segment firm and of a focus-decreasing purchase by a multisegment firm are also higher when aggregate industrial output is high. Focus-increasing mergers by multisegment firms are not as sensitive to changes in aggregate industrial production.

V. Are There Productivity Gains and What Determines the Gains?

In this section, we examine the productivity change (industry adjusted in each year) surrounding the asset sales—both for full-firm mergers and sales and for partial-firm sales. To begin the analysis, we first present simple summary statistics on the change in productivity for the manufacturing plants involved in purchases subsequent to the transactions.

In Table X, we analyze the changes in productivity using a three-by-three matrix to capture the internal organization characteristics of the buyer and the seller. We classify both the buyer and the seller as a single-segment firm, or as a main or peripheral division of a multisegment firm. Because the results in Table VII suggest that single-plant firms may behave differently than the rest of the firm population, in the case of mergers we further subclassify single-segment sellers into firms with one plant and firms with more than one plant.

In this table, and in our subsequent tables analyzing productivity changes, we require that both buyer and seller ex ante data exist for each transaction. Transactions for which we have no ex ante data for buying firms include foreign firms purchasing assets for the first time in the United States, non-manufacturing firms purchasing manufacturing assets, new firms formed to purchase existing assets, assets spun off or carved out from existing firms,

Table X

Summary Statistics for Change in Productivity for Assets Sold or Merged

The change in productivity, industry and year adjusted, for three years surrounding asset sales, mergers, or full-firm sales (year −1 to year +2). Values represent sample means for transactions between buyers and sellers. (Standard error of the mean in parentheses.) Third row is the number of plants transacted.

Panel A: Partial-Firm Sales

	Selling Firm Characteristics		
	Multidivision Firm		
	Main Division	Peripheral Division	Single-segment Firm
Buying firm characteristics			
Multidivision buyer adds to			
Main division	0.062	0.103*	0.127
	(0.039)	(0.036)	(0.092)
	444	580	87
Peripheral division	−0.008	0.047**	0.033
	(0.027)	(0.021)	(0.076)
	857	1,544	122
Single-segment buyer	0.019	0.107**	−0.038
	(0.052)	(0.042)	(0.069)
	275	382	126

Panel B: Full-Firm Mergers and Acquisitions

	Selling Firm Characteristics			
	Multidivision Firm		Single-segment Firm	
	Main Division	Peripheral Division	with 1 Plant	with >1 Plant
Buying firm characteristics				
Multidivision buyer adds to				
Main division	0.087**	0.143***	−0.020	−0.039
	(0.041)	(0.083)	(0.039)	(0.043)
	396	89	420	234
Peripheral division	−0.017	−0.020	−0.051***	0.058
	(0.020)	(0.025)	(0.028)	(0.039)
	1,278	914	723	401
Single-segment buyer	−0.044	0.037	0.053	−0.011
	(0.049)	(0.067)	(0.029)	(0.050)
	237	108	677	219

*, **, *** Significantly different from zero at the 1 percent, 5 percent, and 10 percent levels, respectively, using a two-tailed test.

and small firms outside of the ASM sample that purchase larger plants. Given that our subsequent regressions analyze the effect of differences between ex ante buyer and seller productivity, we also only analyze transactions for which we have ex ante productivity data for both buying and selling firms.[25] After these requirements are taken into account, we are able to analyze productivity changes for 10,109 transactions.

We calculate the industry adjusted change in productivity from the year before the transaction to two years after the transaction, year −1 to year +2, where year 0 is the year of the transaction. For our sample, the mean industry adjusted change in productivity is 0.02, and is significantly different from zero at the one percent significance level. The median change in productivity is also positive. Thus, the majority of the transactions in our sample have led to increases in productivity. Productivity changes for the transaction types are given in Table X.

Panel A of Table X presents the change in productivity for partial-firm asset sales. We find that all sales from peripheral divisions have significant positive ex post changes in productivity, regardless of the buyer's organizational characteristics. For single-segment sellers, no transactions resulted in a significant increase in productivity. There is no evidence that any category of transactions leads to significant declines in productivity of the assets sold.

Panel B presents the change in productivity for full-firm sales and mergers. Several facts emerge: We find significant productivity gains only when buyers add capacity to their main divisions—increasing the focus of their firm. Purchases by single-segment firms, although very frequent, do not result in increased productivity of the purchased assets. Thus, there is evidence that restructuring that involves sales from multisegment firms to single-segment firms does not result in gains. Productivity significantly decreases in only one class of transactions: purchases of single-plant firms by the peripheral divisions of multisegment firms.

The differences in the observed gains in Table X may exist because some types of buyers are more efficient in improving assets. The differences may also occur if, in some types of transactions, there is a higher incidence of inefficient sellers and efficient buyers, who have the expertise or resources to improve the assets. To examine the latter possibility, we classify transactions into those where the productivity of the buyer's assets in the industry exceeds that of the acquired plants, and into those where it does not.

For partial-firm asset sales, the buyer's existing plants are more productive than the acquired plants in 59.6 percent of the transactions. For mergers and acquisitions, 57.2 percent of the total transactions have buyers that are more productive than the plants they purchase. These proportions are significantly different from each other at the 1.5 percent level. Looking at differences based on firm organization, we also find significant differences. For example, for asset sales, we find that when firms add assets to their main divisions, their existing plants are more productive in 62.9 percent of the transactions. By contrast, for peripheral divisions 59.6 percent of buyers are more productive than purchased plants and for single segment firms

[25] This also eliminates transactions occurring prior to 1979, given that we calculate productivity in each industry using five years of lagged data.

54.9 percent are more productive than the purchased plants. In all cases the proportion of transactions is significantly greater than 50 percent at the 1 percent level.

We next examine if these differences between the buyer's and seller's productivity significantly affect productivity gains of the purchased plants in a multivariate regression. To test whether the transaction type affects productivity gains after controlling for productivity differences, we also allow for a differential effect for the difference in seller and buyer productivity based on the type of transaction. We regress the change in productivity of the purchased plants on the difference between the initial productivity of the buyer and the productivity of the plants purchased, buyer's and the seller's respective firm sizes, and the selling firm's initial productivity.

We expect the productivity of acquired plants to increase when they are acquired by a buyer who has higher productivity. However, the productivity of acquired plants may not increase when the buyer's productivity is lower. To examine whether this occurs, we interact the difference between buyer and seller productivity with an indicator variable that equals one when the purchased plant is more productive than the buyer. This variable allows the slope coefficient on the difference in buyer and seller productivity to change when buyers are less productive than the plants they purchase.

Lastly, to test whether there is a differential affect by type of transaction, we interact the difference in productivity between the buyer and seller with indicator variables identifying the different transaction categories from Table X. The interaction variables measure how the effect of the difference between the buyer's and seller's initial productivity on the asset's change in productivity depends on whether the transaction is a partial sale or a merger, and on the organizational structure of the buyer and the seller. The interaction variables thus allow different types of transactions to have larger or smaller sensitivities to the difference between initial buyer and seller productivity.

Table XI shows that the productivity gain following a transaction depends on the productivities of the selling and buying firms. Assets increase in productivity when the productivity of the buying firm is higher than the productivity of the assets purchased. This finding suggests that the earlier stock market evidence of Lang, Stulz, and Walkling (1989), which shows total stock market gains of tender offers when high q firms acquire low q targets, is not caused just by tax differences or by purely financial gains. However, when assets are purchased by a buyer with a lower productivity, the purchased assets' productivity falls. Gains in productivity are positively related to the seller's size and inversely related to the initial seller productivity.

None of the 17 estimated transaction interaction variables is statistically significant. Thus, there is little evidence that the type of transaction affects productivity gains, after controlling for the initial buyer's and seller's productivity.

The fact that some buyers acquire assets that are more productive than their existing assets, and that the acquired assets' productivity declines subsequently, may initially appear puzzling. One possible explanation is that

Table XI

Change in Productivity Based on Buying & Selling Firm Characteristics

This table presents a single regression that tests the joint effects of buyer and selling firm organization characteristics on the change in plant productivity over a three-year horizon from the year prior to the asset sale or merger (year −1) to the end of the second year (year +2) after the transaction. Total Factor Productivity (TFP) variables are calculated using a translog production function. Lagged firm productivity variables are aggregated up from individual plants. All productivity variables are industry and year adjusted. Transaction type variables are indicator variables that show whether the transaction was from a seller's main or peripheral division or from a single-segment firm to a buyer's main, peripheral, or to a single-segment buyer. Transaction type dummy variables are then interacted with the difference in productivity between the buying firm and the assets purchased. We estimate the regressions using ordinary least squares. Significance tests are conducted using heteroskedasticity-consistent standard errors. (*p*-values in parentheses.)

	Dependent Variable: Change in Productivity Year −1 to +2	
	Transaction Type	
Variable	Partial Firm Sale	Merger/Acquisition
Productivity and transaction size		
Lagged productivity (year −1)	−0.453	
of selling firm's plants	(0.000)*	
Difference in productivity (year −1)	0.399	
buying firm—productivity of plants purchased	(0.000)*	
Difference in productivity (year −1) * Indicator	−0.084	
variable for negative difference in productivity	(0.004)*	
Buyer size (coefficient * 10,000,000)	−0.003	
	(0.834)	
Seller size (coefficient * 10,000,000)	0.123	
	(0.000)*	
Difference in productivity interacted with transaction characteristics		
Sale from seller's main division	−0.009	0.000
to buyer's main division	(0.931)	(0.907)
Sale from seller's main division	−0.014	−0.043
to buyer's peripheral division	(0.894)	(0.676)
Sale from seller's main division	−0.032	−0.119
to a single segment buyer	(0.776)	(0.282)
Sale from seller's peripheral division	0.119	omitted
to buyer's main division	(0.268)	
Sale from seller's peripheral division	−0.002	−0.058
to buyer's peripheral division	(0.987)	(0.572)
Sale from seller's peripheral division	−0.090	−0.165
to a single segment buyer	(0.400)	(0.179)
Sale from single segment firm	0.021	−0.034
to buyer's main division	(0.883)	(0.750)
Sale from single segment firm	0.065	−0.045
to buyer's peripheral division	(0.620)	(0.662)
Sale from single segment firm	−0.034	−0.155
to a single segment buyer	(0.786)	(0.131)
Constant		−0.066
		(0.000)*
Total transactions:		
Partial firm sales and merger and acquisitions	10,109	
R^2	0.21	
F-test all coefficients = 0 (p-value)	<1%	

* Significantly different from zero at the 1 percent levels using a two-tailed test.

Table XII

Change in Buyer Productivity

Buyer's change in productivity, industry and year adjusted, for three years surrounding asset purchases, mergers, or acquisitions (year −1 to year +2). Values represent sample means for transactions. We construct a firm-level weighted average of buyer's plants, with weights equal to an individual plant's value of shipments. For the existing assets' change in productivity, we present the weighted average change in productivity for plants in the same industry as the purchased assets. (Standard error of the mean is in parentheses.)

		Cases where	
	Overall Change in Productivity	Initial Buyer Productivity > Productivity of Assets Purchased	Initial Buyer Productivity < Productivity of Assets Purchased
Panel A: Change in Productivity of Buyer's Existing Assets (Excluding Purchased Assets)			
All transactions	0.004	−0.027**	0.053*
	(0.009)	(0.011)	(0.015)
Asset purchases	0.008	−0.028***	0.065*
	(0.014)	(0.016)	(0.023)
Mergers & acquisitions	0.000	−0.027***	0.044**
	(0.012)	(0.016)	(0.019)
Panel B: Change in Productivity of All Assets of Buyer (Including Purchased Assets)			
All transactions	0.020*	0.028*	−0.010
	(0.006)	(0.008)	(0.011)
Asset purchases	0.048*	0.056*	0.002
	(0.009)	(0.010)	(0.014)
Mergers & acquisitions	−0.003	0.004	−0.028**
	(0.007)	(0.009)	(0.013)
Number of buying firms	6905	5366	1539

*, **, *** Significantly different from zero at the 1 percent, 5 percent, and 10 percent levels, respectively, using a two-tailed test.

managers of these buying firms are destroying value by making inefficient acquisitions. However, such a conclusion would be unwarranted if the acquired assets provide synergies that increase the value of the buyers' existing assets.

To check whether this is the case, we calculate the industry- and year-adjusted changes in productivity of the buyer's assets for three years surrounding asset purchases (year −1 to year + 2). In Panel A of Table XII we present the changes in the productivity of buyers' existing plants in the same industry in which plants are acquired. The data is broken down into three categories: all transactions, partial-firm purchases, and whole-firm purchases. We further present productivity changes for transactions for the case in which the buyer's initial productivity exceeds that of the assets purchased, and for the case in which it does not.

Panel A shows that for all transactions, and for partial- and whole-firm transactions taken separately, there is no overall change in the productivity of the buyers' existing assets in the same industry. However, the buyers' assets exhibit a significant decline in productivity in those cases where the initial buyers' productivity exceeds that of the purchased assets. By contrast, buyers' existing assets in a segment show a significant increase in productivity when more productive plants are acquired in that segment.

The pattern of gains is consistent with the notion that the addition of a less productive plant to a segment increases control costs and lowers the productivity of existing assets. A majority of transactions are of this type. The fact that the acquisition of a more productive plant results in gains to the existing assets and a decline in productivity of the acquired plants is consistent with buyer purchasing expertise or productive ability that can be transferred to existing assets.

To determine whether the total gains in productivity outweigh the losses, we compute the total changes in the productivity of the buying firm around the period of the transaction. This calculation, which includes the purchased assets, shows the full effect of the purchase on all of the buyer's manufacturing operations. To get a firm-level measure of the productivity gain, we construct a weighted average of all plants of the buyer. We weight each plant's productivity by its initial value of shipments.

Panel B shows the buyers' total productivity gains at the firm level. The results show that there is a significant firm-level productivity gain in partial-firm sales when the buyer's productivity exceeds the productivity of the acquired plants. Thus, the productivity gain of the acquired plant(s) outweighs the productivity loss on the firm's existing assets. Panel B also shows that a significant firm-level productivity loss only occurs in the case when less productive firms acquire more productive firms. In this case, the productivity gain that the buying firm experiences is outweighed by the loss in productivity of the assets purchased. There are no significant firm-level productivity effects in whole-firm sales when the buyer is more efficient than the seller, or in partial-firm sales when the buyer acquires more efficient plants.

These results, combined with the summary statistics that show significant increases in productivity, are consistent with the hypothesis that the market for assets works well for asset sales and for the majority of mergers. Assets that are transacted result in significant gains, consistent with Hypothesis 1 presented earlier. Contrary to the hypothesis that these divisions get subsidized by their parent firms, multidivisional firms are more likely to sell less productive divisions and these sales to other firms result in subsequent productivity increases. Our results support the conclusion that assets change hands as the prospects in the overall economy and in their other industries improve and their owners discover that they do not have a comparative advantage in running these assets. There is significant firm-level fall in productivity surrounding a transaction in cases where more efficient firms are acquired by less efficient firms—a minority of transactions.[26]

Overall these results show that, as suggested by our first hypothesis, there are significant gains for assets being redeployed from less productive sellers to productive buyers. The results on the timing of transactions are consistent with our second hypothesis, which predicts that more productive firms will expand their operations in good times and when their prospects in a given industry look better than the other industries in which they operate.

VI. Conclusions

In this paper, we analyze the market for corporate assets (plants, divisions, and whole firms) in manufacturing industries. We analyze both the buyers and sellers. We show that the market for both full and partial firms is extensive. On average, 3.89 percent of plants change ownership in each year in our study. The total number of transactions varies with the economy and is strongly procyclical. In expansion years, close to 7 percent of plants annually change ownership. Approximately the same number of plants are sold through partial-firm asset sales as in mergers and acquisitions. The buyers and sellers in the partial-firm asset sale market are typically large multisegment firms, in contrast to the merger and acquisition market where the buyers are much bigger than the sellers.

We analyze the factors that are associated with the probability that assets transfer ownership. We have three main results on the probability assets are sold:

1. For multiple-division firms, the probability of a firm selling assets decreases with both the asset's and the segment's productivity. The probability that assets are sold is higher for peripheral divisions. The probability of mergers and firm sell-offs is higher when the selling firm is less productive and the industry experiences a positive demand shock.
2. The selling firm's productivity in other divisions impacts the probability of a sale. A division is more likely to be sold the better the prospects of the other divisions.
3. We find that the probability that a firm is a buyer of additional assets increases with its efficiency and size.

[26] In unreported results, we have also calculated the total effect of acquisitions at the segment level. These calculations measure the changes of productivity of the new and existing assets of the segment that acquires the new assets. The qualitative results at the segment level are the same as the results at the firm level.

In addition, we show that ex post productivity changes occur for assets transacted and these productivity changes are associated with buyer and seller initial productivity and firm organization. We also examine the overall changes in buyer productivity for purchasing firms. Our primary findings for changes in productivity for assets transacted are:

1. The gain in productivity of assets under new ownership is higher when the selling firm's productivity is low and is higher the more productive the buyer.
2. A firm's internal organization is also associated with observed changes in productivity of the asset sold. Asset sales from peripheral divisions of sellers to both main and peripheral divisions of buyers show significant productivity gains. For mergers and acquisitions, assets that are acquired by the buyer's main divisions from other multiple-segment firms show significant gains. These gains are primarily explained by the differences in the initial productivity of buying and selling divisions.
3. When we take into account both the purchased and existing assets, the change in productivity is positive for partial-firm asset purchases and is insignificantly different from zero for mergers and acquisitions.
4. When firms purchase assets of lower productivity, existing assets increase in productivity but the acquired assets decline in productivity. At the firm level, these losses on the acquired assets are offset by the productivity increases of the purchased assets. Overall firm productivity increases for partial-firm purchases and is insignificant for mergers and acquisitions.
5. When firms purchase assets of higher productivity, the acquired assets decline and the existing assets increase in productivity. At the firm level, the change in productivity is not significantly different from zero for partial-firm purchases by less efficient producers. Firm-level productivity declines for one category of transactions: mergers and acquisitions by less efficient firms.

These findings suggest that firms have differing levels of ability to exploit assets, and that their comparative advantage is in their main industries. The low productivity of firms' peripheral divisions prior to the sale, however, does not necessarily imply inefficient ownership. They may optimally operate these divisions until demand is high, at which point more efficient buyers acquire these assets.

The productivity gains we document are consistent with buying firms being able to offer a premium in part because of the gains in real productivity that occur. The results are also consistent with more skilled buying firms being able to transfer skill and improve the assets they purchase. There is no evidence that managers of conglomerate firms are less willing to sell assets than managers of single-segment firms.

The timing of sales and the pattern of productivity gains suggests that most transactions that occur in the market for plants and divisions tend to improve the allocation of resources and are consistent with profit maximizing by firms across the divisions they operate. Thus, the pattern is consistent with profit-maximizing behavior. However, our results do not disprove the existence of agency conflicts within firms. We identify one category of transactions, full-firm acquisitions by buyers with lower productivity than that of the assets they purchase, for which overall firm productivity declines. Moreover, if managers are able to appropriate the gains of productivity from any acquisitions, there might not be a gain to shareholders.

Our results would indicate that efficient firms refocusing in booms may produce the highest gains to transactions. Boards of directors should be more willing to accept productivity explanations for these types of transactions, particularly for partial firm acquisitions.

Despite our finding that most transactions result in gains in productivity, this does not refute the proposition that sometimes managers undertake transactions that, even given rational expectations, reduce value at the time the transaction is undertaken. For example, our research would also suggest that mergers and acquisitions by inefficient firms, presumably with lower stock market valuations relative to industry peers, should receive closer scrutiny by boards of directors. Further research should examine the link between acquirer and seller stock market valuations and subsequent productivity gains.

Overall, our results suggest that most transactions in the market for assets result in an increase in productive efficiency. We conclude that the market for corporate assets facilitates the redeployment of assets from firms with a lower ability to exploit them to firms with higher ability.

Appendix

In estimating the TFPs in our sample, we use data for approximately 50,000 plants each year. We are able to calculate lagged productivity for plants from 1979 to 1992 as we use five years of lagged data to calculate productivity. In the productivity regression for each industry, we include three different types of inputs: capital, labor, and materials, as explanatory variables for each plant. All these data exist at the plant level. We include plants if plants have at least two years of data. In addition, all observations must have nonzero values for all inputs and outputs. After productivity is calculated, we report and use these numbers in regressions after excluding the top and bottom one percent of the calculated productivities. We also only include plants if the total value of firm shipments is at least 10 million real 1982 dollars.[27] After imposing these restrictions, we end up with over 400,000 plant-level productivity measures.[28] In calculating productivity, the capital variable used

[27] We also find similar results changing this requirement to one million real 1982 dollars.

[28] The regressions in Table IV use 305,024 observations. Single-plant firms, representing 95,916 observations, are not included in Table IV. In addition, 15,874 observations are excluded as we also exclude outliers based on alternative measures of efficiency presented in Table V. The tables for mergers use firm-level observations obtained by aggregating these plant-level observations up to the firm level.

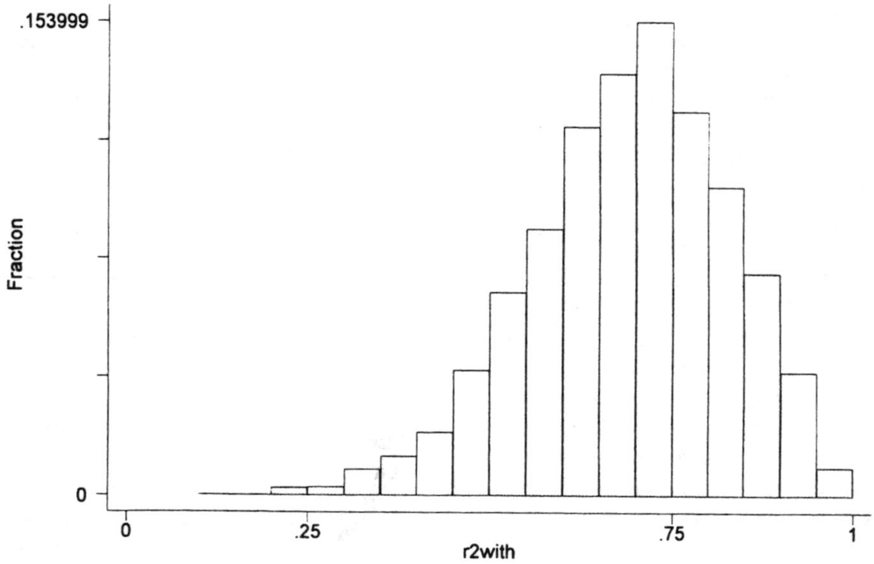

Figure A1. Histogram of *R*-squares from TFP within regressions run each year using five years of lagged data.

is plant's capital stock that is available to be used in production. To account for depreciation of beginning of period capital stock, we use data from the Bureau of Economic Analysis to make depreciation adjustments for beginning period capital stock at the two-digit level. To the beginning of period capital stock, we add the real dollars (in real 1982 dollars) spent on capital expenditures for additions to the capital stock. In addition, to capture vintage effects of capital, we include plant age in our productivity calculations. Plant age is either the first year in which the plant appeared in the database, or 1972 (the first year of the database), if the plant existed in 1972. For the dependent variable, output, the ASM does not state the actual quantity shipped by each plant, but shows only the value (in current period dollars) of shipments. We adjust all nominal dollar variables for inflation by using four-digit SIC code price deflators for output, materials, and capital from the Bartelsman and Gray (1994) database. Kovenock and Phillips (1997) describe these inputs and the method for accounting for inflation and depreciation of capital stock in more detail.

To measure the productivity for a firm's entire business segment, we construct a weighted average of individual plant productivity, in which the weights are the predicted plant-level real value of shipments. The variable for the productivity of the firm's other segments is the weighted average of all of the firm's other plants outside of the segment in question. Again, the weights are the predicted plant-level real value of shipments.

Table AI

Total Factor Productivity

Table reports mean coefficients from yearly regressions by industry. Each regression is repeated in each year for each industry using the last five years of data. Coefficients in column one represent the average coefficients from regressions estimated in each year for each industry (1,726 total regressions). Columns two and three represent illustrative industries for 1978. In each year, productivity is the residual plus the firm-specific fixed effect obtained from regressing the real value (deflated) of output on a plant's age, the value of materials and inputs, the real value of a plant's capital stock and the hours of labor utilized. Adjustments for depreciation for capital stock are made each year using depreciation deflators from the Bureau of Economic Analysis. All dollar amounts are deflated to 1982 dollars using deflators for the National Bureau of Economic Research. (p-values in parentheses).

Independent Variable: Real Value of Output			
Variable	Mean Coefficient	Meat Packing SIC 2011	Oil Refining SIC 2911
Age	0.013	0.019	0.169
	(0.061)***	(0.587)	(0.009)*
Inputs	0.108	0.003	1.661
	(0.000)*	(0.972)	(0.000)*
Capital stock	0.044	0.084	0.306
	(0.000)*	(0.124)	(0.001)*
Labor	0.674	0.773	−0.072
	(0.000)*	(0.000)*	(0.600)
$(\text{Inputs})^2$	0.074	−0.001	0.009
	(0.000)*	(0.825)	(0.043)**
$(\text{Capital stock})^2$	0.000	0.075	0.007
	(0.631)	(0.000)*	(0.411)
$(\text{Labor})^2$	0.020	0.085	−0.024
	(0.000)*	(0.000)*	(0.039)**
Inputs * capital stock	−0.029	−0.005	0.003
	(0.000)*	(0.640)	(0.856)
Inputs * labor	−0.110	−0.005	−0.040
	(0.000)*	(0.503)	(0.003)*
Capital stock * labor	0.044	−0.144	−0.000
	(0.000)*	(0.000)*	(0.999)
Constant	3.352	2.819	−3.765
	(0.000)*	(0.000)*	(0.000)*
R^2		0.92	0.74

*, **, *** For column one mean value of the coefficient is significantly different from zero at the 1, 5, 10 percent levels, respectively, using a two-tailed t-test. For columns two and three, significance test is whether coefficient is significantly different from zero using a two tailed t-test.

We also include other firm and segment-level variables in our regressions to provide additional controls for unmeasured productivity differences and other factors, such as size, that can influence firm growth. We include the lagged firm size and the number of plants operated by a firm at the beginning of the year. We define firm size as the total value of shipments in real 1982 dollars. We exclude all industry segments with real value of shipments smaller than one million dollars from our regressions.

To allow for technical change, each regression is repeated for each industry for each year using data for the current year and the preceding four years, giving us a rolling panel of data for each year. Thus we can calculate productivity for the 1978 to 1992 period. We use the earlier years of data, 1974 to 1977, only for calculating the first year of productivity.[29] Thus, there are 1,726 separate regressions. Figure A1 shows the distribution of adjusted R^2 for the regressions.

In Table AI we present the means of the coefficients for the 1,726 separate regressions covering the whole sample and also the coefficients for two sample industries.

The coefficients for the sample industries are for 1979, the first year for which a five-year panel is available. The first industry, SIC 2011 Meat Packing, was selected because it is the first industry in our sample when industries are ranked by SIC codes. Because meat packing is labor intensive, the second industry, SIC 2911 Oil Refining was selected to illustrate a capital intensive industry. The means of the coefficients in the whole sample are significantly different from zero. The coefficients of the two sample industries reflect their technologies. As expected, labor inputs have a more significant role in the meat packing equation and capital stock inputs are more important in oil refining.

REFERENCES

Alexander, Gordon J., George P. Benson, and Joan M. Kampmeyer, 1984, Investigating the valuation effects of announcements of voluntary corporate selloffs, *Journal of Finance* 39, 503–517.

Andrade, Gregor, and Erik Stafford, 1999, Investigating the economic role of mergers, Working paper, Harvard Business School.

Baily, Martin Neil, Eric J. Bartelsman, and John Haltiwanger, 1998, Labor productivity: Structural change and cyclical dynamics, Working paper 98-7, Center for Economic Studies.

Bartelsman, Eric J., Ricardo J. Caballero, and Richard K. Lyons, 1994, Customer and supplier-driven externalities, *American Economic Review* 84, 1075–1084.

Bartelsman, Eric J., and Wayne Gray, 1994, The NBER Manufacturing Productivity Database, Working paper, The Center for Economic Studies.

Caves, Richard E., and David R. Barton, 1990, Efficiency in U.S. manufacturing. (MIT Press, Cambridge, MA)

Chevalier, Judith, 1999, Why do firms undertake diversifying mergers? An examination of the investment policies of merging firms, Mimeo, University of Chicago.

Fluck, Zsuzsanna, and Anthony W. Lynch, 1999, Why do firms merge and then divest: A theory of financial synergy, *Journal of Business* 72, 319–346.

Graham, John, Michael Lemmon, and Jack Wolf, 2002, Does corporate diversification destroy value? forthcoming, *Journal of Finance* 57.

Hart, Oliver, and John Moore, 1995, Debt and seniority: An analysis of the role of hard claims in constraining management, *American Economic Review* 85, 567–585.

[29] In an earlier version of this paper, we calculated TFPs using the entire sample period for each industry. The two methodologies yielded very similar qualitative results.

Hite, Gailen, James E. Owers, and Ronald C. Rogers, 1987, The market for interfirm asset sales: Partial sell-offs and total liquidations, *Journal of Financial Economics* 18, 229–252.

Jain, Prem C., 1985, The effect of voluntary sell-offs announcements on shareholder wealth, *The Journal of Finance* 40, 209–224.

Jensen, Michael C., 1986, The agency costs of free cash flow: Corporate finance and takeovers, *American Economic Review* 76, 323–329.

Jensen, Michael C., and Richard S. Ruback, 1983, The market for corporate control: The scientific evidence, *Journal of Financial Economics* 11, 5–50.

John, Kose, and Eli Ofek, 1995, Asset sales and the increase in focus, *Journal of Financial Economics* 37, 105–126.

Jorgenson, Dale W., 1986, Econometric methods for modeling producer behavior; in Zvi Griliches and Michael D. Intriligator, eds.: *Handbook of Econometrics*, vol. 3. (North Holland, Amsterdam).

Kaplan, Steven N., and Michael Weisbach, 1992, The success of acquisitions: Evidence from divestitures, *The Journal of Finance* 47, 107–138

Kovenock, Daniel, and Gordon Phillips, 1997, Capital structure and product market behavior: An examination of plant exit and investment behavior, *Review of Financial Studies* 10, 767–804.

Lamont, Owen, 1997, Cash flow and investment: Evidence from internal capital markets, *Journal of Finance* 52, 83–109.

Lang, Larry H. P., Annette Poulsen, and René Stulz, 1995, Asset sales, firm performance, and the agency costs of managerial discretion, *Journal of Financial Economics* 37, 3–38.

Lang, Larry H. P., René Stulz, and Ralph A. Walkling, 1989, Managerial performance, Tobin's *q*, and the gains from successful tender offers, *Journal of Financial Economics* 24, 137–155.

Lang, Larry H. P., René Stulz, and Ralph A. Walking, 1991, A test of the free cash flow hypothesis: The case of bidder returns, *Journal of Financial Economics* 29, 315–335.

Lichtenberg, Frank R., and Donald Siegel, 1992, Takeovers and corporate overhead; in Frank R. Lichtenberg, ed.: *Corporate Takeovers and Productivity* (MIT Press, Cambridge, MA).

Lucas, Robert, 1978, On the size distribution of business firms, *Bell Journal of Economics* 9, 508–523.

Maksimovic, Vojislav, and Gordon M. Phillips, 1998, Asset efficiency and reallocation decisions of bankrupt firms, *Journal of Finance* 53, 1619–1643.

Maksimovic, Vojislav, and Gordon M. Phillips, 2002, Do conglomerate firms allocate resources efficiently across industries: Theory and evidence, forthcoming, *Journal of Finance* 57.

Matsusaka, John G., 1993, Takeover motives during the conglomerate merger wave, *RAND Journal of Economics* 24, 357–379.

McGuckin, Robert H., and Sang V. Nguyen, 1995, On productivity and plant ownership change: New evidence from the LRD, *RAND Journal of Economics* 26, 257–276.

McGuckin, Robert H., and Sang V. Nguyen, 1999, Exploring the role of acquisition in the performance of firms: Is the "firm" the right unit of analysis; in Silvia Biffignandi, ed.: *Micro- and Macrodata of Firms* (Physica-Verlag, New York).

McGuckin, Robert H., and George Pascoe, 1988, The longitudinal research database: Status and research possibilities, *Survey of Current Business* 68, 30–37.

Mitchell, Mark L., and Harold J. Mulherin, 1996, The impact of industry shocks on takeover and restructuring activity, *Journal of Financial Economics* 41, 193–229.

Morck, Randall, Andrei Shleifer, and Robert W. Vishny, 1990, Do managerial objectives drive bad acquisitions? *Journal of Finance* 45, 31–48.

Rajan, Raghuram G., Henri Servaes, and Luigi Zingales, 2000, The cost of diversity: The diversification discount and inefficient investment, *Journal of Finance* 55, 35–80.

Ravenscraft, David, and F. M. Scherer, 1987, *Mergers, Sell-offs, and Economic Efficiency* (Brookings Institution, Washington, DC).

Scharfstein, David S., 1997, The dark side of internal capital markets II, Mimeo, MIT.

Scharfstein, David S., and Jeremy C. Stein, 2000, The dark side of internal capital markets: Divisional rent-seeking and inefficient investment, *Journal of Finance* 55, 2537–2564.

Schlingemann, Frederik, P., René M. Stulz, and Ralph A. Walkling, 2002, Asset liquidity and segment divestitures, forthcoming , *Journal of Financial Economics*.
Shea, John, 1993, Do supply curves slope up? *Quarterly Journal of Economics* 108, 1–32.
Shleifer, Andrei, and Robert W. Vishny, 1992, Liquidation values and debt capacity: A market equilibrium approach, *Journal of Finance* 47, 1343–1365.
Williamson, Oliver, 1985, *The Economic Institutions of Capitalism: Firms, Markets, Relational Contracting*, The Free Press, New York.

Part II
Distressed Restructurings

[14]

Journal of Financial Economics 27 (1990) 315–353. North-Holland

Troubled debt restructurings

An empirical study of private reorganization of firms in default*

Stuart C. Gilson
The University of Texas at Austin, Austin, TX 78712, USA

Kose John and Larry H.P. Lang
New York University, New York, NY 10003, USA

Received November 1989, final version received May 1990

This study investigates the incentives of financially distressed firms to restructure their debt privately rather than through formal bankruptcy. In a sample of 169 financially distressed companies, about half successfully restructure their debt outside of Chapter 11. Firms more likely to restructure their debt privately have more intangible assets, owe more of their debt to banks, and owe fewer lenders. Analysis of stock returns suggests that the market is also able to discriminate *ex ante* between the two sets of firms, and that stockholders are systematically better off when debt is restructured privately.

1. Introduction

With the proliferation of leveraged buyouts (LBOs) and other highly leveraged transactions, there has been growing popular concern that the corporate sector is being burdened with too much debt. Much of this concern

*We would like to thank Edward Altman, Yakov Amihud, Sugato Bhattacharya, Keith Brown, Robert Bruner, T. Ronald Casper, Charles D'Ambrosio, Larry Dann, Oliver Hart, Gailen Hite, Max Holmes, Scott Lee, Gershon Mandelker, Scott Mason, Robert Merton, Wayne Mikkelson, Megan Partch, Ramesh Rao, Roy Smith, Chester Spatt, Gopala Vasudevan, and Richard West for their helpful comments. We are especially grateful to Michael Jensen (the editor) and Karen Wruck (the referee) for their many detailed and thoughtful suggestions. This paper has also benefited from the comments of participants at the 1989 American Economic Association Meetings, the conference on 'The Structure of Governance of Enterprise' at the Harvard Business School, and seminars at Dartmouth College, the Harvard Business School, the University of Oregon, and the University of Pittsburgh. The second author acknowledges support from the Yamaichi Faculty Fellowship and the Garn Institute of Finance.

is founded in the belief that highly levered firms could default in large numbers in a major recession (*Wall Street Journal*, 25 October 1988). At issue is whether corporate default is costly, and whether, as recently suggested by Jensen (1989a, b), private contractual arrangements for resolving default represent a viable (and less costly) alternative to the legal remedies provided by Chapter 11.

This study investigates the incentives of financially distressed firms to choose between private renegotiation and Chapter 11. We analyze the experience of 169 publicly traded companies that experienced severe financial distress during 1978–1987. Our investigation yields a number of insights into the corporate debt restructuring decision. In about half of all cases, financially distressed firms successfully restructure their debt outside of Chapter 11. Financial distress is more likely to be resolved through private renegotiation when more of the firm's assets are intangible, and relatively more debt is owed to banks; private negotiation is less likely to succeed when there are more distinct classes of debt outstanding.

An analysis of common stock returns provides complementary evidence on firms' incentives to settle out of court. Abnormal stock-price performance suggests stockholders generally fare better under private renegotiation than bankruptcy. In advance of the outcome, the market appears to be able to identify which firms are more likely to succeed at restructuring their debt outside of Chapter 11.

Finally, we present detailed descriptive evidence of how debt is restructured outside of bankruptcy. Previous empirical research in corporate financial distress has dealt largely with formal reorganization in Chapter 11. Detailed case analyses of selected firms in our sample provide additional insights into firms' incentives to choose between private renegotiation and Chapter 11.

The study is organized as follows. Section 2 discusses firms' incentives to choose between private renegotiation and bankruptcy as alternative mechanisms for dealing with default. Section 3 describes the data and methodology. Section 4 presents the empirical analysis of troubled debt restructurings. Section 5 concludes with a summary of the results. The appendix presents ten detailed case studies of firms that attempted to restructure their debt privately.

2. Corporate default and debt restructuring

A firm that must restructure the terms of its debt contracts to remedy or avoid default is faced with two choices; it can either file for bankruptcy or attempt or renegotiate with its creditors privately in a 'workout'. The alternatives are similar in that relief from default is obtained when creditors consent to exchange their impaired claims for new securities in the firm. Sometimes this exchange is implicit, as when the terms of a debt contract are modified.

If bankruptcy is the alternative to private renegotiation, then firms' incentives to settle with creditors out of court, and the settlement terms, will reflect the legal and institutional constraints of the bankruptcy process. The remainder of this section briefly describes relevant bankruptcy law, and identifies some important economic factors that affect the choice between bankruptcy and private debt renegotiation.

2.1. Rules and procedures of bankruptcy

For most companies, bankruptcy practices are governed by Chapter 11 of the U.S. Bankruptcy Code (henceforth, the 'Code'). Filings under Chapter 11 are treated as corporate reorganizations, and the bankrupt firm is expected to continue as a going concern after leaving bankruptcy. To protect the firm from creditor harassment while it tries to reorganize, Chapter 11 imposes an automatic stay that prevents creditors from collecting on their debt or foreclosing on their collateral until the firm leaves bankruptcy.[1]

In Chapter 11, an exchange of securities is formally proposed in a reorganization plan. The plan assigns claimholders to various classes, and a separate exchange is proposed for each class. All claims placed within a given class must be substantially similar. Thus, for example, trade debt might be placed in one class, secured bank debt in another, and so forth, although finer partitioning of claims is possible.

The value of new securities distributed to any class is in principle determined by the absolute priority rule, under which each creditor class is compensated for the face value of its prebankruptcy claims only after all other classes designated as senior are paid in full. Franks and Torous (1989), Eberhart et al. (1990), and Weiss (1990) show that significant deviations from absolute priority occur in practice. All three studies document cases where stockholders participate in a reorganization plan that provides for less than full payment of senior claims.

The filing firm, or debtor, has the exclusive right to propose the first plan. If this plan is not filed within 120 days of the initial Chapter 11 filing, or accepted by creditors within 60 additional days, any claimholder class can propose its own plan. Acceptance of the plan requires an affirmative vote by a majority (two-thirds in value and one-half in number) of the claimholders in each impaired class. To break deadlocks, the court can unilaterally impose or 'cram down' the plan on dissenting classes if the plan is 'fair and

[1]Alternatively, firms can elect to liquidate by filing under Chapter 7 of the Code. Before the Code was enacted on October 1, 1979, bankruptcy practices were governed by the Bankruptcy Act, under which corporations could choose to either liquidate under Chapter VII, or reorganize under Chapters X or XI. Filing for Chapter 11 is not always the exclusive right of stockholders. Creditors may file an 'involuntary' Chapter 11 petition, if they can demonstrate that the firm has been delinquent in making payments on its debt. Following a default, creditors can generally accelerate full payment on their debt after 30 days have elapsed, thus giving the firm little option but to file for bankruptcy.

equitable' – that is, if the market value of new securities distributed to each class under the plan at least equals what the class would receive a liquidation. In practice, cram-downs are extremely rare [Klee (1979)]. It is in the joint interest of all classes to avoid a cram-down, because application of the fair and equitable standard requires the court to determine the firm's liquidation value and going-concern value in a special hearing. These hearings are considered extremely time-consuming and costly. Avoidance of cram-down also explains observed deviations from absolute priority, since classes that receive nothing under the plan (including stockholders) are deemed not to have accepted the plan, giving creditors an incentive to voluntarily relinquish part of their claims.

Chapter 11 also provides for the appointment of committees to represent the interests of certain claimholder classes before the court. Committees normally consist of the seven largest members of a particular class who are willing to serve, and are empowered to hire legal counsel and other professional help. Committees' operating expenses are paid out of the bankrupt firm's assets. Appointment of a committee of unsecured creditors is mandatory in Chapter 11 cases; additional committees can be appointed to represent other classes, including stockholders, at the discretion of the judge [DeNatale (1981)].

2.2. *Determinants of the choice between bankruptcy and private renegotiation*

Whether financial distress is resolved through bankruptcy or private renegotiation depends on two factors. First, stockholders and creditors will collectively benefit from settling out of court when private renegotiation generates lower costs than bankruptcy. Under the lower-cost alternative, the resulting value of the firm will be higher, and the firm's claims can be restructured on terms that leave each of the original claimholders better off. Claimholders' incentives to settle privately will increase with the size of the potential cost savings from recontracting outside of Chapter 11. Second, the lower-cost alternative will be adopted only if claimholders can agree on how to share the cost savings. Attempts to settle privately are more likely to fail when individual creditors have stronger incentives to hold out for more favorable treatment under the debt restructuring plan.

The remainder of the section develops this simple economic model of the corporate debt-restructuring decision, and derives empirical proxies for firms' incentives to restructure their debt privately.[2]

[2]Previous empirical studies of out-of-court restructuring include Gilson (1989, 1990), who analyzes changes in corporate ownership and governance structure during financial distress, and Hoshi et al. (1990), who investigate the resolution of financial distress in Japan. Previous theoretical research into the choice between bankruptcy and private renegotiation includes

2.2.1. *Relative cost of formal bankruptcy versus private renegotiation*

Although attempts have been made to measure the costs of Chapter 11 empirically [Warner (1977b), Ang et al. (1982), Altman (1984), Weiss (1990)], we currently know little about how these costs compare with the costs of private renegotiation. In analyzing the costs of financial distress, it has become common to distinguish between direct and indirect costs. Direct costs are out-of-pocket transactions cost (such as charges for legal and investment banking services). Indirect costs include all other costs related to the firm's bankruptcy or debt restructuring. For example, managers may forego profitable investment opportunities because they are distracted by dealings with creditors or the bankruptcy court. Indirect costs also include the value of managers' time spent in such dealings.

It is widely believed among practitioners that direct costs are significantly higher for bankruptcy than private renegotiation, because the procedural demands and legal complexity of Chapter 11 result in inflated lawyers' fees [Stein (1989)]. Formal legal motions must be drafted and argued before the bankruptcy judge at each step of the reorganization. An inordinate amount of time may be required to make any decision that lies outside the ordinary course of the firm's business.[3] When debt is restructured privately, legal costs are reduced because such decisions can be made more quickly. In addition, bankruptcy lawyers have an incentive to prolong the firm's stay in Chapter 11, because their compensation is treated as a priority claim, which entitles them to be paid before any of the firm's general unsecured creditors or shareholders. These arguments suggest that indirect costs (as measured by the expenditure of managers' time) are also higher for bankruptcy than for private renegotiation.

The relative cost disadvantage of bankruptcy is offset by two factors. First, the Code's automatic stay provision ameliorates the common pool problem inherent in distressed situations, by imposing a well-defined queuing order on creditors (who would otherwise rush to be first in line to collect payment on

---

Haugen and Senbet (1978), Bulow and Shoven (1978), White (1983), Aivazian and Callen (1983), Green and Laffont (1987), Roe (1987), Kahn and Huberman (1988), Brown (1989), Giammarino (1989), Hart and Moore (1989), and Mooradian (1989). Much of this research views the firm's bankruptcy decision as the outcome of a strategic game played between stockholders and creditors. An analogous problem is addressed in the 'theory of litigation', which analyzes the choice faced by plaintiffs and defendents between settling out of court or going to trial [Gould (1973)].

[3]For example, if a debtor wishes to retain the services of an investment bank, it must first file an application with the bankruptcy court. Applications can be made only after appropriate 'notice and hearing' has been given, which requires the firm to inform all creditors of the application in writing, and allow sufficient time for any objections to be filed. The court rules on the application at a special hearing. The time required for approval can be shortened if the debtor requires creditors to show cause, allowing the application to be approved within a few days if no objections are raised.

their debt and seize collateral). Such activity will be wasteful if it results in costly duplication of effort or creates additional distraction for management [Jackson (1986)].

Second, firms in Chapter 11 can grant new lenders superpriority status, or a security interest equal or senior to that of existing debt (also known as debtor-in-possession financing). In the absence of this provision, firm value could be reduced because stockholders have an incentive to underinvest in positive-NPV projects that enrich senior claimholders [Myers (1977), Smith and Warner (1979)]. In principle, an equivalent provision could be negotiated among creditors and stockholders privately; however, senior creditors would have to voluntarily consent to subordinate their claims. The option to grant new lenders superpriority status will be especially valuable for firms that are in need of short-term trade financing and have few free assets to pledge as security.

Data limitations preclude direct measurement of relative recontracting costs (see section 3). In the following analysis, we assume that firms and creditors expect private renegotiation to be less costly than bankruptcy. Empirical justification for this assumption is provided in section 4, although we recognize that bankruptcy will dominate private renegotiation for some firms. The importance of relative recontracting costs is assessed by relating the firm's choice of recontracting method (i.e., private or legal) to a variable that measures cross-sectional variation in this assumed cost difference.

Such a test requires us to discriminate among firms on the basis of their expected cost savings from settling privately. This forced us to exclude certain costs (for example, legal fees and management's time costs) for which we were unable to find suitable empirical proxies. The cost that we use to test our model is the destruction of going-concern value that occurs when assets are sold to pay down debt and remedy default [Jensen (1989a, b)]. This loss of value will be greater for intangible assets and assets that generate firm-specific rents (e.g., growth opportunities, managerial firm-specific human capital, monopoly power, and operating synergies whose value depends on the firm's assets being kept together). If, as argued below, assets are more likely to be sold when debt is restructured in Chapter 11 rather than privately, then Chapter 11 will be relatively most costly for firms whose assets are more intangible or firm-specific. We measure the potential loss of going-concern value due to asset sales by the ratio of the firm's market value to the replacement cost of its assets; replacement cost approximates what the firm's assets could be sold for piecemeal. Firms with a higher market value/replacement cost ratio will be more likely to restructure their debt privately, because Chapter 11 is relatively more costly for such firms.

For several reasons, assets are more likely to be sold when debt is restructured in Chapter 11 rather than privately. First, automatic stay gives the debtor more power over the disposition of the firm's assets, by enjoining creditors from exercising their nonbankruptcy right to sue the firm and seize collateral. Asset sales that would normally be in violation of the firm's debt covenants will be allowed if the firm can convince the bankruptcy judge that such sales are necessary for the continued operation of the business.

Second, since the debtor can undermine the value of lenders' collateral and grant new lenders superpriority standing, fully secured lenders will in general prefer liquidation over reorganization. This may create additional pressure for asset sales in bankruptcy. In Chapter 11, creditors can initiate asset sales by 'making a motion to sell assets' before the court. In addition, Chapter 11 cases can be converted into Chapter 7 liquidations. Although conversion to Chapter 7 occurs for only about 5% of the bankruptcies that we examine, other studies have found much higher rates of liquidation. For a sample of Chapter 11 filings in the Southern District of New York (including nonpublic firms), White (1989) finds that about one-third either end up in Chapter 7 or as liquidating reorganizations.

Finally, purchasing assets from a financially distressed firm is less risky in Chapter 11, because asset sales are executed by a court order and are thus free from legal challenge. In addition, assets that are purchased from an insolvent firm that subsequently files for Chapter 11 may have to be returned as a 'voidable preference' or 'fraudulent transfer'. Given the costs incurred if an asset sale is later challenged or cancelled, potential purchasers of an asset will prefer to deal with firms in Chapter 11.

2.2.2. Factors affecting creditors' willingness to settle outside of Chapter 11

Even if stockholders and creditors believe that their combined wealth will be higher if debt is restructured outside of Chapter 11, negotiations can break down if particular creditors hold out for more generous terms. The severity of the holdout problem will depend on the voting rules for determining acceptance of the plan, the number of creditors who participate in the plan, and the type of debt that is restructured (bank loans, publicly traded debt, etc.). In addition, creditors may withhold their consent from a restructuring plan if they dispute the value of the new securities being offered under the plan.

Adopting a debt restructuring plan outside of bankruptcy generally requires the unanimous consent of all creditors whose claims are in default. Impaired creditors who are excluded from the plan can accelerate payment of their claims, or force the firm into bankruptcy by filing an involuntary Chapter 11 petition. Cross-default provisions in the firm's debt contracts will increase the proportion of creditors who participate in the plan. Thus in a typical workout the potential holdout problem is quite severe because of the veto power held by individual creditors. This problem is less severe in Chapter 11, where approval for a reorganization plan is required only from a specified majority of the creditors in each class of claims, and dissenting classes can be forced to comply with the plan under the Code's cram-down provision.

We hypothesize that the holdout problem is more severe (and the probability of successful private renegotiation, lower) when relatively more creditors are allowed to participate in the restructuring plan. An increase in the number of total votes to be cast increases the probability that at least one of the votes will be negative. Reasoning along similar lines, Smith and Warner (1979) conjecture that private negotiation of debt will be easier when the debt is privately placed (and owed to fewer lenders). On the other hand, having fewer creditors could result in more frequent bargaining deadlocks, if smallness of numbers causes individual creditors to feel more powerful and perceive greater dollar benefits to holding out. When there are few creditors – as in any bilateral bargaining situation involving few buyers and sellers – mutually beneficial trades will not always take place. If a negotiated solution is not forthcoming, the only way to break the deadlock may be to file for bankruptcy.

A related consideration is the heterogeneity of the firm's financial claims, or the complexity of its capital structure. Firms with more complex capital structures are hypothesized to succeed less often at restructuring their debt privately. The more that creditors' claims differ in seniority rights, security, and other features, the more likely different claims are to be treated differently under any proposal restructuring plan (in the package of new securities offered to holders of each type of claim). As a result, there may be greater disagreement over whether the plan is equitable in its treatment of different claims. In practice, inter-creditor disputes are extremely common, even among creditors who hold the same general type of security (for example, members of a bank lending consortium).

Achieving a consensus among creditors outside of bankruptcy will also depend upon what type of debt is being restructured. The holdout problem is especially severe for publicly traded bonds. Under the Trust Indenture Act of 1939, firms are prohibited from changing any of the 'core' terms of the bond indenture (the principal amount, interest rate, or stated maturity) unless every bondholder gives his/her consent. Although only a simple or two-thirds majority is generally required to change other covenants in the bond, amendment of the core terms is often critical to resolving financial distress.

As a result, restructuring of publicly traded debt almost always takes the form of an exchange offer. In return for tendering their old bonds, bondholders receive a package of new securities (often including some form of equity) that offers a lower cash payout. Since participation in the offer is voluntary, bondholders will have incentives to hold out if their individual tendering decision has little impact on whether the offer is successful; such incentives will be stronger when the bonds are more widely held. To encourage bondholders to tender, exchange offers are structured to penalize holdouts. The new bonds are generally more senior, and mature sooner, than the old bonds. In addition, holders can be asked to jointly tender their bonds and vote for the elimination of protective covenants in the old bonds; for this reason the success of an exchange offer is often conditional on a stipulated voting majority of bonds being tendered.

In our sample, publicly traded debt is always restructured through exchange offers. These offers are typically completed in under two months. This time can be further reduced if the firm qualifies under Section 3(a)(9) of the 1933 Securities Act for an exemption from ordinary registration requirements for any new securities issued under the offer. These so-called 3(a)(9) offers were pioneered by Drexel Burnham Lambert in the early 1980s. A company will generally qualify to make such an exchange if it is not paying anyone to solicit the exchange, and if both new and old securities involved in the offer have the same issuer. These offers can be made by any firm that qualifies, even if it is not financially distressed. Over the period 1981–1986, approximately 30% of the 184 offers for which Drexel served as advisor were made by financially distressed companies. Currently, virtually all exchange offers made by distressed companies are structured as 3(a)(9) offers.

Bankruptcy practitioners assert that attempts to settle outside of Chapter 11 are more likely to succeed when relatively less debt is owed to trade creditors, and more is owed to bank lenders. The holdout problem is particularly severe for trade debt because the number of trade creditors is often quite large, and their claims are relatively heterogeneous, precluding the use of exchange offers to restructure this debt in the same manner as publicly traded bonds. Securing a consensus among trade creditors is also thought to be more difficult because they tend to be 'acrimonious' and 'unsophisticated'. By similar reasoning, private renegotiation is less likely to succeed when the firm has significant contingent liabilities, such as those arising from product liability suits, where individual tort claims can number in the tens of thousands. Bank lenders, in contrast, tend to be more sophisticated and fewer in number than other kinds of lenders, and are more amenable to settling outside of Chapter 11 [Stein (1989)]. Similar arguments would seem to apply to insurance companies that hold privately placed debt.

Finally, creditors' consent to a restructuring plan will be harder to obtain when there is greater asymmetry in the information used by stockholders and creditors to value the firm. Through their control over the supply of such information, stockholders have incentives to influence creditors' perception of firm value to gain more favorable terms in the restructuring plan. DeAngelo et al. (1990) present evidence that is consistent with financially distressed firms using accounting accruals to influence their negotiations with bank lenders. Since rational creditors are aware of stockholders' incentives to misstate the value of the firm, private renegotiation may fail because of the resulting 'lemons' problem. In Chapter 11, stockholders have a much smaller information advantage over creditors. Firms are required to make extensive, regular disclosures of their financial and operating data to the court. Additional information is contained in the court testimony of expert witnesses and management, and creditors can exercise their 'rights of discovery' to require additional disclosures from the debtor. Any continuing disputes over value can be arbitrated by the court.

We use three variables as proxies for the severity of the holdout problem. First, troubled debt is more likely to be restructured outside Chapter 11 when there are fewer creditors. Second, debt is more likely to be restructured privately when relatively more of the debt is privately held by banks and insurance companies. In addition to the reasons discussed above, bank and insurance company debt is hypothesized to have this effect because such debt reduces the amount of information asymmetry between stockholders and creditors. Since these lenders are generally few in number, they have stronger incentives to monitor the firm than other kinds of creditors. Also, privately placed debt typically includes more financial covenants than other types of debt; even when firms are fully in compliance with these covenants, more information is implicitly revealed about firms' financial and operating characteristics.

Finally, holdouts by junior creditors will be less common when the firm's market value is high in relation to the replacement cost of its assets. As discussed in section 2.2.1, more going-concern value is dissipated in bankruptcy than in private workouts when more of the firm's assets are sold in bankruptcy. Junior creditors' position in the absolute priority ranking ensures that they bear most of this cost, and they will offer less resistance to any proposed restructuring plan. Thus, firms with a higher market value/replacement cost ratio will be more likely to restructure their debt outside of Chapter 11.

2.3. *'Prepackaged' Chapter 11*

The preceding analysis is based on a simple dichotomy between bankruptcy and private renegotiation. However, the Code also permits firms to make a 'prepackaged' Chapter 11 filing, in which the bankruptcy petition and reorganization plan are filed together. Terms of the plan are negotiated in advance between the firm and its creditors, and a vote is taken almost immediately.[4]

[4]Under section 1126(b) of the Code, any claimholder who accepts or rejects a reorganization plan that is proposed prior to filing for Chapter 11 is deemed also to have accepted or rejected the plan for purposes of plan confirmation, provided that the debtor has disclosed all relevant information for making an informed decision as provided under nonbankruptcy law.

Prepackaged Chapter 11 is thus a hybrid of conventional bankruptcy and private renegotiation that incorporates certain features of each recontracting alternative. In practice, successful prepackaged filings are extremely rare. Although prepackaged filings can significantly reduce the time that firms spend in court and obviate the need for costly creditors' committees, disputes involving the plan are still possible after filing. We were informed by a professional bankruptcy consultant that only 5% to 10% of the largest bankruptcies begin as prepackaged filings, and that fewer than half of these are successful (the original plan is accepted). Only one firm in the sample made a prepackaged Chapter 11 filing [see the case of Crystal Oil in the appendix]. The company spent a total of only three months in bankruptcy, compared with a median of eighteen months for all bankrupt firms in the sample.

3. Data and sample selection

Although identifying bankrupt firms is fairly straightforward, there are few legal or institutional guideposts for deciding what constitutes a debt restructuring. In contrast to Chapter 11 cases, most debt restructurings do not have a well-defined beginning or ending date. Restructuring rarely begins or ends with a formal public announcement, and no special documents have to be filed with any government agency. Information about the restructuring disclosed in normal Securities and Exchange Commission (SEC) filings often lacks detail. Sometimes the same debt is restructured on a number of successive occasions, or different classes of debt are restructured concurrently as separate transactions.

This study uses the same sampling procedure and definition of a debt restructuring as Gilson (1989, 1990). This definition emphasizes the economic similarities between Chapter 11 and private renegotiation as alternative mechanisms for dealing with financial distress. A firm is financially distressed if it has insufficient cash flows to meet the payments on its debt. To avoid or remedy a default, the firm must reduce or defer the payments, or replace the debt with securities having residual rather than fixed payoffs. Consistent with this simple intuition, a debt restructuring is defined as a transaction in which an existing debt contract is replaced by a new contract, with one of the following consequences: (i) required interest or principal payments on the debt are reduced; (ii) the maturity of the debt is extended; or (iii) creditors are given equity securities (common stock or securities convertible into common stock). In addition, the restructuring must be undertaken in response to an anticipated or actual default. This last requirement ensures that the sample includes only restructurings that are undertaken by financially distressed firms. As reported later in table 3, approximately two-thirds of sampled firms that privately restructure their debt are in default at some point during their restructuring.[5]

A debt restructuring is assumed to take place over the interval defined by the first and last reference to the restructuring in the *Wall Street Journal* (*WSJ*), unless more accurate dates are available from other sources. Event-study tests undertaken below measure stock returns in relation to these two dates. If a firm restructures its debt in several discrete periods, these are treated as a single restructuring transaction if less than a year separates adjoining periods. A debt restructuring plan is considered successful if the firm does not file for bankruptcy within a year of the last reference to the restructuring.[6] Consistent with the joint reorganization of claims under Chapter 11, concurrent restructuring of the firm's publicly traded and privately placed debt is treated as a single debt restructuring.

This study analyzes a sample of 169 exchange-listed companies that were in severe financial distress during 1978–1987; 80 firms privately restructured their debt, and 89 firms filed for Chapter 11. Selection of the sample was a two-step process. First, for a given year, firms listed on the New York and American Stock Exchanges were ranked by unadjusted common stock returns at year-end (cumulated over three years), and a stratum was formed consisting of those firms in the bottom five percent. Second, financially distressed firms within this stratum were identified by searching through the *WSJ Index* for any reference to a default, bankruptcy, or debt restructuring in each of the surrounding five years. This two-step procedure was repeated for each of the years 1979–1985, resulting in an initial stratified sample of 793 firm-years (447 firms). Under the assumption that extreme stock-price declines reflect extreme declines in firms' cash flows, this sampling procedure replicates the sequence of actual events that lead to financial distress.

This sampling method has two principal advantages. First, since we are interested in contrasting private renegotiation and bankruptcy as alternative mechanisms for dealing with extreme financial distress, we want to exclude debt restructuring by nondistressed firms. For example, a highly levered but

[5]Defaults on technical convenants (for example, those requiring firms to maintain a minimum level of net worth) are not explicitly considered in this definition because such covenants are frequently renegotiated by financially healthy firms when debt is privately placed. As Zinbarg (1975, p. 35) notes: 'My own institution's experience (Prudential Insurance Company of America) may serve as an illustration. In any given year, we will, on average, receive one modification request per loan on the books. In no more than five percent of these cases will we refuse the request or even require any quid pro quo, because the vast majority of corporate requests are perfectly reasonable and do not increase our risk materially.' For a detailed discussion of the economic function of covenants, see Smith and Warner (1979).

[6]Thus, for example, if the last reference to an ongoing restructuring of a firm's bank debt was on June 15, 1982, and the next such reference occurs on September 12, 1983, these would be treated as references to two separate restructurings. Similarly, if a firm's bank debt is successfully restructured on March 22, 1980, and it begins to restructure its publicly traded debt on November 2, 1980, these would be treated as two references to the same ongoing restructuring. Five firms in the sample appear twice as two separate restructurings, and four firms appear as both a debt restructuring and a bankruptcy.

profitable firm may wish to amend certain terms in its debt to enable it to invest in a positive-NPV project. Extreme negative stock returns are a relatively unambiguous indicator of poor financial performance. Inspection of the source documents reveals that 56% of firms in the sample explicitly restructured their debt to avoid bankruptcy. The remaining firms either received a going concern qualification from their auditors during the restructuring, where in default, or experienced a change in control at the hands of creditors (as evidenced by a creditor-initiated senior-management change or placement of stock with creditors).

A second advantage is that the sample contains a more representative cross-section of debt restructurings than if the search had been based on reported cases of default. The latter criterion would exclude firms that restructure their debt to avoid default; evidence reported in the next section suggests that such preemptive restructuring is fairly common. Similarly, a sample that consists of defaults reported by *Moody's* or *Standard and Poor's* would exclude firms that have no publicly traded debt; such firms make up 54% of the current sample. Potential biases inherent in the sampling procedure are discussed in the next section.

Information on debt restructuring plans and other relevant data are obtained from the *WSJ*, the *Moody's* manuals, the *Capital Changes Reporter*, and the *Q-File* directory of 10k reports and proxy statements. Additional data are obtained from the exchange-offer circulars issued by firms that restructured their publicly traded bonds. The market value/replacement cost ratio is constructed using data from the COMPUSTAT data base, and is described in Lang et al. (1989). Because stock returns (and market values) of highly levered firms are extremely volatile, we use a three-year average of this variable in the empirical analysis. The bank-debt ratio is defined as the book value of debt owed to banks and insurance companies divided by the book value of total liabilities. Eighty-five percent of all firms in the sample owe debt to banks, while only eleven percent owe debt to insurance companies; results are qualitatively the same when the numerator includes only bank debt. The number of creditors is approximated by the number of distinct classes of debt referenced in the long-term debt section of *Moody's*. Data used to construct these variables predate as closely as possible the start of the firm's debt restructuring or bankruptcy.

4. Results

4.1. Sample characteristics

Most of the debt-restructuring activity in the sample is clustered in the years 1981–1985 (see table 1). This is consistent with the timing of the general economic recession of the early 1980s, when one would expect there

Table 1

Time series of corporate debt-restructuring activity, by starting date and eventual outcome of restructuring. Sample consists of 80 firms that successfully avoid bankruptcy by restructuring their debt out of court, and 89 firms that are unsuccessful in restructuring their debt and file under Chapter 11 of the U.S. Bankruptcy Code. The sample period is 1978–1987.[a]

Year	Number of attempted debt restructurings	Percentage of restructuring attempts that end in bankruptcy
1978	9	11.1
1979	8	50.0
1980	11	63.6
1981	18	66.7
1982	38	47.4
1983	28	46.4
1984	25	60.0
1985	20	60.0
1986	10	50.0
1987	2	100.0
Total	169	52.7

[a]A debt restructuring is defined as a transaction in which an existing debt contract is replaced by a new contract, with one of the following consequences: (i) required interest or principal payments on the debt are reduced, (ii) the maturity of the debt is extended, or (iii) creditors are given equity securities (common stock or securities convertible into common stock). All restructurings are undertaken in response to an anticipated or actual default. Sources used to determine firms' financial status include the *WSJ*, Commerce Clearing House's *Capital Changes Reporter*, the *Moody's* manuals, and the *Q-file* directory of annual 10k reports and proxy statements.

to be relatively more reported cases of financial distress. Seventy-six percent of the debt restructurings in the sample begin in this period. Also indicated is the percentage of restructuring attempts that eventually fail, and end with a Chapter 11 filing. The sample is about evenly divided between successful and failed attempts. Except in the first and last years of the sample period (when the number of events is extremely small), there does not appear to be any time trend in the observed failure rate.

The frequency of events corresponding to the beginning and conclusion of debt restructurings is listed in table 2. Separate figures are reported for successful and failed restructuring attempts. Primary sources used to identify these events include the *WSJ* and firms' 10k reports. Panel A of the table reveals that in a number of cases, negotiations took place prior to the starting date identified from public sources. Forty-seven initial references in fact pertain to the final resolution of a debt restructuring. We believe that we have come reasonably close to identifying the true starting dates for 90 firms (53 percent of the sample), where the initial event either takes the form of a default (52 firms) or an announcement that the firm has just commenced (or

Table 2

Frequency distribution of events used to identify the beginning and conclusion of 80 successful and 89 unsuccessful attempts by firms to restructure their debt privately to avoid bankruptcy. All transactions take place between 1978 and 1987. Figures in the table are based on information contained in the *Wall Street Journal*, the *Moody's* manuals, Commerce Clearing House's *Capital Changes Reporter*, and the *Q-file* directory of annual 10k reports and proxy statements.[a]

	Outcome of debt-restructuring attempt	
	Successful	Unsuccessful
Panel A: Events that identify the beginning of debt restructuring		
Default	29	23
Final resolution of debt restructuring announced	20	27
Initial announcement of debt restructuring	18	20
Reference to a debt restructuring that is already in progress	11	16
Creditor-initiated senior-management change	1	1
Firm receives a going-concern qualification from its auditors	1	0
Firm engages investment banker to lead debt restructuring	0	1
Senior management denies that bankruptcy is imminent	0	1
Panel B: Events that identify the conclusion of debt restructuring		
Restructuring agreement formally consummated	46	0
Last public reference to an ongoing restructuring in progress	13	0
Sale of equity or debt securities as part of restructuring plan	10	0
Merged into another company	4	0
Creditors receive equity securities under restructuring plan	4	0
Shareholder approval obtained for restructuring plan	3	0
Chapter 11 filing	0	89
Totals	80	89

[a]See table 1 for a definition of debt restructuring and bankruptcy.

will shortly commence) restructuring its debt (38 firms). Of the 52 default announcements, 34 refer to payment defaults and 18 to technical defaults on financial covenants. Over the course of a restructuring, firms can be associated with more than one event listed in panel A. Although a default normally allows the debtor a 30-day grace period before creditors can exercise their right to accelerate full payment of the debt, negotiations to restructure the debt are assumed to begin immediately after the firm defaults.

Panel B of table 2 reports the frequency of events used to identify the conclusion of a debt restructuring. By definition, all 89 restructuring attempts that fail end with a Chapter 11 bankruptcy filing. Of the remaining 80 successful debt restructurings, for 44 firms it was possible to identify the date on which the restructuring agreement was formally consummated. For 13 firms there was no clear concluding date, only some final reference in the *WSJ* to a restructuring that was still in progress. For ten firms the restructur-

Table 3

Selected attributes of 80 successful corporate debt restructurings undertaken to avoid bankruptcy between 1978 and 1987.[a]

Attribute	Percentage of sample
Panel A: Incidence of default during debt restructuring[b]	
Payment default	36.3
Technical default	21.3
Unspecified default	17.5
All defaults	66.3
Panel B: Stockholder approval for restructuring plan	
Approval for issuance of new common stock specified under plan	17.5
Approval of asset sales specified under plan	1.3
No stockholder approval required	81.2
Panel C: Type of debt restructured	
Bank debt (by firms that have bank debt outstanding)	90.0
Publicly traded debt (by firms that have publicly traded debt outstanding)	69.8

[a]See table 1 for a definition of debt restructuring and bankruptcy.

[b]A *payment default* is defined as a default on an interest or principal payment; included are cases where a firm unilaterally suspends payment on its debt, even though no default is formally declared by creditors. A *technical default* is defined as a default on a financial covenant in the firm's debt. Sources used to determine whether debt is in default include the *Moody's* manuals, Commerce Clearing House's *Capital Changes Reporter*, the *Q-file* directory of annual 10k reports and proxy statements, and Standard and Poor's *Bond Owner's Guide*.

ing concluded with the sale of new debt or equity securities, with the issue proceeds used to help finance the restructuring. In four additional cases the restructuring ended with creditors receiving an equity interest in the firm, either directly or as a result of interest being paid in equity securities instead of cash.

Starting and ending dates for bankruptcy are generally better defined. Of the 89 firms in the sample that filed for Chapter 11, 42 leave bankruptcy when their reorganization plans are formally confirmed by the court. An additional ten firms are merged into nonbankrupt firms, and four are liquidated following the conversion of their cases to Chapter 7 proceedings. For the remaining 33 firms, either bankruptcy was still in progress at the time of this writing (eight firms), or it was not possible to determine precisely when or how the firm emerged from Chapter 11.

Some general attributes of the 80 successful debt restructurings in the sample are presented in table 3. Reported default rates in panel A indicate whether any of the firm's outstanding debt is in default; data limitations preclude a finer breakdown by particular classes of debt (secured debt, trade debt, etc.). Although defaults on senior securities and related 'material' events must be reported in the firm's 10k report, the amount and detail of disclosure vary significantly. For example, a firm is not required to report when it first started to restructure its debt, or that it has been in discussion with creditors concerning a possible default. A firm might disclose that it has restructured its 'subordinated debt', without specifying how particular claims in this category have been restructured. A default may go unreported if the firm does not file its 10k report; filing omissions by financially distressed firms are fairly common [Gilson (1990)]. As well, firms and creditors exhibit a penchant for secrecy in these transactions. For example, the debt restructuring of Tiger International Inc. (included in the appendix) began when the *WSJ* reported that the firm unilaterally suspended payments on about half of its $1.8 billion in debt:

> Tiger said that a total of $350 million in interest and principal on its bank and institutional debt is scheduled for payment in 1983. But the company wouldn't disclose how much of the $350 million would be affected by its decision to 'temporarily defer' debt service on $900 million of its total debt. Tiger also wouldn't disclose when specific payments were due on any of the $350 million. Asked for elaboration... a company spokeswoman said she didn't know whether the company had missed a deadline for any payments on the $900 million in debt.... Tiger's lenders, whom the company declined to identify, were informed of the decision at yesterday's meeting.
>
> (*WSJ*, 15 February 1983, 5)

Fifty-three firms (66.3 percent of the sample) were in default before successfully restructuring their debt. Since 29 of these restructurings begin with a default (see table 2), 24 firms did not default until after entering negotiations with creditors to restructure their debt. In 51 firms (64 percent of the sample), no default occurred, or occurred after the debt restructuring began. Thus, firms often begin restructuring their debt before any actual default (or without any default occurring).

Explicit stockholder approval was required for only 18.8 percent of all restructuring plans that were adopted (panel B). In most of these cases, approval was required to issue common stock under the plan, either as a requirement imposed by the firm's stock exchange, or because it was necessary to increase the number of authorized shares. For the remaining 81.2 percent of all cases where such approval was not obtained, the possibility exists that adoption of these plans was not always in the best interests of stockholders. Where managers have the authority to accept or reject a restructuring plan, there is no assurance that they will make the decision that maximizes stockholders' wealth. Gilson (1989, 1990) finds that turnover of senior managers and directors is lower when firms restructure their debt outside of Chapter 11. Thus, managers could have incentives to settle with

Table 4

Summary of restructuring terms for 80 successful corporate debt restructurings undertaken between 1978 and 1987, by general class of debt restructured (bank, publicly traded, and other debt).[a]

	Percentage of debt within a given class restructured on specified terms			Percentage of firms that restructure any debt on specified terms
Restructuring terms	Bank	Public	Other	
Extension of maturity	48.6	6.7	25.0	48.8
Reduction of interest or principal	54.2	56.7	75.0	72.5
Distribution of equity securities	51.4	86.7	75.0	73.8
Percentage of firms that restructure debt in a given class	90.0	37.5	20.0	

[a]*Extension of maturity* includes deferral of promised interest or principal payments. *Reduction of interest or principal* includes foregiveness of overdue or future promised payments, in addition to reductions in the stated rate of interest. *Distribution of equity securities* includes distributions of common or preferred stock, as well as securities that can be converted into either class of stock (e.g., warrants and convertible bonds); also included are provisions in the debt contract that give firms the option to make payments either in cash or in equity securities. *Bank debt* includes debt owed to commercial banks and insurance companies. *Other debt* includes debt owed to suppliers, trade creditors, and other nonbank companies.

creditors on overly generous terms to secure their consent to a plan, even though stockholders would be better off in bankruptcy. Stock-return evidence presented below, however, suggests that the market on average reacts positively to events that increase the probability of successful private renegotiation and negatively to events that increase the probability of bankruptcy. This suggests that potential agency conflicts between managers and stockholders are not a deciding factor in whether firms privately restructure or file for Chapter 11.

Finally, firms that restructure their debt privately sometimes restructure only a subset of their outstanding debt contracts (panel C). Only 90.0 percent of firms in the sample with bank debt outstanding, and 69.8 percent of firms with publicly traded debt, actually restructure such debt. In contrast, Chapter 11 cases necessarily require participation by all impaired claimholder classes, which in practical terms generally means all of the firm's outstanding claims. This suggests that private renegotiation may be less costly than Chapter 11 if the firm is able to recontract only with those creditors whose claims are in default, thus conserving on transactions costs.

Table 4 summarizes the principal terms on which firms in the sample restructure their debt, based on the three criteria used to define a debt restructuring (that is, there must either be a reduction in interest or principal payments, an extension of the debt's maturity, or a distribution of equity securities to creditors). Since firms do not always disclose the exact terms on which debt is restructured, figures in the table represent lower bounds on the frequency with which these terms are actually incorporated in restructuring plans.

New equity securities are distributed to creditors in almost 74 percent of all successful restructurings. A similar percentage of restructurings results in a reduction in promised payments on the debt. The least common provision in these agreements is an extension of maturity. Different classes of debt also appear to be restructured on substantially different terms. Approximately 49 percent of bank debt restructurings provide for an extension of maturity, compared with only 6.7 percent of restructurings of publicly traded debt; this latter result is consistent with firms offering shorter-maturity debt in exchange offers to discourage holdouts (see section 2.2.2). Although 51.4 percent of bank debt restructurings result in bank lenders receiving equity in the firm, holders of publicly traded debt are given equity securities 86.7 percent of the time. The latter difference is a likely consequence of various legal and regulatory factors that make it prohibitively costly for banks to hold large amounts of equity in publicly traded companies.

In particular, banks are constrained from holding significant blocks of stock in other firms by section 16 of the Glass-Steagall Act, the Bank Holding Company Act and the Federal Reserve Board's Regulation Y, although temporary exceptions are granted when stock is obtained in a debt restructuring. In general, banks must divest their stockholdings after approximately two years, although extensions are possible. Second, creditors can be held legally liable to other claimholders if the firm's financial condition deteriorates subsequent to their assuming a controlling interest in the firm and exercising 'undue influence' over its business [Douglas-Hamilton (1975), Smith and Warner (1979)]. A given percentage equity ownership in a firm might, for purposes of proving legal liability, be assumed to confer greater control on a small group of bank lenders than a dispersed group of public bondholders. Finally, a controlling shareholding in a firm could be construed as an 'insider relationship', thus obliging banks to return any monetary consideration received from the firm as a 'preference item' if it later files for bankruptcy. Banks may prefer to receive relatively less equity in a debt restructuring if they assess a high probability that the firm will subsequently become bankrupt.

The preceding simple classification of restructuring terms provides a general overview of how these deals are structured. Given the complexity and idiosyncratic nature of these transactions, some useful insights can also be gained by direct examination of individual cases. The appendix presents detailed case descriptions of ten debt restructurings in the sample. The cases are intended to be a representative cross-section of various restructuring plan types and outcomes. These case descriptions provide evidence that complements evidence presented in the next section, where we attempt to identify factors conducive to restructuring debt outside of Chapter 11.

Table 5 contrasts selected characteristics of firms by whether or not they successfully restructure their debt outside of Chapter 11. Firms that privately restructure their debt have a higher market value/replacement cost ratio and have relatively more bank debt than firms in Chapter 11. The means and medians of both variables are significantly different between subsamples at the 1 percent level of significance. Both differences are consistent with the theory developed in section 2. Firms with a higher market value/replacement cost ratio are hypothesized to find bankruptcy more costly than private renegotiation, and to be less prone to holdouts by junior creditors. Firms with more bank debt outstanding can more easily renegotiate their debt because banks are more sophisticated and less numerous than other kinds of creditors, resulting in fewer holdouts.

The mean number of debt contracts (approximated by the number of entries in the long-term debt section of *Moody's*) is marginally higher for firms that restructure their debt privately, but the difference is not statistically significant, and the medians are identical. Alternatively, we define the standardized number of debt contracts as the number of contracts divided by the book value of total liabilities. This variable is significantly lower for firms that restructure successfully; mean and median differences (not shown) are significant at the 2 percent and 7 percent levels, respectively. The standardized number of debt contracts, or the number of creditors per dollar of debt, is arguably a better proxy for creditors' incentives to hold out. Anecdotal evidence suggests that holdouts are relatively more common among smaller creditors, possibly because they have less wealth at risk if the restructuring attempt fails.

Firms that restructure their debt privately are also generally larger, as measured by the book value of assets and the number of shareholders and employees. Both mean and median book values of assets are higher for firms that restructure successfully, although only the difference in medians is statistically significant using a Wilcoxon rank-sum test (p-value of 0.02). Firm size may be a proxy for the number of creditors or the complexity of the firm's capital structure; the simple correlation between the book value of assets and the (nonstandardized) number of debt contracts is positive and significant (0.72, with a p-value of 0.00).

The two groups of firms are fairly similar in overall leverage (measured by the ratio of total liabilities or long-term debt to total assets), and mean stock-price performance (measured over the current and preceding two years). On the other hand, median unadjusted and net-of-market returns are significantly higher for the firms that restructure privately, according to a Wilcoxon rank-sum test for differences in medians (p-values of 0.04 and 0.05,

Table 5

Selected firm and debt characteristics for 80 firms that successfully restructure their debt out of court, and 89 firms that are unsuccessful in restructuring their debt and file under Chapter 11 of the U.S. Bankruptcy Code. Beginning dates for attempted debt restructurings all take place between 1978 and 1987.[a]

Characteristic	80 successful restructurings				89 unsuccessful restructurings				p-value of t-test (Wilcoxon rank sum test) for difference in:	
	Mean	Median	Min.	Max.	Mean	Median	Min.	Max.	Mean	Median
Market value/replacement cost ratio	0.83	0.65	0.23	2.92	0.61	0.56	0.20	1.75	0.01	0.01
Debt ÷ total liabilities (book values)										
(i) Bank debt	0.40	0.36	0.00	0.88	0.25	0.20	0.00	0.83	0.00	0.00
(ii) Public debt	0.13	0.02	0.00	0.66	0.08	0.00	0.00	0.61	0.08	0.08
(iii) Secured debt	0.14	0.00	0.00	0.82	0.12	0.00	0.00	0.70	0.51	0.91
(iv) Convertible debt	0.07	0.00	0.00	0.68	0.06	0.00	0.00	0.77	0.67	0.65
Number of debt contracts outstanding	7.0	5.0	1.0	28.0	6.0	5.0	1.0	31.0	0.22	0.18
Book value of total assets ($millions)	633	101	9	10,209	317	49	6	9,383	0.15	0.02
Number of shareholders (1,000s)	14	4	1	207	5	3	1	34	0.04	0.08
Number of employees (1,000s)	5	1	0	76	3	2	0	32	0.26	0.88
Total liabilities ÷ book value of assets	0.94	0.83	0.43	4.92	1.01	0.86	0.39	10.00	0.65	0.99
Long-term debt ÷ book value of assets	0.64	0.55	0.00	4.23	0.58	0.45	0.00	8.70	0.63	0.02
Prior 3-year common stock return (%)										
(i) Unadjusted	−36.4	−50.3	−93.3	360.0	−48.6	−60.7	−98.0	179.3	0.17	0.04
(ii) Less market return	−134.0	−142.0	−230.4	273.8	−147.7	−160.4	−249.9	62.0	0.15	0.05
Length of debt restructuring attempt (months)	15.4	11.0	1.0	72.0	8.1	3.0	1.0	42.0	0.00	0.00
Length of bankruptcy proceedings after unsuccessful restructuring attempt (months)	—	—	—	—	20.4	18.0	3.0	43.0	—	—

[a]See table 1 for a definition of debt restructuring and bankruptcy. When applicable, figures are those that most closely predate the beginning of firms' debt restructuring or bankruptcy. Figures defined in terms of firms' assets and liabilities are all based on reported book values in the *Moody's* manuals. *Bank debt* includes outstanding liabilities to both commercial banks and insurance companies. The *market value/replacement cost ratio* equals the three-year average ratio of the market value of assets to their replacement value. The *number of debt contracts* equals the number of separate descriptive headings in the long-term debt section of the *Moody's* manuals. The *market return* is the equally weighted market portfolio return in the CRSP daily returns file.

respectively). A comparison of medians is probably more appropriate given the extreme nonnormality of the sample (drawn from the left-hand tail of unconditional returns distribution). One explanation for this difference is that superior performance is associated with a smaller reduction in going-concern value, resulting in a higher market value/replacement cost ratio and increased incentives to renegotiate debt privately. Consistent with this posited relationship, the correlation between prior unadjusted stock returns and the market value/replacement cost ratio is positive and significant (0.19, with a p-value of 0.04).

Finally, firms that restructure their debt privately require an average of 15.4 months, and a median of 11 months, to complete the restructuring. Restructuring of publicly traded debt is completed in a much shorter time than restructuring of nontraded debt. The 30 exchange offers in the present sample take an average of 6.6 months to complete (not shown), compared with 15.9 months for all other debt; corresponding median times are 2 and 10.5 months. Differences in both means and medians are statistically significant using a t-test and Wilcoxon rank sum test (p-values of less than 0.01).

Firms that file for Chapter 11 spend an average of 8.1 (median of 3) months attempting to restructure their debt before seeking bankruptcy protection, and an average of 20.4 (median of 18) additional months in Chapter 11. In the present sample, Chapter 11 cases take significantly longer to complete than successful debt restructurings; differences in the mean and median number of months elapsed under each alternative are significantly different from zero (p-values of less than 0.01).

4.2. *Direct measurement of debt-restructuring costs*

We argued in section 2 that relative restructuring costs are an important determinant of whether firms restructure their debt privately or in Chapter 11. Because firms are generally not required to disclose the total costs incurred in a private workout, explicit measurement of these costs is generally not possible. Only four firms in the present sample reported debt-restructuring expenses in their 10k reports (and only for restructuring of publicly traded debt). Data on bankruptcy costs are available only at considerable expense, by direct examination of court records [Weiss (1990)].

It is possible, however, to estimate the direct costs of exchange offers for publicly traded debt. Firms must provide an estimate of offer-related costs in the exchange offer circular distributed to bondholders. We obtained the circulars for 26 of the 32 exchange offers in the sample (including two made by firms that ultimately went bankrupt). For 18 of these offers, the circular provided an estimate of out-of-pocket costs (including payments made to the exchange and information agent, and related legal, accounting, brokerage, and investment banking fees). Firms were omitted when only a subset of the

Table 6

Direct costs of troubled exchange offers for publicly traded debt. Sample consists of 18 exchange offers undertaken between 1981 and 1988. Costs consist of compensation paid to the exchange and information agent, and all legal, accounting, brokerage, and investment banking fees incurred by the firm in connection with the offer.[a]

	Mean	Median	Min.	Max.
Exchange offer costs ($1,000s)	799	424	200	2,500
Offer costs as a percentage of the book value of assets	0.65	0.32	0.01	3.40
Offer costs as a percentage of the face value of bonds restructured under offer	2.16	2.29	0.27	6.84

[a]These 18 exchange offers represent all offers in the sample for which an estimate of total offer-related costs was disclosed in either the exchange offer circular of the firm's 10k report. Such documentation was obtained for 26 of the 32 exchange offers in the entire sample (two of which were undertaken by firms that ultimately filed for bankruptcy). The book value of assets and the face amount of debt are the figures that most closely predate the commencement of the offer.

offer's total costs were presented, to avoid biasing the cost estimates downward (several circulars reported only that certain costs would be of some 'customary' amount; another circular contained only blank spaces where offer costs were to have been reported). Firms were also omitted if the investment bank that served as financial advisor to the offer was paid in warrants or common stock, unless a dollar estimate of the value of this payment was provided in the circular.

In economic terms, exchange-offer costs appear to be trivial (table 6). Mean and median exchange-offer costs as a percentage of the book value of assets prior to the offer are only 0.65 and 0.32 percent, respectively. In relation to the face amount of the debt involved in the exchange offer, the corresponding figures are 2.16 and 2.29 percent. These estimates do not include any indirect costs of exchange offers or the costs of restructuring nonpublic debt.

There is evidence that direct bankruptcy costs are also relatively small. Warner (1977b) reports that direct costs for a sample of 11 railroad bankruptcies from the period 1933–1955 represent, on average, 5.3 percent of firms' market value at the time of the bankruptcy filing. Ang et al. (1982) investigate a sample of 86 firms that filed for bankruptcy (and eventually liquidated) in the Western District of Oklahoma between 1963 and 1979. They report mean and median direct costs (as a percentage of total liquidation proceeds) of 7.5 and 1.7 percent, respectively. Weiss (1990) analyzes a sample of 37 New York- and American Stock Exchange-listed firms that filed for bankruptcy between 1980 and 1986, and finds that average direct costs are, on average, 2.9 percent of the book value of assets prior to filing.

Direct costs of exchange offers in our sample also exhibit economies of scale. Average offer costs decline with both the book value of assets and the face value of debt involved in the offer. The correlation between average costs and the book value of assets (not shown) is −0.42 (p-value of 0.08); the correlation between average costs and the face value of debt is −0.57 (p-value of 0.01). A statistically significant negative relation is also found when average costs are regressed against each deflator in ordinary least-squares regressions. Economies of scale have previously been documented for direct bankruptcy costs [Warner (1977b), Ang et al. (1982)].

4.3. Prediction of successful private renegotiation

This section presents a logit regression analysis that relates the probability of successful private renegotiation to our empirical proxies for relative bankruptcy costs and the magnitude of the potential holdout problem. The dependent variable equals 1 if a firm successfully restructures its debt without entering Chapter 11, and equals 0 if the restructuring attempt fails and the firm files for bankruptcy. Thus, a positive coefficient on an independent variable in the regressions implies that firms for which this variable takes on a higher value are more likely to settle with creditors privately. Our explanatory variables are the firm's market/replacement cost ratio, the bank-debt ratio, and the standardized number of debt contracts outstanding (scaled by the book value of total liabilities).

Four estimated specifications of the model are shown in table 7; in the first, all three explanatory variables are included, and in the remaining three, the variables are included separately. In general, all three variables have significant explanatory power, and are consistent with the univariate comparisons made in table 5. The estimated coefficient on the market value/replacement cost ratio is positive and highly significant in both the combined and univariate regressions (both coefficients have p-values of 0.01). The positive coefficient has two non-mutually-exclusive interpretations, since this ratio is a proxy for both relative recontracting costs and the magnitude of junior creditors' losses if the firm files for Chapter 11 (greater expected losses will increase creditors' willingness to settle privately). The logit regression tests do not allow us to distinguish between these two hypotheses.

The estimated coefficient on the bank debt ratio is positive and significant in both of the regressions in which it appears, although it is somewhat more significant when included separately (with a p-value of 0.00, versus 0.05 for the combined regression). The standardized number of debt contracts is negatively related to the probability of successful private renegotiation, although the estimated coefficient is only marginally significant when included in the combined regression (p-value of 0.12). When this variable appears alone, the estimated coefficient is negative and significant (p-value

Table 7

Logit regressions relating firm characteristics to outcome of debt restructuring. Sample consists of 80 firms that successfully avoided bankruptcy by restructuring their debt out of court, and 89 firms that were forced to seek protection under Chapter 11 of the U.S. Bankruptcy Code. All transactions take place between 1978 and 1987. The dependent variable equals 1 if a firm successfully restructures its debt out of court, and equals 0 if the restructuring attempt fails and the firm files for bankruptcy. Asymptotic p-values are shown in parentheses.[a]

Independent variables	(1)	(2)	(3)	(4)
Intercept	−1.40[b] (0.01)	−1.16[b] (0.01)	−0.82[b] (0.00)	0.21 (0.33)
Market value/replacement cost ratio	1.51[b] (0.01)	1.49[b] (0.01)	—	—
Bank-debt ratio	1.59[c] (0.05)	—	2.20[b] (0.00)	—
Number of debt contracts outstanding	−2.60 (0.12)	—	—	−2.91[c] (0.03)
Sample size	112	119	159	157
Model p-value	0.0012	0.0030	0.0005	0.0163
Pseudo R-square	0.051	0.026	0.026	0.013

[a]See table 1 for a definition of debt restructuring and bankruptcy. Explanatory variables predate as closely as possible the start of each firm's debt restructuring or bankruptcy. The *market value/replacement cost ratio* equals the three-year average ratio of the market value of assets to their replacement value. The *bank-debt ratio* equals the book value of debt owed to banks and insurance companies, divided by the book value of total liabilities. The *number of debt contracts outstanding* equals the number of distinct descriptive headings under the long-term debt section of the *Moody's* manuals, divided by the book value of total liabilities; to facilitate reporting in the table, the estimated coefficient on this variable is divided by 1,000.

[b]p-value ≤ 0.01.

[c]p-value ≤ 0.05.

of 0.03). These results suggest that creditor holdouts are less common when relatively more debt is owed to banks, and there are fewer creditors.

The results in table 7 hold with the addition of alternative explanatory variables. Earlier, we hypothesized that private renegotiation is less likely to succeed when relatively more debt is owed to trade creditors, because it is more difficult to obtain their unanimous consent to a restructuring plan. In addition, firms that are more reliant on trade credit may view Chapter 11 more favorably, because the Code's superpriority provision makes it easier to raise new working capital. As a proxy for the importance of trade credit, we use the ratio of accounts payable to total liabilities observed before restructuring activity begins. The trade-debt ratio is negatively correlated with the bank-debt ratio (not shown), and positively correlated with the standardized number of debt contracts (correlations are −0.29 and 0.31, respectively, with p-values of 0.00). It is insignificant in the regressions, however, whether included alone or in combination with other variables.

Although the estimated coefficients are consistent with the hypotheses developed in section 2, the overall explanatory power of the regressions is small. 'Pseudo' R-squares [Madalla (1983)] calculated for each regression indicate that the logit regressions explain no more than about 5 percent of the total variation in the dependent variable, although model p-values are generally less than 1 percent. The lack of overall power may be due to the relatively small sample size and the use of cross-sectional data. In addition, a number of other economic factors that may be critical to the success of private renegotiation are either unsystematic or impossible to quantify (e.g., the relative bargaining abilities and personalities of the parties involved). This last consideration underlies the analysis of stock returns in the next section.

A final concern is that the logit results may be subject to two possible biases. First, our empirical tests assume that private renegotiation is less costly than bankruptcy. Although we do not presume this to be true for all firms, general support for this assumption is found in anecdotal accounts of the bankruptcy process [Stein (1989)] and in stock-return evidence presented in the next section. In addition, a bankruptcy filing represents the first public announcement of financial distress for only 27 firms in the sample (see table 2); for 14 of these firms the *WSJ* report of the filing refers to a previous failed restructuring attempt. Thus 92 percent of firms in the sample first attempted to settle privately with creditors. It can be shown that creditors and stockholders will never attempt to settle privately if bankruptcy is less costly (assuming full participation by all creditors).

A second possible source of bias is the use of a nonrandom sample to estimate the logit regressions. The coefficient estimates in table 7 will be biased if the relative frequency of private restructuring and Chapter 11 in the sample differs from the population frequency [Manski and McFadden (1983)]. Since firms are sampled on extreme negative stock returns, these relative frequencies could differ if the probability of successful private renegotiation depends on prior stock-price performance. Prior stock returns are insignificant when added to the regressions, however, and the remaining coefficient estimates are qualitatively unchanged.

4.4. Evidence from stock returns

Ideally, claimholders' incentives to choose between private renegotiation and bankruptcy could be assessed directly by comparing the value of the securities distributed under each alternative to various claimholder classes (secured lenders, public bondholders, etc.). Although such direct comparisons are precluded by a lack of relevant price data, analysis of common stock returns provides some insights into what determines claimholders' incentives to settle privately.

Given evidence in the last section that certain firm characteristics can be used to predict whether attempted private renegotiation will be successful, we are interested in knowing whether the stock market also forms such a prediction. By examining abnormal stock returns around the initial announcement of a restructuring attempt, one can assess whether the market uses similar information to predict the likelihood of successful private renegotiation.

To investigate this possibility, we perform two related analyses of stock returns. First, we partition the sample by whether or not firms are ultimately successful in privately restructuring their debt. If the market is correct on average in predicting this outcome, we should observe a different stock-price reaction for the two subsamples. This approach imposes no prior constraints on the information set that the market uses in making its forecast. The same approach is used by Bradley et al. (1983) in analyzing target companies' stock-price performance following a failed tender offer. Second, we use cross-sectional regression analysis to relate announcement-day returns to variables that were used in the logit analysis to predict the success of private renegotiation. This approach implicitly constrains the market's information set to contain only some subset of these variables.

By analyzing cumulative stock returns over the entire restructuring interval, it is also possible to make certain inferences about relative recontracting costs. Positive cumulative abnormal returns for successful restructurings are consistent with the hypothesis that fewer total costs are incurred (firm value is higher) under private renegotiation than bankruptcy. This allows us to contrast the costs of private renegotiation and bankruptcy without having to measure these costs directly. Baldwin and Mason (1983) undertake a similar analysis of the debt restructuring of Massey Ferguson (included in the current sample).

Stock returns observed around the outcome announcement will contain more information about relative recontracting costs when more of the firm's debt is restructured under the plan. If the unanimous consent of all creditors is required, abnormal returns at the announcement of a successful restructuring must reflect total savings in recontracting costs from avoiding bankruptcy. Given that all creditors (and stockholders) consent to the plan, the wealth of each claimholder, and thus the value of the firm, will be higher under private renegotiation than bankruptcy.

If only a subset of the firm's debt is restructured, adoption of a restructuring plan could in principle reduce the wealth of nonparticipating creditors (by granting participating creditors increased seniority interests, for example). The size of these wealth transfers will be limited, however, by the right of nonparticipating creditors to sue the firm (and other creditors), covenants that restrict the issuance of more senior debt, and cross-default provisions that restrict the firm's ability to exclude certain creditors from participation in the plan.

Abnormal common stock returns around the initial announcement of a restructuring attempt are reported in table 8. We exclude the 27 bankrupt firms in the sample (see table 2) for which the Chapter 11 filing was the first public announcement of financial distress, since it is not known for these firms when (or whether) private renegotiation was attempted before the bankruptcy filing. Reported returns are two-day mean market-model residuals, estimated using Center for Research in Security Prices (CRSP) daily returns for the period 250 days to 50 days prior to the announcement date, and the equally weighted market return. Since infrequent trading is an especially common problem for measuring stock returns of financially distressed firms, abnormal returns are based on Scholes–Williams estimates of the market-model parameters [Scholes and Williams (1977)].

Separate results are presented for the total sample, and for a subsample of 90 restructuring attempts (including 38 successful and 52 failed restructurings) where the initial public announcement contains a reference to either a default or what appears to be the actual commencement of negotiations with lenders. Announcements in the latter sample may contain relatively more surprise, and therefore provide a more powerful test of the market's ability to discriminate between firms that ultimately either succeed or fail to restructure their debt privately.

For the total sample, two-day average returns associated with the initial announcement of a debt restructuring equal −1.6 percent for firms that successfully restructure their debt, and −6.3 percent for firms whose restructuring attempt ultimately fails. These returns are significantly different at the 5 percent level (t-statistic of 2.50). Corresponding returns estimated for the sample of 'surprise' announcements are −3.0 and −8.7 percent, and are significantly different at the 10 percent level (t-statistic of 1.90). Although less significant results are obtained for the 'surprise' sample (which may be attributable to the smaller sample size), both sets of results are consistent with the market being able to distinguish in advance which firms are more likely to be successful at restructuring their debt privately. As pointed out above, these results do not allow us to identify what specific information the market uses in forming its prediction.

Table 8 also reports two-day abnormal returns for the announcement of the outcome of a debt restructuring. For unsuccessful attempts to restructure, this is the announcement of a firm's Chapter 11 filing. For successful restructurings, abnormal returns around the outcome announcement are insignificantly different from zero, for both samples. For unsuccessful restructurings, abnormal returns are significantly negative around the announce-

Table 8

Two-day average returns associated with the initial announcement of a private debt restructuring, and of the first announcement of the restructuring's resolution. Figures are based on a sample of 80 firms that successfully restructured their debt to avoid bankruptcy, and 89 firms that were ultimately unsuccessful in restructuring their debt and filed under Chapter 11 of the U.S. Bankrutpcy Code. Announcement dates are determined from the *Wall Street Journal*. All announcements take place between 1978 and 1988. In panel B, results are based on a subsample of 90 debt restructurings (47 successful and 43 unsuccessful) that begin with the announcement of a default or for which the actual commencement date of the restructuring is known. *t*-statistics are given in parentheses.[a]

Announcement type	(1) Successful debt restructuring	(2) Unsuccessful debt restructuring	*t*-statistic of (2) minus (1)
	Panel A: Total sample		
(A) Initiation of debt restructuring	−0.016 (1.53)	−0.063 (4.03)[b]	(2.50)[c]
Sample size	68	57	
(B) Resolution of debt restructuring	0.007 (0.63)	−0.167 (6.68)[b]	(6.37)[b]
Sample size	66	38	
t-statistic of (A) minus (B)	(1.51)	(3.53)[b]	
	Panel B: Restructurings that begin with a default or for which actual commencement date is known		
(A) Initiation of debt restructuring	−0.030 (1.94)[d]	−0.087 (3.39)[b]	(1.90)[d]
Sample size	37	31	
(B) Resolution of debt restructuring	−0.009 (0.70)	−0.166 (5.98)[b]	(5.16)[b]
Sample size	34	19	
t-statistic of (A) minus (B)	(1.07)	(2.09)[c]	

[a]See table 1 for a definition of debt restructuring and bankruptcy. The two-day average return is an average of daily returns realized on the *Wall Street Journal* announcement day and the preceding day. Stock returns are obtained from the 1988 CRSP daily returns file.

[b]*p*-value ≤ 0.01.

[c]*p*-value ≤ 0.05.

[d]*p*-value ≤ 0.10.

ment of the Chapter 11 filing, again for both samples (respective abnormal returns are −16.7 and −16.6 percent, with corresponding *t*-statistics of 6.68 and 5.98).

When these results are combined with the initial-announcement returns, it appears that stockholders do better over the entire restructuring interval when their firms ultimately settle with creditors out of court. This impression

Table 9

Average cumulative returns for successful and unsuccessful debt restructurings. Returns are measured from one day before the commencement of restructuring to day on which success of restructuring attempt is determined. Figures are based on a sample of 80 firms that successfully restructured their debt to avoid bankruptcy, and 89 firms that were ultimately unsuccessful in restructuring their debt and filed under Chapter 11 of the U.S. Bankruptcy Code. Announcement dates are determined from the *Wall Street Journal*. All announcements take place between 1978 and 1988. In panel B, results are based on a subsample of 90 debt restructurings (47 successful and 43 unsuccessful) that begin with the announcement of a default or for which the actual commencement date of the restructuring is known. *t*-statistics are given in parentheses.[a]

Outcome of debt restructuring	Average cumulative return
Panel A: Total sample	
(A) Successful	0.414 (2.71)[c]
Sample size	69
(B) Unsuccessful	−0.399 (3.28)[b]
Sample size	55
t-statistic of (A) minus (B)	(4.17)[b]
Panel B: Restructurings that begin with a default or for which actual commencement date is known	
(A) Successful	0.713 (3.21)[b]
Sample size	38
(B) Unsuccessful	−0.361 (2.19)[c]
Sample size	30
t-statistic of (A) minus (B)	(3.88)[b]

[a]See table 1 for a definition of debt restructuring and bankruptcy. Stock return data are obtained from the 1988 CRSP daily returns file.

[b]p-value ≤ 0.01.

[c]p-value ≤ 0.05.

is confirmed in table 9, which reports average cumulative abnormal returns for the entire restructuring interval. For the total sample, stockholders of firms that successfully restructured realized average abnormal returns of 41.4 percent over the restructuring interval, whereas stockholders of ultimately bankrupt firms realized abnormal returns of −39.9 percent. Corresponding returns for the 'surprise' subsample are 71.3 and −36.1 percent. For both panels, differences in returns are significant at the 5 percent level. These results are not driven by outliers. Seventy-two percent of cumulative returns are negative for firms that ultimately file for Chapter 11, and 58 percent are positive for firms that successfully restructure. The percentage of negative returns is significantly different between the two subsamples at the 5 percent level.

These results suggest that, for whatever reason, stockholders on average fare less well in bankruptcy than in private renegotiation, and thus have incentives to settle with creditors privately. Consistent with this possibility, stockholders seldom exercise their option to file for Chapter 11 without first attempting to restructure the firm's debt privately (see table 2). An alternative interpretation, however, is that firms that file for bankruptcy experience unexpectedly worse operating performance than firms that ultimately restructure their debt privately. Thus larger stock-price declines for bankrupt firms may not be due to the recontracting process itself, but instead reflect a selection bias resulting from the fact that bankrupt firms are inherently less profitable (subsequent to the bankruptcy filing).

Finally, attempts to relate abnormal stock returns to the explanatory variables used in the logit regressions yielded insignificant results. Cross-sectional regressions of abnormal returns against various combinations of these variables generally produced adjusted R-squares of less than 5 percent, and individual coefficient estimates were almost always insignificant. The insignificant results cannot be attributed to multicollinearity or heteroskedasticity of the error terms. The low explanatory power of these regressions is consistent with the market's using more information to forecast the outcome of private renegotiation than is captured by the explanatory variables.

5. Conclusion

In this study we investigate how financially distressed firms restructure their debt. For a sample of 169 distressed companies, we investigate firms' economic incentives to choose between private renegotiation and formal bankruptcy as alternative mechanisms for dealing with default. In about half of all cases, financially distressed firms successfully restructure their debt outside of Chapter 11. Financial distress is more likely to be resolved through private renegotiation when more of the firm's assets are intangible, and relatively more debt is owed to banks; private renegotiation is less likely to succeed when there are more distinct classes of debt outstanding. Analysis of stock returns suggests that the market is also able to identify in advance which firms are more likely to succeed in restructuring their debt privately. Cumulative stock returns are significantly higher when debt is restructured privately; thus on average stockholders have incentives to avoid bankruptcy and settle out of court.

One implication of our results is that troubled companies are likely to find informal alternatives to bankruptcy increasingly attractive in dealing with financial distress. As recently argued by Jensen (1989a, b), companies that have relatively more debt outstanding will default sooner if they are being mismanaged. This has the virtue of forcing management to undertake corrective changes in corporate policy sooner, thus preserving more of the firm's going-concern value. Consistent with this, the present study finds that insolvent firms with relatively high going-concern value are more likely to restructure their debt privately, because more of this value tends to be lost for a variety of reasons (including through asset sales) when debt and the firm's operations are reorganized in Chapter 11. Thus, future defaults by the current generation of highly levered companies may be increasingly resolved through private renegotiation.

Our results also have important implications for interpreting recent evidence that shows an increase in the default rate of high-yield publicly traded bonds [Altman (1989), Asquith et al. (1989)]. We present evidence that restructuring of publicly traded debt almost always takes the form of an exchange offer, and is generally completed within two months. The out-of-pocket costs incurred in connection with these offers are economically insignificant (amounting on average to less than 1 percent of the firm's book value of assets). It remains an unanswered empirical question whether other default-related costs are sufficiently high to warrant continued concern over the recent rise in defaults.

Appendix

Case studies of attempts by ten firms to restructure their debt privately to avoid bankruptcy

This appendix presents brief case studies describing the experience of ten firms that attempted to restructure their debt privately to avoid bankruptcy. Each case study describes major events relating to the restructuring, general terms (either proposed or adopted) for restructuring the firm's debt, and other relevant information. The cases are based on information contained in published reports in the *Wall Street Journal* and disclosed in firms' 10k reports, shareholder proxy statements, and exchange-offer prospectuses. The ten firms examined here represent a cross-section of various possible restructuring plan types and outcomes. At the beginning of each case we classify the debt restructuring according to the principal types of debt involved, and whether the restructuring attempt was successful (i.e., whether the firm avoided having to file for Chapter 11). In addition, for each case we report (i) the period over which the restructuring took place (as defined in section 3 of the text), (ii) the Scholes–Williams cumulative abnormal common stock return over the restructuring interval (labeled *car*), and (iii) the firm's common stock price at the beginning and end of the restructuring, or the most recent prices reported inside the restructuring interval (labelled *p0* and *p1*, respectively). Stock prices are obtained from Standard and Poor's *Daily*

Stock Price Record. Reported time intervals are all rounded to the nearest month. 'n.a.' means that cumulative abnormal returns could not be calculated because there were insufficient stock returns available as a result of nontrading.

Brock Hotel Corporation Classification: *Successful restructuring of bank and publicly traded debt, accompanied by stock placement with financial advisor to restructuring and common stock rights offering (6/28/85–6/26/86; car* = n.a.; $p0 = 2\frac{7}{8}$, $p1 = \frac{2}{8}$).

The company made an exchange offer to holders of its eight publicly traded debenture issues, offering a package of common stock and new debentures (having a lower coupon rate, payable in cash or common stock). Although 86 percent of the debentures were tendered under the offer, it was decided that the offer would not be sufficient to resolve the company's financial problems. As a result, the company implemented a comprehensive plan to restructure all of its long-term debt. Under the plan, all of the new debentures issued under the previous exchange offer were converted into various amounts of common and preferred stock, common stock options, and cash. In addition, the company acquired the bank debt and capitalized lease obligations of its operating subsidiaries (using a combination of cash, warrants, and common stock options), and exchanged new debentures for all of the preferred stock of a partly owned subsidiary. Various other debt was also restructured, including liabilities arising from canceled operating leases and company guarantees, and the lease agreement on the company's headquarters building. A critical feature of the plan was a rights offering of 266 million common shares to current stockholders (only about 13 million shares were outstanding before the offering). Following a vote of the common stockholders, the plan was adopted one year from the announcement of the initial exchange offer. A major role in the restructuring was played by The Hallwood Group Inc., which the company engaged as a financial advisor to the restructuring. In addition to managing the rights offering, Hallwood obtained secured lenders' consent to the plan by agreeing to guarantee the minimum proceeds that would be realized from selling various assets under the plan. In return for providing these and other services. Hallwood received the right to elect a majority of the company's board of directors (including its chairman), and was issued 14 percent of the company's common stock.

Crawford Energy Inc. Classification: *Unsuccessful restructuring of bank and trade debt (10/20/83–9/30/85; car* = −63.3%; $p0 = 3\frac{1}{8}$, $p1 = \frac{2}{8}$).

Following eight months of negotiations, the company eliminated most of its $10 million in trade debt by offering new common stock to its 44 trade creditors in a negotiated exchange offer. In return for canceling almost half of the debt, trade creditors received 21 percent of the company's common stock. Also participating in the plan was A. Gail Crawford, the company's founder, chairman, and CEO. Mr Crawford, who before the offer held 79 percent of the company's stock, was issued new stock representing 33 percent of the total shares outstanding after the offer, in return for his personally assuming the remainder of the debt. Four months later, the company announced an agreement in principle with its two banks to restructure its bank loans. Although payment on these loans was four months overdue, neither bank had yet formally declared the company in default. This agreement, which provided for an extension of the loans' due date, was in default eight months later. The banks then agreed to fund the company on a monthly basis while it sought to sell off assets or obtain an infusion of outside equity. Four months after that, the company filed for Chapter 11.

Crystal Oil Company Classification: *Unsuccessful restructuring of bank, trade, and publicly traded debt (6/11/85–10/1/86; car* = n.a.; $p0 = 2$, $p1 = \frac{3}{8}$).

The company entered into an agreement with a major supplier to extend payment on its trade debt, in return for issuing the supplier a secured note. As disclosed in the company's 10k report, it was also in technical default on a secured mortgage note held by a bank, although details concerning how (or whether) the default was resolved were not reported. At the same time, the company undertook an exchange offer for its six publicly traded debenture issues, offering a package of common stock and new secured notes (having a higher coupon rate, payable in either cash or common stock). The old debentures represented approximately 80 percent of the company's long-term debt. Four months later, after extending and sweetening the offer seven times, the company accepted all 70 percent of the debentures that were tendered, resulting in the issuance to noteholders of approximately 26 percent of the company's common stock (following payment of interest on the new notes with common stock, noteholders' ownership increased to 59 percent within three months). Despite the success of the exchange offer, the company subsequently found it necessary to again restructure its debt. Within approximately a year of the conclusion of its exchange offer, the company made a 'prepackaged' Chapter 11 filing, after having first obtained creditors' consent to a reorganization plan. The company emerged from Chapter 11 after only three months.

Dunes Hotels and Casinos Inc. Classification: *Successful restructuring of bank and other privately-placed debt, accompanied by outside stock placement (8/31/83–2/6/84; car* = 102.9%; $p0 = 4\frac{4}{8}$, $p1 = 6\frac{4}{8}$).

For six months, the company attempted to restructure a $30 million debt held by two private investors, Ronald and Stuart Perlman. Initially, the Perlmans agreed to acquire the company for $80 million in notes and the assumption of $105 million in debt. This agreement was replaced by another under which the Perlmans were to convert their debt into approximately 45 percent of the company's common stock. The restructuring of this and other debt was deemed essential to avert a bankruptcy filing. Finally, the company reached an agreement to place 41 percent of its common stock with John Jack Anderson, a private investor with prior management experience in the industry. At about the same time, the company restructured approximately $80 million of debt owed to its three institutional lenders (a bank, a leasing company, and American Financial Corporation), resulting in various payment deferrals. Terms of the agreement gave Mr. Anderson effective voting control over additional shares held by management, increasing the percentage of common shares he either owned or controlled to 51 percent. Mr. Anderson was named chairman of the company, succeeding Morris Shenker, who prior to the restructuring held 41 percent of the company's stock. Mr. Shenker, who remained CEO, had filed for personal bankruptcy four months previously.

Lamson & Sessions Co. Classification: *Successful restructuring of bank debt, accompanied by new private debt placement (12/31/82–4/29/85; car* = 51.3%; $p0 = 3\frac{1}{8}$, $p1 = 3\frac{6}{8}$).

The company disclosed in its annual report that it was not in compliance with 'certain' covenants in its loan agreements, and had been attempting to restructure its debt to 24 bank and insurance company lenders. The company had no publicly traded debt. Ten months into the negotiations, the company announced that the restructuring effort had stalled because of disagreements among lenders over terms. The company refused to explain what the differences were, or disclose the identity of the lenders. A debt restructuring plan was announced five months later. Under the plan, the company's institutional debt was to be converted into cash, new secured notes, and convertible preferred stock (with dividends payable in either cash or common stock). Assuming full conversion of the preferred stock, the lenders would hold 34 percent of the firm's common stock. The cash payment, representing 24 percent of the balance owed, was raised through a new short-term secured credit facility with Congress Financial Corp. As part of the plan, borrowings under this facility were to be reduced by applying part of the proceeds raised from the subsequent divestiture of an operating subsidiary. The plan was adopted three months later at the company's annual meeting, where stockholders approved a requisite increase in the number of authorized common shares. At the same meeting, the company's chairman relinquished the post of CEO to the company president, and announced that he would soon also step down as chairman. Ten months later, the company repurchased (with cash) all of the new notes for 60 percent of their face value, and exchanged new common stock warrants for approximately a third of the preferred stock held by lenders.

Oak Industries Inc. Classification: *Successful restructuring of publicly traded debt, accompanied by outside stock placement* (*2/11/85–5/6/86; car* = −33.3%; $p0 = 2\frac{1}{8}$, $p1 = 1\frac{4}{8}$).

The company, which had no bank debt, offered to exchange a package of notes, warrants, and common stock for its three outstanding publicly traded debenture issues. The new notes had a lower promised coupon rate and identical face value, and were to mature approximately ten years before the old debentures. The notes also allowed payment of interest in either cash or common stock (the company indicated that interest would be paid in common stock for the 'foreseeable future'). After extending the offer three times, the company accepted all 79 percent of the old debentures tendered, two months following the initial announcement of the offer. Approximately one week before the offer's expiration, the company's president resigned to 'pursue other business interests', amid an SEC investigation into alleged disclosure violations by the company. Seven months after the first exchange offer concluded, the company announced a new exchange offer for all of its publicly traded debt, in which holders were offered a package of cash and common stock. The cash part of the offer was financed by the sale of a major operating division and block of new equity securities to Allied-Signal Inc. (not previously a stockholder). The equity placement, which was made conditional on the success of the debt restructuring, consisted of common stock and warrants, representing about 20 percent of the company's common stock outstanding at the conclusion of the offer (assuming full exercise of the warrants). As part of the agreement, Allied-Signal also received three seats on the company's seven-member board of directors. The second exchange offer and the transaction with Allied-Signal were completed five months later, resulting in a doubling of the total number of common shares outstanding.

Petro Lewis Corp. Classification: *Successful restructuring of publicly traded debt, effected through acquisition of the company* (*3/28/85–12/31/86; car* = −50.2%; $p0 = 4\frac{1}{8}$, $p1 = 2\frac{1}{8}$).

The company attempted to restructure its publicly traded debt through a series of three exchange offers. Approximately 75 percent of the company's long-term debt was publicly traded. In the first offer, which took two months to complete, the company sought to exchange new (secured and unsecured) notes and common stock for one of its note issues and three issues of preferred stock. Approximately 80 percent of the notes, and on average 58 percent of the preferred-stock issues, were tendered and accepted. Five months later, the company undertook a new exchange offer for four of its outstanding issues of subordinated notes and debentures. Holders were offered a package of new secured notes (carrying a higher coupon rate but lower face value), common stock, and cash. After several extensions of the expiration date, the offer concluded two months later, with about 50 percent of holders tendering. The third and final offer was announced five months later, and consisted of an offer to exchange a package of new secured and convertible notes and common stock for all nine of the company's publicly traded debt issues outstanding (including those that were issued under the earlier exchange offers). The company terminated this offer four months later, after deciding that it did not 'represent a viable alternative for the company'. Two months previously, an agreement had been announced in which Freeport-McMoRan Inc. would acquire the company to enable it to avert a bankruptcy filing, for a total price of about $770 million. Ultimately Freeport purchased the company by making a public tender offer for all of its outstanding publicly traded securities (debt as well as equity). The time that elapsed between the initial exchange offer and the consummation of the merger was approximately 20 months.

Seiscom Delta Inc. Classification: *Successful restructuring of bank debt, followed by bankruptcy more than one year later* (*5/12/83–4/26/85*; *car* = −65.3%; *p0* = $5\frac{3}{8}$, *p1* = $1\frac{1}{8}$).

The company announced that it restructured its bank debt by obtaining a one-year extension of the date on which its revolving bank loans would convert to term loans. In the *WSJ* story that reported the restructuring, the company refused to identify which banks were involved, and no mention of the transaction was made in the firm's 10k report for that year. The company had no publicly traded debt outstanding. Fourteen months later, the company was granted a 'second' waiver on a bank loan covenant (the first was not reported) that was in default because the company had exceeded the borrowing limit specified in its revolving credit agreement. Two weeks later, D. Gale Reese, chairman and CEO of the company, resigned under pressure from its banks. The *WSJ* quoted a company spokesman as saying: 'It's just a matter of the bank being willing to do certain things provided Gale Reese was not on the team.' In the same story that reported Mr. Reese's resignation, it was revealed that one of the company's banks granted a third waiver of the same loan covenant. Nine months later, a definitive agreement was reached to restructure the company's bank debt. The agreement provided for the banks to forgive 52 percent of the outstanding bank-loan balance, and grant a seven-month waiver of interest and nineteen-month waiver of principal owed on the remaining balance. In return, the banks were given a package of common stock, convertible preferred stock, and warrants, which together represented 77 percent of the company's outstanding common stock (assuming full conversion of preferred stock and warrants). In addition, the banks were granted an increased security interest in all of the company's assets. The agreement also provided for forgiveness of certain lease payments owed on the company's headquarters building. Seventeen months later, the company and four of its wholly owned subsidiaries filed for Chapter 11.

Tiger International Inc. Classification: *Successful restructuring of bank and publicly traded debt by parent company, accompanied by bankruptcy of subsidiary* (*2/14/83–3/25/85*; *car* = 18.3%; *p0* = $7\frac{1}{8}$, *p1* = $8\frac{6}{8}$).

The company and its bank lenders agreed on a tentative restructuring plan four months following the company's decision to unilaterally suspend interest and principal payments on about half of its total $1.8 billion in debt. Regarding the company's decision to suspend payments on its debt, a company spokesman was paraphrased by the *WSJ* as saying that 'the company chose to announce suspension of interest and principal on debt, rather than issue a joint release with lenders, because of the large number of banks involved (60, including certain other unspecified 'lending institutions') and the complexity of the loan agreements'. Under the proposed plan, the company was to be granted an extension on scheduled payments owed by three operating subsidiaries, receive a new revolving credit line from an existing lender, and implement an exchange offer for its two publicly traded issues of debentures. Regarding lenders' reaction to the plan, the firm's chairman noted: 'It's in the lenders' interest to do this. All of them agree that the going concern is the important thing.' On the day before the announcement of the plan, it was announced that the company's president and financial vice president had both resigned; the company denied allegations that this action had been prompted by its lenders. Interest on the new credit line was tied to the company's future earnings performance. The exchange offer took three months to complete, with approximately 81 percent of all bonds being tendered. Tendering debenture-holders received a package of new debentures (having a lower face value, shorter average maturity, and identical coupon rate), common stock, and warrants; interest on the new debentures was payable in either cash or common stock. Final agreement on the restructuring of subsidiary debt was reached by two of the subsidiaries seven months after the initial plan was proposed, and by the third, a year after the plan proposal date. Shortly thereafter the company undertook an additional exchange offer for two issues of publicly traded debt owed by one of its subsidiaries, offering a package of common stock and warrants. Fourteen months following the initial suspension of debt payments, the company revealed in its annual report that it was still attempting to restructure the debt of a subsidiary. Eight months later, the subsidiary independently filed for Chapter 11, after it failed to reach a standstill agreement with its banks on a $132 million secured note that was in default.

Verna Corp. Classification: *Successful restructuring of bank and privately placed debt (12/31/82–4/29/85; car* = −136.7%; *p0* = $4\frac{7}{8}$, *p1* = $\frac{13}{16}$).

After reporting a quarterly loss, the company granted its two banks a security interest in 39 drilling rigs (although no default was reported). Six months later the company announced that it had restructured its bank debt. The banks, which were owed approximately $28 million, were given warrants convertible into 13 percent of the company's common stock, a security interest in accounts receivable, and a 'fee' of $850,000. In return, the company was granted a thirteen-month deferral of interest and principal payments, and an increase in its borrowing limit under an existing revolving loan. Concurrently with the bank debt restructuring, the company privately placed $1 million of new secured subordinated notes with a group of three venture capital companies. In return for purchasing the notes, said companies were given common stock warrants for 8 percent of the common stock and three permanent seats on the board of directors. Ten months later, both the bank debt and new notes hadto be restructured, resulting in various payment deferrals and increased grants of security. Among other things, the banks were given the right to force certain asset sales to effect repayment of the debt. Eighteen months later, the company restructured its debt for a third and final time, following stockholder approval of the transaction. Debt owed to the two banks was converted into an issue of new secured notes, convertible preferred stock, and preferred stock warrants, representing 56 percent of the company's common stock (assuming full conversion of the banks' claims). The notes held by the three venture capital lenders were exchanged for new common stock, representing 24 percent of the common stock then outstanding. Three months later, four of the firm's five outside directors resigned after the company's insurer withdrew its liability coverage.

References

Altman, Edward, 1984, A further investigation of the bankruptcy cost question, Journal of Finance 39, 1067–1089.

Altman, Edward, 1989, Measuring corporate bond mortality and performance, Journal of Finance 44, 909–922.

Ang, James, Jess Chua, and John McConnell, 1982, The administrative costs of corporate bankruptcy: A note, Journal of Finance 37, 219–226.

Asquith, Paul, David Mullins, Jr., and Eric Wolff, 1989, Original issue high yield bonds: Aging analyses of defaults, exchanges and calls, Journal of Finance 44, 923–952.

Aivazian, Varouj and Jeffrey Callen, 1983, Reorganization in bankruptcy and the issue of strategic risk, Journal of Banking and Finance 7, 119–133.

Baldwin, Carliss and Scott Mason, 1983, The resolution of claims in financial distress: The case of Massey Ferguson, Journal of Finance 38, 505–516.

Bradley, Michael, Anand Desai, and E. Han Kim, 1983, The rationale behind interfirm tender offers, Journal of Financial Economics 11, 183–206.

Brown, David, 1989, Claimholder incentive conflicts in reorganization: The role of bankruptcy law, Review of Financial Studies 2, 109–123.

Bulow, Jeremy and John Shoven, 1978, The bankruptcy decision, Bell Journal of Economics 9, 436–445.

DeAngelo, Linda, 1988, Managerial competition, information costs, and corporate governance: The use of accounting performance measures in proxy contests, Journal of Accounting and Economics 10, 3–36.

DeAngelo, Harry, Linda DeAngelo, and Douglas Skinner, 1990, An empirical investigation of the relation between accounting choice and dividend policy in troubled companies, Unpublished paper (University of Michigan, Ann Arbor, MI).

DeNatale, Andrew, 1981, The creditors' committee under the Bankruptcy Code: A primer, American Bankruptcy Law Journal 55, 43–62.

Douglas-Hamilton, Margaret, 1975, Creditor liabilities resulting from improper interference with the management of a financially troubled debtor, Business Lawyer 31, 343–365.

Eberhart, Allan, William Moore, and Rodney Roenfeldt, 1990, Security pricing and deviations from the absolute priority rule in bankruptcy proceedings, Journal of Finance, forthcoming.

Franks, Julian and Walter Torous, 1989, An empirical investigation of U.S. firms in reorganization, Journal of Finance 44, 747–769.

Giammarino, Ronald, 1989, The resolution of financial distress, Review of Financial Studies 2, 25–47.

Gilson, Stuart, 1989, Management turnover and financial distress, Journal of Financial Economics 25, 241–262.

Gilson, Stuart, 1990, Bankruptcy, boards, banks, and blockholders, Journal of Financial Economics, this volume.

Gould, John, 1973, The economics of legal conflicts, Journal of Legal Studies 2, 279–300.

Green, Jerry and Jean-Jacques Laffont, 1987, Renegotiation and the form of efficient contracts, Unpublished paper (Harvard University, Cambridge, MA).

Hart, Oliver and John Moore, 1989, Default and renegotiation: A dynamic model of debt, Unpublished paper (Massachusetts Institute of Technology, Cambridge, MA).

Haugen, Robert and Lemma Senbet, 1978, The insignificance of bankruptcy costs to the theory of optimal capital structure, Journal of Finance 33, 383–393.

Hoshi, Takeo, Anil Kashyap, and David Scharfstein, 1990, The role of banks in reducing the costs of financial distress in Japan, Journal of Financial Economics, this volume.

Jackson, Thomas, 1986, The logic and limits of bankruptcy law (Harvard University Press, Cambridge, MA).

James, Christopher, 1987, Some evidence on the uniqueness of bank loans, Journal of Financial Economics 19, 217–235.

Jensen, Michael, 1989a, Active investors, LBOs, and the privatization of bankruptcy, Journal of Applied Corporate Finance 2, 35–44.

Jensen, Michael, 1989b, Eclipse of the public corporation, Harvard Business Review, Sept./Oct., 61–74.

Huberman, Gur and Charles Kahn, 1988, Default, foreclosure, and strategic renegotation, Unpublished paper (Columbia University, New York, NY).

King, Lawrence, 1979, Chapter 11 of the 1978 Bankrutpcy Code, American Bankruptcy Law Journal 53, 107–131.

Klee, Kenneth, 1979, All you ever wanted to know about cram down under the new bankruptcy code, American Bankruptcy Law Journal 53, 133–171.

Lang, Larry, Rene Stulz, and Ralph Walkling, 1988, Managerial performance, Tobin's q and the gains from successful tender offers, Journal of Financial Economics 24, 137–154.

Maddala, G., 1983, Limited-dependent and qualitative variables in econometrics (Cambridge University Press, Cambridge).

Manski, Charles and Daniel McFadden, 1983, Alternative estimators and sample designs for discrete choice analysis, in: Charles Manski and Daniel McFadden, eds., Structural analysis of discrete data with econometric applications (MIT Press, Boston, MA).

Mooradian, Robert, 1989, Recapitalizations and the free-rider problem, Unpublished paper (University of Florida, Gainesville, FL).

Myers, Stewart, 1977, Determinants of corporate borrowing, Journal of Financial Economics 5, 147–176.

Roe, Mark, 1987, The voting prohibition in bond workouts, The Yale Law Journal 97, 232–279.

Scholes, Myron and Joseph Williams, 1977, Estimating betas from non-synchronous data, Journal of Financial Economics 5, 309–327.

Smith, C. and Jerold Warner, 1979, On financial contracting: An analysis of bond covenants, Journal of Financial Economics 7, 117–161.

Stein, Sol, 1989, A feast for lawyers (M. Evans and Company, Inc., New York, NY).

Titman, Sheridan, 1984, The effect of capital structure on a firm's liquidation decision, Journal of Financial Economics 13, 137–151.

Trost, Ronald, 1979, Business reorganizations under Chapter 11 of the new Bankruptcy Code, Business Lawyer, April, 1309–1346.

Wall Street Journal, 1988, Corporate finance, 'leveraged to the hilt', October 25, p. A11.

Warner, Jerold, 1977a, Bankruptcy, absolute priority and the pricing of risky debt claims, Journal of Financial Economics 4, 239–276.

Warner, Jerold, 1977b, Bankruptcy costs: Some evidence, Journal of Finance 32, 337–347.

Weiss, Lawrence, 1990, Bankruptcy resolution: Direct costs and violation of priority of claims, Journal of Financial Economics, this volume.

White, Michelle, 1989, The corporate bankruptcy decision, The Journal of Economic Perspectives 3, 129–151.

Zinbarg, Edward, 1975, The private placement loan agreement, Financial Analysts Journal 31, 33–52.

[15]

ELSEVIER Journal of Financial Economics 46 (1997) 29–65

JOURNAL OF Financial ECONOMICS

Corporate restructuring during performance declines in Japan[1]

Jun-Koo Kang[a], Anil Shivdasani*,[b]

[a] *College of Business Administration, Korea University, Seoul 136-701, South Korea*
[b] *Kenan-Flagler Business School, University of North Carolina, Chapel Hill, NC 27599, USA*

Received 16 November 1993; received in revised form 4 February 1997

Abstract

This paper documents the restructuring of 92 Japanese corporations that experienced a substantial decline in operating performance between 1986 and 1990. These firms implement a number of downsizing measures such as asset sales, plant closures, and employee layoffs. Firms also expand and diversify, and often restructure their internal operations. Compared to US firms with a similar decline in performance, however, Japanese firms are less likely to downsize, and layoffs affect a smaller fraction of their workforce. The frequency of asset downsizing and layoffs in Japanese firms increases with the ownership by the firm's main bank and other blockholders. Blockholders also increase the probability of management turnover, outside director removals and outside director additions, but decrease the likelihood of acquisitions. We document improvements in operating performance following downsizing actions in Japan.

Keywords: Restructuring; Financial distress; Japanese corporate governance; Ownership structure; Main bank system

JEL classification: G32; G33; G34; L14

* Corresponding author. Tel.: + 1 919 962 3182; E-mail: shivdasa@icarus.unc.edu

[1] We thank David Denis, Geoffrey Lysaught, Steve Kaplan (the referee), Bill Schwert (the editor) and seminar participants at Arizona, Indiana, Michigan State, North Carolina, Pittsburgh, and Purdue universities, the 1997 American Finance Association, and the 1997 Association of Financial Economists for helpful comments. We are grateful to Terry Ursacki for assisting in collecting some of the data used in this study. Shivdasani acknowledges support from the Center for International Business Education and Research and an All-University Research Grant at Michigan State University.

PII S0304-405(97)00024-X

1. Introduction

The ability of firms to respond to a decline in performance, and the nature of these responses, are important factors that affect their organizational efficiency. In this paper, we investigate the nature of corporate reorganization activities during poor performance for a sample of Japanese corporations. While there is an extensive literature on the restructuring activities of US corporations, relatively little systematic evidence exists for Japanese firms.[2]

Our analysis is motivated by the dramatically different nature of contractual relationships that govern Japanese corporations. In the United States, banks are restricted from owning equity of other firms.[3] In contrast, Japanese banks are permitted to own up to 5% of the outstanding shares of their client firms.[4] Most Japanese firms maintain ties to a main bank, which is typically the firm's largest lender and also has a substantial equity ownership stake. In addition, firms also maintain close trading and ownership ties with other corporations. Sometimes, these lending, ownership, and trading ties arise from a firm's affiliation to an industrial group known as a keiretsu, although firms not affiliated with a keiretsu also maintain ties to a main bank and other shareholders.

The extent of external takeover activity also differs dramatically between the US and Japan. In contrast to the extensive takeover market in the US, tender offers, mergers, and proxy contests are virtually unknown among large Japanese corporations.[5] Several authors have argued that the external takeover market plays an important role in the restructuring of US firms. Bhagat et al. (1990) and Berger and Ofek (1996a) document that successfully acquired firms usually undergo an extensive restructuring involving asset sales, plant closures, and layoffs. Mitchell and Lehn (1990) find that targets of takeover attempts often divest prior acquisitions that were viewed unfavorably by the market. In addition, Berger and Ofek (1996b), and Denis et al. (1997) argue that firms that implement corporate refocusing programs often do so in the presence of external control pressures such as takeover attempts and block share purchases.

Given the importance of external corporate control activity in the restructuring of US corporations and the absence of such activity for Japanese firms, we examine how the extent and nature of restructuring activities among Japanese

---

[2] See for example, Gilson (1990), Gilson et al. (1990), John et al. (1992), Ofek (1993), Brown et al. (1993, 1994), Asquith et al. (1994), and Lang et al. (1995).

[3] Roe (1990) provides a detailed discussion.

[4] Prior to 1987, the Japanese Anti-Monopoly Law allowed banks to own up to 10% of a firm's outstanding equity. Since 1987, the legal limit has been lowered to 5% of the outstanding shares.

[5] See Kester (1991), Kaplan (1994), and Kang and Yamada (1996) for evidence on the takeover market in Japan.

firms compares with that of US firms. Our analysis compares 92 publicly traded Japanese manufacturing firms and 114 publicly traded US manufacturing firms that were initially healthy, but suffered a substantial decline in their operating performance in a given year during 1985 to 1990.

We find that, in many respects, the responses of Japanese firms are surprisingly similar to those of US firms. Over 20% of the Japanese firms engage in some form of contraction of their assets or operations, such as asset sales, plant closures, or the withdrawal from a line of business. Almost 30% of the firms implement significant changes in their employment practices such as layoffs, early retirement incentives, or the reduction in salary and bonuses. One-third of the firms experience turnover of the top executive, and in one-third of these cases, the successor is appointed from outside the firm. There is however, heterogeneity in the manner in which firms react. Some firms expand their operations, while some downsize, and several do both. Some firms undertake actions to reduce operating costs and increase production efficiencies, while others respond by cutting inventories and selling marketable securities. These changes occur in the absence of takeover attempts or threats, and outside of formal workouts and court-supervised proceedings.

Comparison of the Japanese responses to those of US firms also suggests some important differences. First, while downsizing of assets occurs in about 23% of the Japanese firms, the corresponding frequency is almost 50% for US firms. In addition, layoffs in Japanese corporations result in a smaller change in firm employment than do layoffs in US firms. For US firms that announce layoffs, employment drops by almost 15% in the two years surrounding the performance drop; the comparable drop is only 4.7% for Japanese firms. Japanese firms also appear more likely to expand their operations than US firms. Of the Japanese firms in the sample, 76% undertake some expansion activity, compared to 55% for the US sample. There is also some evidence that the Japanese expansions, particularly those that occur by means of an acquisition, are likely to represent diversification activities. In contrast, the majority of acquisitions by US firms occur in related industries.

Consistent with prior studies on restructuring of US corporations, we find that our sample of US firms experiences a high incidence of external takeover activity. Given the absence of this activity for Japanese firms, we investigate whether alternative mechanisms that facilitate restructuring exist in Japan. Our results suggest that the Japanese actions are systematically related to the distribution of ownership claims. Firms with greater equity ownership by the main bank are more likely to engage in contraction policies by the use of asset sales, plant closures, and discontinuation of operations. In addition, greater equity ownership by the main bank also increases the probability of employee layoffs and the removal of outside directors from the board. We also find that blockholders other than the main bank play a very important role in influencing the probability that certain operational actions will be taken in response to the performance decline. Increased blockholder ownership is associated with a greater likelihood of downsizing, and a reduction in the likelihood of making acquisitions. Blockholders also play an important role in the likelihood of control change in our sample firms. We document that ownership by blockholders increases the likelihood of management change, the likelihood that the incumbent president is replaced with a successor from outside the firm, the probability of removal of outside members of the board, and the probability that new outside directors are appointed to the board.

Our evidence is consistent with recent theoretical arguments. Admati and Pfleiderer (1994) consider an entrepreneur who has an incentive to continue projects even when it is optimal to terminate them. They demonstrate that such suboptimal decisions will be avoided with a presence of an informed creditor with a fixed fraction claim, such as equity. Admati and Pfleiderer (1994) suggest that venture capital organizations and Japanese banks and blockholders represent examples of such informed investors. In a similar vein, Jensen (1989) compares the Japanese main bank system to that of LBO partnerships in the US. He argues that the joint ownership of debt and equity claims by informed investors results in stringent managerial monitoring and creates strong incentives for managers to make value-maximizing decisions.

Our analysis confirms and extends related work by Kaplan (1994), Kaplan and Minton (1994), and Kang and Shivdasani (1995) who examine changes in the control rights in Japanese firms. Kaplan (1994) finds that the probability of top management turnover in Japan is negatively and significantly related to various measures of firm performance. Kang and Shivdasani (1995) find that the relation between turnover and performance is stronger for firms with close ties to a main bank. Kaplan and Minton (1994) document that appointments of outsiders to the boards of Japanese corporations are more likely to occur when performance is poor. This paper extends this literature by examining how the investment and operating decisions of Japanese corporations compare to US firms during poor performance. Consistent with the role of Japanese banks and blockholders during turnover events documented by these prior studies, we find that they also have an important influence on operating and investment decisions during periods of poor performance. In this respect, Japanese banks and blockholders perform some of the functions generally thought to be performed by the takeover market in the US.

Our paper is also related to previous work by Hoshi et al. (1990) and Sheard (1994) who examine the role of Japanese banks when firms are financially distressed. Both studies document that the main bank plays a crucial role in restructuring client firms during periods of prolonged financial distress. Unlike these studies however, our sample firms experience at least one year of poor operating performance but most do not experience a prolonged bout of financial distress. Further, our results continue to hold when we exclude the six firms in our sample that become financially distressed as a result of the performance decline. To the extent that observed actions such as downsizing and layoffs represent optimal responses to a shrinking investment opportunity set, our results suggest that main banks and blockholders help preserve firm value by triggering responses even when firms are not financially distressed. Thus, while main banks unarguably assume a critical role during financial distress in Japan, our results imply that the role of main banks is important even when firms are not in financial distress. This interpretation accords with Kaplan (1994) and Kaplan and Minton (1994) who also suggest that main bank monitoring can be important even when firms earn enough to satisfy debt payments.

The paper is organized as follows. Section 2 describes the data. The responses of firms subsequent to the earnings shock are described in Section 3. In Section 4 we conduct a multivariate analysis of firm responses. Section 5 examines the changes in performance of Japanese firms subsequent to the performance drop. Section 6 concludes.

2. Data

In this section, we discuss our sample selection criteria for Japanese and US firms and describe the performance of the sample firms.

2.1. Sample

We construct our sample using data from the Pacific-Basin Capital Markets (PACAP) Research Center data base. Our objective is to identify a set of firms that were initially healthy, but suffer a material drop in performance. Since we are interested in documenting the nature of firm responses, it is important to identify firms at the onset of their poor performance. With this objective in mind, we first identify all manufacturing firms listed on the First Section of the Tokyo Stock Exchange (TSE) during 1985 to 1989 that have a ratio of pretax operating income to assets that exceeds the industry median. To avoid including firms that may be financially distressed prior to the performance shock, we also require that the ratio of operating income to interest expense be greater than one. For this set of 'healthy' firms in a particular year, we examine the subset of firms that experienced a decline of at least 50% in their pretax operating income in the subsequent year. Thus, sample firms experience a performance decline in at least one year in the 1986 to 1990 period. Henceforth, we also refer to the year of the performance decline as the shock year, and the year prior as the base or the pre-shock year.

This procedure results in a sample of 92 firms. Although we do not impose any such a priori restriction, no firm enters our sample twice. Using the ratio of operating income to interest expense as an indicator of financial distress, 6 firms become financially distressed as a result of the performance decline. Of these, 5 firms have negative operating income in the year of the performance shock.

Thus, fewer than 7% of our sample firms become financially distressed in the year of performance shock. In this regard, our sample differs substantially from that of Hoshi et al. (1990), who examine a sample of only financially distressed firms. Our sample selection allows the inclusion of firms that performed poorly, but were possibly able to avoid becoming financially distressed due to subsequent restructuring.

We use an accounting measure of performance, rather than stock returns, to identify the onset of poor performance for two reasons. First, in principle, stock returns can incorporate the ability of certain governance structures to recover from performance declines. For example, if firms with strong ties to a main bank recover quickly from performance shocks, and if this information is reflected in stock returns, then, ceteris paribus, firms with strong bank ties will experience a smaller decline in stock returns, and are less likely to be represented in a sample selected according to stock return performance. Second, as documented in French and Poterba (1991), during our sample period, the average level of the Japanese stock market first rose appreciably, and then experienced a rapid drop. Several observers, referring to this as a 'bubble effect', have questioned the reliability of stock prices in Japan as an accurate measure of firm performance during this period.

One issue of potential concern is whether our sampling procedure introduces any selection bias. Since the PACAP data base does not contain information on firms that were acquired, went bankrupt, or were delisted, there is potential for survivorship bias in our sample. To investigate this issue, we identify firms that were delisted from the TSE by examining issues of the Japan Company Handbook from 1985 to 1990. Over this period, 10 firms were delisted from the First Section of the TSE. Of these, 6 firms were merged, 3 went bankrupt, and 1 changed listing to the Second Section of the TSE. However, using data from the Japan Company Handbook prior to their delisting, none of these firms satisfied the criterion for inclusion in the sample. Thus, our sample appears to be free from survivorship bias.

Table 1 presents summary statistics on the sample firms for the year prior to (Year − 1), and the year of (Year 0) the performance shock. For interpretational convenience, values in Japanese yen are converted to US dollars using the month-end exchange rate at the end of the firms' fiscal year. In the pre-shock year, the mean (median) value of assets is $1017 ($368) million, and the mean (median) market value of outstanding equity is $869 ($438) million. The market value of equity of the largest firm in our sample is $9069 million, while that for the smallest firm is $56 million. While the median firm size is small, our sample includes several well known firms, such as Toshiba Ceramics, Suzuki Motors, Kawasaki Steel, and Nippon Steel.

Using the ratio of pretax operating income to assets as an accounting measure of performance, the sample firms appear profitable prior to the performance shock. The median return on assets for Year − 1 is 6.9%, and the sample firms

Table 1

Descriptive statistics for firm characteristics and firm performance. The sample consists of 92 Japanese manufacturing firms listed on the First Section of the Tokyo Stock Exchange and 114 US manufacturing firms listed on the New York or American Stock Exchange during 1986 to 1990. Sample firms have a ratio of pretax operating income to assets that exceeds the industry median in a given year and experience a decline of at least 50% in operating income in the subsequent year. Year 0 denotes the year of the decline in pretax operating income, and Year − 1 denotes the year prior to the decline in pretax operating income. Return on assets (ROA) is computed as the pretax operating income divided by total assets. For Japanese firms, values of assets and market value of equity are converted to US dollars using the month-end exchange rate at the end of the fiscal year. Data on Japanese firms are obtained from the Pacific-Basin Capital Markets Research Center data base. Data on US firms are obtained from Compustat

	Japanese firms				US firms			
	Year − 1		Year 0		Year − 1		Year 0	
Characteristic	Mean	Median	Mean	Median	Mean	Median	Mean	Median
Assets ($ million)	1017	368	1005	380	642	114	650	109
Market value of equity ($ million)	869	438	805	356	451	115	379	78
Book to market equity	0.40	0.36	0.46	0.45	0.56	0.62	0.64	0.86
Operating income/interest expense	12.87	4.76	4.90	1.26	54.02	8.18	11.83	2.03
Current ratio	1.72	1.42	2.02	1.48	2.89	2.28	2.91	2.09
ROA[a]	0.081	0.069	0.026	0.025	0.182	0.167	0.052	0.056
ROA less median industry ROA[a]	0.027	0.016	− 0.014	− 0.013	0.057	0.038	− 0.046	− 0.040

[a] All performance variables are significant at the 0.0001 level using a *t*-test and a sign rank test.

outperform the industry by 1.6% using this measure. In Year 0, median return on assets declines substantially to 2.5%, and the sample firms underperform the industry by 1.3%. The performance shock appears to alter the probability of encountering financial distress. The median ratio of operating income to interest expense in Year −1 is 4.76; this ratio drops to 1.26 in the year of the performance shock. Interestingly, the current ratio actually increases in the shock year. One explanation for this increase is that firms engage in actions to improve their liquidity in response to the shock. Overall, these statistics suggest that the sample contains firms that are initially healthy, but suffer a significant decline in performance in Year 0.

As a basis for comparison, we also construct a sample of US manufacturing corporations listed on the NYSE or AMEX that experienced a similar performance decline between 1986 and 1990. To enter into the sample, we require that a firm have an operating income to assets ratio that exceeds the industry median in the base year, have an interest coverage ratio that exceeds one in the base year, and that operating income decline by at least 50% in the shock year. The performance data for US firms is obtained from Compustat. As with the Japanese sample, no US firm enters our sample twice.

Table 1 shows that the US firms are smaller than the Japanese firms with mean (median) assets of $642 ($114) million. As with the Japanese sample, US firms experience a substantial drop in performance during the shock year. US firms have median operating return on assets of 16.7% in the base year, and this declines to 5.6% in the performance shock year. The median firm outperforms the industry by 3.8% in the base year, but underperforms the industry by 4% in the performance shock year. Using the ratio of operating income to interest expense as an indicator of financial distress, 39 US firms become distressed as a result of the performance decline. Of these, 20 firms experience negative operating income in Year 0. Thus, compared to the Japanese sample, the US sample consists of a much larger proportion of firms that become financially distressed as a result of the performance decline.

2.2. *Data on firm responses*

To examine the responses of Japanese firms during the performance decline, we collect data on corporate actions from a variety of sources, including the Nihon Keizai Shinbun, Nihon Sangyo Shinbun, Asian Wall Street Journal, Japan Economic Times, Lexis-Nexis, and the Wall Street Journal. Of these sources, the Nihon Keizai Shinbun and Nihon Sangyo Shinbun appear to provide the most detail on firm responses.[6] All sources are examined for stories

[6] Nonetheless, the level of detail appears to be less than what is typically available for US corporations. For example, in several cases, the newspaper articles do not specify which assets are

in the year of, and the year subsequent to the performance shock. Similar data on US firms is obtained from the Wall Street Journal, Dow Jones News Retrieval Service, and Lexis-Nexis.

We also collect data on the reported reasons for the performance decline. These reasons are summarized in Table 2. While some firms identify a single primary cause for the earnings shock, several firms report multiple reasons. Thus, the classifications are not mutually exclusive.

For Japanese firms, the appreciation in the strength of the yen is cited with the highest frequency. This reason is noted in 55 of the 92 cases, representing almost 60% of the sample. In 42 instances, firms blame other exogenous factors such as poor economy-wide or industry conditions, a low demand, or a low price for their products. In 4 cases, firms identify the poor performance of their major customers as a reason for the shock. Overall, 70 Japanese firms, representing 76% of the sample, cite an exogenous reason for the decline.

Nonetheless, the performance drop in Japanese firms is not solely due to exogenous factors. Several firms note other factors contributing to the decline. In 12 cases, high operating, distribution, depreciation, or inventory costs are blamed. In 2 cases (Toshiba Machine and Kyocera Corp.), the performance decline is due to aftershocks of illegal trading practices at the firm.[7] Two pharmaceutical firms in the sample attribute the decline to poor performance of certain key drug products. Finally, one firm reports substantial cost overruns at a new plant, while lawsuits and losses on foreign exchange forward contracts are blamed by another three firms. Endogenous factors are cited by 17% of the firms, while in 4 of the firms, an endogenous factor is the only reason mentioned in the newspaper articles. While managers probably have an incentive to blame the performance shock on exogenous factors, analysis of the reasons nonetheless indicates that a wide variety of factors is likely responsible for the performance decline of our sample firms.

Consistent with the findings of John et al. (1992), a substantial fraction of the US firms also blame exogenous factors such as poor economy or industry conditions for the drop in performance. The impact of such exogenous factors are noted by 68 (61%) of the US firms. However, 23% of the firms also state high operating costs as a factor contributing to poor performance. Overall, 35 (31%)

---

sold, the proceeds from asset sales, or the intended use of the proceeds. These omissions complicate the analysis because when several data sources cite asset sales, we are unable to verify whether they all refer to the same set of assets, or refer to several independent events. Thus, we are typically only able to determine whether or not a particular firm engages in a given action such as an asset sale, but not the exact numbers of events involved or the magnitude of the transaction.

[7] In the most notorious of these, Toshiba Machine Corp. was accused of violating Coordinating Committee for Controls on Exports to Communist Block (COCOM) rules due to clandestine sales of US submarine propeller technology to the Soviet Union. In response to these violations, the US Senate passed a bill calling for sanctions on Toshiba Machine, and banning its exports to the US.

Table 2
Reported reasons for performance decline. The sample consists of 92 Japanese manufacturing firms listed on the First Section of the Tokyo Stock Exchange and 114 US manufacturing firms listed on the New York or American Stock Exchange during 1986 to 1990. Sample firms have a ratio of pretax operating income to assets that exceeds the industry median in a given year and experience a decline of at least 50% in operating income in the subsequent year. Data on reported reasons for Japanese firms are obtained from the Nihon Keizai Shinbun, Nihon Sangyo Shinbun, Asian Wall Street Journal, Japan Economic Times, and Lexis-Nexis. Data on reported reasons for US firms are obtained from the Wall Street Journal, Dow Jones News Retrieval, and Lexis-Nexis. The classification of reasons is not mutually exclusive, so firms reporting multiple reasons are indicated more than once in the table

	Japanese firms		US firms	
Reason	Number	(%)	Number	(%)
Exogeneous factors				
Unfavorable exchange rates	55	(59.8)	2	(1.8)
Declining demand/low sales of products	14	(15.2)	26	(22.8)
Poor economy or industry conditions	13	(14.1)	37	(32.5)
Lower prices for products	15	(16.3)	20	(17.5)
Poor performance of major customers	4	(4.3)	0	(0.0)
Competition	2	(2.2)	8	(7.0)
Endogeneous factors				
High depreciation costs	5	(5.4)	1	(0.1)
High operating costs	3	(3.3)	26	(22.8)
High distribution costs	2	(2.2)	3	(2.6)
Excessive inventories	2	(2.2)	7	(6.1)
Illegal business practices	2	(2.2)	1	(0.1)
Efficiency of drug downgraded	2	(2.2)	0	(0.0)
Losses in forward markets	2	(2.2)	0	(0.0)
Startup costs at new plant	1	(1.1)	0	(0.0)
Lawsuits	1	(1.1)	2	(1.8)
Past acquisitions	0	(0.0)	1	(0.1)

of the US firms mention an endogenous factor, and in 16 (14%) firms, an endogenous factor is the only reason identified for the decline in performance.

3. Responses to performance shock

In this section, we describe the operational actions of the Japanese and US firms that we study, and discuss the actions taken by the sample firms. We analyze changes in firm size and employment surrounding these operational responses, and also compare the changes in financial structure that occur around the performance decline.

3.1. Operational actions

We classify the actions that the sample firms take in response to the performance decline into seven broad categories.

(1) *Asset contraction policies*: These include the sale of assets, spinoffs of units, plant closures, and product or line withdrawals. Because the performance shock is likely due to either poor performance of some assets or operations, or due to a substantial shift in the firm's investment opportunity set, or both, we expect that some of the firm's operations are likely to be rendered economically unviable. Under this scenario, some contraction of the firm's operations is likely to be warranted. Using data on US firms, John and Ofek (1995) find that firms that sell assets experience subsequent improvements in operating performance.

(2) *Changes in employment policies*: These include employee layoffs, reductions in compensation or bonuses, and other actions that significantly affect the composition or compensation of the firm's employees. Layoffs of employees and other similar changes are likely to occur when firms downsize, or adopt more efficient or capital intensive production techniques.

(3) *Expansion policies*: We document actions that enhance the scale or scope of operations for our sample firms. Such actions include joint ventures, acquisitions, construction of new plants, increased output or capital expenditures, etc. Expansion will be an optimal action if it represents a valuable investment opportunity such as a strategic acquisition, or a strengthening of distribution channels in response to declining sales. However, as suggested by Jensen (1986), expansion activities that represent diversification strategies or result in a loss of focus can be detrimental to firm value.

(4) *Internal reorganizations*: Actions included in this category represent responses that involve a restructuring without a downsizing or enhancement of the scale of the firm's operations. Examples of such actions include changing production methods, incorporating technological advances in product development and design, and cost-cutting efforts.

(5) *Changes in control*: We identify changes in control of the corporation by collecting data on the identity of the President for Japanese firms, who is similar to the CEO in US firms. For US firms, we track the identity of the CEO. Kaplan (1994) finds that the probability of management turnover in large Japanese firms is inversely related to firm performance. In addition, we examine the addition and removal of outside directors to the board. Kaplan and Minton (1994) provide evidence that such directors perform an important governance function in Japanese corporations. We use the definition of outside directors adopted by Aoki et al. (1994) and Kaplan and Minton (1994) and consider those directors that have prior experience at other organizations to be outsiders. Retired government officials, non-Japanese directors, and auditors are not considered to be outside directors. Our results are unchanged if auditors are considered to be outsiders. For US firms, we define outside directors to be directors that are not

employees of the firm, nor have reported business, family, or prior employment ties with the firm. Unlike data on other responses that are collected from newspaper stories, data on board changes for Japanese firms are obtained from issues of Yakuin Shikiho and Kigyo Keiretsu Soran. For US firms, these data are obtained from proxy statements.

(6) *External takeover activity*: We document instances where firms are the target of external takeover pressures. This includes successful and unsuccessful tender offers, merger and LBO proposals, and proxy contests. Because some firms may restructure in response to a takeover threat that does not materialize, we also tabulate the incidence of offers that are reported to be contemplated or in negotiation, as well as large block purchases of a company's stock.

(7) *Miscellaneous actions*: This is a residual category of actions that do not fall in any of the categories above, and includes responses such as the sale of marketable securities, and corporate name changes.

3.1.1. Japanese responses

The responses for Japanese firms are reported in Table 3. Of the various responses indicating a contraction, the reduction of capital expenditures occurs most frequently. Seven firms respond in this manner, and an additional four cut their production capacity, while two firms also suspend production. Four firms engage in asset sales, and five firms engage in plant closures. Withdrawal from a line of business occurs in four firms, and in one case, a firm conducts a spinoff. Of the 92 firms in the sample, 21 (22.8%) engage in some form of asset contraction.

Japanese firms also make substantial changes in their employment and compensation policies. The most frequently occurring form of such adjustments is via layoffs. This happens in 16 of the sample firms. In most cases, the number of employees laid off represents a substantial fraction of the workforce. We are able to reliably assess the number of employees laid off for 15 firms. In these instances, the average number of employees laid off is 2521 and the median number of employees laid off is 440. For these firms, layoffs represent a mean of 20.9%, and a median of 20%, of their total workforce. The layoffs in our sample are typically implemented through early retirement programs and by the transfer of employees to affiliated firms. In some instances, the layoffs represent an important component of the restructuring program. For example, in the case of Nippon Steel, 19,000 of its 65,000 workers were laid off, 1500 of its blast furnace workers were reassigned to other divisions, and head office staff was reduced by 33%. The firm also simultaneously implemented a productivity wage system to tie worker salaries to productivity. The incidence of layoffs in our sample is, of course, correlated with the incidence of asset sales and plant closures. Of the 16 firms where employees are laid off, two firms sell assets and three firms close plants. However, such changes in asset structure are not a necessary condition for layoffs to occur in our sample. Nine of our sample firms layoff employees without engaging in any form of asset downsizing.

Table 3
Frequency of operational responses during the year of and the year following the performance decline. The sample consists of 92 Japanese manufacturing firms listed on the First Section of the Tokyo Stock Exchange and 114 US manufacturing firms listed on the New York or American Stock Exchanges during 1986 to 1990. Sample firms have a ratio of pretax operating income to assets that exceeds the industry median in a given year and experience a decline of at least 50% in operating income in the subsequent year. Data on reported actions for Japanese firms are obtained from the Nihon Keizai Shinbun, Nihon Sangyo Shinbun, Asian Wall Street Journal, Japan Economic Times, and Lexis-Nexis. Data on reported actions for US firms are obtained from the Wall Street Journal, Dow Jones News Retrieval, and Lexis-Nexis. The classification of actions is not mutually exclusive, so firms reporting multiple actions are indicated more than once in the table

	Japanese firms		US firms	
Action	Number	(%)	Number	(%)
Asset contraction actions				
Cut or postpone capital expenditures	7	(7.6)	4	(3.5)
Withdraw from line of business	4	(4.3)	4	(3.5)
Close plant	5	(5.4)	18	(15.8)
Cut production capacity	4	(4.3)	3	(2.6)
Asset sale	4	(4.3)	42	(36.8)
Suspend production operations	2	(2.2)	10	(8.8)
Spinoff unit	1	(1.1)	4	(3.5)
Shutdown of offices/branch	1	(1.1)	4	(3.5)
Total	21	(22.8)	56	(49.1)
Employment changes				
Layoffs	16	(17.4)	36	(31.6)
Reduce director salary or bonus	12	(13.0)	2	(1.8)
Pay cut for managers or employees	8	(5.4)	7	(6.1)
Lower mandatory retirement age or offer early retirement incentives	3	(3.3)	4	(3.5)
Total	26	(28.3)	42	(36.8)
Expansion actions				
Joint venture	31	(33.7)	17	(14.9)
Increase output or expand existing production facilities	25	(27.2)	3	(2.6)
New facility construction	19	(20.7)	9	(7.9)
Establish subsidiary	17	(18.5)	5	(4.4)
Increase capital expenditures	12	(13.0)	4	(3.5)
New production	11	(12.0)	5	(4.4)
Partial acquisition	10	(10.9)	7	(6.1)
Full acquisition	9	(9.8)	37	(32.5)
Expand distribution channels	8	(8.7)	3	(2.6)
Diversify	6	(6.5)	0	(0.0)
Setup research lab or increase R&D	4	(4.3)	3	(2.6)
Total	70	(76.1)	63	(55.3)

Table 3. (Continued).

	Japanese firms		US firms	
Action	Number	(%)	Number	(%)
Internal reorganization actions				
Cut operating costs	16	(15.2)	16	(14.4)
Modernize production techniques/equipment	10	(10.9)	8	(7.0)
Reorganize existing production processes	11	(12.0)	11	(9.7)
Reorganize subsidiaries/units	9	(9.8)	3	(2.6)
Input acquisition policy changed	8	(8.7)	1	(0.9)
Change product design or line	5	(5.4)	2	(1.8)
Lower inventory	6	(6.5)	1	(0.9)
More in-house production	2	(2.2)	0	(0.0)
More efficient asset management	1	(1.1)	2	(1.8)
Change pricing policy	3	(3.3)	5	(4.4)
Improve product or production quality	2	(2.2)	0	(0.0)
Improve distributional efficiency	1	(1.1)	8	(7.0)
Total	47	(51.1)	35	(30.7)
Changes in internal control				
Turnover of the president/CEO	30	(33.0)	22	(19.3)
Turnover of president/CEO without assuming position of board chairman	13	(14.3)	9	(7.9)
Outside successor appointed	11	(12.1)	7	(6.7)
Outside director(s) added to the board	28	(32.6)	43	(42.6)
Outside director(s) removed from the board	30	(40.0)	46	(50.6)
Total	56	(60.9)	66	(57.9)
External control activity				
Takeover rumors or negotiation	0	(0.0)	6	(5.3)
Shareholder activism	0	(0.0)	2	(1.8)
Proxy contest	0	(0.0)	4	(3.5)
Successfully acquired	0	(0.0)	8	(7.0)
Unsolicited offers	0	(0.0)	10	(8.8)
Block purchases	0	(0.0)	21	(18.4)
Unsuccessful LBO offers	0	(0.0)	2	(1.8)
Chapter 11 filing	0	(0.0)	1	(0.9)
Total	0	(0.0)	42	(36.8)
Miscellaneous actions				
Sold marketable securities	6	(6.5)	6	(5.3)
Lower bank debt or interest payments	4	(4.3)	6	(5.3)
Cancel bond or equity issue	3	(3.3)	0	(0.0)
Change company name	3	(3.3)	4	(3.5)
Change accounting system	1	(1.1)	0	(0.0)
Total	17	(18.5)	15	(13.2)

In 12 instances, firms announce that they are reducing compensation for top level managers and directors, or both. In eight firms, such compensation cuts affect managers and employees that are below the level of the board of directors. Finally, three firms reduce their mandatory retirement age to downsize their workforce through attrition.

While reducing asset size, production, and employment are common responses, expansionary actions occur with the highest frequency in the sample. In the sample, 70 firms report some form of expansionary response. Of these, formation of joint ventures is the most frequent response, and occurs in 31 firms. The second most frequent response, evident in 25 cases, is increased production or enhancement of existing production facilities. Nineteen firms engage in the construction of new plants and production facilities, while 17 firms establish non-manufacturing subsidiary operations. Over 20% of the sample firms also engage in some acquisition activity. Interestingly, six firms explicitly mention that they are expanding for diversification reasons. Comment and Jarrell (1995), Lang and Stulz (1994), Berger and Ofek (1995), and Servaes (1996), however, document that diversification activities adversely impact firm value in the US, and Lins and Servaes (1997) find that diversification is also detrimental to firm value in Japan. Since acquisitions provide a natural mechanism for managers to pursue diversification policies, this observation raises the possibility that some of the acquisitions by our sample firms may not represent value-maximizing decisions.[8]

The expansionary and contractionary policies evidenced by the sample of Japanese firms are not mutually exclusive. Of the 21 firms that engage in some form of contraction, 19 firms also respond by expanding. Of these, eight firms make an acquisition. Thus, in some instances, firms that we consider to be downsizing may actually experience increases in firm size, if, for example, they also make a large acquisition. Therefore, in the subsequent analysis, we also consider the subset of firms that downsize but do not make any acquisitions.

Firms also respond with significant changes in board-level control rights. Thirty (33%) firms experience a change in the president over the two year interval. For comparison, Kaplan (1994) reports that for a sample of the largest Japanese firms, the average likelihood of president turnover during a two-year interval is 30.5%. Thus, the level of overall turnover activity does not appear to be particularly high.

Kaplan (1994) suggests that president tenure follows a conveyer belt property in Japan, where presidents retire at regular intervals without regard to firm

---

[8] Ideally, we would like to compare the industries of the targets to those of the bidders to classify the Japanese acquisitions as related or unrelated. However, since most of the acquired entities are privately held firms, units, divisions, and foreign corporations, data limitations preclude us from investigating the industrial classifications of the targets and bidders for the Japanese firms.

performance. He also finds that it is customary for the retiring president to become the chairman of the board. Accordingly, we examine instances where the president is removed and does not assume the position of chairman, as indicators of disciplinary turnover events. There are 13 (14%) such cases in our sample. This is markedly higher than the 3.86% frequency reported by Kaplan (1994). As an alternative measure of disciplinary turnover, we also examine outside succession events. Following Kang and Shivdasani (1995), we consider a successor to be an outside appointment if he has been with the firm for three years or less. They find that the frequency of outside appointments in Japanese firms is approximately 2.7% over a two year interval. There are 11 such outside appointments in our sample, implying a outside succession frequency of 12%. Thus, outside succession is approximately four times as likely to occur in our sample. In summary, although the overall extent of turnover does not appear to be different, the turnover experienced by our sample firms appears more likely to be disciplinary in nature.

We also examine board-level changes other than the president. Twenty-eight (33%) of our sample firms add outside directors to the board. Kaplan and Minton (1994) for comparison, document that 12.9% of their sample firms appoint outside directors in a given firm-year. This suggests that the frequency with which firms appoint outside directors is relatively high in our sample. If these additions represent the functioning of disciplinary mechanisms, we would expect that they are also associated with removals of incumbent outside directors. We are able to obtain data on outside director removals for 75 of our sample firms. Of these, outside directors depart in 30 (40%) firms. While we are not aware of a benchmark for comparison, this frequency of departures appears to be high. The incidence of outside director appointments is correlated with departures of incumbent outside directors. In 30 firms where outside directors are dropped, 18 (60%) firms appoint new outside directors. However, outside director appointments occur in only 8 (18%) of the 45 firms that do not experience removals of incumbent outside directors.

Our sample firms also respond by taking other actions to reorganize their operations. Sixteen firms mention efforts to reduce their operating costs, and 11 firms discuss reorganization of their existing production processes. Ten firms also implement improved production techniques or modernize their equipment. The sample firms also take a number of other actions, such as changing product design, and changing input acquisition, asset management, inventory, distributional, and product pricing policies.

3.1.2. Comparison to US responses

Table 3 also summarizes the responses of US firms during poor performance. As we discuss below, eight US firms are successfully acquired in the year subsequent to the performance drop. For these firms, we collect data on restructuring activities up to the point that they are acquired, but not subsequent to the acquisition.

Almost 50% of the US firms engage in some form of downsizing. Asset sales represent the most frequently observed response (42 firms), followed by plant closures (18 firms), and the suspension of production (10 firms). Twelve firms also spinoff units, withdraw from a line of business or cut capital expenditures. Overall, 56 firms (49%) undertake asset contraction measures. Thus, US firms are over twice as likely to engage in some form of asset contraction compared to Japanese firms, and certain actions, such as asset sales, occur almost 7 times more frequently among US firms.

Layoffs are a frequent response among US firms, occurring in 36 (32%) firms. Six US firms also take other actions affecting their employees, such as pay reductions, or offering early retirement incentives. Overall, 37% of US firms make adjustments to their employment policies, compared to 28% for Japanese firms.

US firms also frequently undertake expansionary actions, of which acquisitions are the most frequent form, occurring in 44 firms. We are able to obtain data on the Standard Industrial Classification (SIC) codes on both the bidder and the acquired firm, unit, division, or plant, for 30 acquisitions made by 25 firms.[9] Of these, the bidder and the acquired entity share the same four digit SIC code in 16 cases, the same three digit SIC code in 20 cases, and the same two digit SIC code in 22 cases. In an additional four cases, newspaper stories indicate that the operations of the acquired entity will be merged or integrated into the firm's existing operations. Further, we do not find any reference in newspaper reports indicating that these acquisitions reflect diversification strategies. Thus, unlike Japan, the majority of US acquisitions appear to be related to the bidder's existing line of business.

Twenty-two (19%) firms in the sample experience CEO turnover. For comparison, Weisbach (1988) documents an annual CEO turnover rate of 7.8%, Denis and Denis (1995) find a 9.3% rate, and Kaplan (1994) documents a 9.7% annual CEO turnover rate for unconditional samples of US firms, while John et al. (1992) find a 12.5% annual CEO turnover rate for poorly performing US firms. Thus, our sample of US firms does not appear to display an abnormally high frequency of CEO turnover.

There are nine cases where the outgoing CEO does not become chairman of the board. In seven firms, the new CEO is hired from outside the firm. Outside directors depart in over 50% of the sample firms, while in 43% of the firms, an outside director is added to the board. The frequency of outside director appointments in the sample is comparable to those reported by Hermalin and

[9] Data on SIC codes are obtained from Dun and Bradstreet's Million Dollar Directory, Directory of Corporate Affiliations, Ward's Business Directory, Dun's Industrial Guide – The Metalworking Directory, and Manufacturing Directories Microfiche. Most of the acquired entities are units, divisions, subsidiaries, or plants of other firms.

Weisbach (1988) and Kaplan and Minton (1994) for US firms. Thus, unlike Japanese firms, US firms in the sample do not display evidence of abnormally high levels of turnover among outside directors.

Unlike Japan, where we find no indication of any explicit corporate control actions, such takeover activity is prevalent among our sample of US firms. Eight firms are successfully acquired via a merger or tender offer, while four are targets of proxy contests. An additional 12 firms receive leveraged buyout proposals or unsolicited offers (some of which result in a formal tender offer or proposal) that do not succeed. Twenty-one firms experience unsolicited block purchases of their equity, while one firm in the sample files for Chapter 11. Overall, 37% of the firms experience some explicit external takeover pressures.

In summary, the analysis of responses indicates that Japanese firms frequently respond to poor performance by downsizing their assets and operations, engaging in employee layoffs, removing top executives and directors, and implementing a variety of internal reorganization actions. While they are frequent responses, downsizing and layoffs do not occur with the same frequency in Japanese firms as they do for US firms. US firms are at least twice as likely to engage in an asset contraction, and almost twice as likely to lay off employees. US and Japanese firms also differ in the nature of their expansion policies during poor performance. We find some evidence to suggest that Japanese firms make diversifying acquisitions. While US firms also frequently make acquisitions, acquired entities are often in industries related to the acquirer.

3.2. Operational responses and changes in firm size and employment

In this section, we examine changes in firm size and employment to assess the magnitude of the firm responses to poor performance. Panel A of Table 4 reports changes in firm size, and Panel B reports changes in employment for firms according to the observed responses. Because of the relatively small sample sizes in some of the categories, we concentrate our discussion on median changes.

Firm size declines by 4.64% from Year −1 to Year 0 for Japanese firms that downsize. In comparison, changes in firm size over this interval are not significant for firms that do not downsize. When the change in firm size is measured over the Year −1 to Year +1 interval, however, we find no evidence of a reduction in firm size for downsizing firms, whereas there is a significant increase in size for firms that do not downsize.

Firms that announce layoffs also experience a significant drop in firm size. For these firms, total assets drop by 7.3% during the performance shock year and by 8.6% for the two years surrounding the performance shock. In comparison, firm size increases by 8.6% over the two years for firms not announcing layoffs. As a broader measure of downsizing, we also consider firms that either engage in asset contraction or layoffs. For the median firm in this category, firm

Table 4
Changes in firm size and employment during performance decline. The sample consists of 92 Japanese manufacturing firms listed on the First Section of the Tokyo Stock Exchange and 114 US manufacturing firms listed on the New York or American Stock Exchanges during 1986 to 1990. Sample firms have a ratio of pretax operating income to assets that exceeds the industry median in a given year and experience a decline of at least 50% in operating income in the subsequent year. Data on Japanese firms is obtained from the Pacific-Basin Capital Markets Research Center data base and the Daiwa Analyst Guide. Data on US firms is obtained from Compustat. Year − 1, 0, and + 1 denote the year prior to, the year of, and the year after, the decline in pretax operating income, respectively. ***, **, and * denote significance at the 1%, 5%, and 10% level, respectively, using a two-tailed t-test for means and sign rank test for medians

	Japanese firms				US firms			
	Year − 1 to Year 0		Year − 1 to Year + 1		Year − 1 to Year 0		Year − 1 to Year 0	
Action	Mean	Median	Mean	Median	Mean	Median	Mean	Median
Panel A: Percentage change in assets								
All firms	− 1.57	− 2.05*	4.79***	4.82***	5.00	0.58	3.37	1.00
Asset contraction	− 5.31**	− 4.64*	− 1.86	4.82	8.21	0.16	5.21	− 2.47
No asset contraction	− 0.46	− 1.56	6.97**	3.88***	1.91	1.00	1.64	2.50
Layoffs	− 7.50***	− 7.26***	− 11.44**	− 8.62**	11.26	− 0.69	10.34	− 0.54
No Layoffs	− 0.32	− 1.18	8.27***	8.58***	2.12	1.22	− 0.01	2.42
Asset contraction or layoffs	− 4.92	− 5.06**	− 2.34	− 3.52	6.46	− 0.24	4.26	− 1.47
No asset contraction or layoffs	0.06	− 1.49	8.48***	7.45***	2.93	1.64	2.16	3.03
Acquisition	1.56	0.55	11.21***	14.33***	18.75	5.12*	19.13	6.71*
Asset contraction or layoffs but no acquisition	− 7.42***	− 7.14***	− 7.03*	− 7.43*	− 3.10	− 3.30*	− 6.50**	− 7.35**
Panel B: percentage change in employment								
All firms	0.73	0.69**	− 1.19	− 1.34	− 5.33**	− 5.71	− 7.71***	− 8.77***
Asset contraction	1.00	0.44	− 2.25	− 1.47	− 5.37*	− 6.54***	− 13.17***	− 11.64***
No asset contraction	0.66	0.68*	− 0.86	− 1.34	1.91	1.00	1.64	2.50
Layoffs	− 4.47**	− 2.33***	− 11.38***	− 7.42***	− 6.03	− 8.22***	− 7.04	− 8.64***
No Layoffs	1.76***	1.24***	0.88	1.45	− 5.01*	− 3.97***	− 8.03**	− 9.09***
Asset contraction or layoffs	− 0.78	− 0.89	− 5.15**	− 3.90**	− 6.00**	− 6.59***	− 11.57***	− 10.60***
No asset contraction or layoffs	1.44***	1.14***	0.82	− 0.09	− 4.41	− 2.46**	− 2.56	− 1.42
Acquisition	2.46***	3.15**	1.54	− 0.09	1.07	− 0.86	− 2.40	− 2.82
Asset contraction or layoffs but no acquisition	− 2.18	− 1.50	− 7.58***	− 4.69***	− 11.13***	− 9.38***	− 17.83***	− 14.78***

size declines by 5.1% during Year − 1 to Year 0, and by 3.5% during Year − 1 to Year + 1. Firms that do not downsize, in contrast, experience a median increase of 7.5% in firm size during Year − 1 to Year + 1.

Increases in size are evident for firms making acquisitions. Acquiring firms have a median increase in firm size of 14.3% from Year − 1 to Year + 1. There are nine firms that both downsize by asset contraction or layoffs and also make an acquisition. An alternative way to identify firms that downsize is to consider the set of firms that contract assets or lay off employees without engaging in an acquisition. There are 21 such firms in the sample. For these firms, firm size declines by 7.1% during the one year, and by 7.4% during the two years surrounding the performance decline. Thus, this latter group of firms makes substantial reductions in the size of their operations.

Panel B shows that firms engaging in layoffs have a median reduction in employment of 2.3% during the year of performance decline and a 7.4% decline over two years. In comparison, firms that do not make layoffs experience a median increase of 1.2% in the performance shock year, but a statistically insignificant change over the two year interval. The reduction in employment is also pronounced for firms that engage in asset contractions or layoffs without making an acquisition. For these firms, employment declines by 4.7% during Year − 1 to Year + 1.

Changes in firm size for US firms announcing asset contraction, layoffs, or both, are statistically insignificant. There is marginally significant evidence of increases in firm size for US firms that make acquisitions. For these firms, size increases by 5.1% during Year − 1 to Year 0, and by 6.7% during Year − 1 to Year + 1; these increases are significant at the 10% level. US firms that downsize without making an acquisition experience a significant 7.35% drop in size from Year − 1 to Year + 1. For this category of firms, the magnitude of reduction in firm size is similar across US and Japanese firms.

Employment drops by 8.6% over two years for US firms announcing layoffs. US firms that downsize by asset contraction or layoff without making an acquisition experience a 14.8% reduction in employment over this period. This drop is approximately three times the change in employment experienced by Japanese firms that downsize without making acquisitions. Thus, layoffs in US firms that downsize affect a larger fraction of the workforce than in Japan.

In summary, Japanese firms announcing contraction in assets and operations, and those implementing layoffs, experience statistically significant reductions in firm size in the years surrounding the drop in performance. Similar reductions are not observed for firms that do not take such actions. Japanese firms making acquisitions experience an increase in firm size. Thus, the decline in firm size is most pronounced for firms that downsize without a concurrent acquisition. Significant declines in employment are also observed for Japanese firms with reported layoffs, and those that engage in contraction or layoffs without making an acquisition.

3.3. Capital structure and governance changes

In this section, we describe the firm-specific variables that we use in the subsequent analysis to explain the likelihood that certain restructuring actions will be observed. Table 5 reports summary statistics on these explanatory variables, and the changes in these variables over the pre- and post-shock years.

3.3.1. Leverage

Jensen (1989) argues that highly leveraged firms are more likely to restructure when their value declines. We calculate leverage as the ratio of total debt to total assets.

3.3.2. Bank ties

Bulow and Shoven (1978) and Gertner and Scharfstein (1991) note that free-rider problems faced by diffuse investors eliminate the incentive for such debtholders to bear monitoring costs. The joint ownership of substantial debt and equity by main banks can, however, provide monitoring incentives that are lacking in diffuse investors. Following Kaplan (1994), we use the ratio of bank borrowings to total assets to measure the strength of a firm's ties to a main bank. In unreported tests, we also consider the fraction of bank debt from the largest lender, and obtain similar results. We also use the equity ownership by the firm's main bank to measure its financial incentive to monitor. Data on bank ties is collected from annual issues of Kigyo Keiretsu Soran.

3.3.3. Ownership structure

Jensen and Meckling (1976) argue that increased equity ownership by managers provides them with incentives to make value-maximizing decisions. Accordingly, we use the equity ownership by the board of directors as an explanatory variable. In addition, Demsetz and Lehn (1985), Shleifer and Vishny (1986) and Jensen (1989) note that large shareholders have incentives to take actions that enhance firm value. Blockholders are often trading partners in Japan, and thus hold a stake in the firm similar to that of debt (Berglof and Perotti, 1994). Such a joint stake as trade creditors and large shareholders should, in theory, provide incentives for blockholders to take actions that preserve or enhance firm value. We measure the importance of blockholders by the ownership of the firm's ten largest shareholders. Because main banks are also typically blockholders, we exclude ownership by the main bank since the effect of their ownership is examined separately. Henceforth, any unqualified reference to blockholders refers to those other than the main bank.

3.3.4. Keiretsu affiliation

We categorize the Japanese firms as either belonging to a keiretsu or as being independent of corporate groupings. We focus on the six major keiretsus of Mitsubishi, Mitsui, Sumitomo, Fuyo, DKB, and Sanwa. In unreported tests, we

Table 5

Structure of financing and ownership ties prior to performance decline, and changes in financial and ownership ties during the year prior to the performance decline to the year subsequent to performance decline. The sample consists of 92 Japanese manufacturing firms listed on the First Section of the Tokyo Stock Exchange and 114 US manufacturing firms listed on the New York or American Stock Exchange during 1986 to 1990. Sample firms have a ratio of pretax operating income to assets that exceeds the industry median in a given year and experience a decline of at least 50% in operating income in the subsequent year. Year − 1 denotes the year prior to the decline in pretax operating income and Year + 1 denotes the year after the decline in pretax operating income. Data for Japanese firms is obtained from the Pacific-Basin Capital Markets Research Center data base, Kigyo Keiretsu Soran, and Yakuin Shikiho. Data on US firms is obtained from Compustat and proxy statements. ***, **, and * denote significance at the 1%, 5%, and 10% level respectively, using a two-tailed t-test for means and sign rank test for medians

	Japanese firms				US firms			
	Level in year − 1		Change from Year − 1 to Year + 1		Level in year − 1		Change from Year − 1 to Year + 1	
Characteristic	Mean	Median	Mean	Median	Mean	Median	Mean	Median
Total debt/assets	0.603	0.609	0.009	0.001	0.249	0.226	0.032**	0.007
Bank debt/assets	0.152	0.111	0.027	0.000*	0.064	0.036	0.013	0.000
Non-bank debt/assets	0.451	0.456	− 0.027	− 0.010	0.180	0.173	0.033	0.003
Main bank debt[a]/assets	0.034	0.026	0.003	0.000*	—	—	—	—
Fraction of bank debt from main bank	0.204	0.207	0.348	0.000*	—	—	—	—
Equity ownership by main bank	0.035	0.038	− 0.005	0.000	—	—	—	—
Equity ownership by directors	0.039	0.005	− 0.005***	− 0.001***	0.244	0.192	0.003	0.000
Equity ownership by blockholders[b]	0.461	0.430	− 0.004	− 0.004	0.101	0.063	0.031**	0.000**
Keiretsu affiliation[c]	0.304	—	—		—	—	—	—

[a] The main bank is defined as the largest bank lender to the firm.

[b] The firm's ten largest shareholders are considered to be blockholders for Japanese firms. For US firms, shareholders owning 5% or more of a firm's voting securities are considered to be blockholders.

[c] A firm is considered to be affiliated with a keiretsu if it belongs to the Mitsubishi, Mitsui, Sumitomo, Fuyo, DKB, or Sanwa groups.

also consider firms to be part of a keiretsu if they are members of the group's president's council, or part of the Tokai, IBJ, Nippon Steel, Hitachi, Nissan, Toyota, Matushita, Toshiba, Tokyu or Seibu Saisan groups. Using both approaches, we obtain results similar to those presented in the paper. Data on keiretsu membership is obtained from Industrial Groupings in Japan (1985).

Table 5 shows the median leverage ratio for Japanese firms in the pre-shock year is 61%, and bank debt represents 11% of the book value of assets. The mean equity ownership by the main bank is 3.5%, with a median of 3.8%. The main bank is among the firm's ten largest shareholders in 63 firms. Of these, it is the largest shareholder in 12 firms, the second largest shareholder in 17 firms, and the third largest shareholder in 14 firms. Although main banks are usually important stockholders, they do not always own substantial equity stakes. In 24 instances (or 26%), the main bank owns no equity in our sample firms. The average equity ownership by the board of directors in the sample is 3.9%, but board ownership is highly skewed with a median of only 0.5%. On average, the non-main bank blockholders own over 46% of the firm's equity. Finally, 30% of the firms belong to a keiretsu.

While operational actions are a common response to poor performance in Japan, changes in financial and ownership structure do not appear to be a common response. Significant changes are observed for only the equity ownership by directors, which declines by an average of 0.5%. There is some statistically weak evidence of an increase in firm borrowings from the main bank. However, these changes do not appear to be economically large. Median changes in the ratio of bank debt to assets, main bank debt to assets, and fraction of bank debt from the main bank are all close to zero.

For comparison, Table 5 also reports changes in financial and ownership structure for US firms. For US firms, we use the ratio of short-term debt to assets as a proxy for bank debt. As with the Japanese firms, there do not appear to be substantial changes in the financial structure of US firms surrounding the decline in earnings. However, consistent with the high incidence of block share purchases and takeover attempts for US firms, we find a significant increase in the fraction of equity held by 5% blockholders.

4. The likelihood of Japanese firm responses

In this section we investigate whether the likelihood of Japanese actions during performance declines is influenced by the distribution of the firm's debt and equity claims.

4.1. Multivariate results

Table 6 reports the results from logistic regressions where the dependent variable equals one if a particular action occurs, and is zero otherwise. The

Table 6
Logit estimates of the likelihood of restructuring activities subsequent to performance decline. The sample consists of 92 Japanese manufacturing firms listed on the First Section of the Tokyo Stock Exchange during 1986 to 1990 that had a ratio of pretax operating income to assets that exceeds the industry median in a given year and experience a decline of at least 50% in operating income in the subsequent year. Performance variables are measured as of the year of the performance decline, while other variables are measured for the year prior to the decline. Firm size is measured as the logarithm of the book value of assets. Data are obtained from the Pacific-Basin Capital Markets Research Center data base, Kigyo Keiretsu Soran, and Yakuin Shikiho. *p*-values are in parentheses

Actions	Asset contraction (1)	Layoffs (2)	Asset contraction or layoffs (3)	Asset expansion (4)	Partial or full acquisition (5)	Asset contraction or layoffs and no acquisition (6)
Intercept	– 20.59	– 10.97	– 14.96	– 9.34	– 9.56	– 7.59
	(0.00)	(0.02)	(0.00)	(0.02)	(0.04)	(0.05)
Log (size)	1.60	0.83	1.26	0.91	0.78	0.60
	(0.00)	(0.02)	(0.00)	(0.01)	(0.02)	(0.04)
Return on assets[a]	0.05	– 0.56	– 0.16	0.07	0.27	– 0.31
	(0.94)	(0.03)	(0.32)	(0.71)	(0.16)	(0.10)
Industry return on assets[b]	– 0.18	– 0.15	– 0.13	0.46	– 0.19	– 0.29
	(0.58)	(0.68)	(0.65)	(0.07)	(0.52)	(0.33)
Total debt/assets	– 4.24	– 1.92	– 4.66	– 4.57	6.90	– 5.42
	(0.23)	(0.65)	(0.13)	(0.16)	(0.07)	(0.09)
Bank debt/assets	3.44	5.25	3.91	0.51	– 7.71	4.03
	(0.29)	(0.18)	(0.22)	(0.86)	(0.06)	(0.20)
Keiretsu membership[c]	0.83	– 1.85	– 0.06	0.53	0.72	– 0.06
	(0.30)	(0.06)	(0.93)	(0.49)	(0.42)	(0.94)

continued over

Board ownership	0.04	– 0.13	0.00	0.03	– 0.03	0.00
	(0.37)	(0.22)	(0.97)	(0.62)	(0.63)	(0.94)
Main bank ownership[d]	0.31	0.21	0.36	– 0.02	– 0.15	(0.34)
	(0.01)	(0.06)	(0.01)	(0.80)	(0.38)	(0.03)
Blockholder ownership[e]	0.05	0.05	0.04	0.03	– 0.08	0.07
	(0.05)	(0.11)	(0.05)	(0.26)	(0.01)	(0.01)
Firms involved	21	16	30	66	19	21
Pseudo R^2	0.35	0.37	0.30	0.20	0.31	0.23
Model p-value	0.00	0.00	0.00	0.02	0.00	0.00

[a]Return on assets is computed as the pretax operating income divided by total assets.
[b]Industry return on assets is computed as median return on assets for firms in the industry.
[c]A firm is considered to be affiliated with a keiretsu if it belongs to the Mitsubishi, Mitsui, Sumitomo, Fuyo, DKB, or Sanwa groups.
[d]Ownership by the main bank is the fraction of equity held by the firm's largest bank lender.
[e]Ownership by blockholders is the fraction of equity held by the firm's ten largest shareholders other than the main bank.

regressions control for firm size, measured as the logarithm of the book value of assets. We include firm size in the regressions because we classify firms according to whether or not they take a particular action. Thus, for larger firms that operate more plants and have higher employment, ceteris paribus, a plant closure or layoff is more likely to be observed. Since firm size is also correlated with several other explanatory variables, controlling for size helps avoid an omitted variables bias in other coefficient estimates. We also control for firm performance in the year of the performance shock by including the ratio of pretax operating income to total assets in the regressions. In addition, we control for industry performance by including the median ratio of pretax operating income to total assets for the industry.

In column (1) of Table 6, we examine the factors that influence the probability that a firm downsizes its assets or operations in response to the performance shock. The dependent variable in this model equals one if a firm sells assets, spins off one or more units, withdraws from a line of business, closes one or more plants, cuts production or reduces its production capacity, or shuts down stores or offices. The most striking result is that contraction likelihood increases with equity ownership by the firm's main bank, and with the equity ownership by the firm's blockholders. The coefficient on equity ownership by the main bank is positive and statistically significant at the 1% level. Thus, controlling for other factors, firms are more likely to downsize when the main bank holds a significant equity stake. Alternatively, if the equity ownership by the main bank is a proxy for the strength of the ties a firm has to a main bank, this result suggests that firms with close main bank ties are more likely to respond by asset contraction policies. Our results also indicate that blockholders perform an important role by increasing the likelihood of asset contractions. This observation is consistent with theoretical work on the role of blockownership by Demsetz and Lehn (1985) and Shleifer and Vishny (1986), and with the empirical evidence on the role of blockholders in Japan by Kaplan and Minton (1994) and Kang and Shivdasani (1995).

The probability that a firm engages in layoffs is examined in column (2) of Table 6. As with the results on asset contraction, the probability of layoffs is positively related to the equity ownership by the firm's main bank. The coefficient on this variable is positive and marginally significant with a p-value of 0.06. Layoffs are more likely when ownership by the firm's blockholders is high; however, this relation is significant at only the 11% level. Layoffs are also more likely when firms perform poorly and are less likely when firms belong to a keiretsu.

As a broader measure of downsizing, we examine the probability that a firm engages in either a contraction of its assets or layoffs. These results are presented in column (3) of Table 6. As with the previous results, equity ownership by the main bank is positively and significantly related to the likelihood of downsizing. The results on ownership by blockholders are also corroborated. Firms are more likely to downsize when ownership by blockholders is high. These results suggest that firms with strong ties to banks and blockholders are more likely to take actions that reduce the scale of their operations.

Column (4) of Table 6 presents regression results for the probability of an expansion. The only variable that enters the regression significantly is firm size. The coefficient on firm size is positive and significant at the 1% level. Industry performance also has a positive and marginally significant coefficient with a *p*-value of 0.07, suggesting that firms are more likely to expand during favorable industry conditions. None of the other variables measuring ties to banks and blockholders are statistically significant. Thus, the decision to expand does not appear to be systematically related to the financial or ownership structure of our sample firms.

Our results on expansion likelihood differ from Hoshi et al. (1990) who find that firms belonging to a keiretsu or those that maintain close ties with a main bank invest more during financial distress. They interpret this finding as evidence that keiretsu and main bank ties overcome Myers' (1977) underinvestment problem during periods of financial distress. One possible explanation for this difference is that not all expansionary actions in our sample may be enhance firm value. As discussed in Section 3.1.1, several firms explicitly cite a desire for diversifying the firm's operations as a motive underlying the expansion. If, as suggested by Lins and Servaes (1997), the value-reducing consequences of diversification documented for US firms also extend to Japan, some of the expansionary actions by our sample firms may be detrimental to shareholder wealth.

In column (5) of Table 6, we investigate this issue in more detail. We assume that responses such as acquisitions are more likely to represent diversification strategies than other expansionary responses that simply expand the scale of the firm's existing operations, such as enhancing production capacity, increasing research and development and capital expenditures, and engaging in joint ventures. Thus, we are interested in determining whether main bank and blockholder ties control the proclivity of Japanese managers to diversify by means of an acquisition. The results in column (5) suggest that this is indeed the case. The coefficient on ownership by blockholders is negative and statistically significant, suggesting that blockholders reduce the probability of an acquisition. The coefficient on ownership by the main bank is also negative, but statistically insignificant.[10]

As previously discussed, downsizing may not be a meaningful response if a firm simultaneously makes a large acquisition. Thus, in column (6) of Table 6

[10] In unreported tests, we also estimate models for the likelihood that a firm will undertake an internal reorganization. None of the explanatory variables are significant in these regressions. For the sake of brevity, these results are not reported.

Table 7
Logit estimates of the likelihood of changes in control activities subsequent to performance decline. The sample consists of 92 Japanese manufacturing firms listed on the First Section of the Tokyo Stock Exchange during 1986 to 1990 that had a ratio of pretax operating income to assets that exceeds the industry median in a given year and experience a decline of at least 50% in operating income in the subsequent year. Performance variables are measured as of the year of the performance decline, while other variables are measured for the year prior to the decline. Firm size is measured as the logarithm of the book value of assets. Data are obtained from the Pacific-Basin Capital Markets Research Center data base, Kigyo Keiretsu Soran, and Yakuin Shikiho. Due to missing observations, the sample size is 87 for columns (1), (2), and (3), 82 for column (4), and 71 for column (5). p-values are in parentheses.

Actions	All management turnover (1)	Disciplinary management turnover (2)	Outside succession (3)	Outside director(s) appointed (4)	Outside director(s) departed (5)
Intercept	− 0.03	0.35	5.74	− 7.14	0.39
	(0.99)	(0.94)	(0.49)	(0.09)	(0.92)
Log (size)	− 0.19	− 0.36	− 1.99	− 0.01	− 0.34
	(0.46)	(0.37)	(0.04)	(0.99)	(0.34)
Return on assets[a]	0.14	− 0.00	− 0.03	0.30	0.08
	(0.33)	(0.99)	(0.93)	(0.10)	(0.65)
Industry return on assets[b]	− 0.09	− 0.03	0.24	− 0.12	− 0.42
	(0.67)	(0.92)	(0.53)	(0.64)	(0.17)
Total debt/assets	0.81	− 0.65	9.53	5.26	− 1.44
	(0.75)	(0.84)	(0.10)	(0.06)	(0.64)
Bank debt/assets	− 2.81	− 1.14	− 8.50	− 4.53	0.53
	(0.33)	(0.77)	(0.13)	(0.14)	(0.87)

Keiretsu membership[c]	− 0.22	− 0.70	− 4.71	0.93	0.49
	(0.72)	(0.44)	(0.04)	(0.16)	(0.50)
Board ownership	− 0.03	− 0.01	− 0.22	0.02	− 0.02
	(0.45)	(0.75)	(0.14)	(0.67)	(0.56)
Main bank ownership[d]	− 0.09	− 0.13	− 0.01	0.12	0.33
	(0.31)	(0.39)	(0.94)	(0.34)	(0.06)
Blockholder ownership[e]	0.04	0.06	0.18	0.06	0.09
	(0.04)	(0.03)	(0.01)	(0.01)	(0.00)
Firms involved	30	13	11	26	28
Pseudo R^2	0.13	0.16	0.51	0.21	0.28
Model p-value	0.12	0.06	0.00	0.01	0.01

[a]Return on assets is computed as the pretax operating income divided by total assets.
[b]Industry return on assets is computed as median return on assets for firms in the industry.
[c]A firm is considered to be affiliated with a keiretsu if it belongs to the Mitsubishi, Mitsui, Sumitomo, Fuyo, DKB, or Sanwa groups.
[d]Ownership by the main bank is the fraction of equity held by the firm's largest bank lender.
[e]Ownership by blockholders is the fraction of equity held by the firm's ten largest shareholders other than the main bank.

we examine the likelihood that a firm downsizes by either an asset contraction or layoff without acquiring other assets or firms. As with the previous results on downsizing, this probability increases with the equity ownership by the main bank and by other blockholders. The effects of both main bank and blockholder ownership are significant with p-values of 0.03 and 0.01, respectively. There is also marginally significant evidence that such downsizing is negatively related to firm performance and leverage.

In Table 7, we examine the effect of governance structure on the likelihood of changes in board-level control rights. In column (1) of Table 7 we consider the probability of a change in the identity of the president. The dependent variable in this model equals one if there is a change in the president, and is zero otherwise. In this model, the estimated coefficient on ownership by blockholders is positive with a p-value of 0.04, while none of the other variables are significant.

One potential concern is that some of the observed managerial turnover may represent normal succession. Accordingly, to focus on turnover events that are more likely to be disciplinary, we consider the probability that a president is replaced and does not become chairman, in column (2) of Table 7. As with the results for all turnover, the coefficient on ownership by blockholders is positive and significant with this specification. An alternative way to identify disciplinary turnover events is to examine the origin of the successor, since outside succession is more likely to indicate a disciplinary turnover event. We examine the likelihood of such turnover in column (3) and find that it is also related to blockholder ownership. The coefficient on this variable is again positive and significant. Consistent with Kang and Shivdasani (1996), we also find that outside succession is less likely for larger firms and those that are affiliated with a keiretsu.

In column (4) of Table 7, we examine the probability that an outside director is added to the board. These results show that the probability of outside director additions is positively related to leverage and ownership by blockholders; these effects are significant at the 6% and 1% level, respectively. These results are consistent with Kaplan and Minton (1994) who document that the likelihood of corporate director appointments increases with blockholder ownership. In column (5) of Table 7, we estimate the likelihood that outside directors will be removed from the board in response to the performance shock. We find that equity ownership by both the main bank and the firm's blockholders significantly increases this probability, while none of the other variables are statistically significant. Thus, blockholders play a particularly important role in reorganizing the composition of the board by facilitating both the removal of incumbent outsiders and the appointment of new outside directors.

To provide some perspective on the economic magnitudes of the effects of main bank and blockholder ownership on restructuring activities, Table 8 reports the estimated probabilities from the logit models of Tables 6 and 7 where all variables are set to their median values, while varying ownership by

Table 8
Estimated probabilities of restructuring actions during performance decline. Probabilities are estimated using the logit regressions reported in Tables 6 and 7. The sample consists of 92 Japanese manufacturing firms listed on the First Section of the Tokyo Stock Exchange during 1986 to 1990. Sample firms have a ratio of pretax operating income to assets that exceeds the industry median in a given year and experience a decline of at least 50% in operating income in the subsequent year. Probabilities are computed holding all variables constant at their sample median, and varying the ownership by main banks and blockholders from the 25th to the 75th percentiles, respectively.

Action	Probability when all variables are at median	Probability when all variables are at median and main bank ownership is at		Probability when all variables are at median and blockholder ownership is at	
		25th percentile	75th percentile	25th percentile	75th percentile
Asset contraction	0.069	0.022	0.095	0.044	0.135
Layoffs	0.167	0.082	0.203	0.113	0.292
Asset contraction or layoffs	0.225	0.068	0.304	0.162	0.354
Expansion	0.722	0.738	0.718	0.670	0.794
Acquisition	0.155	0.249	0.134	0.281	0.053
Asset contraction or layoffs and no acquisition	0.170	0.053	0.231	0.098	0.359
Disciplinary turnover	0.110	0.170	0.097	0.067	0.228
Outside succession	0.043	0.045	0.043	0.009	0.375
Outside director appointment	0.206	0.141	0.229	0.130	0.381
Outside director removal	0.345	0.130	0.434	0.188	0.658

main banks and blockholders from the 25th to the 75th percentile (i.e. 0–4.97% and 31.47–55%, respectively). The effect of main bank ownership on the probability of asset sales and layoffs seems economically important. Varying main bank ownership from the 25th to 75th percentile increases the probability of asset contraction from 2.2% to 9.5%, while the probability of layoffs increases from 8.2% to 20.3%. Varying blockholder ownership over the interquartile range increases the probability of an asset contraction from 4.4% to 13.5%, the probability of layoffs from 11.3% to 29.2%, the probability of disciplinary managerial turnover from 6.7% to 22.8%, and reduces the probability of an acquisition from 28.1% to 5.3%. The probability that a firm downsizes without making an acquisition is only 9.7% when blockholder ownership is at the 25th percentile, but increases to almost 36% at the 75th percentile. Thus, the effects of ownership by banks and blockholders on the likelihood of operational responses appear to be economically important.

4.2. Additional tests

To check the robustness of the results, we conduct several checks of model specification in unreported tests. We briefly summarize the results of these tests.

4.2.1. Financially distressed firms

Hoshi et al. (1990), Pascale and Rohlen (1983), and Sheard (1994) show that main banks perform a critical role during the restructuring of firms in financial distress. To examine whether our results are driven by firms in financial distress, we also estimate the logit models excluding the 6 firms that became financially distressed as a result of the performance drop. We obtain qualitatively identical results, suggesting that banks and blockholders in Japan perform an important monitoring function even when firms are not financially distressed.

4.2.2. Controlling for liquidity

We examine whether the inclusion of liquidity changes the nature of the results documented in the previous section. We find that liquidity, measured by either the current ratio, or the quick ratio, in the base year is not significant in any of the regressions, and does not alter the qualitative nature of the other variables in the model.

4.2.3. Controlling for firm size

The reported tests control for firm size since size is correlated with several explanatory variables. When size is excluded from the model, the coefficient on equity ownership by blockholders is not significant at the 5% level in models (1) and (3) of Table 6, but retains statistical significance in models (5) and (6) of Table 6 and all models in Table 7. The estimates of all other explanatory variables in these tables are qualitatively similar.

4.2.4. Nonlinear effects of management ownership

Several studies (e.g., Morck et al., 1988; Wruck, 1989; McConnell and Servaes, 1990, 1995) document that management ownership has a non-monotonic impact on firm value in the US. We test for potential nonlinearities in the effect of ownership by Japanese boards in several ways. First, we include a squared term for board equity ownership. Second, we include a piecewise linear specification using 1% and 5% as turning points. Third, we include a dummy variable if board ownership exceeds 5%. With all approaches, we are unable to detect any evidence of a nonlinear relation, and the qualitative nature of the results is unchanged.

4.2.5. Equity ownership by banks and blockholders

Because of the importance that is generally ascribed to main banks in Japan, the preceding tests separately consider the effects of equity ownership of the main bank and other blockholders. We have also estimated the tests combining the ownership of the main banks and of other blockholders, and obtain results that essentially mirror those of non-main bank blockholders reported in Tables 6 and 7. In addition, we estimate our regressions including an interaction term to test for possible differential effects of ownership by blockholders that are financial institutions and those that are corporations. These tests do not reveal such differences.

4.2.6. Multivariate analysis of US firm responses

We estimate regressions similar to those in Tables 6 and 7 for responses by US firms, using firm size, firm and industry performance, leverage, ownership by boards and blockholders, and a dummy variable to indicate the presence of an external takeover threat. We find that the likelihood that a firm downsizes is inversely related to firm performance, but positively related to industry performance. That downsizing and industry performance are related is consistent with arguments by Shleifer and Vishny (1992) who suggest that firms are less likely to sell assets when the industry is performing poorly. We also find that the likelihood of downsizing is unrelated to blockholder ownership, but is negatively related to ownership by the board of directors. The role of blockholders, therefore, appears to differ between the US and Japan. One potential explanation for this difference is that, as shown in Table 4, the average ownership of Japanese blockholders is much larger than that of US blockholders. Alternatively, as suggested by Jensen (1989) and Admati and Pfleiderer (1994), as informed investors of both debt and equity claims, Japanese blockholders have a stronger incentive to monitor than do blockholders in the US. Finally, the results show that the presence of an external control threat increase the probability that a firm downsizes.

We also estimate regressions to predict the likelihood of expansions, acquisition, CEO turnover, outside succession, and outside director additions and removals. We find no evidence that such actions are related to firms' financial and ownership structure in the US.

5. Firm performance following restructuring actions

In this section, we examine the effect of downsizing actions on the operating performance of Japanese firms. We investigate whether operational actions such as asset contraction and layoffs result in improvements in firm performance subsequent to the performance shock. Improvements in performance could result from the divestiture or closure of relatively unprofitable operations, a reduction in labor expenses, or from eliminating negative synergies between divested and existing operations.

Table 9 compares the changes in the industry-adjusted ratio of operating income to assets for the three years following the performance decline according to reported downsizing actions. Over the three years following the performance shock, industry-adjusted operating return on assets improves by 1.47% for firms announcing asset contraction, and by 1.22% for firms announcing layoffs. A sign-rank test indicates these increases are significant at the 10% level. An

Table 9

Changes in firm performance subsequent to performance decline. The sample consists of 92 Japanese manufacturing firms listed on the First Section of the Tokyo Stock Exchange during 1986 to 1990. Sample firms had a ratio of pretax operating income to assets that exceeds the industry median in a given year and experience a decline of at least 50% in operating income in the subsequent year. The table reports changes in performance for all firms as well as for subsamples classified by restructuring activities. Year 0 denotes the year of the decline in performance. Data is obtained from the Pacific-Basin Capital Markets Research Center data base. Numbers in parentheses report *p*-values from a two-tailed *t*-test for means and sign rank test for medians.

	Change in industry-adjusted ratio of operating income to assets					
	Year 0 to Year + 1		Year 0 to Year + 2		Year 0 to Year + 3	
Firms	Mean	Median	Mean	Median	Mean	Median
All firms	0.24 (0.33)	0.17 (0.11)	1.05 (0.00)	0.74 (0.00)	1.27 (0.00)	1.24 (0.00)
Asset contraction	− 0.22 (0.67)	− 0.37 (0.66)	1.03 (0.14)	0.37 (0.28)	1.48 (0.07)	1.47 (0.05)
Layoffs	− 0.12 (0.79)	− 0.23 (0.68)	0.30 (0.50)	0.37 (0.60)	0.95 (0.06)	1.22 (0.07)
Asset contraction or Layoffs	− 0.15 (0.71)	− 0.32 (0.61)	0.90 (0.08)	0.68 (0.14)	1.44 (0.02)	1.54 (0.01)
Asset contraction or layoffs without acquisition	− 0.25 (0.60)	− 0.21 (0.70)	1.26 (0.03)	1.00 (0.02)	1.85 (0.01)	1.68 (0.01)

improvement in operating performance is also evident for firms that announce either layoffs or asset contraction. These firms experience a median 1.54% increase in performance over the subsequent three years. For the subset of these firms that do not make an acquisition, the median change in operating performance over the subsequent three years is 1.68%, which is statistically significant at the 1% level. Thus, analysis of changes in operating performance indicates that Japanese firms that downsize experience subsequent improvements in performance.

6. Conclusions

In this paper, we compare the restructuring of a sample of Japanese and US manufacturing firms that had a substantial decline in operating performance in a given year. We find several similarities in the operational responses by firms subsequent to the performance decline. Both Japanese and US firms downsize their operations by selling assets, closing plants, reducing capital expenditures and production, and through employee layoffs. Both groups of firms also expand their operations and make acquisitions. The US responses are accompanied by frequent external takeover pressures, while such explicit pressures are absent for Japanese firms. There are also some notable differences in firm responses between Japan and the US. The overall frequency of asset contraction actions among US firms is roughly twice that of Japanese firms, and the frequency of asset sales is almost seven times that of Japanese firms. Layoffs also appear to affect a larger fraction of the firm's workforce in the US than in Japan.

We find that the responses undertaken by Japanese firms are related to the distribution of equity ownership and debt claims. In particular, the likelihood of an asset downsizing, employee layoffs and removal of outside directors increases with ownership by the firm's main bank and by the firm's other blockholders. Increased ownership by blockholders also decreases the likelihood of acquisitions, and increases the probability of top management turnover, outside succession events, and addition of outside directors to the board. These results suggest that the nature of the restructuring process during poor performance is a function of the distribution of claims among the firm's investors and that main banks and blockholders in Japan perform an important role in this process.

While our results provide evidence on the importance of financial and ownership structure on the restructuring process during performance declines in Japan, they also raise some important questions. For example, if concentrated ownership increases the ability to respond during poor performance, why do not all Japanese firms have highly concentrated ownership? Under what circumstances do the costs of strong bank and blockholder ties outweigh the benefits? How does the economic efficiency of the restructuring process in Japanese firms compare with the takeover-induced restructurings observed in the US?

Obtaining a better understanding of these issues represents useful areas for additional work.

References

Admati, A.R., Pfleiderer, P.P., 1994. Robust financial contracting and the role of venture capitalists. Journal of Finance 49, 371–402.

Aoki, M., Hugh, P., Paul, S., 1994. The Japanese main bank system: an introductory overview. In: Aoki, M., Hugh, P. (Eds.), The Japanese Main Bank System: Its Relevancy for Developing and Transforming Socialist Economies. Oxford University Press, Cary, NC.

Asquith, P., Gertner, R., Scharfstein, D., 1994. Anatomy of financial distress: an examination of junk-bond issuers. Quarterly Journal of Economics 109 (3), 625–658.

Berger, P.G., Ofek, E., 1995. Diversification's effect on firm value. Journal of Financial Economics 37, 39–65.

Berger, P.G., Ofek, E., 1996a. Bustup takeovers of value destroying diversified firms. Journal of Finance 51, 1175–1200.

Berger, P.G., Ofek, E., 1996b. Causes and Consequences of Corporate Refocusing Programs. Working Paper. New York University, New York.

Berglof, E., Perotti, E., 1994. The governance structure of the Japanese financial keiretsu. Journal of Financial Economics 36, 259–284.

Bhagat, S., Shleifer, A., Vishny, R., 1990. Hostile takeovers in the 1980s: the return to corporate specialization. Brookings Papers on Economic Activity, pp. 1–72.

Brown, D.T., James, C.M., Mooradian, R.M., 1993. The information content of distressed restructurings involving public and private debt claims. Journal of Financial Economics 33, 93–118.

Brown, D.T., James, C.M., Mooradian, R.M., 1994. Asset sales by financially distressed firms. Journal of Corporate Finance 1, 233–257.

Bulow, J., Shoven, J., 1978. The bankruptcy decision. Bell Journal of Economics 9, 437–456.

Comment, R., Jarrell, G.A., 1995. Corporate focus and stock returns. Journal of Financial Economics 37, 67–87.

Demsetz, H., Lehn, K., 1985. The structure of corporate ownership: causes and consequences. Journal of Political Economy 93, 1155–1177.

Denis, D.J., Denis, D.K., 1995. Performance changes following top management dismissals. Journal of Finance 50, 1029–1057.

Denis, D.J., Denis, D.K., Sarin, A., 1997. Agency problems, equity ownership and corporate diversification. Journal of Finance 52, 135–160.

French, K., Poterba, J., 1991. Were Japanese stock prices too high? Journal of Financial Economics 29, 337–364.

Gertner, R., Scharfstein, D., 1991. A theory of workouts and the effects of reorganization law. Journal of Finance 46, 1189–1222.

Gilson, S., 1990. Bankruptcy, boards, banks, and blockholders: evidence on changes in corporate ownership and control when firms default. Journal of Financial Economics 27, 355–387.

Gilson, S., John, K., Lang, L., 1990. Troubled debt restructurings: an empirical study of private reorganization of firms in default. Journal of Financial Economics 27, 315–353.

Hermalin, B., Weisbach, M.S., 1988. The determinants of board composition. Rand Journal of Economics 19, 589–606.

Industrial Groupings in Japan, 1985. Dodwell Marketing Consultants, Tokyo, Japan.

Hoshi, T., Kashyap, A., Scharfstein, D., 1990. The role of banks in reducing the costs of financial distress in Japan. Journal of Financial Economics 27, 67–88.

Jensen, M.C., Meckling, W.H., 1976. Theory of the firm: managerial behavior, agency costs, and ownership structure. Journal of Financial Economics 3, 305–360.

Jensen, M.C., 1986. Agency costs of free cash flow, corporate finance, and takeovers. American Economic Review 76, 323–329.

Jensen, M.C., 1989. Eclipse of the public corporation. Harvard Business Review 5, 61–74.

John, K., Lang, L.H.P., Netter, J., 1992. The voluntary restructuring of large firms in response to performance decline. Journal of Finance 47, 891–917.

John, K., Ofek, E., 1995. Asset sales and increase in focus. Journal of Financial Economics 37, 105–126.

Kang, J.K., Shivdasani, A., 1995. Firm performance, corporate governance, and top executive turnover in Japan. Journal of Financial Economics 38, 29–58.

Kang, J.K., Shivdasani, A., 1996. Does the Japanese governance system enhance shareholder wealth? Evidence from the stock-price effects of top management turnover. Review of Financial Studies 9, 1061–1095.

Kang, J.K., Yamada, T., 1996. The Japanese market for corporate control and managerial incentives. Working Paper. University of California, Riverside, CA.

Kaplan, S.N., 1994. Top executive rewards and firm performance: a comparison of Japan and the United States. Journal of Political Economy 102, 510–546.

Kaplan, S.N., Minton, B.A., 1994. Appointments of outsiders to Japanese boards: determinants and implications for managers. Journal of Financial Economics 36, 225–258.

Kester, W.C., 1991. Japanese Takeovers: The Global Contest for Corporate Control. Harvard Business School Press, Boston, MA.

Lang, L.H.P., Stulz, R.M., 1994. Tobin's Q, corporate diversification and firm performance. Journal of Political Economy 102, 1248–1280.

Lang, L.H.P., Poulsen, A., Stulz, R., 1995. Asset sales, firm performance, and the agency costs of managerial discretion. Journal of Financial Economics 37, 3–37.

Lins, K., Servaes, H., 1997. International evidence on the value of corporate diversification. Working Paper. University of North Carolina, Chapel Hill, NC.

McConnell, J.J., Servaes, H., 1990. Additional evidence on equity ownership and corporate value. Journal of Financial Economics 27, 595–612.

McConnell, J.J., Servaes, H., 1995. Equity ownership and the two faces of debt. Journal of Financial Economics 39, 131–157.

Mitchell, M.L., Lehn, K., 1990. Do bad bidders become good targets? Journal of Political Economy 98, 372–398.

Morck, R., Shleifer, A., Vishny, R.W., 1988. Management ownership and market valuation: an empirical analysis. Journal of Financial Economics 20, 293–315.

Myers, S.C., 1977. Determinants of corporate borrowing. Journal of Finance 5, 147–175.

Ofek, E., 1993. Capital structure and firm response to poor performance. Journal of Financial Economics 34, 3–30.

Pascale, R., Rohlen, T.P., 1983. The Mazda turnaround. Journal of Japanese Studies 9, 219–263.

Roe, M.J., 1990. Political and legal restraints on ownership and control of public companies. Journal of Financial Economics 27, 7–41.

Servaes, H., 1996. The value of diversification during the conglomerate merger wave. Journal of Finance 51, 1201–1225.

Sheard, P., 1994. Main banks and the governance of financial distress. In: Masahiko, A., Hugh, P. (Eds.), The Japanese Main Bank System: Its Relevancy for Developing and Transforming Socialist Economies. Oxford University Press, Cary, NC.

Shleifer, A., Vishny, R.W., 1986. Large shareholders and corporate control. Journal of Political Economy 95, 461–488.

Shleifer, A., Vishny, R.W., 1992. Liquidation values and debt capacity: a market equilibrium approach. Journal of Finance 47, 1343–1366.

Weisbach, M.S., 1988. Outside directors and CEO turnover. Journal of Financial Economics 20, 431–460.

Wruck, K.H., 1989. Equity ownership concentration and firm value: evidence from private equity financings. Journal of Financial Economics 23, 3–28.

[16]

ELSEVIER Journal of Financial Economics 55 (2000) 391–424

JOURNAL OF Financial ECONOMICS
www.elsevier.com/locate/econbase

Managerial discipline and corporate restructuring following performance declines☆

David J. Denis[a,]*, Timothy A. Kruse[b]

[a]*Krannert Graduate School of Management, Purdue University, West Lafayette, IN 47907-1310, USA*
[b]*School of Business Administration, Loyola University Chicago, 820 N. Michigan Avenue, Chicago, IL 60611, USA*

Received 20 May 1998; received in revised form 19 March 1999; accepted 23 November 1999

Abstract

We examine the incidence of disciplinary events that reduce the control of current managers, and corporate restructuring among firms experiencing a large decline in operating performance during an active takeover period (1985–1988) and a less active period (1989–1992). We document a significant decline in the disciplinary events from the active to the less active period that is driven by a significant decline in disciplinary takeovers, those takeovers that result in a top executive change. Following the performance decline, however, there is a substantial amount of corporate restructuring, and a significant improvement in operating performance, during both the active and the less active takeover period. We conclude that, although some managerial disciplinary events are related to overall takeover activity, the decline in takeover activity does not result in

☆We are grateful for helpful comments received from Jeff Allen, Jim Brickley, Diane Denis, Jon Garfinkel, David Haushalter, Jack Helmuth, John McConnell, Tom Nohel, Raghu Rau, Anil Shivdasani, Steven Todd, Bharathram Thothadri, Sunil Wahal, Marc Zenner, an anonymous referee, participants at the Arizona Finance Symposium, and finance workshop participants at Loyola University at Chicago, Southern Illinois University, Southern Methodist University, and the University of Illinois. We also thank Sunil Wahal for data on companies targeted by the nine largest pension funds, and Marc Zenner for data on companies targeted by the United Shareholders Association.

* Corresponding author. Tel.: 765-494-4434; fax: 765-494-9658.

E-mail address: daviddenis@mgmt.purdue.edu (D.J. Denis)

PII: S0304-405X(99)00055-0

392 D.J. Denis, T.A. Kruse / Journal of Financial Economics 55 (2000) 391–424

fewer performance-enhancing restructurings following performance declines.

JEL classification: G32; G34

Keywords: Management turnover; Takeovers; Restructuring

1. Introduction

Poorly performing managers face disciplinary pressures from both internal and external corporate control mechanisms. An important element of this control process is the threat that if managers deviate from value-maximizing corporate policies, their control will be reduced. Consistent with this view, Jensen and Warner (1988) characterize top executive changes as 'a key variable in understanding the forces disciplining managers'. In this paper, we focus on the three primary disciplinary events that represent explicit attempts to reduce or eliminate the control of current managers. These events are corporate takeovers, board dismissals, and shareholder activism. Using a sample of firms that experience a sharp decline in industry-adjusted operating performance, we provide evidence on (i) the frequency with which managers experience at least one of the above disciplinary events, and (ii) corporate restructuring and changes in operating performance following the performance decline.

Our motivation for pursuing this investigation is threefold. First, although several studies provide evidence on each of these control-reducing disciplinary events individually, none address the more fundamental issue of how frequently managers face some threat to their control when they perform poorly. Second, because the frequency of one of the disciplinary mechanisms, corporate takeovers, fell considerably in the early 1990s, we are interested in whether this decline is associated with a corresponding change in the overall frequency of control-reducing disciplinary events in recent years. Third, because previous studies suggest a strong link between control-reducing disciplinary events and corporate restructuring, we are interested in whether any change in the frequency of disciplinary events over time has changed the manner in which firms address poor performance.

Our sample consists of 350 firms that have total assets greater than $100 million, which achieve measurably high operating performance in one year, followed by a marked decline in performance the following year. The sample period, 1985–1992, encompasses an active takeover period (1985–1988) and a less active takeover period (1989–1992), thus allowing us to examine whether managerial discipline and corporate restructuring are linked with activity in the market for corporate control.

We find that a substantial fraction of the sample firms experience control-reducing disciplinary events in the year of and the three years following the year of performance decline. In our sample, half of the firms are either the target of corporate takeover activity, are targeted by activist shareholders, or experience nonroutine turnover of the firm's top executive. Nonroutine turnover is defined as any change in the top executive of the firm except those due to death or illness, and those that are classified as normal retirements using the definition of Denis and Denis (1995). Defining disciplinary management turnover as either the nonroutine turnover of the top executive or a change in top executive following a takeover, we find that 36% of the sample firms experience disciplinary turnover in their top executive by the end of the third year following the year of poor performance.

More importantly, we document a significant decline in the frequency of control-reducing disciplinary events from the active to the less active takeover period. During the active takeover period, 57% of the sample firms are either the target of corporate control activity, are targeted by shareholder activists, or experience nonroutine turnover of the firm's top executive, while only 44% of the firms in the inactive period experience one or more of these events. This difference is statistically significant at the 0.01 level. This reduction in disciplinary events corresponds with a significant reduction in the rate of disciplinary managerial turnover, from 42% in the active takeover period to 31% in the inactive period. These effects are driven by a substantial decline in takeover activity. While 42% of the sample firms are targets of takeover activity during the active takeover period, only 17% are takeover targets in the less active period. It is notable that the decline in takeover activity is not offset by an increase in public shareholder activism in the less active takeover period. The fraction of firms experiencing shareholder targeting activities, such as proxy fights for board seats, shareholder resolutions, and other non-proxy targeting events, increases only from 8% in the active takeover period to 12% in the less active period. This difference is statistically insignificant. Consequently, there is a significant net reduction in the incidence of external control market events from the first to the second subperiod. We thus conclude that, among our sample firms, the significant decline in takeover activity in the early 1990s is associated with a significant decline in disciplinary events that reduce the control of current managers.

Because several previous studies suggest that market disciplinary events are an important determinant of corporate restructuring activity,[1] we examine

[1] See, for example, Bhagat et al. (1990), Bhide (1990), and Berger and Ofek (1996) for evidence of restructuring following successful takeovers; Dann and DeAngelo (1988) for evidence on defensive asset restructurings; Del Guercio and Hawkins (1999) for evidence of restructuring following shareholder proposals; and Berger and Ofek (1999) and Denis et al. (1997) for evidence on the influence of external control pressures on corporate refocusing activity.

whether the overall decline in disciplinary events from the active to the less active takeover period is associated with a corresponding change in the nature of restructuring activity and other operating changes following poor managerial performance. We find that a large fraction of the sample firms undertake major restructurings following the performance decline. Approximately, two-thirds of the firms either restructure their assets, layoff employees, or initiate major cost-cutting efforts. On average, these restructurings are met with a positive stock price reaction, and are more common among firms experiencing disciplinary events. Nevertheless, there is no significant difference in the frequency of these restructurings across the two subperiods. Moreover, the magnitude of restructuring is similar in the active and less active takeover periods. Among firms that sell assets, the asset sales average 28.2% of the book value of total assets in the first subperiod, and 22.4% in the second subperiod.

We also find that the sample firms exhibit significant improvements in operating performance in the three years following the year of performance decline. These operating improvements are economically large, and do not differ significantly between the two subperiods. Moreover, operating improvements are significantly greater among those firms that initiate asset restructurings immediately following the performance decline than in those that do not. We conclude, therefore, that the decline in takeover activity does not result in fewer performance-enhancing restructurings in the less active takeover period.

There have been many previous studies of managerial discipline and corporate restructuring. The three studies most closely related to ours are Morck et al. (1989), Mikkelson and Partch (1997), and Huson et al. (1997). Morck et al. (1989) examine the sensitivity of takeovers and management turnover to alternative measures of firm performance. However, their sample is limited to a cross-section of Fortune 500 firms in 1980. Because they use a relatively small set of poorly performing firms, Morck et al. are unable to examine time-series variation in disciplinary mechanisms. Further, their study omits the examination of corporate restructuring activity. Mikkelson and Partch (1997) and Huson et al. (1997) examine changes in the sensitivity of management turnover, that is not related to takeover activity, to firm performance, comparing an active takeover period to a less active takeover period. Our study differs in two important respects. First, we include a broader set of control-reducing disciplinary events, thereby allowing us to examine whether other control-reducing disciplinary events substitute for a decline in takeovers. Second, we examine corporate restructuring and operating performance following the initial performance decline. This design allows us to draw inferences regarding whether changes in the frequency of explicit disciplinary events have a net effect on the manner in which firms respond to poor performance.

The remainder of the paper is organized as follows. In Section 2, we review related studies of takeovers, shareholder activism, and management turnover. We also discuss the possible effects of a decline in takeover activity on managerial discipline and corporate restructuring. Section 3 describes the sample selection process and reports descriptive statistics. Section 4 reports the incidence of managerial disciplinary events for the full sample and the two subperiods. Section 5 reports the extent of corporate restructuring and operating improvements following the year of poor performance. Section 6 provides a discussion of our results and Section 7 concludes.

2. Managerial discipline in poorly performing firms

Several mechanisms encourage managers to act in the interests of shareholders. These internal and external corporate controls include, but are not limited to, monitoring by the board of directors, by large blockholders, by the takeover market, and by other managers within the firm. In the event of poor performance, an important outcome of this monitoring process is a reduction in managerial autonomy. The most extreme outcome possible is the outright dismissal of the top executive. In this section, we review prior evidence on the three primary methods of reducing current managers' control: board dismissals, takeovers, and shareholder activism. We then discuss the possible effects of a decline in takeovers on (i) the overall frequency of control-reducing disciplinary events, and (ii) the manner in which firms respond to poor performance.

2.1. Prior evidence on board dismissals, takeovers, and shareholder activism

Several studies analyze the effectiveness of internal monitoring mechanisms by examining top management turnover among firms that have not been taken over. Warner et al. (1988) and Weisbach (1988) document an inverse relation between the likelihood of a top management change and prior stock price performance. In addition, Denis and Denis (1995) find that the forced dismissal of a top executive is associated with subsequent improvements in firm performance. These findings suggest that the board of directors serves an important disciplinary role. However, Denis and Denis (1995) and Warner et al. (1988) both question whether the underlying threat of dismissal is large enough to produce meaningful incentives for top executives.

Prior studies also suggest that poor performance increases the likelihood of a firm becoming the target of a takeover attempt. For example, Morck et al. (1989) find that the probability of hostile takeovers is inversely related to firm performance, while Mitchell and Lehn (1990) find that firms making value-decreasing acquisitions are subsequently more likely to become targets themselves. Martin and McConnell (1991) find that the rate of management turnover increases following corporate takeovers, and find that pre-takeover performance is significantly worse among those takeover targets that undergo a post-takeover management change. These findings suggest that takeovers play a direct role in disciplining poorly performing managers. Other studies suggest that takeovers play an indirect role as well. Denis and Denis (1995) find that forced resignations of top executives are often due to takeover-related pressures. Denis and Serrano (1996) document a high incidence of management turnover following unsuccessful takeover contests, and find that this turnover is concentrated among poorly performing firms in which outside blockholders acquire equity stakes. These findings suggest that there is some interaction between internal and external corporate control mechanisms.

Finally, several recent studies examine the role of shareholder activists in corporate governance. Consistent with shareholder activists serving an important disciplinary role, these studies, in general, find that the likelihood of shareholder targeting is inversely related to prior firm performance. The net effects of this activism are less clear, however. Studies examining the shareholder wealth and operating performance effects of shareholder targeting have produced mixed evidence.[2] In addition, Karpoff (1998, p. 28) reports that 'most evidence indicates that firms attracting activist efforts do not experience unusually high rates of CEO turnover'.

Although the above studies suggest that the board of directors, the takeover market, and shareholder activists play some role in disciplining poorly performing managers, the joint impact of these disciplinary events remains an open empirical issue. One goal of our study, therefore, is to provide evidence on the following question: Conditional on poor performance, what is the probability of at least one control-reducing disciplinary event taking place? Evidence on this issue represents an important contribution to the debate on whether the threat of a reduction in control provides meaningful incentives to top executives.

2.2. Possible effects of a decline in takeover activity on managerial discipline

The late 1980s were characterized by a dramatic decline in takeover activity. Comment and Schwert (1995) report that the percentage of exchange-listed firms receiving takeover bids declined from 1.5% per month in 1988 to less than 0.5% in 1990 and 1991. Because of the relation between takeover activity and management turnover discussed above, the decline in the takeover market in the early 1990s has led some to suggest that the overall level of managerial discipline has fallen in recent years. Jensen (1993), for example, argues that takeovers are more effective than other forms of market monitoring. According to Jensen, existing regulatory and legal systems are too blunt, product markets are too slow, and internal control mechanisms provide inadequate monitoring. He

[2] See, for example, Del Guercio and Hawkins (1999), Karpoff et al. (1996), Opler and Sokobin (1997), Smith (1996), Strickland et al. (1996), and Wahal (1996). Karpoff (1998) provides an excellent survey of the literature on shareholder activism.

argues, therefore, that a decline in the takeover market weakens managerial discipline.

Although Jensen's view is plausible, there are other reasonable arguments regarding why the decline in takeover activity would have little impact on managerial discipline. First, a decline in takeover activity is not necessarily evidence of a decline in disciplinary takeovers. The evidence in Mitchell and Mulherin (1996) suggests that external economic shocks, such as deregulation and changes in input costs, account for a large fraction of takeover activity. Consequently, the decline in takeover activity could have resulted from fewer economic shocks, and is therefore unconnected with the level of managerial discipline.

Second, even if disciplinary takeovers have declined, alternative monitoring mechanisms such as active boards and active shareholders can substitute for the takeover market in forcing the replacement of poorly performing managers. Evidence in Kaplan (1994) and Kang and Shivdasani (1997) suggest that such a substitution takes place in Japan, a market historically characterized by a relatively inactive takeover market. These researchers find that blockholders and main banks play an important monitoring role in Japanese firms. Similarly, the emergence of increased activism by large institutional shareholders, such as the California Public Employees Retirement System (CALPERS), can be viewed as a market solution to the decreased monitoring provided by the takeover market in the early 1990s.

Finally, even if control-reducing disciplinary events decline, managers of poorly performing firms can be pressured to undertake necessary restructurings in the absence of management turnover. Pound (1992a,b), for example, describes a political model of corporate governance. Under this model, activist shareholders maintain an ongoing, but private, dialogue with managers and the board of directors, thereby pressuring poorly performing firms to make necessary structural changes without the upheaval of a corporate takeover. Carleton et al. (1998) analyze the negotiations between one financial institution, TIAA-CREF, and the companies it targeted between 1987 and 1996. Their evidence indicates that these negotiations were effective in bringing about desired changes at the targeted companies. Similarly, Del Guercio and Hawkins (1999) find that shareholder proposals are followed by substantial asset sales and restructurings, despite the lack of any unusual top executive turnover. In addition to activist shareholders, other incentive mechanisms can motivate managers to undertake necessary restructurings in the absence of any overt disciplinary threat against the control of current managers. These incentive mechanisms could include direct equity ownership, compensation contracts, and labor market concerns. Labor market concerns refers to the view that managers derive incentives from the knowledge that if they perform poorly, the demand for their services will decline. In an interesting recent study, Brickley et al. (1998) show that these career concerns include not only current managerial opportunities within and outside the manager's company, but also extend to concerns about post-retirement board service.

It is therefore an open empirical question whether the recent decline in takeover activity has had a net impact on either the frequency of control-reducing disciplinary events or the manner in which firms respond to performance declines. Our study addresses both of these isues. In a related study, Mikkelson and Partch (1997) examine a random sample of firms and find that, among firms not taken over, the sensitivity of top executive turnover to firm performance is greater in the active takeover period occurring between 1984 and 1989.[3] One explanation for their findings is that the decline in takeover activity in the United States in the early 1990s caused a decrease in disciplinary managerial turnover. Alternatively, however, substitute disciplinary mechanisms, such as shareholder activism, may have replaced takeovers in monitoring managers. Moreover, it is possible that the presence of either these substitute monitoring mechanisms or other incentive mechanisms provided sufficient motivation to managers to undertake value-increasing restructuring actions in the absence of management turnover. By examining the combined disciplinary effects of takeovers, board dismissals, and shareholder activism, our analysis provides further evidence on these issues.

3. Sample selection and description of data

Our sample selection process attempts to identify a set of firms exhibiting poor managerial performance. Because managerial performance is unobservable, we employ a firm-specific performance measure as a proxy for managerial performance. We recognize that by doing so, our sample will include some firms for which no managerial discipline or corporate restructuring is required. We measure operating performance as the industry-adjusted ratio of earnings before interest, taxes, depreciation, and amortization (EBITDA) to total assets. We select a sample of firms experiencing a substantial decline in operating performance from a year of positive industry-adjusted operating performance to a year of substandard performance. In this way, the sample consists of firms for which there is a clear starting point for their difficulties, as opposed to firms suffering ongoing performance problems. We employ operating performance, as opposed to stock returns, as the performance measure because share prices incorporate the market's expectation of the value of any restructuring or disciplinary activity following the performance decline. In addition, operating performance, unlike

[3] Using a slightly different sampling procedure and empirical approach, Huson et al. (1997) arrive at a different conclusion. They argue that, if anything, internal monitoring mechanisms became more effective in the early 1990s, after the end of the active takeover period.

net income, is not influenced by special charges. Because we are interested in firms for which the poor performance is isolated to that firm, we adjust the operating performance measure for any market-wide or industry-wide effects.

The sample is constructed as follows. For each firm listed on Compustat's annual, over-the-counter, and research tapes with total assets of at least $100 million, we calculate the ratio of EBITDA to total assets (*Compustat* item #13 divided by *Compustat* item #6) for each of the fiscal years 1984 through 1992. We impose the $100 million asset size requirement to increase the probability that the firm receives coverage in the *Wall Street Journal* and has available proxy statements. Imposing this requirement may cause us to overstate the role of large institutional investors, which typically target larger firms.[4] We adjust each firm's operating performance by subtracting the median ratio of EBITDA to assets for all other companies having the same three-digit Standard Industrial Classification (SIC) code. Firms are included in the sample if their industry-adjusted operating performance exceeds the overall sample median in one year, but is in the bottom quartile of the sample the following year. This process results in an initial sample of 412 observations. After deleting companies for which we are either unable to locate proxy statements or for which there is no *Wall Street Journal* coverage of the firm, we are left with a final sample of 350 observations, representing 339 different firms.

By construction, the sample firms experience a substantial decline in industry-adjusted performance in at least one of the years between 1985 and 1992. We refer to this as the year of poor performance (year 0) and the prior year as the base year (year −1). The distribution of the sample by the calendar year of poor performance is fairly uniform, ranging from a low of 34 firms (10% of the sample) in 1987 to 55 firms (16% of the sample) in 1989. In addition, there does not appear to be any substantial industry clustering within the sample. There are 53 different industries, identified using two-digit SIC codes, represented in the sample, and the distribution of 2-digit SIC codes within the sample is similar to that of the universe of Compustat firms with total assets greater than $100 million.

Table 1 reports measures of operating performance and stock returns over the two-year period that includes the base year and the year of poor performance. As depicted in the first column of Panel A, EBITDA as a proportion of total assets averages 0.16 in the base year, and the sample firms outperform the median industry firm by 0.05. In the year of poor performance, operating performance declines substantially to 0.04, and the sample firms now significantly underperform the median industry firm by 0.06. Overall, the data suggest

[4] For example, John and Klein (1994) find that the likelihood of the firm's receiving a governance proposal is positively related to the size of the firm. Also, the Council of Institutional Investors draws their annual sample of companies to be targeted from the worst performers in the S&P 500.

Table 1
Magnitude of the performance decline

Industry-adjusted operating performance and adjusted holding period stock returns for the period surrounding the year of performance decline. The base year is the year prior to the year of performance decline. The sample includes 350 firms with a book value of assets greater than $100 million that are in the top half of industry-adjusted performance in the base year and in the bottom quartile in the year of poor performance. The performance measure that we use is the ratio of earnings before interest, taxes, depreciation, and amortization (EBITDA) to total assets. Industry-adjusted EBITDA is calculated as the difference between the ratio of EBITDA to total assets of the sample firm and the median ratio of EBITDA to total assets for those firms operating in the same three-digit SIC codes. Adjusted holding period stock returns are calculated as the difference between the buy-and-hold return of the sample firm and the buy-and-hold return of a control firm randomly selected from the same market value decile. The sample period is 1985 to 1992. Significance levels for the test that the means and medians are equal to zero are reported using heteroskedastic t-tests and Wilcoxon signed rank tests, respectively. The last two columns report t-statistics and z-statistics for differences in means and medians, respectively, of each variable across the two subperiods. * indicates significance at the 0.01 level.

	Full sample		1985–1988		1989–1992		Test statistic	
	Mean	Median	Mean	Median	Mean	Median	*t*-stat.	*Z*-stat.
Panel A: Operating performance								
Performance at end of base year	0.160	0.156	0.165	0.160	0.156	0.155	1.593	1.458
Performance at end of year of poor performance	0.039	0.051	0.042	0.052	0.035	0.050	0.882	1.145
Change in performance	– 0.121*	– 0.103*	– 0.122*	– 0.104*	– 0.120*	– 0.103*	– 0.258	0.271
Industry-adjusted performance at end of base year	0.053*	0.041*	0.055*	0.037*	0.052*	0.043*	0.519	– 0.574
Industry-adjusted performance at end of year of poor performance	– 0.059*	– 0.052*	– 0.056*	– 0.052*	– 0.061*	– 0.053*	0.716	0.833
Change in industry-adjusted performance	– 0.112*	– 0.095*	– 0.110*	– 0.096*	– 0.113*	– 0.094*	0.774	1.201
Panel B: Adjusted Holding Period Stock Returns								
Beginning of base year to end of year of poor performance	– 0.360*	– 0.286*	– 0.368*	– 0.336*	– 0.352*	– 0.244*	– 0.173	– 0.572
Beginning of base year to end of base year	0.026	0.001	– 0.006	– 0.031	0.052	0.077	– 0.885	– 1.335

that the sample firms were initially performing well, but suffered an economically large, firm-specific performance shock.

To provide some assurance that we have correctly identified the onset of poor performance, we also examine the operating performance of the sample firms in the two years prior to the base year (i.e. years −2 and −3). These results are not reported in a table. We find that the median EBITDA as a proportion of total assets is 0.15 in both years −2 and −3, an amount that is statistically indistinguishable from the median performance level in the base year (year −1). Thus, it appears that the performance in the base year represents the norm, and that the decline in operating performance in year 0 is unusual. We also examine whether the performance decline in year 0 is connected with changes in the firm's top executive. Previous studies provide some evidence that incoming top executives manage earnings such that reported earnings are lower early in their tenure (see, e.g. Murphy and Zimmerman, 1993; Porciau, 1993). In this sample, 37 firms undergo a change in top executive between year −1 and year 0. However, the performance declines of these firms are statistically indistinguishable from those of the remainder of the sample firms. Thus, the performance declines that we document in year 0 are not driven by the earnings management decisions of incoming top executives.

Panel A of Table 1 also compares the performance declines of the sample firms experiencing their year of poor performance during the active takeover period (1985–1988) and the less active takeover period (1989–1992). The results indicate that the performance declines in the two subperiods are nearly identical. Thus, it does not appear as if differences in disciplinary actions or corporate restructuring across the two subperiods can be attributed to systematic differences in the magnitude of poor performance.

It is possible that the market becomes aware of performance problems well before these problems become evident in accounting performance measures. If so, our sample selection process will identify the starting point of operating difficulties incorrectly, and we will overstate the speed with which market disciplinary events occur following the performance decline. To examine this issue, Panel B of Table 1 reports adjusted holding period stock returns over the base year and the year of poor performance. Adjusted holding period returns are defined as the buy-and-hold return of the sample firm minus the buy-and-hold return of a control firm randomly selected from the same market value decile as the sample firm as of last day of the fiscal year of the sample firm's poor performance. Test statistics using this method are generally well-specified (Barber and Lyon, 1997). We obtain qualitatively similar results if we compute adjusted holding period returns as the difference between the return of the sample firm and that of the value-weighted index.

The evidence shown in Panel B of Table 1 indicates that the market first becomes aware of the poor performance in the year that operating performance declines. Adjusted holding period stock returns are small and statistically insignificant in the base year, but average a statistically significant decline of 36% in the year of poor performance. Moreover, as was the case with operating performance, there are no significant differences in stock price performance for firms experiencing performance declines in the two subperiods. These findings suggest not only that the performance decline is a surprise to the market, but also that the market considers the decline to be an economically important event.

In Table 2, we report descriptive statistics on several firm characteristics that could be related to the likelihood of managerial discipline. These include the book value of total assets, the ratio of long-term debt to total assets, and several equity ownership and board composition characteristics. Financial data are obtained from Compustat, while ownership and board composition data are obtained from corporate proxy statements. Affiliated blockholders are defined as those that have some connection with the company, such as through an Employee Stock Ownership Plan (ESOP), being a family member of an officer, or a shareholder having substantial business dealings with the sample firm. All other blockholders are labeled as unaffiliated. We follow the convention in the literature of labeling directors as insiders if they are currently employees of the firm, as affiliated outsiders if they have substantial business relations with the firm, are related to insiders, or are former employees, and as independent outsiders if they are neither insiders nor affiliated outsiders.

For the full sample, the firms have average total assets of approximately $800 million at the end of the base year and long-term debt totaling approximately 20% of total assets. The average shareholdings of the officers and directors, as a group, are 20.0%, while the median shareholdings for this group is 11.3%. This level is quite similar to the median 11.6% holdings of officers and directors reported by Mikkelson and Partch (1997) for a randomly selected set of firms listed on the NYSE and Amex exchanges in 1988. On average, stockholders with at least a 5% stake, or blockholders, own 15.5% of the firm's shares. Affiliated blockholders own 6.3% of the firm's shares, while 9.2% are held by unaffiliated blockholders. On average, the board of directors consists of nine members, of which 36% are corporate insiders, 48% are independent outsiders, and 16% are affiliated outsiders. These board composition statistics are comparable to those reported by Denis and Sarin (1999) for a random sample of 583 firms.

The data in Table 2 also indicate that the characteristics of the sample firms are very similar in the two subperiods. There is weak evidence that the equity ownership of officers and directors is higher in the second subperiod, and weak evidence that the fraction of the board that is composed of affiliated outsiders is lower in the second subperiod. The only characteristic that is significantly different at the 0.05 level in the two subperiods is the number of directors. Consistent with the findings in Huson et al. (1997), firms in the earlier subperiod have significantly larger boards.

Table 2
Description of the sample

Summary statistics for the sample of 350 companies experiencing performance declines over the period 1985–1992. The sample consists of firms, with a book value of assets greater than $100 million, that are in the top half of industry-adjusted EBITDA/Total assets in the base year and in the bottom quartile in the year of poor performance. All reported data are as of the end of the base year. The base year is the year prior to the year of poor performance. Affiliated blockholders are either Employee Stock Ownership Programs (ESOPs) or shareholders having extensive business dealings with the company. All other blockholders are classified as unaffiliated. Inside directors are current or former officers of the company. Affiliated outside directors are family members of officers or directors having substantial business dealings with the company. All other directors are classified as independent outsiders. Dollar values are expressed in millions. The last two columns report heteroskedastic t-statistics and Wilcoxon z-statistics for differences in means and medians, respectively, of each variable across the two subperiods.

	Full sample		1985–1988		1989–1992		Test statistic	
	Mean	Median	Mean	Median	Mean	Median	t-stat.	Z-stat.
Book value of total assets (millions)	805.27	230.28	802.23	228.24	808.16	233.67	− 0.03	− 0.71
Long-term debt/total assets	0.22	0.19	0.22	0.20	0.21	0.19	0.29	0.39
Proportion of shares held by officers and directors	0.20	0.11	0.18	0.11	0.22	0.11	− 1.77	− 0.78
Proportion of shares held by all blockholders	0.16	0.10	0.15	0.09	0.16	0.12	− 0.68	− 0.99
Proportion of shares held by affiliated blockholders	0.06	0.00	0.05	0.00	0.07	0.00	− 1.04	− 1.29
Proportion of shares held by unaffiliated blockholders	0.09	0.07	0.09	0.06	0.09	0.07	0.29	− 0.63
Number of directors	9.05	9.00	9.69	9.00	8.51	8.00	3.18	3.32
Proportion of the board composed of inside directors	0.36	0.33	0.36	0.33	0.37	0.33	− 0.31	0.07
Proportion of the board composed of independent outside directors	0.48	0.46	0.47	0.46	0.49	0.46	− 0.84	− 0.74
Proportion of the board composed of affiliated outside directors	0.16	0.14	0.17	0.14	0.14	0.13	1.61	1.63

4. The incidence of disciplinary events following performance declines

In this section, we report the incidence of control-reducing disciplinary events occurring at the sample firms in the year of and the three years following the performance decline. We first examine external control events, such as actual and attempted takeovers, and targeting by shareholder activists and blockholders. We then report the incidence of management turnover, including both those turnovers that follow takeovers and those that do not. Finally, we estimate logit models that test for time series variation in the incidence of market disciplinary events, while controlling for other factors that might be related to these disciplinary events.

4.1. External control events

Table 3 reports data on the frequency of external control events occurring at the sample firms. We search the Wall Street Journal over the period that includes the year of and the three years following the year of poor performance. We record any instance of a sample firm having been taken over, been the subject of takeover rumors, or been the target of a takeover attempt. We report a firm as being the subject of a takeover rumor only if it is not also the target of an attempted or actual takeover during the year in which the rumor occurred. However, if the rumor exists during a year prior to the attempt or takeover, we report both the rumor and the subsequent takeover attempt. Similarly, attempted takeovers are reported only if the sample firm is not taken over during that year. We report the frequency of external control events for the full sample period (1985–1992) and for the subperiods representing the active (1985–1988) and less active (1989–1992) takeover periods. The significance of the difference in event frequencies between the two subperiods is measured using a χ^2 test of equal proportions.

The results in the first four rows of Table 3 indicate that a large fraction of the sample firms become the target of a takeover attempt following the onset of poor performance. During the sample period, 29% of the sample firms are subject to at least one type of takeover activity in the year of and the three years subsequent to the year of poor performance. The frequency of takeover events is substantially higher in the first subperiod than in the second subperiod. During the first subperiod, 42% of the firms experience some type of takeover activity, whereas only 17% of the firms experience takeover activity in the second subperiod. The difference between these levels is significant at the 0.01 level. This pattern is repeated when we examine the frequency of actual takeovers, rumors, and attempts. With the exception of rumored takeovers, the frequencies of these events are significantly greater, at the 0.01 level, in the 1985–1988 subperiod. We thus conclude that the marketwide decline in takeover activity in the late 1980s extends to our sample of poorly performing firms.

Table 3
Corporate control events

The frequency of external corporate control events for the sample of 350 poorly performing firms for years 0 through 3 relative to the year of poor performance. The sample includes firms, with a book value of assets greater than $100 million, that are in the top half of industry-adjusted EBITDA/Total assets in the base year and in the bottom quartile in the year of poor performance. Information about takeover activity is taken from the Wall Street Journal. A firm is considered subject to a takeover rumor only if there are no attempted or actual takeovers during the year of the rumor. A firm is considered subject to a takeover attempt only if there are no actual takeovers during the year of the attempt. A firm is considered subject to control activity if it is the subject of a takeover rumor, takeover attempt, or actual takeover at any time from the start of year 0 through the end of year 3. Pension fund targeting is taken from Wahal (1996). Companies targeted by the Council of Institutional Investors are from Opler and Sokobin (1997), Pensions and Investments (Oct. 7, 1994), and the Wall Street Journal. Companies targeted by the United Shareholders Association are from Strickland et al. (1996). The sample period is 1985 to 1992. The chi-squared statistic tests the hypothesis that the proportion of firms experiencing each event is equal in the two subperiods. *, **, *** indicates significance at the 0.10, 0.05, and 0.01 levels, respectively.

Event	Full sample (n = 350)		1985–1988 (n = 170)		1989–1992 (n = 180)		χ^2
	N	%	N	%	N	%	
Firm is taken over	67	19	49	29	18	10	20.01***
Firm is subject to takeover rumors	25	9	14	3	11	7	2.71*
Firm is subject to takeover attempts	26	9	20	16	5	4	13.37***
Firm is subject to corporate control activity	102	29	72	42	30	17	27.93***
Firm is targeted by pension fund	15	4	3	2	12	7	5.12**
Firm is targeted by United Shareholders Association	9	3	1	1	8	4	5.19**
Firm is targeted by Council of Institutional Investors	4	1	0	0	4	2	3.82**
Firm is targeted by other shareholder	18	5	11	6	7	4	1.20
Firm is targeted by any shareholder activist	35	10	14	8	21	12	1.14
Total firms subjected to takeover activity or shareholder targeting	122	35	76	45	46	26	14.12***

To put the frequency of takeover activity in our sample into perspective, we compare the sample takeover rates shown in Table 3 to those reported by Mikkelson and Partch (1997) for a random sample of firms over approximately the same time period. For a random sample of 240 firms selected in 1983, Mikkelson and Partch report that 18.2% were taken over by the end of 1988, an annual takeover rate of approximately 3.6%. For a second set of firms selected in 1989, Mikkelson and Partch report that 7.7% were taken over by the end of 1994, an annual rate of 1.5%. To compare the results for our sample, takeover rates are calculated by dividing the number of firms taken over by the product of number of calendar years in the event window times the number of firms initially in each subsample. Our estimated takeover rate understates the true takeover rate because of the disappearance of firms over time. The annual takeover rate in our sample is 7.3% in the first subperiod and 2.5% in the later subperiod. Thus, our sample firms are targeted for takeover activity at an unusually high frequency, particularly in the earlier subperiod.

As discussed in Section 2, it is possible that monitoring by active shareholders substitutes for takeover activity in the less active takeover period. To examine this possibility, Table 3 also reports the frequency with which the sample firms are targeted by various activist shareholder groups. Data on shareholder targeting is obtained from a variety of sources. Companies targeted by the nine largest activist public pension funds from 1987 through 1993 are from Wahal (1996).[5] Companies targeted by the United Shareholders Association (USA) are from Strickland et al. (1996). A list of the companies targeted by the Council of Institutional Investors (CII) from 1991 through 1993 is provided in the appendix of Opler and Sokobin (1997). Companies targeted by the CII in 1994 and 1995 are from the Oct. 7, 1994 issue of Pensions and Investments (p. 4) and the Oct. 2, 1995 issue of the Wall Street Journal (p. A4), respectively. Companies targeted by other shareholder activists, primarily through proxy fights for board seats and shareholder proposals regarding changes in the structure or management of the firm, are obtained from the Wall Street Journal Index.

Although we find that the incidence of shareholder targeting is greater in the second subperiod, the frequency of these events is relatively low in both the active and the less active takeover period. As reported in rows five through nine of Table 3, 10% of the sample firms are targeted by shareholder activists. This rate is 8% in the first subperiod, and 12% in the second subperiod, a statistically insignificant difference.

In the last row of Table 3, we report the frequency with which the sample firms experience either a takeover event or becoming a target of shareholder activists in the three years following the year of poor performance. We find that 35% of the sample firms are the subject of at least one type of external control activity. In addition, we find that the frequency of these control events is substantially higher in the first subperiod, when 45% of the firms experiencing a year of poor performance are the target of at least one control event. In contrast, only 26% of the firms experiencing their year of poor performance between 1989 and 1992 are targeted by outside firms or shareholders. These findings are inconsistent

---

[5] The pension funds are: California Public Employees Retirement System (Calpers), California State Teachers Retirement System (Calstrs), Colorado Public Employee Retirement System (Colpera), New York City Pension Fund System, Pennsylvania Public School Employee Retirement System (PSERS), State of Wisconsin Investment Board (SWIB), Teachers Insurance and Annuity Association – College Retirement Equities Fund (TIAA-CREF), Florida State Board of Administration (FSBA), New York State Common Retirement System (NYSCR).

with the view that shareholder activism fully substituted for the decline in the takeover market. Rather, our findings are consistent with a net decline in external control events from the active to the less active takeover period.

4.2. Management turnover

Demonstrating a net decline in external control events is not sufficient to conclude that there has been a decline in managerial discipline. It is possible that managers are disciplined in the absence of any overt external control threat. For example, anecdotal evidence suggests that corporate boards have become more active in disciplining poorly performing managers in recent years. (See, for example, Fortune, January 11, 1993, pp. 34–39.) To provide evidence on the frequency with which managers are disciplined following performance declines, we examine the incidence of top executive turnover among our sample firms. We define the top executive to be the CEO, if there is one, and to be the president, otherwise. Management turnover is defined as any change in the top executive, and is identified by searching corporate proxy statements over the period including the year of and the three years following the year of poor performance. In the event of a missing proxy statement, we examine the Standard and Poor's Register of Corporations, Directors, and Executives. Because we are interested in management changes that are due to the performance decline, we exclude those changes that are due to death or illness, and those changes that we classify as normal retirements. Following Denis and Denis (1995) turnovers are classified as normal retirements if the stated reason for the turnover is retirement or normal succession, and the manager is between the ages of 64 and 66. We label the remaining management changes as nonroutine turnovers.

The first row of Table 4 reports the incidence of nonroutine top executive changes among firms not taken over within three years following the year of poor performance. Overall, 27% of the sample firms experience a nonroutine change in its top executive at least once from the beginning of the year of poor performance through the end of year three. Contrary to Mikkelson and Partch (1997), however, we find no evidence that turnover rates differ in the active and inactive takeover periods.

Of course, managers can also be removed from office following the takeover of their firm. As noted earlier, Martin and McConnell (1991) find an unusually high rate of management turnover following corporate takeovers. Accordingly, we investigate the incidence of post-takeover management turnover among those sample firms taken over within three years of the year of poor performance. We track the fate of the firm's top executive using the Wall Street Journal and the Directory of Corporate Affiliations, and classify a takeover as disciplinary if it results in a change in the firm's top executive within two years following the completion of the takeover. Of the 67 sample firms taken over, we are able to track the top executive's fate in all but one case.

Table 4
Management turnover events

The frequency of management turnover events for the sample of 350 poorly performing firms for years 0 through 3 relative to the year of poor performance. The sample includes firms, with a book value of assets greater than $100 million, that are in the top half of industry-adjusted EBITDA/Total assets in the base year and in the bottom quartile in the year of poor performance. Nonroutine turnover is defined as the turnover of the top executive except in those cases in which the turnover is classed as a retirement using the definition of Denis and Denis (1995). Turnover is classed as retirement if either (i) the stated reason is retirement or (ii) the stated reason is normal succession and the departing manager is from 64 to 66 years of age. Following Martin and McConnell (1991), a firm is considered to be the subject of a disciplinary takeover if the top manager of the target firm does not retain his or her position following the takeover. The sample period is 1985 to 1992. The chi-squared statistic tests the hypothesis that the proportion of firms experiencing each event is equal in the two subperiods. *, **, *** indicates significance at the 0.10, 0.05, and 0.01 levels, respectively.

Event	Full sample (n = 350)		1985–1988 (n = 170)		1989–1992 (n = 180)		χ^2
	N	%	N	%	N	%	
Nonroutine turnover of top officer	96	27	44	26	52	29	0.40
Firm is subject to disciplinary takeover	47	13	38	22	9	5	22.65***
Nonroutine turnover of top officer or disciplinary takeover	127	36	71	42	56	31	4.47**
Firm is subject to either corporate control activity or the nonroutine turnover of its top manager	176	50	97	57	79	44	6.07***

As reported in row 2 of Table 4, 13% of the sample firms experience a disciplinary takeover. This rate is substantially higher during the active takeover period. Of the 47 firms experiencing a disciplinary takeover, 38 experienced their year of poor performance during the first subperiod. This represents 79% of the firms taken over and 22% of all of the firms experiencing poor performance during the earlier period. Conversely, the nine takeovers classified as disciplinary during the second subperiod represent only 50% of the takeovers and 5% of all the firms experiencing poor performance during that period. In other words, not only are there more takeovers in the earlier period, but a higher fraction of the takeovers result in a management change. The net effect is a significant reduction in the incidence of takeover-driven top executive turnover from the first to the second subperiod. The decline in the fraction of takeovers classified as disciplinary is significant at the 0.01 level ($\chi^2 = 5.43$).

The third row of Table 4 combines the incidence of nonroutine top executive turnover with the incidence of disciplinary takeovers to provide a measure of the frequency with which managers are removed from office following the year of poor performance. We find that 36% of the sample firms experience either a disciplinary takeover or the nonroutine turnover of its top manager. Again, the incidence of top executive changes is significantly higher during the active takeover period, affecting 42% of the firms, than in the less active takeover period, affecting 31% of the firms.

Finally, we combine the incidence of external control events, both takeover threats and shareholder activism, with the incidence of nonroutine turnover to provide a measure of how often poorly performing firms experience some type of control-reducing disciplinary event. As reported in row 4 of Table 4, 50% of the sample firms are the target of takeover activity, are targeted by shareholder activists, or experience the nonroutine turnover of its top manager. The percentage of firms experiencing these external and internal control events declines from 57% to 44% from the first to the second subperiod. A χ^2 test of equal proportions is rejected at the 1% level. Overall, therefore, our findings are consistent with a significant decline in the incidence of disciplinary events from the active to the less active takeover period.

4.3. Logistic regressions of disciplinary events

To provide further evidence on time series variation in disciplinary events, we estimate logit models relating the likelihood of disciplinary events to a set of financial and governance variables. Previous studies have documented that the likelihood of these events is related to firm size, firm performance, industry performance, the firm's debt ratio, whether or not the firm is in financial distress, equity ownership structure, and the composition of the board of directors. To control for the influence of these factors, we include, as independent variables, the logarithm of the firm's total assets at the end of year -1, the change in the firm's unadjusted operating earnings from the end of year -1 to the end of year 0, the change in operating earnings for the median firm in the same three-digit SIC industry, the firm's ratio of total debt to total assets at the end of year -1, the proportion of shares held by officers and directors, the proportion of outsiders on the board of directors, and a binary financial distress variable. The binary distress variable is adopted from Gilson (1989), and equals one if the firm files for Chapter 11 bankruptcy protection, defaults on its debt obligations, restructures or refinances its debt, or makes a debt exchange offer, and zero otherwise. Overall, 17% of the sample firms experience some form of financial distress between the year of poor performance and the end of year 3. The incidence of financial distress is not significantly different between the active and the less active takeover period (19% vs. 16%). Finally, we include a dummy variable that equals one if the firm experienced its year of poor performance during 1989 to 1992 and zero, otherwise.

The logit results are reported in Table 5. Consistent with prior studies, we find that shareholder targeting is more likely in larger firms, financial distress

410 D.J. Denis, T.A. Kruse / Journal of Financial Economics 55 (2000) 391–424

Table 5
Logistic regressions of disciplinary events

Logistic regressions estimating the relation between the probability of disciplinary events and a set of financial and governance variables, as well as a dummy variable equaling one if the year of poor performance occurred during 1989 to 1992 (p-values are in parentheses). A takeover event occurs if the firm is the subject of takeover rumors, is the target of a takeover attempt, or is taken over. Shareholding targeting is any control event initiated by any shareholder activist group. Nonroutine turnover excludes top executive turnover labeled as normal retirements using the classification scheme of Denis and Denis (1995), and those turnovers due to death or illness. Disciplinary takeovers are those cases in which the firm is taken over and the top executive is replaced within two years of the takeover. The binary financial distress variable equals one if the firm files for Chapter 11 bankruptcy protection, defaults on its debt obligations, restructures or refinances its debt, or makes a debt exchange offer, and zero otherwise. The sample consists of 350 companies having assets greater than $100 million that are in the top half of industry-adjusted EBITDA/Total assets in the base year and in the bottom quartile in the year of poor performance. The sample period is 1985–1992.

	Takeover event (1)	Shareholder targeting (2)	Nonroutine turnover (3)	Nonroutine turnover or disciplinary takeover (4)	(1), (2), or (3)
Intercept	– 6.51	– 17.02	– 0.57	– 2.52	– 4.76
	(0.01)	(0.00)	(0.82)	(0.27)	(0.04)
Log (total assets)	0.31	0.78	– 0.07	0.07	0.25
	(0.02)	(0.00)	(0.60)	(0.53)	(0.03)
Change in EBITDA/ Total assets FROM YEAR – 1 to year 0	– 0.81	0.45	– 2.46	– 1.05	– 1.35
	(0.67)	(0.89)	(0.18)	(0.55)	(0.45)
Change in industry EBITDA/Assets from year – 1 to year 0	– 2.54	– 10.47	2.73	6.77	0.60
	(0.62)	(0.18)	(0.61)	(0.17)	(0.90)
Long-term debt/total assets	0.32	– 1.07	0.69	0.78	0.29
	(0.72)	(0.41)	(0.41)	(0.33)	(0.70)
Dummy equal to 1 if firm encounters financial distress	– 0.06	0.29	1.16	0.88	0.34
	(0.88)	(0.63)	(0.00)	(0.02)	(0.35)
Fractional equity ownership of officers and directors	– 1.63	– 3.98	– 0.49	– 0.87	– 1.19
	(0.06)	(0.05)	(0.50)	(0.22)	(0.07)
Fraction of board comprised of independent outsiders	0.22	0.18	0.10	0.50	0.04
	(0.78)	(0.87)	(0.90)	(0.47)	(0.95)
Dummy equal to 1 if 1989–1992	– 1.26	0.60	0.07	– 0.56	– 0.48
	(0.00)	(0.16)	(0.81)	(0.04)	(0.06)
Pseudo R^2	0.11	0.22	0.06	0.06	0.05

increases the likelihood of management turnover, and higher managerial ownership decreases the likelihood of a takeover-related event.[6] More importantly, in three of the five logit models we find a significant negative coefficient on the dummy variable denoting the second subperiod. Specifically, the likelihood of a takeover-related event, the likelihood of either nonroutine turnover or a disciplinary takeover, and the likelihood of any of the disciplinary events (takeover, shareholder targeting, and turnover) are negatively related to the time period dummy variable. In other words, after controlling for other possible determinants of managerial disciplinary events, there is a significant decline in control-reducing disciplinary events in the less active takeover period.

5. Corporate restructuring and changes in operating performance

Our results to this point suggest that poorly performing managers face disciplinary pressure from takeover markets, active shareholders, and corporate boards of directors. However, the incidence of these disciplinary events is significantly lower in the less active takeover period. Because prior studies suggest that corporate restructuring programs often result from external control pressures, a potential implication of these findings is that the reduction in disciplinary pressure reduces the likelihood that firms will undertake value-increasing restructuring actions following performance declines. Alternatively, however, other incentive mechanisms or improvements in internal corporate governance in the later period could induce managers to restructure, generate operating improvements, or both, in the absence of any overt threat to current managers' control. It is also possible that the threat of takeover remains high in the second subperiod, and that the threat is sufficient to induce restructuring. However, it is difficult to believe that the threat of takeover is as high in the second subperiod given the sudden sharp decline in takeovers reported in Comment and Schwert (1995) and our corresponding finding of a significant decline in disciplinary management turnover from the first to the second subperiod.

In this section, we provide evidence on these issues by documenting restructuring actions, the valuation effects of these restructuring events, and changes in operating performance for the sample firms in the year of and the three years following their performance decline. Our analysis is hindered by the disappearance of firms that are taken over. Although we attempt to document the

[6] See Gilson (1989) and Gilson and Vetsuypens (1993) for evidence on management turnover in financially distressed firms, Mikkelson and Partch (1989) and Song and Walkling (1993) for evidence on the relation between equity ownership structure and the likelihood of takeovers, and John and Klein (1994), Karpoff et al. (1996), Smith (1996), and Strickland et al. (1996) for evidence on the relation between firm size and shareholder targeting.

restructuring actions of all firms, including those taken over, we acknowledge that we may understate the magnitude of restructuring among firms that have been taken over. Because the incidence of takeovers is substantially higher in the first subperiod, our comparison of restructuring actions and operating changes between the two subperiods must be interpreted with caution. Nevertheless, we can assess whether firms experiencing performance declines in the second subperiod undertake performance-enhancing restructurings. In addition, we later attempt to assess the importance of the bias created by time series variation in the rate at which firms are taken over.

5.1. Corporate restructuring events following performance declines

We search the Wall Street Journal and Mergers and Acquisitions, published by Mergers and Acquisitions Inc., Washington D.C., for restructuring events over the period from the start of the base year (year − 1) through the end of the third year following the year of performance decline (year 3). Similar to Ofek (1993) and Kang and Shivdasani (1997), we report the proportion of firms undertaking asset restructurings, such as divestitures, spin-offs, plant closings, and liquidations, and employee layoff and cost-cutting programs. We compare the frequency of restructuring actions following the performance decline to that in the year prior to the performance decline, and compare the frequency of restructuring actions in the active takeover period with that in the less active takeover period.

The results, reported in Table 6, indicate a substantial amount of corporate restructuring activity among the sample firms, beginning with the onset of poor performance. Asset restructurings are the most common action, with 61% of the firms undertaking some type of asset restructuring between the onset of poor performance and third year following the performance decline. With 34% of the sample firms either initiating a cost-cutting program or laying off employees, a total of 69% of the firms undertake some type of restructuring event within three years following the performance decline.

To put these restructuring frequencies into perspective, Table 6 also reports the proportion of sample firms undertaking restructuring actions in the year prior to the year of performance decline. The results indicate that the incidence of restructuring approximately doubles in the year of performance decline (year 0) and the following year (year 1). Restructuring frequencies subsequently decline in years 2 and 3, but still remain slightly above those in the base year, year − 1. Thus, the sample firms restructure at an unusually high frequency in the years immediately following the year of performance decline. These findings are consistent with those of Ofek (1993). In addition, our findings for years 0 and 1 are similar to those of Kang and Shivdasani (1997). Although Kang and Shivdasani focus primarily on Japanese firms, they do find that, among 114 U.S. manufacturing firms suffering operating performance declines between 1986 and

Table 6
Frequency of corporate restructuring actions following performance declines

Proportion of firms undertaking corporate restructuring actions over the period from the year prior to the year of performance decline (year − 1) through the third year following the performance decline (year 3). For each restructuring event, the first row reports the percentage of firms in the full sample undertaking the action, while the second and third rows report the restructuring frequencies of firms in the active takeover period and the less active takeover period, respectively. Restructurings include the sale of assets or divisions, the closing or reorganization of a plant or division, spin-offs, liquidations, and the sale of a stake in the firm. The sample consists of 350 companies having assets greater than $100 million that are in the top half of industry-adjusted EBITDA/Total assets in the base year and in the bottom quartile in the year of poor performance. The sample period is 1985–992. * indicates that the proportion of firms undertaking the restructuring action in the active takeover period (1985–1988) is significantly different (at the 0.10 level) from the proportion of firms in the less active takeover period.

Restructuring action	Year − 1	Year 0	Year 1	Year 2	Year 3	Years 0 and 1	Years 0 to 3
Panel A: Asset restructuring							
Sale of asset or division							
Full sample	0.11	0.15	0.17	0.17	0.14	0.28	0.41
1985–1988	0.11	0.19*	0.17	0.18	0.15	0.29	0.41
1989–1992	0.11	0.12	0.18	0.17	0.14	0.27	0.42
Close or reorganize plant or division							
Full sample	0.04	0.13	0.11	0.10	0.06	0.21	0.31
1985–1988	0.05	0.12	0.11	0.11	0.06	0.20	0.31
1989–1992	0.03	0.14	0.11	0.09	0.06	0.22	0.31
Any asset restructuring							
Full sample	0.15	0.27	0.26	0.25	0.20	0.44	0.61
1985–1988	0.15	0.29	0.27	0.25	0.20	0.45	0.59
1989–1992	0.14	0.26	0.26	0.26	0.21	0.43	0.63
Panel B: Employee layoffs and cost-cutting							
Layoffs							
Full sample	0.04	0.11	0.12	0.10	0.06	0.20	0.28
1985–1988	0.06	0.11	0.11	0.08	0.06	0.19	0.26
1989–1992	0.03	0.11	0.13	0.12	0.06	0.21	0.31
Cost-cutting efforts							
Full sample	0.03	0.09	0.08	0.09	0.03	0.15	0.21
1985–1988	0.03	0.10	0.05	0.07*	0.05	0.15	0.19
1989–1992	0.03	0.09	0.10	0.10	0.02	0.15	0.23
Any layoff or cost-cutting							
Full sample	0.07	0.05	0.16	0.14	0.08	0.25	0.34
1985–1988	0.07	0.15	0.14	0.11*	0.09	0.25	0.31
1989–1992	0.06	0.14	0.17	0.18	0.07	0.26	0.37
Panel C: All restructuring actions							
Any asset restructuring, layoffs or cost-cutting efforts							
Full sample	0.17	0.33	0.35	0.31	0.25	0.53	0.69
1985–1988	0.18	0.35	0.34	0.29	0.25	0.53	0.68
1989–1992	0.16	0.31	0.36	0.33	0.24	0.52	0.71

1990, 37% sell assets, 32% layoff employees, and 14% initiate cost-cutting programs.

Consistent with prior studies, the frequency of restructuring is greater among those firms experiencing disciplinary events. In results not reported in a table, we find that 76% of the firms that are takeover targets, are targets of shareholder activism, or that experience the nonroutine turnover of the top executive undertake some type of restructuring event in the year of and the three years following the performance decline. This rate is significantly greater, at the 0.01 level, than the 63% restructuring frequency among those firms having no disciplinary event. We find similar results if we compare restructuring frequencies in years 1–3 relative to the year of performance decline for those firms experiencing a disciplinary event in years 0 and 1 to those firms having no disciplinary event over this period. Similarly, disciplinary events are associated with a greater magnitude of restructuring. Among firms experiencing a disciplinary event, asset sales average 13.6% of the book value of total assets. For firms with no disciplinary event, asset sales average just 7.1% of the book value of total assets. The difference in asset sales between these groups of firms is significant at the 0.05 level.

To examine whether the decline in disciplinary events from the active to the less active takeover period is associated with a change in the manner in which firms respond to performance declines, Table 6 also reports restructuring frequencies in the two subperiods. The results indicate that the restructuring responses to performance declines are strikingly similar in the two subperiods. Overall, 68% of the firms in the active takeover period initiate restructuring activities between years 0 and 3, while 71% of the firms in the less active takeover period undergo restructuring events. The difference in restructuring frequencies is statistically insignificant using a χ^2 test. Similarly, there is no difference in the proportion of firms engaging in asset restructurings, layoffs, or other cost-cutting programs in the two subperiods.

As noted earlier, one concern with our comparisons of restructuring frequencies across subperiods is that we may be missing data for firms that are taken over. To the extent that we understate the incidence of restructuring actions among firms taken over, our subperiod comparisons over years 0 to 3 are biased because a greater fraction of firms are taken over in the 1985–1988 subperiod. Recall that, of the 350 sample firms, 67 are taken over by the end of year 3. Of these, 49 are from the first subperiod and 18 are from the second subperiod. While it is not possible to completely alleviate this concern, we address this issue in two ways. First, we compare the restructuring frequency of those firms taken over to that of the firms not taken over. We find that 75% of the firms taken over engage in some form of restructuring between years 0 and 3. This rate is higher than the 69% rate documented for the full sample, suggesting that our data sources pick up a high frequency of restructuring even among those firms that are taken over. Second, we compare the frequency of restructuring across the two subperiods under the assumption that every firm taken over engages in some type of restructuring. Under this admittedly strong assumption, we still find no significant difference in restructuring frequencies across the two subperiods. During the active takeover period, 76% of the firms undertake some type of restructuring, while this rate is 73% in the less active takeover period. We thus conclude that our results on the frequency of restructuring are not materially biased by the lack of data for firms that are taken over.

Although restructuring frequencies appear to be similar in the two subperiods, it is possible that the magnitude of the restructurings differ. To examine this possibility, we measure the magnitude of asset restructuring as the total proceeds from asset sales divided by the book value of total assets at the end of year − 1. In results not reported in a table, we find that asset sales average 11.4% of total assets in the 1985–1988 subperiod and 9.3% in the 1989–1992 subperiod, an insignificant difference across the two periods. If we examine only those firms that did undertake some asset restructuring between year 0 and year 3, asset sales average 28.2% of total assets in the active takeover period, and 22.4% of total assets in the less active takeover period. Median asset sales for firms undertaking asset restructurings are 13.3% of total assets in the active period, and 8.1% in the less active period. Here, the difference in medians is significant at the 0.10 level, but the difference in means is not. Thus, there is little evidence that the scope of restructuring differs between the active and the less active subperiods.

5.2. The valuation impact of restructuring announcements

To assess the valuation impact of the restructuring events, we conduct an event-study analysis of the restructuring announcements. We search the Wall Street Journal and Lexis-Nexis for announcement dates for each asset restructuring, layoff, and cost-cutting event. After excluding events for which there is a confounding announcement on either the day of or the day prior to the restructuring announcement, and those for which there is insufficient stock return data, we are left with 377 announcement dates of restructuring events. Of these, 289 are asset restructurings and 88 are announcements of layoffs or cost-cutting actions.

We measure abnormal returns over the two-day period, including the day of and the day prior to the announcement, using the market model techinique. Market model parameters are estimated over the 250 trading-day period ending 40 days prior to the announcement. Our findings, reported in Table 7, indicate that the restructuring announcements are met with a positive stock price reaction, on average. For the full set of 377 announcements, the average abnormal return over the two-day announcement period is 0.59%, significant at the 0.10 level. The positive stock price reaction is driven by the subsample of asset sale announcements. Announcement period abnormal returns average

Table 7
The stock price reaction to restructuring announcements

Two-day announcement period abnormal returns for the set of 377 announcements of asset restructuring and layoff or cost-cutting events. Announcement dates are obtained from the Wall Street Journal Index and from Lexis/Nexis. Abnormal returns are measured using the market model technique, with parameters estimated over the 250 trading day period ending 40 days prior to each announcement. The test statistics are heteroskedastic t-tests of equal means and Wilcoxon signed-rank tests of equal medians across the two subperiods. ***, **, and * denote significance at the 0.01, 0.05, and 0.10 levels, respectively.

Type of restructuring	Full sample			1985–1988			1989–1992			Test statistic	
	Mean	Median	N	Mean	Median	N	Mean	Median	N	t-stat.	Z-stat.
All events	0.0059*	0.0025**	377	0.0013	0.0007	195	0.0108**	0.0041**	182	−1.317	−1.131
Asset sales	0.0175***	0.0068***	189	0.0111**	0.0054***	103	0.0251***	0.0108***	86	−1.470	−1.092
Asset reorganizations	−0.0099	−0.0062	70	−0.0126	−0.0080	40	−0.0062	−0.0038	30	−0.374	−0.095
All asset restructurings	0.0088**	0.0036***	289	0.0039	0.0021	159	0.0149*	0.0049***	130	−1.266	−1.293
Layoffs/Cost-cutting	−0.0039	−0.0053	88	−0.0103	−0.0039	36	0.0005	−0.0067	52	−0.769	−0.535

1.75% for asset sales, significant at the 0.01 level and a statistically insignificant −0.39% for cost cutting or layoff announcements. Moreover, we find no difference in average or median stock price reactions across the two subperiods. We thus conclude that the asset restructurings announced in the year of and the three years following performance declines are value-enhancing events for the sample firms.

5.3. Changes in operating performance following performance declines

To examine whether the sample firms generate operating improvements following performance declines, Table 8 reports industry-adjusted operating performance over the period from one year prior to the performance decline (year −1) through three years following the performance decline (year 3). Industry-adjusted operating performance is measured as the ratio of EBITDA to total assets minus the same ratio for the median firm having the same three-digit SIC code.

As noted earlier, industry-adjusted operating performance is significantly positive in year −1, and signficantly negative in year 0. More importantly, industry-adjusted operating performance improves substantially in the three years following the performance decline. By the end of year 3, the operating performance of the sample firms does not differ from that of the median firm in the industry. Moreover, the results are nearly identical in the two subperiods.

It is possible, however, that the improvement in operating performance simply reflects normal reversion to the mean in operating performance measures.[7] Therefore, to assess the significance of changes in operating performance between years 0 and 3, we follow the procedure described in Barber and Lyon (1996), and compare the change in operating performance for each sample firm to the median change for a set of firms matched by industry and performance in year 0. Our comparison sample includes those firms having the same two-digit SIC code, and whose ratio of EBITDA-to-total assets falls between 90% and 110% of the sample firm as of the end of year 0. We initially attempted to match on the basis of performance and 3-digit SIC code. However, because we were unable to identify industry matches for a large number of firms, we employed 2-digit SIC matches instead.

The results, reported in Table 9, indicate that, following the year of poor performance, operating performance improves significantly for the sample firms. Between year 0 and year 3, the median adjusted change in operating performance is 0.032, which represents a 61.5% increase over the ratio of operating

[7] See Barber and Lyon (1996) for a discussion of this issue, and Penman (1991) and Fama and French (1995) for evidence that accounting earnings are mean-reverting.

Table 8
Industry-adjusted operating performance following performance declines

Mean and median industry-adjusted ratio of EBITDA to total assets for the years − 1 to 3 relative to the year of poor performance. Industry-adjusted performance is measured as the difference in operating performance between the sample firm and the median firm in the same three-digit SIC code. The test statistics are heteroskedastic *t*-tests of equal means and Wilcoxon signed-rank tests of equal medians across the two subperiods. *, **, *** indicates significance at the 0.10, 0.05, and 0.01 levels, respectively.

	Full sample		1985–1988		1989–1992		Test statistic	
	Mean	Median	Mean	Median	Mean	Median	*t*-stat.	*Z*-stat.
Year − 1	0.053***	0.040***	0.055***	0.037***	0.051***	0.043***	0.688	− 0.486
Year 0	− 0.058***	− 0.051***	− 0.055***	− 0.051***	− 0.061***	− 0.051***	0.802	0.716
Year 1	− 0.035***	− 0.015***	− 0.032***	− 0.014***	− 0.037***	− 0.015***	0.341	0.399
Year 2	− 0.016***	0.000	− 0.011	0.001	− 0.020**	− 0.002	0.718	0.861
Year 3	− 0.007	0.004	− 0.004	0.007	− 0.009	0.000	0.475	0.767

Table 9
Performance-adjusted changes in operating performance following performance declines

Mean and median adjusted changes in operating performance, defined as the change in EBITDA/Assets for the sample firm minus the median change for a set of firms matched by industry and year 0 performance. The comparison sample includes those firms having the same two-digit SIC code and whose ratio of EBITDA to total assets is between 90% and 110% of the sample firm. The test statistics are heteroskedastic t-tests of equal means and Wilcoxon signed-rank tests of equal medians across the two subperiods. *, **, *** indicates significance at the 0.10, 0.05, and 0.01 levels, respectively.

	Full sample			1985–1988			1989–1992			Test statistic	
	Mean	Median	N	Mean	Median	N	Mean	Median	N	t-stat.	Z-stat.
Change from year 0 to year 1	0.015*	0.026***	318	0.013	0.021***	149	0.017	0.029***	169	− 0.264	0.816
Change from year 0 to year 2	0.030***	0.034***	304	0.028***	0.034***	139	0.032***	0.034***	165	− 0.364	− 0.010
Change from year 0 to year 3	0.028***	0.032***	287	0.025***	0.031***	130	0.031***	0.034***	157	− 0.565	− 0.479

income-to-total assets in year 0. The results also indicate that the performance improvements do not differ significantly between the two subperiods. We thus conclude that the increased level of operating performance reported in Table 8 represents an improvement in operating performance over and above that which would be expected due to normal mean reversion of accounting earnings.

To this point, we have established that a large fraction of the sample firms restructure during the year of and the three years following a performance decline and that, on average, the sample firms exhibit operating improvements over this period. An interesting remaining question is whether the improved operating performance results in part from the restructuring actions documented in Table 6. To address this issue, we examine the adjusted change in operating performance between years 1 and 3 for those firms that restructure in year 0 with those that do not restructure in year 0. In this way, we examine performance changes over a period following a set of restructuring events. One drawback to this approach, however, is that it ignores those restructurings that take place after year 0, and their potential impacts on performance.

Our results, not reported in a table, suggest that asset restructurings are linked with subsequent operating improvements, but that cost-cutting and layoffs are not. Specifically, for those firms with an asset restructuring in year 0, the average adjusted change in operating performance over years 1–3 is 0.026, and the median change is 0.010. The average change is significantly different from zero, and from the statistically insignificant change of − 0.009 for those firms with no asset restructuring in year 0. We find no significant adjusted changes in operating performance for either those firms with or without cost-cutting or layoff events in year 0.

We note two caveats in interpreting our findings with respect to changes in operating performance. First, as noted previously, we are able to report operating performance only for those firms that remain independent. Because more firms are taken over in the first subperiod, our comparison of operating improvements between subperiods must be interpreted with caution. We examined both the level of industry-adjusted operating profitability in year 0 and the change in industry-adjusted operating profits from year − 1 to year 0 for evidence that operating profits are systematically different among those firms that are subsequently taken over. We found no signficant differences. Second, it is possible that we observe operating improvements partly because the sample firms sell off their least profitable assets. This argument would suggest that the findings reported in Tables 8 and 9 overstate the real improvements in operating performance within the sample firms. Nonetheless, the fact the sample restructurings are met with a positive stock price reaction suggests that, on average, the restructurings are value-enhancing events.

6. Discussion

Our overall findings are broadly consistent with those of Mikkelson and Partch (1997) in that we find that disciplinary events are linked with activity in the takeover market. As noted in Section 2, a decline in the frequency of those disciplinary events that reduce the control of current managers could reduce the incentives of managers to maximize firm value. Under this hypothesis, disciplinary events are an important force in motivating managers to make value-enhancing restructuring decisions. Following a decline in disciplinary events, therefore, one might expect to observe fewer value-enhancing restructurings.

Contrary to this hypothesis, however, we find no difference in either the frequency of restructurings or subsequent operating improvements between the active and the less active takeover period. A possible interpretation of these results is that the disciplinary events that we study are not important in eliciting performance-enhancing restructurings. However, we also find that performance-enhancing restructurings are more likely in firms facing disciplinary events than in those firms with no disciplinary event. This observation raises a puzzle. If restructurings are linked with disciplinary events, and the frequency of disciplinary events declines from the active to the less active takeover period, how is it that firms suffering performance declines restructure with equal frequency in the two subperiods?

We conjecture that other incentive mechanisms, such as the increased use of stock-based compensation, or other forms of managerial monitoring, such as more active boards of directors and active shareholders, substitute for the takeover market in ensuring that performance-enhancing restructurings take place following substantial declines in operating performance. Our findings suggest that these other control mechanisms are less public and do not involve the replacement of the CEO as often as does the takeover market, but appear to nonetheless generate improvements in performance. This view is consistent with Pound's (1992a,b) political model of corporate governance in which active shareholders maintain ongoing, but mostly private dialogues with managers and the board of directors. Moreover, our findings complement those of Carleton et al. (1998), who find that the private negotiations between one large institutional investor, TIAA-CREF, and a set of targeted companies are remarkably effective in bringing about the changes desired by TIAA-CREF.

Our conjecture is also consistent with Kaplan's (1997) views on why hostile leveraged buyouts (LBOs) and corporate raiders have not reappeared despite the resurgence in takeover activity in the mid-1990s. Kaplan argues that shareholders, boards, and managers have applied the insights learned from LBOs in the 1980s to improve corporate governance practices in U.S. corporations. Our findings fit well with this view in the sense that poorly performing firms in the less active takeover period appear to undertake performance-enhancing restructurings just as frequently as firms in the active takeover period, despite a substantial decline in disciplinary events.

Nevertheless, even if this substitution from takeovers to other incentive and monitoring mechanisms takes place, we cannot conclude from our evidence that takeovers are unimportant as a disciplinary force. It is possible that restructurings following takeovers improve performance to a greater extent than restructurings that take place in the absence of a takeover. Because the firms cease to exist as independent entities, we cannot observe the performance effects of those restructurings that take place following takeovers. Therefore, we cannot fully address this possibility. At a minimum, though, our evidence suggests that the decline in disciplinary events from the first to the second subperiod does not result in fewer performance-enhancing restructurings.

7. Conclusion

We examine the incidence of those disciplinary events that reduce current managers' control, and the extent of corporate restructuring among firms experiencing a substantial decline in industry-adjusted operating performance. We find that approximately one-half of the sample firms are the target of some control-reducing disciplinary event in the year of and the three years following the year of poor performance. These disciplinary events include takeover attempts, shareholder activism, and board dismissals. The high frequency of these events suggests that the threat of a control reduction provides meaningful incentives to top executives. In addition, there is a significant decline in the incidence of control-reducing disciplinary events from the active takeover period (1985–1988) to the less active takeover period (1989–1992). This decline suggests that, during the less active takeover period, other monitoring mechanisms do not fully substitute for takeovers in forcing the dismissal of top executives of poorly performing firms. Despite the decline in control-reducing disciplinary events, however, we find evidence of significant increases in corporate restructuring following performance declines in both subperiods. Asset restructuring announcements are more likely in firms experiencing disciplinary events, are met with positive stock price reactions, and are associated with subsequent improvements in operating performance. We thus conclude that the decline in disciplinary events from the active to the less active takeover period does not lead to fewer value-enhancing corporate restructurings. Further studies that provide direct evidence on the process through which boards of directors, active shareholders, and managers interact to produce such changes would represent an important contribution to the corporate governance literature.

References

Barber, B.M., Lyon, J.D., 1996. Detecting abnormal operating performance the empirical power and specification of test statistics. Journal of Financial Economics 41, 313–358.

Barber, B.M., Lyon, J.D., 1997. Detecting long run abnormal stock returns: the empirical power and specification of test statistics. Journal of Financial Economics 43, 341–372.

Berger, P.G., Ofek, E., 1996. Bustup takeovers of value-destroying diversified firms. Journal of Finance 51, 1175–1200.

Berger, P.G., Ofek, E., 1999. Causes and effects of corporate refocusing programs. Review of Financial Studies, forthcoming.

Bhagat, S., Shleifer, A., Vishny, R., 1990. Hostile takeovers in the 1980's: the return to corporate specialization. Brookings Papers on Economic Activity: Microeconomics Volume, 1–72.

Bhide, A., 1990. Reversing corporate diversification. Journal of Applied Corporate Finance 3, 70–81.

Brickley, J.A., Coles, J.L., Linck, J.S., 1998. What happens to CEOs after they retire? New evidence on career concerns, horizon problems, and CEO incentives. Journal of Financial Economics 52, 341–378.

Carleton, W.T., Nelson, J.N., Weisbach, M.S., 1998. The influence of institutions on corporate governance through private negotiations: evidence from TIAA-CREF. Journal of Finance 53, 1335–1362.

Comment, R., Schwert, G.W., 1995. Poison or placebo? Evidence on the deterrence and wealth effects of modern antitakeover measures. Journal of Financial Economics 39, 3–44.

Dann, L.Y., DeAngelo, H., 1988. Corporate financial policy and corporate control: a study of defensive adjustments in asset and ownership structure. Journal of Financial Economics 20, 87–127.

Del Guercio, D., Hawkins, J., 1999. The motivation and impact of pension fund activism. Journal of Financial Economics 52, 293–340.

Denis, D.J., Denis, D.K., 1995. Performance changes following top management dismissals. Journal of Finance 50, 1029–1057.

Denis, D.J., Denis, D.K., Sarin, A., 1997. Agency problems, equity ownership, and corporate diversification. Journal of Finance 52, 135–160.

Denis, D.J., Serrano, J.M., 1996. Active investors and management turnover following unsuccessful control contests. Journal of Financial Economics 40, 239–266.

Denis, D.J., Sarin, A., 1999. Ownership and board structures in publicly traded corporations. Journal of Financial Economics 52, 187–224.

Fama, E.F., French, K., 1995. Size and book-to-market factors in earnings and returns. Journal of Finance 50, 131–155.

Gilson, S.C., 1989. Management turnover and financial distress. Journal of Financial Economics 25, 241–262.

Gilson, S.C., Vetsuypens, M.R., 1993. CEO compensation in financially distressed firms: an empirical analysis. Journal of Finance 48, 425–458.

Huson, M.R., Parrino, R., Starks, L., 1997. The effectiveness of internal monitoring mechanisms: evidence from CEO turnover between 1971 and 1994. Unpublished working paper. University of Texas, Austin.

Jensen, M.C., 1993. The modern industrial revolution, exit, and the failure of internal control systems. Journal of Finance 48, 831–880.

Jensen, M.C., Warner, J.B., 1988. The distribution of power among corporate managers, shareholders, and directors. Journal of Financial Economics 20, 3–24.

John, K., Klein, A., 1994. Shareholder proposals and corporate governance. Unpublished working paper. New York University.

Kang, J., Shivdasani, A., 1997. Corporate restructuring during performance declines in Japan. Journal of Financial Economics 46, 29–66.

Kaplan, S.N., 1994. Top executive rewards and firm performance: a comparison of Japan and the United States. Journal of Political Economy 102, 510–546.

Kaplan, S.N., 1997. The evolution of corporate governance: we are all Henry Kravis now. Journal of Private Equity (Fall), 7–14.

Karpoff, J., 1998. The impact of shareholder activism on target companies: a survey of empirical findings. Unpublished working paper. University of Washington, Seattle.

Karpoff, J., Malatesta, P., Walkling, R., 1996. Corporate governance and shareholder initiatives: empirical evidence. Journal of Financial Economics 42, 365–395.

Martin, K.J., McConnell, J.J., 1991. Corporate performance, corporate takeovers, and management turnover. Journal of Finance 46, 671–687.

Mikkelson, W., Partch, M., 1989. Managers' voting rights and corporate control. Journal of Financial Economics 25, 263–290.

Mikkelson, W., Partch, M., 1997. The decline of takeovers and disciplinary managerial turnover. Journal of Financial Economics 44, 205–228.

Mitchell, M.L., Lehn, K., 1990. Do bad bidders become good targets? Journal of Political Economy 98, 372–398.

Mitchell, M.L., Mulherin, J.H., 1996. The impact of industry shocks on takeover and restructuring activity. Journal of Financial Economics 41, 193–229.

Morck, R., Shleifer, A., Vishny, R.W., 1989. Alternative mechanisms for corporate control. American Economic Review 79, 842–852.

Murphy, K.J., Zimmerman, J.L., 1993. Financial performance surrounding CEO turnover. Journal of Accounting and Economics 16, 273–316.

Ofek, E., 1993. Capital structure and firm response to poor performance. Journal of Financial Economics 34, 3–30.

Opler, T., Sokobin, J., 1997. Does coordinated institutional activism work? An analysis of the activities of the Council of Institutional Investors. Unpublished working paper, Ohio State University, Columbus.

Penman, S., 1991. An evaluation of accounting rate of return. Journal of Accounting, Auditing, and Finance 6, 233–255.

Porciau, S., 1993. Earnings management and nonroutine executive changes. Journal of Accounting and Economics 16, 317–336.

Pound, J., 1992a. Beyond takeovers: politics comes to corporate control. Harvard Business Review 70, 83–93.

Pound, J., 1992b. Raiders, targets, and politics: the history and future of American corporate control. Journal of Applied Corporate Finance 5, 6–18.

Smith, M., 1996. Shareholder activism by institutional investors: evidence from CalPERS. Journal of Finance 51, 227–252.

Song, M.H., Walkling, R.A., 1993. The impact of managerial ownership on acquisition attempts and target shareholder wealth. Journal of Financial and Quantitative Analysis 28, 439–457.

Strickland, D., Wiles, K.W., Zenner, M., 1996. A requiem for the USA: is small shareholder monitoring effective? Journal of Financial Economics 40, 319–338.

Wahal, S., 1996. Pension fund activism and firm performance. Journal of Financial and Quantitative Analysis 31, 1–23.

Warner, J.B., Watts, R.L., Wruck, K.H., 1988. Stock prices and top management changes. Journal of Financial Economics 20, 461–492.

Weisbach, M.S., 1988. Outside directors and CEO turnover. Journal of Financial Economics 20, 431–459.

THE JOURNAL OF FINANCE • VOL. LIII, NO. 5 • OCTOBER 1998

Asset Efficiency and Reallocation Decisions of Bankrupt Firms

VOJISLAV MAKSIMOVIC and GORDON PHILLIPS*

ABSTRACT

This paper investigates whether Chapter 11 bankruptcy provides a mechanism by which insolvent firms are efficiently reorganized and the assets of unproductive firms are effectively redeployed. We argue that incentives to reorganize depend on the level of demand and industry conditions. Using plant-level data, we find that Chapter 11 status is much less important than industry conditions in explaining the productivity, asset sales, and closure conditions of Chapter 11 bankrupt firms. This suggests that firms that elect to enter into Chapter 11 incur few real economic costs.

A KEY QUESTION IN CORPORATE FINANCE LITERATURE is whether Chapter 11 bankruptcy provides a mechanism by which insolvent firms can be efficiently reorganized and the assets of unproductive firms effectively redeployed. Several studies have identified possible costs and benefits associated with Chapter 11 bankruptcy reorganizations. Of these costs, indirect or real costs represent a deadweight loss and are therefore considered most significant.[1]

In this paper, we examine the importance of these costs and the effect of plant-level efficiency, firm characteristics, and industry demand on the decisions to redeploy assets or close manufacturing plants in bankruptcy. Our approach differs in two ways from previous studies. First, our empirical de-

*The authors are at the University of Maryland Business School, College Park. We thank Judy Chevalier, John Graham, Charles Hadlock, Kathleen Weiss Hanley, Marc Lipson, Colin Mayer, Pegaret Pichler, Jay Ritter, David Scharfstein, Alex Triantis, Henri Servaes, Sheridan Titman, Luigi Zingales, an anonymous referee, and the editor René Stulz. We are grateful to seminar participants at Boston College, the University of Chicago, Columbia University, the Board of Governors of the Federal Reserve System, the University of Georgia, the University of Maryland, MIT, the University of North Carolina, New York University, Southern Methodist University, the University of Texas at Austin, Tulane University, the University of British Columbia, the University of Utah, Vanderbilt University, the University of Virginia, and the Wharton School of Business for helpful comments. We are also grateful to participants at the meetings of the American Finance Association, the Center for Policy Research, and at the National Bureau for Economic Research. We also thank SuZanne Peck, Bob McGuckin, and researchers at the Center for Economic Studies for data help and discussions on this project. This work was conducted at the Center for Economic Studies, U.S. Census Bureau, where Phillips was an ASA/NSF research fellow.

[1] Bankruptcy costs can be both direct and indirect. Legal and administrative costs are commonly called direct costs of bankruptcy. For a review of the literature on bankruptcy costs see Altman (1993) or Senbet and Seward (1995). Warner (1977) and Weiss (1990) examine the direct costs (lawyers, accountants) of bankruptcy.

sign explicitly recognizes that if an important function of bankruptcy is to facilitate the redeployment of assets to more productive uses, then both its incidence and its effectiveness should differ systematically with industry conditions. Second, we use detailed plant-level operating data from a sample of 1195 plants of 302 firms that declared Chapter 11 and over 50,000 plants of nonbankrupt firms – representing both public and private firms in the U.S. manufacturing sector. These plant-level data enable us to track changes in composition of firms as they sell or close plants. Thus, our evaluation of reorganizations is not subject to sample selection bias inherent in the use of firm-level data from survivor firms.

There has been a major debate in the literature about the likely significance of the costs of bankruptcy reorganizations. Haugen and Senbet (1978) argue that bankruptcy costs per se are unlikely to be significant, since many of these costs would be associated with reorganizations outside of bankruptcy in which assets are reallocated to new users. Several recent papers, among them Harris and Raviv (1990), Diamond (1993), Jensen (1993), and Hart and Moore (1995), argue that bankruptcy can even be beneficial, triggering a change in control of the firm and the termination of unprofitable projects. By contrast, Bulow and Shoven (1978), Giammarino (1989), Bergman and Callen (1991), and Gertner and Scharfstein (1991) identify potential conflicts that, if unresolved, may cause the firm not to maintain, sell, or close assets optimally in bankruptcy.

The tests and evidence in this paper help resolve some of these debates. Central to our tests is the idea that industry conditions affect the marginal product of capital, and thus the incentives to disinvest and redeploy assets.[2] Therefore, if an important function of bankruptcy is to facilitate the redeployment of assets into more productive uses, both its incidence and its effectiveness in promoting value-enhancing transfers should also differ systematically with industry conditions.[3]

Our empirical results show that industry effects are important determinants of the frequency of bankruptcy and of economic decisions in bankruptcy. We find that in declining industries the proportion of plants in Chapter 11 is as much as three times higher than in high-growth industries. However, in declining industries the productivity of plants in Chapter 11 bankruptcy and subsequent to emerging does not significantly differ from that of their industry counterparts, nor does it decline during Chapter 11. This find-

[2] Related literature has considered asset sales by firms. Rajan (1992), Diamond (1993), and Brown, James, and Mooridian (1993) study how the presence of financial intermediaries (who have a comparative advantage in monitoring) among debtors in bankruptcy can affect the resolution of claims and the disposal of the bankrupt firm's assets.

[3] We do not examine costs that can arise outside bankruptcy in times of cash flow shortages or financial distress. Opler and Titman (1994) examine whether firms with high leverage lose market share relative to industry counterparts in industry downturns. Pulvino (1998) examines asset sales by financially distressed airlines. Andrade and Kaplan (1998) examine firms from a sample of highly leveraged transactions that become distressed. Gilson, John, and Lang (1990) examine private reorganizations of firms in default.

ing remains when we control for the changing composition of bankrupt firms as they make decisions to retain, sell, or close plants. Thus, Haugen and Senbet's (1978) contention that there are no indirect bankruptcy costs is supported in declining industries where most Chapter 11 bankruptcies occur. In high-growth industries, when we control for asset sales and closures, we find significant declines in productivity only for plants that immediately exit Chapter 11, or that remain in Chapter 11 for four or more years.

Analysis of plant sales and closures provides little evidence that Chapter 11 facilitates asset sales by less efficient firms. Bankrupt firms sell plants at a higher rate than nonbankrupt firms. However, for the most part, this difference is accounted for by sample selection and industry conditions, not by bankruptcy status. Although the probability of an asset sale is not strongly affected by bankruptcy status, we find that in high-growth industries, the plants that are sold by bankrupt firms experience a subsequent increase in productivity.

In declining industries, Chapter 11 status is associated with a higher probability of closing a plant. However, this higher probability is not caused by an increased tendency to weed out inefficient plants. Instead, it is caused by a higher rate of plant closures by Chapter 11 firms in response to declines in industry shipments.

Our analysis suggests that in declining demand industries, in which the marginal product of capital is low, firms can go bankrupt as a result of industry-wide excess capacity. The gains in redeploying assets in such industries are relatively small.

In high-growth industries, bankruptcy is more likely to be triggered by firm-specific inefficiency, and here the gains from redeploying assets of inefficient firms are greater. However, the effectiveness of bankruptcy in facilitating redeployment in high-growth industries might be limited because inefficient firms could have sufficient cash flows to continue to operate despite gains from asset transfers. Thus, Chapter 11 bankruptcy has a greater role in promoting the exit of capacity from declining industries than in changing firms' incentives to sell plants to more efficient producers.[4] More generally, our results suggest that we cannot evaluate other endogenous changes in corporate governance (boards of directors and managers) of bankrupt firms without explicitly considering the industry environment.

Our paper is part of a group of studies that considers the industry environment and the interaction of firms' asset sale and exit decisions with their environment.[5] The effect of demand conditions on the reorganization of insolvent firms has been recognized by Shleifer and Vishny (1992). They focus on asset sales and on how liquidation value depends on the cash reserves of firms in

[4] A related finding by Morck, Shleifer, and Vishny (1989) is that hostile takeovers are used to discipline managers in poorly performing industries, but alternative mechanisms are used in healthy industries.

[5] Papers in this group include Maksimovic and Zechner (1991), Chevalier (1995), and Kovenock and Phillips (1997).

the same industry. In their model, bankruptcies occur during industry downturns. As a result, the most efficient potential purchasers may also be in financial distress.[6] Thus, inefficient transfers by bankrupt firms are likely to be severe in times of low demand. Our approach differs because the optimal distribution of assets changes with demand. Higher potential costs of bankruptcy occur when firms fail to transfer assets at higher levels of demand.

The empirical analysis in our paper is related to the study of bankruptcy outcomes by Hotchkiss (1995), and the study of prebankruptcy asset sales by Khanna and Poulsen (1995). We differ from these papers in several key respects: First, we take into account the effect of industry conditions on the frequency and resolution of bankruptcy. Second, our data enable us to examine the performance and track the closures and sales of individual plants, rather than of the firm as a whole. Third, our sample also includes firms that do not emerge from Chapter 11 bankruptcy protection.

The paper is organized as follows. Our framework is discussed in Section I. We discuss data and our methodology in Section II. Section III contains results on firm productivity and the bankruptcy process. Section IV concludes the paper.

I. Bankruptcy and Reallocation in an Industry Equilibrium

Chapter 11 bankruptcy allows a reorganization of an insolvent firm's assets. How do industry conditions affect which firms enter bankruptcy and their bankruptcy costs?

Most studies of reorganization in finance analyze how a firm's capital structures induces it to liquidate unproductive capacity.[7] In single-firm analysis, the opportunity cost of capacity is taken as exogenous. The firm optimally scraps a plant when the plant's productivity falls below the firm's marginal gain from operating it. Hence, these studies suggest that there is a critical value of the asset's marginal product below which the asset should be liquidated, and above which it should be retained.

In multifirm industry settings, the firm's liquidation decision is more complex because the productivity of an individual plant may depend on the firm to which the plant belongs. Some firms are better than others at managing plants. Those firms that we term more productive get more output per unit of input from each of their plants. However, all firms face costs of internal control. These costs induce diminishing returns to scale at the firm level.[8]

[6] Shleifer and Vishny (1992) argue that firms trade off the benefits of a reduction of agency costs due to high debt against the expected loss from asset sales to inefficient firms which occur when highly leveraged firms become bankrupt during industry downturns.

[7] Important papers that take this approach include Harris and Raviv (1990), Diamond (1993), and Hart and Moore (1995).

[8] See Coase (1937) and Lucas (1978), for example, for analyses of optimal firm size that explore decreasing returns to scale that occur because of control costs. For empirical support of decreasing returns to scale, see Brock and Evans (1986). For a formal treatment of the trade in capacity in response to changes in industry conditions, see Maksimovic and Phillips (1996).

Firms trade plants until an equilibrium is reached in which marginal plants have the same total productivity in each firm.

When demand and output prices are high, the ability to get more output from inputs at the plant level is very valuable. Hence, firms that are better at managing plants can afford to pay larger costs of control. They increase in size by buying capacity from less productive firms. When demand is low, the ability to manage plants efficiently is less valuable relative to control costs. The gains from transferring plants from less productive but smaller firms to more productive firms will be smaller. Thus, a firm's decision to liquidate capacity depends both on its productivity and on industry conditions.

As the existing literature implies, highly productive firms liquidate capacity by selling it for scrap when demand falls below a critical level. However, less productive firms may have two optimal liquidation regions. Like the more productive firms, they can scrap plants when demand is low. They can also liquidate by selling out to more productive firms when demand is at higher levels. When demand is high, such sales are advantageous because the higher value of additional output that more efficient firms produce compensates for the additional control costs of operating the newly acquired assets.

The relation between the firm's cash flows and the optimal amount of capacity can also be different for high and low productivity firms. With high productivity firms, the cash flows and the optimal amount of capacity increases monotonically with demand. By contrast, for low productivity firms, value is maximized by selling off capacity when capacity is most valuable. This occurs when both demand and cash flows are high. Thus, if the compensation of a firm's managers depends on the amount of capacity they control, the interests of the managers and owners will be directly opposed when demand is high and the firm is of low productivity.

We examine how industry conditions affect both the incidence of bankruptcy and the productivity of firms entering bankruptcy. Because cash flows vary with output prices, we would expect that for a given debt level the productivity of the firms that go bankrupt is inversely related to industry demand. Bankrupt firms in high-demand industries are likely to be less productive than other industry firms, but the productivity of bankrupt firms in declining industries is likely to be closer to the industry average.

The relation between the productivity of bankrupt firms and demand also has implications for the view that bankruptcy triggers firms to optimally liquidate their assets. Liquidation policy must address two different outcomes, closures when demand is low and asset transfers when demand is high. If debt levels are set to bankrupt low-productivity firms when demand is high, then they will also bankrupt high-productivity firms when demand is low. Thus, if there are costs to bankruptcy, then bankruptcy is likely to be an ineffective method of enforcing optimal liquidation of low-productivity firms in high-demand industries. Bankruptcy can be effective in forcing firms to scrap assets when demand is low. However, when demand is low, both the value of the assets and the difference in value between efficient and inefficient firms is also likely to be lower. As a result, the value of high leverage in weeding out inefficient firms might not be high.

In the empirical tests that follow, we use plant-level manufacturing data to test for the existence of indirect bankruptcy costs. We distinguish between two types of potential indirect bankruptcy costs. The first type we consider is the effect of bankruptcy on the efficiency of a firm's plants. In both high- and low-demand industries, once a firm is in bankruptcy, it might have no incentive to maintain the value of its assets.[9] These assets include the value of a firm's reputation, which affects its ability to contract optimally with customers (Titman (1984) and Maksimovic and Titman (1991)). If these costs are significant, a bankrupt firm's productivity might decline relative to competitors. At each level of productivity, in high-demand industries, bankrupt firms are likely to have higher cash flows and thus may be able to maintain assets. However, opportunities for cost-saving investments are also likely to be greater when demand is high. Thus, the effect of the level of demand on the relative productivity of bankrupt firms is an empirical question that we investigate below.

The second type of indirect bankruptcy cost is an increased reorganization cost associated with a firm's bankruptcy status. We consider whether firms' asset sales and closure decisions are different from those of industry competitors. In high-demand industries managers could fail to sell assets when it is best to do so. This cost is potentially significant because assets in high-demand industries have high opportunity costs. Moreover, even unproductive firms in such industries have high cash flows, giving to the debtor in possession the resources to operate the firm. The bankrupt firm could also fail to liquidate assets by closing plants as soon as it is efficient to do so. This is especially apt to happen in low-demand industries.

In addition, we use our data to test aspects of a related model proposed by Shleifer and Vishny (1992). They argue that an important cost of bankruptcy is the cost of being forced to sell assets to less efficient producers in order to raise capital. In our context, there are three predictions based on their model. First, highly leveraged firms, which become bankrupt in industry downturns, have lower agency costs prior to bankruptcy, and therefore are at least as efficient as nonbankrupt firms. Second, bankrupt firms sell more assets than nonbankrupt firms. Third, all other factors being equal, bankrupt firms' assets sold may decrease in productivity under new owners.

II. Empirical Analysis: How Important Are Industry Conditions?

We explore the previous predictions on how industry demand and supply conditions, along with firm factors, influence the productivity and the reallocation decisions of firms in Chapter 11. Our null hypothesis is that value-

[9] In our empirical tests we follow firms for four years after they declare bankruptcy. Thus, we capture forgone opportunities to the extent that the bankrupt firms' failure to exploit opportunities is reflected in the cash flows of their existing plants during this period. We do not observe if bankrupt firms forgo entirely new projects as a result of bankruptcy status. If they exist, such costs are more likely to be significant in growing than in declining industries.

maximizing transfers occur and are related to demand and productivity conditions, and that there are no indirect bankruptcy costs. To examine whether industry demand and supply conditions influence indirect costs of bankruptcy, we investigate both long-run changes in industry shipments and short-run changes in aggregate industry investment. The detailed micro-level plant data we use allow us to control for this changing asset composition and compare the productivity of assets before, during, and after firms emerge from Chapter 11.

A. Data

We examine a sample of 302 firms that filed for Chapter 11. For inclusion in our sample, firms must satisfy two basic criteria. First, the firm must be a manufacturing firm producing products in SIC codes 2000 to 3999. Second, the bankruptcy had to occur in the years 1978 to 1989. We require that firms meet these criteria because of the unique nature of the microlevel data that we use to analyze plant-level productivity.

Our sample and tests include firms that declare Chapter 11 reorganization and subsequently change status to Chapter 7. We include all firms in Chapter 11, regardless of whether or not they emerge, thus avoiding survivorship bias.[10] The Chapter 11 bankrupt firms were identified from several sources. We use a comprehensive list compiled by the Securities and Exchange Commission.[11] Our sample also includes firms contained in Betker (1995) and Altman (1984). We also examined the *Wall Street Journal* Index for additional firms. We found 393 firms that satisfied our criteria for sample inclusion. We then verified the outcome of the bankruptcy process using LEXIS-NEXIS and the *Wall Street Journal* Index. We classify the outcome of the bankruptcy process as one of the following: plan confirmed and emerged, firm still in Chapter 11, or status changed to Chapter 7 liquidation.[12] For firms for which we were unable to find a bankruptcy resolution date, we located phone numbers from *Wards Business Directory* and called the firms. We were able to verify the resolution of the bankruptcy process for an additional 20 of these firms.

We use data from the Longitudinal Research Database (LRD), maintained by the Center for Economic Studies at the Bureau of the Census.[13] The LRD database contains detailed plant-level data on the value of shipments pro-

[10] We do not study firms that begin bankruptcy in Chapter 7. Conversations with Michael Berman, Bankruptcy Counsel, Office of General Counsel, at the Securities and Exchange Commission confirmed that the normal procedure for public firms in manufacturing that are liquidated is to first declare Chapter 11 and later convert to Chapter 7. In a subsample of Chapter 7 firms, we confirmed that all firms we examined that begin bankruptcy in Chapter 7 were either outside manufacturing or too small to be in our database.

[11] The list was kindly provided to us by Michael Berman.

[12] When a firm transfers to Chapter 7, we exclude it from that point onward in our analysis of the Chapter 11 period, because the incentives and decision rights of management and investors change in Chapter 7. We examine the Chapter 7 period for these firms in a separate table.

[13] For a more detailed description of the Longitudinal Research Database (LRD), see McGuckin and Pascoe (1988).

duced by each plant, investments broken down by equipment and buildings, and the number of employees. There are several advantages to this database. First, it covers both public and private firms in manufacturing industries. This mix is especially helpful for examining firms in bankruptcy. We can examine public firms that either did not emerge from Chapter 11, or emerged as private firms. Second, coverage is at the plant level and output is assigned by plants at the four-digit industry SIC code level. Thus, firms that produce under multiple SIC codes are not assigned to just one industry. Third, plant-level coverage means that we can track plants even as they change owners. Fourth, the database identifies when plants actually closed and not merely changed ownership.[14]

The LRD covers approximately 50,000 manufacturing plants every year in the Annual Survey of Manufacturers (ASM). The ASM covers all plants with more than 250 employees. Smaller plants are randomly selected every fifth year to complete a rotating five-year panel.

We confine our analysis to 1977 through 1990. We use 1977 as the starting year of our analysis because it is a complete census year. Earlier name records for the firms in this panel are incomplete, which makes it difficult to identify bankrupt firms in the early 1970s. 1990 is the most recent year of data available to us.

We match our sample of bankrupt firms to name records from the LRD. We are unable to match the names of several firms, either because they are not manufacturing firms or because we cannot find records for them in the LRD. Name records can be hard to match for several reasons: The bankrupt firm might be part of a larger corporation, and since the name records in the LRD are frequently at the division level, name changes at the firm level might not be updated in the LRD; or because abbreviations in firm names preclude unique identification. Because the remaining firms for which we were unable to find a resolution date were generally small firms that changed names, we use the LRD to locate subsequent name changes for them. Of the original 393 firms, we are able to verify for 302 firms that there was either a resolution of bankruptcy or that the firm remained in bankruptcy, and therefore keep these for our final sample of matched firms.

B. Variable Selection

We use both plant-level efficiency and industry-level variables to test our hypotheses that there are no bankruptcy costs, and that value-maximizing transfers occur for bankrupt firms. We examine whether plant-level efficiency, and asset sale and closure decisions are different from the decisions of industry competitors.

[14] One disadvantage of this database is that it does not have capital structure data. However, we identify bankruptcy status, and thus can test our null hypotheses of no bankruptcy costs, and that transfers and closures are unaffected by bankruptcy status.

B.1. Productivity and Cash Flow Variables

We calculate productivity and a measure of plant cash flow for both the bankrupt and nonbankrupt industry firms. Our primary measure of performance is Total Factor Productivity (TFP), which takes the actual amount of output produced for a given amount of inputs and compares it to a predicted amount of output. Predicted output is what the plant should have produced, given the amount of inputs it used. A plant that produces more than the predicted amount of output, given its actual inputs, has a greater-than-average productivity. This measure is much more flexible than the cash flow measure, and does not impose the restrictions of constant returns to scale and constant elasticity of scale that a "dollar-in dollar-out" cash flow measure requires.

In calculating the predicted output of each plant, we assume a functional form of the firm's production function that defines the relation between the plant's inputs and outputs. Then, using all plants in the industry from 1977 to 1990, we obtain TFP as the residual from the estimation of a production function.[15]

We assume that the plants in our sample have a translog production function. This functional form is a second-degree approximation to any arbitrary production function, and therefore takes into account interactions between inputs.[16] To estimate predicted outputs, we take the translog production function and run a regression of log of total value of shipments on log of inputs, including cross-product and squared terms:

$$\ln Q_{it} = A + a_j \ln L_{jit} + \sum_{j=1}^{N} \sum_{k=j}^{N} a_{jk} \ln L_{jit} \ln L_{kit}, \tag{1}$$

where Q_{it} represents output of plant i in year t, L_{jit} denotes the quantity of input j used in production for plant i for time period t. A is a technology shift parameter, assumed to be constant by industry, and $a_j = \Sigma_{i=1}^{N} a_{ji}$ indexes returns to scale. We standardize plant-level TFP by dividing by the standard deviation of TFP for each industry. Thus, our results are not driven by differences across industries in the dispersion of productivity in each industry.

In estimating the TFPs in our sample, we use data for more than 500,000 plant years, and approximately 50,000 plants each year. More than 90 percent of the plants in the ASM during this period are in an industry in which

[15] Our approach follows that of Kovenock and Phillips (1997). Alternatively, we could predict outputs for each plant by using averages of all the inputs in the industry and the plant's own inputs. In our regression approach, the calculated average TFP is also zero for each industry. Thus, the TFP numbers we present describe the plant's productivity relative to others in the industry. Another additional advantage is that our approach does not impose constant returns to scale or constant elasticity of substitution. Including fixed effects in the TFP regressions does not qualitatively alter the reported changes in productivity.

[16] The translog production function is used by Kim and Maksimovic (1990) in their study of agency costs and airline productivity and by Caves and Barton (1991).

a firm has filed for Chapter 11. We include three types of inputs—capital, labor, and materials—as explanatory variables in the productivity regression for each industry. All of these data exist at the plant level. However, the ASM does not state the actual quantity shipped by each plant, but shows only the value of shipments. As a result, we take the difference between actual and predicted shipments as our measure of TFP. We adjust for inflation by using four-digit SIC code data from the Bartelsman and Gray (1994) database. We make depreciation adjustments at the two-digit level using data from the Bureau of Economic Analysis. Kovenock and Phillips (1997) describe these inputs and the method for accounting for inflation and depreciation of capital stock in more detail.

We also calculate operating cash flow at the plant level as an alternative measure of performance. Operating cash flow is calculated as the value of shipments less labor, materials, and energy costs, divided by the value of shipments. We calculate this measure at both plant and firm level, noting that at neither level do we have corporate overhead or selling, or general and administrative expense. The cash flow measure is thus an operating margin.

In our logistic regressions, we also include other firm and plant-level variables to provide additional control for unmeasured productivity differences and other factors, such as size, that can influence the asset sale and closure decision. We include the log of firm size, relative plant scale, plant age, and the number of plants a firm operates. We define firm size as the total value of shipments. The number of plants and size can influence the closure decision, because firms can reallocate production to other plants if there is underutilized capacity. Plant scale is the plant's asset size divided by the average asset size for plants in each industry. Plant age is calculated as the current year less the first year the plant appeared in the database.

B.2. Industry Variables: Shipments and Capacity Utilization

We focus on industry conditions and shipment or output growth for two reasons. First, the value of capital and the value of transferring assets in an industry depend on industry growth. Second, firms' cash constraints may depend on industry conditions. If bankrupt firms in high-growth industries are less cash constrained than those in declining industries, then managers might not sell or close assets at the optimal time.

We calculate several different measures of industry demand and supply conditions. Our central variables are the yearly and long-run changes in industry shipments, industry-level research and development (R&D), and capacity utilization. For industry shipments, we use the Bartelsman and Gray (1994) database at the National Bureau of Economic Research (NBER) at the three-digit SIC code level. We use industry shipments and investment data to investigate if long-run changes in an industry affect the number of firms entering and leaving bankruptcy, and the relative performance of these firms.

We include industry research and development to capture variation in the difficulty of valuing businesses that produce unique products or rely on proprietary technology or brand names. We calculate industry research and development expenditures from COMPUSTAT firm-level data. Our calculations represent R&D and advertising, weighted by the firm's percentage of industry sales, aggregated up to the three-digit SIC code level.

We obtain data on capacity utilization from the Bureau of the Census publication, *The Annual Survey of Capacity Utilization*. Our capacity utilization measure is output as a percentage of normal full production at the three-digit SIC code level. We include capacity utilization to capture changes in the supply relative to demand conditions, and to examine whether excess capacity might exist in industries and perhaps cause firms to optimally close down plants.

To examine whether the level of industry demand alters the relation between the explanatory variables and actions (closures, asset sales), we divide our sample of industries into quartiles according to level of demand. Where appropriate, we report results for both the entire sample and the quartiles.

We classify industries into "demand" or change-in-shipment quartiles by constructing an index of long-run changes in real industry shipments over a ten-year period. We include *all* industries in constructing these quartiles, not just those that have firms entering bankruptcy. We measure the change by using the log of a three-year average of total shipments during the years 1986 to 1988, divided by the three-year average from 1977 to 1979. We use the total value of shipments, a production-based number, for U.S. producers. Thus, this measure captures both cost shifts from increased foreign imports or shocks to production costs, and demand changes in the industry. We use three-year averages as the endpoints to avoid short-term changes in demand. We classify all the three-digit SIC industries in our database into quartiles based on our index of long-run changes in industry shipments. We use three-digit SIC industries to prevent smaller, four-digit, industries from being overrepresented in any quartile. Then, we examine the productivity of the bankrupt firms' plants in these quartiles.

Note that, by design, we do *not* have a similar number of firms in each quartile. If certain industries have more firms and also more bankruptcies, then the quartile containing these industries has more firms represented. Thus, we can examine whether declining industries have a higher frequency of bankruptcies, and whether productivity of these firms is both significantly different from other firms in their quartile and from firms in other quartiles.

In addition to shipment growth quartiles, we also classify industries into quartiles by annual changes in aggregate investment. We examine investments expressed in real 1982 dollars divided by total industry assets, again in real 1982 dollars. We use the Bartelsman and Gray (1994) data for investment and assets, and also their constructed price deflators. Classifying industries this way provides an aggregate industry-level measure of investment in an industry. These investment changes are proxies for the marginal productivity of capital and the expectation of future returns in the industry.

We then examine the relative number and productivity of plants for the bankrupt firms in each quartile. Again, we do *not* have a similar number of firms in each quartile. Using this procedure, we examine whether bankrupt firms with high investment have lower productivity than nonbankrupt firms in the same industry and whether investment rates are lower than for industry nonbankrupt firms. For firms in each investment quartile, we also examine whether productivity decreases while the firms are under Chapter 11 bankruptcy protection. The results are similar using this classification and are available from the authors.

III. Results

A. Summary Statistics

Table I presents summary statistics for our total sample. Panel A shows that in our sample, the plants of bankrupt firms are, on average, bigger than those of nonbankrupt firms (average value of plant-level shipments of $61.95 million and $29.76 million, respectively) and somewhat older (11.5 and 8.2 years, respectively). In the whole sample, the average standardized TFP of plants of firms that filed for bankruptcy, calculated the year prior to filing of Chapter 11, is −0.048. Thus, these plants show a lower productivity than their industry averages. The difference across all industries and all shipment growth quartiles is statistically significant at the 10 percent level.

Panel B shows the median growth in real industry shipments for each industry quartile, and the summary statistics of the frequency of Chapter 11 bankruptcies across quartiles. There is a considerable difference in the real growth of industry shipments between quartiles 1 and 4. In quartile 4, shipments increase by 23.14 percent over the ten-year period, but in quartile 1 they decrease by 33.93 percent. In addition to the full sample, we present results for quartiles 1 to 4 separately. Quartile 1 we label the declining industry quartile, and quartile 4 the high-growth industry quartile.

There is also a substantial difference in the frequency of Chapter 11 across quartiles. This difference in frequency is consistent with a paper by Berkovitch and Israel (1997) in which they model the decision to declare Chapter 11 as a strategic choice variable. In their model, the proportion of firms entering Chapter 11 is higher in mature industries, because underinvestment problems are less important. We find that the proportion of plants in Chapter 11 falls monotonically from 3.23 percent to 0.98 percent as we move from declining industries to high-growth industries, suggesting that the incidence of bankruptcy depends on industry demand.

B. Industry Conditions and Bankruptcy

Table II tests whether the population of bankrupt firms differs across high- and low-growth industries. It provides evidence on the relative productivity of Chapter 11 plants before, during, and after emergence from bankruptcy.

Table I

Chapter 11 Bankruptcy Sample Characteristics

Sample characteristics of plants of bankrupt firms that declared Chapter 11 in the years 1978 to 1989. We obtain plant-level data from the Annual Survey of Manufacturers (ASM), Bureau of the Census, U.S. Department of Commerce. Total factor productivity (TFP) statistics are given for the year prior to the declaration of Chapter 11 for each of the bankrupt firms. TFP is a relative measure of productivity calculated such that average TFP over time equals 0. TFPs are standardized by dividing each TFP by the standard deviation of the industry's TFP at the four-digit level. Shipment or output change is determined by using aggregate industry data from the NBER for manufacturing industries. We determine quartiles by computing the change in the real value of shipments over 10 years at the three-digit SIC code level. We use the year of the first bankruptcy in an industry when there are multiple bankruptcies in an industry for the number of nonbankrupt industry firms and industry plants. Average plant age is calculated as the year before Chapter 11 less the time the plant first appeared in the database, beginning with 1972. (Standard errors of the means are in parentheses.)

	Sample of Firms	
	Bankrupt Firms	Nonbankrupt Industry Firms
Panel A: Characteristics of Plants of Bankrupt and Nonbankrupt Firms		
Number of plants (302 bankrupt firms)	1,075	56,256
Average plant size (Value of shipments in $ millions)	61.954	29.764
Average plant age (years)	11.5	8.24
	(0.154)	(0.025)
Total factor productivity: Year before Chapter 11		
Avg. standardized TFP (bankrupt - industry avg.)	−0.048*	
	(0.028)	
Panel B: Industry Characteristics: Growth in Industry Shipments Quartiles		
Quartile 1: Number of plants	259	8,021
% of industry plants in bankruptcy	3.23%	
Median growth in real industry shipments	−33.93%	
Quartile 2: Number of plants	457	18,089
% of industry plants in bankruptcy	2.53%	
Median growth in real industry shipments	−4.12%	
Quartile 3: Number of plants	199	12,978
% of industry plants in bankruptcy	1.53%	
Median growth in real industry shipments	8.11%	
Quartile 4: Number of plants	160	16,295
% of industry plants in bankruptcy	0.98%	
Median growth in real industry shipments	23.14%	

* Significantly different from zero at the 10 percent level using a two-tailed test for the difference of the mean from zero.

This table includes plants of firms that do not emerge from Chapter 11 as well as those plants that eventually emerge, are sold off, closed, or transferred to Chapter 7, for the years in which they are in Chapter 11. Thus, these initial data do not control for changes over time in the composition of firms as they make asset sale and closure decisions.

Table II

Industry-Adjusted Productivity of Plants of Chapter 11 Firms

This table presents summary statistics that examine whether the productivity and number of plants of bankrupt firms varies over aggregate industry quartiles. Quartiles are defined by change in industry demand over the 10-year period, using the change in three-year averages for 1977–1979 to 1986–1988. Numbers are average relative total factor productivity (TFP) less the industry average TFP for firms that declared Chapter 11 in the years 1978 to 1989. We standardize TFPs by dividing each TFP by the standard deviation of the industry TFPs at the four-digit code level. We determine quartiles by using aggregate industry shipment data from the NBER for manufacturing industries. The industry shipment data is the real value of shipments at the three-digit SIC code level. Q1 is productivity for quartile 1, Q4 is productivity for quartile 4. (*t*-statistics for significant differences from zero are in parentheses.)

	Average Productivity		Average Productivity by Industry Growth Quartile				*t*-statistics for Significant Difference for Q4 − Q1
	All Firms	*n*	Q1 (lowest quartile)	*n*	Q4	*n*	
Panel A: Years Before Chapter 11							
Year −2	−0.044	1188	−0.052	308	−0.009	196	(0.47)
	(−1.53)		(−1.04)		(−0.12)		
Year −1	−0.048[c]	1075	−0.032	259	−0.151[c]	160	(−1.14)
	(−1.70)		(−0.53)		(−1.70)		
Panel B: In Chapter 11							
Year 0	−0.092[a]	873	−0.118[c]	207	−0.188	154	(−0.56)
t-stat for average	(−2.51)		(−1.73)		(−1.46)		
t-stat for −1 to 0	(−0.89)		(−0.98)		(−0.24)		
Year +1	0.036	639	0.086	156	0.015	102	(−1.26)
t-stat for average	(0.86)		(1.06)		(0.13)		
t-stat for −1 to +1	(1.67)		(1.20)		(1.14)		
Year +2	−0.024	345	0.072	99	−0.237[b]	61	(−1.98)[b]
t-stat for average	(−0.51)		(0.72)		(−1.74)		
t-stat for −1 to +2	(0.42)		(1.04)		(−0.53)		
Year +3	−0.071	200	0.027	72	−0.369[a]	29	(−2.62)[a]
t-stat for average	(−1.14)		(0.31)		(−2.47)		
t-stat for −1 to +3	(−0.33)		(0.57)		(−1.26)		
Year +4	−0.023	143	0.093	56	−0.335[a]	24	(−2.40)[a]
t-stat for average	(−0.31)		(0.87)		(−2.66)		
t-stat for −1 to +4	(0.33)		(1.03)		(−1.19)		
Panel C: After Emerging from Chapter 11							
Year +1	−0.123[c]	372	−0.055[c]	75	0.022	49	(0.44)
t-stat for average	(−1.89)		(−0.48)		(0.17)		
t-stat for −1 to +1	(−0.83)		(−0.18)		(1.13)		
Year +2	−0.093	213	−0.040	56	−0.003	34	(0.65)
t-stat for average	(−1.48)		(−0.31)		(0.02)		
t-stat for −1 to +2	(−0.65)		(−0.06)		(0.90)		
Year +3	−0.165[c]	124	−0.003	28	−0.288	30	(−0.63)
t-stat for average	(−1.63)		(−0.01)		(−1.47)		
t-stat for −1 to +3	(−1.11)		(0.10)		(−0.64)		

[a,b,c] Significantly different from zero at the 1 percent, 5 percent, and 10 percent levels, respectively, using a two-tailed *t*-test.

Table II presents industry-adjusted productivity per-year statistics relative to the year the firm filed for Chapter 11, which we call year 0. In the interest of space, we present data only for the total sample and quartiles 1 and 4.[17] The last column of the table tests whether there is a significant difference between the productivity of plants in quartiles 1 and 4.

Panel A reports average total factor productivity of bankrupt firms' plants relative to their industry counterparts for the two years prior to filing for Chapter 11 protection. In Panel B, we present average industry-adjusted productivity for years while the firm is in Chapter 11, and in Panel C for the years after emerging from Chapter 11. These panels also report t-statistics for this average and for the unreported change in productivity relative to the year prior to Chapter 11. The unreported changes can be calculated by subtracting the average productivity in the year prior to Chapter 11 from the productivity for the year in question.

Column 1 in Panel A reveals that for the sample as a whole, in the year before bankruptcy the average productivity of Chapter 11 plants is significantly lower than that of their industry counterparts. Columns 2 and 3, however, show that this significant negative productivity is concentrated in quartile 4. The average productivity of quartile 1 plants in the year prior to Chapter 11 is not significantly different from their industry counterparts. Although quartile 1 firms have a lower average productivity than their industry counterparts, this difference is smaller than the difference for those plants in quartile 4.

In Panel B, we test whether the average productivity is significantly different from zero. For the full sample, the average industry-adjusted productivity in year 0 is negative and significant. All other industry-adjusted levels are insignificant.

However, we find very different results when we subdivide by quartiles in columns 2 and 3. In quartile 1, while the firm is under Chapter 11 bankruptcy protection, the average levels are positive, albeit insignificant, for four of the five years covered. In quartile 4, the average industry-adjusted productivity is negative, and significant in four of the five years.

Panel B also tests whether firms under Chapter 11 protection experience changes in productivity. The table presents the t-statistic for this change in productivity. For the full sample and for quartiles 1 and 4, there is no evidence of significant changes in industry-adjusted productivity. Thus, we cannot reject the hypothesis that bankrupt firms' plants do not decline in productivity while in Chapter 11, either for the whole sample or for the quartiles. These results are consistent with the hypothesis that declining productivity is not a cost for firms that enter Chapter 11 bankruptcy.

In the last column, we test for equality of means across quartiles. We find significantly lower productivity in quartile 4 than in quartile 1. In three out of five years during Chapter 11, the average industry-adjusted productivity

[17] The largest differences in average plant productivities are between quartiles 1 and 4. The results for quartiles 2 and 3 are available from the authors.

in quartile 4 is significantly lower than it is in quartile 1. These findings show that differences between industries are important in determining the relative productivity during Chapter 11. Thus, we find differences across quartiles in the frequency of bankruptcies, and in the productivity during bankruptcy. The differences in the populations of bankrupt firms across quartiles are consistent with firms in quartile 4 deciding not to enter Chapter 11 because of potential indirect bankruptcy costs.

Panel C shows the productivity of the plants of firms that emerge from Chapter 11. The number of plants that emerge from Chapter 11 bankruptcy and remain under the same ownership is low, both because plants and firms are liquidated during the bankruptcy process, and because some remained in bankruptcy at the end of the sample period. Average productivity of firms that emerge is negative and significant at the 10 percent level for both the whole sample and for those in quartile 1. Only in the year of emergence do we find that industry-adjusted average productivity is significantly different from zero. In no years do we find that the change in industry productivity, relative to the year prior to Chapter 11, is significantly different from zero.

In Table III we examine cash flows of plants of Chapter 11 firms. The overall findings are consistent with Table II. We find some interesting patterns when we look at average cash flow that is *not* adjusted for industry averages in the year prior to bankruptcy. Average cash flows of plants (0.212 in year $t - 1$) with negative industry-adjusted productivity in quartile 4, year $t - 1$ (Table II) are significantly higher (t-statistic = 2.75) than cash flows of plants of firms in quartile 1 (0.144 in year $t - 1$) whose productivity is not lower than that of the industry. Plants of less than average productivity in high-growth industries have higher cash flows than plants of firms that are of above average productivity in declining industries. This tells us that industry effects are likely to be very important in understanding which plants enter bankruptcy.

Table IV directly controls for the changing asset composition of Chapter 11 firms' assets. We present data on productivity in the year prior to Chapter 11, and for the change in productivity relative to that year. Each row of Table IV follows the same set of plants over time, based on the number of years the plants are in Chapter 11. For example, in the two-year row, we exclude all plants that are sold or closed prior to the end of year 2, or that are retained for three or more years. We present results for quartiles 1 and 4 in this table. In Panel A we show results for quartile 1 and in Panel B the results for quartile 4.

Table IV reveals significant differences between quartiles 1 and 4. In quartile 1, the industries with the lowest output growth, there is no significant decline in industry-adjusted productivity during Chapter 11. Thus, in the low-growth quartile there is no evidence of costs in the form of declines in productivity while firms are in bankruptcy status. There is evidence that plants in quartile 1 that exit within a year are on average less productive than their industry counterparts in year $t - 1$, but they do not suffer sig-

Table III

Plant-level Operating Cash Flows of Chapter 11 Firms

This table presents the cash flow of plants of bankrupt firms by aggregate industry quartiles. Quartiles are defined by the real value industry shipments over a ten-year period. Cash flow numbers are plant-level values of shipments less materials, energy, and labor costs. We present changes relative to the year prior to bankruptcy, as all averages (levels) are significantly different from zero at the 1 percent level. We determine quartiles by using aggregate industry shipment data from the NBER for manufacturing industries. The change in shipments is calculated over a ten-year period at the three-digit SIC code level, using the change in three-year averages for 1977–1979 to 1986–1988. Q1 is productivity for quartile 1, Q4 is productivity for quartile 4. (*t*-statistics for significant differences from zero are in parentheses.)

			Cash Flows by Industry Growth Quartile				*t*-statistics for Significant Difference for
	All Firms	*n*	Q1 (lowest quartile)	*n*	Q4	*n*	Q4 − Q1
Panel A: Years Before Chapter 11—Average Cash Flow							
Year −2	0.190[a]	1188	0.167[a]	308	0.233[a]	196	(2.81)[a]
	(19.19)		(10.17)		(13.73)		
Year −1	0.203[a]	1075	0.144[a]	259	0.212[a]	160	(2.75)[a]
	(24.38)		(7.36)		(13.90)		
Panel B: In Chapter 11—Change in Cash Flow from Year before Chapter 11							
Change Year −1 to 0	−0.007	607	0.023	207	−0.002	13	(−0.68)
	(−0.48)		(0.81)		(−0.08)		
Year −1 to +1	0.039[a]	639	0.080[a]	156	0.027	102	(−1.85)[c]
	(2.96)		(2.82)		(1.21)		
Year −1 to +2	0.021	345	0.067[a]	99	−0.020	61	(−2.12)[b]
	(1.42)		(2.40)		(−0.75)		
Year −1 to +3	−0.016	200	0.049[c]	72	−0.043[c]	29	(−1.69)[c]
	(−0.90)		(1.68)		(−1.64)		
Year −1 to +4	0.014	143	0.051	56	−0.016	24	(−1.48)
	(0.69)		(1.57)		(−0.75)		
Panel C: After Emerging from Chapter 11							
Year −1 to +1	0.013	372	0.056	75	0.043	49	(−0.26)
	(1.29)		(1.32)		(1.27)		
Year −1 to +2	−0.010	213	0.101[b]	56	−0.024	34	(−1.93)[c]
	(−0.41)		(1.96)		(−0.51)		
Year −1 to +3	−0.054	124	0.034	28	−0.017	30	(−0.43)
	(−1.29)		(0.31)		(−0.34)		

[a,b,c] Significantly different from zero at the 1 percent, 5 percent, and 10 percent levels, respectively, using a two-tailed *t*-test.

nificant declines while in Chapter 11. In quartile 4, the productivity of bankrupt firms' plants shows a different pattern. After controlling for composition changes, the productivity of firms' plants that remain in Chapter 11 for four

Table IV

Productivity Controlling for Composition Changes

This table presents the prior productivity of plants by the number of years in Chapter 11, for industry growth quartiles 1 and 4. The table thus directly controls for changing asset composition. Plants leave Chapter 11 because they are sold off or closed down, or because the firm emerges from Chapter 11. Numbers are plant-level total factor productivity (TFP) less the industry average TFP for firms that declared Chapter 11 in the years 1978 to 1989. TFPs are standardized by dividing each TFP by the standard deviation of the industry TFPs at the four-digit SIC code level. We determine quartiles by using the change in ten-year shipments at the aggregate three-digit SIC code level for all industries. Plant counts do not add up exactly to the yearly changes in plants in Table II because of missing plant-year data. Q1 represents productivity of plants in quartile 1, Q4 for quartile 4, respectively. Q4 − Q1 represents the difference in means between quartle 4 and quartile 1. (*t*-statistics for significant differences from 0 are in parentheses.)

Number of Years in Chapter 11	Average Year −1	Change: Year −1 to 0	Change: −1 to 1	Change: −1 to 2	Change: −1 to 3	Change: −1 to 4
Panel A: Industry Quartile 1: Productivity in Bankruptcy						
< 1 year, $n = 47$	−0.293[b]	0.068				
t-stat for Q1	(−2.14)	(0.31)				
1 year, $n = 54$	−0.287[b]	0.187	0.312			
t-stat for Q1	(−2.19)	(0.96)	(1.48)			
2 years, $n = 27$	−0.086	−0.110	0.252	0.240		
t-stat for Q1	(−0.67)	(−0.55)	(1.18)	(0.23)		
3 years, $n = 13$	0.286	−0.266	−0.172	−0.162	0.001	
t-stat for Q1	(1.44)	(−0.86)	(−0.63)	(−0.53)	(0.01)	
4 or more years, $n = 56$	−0.078	−0.023	0.148	0.087	0.107	0.176
t-stat for Q1	(−0.71)	(−0.21)	(1.18)	(0.88)	(1.02)	(1.55)
Panel B: Industry Quartile 4: Productivity in Bankruptcy						
< 1 year, $n = 20$	−0.306	−0.517				
t-stat for Q4	(−1.61)	(−1.71)[c]				
t-stat for Q4 − Q1	(−0.09)	(−1.67)[c]				
1 year, $n = 39$	−0.159	0.233	0.212			
t-stat for Q4	(−0.68)	(0.66)	(0.68)			
t-stat for Q4 − Q1	(0.94)	(0.12)	(0.14)			
2 years, $n = 29$	0.247	0.057	0.055	−0.352		
t-stat for Q4	(0.99)	(0.18)	(0.17)	(−1.02)		
t-stat for Q4 − Q1	(1.40)	(0.45)	(−0.52)	(−0.54)		
3 years, $n = 6$	−0.541	−0.239	−0.251	0.029	0.128	
t-stat for Q4	(−1.51)	(−0.60)	(−0.64)	(0.07)	(0.34)	
t-stat for Q4 − Q1	(−2.26)[b]	(0.06)	(−0.17)	(0.40)	(0.29)	
4 or more years, $n = 24$	−0.076	−0.037	−0.048	−0.228	−0.274	−0.258
t-stat for Q4	(−0.69)	(−0.27)	(−0.37)	(−1.78)[c]	(−2.35)[b]	(−2.11)[b]
t-stat for Q4 − Q1	(0.02)	(−0.08)	(−0.96)	(−1.84)[c]	(−2.16)[b]	(−2.32)[b]

[a,b,c] Significantly different from zero at the 1 percent, 5 percent, and 10 percent levels, respectively, using a two-tailed *t*-test.

or more years significantly declines for years −1 to +2, −1 to +3, and −1 to + 4. These declines are also significantly different from the productivity changes in quartile 1.

We cannot come to any conclusion from the results in Tables II to IV about whether or not bankrupt firms in the highest quartile should be making different economic decisions. However, we can conclude that in high-growth industries, bankrupt firms' plant-level productivity significantly declines when the firms remain in Chapter 11 for four or more years. The evidence also suggests that the populations of bankrupt firms in high- and low-growth industries differ.

C. Chapter 11 Outcomes: Asset Sales and Plant Closures

In this section we examine asset sale and closure decisions of Chapter 11 and industry firms.

C.1. Asset Sales

We examine asset sales for bankrupt firms before, during, and after Chapter 11. Using the plant-level focus of the database, we can examine the productivity of the individual plants under new ownership.

We test three predictions from our analysis about asset sales. First, relatively more asset sales will occur in high-growth industries. Second, for bankrupt firms, if there are increased conflicts of interest in bankruptcy, the frequency of asset sales will be reduced in these industries. Third, for those asset sales by bankrupt firms that do occur, in high-growth industries the increase in the productivity of assets sold will be greater under new ownership. We also test whether the average productivity of the firms' remaining assets is lower because the firm has sold off its more productive assets.

Table V shows by quartile the productivity of sold and retained plants for bankrupt and industry firms' plants. The results are presented in four panels, each of which presents results combining the top two and bottom two quartiles. We do this because there are too few asset sales by quartiles for some bankruptcy periods to allow disclosure of results by individual quartile under U.S. Census Bureau regulations.

Panels A, B, and C examine the assets sold off by Chapter 11 firms and their industry counterparts, before, during, and after Chapter 11 respectively. We construct a matching set of industry asset sales for each of these periods by getting all asset sales for the four-digit SIC code of the bankrupt firm. We assign these industry asset sales to the before, during, and after Chapter 11 periods based on the status of the bankrupt firm in that industry. Panel D examines the productivity of the plants of the purchasers in the industry, excluding the plants that they purchase.

Table V shows several findings. First, there are more asset sales by Chapter 11 firms in high-growth industries. Panel A shows that prior to Chapter 11, conditional on selling a plant, in the high-growth quartiles bankrupt firms sell 52.4 percent of their plants, compared to 41.3 percent in low-

Table V

Asset Sales by Chapter 11 Firms

This table examines the productivity of firms' plants that were sold by Chapter 11 firms and industry plants in the same four-digit SIC code. For industry quartiles, we use external industry data from the NBER and represent the change in shipments over a ten-year period at the three-digit SIC code level. Total factor productivity (TFP) is standardized by dividing each TFP by the standard deviation of the industry TFPs at the four-digit SIC code level. Years after emergence are combined for the lowest two and highest two quartiles because of disclosure restrictions. Industry numbers do not include takeovers or mergers. Asset sale firms are defined as firms selling assets while remaining in business. (t-statistics are in parentheses.)

Panel A: Before Chapter 11

	Lowest Two Quartiles				Highest Two Quartiles			
	Bankrupt Firms		Industry Firms		Bankrupt Firms		Industry Firms	
	Old Owners	New Owners	Old Owners	New Owners	Old Owners	New Owners	Old Owners	New Owners
Asset sale firms: TFP of sales	−0.014	−0.027	−0.015	0.017	−0.065	−0.052	−0.032	−0.020
t-stat for average TFP = 0	(−0.26)	(−0.46)	(−0.98)	(1.23)	(−0.91)	(−0.60)	(−2.07)[b]	(−1.16)
t-stat for improvement under new owners, relative to industry		(−2.18)[b]				(0.03)		
Number of plants [percent sold off]	193 [41.3%]		706 [18.4%]		122 [52.4%]		502 [13.1%]	
[percent based on total plant years]	[11.1%]		[6.2%]		[14.9%]		[5.8%]	
Assets retained: TFP	−0.049		0.029		−0.057		0.040	
t-stat for average TFP = 0	(−1.26)		(1.50)		(−1.25)		(2.28)[b]	
t-stat for retained–sold	(−0.54)		(1.78)[c]		(0.09)		(3.08)[a]	
Number of plants	274		3124		111		3324	
Nonasset sale firms: TFP	−0.070		−0.008		−0.016		−0.009	
t-stat for average TFP = 0	(−1.63)		(−1.15)		(−0.57)		(−1.23)	
Number of plants	434		19664		251		16967	

Panel B: Chapter 11 Period

	Lowest Two Quartiles				Highest Two Quartiles			
	Bankrupt Firms		Industry Firms		Bankrupt Firms		Industry Firms	
	Old Owners	New Owners	Old Owners	New Owners	Old Owners	New Owners	Old Owners	New Owners
Asset sale firms: TFP of sales	−0.030	−0.057	−0.033	−0.008	0.011	0.080	−0.009	−0.051
t-stat for average TFP=0	(−0.36)	(−1.45)	(−2.24)[b]	(−0.44)	(0.11)	(1.72)[c]	(−0.65)	(−3.33)[a]
t-stat for improvement under new owners, relative to industry		(−1.20)				(2.29)[b]		
Number of plants [percent sold off]	138 [44.4%]		437 [20.2%]		47 [58.8%]		466 [19%]	
[percent based on total plant years]	[16.5%]		[8.8%]		[24.4%]		[9.9%]	
Assets retained: TFP	0.053		0.046		−0.209		0.035	
t-stat for average TFP = 0	(1.56)		(1.53)		(−2.37)[b]		(2.66)[a]	
t-stat for retained–sold	(0.93)		(2.36)[a]		(−1.66)[c]		(2.34)[b]	
Number of plants	172		1726		33		1983	
Nonasset sale firms: TFP	0.064		−0.002		−0.154		−0.005	
t-stat for average TFP = 0	(1.19)		(−0.26)		(−1.38)		(−0.68)	
Number of plants	258		21592		120		19738	

Panel C: After Chapter 11

	Lowest Two Quartiles				Highest Two Quartiles			
	Bankrupt Firms	Number of Plants	Industry Firms	Number of Plants	Bankrupt Firms	Number of Plants	Industry Firms	Number of Plants
Productivity of Assets Retained	0.006	167	0.027	1472	−0.167	85	0.020	1807
t-stat for average TFP = 0	(0.15)		(2.50)[a]		(−1.72)[c]		(2.50)[a]	

continued over

Table V—*Continued*

Panel D: Productivity of Purchasers' Existing Assets (for the four years surrounding purchase)				
	Lowest Two Quartiles		Highest Two Quartiles	
	Quartiles 1 and 2	Number of Plants	Quartiles 3 and 4	Number of Plants
Productivity of Purchaser				
TFP before purchase	0.069	1396	0.055	1554
t-stat for average TFP = 0	(2.83)[a]		(2.74)[a]	
TFP after purchase	0.055	1274	0.030	1405
t-stat for average TFP = 0	(2.07)[b]		(1.18)	

[a,b,c] Significantly different from 0 at the 1 percent, 5 percent, and 10 percent levels, respectively, using a two-tailed *t*-test for the difference of the mean from zero.

growth quartiles. Panel B shows that during Chapter 11, bankrupt firms sell 58.75 percent of their plants, compared to 44.37 percent in the bottom two quartiles. Both of these proportions are higher than their industry counterparts.

Second, Panel B shows that the productivity of plants sold only improves in the two high-growth industry quartiles. In Chapter 11, the productivity of the 47 plants sold in quartiles 3 and 4 significantly increases under the new owners.

In both Panels A and B, we examine the plants that are retained by the firms and not subsequently sold off. We find that the plants retained by firms in high-growth industries have lower productivity than the ones sold off. For industry firms, plants retained have significantly higher productivity than those sold.[18]

In Panel D, we find that purchasing firms' existing plants are more productive than the industry average, both before and after the purchase. This finding does not differ much by quartiles.

These results show how important changes to industry output are to the asset sale decisions for all firms. More asset sales occur in high-output growth industries. Second, bankrupt firms in high-growth industries sell their relatively more productive plants and these plants improve productivity under their new owners. This evidence is consistent with a higher value of asset reallocations in high-growth industries.

In Table VI we investigate the asset sale process further by examining whether the probability of selling a plant, conditional on industry and productivity variables, is different for bankrupt and nonbankrupt firms. The logistic regressions include industry-, plant-, and firm-level explanatory variables, and interact several of these variables with indicators of bankruptcy status. We run regressions for the full sample and also for quartiles 1 and 4 of our long-run, ten-year change in industry shipments.[19]

The last column presents a test of whether coefficients are significantly different between quartiles 1 and 4. We test for differences by running a regression for all quartile 1 and 4 firms with a quartile 4 dummy variable interacted with the independent variable, and present the *p*-values for these interaction variables.

Column 1 of Table VI shows that, for the sample as a whole, there are only limited differences in the asset sale decisions of Chapter 11 and industry firms. For both firms, bankrupt and nonbankrupt, the industry variables

[18] We do not present data on the productivity of plants sold off after Chapter 11, because there are few partial firm asset sales in quartiles 3 and 4. Census rules prevent these numbers from being disclosed.

[19] As a robustness check we also estimate both the current asset sale equation and the subsequent closure equation for quartiles 1 and 4 using a random effects panel probit model (see Butler and Moffitt (1982)). We find that there are no changes in the interpretation or significance levels of the bankruptcy variables when estimating using the random probit. Only one industry variable, lagsize, changed in significance from the 8 percent level to the 14 percent level. Thus we do not report the results of this estimation.

Table VI

Asset Sale Decisions

Regressions test the effects of plant-level productivity and industry-level demand and supply variables on asset sale decisions of bankrupt firms and other nonbankrupt industry firms. We estimate the regressions using a logistic-limited dependent variable model. The dependent variable equals 1 if a plant is sold in that year. The change in industry shipments and capacity utilization are yearly at the four-digit SIC code level. Weighted industry R&D is from COMPUSTAT firm-level data and represents R&D and advertising expense divided by firm sales aggregated up to the three-digit SIC code. We calculate total factor productivity (TFP) using a translog production function. Operating cash flow is the value of shipments less labor, materials, and energy costs divided by value of shipments. Plant scale is the plant's asset size divided by the average assets for plants in each industry. Data are yearly from 1977 to 1990. (p-values are in parentheses.)

	Dependent Variable: Plant Asset Sale			Test for Significant Difference: Quartile 4 − Quartile 1 (p-value)
	Logit A: Full Sample	Logit B: Quartile 1	Logit C: Quartile 4	
Industry-level variables				
Change in industry shipments	1.141	0.983	0.538	
	(0.000)[a]	(0.006)[a]	(0.161)	(0.000)[a]
Weighted industry R&D	1.935	9.675	0.256	
	(0.000)[a]	(0.000)[a]	(0.773)	(0.000)[a]
Capacity utilization	−0.015	−0.010	−0.005	
	(0.000)[a]	(0.000)[a]	(0.129)	(0.135)
Standard deviation of industry shipments	−4.744	1.381	−3.489	
	(0.000)[a]	(0.170)	(0.001)[a]	(0.002)[a]
Plant- and firm-level variables				
Number of plants owned by firm	−0.005	−0.009	0.000	
	(0.000)[a]	(0.000)[a]	(0.839)	(0.000)[a]
Log of firm shipments	0.382	0.404	0.378	
	(0.000)[a]	(0.000)[a]	(0.000)[a]	(0.399)
Total factor productivity (TFP)	−0.168	−0.130	−0.132	
(Lagged one year)	(0.000)[a]	(0.005)[a]	(0.000)[a]	(0.207)
Plant-level operating cash flow	0.173	0.017	0.339	
(Lagged one year)	(0.007)[a]	(0.901)	(0.010)[a]	(0.115)
Relative plant scale	−0.154	−0.167	−0.171	
	(0.000)[a]	(0.000)[a]	(0.000)[a]	(0.905)
Plant age	0.020	0.037	0.019	
	(0.000)[a]	(0.000)[a]	(0.000)[a]	(0.006)
Bankruptcy variables				
Before Chapter 11 dummy variable	0.602	0.275	0.266	
(=1 for years before firm is in Ch. 11)	(0.000)[a]	(0.073)[c]	(0.209)	(0.751)
In Chapter 11 dummy variable	0.409	−0.068	0.654	
(=1 while firm is in Ch. 11)	(0.198)	(0.963)	(0.321)	(0.332)
After Chapter 11 dummy variable	−0.119	−0.950	−0.465	
(=1 after firm emerges from Ch. 11)	(0.583)	(0.184)	(0.474)	(0.693)
In Chapter 11*TFP	0.251	0.483	0.680	
	(0.135)	(0.214)	(0.082)[c]	(0.900)
In Chapter 11*cash flow	−0.737	−1.368	−3.209	
	(0.163)	(0.115)	(0.042)[b]	(0.146)

Table VI—*Continued*

	Dependent Variable: Plant Asset Sale			Test for Significant Difference: Quartile 4 − Quartile 1 (*p*-value)
	Logit A: Full Sample	Logit B: Quartile 1	Logit C: Quartile 4	
Bankruptcy variables				
In Chapter 11*industry R&D	0.757	22.800	−14.718	
	(0.845)	(0.080)[c]	(0.088)[c]	(0.010)[a]
In Chapter 11*change in shipments	0.467	−2.786	5.259	
	(0.801)	(0.358)	(0.012)[b]	(0.014)[b]
In Chapter 11*capacity utilization	−0.004	−0.010	0.009	
	(0.315)	(0.581)	(0.369)	(0.365)
Total plant years	371,373	60,477	85,148	
χ^2 statistic	4370.57	653.20	1255.57	
Significance level (*p*-value)	<1%	<1%	<1%	

[a,b,c] Significantly different from zero at the 1 percent, 5 percent, and 10 percent levels, respectively, using a two-tailed *t*-test.

(change in industry shipments, capacity utilization, industry R&D, and the standard deviation of industry shipments) are highly significant at less than the 1 percent level. These results show that growth in industry output positively affects both the frequency of asset sales and the productivity gain from asset sales, both outside and inside bankruptcy. Consistent with the importance of demand on asset sales, plant-level cash flows are highly significant and positively related to the probability of selling a plant.

The results in Table VI also show that asset sales are more frequent in industries with high R&D. Therefore, there is no evidence that the presumed greater asymmetry of information in these industries impedes the efficient transfer of assets.

When we examine the effect of Chapter 11 status, we find some differences between the bankrupt firms and nonbankrupt firms. The coefficient on the dummy variable for the years before Chapter 11 is positive and highly significant. Chapter 11 firms sell assets at a higher rate before they enter Chapter 11. However, the dummy variables for the during- and after-Chapter 11 periods are insignificant. This finding shows that although firms that go bankrupt sell assets at a higher rate before bankruptcy, there is no evidence that bankruptcy either increases or decreases asset sales.

We also investigate whether asset sales of bankrupt firms are more sensitive to industry and productivity variables. We interact the before- and the in-Chapter 11 dummy variables with total factor productivity, industry R&D, change in shipments, and capacity utilization. There are no significant interactions between the before-Chapter 11 dummy and our independent variables. For the full sample of bankrupt firms, there are also no significant interactions between the in-Chapter 11 dummy and the independent variables.

In columns 2 and 3 of Table VI, we present the results of asset sale logistic regressions by shipment growth quartiles. We do find differences in the in-bankruptcy interaction variables when we split our sample by quartiles. In quartile 1, plants of Chapter 11 firms in industries with high R&D are more likely to be sold, but in quartile 4 they are less likely to be sold. These results suggest that there exist differences in the types of firm that goes bankrupt in quartiles 1 and 4. The differences in the coefficient of the R&D interaction variable across quartiles are consistent with either an indirect cost of bankruptcy in quartile 4, or that R&D programs of bankrupt firms were not successful. For all firms in quartile 4, high R&D in the industry is associated with increased asset sales, for bankrupt firms the rate is lower.

Other significant interactions show up in quartile 4: Plants that are both more productive and in industries experiencing greater growth are more likely to be sold. This is consistent with our findings in Table V.[20] We also find a significant negative interaction between firm-level cash flow and the in-Chapter 11 dummy variable. These findings are also consistent with bankrupt firms in the high-growth quartile selling off their more-efficient plants to raise cash.

The last column of this table reports *p*-values for tests of the equality of coefficients between quartiles 1 and 4. The firm- and plant-specific productivity variables have a similar effect in high- and low-growth quartiles for both bankrupt and nonbankrupt firms. The only two firm-specific variables that have a differential effect by quartiles are the number of plants a firm operates and plant age. It is mainly the industry variables, including the industry variables interacted with the in-Chapter 11 dummy variable, that have significantly different effects in the high- and low-growth quartiles.

In Table VII, we report the economic significance of our results by calculating the estimated probabilities of asset sales by bankrupt and nonbankrupt firms. The probabilities are computed at the means of all variables for the bankrupt sample and at the means of the nonbankrupt sample variables.[21] TFP is then varied from the 10th to the 90th percentile to examine how productivity differences affect the probability of asset sales for both of these samples. Panel A illustrates that transition into bankruptcy does not have an important economic effect on the probability of asset sales. The probability of asset sales is slightly higher in prebankrupt year $t-1$ versus

[20] Recall that industries are classified into quartiles by growth over the whole sample period, but the change in industry shipments is calculated annually.

[21] When we calculate the probability of an asset sale for the same subsample of data, the only difference between bankrupt and nonbankrupt firms' probability in year $t-1$ will be the effect of the bankrupt firm dummy. In year $t+1$ for the bankrupt firm, we add the in-Chapter 11 variable and its interactions. This procedure thus controls for differential data, such as productivity differences.

Table VII

Plant Asset Sales: Estimated Probabilities

Estimated probabilities of an asset sale by bankrupt and nonbankrupt firms at the 10th, 25th, 50th, and 90th percentiles of total factor productivity (TFP). We compute estimated probabilities using the coefficients from the logit regressions from Table VI predicting asset sales. Panel A uses the coefficients from logit regression A from Table VI and the data for the full sample. Panel B is for quartiles 1 and 4 and uses the coefficients from logit regresssions B and C from Table VI. We compute these probabilities holding all other variables besides TFP and TFP interaction terms at the sample means of the nonbankrupt and bankrupt firms. For the year $t - 1$, nonbankrupt firms and the bankrupt firms probabilities are computed with the before-bankruptcy indicator variable equal to 0 and 1 respectively. For the year $t + 1$ for the bankrupt firm, we include the during-bankruptcy indicator variable and the interactions with the industry and productivity variables. For quartiles, the percentiles refer to that specific subsample. Thus the 50th percentile for quartile 1 is the 12.5th percentile of the overall sample.

		Probability of Plant Asset Sale at TFP:			
		10th Percentile	25th Percentile	50th Percentile	90th Percentile
	Panel A: Full Sample				
Bankrupt firm:	Year $t - 1$	7.65%	7.06%	6.57%	5.59%
(data from bankrupt sample)	Year $t + 1$	4.91%	5.16%	5.39%	5.88%
Bankrupt firm:	Year $t - 1$	3.15%	2.91%	2.70%	2.25%
(data from nonbankrupt sample)	Year $t + 1$	2.16%	2.25%	2.33%	2.54%
Nonbankrupt firm:	Year $t - 1$	1.75%	1.62%	1.50%	1.25%
(data from nonbankrupt sample)	Year $t + 1$	1.85%	1.70%	1.57%	1.31%
Nonbankrupt firm:	Year $t - 1$	4.34%	3.99%	3.71%	3.14%
(data from bankrupt sample)	Year $t + 1$	4.46%	4.02%	3.68%	3.06%
	Panel B: Quartiles 1 and 4				
Quartile 1: Bankrupt firm	Year $t - 1$	4.90%	4.62%	4.35%	3.74%
	Year $t + 1$	2.55%	3.23%	3.93%	5.70%
Quartile 1: Nonbankrupt firm	Year $t - 1$	4.48%	4.14%	3.81%	3.14%
	Year $t + 1$	3.64%	3.28%	2.90%	2.22%
Quartile 4: Bankrupt firm	Year $t - 1$	8.09%	7.51%	6.92%	5.74%
	Year $t + 1$	3.74%	4.22%	4.87%	6.64%
Quartile 4: Nonbankrupt firm	Year $t - 1$	4.78%	4.51%	4.25%	3.66%
	Year $t + 1$	4.86%	4.45%	4.15%	3.61%

bankrupt year $t + 1$. This higher probability results from the large, statistically significant pre-Chapter 11 indicator variable.

Bankrupt firms have a higher probability of selling assets than do nonbankrupt firms. However, this increased probability is driven mainly by differences in the mean values of our explanatory productivity, firm-level cash flows, and industry variables for bankrupt and nonbankrupt firms. Evaluating the probability of asset sales by bankrupt firms at the mean of the data of the nonbankrupt sample, we find that there is a 3 to 4 percentage points lower probability of asset sale. Evaluating the nonbankrupt firm's probability of sale at the mean of the bankrupt sample, there is a 2 to 2 1/2 percentage points increase in the probability of an asset sale. Thus, approximately two-thirds of the increased probability of sales by bankrupt firms is accounted for by differences in the sample means, and one-third by the before- and in-Chapter 11 dummy variables. The in-Chapter 11 interaction variables do not contribute significantly to the results.

The one case where an economically important difference for asset sales in bankruptcy occurs is in quartile 4. When we examine the probability of an asset sale by quartiles in Panel B, we find that for quartile 4 firms, the probability of an asset sale in the year subsequent to bankruptcy increases with TFP. This is consistent with our earlier finding that quartile 4 firms sell their better assets in bankruptcy.

The results support the prediction of a higher value of reallocation for all firms, both bankrupt and nonbankrupt, in high-growth industries. More asset sales occur for bankrupt firms but the industry and plant productivity variables are highly significant in explaining these sales. We find no evidence of an indirect bankruptcy cost in the form of a failure to sell assets. In fact, asset sales occur at a higher rate in the high-growth quartile. Thus, there is no evidence that reorganization costs are higher inside than outside of bankruptcy. However, we do find evidence that the bankrupt firms in the high-growth quartiles did not operate the sold plants as efficiently as the new owners. Thus, our evidence does not support the prediction of Shleifer and Vishny (1992) that assets of bankrupt firms are sold to less-efficient buyers.

C.2. Plant Closures and Liquidations

To analyze plant closures by and liquidations of bankrupt firms, we first present average productivity numbers for closed plants and frequencies of closures for both bankrupt and industry firms. Next, we examine whether the industry-, firm-, and plant-level factors are associated with the decision to close a plant. We examine if there is any delay in closing plants by bankrupt firms—a potential bankruptcy cost if conflicts of interest are higher in bankruptcy.

We investigate whether industry characteristics can explain the probability of plant closure using logistic regressions. Our regressions include industry-, plant- and firm-level variables, and interactions of several of these variables with indicators of bankruptcy status. We present logistic results for the full sample and for quartiles 1 and 4. As in Table VI, the last column presents a test of whether coefficients are significantly different between quartiles 1 and 4. We test for differences by running a regression for all firms in quartiles 1 and 4 with a quartile 4 dummy variable interacted with the independent variables, and present the p-value for this interaction variable.

In the results for all quartiles, presented in column 1 of Table VIII, we do not find evidence of costs of bankruptcy in the form of delay or failure to close plants. The logistic regressions in column 1 show that for all firms, the industry-level variables—change in industry shipments and weighted industry R&D—are highly significant at less than 1 percent. We find that the probability of closure is negatively related to the change in industry shipments. Plant-level cash flows and productivity are also significantly and negatively related to closures. Both results are consistent with economic efficiency.

Though there are some differences between firms that experience and firms that do not experience bankruptcy, we find limited evidence that Chapter 11 status affects closing decisions. After controlling for other variables, firms that experience bankruptcy have increased rates of closures before and after, but not during, Chapter 11. The coefficients on the dummy variables for before- and after-Chapter 11 are positive and highly significant. However, the variable indicating that the firm is in Chapter 11 is not significant.

We interact the before-, in-, and after-Chapter 11 dummy variables with total factor productivity, cash flow, industry R&D, change in shipments, and capacity utilization. There are no significant interactions between the before- and after-Chapter 11 bankrupt-firm dummy variables and the industry variables. We do not report these interactions.

There are significant interactions between the in-Chapter 11 dummy variable and our independent variables. While they are in Chapter 11, firms' closing decisions are more sensitive to the change in industry shipments and the level of industry R&D. The interaction with the change in industry shipments is negative and significant, showing that a decline in shipments causes the probability of closure to increase. The increased sensitivity to industry shipments suggests that the bankrupt firms' plants are marginal in the industry. The negative association between the interaction of bankruptcy and industry R&D shows that firms in industries with low R&D close more plants. This finding is consistent with the perception of fewer growth options in these industries.

In columns 2 and 3 of Table VIII, we investigate closing decisions by quartiles. Except for the case of quartile 4 firms, we find no evidence that the productivity of plants closed by bankrupt firms differs from that of plants closed by other industry firms. In quartile 4, there is a negative interaction, significant at the 10 percent level, between total factor productivity and the in-Chapter 11 variable: As productivity increases, these plants are less likely to be closed. There are no significant interactions between firm cash flow and the in-Chapter 11 variable. This indicates that cash flows do not affect closure decisions of bankrupt firms differently.

The last column of this table tests whether coefficients are significantly different between quartiles 1 and 4. We report p-values for this test in the last column. For bankrupt firms, we find significant differences between quartiles 1 and 4 for the effect of the industry R&D. In high-growth quartiles, increased industry R&D is associated with a lower probability of closing a plant.

Table VIII

Plant Closing Decisions

Regressions test the effects of plant-level productivity and industry-level demand and supply variables on plant closing of bankrupt firms and other nonbankrupt industry firms. We estimate the regressions using a logistic-limited dependent variable model. The dependent variable equals 1 if a plant is closed in that year. The change in industry shipments and capacity utilization are yearly at the 4-digit SIC code level. Weighted industry research and development (R&D) is from COMPUSTAT firm-level data and represents R&D and advertising expense divided firm sales aggregated up to the 3-digit SIC code. Total Factor Productivity (TFP) is calculated using a translog production function. Operating cash flow is the value of shipments less labor, materials and energy costs divided by value of shipments. Relative plant scale is the plant's asset size divided by the average assets for plants in each industry. Capacity utilization is at the 4-digit SIC code and is from the Bureau of the Census. Data are yearly from 1977 to 1990. (p-values are in parentheses.)

	Dependent Variable: Plant Closing			Test for Significant Difference: Quartile 4 − Quartile 1
	Logit A: Full Sample	Logit B: Quartile 1	Logit C: Quartile 4	(p value)
Industry-level variables				
Change in industry shipments	−1.581	−1.304	−2.135	
	(0.000)[a]	(0.002)[a]	(0.000)[a]	(0.018)[b]
Weighted industry R&D	−7.360	−3.286	−2.904	
	(0.000)[a]	(0.014)[b]	(0.038)[b]	(0.015)[b]
Capacity utilization	−0.006	−0.007	0.001	
	(0.000)[a]	(0.006)[a]	(0.214)	(0.396)
Standard deviation of industry shipments	3.783	3.256	12.00	
	(0.000)[a]	(0.000)[a]	(0.000)[a]	(0.000)[a]
Plant- and firm-level variables				
Number of plants owned by firm	0.006	0.005	0.007	
	(0.000)[a]	(0.000)[a]	(0.000)[a]	(0.556)
Log of firm shipments	−0.048	−0.066	−0.027	
	(0.000)[a]	(0.000)[a]	(0.160)	(0.429)
Total factor productivity (TFP)	−0.173	−0.162	−0.279	
(Lagged one year)	(0.000)[a]	(0.000)[a]	(0.000)[a]	(0.000)[a]
Plant-level operating cash flow	−0.147	−0.158	−0.097	
(Lagged one year)	(0.002)[a]	(0.014)[b]	(0.296)	(0.226)
Relative plant scale	−0.276	−0.286	−0.463	
	(0.000)[a]	(0.000)[a]	(0.000)[a]	(0.000)[a]
Plant age	−0.022	−0.026	−0.030	
	(0.000)[a]	(0.000)[a]	(0.000)[a]	(0.261)
Bankruptcy variables				
Before Chapter 11 dummy variable	0.681	0.692	0.944	
(=1 for years before firm is in Ch. 11)	(0.000)[a]	(0.000)[a]	(0.000)[a]	(0.663)
In Chapter 11 dummy variable	−0.123	−2.019	−0.473	
(=1 while firm is in Ch. 11)	(0.916)	(0.384)	(0.889)	(0.899)
After Chapter 11 dummy variable	0.382	−0.136	0.529	
(=1 after firm emerges from Ch. 11)	(0.007)[a]	(0.787)	(0.002)[a]	(0.056)[b]
In Chapter 11*TFP	−0.543	−0.394	−0.808	
	(0.146)	(0.351)	(0.047)[b]	(0.417)

Table VIII—*Continued*

	Dependent Variable: Plant Closing			Test for Significant Difference: Quartile 4 − Quartile 1 (p value)
	Logit A: Full Sample	Logit B: Quartile 1	Logit C: Quartile 4	
Bankruptcy variables				
In Chapter 11*cash flow	−0.804	−0.293	−0.418	
	(0.189)	(0.751)	(0.351)	(0.966)
In Chapter 11*industry R&D	−23.915	−70.289	−41.85	
	(0.015)[b]	(0.008)[a]	(0.069)[c]	(0.008)[a]
In Chapter 11*change in shipments	−3.072	−9.213	−10.51	
	(0.035)[b]	(0.054)[c]	(0.025)[b]	(0.393)
In Chapter 11*capacity utilization	0.007	0.032	0.031	
	(0.216)	(0.262)	(0.452)	(0.337)
Total plant years	371,373	60,477	85,148	
χ^2 statistic	1299.79	145.33	463.81	
Significance level (p-value)	<1%	<1%	<1%	

[a,b,c] Significantly different from zero at the 1 percent, 5 percent, and 10 percent levels, respectively, using a two-tailed t-test.

In Table IX we investigate the economic significance of our results. As with asset sales, we compute the estimated probabilities of plant closures at the means of all variables for the bankrupt sample, and at the means for the nonbankrupt sample. We examine how the change in industry shipments affects the probability of closure for the bankrupt and nonbankrupt samples, and find that the probability of closure is higher for bankrupt firms. At the 50th percentile, the probability of closing in the year prior to bankruptcy is 3.23 percent for bankrupt firms and 1.65 percent for nonbankrupt firms. We evaluate both at the mean of the variables of the bankrupt firm sample. The increased probability relates to the higher sensitivity of bankrupt firms' closure decisions to the industry variables interacted with the during-bankruptcy dummy variable.

We also find a striking difference between quartile 1 and quartile 4. At the 50th percentile of these quartiles, the probability of closing is 9.5 percent for quartile 1 and only 0.25 percent for quartile 4. These results show that average closure rates are significantly higher and economically more important for bankrupt firms in the declining quartile. In declining industries, Chapter 11 appears to be a mechanism for fostering the exit of capacity.

We also explore how asset sales and closures may relate to each other. First, we estimate a multinomial logit for quartiles 1 and 4. The differences between the multinomial estimates and the ones we present in the paper are immaterial: They are in the third decimal place. This is consistent with our priors that the shocks that affect closing and asset sales are different.

Table IX

Plant Closures: Estimated Probabilities

Estimated probabilities of a plant closure by bankrupt and nonbankrupt firms at the 10th, 25th, 50th, and 90th percentiles of change in industry shipments. We compute estimated probabilities using the coefficients from the logit regressions from Table VIII using logit regression A for the full sample and logit regressions C and D for the quartiles. We compute these probabilities holding all other variables besides change in industry shipments and its interaction terms at the sample means of the nonbankrupt and bankrupt firms. For the year $t - 1$, nonbankrupt firms and the bankrupt firms' probabilities are computed with the before-bankruptcy indicator variable equal to 0 and 1 respectively. For the year $t + 1$ for the bankrupt firm, we include the during-bankruptcy indicator variable and the interactions with the industry and productivity variables. For quartiles, the percentiles refer to that specific subsample. Thus the 50th percentile for quartile 1 is the 12.5th percentile of the overall sample.

		Probability of Plant Closure Varying Change in Industry Shipments			
		10th Percentile	25th Percentile	50th Percentile	90th Percentile
Bankrupt firm: All quartiles	Year $t - 1$	3.65%	3.38%	3.23%	2.86%
(data from bankrupt sample)	Year $t + 1$	1.92%	1.62%	1.43%	1.22%
Quartile 1	Year $t + 1$	12.69%	9.81%	9.50%	6.29%
Quartile 4	Year $t + 1$	0.46%	0.30%	0.25%	0.15%
Bankrupt firm: All quartiles	Year $t - 1$	3.23%	3.04%	2.89%	2.45%
(data from nonbankrupt sample)	Year $t + 1$	1.66%	1.33%	1.19%	1.04%
Quartile 1	Year $t + 1$	11.76%	8.55%	8.60%	6.09%
Quartile 4	Year $t + 1$	0.39%	0.29%	0.19%	0.05%
Nonbankrupt firm:	Year $t - 1$	1.65%	1.55%	1.48%	1.25%
(data from nonbankrupt sample)	Year $t + 1$	1.57%	1.45%	1.40%	1.23%
Nonbankrupt firm:	Year $t - 1$	1.87%	1.73%	1.65%	1.45%
(data from bankrupt sample)	Year $t + 1$	1.83%	1.73%	1.66%	1.47%

Second, we estimate the interaction between asset sales and closures over time. We include two variables to capture the extent of past closures and asset sales. These variables measure the percentages closed and sold, respectively, in the previous five years. We interact these variables with the bankruptcy indicator variable to test if bankrupt firms are affected differently by past sales and closures.

Including these variables does not change the significance or sign on the other variables in our previous regressions. For all firms, past asset sales and closures reduce the probability of a current asset sale, but past closures increase the likelihood of a current closure. There is a very limited difference between bankrupt and nonbankrupt firms. The bankruptcy interaction variables are not significant in quartiles 1 and 4 for asset sales. For closures, the bankruptcy interaction variable with past asset sales is significant at 4.9 percent only in quartile 4, and insignificant in quartile 1.

Table X compares the subsample of bankrupt firms that convert to Chapter 7 from Chapter 11 with Chapter 11 firms that do not convert to Chap-

Table X

Transfers to Chapter 7 Liquidation

This table examines the productivity of firms' plants that transferred into Chapter 7 liquidation from Chapter 11 compared to the remaining Chapter 11 firms that did not enter Chapter 7. Numbers are relative total factor productivity (TFP) for plants less the industry-average TFP for each year. TFPs are standardized by dividing by the standard deviation of industry TFP at the four-digit SIC code level. Quartiles are determined by using the change in the real value of shipments at the three-digit SIC code from the NBER. Productivity (TFP) numbers are presented combining the lowest two and highest two quartiles to obtain sufficient numbers of plants to allow disclosure under government criteria. — means that the cell cannot be disclosed because there are too few plants in this relative year. The Chapter 11 firms in columns 1 and 3 are the subset of Chapter 11 firms that do not transfer to Chapter 7. Columns 2 and 4 represent the years in Chapter 7 after transferring from Chapter 11, for the lowest two and highest two quartiles, respectively. We assign firms to Chapter 7 based on the year-end status; thus some firms transfer to Chapter 7 in the same year they declare Chapter 11. (*t*-statistics for significant differences from zero are in parentheses.)

	Growth in Shipments							
	Lowest Two Quartiles				Highest Two Quartiles			
	Chapter 11 Firms	*n*	Ch. 11 Firms transferred to Chapter 7	*n*	Chapter 11 Firms	*n*	Ch. 11 Firms transferred to Chapter 7	*n*
Panel A: Years before Chapter 11								
Year −2	−0.031	636	−0.219	146	0.046	330	−0.198	76
	(−0.82)		(−2.81)[a]		(0.88)		(−1.75)[c]	
Year −1	−0.036	607	−0.098	109	−0.019	295	−0.189	64
	(−1.04)		(−1.20)		(−0.33)		(−1.38)	
Panel B: After Declaration of Chapter 11								
Year 0	−0.100	514	−0.070	24	−0.046	299	−0.347	36
t-stat for average	(−2.35)[c]		(−0.40)		(−0.77)		(−2.58)[a]	
t-stat for −1 to 0	(−1.15)		(0.15)		(−0.32)		(−0.82)	
Year +1	0.046	412	−0.105	13	0.016	209	—	
t-stat for average	(0.89)		(−0.41)		(0.19)			
t-stat for −1 to +1	(1.32)		(−0.03)		(0.37)			
Year +2	0.026	208	—		−0.073	129	—	
t-stat for average	(0.46)				(−0.78)			
t-stat for −1 to +2	(0.93)				(−0.58)			
Year +3	0.048	133	—		−0.336	59	—	
t-stat for average	(0.62)				(−2.49)[a]			
t-stat for −1 to +3	(0.99)				(−2.96)[a]			
Year +4	0.072	85	—		−0.177	49	—	
t-stat for average	(0.76)				(−1.32)			
t-stat for −1 to +4	(1.07)				(−1.28)			

Table X—*Continued*

	Growth in Shipments							
	Lowest Two Quartiles				Highest Two Quartiles			
	Chapter 11 Firms	n	Ch. 11 Firms transferred to Chapter 7	n	Chapter 11 Firms	n	Ch. 11 Firms transferred to Chapter 7	n
Panel C: After Leaving Chapter 11, Emerged Firms versus Firms Transferred to Chapter 7								
Year +1	−0.087	260	−0.274	80	−0.207	112	−0.131	38
t-stat for average	(−1.41)		(−2.89)[a]		(−2.32)[b]		(−0.97)	
t-stat for −1 to +1	(−0.71)		(−1.40)		(−1.78)[c]		(0.31)	
Year +2	−0.104	136	−0.197	69	−0.073	77	−0.409	17
t-stat for average	(−1.21)		(−1.65)[c]		(−0.86)		(−1.99)[c]	
t-stat for −1 to +2	(−0.73)		(−0.68)		(−0.53)		(−0.64)	
Year +3	−0.126	75	−0.389	69	−0.226	49	−0.583	15
t-stat for average	(−0.92)		(−3.50)[a]		(−1.51)		(−2.67)[a]	
t-stat for −1 to +3	(−0.63)		(−2.11)[b]		(−1.29)		(−1.53)	

[a,b,c] Significantly different from zero at the 1 percent, 5 percent, and 10 percent levels, respectively, using a two-tailed t-test.

ter 7. Columns 1 and 3 represent the firms that never switch to Chapter 7, for the top and bottom two quartiles, respectively. Columns 2 and 4 represent the firms that do convert to Chapter 7 from Chapter 11.[22] The firms in the Chapter 7 subsample do not emerge. Eventually they either sell or close all their plants. We assign firms to Chapter 7 based on the year-end status, thus some firms transfer to Chapter 7 within the same year of declaring Chapter 11. Year 0 is not included in this table because in this year firms spend part of the year in Chapter 11 and part of the year in Chapter 7. Panel A covers the years before declaring Chapter 11 and separates out those firms that eventually switch to Chapter 7 from Chapter 11. Panel B covers the years while the firms are in Chapter 11, again separating out firms that switch to Chapter 7. Panel C covers the years after firms leave Chapter 11, either emerging from bankruptcy (columns 1 and 3) or transferring to Chapter 7 (columns 2 and 4).

Panel B shows that while firms are in Chapter 11, the productivity of plants of those firms that eventually convert to Chapter 7 is much lower than the productivity of plants of firms that do not. Panel C shows that the productivity of those that convert to Chapter 7 is also much lower than the productivity of those that emerge from Chapter 11. There are also more Chapter 7 liquidations in the lowest two shipment growth quartiles. The

[22] All the prior tables include these Chapter 7 firms while they are in Chapter 11, thus avoiding survivorship bias.

lower productivity of Chapter 7 plants shows that, consistent with economic efficiency, plants selected for liquidation are indeed significantly less productive than their industry counterparts. This suggests that the bankruptcy process does discriminate between inefficient and efficient firms. Overall, we find a higher incidence of Chapter 7 liquidations, and a higher probability of closure and Chapter 11 bankruptcies in the declining-industry quartiles. This emphasizes the importance of industry effects in determining which firms become bankrupt.

IV. Conclusions

We investigate how industry shipments and other industry characteristics affect firms' performance in bankruptcy and the decision to redeploy assets. We do not find much evidence of indirect bankruptcy costs. Chapter 11 bankruptcy status is relatively less important than industry and plant-level productivity factors in influencing bankrupt firms' decisions.

Our evidence shows that the decision to sell and close plants depends on industry demand and capacity utilization, which determine the opportunity costs of assets. Firms can enter bankruptcy and sell and/or close plants because the number of plants that can operate profitably in the industry can change. Under plausible assumptions, the value of reorganizing is highest when industry growth is highest. However, in these industries, the likelihood of bankruptcy could be lowest because the overall level of industry cash flows is high.

Our results show that the frequency of bankruptcy is indeed lowest in high-growth industries. We find that the proportion of plants going bankrupt is more than three times higher in declining industries than in high-growth industries. However, the productivity of plants in declining industries does not significantly decrease relative to their industry counterparts. Thus, we find no evidence of any bankruptcy costs in these industries. For firms in declining industries, Chapter 11 protection does not seem to be used by low-productivity firms to avoid closing or selling inefficient plants.

The results are different for plants belonging to firms that declare Chapter 11 in high-growth industries. Although these represent a lower proportion of plants in their industries, their average productivity is significantly lower than that of their industry counterparts. After correcting for survivorship bias because of plant sales and closures, the productivity of plants of bankrupt firms in high-growth industries, although low, decreases over time only for those firms that remain in Chapter 11 for four or more years. These findings show that asset composition and survivorship bias are serious problems that must be accounted for before comparisons can be made between ex post and ex ante performance. Changes in bankrupt firms' performance can be explained for the most part by asset sales and closures, not by changes in the efficiency of retained assets. As a result, the evaluation of the bankruptcy process must track all of these outcomes and must not focus solely on the productivity of survivor firms.

When we analyze the redeployment of plants of Chapter 11 firms, several conclusions emerge. First, in high-growth industries, the productivity of purchased plants increases under new ownership, but in declining industries it does not. This finding is consistent with the hypothesis that the value of asset transfers is higher in high-growth industries. Second, the purchasers of bankrupt firms' plants are more efficient than the average firm in their industry. Overall, there is no evidence that indirect reorganization costs in Chapter 11 are higher than outside of bankruptcy.

The logistic regressions show that for both bankrupt and nonbankrupt firms, the probabilities of closures and asset sales are significantly related to the change in industry output and productivity. Bankruptcy status has a minimal effect on the probability of selling a plant. The probability of closures is higher for bankrupt firms in declining industries. This higher probability arises from the increased sensitivity of closures to changes in industry shipments during Chapter 11.

Our logistic regressions also show that industry-level research and development is significant in explaining the asset sale and closure decisions. In industries with high R&D and high growth in shipments, firms in bankruptcy are less likely to close and sell plants. These results suggest that asset specificity and technological change might affect the value of assets and whether these assets are sold.

The results suggest that in industries in which the opportunity costs of assets are high and positively correlated with cash flows, mechanisms other than bankruptcy might have a more important role in restructuring inefficient firms. The small size of realized indirect costs for firms that elect to enter bankruptcy does not necessarily imply that other distressed firms would not incur indirect bankruptcy costs if they enter Chapter 11. The differences across quartiles in the frequency of bankruptcy, in the efficiency of firms prior to bankruptcy, and in the population of bankrupt firms suggest that some firms in high-growth industries may not take advantage of Chapter 11 reorganization because of indirect costs. In future research we plan to examine these factors, and whether financial distress and the threat of bankruptcy affect the asset redeployment process under different demand conditions.

REFERENCES

Altman, Edward I., 1984, A further investigation of the bankruptcy cost question, *Journal of Finance* 39, 1067–1089.

Altman, Edward I., 1993, *Corporate Financial Distress and Bankruptcy* (John Wiley, New York).

Andrade, Gregor, and Steven N. Kaplan, 1998, How Costly Is Financial (not Economic) Distress? Evidence from Highly Leveraged Transactions that Became Distressed, *Journal of Finance* 53, 1443–1493.

Bartelsman. Eric J., and Wayne Gray, 1994, *The NBER Manufacturing Productivity Database*.

Bergman, Yaacov Z., and Jeffrey L. Callen, 1991, Opportunistic underinvestment in debt renegotiation and capital structure, *Journal of Financial Economics* 29, 137–171.

Berkovitch, Elazar, and Ronen Israel, 1997. The bankruptcy decision and debt contract renegotiations, Working paper, University of Michigan.

Betker, Brian L., 1995, Management's incentives, equity's bargaining power and deviations from absolute priority in Chapter 11 bankruptcies, *Journal of Business* 68, 161–184.

Brock, William A., and David S. Evans, 1986, *The Economics of Small Business: Their Role and Regulation in the U.S. Economy* (Holmes and Meier, New York).

Brown, David T., Chris James, and Robert Mooridian, 1993, The information content of distressed restructurings involving public and private debt claims, *Journal of Financial Economics* 33, 93–118.

Bulow, Jeremy I., and John B. Shoven, 1978, The bankruptcy decision, *Bell Journal of Economics* 9, 437–456.

Butler, J. S., and Robert Moffitt, 1982, A computationally efficient quadrature procedure for the one-factor multinomial probit model, *Econometrica* 50, 761–764.

Caves, Richard E., and David R. Barton, 1991, *Efficiency in U.S. Manufacturing* (MIT Press, Cambridge, Mass.).

Chevalier, Judith, 1995, Debt and product market competition: Local market entry, exit, and expansion decisions of supermarket chain, *American Economic Review* 85, 415–435.

Coase, Ronald, 1937, The nature of the firm, *Economica* 4, 386–405.

Diamond, Douglas W., 1993, Seniority and maturity of debt contracts, *Journal of Financial Economics* 33, 341–368.

Gertner, Robert, and David Scharfstein, 1991, A theory of workouts and the effects of reorganization law, *Journal of Finance* 46, 1189–1222.

Giammarino, Ronald, 1989, The resolution of financial distress, *Review of Financial Studies* 2, 25–47.

Gilson, Stuart, Kose John, and Larry Lang, 1990, Troubled debt restructurings: An empirical study of private reorganization of firms in default, *Journal of Financial Economics* 26, 315–353.

Harris, Milton, and Artur Raviv, 1990, Capital structure and the informational role of debt, *Journal of Finance* 45, 321–349.

Hart, Oliver, and John Moore, 1995, Debt and seniority: An analysis of hard claims in constraining management, *American Economic Review* 85, 567–587.

Haugen, Robert A., and Lemma W. Senbet, 1978, The insignificance of bankruptcy costs to the theory of optimal capital structure, *Journal of Finance* 33, 383–393.

Hotchkiss, Edith S., 1995, Post-bankruptcy performance and management turnover, *Journal of Finance* 50, 3–21.

Jensen, Michael C., 1993, The modern industrial revolution, exit, and the failure of internal control systems, *Journal of Finance* 48, 831–880.

Khanna, Naveen, and Annette Poulsen, 1995, Managers of financially distressed firms: Villains or scapegoats? *Journal of Finance* 50, 919–940.

Kim, Moshe, and Vojislav Maksimovic, 1990, Debt and input misallocation, *Journal of Finance* 45, 795–816.

Kovenock, Daniel, and Gordon Phillips,1997, Capital structure and product market behavior: An examination of plant exit and investment behavior, *Review of Financial Studies* 10, 767–804.

Lucas, Robert, 1978, On the size distribution of business firms, *Bell Journal of Economics* 9, 508–523.

Maksimovic, Vojislav, and Gordon Phillips, 1996, The efficiency of bankrupt firms and industry conditions: Theory and evidence, Working paper, #96-12, Center for Economic Studies, Department of Commerce, Washington DC.

Maksimovic, Vojislav, and Sheridan Titman, 1991, Financial policy and reputation for product quality, *Review of Financial Studies* 2, 175–200.

Maksimovic, Vojislav, and Josef Zechner, 1991, Debt, agency costs, and industry equilibrium, *Journal of Finance* 46, 1619–1643.

McGuckin, Robert H., and George Pascoe, 1988, The longitudinal research database: Status and research possibilities, *Survey of Current Business* 68, 30–37.

Morck, Randall, Andrei Shleifer, and Robert W. Vishny, 1989, Alternative mechanisms for corporate control, *American Economic Review* 79, 842–852.

Opler, Tim C., and Sheridan Titman, 1994, Financial distress and corporate performance, *Journal of Finance* 49, 1015–1040.

Pulvino, Todd C., 1998, Do asset fire sales exist? An empirical investigation of commercial aircraft transactions? *Journal of Finance*, 53, 939–978.

Rajan, Raghuram G., 1992, Insiders and outsiders: The choice between relationship and arms-length debt, *Journal of Finance* 47, 1367–1400.

Senbet, Lemma, and James Seward, 1995, Financial distress, bankruptcy and reorganization; in R. Jarrow, V. Maksimovic, and W. Ziemba, eds.: *Handbook of Finance* (North-Holland, Amsterdam).

Shleifer, Andrei, and Robert W. Vishny, 1992, Liquidation values and debt capacity: A market equilibrium approach, *Journal of Finance* 47, 1343–1365.

Titman, Sheridan, 1984, The effect of financial structure on a firm's liquidation decision, *Journal of Financial Economics* 13, 137–151.

Warner, Jerold B., 1977, Bankruptcy, absolute priority, and the pricing of risky debt claims, *Journal of Financial Economics* 4, 239–276.

Weiss, Lawrence, 1990, Bankruptcy resolution: Direct costs and the violation of priority of claims, *Journal of Financial Economics* 27, 285–314.

[18]

ELSEVIER Journal of Financial Economics 58 (2000) 337–368

JOURNAL OF Financial ECONOMICS

www.elsevier.com/locate/econbase

Bankruptcy auctions: costs, debt recovery, and firm survival☆

Karin S. Thorburn

Amos Tuck School of Business Administration, Dartmouth College, Hanover, NH 03755, USA

Abstract

This paper provides some first, large-sample evidence on the Swedish auction bankruptcy system. Compared to U.S. Chapter 11 cases, the small-firm bankruptcy auctions examined here are substantially quicker, have lower costs, and avoid deviations from absolute priority. Three-quarters of the firms are auctioned as going concerns, which is similar to Chapter 11 survival rates. Moreover, based on market values, creditors in going-concern auctions recover a similar fraction of face value as creditors of much larger firms in Chapter 11 reorganizations. The evidence presented here suggests that the auction bankruptcy system is a surprisingly efficient restructuring mechanism for small firms. © 2000 Elsevier Science S.A. All rights reserved.

JEL classification: G33; G34; K22

Keywords: Auctions; Bankruptcy costs; Debt recovery; Prepacks; Chapter 11

☆This work is derived from my doctoral dissertation at the Stockholm School of Economics. I wish to thank, in particular, B. Espen Eckbo for valuable comments. I am also grateful for the comments by Peter Björnram, Ted Eisenberg, Julian Franks (the referee), Ron Giammarino, Jonathan Karpoff, Kai Li, Wayne Mikkelson, Todd Pulvino, Stefan Sundgren, Liz Tashjian, Larry Weiss, the finance seminar participants at Dartmouth College, Duke University, Harvard Business School, the Norwegian School of Economics, the Norwegian School of Management, Penn State University, the Stockholm School of Economics, the universities of Illinois, Toronto, and Vienna, the meetings of the 1997 European Finance, the 1998 Western Finance, and the 1999 American Law and Economics associations, and the 1998 Utah Winter Finance Conference. This research has received financial support from Bankforskningsinstitutet, NÖDFOR, Sparbankernas Forskningsstiftelse, and the Norwegian Research Council (Norges Forskningsråd), Grant no. 125105/510.

E-mail address: karin.s.thorburn@dartmouth.edu (K.S. Thorburn).

PII: S0304-405X(00)00075-1

1. Introduction

Different bankruptcy procedures allocate different sets of control rights to incumbent managers and the security holders of a firm, thus affecting both the timing and form of management's choice of bankruptcy venue. For example, Chapter 11 of the U.S. bankruptcy code allows managers to retain a certain degree of control over the firm's assets and operations while in bankruptcy. Managers are thus encouraged to select a court-supervised debt renegotiation under Chapter 11 rather than file for liquidation in Chapter 7. In contrast, the Swedish bankruptcy code, which constitutes the empirical laboratory of this study, has no effective reorganization provisions and all bankruptcy filings are resolved through a public auction requiring payment in cash. In this auction, the firm is either liquidated piecemeal or survives as a going concern. The auction is run by an independent, court-appointed trustee, and incumbent management and shareholders immediately lose their control rights.

The relative efficiency of court-supervised reorganizations and bankruptcy auctions is a largely unexplored empirical issue, and systematic evidence on the outcomes of auction bankruptcy is sparse.[1] In this study, I present evidence on 263 small-firm bankruptcy auctions in Sweden and perform a systematic comparison with extant evidence on Chapter 11 cases.[2] To enhance comparability with the U.S. evidence, which is generally based on large firms, the analysis includes control variables reflecting firm size, financing structure, and ownership structure. The paper further adds to the bankruptcy literature by including controls for industry distress, asset uniqueness, and operating profitability relative to the filing firm's competitors. Furthermore, the paper is the first to examine prepackaged bankruptcy filings under an auction system, which I refer to as auction prepacks.

There is an ongoing debate as to the merits of an auction bankruptcy system. Proponents point to the benefits of market valuation over court-administered value assessment.[3] Sale to the highest-valuation bidder also reduces the scope for agency conflicts and disagreement among existing claimholders, and thus lowers bankruptcy costs. Moreover, the requirement for cash payment allows settlement of debt claims strictly according to absolute priority rules (APR). On

---

[1] Exceptions are Ravid and Sundgren (1998), who examine 72 bankruptcy auctions in Finland, and Strömberg (2000).

[2] There is no comparable evidence on Chapter 7 cases. Also, although 99.5% of all Chapter 11 filings are by small, privately held firms of the type studied here (Altman, 1993), available studies of Chapter 11 bankruptcies focus on large, publicly traded companies. Note also that the prospect of empirical biases due to self-selection of firms filing for alternative bankruptcy chapters (such as Chapter 11 vs. Chapter 7) is not a concern in the Swedish, single-chapter environment.

[3] See, e.g., Roe (1983), Baird (1986), Bebchuk (1988), Jensen (1991), and Bradley and Rosenzweig (1992).

the other hand, opponents of the auction system warn that it is likely to induce delayed filing and costly pre-filing asset substitution due to adverse managerial incentives and agency conflicts between holders of equity and holders of debt. Moreover, it has been argued that auctions involve a substantial risk of losses due to asset "fire-sales".[4]

The empirical analysis below addresses this debate by focusing on three important characteristics of the outcomes of bankruptcy auctions. First, I provide evidence on firm survival rates to address the extent to which the auction system promotes continuation of the bankrupt firm as a going concern. Of the 263 cases, 75% survive as a going concern, either through pre-filing auction prepack (20%) or through post-filing auction sale. In the remaining 25% of the cases, the firm's assets are liquidated piecemeal. The 75% survival rate is similar to the percentage of small firms that survive as a going concern through Chapter 11 proceedings, as reported by White (1984). I also find that, as expected, the probability of a firm being sold as a going concern increases with the proportion of intangible assets. Auction prepacks are more likely to occur the larger the firm and, interestingly, when the firm is run by an owner-manager. While shareholders themselves have few incentives to initiate a prepack, which eradicates their equity claims, owner-managers may use a prepack to maintain control benefits and to enhance their market value as managers with the new owners.

Second, I provide evidence on bankruptcy costs. Direct costs in percent of pre-filing book value of assets average 6.4% across the sample of firms undergoing auctions in bankruptcy, and 3.7% for the one-third largest firms. Auction prepacks are generally low-cost with an average direct cost of 2.5%. Regressions indicate that direct costs have a significant fixed component, which probably accounts for the size effect, and are lower for piecemeal liquidations. Interestingly, direct costs are increasing in industry distress, where distress is measured as the proportion of firms sharing the same 4-digit Standard Industrial Classification (SIC) code that either have an interest coverage ratio of less than one or file for bankruptcy that year. One possible explanation for this result is that the trustee increases marketing efforts in response to lower auction demand induced by industry distress. The direct cost estimate for the largest firms in my sample corresponds closely to the typical cost of large-firm Chapter 11 cases reported by Weiss (1990) and Betker (1997). Averaging across the samples studied by Weiss (1990) and Betker (1997), the sample-size weighted mean of direct costs for publicly traded firms undergoing Chapter 11 reorganization is 3.6%. Moreover, there is reason to believe that total costs, calculated as the sum of direct and indirect costs, are lower in Sweden. Indirect costs increase with the length of time spent in bankruptcy, and Swedish bankruptcy auctions are unquestionably

---

[4] For example, Shleifer and Vishny (1992), Aghion et al. (1994), Berkovitch and Israel (1995), White (1996), and Pulvino (1998). Eckbo and Thorburn (2000a) fail to find support for asset fire-sales in Swedish bankruptcy auctions.

speedy. On average, two months pass from filing for bankruptcy to sale as a going concern. In contrast, it typically takes about two years to resolve small-firm reorganizations under Chapter 11 (see, e.g., Flynn, 1989).

Third, I report evidence on debt recovery rates. Importantly, the cash settlement from the auction directly yields the market value of the recovery. Overall, debtholders recover 35% of the face value of their claims, with a 27% mean recovery rate for piecemeal liquidations and 39% recovery for going concern sales. In comparison, Franks and Torous (1994) provide market-value estimates for a subsample of 12 Chapter 11 cases which resulted in successful reorganizations, and find that the median overall recovery is 41%, similar to that of firms auctioned as going concerns. Franks and Torous (1994) is, to my knowledge, the only study that reports recovery rates in Chapter 11 that are based entirely on market values. Given the default rates of firms emerging from Chapter 11 bankruptcy (Hotchkiss, 1995), debt face values tend to overstate market values of debt, and thus overstate recovery rates. I find that secured debtholders receive on average 69% of their claims, while junior unsecured creditors recover only 2% on average. The distribution of recovery rates is skewed, with a median of 82% for secured debt and 0% for unsecured creditors. As expected, recovery rates are lower the greater the fraction of intangible assets and in years with a general economic downturn. Interestingly, secured debtholders recover more when the original owner buys back the firm and when the old bank finances the buyer in the auction. While not pursued here, this evidence suggests that the decision to repurchase or refinance the bankrupt firm in part reflects private information about firm value.

This study concludes that the Swedish auction bankruptcy system promotes firm survival rates, bankruptcy costs, and debt recovery rates that compare favorably with the reorganization system in the U.S. Overall, the evidence presented here suggests that auctions constitute a surprisingly efficient mechanism for restructuring small firms in bankruptcy.

The rest of the paper is organized as follows. Highlights of the Swedish bankruptcy code, data sources and sampling procedures are contained in Section 2. Section 3 presents evidence on the use of auction prepacks, and firm survival in bankruptcy auctions. Section 4 examines direct bankruptcy costs, while debt recovery rates are discussed in Section 5. Section 6 concludes the paper.

2. Legal rules summary and sample characteristics

2.1. *Highlights of the Swedish auction bankruptcy code*

Table 1 summarizes central characteristics of the legal rules under Swedish auction bankruptcy and shows the comparable rules under Chapter 11 in the

Table 1
Legal rules under Swedish auction bankruptcy and Chapter 11 of the U.S. Bankruptcy Code

Summary characteristics of legal rules under Swedish auction bankruptcy and under Chapter 11 of the U.S. Bankruptcy Code. A "cram down" refers to a setting in which the Chapter 11 bankruptcy judge forces an opposing class of debtholders to accept a proposed reorganization plan.

Characteristic	Rules under Swedish auction bankruptcy	Rules under U.S. Chapter 11
Right to file for bankruptcy:	The firm, or any individual creditor.	The firm, or a joint filing of at least 3 creditors with unsecured claims exceeding $5,000.
Control right to firm in bankruptcy:	An independent court-appointed trustee. Firm is auctioned off either piecemeal or as a going concern.	Incumbent management. A trustee takes control only in cases of mismanagement or fraud. Management has exclusive right to propose a reorganization plan during the first 120 days, plus an additional 60 days to seek acceptance for the plan.
Voting rules to approve of reorganization:	None. Firm is auctioned off.	1/2 in number of votes and 2/3 in value of claims in each debt class.
Possibility of "cram down":	No. Firm is auctioned off.	Yes. Each debt class must get at least what the creditors would receive in liquidation.
Settlement of claims:	Cash only.	Cash and securities, including common stock.
Absolute priority rules:	No deviations allowed.	Deviations frequently observed.
Seizure of collateral by secured creditors:	No seizure, except in limited circumstances when collateral is in creditor's physical possession.	No seizure. All creditors are stayed.
Service of debt during the proceeding:	No. Interest and principal payments stop.	No. Interest and principal payments stop.
Accrual of interest during the proceeding:	Yes, on secured debt, if the value of collateral is sufficiently high.	Yes, on secured debt, if the value of the collateral is sufficiently high.
Debtor-in-possession financing:	Yes. New debt issued in bankruptcy gets super-priority.	Yes, debtor-in-possession financing allows new debt with super-priority to be issued.
Government wage guarantee:	Yes, up to a certain limit.	No guarantee.

U.S. In Sweden, as an alternative to auction bankruptcy, an insolvent firm can file for composition, or "ackord", which is a court-supervised procedure for renegotiation of unsecured (junior) debt claims. The composition procedure, however, provides no protection for the firm against its secured debtholders and holders of priority claims, and is therefore almost never used. In preliminary work, Eckbo and Thorburn (2000b) find that in a sample of 1,650 financially distressed firms, only 4 firms file for composition over the next two years, while almost 300 firms file for bankruptcy.

In Swedish bankruptcy, the incumbent management team is immediately replaced by an independent, court-appointed trustee with a fiduciary responsibility towards creditors. The trustee organizes the sale of the firm's assets in an open ascending English-style auction, either piecemeal or as a going concern. A going concern sale takes place by merging the assets and operations of the firm into a receiving company which is either established or held by the buyer. The auction typically attracts 3–4 bidders, and payments are restricted to cash only. The bulk of cash represents bank debt financing provided to the buying corporation, much like in a leveraged buyout. As under Chapter 11, the operations of a firm in auction bankruptcy are protected through automatic stay of creditors. In other words, once the trustee takes over, debt service is halted and creditors cannot seize collateral. Furthermore, the code permits debtor-in-possession financing such that the firm can issue new debt claims with super-priority status over all existing debt claims. In practice, bankrupt firms tend to cover operating expenses by increasing their debt obligations in the form of trade credits which get super-priority, while new debt issues or bank loans are almost never observed.

The bankruptcy auction is supervised by the provincial supervisory authority, known as "Tillsynsmyndigheten i Konkurs" (TSM). This supervision, the legal constraints on the trustee, and the value of the trustee's own reputation all increase the trustee's incentives to fulfill his or her responsibility to the filing firm's creditors. This setting contrasts with the U.S. reorganization code which provides a strong protection of managers and equityholders. During the Chapter 11 proceeding, incumbent managers usually remain in control of the firm. Management has an exclusive right to propose a reorganization plan during the first four months, and receive another two months to seek approval of the plan. Moreover, shareholders participate in the voting of the proposed plan and are often allowed to retain some equity.

The cash proceeds from the bankruptcy auction are distributed to creditors strictly according to APR. Payment of administrative and advisory costs of the bankruptcy proceeding has super-priority along with any new debtor-in-possession financing. Secured claims are entitled to the proceeds from sale of collateral, and any unpaid part of the claim is treated as an unsecured claim. The vast majority of firms have floating charge secured claims, pledging as collateral the movable property of the firm, such as machinery, inventory, and accounts receivables. Prior to filing, the floating charge asset base can shrink, or grow, at the discretion of the firm's manager, by selling or purchasing machinery, for example, or decreasing or increasing inventory. Moreover, individual assets, like a machine or inventory, contained in the floating charge asset base can be taken as collateral for a fixed charge claim. In contrast, fixed charge debt have a claim to a specific asset that cannot be sold without creditor approval. Floating charge claimholders thus have less control rights than fixed charge claimholders.

Debt claims are paid in the following order: super-priority claims, secured claims, both fixed and floating charge, certain audit claims, tax claims, wage claims, and, lastly, unsecured or junior claims. Audit, tax, and wage claims have statutory priority to the unsecured claims, and are classified as priority claims in this paper. Note that the Swedish government guarantees the payment of wage claims up to a certain limit, while there is no corresponding guarantee in the U.S. Since Swedish priority rules prescribe equal treatment of all unsecured claims, firms effectively cannot issue different classes of unsecured debt. I therefore use the term unsecured debt and junior debt interchangeably.

2.2. Data sources

I analyze a sample of Swedish bankruptcies compiled by Strömberg and Thorburn (1996) that are restricted to firms with at least 20 employees. This sample is identified from UpplysningsCentralen AB's database (UC), which contains a total of 1,159 bankruptcy filings from January 1, 1988 through December 31, 1991. The UC database, which is restricted to bankruptcy cases that remained open on December 31, 1991, covers virtually the entire population of filings over the sample period. The reason is that a bankruptcy case cannot be formally closed until all claims owned by the filing firm are fully collected, which can take several years. The data collection was restricted to the four largest administrative provinces in Sweden, which are Stockholms län, Göteborg- och Bohus län, Malmöhus län, and Upplands län. Of the total 1,159 filings, the sampling procedure eliminates the following cases: 581 firms located outside the selected geographical area, 145 cases which are pending in bankruptcy on June 30, 1995, 59 cases that are related to tax fraud charges, and 111 cases for which the bankruptcy file is either missing or incomplete. The final sample consists of 263 cases, of which 9 filed in 1988, 27 in 1989, 71 in 1990, and 156 in 1991.

For each firm in the sample, information on firm characteristics and case-specific characteristics is collected from the bankruptcy file kept by the provincial supervisory authority. Pre-bankruptcy financial statements are obtained from UC. Moreover, UC also provides annual financial statements from the period 1987–1994 for the Swedish population of more than 15,000 firms that had at least 20 employees and were in operation on December 31, 1991. This information is used below to construct industry distress and profitability measures.

The paper extends the original dataset and compiles information on the identity of the financing source of the buyer in the auction, typically a bank, as well as the stock ownership of the incumbent CEO. The former is from the national register of corporate floating charge claims (Inskrivningsmyndigheten för företagsinteckning), and allows classification of each case as to whether or not the filing firm's bank participates in the financing of the successful buyer in the auction. Of the 195 going concern sales, the role of the old bank is identified for 108 cases. CEO stock ownership is compiled by matching the information on management and owners in the bankruptcy file, with board information provided by UC. This matching process produces the stock ownership for 215 CEOs.

2.3. Sample characteristics

Of the 263 bankrupt firms, 63 (24%) are liquidated piecemeal and 195 (74%) are sold as a going concern. In the remaining 5 cases (2%), there is insufficient information to classify the case as either a going concern sale or a piecemeal liquidation. In this classification, a going concern sale is a joint sale of the firm's core assets, defined as assets essential for the continued operations, such as inventories, machinery, vehicles, unfinished products, intangible assets, industrial estate, and rental contracts. The classification of each firm into piecemeal liquidation, going concern sale, and auction prepack has been confirmed by the respective trustee. Firms sold as going concerns are repurchased by the original owner in 54% of the cases.

The firms in the sample represent the larger firms in Sweden. Only 6% of Swedish corporations have 20 employees or more, and 90% of firms have less than 10 employees (source, Statistics Sweden). If liquidation rates are higher for the very small firms, which constitute the bulk of businesses, the liquidation rate across all business bankruptcies in Sweden may be significantly higher than the 24% found here. In the U.S., for example, Altman (1993) reports that 60% of all business bankruptcies are Chapter 7 filings.

The sample firms represent more than 30 different 2-digit SIC groups. The largest number of cases, 76 firms, occur in the manufacturing industry. Of the remaining cases, 33 are in the construction industry, 30 firms are wholesale companies, 26 firms are hotels and restaurants, while 26 cases are from the transportation industry. All firms are privately held, and most have concentrated ownership. Of the 181 sample firms with information available regarding shareownership, 56% are wholly owned by one individual or family. For another 31%, at least half of the equity is controlled by a single shareholder. Moreover, three-quarters of the firms are run by an

Table 2
Pre-filing characteristics of Swedish and U.S. firms filing for bankruptcy or initiating a workout, 1978–1990

Table shows pre-filing financial characteristics of 263 privately held Swedish firms filing for auction bankruptcy in 1988–1991, and for publicly traded U.S. firms filing for Chapter 11 or initiating workouts during 1978–1990. For the sample of Swedish firms, the numbers shown are book values, denoted in 1991 prices, from the last financial statement reported prior to bankruptcy filing, dated on average 16.5 months before filing. Data for the Swedish firms are from the database of UpplysningsCentralen AB (UC). The information on publicly traded firms in Chapter 11 is from Weiss (1990), Gilson et al. (1990), Franks and Torous (1994), and Hotchkiss (1995). The numbers shown for the U.S. firms are from the financial statement of the last fiscal year prior to bankruptcy filing. The sample size for the U.S. firms is an average of the sample sizes in the four studies listed above, and data in the table reflect sample-size weighted averages of the results from these studies. The debt-to-assets ratio is defined as book value of total liabilities divided by the market value of equity (book value of equity for the Swedish companies and for the firms studied by Gilson et al., 1990) plus the face value of debt. Current ratio is the ratio of current assets to short term debt. Percentage of firms with negative earnings before interest and taxes (EBIT) is also shown.

	Swedish firms			Publicly traded U.S. firms	
	Mean	Median	Standard deviation	Mean	Median
Sample size	263			90	
Book value of assets ($ million)	2.4	1.3	3.6	288	46
Number of employees	43	29	48	3,000	2,000
Debt-to-assets ratio	0.92	0.93	0.21	0.91	0.84
Long-term debt/book-value of assets	0.34	0.35	0.24	0.58	0.45
Current ratio	1.39	1.23	0.97	1.06	0.99
Fraction firms with negative EBIT	46%	—	—	62%	—

owner-manager, defined as a CEO holding 10% or more of the firm's equity, while the remaining firms are managed by an external CEO.

Table 2 lists selected pre-bankruptcy characteristics for the sample firms based on their last reported financial statement. On average, these financial statements were created 16.5 months before filing. For comparison purposes, Table 2 also presents the corresponding information for much larger, publicly traded U.S. firms that file for Chapter 11, as reported by Weiss (1990), Gilson et al. (1990), Franks and Torous (1994), and Hotchkiss (1995). In the Swedish sample, the average book value of total assets one year prior to filing is only $2.5 million, with median assets totaling $1.3 million. The average number of employees for the Swedish firms is 43, and the median number of employees is 29.

The sample firms are highly leveraged with an average pre-filing debt-to-assets ratio of 92%. Interestingly, this ratio is almost identical to the 91% average debt ratio measured across the Chapter 11 samples. Moreover, reflecting the extensive use of short-term bank financing, the Swedish firms have on average only 34% of long-term debt in their capital structure, as opposed to 58% for U.S. firms. Capturing liquidity, the current ratio, defined as current assets to short-term debt, is on average 1.39 for the Swedish sample, as compared to 1.06 for Chapter 11 firms. Also, just less than half of sample firms, 46%, report negative earnings before interest and taxes (EBIT) in the year prior to filing. This level, again, is less than the 62% of firms with negative EBIT in Hotchkiss' (1995) sample of Chapter 11 cases. Overall, the statistics indicate that, prior to filing, the firms filing for auction bankruptcy are in a comparable financial condition as the firms filing for Chapter 11.

The financial characteristics of the sample firms after filing for bankruptcy are shown in Table 3. The realized auction value for these firms averages $0.8 million, with median auction value of $0.4 million, and is similar to the book value reported for private U.S. firms in Chapter 11.[5] The auction value, which is reported in the filing documents, is the sum of the total proceeds from the sale of assets in the auction, accounts receivables, and other claims owned by the firm and collected by the trustee. This value is only one-third of the average pre-filing book value of assets reported in Table 2 above, and the difference reflects a combination of pre-filing asset sales and book values overstating market values for financially distressed firms. In my sample, one-third of the firms report that they sold non-core assets over the two-year period prior to filing. Asset sales in the two years prior to bankruptcy filing are qualitatively different from auction prepacks. First, these sales occur prior to the firm being bankrupt and second, they do not involve core assets which are the object of the prepackaged going concern sale.

Table 3 also provides information on the debt structure of the sample firms and, for comparison, of U.S. firms in Chapter 11. For the average firm in the sample, 39% of the total liabilities is secured debt, of which 80% is floating charge debt and the remainder is fixed charge debt. The proportion of secured debt is similar to the 42% mean fraction of secured debt reported by White (1984) for privately held firms in Chapter 11. Moreover, on average 88% of the sample firms' secured debt is held by banks, with a median of 100%. This amount constitutes the bulk of the bank debt, given that only 6% of claims held by banks are unsecured. Thus, the sample firms' 39% mean fraction of secured debt, which includes practically all bank debt, is comparable to the 37% average

[5] The evidence on privately held firms in Chapter 11 is from LoPucki (1983), White (1984), and Lawless et al. (1994). For the evidence on publicly traded firms in Chapter 11, see the references in Table 2, as well as LoPucki and Whitford (1993) and Betker (1997).

Table 3
Debt structure and total assets of Swedish and U.S. firms in bankruptcy, 1978–1993

Table shows debt structure and total assets of 263 privately held Swedish firms filing for auction bankruptcy in 1988–1991, and for publicly traded and privately held U.S. firms filing for Chapter 11 in 1978–1993. Data for the Swedish firms are from the bankruptcy file kept with the supervisory authority, or Tillsynsmyndigheten i Konkurs (TSM). The information on publicly traded firms in Chapter 11 is from Weiss (1990), Gilson et al. (1990), LoPucki and Whitford (1993), Franks and Torous (1994), Hotchkiss (1995), and Betker (1997). The evidence on private firms in Chapter 11 is from LoPucki (1983), White (1984) and Lawless, Ferris, Jayaraman, and Makhija (1994). The sample sizes shown for U.S. firms are averages of the sample sizes in the studies listed above of publicly traded and privately held firms, respectively, and data in the table reflect sample-size weighted averages of the results from these studies. Auction value is the sum of total proceeds from the sale of the firm's assets in the bankruptcy auction, and the value of accounts receivables and other claims owned by the firm and collected by the trustee. For the Swedish firms, bank debt constitutes on average 88% of the secured debt, median 100%, and banks hold on average 36% of the total liabilities.

	Swedish firms			Publicly traded U.S. firms		Privately held U.S. firms	
	Mean	Median	Standard deviation	Mean	Median	Mean	Median
Sample size	263			79		46	
Book value of assets ($ million)	—	—	—	—	—	1.2	0.3
Auction value ($ million)	0.8	0.4	1.2	—	—	—	—
Secured debt/total liabilities	0.39	0.38	0.25	0.12	0.00	0.42	—
Bank debt/total liabilities	—	—	—	0.25	0.20	—	—
Priority claims/total liabilities	0.29	0.24	0.21	—	—	—	—
Senior debt/total liabilities	—	—	—	—	—	0.05	—
Junior debt/total liabilities	0.33	0.28	0.21	—	—	0.54	—

fraction of the sum of secured debt and bank debt reported for publicly traded U.S. firms. Furthermore, of the Swedish firms' total debt, on average 29% is priority claims, i.e., audit, tax and wage claims, and 33% is junior unsecured debt. In comparison, White (1984) reports a higher fraction of junior debt, with a mean of 54%, for small firms in Chapter 11.

3. Auction prepacks, in-bankruptcy auctions, and firm survival

This section examines the firm's choice of a pre-negotiated auction prepack versus filing for an in-bankruptcy auction. Moreover, I present evidence on the degree to which the in-bankruptcy auction leads to a going concern sale versus piecemeal liquidation. This analysis sheds light on the extent to which the auction bankruptcy system promotes survival of the filing firms.

3.1. Auction prepacks

In the total sample of 195 going concern sales, 53 sales (27%) were arranged just prior to filing for bankruptcy. These cases are labeled prepackaged going concern sales, and referred to as simply auction prepacks. In an auction prepack, a buyer has been found and the rights to the distressed firm's core assets have been transferred to the buyer in return for cash. However, since the amount of cash is less than the sum of the firm's liabilities, the selling firm still must file for bankruptcy. Moreover, for the prepack sales agreement to take effect after filing, it must be formally approved by all secured creditors whose collateral is included in the prepack sale, as well as the bankruptcy trustee. In my sample, there is no evidence of prepacks being overturned. In the case of prepacks, however, the trustee need not open an auction since the assets of the bankrupt firm are now primarily made up of cash. Thus, the trustee can proceed with the distribution of the cash to creditors on an absolute priority basis.

There are several incentives for firms to arrange a prepack. Shareholder claims are eradicated in both auction prepacks and in bankruptcy auctions. This feature makes auction prepacks different from prepackaged Chapter 11 filings, where shareholders retain some equity in the reorganized firm. Nevertheless, certain shareholders, such as those with valuable private information about the firm, or with substantial private benefits of control, may see an advantage in repurchasing the bankrupt company. It is possible that the terms of the repurchase are more favorable to the buyer in a prepack agreement than in the open bankruptcy auction. If this benefit occurs systematically, one would expect the frequency of owner repurchases to be highest in the sample of prepacks. However, I find no support for this proposition in my database. No significant difference exists in the proportion of owner repurchases between the samples of prepacks and going concern bankruptcy sales.

The distressed firm's managers and debtholders may also have a preference for the prepack option. For example, if prepacks have lower direct bankruptcy costs, they benefit debtholders. In fact, as discussed below, there is significant evidence that auction prepacks have lower costs. Furthermore, managers concerned with their prospects for being rehired by the new owners have an incentive to choose the bankruptcy venue with the lowest cost, thus building a reputation for value-maximizing behavior. While not a topic of this paper, Thorburn (2000) shows that CEOs undertaking auction prepacks on average suffer smaller compensation losses when their firms file for bankruptcy.

Firms that select an auction prepack share several characteristics. Table 5 shows the results of a probit regression for the probability that a sample firm files a prepack ($y = 1$) versus files for an auction in bankruptcy ($y = 0$). The estimation uses 205 observations, of which 35 cases are auction prepacks. The regression eliminates the remaining 18 auction prepack cases due to missing information on one or more of the explanatory variables. The probit model is described by the following equation:

$$\begin{aligned} Prob(Prepack) = {} & \alpha_0 + \alpha_1 Secured + \alpha_2 Float + \alpha_3 Distress + \alpha_4 Unique \\ & + \alpha_5 Ownermgr + \alpha_6 Profmarg + \alpha_7 Size \\ & + \alpha_8 Industry + \varepsilon. \end{aligned} \quad (1)$$

The explanatory variables are defined in Table 4. Firms with a high proportion of intangibles are more difficult to value, and thus have higher expected auction costs. The variable Secured, which measures the proportion of secured debt in the firm's capital structure, is used as a proxy for the fraction of tangible assets. The expected auction costs are thus higher the lower the value of Secured, and the higher the auction costs the greater the incentive to set up a prepack agreement. Also, the value of intangible assets tends to become diminished if the firm is liquidated piecemeal, which can be avoided through a prepackaged filing. Both arguments predict that the proportion of tangible assets will enter the regression with a negative coefficient, such that $\alpha_1 < 0$. Furthermore, the execution of an auction prepack requires approval by the creditors holding claims secured by core assets. The probability of a prepack is therefore expected to decrease with the number of creditors holding claims secured by floating-charge collateral, labeled Float in Eq. (1), producing $\alpha_2 < 0$.

Industry distress reduces liquidity among competitors and increases the chance that asset will be unloaded in fire sales, thus increasing the incentive creditors have to restructure the company out of court. The variable Distress, defined as the fraction of financially distressed firms in the industry, is therefore predicted to produce a positive coefficient, $\alpha_3 > 0$. A related argument is that firm assets that can be classified as unique within the industry are of a relatively low value to industry outsiders, and will sell at a substantial discount in a piecemeal liquidation. The variable Unique measures the fraction of assets that are classified as industry unique, defined as machinery, equipment, inventory, intangible assets, and work in progress. This variable is expected to have a positive impact on the likelihood that an auction prepack is selected, such that $\alpha_4 > 0$. The value of the unique assets is estimated by the trustee to be on average one-third of total firm value. Non-unique assets include liquid assets, accounts receivables, other financial claims, vehicles, and real estate.

The model also includes a binary variable, Ownermgr, indicating that the firm is run by an owner-manager, holding at least 10% of the equity in the firm. Owner-managers have both the incentives and the control rights to execute auction prepacks, suggesting that the variable Ownermgr should enter the regression with a positive sign, $\alpha_5 > 0$. The probit model further contains a measure for the firm's pre-filing operating profitability relative to its industry competitors, Profmarg, predicted to increase the probability of a prepackaged going concern sale, such that $\alpha_6 > 0$. Moreover, relatively large firms with

Table 4
Definition of variables in the regression models

Variable label	Variable definition
Panel A: Firm characteristics	
Size	Log of book value of total assets in the firm's last financial statement prior to filing.
Large	Binary variable indicating that the firm belongs to the one-third of sample firms (88 firms) with the largest pre-filing book-value of total assets, ranging from $2.1 million to $4.2 million.
Medium	Binary variable indicating that the firm belongs to the one-third of sample firms (88 firms) in the middle range of pre-filing book-value of total assets, ranging from $0.9 million to $2.1 million.
Profmarg	Pre-filing operating profitability, defined as earnings before interest, taxes, amortization and depreciation, EBITDA, divided by total sales, minus the contemporaneous median operating profitability of all Swedish firms with more than 20 employees that shares the same 4-digit SIC code as the sample firm.
Unique	Fraction of firm's assets that are unique to the industry, defined as machinery, equipment, inventory, intangible assets and work in progress, as estimated by the trustee upon bankruptcy filing.
Secured	Fraction of secured debt to total debt in the firm's capital structure at bankruptcy filing.
Float	Number of debt holders secured with floating-charge collateral.
Ownermgr	Binary variable indicating that the CEO owns at least 10% of the firm's equity, vs. less than 10% of the equity.
Distress	Fraction of Swedish firms with over 20 employees sharing the same 4-digit SIC code as the sample firm that either report an interest coverage ratio of less than one in the year of bankruptcy filing, or file for bankruptcy during the next calendar year.
Panel B: Auction characteristics	
Creditor	Binary variable indicating that a creditor, vs. the firm, files the bankruptcy petition.
Filing91	Binary variable indicating that the firm files for bankruptcy in 1991, vs. in 1988–1990.
Prepack	Binary variable indicating that a going concern sale of the firm's core assets is negotiated by the firm prior to bankruptcy filing, vs. a sale is arranged in bankruptcy by the trustee.
Piecemeal	Binary variable indicating that the firm's assets are sold piecemeal in the bankruptcy auction, vs. are sold as a going concern.
Bank	Binary variable indicating that the filing firm's bank, vs. a new bank, finances the buyer in the auction of the bankrupt firm's assets.
Repurchase	Binary variable indicating that the pre-filing owner buys back, vs. a new owner buys, the assets of the firm. Pre-filing owner is defined as an equity holder or a group company of the filing firm, or, if the ownership of the acquirer is unknown, cases where the acquiring firm's board includes all member of the filing firm's board.
Length	Number of months that the firm's legal corporate existence is kept on file with the court as an open bankruptcy case. The firm typically continues to exist as a legal entity in bankruptcy for several years after the assets have been sold.

multiple divisions may have synergies that are lost in a piecemeal liquidation, hence increasing expected auction costs. The variable Size, measured as the log of pre-filing book value of assets, is therefore predicted to produce a positive coefficient, $\alpha_7 > 0$. Finally, the probit estimation adds a number of industry indicators, described by the vector Industry.

As shown in Table 5, the probability of an auction prepack decreases with the amount of secured debt in the firm's capital structure, as expected. Firms with a higher proportion of intangibles, and thus high expected bankruptcy costs, are more likely to choose the prepack option. This result is consistent with Gilson et al. (1990), who find that firms restructuring their debt in a private workout tend to have relatively more intangible assets than firms filing for Chapter 11. Moreover, the coefficient for firm size is positive, again suggesting that prepackaged bankruptcy is more predominant among firms facing relatively high expected auction costs. In contrast, Betker (1997) reports that firms in traditional Chapter 11 proceedings on average have larger pre-filing assets than firms in Chapter 11 prepacks. As predicted, the variable indicating that the firm is run by an owner-manager produces a positive coefficient, perhaps reflecting the reputational concerns of managers in the selection of auction prepacks. Similarly, prepackaged bankruptcy filings in the U.S. are often characterized by substantial managerial equity ownership. Approximately 40% of Chapter 11 prepacks involve failed LBO firms in which management typically has significant shareholdings (see, e.g., Jensen, 1989; Betker, 1995).

The coefficients for Float, Unique and Distress, shown in Table 5, are all insignificant, suggesting that the prepack decision is not affected by the number of secured debtholders, asset uniqueness, and industry distress. Also, the relative profitability of the firm has no statistically discernible impact for the probability of an auction prepack. Overall, the regression model is significant with a pseudo-R^2 of 10.2% and a likelihood ratio test statistic with a p-value of 0.08. While not shown here, a separate estimation using a subsample of going concern sales produces similar results.

3.2. *Firm survival*

A central issue concerns whether managers facing auction bankruptcy and possible job losses will delay filing.[6] A delay means that going concern value is destroyed while the restructuring of the firm is postponed, causing the firm to be of relatively low value when entering bankruptcy. In this paper, more than 90% of the bankruptcy filings are made by the distressed firm. Since the creditor can also file, at first sight this may seem to contradict the hypothesis of delayed filing. However, managers generally have an informational advantage

[6] See, e.g., Franks et al. (1996) and White (1996).

Table 5
Comparison of bankruptcy outcomes, Swedish firms, 1988–1991

Parameter estimates in probit regressions for the probability of auction prepack vs. in-bankruptcy auction, and of in-bankruptcy going concern sale vs. piecemeal liquidation. Sample of 205 Swedish firms filing for auction bankruptcy in 1988–1991. In the regressions, the dependent variable is a binary variable, y, indicating type of bankruptcy outcome. The first equation compares auction prepacks to in-bankruptcy auctions, with y set to 1 for prepacks and 0 for auctions in bankruptcy. The second equation compares going concern sales in bankruptcy ($y = 1$) to piecemeal liquidations ($y = 0$). An auction prepack is a going concern sale of the distressed firm's core assets that is negotiated by the firm prior to bankruptcy filing. Industry indicators were included for manufacturing, construction, wholesale and retail, hotels and restaurants, and transportation. See Table 4 for variable definitions.

	Auction prepack vs. in-bankruptcy auctions			In-bankruptcy going concern sale vs. piecemeal liquidation		
	Expected sign of coefficient	Coefficient	p-value	Expected sign of coefficient	Coefficient	p-value
Constant		− 6.62	0.005		− 0.07	0.971
Explanatory variables:						
Secured	< 0	− 1.25	0.023	< 0	− 0.91	0.058
Float	< 0	− 0.13	0.522	—	—	—
Creditor	—	—	—	< 0	− 0.69	0.058
Distress	> 0	− 0.76	0.305	< 0	− 0.72	0.333
Unique	> 0	0.24	0.459	> 0	0.01	0.986
Ownermgr	> 0	0.48	0.099	> 0	− 0.29	0.278
Profmarg	> 0	0.16	0.849	> 0	0.38	0.600
Size	> 0	0.38	0.008	> 0	0.11	0.367
Industry indicators with p-values less than 0.10:						
None	—	—	—	—	—	—
Sample size:						
$y = 1$		35			117	
$y = 0$		170			49	
Pseudo R^2		0.102			0.059	
Likelihood ratio test		19.16	0.084		11.79	0.463

concerning the financial status of the firm, and may effectively delay filing by withholding such information from creditors. In the U.S., managers have potentially fewer incentives to delay a Chapter 11 filing since they retain substantial control rights throughout the bankruptcy proceeding. Thus, the delayed filing hypothesis predicts that firms filing for auction bankruptcy are less likely to survive as going concerns than firms filing for Chapter 11.

In the total sample of auction bankruptcies, 74% of firms survive as going concerns. Excluding auction prepacks, which are all going concern sales, and focusing on the 205 firms sold by the trustee in a public auction, 63 firms (31%) are liquidated piecemeal and 142 firms (69%) are sold as going concerns. The fifth column of Table 5 reports the estimated coefficients in a model for the probability that the firm survives as a going concern as opposed to being liquidated piecemeal in the auction. The estimation uses a subsample of 166 firms sold by the trustee in bankruptcy, of which 49 firms were liquidated piecemeal. The probability of a going concern sale is defined as follows:

$$\begin{aligned} \mathit{Prob(Survival)} = {} & \alpha_0 + \alpha_1 \mathit{Secured} + \alpha_2 \mathit{Creditor} + \alpha_3 \mathit{Distress} + \alpha_4 \mathit{Unique} \\ & + \alpha_5 \mathit{Ownermgr} + \alpha_6 \mathit{Profmarg} + \alpha_7 \mathit{Size} \\ & + \alpha_8 \mathit{Industry} + \varepsilon. \end{aligned} \tag{2}$$

In formulating the model expressed in Eq. (2), I expect a going concern sale to be driven by the same factors as an auction prepack. Thus, the model in Eq. (2) contains the same variables as the prepack model in Eq. (1), with the exception of Float, which is omitted from Eq. (2). Moreover, Eq. (2) includes a binary variable, Creditor, indicating whether a creditor, as opposed to the firm, files the bankruptcy petition. If firms that are forced into bankruptcy by a creditor are of lower quality, this setting should reduce the probability of survival, such that $\alpha_2 < 0$. Furthermore, since a piecemeal liquidation would dissipate the value of intangible assets, the probability of a going concern sale is expected to decrease with Secured, or $\alpha_1 < 0$. The likelihood of firm survival is also predicted to be lower in down-sizing or distressed industries, captured by Distress, thus $\alpha_3 < 0$. To the extent the firm's equityholders can influence the trustee's sales effort, the variable Ownermgr is expected to produce $\alpha_5 > 0$, reflecting a greater expected loss of managerial private benefits when the firm is liquidated piecemeal. The model also contains the variables Unique, Profmarg, and Size, which are all expected to increase the likelihood of a going concern sale.

As predicted, the coefficient for Secured is negative, suggesting that firms with a large fraction of intangible assets tend to be auctioned as going concerns. This result is consistent with the earlier finding that auction prepacks are more common for firms with a significant part of their value in intangibles, reflecting higher expected bankruptcy costs. Moreover, the coefficient for Creditor, α_2, is negative and significant. Thus, firms for which a creditor files the bankruptcy petition seem to have a lower chance of survival, as expected. While the probability of an auction prepack is increasing in the indicator for owner-manager, this variable has no significant impact on the outcome of the bankruptcy auction, possibly indicating that the trustee acts independently of equityholders and managers during the auction. As before, the coefficients for the proportion assets that are industry unique and the level of distress in the industry are insignificant, suggesting that neither asset uniqueness nor industry distress affect the choice of going concern sale versus piecemeal liquidation. Finally, the variables capturing industry-adjusted operating profitability and size produce insignificant coefficients, as do the industry indicators. The overall significance of this regression is lower than for the above prepack regression, with a pseudo-R^2 of 5.9%.

Interestingly, the three-quarter survival rate in Swedish bankruptcy is close to survival rates reported for Chapter 11 filings by privately held firms. White (1984) finds that in a sample of 64 small corporations filing for Chapter 11, 47% of firms adopt reorganization plans, 23% are sold as going concerns, and the remaining 30% are subsequently liquidated under Chapter 7. Thus, in White's sample, 70% of the firms continue operating with their assets in their current use. This survival rate is also similar to the finding of Flynn (1989), who reports that, in a sample of 2,395 small Chapter 11 cases with confirmed reorganization plans from 1979 to 1989, 25% had plans to liquidate the firm, which implies a conditional survival rate of 75%. Jensen-Conklin (1992) also study confirmed plans by small firms in Chapter 11, and finds that 25% were liquidation plans. LoPucki (1983) reports that 27% of his sample of 48 firms obtain confirmation of a reorganization plan and are still operating three years later. Since this post-to Chapter 11 rate reflects firm-specific economic conditions over the three-year post-bankruptcy period, it understates actual survival rates. Also, LoPucki does not include going concern sales in Chapter 11, which leads to a further understatement of actual survival rates. As to Chapter 11 filings by publicly traded firms, Weiss (1990) reports that in a sample of 35 cases, 86% successfully reorganize, while LoPucki and Whitford (1993) report a 74% survival rate for their 43 cases.

In sum, the survival rate in auction bankruptcy is largely indistinguishable from the fraction of firms surviving Chapter 11 filings. One interpretation of this result is that U.S. firms filing for Chapter 11 tend to be in a similar economic condition as the Swedish firms studied here, an explanation that is also consistent with the discussion in Section 2.3, above. If one assumes that only the lowest-quality firms are liquidated piecemeal, this finding also fails to support the hypothesis that managers delay filing under an auction bankruptcy code relative to what is observed under a reorganization code. In contrast, as shown by Thorburn (2000), managers may have incentives to file early to increase the chance of retaining control of the firm after bankruptcy.

4. Bankruptcy costs

Total bankruptcy costs are the sum of direct costs, such as lawyer fees, consulting fees, administrative costs, for example, and indirect costs, which include the opportunity cost of management's time and potentially adverse reputational effects in product and capital markets. In this section, I report estimates of direct costs as well as the length of time the firm spends in auction bankruptcy.[7]

4.1. Direct bankruptcy costs

As shown in Panel A of Table 6, direct costs in bankruptcy auctions, excluding prepacks, average 6.4% of pre-filing assets. The median level of direct costs in bankruptcy auctions is 4.5%. Note that costs based on pre-filing book value of assets are biased downwards. However, market values of assets prior to filing are generally not available. Moreover, as presented in Panel B of Table 6, auction prepacks are relatively inexpensive. The average direct costs for auction prepacks are 2.5%, with median costs measuring 1.5%. As expected, scaling costs with market value of assets in bankruptcy, using the realized auction proceeds, produces a much higher cost estimate for bankruptcy auctions of on average 19.1%, with median 13.2%. This estimate may contain a potential upward bias if the auction produces an asset fire sales. To make the Swedish results comparable to U.S. studies, I focus in the following primarily on costs measured as a fraction of pre-filing book value of assets.

Table 7 contains ordinary least squares (OLS) estimates of the parameters in two cross-sectional regressions explaining direct bankruptcy costs in percent of pre-filing assets. I choose this scaling rather than realized auction proceeds since the latter is likely to vary with several of the explanatory variables. The regression model is defined as

$$Costs = \alpha_0 + \alpha_1 Large + \alpha_2 Medium + \alpha_3 Piecemeal + \alpha_4 Prepack$$
$$+ \alpha_5 Secured + \alpha_6 Unique + \alpha_7 Distress + \alpha_8 Length$$
$$+ \alpha_9 Industry + \varepsilon. \quad (3)$$

As before, the explanatory variables are defined in Table 4. The model contains two binary variables for firm size, one covering the one-third largest firms in the sample (Large), and the second the one-third intermediate-sized firms (Medium). In the presence of fixed bankruptcy costs, these two variables should have negative signs, thus I expect $\alpha_1 < 0$ and $\alpha_2 < 0$. The regressions further include a binary variable indicating piecemeal liquidation (Piecemeal), and, for the extended sample, an indicator for auction prepack (Prepack). Both of these outcomes are likely to incur lower direct costs than going concern sales in bankruptcy, hence Piecemeal and Prepack are predicted to enter with negative coefficients, or $\alpha_3 < 0$ and $\alpha_4 < 0$.

---

[7] The magnitude of bankruptcy costs is an important determinant of the firm's capital structure. See e.g. Miller (1977), Warner (1977), Haugen and Senbeth (1978, 1988) and Harris and Raviv (1991).

356 K.S. Thorburn / Journal of Financial Economics 58 (2000) 337–368

Table 6
Direct bankruptcy costs and time in bankruptcy for Swedish and U.S. firms, 1978–1993

Direct bankruptcy costs and time in bankruptcy for 263 private Swedish firms filing for auction bankruptcy in 1988–1991, and for public and private U.S. firms filing for Chapter 11 during 1978–1993. The information on publicly traded firms in Chapter 11 is from Weiss (1990), Gilson et al. (1990), LoPucki and Whitford (1993), Franks and Torous (1994), Hotchkiss (1995), and Betker (1997), and, on Chapter 11 prepacks, from Betker (1995) and Tashjian et al. (1996). The evidence on privately held firms in Chapter 11 is from LoPucki (1983), White (1984), Flynn (1989), and Lawless et al. (1994). The sample sizes shown for the U.S. firms are averages of the sample sizes in the studies listed above of public and private firms, respectively, and data in the table reflect sample-size weighted averages of the results from these studies. Data for the Swedish firms are from the database of UC and the bankruptcy file kept with TSM. For Swedish firms, the time in bankruptcy is measured as the time from filing to sale of the core assets as a going concern. In Sweden, prepack is a going concern sale that is negotiated prior to bankruptcy filing. For U.S. firms, prepack is a bankruptcy filing in which a reorganization plan is negotiated out-of-court.

	Swedish firms			Publicly traded U.S. firms		Privately held U.S. firms	
	Mean	Median	Standard deviation	Mean	Median	Mean	Median
Panel A: Auctions and reorganizations in bankruptcy							
Sample size	210			79		46	
Direct costs/book-value of pre-filing assets	0.064	0.045	0.057	0.036	0.031	—	—
Direct costs/market value of assets in bankruptcy	0.191	0.132	0.189	—	—	—	—
Direct costs/book-value of assets in bankruptcy	—	—	—	—	—	0.145	—
Time in bankruptcy (months)	2.4	1.5	3.4	23	19	25	22
Panel B: Prepacks							
Sample size	53			49			
Direct costs/book-value of pre-filing assets	0.025	0.015	0.027	0.024	0.020	—	—
Time in bankruptcy (months)	−2.2	−0.2	4.1	2.9	1.9	—	—

To capture the effects of market illiquidity on the trustee's level of involvement in the auction sale, the regression includes the variables Secured, Unique and Distress. The higher the fraction of tangible assets, or the higher the value of Secured, the greater its asset liquidity and the lower are expected bankruptcy costs, thus $\alpha_5 < 0$. Moreover, the higher the levels of Unique and Distress, the lower is the expected demand for the assets in the auction, which in turn is expected to lead to higher bankruptcy costs. Both Unique and Distress are therefore predicted to enter with positive coefficients, $\alpha_6 > 0$ and $\alpha_7 > 0$. The model also contains a variable, Length, measuring the number of months that the firm's corporate shell is kept on file with the court as an open bankruptcy case. The longer the case is administered in bankruptcy, the more time the trustee tends to spend on the case, thus increasing the overall costs, such that $\alpha_8 > 0$. The time the case is kept on file with the court should not be confused with the time the firm operates in bankruptcy before being auctioned off. Importantly, the Pearson correlation between the time the case is kept on file and the time between filing and going concern sale is a low 0.056 (2-tailed p-value of 0.481). I found no data available on the length of the piecemeal auctions. Finally, the probit regression includes a vector of industry dummy variables, Industry.

I also examined an alternative model specification which includes the dummy variable Repurchase, indicating whether or not the old owner repurchases the firm in the auction. While not reported in Table 7, this variable produces an insignificant coefficient. This result is inconsistent with the conjecture that the trustee sells the assets back to the old owner to reduce the trustee's own sales effort.

The second column of Table 7 reports the coefficient estimates from a regression using a subsample of 171 in-bankruptcy auctions, excluding auction prepacks. The regression is significant with an adjusted R^2 of 25.5%. As indicated by the negative coefficients for the dummy variables capturing size of firm, α_1 and α_2, direct bankruptcy costs have significant fixed components. The constant term produced in the model is 6.7% for the one-third smallest firms in the sample, and decreases by 3.7% for intermediate-sized firms and 6.1% for the one-third largest firms.[8] Consistently, the unconditional direct costs for the one-third largest firms in my sample, excluding prepacks, are on average 3.7% of pre-filing assets, with median costs measuring 2.5% of the pre-filing assets. Measured in percent of market value of assets in bankruptcy, the direct costs for the one-third largest firms are on average 14.4%, with a median of 9.7%.

The indicator of a piecemeal sale also produces a negative and significant coefficient, α_3, suggesting that piecemeal liquidations have lower direct costs than going concern sales, as expected. Interestingly, the regressions in Table 7 imply that bankruptcy costs are increasing in the degree of industry distress, possibly because the bankruptcy trustee must increase sales efforts to find a high-valuation bidder in distressed industries. Moreover, the coefficient for Length, α_8, is positive and significant, suggesting that the direct costs increase with the time that the case is administered in bankruptcy. This result may raise

[8] Direct bankruptcy costs in dollar terms are found to be concave also in the U.S., see, e.g., Warner (1977), Ang et al. (1982) and Betker (1997).

Table 7
Comparison of direct bankruptcy costs, Swedish firms, 1988–1991

OLS coefficient estimates in regressions of direct bankruptcy costs for 213 Swedish firms filing for auction bankruptcy in 1988–1991. Direct costs are the administrative, advisory and legal fees incurred in bankruptcy, in percent of the book value of total assets, as reported in the last financial statement prior to filing. The first regression uses a sample of in-bankruptcy going concern sales and piecemeal liquidations, while the second regression also comprises auction prepacks, which are going concern sales that are negotiated prior to bankruptcy filing. Industry indicators were included for manufacturing, construction, wholesale and retail, hotels and restaurants, and transportation. See Table 4 for variable definitions.

Sample criteria:	Sample of in-bankruptcy auctions			Sample of all filings		
	Expected sign of coefficient	Coefficient	p-value	Expected sign of coefficient	Coefficient	p-value
Constant	> 0	0.067	0.001	> 0	0.077	0.000
Explanatory variables:						
Large	< 0	− 0.061	0.000	< 0	− 0.055	0.000
Medium	< 0	− 0.037	0.000	< 0	− 0.034	0.000
Piecemeal	< 0	− 0.019	0.021	< 0	− 0.017	0.025
Prepack	—	—	—	< 0	− 0.035	0.000
Secured	< 0	− 0.003	0.880	< 0	− 0.006	0.689
Unique	> 0	0.003	0.542	> 0	0.005	0.356
Distress	> 0	0.059	0.026	> 0	0.042	0.054
Length	> 0	0.001	0.029	> 0	0.001	0.092
Industry indicators with p-values less than 0.10:						
None	—	—	—	—	—	—
Sample size		171			213	
R^2 adjusted		0.255			0.277	
F-value		5.85	0.000		7.24	0.000

the issue of whether the cost estimates presented in this paper are biased, since the sample selection procedure eliminates 145 open bankruptcy cases (see Section 2.2). However, within the sample, the unconditional Pearson correlation between the percentage direct costs and time on file is a low 0.073, producing a 2-tailed p-value of 0.274, providing no support for the existence of such bias in the cost estimates. Furthermore, there is no evidence that the measures for asset type and uniqueness affect direct costs.

Column 5 of Table 7 reports the coefficient estimates based on a sample of 213 firms that also includes 42 auction prepacks. The regression is again significant, and the coefficient estimates are generally consistent with the above results for the subsample of auctions in bankruptcy. The direct costs decrease with firm size and increase with industry distress and the length of the bankruptcy case, with no detectable impact of the proportion tangible assets and the degree to which assets are unique to the industry. As expected given the results in Table 6, the coefficient for Prepack, α_4, is negative and significant. The one-third largest Swedish firms undertaking auction prepacks have unconditional average direct costs of 1.9% of pre-bankruptcy assets, with median costs of 1.3%.

For comparison purposes, Table 6 also contains extant evidence on costs for much larger, publicly traded firms reorganizing in Chapter 11. The direct costs for Chapter 11 cases, in percent of book value of pre-filing assets, is estimated at 3.6%, with median direct costs measuring 3.1%. These calculations represent a sample-size weighted average of the cost estimates in Weiss (1990) and Betker (1997).[9] This average cost estimate corresponds closely to the 3.7% average costs reported for the one-third largest cases in my auction bankruptcy sample. Moreover, for a sample of 22 privately held small firms in Chapter 11, Lawless et al. (1994) report average direct costs, measured as a fraction of book value of assets in bankruptcy, of 14.5%. In light of the fixed cost components, the statistics indicate that the auction procedure may provide a relatively low-cost mechanism for restructuring firms in bankruptcy. Hansen and Thomas (1998) argue that a conservative estimate of total direct costs for auctioning off large firms in bankruptcy is 2% of assets.

As in Sweden, prepacks in the U.S. incur lower direct costs than traditional bankruptcy cases. Panel B of Table 6 shows direct costs for prepackaged Chapter 11 filings by publicly traded firms, averaged across the samples in Betker (1995) and Tashjian et al. (1996). The direct costs for Chapter 11 prepacks, measured as a fraction of pre-filing assets, are on average 2.4%, with median costs of 2.0%. This measure is somewhat higher than the direct costs reported for the one-third largest firms executing auction prepacks, which have a mean of 1.9%. Note, however, that the U.S. estimates include costs incurred prior to bankruptcy, while the Swedish estimate does not include pre-filing costs. Overall, prepackaged filings are relatively low-cost options under either bankruptcy system.

4.2. Time in bankruptcy

Table 7 and the above comparison with the costs of Chapter 11 proceedings leave out one important fundamental, namely the total time firms operate under bankruptcy protection. Indirect costs, in terms of the opportunity cost of managerial time and negative reputational effects in product and capital markets, increase with the time the firm spends in bankruptcy. For firms sold as going concern in an in-bankruptcy auction, excluding prepacks, the average

[9] The results of Warner (1977), Ang et al. (1982), and Altman (1984) are not reported here, since they study firms filing for bankruptcy prior to the 1978 enactment of Chapter 11.

time from filing to the date the assets are sold is 2.4 months, with a median of 1.5 months. Panel A of Table 6 displays these results. Moreover, only one of the 142 firms surviving the bankruptcy auction as going concerns was operating for more than one year in bankruptcy before a buyer was found. Not surprisingly, auction prepack procedures are much shorter than the typical auction bankruptcy case (Panel B of Table 6). Auction prepacks are executed a median of four days before filing for bankruptcy, and incur no further delay due to filing. Because of two outliers which represent prepacks executed very early, the average prepack is executed 2.2 months prior to filing.

The time spent in auction bankruptcy is significantly lower than the average length of a Chapter 11 proceeding. For the 2,395 small firm cases in Flynn (1989), the average time in bankruptcy is reported to be 25 months, with a median of 22 months. Jensen-Conklin (1992) reports 22 months for her sample of 45 small-firm Chapter 11 cases, while, in the sample of 20 small firms studied by LoPucki (1983), the court confirms the reorganization plan on average 10 months after filing. The average time in Chapter 11 appears to be similar for large publicly traded and small privately held firms (see, e.g., Gilson et al., 1990; Weiss, 1990; Franks and Torous, 1994; Betker, 1997; Hotchkiss, 1995). Prepackaged Chapter 11 filings are also less time-consuming than the traditional Chapter 11 proceeding. Betker (1995) and Tashjian et al. (1996) find that the average Chapter 11 prepack for publicly traded firms lasts three months, with a median of two months, from filing until the plan is confirmed by court. Moreover, it takes on average 17 months for a Chapter 11 prepack to be set up prior to filing. Thus, there are strong indications that large firm Chapter 11 prepacks require more time than the typical small firm auction bankruptcy case in Sweden.

5. Debt recovery rates

A creditor's expected payoff in bankruptcy affects his or her incentives to renegotiate debt outside of formal bankruptcy proceedings. Moreover, debt recovery rates provide important information on the economic value of firms filing for bankruptcy as well as indirect and direct costs imposed by the bankruptcy proceeding itself. This section examines creditors' recovery rates in Swedish auction bankruptcy cases.

Panel A of Table 8 presents recovery rates, measured as the proportion of the debt's face value repaid in bankruptcy, excluding prepacks. Importantly, recovery rates in my sample are based entirely on market values since the cash settlement in the auction permits a cash distribution to creditors. The overall recovery rate for Swedish firms, averaged across both secured and unsecured debt, is 35%, with median of 34%. Focusing on the different classes of debt, secured creditors receive on average 69%, or median 83%, of the face value of

Table 8
Debt recovery rates for Swedish and U.S. firms filing for bankruptcy, 1985–1993

Debt recovery rates for 263 private Swedish firms filing for auction bankruptcy in 1988–1991, and for publicly traded U.S. firms filing for Chapter 11 in 1985–1993. Debt recovery rate is defined as the payment to a class of debtholders, measured as a fraction of the face value of claims held by that debt class. The information on firms in traditional Chapter 11 proceedings is from Franks and Torous (1994). The evidence on Chapter 11 prepacks is from Tashjian et al. (1996). Data on the Swedish firms are from the database of UC and the bankruptcy file kept with TSM. The subsample of Swedish going concern sales shown in Panel C comprises 142 firms that were auctioned as going concerns in bankruptcy. The subsample of U.S. firms shown in Panel C consists of 12 firms that completed their Chapter 11 restructuring in 1985–1990, and for which market values were available for all claims distributed in the reorganization. For Swedish firms, auction prepack is a going concern sale that is negotiated prior to bankruptcy filing. For U.S. firms, prepack is a Chapter 11 filing in which a reorganization plan is negotiated out-of-court.

	Swedish firms			Publicly traded U.S. firms		
	Market values			Face values		Market values
	Mean	Median	Standard deviation	Mean	Median	Median
Panel A: In-bankruptcy auctions						
Sample size	210					
All debt classes	0.35	0.34	0.21	—	—	—
Secured debt	0.69	0.83	0.33	—	—	—
Priority claims	0.27	0.19	0.28	—	—	—
Junior debt	0.02	0.00	0.11	—	—	—
Panel B: Piecemeal liquidations						
Sample size	63					
All debt classes	0.27	0.25	0.24	—	—	—
Secured debt	0.50	0.45	0.36	—	—	—
Priority claims	0.21	0.14	0.26	—	—	—
Junior debt	0.02	0.00	0.12	—	—	—
Panel C: Going concern sales and successful reorganizations						
Sample size	142				38	12
All debt classes	0.39	0.38	0.19	—	0.51	0.41
Secured debt	0.77	0.87	0.28	—	0.80	—
Priority claims	0.30	0.20	0.29	—	—	—
Senior debt	—	—	—	—	0.47	—
Junior debt	0.02	0.00	0.11	—	0.29	—
Panel D: Prepacks						
Sample size	53			49		
All debt classes	0.32	0.31	0.22	0.73	—	—
Secured debt	0.74	0.89	0.32	0.99	—	—
Priority claims	0.26	0.19	0.28	—	—	—
Senior debt	—	—	—	1.00	—	—
Junior debt	0.01	0.00	0.07	0.64	—	—

their debt, and priority claims receive on average 27%, with a median of 19%. Unsecured creditors, however, on average recovers only 2%, with median value of zero, reflecting the strict adherence to APR in auction bankruptcy.

The distributions to creditors are significantly lower in auctions where the firm is closed down and its assets sold piecemeal. As shown in Panel B, the overall recovery rate for the subsample of 63 firms that were liquidated piecemeal is on average 27%, with a median of 25%. Also, secured creditors recover less money in these auction cases, with an average payback of 50%, with a median of 45%.

All claimholders seem to recover a higher proportion when the auction preserves the firm as a going concern. Panel C of Table 8 reports recovery rates for the subsample of 142 firms auctioned in bankruptcy as going concerns. The average overall recovery rate is 39%, with median 38%, such that secured debtholders receive an average of 77%, median 87%, and junior unsecured creditors 2%, median 0%. For a subsample of 58 firms auctioned as going concerns prior to the economic downturn in 1991, the overall recovery rate averages 40%, with median 40%.

Moreover, Panel D of Table 8 shows recovery rates for the 53 auction prepacks. The overall recovery rate in Swedish prepacks is slightly lower than that reported above for auctions in bankruptcy, with a mean of 32% and median of 31%. Secured creditors receive on average 74%, median 89%, while junior creditors again receive basically nothing.

Table 9 reports OLS estimates of coefficients in two regressions with total recovery rates and recovery rates for secured debt as dependent variables. The sample includes 168 observations of the first type, and 162 observations of the second type. The regression model has the following specification:

$$\begin{aligned} Recovery = {} & \alpha_0 + \alpha_1 Profmarg + \alpha_2 Secured + \alpha_3 Creditor + \alpha_4 Piecemeal \\ & + \alpha_5 Prepack + \alpha_6 Size + \alpha_7 Unique + \alpha_8 Distress \\ & + \alpha_9 Filing91 + \alpha_{10} Repurchase + \alpha_{11} Bank \\ & + \alpha_{12} Industry + \varepsilon. \end{aligned} \tag{4}$$

Firms with a high pre-filing cash flow performance, captured by Profmarg, are likely to have a higher going concern value, thus I predict $\alpha_1 > 0$. Because the value of intangible assets may get dissipated in the bankruptcy auction, recovery rates are expected to increase in Secured, such that $\alpha_2 > 0$. Moreover, to the extent creditor filing implies lower firm quality, the variable Creditor will produce a negative coefficient, or $\alpha_3 < 0$. Debtholders are further expected to recover less in piecemeal liquidations, Piecemeal, reflecting loss of going concern value, or $\alpha_4 < 0$. Debt recovery is also assumed to decrease with firm size, the fraction industry unique assets and industry distress.

Sweden experienced an economy-wide downturn in 1991, which led to a general decline in asset prices in the later years of the sample period. To account for the effects of this recession, the regression includes a binary variable indicating that the firm filed for bankruptcy in 1991, Filing91, which is expected to have a negative impact on recovery rates, thus $\alpha_9 < 0$. The model further contains a binary variable for the case that the pre-filing owner buys back the assets of the firm, Repurchase. In 54% of the going concern sales, the old owner wins the auction and repurchases the firm. If owners tend to repurchase the firm when they have private information that it is of relatively high quality, Repurchase should enter with a positive coefficient, or $\alpha_{10} > 0$. Similarly, the financing of the successful buyer in the auction by the filing firm's bank, represented by Bank, is expected to be associated with higher recovery rates, thus $\alpha_{11} > 0$. The model also controls for auction prepacks and industry characteristics, described by the vector Industry.

The regressions reported in Table 9 are significant, with adjusted R^2 of 12.2% and 22.1%, respectively, and several of the sign predictions are borne out. Recovery rates are increasing in the proportion of secured debt in the firm's capital structure, possibly reflecting a lower liquidity for intangible assets. As expected, the coefficient for bankruptcy filings in 1991, α_9, is negative and significant, indicating generally lower auction prices during the period of economic recession. Moreover, consistent with Table 8, the estimated coefficient for piecemeal sales, α_4, is negative, suggesting that recovery rates tend to be lower in piecemeal liquidations than in going concern sales, which do not enter with a separate dummy in the regression, while α_5 for auction prepacks is insignificant.

Recovery rates are higher when the old bank refinances the buyer in the auction, yielding $\alpha_{11} > 0$. Furthermore, the coefficient for a repurchase of the firm, α_{10}, is positive in the second regression, indicating that secured creditors, usually banks, on average recover more when the original owner buys back the firm. This occurrence may simply reflect the on average somewhat lower proportion of secured debt in these cases. Contrary to expectations, there is little evidence that recovery rates depend on pre-filing operating profitability, creditor filing, industry distress, or asset uniqueness. Also, Size produces a statistically insignificant coefficient, α_6, failing to indicate any systematic variation in recovery rates with firm size.

Before turning to the U.S. evidence, a caveat on measurement issues. In a Chapter 11 reorganization, the claims on the bankrupt firm are settled mainly with new financial securities, as opposed to cash. In the average Chapter 11 reorganization studied by Franks and Torous (1994), 71% of creditors' total payments are received in the form of new financial securities, and 29% in cash. Recovery rates reported for Chapter 11 are therefore based largely on the face value of non-traded claims. In light of the significant default rates following Chapter 11 shown by Hotchkiss (1995), the face value of debt significantly overstates its market value. Consistent with this, Eberhart et al. (1990) report a value-weighted ratio of market-to-face value of 80% for debt claims distributed in Chapter 11 to the creditors of Wickes Companies.

Table 9
Comparison of debt recovery rates, Swedish firms, 1988–1991

OLS estimates of coefficients in regressions of debt recovery rates. Sample of 168 firms filing for Swedish auction bankruptcy in 1988–1991. In the first regression, the independent variable is the overall debt recovery rate for the firm, and in the second regression the independent variable is the recovery rate for secured debtholders. Debt recovery rate is the payment in bankruptcy to a class of debtholders divided by the face value of claims held by that debt class. Industry indicators were included for manufacturing, construction, wholesale and retail, hotels and restaurants and transportation. See Table 4 for a definition of the variables.

	Overall recovery rate			Recovery rate for secured debt		
	Expected sign of coefficient	Coefficient	p-value	Expected sign of coefficient	Coefficient	p-value
Constant		0.498	0.087		1.185	0.005
Explanatory variables:						
Profmarg	> 0	– 0.107	0.322	> 0	– 0.224	0.146
Secured	> 0	0.301	0.001	—	—	—
Creditor	< 0	– 0.059	0.306	< 0	– 0.128	0.138
Piecemeal	< 0	– 0.094	0.042	< 0	– 0.110	0.098
Prepack	> 0	– 0.026	0.569	> 0	– 0.034	0.609
Size	< 0	– 0.008	0.644	< 0	– 0.022	0.376
Unique	< 0	– 0.003	0.901	< 0	0.018	0.595
Distress	< 0	– 0.112	0.480	< 0	– 0.351	0.130
Filing91	< 0	– 0.099	0.035	< 0	– 0.138	0.045
Repurchase	> 0	0.016	0.706	> 0	0.114	0.060
Bank	> 0	0.070	0.087	> 0	0.195	0.001
Industry indicators with p-values less than 0.10:						
None	—	—	—		—	—
Sample size		168			162	
R^2 adjusted		0.122			0.221	
F-value		2.46	0.001		4.05	0.000

Only one existing study reports recovery rates for Chapter 11 cases entirely based on market values. Franks and Torous (1994) provide market-value based estimates of recovery rates for a subsample of 12 publicly traded firms that successfully completed their Chapter 11 reorganization, as shown in Panel C of Table 8. They find a median overall recovery rate of 41%, which compares to the 39% recovery rate for Swedish firms auctioned as going concerns. For the full sample of 38 Chapter 11 cases, Franks and Torous (1994) report a median overall recovery rate of 51%, based largely on face values. If the firms in their two samples have similar economic values and default probabilities, the difference in recovery rates provides further indirect evidence that face values overstate market values. Moreover, for the latter sample, Franks and Torous report a median recovery of 80% for secured debtholders and 29% for junior debt. The substantial payment promised to junior debtholders in Chapter 11 represents a deviation from APR.[10] In contrast, as pointed out earlier, the cash payment in the auction ensures that claims are settled according to absolute priority, an arguably attractive feature of auction bankruptcy. Jensen (1991) claims that the observed deviations from APR under the U.S. Chapter 11 generate large inefficiencies by increasing firms' cost of capital. Others, however, have argued that ex post deviations from APR are potentially beneficial in terms of reducing underinvestment inefficiencies as well as the time spent in bankruptcy reorganization (see, e.g., Franks and Torous, 1989; Weiss, 1990).

While recovery rates are similar across auction prepacks and in-bankruptcy auctions, debtholders seem to recover substantially more in prepackaged than in traditional Chapter 11 filings. Tashjian et al. (1996) report that creditors of publicly traded firms filing Chapter 11 prepacks recover on average 73% of the face value of their debt claims. Moreover, the mean recovery rate of secured creditors is a high 99%, and for unsecured creditors it is 64%. While not explored here, this difference between the Swedish and the U.S. evidence possibly reflects the different selection processes behind prepacks under the two bankruptcy systems alluded to in Section 3.1, above.

6. Conclusions

There is an international trend away from pure auction bankruptcy systems towards Chapter 11 style reorganization codes. During the last 20 years, several European countries, including the U.K., Germany, France, Finland, Norway, and Sweden, have changed or are proposing changes to, their bankruptcy regulation, much in the direction of the U.S. Chapter 11. This trend takes place despite a largely unresolved empirical debate as to the relative efficiency of bankruptcy auctions. In this study, I examine 263 small firms filing for auction bankruptcy in Sweden over the period 1988–1991, and make systematic comparisons to extant evidence on U.S. Chapter 11 cases. However, while U.S. firms may choose a court-supervised reorganization under Chapter 11, no such provisions effectively exist in Sweden, where the bankruptcy code is an auction procedure. Thus, every Swedish firm filing for bankruptcy is subsequently auctioned off, either as a going concern or piecemeal, under the supervision of an independent, court-appointed trustee.

The analysis yields several interesting results. First, three-quarters of firms survive the bankruptcy auction as going concerns. This survival rate is similar to

[10] See, e.g., Franks and Torous (1989), Eberhart et al. (1990) and Weiss (1990).

the survival rates observed for U.S. Chapter 11 filings for small and large firms. Moreover, in Sweden, one-quarter of the going concern sales, comprising 20% of all filings, are auction prepacks, in which the buyer negotiates the purchase of the firm's assets prior to filing for bankruptcy. The probability of a going concern sale increases with the fraction of intangible assets. Interestingly, auction prepacks are more likely to occur when the firm is run by an owner-manager, perhaps reflecting managerial concerns with post-bankruptcy reputation.

Second, direct bankruptcy costs are found to decrease with firm size, and to be lower in piecemeal liquidations and auction prepacks. The percentage costs, measured as a fraction of pre-filing assets, average 6.4% for the total sample and 3.7% for the one-third largest firms. The latter estimate is similar to costs reported for much larger publicly traded U.S. firms in Chapter 11. Direct costs are also increasing in industry distress, possibly reflecting a higher sales effort by the trustee when industry demand is low. Importantly, indirect costs are almost certainly lower under auction bankruptcy, due to the significantly shorter time firms operate in bankruptcy. This period can last from 1 to 2 months in Sweden, and can extend to approximately two years in the U.S.

Third, debtholders recover on average 35% of their debt in auction bankruptcy. Secured creditors recover approximately 70% on average, with median amount of 80%, while junior unsecured creditors recover almost nothing. Using market values, and avoiding a potential upward bias in face values, overall debt recovery rates seem to be similar across small firms in auction bankruptcy and publicly traded firms filing for Chapter 11. For firms surviving as going concerns under both set of circumstances, the average recovery rate is approximately 40%. However, junior creditors receive a relatively smaller piece of the pie in auction bankruptcy, reflecting the strict adherence to absolute priority made possible by the cash settlement in the auction.

Easterbrook (1990) suggests that if auctions are more efficient than court supervised debt reorganizations, one should observe firms being sold under Chapter 11 proceedings. In fact, the 1980s saw the emergence of an active market for claims of firms in Chapter 11. During the last decade, vulture funds specializing on claims of distressed firms have taken significant positions in most of the large Chapter 11 cases.[11] Moreover, Hotchkiss and Mooradian (1998) find positive abnormal stock returns on acquisition announcements for both target firms in Chapter 11 and bidders, signaling a positive market reaction to the ending of the Chapter 11 proceeding. The emergence of vulture funds as well as other out-of-court solutions such as prepacks and public debt exchanges is further evidence that market transactions, such as auctions, often dominate court supervised reorganizations in the U.S. environment.

[11] See, e.g., Lieb (1993), and Hotchkiss and Mooradian (1997).

The results in this paper suggest that auction bankruptcy is a speedy, low cost procedure compared to reorganizations under the U.S. Chapter 11. Moreover, firm survival rates, debt recovery rates, and pre-filing financial characteristics are comparable across the two systems. Overall, the evidence indicates that auction bankruptcy in fact provides an efficient mechanism for restructuring small firms.

References

Aghion, P., Hart, O., Moore, J., 1994. The economics of bankruptcy reform. Journal of Law, Economics and Organization 8, 523–546.

Altman, E., 1984. A further empirical investigation of the bankruptcy cost question. Journal of Finance 39, 1067–1089.

Altman, E., 1993. Corporate Financial Distress and Bankruptcy. Wiley, New York.

Ang, J., Chua, J., McConnell, J., 1982. The administrative costs of corporate bankruptcy: a note. Journal of Finance 37, 219–226.

Baird, D., 1986. The uneasy case for corporate reorganizations. Journal of Legal Studies 15, 127–147.

Bebchuk, L., 1988. A new approach to corporate reorganizations. Harvard Law Review 101, 775–804.

Berkovitch, E., Israel, R., 1995. The bankruptcy decision and debt contract renegotiation. Unpublished working paper, University of Michigan, Ann Arbor, MI.

Betker, B., 1995. An empirical examination of prepackaged bankruptcy. Financial Management 24, 3–18.

Betker, B., 1997. The administrative costs of debt restructurings: some recent evidence. Financial Management 26, 56–68.

Bradley, M., Rosenzweig, M., 1992. The untenable case for Chapter 11. Yale Law Journal 101, 1043–1095.

Easterbrook, F., 1990. Is corporate bankruptcy efficient? Journal of Financial Economics 27, 411–418.

Eberhart, A., Moore, W., Roenfeldt, R., 1990. Security pricing and deviations from the absolute priority rule in bankruptcy proceedings. Journal of Finance 45, 1457–1469.

Eckbo, E., Thorburn, K., 2000a. Toeholds and fire-sales in bankruptcy auctions. Unpublished working paper, Dartmouth College, Hanover, NH.

Eckbo, E., Thorburn, K., 2000b. The resolution of financial distress in a cash auction bankruptcy environment. Unpublished mimeo, Dartmouth College, Hanover, NH.

Flynn, E., 1989. Statistical analyses of Chapter 11. Unpublished study. Administrative Office of the U.S. Courts, Washington, DC.

Franks, J., Nyborg, K., Torous, W., 1996. A comparison of US, UK and German insolvency codes. Financial Management 25, 86–101.

Franks, J., Torous, W., 1989. An empirical investigation of U.S. firms in reorganization. Journal of Finance 44, 747–770.

Franks, J., Torous, W., 1994. A comparison of financial recontracting in distressed exchanges and Chapter 11 reorganizations. Journal of Financial Economics 35, 349–370.

Gilson, S., John, K., Lang, L., 1990. Troubled debt restructurings: an empirical study of private reorganization of firms in default. Journal of Financial Economics 27, 315–353.

Hansen, R., Thomas, R., 1998. Auctions in bankruptcy: theoretical analysis and practical guidance. International Review of Law and Economics 18, 159–185.

Harris, M., Raviv, A., 1991. The theory of capital structure. Journal of Finance 46, 297–355.

Haugen, R., Senbeth, L., 1978. The insignificance of bankruptcy costs to the theory of optimal capital structure. Journal of Finance 33, 383–393.

Haugen, R., Senbeth, L., 1988. Bankruptcy and agency costs: their significance to the theory of optimal capital structure. Journal of Financial and Quantitative Analysis 23, 27–38.

Hotchkiss, E., 1995. Post-bankruptcy performance and management turnover. Journal of Finance 50, 3–21.

Hotchkiss, E., Mooradian, R., 1997. Vulture investors and the market for control of distressed firms. Journal of Financial Economics 43, 401–432.

Hotchkiss, E., Mooradian, R., 1998. Acquisitions as a means of restructuring firms in Chapter 11. Journal of Financial Intermediation 7, 240–262.

Jensen, M., 1989. Active investors, LBOs, and the privatization of bankruptcy. Journal of Applied Corporate Finance 2, 35–44.

Jensen, M., 1991. Corporate control and the politics of finance. Journal of Applied Corporate Finance 4, 13–33.

Jensen-Conklin, S., 1992. Do confirmed Chapter 11 plans consummate? the results of a study and analysis of the law. Commercial Law Journal 97, 297–331.

Lawless, R., Ferris, S., Jayaraman, N., Makhija, A., 1994. A glimpse at professional fees and other direct costs in small firm bankruptcies. University of Illinois Law Review 4, 847–888.

Lieb, R., 1993. Vultures beware: risks of purchasing claims against a Chapter 11 debtor. The Business Lawyer 48, 915–941.

LoPucki, L., 1983. The debtor in full control – systems failure under Chapter 11 of the bankruptcy code? American Bankruptcy Law Journal 57, 99–126 and 247–273.

LoPucki, L., Whitford, W., 1993. Patterns in the bankruptcy reorganization of large, publicly held companies. Cornell Law Review 78, 597–618.

Miller, M., 1977. Debt and taxes. Journal of Finance 32, 261–275.

Pulvino, T., 1998. Do asset fire-sales exist? an empirical investigation of commercial aircraft transactions. Journal of Finance 53, 939–978.

Ravid, A., Sundgren, S., 1998. The comparative efficiency of small-firm bankruptcies: a study of the U.S. and Finnish bankruptcy codes. Financial Management 27, 28–40.

Roe, M., 1983. Bankruptcy and debt: a new model for corporate reorganization. Columbia Law Review 83, 527–602.

Shleifer, A., Vishny, R., 1992. Liquidation values and debt capacity: a market equilibrium approach. Journal of Finance 47, 1343–1366.

Strömberg, P., 2000. Conflicts of interest and market illiquidity in bankruptcy auctions: theory and tests. Journal of Finance, forthcoming.

Strömberg, P., Thorburn, K., 1996. An empirical investigation of Swedish corporations in liquidation bankruptcy. EFI Research Report, Stockholm School of Economics, Sweden.

Thorburn, K., 2000. Auction bankruptcy and the CEO. Unpublished working paper, Dartmouth College, Hanover, NH.

Tashjian, E., Lease, R., McConnell, J., 1996. An empirical analysis of prepackaged bankruptcies. Journal of Financial Economics 40, 135–162.

Warner, J., 1977. Bankruptcy costs: some evidence. Journal of Finance 32, 337–347.

Weiss, L., 1990. Bankruptcy resolution: direct costs and violation of priority of claims. Journal of Financial Economics 27, 285–314.

White, M., 1984. Bankruptcy liquidation and reorganization. In: Logue, D., Seward, J. (Eds.), Handbook of Modern Finance. Warren, Gorham & Lamont, Boston, pp. E7-1–E7-44.

White, M., 1996. The costs of corporate bankruptcy: a U.S. – European comparison. In: Bhandari, J., Weiss, L. (Eds.), Corporate Bankruptcy: Economic and Legal Perspectives. Cambridge University Press, England, pp. 467–500.

[19]

ELSEVIER Journal of Financial Economics 52 (1999) 151–186

JOURNAL OF Financial ECONOMICS

Effects of bankruptcy court protection on asset sales☆

Todd C. Pulvino*

Kellogg Graduate School of Management, Northwestern University, Evanston, IL 60208, USA

Received 2 January 1997; received in revised form 27 March 1998; accepted 1 January 1999

Abstract

This paper uses commercial aircraft transactions to determine whether prices obtained from asset sales are greater under Chapter 11 reorganization than under Chapter 7 liquidation. Results indicate that prices obtained under both bankruptcy regimes are substantially lower than prices obtained by non-distressed airlines. Furthermore, there is no evidence that prices obtained by firms reorganizing under Chapter 11 are greater than those obtained by firms liquidating under Chapter 7. An analysis of aircraft sales indicates that Chapter 11 is also ineffective in limiting the number of aircraft sold at discounted prices. © 1999 Elsevier Science S.A. All rights reserved.

JEL classification: G33

Keywords: Bankruptcy; Asset sales

1. Introduction

When a firm files for protection under Chapter 11 of the U.S. Bankruptcy Code, an automatic stay is imposed on creditors. Payments to creditors and

* Corresponding author. Tel.: 847-491-8337; fax: 847-491-5719.

E-mail address: tpulvino@nwu.edu (T.C. Pulvino)

☆I am grateful to George Baker, Ben Branch, Charles Calomiris, Miguel Cantillo, Richard Caves, Ken Froot, Bill Schwert (the editor), Andrei Shleifer and Jerry Warner (referee) for helpful comments. I would also like to thank Chris Allen for helping with data collection. Financial support from the Harvard Business School Division of Research is gratefully acknowledged.

PII: S0304-405X(99)00007-0

suppliers are suspended until management generates, and creditors approve, a plan of reorganization. This removes much of the pressure to meet principal and interest payments with cash raised via quick liquidation of assets.

Whether the reduction in the pressure to liquidate provided by the automatic stay is desirable has been the subject of debate by both policymakers and academicians. On one side of the debate are those who argue that the current U.S. reorganization law (Chapter 11) fails to provide adequate incentives for managers to sell assets to higher-value users (Bradley and Rosenzweig, 1992; Wruck, 1990). According to this view, distressed firms' managers faced with the prospect of unemployment have strong incentives to keep their firms operating, whether profitably or not. The complex bargaining process fostered by the current reorganization law creates severe hold-up problems and allows incumbent managers to avoid liquidation, even if liquidation would maximize firm value. Consequently, in addition to direct bankruptcy costs, reorganization (rather than liquidation via Chapter 7) often results in gross investment inefficiencies and substantial wealth transfers from creditors to managers and equityholders (Warner, 1977; Altman, 1984; Weiss, 1990; Wruck, 1990; Weiss and Wruck, 1998; Betker, 1995; Altman, 1993; Franks and Torous, 1994). Some authors argue that immediate cash liquidation of insolvent firms' assets would result in a superior allocation of resources compared to the allocation obtained by allowing managers to choose the lengthy and potentially costly option of reorganization (Baird, 1986; Thorburn, 1997).

On the other side of the debate are those who argue that forced liquidation of insolvent firms' assets would result in an inefficient allocation of resources. They point out that forced liquidation can result in the dismantling of economically viable firms. Furthermore, they argue that in the presence of capital market imperfections, assets will not necessarily be allocated to the highest-value users. This will be particularly true when forces that caused the insolvent firm's distress also affect others in the industry. In this case, direct competitors might not be able to pay fundamental value for the insolvent firm's assets. Assets will then be allocated to firms outside the industry who, if the assets are industry specific, are lower-value users. Not only will this result in a socially inefficient allocation of resources, but it can also fail to maximize the amount of cash available for distribution to the insolvent firm's creditors (Shleifer and Vishny, 1992; Aghion et al., 1992). Evidence from commercial aircraft transactions presented in Pulvino (1998) supports these concerns. Outside of bankruptcy, financially distressed airlines receive lower prices when selling assets; they are also more likely to sell to firms outside the industry. Brown (1997) and Strömberg (1998) provide additional evidence that liquidation is costly for distressed firms that have industry specific assets. Conversely, Thorburn (1997) finds no evidence that distressed firms liquidate assets at discounted prices. However, her analysis does not focus on industries with industry specific assets.

This paper makes further use of data on commercial aircraft sales by U.S. airlines to assess the effects of both Chapters 11 and 7 protection on asset sale revenues. Asset sale revenues can be affected by bankruptcy court protection by (1) increasing prices at which assets are sold and (2) reducing the quantity of assets sold at distress-sale discounts. This paper examines both of these effects.

The advantage of using aircraft transactions to assess the effect of bankruptcy court protection on asset sale revenues is that transaction data are readily available. Prior to 1992, prices at which U.S. airlines sold their aircraft had to be disclosed to the Department of Transportation. Thus, both prices and quantities of sales are available. Another advantage of using aircraft transactions is that bankruptcy is common in the U.S. airline industry. Analyses presented in this paper are based on nine bankruptcy filings by major U.S. airlines between 1978 and 1992: Air Florida (July 1984), America West (June 1991), Braniff (May 1982), Continental (September 1983), Continental (December 1990), Eastern (March 1989), Midway (March 1991), Pan Am (January 1991), and TWA (January 1992).

Analyses of transaction prices suggest that prices obtained by airlines reorganizing under Chapter 11 are not significantly higher than those obtained by airlines liquidating under Chapter 7. Bankrupt carriers, whether operating under Chapter 11 or liquidating under Chapter 7, sell assets at discounts that average between 14% and 46%. Because aircraft account for a large portion of airlines' total assets, the dollar magnitude of this discount can be substantial. For example, net flight equipment (flight equipment less depreciation) accounted for more than $700 million of Braniff Airlines' $1 billion in pre-bankruptcy assets. An average discount of only 15% would have reduced the amount available for distribution to creditors by more than $100 million. Moreover, because airplanes are among airlines' most liquid assets, these discounts are likely to underestimate the average discount associated with a complete liquidation of an airline's assets.

Regardless of bankruptcy venue (i.e., Chapter 7 or Chapter 11), prices that bankrupt airlines receive for their used aircraft are generally lower than prices received by distressed but nonbankrupt firms. For example, distressed but nonbankrupt airlines sell aircraft at discounts ranging from 12% to 28%. The magnitude of this discount increases as the rate of aircraft sales increases. Consistent with the literature on the price impact of large-block stock transactions, evidence presented in this paper and in Pulvino (1998) suggests that the price decreases by 1.5% for each additional aircraft sold in the calendar quarter.[1] Because it is not uncommon for distressed firms to

[1] In stock transactions, the large-block discount is usually associated with asymmetric information. However, information asymmetries are not likely to be severe for used aircraft transactions. Liquidity costs have also been suggested as an explanation for price declines around large-block trades; this explanation is likely to be more applicable to used aircraft. Effects of large-block transactions are discussed in Holthausen et al. (1987,1990), Chan and Lakonishok (1993,1995), Mikkelson and Partch (1985), and Kraus and Stoll (1972).

sell 10 or more aircraft per quarter, this incremental discount can be substantial. However, once bankruptcy court protection is obtained, the sensitivity of the price discount to the number of sales disappears in that bankrupt airlines sell aircraft at substantial discounts regardless of the number of aircraft being sold.

There are at least two reasons that bankrupt airlines receive lower prices for their aircraft than distressed but non-bankrupt carriers. First, bankruptcy status attracts 'low-ball' bids from opportunistic buyers. Second, the structure of the bankruptcy law encourages managers to accept these low bids. For 120 days after filing for Chapter 11, incumbent management has the exclusive right to propose a reorganization plan. Acceptance of the plan requires approval by each *impaired* creditor class (including shareholders) or a decision by the bankruptcy judge to force the plan on dissenting classes (commonly referred to as a 'cram down'; see Section 1126 of Chapter 11 of the U.S. bankruptcy code for a complete discussion of the conditions under which this option is viable). As Wruck (1990, p. 441) points out, the fact that only impaired creditors and shareholders vote means that 'the plan determines who votes and which claimants vote together'. Thus, managers interested in securing their jobs have a strong incentive to raise capital so that they can satisfy certain claims (within the confines of the bankruptcy code), thereby selecting the most favorable voters to pass judgment on the reorganization plan.

Furthermore, proceeds from asset sales can be used to finance operations. Weiss and Wruck (1998) describe Eastern Airline's use of asset-sale proceeds to fund operations while operating under Chapter 11 protection. Bankrupt firms that are severely cash constrained can avoid immediate shutdown by accepting low bids, even if doing so fails to maximize firm value.

The rate of asset sales provides additional evidence that Chapter 11 is ineffective in helping distressed firms search for high-value buyers for their assets. Rather than decreasing, the rate of asset sales increases after firms file for Chapter 11 protection. This is particularly true for firms that eventually liquidate under Chapter 7. These firms experience very high rates of asset sales in the two years preceding Chapter 11 filing, and an increased rate of sales after the filing date. For firms that eventually emerge from bankruptcy, the rate of asset sales is low in the two years preceding bankruptcy and increases slightly after bankruptcy court protection is obtained. Results from both this analysis and the pricing analysis suggest that providing sellers with time to find high-value buyers for their assets is not a benefit provided by Chapter 11 protection.

The remainder of this paper proceeds as follows. Section 2 describes the sample of aircraft transactions used in the empirical analyses. Section 3 examines the effect of bankruptcy court protection on prices that airlines receive for their assets. Section 4 presents an analysis of the effect of bankruptcy court protection on the rate of asset sales and Section 5 concludes.

2. Data description

Department of Transportation and Federal Aviation Administration records of used commercial aircraft transactions between 1978 and 1991 are used to examine asset sales in bankruptcy. These data were collected by Avmark, Inc., an aircraft appraisal firm, and consist of transaction date, aircraft model, serial number, transaction price, engine type, seller identity, and buyer identity.

Using aircraft transactions has a number of advantages. First, bankruptcy filings are common in the U.S. airline industry. Of the 27 major U.S. airlines examined in this paper, eight went bankrupt between 1978 and the end of 1992 (Continental filed for Chapter 11 protection twice during this period). Second, compared to other observable asset sales by distressed firms (for example, sales of manufacturing plants or corporate divisions), aircraft are relatively homogeneous. This makes it much easier to isolate the effects of bankruptcy on transaction prices and quantities. Finally, because the Department of Transportation required price disclosure for aircraft transactions that occurred prior to 1992, aircraft sales provide a sample that is free from selection bias.

This paper presents two analyses. The first examines prices that bankrupt airlines receive for their assets and the second analyzes the rate of aircraft sales. The first analysis includes only aircraft models for which at least 15 transactions occurred between 1978 and 1991 and for which transactions are not dominated by a single airline. For example, Airbus 300B4-100s are omitted because 13 of the 16 transactions that occurred were sales by Eastern Airlines. Eliminating infrequently traded models helps to ensure accuracy in estimating market prices.

Table 1 presents the airlines and number of aircraft sales included in the pricing analysis. The sample comprises 582 (87%) narrow-body transactions and 86 (13%) wide-body transactions. Bold-faced airlines in Table 1 filed for bankruptcy protection sometime in the 1978–1992 time period. Of the bankrupt airlines, Eastern Airlines has the greatest number of sales (21% of the total sample). In addition to sales by airlines listed in Table 1, sales by non-U.S. airlines (i.e., leasing companies, banks, and regional airlines) are used to estimate asset prices. However, these transactions are not used to assess the effects of bankruptcy status on prices.

Table 2 presents the number and timing of aircraft sales by bankrupt airlines. It lists the number of sales by firms operating under Chapters 7 and 11 as well as transactions that occurred up to two years prior to the Chapter 11 filing date. There are two numbers in each cell of Table 2. The first number is the total number of aircraft sales and the number in parentheses is the number of sales included in the pricing analysis. Differences between the two numbers represent sales of aircraft models for which there were few transactions. For example, two calendar quarters before filing for Chapter 11 protection, Eastern Airlines sold 13 aircraft. Only four of these aircraft are used to examine the effects of bankruptcy on asset sale prices. The other nine transactions consist of sales of

Table 1
Numbers of narrow-body and wide-body aircraft sales (not including sale/leasebacks) for selected airlines and aircraft models, 1978–1991. Only aircraft models for which at least 15 transactions occurred over the 1978–1991 time period are included. Airlines that filed for bankruptcy at least once between 1978 and 1992 are in bold face.

	Number of narrow-body sales (1978–1991)	Number of wide-body sales (1978–1991)	Total number of sales (1978–1991)
Air Florida	10	0	10
Alaska	6	0	6
Aloha	2	0	2
America West	8	0	8
American	38	3	41
Braniff	54	1	55
Braniff Liq. Trust	26	0	26
Continental	12	0	12
Delta	50	16	66
Eastern	123	20	143
Hawaiian	4	0	4
Midway	6	0	6
Northwest	38	0	38
Ozark	2	0	2
PSA	17	0	17
Pan Am	33	30	63
People Express	0	1	1
Piedmont	5	0	5
Republic	4	0	4
TWA	40	4	44
United	54	8	62
US Air	25	0	25
Western	25	3	28
TOTAL	**582**	**86**	**668**

Airbus 300B4-100 aircraft. As noted above, there are an insufficient number of non-Eastern sales of this particular model to establish reliable market prices.

Bankruptcy sales are dominated by Eastern and Braniff. Table 2 shows that, of the 130 bankruptcy sales analyzed in this paper, 73 (56%) were by Eastern and 49 (38%) by Braniff (including Braniff Liquidating Trust). Table 2 also shows that the majority of sales by airlines that filed for bankruptcy occurred after the Chapter 11 filing date. The general pattern revealed in Table 2 is that bankrupt firms that are eventually liquidated sell large numbers of aircraft both before and after filing for bankruptcy court protection. Conversely, bankrupt airlines that eventually emerge sell few aircraft, regardless of their bankruptcy status.

Table 2
Number of aircraft sales before and during bankruptcy for airlines that filed for bankruptcy court protection between 1978 and the end of 1992. Transactions listed under 'Chpt. 11' occurred while the firm was operating under Chapter 11 protection; those listed under 'Chpt. 7' occurred while the firm was liquidating under Chapter 7 of the bankruptcy code. Numbers of pre-bankruptcy sales in each of the eight calendar quarters preceding the Chapter 11 filing date are also presented. For example, transactions listed under the heading '1' occurred no more than three months prior to Chapter 11 filing; those listed under '2' occurred between three months and six months prior to filing. There are two numbers per cell in this table. The first number is the total number of sales. The second number (in parentheses) is the number of sales used in the pricing analyses presented in Tables 4 and 5. Differences between the two numbers result from omitting aircraft models for which there were an insufficient number of sales to estimate marketprices. Bold-faced airlines are those that were eventually liquidated.
Table Entries: Total number of aircraft sales (Number of sales for models included in pricing analysis)

Airline(Chapter 11 Date)	*Chpt. 7*	*Chpt. 11*	Number of Calendar Quarters Prior to Chapter 11 Filing							
			1	*2*	*3*	*4*	*5*	*6*	*7*	*8*
Air Florida (7/84)	3 (3)	0 (0)	2 (2)	2 (2)	0 (0)	0 (0)	0 (0)	0 (0)	0 (0)	1 (0)
America West (6/91)	n.a.	0 (0)	0 (0)	0 (0)	0 (0)	0 (0)	1 (1)	0 (0)	0 (0)	0 (0)
Braniff (5/82)	9 (9)	15 (14)	1 (1)	1 (1)	7 (7)	0 (0)	5 (5)	9 (8)	3 (2)	1 (1)
Braniff Liquidating Trust (n.a.)	26 (26)	n.a.	n.a.	n.a.	n.a.	n.a.	n.a.	n.a.	n.a.	n.a.
Continental (9/83 and 12/90)	n.a.	7 (3)	1 (1)	1 (0)	0 (0)	0 (0)	0 (0)	0 (0)	0 (0)	0 (0)
Eastern (3/89)	2 (2)	83 (71)	3 (3)	13 (4)	7 (4)	5 (5)	3 (1)	0 (0)	0 (0)	2 (2)
Midway (3/91)	0 (0)	2 (2)	0 (0)	0 (0)	0 (0)	0 (0)	0 (0)	0 (0)	0 (0)	0 (0)
Pan Am (1/91)	3 (0)	0 (0)	2 (2)	0 (0)	0 (0)	0 (0)	0 (0)	0 (0)	0 (0)	0 (0)
TWA (1/92)	n.a.	0 (0)	0 (0)	0 (0)	0 (0)	1 (1)	0 (0)	1 (1)	3 (3)	0 (0)
TOTAL	*43 (40)*	*107 (90)*	*9 (9)*	*17 (7)*	*14 (11)*	*6 (6)*	*9 (7)*	*10 (9)*	*6 (5)*	*4 (3)*

In addition to aircraft prices, data describing airlines' fleets, financial characteristics, operating statistics, and bankruptcy filing dates are used (quarterly data when available and annual data otherwise). Fleet descriptions are obtained from companies' annual and quarterly reports. Financial data are obtained from Compustat, and operating statistics are obtained from *Air Carrier Traffic Statistics* published by the Department of Transportation and the Civil Aeronautics Board. Bankruptcy filing dates are obtained from the *Capital Changes Reporter* (published by Commerce Clearing House).

3. Effect of bankruptcy court protection on asset prices

The analysis presented in this section assesses the degree to which bankruptcy laws affect prices that distressed sellers receive for their assets. If reorganization laws like Chapter 11 of the U.S. bankruptcy code are better at promoting orderly dispositions of assets than are liquidation proceedings such as Chapter 7, then we should observe smaller price discounts for asset sales conducted under Chapter 11 than for those conducted under Chapter 7. Furthermore, because the bankruptcy code's automatic stay provision reduces pressure to meet debt obligations via quick asset sales, we should observe smaller discounts for transactions by bankrupt airlines than for transactions by distressed but non bankrupt airlines. In order to make this comparison, sellers' levels of distress must be characterized. Consequently, this section proceeds in three steps. First, price discounts are calculated. Second, the degree of seller distress is characterized. Third, the effects of bankruptcy status and distress on price discounts are estimated.

3.1. Step #1 – hedonic price calculation

The first step involves calculating 'hedonic prices', that is, prices that are functions of only aircraft attributes and time. Hedonic regressions are often used to study real estate prices. They also have been used in a number of other industries including rigid disk drives (Lerner, 1995), automobiles (Ohta and Griliches, 1986), and computers (Chow, 1967). Essentially, this procedure estimates an equilibrium price for each aircraft model in every calendar quarter between 1978 and the end of 1991. The following specification is used to calculate hedonic prices:

$$\log(\text{PRICE}) = \beta_0 + \sum_1^I \beta_i \,\text{QTR}_i + \sum_1^J \beta_j \,\text{MODEL}_j + \sum_1^K \beta_k \,\text{STAGE}_k + \beta_{\text{AGE}} \log(1 + \text{AGE}) + \varepsilon, \qquad (1)$$

where PRICE is the transaction price, QTR are the dummy variables representing calendar quarters, MODEL are the dummy variables representing aircraft models, STAGE are the dummy variables representing engine stage categories, and AGE is the aircraft age at time of transaction.

All aircraft sales, including those by non-U.S. airlines (i.e., leasing companies, banks, and regional airlines) but excluding sale/leasebacks, are used to estimate Eq. (1). The logarithm of transaction price is used as the dependent variable to impose a (price) nonnegativity constraint on the model. Price levels depend significantly on the aircraft model. For example, the average transaction price for 727-100s is \$3 million (in 1992 dollars). The average price for 747-200s is \$39 million. In general, wide-body aircraft and late-model aircraft with quiet engines command the highest prices. All prices are in 1992 dollars. Inflation adjustments are made using the producer price index. Including additional dummy variables to represent engine type substantially reduces the number of degrees of freedom but increases the adjusted R^2 by less than 0.5%. Therefore, engine variant dummies are omitted from the analysis. Stage categories refer to engine noise output characteristics. Stage 1 aircraft are the loudest – they are no longer allowed to fly in the U.S. Stage 2 engines are quieter, but they too will be outlawed by the year 2000. Stage 3 aircraft are the quietest.

Eq. (1) is estimated separately for narrow-body and wide-body aircraft. Segmenting the data in this way allows coefficients on calendar quarter dummies, stage dummies, and the age variable to differ for these two aircraft classes, thus improving the accuracy of hedonic price estimates. Appendix A presents results from this regression for both narrow- and wide-body aircraft. Both regression models have significant explanatory power – the adjusted R^2 is 0.76 for the narrow-body regression and 0.74 for the wide-body regression. The AGE coefficient of -0.16 in the narrow-body regression implies that narrow-body aircraft depreciate by 16% per year in the first year of operation and by 1% per year after ten years. The coefficient is slightly larger in absolute value for wide-body aircraft, suggesting that they depreciate at a more rapid rate than narrow-body aircraft. Calendar quarter dummies are highly variable and generally signify the health of the airline industry. For example, dummy variables representing calendar quarters between 1982 and the middle of 1984 are small. During this time period, the U.S. airline industry was ailing and aircraft values were low. In the later 1980s, the airline industry was relatively healthy. Aircraft values, represented by the calendar quarter dummy variables from 1985 through 1989, were relatively high during this period. When a severe recession hit the airline industry in 1991, aircraft values dropped significantly.

Residuals from estimation of Eq. (1) are used as the dependent variable in many of the analyses that follow. A positive residual implies that the aircraft sold for a premium whereas a negative residual indicates that the aircraft sold at a discount to the hedonic price. Because of the logarithmic specification, residuals can be interpreted (approximately) as percentages. For example, a residual of -0.15 implies that the actual transaction price is 14% ($= 1 - e^{-0.15}$) lower than the hedonic price. An alternative to the two-stage analysis presented in this paper would be to perform a single-stage analysis by including explanatory variables from the second stage directly in the hedonic regression. The primary problem with this approach is that transactions for which second-stage explanatory variables are unavailable (e.g., leasing companies) would have to be omitted. Omission of these transactions would result in less accurate hedonic prices.

3.2. Step #2 – characterizing sellers' distress levels

The second step of the analysis consists of classifying transactions according to the level of distress of the seller. The following categories are constructed:

1. *Chapter 7 transactions:* Transactions that occur while the seller is liquidating under Chapter 7.
2. *Chapter 11 transactions:* Transactions that occur while the seller is operating under Chapter 11.
3. *Pre-Bankruptcy transactions:* Transactions that occur during the two years preceding the seller's Chapter 11 filing date.
4. *Nonbankruptcy transactions:* Transactions that occur more that two years prior to the seller's Chapter 11 filing date or transactions by firms that never file for bankruptcy court protection.

Transactions classified under Category 4 are further segmented according to the selling firm's bankruptcy probability. This is accomplished by estimating the following airline-specific probit model, where each observation consists of one firm-quarter:

$$\begin{aligned}\Pr(\text{BKRPT} = 1) = \alpha &+ \beta_1\,\text{NETLEV} + \beta_2\,\text{ISS} + \beta_3\,\text{OPINC} \\ &+ \beta_4\,\text{COST} + \beta_5\,\text{REV} + \beta_6\,\ln(\text{ASSETS}) \\ &+ \beta_7\,\text{INDEX} + \beta_8\,(\text{Med.NETLEV}) \\ &+ \beta_9(\text{Med.COST}) + \beta_{10}\,(\text{Med.REV}) + \varepsilon, \qquad (2)\end{aligned}$$

where BKRPT is one if the firm files for bankruptcy in the following quarter and zero otherwise, NETLEV is the book value of long-term debt less working capital divided by the sum of book value of debt and market value of equity, ISS are the number of debt issues outstanding, OPINC is the operating income divided by sales, COST is the cost of goods sold divided by available seat-miles, REV is the load factor multiplied by revenue per revenue-passenger-mile, ASSETS is the book value of assets, INDEX is the index of narrow-body prices,

Med.NETLEV is the median of NETLEV across firms in each calendar quarter, Med.COST is the median of COST across firms in each calendar quarter, and Med.REV is the median of REV across firms in each calendar quarter.

Explanatory variables in Eq. (2) fall into three categories: (1) proxies for financial distress, (2) proxies for economic distress, and (3) control variables. Proxies for financial distress include NETLEV and ISS. NETLEV measures the effect of financial condition on bankruptcy probability. The coefficient on NETLEV should be positive; as financial leverage increases and financial liquidity decreases, bankruptcy probability increases. ISS proxies for creditor dispersion. Because debt renegotiation is likely to be more difficult as the number of creditors increases, the likelihood of bankruptcy should increase as creditor dispersion increases (Gertner and Scharfstein, 1991; Asquith et al., 1994). Thus, the sign on ISS should be positive.

OPINC, COST, and REV are all intended to measure economic distress. Firms with favorable economic prospects are likely to have low bankruptcy probabilities, whereas firms with poor economic prospects are likely to have high bankruptcy probabilities. Thus, we would expect coefficients on OPINC and REV to be negative and the coefficient on COST to be positive.

Control variables include firm size, INDEX, Med.NETLEV, Med.COST, and Med.REV. Including firm size, measured by ln(ASSETS), controls for the possibility that firms of different sizes have inherently different bankruptcy probabilities. The remaining variables control for the effect of the overall condition of the airline industry on the probability of bankruptcy. INDEX is calculated from the calendar quarter dummy variables in the narrow-body hedonic regression presented in Appendix A.

Eq. (2) is estimated for 27 airlines over the 1978–1991 time period. Because of mergers, entry, and liquidations, not all airlines are represented in every calendar quarter. The final sample consists of 980 firm-quarters. High predicted values from this regression correspond to firm-quarters in which the chances of bankruptcy in the near future are high. Low predicted values correspond to firm-quarters in which bankruptcy is unlikely.

Table 3 presents results from estimating Eq. (2). As expected, the NETLEV coefficient is positive and statistically significant, implying that bankruptcy probability increases as the level of financial distress increases. Airlines' cost efficiencies and revenue-generating capabilities also significantly influence bankruptcy probability. The coefficient on COST indicates that as cost of goods sold per available seat-mile increases, bankruptcy probability increases. Similarly, the coefficient on REV in Table 3 indicates that bankruptcy probability decreases as airlines' abilities to fill their planes with high-revenue passengers increases. Although none of the other coefficients are statistically significant at conventional levels, most have the expected signs. Furthermore, the pseudo-R^2 of 0.58 indicates that the model has substantial explanatory power.

Table 3
Probit analysis used to estimate the bankruptcy probability for 27 airlines between 1978 and 1991:

$$\Pr(\text{Bankrupt} = 1) = \alpha + \beta_1\,\text{NETLEV} + \beta_2\,\text{ISS} + \beta_3\,\text{OPINC} + \beta_4\,\text{COST} + \beta_5\,\text{REV} + \beta_6\,\ln(\text{ASSETS}) + \beta_7\,\text{INDEX} + \beta_8\,(\text{Med.NETLEV}) + \beta_9\,(\text{Med.COST}) + \beta_{10}\,(\text{Med.REV}) + \varepsilon.$$

Total sample size is 980 firm-quarters. The dependent variable takes a value of one if the firm files for Chapter 11 protection in the calendar quarter and zero otherwise. NETLEV equals long-term debt plus current liabilities minus current assets all divided by the sum of book value of debt and market value of equity; ISS equals number of outstanding debt issues; OPINC equals operating income divided by sales; COST equals cost of goods sold divided by available seat-miles; REV equals load factor times revenue per revenue-passenger-mile; ASSETS equals book value of assets; INDEX measures relative prices of used aircraft; Med.NETLEV equals the median net leverage across firms in the calendar quarter; Med.COST equals median cost of goods sold divided by available seat miles in each quarter; Med.REV equals median load factor times revenue per revenue-passenger-mile in each quarter. All independent variables are lagged one calendar quarter. Standard errors are in parentheses.

Dependent variable equals one in the calendar quarter in which Chapter 11 filing occurs, zero otherwise; 980 observations.

Net Leverage	ISS	OPINC	COST	REV	ln(Assets)	INDEX	Med. Net Leverage	Med.COST	Med.REV	Constant	Adj. R^2
10.53 (3.89)[b]	– 0.05 (0.052)	3.51 (6.14)	118.64 (50.99)[a]	– 90.18 (43.28)[a]	– 0.14 (0.368)	0.19 (0.437)	4.81 (4.24)	– 56.74 (84.36)	17.19 (76.85)	– 12.71 (7.19)	0.58

[a]Significant at 0.05 level.
[b]Significant at 0.01 level.

3.3. Step #3 – price comparisons

The third and final step of the analysis involves comparing price residuals from the hedonic regressions for each of the four transaction categories listed above, i.e., Chapters 11 and 7, pre-bankruptcy, and nonbankruptcy. This comparison is made by regressing hedonic regression residuals on indicator variables that represent each category. To control for potential misspecification associated with omitted variables in Eqs. (1) and (2), the regression also includes firm-specific indicator variables. Southwest Airlines provides a good example of why firm effects should be included. Because their planes do not have kitchens, Southwest aircraft would likely sell at a discount compared to sales of otherwise similar aircraft by other airlines (since the Avmark database contains no records of used aircraft sales by Southwest Airlines between 1978 and the end of 1991, the expected effect of Southwest's unique aircraft configuration on transaction price cannot be verified). Another example of a firm-specific effect involves airlines' abilities to find high-value buyers for their assets. Until the mid-1990s, there was no organized market for used airplanes. Transactions were privately negotiated and the prices that airlines received for their planes were affected, at least in part, by the talents of those responsible for negotiating the sales. Many smaller airlines relied on third-party brokers to locate potential buyers. Conversely, George 'Bud' Dutton of Eastern Airlines was reputed to be a particularly talented aircraft salesman (based on discussions with Morten Beyer of Morten Beyer Associates). Therefore, ceteris paribus, Eastern would be expected to receive relatively high prices for their aircraft. The mid-1990s saw the development of organized auctions of used aircraft, but these auctions have not been particularly successful. Most aircraft transactions continue to be privately negotiated deals.

Given a large enough sample of transactions by bankrupt carriers, the 'Eastern' effect would not bias the relation between asset prices and bankruptcy status. Hence, there would be no need to control for firm-specific effects. However, as previously discussed, Chapter 11 transactions are dominated by Eastern Airlines (71 out of 90) and Chapter 7 transactions are dominated by Braniff and its liquidating trust (35 out of 40). Including firm-specific dummy variables allows bankruptcy effects to be isolated from the 'Eastern' and 'Braniff' effects. Therefore, the following model is estimated:

$$\begin{aligned} \mathrm{RES} = \alpha &+ \beta_1\,\mathrm{Ch7} + \beta_2\,\mathrm{Ch11} + \beta_3\,T_{-1} + \beta_4\,T_{-2} + \beta_5\,\mathrm{PBR}_5 \\ &+ \beta_6\,\mathrm{PBR}_4 + \beta_7\,\mathrm{PBR}_3 + \beta_8\,\mathrm{PBR}_2 + \beta_9\,\mathrm{NSALE} \\ &+ \mathrm{FirmEffects} + \varepsilon, \end{aligned} \tag{3}$$

where RES is the residual from hedonic regressions, Ch. 7 is a dummy variable equal to one if the transaction occurred under Chapter 7 liquidation, Ch. 11 is a dummy variable equal to one if the transaction occurred when the selling firm was operating under Chapter 11 protection, T_{-1} is a dummy variable equal to one if the transaction occurred in the year preceding the seller's Chapter 11 filing date, T_{-2} is a dummy variable equal to one if the transaction occurred between one and two years prior to the seller's Chapter 11 filing date, PBR_j are the dummy variables indicating bankruptcy probability quintiles based on predicted values from Eq. (2); PBR_5 takes the value of one if the firm-quarter is in the highest bankruptcy probability quintile and zero otherwise and PBR_2 takes the value of one if the firm-quarter is in the second lowest bankruptcy probability quintile and zero otherwise (PBR_1 is omitted to avoid collinearity) and, NSALE is the number of used aircraft sold by the airline in the current calendar quarter.

To test statistically for the effects of bankruptcy court protection on asset sale prices, this regression is estimated in both restricted and unrestricted forms. The restricted form imposes the condition that coefficients on the Ch. 7 dummy variable, the Ch. 11 dummy variable, and dummy variables representing distressed (but not bankrupt) airlines are equal (i.e., H_0: $\beta_1 = \beta_2 = \beta_3 = \beta_5$). An F-test is used to determine the statistical significance of this restriction.

3.3.1. Univariate results

Table 4 presents average price residuals for various categories of transactions. Panel A contains price residuals for bankrupt firms and Panel B contains residuals for nonbankrupt firms. Because the dependent variable in the hedonic regression used to calculate residuals is the logarithm of price, entries in Table 4 approximate percentage deviations from the hedonic price. For example, Panel A shows that sales by Chapter 7 and Chapter 11 firms are transacted at average discounts of 11% and 10% from the hedonic price, respectively.[2] Although both of these average discounts are significantly different from zero at the 0.1% level, they are not different from each other. This evidence suggests that the current reorganization law is no more effective than court-supervised liquidation in helping distressed sellers locate high-value buyers for their assets. Prior to entering Chapter 11, there is no discernible pattern (over time) in prices that airlines receive for their assets. However, as will be reported in subsequent regressions that control for firm effects, there is evidence of substantial price discounting in the year preceding Chapter 11 filing.

Panel B uses predicted values from the airline-specific bankruptcy probability model of Eq. (2) to summarize price residuals according to the bankruptcy probability of the seller. Only transactions by firms that do not file for Chapter 11 protection within two years of the transaction are included in Panel B.

[2] Table 4 entries approximate price discounts. To get an exact estimate of the discount requires exponentiating the table entries. For example, Chapter 7 transactions occur at a discount of $1 - e^{-0.11}$ or 10.4%. As this example shows, the approximation is accurate for small residuals.

Transactions by firms with bankruptcy probabilities in the lowest quintile receive prices that average 5% above the hedonic price. This premium decreases, although not monotonically, with bankruptcy probability. Sales by firms in the second-highest bankruptcy-probability quintile and the highest bankruptcy-probability quintile are transacted at discounts of 11% and 8%, respectively. The null hypothesis that average residuals are the same for the low and high bankruptcy-probability quintiles is rejected at the 5% level. Similarly, tests that average residuals are the same for sales by bankrupt firms (Chapters 11 and 7) and sales by firms in the low bankruptcy-probability quintile reject at the 0.1% level. However, there is no evidence of differences in discounts for bankrupt airlines and distressed (but not bankrupt) airlines. Discounts for all of these groups average between 8% and 11%. Differences between groups are not statistically significant at conventional levels. Thus, simply comparing price residuals indicates that although distressed airlines receive lower prices for their aircraft, this particular cost of distress is mitigated neither by Chapter 11 nor Chapter 7 protection.

3.3.2. Multivariate results

As previously discussed, simply comparing average residuals across groups controls for neither the number of aircraft sold in a calendar quarter (the large-block effect) nor firm fixed effects. Results from estimating Eq. (3), which includes these controls, are presented in Panel A of Table 5. To account for the possible lack of independence of the error terms, standard errors presented in Table 5 are calculated assuming that observations are independent across firms. No assumptions are made regarding independence of observations across or within firm-quarters. The effect of this assumption is that standard error estimates are conservatively high. True standard errors are likely to be smaller than those reported in Table 5.

Specification 1 in Table 5 controls for the rate of asset sales but does not include firm fixed effects. Results indicate that after controlling for the rate of asset sales, the difference in price residuals between bankrupt and distressed (but solvent) firms is slight. More importantly, there are no significant differences in prices obtained by firms operating under Chapter 11 and those liquidating under Chapter 7. A test of the null hypothesis that coefficients on the Chapters 7, 11, T_{-1}, and Bankruptcy Quintile 5 variables are equal fails to reject at conventional levels. The effect of the number of aircraft sales in a calendar quarter contributes only slightly to the price discount. For each additional aircraft sold, the price decreases by approximately one-half of one percent.

Specification 2 in Panel A of Table 5 controls for the rate of asset sales as well as firm fixed effects. Results from this specification indicate that firms with low bankruptcy probabilities receive higher prices for their aircraft than do firms with high bankruptcy probabilities. Transactions that occur in the year preceding bankruptcy filing occur at an average discount of 32% compared to sales by

Table 4

Average residuals (ε) from the following hedonic price regression using aircraft transactions that occurred between 1978 and 1991:

$$\log(\text{PRICE}) = \beta_0 + \sum_1^I \beta_i \,\text{QTR}_i + \sum_1^J \beta_j \,\text{MODEL}_j + \sum_1^K \beta_k \,\text{STAGE}_k + \beta_{\text{AGE}} \log(1 + \text{AGE}) + \varepsilon$$

where PRICE equals transaction price, QTR_i are a series of 56 dummy variables representing calendar quarters between 1978 and 1991, MODEL_j are dummy variables representing aircraft models, STAGE_k are dummy variables representing engine noise categories, and AGE is aircraft age (in years) at the time of the transaction. Results from estimating the hedonic regression using 1333 used-aircraft transactions are presented in Appendix A. Residuals (ε) summarized in this table can be interpreted as percent deviations from hedonic price. Positive residuals imply that the aircraft were sold for prices above the hedonic price; negative residuals imply that the aircraft were sold for prices below the hedonic price. Panel A presents average residuals for transactions by airlines that are liquidating under Chapter 7, reorganizing under Chapter 11, and transactions that occur within two years prior to Chapter 11 filing. Panel B presents residuals for transactions by airlines that remained solvent throughout the 1978–1992 time period. Bankruptcy probability is calculated using predicted values from the bankruptcy model presented in Table 3.

Panel A: mean price residuals for bankrupt firms

	While In		Number of Calendar Quarters Prior to Chapter 11 Filling							
	Ch 7	Ch 11	1	2	3	4	5	6	7	8
Mean price residual	− 0.11	− 0.10	− 0.002	0.05	− 0.24	0.08	0.07	0.06	− 0.06	− 0.06
Standard deviation of mean	0.020[c]	0.026[c]	0.056	0.042	0.081[a]	0.065	0.011[c]	0.016[b]	0.058	0.002
No. of observations	40	90	9	7	11	6	7	9	5	3

Panel B: mean price residuals for nonbankrupt firms

	Bankruptcy probability quintile				
	High probability				Low probability
	5	4	3	2	1
Mean price residual	– 0.08	– 0.11	– 0.04	0.03	0.05
Standard deviation of mean	0.048	0.051[a]	0.040	0.022	0.035
No. observations	97	98	94	96	96

[a]Significant at 0.05 level.
[b]Significant at 0.01 level.
[c]Significant at 0.001 level.

Table 5

Ordinary least-squares regressions of the effect of bankruptcy court protection on transaction price, 1978–1991. The dependent variable is the residual from estimating the following hedonic price regression:

$$\log(\text{PRICE}) = \beta_0 + \sum_1^I \beta_i \,\text{QTR}_i + \sum_1^J \beta_j \,\text{MODEL}_j + \sum_1^K \beta_k \,\text{STAGE}_k + \beta_{\text{AGE}}\log(1 + \text{AGE}) + \varepsilon,$$

where PRICE equals transaction price, QTR_i are a series of 56 dummy variables representing calendar quarters between 1978 and 1991, MODEL_j are dummy variables representing aircraft models, STAGE_k are dummy variables representing engine noise categories, and AGE is aircraft age (in years) at the time of the transaction. Results from estimating the hedonic regression using 1333 used-aircraft transactions are presented in Appendix A. Independent variables characterize the selling firm's bankruptcy status and are defined as follows: Ch 7 is a dummy variable equal to one if the transaction occurred while the firm was liquidating under Chapter 7 of the bankruptcy code; Ch 11 is a dummy variable equal to one if the firm was operating under Chapter 11 of the code; T_{-1} is a dummy variable equal to one if the transaction occurred within one year prior to Chapter 11 filing; T_{-2} is a dummy variable equal to one if the transaction occurred more than one year but less than two years prior to Chapter 11 filing; bankruptcy probability quintile dummies correspond to predictions from the Probit regression in Table 3; INDEX measures the relative strength of the used aircraft market at the time of the transaction and is obtained from the calendar quarter dummy variable coefficients in the hedonic regression; Number of Sales equals the total number of used aircraft sales by the selling firm in the quarter. Panel A presents OLS regressions; Panel B presents results after inclusion of the Inverse Mills Ratio to control for sample selection bias. The dummy variable representing the lowest bankruptcy probability quintile is omitted to avoid collinearity. Standard errors (in parentheses) are calculated assuming independence across firms. No assumptions are made regarding the independence of transactions that have common sellers.

Panel A: OLS regression, dependent variable is hedonic price residual; 668 observations

Specification	While In:		Years before Chapter 11 filing:		Bankruptcy probability quintile				Number of sales	Ch 7 X Number of sales	Ch 11 X Number of sales	Const.	Adj. R^2
	Ch 7	Ch 11	T_{-1}	T_{-2}	(High probability) 5	4	(Low probability) 3	2					
1	−0.15	−0.08	−0.09	−0.002	−0.13	−0.16	−0.08	−0.01	−0.006			0.07	0.02
	(0.102)	(0.143)	(0.142)	(0.103)	(0.168)	(0.111)	(0.067)	(0.094)	(0.007)			(0.089)	
2	−0.48	−0.35	−0.38	−0.17	−0.34	−0.30	−0.12	−0.03	−0.01			Firm	0.26
	(0.186)[a]	(0.195)	(0.169)[a]	(0.177)	(0.213)	(0.145)	(0.137)	(0.102)	(0.009)			effects	
3	−0.22	−0.23	−0.08	0.02	−0.13	−0.16	−0.06	0.01	−0.01	0.02	0.02	0.10	0.03
	(0.129)	(0.118)	(0.148)	(0.117)	(0.166)	(0.111)	(0.063)	(0.098)	(0.011)	(0.016)	(0.011)	(0.083)	
4	−0.62	−0.52	−0.35	−0.14	−0.33	−0.28	−0.10	−0.004	−0.02	0.03	0.02	Firm	0.27
	(0.200)[b]	(0.228)[a]	(0.153)[a]	(0.161)	(0.195)	(0.133)[a]	(0.120)	(0.093)	(0.009)[a]	(0.017)	(0.09)[a]	effects	

Panel B: Heckman two-step second-stage regression, dependent variable is Hedonic price residual; 668 observations

Specfication	While In:		Years before Capter 11 filing:		Bankruptcy probability quintile				Number of sales	Ch 7 X Number of sales	Ch 11 X Number of sales	Inverse Mills ratio	Const.	Adj. R^2
	Ch 7	Ch 11	T_{-1}	T_{-2}	(High probability) 5	4	(Low probability) 3	2						
1	−0.27	−0.01	−0.07	−0.005	−0.08	−0.14	−0.06	−0.004	−0.003			0.22	−0.20	0.05
	(0.101)[a]	(0.153)	(0.148)	(0.095)	(0.163)	(0.098)	(0.065)	(0.094)	(0.007)			(0.089)[a]	(0.032)	
2	−0.45	−0.33	−0.36	−0.16	−0.32	−0.28	−0.12	−0.02	−0.01			0.05	Firm	0.26
	(0.260)	(0.258)	(0.198)	(0.206)	(0.248)	(0.193)	(0.156)	(0.107)	(0.009)			(0.181)	Effects	
3	−0.26	−0.15	−0.06	0.02	−0.07	−0.14	−0.05	0.01	−0.01	0.002	0.01	0.22	−0.17	0.05
	(0.099)[a]	(0.123)	(0.155)	(0.110)	(0.161)	(0.098)	(0.061)	(0.097)	(0.011)	(0.021)	(0.012)	(0.088)[a]	(0.135)	
4	−0.61	−0.51	−0.35	−0.13	−0.32	−0.28	−0.10	−0.003	−0.02	0.03	0.02	0.01	Firm	0.26
	(0.275)[a]	(0.296)	(0.185)	(0.193)	(0.235)	(0.188)	(0.143)	(0.100)	(0.010)[a]	(0.017)[a]	(0.009)[a]	(0.183)	effects	

[a]Significant at 0.05 level.
[b]Significant at 0.01 level.

airlines with the lowest bankruptcy probabilities. Discounts are slightly smaller for transactions by airlines selling while in Chapter 11 (30%) and slightly larger for airlines liquidating under Chapter 7 (38%). While it appears that firms liquidating under Chapter 7 receive lower prices than firms operating under Chapter 11, the difference is not statistically significant. The effect of the number of sales per calendar quarter increases slightly when firm-specific effects are included, but the effect is not statistically significant.

To further examine the effects of Chapters 11 and 7 protection on distress-sale discounts, the effect of the number of sales per quarter is allowed to vary depending on bankruptcy venue (Chapter 11 versus Chapter 7). Specifications 3 and 4 of Panel A in Table 5 include interaction terms to accomplish this. The effect of these interactions is most significant when firm-specific effects are included in the model (Specification 4). Discounts associated with Chapters 11 and 7 are higher, but again, they are not significantly different from one another. In addition, discounts increase with the number of aircraft sales per quarter, but only when the seller is without bankruptcy court protection. For each additional aircraft sold in the calendar quarter, the price discount increases by approximately 1.5%. When the firm has either Chapter 11 or Chapter 7 protection, the increased discount associated with large-block sales disappears. However, this is not as much of a benefit as it might first appear. Regression coefficients in Specification 4 of Panel A in Table 5 imply that, because of the large 'fixed' discount associated with bankruptcy, only firms selling more than 9 aircraft per calendar quarter would receive higher prices with bankruptcy court protection than without it. This is true regardless of bankruptcy venue – there is little evidence that reorganization proceedings allow firms to obtain better prices for their assets than liquidation proceedings.

Firm fixed effects (not reported) are highly variable and range in magnitude from a statistically insignificant −0.21 (American Airlines) to a significant 0.55 (Pacific Southwest Airlines). Only two firms (American and U.S. Air) have negative intercepts. Of the bankrupt airlines, TWA has the smallest intercept (0.10) and Air Florida has the largest (0.53). Both Eastern and Braniff have positive intercepts (0.47 and 0.34, respectively). The variability in firm effects suggests that, because the other independent variables in Eqs. (1) and (2) do not fully explain variation in price, firm effects should be included in the specification. Furthermore, the fact that all of the bankrupt firms have positive intercepts is inconsistent with the notion that airlines that file for bankruptcy are inherently more likely to sell aircraft at discounted prices, regardless of their financial condition.

3.4. Specification tests

This section describes three specification tests used to assess the robustness of the conclusions drawn from the pricing analysis summarized in Tables 4 and 5.

The first test involves an assessment of the degree to which the results depend on the specific bankruptcy model used to define firm-quarter bankruptcy-probability quintiles. The second tests for sample selection biases. The third test assesses the degree to which predicted prices obtained from the hedonic regressions described by Eq. (1) are affected by the large number of Eastern and Braniff sales.

Because there are only nine bankruptcies in this analysis, there is a possibility that the bankruptcy probability model described by Eq. (2) inaccurately places firms into bankruptcy probability quintiles. To determine whether results presented in Tables 4 and 5 are dependent on the specific bankruptcy probability model used, bankruptcy probabilities are calculated using two alternative approaches. Both of the alternative approaches are based on Altman's (1993) Z-score methodology. The first uses Z-scores to categorize firm-quarters into bankruptcy probability quintiles:

$$Z = 1.2X_1 + 1.4X_2 + 3.3X_3 + 0.6X_4 + 1.0X_5, \tag{4}$$

where X_1 is working capital/total assets, X_2 is the retained earnings/total assets, X_3 is the earnings before interest and taxes/total assets, X_4 is market value equity/book value of liabilities, and X_5 is sales/total assets.

Firm-quarters with low Z-scores are assumed to have high bankruptcy probabilities; those with high Z-scores are assumed to have low bankruptcy probabilities.

The second approach uses a probit model similar to that described by Eq. (2), except that Altman's (1993) independent variables (X_1–X_5) are used:

$$\Pr(\mathrm{BKRPT} = 1) = \alpha + \beta_1 X_1 + \beta_2 X_2 + \beta_3 X_3 + \beta_4 X_4 + \beta_5 X_5. \tag{5}$$

All three of the bankruptcy probability models provide reasonable assessments of relative bankruptcy probabilities. Regardless of the model used, airlines approaching bankruptcy (e.g., Eastern Airlines in 1988) are consistently in the highest bankruptcy-probability quintiles and financially healthy airlines (e.g., Southwest Airlines) are consistently in the lowest bankruptcy-probability quintiles. Furthermore, pricing analyses using all of the bankruptcy-probability models yield similar results. Therefore, there is no evidence that observed similarities in price discounts for Chapters 7 and 11 transactions are driven by the specific bankruptcy model used.

The second specification issue addressed in this section involves sample selection bias. Although bankruptcy court protection fails to mitigate discounts at which distressed firms sell assets, it can help firms avoid liquidation in the first place (liquidation avoidance is addressed in more detail in the following section). This raises questions concerning the accuracy of the price discount analyses presented in Table 5. In particular, since we only observe discounts for airlines that choose to sell, previously reported coefficient estimates might be biased because of the sample selection procedure. To address this possibility,

Heckman's (1979) two-step correction is implemented. In the first step, the inverse Mills ratio is calculated from a probit model that predicts the probability that an airline will sell an aircraft in a given calendar quarter. In the second step, the inverse Mills ratio is included as a regressor in Eq. (3), the price discount regression. The inverse Mills ratio is calculated using the following probit model, estimated over 1021 firm-quarters:

$$\begin{aligned}\Pr(\text{SALE} = 1) = \alpha + \sum_{j=2}^{5} \beta_j \Pr(\text{BR})_j + \beta_6 T_{-1} + \beta_7 T_{-2} + \beta_8\, \text{BKRPT} \\ + \beta_9\, \text{INDEX} + \beta_{10}\, \text{NDEL} + \beta_{11}\, \text{NBUY} \\ + \beta_{12} \log(\text{NOWN}), \qquad (6)\end{aligned}$$

where SALE is one if the firm sells at least one aircraft in the calendar quarter and zero otherwise, $\Pr(\text{BR})_j$ are dummy variables indicating bankruptcy probability quintiles, calculated using Eq. (2), BKRPT is one if the transaction occurred when the firm was operating under Chapter 11 or liquidating under Chapter 7 and zero otherwise, INDEX is the used aircraft price index calculated from hedonic regression calendar quarter dummy variable coefficients, NDEL is the number of new aircraft delivered in the quarter, NBUY is the number of used aircraft purchased in the quarter, and NOWN is the number of aircraft owned at the beginning of the quarter.

Estimation results from Eq. (6) are presented in Appendix B.

Panel B of Table 5 presents analyses of hedonic regression residuals when the inverse Mills ratio is included as a regressor. Results are very similar to those obtained when the inverse Mills ratio is excluded (Panel A), especially if firm effects are included in the model. A test of the null hypothesis that Chapters 7, 11, T_{-1}, and Bankruptcy Quintile 5 coefficients are equal still fails to reject at conventional levels. This suggests that sample selection bias is not driving the conclusion that there is little difference in the effects of Chapters 11 and 7 protection on asset sale prices.

The third and final specification test addresses the possibility that similarities in price discounts for Chapters 7 and 11 transactions are caused by the hedonic regression methodology. Specifically, because Chapters 7 and 11 sales are dominated by Braniff and Eastern, respectively, these transactions may be causing a downward bias in hedonic prices. Therefore, even if bankruptcy transactions occur at severe discounts to true fundamental value, discounts from hedonic prices would not be detected, additionally impeding the ability to detect differences in price discounts for Chapters 7 and 11 transactions. To determine whether this concern is valid, analyses presented in Tables 4 and 5 are repeated after omitting Eastern and Braniff transactions from the hedonic regression. Results are similar to those reported in Tables 4 and 5. Even when Braniff and Eastern sales are omitted from the hedonic regression, there is little statistical evidence that discounts are different for Chapters 7 and 11 transactions.

3.5. Aircraft quality

An alternative explanation for observed effects of bankruptcy status on price is that bankrupt airlines sell aircraft of lower quality. Although the FAA enforces maintenance requirements, airlines are nevertheless able to choose which aircraft in their fleets to sell. To reduce maintenance expenses, bankrupt airlines might choose to sell aircraft that have little time remaining until the next maintenance overhaul. In this case, we would see lower transaction prices for bankrupt sellers simply because of aircraft quality differences. To control for this possibility, one would need information describing time until next airframe overhaul, number of hours on engines, and compliance with FAA airworthiness directives for each aircraft at the time of the transaction. Unfortunately, these data are generally unavailable. Aircraft maintenance records are transferred to aircraft buyers; duplicates are maintained neither by the selling airline nor the FAA. Maintenance expense is reported to the Department of Transportation on a quarterly basis, but after controlling for aircraft type and calendar quarter, maintenance expense is an insignificant predictor of price. Furthermore, bankruptcy and distress variable coefficients are not substantially affected by including maintenance expense as an independent variable.

Although quality-adjusted prices are not available for the entire sample, they are available for a small subsample of Braniff sales that occurred in April 1984 when that airline was operating under Chapter 7 protection. Braniff sold 11 727-200 ADV aircraft to People Express Airlines, which financed the $54.3 million purchase by issuing secured debt. Included in the prospectus for this secured debt issue are appraised values for each of the 11 Braniff aircraft. Appraised values, provided by Avmark, Inc., an independent aircraft appraisal firm, take variability in aircraft quality into consideration. Based on Avmark's appraisals, values for these 11 727-200 ADVs averaged $7.3 million. Braniff sold the airplanes for an average price of $4.9 million, corresponding to a 32.6% discount. This discount, which is in excess of the cost of refurbishment incurred by People Express Airlines, is close to the 24% discount implied by predicted values from Specification 4 of Panel A in Table 5. Thus, based on this small subsample of aircraft, controlling for aircraft quality variation would not significantly alter reported results.

Institutional details also help to alleviate the concern that quality differences are driving results presented in Table 5. Because FAA-approved maintenance plans are carrier specific, airlines have an incentive to sell used aircraft that are in need of scheduled overhauls. By doing so, the buyer's (rather than the seller's) maintenance procedures can be followed, thereby avoiding costly duplication of maintenance. Therefore, it is likely that even financially healthy airlines are prone to sell aircraft in need of maintenance. This reduces the likelihood that differences in observed prices are driven by differences in aircraft quality.

4. Effect of bankruptcy court protection on the rate of sales

The rate of asset sales provides further evidence that bankruptcy court protection is ineffective in helping distressed firms conduct orderly dispositions of their assets. Although firms reorganizing under Chapter 11 receive prices that are no greater than prices received by firms liquidating under Chapter 7, Chapter 11 protection may help airlines limit the number of aircraft sold at discounted prices. The number of aircraft sales in a given calendar quarter for firms operating under Chapter 11 protection is compared to the number of sales for the same firms prior to Chapter 11 filing. If Chapter 11 is effective, there should be a noticeable drop in the rate of sales after the filing date.

Table 2 shows the number of sales for each of the bankrupt airlines both during bankruptcy and in the two years preceding bankruptcy filing. The pattern revealed in Table 2 is that firms that eventually enter liquidation proceedings (Air Florida, Braniff, Eastern, Midway, and Pan Am) also sell a significant number of aircraft in the two years preceding bankruptcy. After these firms file for Chapter 11, the number of aircraft sales *increases*. However, airlines that eventually emerge from bankruptcy (America West, Continental, and TWA) sell few aircraft in the months leading up to bankruptcy and experience only a slight increase in the number of sales after bankruptcy filing. Therefore, it does not appear that Chapter 11 protection allows firms to reduce the number of aircraft sales. The data are more consistent with sample selection, whereby the sickest airlines liquidate and the healthier airlines restructure their liabilities (not their assets) in Chapter 11.

There are two potential problems with conclusions drawn from Table 2. The first is that, while Table 2 documents the total number of sales in bankruptcy, it does not document the *rate* of sales for bankrupt firms. The second problem is that there are no controls for other factors that contribute to the rate of sales. For example, larger airlines are likely to sell more aircraft per quarter, as are airlines in the process of upgrading their fleets. To control for these factors, a regression model of the number of aircraft sold in a calendar quarter is constructed.

The dependent variable in the analysis that follows is the number of aircraft sales by a particular firm in a given quarter. Because the dependent variable is a 'count' variable with many observations equal to zero, I assume a Poisson model for aircraft sales. Unlike ordinary least squares (OLS), this specification is particularly well suited to modeling nonnegative integers. Another approach would be to use a probit estimation where the dependent variable takes the value of one if the airline sold a positive number of aircraft in the quarter and zero otherwise. This approach suppresses information contained in the number of sales per quarter. Nevertheless, it yields results similar to those presented. A drawback of the Poisson model is its assumption that the mean and variance of the dependent variable are equal. To avoid imposing this restriction on the data, I use a negative-binomial maximum likelihood procedure pioneered by Hausman et al. (1984, p. 922, Eq. (3.1)). Pulvino (1998), Appendix C, uses the same approach to analyze aircraft purchases. Following this approach, the expected number of sales by firm i during quarter t, $E(n_{it})$, equals the parameter λ_{it}, which is gamma distributed with a mean of γ_{it} and variance δ_{it}. Because the expected number of sales is nonnegative, I assume the following exponential form:

$$\gamma_{it} = e^{(X_{it-1}\beta)}. \qquad (7)$$

X is a matrix of the following explanatory variables:

PBR_j	= dummy variables indicating bankruptcy probability quintiles per Eq. (2), which only take the value of one if the firm is solvent and does not go bankrupt within the next two years,
Ch7	= dummy variable equal to one if the firm is currently liquidating under Chapter 7,
LIQ	= dummy variable equal to one if the firm is currently operating under Chapter 11 and is eventually liquidated,
LIQ_{-1}	= dummy variable equal to one if the calendar quarter is within one year preceding the seller's Chapter 11 filing date and the seller is eventually liquidated,
LIQ_{-2}	= dummy variable equal to one if the calendar quarter is within two years, but more than one year, preceding the seller's Chapter 11 filing date and the seller is eventually liquidated,
NOLIQ	= dummy variable equal to one if the firm is currently bankrupt but eventually emerges from bankruptcy,
$NOLIQ_{-1}$	= dummy variable equal to one if the calendar quarter is within one year preceding the seller's Chapter 11 filing date and the seller eventually emerges from bankruptcy,
$NOLIQ_{-2}$	= dummy variable equal to one if the calendar quarter is within two years, but more than one year, preceding the seller's Chapter 11 filing date and the seller eventually emerges from bankruptcy,
INDEX	= used aircraft price index calculated from calendar quarter dummy variable coefficients in the narrow-body hedonic regression,
NBUY	= number of used aircraft purchased in the quarter,
NDEL	= number of new aircraft delivered in the quarter, and
log(NOWN)	= logarithm of the number of aircraft owned at the beginning of the quarter.

The effect of bankruptcy court protection on the rate of asset sales can be inferred by examining differences in the coefficients multiplying the bankruptcy

Table 6
This table presents determinants of the number of aircraft transactions. The dependent variable in Panel A is the number of aircraft sold in a calendar quarter. In Panel B, the dependent variable is the number of net sales (sales minus the sum of new and used aircraft purchases) per calendar quarter. Independent variables are defined as follows: Ch 7 is a dummy variable equal to one if the firm is liquidating under Chapter 7 in the current calendar quarter; LIQ is a dummy variable equal to one if the firm is operating under Chapter 11 in the calendar quarter and is eventually liquidated; LIQ_{-1} is a dummy variable equal to one if the calendar quarter is within one year preceding the Chapter 11 filing date and the firm is eventually liquidated; LIQ_{-2} is a dummy variable equal to one if the calendar quarter is within two years, but more than one year, preceding the Chapter 11 filing date and the firm is eventually liquidated; NOLIQ equals one if the firm is operating under Chapter 11 in the current calendar quarter but eventually emerges from bankruptcy; $NOLIQ_{-1}$ is a dummy variable equal to one if the calendar quarter is within one year preceding the Chapter 11 filing date and the firm eventually emerges from bankruptcy; $NOLIQ_{-2}$ is a dummy variable equal to one if the calendar quarter is within two years, but more than one year, preceding the Chapter 11 filing date and the firm eventually emerges from bankruptcy; and bankruptcy probability quintile dummies (lagged one period) correspond to predictions from the Probit regressions reported in Table 3. Index, calculated from hedonic regression calendar quarter dummy variables, measures the relative strength of the used aircraft market in the given calendar quarter. NBUY equals the number of used aircraft purchases in the quarter; NDEL equals the number of new aircraft delivered in the firm-quarter; NOWN equals the number of aircraft owned at the beginning of the quarter. Low probability of bankruptcy firm-quarters are omitted to avoid collinearity. Panel A presents maximum likelihood estimates, based on a Poisson specification with an adjustment to allow for differences in the distribution's mean and variance. The estimated variance/mean ratio equals $(1 + \delta)/\delta$. Standard errors are in parentheses.

Panel A: Maximum likelihood estimates of the determinants of the number of used aircraft sales per calendar quarter; 1021 observations

Ch 7	Liquidating firms			Emerging firms			Bankruptcy probability quintile				Index	NBUY	NDEL	ln(NOWN)	ln(δ)	Const.
	LIQ	LIQ_{-1}	LIQ_{-2}	NOLIQ	$NOLIQ_{-1}$	$NOLIQ_{-2}$	(High probability) 5	4	(Low probability) 3	2						
2.18	2.03	1.74	1.12	0.58	0.09	0.09	0.76	0.54	−0.01	0.36	0.02	0.07	0.02	0.65	−0.98	−4.73
(0.38)[c]	(0.32)[c]	(0.34)[c]	(0.39)[b]	(0.42)	(0.70)	(0.59)	(0.21)[c]	(0.21)[a]	(0.25)	(0.21)	(0.07)	(0.03)[a]	(0.02)	(0.07)[c]	(0.13)[c]	(0.42)[c]

Panel B: OLS estimates of the determinant of the number of 'net sales' per calendar quarter; 1021 observations

Ch 7	Liquidating firms			Emerging firms			Bankruptcy probability quintile				Index	ln(NOWN)	Const.	Adj. R^2
	LIQ	LIQ_{-1}	LIQ_{-2}	NOLIQ	$NOLIQ_{-1}$	$NOLIQ_{-2}$	(High Probability) 5	4	(Low Probability) 3	2				
5.33	7.80	4.21	2.69	2.44	2.45	2.24	1.91	1.62	0.34	0.37	0.18	−0.64	−0.40	0.16
(1.09)[c]	(0.88)[c]	(0.82)[c]	(0.82)[c]	(0.84)[b]	(0.91)[b]	(0.90)	(0.37)[c]	(0.37)[c]	(0.37)	(0.36)	(0.14)	(0.09)[c]	(0.60)	

[a]Significant at 0.05 level.
[b]Significant at 0.01 level.
[c]Significant at 0.001 level.

variables (Ch7, LIQ, NOLIQ) and the pre-bankruptcy variables (LIQ_{-1}, LIQ_{-2}, $NOLIQ_{-1}$, $NOLIQ_{-2}$). For example, a finding that the NOLIQ coefficient is significantly smaller than the $NOLIQ_{-1}$ coefficient would imply that bankruptcy court protection reduces the rate of asset sales.

Control variables in the negative binomial model include INDEX, NBUY, NDEL, and NOWN. INDEX is included to control for the effect of the strength of the used aircraft market on firms' propensities to sell aircraft. NBUY and NDEL control for the possibility that airlines sell used airplanes because they have commitments to buy other planes, and NOWN controls for the possibility that firms that own more aircraft tend to sell more aircraft.

Panel A of Table 6 presents results from estimating the negative binomial model. These results are consistent with patterns observed in Table 2. Coefficients on the bankruptcy probability dummy variables indicate that the rate of asset sales is positively related to the degree of distress. Compared to firm-quarters in the lowest bankruptcy probability quintile, those in the highest quintile sell approximately twice as many aircraft per quarter ($e^{0.76} = 2.14$). For firms that are eventually liquidated, the rate of sales increases dramatically in the two years before the Chapter 11 filing. Further increases in the rate of sales are evident during Chapter 11. The rate of sales in Chapter 11 is seven times greater than the rate observed for financially healthy firms ($e^{2.03} = 7.61$) and is almost identical to the rate observed in Chapter 7 liquidation.

Results are much less dramatic for firms that emerge from bankruptcy. In the two years prior to filing for bankruptcy, the rate of sales for these firms is indistinguishable from the rate at which healthy airlines sell aircraft. After Chapter 11 filing, the rate of sales jumps to a rate that is 1.8 times greater than the rate at which the most healthy airlines sell assets, but this effect is not statistically significant at conventional levels. The bottom line is that there is no evidence that Chapter 11 protection *reduces* the rate of asset sales.

To determine whether the negative binomial results presented in Panel A are sensitive to specification, I use OLS to assess the effect of bankruptcy status on 'net sales', defined to be the number of used aircraft sales per calendar quarter minus the sum of new and used aircraft purchases in the same calendar quarter. Results from the OLS analysis are presented in Panel B of Table 6. Consistent with results from the negative binomial model, Chapter 11 does not reduce the rate of aircraft sales.

5. Conclusions

This paper uses a sample of commercial aircraft transactions to assess the effects of reorganization and liquidation proceedings on revenues from asset sales. The evidence indicates that neither protection under Chapter 11 of the bankruptcy code nor court-supervised liquidation under Chapter 7 of the code are effective at eliminating distress-sale discounts. Airlines operating under supervision of the bankruptcy court sell assets at greater discounts than do distressed but nonbankrupt carriers. Furthermore, the magnitude of the discount is not significantly lower for transactions occurring in reorganization proceedings than in liquidation proceedings. Therefore, the data do not support the contention that Chapter 11 of the current bankruptcy law (rather than liquidation via Chapter 7) helps to mitigate distress-sale discounts and improve resource allocation.

Bankruptcy court protection also does not appear to affect the rate of asset sales. Distressed firms that eventually liquidate experience a high rate of asset sales prior to entering bankruptcy and an even higher rate after Chapter 11 filing. Airlines that eventually emerge from bankruptcy refrain from selling assets before filing for Chapter 11 and experience a slight increase in selling activity during bankruptcy proceedings. As far as asset sales are concerned, Chapter 11 does not appear to provide significant benefits to distressed firm's claimholders – it neither increases prices at which assets are sold nor limits the number of aircraft sold at discounted prices. Therefore, whether bankruptcy systems that encourage reorganization are superior to those that require liquidation depends on the ability of reorganization laws to allow the continuation of financially distressed firms and promote liquidation of economically distressed firms. To date, studies that have examined this question have failed to reach a consensus. Hotchkiss (1995), p. 3, concludes that the current bankruptcy code provides '... economically important biases toward continuation of unprofitable firms'. The opposite conclusion is reached by Alderson and Betker (1995), who find that of 88 firms that reorganized under Chapter 11, over 80% created more wealth by continuing rather than liquidating. Additional research on the relative efficiencies of reorganization and liquidation bankruptcy venues is clearly needed.

Appendix A

This table presents results from estimating the following hedonic regression:

$$\log(\text{PRICE}) = \beta_0 + \sum_{1}^{I} \beta_i\, \text{QTR}_i + \sum_{1}^{J} \beta_j\, \text{MODEL}_j + \sum_{1}^{K} \beta_k\, \text{STAGE}_k + \beta_{\text{AGE}} \log(1 + \text{AGE}) + \varepsilon.$$

The dependent variable is the natural logarithm of transaction price. Panel A presents results using narrow-body transactions; Panel B presents results using wide-body transactions. Dummy variables for Airbus 300B4-200 for the narrow-body regression and B-747-100 for the wide-body regression, Stage 3 engines, and the third quarter of 1991 are omitted to avoid collinearity.

Standard errors are in parentheses and are corrected for heteroskedasticity using the methods of Huber (1967) and White (1980). Missing entries are due to a lack of transactions and collinearity (e.g., B-737-100 and B-707-320C are the only Stage 1 narrow-body aircraft in the sample). Significance at the 0.001, 0.01 and 0.05 levels is denoted by ***, **, and * respectively.

	Independent variables	Panel A: narrow-body sales	Panel B: wide-body sales
Model dummies (Narrow-Body/ Wide-Body)	DC-9-10/DC-10-10	− 0.40 (0.073)***	0.17 (0.071)*
	DC-9-30/DC-10-30	0.19 (0.066)**	0.38 (0.079)***
	DC-9-50/B-747-100	0.76 (0.092)***	—
	B-707-320C/B-747-200	− 0.71 (0.151)***	0.49 (0.072)***
	B-727-100/L-1011-1	− 0.63 (0.069)***	− 0.51 (0.088)***
	B-727-100QC/L-1011-500	− 0.34 (0.071)***	0.11 (0.110)
	B-727-200	− 0.07 (0.081)	—
	B-727-200 ADV	0.46 (0.077)***	—
	B-737-100	—	—
	B-737-200	0.14 (0.073)*	—
	B-737-200 ADV	0.77 (0.110)***	—
	B-737-300	− 0.51 (0.170)***	—
Quarter dummies	1978.1	1.34 (0.221)***	—
	1978.2	1.32 (0.205)***	0.95 (0.166)***
	1978.3	1.54 (0.247)***	1.01 (0.175)***
	1978.4	1.23 (0.199)***	0.74 (0.171)***
	1979.1	1.62 (0.230)***	—

Appendix. Continued.

Independent variables	Panel A: narrow-body sales	Panel B: wide-body sales
1979.2	1.34 (0.214)***	—
1979.3	1.40 (0.219)***	—
1979.4	1.52 (0.211)***	—
1980.1	1.28 (0.200)***	—
1980.2	1.36 (0.198)***	0.82 (0.159)***
1980.3	1.49 (0.230)***	—
1980.4	1.22 (0.192)***	—
1981.1	1.05 (0.192)***	0.66 (0.170)***
1981.2	1.16 (0.197)***	0.03 (0.210)
1981.3	1.14 (0.202)***	0.20 (0.158)
1981.4	1.03 (0.200)*	—
1982.1	0.65 (0.226)**	0.57 (0.150)***
1982.2	0.95 (0.208)***	—
1982.3	0.92 (0.223)***	– 0.15 (0.161)
1982.4	0.75 (0.240)***	– 0.12 (0.150)
1983.1	0.88 (0.226)***	0.29 (0.148)*
1983.2	0.98 (0.202)***	– 0.19 (0.146)
1983.3	0.57 (0.220)**	– 0.08 (0.165)
1983.4	0.73 (0.194)***	0.11 (0.164)

continued over

Appendix. Continued.

Independent variables	Panel A: narrow-body sales	Panel B: wide-body sales
1984.1	0.75 (0.191)***	− 0.21 (0.147)
1984.2	0.90 (0.193)***	0.09 (0.166)
1984.3	0.94 (0.211)***	0.14 (0.172)
1984.4	1.00 (0.192)***	0.30 (0.157)
1985.1	1.11 (0.190)***	0.38 (0.147)**
1985.2	1.04 (0.192)***	0.24 (0.146)
1985.3	1.40 (0.193)***	0.39 (0.146)**
1985.4	1.31 (0.193)***	0.49 (0.164)**
1986.1	1.40 (0.206)***	0.40 (0.144)**
1986.2	1.08 (0.243)***	0.41 (0.163)*
1986.3	1.30 (0.221)***	0.41 (0.141)**
1986.4	1.20 (0.195)***	0.52 (0.150)***
1987.1	1.38 (0.191)***	0.54 (0.181)**
1987.2	1.42 (0.206)***	0.56 (0.171)***
1987.3	1.23 (0.186)***	0.43 (0.154)**
1987.4	1.34 (0.190)***	0.56 (0.157)***
1988.1	1.22 (0.236)***	0.39 (0.170)*
1988.2	1.28 (0.200)***	0.46 (0.145)**
1988.3	1.28 (0.191)***	0.37 (0.171)*
1988.4	1.17 (0.196)***	0.29 (0.170)

Appendix. Continued.

Independent variables	Panel A: narrow-body sales	Panel B: wide-body sales
1989.1	1.14 (0.195)***	0.41 (0.151)**
1989.2	1.09 (0.189)***	0.39 (0.166)*
1989.3	1.20 (0.197)***	0.49 (0.170)**
1989.4	1.24 (0.185)***	0.74 (0.142)***
1990.1	0.96 (0.222)***	0.71 (0.139)***
1990.2	1.10 (0.192)***	0.55 (0.146)***
1990.3	1.03 (0.203)***	0.63 (0.163)***
1990.4	1.05 (0.214)***	0.04 (0.219)
1991.1	0.90 (0.195)***	0.30 (0.173)
1991.2	0.69 (0.214)**	0.45 (0.234)
1991.4	– 0.08 (0.409)	0.17 (0.198)
log(AGE + 1)	– 0.16 (0.057)***	– 0.33 (0.089)***
St1 Dummy	– 2.16 (0.277)***	—
St2 Dummy	– 1.73 (0.146)***	—
Constant	2.83 (0.247)***	3.61 (0.309)***
Number of observations	1079	254
Adjusted R^2	0.76	0.74

Appendix B. Heckman two-stage regression

This table presents results from the first-stage probit estimation used in the Heckman two-stage sample selection correction procedure:

$$\Pr(\text{SALE}=1) = \alpha + \sum_{j=2}^{5} \beta_j\,\text{PBRj} + \beta_6 T_{-1} + \beta_7 T_{-2} + \beta_8\,\text{BKRPT} + \beta_9\,\text{INDEX} + \beta_{10}\,\text{NDEL} + \beta_{11}\,\text{NBUY} + \beta_{12}\log(\text{NOWN}).$$

The dependent variable takes the value of one if the airline sold at least one airplane in the calendar quarter and zero otherwise. PBR2, PBR3, PBR4, and PBR5 are dummy variables representing bankruptcy probability quintiles generated from Eq. (2). PBR1 is omitted from the regression to avoid collinearity. T_{-1} and T_{-2} are dummy variables indicating whether the firm files for bankruptcy within the next one and two years, respectively; BKRPT takes the value of one if the firm is bankrupt in the quarter, zero otherwise; INDEX uses the hedonic regression calendar quarter dummy coefficients to measure the relative strength of the used aircraft market in the calendar quarter; NDEL equals the number of new aircraft deliveries and NBUY equals the number of used aircraft purchases in the calendar quarter; and NOWN equals the number of aircraft owned at the beginning of the calendar quarter. All independent variables, except for NDEL and NBUY, are lagged one period. Predicted values from this regression are used to calculate the Inverse Mills Ratios:

$$\text{Inverse Mills Ratio} = \frac{\phi(\alpha)}{1-\Phi(\alpha)},$$

where α = predicted value from the probit regression, ϕ = probability density function for the normal distribution, and Φ = cumulative function for the normal distribution. Standard errors are in parentheses.

Heckman 1st-stage probit: dependent variable equals one if number of sales is positive, zero otherwise. Significance at the 0.001, 0.01 and 0.05 levels is denoted by ***, **, and * respectively.

Independent variables	
PBR1	—
PBR2	0.33 (0.155)*
PBR3	0.01 (0.168)
PBR4	0.51 (0.156)***
PBR5	0.62 (0.155)***
T_{-1}	0.63 (0.259)*

Independent variables	
T_{-2}	0.44 (0.262)
BKRPT	1.00 (0.227)***
INDEX	0.04 (0.057)
NDEL	0.02 (0.015)
NBUY	0.05 (0.027)
log (NOWN)	0.37*** (0.044)
Constant	− 2.70 (0.283)***
No. of observations	1021
Pseudo-R^2	0.13

References

Aghion, P., Hart, O., Moore, J., 1992. The economics of bankruptcy law reform. Journal of Law, Economics, and Organization 8, 523–546.

Alderson, M., Betker, B., 1995. Liquidation versus continuation: did reorganized firms do the right thing? Unpublished working paper, Ohio State University.

Altman, E., 1984. A further empirical investigation of the bankruptcy cost question. Journal of Finance 39, 1067–1089.

Altman, E., 1993. Corporate Financial Distress and Bankruptcy, second ed., Wiley, New York.

Asquith, P., Gertner, R., Scharfstein, D., 1994. Anatomy of financial distress: an examination of junk-bond issuers. Quarterly Journal of Economics 109, 625–658.

Baird, D., 1986. The uneasy case for corporate reorganizations. Journal of Legal Studies 15, 127–147.

Betker, B., 1995. Management's incentives, equity's bargaining power, and deviations from absolute priority in Chapter 11 bankruptcies. Journal of Business 68, 161–183.

Bradley, M., Rosenzweig, M., 1992. The untenable case for Chapter 11. Yale Law Journal 101, 1043–1095.

Brown, D., 1997. Liquidity and liquidation: evidence from real estate investment trusts. Journal of Finance, forthcoming.

Chan, L., Lakonishok, J., 1993. Institutional trades and intraday stock price behavior. Journal of Financial Economics 33, 173–199.

Chan, L., Lakonishok, J., 1995. The behavior of stock prices around institutional trades. The Journal of Finance 50, 1147–1174.

Chow, G., 1967. Technological change and the demand for computers. American Economic Review 57, 1117–1130.

Franks, J., Torous, W., 1994. A comparison of financial recontracting in distressed exchanges and Chapter 11 reorganizations. Journal of Financial Economics 35, 349–370.

Gertner, R., Scharfstein, D., 1991. A theory of workouts and the effects of reorganization law. The Journal of Finance 46, 1189–1222.

Hausman, J., Hall, B., Griliches, Z., 1984. Econometric models for count data with an application to the patents–R&D relationship. Econometrica 52, 909–938.

Heckman, J., 1979. Sample selection bias as a specification error. Econometrica 47, 153–162.

Holthausen, R., Leftwich, R., Mayers, D., 1987. The effect of large block transactions on security prices. Journal of Financial Economics 19, 237–267.

Holthausen, R., Leftwich, R., Mayers, D., 1990. Large block transactions, the speed of response, and temporary and permanent stock-price effects. Journal of Financial Economics 26, 71–95.

Hotchkiss, E., 1995. Postbankruptcy performance and management turnover. Journal of Finance 50, 3–21.

Huber, P., 1967. The behavior of maximum likelihood estimates under non-standard conditions. Proceedings of the Fifth Berkeley Symposium on Mathematical Statistics and Probability 1, 221–233.

Kraus, A., Stoll, H., 1972. Price impacts of block trading on the New York Stock Exchange. Journal of Finance 27, 569–588.

Lerner, J., 1995. Pricing and financial resources: an analysis of the disk drive industry, 1980–1988. Review of Economics and Statistics 77, 585–598.

Mikkelson, W., Partch, M., 1985. Stock price effects and costs of secondary distributions. Journal of Financial Economics 14, 165–194.

Ohta, M., Griliches, Z., 1986. Automobile prices and quality: did the gasoline price increases change consumer tastes in the US? Journal of Business and Economic Statistics 4, 187–198.

Pulvino, T., 1998. Do asset fire-sales exist?: an empirical investigation of commercial aircraft transactions. Journal of Finance 53, 939–978.

Shleifer, A., Vishny, R., 1992. Liquidation values and debt capacity: a market equilibrium approach. Journal of Finance 47, 1343–1366.

Strömberg, P., 1998. Conflicts of interest and market illiquidity in bankruptcy auctions: theory and tests. Unpublished working paper, University of Chicago.

Thorburn, K., 1997. Cash auction bankruptcy: costs, recovery rates and auction premiums. Unpublished working paper, Stockholm School of Economics.

Warner, J., 1977. Bankruptcy costs: some evidence. Journal of Finance 32, 337–347.

Weiss, L., 1990. Bankruptcy resolution: direct costs and violation of priority claims. Journal of Financial Economics 27, 285–314.

Weiss, L., Wruck, K., 1998. Information problems, conflicts of interest, and asset stripping: Chapter 11's failure in the case of Eastern Airlines. Journal of Financial Economics 48, 55–97.

White, H., 1980. A heteroskedasticity-consistent covariance matrix estimator and a direct test for heteroskedasticity. Econometrica 48, 817–830.

Wruck, K., 1990. Financial distress, reorganization, and organizational efficiency. Journal of Financial Economics 27, 419–444.

[20]

THE JOURNAL OF FINANCE • VOL. LIV, NO. 5 • OCTOBER 1999

The Equity Performance of Firms Emerging from Bankruptcy

ALLAN C. EBERHART, EDWARD I. ALTMAN, and REENA AGGARWAL*

ABSTRACT

This study assesses the stock return performance of 131 firms emerging from Chapter 11. Using differing estimates of expected returns, we consistently find evidence of large, positive excess returns in 200 days of returns following emergence. We also examine the reaction of our sample firms' equity returns to their earnings announcements after emergence from Chapter 11. The positive and significant reactions suggest that our results are driven by the market's expectational errors, not mismeasurement of risk. The results provide an interesting contrast, but not a contradiction, to previous work that has documented poor operating performance for firms emerging from Chapter 11.

WITH LARGE CORPORATE BANKRUPTCIES being commonplace during the late 1980s and early 1990s, there has been a notable increase in the number of firms emerging from bankruptcy (Altman (1991, 1993)). When firms emerge from bankruptcy, they often cancel the old stock and distribute an entirely new issue of common stock.

The stocks of firms emerging from a Chapter 11 bankruptcy are often called "orphan" equities among practitioners and there have been reports in the popular press about spectacular returns in this market. For example, as Sandler (1991, p. C1) states:

> While initial public offerings have been grabbing all the glory, there's a shadow market for new stocks that is doing nicely too. It's where people trade shares of companies coming out of bankruptcy or reorganization.

* Allan Eberhart and Reena Aggarwal are from Georgetown University and Edward Altman is from New York University. We acknowledge helpful comments received from Edie Hotchkiss, Lisa Fairchild, René Stulz, an anonymous referee, and seminar participants at the Hong Kong University of Science and Technology, the IBC Conference, the University of North Carolina at Chapel Hill, and the University of British Columbia. We thank the Georgetown University Capital Markets Research Center for providing support. Aggarwal and Eberhart received support from a Georgetown University Summer Research Grant. Eberhart also received support from a Goldman Sachs Fellowship and worked on parts of this paper as a Visiting Assistant Professor at the New York University Stern School of Business. Aggarwal worked on parts of this paper as an Academic Scholar at the Securities and Exchange Commission. We thank Christopher McHugh of New Generation Research (Boston) for generously supplying part of the data for this study and our research assistants for excellent research assistance.

> In recent months, some investors have made 50% to 100% on their money by trading the new shares of Republic Health, Southland Corp. and Maxicare Health Plans after those companies finished reorganizing their business.

The primary purpose of this paper is to test the efficiency of the market for stocks of firms emerging from Chapter 11. Our sample includes 131 firms emerging from Chapter 11 between 1980 and 1993 and we test whether the long-term—that is, the first 200 days of returns after emergence—average cumulative abnormal returns (ACARs) are significantly different from zero. We find significant ACARs that—depending on how the expected returns are estimated—have a lower bound of 24.6 percent (the median CARs, though lower, are also positive and significant).[1]

We investigate several explanations for these findings. Since our tests are joint tests of efficiency and the model we use to estimate expected returns, our results may reflect a mismeasurement of the stocks' riskiness rather than an inefficient market. The results' robustness with respect to different ways of estimating expected returns casts doubt on this explanation, however.

We also examine the reaction of our sample firms to their earnings announcements after emergence. La Porta et al. (1995) argue that the positive excess returns on "value" stocks are due to expectational errors made by the market. Consistent with this assertion, they find that value stocks have unexpectedly good earnings as shown by the positive abnormal returns around their earnings announcements. For our sample, the average and median excess returns are positive and significant around the sample firms' earnings announcements, providing more evidence that our results are driven by expectational errors made by the market, not a mismeasurement of risk.

We also analyze cross-sectional differences in the returns. Specifically, we examine the firms' stock prices upon emergence, changes in their primary line of business, whether the firm had a prepackaged bankruptcy and the willingness of institutional investors to accept only equity in the reorganized firm (in exchange for their old claims).

Low-priced stocks often have higher transaction costs and may have higher estimation risks than captured by our estimates of expected returns.[2] We find no evidence, however, that our positive excess returns are concentrated in low-priced stocks.

Firms that change their primary line of business in bankruptcy may also have higher estimation risks because the historical information on the firm

[1] The emergence of a firm from bankruptcy is loosely analogous to an IPO. In contrast to our long-term positive excess returns, Aggarwal and Rivoli (1990) and Ritter (1991) report long-term negative excess returns for IPOs. Field (1997) finds that IPOs with larger institutional holdings do not underperform a control sample in the long run, ceteris paribus.

[2] Barry and Brown (1984) argue that small firms have higher estimation risk and this explains much, though not all, of the small-firm effect identified by Banz (1981). For our sample, the correlation between the log of price at emergence and the log of equity capitalization at emergence is 0.73.

is less helpful in predicting the firm's future performance. Our results, though, show no consistent difference in returns between firms that change their primary line of business and those that do not.

Because of their shorter duration, prepackaged bankruptcies may have risk characteristics that differ from the nonprepackaged bankruptcies. However, we find no consistent evidence of a significant relation between returns and a dummy variable equal to one if the firm had a prepackaged bankruptcy and zero otherwise.

Finally, Brown, James, and Mooradian (1993) argue that the acceptance of equity in a reorganized firm by informed investors, such as banks, conveys favorable private information. We find some evidence that when institutional investors accept only equity (including warrants) in exchange for their claims, the long-term returns are higher.[3]

Our results are of broad interest for two main reasons. First, they cast doubt on the informational efficiency of this market and are consistent with recent studies documenting long-term abnormal returns (e.g., Loughran and Ritter (1995), Spiess and Affleck-Graves (1995)). Second, the results provide an interesting contrast, but not a contradiction, to prior work that suggests the Chapter 11 process does not efficiently screen out economically inefficient firms (e.g., Hotchkiss (1995)). Our results suggest that, although these firms may not achieve strong operating performance, their performance is better than the market expected at the time they emerged from Chapter 11. Most firms emerging from bankruptcy, however, do not emerge with stock trading on the NYSE/AMEX or Nasdaq and the sample in Hotchkiss includes some of these firms. Therefore, direct comparisons with the sample in Hotchkiss must be tempered by this caveat.

A brief review of the bankruptcy process and related literature is presented in the next section. The data and methods are discussed in Section II. The empirical results are presented in Section III and the summary in Section IV.

I. The Bankruptcy Process and Related Work

Often, as noted earlier, when the formerly bankrupt firm emerges as a public company the old stock is canceled and new stock is issued. If the value of the debt claims exceeds the value of the firm and the absolute priority rule (APR) is followed, then the old shareholders' claim is worthless. In approximately 75 percent of corporate bankruptcy cases, however, the APR is violated (e.g., Eberhart, Moore, and Roenfeldt (1990), Eberhart and Sweeney (1992), Weiss (1990)). Nevertheless, Altman and Eberhart (1994) show that,

[3] Brown et al. (1993) focus on the valuation effects around offer announcements. Therefore, they do not explicitly predict that the market fails to fully account for this information in the stock price after it is publicly known. Nevertheless, their model provides a useful motivation for our test of the market's ability to efficiently incorporate this information.

on average, higher seniority still implies higher payoffs upon emergence from bankruptcy. Creditors usually receive part of their payoff as new stock in the firm, frequently giving them majority ownership.

During the bankruptcy process, the estimate of the firm's going concern value that will be used to set the payoffs to each class of claimants is debated. Depending on its priority, each class of claimants has an incentive to present a biased estimate of firm value. It is in the interest of junior claimants to argue for upwardly biased estimates of firm value because this increases the proportion of firm value they receive. Conversely, senior claimants—who are often the institutional investors—usually push for a lower estimate of firm value so that they can retain a greater portion of the firm and reap the rewards if the firm's subsequent equity value is higher than would be expected given the riskiness of the stock. Perhaps most important is the bias of management; they have an incentive to value the firm above its liquidation value (to maintain their jobs) but below its true value, assuming its true value is above the estimate of its liquidation value. Therefore, if the market is persuaded by the manager's forecast, the postemergence stock performance of the firm will seem superior relative to the equilibrium expected returns and the manager's performance will look abnormally good.

Hotchkiss (1995) documents the operating performance of firms emerging from bankruptcy that filed for Chapter 11 between October 1979 and September 1988. Overall, she finds the median operating performance to be positive. More than 40 percent of the firms, however, continue to experience operating losses in the three years after emergence and 32 percent subsequently file for bankruptcy again or restructure their debt. Moreover, the median industry-adjusted operating performance is negative.

More recent evidence by Alderson and Betker (1996) suggests that the operating performance of firms is abnormally positive following emergence from Chapter 11. They examine 89 firms emerging between 1983 and 1993. In contrast to the focus by Hotchkiss (1995) on accounting measures of performance, they focus on the total cash flows provided by the firm. They report that the total cash flow returns for their sample are significantly higher than the returns on the S&P 500 index.

In summary, the results in Hotchkiss (1995) suggest that the bankruptcy code is biased toward letting economically inefficient, or poorly restructured, firms reorganize instead of liquidating. Alderson and Betker argue that total cash flow measures and comparisons to the alternative of liquidation are better means of assessing the success of firms emerging from Chapter 11. By their metrics, the Chapter 11 process looks more efficient.[4] Though the focus of this paper is on the efficiency of the stock market, our results are indirectly supportive of Alderson and Betker (1996).

[4] See Gilson (1997) for some additional evidence on the efficiency of Chapter 11. Andrade and Kaplan (1998) also examine 20 stocks of firms emerging from bankruptcy or financial distress and find that they perform abnormally well after emergence.

II. Data and Methods

Our primary source of information on firms emerging from bankruptcy is New Generation Research (Boston). New Generation is a firm that specializes in collecting bankruptcy data. Because New Generation's list of firms emerging from bankruptcy becomes more thorough in the 1990s, we construct our sample in two phases.

The first phase is for a list of firms, provided by New Generation, that file and complete a Chapter 11 bankruptcy between January 1980 and December 1989. We supplement this list with a search on the *Dow Jones News Retrieval* using the keywords "bankruptcy" and "emerge." There are 350 firms in this sample. For the second phase, we use a more comprehensive list provided by New Generation. This list contains 196 firms that emerge from Chapter 11 between January 1990 and December 1993, bringing the total sample to 546 firms.

Among the 546 firms, 131 emerge with equity trading on the NYSE, AMEX, or Nasdaq.[5] When the firms emerge from bankruptcy, 71 begin trading on the Nasdaq, 37 on the NYSE, and 23 on the AMEX; 76 of the stocks trade throughout the bankruptcy process. Though we cannot rule out the possibility that our sample is less than the population, we are confident that we have assembled the vast majority of firms.[6]

The average closing price on the first day of trading (postemergence day 0) following emergence is \$6.32 and the median is \$3.75. Similar to other studies (e.g., Altman (1993)), we find that the average time spent in bankruptcy (measured, in our case, from the bankruptcy announcement date through the first trading date after emergence) is close to two years, with an average of 22.39 months and a median of 20.17 months.

There are 78 firms for which we have some information provided by New Generation on the payoffs to each claimant in the formerly bankrupt firms. Over the past several years, New Generation has gathered information on the payoffs from disclosure statements, discussions with attorneys, and other sources. With this information, we can distinguish between cases where institutional investors accept only equity (including warrants) in the newly emerged firm and cases where they demand another form of payment; 10 firms had their institutional investors accept only equity.

[5] Two firms in our sample stop trading during the 200 days of returns following emergence. As a robustness check, we assume that these stocks are worthless on the last trading day and find qualitatively similar results to those reported below (see Shumway (1997) for a discussion of the delisting bias in CRSP data).

[6] Hotchkiss (1995) has an overall sample that is larger than our sample but, in an earlier version of her paper, she reports that only 41 of the firms in her sample have sufficient data on CRSP (Center for Research in Security Prices) to compute returns for the first year following bankruptcy. Moreover, Alderson and Betker (1996) require some market data for their tests and their sample size is 89 firms (we have 126 firms over the 1983 to 1993 period covered in the Alderson and Betker sample).

A. Definition of the First Trading Date

Because the emergence procedure varies across firms, so does the appropriate starting point for our efficiency tests. For example, as mentioned earlier, 76 of the sample firms' stocks trade throughout the Chapter 11 period. The stock may trade up to the day the new stock is issued and the old stock is then canceled. Alternatively, additional shares may or may not be issued and the "new" stock often trades under the old name. If the old stock is canceled and new stock is issued, then the first trading date is simply the first day the new stock trades following emergence. If additional stock is issued, then the first trading day is the first day the "new" stock (i.e., with the additional shares) trades following emergence. If no new stock is issued, then the first trading date is defined as the emergence date for the firm (recall that the first return day is for the second day of trading). Our sources for the emergence dates include New Generation, *Capital Changes Reporter*, *Wall Street Journal Index* (if we do not have information from the *Dow Jones News Retrieval)*, and *Bloomberg*.

There are only two firms where we know the shareholders retain their shares in the old firm and no additional stock is issued. As noted above, the other two categories are where the shareholders retain their shares and additional stock is issued to pay the debtholders or the old stock is canceled and new stock is issued. The difference between these two categories is not substantive; the old shareholders can have their ownership diluted equally by retaining their shares and having the firm issue additional stock to the old debtholders or by having the firm cancel the old stock and giving the old shareholders a fraction of the new stock.

The Center for Research in Security Prices (CRSP) does not always pick up the stock when it first begins trading. So, we hand-collect data from the *Standard and Poor's Daily Stock Price Record* (SPDSPR) for the 28 firms where the first trading date in the SPDSPR precedes the first trading date on CRSP. The reason for this gap is that all these firms begin trading on a "when-issued" basis (i.e., trading of stock before it is issued). When-issued trading begins after the reorganization plan is confirmed. The exchanges and Nasdaq allow when-issued trading when they are certain the shares will be mailed out by the firm and it will be possible to settle shortly afterward.[7] Therefore, though there can be some liquidity and settlement day differences between when-issued and "regular" stock trading (e.g., Lamoureux and Wansley (1989)), the first trading date can be for when-issued or

[7] The stock is listed when it first begins trading, whether on a when-issued or "regular" basis. For an analysis of the listing effect, see Dharan and Ikenberry (1995). Our sample differs substantially from the sample in Dharan and Ikenberry because our firms typically have restructured their operating and financial structure in a way that firms do not do when they just change their listing. Moreover, many firms in our sample trade continuously and do not change their listing.

regular trading, whichever comes first.[8] To check if the 28 firms with SPDSPR prices (preceding the CRSP prices) perform differently from the other 103 firms, we compare the average and median excess returns of the two subsamples over the 200-day period and find that they are insignificantly different.

B. Estimation of Expected Returns

Our primary method of estimating expected returns is to use matched firms.[9] For each sample firm, we choose a matched firm that has the same primary two-digit SIC code as the sample firm and is closest in equity capitalization as of the first trading date for the sample firm. We call this sample the size- and industry-matched (SIM) sample.

We also match firms in the same industry by size and book-to-market ratios. First, we form size deciles within the two-digit primary SIC code for each sample firm, where size is defined above. Next, we choose the firm in the same size decile as the sample firm that has the closest book-to-market ratio. Seven of the matched firms delist during the 200-day period following emergence from Chapter 11 for our sample firms. In these cases, we fill in the remaining days with the next closest matched firm (where the matching is done as of the first trading day for the sample firm).

Because our sample firms have often undergone dramatic restructurings, their book values reported before their emergence cannot be used. Therefore, we use the book values reported in the first annual report following emergence;[10] for the sake of consistency, we use book values for the matched firms as reported in their first annual reports following the emergence dates for the sample firms. We call this the book-to-market, size- and industry-matched (BMSIM) sample. Because six of our sample firms do not report book values during the 200-day period following emergence, these firms are not included in the sample. As a robustness check, we compute the median book-to-market ratio for our sample firms and match firms to these six firms using this median ratio. The excess returns with this full sample are qualitatively very similar to those reported below.

Finally, as an additional robustness check, we use the market model to estimate expected returns with the NYSE/AMEX and Nasdaq value-weighted indices as the market returns. We estimate the market model parameters over days 201 through 274.

[8] In one case (Maxicare Health Plans, Inc.), the *Capital Changes Reporter* states the firm began trading on a when-issued basis on December 19, 1990 at $4 per share. However, the SPDSPR and CRSP do not note any trading until April 30, 1991 and this is the date we use. The price on April 30 was $8.875. If the *Capital Changes Reporter* is correct, then we have biased downward our estimate of the excess returns.

[9] Spiess and Affleck-Graves (1995) employ the use of matched firms in their study of the performance of stocks subsequent to seasoned equity offerings. Barber and Lyon (1997) also recommend the use of matched firms.

[10] Because of this estimation problem, we perform this test merely as a robustness check.

C. Efficiency Tests

Our first efficiency test is the well-known test of whether the average cumulative abnormal return (ACAR) is significantly different from zero. The ACAR tests whether the average actual return equals the average expected rate of return.

$$\text{ACAR} = \left(\frac{1}{N}\right)\sum_{i=1}^{N}\left(\left(\prod_{t=1}^{T}(1+r_{it})\right)-1\right) - \left(\frac{1}{N}\right)\sum_{i=1}^{N}\left(\left(\prod_{t=1}^{T}(1+E(r_{it}))\right)-1\right) = \left(\frac{1}{N}\right)\sum_{i=1}^{N}\text{CAR}_i, \quad (1)$$

where r_{it} = the actual rate of return for stock i on day t, $E(r_{it})$ = the expected rate of return for stock i on day t (see Section II.B), T = the number of days in the event period, N = the number of stocks, and CAR_i = the cumulative abnormal return for stock i.

We also compute a closely related measure of abnormal performance called the wealth relative (WR) (e.g., Ritter (1991)):

$$\text{WR} = \left(\sum_{i=1}^{N}\frac{\left(\prod_{t=1}^{200}(1+r_{it})\right)}{\left(\prod_{t=1}^{200}(1+E(r_{it}))\right)}\right)\Bigg/ N. \quad (2)$$

A WR greater than one implies that the sample firms earned abnormal profits and a WR less than one implies abnormal losses.

D. Cross-Sectional Tests

Recall that firms with low stock prices may have higher returns because of estimation risk (e.g., Barry and Brown (1984)) or transaction costs. Firms that change their primary two-digit SIC code may have greater estimation risk because the historical information on the firm is less helpful in predicting the firm's future performance and prepackaged bankruptcies may have different risk characteristics from the more lengthy nonprepackaged bankruptcies. Finally, the willingness of institutional investors to accept only equity in the new firm—in exchange for their old claim—may portend good future performance that is not fully reflected in the stock price upon emergence.

We use the four variables described above (that are known at the close of the first trading day upon emergence from Chapter 11) and the estimate of expected returns in our cross-sectional tests,

$$R_i = \beta_0 + \beta_1 E(R_i) + \beta_2 P_{i0} + \beta_3 \text{SICCH}_i + \beta_4 \text{PREPACK}_i + \beta_5 \text{ISTKDUM}_i + \epsilon_i, \quad (3)$$

where R_i = the compounded actual rate of return for stock $i(\prod(1 + r_{it}) - 1)$; $E(R_i)$ = the compounded expected rate of return for stock $i(\prod(1 + E(r_{it})) - 1)$; P_{i0} = the (log of) price of stock i at the close of the first trading day upon emergence from Chapter 11 (day 0); $SICCH_i$ = the dummy variable equal to one if the firm changes its primary two-digit SIC code during the bankruptcy process, zero otherwise; $PREPACK_i$ = the dummy variable equal to one if the firm's Chapter 11 filing is a prepackaged bankruptcy, zero otherwise;[11] and $ISTKDUM_i$ = the dummy variable equal to one if institutional investors accept only equity in the emerging firm (in exchange for their old claim), zero otherwise.

E. Earnings Announcement Tests

There are 99 firms with at least one earnings announcement during the 200-day period following emergence. To check if this subsample is biased toward the better-performing firms, we compute the long-term excess returns for the 32 firms without an earnings announcement and find that they do not have a significantly lower ACAR and median CAR than the stocks with at least one earnings announcement. On average, there are 2.6 earnings announcements for each firm with an announcement.

For the earnings announcement tests, the (compounded) CARs—using the matched firms—are computed over the 21-day period surrounding the announcement (−10 to +10; where day 0 is the earnings announcement date). The CARs are computed for up to four earnings announcements over the 200-day period for each firm that had an announcement.

The ACARs are computed two ways. First, we assume independence among CARs computed for the same firm and average all the CARs; we call this the "All Firm Announcement Effects" sample. Second, we average the CARs for each firm with multiple announcements and use this average to compute the ACAR; this method assumes that CARs from the same firm are perfectly correlated and we call this the "Average Firm Announcement Effects" sample. We also compute median CARs for both samples.

III. Empirical Results

The ACAR results are presented in Table I. For the first two days of returns following emergence—the postemergence period (1, 2)—the ACAR ranges from 3.0 percent to 3.8 percent but the statistical significance is weak. Moreover, the median CARs are smaller (0 percent to 0.3 percent) and insignificant.

[11] We have 25 prepackaged bankruptcies. The median time in Chapter 11 is 7.237 months for our prepackaged bankruptcies and 22.83 for our nonprepackaged bankruptcies (recall that we measure time in Chapter 11 from the bankruptcy announcement date through the first trading date). The samples in Betker (1995) and Chatterjee, Dhillon, and Ramirez (1996) are helpful in identifying which of our sample firms are prepackaged bankruptcies.

Table I

Average Cumulative Abnormal Returns

Average cumulative abnormal returns (ACARs) are computed for the sample of 131 firms emerging from Chapter 11 from 1980 through 1993. Postemergence day 0 is defined as the first trading day upon emergence from Chapter 11. The size- and industry-matched (SIM) sample is the sample with matching firms that have the same two-digit SIC code as the formerly bankrupt firms and are closest in size (i.e., equity capitalization). The book-to-market, size- and industry-matched (BMSIM) sample is the sample with matching firms that have the same two-digit SIC code as the formerly bankrupt firm, are within the same (industry) size decile, and are closest in the book-to-market ratio. The market model adjusted returns are based on alpha and beta coefficients estimated in the (201, 274) interval using the NYSE/AMEX market index and the Nasdaq index. The ACAR and median cumulative abnormal return (CAR) are based on daily compounded returns. The Wealth Relative is the average of the daily compounded actual rate of return divided by the daily compounded expected rate of return. *p*-values are in parentheses.

Event Period	Matched Firm Sample	ACAR	Wealth Relative	Median CAR
(1, 2)	SIM	0.038***	1.038	0.000
		(0.059)		(0.184)
(1, 200)	SIM	0.246*	1.249	0.063**
		(0.004)		(0.025)
(1, 2)	BMSIM	0.030	1.030	0.000
		(0.150)		(0.671)
(1, 200)	BMSIM	0.600**	1.603	0.084**
		(0.050)		(0.022)
(1, 2)	Mkt. model	0.033	1.033	0.002
	(NYSE/AMEX)	(0.112)		(0.112)
(1, 200)	Mkt. model	1.385**	2.384	0.072*
	(NYSE/AMEX)	(0.016)		(0.009)
(1, 2)	Mkt. model	0.033	1.033	0.003
	(Nasdaq)	(0.114)		(0.497)
(1, 200)	Mkt. model	1.388**	2.387	0.051**
	(Nasdaq)	(0.028)		(0.013)

*, **, and *** indicate significant difference from zero at the 1-, 5-, and 10-percent levels, respectively.

The results become unambiguous when the postemergence period is extended to day 200. Under every method of estimating expected returns, the ACARs are large, positive, and significant (from 24.6 percent to 138.8 percent). Though lower, the median CARs are also positive and significant (from 5.1 percent to 8.4 percent). The wealth relatives are greater than unity every time.

Table II shows the excess returns around the earnings announcements. In each case, the ACAR is large, positive, and significant. The median CARs are also positive and significant, though the median CAR is marginally significant for the "All Firm Announcement Effects" sample using the size- and industry-matched firm sample. These results suggest that the market is surprised by the performance of our sample firms over the 200-day period following emergence.

Table II

Earnings Announcement Tests

Average cumulative average returns (ACARs) are calculated around earnings announcement dates. The (compounded) cumulative abnormal returns (CARs)—using the matched firms—are computed over the 21-day period surrounding the announcement (−10 to +10; where day 0 is the earnings announcement date). The CARs are computed for up to four earnings announcements over a 200-day period for each firm that had an announcement. The ACARs are computed two ways. First, we assume independence among CARs computed for the same firm; we call this the "All Firm Announcement Effects" sample. Second, we average the CARs for each firm with multiple announcements and use this average to compute the average CAR across firms; this method assumes that CARs from the same firm are perfectly correlated and we call this the "Average Firm Announcement Effects" sample. The size- and industry-matched (SIM) sample is the sample with matching firms that have the same two-digit SIC code as the formerly bankrupt firms and are closest in size (i.e., equity capitalization). The book-to-market, size- and industry-matched (BMSIM) sample is the sample with matching firms that have the same two-digit SIC code as the formerly bankrupt firm, are within the same (industry) size decile, and are closest in the book-to-market ratio. *p*-values are in parentheses.

Matched Firm Sample	ACAR	Median CAR
All firm announcement effects		
SIM	0.068**	0.009
	(0.043)	(0.136)
BMSIM	0.079*	0.023*
	(0.010)	(0.004)
Average firm announcement effects		
SIM	0.045***	0.026***
	(0.100)	(0.095)
BMSIM	0.062**	0.032*
	(0.013)	(0.003)

*, **, and *** indicate significant difference from zero at the 1-, 5-, and 10-percent levels, respectively.

The cross-sectional results are shown in Table III (the standard errors are corrected using White's (1980) method). For the first two return days, there is no variable that consistently explains the cross-sectional differences in returns; therefore, the excess returns do not appear to be concentrated in stocks with higher estimation risks or transaction costs. Because our primary method of estimating expected returns is to use a matched firm of similar size to the sample firm, the transaction costs and estimation risks for these matched firms are likely to be similar anyway.

The variable $ISTKDUM_i$ is positive but only marginally significant. With the 200-day return regressions, $ISTKDUM_i$ is positive and significant with the BMSIM sample. On the other hand, with the SIM sample, this variable—though positive—is not significant. Therefore, we find mixed evidence that the willingness of institutional investors to accept only equity in exchange for their old claims on the formerly bankrupt firm portends abnormally good long-term performance that is not fully reflected in the stock prices upon emergence. More generally, we find no consistent evidence that any of the

Table III

Cross-Sectional Tests

Regression estimates of the models,

$$R_i = \beta_0 + \beta_1 E(R_i) + \beta_2 P_{i0} + \beta_3 \text{SICCH}_i + \beta_4 \text{PREPACK}_i + \epsilon_i$$

and

$$R_i = \beta_0 + \beta_1 E(R_i) + \beta_2 P_{i0} + \beta_3 \text{SICCH}_i + \beta_4 \text{PREPACK}_i + \beta_5 \text{ISTKDUM}_i + \epsilon_i,$$

where R_i is the compounded rate of return for firm i; $E(R_i)$ is the compounded expected rate of return for firm i; P_{i0} is the log of the closing price on day 0 for firm i; SICCH_i is a dummy variable that equals one if the firm changes its primary two-digit SIC code during the bankruptcy process, zero otherwise; PREPACK_i is a dummy variable that equals one if the firm's Chapter 11 is a prepackaged bankruptcy, zero otherwise; ISTKDUM_i is a dummy variable equal to one if institutional investors accept only equity (including warrants) in the firm emerging from bankruptcy, zero otherwise. The size- and industry-matched (SIM) sample (columns A through D) is the sample with matching firms that have the same two-digit SIC code as the formerly bankrupt firms and are closest in size (i.e., equity capitalization). The book-to-market, size- and industry-matched (BMSIM) sample (columns E through H) is the sample with matching firms that have the same two-digit SIC code as the formerly bankrupt firm, are within the same (industry) size decile, and are closest in the book-to-market ratio. The *p*-values of the coefficient estimates are shown in parentheses. (1, 2) is for the first two return days following emergence from Chapter 11; (1, 200) is for the first two hundred returns days following emergence.

	SIM				BMSIM			
	A	B	C	D	E	F	G	H
Variable	(1, 2)	(1, 2)	(1, 200)	(1, 200)	(1, 2)	(1, 2)	(1, 200)	(1, 200)
Intercept	0.036	−0.041	0.227	0.331	0.036	−0.036	0.326***	0.381
	(0.261)	(0.297)	(0.103)	(0.144)	(0.260)	(0.328)	(0.066)	(0.192)
$E(R_i)$	0.287**	0.068*	0.295*	0.359**	0.572	0.566	0.429***	0.588
	(0.016)	(0.000)	(0.000)	(0.030)	(0.162)	(0.169)	(0.036)	(0.192)
P_{io}	−0.020	0.009	−0.091	−0.095	−0.020	0.010	−0.121	−0.121
	(0.222)	(0.617)	(0.209)	(0.346)	(0.206)	(0.540)	(0.158)	(0.337)
PREPACK_i	0.169**	−0.088	0.045	0.233	0.160**	−0.108***	0.035	0.215
	(0.026)	(0.140)	(0.770)	(0.312)	(0.031)	(0.080)	(0.824)	(0.582)
SICCH_i	−0.095**	0.097***	0.163	−0.188	−0.106*	0.094***	0.111	−0.235
	(0.017)	(0.072)	(0.305)	(0.276)	(0.008)	(0.075)	(0.590)	(0.224)
ISTKDUM_i		0.115		0.147		0.089		0.406***
		(0.249)		(0.704)		(0.360)		(0.034)
Adj. R^2	0.083	0.088	0.118	0.107	0.118	0.107	0.060	0.104

*, **, and *** indicate significant difference from zero at the 1-, 5-, and 10-percent levels, respectively.

other variables that may be associated with risks or transaction costs not fully captured in our expected return estimates explain our long-term excess returns.[12]

IV. Summary and Conclusions

We investigate the efficiency of the market for stocks of firms emerging from bankruptcy. We find weak evidence of positive excess returns in the short-term and strong evidence of positive excess returns in the long-term. Specifically, over the first 200 days of returns after emergence, the ACAR varies from 24.6 percent to 138.8 percent depending on how the expected returns are estimated. The median CARs, though lower, are significant and range from 5.1 to 8.4 percent.

Transaction costs or risk characteristics not captured in our expected return estimates could explain the results. We investigate these possibilities using differing estimates of expected returns and check for whether other risk or transaction cost proxies explain the excess returns. We continue to find excess returns after conducting these investigations. There is some evidence, however, that the willingness of institutional investors to accept only equity (in exchange for their old claims on the formerly bankrupt firm) in the newly emerged firm is positively associated with long-term excess returns. This result suggests the type of securities accepted by these informed investors may reflect information on the stock's intrinsic value that is not fully reflected in the stock price upon emergence from Chapter 11.

We also find the average and median excess returns are positive when our sample firms make their earnings announcements. These results are consistent with La Porta et al. (1997) and suggest that our findings are the result of the market being surprised by the postemergence performance of our sample firms.

In summary, our results cast doubt on the informational efficiency of this market. The results also present an interesting contrast, but not a contradiction, to the poor operating results of firms emerging from bankruptcy as reported in previous work. Our results suggest that, although these firms may not do well in their post-Chapter 11 accounting performance, they appear to do better than the market had expected at the time of emergence from Chapter 11.

REFERENCES

Aggarwal, Reena, and Pietra Rivoli, 1990, Fads in the initial public offering market?, *Financial Management* 19, 58–67.

Alderson, Michael J., and Brian L. Betker, 1996, Assessing postbankruptcy performance: An analysis of reorganized firms' cash flows, Working paper, Saint Louis University.

[12] To check further whether our long-term positive excess returns are concentrated among low-priced stocks, we compute the 200-day average and median excess returns (with the SIM and BMSIM sample) for stocks with a first trading day price of $4 or less and for stocks with a price of more than $4; the average and median excess returns for the low-price stocks are not significantly higher than for the high-price stocks.

Altman, Edward I., 1991, *Distressed Securities* (Probus Publishing Company, Chicago).

Altman, Edward I., 1993, *Corporate Financial Distress and Bankruptcy* (John Wiley and Sons, New York).

Altman, Edward I., and Allan C. Eberhart, 1994, Do seniority provisions protect bondholders' investments?, *Journal of Portfolio Management* 20, 67–75.

Andrade, Gregor, and Steven N. Kaplan, 1998, How costly is financial (not economic) distress? Evidence from highly leveraged transactions that became distressed, *Journal of Finance* 53, 1443–1493.

Banz, Rolf W., 1981, The relationship between return and market value of common stock, *Journal of Financial Economics* 9, 3–18.

Barber, Brad M., and John D. Lyon, 1997, Detecting long-run abnormal stock returns: The empirical power and specification of test statistics, *Journal of Financial Economics* 43, 341–372.

Barry, Christopher B., and Stephen J. Brown, 1984, Differential information and the small firm effect, *Journal of Financial Economics* 13, 283–294.

Betker, Brian L., 1995, An empirical examination of prepackaged bankruptcy, *Financial Management* 24, 3–18.

Brown, David T., Christopher M. James, and Robert M. Mooradian, 1993, The information content of exchange offers made by distressed firms, *Journal of Financial Economics* 33, 93–118.

Chatterjee, Sris, Upinder S. Dhillon, and Gabriel G. Ramirez, 1996, Resolution of financial distress: Debt restructurings via Chapter 11, prepackaged bankruptcies, and workouts, *Financial Management* 25, 5–18.

Dharan, Bala G., and David L. Ikenberry, 1995, The long-run negative drift of post-listing stock returns, *Journal of Finance* 50, 1547–1574.

Eberhart, Allan C., William T. Moore, and Rodney L. Roenfeldt, 1990, Security pricing and deviations from the absolute priority rule in bankruptcy proceedings, *Journal of Finance* 45, 1457–1469.

Eberhart, Allan C., and Richard J. Sweeney, 1992, Does the bond market predict bankruptcy settlements?, *Journal of Finance* 47, 943–980.

Field, Laura C., 1997, Is institutional investment in initial public offerings related to the long-run performance of these firms?, Working paper, Pennsylvania State University.

Gilson, Stuart, 1997, Transaction costs and capital structure choice: Evidence from financially distressed firms, *Journal of Finance*, 52, 161–197.

Hotchkiss, Edith S, 1995, The post-emergence performance of firms emerging from Chapter 11, *Journal of Finance* 50, 3–21.

Lamoureux, Christopher G., and James W. Wansley, 1989, The pricing of when-issued securities, *Financial Review* 24, 183–198.

La Porta, Rafael, Josef Lakonishok, Andrei Shleifer, and Robert Vishny, 1997, Good news for value stocks: Further evidence on market efficiency, *Journal of Finance* 52, 859–874.

Loughran, Tim, and Jay R. Ritter, 1995, The new issues puzzle, *Journal of Finance* 50, 23–51.

Ritter, Jay R., 1991, The long-run performance of initial public offerings, *Journal of Finance* 46, 3–48.

Sandler, Linda, 1991, Post-bankruptcy shares: next big play?, *Wall Street Journal*, May 16.

Shumway, Tyler, 1997, The delisting bias in CRSP data, *Journal of Finance* 52, 327–340.

Spiess, D. Katherine, and John Affleck-Graves, 1995, Underperformance in long-run stock returns following seasoned equity offerings, *Journal of Financial Economics* 38, 243–267.

Weiss, Lawrence A., 1990, Bankruptcy costs and violation of claims priority, *Journal of Financial Economics* 27, 285–314.

White, H., 1980, A heteroskedasticity-consistent covariance matrix estimator and a direct test for heteroskedasticity, *Econometrica* 48, 817–838.

Name Index

The International Library of Critical Writings in Financial Economics

1. The Theory of Corporate Finance
(Volumes I and II)
Michael J. Brennan
2. Futures Markets
(Volumes I, II and III)
A.G. Malliaris
3. Market Efficiency: Stock Market Behaviour in Theory and Practice
(Volumes I and II)
Andrew W. Lo
4. Microstructure: The Organization of Trading and Short Term Price Behavior
(Volumes I and II)
Hans R. Stoll
5. The Debt Market
(Volumes I, II and III)
Stephen A. Ross
6. Options Markets
(Volumes I, II and III)
George M. Constantinides and A.G. Malliaris
7. Empirical Corporate Finance
(Volumes I, II, III and IV)
Michael J. Brennan
8. The Foundations of Continuous Time Finance
Stephen M. Schaefer
9. International Securities
(Volumes I and II)
George C. Philippatos and Gregory Koutmos
10. Behavioral Finance
(Volumes I, II and III)
Hersh Shefrin
11. Asset Pricing Theory and Tests
(Volumes I and II)
Robert R. Grauer
12. International Capital Markets
(Volumes I, II and III)
G. Andrew Karolyi and René M. Stulz
13. Financial Forecasting
(Volumes I and II)
Roy Batchelor and Pami Dua
14. Emerging Markets
Geert Bekaert and Campbell R. Harvey
15. Corporate Restructuring
(Volumes I and II)
John J. McConnell and David J. Denis
16. Recent Developments in Corporate Finance
(Volumes I and II)
Jay R. Ritter

Future titles will include:

Foreign Exchange Markets
Richard J. Sweeney

Financial Econometrics
Andrew W. Lo

Financial Markets and the Real Economy
John H. Cochrane